BATH SPA UNIVERSITY
LIBRARY

International Business

Environments & Operations

Sixteenth Edition

Global Edition

John D. Daniels

University of Miami

Lee H. Radebaugh

Brigham Young University

Daniel P. Sullivan

University of Delaware

Pearson

Harlow, England • London • New York • Boston • San Francisco • Toronto • Sydney • Dubai • Singapore • Hong Kong

Tokyo • Seoul • Taipei • New Delhi • Cape Town • Sao Paulo • Mexico City • Madrid • Amsterdam • Munich • Paris • Milan

B.S.U. - LIBRARY

00364636

Vice President, Business Publishing: Donna Battista
Director of Portfolio Management: Stephanie Wall
Portfolio Manager: Daniel Tylman
Associate Acquisitions Editor, Global Edition: Ishita Sinha
Associate Project Editor, Global Edition: Paromita Banerjee
Assistant Editor, Global Edition: Tahnee Wager
Editorial Coordinator: Linda Albelli
Vice President, Product Marketing: Roxanne McCarley
Director of Strategic Marketing: Brad Parkins
Strategic Marketing Manager: Deborah Strickland
Product Marketer: Becky Brown
Field Marketing Manager: Lenny Ann Kucenski
Product Marketing Assistant: Jessica Quazza
Vice President, Production and Digital Studio, Arts and Business: Etain O'Dea
Director of Production, Business: Jeff Holcomb
Managing Producer, Business: Ashley Santora

Operations Specialist: Carol Melville
Senior Manufacturing Controller, Global Edition: Jerry Kataria
Content Producer, Global Edition: Sudipto Roy
Creative Director: Blair Brown
Manager, Learning Tools: Brian Surette
Content Developer, Learning Tools: Lindsey Sloan
Managing Producer, Digital Studio, Arts and Business: Diane Lombardo
Digital Studio Project Manager: Darren Cormier
Digital Studio Project Manager: Alana Coles
Manager, Media Production, Global Edition: Vikram Kumar
Full-Service Project Management and Composition: Integra Software Services Pvt. Ltd.
Interior Designer: Integra Software Services Pvt. Ltd.
Cover Designer: Lumina Datamatics.
Cover Art: Avigator Thailand / Shutterstock

Acknowledgments of third-party content appear on the appropriate page within the text.

PEARSON, ALWAYS LEARNING, and MYMANAGEMENTLAB® are exclusive trademarks owned by Pearson Education, Inc. or its affiliates in the U.S. and/or other countries.

Pearson Education Limited
KAO Two
KAO Park
Harlow
CM17 9NA
United Kingdom

and Associated Companies throughout the world

Visit us on the World Wide Web at: www.pearsonglobaleditions.com

© Pearson Education Limited 2019

The rights of John D. Daniels, Lee H. Radebaugh, and Daniel P. Sullivan to be identified as the authors of this work have been asserted by them in accordance with the Copyright, Designs and Patents Act 1988.

Authorized adaptation from the United States edition, entitled International Business: Environments & Operations, 16th Edition, ISBN 978-0-13-420005-7 by John D. Daniels, Lee H. Radebaugh, and Daniel P. Sullivan, published by Pearson Education © 2018.

All rights reserved. No part of this publication may be reproduced, stored in a retrieval system, or transmitted in any form or by any means, electronic, mechanical, photocopying, recording or otherwise, without either the prior written permission of the publisher or a license permitting restricted copying in the United Kingdom issued by the Copyright Licensing Agency Ltd, Saffron House, 6–10 Kirby Street, London EC1N 8TS.

All trademarks used herein are the property of their respective owners. The use of any trademark in this text does not vest in the author or publisher any trademark ownership rights in such trademarks, nor does the use of such trademarks imply any affiliation with or endorsement of this book by such owners.

ISBN 10: 1-292-21473-2
ISBN 13: 978-1-292-21473-3

British Library Cataloguing-in-Publication Data
A catalogue record for this book is available from the British Library

10 9 8 7 6 5 4 3 2 1

Typeset in Times NR MT Pro by Integra Software Services Pvt. Ltd.
Printed and bound by Vivar in Malaysia

Brief Contents

Contents

16 The Organization and Governance of Foreign Operations   471

Preface

This textbook is one of the best-selling U.S. and worldwide international business (IB) textbooks. Widely used in both undergraduate and MBA level courses, this text has had authorized translations into Albanian, Chinese, Macedonian, Russian, Spanish, Korean, and Thai. Its first edition in 1976, according to many professors, defined the IB field. Its subsequent 14 editions have set the global standard for studying IB's environments and operations. Students, faculty, and managers have praised our text for its compelling balance between rigorous, authoritative theory and meaningful practice within the context of a fresh, current analysis of IB. The elements of success that have driven this performance anchor our efforts to make this 16th edition the best version yet. We believe these efforts result in a textbook that provides you and your students the best possible understanding of what is happening and is likely to happen in the world of business.

WHAT'S NEW TO THE SIXTEENTH EDITION?

Ongoing trends and new development in the global business environment called for us to rethink and revise our interpretations of the environments of operations of international business. Incorporating the corresponding changes convinced the publishers and the authors of the usefulness of publishing a 16th edition.

- **Global Changes**

IB, probably more so than any other subject, needs updating because of the number of and rapidity of global changes. The period since our last edition was no exception. Among the many changes we have referenced in our text are the spread of mosquito-borne epidemics (Zika, Ebola, dengue fever, and yellow fever); changes in national borders (e.g., Crimea now a part of Russia rather than the Ukraine); the rise of ISIS and its extended terrorism; the expanding scale and scope of technology; oil technology that has altered global supply locations and prices; the evolving role of Bitcoins for international currency exchange and investment opportunities; the emergence of disruptive technologies such 3-D printers, robotics, and artificial intelligence; the opening of U.S.–Cuban diplomatic exchanges; the advent of negative interest-rate policies in many Western markets; the termination of an embargo on Iran; the near breakup of certain countries (e.g., the United Kingdom and Spain); the use of corporate inversions to reduce taxes; ongoing ups and downs by prominent emerging markets; accelerating sophistication of communication systems; decreasing degrees of political and economic freedom throughout the world; greater agreement that the global climate is warming; the game changing implications of social media; an almost unprecedented refugee movement into Europe; and greater support in many countries for more national sovereignty leading to the possible breakup of regional economic groups.

- **Theories and Evidence to Explain IB and Globalization**

It is now over 40 years since we started writing this text's first edition. We can remember when the Academy of International Business (AIB), the main IB academic organization, attracted fewer than 40 attendees for its annual meeting; now it routinely draws more than a thousand. Journals with an emphasis on international business were virtually nonexistent; thus the few people working directly in the field had to depend on discipline- and functional-based journals as outlets for their research. We all know how this has changed, which has, on the one hand, helped us to understand the global business environment in innovative, exciting ways. Nevertheless, the expanding scale of globalization and IB growth fuels such an abundance of published materials that academicians have had to specialize in narrower areas to stay abreast of relevant research. The growth has also created a challenge for authors, such as us, to keep sufficiently up to date on the breadth of research being published on all the functional and disciplinary topics we cover in an introductory text. We are the first to admit that we cannot, but, at the same time, when we have revised for each new edition, we have discovered work that goes well beyond a slight movement in existing knowledge frontiers. It is gratifying for us to delve deeper into emerging trends such as those we described above, and thus we have added significant new material to the 16th edition.

• Reduced Length

Over the years, we received sporadic objections to the length of our text. And complicating matters was the sense that as the text expanded, students increasingly preferred learning in shorter, focused bursts. Hence, we set a goal of reducing the text length by 200 pages without sacrificing content, coverage, or quality; we more than met our goal. We did this partially by shifting end notes to an easily-accessed online location, removing all cartoons because they did not sufficiently enhance students' learning, and reducing tables of data that quickly became obsolete. However, to our surprise, our biggest reduction by far was from tightening our prose. Completing chapters very quickly to reach a deadline for a two-year cycle had caused us to be much too wordy and to lead us to undue redundancy among our chapters. We quickly learned that reducing 200 pages was more time consuming than adding 200, but we feel that the text is now far more engaging, interesting, and readable.

• Improved In-Text Learning Aids

1. We aligned our objectives at each chapter's opening with major headings within the chapters. This meant, in many cases, reorganizing the materials within the chapter. However, this should help students master materials more effectively and efficiently. Further, the change has permitted the generators of the corresponding test bank to key questions better with learning objectives.

2. We already had marginal notes to refer back to previous chapters. We expanded those considerably and now refer to the specific pages where students can find earlier materials.

3. We dropped the "Geography and International Business" feature. It had not appeared in all the chapters, and we incorporated the coverage into specific parts of the chapters.

4. We dropped the "Summary" and "Key Terms" sections from the end of our chapters. Our reasoning is that our marginal notes cover all the summary points in greater detail and next to the material being covered. All key terms are shown in bold and included in the glossary, thus we eliminated this redundancy.

5. We updated all of our cases. In addition, we replaced seven cases with new ones as follows:

> *Chapter 5:* South Korea's Success Story in the Post-WWII International Economy
> *Chapter 6:* The Case of REEs: Trade Disputes and Protectionist Measures for Strategic Materials
> *Chapter 7:* Regional Integration and the Different Modalities of a Custom Union Divorce
> *Chapter 9:* Venezuela's Rapidly Changing Currency
> *Chapter 13:* The Lego Group Case
> *Chapter 14:* The Borderfree Option: Going Global—Simplified
> *Chapter 16:* Organizing Global Operations: The "Gore Way"

- **Limiting Authors' Names**

Early on, we observed that students too often thought that they needed to memorize the names of all the authors who were cited. Thus, we have made it a point to cite only classic authors, such as Adam Smith. If students (or instructors) want to know the origin of materials, they can find this information in the end note section.

BUILDING ON SUCCESS

For the record, fewer than one percent of textbooks reach 16 editions. The longevity of this text signifies its successful adaptation to the changing domain of globalization and IB. Indeed, sustainability has become a byword within the global economy. Sustainability, such as for a text, calls for building on what works well and eliminating what does not. Here are some highlights of the 16th edition building blocks.

FOCUSING ON BOTH MACRO AND MICRO PERFORMANCE

We have always, and steadfastly continue to present materials from a broader perspective than company performance. First, although IB affects nearly all business, many students will be only tangentially involved. Second, knowledge of IB supports good citizenship, helping students interpret macro policies that affect their personal lives and career ambitions.

RESPONDING TO UPDATED LITERATURE

From the beginning, we have constantly assessed academic and practitioner publications to stay abreast of relevant issues and events. We have made no exception for this edition. A review of our exhaustive endnotes shows a citation mix of classic treatises along with significant IB materials that have been published since the preceding edition. Further, the companies cited in the "Company Index and Trademarks" section come from a variety of industries—large and small, U.S. and non-U.S.—and the list continues to be comprehensive and contemporary.

RELAYING PERSONAL EXPERIENCES

We regularly interact with IB stakeholders—managers, students, professors, and people affected by trade and other international events—through our teaching of degree-earning and executive students, attendance at academic and civic meetings, and foreign travel. For example, since the 15th text edition was published, we have traveled collectively to 25 countries, largely dealing with IB managers in each. These exchanges, taking place in every region of the world, provide insights and anecdotes that develop new materials and prioritize coverage via chapter content and cases. We believe no other textbook comes as close to effectively blending a comprehensive review of international business theory with exhaustive attention to what happens in the many parts of the world.

INCORPORATING CASES

We maintain the inclusion of a case to open and close each chapter. With few exceptions, we wrote the cases ourselves. When we did not, we worked closely with the authors to assure that the focus of each fit precisely with chapters' materials. These cases span the globe and engage an extensive range of topics from environmental, institutional, country, industry, company, and individual perspectives. They also include a wide range of company perspectives, from large MNEs to small exporters, from old-line manufacturers to emergent cyber businesses, and from product manufacturers to service providers.

The opening cases set the stage for the chapters' major issues, highlighting themes and ideas that are then covered throughout the chapter. These also include questions to guide students to real situations as they read the chapters. The closing cases, also anchored with questions, integrate the ideas and tools presented in the chapter and call upon the students to analyze issues and propose actions.

POINT-COUNTERPOINT

To reinforce our strong applications orientation, we carry on a feature in every chapter that brings to life a major debate in contemporary IB and globalization. We use a point-counterpoint style to highlight opposing viewpoints that managers and policymakers face when trying to make sense of vital issues. The give and take between two sides reinforces this textbook's effort to link theory and practice.

LOOKING TO THE FUTURE

As in previous editions, each chapter offers future scenarios that are important to managers, companies, or the world. The topic of each *Looking to the Future* feature alludes to the ideas discussed in the chapter in a way that prompts students to engage their imagination about the future of the world.

MAPS

Geographic literacy is essential in international business. Thus, we have maintained an Atlas, now located immediately after this Preface. Not only does it show locations, it includes the almost equally important pronunciations of the countries and territories that are included. In addition to the Atlas, we have an abundance of maps throughout that are visual presentations of materials, such as the major locations of a country's export markets.

ENGAGING IN-TEXT LEARNING AIDS

To support students' concentration on fundamental information and lessons, we introduce each new major term in bold. These terms are also included in a Glossary to help them recall definitions when they see these terms in later chapters. We use marginal notes to summarize discussions, and we include marginal chapter review notes to lead students back to earlier material that helps them fathom later discussions.

INSTRUCTOR SUPPLEMENTS

Instructors can access the following downloadable supplemental resources by signing into the Instructor Resource Center at www.pearsonglobaleditions.com/Daniels.

- **Instructor's Manual**
- **Test Item File and TestGen® Computerized Test Bank**—includes multiple choice, true/false, short answer, and essay questions that are tagged to Learning Objectives, Skill, Difficulty, Learning Outcomes, and AACSB Learning Standards to help measure whether students are grasping the course content that aligns with AACSB guidelines.
- **PowerPoint Slides**
- **Image Library**

Need help? Our dedicated Technical Support team is ready to assist instructors with questions about the media supplements that accompany this text. Visit **support.pearson.com/getsupport** for answers to frequently asked questions and toll-free user-support phone numbers.

ACKNOWLEDGMENTS

PINPOINTING OUR REVIEWS

Although we have always depended on outside reviewers to give us advice, the process had several shortcomings in terms of our recent needs. The most basic one is that instructors were asked to comment on the entire book, which led to responses that were too general to help us sufficiently, such as "I've used the book for several years and am happy with it." Or, reviewers had never adopted the book, thus the responses were obviously based on a mere scanning of materials without any specific substantive suggestions. There was a tendency to propose additions without eliminations that would compensate for them. In addition, some of the recommendations were made by users who to go into greater depth in an area without considering the breadth required for our book. Given that the reviews came to us anonymously, we could not speculate on the type of student market about which they were evaluating the text.

For our present edition, we received early on three anonymous reviews, thus we cannot acknowledge them by name. We then solicited people who are well-known scholars to review only one chapter that corresponded to their major expertise. We asked them to not only inform us of errors, but also to suggest important omissions. In addition, we needed their recommendations on where we could cut material in order to meet the demands of the market in terms of length. We cannot thank the following people enough for making thorough, practical, and insightful recommendations.

Benjamin Bader, Lüneburg University (Germany)
Mary Yoko Brannen, University of Victoria (Canada)
F. Greg Burton, Brigham Young University (USA)
Jean J. Boddewyn, Baruch College (USA)
Fidel León Darder, Universitat de València (Spain)
Tom Foster, Brigham Young University (USA)
Simon Greathead, Brigham Young University (USA)
Lichung Jen, National Taiwan University (Taiwan)
Steve Katsaros, Founder and CEO of Nokero (USA)
Jeffrey A. Krug, Bloomsburg University (USA)
Sumit K. Kundu, Florida International University (USA)
Shige Makino, Chinese University of Hong Kong (Hong Kong)
Ali R. Manbeian, Managing Partner, GPS Capital Markets Inc. (USA)
Kurt Norder, University of Delaware (USA)
Jon Jungbien Moon, Korea University (Korea)
Terence Mughan, Royal Roads University (Canada)
Daniel Rottig, Florida Gulf Coast University (USA)
Manuel G. Serapio, University of Colorado Denver (USA)
Saeed Samiee, University of Tulsa (USA)
Cristina Villar, Universitat de València (Spain)
Sharon Watson, University of Delaware (USA)

In addition to the reviewers cited above, there have been countless individuals who have helped us through the years. Because this is the culmination of several previous editions, we would like to acknowledge everyone's efforts. However, many more individuals than we can possibly list have helped us. To those who must remain anonymous, we offer our sincere thanks.

We would also like to acknowledge people whom we interviewed in writing cases. Omar Aljindi, Nora al Jundi, and Talah Tamimi (Saudi Arabia's Dynamic Culture); Jonathan Fitzpatrick, Julio A. Ramirez, Arianne Cento, and Ana Miranda (Burger King); several executives at American Airlines and oneworld who wish to remain anonymous (The oneworld Airline Alliance); and Ali R. Manbien (GPS Capital Markets Inc). In addition, we would like to thank several people who authored or coauthored cases for us: Mary Yoko Brannen and Terence Mughan at the University of Victoria and Royal Roads University for Tesco PLC: Leveraging Global Knowledge (Chapter 2), Fidel León-Darder and Cristina Villar at Universitat de València for Meliá Hotels International (Chapter 15), Jon Jungbien Moon at Korea University for Grameen Danone Foods in Bangladesh (Chapter 17), and Manuel Serapio at the University of Colorado Denver and Steve Katsaros, founder and CEO of Nokero for Nokero: Lighting the World (Chapter 18); others who helped with administrative and research matters include Ian G. Daniels, Maddison Daines, Lisa Curlee, Allison Johnson, and Katie Cooper Redding.

It takes a dedicated group of individuals to take a textbook from first draft to final manuscript. We would like to thank our partners at Pearson Education for their tireless efforts in bringing the 16th edition of this book to fruition. Our thanks go to Director of Portfolio Management, Stephanie Wall; Portfolio Manager, Daniel Tylman; Managing Producer, Ashley Santora; Production Director, Jeff Holcomb; Managing Producer, Alison Kalil; Product Marketer, Becky Brown; Editorial Coordinator, Linda Albelli; Project Manager, Karin Williams; and Project Manager at Integra, Preetha Menon.

Our sincerest thanks also go out to Lisa Cherivtch at Oakton Community College, Mamoun Benmamoun at Saint Louis University, and Susan Leshnower at Midland College, as well as Meg O'Rourke and Emily Yelverton, for their contributions to the instructor resources and MyLab Management content.

GLOBAL EDITION ACKNOWLEDGMENTS

We want to thank the following people for their contributions:

Javier Calero Cuervo, University of Macau
Stefania Paladini, Birmingham City University
Krish Saha, Birmingham City University

We would also like to thank the following people for reviewing the Global Edition and sharing their insightful comments and suggestions:

Fuad Aliyev, Georgia State University
Bernard Bouwman, Freelance Writer
Susan Chin, Freelance Writer
Jacques Couvas, Lucerne School of Business, Switzerland
Marios I Katsioloudes, Qatar University
Yukari Iguchi, University of Derby Online Learning

About the Authors

From left to right: **Daniel Sullivan, John Daniels, and Lee Radebaugh.**

Three respected and renowned scholars show your students how dynamic, how real, how interesting, and how important the study of international business can be.

John D. Daniels, the Samuel N. Friedland Chair of Executive Management emeritus at the University of Miami, received his BBA, MBA, and PhD respectively at the University of Miami, University of the Americas, and the University of Michigan. He also holds an honorary doctorate from UPAO in Peru. His dissertation won first place in the award competition of the Academy of International Business. Since then, he has been an active researcher and won a decade award from the *Journal of International Business Studies.* His articles have appeared in such leading journals as *Academy of Management Journal, Advances in International Marketing, California Management Review, Columbia Journal of World Business, International Marketing Review, International Trade Journal, Journal of Business Research, Journal of High Technology Management Research, Journal of International Business Studies, Management International Review, Multinational Business Review, Strategic Management Journal, Transnational Corporations,* and *Weltwirtschaftliches Archiv.* Professor Daniels has published 15 books, most recently *Multinational Enterprises and the Changing World Economy* (coedited with Ray Loveridge, Tsai-Mei Lin, and Alan M. Rugman), three volumes on *Multinational Enterprise Theory,* and three volumes on *International Business and Globalization* (all coedited with Jeffrey Krug). On its 30th anniversary, *Management International Review* referred to him as "one of the most prolific American IB scholars." He served as president of the Academy of International Business and dean of its Fellows. He also served as chairperson of the international division of the Academy of Management, which named him Outstanding Educator of the Year in 2010. Professor Daniels has worked and lived a year or longer in 7 different countries, worked shorter stints in approximately 30 other countries on 6 continents, and traveled in many more. His foreign work has been a combination of private sector, governmental, teaching, and research assignments. He was formerly a faculty member at Georgia State University and The Pennsylvania State University, director of the Center for International Business Education and Research (CIBER) at Indiana University, and holder of the E. Claiborne Robins Distinguished Chair at the University of Richmond.

Lee H. Radebaugh is the emeritus Kay and Yvonne Whitmore Professor of International Business and former Director of the Whitmore Global Management Center/CIBER at Brigham Young University. He received his MBA and DBA from Indiana University. He was a faculty member at The Pennsylvania State University from 1972 to 1980. He also has been a visiting professor at Escuela de Administración de Negocios para Graduados (ESAN) in Lima, Peru. In 1985, Professor Radebaugh was the James Cusator Wards visiting professor at Glasgow University, Scotland. His other books include *International Accounting and Multinational Enterprises* (John Wiley and Sons, 6th edition) with S. J. Gray and Erv Black; *Introduction to Business: International Dimensions* (South-Western Publishing Company) with John D. Daniels; and seven books on Canada–U.S. trade and investment relations, with Earl Fry as coeditor. He has also published several other monographs and articles on international business and international accounting in journals such as the *Journal of Accounting Research, Journal of International Financial Management and Accounting, Journal of International Business Studies*, and the *International Journal of Accounting*. He is the former editor of the *Journal of International Accounting Research* and area editor of the *Journal of International Business Studies*. His primary teaching interests are international business and international accounting. Professor Radebaugh has been an active member of the American Accounting Association, the European Accounting Association, the International Association of Accounting Education and Research, and the Academy of International Business, having served on several committees as the president of the International Section of the AAA and as the secretary treasurer of the AIB. He is a member of the Fellows of the Academy of International Business. In 2007, Professor Radebaugh received the Outstanding International Accounting Service Award of the International Accounting Section of the American Accounting Association, and in 1998, he was named International Person of the Year in the state of Utah and Outstanding International Educator of the International Section of the American Accounting Association. In 2012, Lee was honored when the award for the top article published in the *Journal of International Accounting Research* in the past decade was named the Lee H. Radebaugh Notable Contribution to International Accounting Research.

Daniel P. Sullivan, Professor of International Business at the Alfred Lerner College of Business of the University of Delaware, received his PhD from the University of South Carolina. He researches a range of topics, including globalization and business, international management, global strategy, competitive analysis, and corporate governance. His work on these topics has been published in leading scholarly journals, including the *Journal of International Business Studies, Management International Review, Law and Society Review*, and *Academy of Management Journal*. In addition, he has served on the editorial boards of the *Journal of International Business Studies* and *Management International Review*. Professor Sullivan has been honored for both his research and teaching, receiving grants and winning awards for both activities while at the University of Delaware and, his former affiliation, the Freeman School of Tulane University. He has been awarded numerous teaching honors at the undergraduate, MBA, and EMBA levels—most notably, he has been voted Outstanding

Teacher by the students of 18 different executive, MBA, and undergraduate classes at the University of Delaware and Tulane University. Professor Sullivan has taught, designed, and administered a range of in-class and online graduate, undergraduate, and nondegree courses on topics spanning globalization and business, international business operations, international management, strategic perspectives, executive leadership, and corporate strategy. In the United States, he has delivered lectures and courses at several university sites and company facilities. In addition, he has led courses in several foreign countries, including China, Hong Kong, Bulgaria, the Czech Republic, France, South Korea, Switzerland, Taiwan, and the United Kingdom. Finally, he has worked with many managers and consulted with several multinational enterprises on issues of international business.

An Atlas

Satellite television transmission now makes it commonplace for us to watch events as they unfold in other countries. Transportation and communication advances and government-to-government accords have contributed to our increasing dependence on foreign goods and markets. As this dependence grows, updated maps are a valuable tool. They can show the locations of population, economic wealth, production, and markets; portray certain commonalities and differences among areas; and illustrate barriers that might inhibit trade. In spite of the usefulness of maps, a substantial number of people worldwide have a poor knowledge of how to interpret information on maps and even of how to find the location of events that affect their lives.

We urge you to use the following maps to build your awareness of geography.

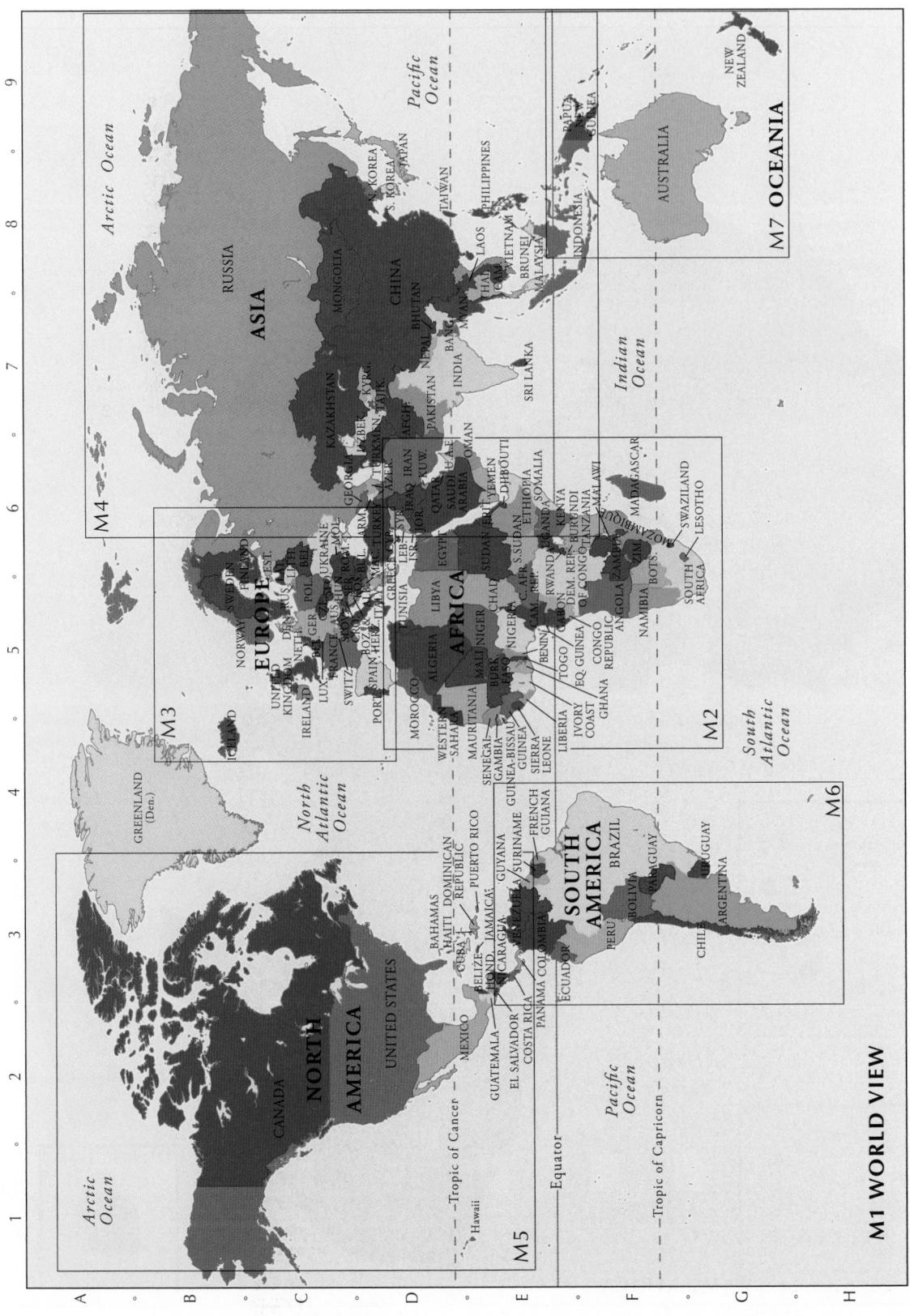

M1 WORLD VIEW

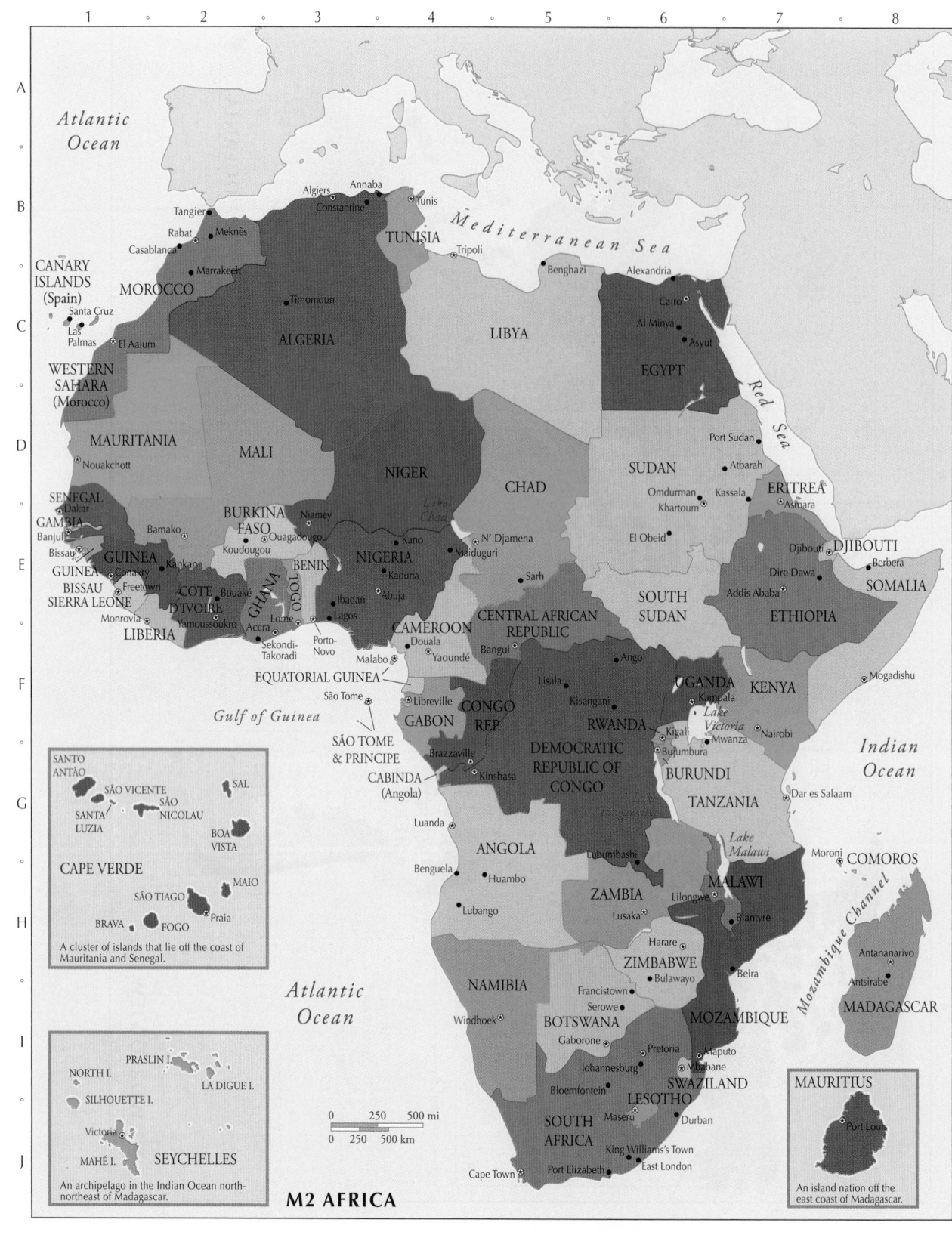

1   2   3   4   5   6   7   8

A

Atlantic Ocean

B

Algiers   Annaba
Tangier   Constantine   Tunis
Rabat   Meknès
Casablanca   TUNISIA
Tripoli
Mediterranean Sea
Benghazi   Alexandria
Marrakech   Cairo
CANARY ISLANDS (Spain)   Al Minya
Santa Cruz   Timomoun   Asyut
Las Palmas   El Aaiun   ALGERIA   LIBYA   EGYPT

C

MOROCCO

WESTERN SAHARA (Morocco)

Red Sea

D

MAURITANIA   MALI   Port Sudan
Nouakchott   NIGER   CHAD   SUDAN   Atbarah
Omdurman   Kassala   ERITREA
SENEGAL   BURKINA   Khartoum   Asmara
Dakar   FASO   Niamey   N' Djamena   El Obeid   Djibouti   DJIBOUTI
GAMBIA   Bamako   Ouagadougou   Kano   Maiduguri   Dire Dawa   Berbera
Banjul   Koudougou   NIGERIA   Sarh   Addis Ababa   SOMALIA
GUINEA   Kankan   Kaduna   SOUTH   ETHIOPIA
GUINEA   Conakry   Bouaké   Abuja   CENTRAL AFRICAN   SUDAN
BISSAU   Freetown   COTE   Ibadan   REPUBLIC   Mogadishu
SIERRA LEONE   D'IVOIRE   Lagos   Ango
Monrovia   Yamoussoukro   Accra   Lomé   CAMEROON   Bangui   UGANDA   KENYA
LIBERIA   Sekondi-   Porto-   Douala   Lisala   Kampala   *Lake*
Takoradi   Novo   Malabo   Yaoundé   Kisangani   *Victoria*   Nairobi
EQUATORIAL GUINEA   CONGO   RWANDA   Kigali   Mwanza   *Indian Ocean*
São Tomé   REP.   Bujumbura
Gulf of Guinea   Libreville   GABON   DEMOCRATIC   BURUNDI
SÃO TOME   REPUBLIC OF   Dar es Salaam
& PRINCIPE   Brazzaville   CONGO   TANZANIA
CABINDA   Kinshasa   *Lake*   *Lake*   Moroni   COMOROS
(Angola)   *Tanganyika*   *Malawi*
Luanda   MALAWI   Antananarivo
ANGOLA   Lubumbashi   Lilongwe   Antsirabe
Benguela   Huambo   ZAMBIA   Blantyre   MADAGASCAR
Lubango   Lusaka   Beira
Harare
ZIMBABWE   *Mozambique Channel*
Bulawayo
Atlantic Ocean   NAMIBIA   Francistown
Serowe   MOZAMBIQUE
Windhoek   BOTSWANA   Maputo
Gaborone   Pretoria   Mbabane
Johannesburg   SWAZILAND   MAURITIUS
Bloemfontein   LESOTHO   Port Louis
SOUTH   Maseru   Durban
AFRICA   King Williams's Town   An island nation off the
Cape Town   Port Elizabeth   East London   east coast of Madagascar.

E

F

G

H

I

J

SANTO ANTÃO   SAL
SÃO VICENTE   SÃO
SANTA   NICOLAU
LUZIA   BOA
VISTA
CAPE VERDE
MAIO
SÃO TIAGO
BRAVA   FOGO   Praia
A cluster of islands that lie off the coast of
Mauritania and Senegal.

PRASLIN I.
NORTH I.   LA DIGUE I.
SILHOUETTE I.
Victoria
MAHÉ I.   SEYCHELLES
An archipelago in the Indian Ocean north-
northeast of Madagascar.

0   250   500 mi
0   250   500 km

M2 AFRICA

M3 EUROPE

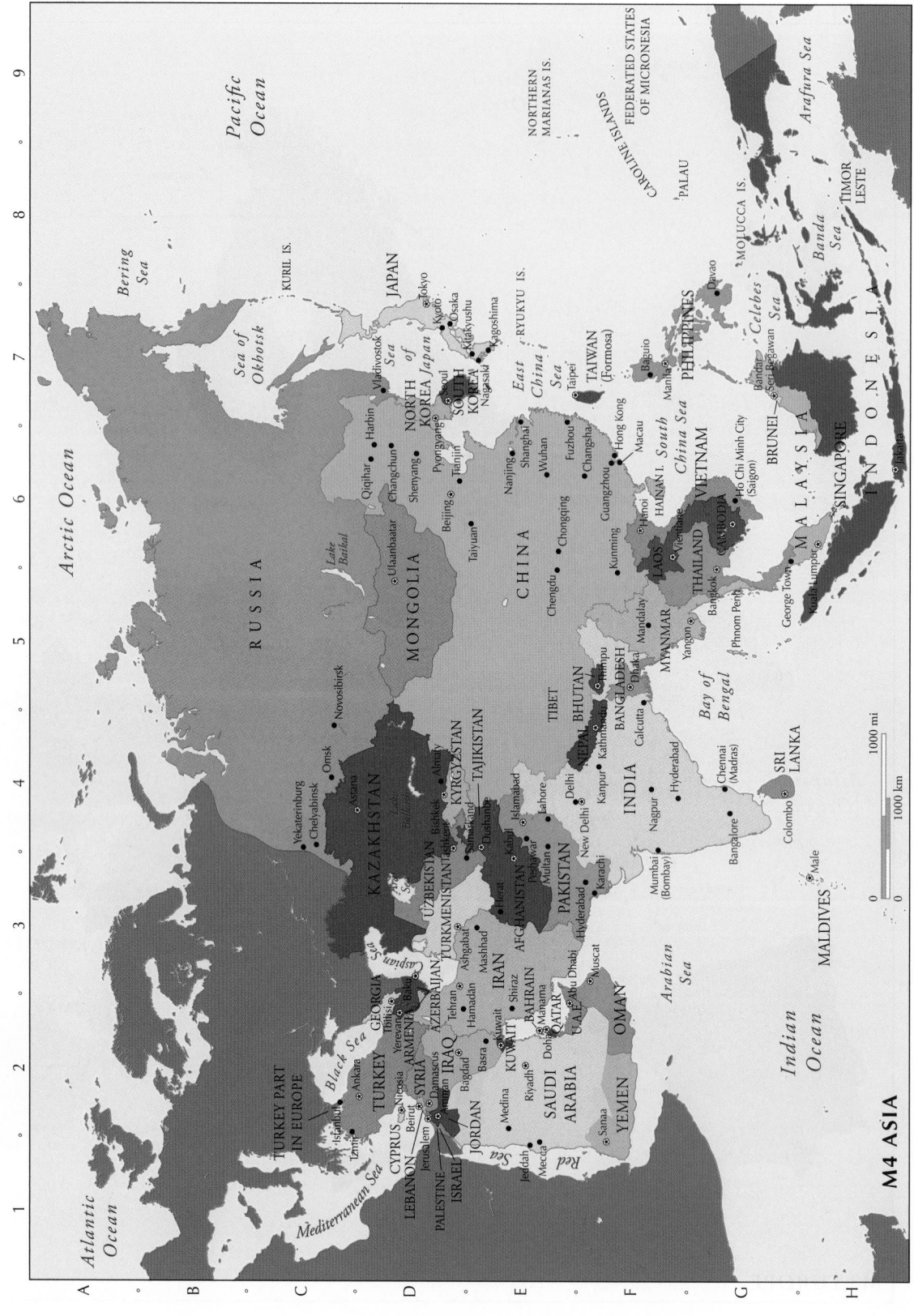

M4 ASIA

Atlantic Ocean

Arctic Ocean

Pacific Ocean

Bering Sea

Sea of Okhotsk

KURIL IS.

RUSSIA

Lake Baikal

Novosibirsk

Omsk

Chelyabinsk

Yekaterinburg

Vladivostok

JAPAN

Sea of Japan

Tokyo

Kyoto

Osaka

Kitakyushu

Nagasaki

Kagoshima

RYUKYU IS.

NORTH OF KOREA

Harbin

Qiqihar

Changchun

Shenyang

Pyongyang

SOUTH KOREA

Seoul

Tianjin

Beijing

Ulaanbaatar

MONGOLIA

Taiyuan

CHINA

Nanjing

Shanghai

Wuhan

Chengdu

Chongqing

Kunming

Fuzhou

Changsha

Guangzhou

Hong Kong

Macau

East China Sea

South China Sea

TAIWAN (Formosa)

Taipei

PHILIPPINES

Baguio

Manila

Davao

NORTHERN MARIANAS IS.

CAROLINE ISLANDS

PALAU

FEDERATED STATES OF MICRONESIA

Arafura Sea

Banda Sea

Celebes Sea

MOLUCCA IS.

TIMOR LESTE

INDONESIA

SINGAPORE

MALAYSIA

Kuala Lumpur

George Town

BRUNEI

Bandar Seri Begawan

Jakarta

VIETNAM

Ho Chi Minh City (Saigon)

Hanoi

HAINAN I.

LAOS

Vientiane

CAMBODIA

Phnom Penh

THAILAND

Bangkok

MYANMAR

Yangon

Mandalay

Naypyidaw

BANGLADESH

Dhaka

BHUTAN

Thimpu

NEPAL

Kathmandu

TIBET

Bay of Bengal

Calcutta

Kanpur

New Delhi

Delhi

INDIA

Nagpur

Hyderabad

Chennai (Madras)

Bangalore

SRI LANKA

Colombo

MALDIVES

Male

Mumbai (Bombay)

Indian Ocean

Arabian Sea

Karachi

Hyderabad

PAKISTAN

Multan

Lahore

Islamabad

Peshawar

Kabul

AFGHANISTAN

Herat

Mashhad

IRAN

Tehran

Hamadan

Shiraz

Muscat

OMAN

U.A.E.

Abu Dhabi

QATAR

Doha

BAHRAIN

Manama

KUWAIT

Kuwait

Basra

Baghdad

IRAQ

Riyadh

SAUDI ARABIA

Medina

Mecca

Jeddah

YEMEN

Sanaa

Red Sea

JORDAN

ISRAEL

PALESTINE

Jerusalem

Amman

Damascus

SYRIA

LEBANON

Beirut

CYPRUS

Nicosia

TURKEY

Ankara

Istanbul

Izmir

TURKEY PART IN EUROPE

Black Sea

Mediterranean Sea

GEORGIA

Tbilisi

ARMENIA

Yerevan

AZERBAIJAN

Baku

Caspian Sea

TURKMENISTAN

Ashgabat

UZBEKISTAN

Tashkent

Samarkand

Dushanbe

TAJIKISTAN

KYRGYZSTAN

Bishkek

Almaty

Aral Sea

Astana

KAZAKHSTAN

Lake Balkhash

1000 mi

1000 km

0

1 2 3 4 5 6 7 8

Arctic Sea

GREENLAND

ELLESMERE I.

PARRY IS.

Baffin Bay

Beaufort Sea

BANKS I.

BAFFIN I.

Davis Strait

Bering Sea

VICTORIA I.

Fairbanks

Anchorage

Labrador Sea

Gulf of Alaska

Juneau

CANADA

Hudson Bay

NEWFOUNDLAND

St. John's

Gulf of St. Lawrence

Edmonton

Calgary   Regina   Winnipeg

Quebec   Halifax

Montréal

Vancouver   Ottawa   Burlington

Pacific Ocean

Seattle   Toronto   Boston

Tacoma   Spokane   Hartford   Providence

Portland   Helena   Bismarck   Buffalo   New York

Minneapolis   Detroit   Philadelphia

UNITED STATES   Milwaukee   Pittsburgh   Baltimore

Chicago   Cleveland   Washington, D.C.

Great Salt Lake   Salt Lake City   Omaha   Des Moines   Cincinnati   Richmond

Sacramento   Provo   Kansas City   Indianapolis   Norfolk

Boulder   St. Louis   Louisville   Winston-Salem

San Francisco   Denver   Wichita   Charlotte   **Atlantic Ocean**

Las Vegas   Tulsa   Little Rock   Memphis   Columbia   BERMUDA

Los Angeles   Albuquerque   Oklahoma City   Atlanta   Savannah

Phoenix   Dallas   Jackson   Jacksonville

San Diego   Fort Worth   Shreveport   Mobile   Orlando

Tijuana   Tucson   El Paso   New Orleans

Ciudad   San Antonio   Houston   St. Petersburg   **BAHAMAS**   Turks and Caicos Islands

Juárez   Corpus Cristi   Miami

HAWAIIAN ISLANDS (U.S.)   *Gulf of Mexico*   **WEST INDIES**   DOMINICAN REPUBLIC

Torreón   Havana   CUBA   HAITI

MEXICO   Monterrey   Nassau   Santo Domingo

EASTERN CARIBBEAN   Mérida   Cancún   Port-au-Prince

VIRGIN ISLANDS (U.S. & Br.)   SAINT MARTIN   Guadalajara   León   JAMAICA   Kingston

DOMINICAN REPUBLIC   ANGUILLA   ANTIGUA & BARBUDA   Mexico City   BELIZE   *Caribbean Sea*

San Juan   Puebla   Belmopan

Santo Domingo   PUERTO RICO   ST. KITTS & NEVIS   MONTSERRAT (Br.)   Acapulco   GUATEMALA   HONDURAS

Caribbean   DOMINICA   GUADELOUPE (Fr.)   Tegucigalpa   NICARAGUA

CURAÇAO (Neth.)   MARTINIQUE (Fr.)   ST LUCIA   Guatemala   EL SALVADOR   Managua

BONAIRE (Neth.)   ST VINCENT & THE GRENADINES   BARBADOS   COSTA RICA   Panama

GRENADA   San José   PANAMA

ARUBA (Neth.)   Port of Spain   TRINIDAD & TOBAGO

0   2000 mi

0   2000 km

M5 NORTH AMERICA

M6 SOUTH AMERICA

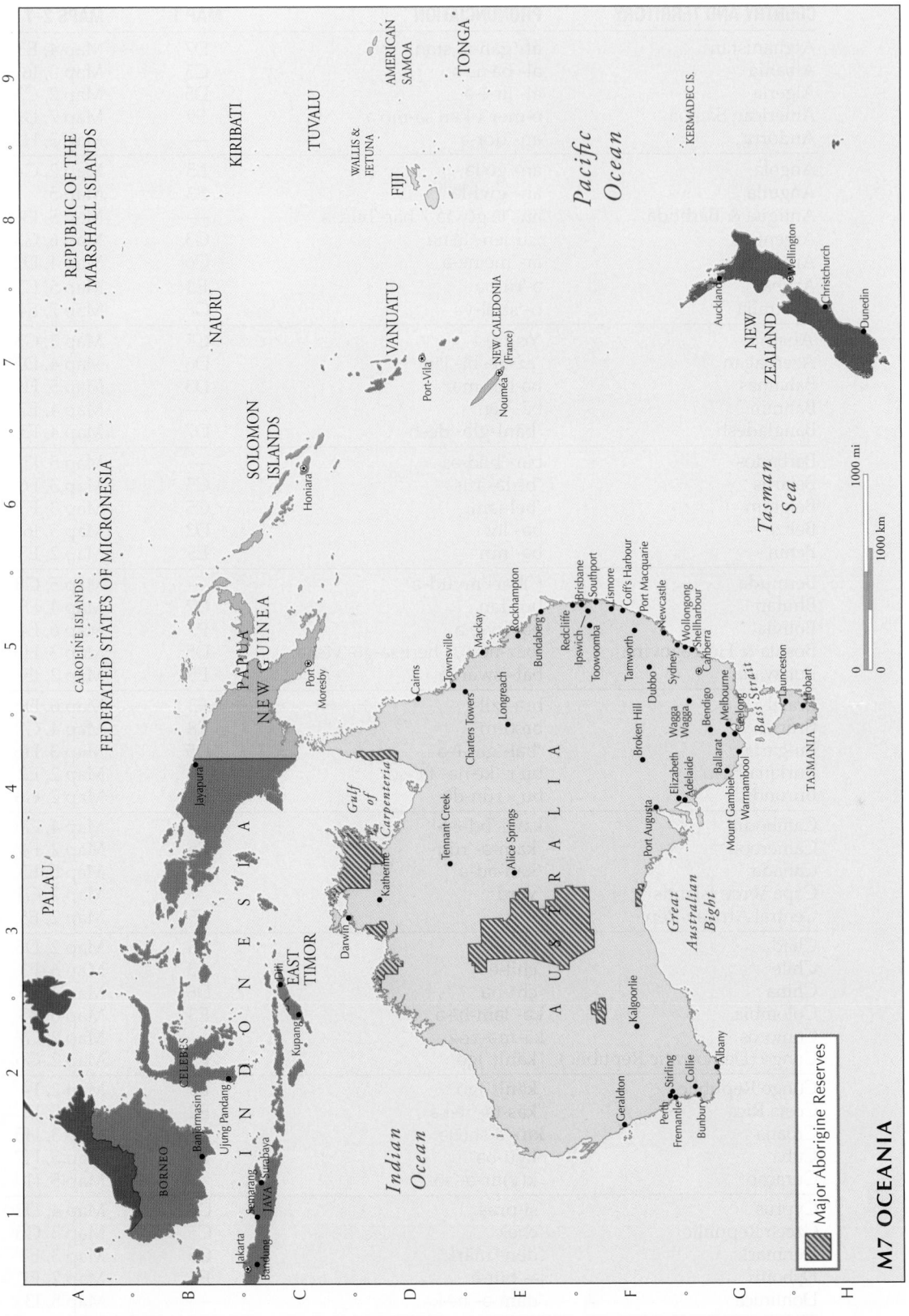

M7 OCEANIA

Major Aborigine Reserves

COUNTRY AND TERRITORY	PRONUNCIATION	MAP 1	MAPS 2–7
Afghanistan	af-ˈgan-ə-ˌstan	D7	Map 4, E3
Albania	al-ˈbā-nē-ə	C5	Map 3, I6
Algeria	al-ˈjir-ē-ə	D5	Map 2, C3
American Samoa	ə-merˈi-kən sə-mōˈə	F9	Map 7, D9
Andorra	an-ˈdȯr-ə	—	Map 3, H2
Angola	an-ˈgō-lə	E5	Map 2, G4
Anguila	an-ˈgwi-lə	E3	Map 5
Antigua & Barbuda	an-ˈtē-g(w)ə / bär-ˈbüd-ə	—	Map 5, I3
Argentina	ˌär-jen-ˈtē-nə	G3	Map 6, G3
Armenia	är-ˈmē-ne-ə	C6	Map 4, D2
Aruba	ə-ˈrü-bə	E3	Map 5, I7
Australia	ȯ-ˈstrāl-yə	G8	Map 7, E4
Austria	ˈȯs-trē-ə	C5	Map 3, G5
Azerbaijan	ˈaz-ər-ˈbī-ˈjän	D6	Map 4, D2
Bahamas	bə-häˈ-məz	D3	Map 5, H7
Bahrain	bä-ˈr ān	—	Map 4, E2
Bangladesh	ˈbänJ-glə-ˈdesh	D7	Map 4, F5
Barbados	bär-ˈb ād-əs	—	Map 5, J3
Belarus	ˈbē-lə-ˈrüs	C5	Map 3, F6
Belgium	ˈbel-jəm	C5	Map 3, F3
Belize	bə-ˈlēz	D2	Map 5, I6
Benin	bə-ˈnin	E5	Map 2, E3
Bermuda	(ˈ)bər-ˈmyüd-ə	—	Map 5, G8
Bhutan	bü-ˈtan	D7	Map 4, F5
Bolivia	bə-ˈliv-ē-ə	F3	Map 6, E4
Bosnia & Herzegovina	ˈbäz-nē-ə / ˈhert-sə-gō-ˈvē-nə	D5	Map 3, H5
Botswana	bät-ˈswän-ə	F5	Map 2, I5
Brazil	brə-ˈzil	F3	Map 6, D6
Brunei	brōo-nīˈ	E8	Map 4, G7
Bulgaria	ˈbəl-ˈgar-ē-ə	D5	Map 3, H6
Burkina Faso	buˈr-ˈkē-nə-ˈfaˈ-sō	E5	Map 2, E2
Burundi	buˈ-ˈrün-dē	E6	Map 2, G6
Cambodia	kam-ˈbd-ē-ə	E7	Map 4, G6
Cameroon	ˈkam-ə-ˈrün	E5	Map 2, F4
Canada	ˈkan-əd-ə	C2	Map 5, E5
Cape Verde Islands	ˈvard	—	Map 2, G1
Central African Rep.		E5	Map 2, E5
Chad	ˈchad	E5	Map 2, D5
Chile	ˈchil-ē	G3	Map 6, F3
China	ˈchī-nə	D8	Map 4, E5
Colombia	kə-ˈləm-bē-ə	E3	Map 6, B3
Comoros	kä-mə-ˌrōz	—	Map 2, G7
Congo (Democratic Republic)	ˈkänJ(ˈ)gō	E5	Map 2, G5
Congo Republic	ˈkänJ(ˈ)gō	E5	Map 2, F4
Costa Rica	ˈkäs-tə-ˈrē-kə	E2	Map 5, J7
Croatia	krō-ˈā-sh(ē)ə	D5	Map 3, H5
Cuba	ˈkyü-bə	E3	Map 5, H7
Curaçao	ˈk(y)ür-ə-ˈsō	—	Map 5, J1
Cyprus	ˈsī-prəs	D6	Map 4, D2
Czech Republic	ˈchek	C5	Map 3, G5
Denmark	ˈden-ˈmärk	C5	Map 3, E4
Djibouti	jə-ˈbüt-ē	E6	Map 2, E7
Dominica	ˈdäm-ə-ˈnē-kə	—	Map 5, I3
Dominican Republic	də-ˈmin-i-kən	E3	Map 5, H8
Ecuador	ˈek-wə-ˈdȯ(ə)r	E3	Map 6, C2
Egypt	ˈē-jəpt	D5	Map 2, C6
El Salvador	el-ˈsal-və-ˈdȯ(ə)r	E2	Map 5, I6
Equatorial Guinea	ē-kwaˈ-tōr-ēal ˈgi-nē	E5	Map 2, F4

COUNTRY AND TERRITORY	PRONUNCIATION	MAP 1	MAPS 2–7
Eritrea	´er-ə-´trē-ə	E6	Map 2, D7
Estonia	e-´stō-nē-ə	C5	Map 3, D6
Ethiopia	´ē-thē-´ō-pē-ə	E6	Map 2, E7
Falkland Islands	´fȯ(l)-klənd	—	Map 6, J4
Faroe Islands	fer -(ˌ)ō	—	Map 3, C2
Fiji	´fē-jē	—	Map 7, D8
Finland	´fin-lənd	B5	Map 3, C6
France	´fran(t)s	C5	Map 3, G3
French Guiana	gē-´an-ə	E3	Map 6, B5
Gabon	ga-´bōn	E5	Map 2, F4
Gambia	´gam-bē-ə	E4	Map 2, E1
Georgia	´jȯr-jə	C6	Map 4, D2
Germany	´jerm-(ə-)nē	C5	Map 3, F4
Ghana	´gän-ə	E5	Map 2, E2
Greece	´grēs	D5	Map 3, I6
Greenland	´grēn-lənd	A4	Map 5, B7
Grenada	grə-nā´də	—	Map 5, J3
Guam		—	
Guatemala	´gwät-ə-´mäl-ə	E2	Map 5, I6
Guinea	´gin-ē	E4	Map 2, E1
Guinea-Bissau	´gin-ē-bis-´au˙	E4	Map 2, E1
Guyana	gī-´an-ə	E3	Map 6, B4
Haiti	´hāt-ē	E3	Map 5, H8
Honduras	hän-´d(y)u˙r-əs	E2	Map 5, I7
Hong Kong	´hänJ-´känJ	—	Map 4, F6
Hungary	´hənJ-g(ə)rē	C5	Map 3, G5
Iceland	´ī-slənd	B4	Map 3, B1
India	´in-dê-ə	D7	Map 4, F4
Indonesia	´in-də-´nē-zhə	E8	Map 4, H7; Map 7, B3
Iran	i-´rän	D6	Map 4, E3
Iraq	i-´räk	D6	Map 4, D2
Ireland	´ī(ə)r-lənd	C5	Map 3, F1
Israel	´iz-rē-əl	D6	Map 4, D2
Italy	´it-əl-ē	D6	Map 3, H4
Ivory Coast (Cote D'Ivoire)	ī´və-rē	E5	Map 2, E2
Jamaica	jə-´mā-kə	E3	Map 5, I7
Japan	jə-´pan	D8	Map 4, D7
Jordan	´jȯrd-ən	D6	Map 4, D2
Kazakhstan	kə-´zak-´stan	D7	Map 4, D4
Kenya	´ken-yə	E6	Map 2, F7
Kiribati	kîr-ì-bàs´	—	Map 7, B8
Korea, North	kə-´rē-ə	D8	Map 4, D7
Korea, South	kə-´rē-ə	D8	Map 4, D7
Kosovo	´Ko-sō-vō	C5	Map 3, H6
Kuwait	kə-´wāt	D6	Map 4, E2
Kyrgyzstan	kîr-gē-stän´	D7	Map 4, D4
Laos	´lau˙s	D7	Map 4, F5
Latvia	´lat-vē-ə	C5	Map 3, E6
Lebanon	´leb-ə-nən	D6	Map 4, D2
Lesotho	lə-´sō-(´)tō	F6	Map 2, J6
Liberia	lī-´bir-ē-ə	E5	Map 2, F2
Libya	´lib-ē-ə	D5	Map 2, C4
Liechtenstein	lìk´tən-stīn´	—	Map 3, G4
Lithuania	´lith-(y)ə-´wā-nē-ə	C5	Map 3, E6
Luxembourg	´lək-səm-´bərg	C5	Map 3, G3
Macao SAR	mə- ´kau˙	—	Map 4, F6

COUNTRY AND TERRITORY	PRONUNCIATION	MAP 1	MAPS 2–7
Macedonia	′mas-ə-′dō-nyə	D6	Map 3, H6
Madagascar	′mad-ə-′gas-kər	F6	Map 2, I8
Malawi	mə-′lä-wē	F6	Map 2, H6
Malaysia	mə-′lā-zh(ē-)ə	E8	Map 4, G6
Maldives	môl′dīvz	—	Map 4, H3
Mali	′mäl-ē	D5	Map 2, D2
Malta	′mȯl-tə	—	Map 3, J5
Marshall Islands	mär′shəl	—	Map 7, A8
Mauritania	′mȯr-ə-′tā-nē-ə	D5	Map 2, D1
Montenegro	′män-tə-′nē-grō	—	
Mauritius	mȯ-′rish′əs	—	Map 2, J8
Mexico	′mek-si-′kō	D2	Map 5, I5
Micronesia	mī′krō-nē′zhə	—	Map 7, A5
Moldova	mäl-′dō-və	D6	Map 3, G7
Mongolia	män-′gōl-yə	D8	Map 4, D5
Morocco	mə-′räk-(′)ō	D5	Map 2, B2
Mozambique	′mō-zəm-′bēk	F6	Map 2, H6
Myanmar	′myän-′mär	E7	Map 4, F5
Namibia	nə-′mib-ē-ə	F5	Map 2, I4
Naura	nä′-ü-rü	—	Map 7, B7
Nepal	nə-′pȯl	D7	Map 4, F4
Netherlands	′neth-ər-lən(d)z	C5	Map 3, F3
New Caledonia	′kal-ə-′dō-nyə	—	Map 7, E7
New Zealand	′zē-lənd	G9	Map 7, H7
Nicaragua	′nik-ə-′räg-wə	E3	Map 5, I7
Niger	′nī-jər	E5	Map 2, D4
Nigeria	nī-′jir-ē-ə	E5	Map 2, E4
Norway	′nȯ(ə)r-′wā	C5	Map 3, D4
Oman	ō-′män	E6	Map 4, F2
Pakistan	′pak-i-′stan	D7	Map 4, E3
Palau	pä-lou′	—	Map 7, A3
Palestine	pa-lə-′stīn	—	Map 4, D1
Panama	′pan-ə-′mä	E3	Map 5, J8
Papua New Guinea	′pap-yə-wə	F9	Map 7, C5
Paraguay	′par-ə-′gwī	F3	Map 6, E4
Peru	pə-′rü	F3	Map 6, D2
Philippines	′fil-ə-′pēnz	E8	Map 4, F7
Poland	′pō-lənd	D5	Map 3, F5
Portugal	′pōr-chi-gəl	D5	Map 3, I1
Puerto Rico	′pōrt-ə-′rē(′)kō	E3	Map 5, I2
Qatar	′kät-ər	D6	Map 4, E2
Romania	rō-′ā-nē-ə	D5	Map 3, H6
Russia	′rəsh-ə	C7	Map 3, D7; Map 4, C5
Rwanda	ru′-′än-də	E6	Map 2, F6
St. Kitts & Nevis	′kits / ′nē-vəs	—	Map 5, I3
St. Lucia	sānt-′lü-shə	—	Map 5, I3
St. Martin	sānt- ′mär-tᵗn	—	Map 5
St. Vincent and the Grenadines	grèn′ə-dēnz′	—	Map 5, J3
San Marino	sàn mə-rē′nō	—	Map 3, H4
São Tomé and Príncipe	soun tōə-mè′prēn′-sēpə	—	Map 2, F3
Saudi Arabia	′sau′d-ē	E6	Map 4, E2
Senegal	′sen-i-′g′l	E4	Map 2, D1
Serbia	′sər-bē-ə	D5	Map 3, H6
Seychelles	sā-shèlz′	—	Map 2, J1
Sierra Leone	sē-′er-ə-lē-′ōn	E4	Map 2, E1
Singapore	′sinJ-(g)ə-′pō(ə)r	—	Map 4, H6
Slovakia	slō-′väk-ē-ə	C5	Map 3, G5
Slovenia	slō-′vēn-ē-ə	C5	Map 3, H5

COUNTRY AND TERRITORY	PRONUNCIATION	MAP 1	MAPS 2–7
Solomon Islands	´säl-ə-mən	—	Map 7, C6
Somalia	sō-´mäl-ē-ə	E6	Map 2, F8
South Africa	´a-fri-kə	F6	Map 2, J5
South Sudan	sü-´dan	E6	Map 2, E6
Spain	´spān	C5	Map 3, I1
Sri Lanka	(´)srē-´länJ-kə	E7	Map 4, G4
Sudan	sü-´dan	E6	Map 2, E6
Suriname	su˙r-ə-´näm-ə	E3	Map 6, B5
Swaziland	´swäz-ē-´land	F6	Map 2, I6
Sweden	´swēd-ən	B5	Map 3, C5
Switzerland	´swit-sər-lənd	C5	Map 3, G4
Syria	´sir-ē-ə	D6	Map 4, D2
Taiwan	´tī-´wän	D8	Map 4, E7
Tajikistan	tä-´ji-ki-´stan	D7	Map 4, E4
Tanzania	´tan-zə-´nē-ə	F6	Map 2, G6
Thailand	´tī-land	E8	Map 4, F5
Timor Leste	tē-mōr-´lesh-ˌtā	—	Map 4, H8
Togo	´tō(´)gō	E5	Map 2, E3
Tonga	´tän-gə	—	Map 7, D9
Trinidad & Tobago	´trin-ə-´dad / tə-´bā-(´)gō	—	Map 5, J3
Tunisia	t(y)ü-´nē-zh(ē-)ə	D5	Map 2, B4
Turkey	´tər-kē	D6	Map 4, D2
Turkmenistan	tûrk´-men-i-stàn´	D6	Map 4, D3
Turks and Caicos Islands	tərks-ənd-´kā-kəs	—	Map 5, H8
Tuvalu	tü´-vä-lü	—	Map 7, C9
Uganda	(y)ü-´gan-də	E6	Map 2, F6
Ukraine	yü-´krān	C6	Map 3, F7
United Arab Emirates	yoo-nī´tid à r´əb i-mîr´its	D6	Map 4, E2
United Kingdom	king´dəm	C5	Map 3, F2
United States	yu˙-´nīt-əd-´stāts	D2	Map 5, F5
Uruguay	´(y)u˙r-ə-gwī	G3	Map 6, G5
Uzbekistan	(´)u˙z-´bek-i-´stan	C6	Map 4, D3
Vanuatu	van-ə-´wät-(´)ü	—	Map 7, D7
Vatican City	vàt´ ì-kən	—	Map 3, H4
Venezuela	´ven-əz(-ə)-´wā-lə	E3	Map 6, A4
Vietnam	vē-´et-´näm	E8	Map 4, G6
Virgin Islands (U.S.–Br.)		—	Map 5
Western Sahara	sə-hâr´ə	D4	Map 2, C1
Yemen	´yem-ən	E6	Map 4, F2
Zambia	´zam-bē-ə	F5	Map 2, H5
Zimbabwe	zim-´bäb-wē	F6	Map 2, H6

CHAPTER 1
International Business and Globalization

OBJECTIVES

After studying this chapter, you should be able to

1-1 Relate *globalization* and *international business* (IB) to each other and explain why their study is important

1-2 Grasp the forces driving globalization and IB

1-3 Discuss the major criticisms of globalization

1-4 Assess the major reasons companies seek to create value by engaging in IB

1-5 Define and illustrate the different operating modes for companies to accomplish their international objectives

1-6 Recognize why national differences in companies' external environments affect how they may best improve their IB performance

MyLab Management®
Improve Your Performance
When you see this icon ✪, visit
www.mymanagementlab.com for
activities that are applied, personalized,
and offer immediate feedback.

*The world's a stage; each plays his part,
and takes his share.*

—Dutch proverb

Source: Ahmad Faizal Yahya. Shutterstock

A group of cyclists in action during ▶
a cycling tour

The Globalized Business of Sports

Sports may be the world's most globalized business.[1] Fans demand to see the best, and "best" has become a global standard of competition. (The opening photo shows a marathon in Berlin, Germany that had runners from over 130 nations and more than a million spectators.) Satellite TV brings live events from just about anywhere in the world to fans just about anywhere else. This gives the key sports-business participants—athletes, team owners, league representatives, and sports associations—broadened audience exposure, expanded fan bases, and augmented revenues.

National sports federations' sponsorship of international competitions are common, most notably the longstanding World Cup in football (soccer) and the Olympics. More national organizations participate in these events than there are United Nations (UN) members, and probably more people follow them than follow most of the UN's activities. How do these international competitions relate to business? Cities and countries compete to host events to attract tourists and publicize their business opportunities. In turn, companies pay for marketing rights as sponsors. Finally, individual athletes, such as Michael Phelps in swimming, compete not only for medals, but also for lucrative contracts to endorse products.

While the Olympics and the World Cup participations have long been global, the competitive location has been less so. This has recently changed with the 2010 World Cup in South Africa, the 2016 Olympics in Brazil, and the 2022 World Cup in Qatar.

THE INTERNATIONAL JOB MARKET

The search for talent has become worldwide. Professional basketball scouts search remote areas of Nigeria for tall high-potential youngsters. Baseball agents provide live-in training camps for Dominican Republic teenagers in exchange for a percentage of their future professional signing bonuses. However, assembling talent is necessary but insufficient for making a sports business successful. Shrewd marketing and financial management are crucial too. For instance, Fútbol Barcelona, one of recent years' best professional soccer teams, turned to young business graduates to help reduce its financial problems.

Most of today's top-notch athletes are willing to follow the money anywhere. About two-thirds of the players in England's professional soccer league (Premiership) are from other countries, which helps improve the caliber of play and increase the TV fan base outside England.

How the ATP Courts Worldwide Support

You've probably noticed that individual sports professionals are globe hoppers. Take tennis. No country boasts enough fans to keep players at home for year-round competition, yet today's top-flight tennis pros come from every inhabited continent. For 2017 the Association of Tennis Professionals (ATP) sanctioned 68 tournaments in 33 countries. It also requires pros to compete in a certain number of events—and thus play in a number of countries—to maintain international rankings.

Because no tennis pro can possibly play in every tournament, organizers compete for top draws to fill stadium seats and land lucrative TV contracts. Prizes can be extremely generous (about US $2.7 million for each of the 2016 Australian Open singles champions).

Tournaments earn money through ticket sales, corporate sponsorship agreements, television contracts, and leasing of advertising space. The larger the stadium and TV audiences, the more backers and advertisers will pay to get their attention. Moreover, international broadcasts attract sponsorship from companies in various industries and countries.

From National to International Sports Pastimes

Some countries have legally designated a national sport as a means of preserving traditions; others effectively have one. Map 1.1 shows a sample of these. However, other sports have sometimes replaced national sports in popularity, such as cricket replacing field hockey as India's most popular sport.

Baseball was popular only in its North American birthplace for most of its history, but the International Baseball Federation now has over 100 member countries. As TV revenues flattened in North America, Major League Baseball (MLB) broadened its fan base by broadcasting games to international audiences, which also showed youngsters all over the world how the game was played. The average MLB clubhouse is now a bastion of multilingual camaraderie, with players and coaches talking baseball in Spanish, Japanese, Mandarin, and Korean as well as English.

THE WIDE WORLD OF TELEVISED SPORTS

Not surprisingly, other professional sports have expanded their global TV coverage (and marketing programs). Most viewers of Stanley Cup hockey watch from outside North America. Fans can watch NASCAR races (National Association for Stock Car Auto Racing) and NBA games in most countries.

TV isn't the only means by which sports organizations are seeking foreign fan bases and players. The National Football League (NFL) of the United States underwrites football programs in Chinese schools and plays some regular games in Europe. The NBA is helping to build basketball youth leagues in India.

MAP 1.1   Examples of National Sports

Some 63 countries have either defined a national sport by law or de facto have a national sport. Some national sports are shared by more than one country, such as cricket by England and seven of its former colonies. Some others have been established to protect an historical heritage, such as tejo in Colombia and pato in Argentina. Note also that Canada has two designations, one for winter and one for summer.

Source: The information on sports was taken from Wikipedia, http://en.wikipedia.org/wiki/National_sport (accessed March 18, 2016).

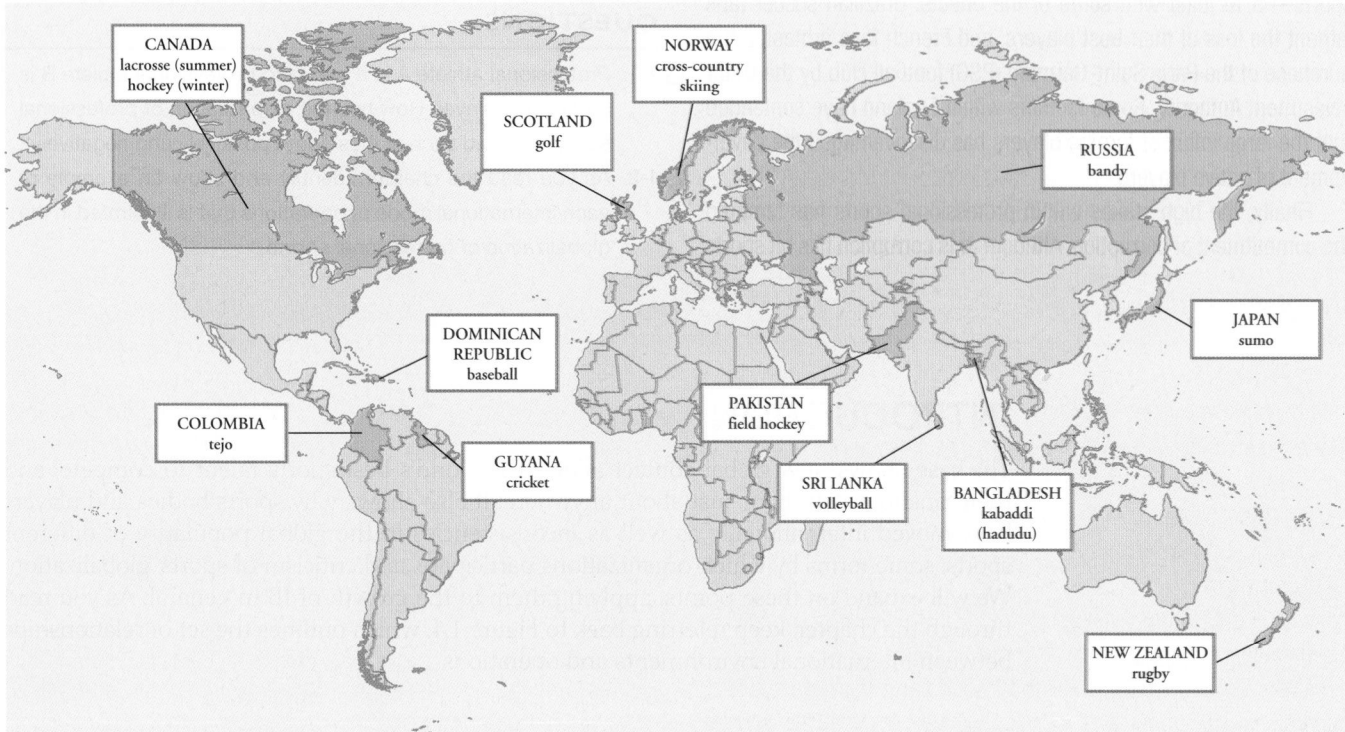

The Top-Notch Pro as Upscale Brand

Many top players are effectively global brands, such as U.S. tennis pro Serena Williams and Portuguese soccer forward Cristiano Ronaldo. Because of their sports success and charisma, companies within and outside the sports industry pay them handsomely for endorsing clothing, equipment, and other products.

Promotion as Teamwork

A few teams, such as the New York Yankees in baseball, the New Zealand All Blacks in rugby, and Manchester United (Man U) in soccer also have enough brand-name cachet to be global brands for selling clothing and other items. Just about every team can get something for the rights to use its logo, while some have enough name recognition to support global chains of retail outlets. Similarly, companies both sponsor and seek endorsements from well-known teams, such as the placement of "Fly Emirates" on Real Madrid's soccer jerseys.

Still others pay for naming rights to arenas and other venues. Of course, teams themselves can be attractive international investments. For instance, U.S. investors bought the Liverpool Football Club of the United Kingdom.

The Upsides and Downsides of Globalized Sports

What does all this mean to a sports fan? Now that pro sports have become a global phenomenon, fans can enjoy a greater variety—and a higher level of competition—than any former generation. That's the upside, but people don't always take easily to another country's sport. Despite many efforts, cricket, although popular in countries that were British colonies for centuries, is not popular elsewhere. Nor has American football gained much popularity outside the United States. One possible reason is that rules for cricket and American football are so complicated. However, basketball and soccer have traveled to new markets more readily because they are easier to understand and require little specialized equipment.

Further, there is disagreement about the economic effect of successfully winning a bid to host big international competitions such as the World Cup and Olympics. On the one hand, they help spur tourism, foreign investment, infrastructure construction, and improvement of blighted areas that will speed future economic growth. On the other hand, in light of threats from global terrorism, the cost of security has skyrocketed, while hosts may have to spend on stadiums and facilities that have no use afterward. Many competitions have ended with substantially increased local and national debt. Critics, therefore, often believe the funds would have been better spent on social services.

Nor is everyone happy with the unbridled globalization of sports—or at least with some of the effects. Brazilian soccer fans lament the loss of their best players, and French fans protested the purchase of the Paris Saint-Germain (PSG) football club by the Qatar Investment Authority. Some factions within England have contended that the large influx of foreign players has disadvantaged the development of native players.

Finally, the high stakes within professional sports has tempted the commitment of corruption. Although this corruption has hit sports as obscure as handball, the most notable recent instances have involved bribes to officials of FIFA (the soccer governing body) and the fixing of cricket matches in India. ■

QUESTIONS

★ **1-1.** Professional athlete A is a star, and professional athlete B is an average player. How has the globalization of professional sports affected each of these both positively and negatively?

★ **1-2.** As you read the chapter, identify and show an example of each international mode of operations that is illustrated in the globalization of professional sports.

INTRODUCTION

The case shows how global contact allows the world's best sports talent to compete, and their fans to watch them, just about anywhere. It also shows why sports bodies and players have moved internationally as well as inconsistencies in the global popularity of different sports, some forms by which organizations participate, and criticism of sports' globalization. We will expand on these points, applying them to the growth of IB in general. As you read through the chapter, keep referring back to Figure 1.1, which outlines the set of relationships between international environments and operations.

FIGURE 1.1   Factors in IB Operations

The conduct of a company's international operations depends on two factors: its objectives and the means by which it intends to achieve them. Likewise, its operations affect, and are affected by, two sets of factors: physical/social and competitive.

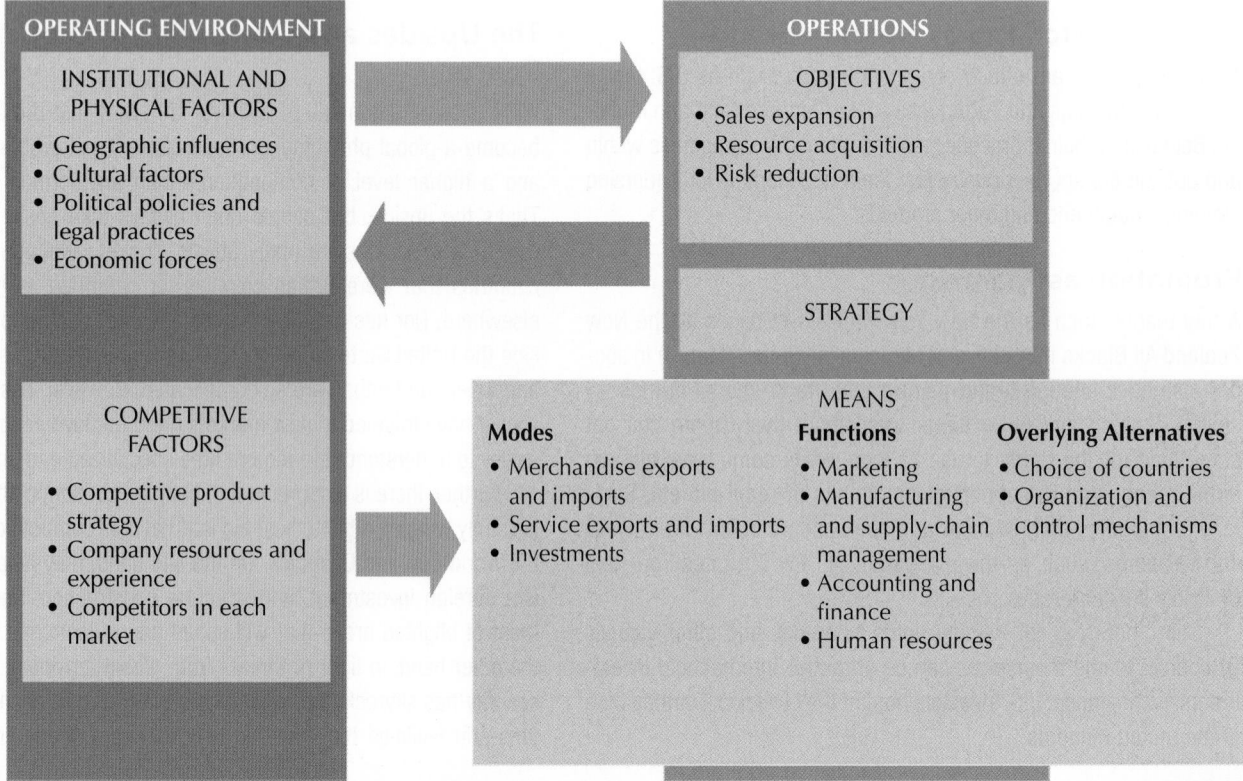

WHY STUDY ABOUT GLOBALIZATION, IB, AND THEIR RELATIONSHIP?

Globalization is the widening and deepening of interdependent relationships among people from different nations. The term sometimes refers to the elimination of barriers to international movements of goods, services, capital, technology, and people that influence the integration of world economies.[2] Throughout history, expanded human connections have extended people's access to more varied resources, products, services, and markets. We've altered the way we want and expect to live, and we've become more deeply affected (positively and negatively) by conditions outside our immediate domains.

Industries have expanded to distant places to gain supplies and markets. As consumers we know from "Made in" labels that we commonly buy products from all over the world, but these labels do not tell us everything. For instance, a Belgian Neuhaus bonbon and an American Ford automobile contain so many different components, ingredients, and specialized business activities from diverse countries that pinpointing where they were made is challenging.[3] Although Apple ships its iPhones from China and they appear to be Chinese products, less than 4 percent of their value is created in China.[4]

Globalization enables us to get more variety, better quality, or lower prices. Our meals contain spices that aren't grown domestically and fresh produce that may be out of season in the local climate. Our cars cost less than they would if all the parts were made and the labor performed in one place.

HOW DOES *IB* FIT IN?

IB consists of all commercial transactions between two or more countries.

- **The IB goal of private business is to make profits.**
- **Government IB may or may not be motivated by profit.**

The Relation to Globalization   The global connections between supplies and markets result from the activities of IB, which are all commercial transactions (including sales, investments, and transportation) that take place among countries. Private companies undertake such transactions for profit; governments may undertake them either for profit or for other reasons.

THE STUDY OF IB

Studying IB is important because

- **most companies are either international or compete with international companies,**
- **modes of operations may differ from those used domestically,**
- **it helps managers to decide where to find resources and to sell,**
- **the best way of conducting business may differ by country,**
- **an understanding helps you make better career decisions,**
- **an understanding helps you decide what governmental policies to support.**

Why should you study IB? Simply, it makes up a large and growing portion of the world's business. Global events and competition affect almost all industries and companies, large and small. Not only do companies sell output and secure supplies and resources abroad, they compete against products, services, and companies from foreign countries. Thus, most managers need to take into account IB when setting their operating strategies and practices. As a manager in almost any company you'll need to consider (1) where you can obtain the best inputs at the best possible price for your production and (2) where you can best sell the product or service you've put together from those inputs.

Understanding the Environment/Operations Relationship   The best way to do business abroad may not be the same as the best way within your domestic market. Why? First, when your company operates internationally, it will engage in *modes* of business, such as exporting and importing, which differ from those it uses domestically. Second, physical, institutional, and competitive conditions differ among countries and affect the optimum ways to conduct business. Thus, international companies have more diverse and complex operating environments than purely domestic ones.

Making Nonbusiness Decisions   Even if you never have direct IB responsibilities, understanding some of the complexities may be useful to you. Companies' international operations and their governmental regulations affect overall national conditions—economic growth, employment, consumer prices, national security—as well as the success of individual industries and firms. A better understanding of IB will help you make more informed decisions, such as where to work and what governmental policies to support.

THE FORCES DRIVING GLOBALIZATION AND IB

Although hard to measure, globalization

- has been growing,
- is less pervasive than generally thought,
- has economic and noneconomic dimensions,
- is stimulated by several factors.

Measuring globalization is problematic, especially for historical comparisons. First, a country's interdependence must be measured indirectly.[5] Second, when national boundaries shift, such as in the breakup of Ukraine, domestic business transactions can become international ones and vice versa. Nevertheless, various reliable indicators assure us that economic interdependence has been increasing, although sporadically, at least since the mid-twentieth century. Currently, about a quarter of world production is sold outside its country of origin, compared to about 7 percent in 1950. Restrictions on imports have generally been decreasing, and output from foreign-owned investments as a percentage of world production has increased. In periods of rapid economic growth, such as most years since World War II, world trade grows more rapidly than world production. However, in recessionary periods, global trade and investment shrink even more than the global economy.

At the same time, however, globalization is less pervasive than you might suppose. In fact, many Americans are surprised to learn that only about 15 percent of the value of U.S. consumption comes from other countries. In much of the world (especially in poor rural areas), people lack the resources to connect much beyond their isolated domains. Such isolation is changing quickly, though, especially since the advent of mobile phones.[6] (The below photo shows a solar-powered Internet café in Kenya, thus illustrating how innovation is enabling people in remote areas to access the rest of the world.) Only a few countries—mainly very small ones—either sell over half their production abroad or depend on foreign output for more than half their consumption. This means that most of the world's goods and services are still sold in the countries where they're produced. Moreover, the principal source of capital in most countries is domestic rather than international.

This solar-powered Internet café within a shipping container in a rural area of Kenya enables people in an impoverished village to have access to the rest of the world.

Source: Tony Karumba/Stringer/Getty Images

Granted, these measurements address only *economic* aspects of globalization. Various studies have made more comprehensive comparisons by including, say, people-to-people contacts through travel and communications, technological interchanges, government-to-government relationships, and acceptance and adaptation of attributes from foreign cultures such as words from other languages.[7] The studies' results have several commonalities:

- *Size of countries*—Smaller countries tend to be more globalized than larger ones, mainly because their smaller land masses and populations permit a lower variety of production.
- *Per capita incomes*—Countries with higher per capita incomes tend to be more globalized than those with lower ones because their citizens can better afford foreign products, travel, and communications.
- *Variance among globalization aspects*—Although a country may rank as highly globalized on one dimension, it may be low on another, such as the United States being high on technological scales but low on economic ones.

FACTORS IN INCREASED GLOBALIZATION

What factors have contributed to the growth of globalization in recent decades? Most analysts cite the following interrelated factors:

1. Rise in and application of technology
2. Liberalization of cross-border trade and resource movements
3. Development of services that support IB
4. Growth of consumer pressures
5. Increase in global competition
6. Changes in political situations and government policies
7. Expansion of cross-national cooperation

Rise in and Application of Technology   Many of the proverbial "modern marvels" and efficient means of production have come about fairly recently. These include new products, such as handheld mobile communications devices, as well as new applications of old products, such as Indian guar beans in oil and natural gas mining.[8] Thus, much of what we trade today either did not exist or was unimportant in trade a decade or two ago. Why have technical developments increased so much? More than half the scientists who have ever lived are alive today. One reason, of course, is population growth. But another is rising productivity—taking less time to produce the same thing—which frees up more people to *develop* new products because fewer people are necessary to *produce* them. This rising productivity also means that on average people can buy more, including the new products, by working the same number of hours. The entry of new products into the market creates a need for other complementary products (such as cases and apps for smartphones), thus accelerating the need for scientists and engineers.

Construction of many new products cannot successfully take place in a single country. Much new technical innovation takes so many financial and intellectual resources that companies from different countries must cooperate to take on portions of development. Further, when new products are developed, the optimum scale size of production seldom corresponds with the market demand in a single country. Consequently, companies may need to sell both domestically and internationally in order to spread the fixed developmental and production costs over more units of production.

Advances in Communications and Transportation   Strides in communications and transportation now allow us to discover, desire, and demand goods and services from abroad. Meanwhile, the costs of these strides have risen more slowly in most years than costs in general, thus increasing affordability. A three-minute phone call from New York to London that cost $10.80 in 1970 costs less than $0.20 today, while a call using Voice over Internet Protocol (VoIP) is virtually free.

Innovations in transportation mean that more countries can compete for sales to a given market. U.S. purchases of foreign-grown flowers used to be largely impractical and aimed only at high-income consumers; today, however, flower producers from as far away as Ecuador, Israel, the Netherlands, and New Zealand compete with each other for the U.S. market because growers can ship flowers quickly and economically.

Improved communications and transportation also enhance a manager's ability to oversee foreign operations, such as more easily visiting foreign facilities and communicating with managers therein. Thanks to the Internet, companies can instantly exchange pictures of samples. Even small companies can reach global customers and suppliers. However, you may ponder the following question: Has the Internet been a bigger force in globalization than the laying of the first transoceanic cable across the Atlantic in 1858 that reduced communication time from 10 days to a matter of a few minutes?

Liberalization of Cross-Border Trade and Resource Movements To protect its own industries, every country restricts the entry and exit of not only goods and services but also the resources—workers, capital, tools, and so on—needed to produce them. Such restrictions, of course, set limits on IB activities and, because regulations can change at any time, contribute to uncertainty. Over time, however, most governments have reduced such restrictions, primarily for three reasons:

1. Their citizens want a greater variety of goods and services at lower prices.
2. Competition spurs domestic producers to become more efficient.
3. They hope to induce other countries to lower their barriers in turn.

Services that Support IB Companies and governments have developed services that facilitate global commerce. For example, because of bank credit agreements—clearing arrangements that convert one currency into another and insurance that covers such risks as nonpayment and damage en route—most producers can be paid relatively easily for their sales abroad. When Nike sells sportswear to a French soccer team, a bank in France collects payment in euros from the soccer team when the shipment arrives at French customs and pays Nike in U.S. dollars through a U.S. bank.

Growth in Consumer Pressures More consumers know more today about products and services available in other countries, can afford to buy them, and want the greater variety, better quality, and lower prices offered by access to them. However, this demand is spread unevenly because of uneven affluence, both among and within countries as well as from year to year.

Consumer pressure has also spurred companies to spend more on research and development (R&D) and to search worldwide for innovations and products they can sell to ever-more-demanding consumers. By the same token, consumers are more proficient today at scouring the globe for better deals, such as searching the Internet for lower-priced prescription drugs abroad.

Increase in Global Competition Increased competitive pressures can persuade companies to buy or sell abroad. For example, a firm might introduce products into markets where competitors are already gaining sales, or seek supplies where competitors are getting cheaper or more attractive products. Once a few companies respond to foreign opportunities, others inevitably follow suit. And they learn from each other's foreign experiences. As the opening case suggests, the early success of foreign-born baseball players in U.S. leagues undoubtedly spurred U.S. basketball and football organizations to look for and develop talent abroad.[9]

So-called **born-global companies** start out with a global focus because of their founders' international experience[10] and because advances in communications give them a good idea of the location for global markets and supplies. Take SoundCloud, a Swedish audio-sharing web service. Its cofounders—one born in England and one in Sweden—were previously knowledgeable enough about the German and U.S. markets to move into both within months of starting up.[11] Regardless of industry, most firms and individuals have to become more global; in today's competitive business environment, failure to do so can be disastrous.

Changes in Political Situations and Government Policies   For nearly half a century after World War II, business between Communist countries and the rest of the world was minimal. Today, only a few countries are heavily isolated economically or do business almost entirely within a political bloc. In fact, political changes sometimes open new frontiers, such as diplomatic relations between the United States and Cuba. Nevertheless, governments still deny business with others for political reasons, such as many countries' sanctions against doing business with North Korea.

Governments support programs, such as improving airport and seaport facilities, to foster efficiencies for delivering goods internationally. They also now provide an array of services to help domestic companies sell more abroad, such as collecting information about foreign markets, furnishing contacts with potential buyers, and offering insurance against nonpayment in the home-country currency.

Expansion of Cross-National Cooperation   Governments have come to realize that their own interests can be addressed through international cooperation by means of treaties, agreements, and consultation. The willingness to pursue such policies is due largely to these three needs:

1. To gain reciprocal advantages
2. To attack problems jointly that one country acting alone cannot solve
3. To deal with areas of concern that lie outside the territory of any nation

Gain Reciprocal Advantages   Essentially, companies don't want to be disadvantaged when operating internationally, so they lobby their governments to act on their behalf. Thus, governments join international organizations and sign treaties and agreements with other governments for a variety of commercial activities. For instance, some treaties and agreements allow countries' commercial ships and planes to use each other's seaports and airports; some cover commercial-aircraft safety standards and flyover rights; and some protect property, such as foreign-owned investments, patents, trademarks, and copyrights. Countries also enact treaties for reciprocal reductions of import restrictions.

Multinational Problem Solving   Governments often act to coordinate activities along their mutual borders by building highways, railroads, and hydroelectric dams that serve the interests of all parties. (However, there are still border inefficiencies. For instance, trains between Italy and Sweden must change locomotives three or four times because of different national systems.)[12]

They also cooperate to solve problems that they either can't or won't solve alone. First, the needed resources may be too great for one country to manage. Further, sometimes no single country is willing to pay all the cost for a project that will also benefit another country. In any case, many problems are inherently global—think of countering global climate change or terrorism.

Second, one country's policies may affect those of others. Higher real-interest rates in one country, for example, can attract funds very quickly from individuals and firms in countries with lower rates, thus creating a shortage of investment funds in the latter. This movement is particularly disruptive to small developing economies.[13] Similarly, a country may weaken the value of its currency so that its products are cheaper in foreign markets. Thus buyers may switch to the newly cheaper country, hence contributing to unemployment in the country they forsook. To coordinate economic policies in these and other areas, the most economically important countries meet regularly to share information and pool ideas. The most notable coordination, known as the G20 countries, consists of 19 of the world's most economically important countries plus representation from the European Union of its members not included in the 19. These countries account for over 85 percent of the world's production, 80 percent of world trade, and about two-thirds of the world's population.

Areas Outside National Territories   Three global areas belong to no single country: the noncoastal areas of the oceans, outer space, and Antarctica. Until their commercial viability was demonstrated, they excited little interest for either exploitation or multinational cooperation. The oceans, however, contain food and mineral resources and constitute the surface over which much international commerce passes. Today, we need agreements to specify the amounts and methods of fishing, to address questions of oceanic mineral rights (such as on oil resources below the Arctic Ocean), and to deal with the piracy of ships.[14]

Likewise, there is disagreement on the commercial benefits to be reaped from outer space. Commercial satellites, for example, pass over countries that receive no direct benefit from them but argue that they should. If that sounds a little far-fetched, remember that countries do charge foreign airlines for flying over their territories.[15]

Antarctica, with minerals and abundant sea life along its coast, attracts thousands of tourists each year, has a highway leading to the South Pole and a Russian Orthodox church. Thus, it has been the subject of agreements to limit commercial exploitation. However, there is still disagreement about the continent's development—how much there should be and who does it.

THE CRITICISMS OF GLOBALIZATION

Critics of globalization claim

- countries' sovereignty is diminished,
- the resultant growth hurts the environment,
- some people lose both relatively and absolutely,
- greater insecurity increases personal stress.

Although we've discussed interrelated reasons for and the benefits from the rise in IB and globalization, the consequences of the rise are controversial. *Antiglobalization* forces regularly protest international conferences and governmental policies—sometimes violently. We focus here on three issues: *threats to national sovereignty, environmental stress,* and *growing income inequality and personal stress.*

THREATS TO NATIONAL SOVEREIGNTY

You've probably heard the slogan "Think globally, act locally," which means to accommodate local interests before global ones. Some observers worry that the proliferation of international agreements, particularly those that undermine local regulations on how goods are produced and sold, will diminish a nation's **sovereignty**—its freedom to "act locally" and without externally imposed restrictions.

The Question of Local Objectives and Policies   Countries seek to fulfill their citizens' objectives by setting policies reflecting national priorities, such as those governing worker protection and environmental practices. However, critics argue that these priorities are undermined by opening borders to trade. For example, if a country has stringent regulations on labor conditions and requires clean production methods, it may not be able to compete with countries that have less rigorous rules. By opening its borders to trade, it may either have to forgo its labor and environmental priorities to be competitive or face the downside of fewer jobs and economic output.

The Question of Small Economies' Overdependence   Critics complain that economically small countries depend too much on larger ones for supplies and sales. Thus, they are vulnerable to foreign mandates, including everything from defending certain UN positions to supporting a large economy's foreign military or economic actions. Nobel economist George Akerlof has noted that this dependence is intensified by poor countries' inadequate administrative capacity to deal with globalization.[16] Similarly, critics complain that large international corporations are powerful enough to dictate their operating terms (say, by threatening to relocate), exploit legal loopholes to avoid political oversight and taxes, and counter the small economies' best interests by favoring their home countries' political and economic interests.

The Question of Cultural Homogeneity   Finally, critics charge that globalization homogenizes merchandise, production methods, social structures, and even language, thus undermining the cultural foundation of sovereignty. In essence, they argue that countries have difficulty maintaining the traditional ways of life that unify and differentiate them. Fundamentally, they claim helplessness in stopping the incursion of foreign influences by such means as satellite television, print media, and Internet sites.[17]

ENVIRONMENTAL STRESS

Much critique of globalization revolves around the economic growth it brings. One argument is that growth in both production and international travel consumes more nonrenewable natural resources and increases environmental damage—despoliation through toxic runoff into rivers and oceans, air pollution from factory and vehicle emissions, and deforestation that can affect weather and climate. In addition, critics contend that buying from more distant locations increases transportation, hence increasing the *carbon footprint*, which refers to the total set of greenhouse gases emitted.[18] They point further to the more than 1000 container ships plying the seas and relying on heavy oil as a fuel; each pollutes as much as 50 million cars do.[19]

The Argument for Global Growth and Global Cooperation   However, other factions assert that globalization is positive for conserving natural resources and maintaining an environmentally sound planet—the former by fostering superior and uniform environmental standards and the latter by promoting global competition that encourages companies to seek resource-saving and eco-friendly technologies. A case in point is the automobile industry that has progressively produced cars that use less gas and emit fewer pollutants.

The positive effects of pursuing *global* interests may, nevertheless, conflict with *national* interests. Consider the effect of global pressure on Brazil to help protect the world's climate by curtailing logging activity in the Amazon region. Unemployed Brazilian workers have felt that job creation in the logging industry is more important than climate protection outside Brazil.

GROWING INCOME INEQUALITY AND PERSONAL STRESS

In terms of economic well-being, we look not only at our absolute situations but also compare ourselves to others. We generally don't find our economic status satisfactory unless we're doing better *and* keeping up with others.[20]

Income Inequality   By various measurements, income inequality, with some notable exceptions, has been growing both among and within many countries. Critics claim that globalization has affected this disparity by helping to develop a global superstar system, creating access to a greater supply of low-cost labor, and developing competition that leads to winners and losers.

The superstar system is especially apparent in sports, where today's global stars (as compared to past years) earn far more than the average professional player or professionals in less popular sports. The system carries over to other professions, such as in business, where charismatic leaders can command many times what others can.

Although globalization has brought unprecedented opportunities for firms to profit by gaining more sales and cheaper or better supplies, critics argue that profits have gone disproportionately to the top executives rather than to the rank and file. Nobel economist Robert Solow has supported this criticism by arguing that greater access to low-cost labor in poor countries has reduced the real wage growth of labor in rich countries.[21] And even if overall worldwide gains from globalization are positive, there are bound to be some absolute or relative losers (who will probably oppose globalization). The speed of global technological and competitive expansion creates more winners and losers along with changing the relative positions of individuals, companies, and countries. As an example, manufacturing and foreign sales growth in China and India have helped them to grow more rapidly than the United States, thus lessening the *relative* economic leadership of the United States over those countries.[22] Likewise, some workers have lost economic and social standing as manufacturing jobs have shifted to other countries. The challenge, therefore, is to maximize the gains from globalization while simultaneously minimizing the costs borne by the losers.

Personal Stress   Some repercussions of globalization can't be measured in strictly economic terms, such as people's stress from real and potential loss of relative economic and social positions.[23] Further, stress, if widespread, goes hand in hand with costly social unrest.[24] Although few of the world's problems are brand new, we may worry about them more now because globalized communications bring exotic sagas of misery into living rooms everywhere.[25]

Point

Is Offshoring of Production a Good Strategy?

Point   **Yes Offshoring** is the dependence on production in a foreign country, usually by shifting from a domestic source. *If offshoring succeeds in reducing costs, it's good.* This is happening with many companies. Most branded clothing companies locate offshore to have work done by cheaper sewing machine operators. Many investment companies, such as Fidelity in India, are hiring back-office workers in lower-wage countries to cut the cost of industry research. What good are cost savings? It's basic. If you can cut your costs, you can cut your prices or improve your product. Thus, by offshoring work to India, Claimpower, a small U.S. medical-insurance billing company, cut costs, lowered the prices it charges doctors, quadrupled its business in two years, and hired more U.S. employees because of the growth.[26]

What's the main complaint about offshoring? Too many domestic jobs end up abroad. As we discuss this, keep in mind that employment results from offshoring are difficult to isolate from other employment changes. Sure, many workers in high-income countries have lost jobs, but this has probably been due mainly to improvements in production technology. Let's try to pinpoint direct results of offshoring.

Samsung is a good example. By offshoring mobile phone assembly from Korea to Brazil, China, India, and Vietnam, the company was able to lower costs and sell more units, thereby maintaining the same number of low-paying domestic jobs while increasing high-paying jobs at home in R&D, engineering, design, and marketing.[27] If Samsung failed to enact such cost savings, its competitors in low-wage countries could underprice it with competitive products and services. In summary, cost savings generate growth, and growth creates more jobs.

Not just any jobs, either: This process lets companies create more *high-value* jobs at home—the ones performed by people like managers and researchers, who draw high salaries. When that happens, demand for qualified people goes up. In the United States, that process has already resulted in a higher percentage of white-collar and professional employees in the workforce. These are *high-income* people, and more of them are employed as a result of sending *low-income* jobs to countries with lower labor costs.[28]

Further, offshoring is a natural extension of *outsourcing*, the process of companies' contracting work to other companies so that they can concentrate on what they do best.[29] This contributes to making a company more efficient. What is the difference, then, of outsourcing to a domestic versus a foreign location?

Admittedly, workers do get displaced from offshoring, but *aggregate* employment figures show that these workers find other jobs, just like workers who get displaced for other reasons. In a dynamic economy, people are constantly shifting jobs, partly due to technology. The prevailing employment for U.S. women was once as telephone operators; direct dialing technology changed that. Attendants used to pump all the gas, but most is now self-service. Passenger aircraft used to carry five cockpit crew members; technology eliminated the need for the navigator, flight engineer, and radio operator. On the near-future horizon, pilotless passenger aircraft and package-carrying drone helicopters will reduce the cockpit crew to one or even zero,[30] while driverless cars will reduce demand for traffic policemen, auto insurers, emergency room personnel, and makers of such products as road signals and guard rails.[31] In fact, a study of 702 U.S. occupations showed that about 47 percent of employment is at risk from computerization.[32]

What all this means is that the shifting of jobs is commonplace, and shifting because of outsourcing is no different from doing so for any other reason. In any case, because there are bound to be upper limits on the amount of outsourcing work a country can do, the direst predictions about job loss are exaggerated: There simply aren't enough unemployed people abroad who have the needed skills *and* who will work at a sufficiently low cost. Further, as production increases in outsourced facilities abroad, wage rates go up there.

Offshoring isn't for all companies or all types of operations. Some firms are bringing many operations *back* from abroad, a situation known as **reshoring** or **rightshoring**, because of miscalculating offshoring advantages to begin with as well as poor quality, consumer pressure, concerns about competitive security, and advantages of locating production near technical development.[33] That brings us back to what we said explicitly at the outset: Offshoring works when you cut operating costs *effectively.*

Is Offshoring of Production a Good Strategy?

Counterpoint **No** Some things are good for some of the people some of the time, and that's *almost* the case with offshoring. Unfortunately, it is good for only a *few* people but not for *most.* I keep hearing about the cost savings, but when I buy goods or services I rarely find anything that's cheaper than it used to be. Whether buying a Ralph Lauren shirt, getting medical services from a doctor who is saving money through Claimpower, or having Fidelity manage my assets, I have seen no lower prices for me. Instead, the lower production costs have resulted in higher compensation for already high-paid managers and for shareholders. Further, Claimpower's growth had to be at the expense of other companies in the business, not because of growth in the number of people getting medical services. In fact, studies show that in aggregate, the percentage of national income going to labor has gone down while the percentage of national income going to profits and upper-level employees has been going up.[34]

Here's a key problem: When you replace jobs by offshoring, you're exchanging *good* jobs for *bad* ones. Most of the workers who wind up with the short end of the offshoring stick struggled for decades to get reasonable work hours and a few basic benefits, such as health-care and retirement plans. More important, their incomes allowed them to send their kids to college, and the result was an upwardly mobile—and productive—generation.

Now many of these employees have worked long and loyally for their employers and have little to show for it in the offshoring era. Yes, I know governments give them unemployment benefits but these never equal what the employees had before, and they run out.[35] On top of everything else, they may have no other usable skills, and at their ages, who's going to foot the bill for retraining them? The increase in what you call "high-value jobs" doesn't do *them* any good. Further, when *reshoring* occurs (usually because managers didn't think through the offshoring decision adequately in the first place), you can bet they rehire domestic

Counterpoint

workers at less cost than before they offshored those jobs.

Offshoring may lead to short-term cost savings, but many studies indicate that it merely diverts companies' attention from taking steps to find innovative means of more efficient production, such as productivity-enhancing technologies.[36] Concentrating on these innovative means may cut costs, increase production, maintain the jobs that are going abroad, and permit incomes of workers to rise.

While we're on the subject of job "value," what kinds of jobs *are* we creating in poor countries? Because countries are competing with lower wages, it encourages them to keep wages from rising, a sort of race to the bottom. However, multinational enterprises (MNEs) no doubt pay workers in low-wage countries more than they could get otherwise, and I'll grant that some of these jobs—the white-collar and technical jobs—are pretty good. But for most people, the hours are long, the working conditions are barbaric, and the pay is barely enough to survive. When you use such suppliers, your reputation can suffer. In Bangladesh, workers were killed when locked doors prevented their escape from a fire, and others were killed when their ramshackle workplace building collapsed. There is also little job security. If salaries creep up where companies are offshoring, the companies merely move to even cheaper places to get the job done.

Admittedly, in a dynamic economy, people have to change jobs more often than they would in a stagnant economy— *but not to the extent caused by offshoring.* There's still some disagreement about the effects of offshoring on a country's employment rate. Researchers are looking into the issue, but what they're finding is that more of the so-called better jobs are also being outsourced, such as in finance and IT. So are we really creating higher-level jobs at home? Here's the bottom line: In countries like the United States, workers simply aren't equipped to handle the pace of change when it means that jobs can be exported faster than the average worker can retrain for different skills.

WHY COMPANIES ENGAGE IN IB

Let's now focus on some of the specific ways firms can create value through IB. Take another look at Figure 1.1, where you'll see three major IB operating objectives:

- Sales expansion
- Resource acquisition
- Risk reduction

Normally, these three objectives guide all decisions about whether, where, and how to engage in IB. Let's examine each in more detail.

SALES EXPANSION

Pursuing international sales usually increases the potential sales and potential profits.

A company's sales depend on consumers' demand. Obviously, there are more potential consumers in the world than in any single country. Now, higher sales ordinarily create value, but only if the costs of making the additional sales don't increase disproportionately. Recall, for instance, the opening case. Televising sports competitions to multiple countries generates advertising revenue in excess of the increased transmission costs. In fact, additional sales from abroad may enable a company to reduce its per-unit costs by covering its fixed costs—say, up-front research costs—over a larger number of consumers. Because of lower unit costs, it can boost sales even more.

So increased sales are a major motive for expanding into international markets, and many of the world's largest companies derive more than half their sales outside their home countries. Bear in mind, though, that IB is not the purview only of large companies. In the United States, 97 percent of exporters are small firms. Further, many sell products to large companies, which install them in finished products slated for sale abroad.[37]

RESOURCE ACQUISITION

Foreign locations may give companies

- lower costs,
- new or better products,
- additional operating knowledge.

Producers and distributors seek out products, services, resources, and components from foreign countries—sometimes because domestic supplies are inadequate (such as industrial diamonds in the United States). They're also looking for anything that will create a competitive advantage. This may mean acquiring any resource that cuts costs. For instance, Rawlings's relies on labor in Costa Rica—a country that hardly plays baseball—to produce baseballs.

Sometimes firms gain competitive advantage by improving product quality or differentiating their products from those of competitors; in both cases, they're potentially increasing market share and profits. Most automobile manufacturers, for example, hire design companies in northern Italy to help with styling. Many companies establish foreign R&D facilities to tap additional scientific resources.[38] Indian firms have recently followed foreign acquisition strategies to gain knowledge needed to compete globally.[39] Further, by operating abroad, companies gain diversity among their employees that can bring them new perspectives.

RISK REDUCTION

International operations may reduce operating risk by

- smoothing sales and profits,
- preventing competitors from gaining advantages.

Selling in countries with different timing of business cycles can decrease swings in sales and profits (e.g., increasing sales stability through operations in countries that enter and recover from recessions at even slightly different times). Moreover, by obtaining supplies of products or components both domestically and internationally, companies may be able to soften the impact of price swings or shortages in any one country.

Finally, companies often go international for defensive reasons. Perhaps they want to counter competitors' advantages in foreign markets that might hurt them elsewhere. By operating in Japan, for instance, Procter & Gamble (P&G) delayed potential Japanese rivals' foreign expansion by slowing their amassment of the resources needed to enter into other international markets where P&G was active. Similarly, Tredegar Industries followed its main U.S. customer into the Chinese market so as to prevent its customer from finding an alternative supplier who might then threaten Tredegar's U.S. position.

IB OPERATING MODES

When pursuing IB, an organization must decide on suitable *modes of operations* included in Figure 1.1. In the following sections, we define and introduce each of these modes.

MERCHANDISE EXPORTS AND IMPORTS

Merchandise exports and imports are the most popular IB modes.

Exporting and importing are the most popular IB modes, especially among smaller companies. **Merchandise exports and imports** are tangible products—goods—that are respectively sent *out* of and brought *into* a country. Because we can actually *see* these goods, they are sometimes called *visible exports* and *imports.* For most countries, the export and import of goods are the major sources of international revenues and expenditures.

SERVICE EXPORTS AND IMPORTS

Service exports and imports are international nonproduct sales and purchases.

- They include travel, transportation, banking, insurance, and the use of assets such as trademarks, patents, and copyrights.
- They are very important for some countries.
- They include many specialized IB operating modes.

The terms *export* and *import* often apply only to *merchandise.* For non-merchandise *international earnings,* the terms are **service exports and imports** and are referred to as *invisibles.* The provider and receiver of payment makes a *service export;* the recipient and payer makes a *service import.* Services constitute the fastest growth sector in international trade and take many forms. In this section we discuss the following:

- Tourism and transportation
- Service performance
- Asset use

Tourism and Transportation Let's say that some U.S. fans take Korean Air to attend the 2018 Winter Olympics. Their tickets on Korean Air and travel expenses in Korea are service exports for Korea and service imports for the United States. Obviously, then, tourism and transportation are important sources of revenue for airlines, shipping companies, travel agencies, and hotels. The economies of some countries depend heavily on revenue from these sectors, such as Greece and Norway from foreign cargo carried on their shipping lines and for the Bahamas from foreign tourists.

Service Performance Some services, including banking, insurance, rental, engineering, and management services, net companies earnings in the form of *fees:* payments for the performance of those services. On an international level, for example, companies receive fees for engineering services rendered in **turnkey operations**, which are construction projects performed under contract and transferred to owners when they're operational. For instance, the Spanish turnkey operator, Sacyr Vallehermosa, constructed the Panama Canal expansion that opened in 2016. Companies also receive fees from **management contracts**—arrangements in which they provide personnel to perform management functions for another, such as Disney's management of theme parks in France and Japan.

Asset Use Companies receive **royalties** from **licensing agreements**, whereby they allow others to use some assets—such as trademarks, patents, copyrights, or expertise. For example, the Real Madrid football team receives a royalty from Adidas' use of its logo on merchandise. Companies also receive royalties from **franchising**, a contract in which a company assists another on a continuous basis and allows use of its trademark. For instance, McDonald's assists individually owned McDonald's trademarked restaurants by providing supplies, management services, technology, and joint advertising programs.

INVESTMENTS

Dividends and interest from foreign investments are also service exports and imports because they represent the use of assets (capital). The investments themselves, however, are treated separately in national statistics. Note that *foreign investment* means ownership of foreign property in exchange for a financial return, such as interest and dividends, and it may take two forms: *direct* and *portfolio.*

Direct Investment   In **foreign direct investment (FDI)**, sometimes referred to simply as *direct investment,* the investor takes a controlling interest in a foreign company. When, for example, U.S. investors bought the Liverpool Football Club, it became a U.S. FDI in the United Kingdom. Control need not be a 100 percent or even a 50 percent interest; if a foreign investor holds a minority stake and the remaining ownership is widely dispersed, no other owner may effectively counter the investor's decisions. When two or more companies share ownership of an FDI, the operation is a **joint venture**. (There are also non-equity joint ventures.)

Portfolio Investment   A **portfolio investment** is a *noncontrolling* financial interest in another entity. It consists of shares in or loans to a company (or country) in the form of bonds, bills, or notes purchased by the investor. They're important for most international companies, which routinely move funds from country to country for short-term financial gain.

Key components of portfolio investment are

- *noncontrolling interest of a foreign operation,*
- *extension of loans.*

TYPES OF INTERNATIONAL ORGANIZATIONS

Basically, an "international company" is any company operating in more than one country, but a variety of terms designate different ways of operating. The term **collaborative arrangements** denotes companies' working together—in *joint ventures, licensing agreements, management contracts, minority ownership,* and *long-term contractual arrangements.* The term **strategic alliance** is sometimes used to mean the same, but it usually refers either to an agreement that is of critical importance to a partner or one that does not involve joint ownership.

Multinational Enterprise   A **multinational enterprise (MNE)** usually signifies any company with foreign direct investments. This is the definition we use in this text. However, some writers use the term only for a company that has direct investments in some minimum number of countries. The term **multinational corporation** or **multinational company (MNC)** is often used as a synonym for MNE, while the United Nations uses the term **transnational company (TNC)**.

A multinational enterprise or MNE (sometimes called MNC or TNC) is a company with foreign direct investments.

Does Size Matter?   Some definitions require a certain size—usually giant. However, a small company can have foreign direct investments and adopt any of the operating modes we've discussed. Note though that, if successful, small companies become medium or large ones.[40] Vistaprint (now Cimpress) is a good example. Founded in 1995, its sales grew to $6.1 million in 2000 and to over $1 billion by 2012 with operations mainly in North America and Europe.

WHY DO COMPANIES' EXTERNAL ENVIRONMENTS AFFECT HOW THEY MAY BEST OPERATE ABROAD?

Let's now turn to the conditions in a company's *external environment* that may affect its international operations. Although there are many anecdotes illustrating operational problems when companies have failed to consider foreign environmental differences, these differences are not so daunting that they prevent success. First, some of the anecdotes are merely myths that have been repeated so often their validity is seldom challenged. Second, gaining start-up success domestically is also problematic almost anywhere in the world; thus, when companies look objectively at their domestic opportunities and risks, foreign entries may

Although foreign external environmental differences are problematic

- *some anecdotes of failures are merely myths,*
- *they must be weighed against domestic opportunities and risks,*
- *understanding institutional factors and how they affect all business functions helps assure success abroad.*

seem less formidable. Third, a good understanding of what one will encounter helps reduce operating risks, and smart companies develop the means to implement international strategies by examining the following conditions abroad that can affect their success:

- *Physical factors* (such as geography or demography)
- *Institutional factors* (such as culture, politics, law, and economy)
- *Competitive factors* (such as the number and strength of suppliers, customers, and rival firms)

In examining these categories, we delve into external conditions that affect patterns of companies' behavior in different parts of the world and that influence companies to alter what they do domestically to fit foreign needs.

PHYSICAL FACTORS

Physical factors can affect how companies produce and market products, employ personnel, and even maintain accounts. Remember that any of these factors may require a company to alter its operation abroad (compared to domestically) for the sake of performance.

Physical factors affect
- where different goods and services can be best produced,
- operating risks.

Geographic Influences   Managers who are knowledgeable about geography are in a position to better determine the location, quantity, quality, and availability of the world's natural resources and conditions. Their uneven global distribution helps explain why different products and services are produced in different places.

Again, take sports. Norway fares better in the Winter Olympics than in the Summer Olympics because of its climate, and except for the well-publicized Jamaican bobsled team (whose members actually lived in Canada), you seldom hear of tropical countries competing in the Winter Olympics. East Africans' domination in distance races is due in part to their ability to train at higher altitudes than most other runners.

Geographic barriers—mountains, deserts, jungles, and land-locked areas—often affect communications and distribution channels. And the chance of natural disasters and adverse climatic conditions can make business riskier in some areas than in others while affecting supplies, prices, and operating conditions in far-off countries. Keep in mind also that climatic conditions may have short- or long-term cycles. For instance, recent melting of Arctic ice floes along with new ship technologies have allowed more ships to use a Northwest Passage to cut transport costs by saving as many as 15 days at sea.[41]

Demographic Influences   Finally, countries' populations differ in many ways, such as density, education, age distribution, and life expectancy. These differences impact IB operations, such as market demand and workforce availability.

INSTITUTIONAL FACTORS

Institutions refer to "systems of established and prevalent social rules that structure social interactions. Language, money, law, systems of weights and measures, table manners and firms (and other organizations) are thus all institutions."[42] We will now examine a sample of these.

Politics often determines where and how IB can take place.

Political Policies   Not surprisingly, a nation's political policies influence how and if IB takes place. For instance, before Cuba and the United States severed diplomatic relations in the 1960s, Havana had a minor league baseball franchise. Not only did that disappear, but also the facility by which Cuban baseball players could join U.S. professional teams. Many of them did so, although most had to defect from Cuba to play abroad. That changed again with the beginning of political normalizations in 2014.[43]

Obviously, political disputes—particularly military confrontations—can disrupt trade and investment. Even conflicts that directly affect only small areas can have far-reaching effects since these areas may produce important components needed for production elsewhere and because tourists' fear prevents their travel to the entire region.

Each country has its own laws regulating business. Agreements among countries set international law.

Legal Policies   Domestic and international laws play a big role in determining how a company can operate abroad. *Domestic law* includes both home- and host-country regulations on such matters as taxation, employment, and foreign-exchange transactions. British law, for example, determines how the U.S.-investor-owned Liverpool Football Club is taxed and which nationalities of people it employs in the U.K. Meanwhile, U.S. law determines how and when the earnings from the operation are taxed in the United States.

International law—in the form of legal agreements between countries—determines how earnings are taxed by *all* jurisdictions. As we point out in our closing case, international agreements permit ships' crews to move about virtually anywhere. When transactions between countries involve disputes, such as whether a French football team must pay Nike for imported uniforms when it questions the quality, the contract usually specifies the country's law that will make the determination.

Finally, the ways in which laws are *enforced* also affect a firm's foreign operations. In the realm of trademarks, patented knowledge, and copyrights, most countries have joined in international treaties and enacted domestic laws dealing with violations. Many, however, do very little to enforce either the agreements or their own laws. This is why companies must determine how fastidiously different countries implement their laws.

Countries' behavioral norms influence how companies should operate there.

Behavioral Factors   The related disciplines of anthropology, psychology, and sociology can help managers better understand different values, attitudes, and beliefs to help them make operational decisions abroad. Let's return once again to the opening case. Although professional sports are spreading internationally, the popularity of specific sports differs among countries, while rules and the customary way of play for the same sport sometimes differ as well. Because of tradition, tennis's grand slam tournaments are played on hard courts in Australia and the United States, on clay in France, and on grass in England. A baseball game in the United States continues until there is a winner, while Japanese games end with a tie if neither team is ahead after 12 innings. Presumably the reason for the baseball difference is that the Japanese value harmony more than Americans do, whereas Americans value competitiveness more than the Japanese do.

Economics explains country differences in costs, currency values, and market size.

Economic Forces   Economics helps explain why countries exchange goods and services, why capital and people travel among countries in the course of business, and why one country's currency has a certain value compared to another's. Recall the internationalization of sports. Non-U.S.-born players make up an increasing portion of major league baseball rosters, and players from the Dominican Republic form the largest share. Obviously, higher incomes in the United States and Canada enable major league teams to offer salaries that attract Dominican players. Further, putting a major league baseball team in the Dominican Republic isn't practical because too few Dominicans can afford the ticket prices necessary to support a team.

Economics also helps explain why some countries can produce goods or services for less. And it provides the analytical tools to determine the impact of an international company's operations on the economies of both host and home countries, as well as the impact of the host country's economic environment on a foreign firm.

THE COMPETITIVE ENVIRONMENT

In addition to its physical and social environments, every globally active company operates within a competitive environment. Figure 1.1 highlights the key competitive factors in the external environment of IB: product strategy, resource base and experience, and competitor capability.

Companies' competitive situations may differ by

- their relative size in different countries,
- the competitors they face by country,
- the resources they can commit internationally.

Competitive Product Strategy   Products compete by means of *cost* or *differentiation strategies*, the latter usually by

- developing a favorable *brand image,* usually through advertising or from long-term consumer experience with the brand; or

- developing *unique characteristics,* such as through R&D efforts or different means of distribution.

Using either approach, a firm may mass-market a product or sell to a niche market (the latter approach is called a *focus strategy*). Different strategies can be used for different products or for different countries, but a firm's choice of strategy plays a big part in determining how and where it will operate. Take Fiat Chrysler Automobiles (FCA) that competes with its best-selling models by using a cost strategy aimed at mass-market sales. This strategy has influenced FCA to shift some fabrication of engine plants to China, where production costs are low, and to sell in India and Argentina, which are cost-sensitive markets. At the same time, FCA has centered its production of its Alfa Romeo and Maserati vehicles in Italy because these compete with a high-priced focus strategy that requires access to both the expertise and image of high technical competence. And it has targeted most sales of these high-priced vehicles in high-income countries.

Company Resources and Experience Other competitive factors are a company's size and resources compared to those of its competitors. A market leader, for example—say, Coca-Cola—has resources for much more ambitious international operations than a smaller competitor like Royal Crown. Royal Crown sells in about 60 countries, Coca-Cola in more than 200.

In large markets (such as the United States), companies have to invest much more to secure national distribution than in small markets (such as Ireland). Further, they'll probably face more competitors in large markets than in small ones. Conversely, national market share and brand recognition have a bearing on operating in a given country. A company with a long-standing dominant national market position uses operating tactics that are quite different from those employed by a newcomer. Such a company, for example, has much more clout with suppliers and distributors. Remember, too, that being a leader in one country doesn't guarantee being a leader anywhere else. For example, in terms of global market share, Toyota and General Motors see-saw in the number one and two positions, but in many countries they hold neither of these top two positions.

Competitors Faced in Each Market Finally, market success, whether domestic or foreign, often depends on the strength of competition and whether it is international or local. Large commercial aircraft makers Boeing and Airbus, for example, compete almost only with each other in every market they serve. What they learn about each other in one country is useful in predicting the other's strategies elsewhere. In contrast, Walmart faces different local competition with customized local strategies in almost every foreign market it enters.

Looking to the Future
Three Major Scenarios on Globalization's Future

At this juncture, opinions differ on the future of IB and globalization. Basically, there are three major scenarios:

- Further globalization is inevitable.
- IB will grow primarily along regional rather than global lines.
- Forces working against further globalization and IB will slow down the growth of both.

Globalization Is Inevitable

The view that globalization is inevitable reflects the premise that advances in human connectivity are so pervasive that consumers everywhere will know about and demand the best products for the best prices regardless of their origins. This view, known as *connectography*, premises that internationally connecting infrastructure will accelerate.[44] Those who hold this view also argue that because MNEs have built so many international production and distribution networks, they'll pressure their governments to place fewer restrictions on international movements of goods and means to produce them.

Even if we accept this view, we must still meet at least one challenge to riding the wave of the future: Because the future is what we make of it, we must figure out how to spread the benefits of globalization equitably while minimizing the hardships placed on those parties—both people and companies—who suffer from increased international competition.

The *Wall Street Journal* posed a question to Nobel Prize winners in economics: "What is the greatest economic challenge for the future?" Several responses addressed globalization and IB. Robert Fogel said it's the problem of getting available technology and food to people who are needlessly dying. Both Vernon Smith and Harry Markowitz specified the need to bring down global trade barriers. Lawrence Klein called for "the reduction of poverty and disease in a peaceful political environment." John Nash felt we must address the problem of increasing the worldwide standard of living while the amount of the earth's surface per person is shrinking.[45] Clearly, each of these responses projects both managerial challenges and opportunities.

More Regional Than Global Growth

The second view—that growth will be largely regional rather than global—is based on studies showing that almost all of the companies we think of as "global" conduct most of their business in home and neighboring countries.[46] Most world trade is regional, and many treaties to remove trade barriers are regional. Transport costs favor regional over global business. And regional sales may be sufficient for companies to gain scale economies to cover their fixed costs adequately. Nevertheless, regionalization of business may be merely a transition stage. In other words, companies may first promote international business in nearby countries and then expand their activities once they've reached certain regional goals.

Globalization and IB Will Slow

The third view argues that the pace of globalization will slow, or may already have begun collapsing.[47] In light of the antiglobalization sentiments mentioned earlier, it's easy to see that some people are adamant and earnest in voicing their reservations. The crux of the antiglobalization movement is the perceived schism between parties (including MNEs) who are thriving in a globalized environment and those who aren't. For example, in 2015, about 14 percent of the developing countries' population was living in extreme poverty. However, the figure was 47 percent in 1990. Most of the improvement came in China.[48]

Antiglobalists pressure governments to promote nationalism by raising trade barriers and rejecting international organizations and treaties. Historically, they have often succeeded (at least temporarily) in obstructing either technological or commercial advances that threatened their well-being. Recently, antiglobalization sentiments have grown in many countries, such as law changes in some U.S. states that hinder activities of undocumented aliens, the deportation by France of ethnic Roma (gypsies), the evacuation in Italy of immigrants to protect them against local residents, and the backlash against accepting refugees in a number of countries. In Brazil and South Africa, the governments have authorized domestic companies to copy pharmaceuticals under global patent protection. Bolivia and Venezuela have nationalized some foreign investments, and Canada prevented the Malaysian state energy firm, Petronas, from buying Progress Energy, a natural gas producer. The sparring between pro- and anti-globalists is one reason why the globalization process has progressed in fits and starts.

Other uncertainties may hamper globalization. First is the question of oil prices, which affect international transportation because they can constitute more than 75 percent of operating costs on large ships.[49] Not only have global oil prices fluctuated widely, but technology for fracking and shale oil conversion have altered production locations when prices are high. Many U.S. companies, such as furniture manufacturers, have responded by reshoring rather than facing transport cost uncertainty. Second, safety concerns—property confiscation, terrorism, piracy of ships, and outright lawlessness—may inhibit companies from venturing abroad as much.

Finally, one view holds that for globalization to succeed, efficient organizations with clear-cut mandates are necessary; however, there is concern that neither the organizations nor the people working in them can adequately handle the complexities of an interconnected world.[50]

Going Forward

Only time will tell, but one thing seems certain: If a company wants to capitalize on international opportunities, it can't wait too long to see what happens on political and economic fronts. Investments in research, equipment, plants, and personnel training can take years to pan out. Forecasting foreign opportunities and risks is always challenging. Yet, by examining different ways in which the future may evolve, a company's management has a better chance of avoiding unpleasant surprises. That's why each chapter of this book includes a feature that shows how certain chapter topics can become subjects for looking into the future of IB. ∎

CASE — Transportation and Logistics: Dubai Ports World

—Hamed Shamma

The world economy and global trade has been gradually growing since the recession of 2008–2009. Growth is coming from Europe and Japan where trade is stronger than expected, from China and India where high growth rates continue to be recorded, and from less developed countries where trade is primarily based on petroleum and basic commodities. The global transportation and logistics industry is one of the most important contributors to the expansion of trade and logistics, making it important to understand how this industry operates and know more about its trends.

Several factors have led to the growth in the transportation and logistics industry: the separation of raw materials, labor and production, decline in tariffs, import restrictions, and exchange rate controls are some of the main factors that led to this growth. These factors have resulted in an increased demand for transporting raw materials, unfinished goods, and finished goods in the global economy. These trends have increased the demand for global transportation and logistics services. According to the World Shipping Council, in 2014, containers handled by ports around the world are estimated at more than 680 million TEU (twenty-foot equivalent units). In 2016, DP World alone handled around 64 million TEU across their portfolio. In 2015, Dubai Ports ranked among the top 10 global ports in container traffic, with Shanghai leading the list.

Trends in the Transportation and Logistics Industry

The "geographic fragmentation of production" has been an important driver of global trade volumes. There has also been a gradual decline in tariffs, import restrictions, and exchange rate controls. The rise in global logistics and supply chain means that governments today have less of an incentive to impose trade barriers than in the past. While many countries thought that putting trade restrictions helps the companies in the domestic market, yet this hinders their growth in the global markets. These trends have increased the demand for global transportation and logistics services.

Competition and rivalry brings constant need for change and improvement. In response to the growing world trade volume, the number of container ships that can accommodate a large capacity has increased over the past few years. This increase in vessel size of containers requires new port infrastructure.

Ports play an important role in the international logistics chain, which includes providing quality services and efficient productivity. In order to be competitive, ports need to use advanced technologies and skilled labor. The World Bank has for some years developed a logistics performance indicator (LPI 2016) that allows for comparisons across 160 countries. The LPI measures the different dimensions of supply chain performance in the different countries such as customs clearance procedures, quality of trade-related infrastructure, quality of transport services, timeliness of delivery, ability to track and trace consignments. The World Bank has also highlighted the importance that government policies have on logistics performance. Countries that attempt to develop policies to improve supply chain activities find themselves scoring higher on the LPI than countries that do not pay attention to such policies.

Transportation and Logistics Industry

Logistics has in the past focused on reducing barriers to trade, and procedures to be followed by governments for getting clearance for goods at customs. While these are important aspects to consider, it is important to develop policies that integrate all the elements of the supply chain so that all the different players can easily manage all the different steps of their business. This aspect has been lacking lately and needs to be given more attention. An approach that centers on all of the policies will have a major impact on productivity and efficiency of logistics business. This requires bringing all the integrators together in the logistics chain: cargo handling, storage, warehousing, freight services, and courier. This should result in improving the global supply chain business.

Developing Logistics Clusters

Governments around the world are investing significant resources in developing logistics clusters. This requires investment in seaports, airports, railroads, and highways. Examples of leading logistics clusters include Singapore, the Netherlands, Los Angeles, Dubai, and Sao Paulo. Other terms that are sometimes used to refer to logistics clusters include logistics parks, transport centers, logistics platform, and logistics centers.

The advantages of logistics clusters include economies of scope, economies of scale, economies of density, better service, and price stability. These benefits create a positive feedback loop that attract more companies to the cluster, which results in further cost reduction and improved efficiency.

MAP 1.2   Dubai Ports World

Dubai Ports World operates in more than 70 terminals across 40 countries, some of which have been indicated in the following map.

Source: The map has been created based on information from the DP World Web site at http://web.dpworld.com/our-business/marine-terminals/ (accessed October 2016)

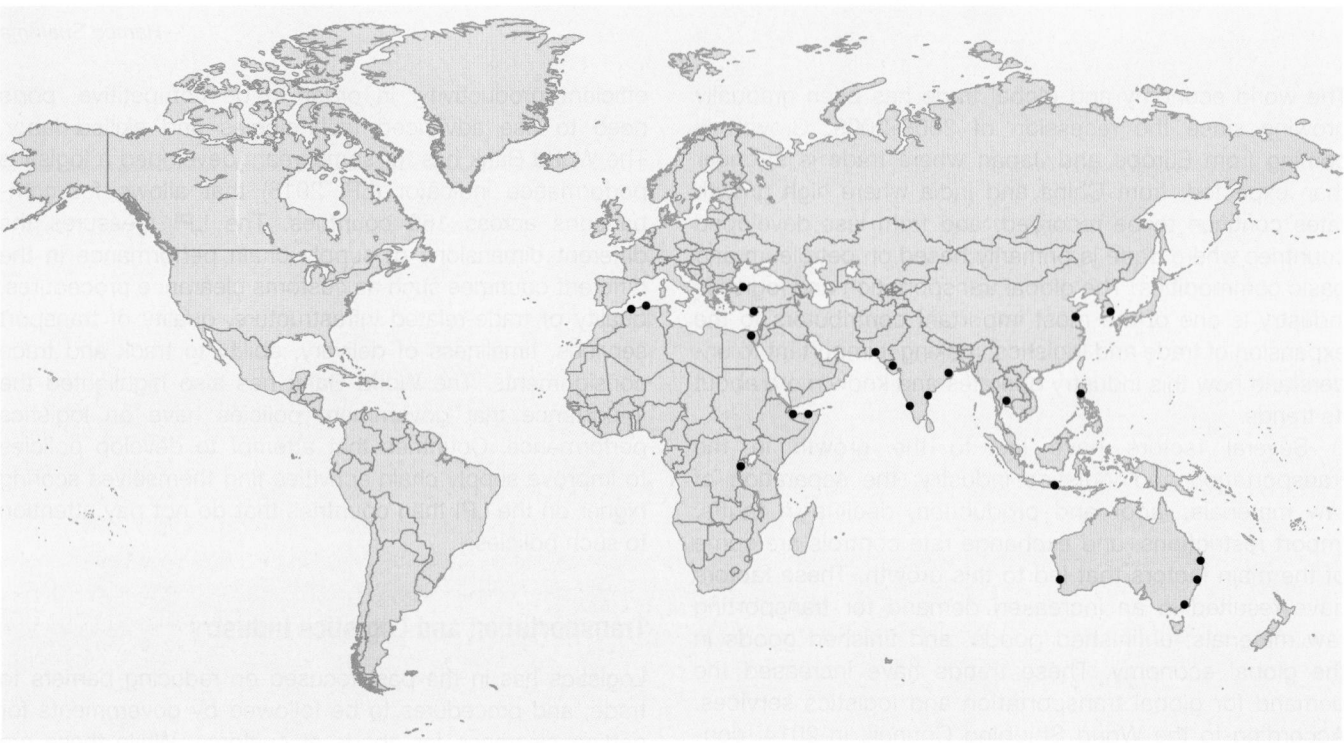

Doing Business in Different Countries

Local or domestic policies may affect the logistics operations in the various markets. Some of these policies may increase costs, reduce efficiency, preferential treatment for local or public owned corporations, a dominating supplier and limitations on investment in certain activities. These policies can significantly impact the supply chain which may add costs to a firm and also affect the business activity.

Foreign countries may introduce restrictive policies such as importing raw material as opposed to processed products where the processing might be more efficient. Other restrictions include bilateral agreements that distort competition, embargoes, business visa restrictions, and security requirements.

About Dubai Ports (DP) World

Headquartered in Dubai, United Arab Emirates, Dubai Ports (DP) World is among the top 3 Global Terminal Operators. It is considered to be one of the new players in the global market, yet has an aggressive growth and acquisition strategy. Founded in 2005 as a result of the merger between Dubai Ports Authority and Dubai Ports International, DP

World's first project was in Jeddah, Saudi Arabia, and has expanded its operations to many other countries like Djibouti, India, and Romania. A large portion of its business is from the emerging markets in South America and Africa. With a team of over 36,000 employees from 103 countries, DP World operates in 77 terminals, marine and inland, across 40 countries.

As DP World's capacity is expected to rise to more than 100 million TEU's by 2020, it continues to invest in its people and technology to provide the better customer service quality to its customers everywhere across the world. This customer-oriented approach has resulted in strong relationships with customers and superior customer service levels. DP World's Jebel Ali facility has been voted as the "Best Seaport in the Middle East" for 19 consecutive years.

In 2006, DP World acquired the Peninsular & Oriental (P&O) Steam Navigation company and expanded its global network and market position in Asia, Africa, Australia, Europe, and the Americas. In the same year, it faced some controversy after purchasing several ports in the United States, but had sold them shortly afterwards.

The organization's mission and vision include leading the future of global trade by adding value, thinking ahead, and building its legacy.

The Overseas Environment

Operating in various markets offer opportunities as well as challenges. The opportunities include access to new markets, larger business, access to resources, and technology leading to innovation. The industry remains to be dynamic and profitable, where emerging markets experience significant growth in business. Governments are usually aspiring to open their ports to logistics companies. Logistics brings with it economic growth and jobs. They offer blue collar, white collar, and no collar jobs. Logistics companies also provide opportunities to open new businesses. Logistics companies also offer value added services on products, and many manufacturers like to locate close of logistics companies. They offer support to a variety of industries.

The challenges include the complexity of operating in certain countries such as Africa, where the supply chain is an expensive and time-consuming activity. Transportation cost comprise up to 75 percent of the retail price in markets such as Malawi, Rwanda, and Uganda. For example, transporting a car from China to Tanzania can cost around $5,000 while transporting the same car from China to Uganda can cost $9,000.

Findings the Right Skills

Although in many cases may be overlooked, the logistics industry is primarily a people business. Around 25 percent of the costs of logistics are labor costs. Thus, it becomes essential to attract, train, and motivate qualified people at all levels. Most companies find it difficult to recruit the right people, especially when they operate in foreign countries and finding the appropriate skills becomes a challenge. There is usually low supply of qualified candidates, in addition to low wages, low profile regarding the industry for many people, and poor working conditions.

Risk Issues

In 2012, President Obama had stated that securing the global supply chain, while ensuring its smooth functioning is essential to our national security and economic prosperity. Addressing risk in supply chain is becoming a priority for business. Supply chain risk can be caused by various disruptions—environmental risk such as natural disasters; geopolitical risk such as threat of attacks and terrorism; economic risk such as currency fluctuations, demand shocks, and supplier failings; and technological risk such as outage in IT and telecommunication systems. Risk can be controlled by conducting scenario analysis, collaborating with the different players by sharing information, identifying vulnerabilities, and synchronizing back up plans.

Technology in Business

DP World has been keen to use advanced information technology tools to facilitate its business. It has been using mobile technology to make life easier for customers by saving time and money. They also use mobile technology for their employees. Issues such as labor deployment, vessel arrival, gate appointments are available on mobile devices. This is linked to the human resources department that assigns labor to points of work, which results in more efficient work. Recently, this technology enabled container shipping lines to access bay and stowage which helped reduce port call time.

Environmental Considerations

Presence of logistics companies may result in a deterioration of air quality, and air pollution. This increases the health hazards around those clusters. Thus, there is always a tradeoff between the economic benefits of logistics operations and the hazards of its effect on the environment and health of the surrounding community. There are "green innovations" in logistics operations and processes that are ultimately minimizing the negative effects of logistics operations on the environment.

Future of Logistics

The logistics industry is a very promising industry that has high prospects for growth as the global economy grows. There are several matters that need attention to support this growth. There is a need for more comprehensive logistics policies that bring the various components of logistics together—land transportation, railway, shipping, commerce, and finance—along with more coordination between these institutions. More investment is required in logistics infrastructure such as roads, rail, and shipping to ease traffic congestion and reduce costs and air pollution. People issues are also becoming essential to ensure the appropriate skills are available to offer the high-quality services.

QUESTIONS

1-3. What factors have contributed to the growth of the transportation and logistics industry and how?

1-4. What steps has DP World taken to benefit from global economic changes?

1-5. What economic factors influence the success of the international transportation and logistics industry?

MyLab Management

Go to **mymanagementlab.com** for the following Assisted-graded writing questions:

1-6   What threats exist for DP World? Explain how you would overcome these threats if you were in charge of DP World.

1-7   How can a logistics company increase its business with countries in Europe, Asia, or Africa?

Endnotes

Scan for Endnotes or go to www.pearsonglobaleditions.com/Daniels

CHAPTER 2
Culture

OBJECTIVES

After studying this chapter, you should be able to

2-1 Explain why culture, especially national culture, is important in IB, but tricky to assess

2-2 Grasp the major causes of national cultural formation and change

2-3 Discuss major behavioral factors influencing countries' business practices

2-4 Recognize the complexities of cross-cultural communications

2-5 Analyze guidelines for cultural adjustment

MyLab Management®
Improve Your Performance!
When you see this icon ✪, visit **www.mymanagementlab.com** for activities that are applied, personalized, and offer immediate feedback.

If you see men stroking their beards, stroke yours.

—*Arab proverb*

Tower in Riyadh, ▶
Saudi Arabia.

Source: Salem Alforaih. Shutterstock

CASE Saudi Arabia's Dynamic Culture

Saudi Arabia (see Map 2.1) can be perplexing to foreign managers as they try to exercise acceptable personal and business behavior.[1] Its mixture of strict religious convictions, ancient social traditions, and governmental economic policies results in laws and customs that often contrast with those in other countries, shift with little advance notice, and vary by industry and region. Thus, foreign companies and employees must determine what these differences are and how to adjust to them. A brief discussion of a sample of Saudi traditions, cultural norms, and foreign operating adjustments should help you understand the importance of culture in IB.

A LITTLE HISTORY AND BACKGROUND

Although the land encompassing the Kingdom of Saudi Arabia has a long history, during most of that history invaders controlled a divided land and most inhabitants had a tribal rather than national loyalty. Nevertheless, the inhabitants have shared a common language (Arabic) and religion (Islam). In fact, Saudi Arabia is the birthplace of Islam and the location of its two holiest cities, Mecca and Medina. (The opening photo shows the Nabawi Mosque at Medina, the second holiest mosque in Islam.) King Ibn Saud, a descendant of Mohamad, took power in 1901, merged independent areas, created a political and religious entity, and legitimized his monarchy and succession by being the defender of Islamic holy areas, beliefs, and values.

The growing importance of oil for Saudi Arabia, particularly since the 1970s, led to rapid urbanization and gave the government the means to offer social services such as free education. These changes have furthered its citizens' sense of a national identity, while diminishing their traditional (particularly nomadic) ways of living. Cities have modernized physically. However, below the physical surface, Saudis hold some attitudes and values that are neither like the norm elsewhere nor easily discerned.

Modernization has been controversial within Saudi Arabia. A liberal group, supported by an elite foreign-traveled segment, wants economic growth to provide more choices in products and lifestyles. A conservative group, supported by religious leaders, is fearful that modernization will upset traditional values and strict Koranic teachings. The government (the Royal Family) must satisfy conservative viewpoints, lest its leadership becomes vulnerable. For instance, Iran's Islamic Revolution was spearheaded in part by dissenters who viewed the Shah's modernization movements as too secular. Meanwhile, liberals have been largely pacified by taking well-paid government jobs and slowly gaining the transformation they wish. The government has sometimes made trade-offs to appease conflicting groups, such as requiring women to wear longer robes (women must wear *abayas* and men customarily wear *thobes*) in exchange for advancing women's education. However, the abayas, traditionally black, are increasingly in more modern designs and bright colors.

THE RELIGIOUS FACTOR

If you are accustomed to fairly strict separation between religion and the state, you will probably find the pervasiveness of religious culture in Saudi Arabia daunting. Religious proscriptions prohibit pork products and alcohol. During the holy period of Ramadan, when people fast during the day, restaurants serve customers only in the evening. Restaurants such as McDonald's dim their lights and close their doors during the five times a day that Muslim men are called to prayer. Many companies convert revenue-generating space to prayer areas; Saudi Arabian Airlines does this in the rear of its planes, the British retailer Harvey Nichols in its department store.

However, there are regional differences. In Riyadh, women customarily wear *niqabs* that cover their faces. But in Jeddah, which has more contact with foreigners and is less conservative, dress codes are more relaxed and fewer women wear them. Nevertheless, merchants routinely remove mannequins' heads and hands and keep them properly clad to prevent public objections. IKEA even erased pictures of women from its Saudi catalogue.

Rules of behavior may also be hard to comprehend because religious and legal rules have sometimes been adapted to contemporary situations. Islamic law, for instance, forbids charging interest and selling accident insurance (strict doctrine holds there are no accidents, only preordained acts of God). In the case of mortgages, the Saudi government offers interest-free mortgage loans instead. It allows accident insurance because Saudi businesses, like businesses elsewhere, need the coverage.

Nor are expected behaviors necessarily the same for locals and foreigners. Non-Muslim foreign women are not required to wear head scarves, although they may be admonished by religious patrols. Saudi Arabian Airlines does not hire Saudi women as flight attendants (being in direct contact with men might tempt promiscuous behavior), but it hires women from other Arab nations. In addition, the government permits residents of compounds, inhabited largely by Americans and Europeans, to dress therein much the way they do back home. However, in an example of a reverse dress code, some compounds prohibit residents and their visitors from wearing *abayas* and *thobes* in their public areas.

MAP 2.1 Saudi Arabia and the Arabian Peninsula

The kingdom of Saudi Arabia comprises most of the Arabian Peninsula in Southwest Asia. The capital is Riyadh. Mecca and Medina are Islam's holiest cities. Jeddah is the most important port. All of the country's adjacent neighbors are also Arabic—that is, the people speak Arabic as a first language. All the nations on the peninsula are predominantly Islamic.

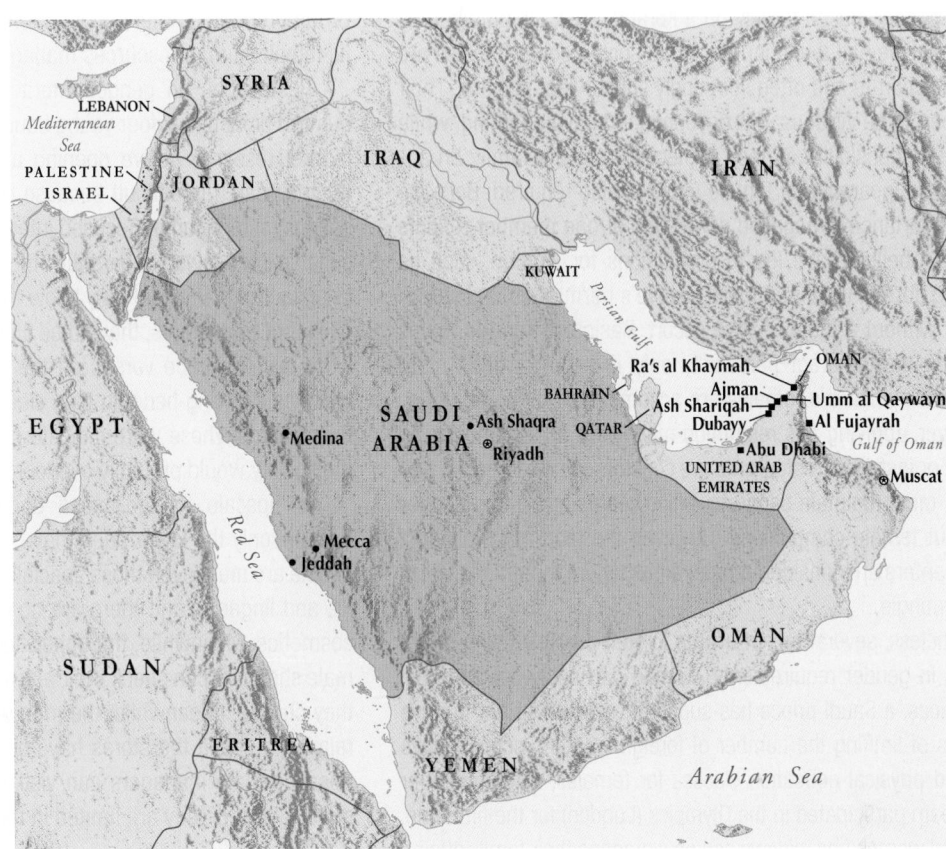

TRADITIONAL FACTORS

Some Saudi Arabian traditions are probably the outgrowth of a tribal and nomadic past. For instance, the oft-quoted saying "Me against my brother, my brothers and me against my cousins, then my cousins and me against strangers" illustrates a family-centered society where trust of others is highly correlated with the degree of familiarity with them.

Given the trust factor, most Saudi businesses have historically been family owned and operated, preferring to hire family members or people they know well even though others might be better qualified technically. However, as companies have needed to partner with foreign firms to gain expertise, the partnering process has usually been lengthy. Saudis take time to know the foreigners well and are reluctant to make full financial disclosures outside the family. They generally prefer to get to know you well, perhaps invite you into their homes, and develop a certain level of friendship before ever turning to business.

Not understanding this norm, a British publisher dispatched two salesmen to Saudi Arabia and paid them on commission. The salesmen moved aggressively to make the same number of calls—and sales—per day as they made in Britain, where they were used to punctual schedules, undivided attention of potential clients, and conversations devoted only to business. To them, time was money. In Saudi Arabia, however, they found that appointments seldom began at the appointed time, usually taking place at cafés over cups of coffee. They felt that Saudis spent too much time in idle chitchat while ignoring business to talk with friends. Eventually, both salesmen showed their irritation, and their Saudi counterparts regarded them as rude and impatient. The publisher had to recall them.

Saudis' preference for dealing with people they know has led to a system known as *wasta*, which roughly translates into English as "connections." Thus, who you know helps a great deal in almost everything, such as moving a résumé to the top of a pile, gaining approval of a zoning request, getting a passport, and obtaining a visa to bring in a visitor from headquarters.

Gender Roles

Perhaps the most baffling aspect of Saudi culture to outsiders is the role of gender. Based largely on a Koranic prescription whereby daughters receive half the inheritance that sons receive, females are placed in a separate and often seemingly subservient position. Their role has been to be virtuous, marry young, and have offspring, while males take responsibility as their protectors and the family breadwinners. The appearance of female virtue is also required. Because of family importance, a negative perception of one member reflects on all. These beliefs have led to prohibitions for women, such as for traveling abroad without a male relative's permission and studying abroad without a male relative escort. Basically, non-kin males and females may interact personally only in "open areas," or in "closed areas" when the females are accompanied by a male relative. However, applying this restriction may seem a bit confusing to outsiders. For instance, restaurants are considered closed areas, and proprietors must maintain separate dining rooms and entrances for men without female companions. However, the food malls at most shopping centers are considered open areas where members of both sexes intermingle.

Nevertheless, several recent events foretell possibly fewer future differences in gender requirements: women can now vote and hold political offices, a Saudi prince has supported women's right to drive as a means of limiting the number of foreign workers, schools have commenced physical education classes for females, a two-member women's team participated in the Olympics (London) for the first time, and divorced women and widows can now manage their family affairs.

Men and women may mix in the workplace, but the situation is complex. Male and female employees within the public sector work in separate buildings. When they must meet together, they do so within special meeting rooms, where they must use separate entrances. Men and women may work together within the private sector, but there are other limitations.

Although females now outnumber males as university graduates, only about 15 percent of the Saudi workforce is female. Why? Some women prefer traditional family roles. Some find driving restrictions to be too much of a hassle. And some families prohibit female members from working because of family honor ("What will people think?"). Economic factors blend with cultural ones as well, such as companies' reluctance to hire women so as to avoid incurring the cost of providing separate entrances and toilet facilities. Nevertheless, the genders do interact in multinational companies as long they adhere to dress codes. However, females are limited in foreign business travel because they need permission from their male relatives. Some multinationals ease this problem by paying the travel costs for a male relative to accompany a woman abroad.

At one time, visas for single women to enter Saudi Arabia were nearly unobtainable. However, Saudi Arabia promotes investments by MNEs, and they need visas to send female executives there. While these visas are not given automatically, they can be obtained—more easily for women over 40, but also possible for younger women, especially with the use of *wasta*. The U.S. consulting company Monitor Group brought in American women in their 20s and L'Oreal has sent its female human resources manager there.

Restrictions on gender interactions also lead to other adjustments. For instance, four young Saudis, who had lived abroad, needed market research before opening an upscale restaurant in Jeddah. Such research is difficult because limitations on male–female interactions restrain family-focused interviews. In this case, however, consultants interviewed apparently affluent families by approaching them in restaurants. How did they know they were affluent? Aside from the caliber of restaurants, they noted clients' comportment, whether they wore custom-made versus off-the-rack robes, the quality of wristwatches showing beneath long sleeves, and how well the men kept their beards. These were indicators that researchers unfamiliar with the society would probably overlook.

At upscale foreign-based department stores like Saks Fifth Avenue, only the lower floors have mixed shopping. There, all salespeople are men (even those specializing in such products as cosmetics and lingerie), and there are no changing rooms or places to try cosmetics. Meanwhile, the upper floors are for women only, and female shoppers can check their *abayas* and shop in jeans or whatever they choose. (Meanwhile, the men who drove the women there can relax in a space the stores have set aside for them.) One problem: Because male managers can visit these upper floors only when a store is closed, they are limited in their ability to observe operations.

CULTURAL DYNAMICS

Almost all aspects of culture evolve, and we have shown that Saudi Arabia is no exception. Since the first public school for girls opened in 1960, there has been a gradual increase in years of study and curriculum for females. On the one hand, economic need has spurred changes in education and its use within the workforce. On the other hand, critics have had to be persuaded that changes for women are compatible with their roles. One of the first acceptances of working women (alongside men) was in the medical field because of the shortage of doctors, the high cost to separate male and female specialists, and the compatibility of healing with women's role as nurturers.

In addition, Saudi opinion and policy has been to reduce the heavy dependence on and cost of foreign workers. Thus, the government pays for foreign university education of its citizens while increasingly recognizing that much female talent is not being exploited.

The Saudi business world has seen much change. Consider that women own about 20 percent of all Saudi businesses, or that a woman is CEO of one of the country's largest concerns, the Olayan

Financing Company. Five things will likely boost Saudi female work-force participation: (1) an increase in inward FDI, (2) more women studying abroad, (3) women's psychological drive to prove them-selves, (4) social media access that connects genders and provides Saudis with more outside information, and (5) the uncertainty of in-come from oil as prices fluctuate. Bear in mind, however, that changes tend to be uneven, particularly among the country's geographic areas and among people with different income and educational levels. ■

QUESTIONS

2-1. Assume you are an MNE manager who needs to send a team to Saudi Arabia to investigate the feasibility of selling your products there. What advice should you give them to help assure that cultural problems do not impede their success?

2-2. Assume your company is from North America or Europe and considering the establishment of an office in Saudi Arabia. What additional operating costs might it have to assume be-cause of the Saudi culture?

CULTURE'S IMPORTANCE IN IB AND TRICKINESS TO ASSESS

CONCEPT CHECK

In Chapter 1 (page 62), we ex-plained that behavioral factors, values, attitudes, and beliefs can be studied as keys to developing suitable business practices abroad.

The nation is a useful definition of society because

- similarity among people is a cause and an effect of national boundaries,
- it is a reference people make to "we" versus "they."

Our opening case illustrates companies' need to understand and be sensitive to the culture where they operate. The adjacent Figure 2.1 shows the relation of culture to IB.

NATIONAL CULTURES AS A POINT OF REFERENCE

Values are learned, and all individuals have them. They are reflected in their attitudes, be-liefs, and actions. Their **core values** are so strong that they are not negotiable, whereas their **peripheral values** are less dominant and more pliable.[2] The shared values, attitudes, and beliefs of a group of individuals constitutes a **culture**.

Culture is an elusive topic to study, partly because people belong to multiple cultures based on their nationality, ethnicity, religion, gender, work organization, profession, age, and income level. We emphasize *national cultures,* but also discuss how major cultural member-ships differ among countries.

The nation provides a workable definition of culture because similarity among people is both a cause and effect of national boundaries. Within a nation's borders, people chiefly share such essential attributes as values and language. The feeling of "we" casts foreigners

FIGURE 2.1 Cultural Factors Affecting IB Operations

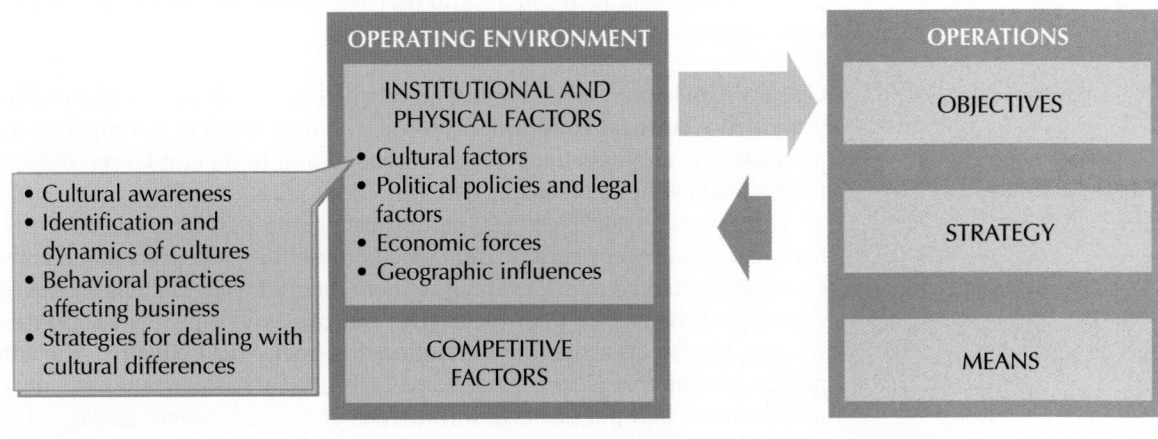

as "they." National identity is perpetuated through rites, symbols, and respect for national heroes, while the preservation of national sites, documents, monuments, and museums promotes a common perception of "we."

The Nation as Cultural Mediator   Obviously, not everyone in a country shares all the same values, nor is each country unique in all respects. Nations include various subcultures, and a nation must be flexible enough to accommodate and mediate its diversity;[3] those that fail sometimes dissolve. Yet a nation's shared and mediated characteristics constitute its national identity and affect the practices of any company that does business there. At the same time, some people (probably a growing number) are **bicultural** or **multicultural**, meaning that they have internalized more than one national culture because of having dual or multiple citizenships, parents or spouses from another country, or lived abroad at an impressionable age.

Groups can hold more similar attitudes with like-groups abroad than with dissimilar groups in their own countries. For instance, urban people in Country A may have more in common with urban people in Country B than with rural people in their own country. As a consequence, when comparing nations culturally, one must be careful to examine *relevant groups*—differentiating between, say, the typical attitudes of rural and urban dwellers, or between managers and production workers.

> Despite using the nation as a cultural reference point
>
> - not everyone therein shares the same values and attitudes,
> - subcultures exist within nations,
> - some people have internalized more than one culture,
> - cultural similarities link groups from different countries.

THE PEOPLE FACTOR

IB involves people from different national cultures, which affects every business function—managing a workforce, marketing and transporting output, purchasing supplies, dealing with regulators, securing funds.

> Cultural diversity can be a competitive advantage, but managing it can be difficult.

Cultural Diversity   As nationalities come together through projects and teams, their diverse perspectives and experiences often enable businesses to gain a deeper knowledge of how to create and deliver products and services. However, successful cultivation of diversity is difficult because individuals may interact as they do within their own cultures. Fortunately, there is an emerging body of research on nationally diverse teams that helps make them more effective. For instance, problems occur when some nationalities are accustomed to compete with team members while others are accustomed to cooperate, when some await precise directions while others take self-initiative, and when some expect to divide tasks while others seek a cooperative solution to each. Similarly, language differences inhibit a common understanding of team roles, priorities, and sentiments.[4] The more successful teams work to understand each other's cultures before dealing with the tasks at hand.[5] When there is an expectation of diversity, team members are more prone to realize the need to prepare to deal with differences, keep open minds, and develop a nonthreatening atmosphere, especially for dealing with others who may feel insecure in the language or threatened when expressing minority and divergent viewpoints.[6]

> Cultural collision may cause
>
> - ineffective business practices,
> - personal distress.

Cultural Collision   When contact among divergent cultures creates problems, the situation is known as **cultural collision**. Such collision may result in a company's implementation of practices that are less effective than intended and to its employees' distress because of difficulty in adjusting to behaviors abroad.

Our opening case illustrates both problems: the publisher failed to meet its sales objectives, and its sales reps became distressed because they wrongly assumed their potential Saudi customers would be punctual and give them their undivided attention. Specifically, the British sales reps came from a **deal-focus (DF) culture**, where people are primarily task-oriented; whereas the Saudis came from a **relationship-focus (RF) culture**.[7] The latter had less compulsion to wrap things up, regarded small talk at a café as a means to identify acceptable business partners, and put dealings with friends ahead of business dealings. **DF** people typically view **RF** people as time-wasters, whereas **RF** people view **DF** people as offensively blunt.

BUILDING CULTURAL AWARENESS

A firm doing business abroad must determine which foreign business practices differ from its own and then decide what adjustments, if any, it should make. Some cultural differences, such as acceptable attire, are fairly obvious; others aren't. And people often react to given situations by expecting the same responses they would likely get in their own countries.

Most cultural variables—daily routines and rules, codes of social relations, language, emotive expression, concepts of luck—exist everywhere; however, the forms they take differ among cultures. Every national culture, for instance, features dancing, but types of and participation in dancing vary among and even within cultures.[8]

No foolproof method exists for building cultural awareness.[9] Travelers remark on cultural differences, experts write about them, and international managers note how they affect operations. Even so, people disagree on what they are, whether they're widespread or limited, and whether they are caused by core versus peripheral values.

Some people have an innate ability to say and do the right thing at the right time, while others offend unintentionally or seem ignorant. Experts note, however, that businesspeople can improve their awareness and sensitivity and, by educating themselves, enhance the likelihood of succeeding abroad. Although research on another culture can be instructive, one must assess information carefully to determine if it perpetuates unwarranted stereotypes, covers only limited segments of a country's culture, or is obsolete. One should also observe the behavior of those people who have garnered the kind of respect and confidence they themselves will need.

Of course, cultural variations are too numerous to memorize completely. Just consider one—the many different ways to address people. Should you use a given name or a surname? Does a surname come before or after a given name? Do people take a parent's name as a surname? If so, is it taken from a parent's first or last name? If so, is it from one or both parents? Does a wife take her husband's name? What titles are appropriate for different professions? Note also that many countries use pronouns and verb forms (familiar and polite) that reflect status and familiarity. Mistakes that may seem minor can be perceived as ignorance or rudeness, thus jeopardizing a business deal. Fortunately, you can consult guidebooks and speak with knowledgeable people at home and abroad. In addition, there are many recent studies on cross-cultural attitudes and practices that concern businesspeople.[10] Nevertheless, many attitudes, practices, and cultures remain insufficiently studied.

SHORTCOMINGS IN CULTURAL ASSESSMENTS

Too often when we can't explain some difference—say, why the Irish consume more cold cereal than the Spanish do—we attribute it to culture without probing why. (Perhaps the difference is simply that cereal companies have marketed more in Ireland.) Nor is it easy to isolate culture from economic and political conditions. Entrepreneurial practices, for example, could be influenced not only by risk-taking values but also by current economic conditions.[11] China's changing preference for male versus female offspring offers an example of cultural and economic interaction. When China had its one-child policy, millions of families aborted female fetuses and put girls up for adoption. Why? Because males could carry on a family name (cultural), help work fields in rural areas (economic), and care for parents in old age (cultural and economic). Recently, however, China has seen a shift toward preference for female offspring. Why? Urbanization requires fewer male workers on farms (economic), while rising property values (economic) have taken a toll on families' tradition (cultural) of buying living quarters for sons before they can marry.[12]

We should also emphasize a few common shortcomings in interpreting cultural research:

1. Comparing countries by what people say can be risky. Responses may be colored by the very culture one tries to understand. Some groups may be happiest when they're complaining; some respond with what they think questioners want to hear. In responding to degrees of agreement, say on a scale of one to five, some cultures are more apt to select the middle point, others the extremes.[13]

Margin notes:

Almost everyone agrees that national cultures differ, but they disagree on what the differences are and the importance of them.

Cultural research can improve a person's awareness and sensitivity.

Sometimes differences are attributed only to culture, although other factors may be influential.

Shortcomings in cultural research include

- erroneous responses to questions,
- relying on averages when there are variations,
- overlooking changes.

2. Researchers focusing on national differences in terms of *averages* may overlook variations within countries. For instance, the *average* Scandinavian may be uncomfortable with bargaining, but assuming that a Swedish buyer for IKEA doesn't expect to bargain on prices could be a grave mistake.[14] And of course, personality differences make some people outliers in their own cultures, with no certainty that they'll eventually integrate and conform to their national norms.[15] Nevertheless, there is a marked difference among countries in the extent that people conform close to the countries' average. When most people are close to the average, it is known as *cultural tightness.* When people are not, it is known as *cultural looseness.*[16]

3. Because cultures evolve, research may be outdated. Our opening case, for instance, details some changing Saudi practices toward gender differences.

INFLUENCES ON CULTURAL FORMATION AND CHANGE

Culture is transmitted in various ways—from parent to child, teacher to pupil, social leader to follower, peer to peer. Developmental psychologists believe that most people acquire their basic value systems, especially core values, as children, including such concepts as evil versus good, dirty versus clean, ugly versus beautiful, unnatural versus natural, abnormal versus normal, paradoxical versus logical, and irrational versus rational.[17]

SOURCES OF CHANGE

Cultural value systems, especially core values, are set early in life but may change through

- choice or imposition,
- contact with other cultures.

Examining individual and collective evolution of values helps explain how cultures come to accept (or reject) certain business practices—a useful examination for companies attempting to introduce their business practices abroad. The important thing here is willingness to accept a *change,* which may result from either *choice* or *imposition.*

Change by Choice   Change by choice may occur because social and economic situations present people with new alternatives. When rural people choose to accept factory jobs, for example, they change some basic customs—notably, by working regular hours they give up work-time social interactions that farm work allowed.

Change by Imposition   Change by imposition—sometimes called **cultural imperialism**—involves imposing certain elements from an alien culture, such as a forced change in laws by a dominant country that, over time, becomes part of the subject culture.

As a rule, contact among countries brings change, known as *cultural diffusion.* When the change results in mixing cultures, we have *creolization.* For example, the U.S. popularity of Mexican tortillas is a result of *cultural diffusion.* Subsequent U.S. innovations to adapt them to U.S. tastes, such as tortilla chips and burritos, are *creolization.* Some groups and governments have tried without full success to protect national cultures. Their efforts have been hampered by their citizens' foreign travel, access to information abroad, and desire to adopt foreign technology that advances them economically. Thus, most countries seek to preserve traditions that help maintain national cohesiveness while being open to changes that grow their economies. South Korea, for example, has recently become more multiethnic because of the influx of foreigners needed to work in its factories. To help maintain traditions, the government now sponsors programs and language centers to "Koreanize" the foreigners.[18]

A common language is a unifying force, but many countries

- have multiple language groups,
- depend on a regional lingua franca.

LANGUAGE AS BOTH A DIFFUSER AND STABILIZER OF CULTURE

Language is probably the most noticeable aspect of culture because it limits contact among people who can't communicate with each other. Although a nation may have a single official language, the reality is much more complex.[19] Many nations contain multiple languages, of which more than one may be official. In fact, the official language(s) may not even be the most prevalent. Further, many people are bilingual or multilingual. Nevertheless, language is at the heart of social identity. When people from different countries speak the same language, culture spreads more easily among them. Commerce also expands, because a common language fosters a sense of shared identity, and, on a practical level, there is less need to translate everything. When a group, especially one with few people, has a language not spoken elsewhere, people therein either learn other languages or they become isolated.

Certain languages have long been a regional lingua franca, such as French in parts of Africa and Russian in Eastern Europe and Central Asia. These languages often become a second language when the regional one is not the official or primary language, such as Russian in Ukraine. This leads native speakers of regional or very widely spoken languages to be complacent about learning foreign languages because they can so often get by without doing so. Further, these languages are often seen as the languages of power, influence, and opportunity. For instance, as English has emerged as the top tier of these lingua francas, there is less foreign language learning in English-speaking countries than in most others. This has made native English speakers more dependent on others (whom they often hardly know) to mediate in multicultural and multilingual business settings. There is a simple business logic to this: If you speak the languages of both parties, you need not depend on an intermediary who may confuse the communication. (Map 2.2 shows the distribution of the world's major language groups.)

English has become the "international language of business" because

- native English language countries account for so much of world production,
- it is the world's most important second language.

Why English Travels So Well Although the countries where English is spoken as a first language have only 6 percent of the global population, they account for 25 percent of the world's output.[20] This difference helps to explain why English is the world's most important *second* language. Remember, too, that MNEs—which are largely headquartered in English-speaking countries—decide on the common language for communication among their

MAP 2.2 Distribution of the World's Major Languages

Globally, people speak about 6000 different languages, but 50 to 90 percent are expected to be extinct by the end of the twenty-first century. Only a few languages remain important in the dissemination of culture. A significant portion of countries, for example, speak English, French, or Spanish. But take a look at Mandarin Chinese. It's important in IB because China comprises a lot of people and has become the world's second-largest economy. The classification "Regional" actually takes in two categories: (1) countries in which the dominant language is not dominant anywhere else (e.g., Japan) and (2) countries in which several different languages are spoken (e.g., India).

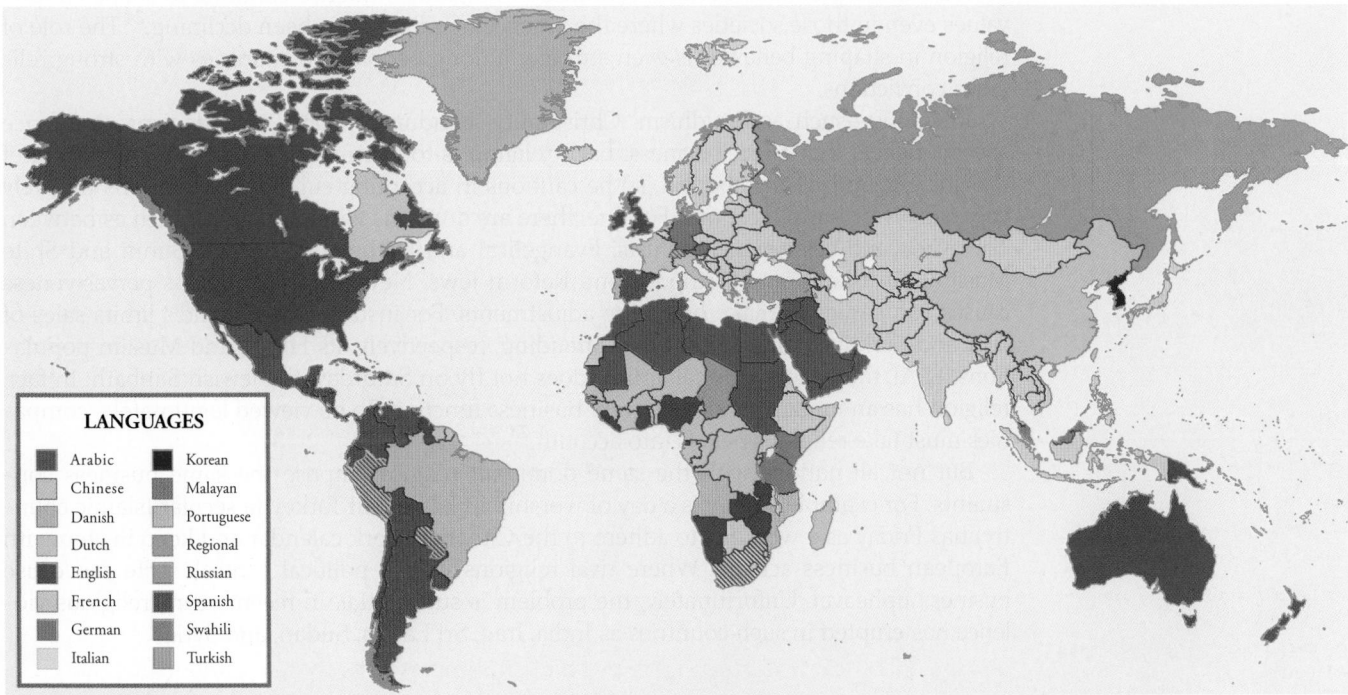

LANGUAGES

Arabic	Korean
Chinese	Malayan
Danish	Portuguese
Dutch	Regional
English	Russian
French	Spanish
German	Swahili
Italian	Turkish

employees in different countries. Not surprisingly, they usually select English, because many of their managers either speak only English or have English as a second language. In addition, some MNEs from non-English-speaking countries have adopted English—the "international language of business"—as their operating language. Nevertheless, this policy can have some negative effects, such as overvaluing people with English language competence.[21] More competent individuals who are less adept at English may not be hired. If hired, they may become marginal in decision-making, lose status, and eventually leave the company. However, at the same time, a common corporate language is often an illusion as individuals continue to use other languages informally.

Monolingual English speakers may eventually experience more difficulty in communicating worldwide. Why? Because the percentage of them will decrease, while the languages of such countries as China and India will grow rapidly along with their economies.[22] As is often the case, history may teach us about this matter: Latin and French were once the languages of scholarship and diplomacy, respectively. Aramaic was once dominant in the Middle East.[23] But the use of these languages has long since been diminished or supplanted.

> The use of English in IB may overvalue people simply because of language competence.

The Evolvement of Languages   Languages add and delete words. Over time, if groups of people become sufficiently isolated from each other, a common language may evolve into more than one, such as occurred with the various Romance languages that developed from Latin. At the same time, languages coexist and influence each other. When, say, a U.S. product enters a foreign market, its vocabulary often enters the language as well—sometimes in a strange form. In a Spanish-speaking country, for instance, you might see a sign announcing *Vendemos blue jeans de varios colores* ("We sell various colors of blue jeans"). It might appear that the use of the word "jeans" in this context is an example only of English predominance. However, the English language adapted the word "Gênes," the French word for the Italian city of Genoa and the fabric (now referred to as denim) that originated there. This cross-pollination of languages is an ongoing phenomenon that coincides with the diffusion of cultures.

RELIGION AS A CULTURAL STABILIZER

> Many strong values are the result of a dominant religion.

Map 2.3 shows the approximate distribution of the world's major religions. Religion has been a cultural stabilizer because centuries of religious influence continue to shape cultural values even in those societies where the practice of religion has been declining.[24] The role of religion in shaping behavior is even stronger among people and countries with strong religious convictions.

Religions—such as Buddhism, Christianity, Hinduism, Islam, and Judaism—influence specific beliefs that affect business. Each religion is too complex to make meaningful brief realistic generalizations about it, so be cautious in accepting cultural explanations that rely very heavily on simplifications. For one, there are divisions within religions, such as between Theravada and Vajrayana Buddhists, Evangelical and Catholic Christians, Sunni and Shite Muslims (in Islam), and Orthodox and Reform Jews. Nevertheless, religious pervasiveness causes companies to make operating adjustments. For instance, McDonald's limits sales of beef and pork in India to keep from offending, respectively, its Hindu and Muslim populations. El Al, the Israeli national airline, does not fly on Saturday, the Jewish Sabbath. In fact, religion has an impact on almost every business function. To be viewed legitimately, companies must take religious beliefs into account.[25]

But not all nations with the same dominant religion impose the same business constraints. For example, Friday is a day of worship in Islam, but Turkey (a secular Islamic country) has Friday as a workday to adhere to the Christian work calendar and keep in step with European business activity. Where rival religions vie for political control, strife can cause business upheaval. Unfortunately, the problem is substantial. In recent years, religious violence has erupted in such countries as India, Iraq, Sri Lanka, Sudan, and Syria.

MAP 2.3 Distribution of the World's Major Religions

About 84 percent of the world's population identifies with a religious group. Most countries are home to people of various religious beliefs, but a nation's culture is typically influenced most heavily by a dominant religion. The practices of the dominant religion, for instance, often shape customary practices in legal and business affairs.

Source: The numbers for adherents are taken from Pew Research Center, "The Global Religious Landscape," (December 18, 2012) http://www.pewforum.org/2012/12/18/global-religious-landscape-exec/?utm_content=bufferf682f&utm_source=buffer&utm_medium=twitter&utm_campaign=Buffer (accessed February 6, 2016).

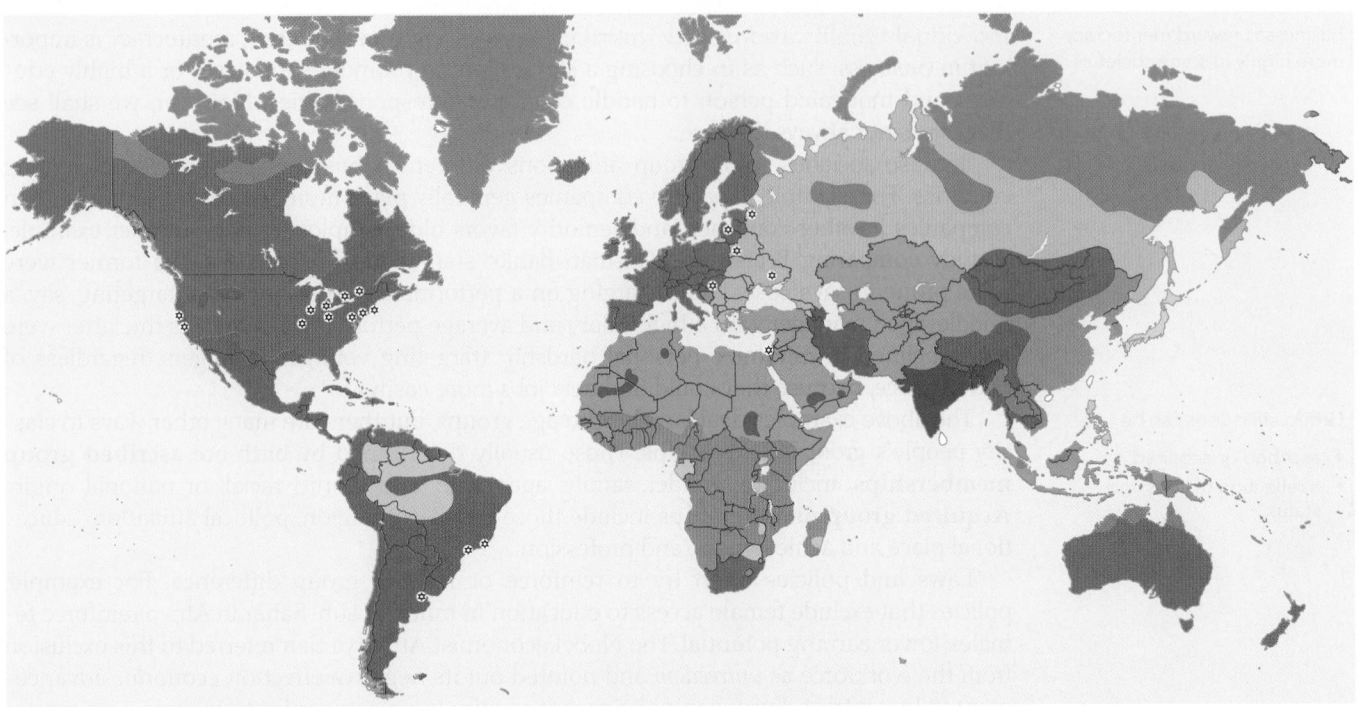

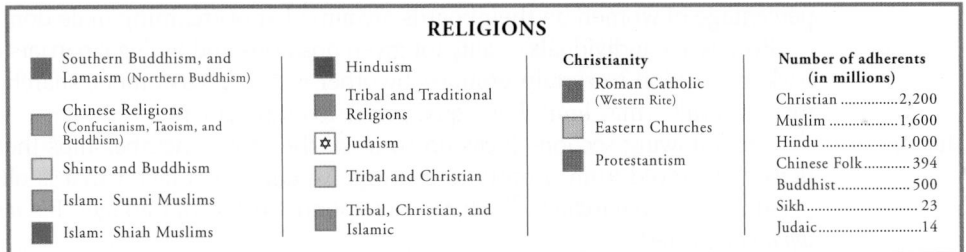

RELIGIONS

- Southern Buddhism, and Lamaism (Northern Buddhism)
- Chinese Religions (Confucianism, Taoism, and Buddhism)
- Shinto and Buddhism
- Islam: Sunni Muslims
- Islam: Shiah Muslims

- Hinduism
- Tribal and Traditional Religions
- ✿ Judaism
- Tribal and Christian
- Tribal, Christian, and Islamic

Christianity
- Roman Catholic (Western Rite)
- Eastern Churches
- Protestantism

Number of adherents (in millions)

Christian 2,200
Muslim 1,600
Hindu 1,000
Chinese Folk........... 394
Buddhist.................. 500
Sikh 23
Judaic.........................14

MAJOR BEHAVIORAL PRACTICES AFFECTING BUSINESS

Cultural variables are sometimes defined differently and with various names given to slightly different and sometimes overlapping concepts. Because of these nuances, there are thousands of possible ways to relate culture to business—far too many to cover in one chapter. We'll settle for hitting the highlights.

ISSUES IN SOCIAL STRATIFICATION

Every culture ranks people. Such *social stratification* creates hierarchies and influences a person's class, status, and financial rewards within that culture. In business, this practice may entail ranking members of managerial groups more highly than production group members. Social stratification is determined by (1) individuals' achievements and talents (*meritocracy*) and (2) their group memberships. These two factors interact, but the importance of one versus the other varies among cultures. Further, more formal cultures expect more status-oriented communications between hierarchical levels. Higher-status individuals, for example, may be offended if people from a lower status address them by a first name or without using a title.

Businesses reward meritocracy more highly in some societies.

Individual Qualifications and Their Limitations
In most societies, meritocracy is important in business, such as in choosing a star athlete to promote sportswear or a highly educated and motivated person to handle competitive responsibilities. However, we shall see that this is not always the case.

Because societies value group affiliations differently, business practices differ among countries. For example, Japanese companies generally place more weight on seniority than companies in other countries, and seniority favors older employees.[26] In another example, a study comparing British and German banks' staff-reduction practices, the former were more prone to save costs by discharging on a performance-to-salary basis (targeting, say, a middle-aged manager with a high salary and average performance), whereas the latter were more inclined to minimize personal hardship (targeting younger managers, regardless of performance, because they could find new jobs more easily).[27]

Group affiliations can be

• ascribed or acquired,
• a reflection of class and status.

The above examples deal largely with age groups, but there are many other ways to classify people's group memberships. Those usually determined by birth are **ascribed group memberships**, including gender, family, age, caste, and ethnic, racial, or national origin. **Acquired group memberships** include those based on religion, political affiliation, educational place and achievement, and profession.

Laws and policies often try to reinforce or remove group difference. For example, policies that exclude female access to education in much of sub-Saharan Africa reinforce females' lower earning potential. The Nobel economist Amartya Sen referred to this exclusion from the workforce as *unfreedom* and pointed out its negative effect on economic advancement.[28] In contrast, European policies that require large companies to include a minimum percentage of women on their boards are aimed at overcoming male dominance therein.[29]

Even when individuals qualify for given positions and no legal barriers exist to hold them back, opposition to certain groups—by other workers, customers, shareholders, or government officials—may limit their equal access to employment.

Country-by-country attitudes vary toward

• social connections,
• race and ethnicity,
• male and female roles,
• rules and expectations based on age,
• family ties.

The following sections focus on some of the group memberships that influence how a person is viewed from country to country. An additional factor that is often important is a person's *social connections*,[30] which corresponds to the old adage, "It's *who* you know, not *what* you know."

Ethnic and Racial Groups
Malaysia, for example, defines political parties and employment quotas explicitly by three ethnic groups——Malays, Chinese, and Indians. The employment quotas are primarily to upgrade the economic position of Malays because the Chinese and Indian minorities long dominated business ownership and the professions, respectively.[31] The system requires companies to maintain expensive record-keeping systems of their hiring.[32] Similarly, Brazilian common language usage has many terms to designate skin color, of which five are official classifications within its census. The country has racial quotas in universities and some groups have pressured to enact quotas for employment as well.[33] (But there has been no pressure for national football team racial quotas, where only competence counts.)

Gender-Based Groups
Country-specific differences in equality and attitudes toward gender are sometimes quite pronounced.[34] In our opening case, we discussed Saudi Arabian cultural attitudes toward gender, resulting in almost seven employed men for every employed woman. Compare that with Norway, where only 1.1 men are employed for every woman. In Lithuania, more than 50 percent of both males and females agreed with the following statement: "When jobs are scarce, men have a better right to a job than women"; in Sweden and Iceland, the number was under 10 percent.[35]

A World Bank study of 173 countries found that 90 percent of them have laws hindering women's ability to work. Although many of these laws are intended to protect women, the results are sometimes discriminatory. For example, France prohibits women from working in jobs requiring them to lift more than 25 kilos (55 pounds), even though that's about the weight of a 5-year-old that they regularly lift. It also cuts them off from working, for example, to deliver FedEx packages.[36] In many places, however, gender barriers in employment practices are coming down because of changes in attitudes and work requirements. A noticeable U.S. change is reflected in the number of people of one gender employed in occupations previously dominated by the other, such as more male nurses and more female physicians. But some of this change may be economic rather than attitudinal as males have gravitated to where there are jobs; even now, few boys say they want to grow up to be nurses.[37] The change in work requirements is reflected in the decrease in jobs requiring brawn and increase in jobs needing specialized education, such as X-ray technology and psychiatric casework.

Age-Based Groups　All countries enforce age-related laws such as on employment, driving privileges, rights to obtain products and services (alcohol, cigarettes, certain pharmaceuticals, bank accounts), and civic duty (voting, serving in the military or on juries). Sometimes the logic of these laws seems paradoxical. For example, Americans can vote, marry, drive, and die for their country before they can legally buy alcohol at age 21. In contrast, Luxembourgers can legally buy distilled alcohol at age 16.[38] U.S. firms bombard children with TV advertising, but Sweden prohibits ads targeted to children.

National differences toward employment age are substantial. Both Finland and the Netherlands enforce mandatory retirement ages, but with few exceptions (e.g., airline pilots) U.S. law specifically prohibits the practice. In Britain, age discrimination laws apply to all ages, whereas U.S. law (except for child labor) protects only people over age 40.[39] When the proposition "When jobs are scarce, people should be forced to retire early" was put to people in different countries, almost three-quarters of Bulgarians agreed, but only 10 percent of Japanese.[40] Why this latter difference? For one thing, Japanese hold strongly to the assumption that there's a correlation between age and wisdom.

Family-Based Groups　In some cultures, such as in much of Latin America, family is the most important group. A person's position in society depends heavily on the family's social status or "respectability" rather than on individual achievement. When family ties are strong, small family-run companies are quite successful; however, they often encounter growth difficulties because owners are reluctant to share responsibility with technically competent professional managers hired from outside the family. When its business culture is thus hampered, a country may lack sufficient numbers of indigenously owned *large-scale* companies that are usually necessary for long-term economic development.[41]

WORK MOTIVATION

Highly motivated employees (toward work) are normally more productive than workers who aren't. Further, higher worker productivity impacts companies' efficiency and countries' economic development. We now summarize major studies showing some differences in how and why nations differ in this motivation.

The desire for material wealth is
- a prime motivation to work,
- positive for economic development.

Materialism and Motivation　When developing his *Protestant work ethic* theory, Max Weber observed that predominantly Protestant countries were the most economically developed. He attributed this to an outgrowth of the Protestant Reformation in sixteenth-century Europe, which reflects the "ethic" that work is a pathway to salvation and that material success does not impede redemption. Although we no longer strictly accept this distinction for Protestants, we do tend to adhere to some of Weber's underlying notions: namely, that self-discipline, hard work, honesty, and a belief in a just world foster work motivation and, thus, economic growth.[42]

On one hand, evidence indicates a positive correlation between the intensity of religious beliefs per se (regardless of specific belief systems) and adherence to some attributes that lead to economic growth (say, confidence in the rule of law and belief in the virtue of thrift).[43] Moreover, individuals' desire for material wealth motivates them to work hard, which in turn leads to community-wide economic development.[44] On the other hand, some religious values, such as predetermination, may lessen work motivation because "what will be, will be."[45] Further, in societies such as Bhutan and Myanmar, a large portion of the population vanishes from the economic workforce temporarily or permanently while pursuing religious activities and being supported by others. (See the adjacent photo in Yangon, Myanmar.)

The Productivity/Leisure Trade-Off Some cultures value leisure time more than others do. They push to work shorter hours, take more holidays and vacations, and generally spend more time and money on leisure activities. In a study of OECD (fairly high-income) countries, France and the United States offered a contrast. The French had 30 days mandated vacation; Americans had none. The French also spent more time per day eating and sleeping than Americans.[46] In the United States, there is still some disdain for people who work very little: people of privilege who appear to contribute too little to society and people who appear to be satisfied to live on social benefits. Americans who give up work (primarily retirees) often complain of doing too little to occupy their time meaningfully.

Expectation of Success and Reward The perceived likelihood of success and its rewards versus failure influence work motivation. Generally, people have little enthusiasm for effort when the likelihood of success seems overly easy or difficult. Few would care to run a race against either a snail or a racehorse; in either case, the outcome is too predictable. Enthusiasm peaks when uncertainty of success is high, such as the challenge of racing another human of roughly equal ability. Likewise, the reward for a successfully completed

> People are more eager to work if
> - rewards for success are high relative to failure,
> - there is some uncertainty of success.

Buddhist monks in Myanmar ▶ (Burma) line up to await lunches that are donated to them.
Source: simo2582/123RF

task—say, winning a fair footrace—may be high or low, and most of us usually exert more effort when the expectation of reward from success is much higher than for failure.

Success and Reward Across Borders Performed in different countries, the same tasks come with different probabilities of success and different rewards for success versus failure. In cultures where the probability of economic failure is almost certain and the perceived rewards of success versus failure are not much different, people tend—not surprisingly—to view work as unsatisfying, mainly because they foresee little benefit to themselves. This attitude may prevail in harsh climates, in very poor areas, or in subcultures subject to discrimination. Likewise, there is less motivation to work hard where public policy allocates output from productive workers to unproductive workers. When high outcome uncertainty is combined with a positive reward for success and little or no reward for failure, we find the greatest work enthusiasm.[47]

Performance and Achievement

A high-masculinity culture prefers to "live to work," and a high-femininity culture prefers to "work to live."	***The Masculinity–Femininity Index*** The **masculinity–femininity index** measures attitudes toward achievement. A high-masculinity score indicates a preference for "live to work," whereas a high-femininity score indicates a preference for "work to live." In essence, high-masculinity individuals show admiration for successful achievers, little sympathy for the unfortunate, preference to be better than others rather than on a par with them, and a money-and-things orientation. (They also strongly prefer role differences between the genders.) A high-femininity score denotes the opposite. It indicates a people orientation rather than work orientation and a preference for quality of life and the environment over economic performance and growth.[48]

This index may help explain national differences in behaviors. Let's say a firm in a high-masculinity country such as Austria sets up operations in a high-femininity country such as Sweden. Purchasing managers in Sweden, if they are high-femininity individuals, probably prefer smooth social relationships, amiable and ongoing dealings with suppliers, and employee and social welfare. Whereas the Austrian firm prefers lower costs, faster delivery, and minimized compensation for workers.

The hierarchy of needs • may differ among countries, • is useful in deciding how to motivate differently among countries.	**Hierarchies of Needs** According to the **hierarchy-of-needs theory** of motivation, people try to fulfill lower-level needs before moving on to higher-level ones.[49] The most basic needs are *physiological*: food, water, and sex. We have to satisfy (or nearly satisfy) those before our *security* needs—safe physical and emotional environments—become motivators. These must be satisfied before triggering *affiliation* needs—peer acceptance. Then we're motivated to satisfy our *esteem* needs—bolstering our self-image through recognition, attention, and appreciation. The highest-order need calls for *self-actualization*—self-fulfillment. Finally, the theory infers that once a need is satisfied, its motivation value diminishes.

This theory helps in distinguishing among employees' reward preferences in different parts of the world. In very poor countries, for example, a large portion of workers are likely engaged in very menial and unskilled jobs;[50] thus, a company may motivate them simply by providing enough compensation to satisfy needs for food and shelter. Elsewhere, a larger portion of workers are motivated by other needs.

Compensation (even at low levels of income) cannot fully explain differences in work motivation. A long-term study among a U.S. airline's back-office employees (almost all female) found that those in the United States and the Dominican Republic saw the job as a stepping-stone to higher-level positions. However, few in Barbados (because of using work largely to help fulfill affiliation needs) wanted a promotion because it would change relationships with friends. U.S. workers dressed very casually because they perceived choice of attire in a back-office job to be insignificant in fulfilling their esteem needs. But Barbadians dressed up to be seen en route to what they considered a prestige job. In fact, the company offered the Barbadians free company-owned bus transport, but they preferred to use slower public transportation where others could see them. The Barbados staff had low absenteeism and turnover rates because Barbados has a history of women working long-term. In the Dominican Republic, however, most female employees stayed on only until they married.[51]

RELATIONSHIP PREFERENCES

So far, we've discussed two categories of behavioral practices affecting business: social stratification systems and work motivation. Next, we examine some of the values underlying interpersonal differences in behavior.

There are national variations in the preference for autocratic versus consultative management.

Power Distance   **Power distance** is a measurement of employee preferences of interaction between superiors and subordinates. Evidence suggests that people perform better when these interactions fit their preferences, thus companies should consider aligning relationship styles effectively.

With *high* power distance, people prefer little consultation between bosses and subordinates. They also prefer management styles that are either *autocratic* (ruling with unlimited authority) or *paternalistic* (regulating subordinate conduct by supplying their needs). With *low* power distance, they prefer "consultative" styles.[52] What might happen, therefore, if a Dutch manager, who typically prefers low power distance, were sent to work in Morocco, where workers typically prefer high power distance? The Dutch manager might consult with Moroccan subordinates, who lose confidence in the manager, believing "Why doesn't the boss know what to do?" Thus, performance deteriorates rather than improves.

Interestingly, managers who prefer an autocratic relationship style are generally willing to delegate and accept decision-making by a majority of subordinates. What they don't accept well is consultative interaction between the two tiers, which implies a more equal relationship between them. Clearly, worker-participation methods may need to be adjusted to fit different countries.

"Safe" work environments motivate collectivists. Challenges motivate individualists.

Individualism Versus Collectivism   *High* **individualism** describes a preference to fulfill leisure time, build friendships, and improve skills independently of the organization. People with high individualism also prefer to receive direct monetary compensation as opposed to fringe benefits, and they prefer to engage in personal decision-making and on-the-job challenges. *High* **collectivism**, in contrast, typifies an employee's penchant for dependence on the organization through training, satisfactory workplace conditions, and good benefits. For example, the United States is a highly individualist country, and employees socialize less with close work colleagues outside of work than employees do in more collectivist societies.[53] In countries with high individualism, a self-actualization opportunity is a prime motivator because employees want challenges. In those with high collectivism, fulfilling security needs is a prime motivator.[54]

Degrees of individualism and collectivism also influence on-the-job interactions. Levi Strauss attempted to introduce team-based production into U.S. plants after its management observed its high productivity within Japan's highly collectivist culture. However, U.S. employees, especially the most skilled workers, detested the system; productivity went down, and Levi Strauss returned to a more individualistic system that better suited its U.S. workforce culture.

RISK-TAKING BEHAVIOR

Risk-taking behavior differs among nationalities because of their

- ease of handling uncertainties,
- degree of trust among people,
- future orientation.
- attitudes of self-determination and fatalism.

Cultures differ in people's satisfaction with the status quo versus taking risks to change situations. The following discussion examines four types of *risk-taking behavior* that reflect these attitudes: *uncertainty avoidance, trust, future orientation,* and *fatalism.*

Uncertainty Avoidance   **Uncertainty avoidance** describes a trait of being uncomfortable with ambiguity. Where this trait is strong, most employees prefer to follow set rules even if they believe that breaking them may be in the company's best interests. They also tend to stay with current employers for a long time, preferring the certainty of present positions over the uncertainty of their future elsewhere.[55] In such situations, superiors may need to be more precise in their directions to subordinates, who typically don't want to be responsible for actions that counter what their superiors want.

Trust Surveys measuring *trust* indicate national differences in responses to such statements as "Most people can be trusted" and "You can't be too careful in dealing with people." Many more Norwegians than Brazilians, for example, regard most people as trustworthy.[56] Where trust is high, business costs tend to be lower because managers spend less time fussing over every possible contingency and noncompliance, thus giving them more time to produce, sell, and innovate.[57] At the same time, trust may differ between people's in-group and others.[58] For instance, we discussed that in some family-oriented societies, people have high trust of other family members, but low trust of people they know less well.

Future Orientation A **future orientation** denotes a willingness to delay gratification in order to reap more in the future. People develop this characteristic as preschoolers and it relates positively to their success as adults. It also relates positively to trust (e.g. belief in whether they'll receive the postponed rewards).[59] Future orientation is more pronounced in, for example, Switzerland, than in Italy.[60] In the former, it may be easier for companies to motivate workers through such delayed-compensation programs as retirement plans.

Fatalism If people are *fatalistic*, they're less likely to accept the basic cause-and-effect relationship between work and reward. Thus, managers are less apt to sway them with cause-and-effect logic than by making personal appeals or offering them rewards for complying with requests.[61]

INFORMATION AND TASK PROCESSING

"Beauty," we're often told, "is in the eye of the beholder." So, apparently, are perceptions and judgments, both of which are based on what people consider accurate *information*. The following discussion examines some of the ways in which people perceive, obtain, and process information.

Differences in perception of cues may result from genetics and language.	**Perception of Cues** As a rule, we're selective in perceiving *cues*—features that inform us about the nature of something. We may identify things through any of our senses, and each sense can provide information in various ways, such as seeing color, depth, and shape through vision. People rely on cues that are partly physiological because evolution and genetics play a role in how different groups perceive.[62] Genetic differences in eye pigmentation, for instance, allow some people to differentiate colors more precisely than others.

Cultural differences, especially language, also reflect perceptual differences. The richness of a language's descriptive vocabulary allows its speakers to note and express very subtle nuances that nonspeakers do not discern. For instance, the Arabic language has many more words for camels, their body parts, and the equipment associated with them than other languages,[63] and Arabic speakers who work around camels can express nuances about them that most other people overlook.

Managers are helped by knowing whether cultures favor

- *focused or broad information,*
- *a particular way of classifying information,*
- *sequential or simultaneous handling of situations,*
- *handling principles versus small issues first.*

Obtaining Information: Low-Context Versus High-Context Cultures Some countries (including the United States and most of northern Europe) are **low-context cultures**, ones where people generally regard as relevant only firsthand information that bears directly on the subject at hand. Businesspeople will spend little time on small talk and tend to get to the point. In **high-context cultures**, people tend to understand and regard indirect information as pertinent. Low versus high context cultural differences even cause misunderstanding in international litigation.[64] Miscommunication can result as well. For example, in Japan, a high-context culture, subordinates typically understand superiors' indirect instructions. But Japanese managers in the United Kingdom, a low-context culture, have been challenged in conveying instructions there because the subordinates expect more explicit explanations.[65]

Information Processing   All cultures process information inasmuch as they categorize, plan, and quantify. However, every culture has its own systems for ordering and classifying information. In U.S. directories, people's names appear in alphabetical order by last (family) name; in Iceland, they're organized by first (given) name. U.S. street numbers are generally odd on one side of the street and even on the other; in much of the Americas, the numbers indicate the distance from where the street begins; in much of Japan, the numbers refer to the construction date; and in Berlin, numbers often go up sequentially on one side of the street and then down the other.[66] To perform efficiently and work amicably in a foreign environment, you need to understand such differences in processing systems. Further, different processing systems create challenges in sharing global data. Even global personnel directories are problematic because of different alphabets, alphabetizing methods, and number systems.

Monochronic Versus Polychronic Cultures   In **monochronic** cultures people normally prefer to work sequentially, such as finishing transactions with one customer before dealing with another. Conversely, **polychronic** people are more comfortable when working simultaneously on a variety of tasks (multitasking), such as dealing simultaneously with multiple customers who need service. Imagine the potential misconceptions when monochronic businesspeople think their polychronic counterparts are uninterested in doing business with them because they don't bother to give them their undivided attention. Further, when teams combine people from both types of cultures, the monochronic members sometimes feel that the polychronic ones delay results by wasting time before finishing with any items in the program.[67]

Idealism Versus Pragmatism   Some cultures tend to focus first on the whole and then on the parts; others do the opposite. When asked to describe an underwater scene in which one large fish was swimming among some smaller fish, most Japanese first described the overall picture, whereas most Americans first described the large fish.[68] Similarly, some cultures prefer to establish overall principles before they try to resolve small issues—an approach sometimes labeled **idealism**. Cultures in which people focus more on details than on abstract principles are said to be **pragmatic**.

These different approaches can affect business in a number of ways. In a pragmatic culture (as in the United States), labor negotiations tend to focus on specifically defined issues—say, hourly pay increases for a specific bargaining unit. In an idealist culture (as in Argentina), labor disputes tend to blur the focus on specific demands as workers are inclined to rely first on mass action, such as general strikes or political activities, to gain support for basic principles.

PROBLEMS IN COMMUNICATING ACROSS CULTURES

We now look at problems in *communicating across cultures*—especially translating, differences in word meanings, and communication that occurs by means other than spoken and written language (a so-called "silent language").

TRANSLATION OF SPOKEN AND WRITTEN LANGUAGE

Cross-border communications do not always translate as intended.

Translating one language into another is not as straightforward as it may seem. Some words simply don't have direct translations. In English, for example, *children* may mean either "young people" or "offspring." In Spanish, *niños* and *hijos* distinguish between the two, and there is no word that encompasses both meanings that exist in English. Thus, despite recent strides in machine translations, many errors still occur. Moreover, many translations—say, Galician into Welsh—go through an intermediate language, usually English.[69]

Language is constantly evolving. When Microsoft purchased a thesaurus code for its Spanish version of Word, the connotations of many synonyms had shifted by the time it implemented the software; some, in fact, were transformed into outright insults that alienated potential customers.[70] Of course, in any language, words mean different things in different contexts. For example, the English word "old" can mean "former" or "long-standing." Imagine the confusion of "We are the old leader in making returns on stock portfolios."

Finally, grammar is complex and the seemingly slight misuse (or even placement) of a word can substantially change the meaning. The following, each originally composed to assist English-speaking guests, have appeared on signs in hotels around the world:

JAPAN: "You are invited to take advantage of the chambermaid."

NORWAY: "Ladies are requested not to have children in the bar."

SWITZERLAND: "Because of the impropriety of entertaining guests of the opposite sex in the bedroom, it is suggested that the lobby be used for this purpose."

These examples offer a comical look at language barriers that usually result in only a chuckle or a little embarrassment. Poor translations, however, can cause commercial disputes; the Shanghai Maritime Court has dealt with thousands of such disputes between Chinese and foreign companies.[71] So choose your words carefully. Although there's no foolproof way of ensuring translations, experienced IB personnel rely on suggestions such as the following:

- Get references for the people who will be translators.
- Make sure your translator knows the technical vocabulary of your business.
- For written work, do *back translations*: Have one person go from, say, English to French and a second from French back to English. If your final message says what you meant originally, it's probably satisfactory.
- Make sure that the tone, not just the words, fit both your own intentions and the expectations of recipients.
- Use simple words whenever possible (such as *ban* instead of *interdiction*).
- Avoid slang. U.S. slang, especially words or phrases originating from sports—*off base, out in left field, threw me a curve, ballpark figure*—are probably meaningless to most businesspeople outside the United States.[72]
- When either you or your counterpart is dealing in a language other than your first language, clarify communications in several ways (repeat things in different words and ask questions) to ensure that all parties have the same interpretation.
- Budget from the start for the extra time needed for translation and clarification.

Be careful with humor because it sometimes lacks universal appeal. A Microsoft executive quipped to Indian executives that he lacked qualifications to speak because he did not complete his MBA. The comment was badly received because most Indians place high importance on education and on persevering rather than dropping out.[73]

Finally, even when all parties to a communication come from countries that share an official language, don't assume that understanding will go smoothly. Table 2.1, for instance, lists a few business terms that have different meanings in British and American English. What could go wrong? When Hershey's launched its Elegancita candy bar in Latin America, it advertised the *cajeta* in the product. Unfortunately, although *cajeta* means "goat's-milk caramel" in Mexico, in much of South America it's vulgar slang for a part of the female anatomy.[74] In addition, marketers have learned that pronunciations and inflections need to be appropriate for the Spanish speaking country they target.[75]

SILENT LANGUAGE

We constantly exchange messages through a host of nonspoken and nonwritten cues that form a **silent language**.[76] Recall from our opening case that in the process of conducting market research for a new restaurant, researchers depended on several such cues to deduce who was affluent.

TABLE 2.1   Dangers of Misspeaking the Language(s) of Business

Below is a short list of business words whose meanings are different in the United States and the United Kingdom—"two countries separated by a common language," as the Irish playwright G.B. Shaw once quipped. There are approximately 4,000 words with the potential to cause problems for people who—in theory—speak the same language.

United States	United Kingdom
turnover	redundancy
sales	turnover
inventory	stock
stock	shares
president	managing director
chapter 11	receivership

Silent language includes color associations, sense of appropriate distance, concept of time, body language, and prestige cues.

Colors   For a product to succeed, its colors must coincide with consumers' frame of reference. Colors invoke distinct connotations in different countries, such as being lucky or unlucky or being associated with a specific business (e.g., yellow cabs in the United States and black ones in the United Kingdom). In most Western countries, black is a color for mourning death; in parts of Africa, it's white. United Airlines' promotion of a new passenger service in Hong Kong backfired because of color. Why? It handed out white carnations to boarding customers, but Hong Kong residents give white carnations in sympathy for a death in the family.

Distance   For example, in the United States people tend to maintain larger distances during conversations or when conducting business than people in Mexico do. And except for handshakes, there is little or no touching in the United States, whereas touching one another in Mexico is quite common.[77] Thus, U.S. and Mexican managers when conducting business with each other may find themselves constantly moving to maintain their accustomed distances and body contact. At the end of the discussion, both parties may well feel uneasy about each other without realizing why.

Time and Punctuality   Different perceptions of time and punctuality also may create confusion. U.S. businesspeople usually arrive before a business appointment time, a few minutes late for dinner at someone's home, and a bit later still for large social gatherings. In another country, the concept of punctuality in any or all of these situations may be different. A Latin American host may be astonished and find U.S. guests perhaps discourteous if they arrive only a few minutes later than the stated time for dinner.

Is time a scarce commodity or an event? People who value time as a scarce commodity believe that if it's lost, it can't be recouped.[78] They tend to stick to schedules, even if taking longer would yield better results. In contrast, people who view time as an event prefer to take as long as necessary to complete a task to their satisfaction. In one case, a U.S. management team was so confident of winning a contract on the basis of better technology that it scheduled a tight, one-day meeting in Mexico City, thinking this was sufficient for its presentation and questions. Unfortunately, the Mexican team arrived one hour after the scheduled start. Then, when an urgent phone call caused a Mexican team member to leave the room, the whole Mexican group got upset when the U.S. team tried to proceed without him. The competing French team, in contrast, allocated two weeks for discussions and won the contract with less sophisticated technology.[79]

Body Language   Body language, or *kinesics*, is the way people walk, touch, and move their bodies. Very few have universal meanings. A Greek, Turk, or Bulgarian may indicate "yes" with a sideways movement of the head that could be construed as "no" in the United States and much of Europe. As Figure 2.2 shows, certain gestures may have several, even contradictory meanings.

Prestige   Another factor in silent language relates to a person's status, particularly in an organizational setting. U.S. managers typically place great faith in physical things as cues to

FIGURE 2.2   Body Language Is Not a Universal Language

The fine line between approval and put-down: Very few gestures have universal meanings. In the United States, you'd probably be safe in approving of another person's statement by forming an O with your thumb and index finger (the so-called high sign). In Germany, Greece, and France, however, you'd be expressing a very different opinion.

Source: The meanings are based on descriptions in Roger E. Axtell, *Gestures* (New York: John Wiley, 1998). Reprinted by permission of John Wiley & Sons, Inc.

United States	**Germany**	**Greece**	**France**	**Japan**
It's fine	You lunatic	An obscene symbol for a body orifice	Zero or worthless	Money, especially change

prestige and may underestimate the status of foreign counterparts who lack large, plush corner offices on high floors. Foreigners may underestimate U.S. counterparts who perform their own services, such as opening doors, fetching coffee, and answering unscreened phone calls.

GUIDELINES FOR CULTURAL ADJUSTMENT

After managers identify key cultural differences abroad, must they alter their customary practices to succeed there? Can people overcome culturally related adjustment problems when working abroad? There are no easy answers to these questions, but the following discussion highlights four issues that affect *degrees* of successful adjustment:

1. The extent to which a culture is willing to accept the introduction of anything foreign
2. Whether key cultural differences are small or great
3. The ability of individuals to adjust to what they find in foreign cultures
4. The general management orientation of the company involved

The following sections address each of these issues in some depth.

HOST SOCIETY ACCEPTANCE

Host cultures do not always expect foreigners to adjust to them.

Although our opening case illustrates the advantages of *adjusting* to a host country's culture, international companies sometimes succeed in introducing new products, technologies, and operating procedures with relatively little alteration. They pull it off because what they're introducing does not run counter to core values and because the host culture is willing to accept foreign products or practices as an agreeable trade-off to its peripheral values. Bahrain needs non-Muslim workers, so it permits the sale of pork products (ordinarily prohibited by religious law) as long as transactions are limited to special places in which Muslims can neither work nor shop.

Sometimes the local society regards foreigners and domestic citizens differently. When staying overnight in Saudi Arabia, Western female flight attendants can wear types of clothing publicly that local women cannot.[80]

DEGREE OF CULTURAL DIFFERENCES

When doing business in a similar culture, companies
- usually have to make fewer adjustments,
- may overlook subtle differences.

Obviously, some countries are much like others, usually because they share many characteristics such as language, religion, geographic location, ethnicity, and level of economic development.

Cultural Distance   A human values study comparing 43 societies on 405 cultural dimensions[81] determined their **cultural distance**, which is the average number of countries they are apart on the dimensions. When a company moves into a culturally close foreign country, such as an Ecuadoran company into Colombia, it should encounter fewer cultural adjustments than when entering a culturally distant country, such as Thailand.

Even among culturally close countries, however, differences could still undermine business dealings. Managers may assume that countries are more alike than they really are, thus overlooking important subtleties or some differences that are not noted in overall cultural distance analysis. For instance, Arab countries are culturally close to each other overall, but women's roles and behavior differ substantially from one Arab country to another.

Hidden Cultural Attitudes   Even if the home and host countries have seemingly similar cultures, people in the host country may reject the influx of foreign practices because they see them as additional steps that threaten their self-identities.[82] And with thousands of *minute* cultural dimensions, it may not be easy to discern operating impediments by comparing countries on the *broad* ones that are both obvious and studied. Disney had much more success in opening a theme park in Japan than in France, even though France is culturally closer to the United States. Why? First, many French were concerned about loss of the country's individuality, especially vis-à-vis the United States because of encroachment of American English words into French, fast-food restaurants' threat to customary long lunches with traditional cuisine, and U.S. companies' acquisition of French firms considered focal to French distinctiveness. Next, subtle differences separated the Japanese from the French. The Japanese were more receptive to Disney because (1) both Japanese children and adults perceived Mickey Mouse as a wholesome, nonthreatening figure, (2) the Japanese had a tradition of buying souvenirs on family excursions, and (3) Disney's reputation for super-cleanliness and smiling faces fit well with Japanese preferences for harmony and order. The French, in contrast, knew Mickey Mouse only as a comic conniver. They regarded Disney souvenirs as tacky and policies requiring personnel to dress uniformly and smile mindlessly as violations of personal dignity.[83]

ABILITY TO ADJUST: CULTURE SHOCK

| Some people get frustrated when entering a different cultural environment.

Some individuals' passages abroad are self-initiated. In other cases, international companies send personnel abroad. In either situation, individuals may be subjected to potentially traumatic foreign practices. In fact, cultural practices all over the world are considered by many outsiders as downright wrong, such as polygamy, child marriage, the punishment of people (sometimes severe) for activities not considered crimes at home, and the public display of executions and executed bodies. Both companies and individuals must decide if they're ready to work in places that countenance such practices.

Even in countries whose practices aren't necessarily traumatic to them, workers who go abroad often encounter **culture shock**—the frustration that results from having to absorb a vast array of new cultural cues and expectations. Even such seemingly simple tasks as using a different type of toilet or finding how to obtain specific merchandise or services can be taxing experiences at first. As such, some people may pass through certain adjustment stages. At first, much like tourists, they're delighted with quaint differences. Later, however, they grow depressed and confused (the *culture shock* phase), so their effectiveness in the foreign environment suffers. Fortunately for most people, culture shock begins to ebb after a month or two as they grow more comfortable. In fact, some people experience **reverse culture shock** when they return, having become partial to aspects of life abroad that are not options back home.

COMPANY AND MANAGEMENT ORIENTATIONS

Whether and how a company and its managers adapt abroad depends not only on the host-country culture but also on their own attitudes. The following sections discuss three such attitudes or orientations: polycentrism, ethnocentrism, and geocentrism.

Polycentric management may be so overwhelmed by national differences that it won't introduce workable changes.

Polycentrism

A *polycentric* organization believes it should act abroad like companies there. Given the uniquely publicized problems of not adapting to foreign cultures, companies' development of polycentric perspectives is not surprising. However, polycentrism may be an overly cautious response to cultural variety, causing a firm to shy away from certain countries or avoid transferring home-country practices or resources that will actually work well abroad.

Look at it this way. To compete effectively, an international company must usually perform some functions differently from its competitors abroad in order to have an advantage over them. They may, for instance, need to sell and market new products or produce old ones differently. Thus, the overly polycentric firm may rely too heavily on imitating proven host-country practices and, in the process, lose the innovative edge it has honed at home.

Ethnocentric management overlooks national differences and

• ignores important factors,
• believes home-country objectives should prevail,
• thinks acceptance by other cultures is easy.

Ethnocentrism

Ethnocentrism reflects the conviction that one's own practices are superior to those of other countries. In IB, the term is usually applied to a company (or individual) so strongly committed to the principle of "What works at home will work abroad" that its foreign practices ignore differences in cultures and markets. In turn, it underestimates the complexity of introducing new management methods, products, or marketing means, which likely leads to poor performance.

However, ethnocentrism isn't entirely an inappropriate way of looking at things. Obviously, much of what works at home will in fact work abroad. Further, concentrating on national differences in terms of *averages* overlooks specific variations within countries. A company may be able to deal with outliers even though the *average* person in the country has a strong cultural bias against what the company does. For example, although the average person in India has a strong cultural bias against eating meat, a company could sell meat products to the many Indians who do eat meat. Likewise, a company may identify partners, suppliers, and employees among a population's minority whose attitudes don't fit the cultural average (there are always individualists in even the most collectivist societies).

Geocentrism

Between the extremes of polycentrism and ethnocentrism, *geocentrism* integrates home- and host-country practices as well as introducing some entirely new ones.[84] In our opening case, Saks Fifth Avenue adjusted to Saudi customs by setting aside women-only floors, introduced many home-country merchandising practices, and introduced the new practice of providing lounges for the drivers of female customers.

Geocentric management often uses business practices that are hybrids of home and foreign norms.

Geocentrism requires companies to balance informed knowledge of their own organizational cultures with home- and host-country needs, capabilities, and constraints. Because it encourages innovation and improves the likelihood of success, geocentrism is the preferred approach for most companies to succeed in foreign cultures and markets.

STRATEGIES FOR INSTITUTING CHANGE

As we've seen, companies may need to compete by operating differently in some ways from other companies abroad (i.e., they introduce some degree of change into foreign markets). Thus, they need to bear in mind that people don't always accept change very readily. The methods they choose for managing such changes are important for ensuring success.

Because people do not necessarily accept change readily, the management of change is important.

Fortunately, we can gain a lot of insight by examining the international experiences of both for-profit and not-for-profit organizations. Moreover, a great deal of material is available on potential methods and so-called *change agents* (people or processes that intentionally cause or accelerate social, cultural, or behavioral change). The following sections discuss both experiences with and approaches to successful change, focusing on the following areas:

• Value systems
• Resistance to too much change
• Participation
• Reward sharing
• Opinion leadership

- Biculturals as mediators
- Timing
- Learning abroad

Value Systems   If something contradicts core values, it will likely not be accepted. But even contradictions to peripheral values face obstacles. In Eritrea, for example, seafood consumption is very low despite its periods of agricultural famine and long coastline rich in seafood. One reason is that Eritrea's Cushitic speakers have religious taboos against eating much of the seafood that is available. Since seafood consumption goes against their core dietary value, the Eritrean government and the United Nations World Food Program have not been fully successful in persuading them to change their eating habits. But non-Cushitic speakers also eat little seafood. Part of the reason is economic. Poverty has prevented most of them from accessing ice and refrigeration to prevent seafood spoilage. Thus many adults have never developed a taste for seafood, worry about its safety, and believe it has a foul taste. Among schoolchildren, however, whose value systems and habits are still flexible, officials have faced little opposition.[85]

Resistance to Too Much Change   The German magazine publisher G + J bought U.S.-based *McCall's* and immediately overhauled the magazine's format: changed editors, eliminated long stories and certain features, increased celebrity coverage, made layouts more robust, supplemented articles with sidebars, and refused discounts for big advertisers. Before long, morale declines led to greater employee turnover. More important, revenues fell because advertisers saw the change in format as too radical.[86] According to most observers, G + J might have received more employee and advertiser acceptance had it phased in its plans for change a little more gradually.

Participation   One way to avoid problems is to discuss proposed changes with stakeholders (employees, suppliers, customers, and the like) in advance. The discussion might help

Point

Does IB Lead To Cultural Imperialism?

Point **Yes** The idea is pretty well accepted: IB influences globalization and globalization influences culture. Now, I have nothing against IB or globalization—at least part of it. What I don't like is modern cultural imperialism, which is what happens when the West, especially the United States, imposes its technical, political, military, and economic supremacy on developing countries.[87]

U.S. firms are in the business of exporting U.S. culture—mostly through tactics that are rarely in the best cultural interests of the nations it targets for economic domination. Because these firms nearly monopolize the international entertainment media, people all over the world are bombarded with U.S. movies and television, not to mention the barrage of accompanying ads from U.S. companies.

And what about the hordes of U.S. tourists who pay more for a night's lodging in a developing country than the hotel maid makes in a year? The fact is they're selling the U.S. lifestyle to a market that can't afford it and that's probably better off without it. The combination of media, advertisements, and tourists means that people in developing countries are exposed to U.S. possessions, practices, and lifestyles to their hearts' content. Never mind that they get an

erroneous impression. According to TV and the movies, the United States is mainly populated by the super-wealthy and by cops and psychotic malcontents whose daily lives are taken up with bullet-spattered body parts, round-the-clock sex, and inane family relationships. The lifestyle is, nevertheless, seductive. That's why people everywhere are eating and consuming soft drinks at U.S. franchised fast-food restaurants and starting to behave and even talk like fictional Americans. Every speech from Manila to Managua is now peppered with U.S. slang. Along the way, people are letting their own cultural identities slip away.

I admit, if a country is rich enough, it can afford to resist most cultural exploitation. Canada says no to foreign investment in culturally sensitive industries and makes sure there's Canadian content in local entertainment media. France shuns outside languages and subsidizes a national motion picture industry. But even rich countries are affected. Some French TV programs and films are now being produced in English to cater to international audiences, and more of their university courses are being taught in English.[88] In the developing world, where there's precious little cash for fighting off cultural extinction, people are at the mercy of foreign culture brokers.

Does IB Lead To Cultural Imperialism?

Counterpoint **No** You imply that people in poor countries passively accept everything they see in movie theaters and on TV. But they've turned their backs on a lot of products that international companies have promoted. Like most of us, they pick and choose.[89] You also imply that cultures in developing countries are the same. They aren't. They interpret what they see and hear—and what they buy—quite differently.

Like cultural purists everywhere, you've overlooked how cultural diffusion works. Through contact, culture heads in both directions and evolves. Of course, American English is seeping into other languages, but Americans have recently added a lot of foreign words as well. If you're a macho (Spanish) guy in charge of the whole enchilada (Spanish), for example, you're probably called the "head honcho" (Japanese).

Similarly, although U.S.-style fast food is almost everywhere, it has not entirely displaced local foods anywhere. When it comes to food, the result of IB is greater diversity for everybody. What we're witnessing is not "cultural imperialism" but cultural hybridization. In most countries, U.S. hamburgers, Japanese sushi, Italian pizza, Mexican tacos, and Middle Eastern pita bread coexist with the local cuisine.

Counterpoint

Mexico's Grupo Bimbo (owner of Sara Lee from the United States) sells tortillas in the United States and U.S.-style bagels in Mexico.[90]

Also, just because people in developing countries have taken a liking to soft drinks and fast food doesn't mean their tastes are permanent. Some evidence suggests that, although young people are most likely to adopt elements from a foreign culture, they tend to revert to traditional values and habits as they get older.[91]

As people seek to fulfill different wants, they must make trade-offs. But are people (and societies) worse off because they give up, say, lunch with the family to be able to afford certain consumer goods that will satisfy the whole family's needs? Globalization simply gives people more options. And tourism is also a two-edged sword. Rather than having a primarily negative effect, quite often it has helped maintain certain features of a traditional culture, such as the revival of traditional Balinese dancing because tourists want to see it.

Rather than simply imposing a foreign culture, a successful business, whether local or foreign-owned, must accommodate itself sufficiently to the culture in which it operates. This may mean revising plans to respond to local demands, which many foreign companies have done.

management assess the strength of the resistance, stimulate stakeholders to recognize the need for change, and ease fears about the consequences. Stakeholders might be satisfied that management has at least listened to them, regardless of the decisions it ultimately makes.[92]

Companies sometimes make the mistake of thinking that stakeholder participation in decision-making is effective only with suitably educated people who can contribute and are willing to speak up. Anyone who has had to deal with foreign aid programs can tell you that participation can be extremely important even in countries where education levels are low and power distance and uncertainty avoidance high.

Reward Sharing Sometimes a proposed change may have no foreseeable benefit for those whose support is needed. Production workers, for example, may have little incentive to try new work practices unless they see some imminent benefit for themselves. What can an employer do? It might develop means of sharing gains with stakeholders. For example, China National Petroleum has faced property damage from angry Iraqi farmers who have perceived problems without gains from living near drilling operations.[93] In contrast, a U.S.–Peruvian gold-mining venture won the support of skeptical Andean villagers simply by donating sheep to them.[94]

Opinion Leadership By making use of channels of influence, or *opinion leaders*, a firm may be able to facilitate the acceptance of change. Opinion leaders may emerge in unexpected places. When Ford wanted to instill U.S. manufacturing methods in a Mexican plant, management relied on Mexican production workers—rather than either Mexican or U.S. supervisors—to observe operations at U.S. plants. The advantage was that the production workers had more credibility with the Mexican workforce who would have to implement the new methods.[95]

Biculturals as Mediators Companies may rely on bicultural or multicultural individuals, especially those within their own ranks, to present and explain changes to stakeholders.[96]

The stakeholders are persuaded not only by the details of proposed changes, but also by their confidence in the presenters' technical qualifications, understanding of host-country constraints, and flexible attitudes toward reaching solutions. Bicultural and multicultural individuals may be especially adept at serving in this mediator role, especially if their cultures are from both the company's home and host countries. Even if the cultures are from other countries, these individuals may understand nuances in the host country culture more easily than unicultural individuals. Further, their demonstrated empathy for divergent viewpoints may be more positively perceived by host country stakeholders simply because they seem less likely to be pushing an ethnocentric agenda.[97]

Timing   Many well-conceived changes fail simply because they're ill-timed. A proposed labor-saving production method, say, might make employees nervous about losing their jobs no matter how much management tries to reassure them. If, however, the proposal is made during a period of labor shortage, the firm will likely encounter less fear and resistance.

In certain cases, of course, crisis precipitates the acceptance of change. In Turkey, for example, where family members have traditionally dominated business organizations, poor performance stimulated a rapid change in this practice: rather than "running" the business, many families now serve in "advisory capacities" (often on the board of directors).

Learning Abroad   Companies' experience in foreign operations enables them to learn as well as impart valuable knowledge—knowledge that proves just as useful at home as in the host country. Such learning may concern any business function; however, access to R&D personnel is a particularly potent advantage in operating abroad. Nevertheless, going abroad with the belief that one already knows everything provides little chance to learn. But there are many examples of good results from being open-minded. For example, the merger between Renault and Nissan brought complementary strengths together. Renault brought its better financial management (typical of French firms) to Nissan. Meanwhile, Nissan brought its superior ability to have functional groups that work well together (typical of Japanese firms) to Renault.[98]

Finally, companies should examine the economies and businesses abroad that are performing well in order to determine practices they can emulate. For example, some large Indian companies have recently performed extremely well because of stressing social missions and investing heavily in their employees.[99] Can non-Indian companies learn from and emulate this experience successfully?

Looking to the Future
Scenarios on The Evolvement of National Cultures

Scenario I: New Hybrid Cultures Will Develop and Personal Horizons Will Broaden

International contact is growing at a rate perhaps unimaginable a few decades ago—a process that should lead to a certain mixing and greater similarity among national cultures. At first glance, that's exactly what's happening. The mixing seems evident when one sees, say, Japanese tourists listening to a Philippine band perform an American pop song at a British hotel in Indonesia. Likewise, combinations of languages such as "Spanglish" have emerged. The growing mix seems apparent when people in every corner of the world wear similar clothing and listen to international recording stars alongside other people wearing local styles and listening to local recording artists. Competitors headquartered in far-flung global areas are increasingly copying each other's operating practices, thus creating a competitive work environment that's more global than national. As companies and people get used to operating internationally, they should continue to gain confidence in applying the benefits of cultural diversity and globally inspired operating procedures to explore new areas in both workplace productivity and consumer behavior.

We'll also likely see people taking advantage of greater mobility and broadening their concepts of what it means to enjoy global or flexible citizenship.[100] Historically, most people who immigrated to foreign countries were able to return to their birthlands perhaps once in their lives. They were thus usually compelled to accept the cultures of their adopted countries, sacrificing much of their native cultural identity in the process. Today, however, many obtain dual citizenship and maintain contact with their native cultures through travel, direct-dial phone calls, and Internet communications. On the one hand, these immigrants tend to transfer culture in both directions, bringing greater diversity to both host and home countries. Further, as people travel more abroad, marriage among different nationalities increases; the number of Americans with foreign-born spouses doubled between 1960 and 2010.[101] Evidence suggests that children in these circumstances are becoming bi- or multicultural, resulting in a class of international managers whose traditional ties to specific cultures are much looser than those of most people (witness CEO Carlos Ghosn of Japan's Nissan and France's Renault, a Brazilian of Lebanese extraction educated in France).[102] On the other hand, multiculturalism appears to be failing in many places because the number of immigrants is so large that they no longer have to assimilate into the culture of their new residency. This may lead to more cultural strife within nations.[103]

Scenario 2: Although the Outward Expressions of National Culture Will Continue to Become More Homogeneous, Distinct Values Will Tend to Remain Stable

Beneath the surface of the visual aspects of culture (including the elements touched on in Scenario 1), people continue to hold fast to some of the basics that distinguish national cultures. In other words, although certain material and even behavioral facets of cultures will become more universal, certain fundamental values and attitudes will continue to vary. Religious differences are as strong as ever; language differences still bolster ethnic identities. What's important is that such differences are still powerful enough to fragment the world culturally and stymie the global standardization of products and operating methods.

Scenario 3: Nationalism Will Continue to Reinforce Cultural Identity

If people didn't perceive the *cultural* differences among themselves and others, they'd be less likely to regard themselves as distinct *national* entities. That's why appeals to cultural identity are so effective in mobilizing people to defend national identity. Typically, such efforts promote the "national culture" by reinforcing language and religion, subsidizing nationalistic programs and activities, and propagandizing against foreign influences on the national culture. Further, even though people will be more internationally mobile, peer pressure will force them to adhere to their national cultures.

Scenario 4: Existing National Borders Will Shift to Accommodate Ethnic Differences

Several countries are showing more evidence of subcultural power and influence. Why? Among basic factors are immigration and the rise of religious fundamentalism. Equally important seems to be the growing desire among ethnic groups for independence from dominant groups where they reside. Both Yugoslavia and Czechoslovakia broke up for this reason, while people within ethnic groups in Britain and Spain (Scots, Catalons, and Basques) are currently pushing for independence. Meanwhile, some subcultures—such as the Inuits in the Arctic and the Kurds in the Middle East—transcend national boundaries and simply resist being "nationalized." Because they have less in common with their "countrymen" than with ethnic brethren in other countries, it's hard to assign them an identity on the basis of geography.

Regardless of the scenario that unfolds in any given arena, IB personnel must learn to examine specific cultural differences if they hope to operate effectively in a foreign environment. In the future, analysis based only on national characteristics won't be sufficient; business will have to pay attention to all the other myriad factors that contribute to distinctions in values, attitudes, and behavior. ∎

CASE Tesco PLC: Leveraging Global Knowledge

—Mary Yoko Brannen and Terry Mughan

David Potts stared out the plane's window as it taxied for takeoff. [104] He had just completed his first visit to China as CEO of Tesco Asia. The visit had been exciting but had posed a number of big questions. The United Kingdom-based retailing giant had been in Asia for a little over a decade and sales and profits were already comfortably outstripping those in the UK and other Tesco areas. Yet it was clear that every Asian market was unique. Thailand, Malaysia, and South Korea had been great successes, yet Tesco had failed completely in Taiwan and operations in Japan were not going well at all. The sheer size of China and India put them in a category of their own. How, then, was Tesco Asia going to develop across such a huge continent? And how could Asian operations strengthen the UK's core operations? Maybe Tesco could find an innovative answer to this challenge. It had done so supremely in other circumstances since its great transformation in the mid-1980s.

Company Background

Tesco originated in the aftermath of World War I by purchasing and selling surplus military supplies. The company became a readily identifiable feature of the UK retail scene. Known as a "Pile it high, sell it cheap" retailer with outlets in almost every town and city, Tesco knew its place in the class-based pecking order of the UK market, in which chains such as Sainsburys and Marks & Spencer met the needs of consumers with more disposable income and more refined tastes.

During the recession of the mid-1980s, a new chairman ushered in a new management team that changed the corporate culture and its market position radically. Relying on a cohort of young, talented executives with an innate understanding of the UK consumer market, Tesco became a store to meet all UK shoppers' needs. It crushed the competition, including the Walmart-backed Asda.

Tesco's approach to become market leader was to improve every aspect of its operations, including distribution, marketing, land acquisition, and product innovation. The key driver was a change in corporate culture to emphasize attention to people. The new management prized loyalty and commitment from staff and was determined to make Tesco the employer of choice in the retailing sector. Such an attitude manifested itself in simple and clear company language: "Treat people how we like to be treated" for customers, "Listen, support and say thank you" among employees.

Tesco took the company language a step further by compiling a "Jargonbuster"—a corporate dictionary that banished obscure terms and acronyms and laid down how simple words make for clear communication. This was increasingly important in Tesco's UK home base because immigrants and people with multicultural backgrounds permeated both the workforce and customer demographics. In the 1990s this dictate of clear and consistent communication extended further as the company increased the size range of stores: the *Super* stores, the smaller *Express* stores in urban centers, and the large *Extra* stores carrying the widest range of merchandise. Tesco bolstered its own branded food product range by adding the "Value" line at the lower end and the "Finest" line at the top end. Tesco embarked on an aggressive marketing campaign dubbed "The Tesco Way," a slogan called "Every Little Helps," as well as a Clubcard incentive scheme. It gained invaluable customer data and overtook its UK competition. During a six-year period, its sales and profits grew by over 300 percent, making it the largest Internet retailer and private sector employer in the country. Thus, it began looking to international markets for the next phase of expansion.

Internationalization

In 1995 Tesco acquired the S-Market chain in Hungary. In 1998 it found a local partner in Thailand and established Tesco-Lotus. An innovative partnership in 1999 with Samsung in South Korea formed Homeplus, thereby creating the bedrock for a sustained Asian presence.

Tesco initially entered most of its foreign markets ethnocentrically by replicating its home success and culture abroad. In the smaller and less distant cultures of central Europe this had worked well—then came France. The setback across the Channel was no great surprise; UK competitors such as Marks & Spencer had also found the British–French cultural gap too wide, even though France was Britain's nearest neighbor. In fact, Tesco made English its operating language, which was more challenging in France than in the other countries where it operated.

Another problem occurred in Taiwan where Tesco paraded its Britishness by displaying Union flags and Beefeaters in front of the store. It had a disastrous £11 billion failure there after it sought to sell all of its Taiwanese sites. But Tesco had to settle on swapping them for stores owned by Carrefour (a major French competitor) in the Czech Republic and Slovakia. The French and Taiwanese experiences taught Tesco a strong lesson about foreign market entry strategy. Determined to banish any signs of imperialism and restore the qualities of hard work, humility, and customer dedication in future ventures, the company moved toward a more locally responsive stance.

Tesco has desired to grow domestically and internationally in a bottom-up fashion. Almost all the young executives who came through the ranks in the 1990s were "lifers"—people who started on the bottom rung of the corporate ladder, stayed with the company, and worked their way up. Some had left school early to join Tesco by stacking shelves on the grocery floor and gradually moving into management. This gave managers a deep understanding of the store, its customers, and the challenges involved in meeting their daily needs. Tesco even institutionalized this learning progress through the practice of TWIST—Tesco Week In Stores—whereby all management must work in a store one week a year so as to always stay close to the customer and the stores' basic operations. All other activities of the company, whether supplier management, executive meetings, or government relations, are built around this key process. Extending this practice abroad was a natural next step. Now, Tesco faced the challenges of operating in 14 countries across Asia, Europe, and North America. (Map 2.4 shows the countries with Tesco operations as of 2015.)

The main challenge for Tesco lay first in identifying the global advantages of its foreign subsidiaries and second in learning from them in ways that would reinvigorate its UK competitive advantage. Although the company had accumulated a vast working knowledge of IB as Tesco rapidly became the world's third-largest food retailer, it faced questions. How could it go about managing flourishing growth in Asia while maintaining and even enhancing the competitive position of Tesco in the UK? Was there a way to transfer Tesco's leading-edge data, purchasing, and distribution resources across its global operations while also learning from the best practices evolving from operations in its foreign subsidiaries? And would it be possible to do all this and still maintain a globally integrated corporate culture? Was this a job for a consulting company? Could outsiders help solve this puzzle?

Thoughts went back to 2010, when, for the first time in over two decades, Tesco was losing its UK competitiveness while sales were down .5 percent for the year. Still, worldwide profits had risen by 12.9 percent, a growth led by the performance in Asia. Clearly there was a lot that Tesco might learn from its Asian subsidiaries. But how?

The Essence of the Tesco Project

Tesco finally came up with a novel solution that was consistent with Tesco's philosophy of building on its internal resources. Aware that declining growth is often a signal of complacency that can go unnoticed by people close to the situation, it decided to bring together a team of Asian managers who would

MAP 2.4   Tesco Locations and Its Cross-Cultural Project

The orange-colored countries on the map show Tesco's operations by country as of 2015. The arrows indicate the countries sending personnel to the United Kingdom to participate in the project. Note that Japan participated, but Tesco has since closed operations there.

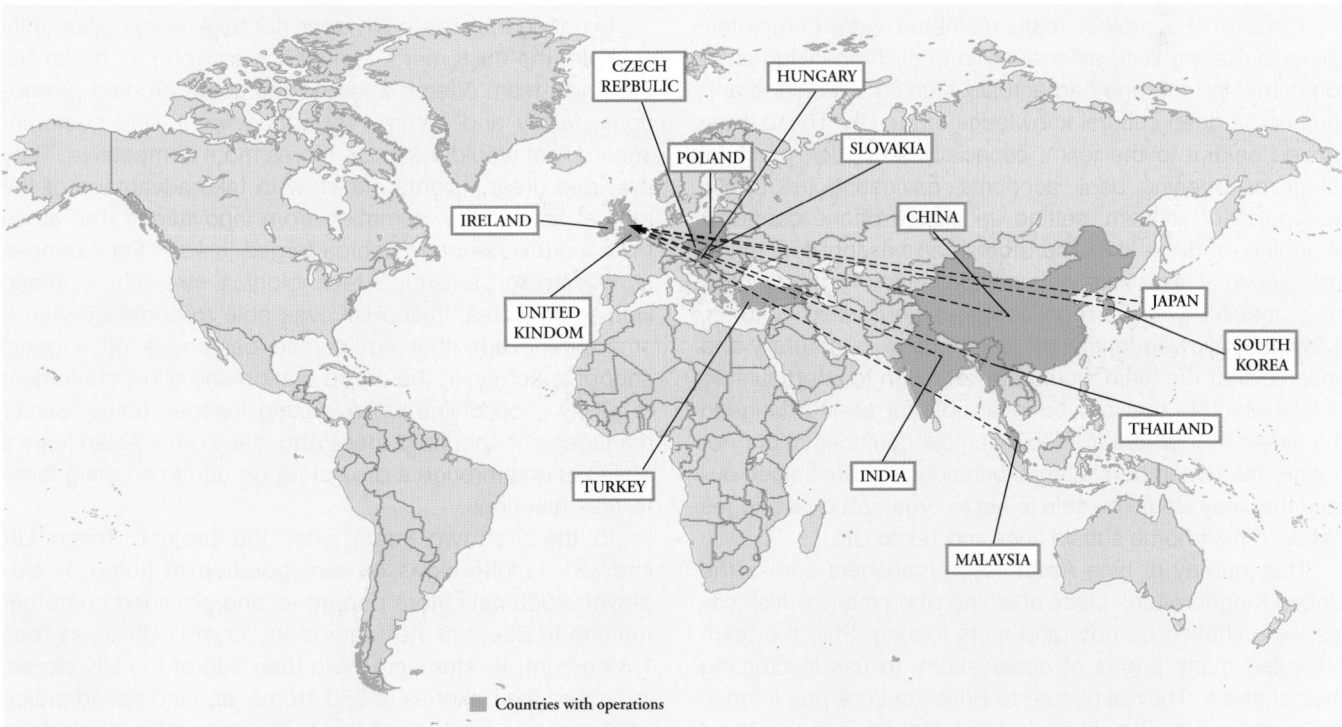

Countries with operations

visit and examine Tesco's operations in the UK. As Tesco insiders, they would be familiar with the company's mission, values, processes, and procedures and thus would be able to feel at home in the store context; as outsiders in the UK, they could see things differently from the British managers, thereby bringing valuable home-country insights and sharing best practices that had evolved in their local markets. The project, "The Essence of Tesco," had a two-pronged strategic purpose: (1) to determine what was and wasn't working by conducting a health-check of Tesco UK's current corporate state; and (2) to compare and contrast that state with what had evolved in Tesco's Asian subsidiaries so as to learn from and leverage them globally.

Tesco chose nine managers from six of its Asian subsidiaries: two each from Thailand, South Korea, and China—its largest Asian markets—and one each from Malaysia, Japan, and India. It brought this Asian project team to the UK; trained its members in skills needed to observe and make sense of organizational behavior, values, and assumptions (a kind of corporate ethnography); and deployed them for a three-month period to observe and work in 52 stores across the UK and Ireland. The task of helping Tesco reinvigorate home operations was not easy; nor was it easy to find nine managers who could leave their jobs for an extended three-month period. In the end, the main criteria stipulated that team members had to have worked for Tesco for at least three years, have a working knowledge of English, and be store-level employees rather than country-level managers. The team was also assessed on various cultural adaptability skills needed to get by in a foreign environment, such as flexibility and openness, emotional resilience, and personal autonomy.

Three of the project team members were completely bilingual, having lived extensively in English-speaking environments; in fact, one had actually studied in England and thus had a deep cultural knowledge of the UK. These three proved helpful to the team, especially with such practical things as opening bank accounts, navigating the public transportation system, setting up mobile phone contacts, shopping, and the like. The others had varying degrees of cross-cultural exposure and competencies in the English language. All were from collectivist, high-context cultures, a fact that allowed teamwork to emerge quite naturally and ensured that the team would pay attention to unarticulated details—factors that proved invaluable for seeing things in the stores that others from low-context countries might not notice. Team members' natural perceptual ability helped ensure that they would be able to act as organizational bridges between their home subsidiaries and Tesco UK.

This journey of nine Asian Tesco managers across the United Kingdom took place at a time when many British cities were shaken by riots and store looting. Still, the team compiled many pages of observations to use in creating their analysis. Their exposure to British culture was intense on many levels. Two of them were locked in a Liverpool store during a riot and, though frightened, were impressed by the store managers' calm manner to handle the situation. The day-to-day experiences, though less exciting, were also very informative and gave rise to many comparisons and contrasts in implementing such core company values as customer focus in the UK and the home countries.

The team exchanged brief anecdotes at the end of each working day and provided some insight into their findings. For instance, while watching a Tesco UK produce handler throw a bunch of bananas onto a display, Thai managers felt that UK standards were below those to which they were accustomed. A Japanese project team member was shocked to learn that a UK fishmonger had only a couple of days' training before taking on the new role of cutting and preparing fresh fish, which was almost an art form in Japan and required several months of intensive training.

Was Tesco still a place where everybody could develop a career? It certainly didn't seem so when the team exchanged stories of how one shop floor worker had never been enrolled in the career advancement program, or how another had been working at the same job-grade level for quite a few years. What were the reasons for this? By engaging with store staff, the project team found out that, although there was a clearly developed "Opportunity to Get On" program, an employee had to be willing to move geographically and/or take up a new job role in order to benefit from the program. The team uncovered many discrepancies between Tesco's espoused corporate culture and its everyday practices in the UK. Noting these discrepancies and asking follow-up questions, the project team members brought new perspectives to the company culture and were able to offer solutions from their own home practices.

In noting that Tesco UK does not take every opportunity to make the customer's experience as good as it can be, the Asian team offered suggestions about product promotions, family and community engagement, and customer service that would make UK stores more competitive. They provided great insights into how to take advantage of the market knowledge stemming from innovations that arose from the diverse partnerships forged in Asia. For example, by leveraging Samsung's technological strengths at Tesco Homeplus Korea, Tesco-UK was able to come up with a smartphone app that could read bar codes off a panel shopping screen in the metro station and allow customers to easily shop online while waiting for their trains. Senior management absorbed these and many other Asian team's observations through a project report and in ongoing face-to-face meetings.

In the first two years after the project, Tesco UK showed definite signs of reinvigoration at home. It employed 8000 new store personnel and provided customer training to 250,000 staff members. Overall UK sales rose 1.8 percent. It refreshed more than 300 of the UK stores, improved the bakeries in 850 stores, and increased online grocery sales by 12.8 percent. The international strategy of the company seems to have moved beyond its ethnocentric past to become locally responsive and to learn from its operations abroad.

2014 was a turbulent year for Tesco. In the midst of the continuing economic recession, the company's share price fell to an 11-year low when it was disclosed that profits had been overstated. This led to the resignation of both the CEO and the chairman. Furthermore, it depleted the company's reserves, caused a pretax loss for the previous year, and resulted in the 2015 sale of its South Korean company to protect and strengthen its balance sheet. (This was Tesco's third foreign divestment in three years, following those in Japan and the United States. However, the Korean operation was the only one that had been a commercial and cultural success.) Commentators saw the South Korean sale as a sad end to a venture that had benefited both Tesco and South Korea. Tesco's successful Korean localization strategies had distinguished it from the approach of its earlier failed competitors, Carrefour and Walmart. By appointing a local businessman to lead, the company adopted a number of successful innovations, such as "Cultural Centres" in stores where customers could receive lessons in cooking or in English and a training academy for teaching retail skills to employees.

Tesco retains its investments in four Asian countries (China, India, Malaysia, and Thailand) as well as those in Central Europe and Turkey. An economic recession, management failings, and rapid international expansion all have a part to play in this story.

QUESTIONS

2-3. The United States and France are more culturally similar to the UK than are Thailand and Malaysia, yet Tesco failed in the former two and has been highly successful in the latter two. How might you explain the difference?

2-4. What is the role of global teams in sharing best practices across a firm's global operations? What advice would you give to make the teams more effective?

2-5. Look at the Tesco PLC website (www.tescoplc.com). What exactly are its businesses and what do you think this tells us about its international strategy today?

2-6. How would Tesco's business model translate into policies of recruitment, training and development, and career management across the Group?

MyLab Management

Go to **mymanagementlab.com** for the following Assisted-graded writing questions:

2-7 What cultural skill sets are needed for individuals from multiple cultures to share best practices across the global group?

2-8 What are some things an MNE can do to facilitate knowledge sharing and global integration across its global businesses?

Endnotes

Scan for Endnotes or go to www.pearsonglobaleditions.com/Daniels

CHAPTER 3
Governmental and Legal Systems

OBJECTIVES

After studying this chapter, you should be able to

3-1 Explain how politics and laws influence business

3-2 Appraise the principles and practices of the political environment

3-3 Discuss the contemporary state of political freedom

3-4 Interpret political risk

3-5 Appraise the principles and practices of the legal environment

3-6 Describe key legal issues facing international companies

3-7 Relate the ideas of politics, law, and the business environment

MyLab Management®
Improve Your Performance!
When you see this icon ⭐, visit **www.mymanagementlab.com** for activities that are applied, personalized, and offer immediate feedback.

Every road has two directions.

—Russian proverb

Source: 123rf.com

CASE   China: Big Opportunities, Complicated Risks[1]

From 1949 to the late 1970s, China was autarkic, championing a self-sufficient economy that relied entirely on its own resources. Leaders of the governing Chinese Communist Party (CCP) feared interaction with foreigners would corrupt China's politics and pollute its culture; hence, they prohibited foreign investment and restricted foreign trade. Near the end of the 1970s, China's increasing economic struggles pushed its leaders to rethink this outlook. In 1978, China instituted the *Law on Joint Ventures Using Chinese and Foreign Investment* and began opening its market to the world. Since then, China's economic liberalization has fueled booming exports and attracted waves of foreign investment. Undeniably, the CCP maintains its monopoly on political power. As one Beijing scholar observed, "The Party (CCP) is like God. He is everywhere. You just can't see him."[2] Free market principles, however, steadily shape the country's business environment.

Transformation yielded astonishing results. Over the past three decades, China has prospered more from globalization than any other country, outsmarting and outperforming many on the world stage. Many of its citizens have moved from mud huts to high rises. China's per capita income increased fivefold between 1990 and 2000, from $200 to $1,000. Between 2000 and 2010, its per capita income rose by the same rate, from $1,000 to $5,000, thereby moving China into the ranks of middle-income countries. Chinese companies have spun from woeful state-owned enterprises into world-class multinationals. Steadily, China has accumulated the greatest financial reserves in the world. Consequently, many see its ascendency as a global event without parallel.

Since the 1980s, MNEs of virtually every sort, size, and nationality have opened Chinese operations. Total FDI in China, literally nonexistent in 1980, headed toward $2 trillion in 2016 on investments in more than 600,000 ventures. Why have so many made huge bets on China? Quite simply, they see stunning opportunities in terms of consumer demand, worker productivity, ingenuity and innovativeness, infrastructure buildouts, and market potential.[3]

THE CALL AND COMPLICATION OF CHINA

Tens of thousands of foreign investors have entered China, opened operations, managed activities, and earned profits. Still, China's political system imposes hardships while its legal system complicates activities. MNEs report that China's political and legal systems can make business operations a hazy, frustrating process. Accustomed to democratic governance in Western markets, in which they have extensive political freedom and legal safeguards, they run into different circumstances in the Middle Kingdom. There, the government, under the control of the CCP, practices "State Capitalism," manipulating market activities to achieve political goals. Consequently, MNEs doing business in China find themselves struggling to make sense of political and legal activities. Ambitious Western firms such as Exxon-Mobil, ABB, Google, Best Buy, Home Depot, Caterpillar, and Vodafone started operations or purchased big stakes in Chinese companies. Political problems and legal difficulties short-circuited their plans. Eventually, like many others, they sold their stakes and reset their strategies.[4]

China's rapid economic emergence accentuates long-running idiosyncrasies. Its mix of ancient and contemporary outlooks creates many gray zones. Some argue that, when it comes to doing business in China, the number one rule is to throw away the rulebook. Foreign investors abandon the notion that Western ideas automatically work in China. For instance, the freedom to form a corporation "for any valid business purpose," commonplace in the United States, does not exist in China. Incorporating in China requires informing the government—in excruciating detail—who you are, what you want to do, how you plan to do it, how much you intend to invest, how many jobs you will create, and on and on. MNEs endure protracted negotiations to get permission to open local units. Each stop along the long march finds national, provincial, and local officials asking how the proposed investment encourages capital formation, promotes exports, creates jobs, and transfers technology. Hitting the right targets, never an easy process, gets the green-light from the government.

DRAGONS AND SNAKES

Many countries, as does China, rely on a centralized state to shape political and legal environments to set the path and pace of economic development. China, however, poses a particularly tough case. The complexity of its political and legal systems imposes time-consuming tasks. China can stack the odds against foreigners who are bold enough to forge ahead in the face of an intricate government bureaucracy and a fledgling legal system.[5] "If the great invention of European civilization was a legal system," quipped an observer, "then China's was bureaucracy."[6]

Exasperated investors often blame a byzantine system that regulates activity based on transparent standards as well as arbitrary agendas. Connections, not competencies, often matter more in righting wrongs and getting deals done. Managers who reason that objective economics should determine the efficient means of doing business see this as illogical. Still, it is utterly logical to Chinese leaders who regard state control of business activity as the most reliable path toward harmonious prosperity—and, one mustn't forget, staying in charge of the show. Consequently, foreign investors navigate often-mysterious political channels.

The long-running conflict between central and local Chinese authorities further confuses matters. The vastness of the country means that local officials, whether headquartered in the smallest village or the largest city, are often left alone by their comrades in Beijing, the capital of China. Certainly, there are national laws, but how they move from Beijing to the other 33 provinces is a different story.[7] "The center," notes one observer, often "has no control over the provinces. When it sends people to investigate illegal pirating of CDs, local governors block access to the factories."[8] As Chinese folklore warns, "The mightiest dragon cannot crush the local snake." This proverb captures the spirit of the enduring power struggle within China. Essentially, even though the central authorities in Beijing may appear to be all-powerful, the politics of powerful local fiefdoms often subvert their authority, to the dismay of foreign investors.

PRECISE LAWS OR AMBIGUOUS GUIDELINES?

China had no formal legal system in 1978 when it launched one of the greatest campaigns of legal reform in history. Ongoing developments have stabilized what had been an unpredictable, periodically chaotic legal environment. Still, China poses legislative gaps, hazy interpretation, and lax enforcement. Legislation is chock-full of ambiguities, says one Beijing-based lawyer, who thinks it will take a generation to iron out the wrinkles.[9] Some are less optimistic, comparing the state of the Chinese legal system with that of the United States in the 1920s—then an antiquated composite of statutes and codes that took several decades to modernize.

Others note that, in the case of the Chinese legal system, bigger problems reflect a difference in the concept of legality. Western legal systems rest on the rule of law and its doctrine of legitimate regulations transparently administered by public officials who are held accountable for their just enforcement. In contrast, China practices the philosophy of the rule of man, seeing the right of the "man" (once in the person of the Emperor, today in the form of the CCP) to act free of checks and balances as long as "he" honors his "mandate of heaven." The latter, an ancient Chinese philosophical idea, holds that *tiān* (heaven) grants an emperor the right to rule unilaterally, as long as he rules virtuously. Hence, besides being the law, the CCP has the legitimacy, based on its mandate of heaven, to operate above the law. So, in practice, rarely does the Chinese criminal court, under the direction of the CCP, end with anything other than a guilty verdict. Explained an FBI Special Agent and legal attaché at the U.S. Embassy in Beijing, "there is really no rule of law here…they (CCP) make a decision ahead of time to make a point."[10]

THE LEGALITY OF ILLEGALITY

China's legal practices, combined with the growing pains of its novel legal institutions and evolving political norms, challenge MNEs. A flashpoint is the protection of intellectual property—patents, trademarks, copyrights, and so on. MNEs complain that relentless, widespread, and sophisticated theft of their intellectual property fuels China's surge. Early on, aggressive estimates linked nearly a third of the Chinese economy to piracy.[11] Its share has declined in tandem with China's expansion. Still, the FBI estimates that American companies lose hundreds of billions annually to counterfeiting. China continues to be the number one source country for counterfeit and pirated goods seized. In the United States, Customs officials report that nearly 90 percent of counterfeits seized originated in China.[12] U.S. authorities, noting the rarity of legal punishment, charge Chinese officials with tolerating, if not encouraging, pirates. The United States, to slight success, has appealed to transnational institutions to redress China's "inadequate enforcement" of intellectual property regulations.[13]

What accounts for China's status as the world's premier counterfeiter? Analysts point to a mix of its quest to catch the West, collectivist orientation, rule-of-man legacy, and dubious enforcement of ambiguous laws—conditions that create a political and legal muddle. Noted an observer, "We have never seen a problem of this size and magnitude in world history….There's more counterfeiting going on in China now than we've ever seen anywhere."[14] Problems threaten to escalate. Government policies have "left a deep impression on companies that intellectual property is there for anyone to use it." Local and provincial authorities look to pirates to power economic growth. Moreover, China excels in making high-quality knockoffs. As some say in Shanghai, "We can copy everything except your mother."[15]

WHAT'S NEXT?

Inevitably, investors question how an opaque, single-party political system, combined with a shadowy legal environment, can protect their property and business rights. Some believe that external institutions will improve transparency. China's 2001 ascension to the WTO, for example, required it to accept rules on all sorts of business matters, including tariffs, subsidies, and intellectual property. China has steadily amended its legal codes to comply with WTO standards. However, the struggle is not a shortage of regulations. Rather, critics charge China's sluggish enforcement, even in cases of outright violation, is the primary problem.

Some point to the CCP's growing support of Confucian ideals foreshadowing its future legal standards. Xi Jinping, CCP chief and China's president, champions Confucian virtues, seeing the homegrown thoughts of the ancient sage, codified in his collected teachings, "The Analects," as useful guides for China's political and legal evolution (the opening photo of this chapter shows a depiction of Confucius found in the Shanghai Confucius Temple). Confucianism holds that people are fundamentally good and, rather than coerced via government regulations and penal law, are better governed through the virtuous abstraction of *Li*—namely, traditional values, ritual, decorum, rules of propriety, customs, and norms. Internalizing the ideals of *Li*, goes this reasoning, culminates in a harmonious social order where all behave properly. Certainly, formal laws need exist, but they apply to individuals who selfishly maximize their self-interests at the expense of the collective. Foreign investors, naturally, wondered how blending Confucian virtues, ideals of *Li*, and social harmony might regulate their rights.[16]

Despite intimidating political difficulties and confusing legal questions, legions of foreign investors profitably answer the siren call of China. Whether driven by bright forecasts, confidence in continued progress, or desperation to ride this megatrend, many foreign companies leave the sanctuary of predictable markets for the distinctive ways of the Middle Kingdom. Then, once they clear immigration, convince skeptical bureaucrats, and cross the modern-day Rubicon, they face the daunting task of interpreting China's political and legal systems. ■

QUESTIONS

✪ **3-1.** Recommend a perspective an MNE could use to make sense of the political situation in China.

✪ **3-2.** How would you advise an MNE to manage the intricacies of China's legal environment?

POLITICS, LAWS, AND OPERATING INTERNATIONALLY

Politics and laws are always and everywhere dynamic. At different times, different parties champion different ideologies that endorse different political systems. Consequently, investing and operating internationally exposes MNEs to risks that arise from change in a country's political system.[17] Map 3.1 identifies the degree of political risk in countries worldwide. We profile political risk later in the chapter, but, at this point, this map highlights an enduring reality of IB: every market in the world has some, with most having high, degree of political risk that

MAP 3.1 Map of Political Risk, 2015

The distribution of political risk worldwide shows that it is a fundamental feature of the global business environment. As we see below, some countries have more, some countries have less, but all pose short- and long-term threats to an MNE's operating decisions and strategic choices.

Source: Based on Marsh Political Risk Map 2015; and AON Political Risk, http://www.aon.com/2016politicalriskmap

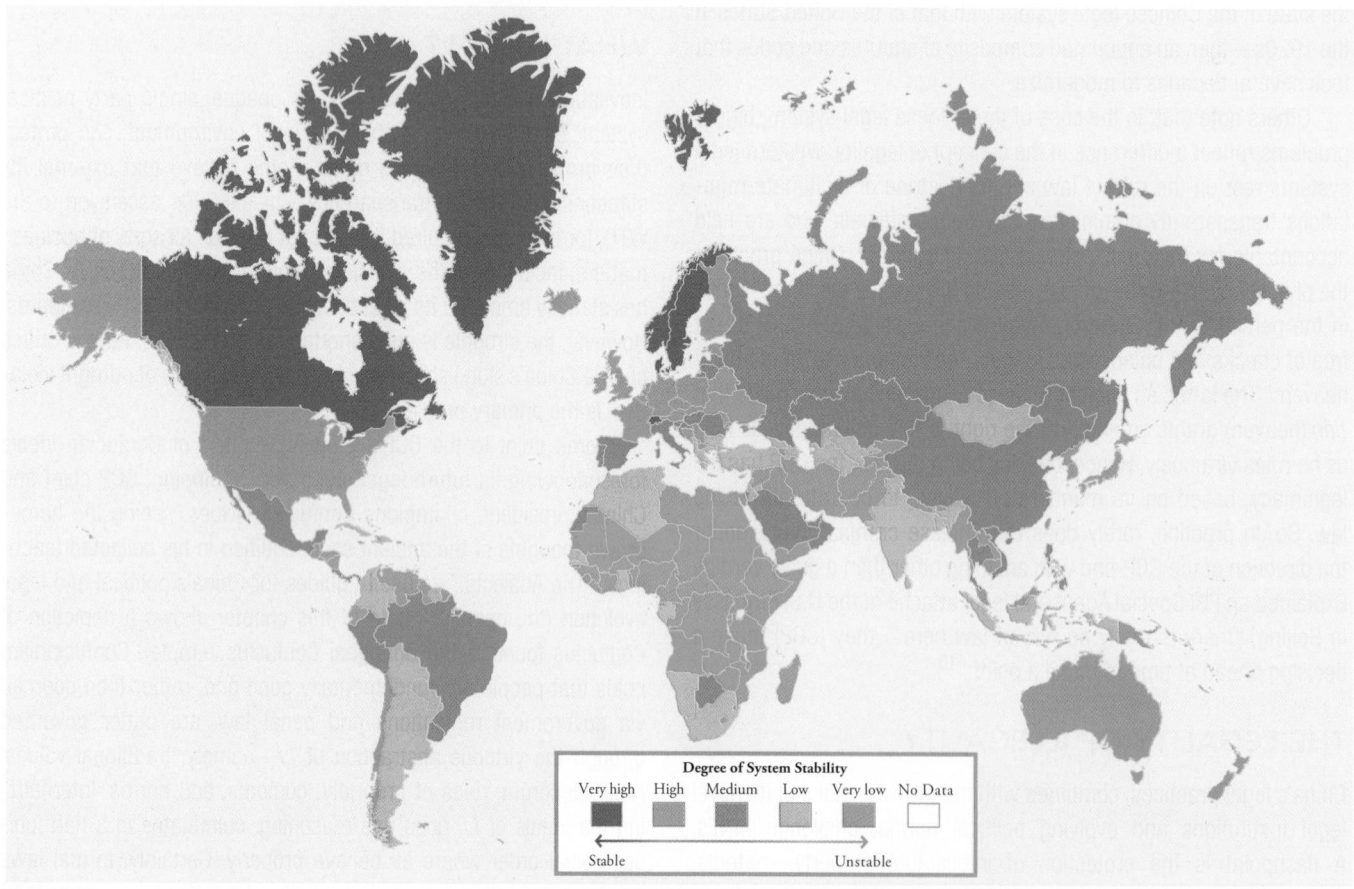

Degree of System Stability

| Very high | High | Medium | Low | Very low | No Data |

Stable ←→ Unstable

threatens the short-term profit and long-term sustainability of business activity.[18] Therefore, managers evaluate politics and law, making sense of the scale and scope of their dynamism, and estimating the resulting risks to the profitability and sustainability of their operations.

Operating internationally exposes managers to diverse, conflicting pressures. Some countries are similar; Australian companies find few surprises in New Zealand, for instance. In other cases, the differences are profound; an ill-prepared U.S. company will hit bumps in China. Consider, for instance, Russia. Home to 144 million people, Russia is the world's largest country in terms of territory. It possesses vast natural resources and its government looks to foreign MNEs to help modernize its energy-dependent economy. Still, political risks pose big problems for foreign investors. An executive at Swedish retailer IKEA explained that the Russian political environment is "a bit of a roller coaster....[Y]ou don't know exactly what will happen tomorrow."[19] For instance, Russian authorities arbitrarily confiscated Motorola's assets, charged PwC Russia with tax evasion on dubious allegations, and closed the McDonald's franchise in retaliation for the U.S. policy on the Ukraine.[20] Doing business in Russia means you had better be "big enough to defend yourself against bureaucratic attacks [and]...ready to hold your nose when elections are rigged and political opposition is crushed."[21] Then again, that might be insufficient—in 2015, Prime Minister Vladimir Putin authorized Russian prosecutors to declare foreign organizations "undesirable" and unilaterally close them. Besides political risk, Russia ranks high in terms of corruption, crony capitalism, and arbitrary governance.[22]

> Managers study political and legal environments in order to fit activities to local circumstances.

Politics and laws vary among the many markets that compose the global business environment.[23] The interplay of political ideologies, conceptions of political freedom, legacies of legality, presumptions of fairness, and standards of accountability in each market makes for challenging business environments. Navigating markets requires studying how political and legal circumstances overlap and differ. Managers evaluate, monitor, and forecast the dimensions and dynamics of foreign political environments. They gauge whether political freedom is a practical ideal or a wishful abstraction. They study how state officials exercise authority, legislate policies, regulate enterprise, and punish wrongdoers. They assess the interplay between the rule of law and man. They monitor how politicians are elected and whether, and how, they depart. Then, based on their analyses, they forecast points of political risk, construct business scenarios, and determine the best ways to acquire resources, make investments, adapt operating modes, and manage threats.

Cross-national variations, as seen in Map 3.1, increase the challenge of interpreting different philosophies, laws, and attitudes on political freedom, property rights, and legal responsibility. Consequently, effective managers begin with the realization that when it comes to politics and laws, different ideas result in different outcomes in different countries. Figure 3.1 identifies the political principles and legal outlooks that define a nation's business environment. This chapter profiles how they influence the predominant political ideology, shape the role of government, moderate the degree of political risk, and define the legal system.

FIGURE 3.1   Political and Legal Factors Influencing IB Operations

The political and legal environments are broad-stroke concepts that defy straightforward classification. Nevertheless, here we see key points that help managers develop useful perspectives.

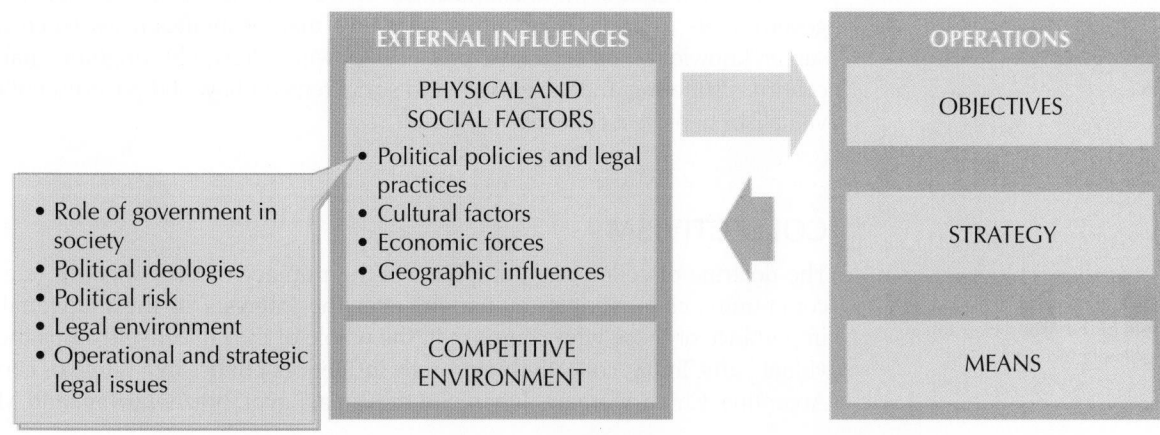

THE POLITICAL ENVIRONMENT

Whether targeting Afghanistan, Zimbabwe, or any of the 200-plus markets in between, managers study a nation's **political system**—namely, the structural dimensions and power dynamics of the government that (1) specify institutions, organizations, and interest groups and (2) define the norms and rules that govern political activities. The mission of a political system is clear-cut: integrate different groups into a functioning, self-governing society. Likewise, its test is sustaining society in the face of divisive viewpoints. Success supports peace and prosperity, as we see in Australia, Botswana, and Sweden. Failure leads to instability, insurrection, and fragility of the sort seen in Afghanistan, Haiti, Libya, and Yemen.[24]

> The goal of the political system is integrating the diverse elements of a society. Its test is uniting society in the face of divisive viewpoints.

Explaining the similarities and differences of political systems has intrigued a long line of thinkers, beginning with Plato and Confucius and moving on to Herodotus, Machiavelli, Smith, Rousseau, Marx, Gandhi, and Friedman.[25] Each wrestled with enduring philosophical issues: How should society balance individual rights versus the needs of the community to sustain a rational, righteous, and harmonious system? What is the basis of the state's authority over its citizens? Should society guarantee an individual the freedom to pursue economic self-interest? Does society fare better when individual rights are subordinated to collective goals? Should society champion equality or institute hierarchy? Are individual rights inalienable or conferred by the collective? Engaging these and like-minded questions, vital to interpreting political environments, directs our attention to the ideas of **individualism** and **collectivism**.

CONCEPT CHECKS

Chapter 2 showed that culture moderates the practices of international business. Many points of interpretation, both from an academic and managerial perspective, follow from the play of collectivism or individualism in a country.

INDIVIDUALISM

> Individualism champions the primacy of the rights and role of the individual over the group.

The doctrine of individualism emphasizes the primacy of individual freedom, self-expression, and personal independence (think of the stipulation in the U.S. Declaration of Independence that we all have "certain inalienable Rights, that among these are Life, Liberty and the pursuit of Happiness").[26] Individualism champions the exercise of one's ambitions while opposing regulations that constrain them. The government protects the liberty of individuals to act as they wish, as long as their actions do not infringe upon the liberties of others.

The business implications of individualism are direct: every person has the right to make decisions free of onerous rules and regulations. Countries with an individualistic orientation, such as Australia, Canada, the Netherlands, and the United States, shape their marketplace with the idea of *laissez-faire* (French for "let go/let do"). It holds that the government should not interfere in business affairs. Rather, the market operates according to the neoliberal principles of free market fundamentalism whereby people (1) regulate themselves in promoting economic prosperity and (2) act fairly and justly to maximize personal performance without threatening the welfare of society.

In practice, gaps between philosophical ideals and opportunistic behaviors fan an adversarial relationship between governments and businesses in individualistic societies. Apprehension that some maximize self-interest at the expense of collective welfare leads governments to apply regulations to reduce market inefficiencies (such as deficient consumer knowledge or excessive producer power). Presently, ongoing market problems in countries suffering anemic growth and social tension have led governments to restrain individualism to protect collective welfare.[27]

COLLECTIVISM

> Collectivism advocates the primacy of the rights and role of the group over the individual.

The doctrine of collectivism emphasizes the primacy of the collective (e.g., a group, party, community, class, society, or nation) over the interests of the individual. No matter the importance of those who compose it, the whole of the collective trumps the sum of its individual parts. Today, collectivism strongly influences politics in a range of countries, including Argentina, China, Vietnam, Japan, South Korea, Egypt, Brazil, Taiwan, and Mexico.

Collectivism in the business world holds that the ownership of assets, the allocation of resources, the structure of industries, the conduct of companies, and the actions of managers share a common goal: make decisions and conduct activities that improve the welfare of the collective. A collectivist outlook encourages political systems to develop regulations that promote social equality, labor rights, income equality, and workplace democracy. Then, the "welfare of the nation takes precedence over the selfishness of the individuals."[28] In extreme cases, such as Venezuela, Iran, or Saudi Arabia, political leaders limit individual property rights and police mass media in order to enforce collective standards. Private ownership of satellite dishes, for instance, is illegal in Iran and Saudi Arabia given the state's view that they let people access media that promotes anti-Islamic individualism.[29]

POLITICAL IDEOLOGY

> A political ideology encapsulates the doctrine of political behavior and change. It outlines the procedures for converting ideas into actions.

A nation's orientation toward individualism or collectivism anchors its political system and, hence, its predominant **political ideology**. In theory, an ideology is an integrated vision that defines a holistic conception of an abstract ideal and its normative thought processes.[30] For example, the ideal of freedom, the foundation of democratic ideologies, carries with it ideas about related principles, doctrines, goals, practices, and symbols. Practically, a political ideology stipulates how society ought to govern itself and outlines the methods by which it will do so. An effective political ideology moves beyond describing a vision of a better, brighter future—it specifies the means to achieve that ideal.[31]

Figure 3.2 interprets prominent political ideologies in terms of a **political spectrum**. By specifying a basic conceptual structure, spectrum analysis guides the assessment of a complex issue—in this case, political ideology. Configuring ideologies along the central axis lets us model different ones relative to the others. The starting point is specifying reasonable endpoints. Once set, one then positions other ideologies. Determining the standard of "reasonable endpoints" is open for interpretation given the range of candidates. Possibilities include anarchism, conservatism, secularism, environmentalism, liberalism, feminism, nationalism, socialism, theocracy, and so on. Culture also moderates interpretation. From a Western perspective, for example, one commonly sets the endpoints as conservative versus

FIGURE 3.2 The Political Spectrum

In practice, purely democratic and totalitarian systems are exceptions. Looking around the world, one sees many variations. For example, democratic systems range from radical on one side (advocates of extreme political reform) to reactionary (advocates of a return to past conditions). Likewise, totalitarian systems emphasize different degrees of state control. Fascism aims to control people's minds, souls, and daily existence, whereas authoritarianism confines itself to political control of the state.

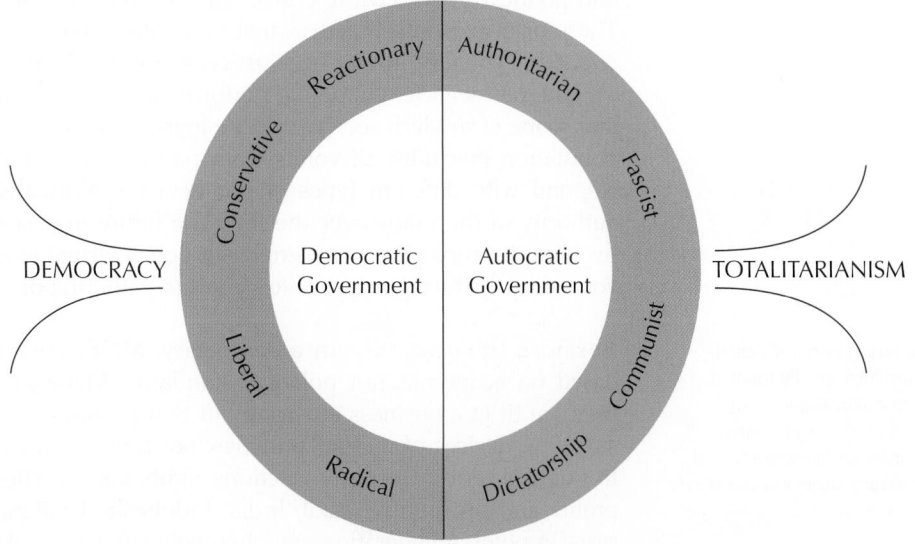

liberal interpretations of democracy (i.e., Republican versus Democrat). Other endpoints command greater relevance in other contexts. A political spectrum in an Islamic country, such as Iran or Saudi Arabia, is bounded by theocracy versus secularism to reflect the role of the clergy in the government. In the case of Taiwan, parties that champion Taiwanese independence oppose those advocating reunification with China. In Belgium, the ends would reflect the ethnic and socioeconomic tensions between the Dutch-speaking Flanders region and the French-speaking Walloon region. In Canada, they would be inclusive nationalism versus Bloc Québécois's call for the sovereignty of predominantly French-speaking Québec.

A common theme anchors how managers interpret a political ideology: namely, its vision of political freedom. The notion of political freedom originated in the practice of politics in ancient Greece and has since been inseparable from interpreting the play of politics and laws. **Political freedom** is the degree to which fair and competitive elections occur, the extent to which individual and group freedoms are guaranteed, the legitimacy ascribed to the rule of law, and the existence of freedom of expression. Rather than an inalienable right, the ideal degree of political freedom is open to debate. Some, like the United States, champion a lot, others, like Saudi Arabia, advocate a little. Consequently, the matters of where, how, and why a company invests and how it manages operations are alienable freedoms, subject to the prevailing political ideology.

Poetical freedom sets the political spectrum that we use in this text (see Figure 3.2). Democracy, and its call to promote and protect individuals' political freedom, anchors one endpoint. Totalitarianism, and its call to control and constrain individuals' political freedom, sets the other.[32] The ideologies that fall between these endpoints interpret political freedom differently. Liberal ideologies, for instance, advocate the right of individuals whereas authoritarian ideologies subordinate individual freedoms to the welfare of the collective. In the former, managers have many options. In the latter, they have far fewer. Hence, managers study how a political system interprets freedom, and gauge its implications for how the state then regulates the market. Unquestionably, each ideology in Figure 3.2 is notable; we lack the space to profile each. Understanding the ideals and the means of the two endpoints, democracy and totalitarianism, supports interpreting the others.

DEMOCRACY

Abraham Lincoln held that **democracy** is a government "of the people, by the people, for the people." Modern-day democracies translate this ideology into the principles that all citizens are politically equal, entitled to freedom of thought, opinion, belief, speech, and association, and command sovereign power over public officials.[33] A democratic government protects personal and political rights, civil liberties, fair and free elections, and independent courts of law.[34] These principles and practices institutionalize political freedoms and civil liberties that, by endorsing equality, liberty, and justice, support individualism.

Different legacies shape the performance of democracy in a nation. Practically, the scale and scope of modern society impose logistical constraints, particularly when the size of the population precludes all voters from participating directly. Table 3.1 shows that countries respond with different types of democracies. Notwithstanding variance, all advocate the authority of the many over the few. The future may see a resurgence of direct democracy. Evolving technologies increasingly support a virtual assembly of citizens who express their votes directly through electronic signature gathering or online polling processes.

Business Implications In a democracy, MNEs have the freedom to invest and operate based on economic, not political, standards. Managers and consumers are free to do as they see fit in a business environment that promotes commerce and encourages trade. The signaling devices of market activities, not bureaucratic regulation, organize resource flows. In political terms, freedom sanctions rights and liberties. In economic terms, it legitimizes profits and prosperity. Brazil, India, Indonesia, Thailand, Colombia, and Malaysia provide cases in point. A generation ago, their belief in central planning run by a strong state had led

Political freedom measures the degree to which fair and competitive elections occur, the extent to which individual and group freedoms are guaranteed, the legitimacy ascribed to the rule of law, and the existence of freedom of the press.

Democracy calls for participation by citizens in a fair and just decision-making process.

Democracy and individualism are intrinsically related and mutually reinforcing; individualism legitimates principles of democracy and democracy supports standards of individualism.

TABLE 3.1 Prominent Types of Democracies

The elemental definition of democracy hails from the Greek *dēmokratía:* "rule by the people." Translating the ideal of the "rule by the people" into a functioning political system can take a variety of forms.

Representative	Originates in a constitution that protects individual freedoms and liberties. The law treats all citizens equally. Elected representatives, while ultimately autonomous, act in the people's interest. Officials represent voters and, while mindful of voters' preferences, have the authority to act as they see fit. Examples include the United States and Japan.
Multiparty	System whereby three or more parties govern, either separately or as part of a coalition. A single party cannot legislate policy without negotiating with opposition parties. Examples include Canada, Germany, Italy, and Israel.
Parliamentary	Citizens exercise political power by electing representatives to a legislative branch, the parliament. The legislature is the source of legitimacy for the various ministers that run the executive branch. Examples include India and Australia.
Social	Applies democratic means to guide the transition from capitalism to socialism. The government promotes egalitarianism while also regulating capitalism's tendency toward opportunism. Examples include Norway and Sweden.

to stagnant, if not failing, economies. Now, these countries are converting the energy of their emerging democracy into dynamic business environments.[35]

TOTALITARIANISM

A **totalitarian system** subordinates the interests of the individual to that of the collective. An agent in whatever form, such as an individual, a committee, an assembly, a junta, or a party, monopolizes political power and uses it to regulate many, if not all, aspects of public and private life. The agent, whether idealistic or delusional, believes it has noble intentions, protecting people from the hazards of individual choice.[36] Fair game includes regulating residents' occupation, income level, interests, religion, and even family structure.[37] A totalitarian government eliminates dissent through indoctrination, persecution, surveillance, propaganda, censorship, and violence. It tolerates few, if any, ideas, interests, or activities that oppose state ideology.[38] In extreme situations, personal survival is linked to that of the ruling regime. These conditions merge the interests of individuals with those of the state. Table 3.2 profiles types of totalitarian systems.

A totalitarian system consolidates power in a single agent who then controls political, economic, and social activities.

TABLE 3.2 Prominent Types of Totalitarianism

First noted in reference to Italian fascism, "totalitario" stood for "complete, absolute," control by a dictatorial one-party state that regulates every realm of life. Here, we see approaches that a ruling agent can take to control society to different degrees.

Authoritarianism	Tolerates no deviation from state ideology. Day-to-day life reflects submission to state authority; resistance incurs punishment. Officials control the political environment, but pay less attention to the economic and social structure of society. Examples include Kazakhstan, North Korea, Chad, and Turkmenistan.
Fascism	Advocates a single-party state that controls, through force and indoctrination, people's minds, souls, and daily existence. Calls for the merger of state and corporate power, applying corporatist perspectives, values, and systems. There have been few fascist political systems; most prevailed during World War II.
Secularism	A single-party government controls elections, tolerates dissent as long as it does not challenge the state, and suppresses other ideologies. The state does not prescribe an all-encompassing ideology. It grants limited individual freedoms provided one does not contest state authority or disrupt social harmony. Examples include China, Vietnam, and Venezuela.
Theocracy	Government is an expression of the favored deity. Leaders profess to represent its interests on earth. The State applies ancient dogma in place of modern principles. Strict social regulation and gender regimentation typically prevails. Examples include Iran, Afghanistan, and Saudi Arabia.

CONCEPT CHECKS

Recall our discussion in Chapter 2 (page 79), of "Major Behavioral Factors Affecting Business." These variables change as people change—or as state authority influences them. Shaping people's behavior to support the state's interests leads an authoritarian government to manipulate norms, including work motivation, risk taking, communication practices, and consumption preferences.

Totalitarianism and collectivism are intrinsically related and mutually reinforcing; collectivism legitimates principles of totalitarianism and totalitarianism supports standards of collectivism.

Authoritarian parties often rely on shadowy politics, skewed elections, and nefarious security agencies.

The dynamics of change in a totalitarian state highlight the means used to enforce its ideology. Rejecting preceding forms of society as corrupt, immoral, and beyond reform, a single leader advocates a new society that corrects wrongs, redresses injustice, and creates harmony. In place of private property, the state allocates power and status to reward supporters (who often monetize privileges through corruption). It uses propaganda, indoctrination, and incarceration to coerce citizens. State-controlled media filters information, state-controlled education filters ideas, and state-controlled courts, police, and security suppress dissent. In extreme cases, the cumulative result is a "virtual mind prison" that fuses leader and the state.[39] An individual conforms or is cast out.

Although remote to citizens in Western democracies, forms of totalitarianism prevail throughout the world. Some 2.6 billion people—roughly one-third of the world's population—live under such rule, with another 1.7 billion people residing in less draconian but still authoritarian political systems.[40] The citizens of such countries as Madagascar, Turkmenistan, Afghanistan, China, Iran, North Korea, and Saudi Arabia have fewer personal freedoms and civil liberties than their counterparts in Japan, Canada, or Denmark. The reemergence of powerful, single-party states worldwide reinforces totalitarianism: Russia suppresses individual freedoms through arbitrary governance; Venezuela restricts dissenting media; Iran corrupts its electoral process; and Saudi Arabia regulates personal choice. Leaders of these and similarly governed states display improving skillfulness. Research spotlights the "growing sophistication of modern authoritarians. They are flexible; they distort and abuse the legal framework; they are adept at the techniques of modern propaganda."[41] In particular, some point to the astute political practices powering China's rise.[42]

Business Implications   Managers in totalitarian systems face radically different markets than those found in democracies. Private enterprise, if permitted, supports state control of the economy. For instance, the Chinese government, under the direction of the CCP, owns and manages large swathes of its economy. The state is the majority owner of many of the largest publicly listed Chinese companies, some of which are among the biggest firms in the world.[43] Similarly, conglomerates in finance, media, mining, metals, transportation, communication, and so on answer to the CCP. Likewise, China's provincial and municipal officials control tens of thousands of medium-sized and smaller ones.[44] Add it all up and you have an authoritarian system that rejects many of the practices found in a democracy.

Managers operating in these sorts of markets adjust decision-making to the fact that government's imperative is sustaining state power, and it sees the market as a powerful tool to do so. Political risks affect all companies, but typically hit foreign investors hardest. The state favors local companies at the expense of foreign competitors, providing them with advantageous financing, special tax programs, relaxed work regulations, and other benefits.[45] The state manipulates markets for political purposes, thereby distorting resource valuations and blurring risk–return relationships. For example, China requires foreign enterprises to accept, if not facilitate, setting up Communist Party cells in their local operations. Local governments can insist private companies contribute a share of their payrolls to finance Party activities.[46] The cells then direct companies to behave lawfully, fulfill their social responsibilities, promote harmonious labor relations, and maintain social stability.

MNEs strike deals in authoritarian states that they avoid elsewhere. Consider General Electric's 50/50 joint venture with Aviation Industry, a Chinese military-jet maker, to produce avionics, the electronic brains of aircraft. The deal required GE to take the risky, but potentially lucrative step of folding pieces of its global operations into a partnership with a state-owned enterprise. Such deals had earlier proved troublesome, souring over concerns that Chinese partners, after gaining access to Western technology and expertise, became potent rivals.[47] Even so, seeing China as its "second home market," GE reasoned the cost of missing the fast-expanding Chinese aviation industry exceeded the potential political risks. Reasoned GE's vice chairperson: "Staying out of China in hopes of keeping our intellectual property safe is obviously not an option."[48]

THE STATE OF POLITICAL FREEDOM

Freedom House identifies three types of political systems:

- Free
- Partly free
- Not free

Since 1972 Freedom House has annually assessed the state of political freedom around the world.[49] It declares that "Freedom is possible only in democratic political systems in which the governments are accountable to their own people; the rule of law prevails; and freedoms of expression, association, and belief, as well as respect for the rights of minorities and women, are guaranteed."[50] Freedom House applies measures derived from the Universal Declaration of Human Rights, a landmark document that defines the 30 rights to which all human beings are inherently entitled, including freedom of speech, religion, from fear, and from want.[51] Freedom House assesses the rights and freedoms enjoyed by individuals, rather than those proclaimed by governments. Performance places a country into one of three classes:

- A *"free" country* exhibits open political competition, respect for civil liberties, independent civic life, and independent media. There are inalienable freedoms of expression, assembly, association, education, and religion. Examples include Australia, Brazil, India, and the United States.

- A *"partly free" country* exhibits limited political rights and civil liberties, corruption, weak rule of law, ethnic and religious strife, unfair elections, and censorship. Often, democracy is a convenient slogan for the single party that dominates within a façade of regulated pluralism. Examples include Guatemala, Pakistan, and Tanzania.

- A *"not free" country* has few to no political rights and civil liberties. The government allows minimal to no exercise of personal choice, relies on the rule of man as the basis of law, constrains religious and social freedoms, and controls a large share, if not all, of business activity. Examples include China, Russia, Saudi Arabia, and Iran.

Map 3.2 shows the distribution of freedom worldwide. In 2015, 86 countries were free, 59 partly free, and 50 not free. Regarding population, approximately 2.9 billion people

MAP 3.2 Map of Freedom

Freedom House, classifying countries in terms of their degree of political freedom, identifies three types—Free, Partly Free, and Not Free. If you live in a country classified as "free," you enjoy a broad range of political rights and civil liberties. If you are a citizen of a "partly free" nation, your share of rights and liberties ranges anywhere from average to just below average. If your homeland is "not free," you have few rights and liberties.

Source: Freedom House, "Map of Freedom 2015," at https://freedomhouse.org/report/freedom-world/freedom-world-2015. Used by permission of Freedom House.

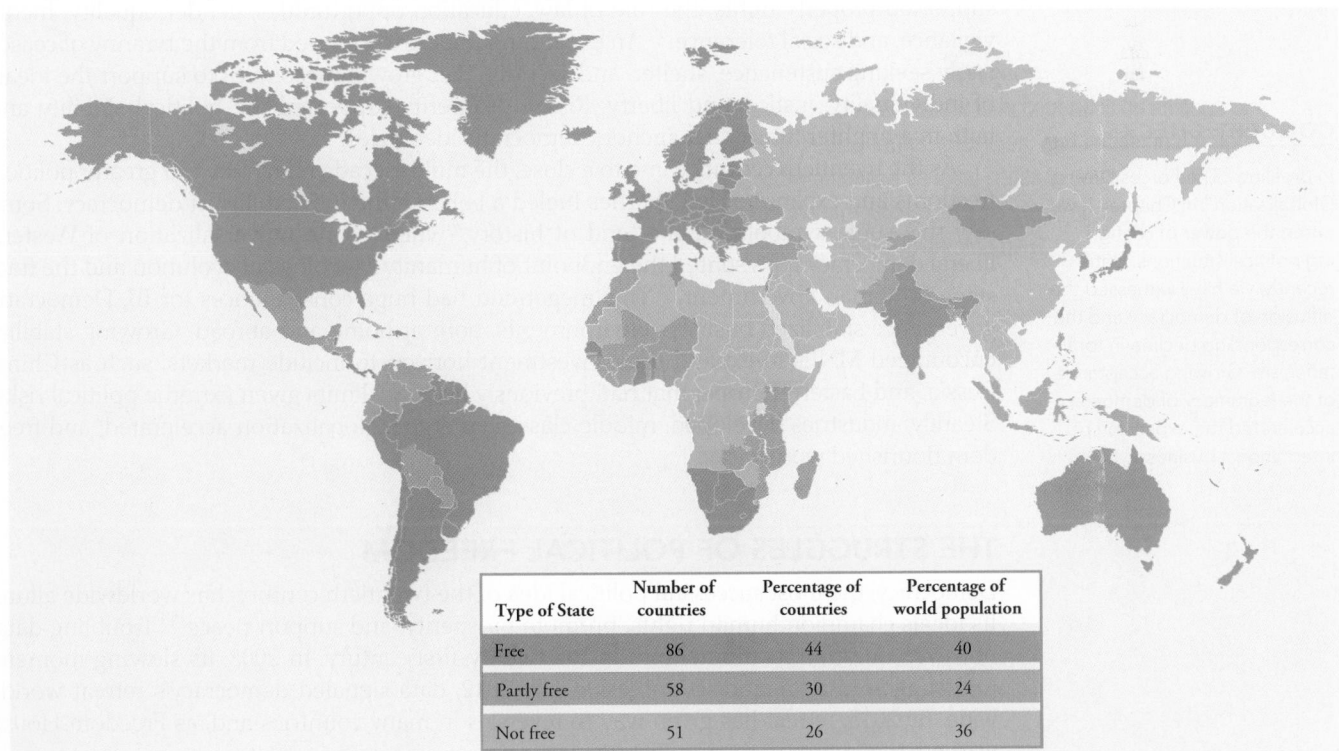

Type of State	Number of countries	Percentage of countries	Percentage of world population
Free	86	44	40
Partly free	58	30	24
Not free	51	26	36

(40 percent of the global population) live in a free country, 1.8 billion live in a partly free country, and 2.6 billion live in a not free country.

THE PREVALENCE OF POLITICAL FREEDOM

The second half of the twentieth century saw the steady diffusion of democracy worldwide. Between 1950 and 2014, the number of electoral democracies grew from 22 to 120 countries. Many had been totalitarian states of some form, but had begun developing democratic governance. This shift signified the so-called **Third Wave of Democratization**, a global movement that expanded individual freedoms and civil liberties.[52] Societies began building just institutions, fair property rights, independent media, and impartial judiciaries. As a result, by 2000, nearly half the world's population, more than at any time in history, lived in a democracy of some sort.

Beginning in the mid-1970s, a confluence of trends began fueling engines that powered the Third Wave of Democratization. Ultimately, they culminated in toppling the Berlin Wall, undoing the Communist Bloc, and closing the Cold War. First, the growing failure of totalitarian regimes to deliver prosperity eroded their legitimacy. Aggrieved citizens, weary of declining standards of life, rebelled. Formerly communist countries, shifting to freer markets, endorsed entrepreneurialism. Shift from collectivism to individualism promoted civil liberties and encouraged political freedom.

Second, improving communications technologies eroded totalitarian regimes' power to control information. Whereas once it took weeks, if ever, for word-of-mouth protests to spread, improving connections quickly circulated news.[53] Images of resistance and rebellion had snowball effects, inspiring pro-democracy campaigns worldwide. People, increasingly aware of their rights and the global march to freedom, challenged the injustice of state control.[54] Expanding access to uncensored news, in light of Thomas Jefferson's belief that "Information is the currency of democracy," fortified calls for civil liberties.

Finally, freedom yielded economic dividends, helping people move from poverty to prosperity.[55] The median per capita gross domestic product, a measure of the standard of living, was nearly seven times greater in free versus not free countries. Growing prosperity supported property rights, the rule of law, education opportunities, gender equality, media vigilance, and social tolerance.[56] An expanding middle class, freed from the tyranny of ceaselessly seeking sustenance, shelter, and security, had growing resources to support the ideals of individuality, justice, and liberty. Rising prosperity supported the political stability and faith in a brighter future that anchors democratic ideologies.[57]

As the twentieth century came to a close, the multi-decade march toward greater political freedoms and expansive civil liberties fueled a belief in the inevitability of democracy. Some saw this surge symbolizing the "end of history," whereby the universalization of Western liberal democracy represented the endpoint of humanity's ideological evolution and the final stage of human government.[58] This megatrend had huge consequences for IB. Democratic governance stabilized business environments, both at home and abroad. Growing stability encouraged MNEs to expand their investment horizon to include markets, such as China, Russia, and Eastern Europe, that had previously been off-limits given extreme political risks. Steadily, industries developed, middle classes emerged, globalization accelerated, and freedom flourished worldwide.

THE STRUGGLES OF POLITICAL FREEDOM

Democracy, the most successful political idea of the twentieth century, has worldwide allure. Its ideals champion human rights, promote prosperity, and support peace.[59] Troubling data, however, question its momentum in the twenty-first century. In 2008, its slowing momentum suggested a "democracy recession." By 2012, data signaled democracy's retreat worldwide. By 2015, retreat has given way to reversals in many countries and, as Freedom House warned, the "return of the iron fist."

The Third Wave of Democratization refers to the third surge of democratically governed states in the twentieth century. Ultimately, as this wave crested, the number of countries led by a democratic government doubled.

Various forces powered past the Third Wave of Democratization:

- Failure of totalitarian regimes to deliver prosperity
- Improving communication technology
- Economic dividends of political freedom

CONCEPT CHECKS

Chapter 1 identifies the "Expansion of Technology" as a driving force of globalization. Advances in telecommunications liberated the flow of information, thereby challenging and changing social and political attitudes in many countries.

CONCEPT CHECKS

In profiling "The Forces Driving Globalization" in Chapter 1, we noted the power of changing political situations. Until recently, we have witnessed the diffusion of democracy and the corresponding decline in totalitarianism. Growing acceptance of the legitimacy of democracy accelerated the expansion of international business.

Several indicators show slowing adoption of democracy throughout the world.

Increasingly, managers qualify their interpretation of rising political risks with the possibility that "history," rather than ending, is just beginning. Granted, the gains in electoral democracies seen during the Third Wave of Democratization have not been erased. Individuals and institutions, however, struggle to promote free elections, defend human rights, constrain state power, and safeguard integrity in public policy. In their place, sham elections, police crackdowns, kangaroo courts, and persecution of dissidents gain traction. All speak to the stance taken by President Lukashenka of Belarus, who declared on the heels of a rigged election victory, "There will be no more mindless democracy in this country."[60] Worldwide, influential totalitarian regimes impose "forceful measures designed to suppress democratic reformers, international assistance to those reformers, and ultimately the very idea of democracy itself."[61] As a result, 2015 marked the ninth consecutive year that political freedom declined worldwide—the longest consecutive period of setbacks in modern times.[62]

The *Economist Intelligence Unit* identifies four types of political systems:

- Full democracy
- Flawed democracy
- Hybrid regime
- Authoritarian regime

Gauging the Scale of Struggle: The Texture of Democracy Democracy, narrowly defined, is easily achieved—if merely holding elections were sufficient, virtually every country would qualify. The *Economist Intelligence Unit* (EIU) resolves this distortion, gauging the electoral process, but also assessing the degree that day-to-day life supports political freedom. Specifically, the EIU evaluates the "texture of democracy" in a country in terms of its public institutions, political processes, public attitudes, pluralism, civil liberties, political participation, and political culture. The EIU translates these dimensions into 60 indicators that measure the texture of democracy in 167 countries. Combined, these countries are home to nearly the entire global population.[63] The EIU classifies a country as a *full democracy, flawed democracy, hybrid regime,* or *authoritarian regime.* Table 3.3 profiles the general characteristics of each. Map 3.3 identifies their distribution worldwide.

TABLE 3.3 Types and Characteristics of Political Systems in the World

Classification	Characteristics[64]	Examples
Full Democracy	• Mature political culture promotes and protects political freedoms and civil liberties. • Government discharges responsibility transparently. • An effective system of checks and balances regulates politics. • The judiciary is independent, its decisions are impartially enforced, and the rule of law prevails. • Media are independent, vigilant, and diverse.	Australia, Austria, Costa Rica, Denmark, Norway, South Korea, United States, Uruguay.
Flawed Democracy	• The State respects basic civil liberties. • Free and fair elections regularly occur but experience fraud or media restrictions. • Governance problems and low political participation make for a weak political culture. • Leadership and policy change occur frequently.	Brazil, Estonia, Hungary, India, Indonesia, Jamaica, Mexico, Namibia, Senegal, Singapore, South Africa, Taiwan.
Hybrid Regime	• Electoral irregularities undermine freedom and justice. • Government limits opposition parties and candidates. • Judicial bias signals the state corrupting the rule of law. • Political culture, public administration, and political participation struggles. • Corruption is extensive, civil society fades, and media are regulated.	Bangladesh, Cambodia, Ecuador, Honduras, Kyrgyzstan, Mozambique, Niger, Pakistan, Tanzania, Thailand, Venezuela.
Authoritarian Regime	• Political pluralism is absent or repressed by the state. • Democratic institutions may exist, but have little substance and the state uses them to legitimate single-party rule. • Elections, if they do occur, are neither free nor fair. • The state systematically disregards civil liberties. • There is no independent judiciary and the rule of man prevails. • Media are typically state-owned or controlled by groups connected to the regime. • Censorship suppresses criticism of the state and propaganda promotes the state ideology.	Afghanistan, Chad, China, Guinea, Kazakhstan, Kuwait, Nigeria, Russia, Saudi Arabia, Swaziland, Zimbabwe.

MAP 3.3   THE DEMOCRACY INDEX

The scale and scope of democracy varies worldwide. Differences in electoral process and pluralism, civil liberties, functioning of government, political participation, and political culture make for different outcomes.

Source: Adapted from "Democracy Index 2014." 2015. The Economist Intelligence Unit. Accessed November 25. http://www.eiu.com/public/topical_report.aspx?campaignid=Democracy0115 .

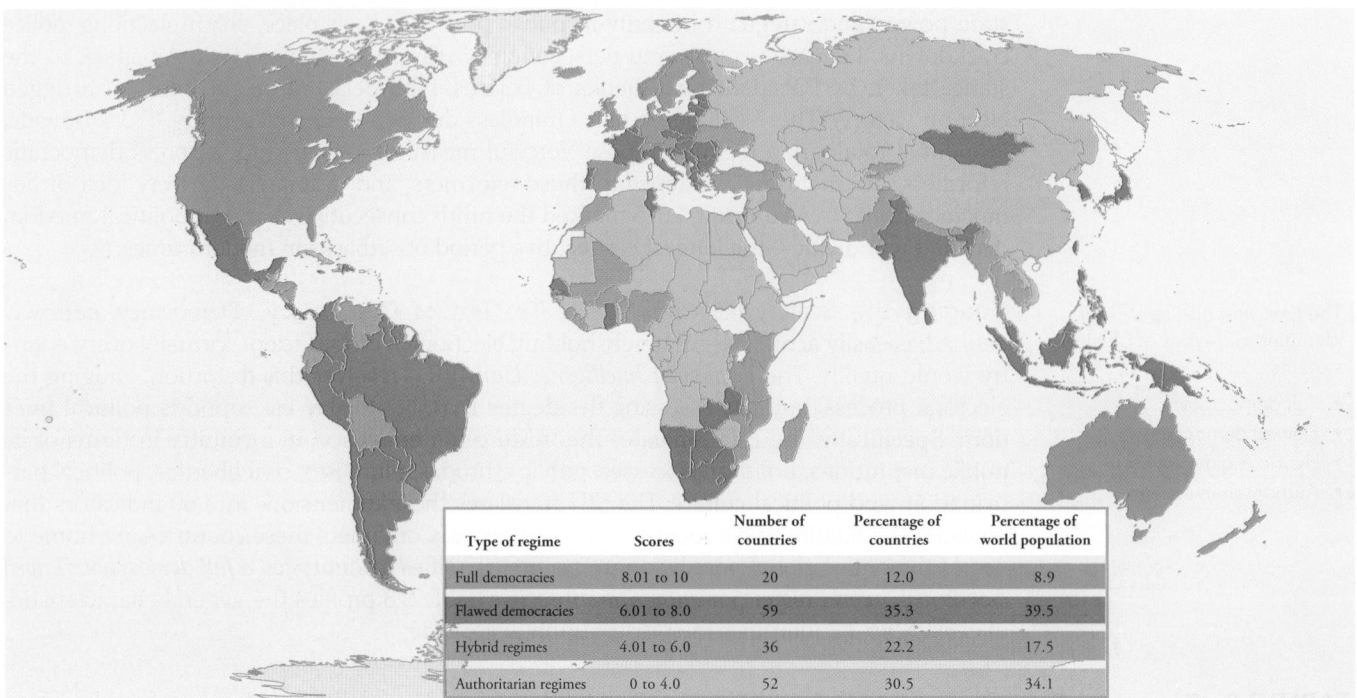

Type of regime	Scores	Number of countries	Percentage of countries	Percentage of world population
Full democracies	8.01 to 10	20	12.0	8.9
Flawed democracies	6.01 to 8.0	59	35.3	39.5
Hybrid regimes	4.01 to 6.0	36	22.2	17.5
Authoritarian regimes	0 to 4.0	52	30.5	34.1

The EIU's analysis reports that many countries are "democracies" in name only. Of the 76 countries commonly regarded as democracies, 24 are full democracies while 52 are flawed democracies. One sees 19 full democracies in the West, with the remainder in Latin America, Eastern Europe, and Africa. Flawed democracies predominate in Latin America and Eastern Europe. The fragility of their institutional structures, political participation, and democratic cultures constrains freedom. Likewise, their governments' response to corruption, terrorism, and drug trafficking worsens the situation.

Of the remaining 89 countries, 39 are hybrid regimes that mix democratic and authoritarian practices. Many hybrid regimes manifest the markings of democracies. Procedural irregularities, by corrupting free and fair processes, undermine freedom. Hong Kong, for example, exemplifies a hybrid regime. It has telltale aspects of a democracy, such as an impartial judiciary, civil liberties, independent media, and political parties. Still, authoritarian policies persist. Consider, for instance, its electoral process. Its Chief Executive (effectively its president) is chosen not by Hong Kong's 7 million residents, but by a 1,200-person "Election Committee" composed of handpicked elites; Hong Kong, by the way, tops the crony-capitalism world league table.[65]

Authoritarian regimes predominate in 52 countries. Like hybrid regimes, most of these states showcase democratic practices, such as popular elections. Fundamentally, they are largely Potemkin designs—citizens have the freedom, for instance, to vote only for candidates that have been preapproved by the ruling elite. Day-to-day life evidences aspects of totalitarianism, including personal restrictions, public corruption, state-owned media, omnipresent state security, pervasive censorship, and a biased judiciary.

Worldwide, few people live in fully functional democracies; many more live in authoritarian states.

Qualifying Democracy by Demography   The distribution of political systems in terms of demography improve our understanding of the play of ideologies worldwide. In broad terms, about half of the world's population lives within some sort of democracy—that is, they meet the minimum expectation, regularly running elections of some sort. However, EIU standards indicate that 12 percent of the world population lives in countries with a functioning full democracy, 36 percent live in flawed democracies, 14 percent live in hybrid regimes, and 38 percent live in authoritarian regimes.[66] Effectively, about 900 million people, or one of eight people, live in a full democracy. Alternatively, some 2.6 billion people, or about a third of the world's population, live in authoritarian states.[67]

THE ALLURE OF AUTHORITARIANISM

Powering the resurgence of totalitarianism is

- strong states support strong performance,
- gaps in the principles and practices of democracy.
- Economic insecurity following slowing growth,
- escalating debate of the meaning of democracy.

Countries, skeptical of the virtues of a multiparty democracy, have translated authoritarian ideologies into single-party political systems. This trend spans the world, including Hungary, Burkina Faso, Russia, Lithuania, Thailand, Venezuela, Turkey, and Malaysia.[68] Authoritarianism reduces political freedom and alters the texture of democracy. Analogous to the engines that powered the Third Wave of Democratization, several contemporary developments promote authoritarianism.

Political Economy of Growth   The modernization hypothesis holds that aspects of economic development—notably, industrialization, urbanization, education, health, and income—support democratic governance. Rising wealth, particularly among an expanding middle class, promotes property rights and individualism, which in turn endorses democracy. Today, data challenges this thesis.[69] Consider China. Many have seen its economic performance since 1980 validating, if not legitimating, its authoritarian, one-party system as an alternative to a liberal, multiparty democracy. For many poverty-stricken, politically unstable countries, patience with the not-yet-realized dividends of the "democracy advantage" thesis has worn thin. Some point to India, noting that more than 65 years of nearly uninterrupted democratic governance rule has failed to improve health, education, or wealth for a majority of its residents. Consequently, China's model of a "people's democratic dictatorship" gains credibility.[70]

Rhetoric Versus Reality   Democracy setbacks in Italy, France, UK, Spain, and the United States give pause to some 70 strategically significant countries at the political crossroads. If democracy can't work there, how could it work here, wonder some in Bangladesh, Ecuador, Mozambique, and Afghanistan.[71] Charges of hypocrisy against Western countries (owing to incursions in Iraq, Libya, and Afghanistan, along with the implications of antiterrorist activities to political freedoms and civil liberties) jumble democratic ideals. Double standards in foreign policy (i.e., some autocratic countries can be allies, such as Saudi Arabia, whereas others are foes, like Venezuela) discredit democracy's promoters.[72] Confidence in institutions has declined throughout the West. Fewer than one in five West Europeans trust political parties, while only one in three regards governments and parliaments as trustworthy.[73] In the United States, 8 percent of Americans, versus 40 percent in 1987, report "a great deal" or "quite a lot" of confidence in Congress; this is the only major U.S. institution, from a set of 15 that includes the military, big business, public schools, banks, newspapers, and the presidency, to score in the single digits.[74]

Economic Problems   High unemployment, slow growth, and rising debt in many Western democracies erodes the effectiveness of democracy. The International Labour Organization reports wavering belief that political policies in democratic states lead to a fairer and brighter future.[75] History shows that right-wing totalitarian movements generally draw popular support from middle-class folks seeking to preserve the status quo. Those who fall into poverty are politically hazardous. Often, the worse the economy, the more people describe themselves as "right-wing."[76] Alternatively, left-wing totalitarianism often develops from working-class movements seeking to overthrow wealthy oppressors—think of the tension between the proletariat and bourgeois in Marxism. Persistent unemployment, debt, and anxiety erode confidence that democracy works.[77]

Who Defines Democracy?   The legitimacy of Western notions of democracy travels poorly to countries that endorse different ideals. Hu Jintao, former CCP chief and China's president, speaks of "democracy" with a different meaning from that used by Westerners. In his view, calls for multiparty democracy are taboo, opposition cannot officially organize, reform must obey the "correct political orientation," and "orderly" change must respect and preserve the authority of the CCP.[78] Hu's successor, Xi Jing Ping, elaborates this view, advising the West that "your democracy is the democracy of Greece and ancient Rome, and that's your tradition. We have our own traditions."[79] Similarly, Prime Minister Vladimir Putin, proclaiming himself "a true democrat," argues the West misinterprets the virtues of authoritarianism. He charges "some of the participants in the international dialogue believe that their ideas [of democracy] are the ultimate truth."[80] Instead Putin has promised a "dictatorship of the law," an approach that appeals to many Russians that prefer strong leadership to a vibrant democracy. Others add that Western-style democracy, rather than promoting individual rights and civil liberties, is an ideological ruse that disguises inequalities. Brazil's former President da Silva contends the advocates of Western-style democracy no longer speak for the world, having lost the moral authority to dictate solutions to developing countries.[81]

The engines of totalitarianism, considered in the context of democracy's reversal, raise vital questions. Our *Looking to the Future* assesses these trends and asks how MNEs might respond.

Looking to the Future
Political Ideology and MNEs' Actions

Managers wonder what a political map of the world might look like in the next decade. Will democracy regain its allure? Will totalitarianism gain momentum? Will new ideologies arise? It's tempting to dismiss these questions as academic distractions. The data indicate they are anything but. As faltering freedom and resurgent authoritarianism accelerate democracy's retreat, countries reset, markets change, and MNEs adjust strategies. Trends spotlight three ideologies competing for supremacy—namely, the Washington Consensus, the Beijing Consensus, and the Clash of Civilizations. What, pray tell, might these mean to managers?

The Washington Consensus

Named after the close of the Cold War for the free-market, pro-trade, and pro-globalization policies promoted by the United States, the Washington Consensus advocates democracy, political freedom, rule of law, and human rights.[82] As Washington became the philosophical center in an America-dominated unipolar world, its idealized Consensus—promoted by executives, politicians, generals, journalists, and institutions—called upon countries to reform in ways that mimic the political economy of the United States. Powering this call was a set of interrelated principles:

right-minded reform led to economic growth, which created a middle class that supported property rights, which, in turn, promoted the rule of law. Making those choices and implementing the requisite policies, in turn, supported individualism and instituted democracy. Navigating this sequence, reasoned the United States, built nations that championed prosperity and peace. A world of nations practicing U.S.-style, pro-peace democracy arguably signified the endpoint of humanity's sociocultural evolution.[83]

The Beijing Consensus

Some see the growing appeal of the Beijing Consensus signaling the next predominant ideology.[84] A euphemism for China's self-proclaimed "people's democratic dictatorship," the Beijing Consensus is a single-party system in which elected representatives, preapproved by the CCP, oversee a nominal democratic system whose citizens, though granted the right to vote, cannot participate in decision-making.[85] Elections, although free, are not fair. The CCP aspires to rule by consent, preferring benevolent persuasion to the iron fist. Still, it swiftly suppresses those who challenge its authority. Spontaneity in a single-party system, no matter how apolitical, symbolizes protest. As CCP officials consistently explain, "Stability trumps everything."[86]

Unlike the ideologically interventionist Washington Consensus, the Beijing Consensus is ideologically agnostic. It prizes economic development and international trade as the means to generate domestic growth, create wealth, and build a harmonious society. It uses fast-growing prosperity to subvert individual political choice, reasoning that people value wage growth, prosperity, and social stability more than political freedom. The Beijing Consensus does not pass judgment on other countries' politics; in turn, it expects not to be judged. It advocates trade with no strings attached—which, in the case of the Washington Consensus, are democracy, freedom, human rights, and the rule of law.[87]

China's policy of harmonious stability within a single-party state finds followers worldwide; said one analyst, "[T]he 'China model' of authoritarian capitalism is gaining currency. Governments from Syria to Vietnam have sung its praises."[88] Some argue that state control that weds liberal economics with single-party authoritarian politics, rather than the union of liberal economics and multiparty democracy, now represents the superior political path to prosperity and harmony.

The Clash of Civilizations

Spreading democracy in the Arab world, which is regularly rated the world's least politically free region, has been a long-running goal of the West. An aim of the Iraq War was to build the luminous "city upon a hill" that would inspire democracy throughout the region. Efforts there, as well as pro-democracy movements in Afghanistan, Egypt, Libya, Yemen, and elsewhere, have had limited success. Moreover, Western military intervention calls into question the legitimacy of democratic ideals. Faltering institutions and changes in political sentiments hinder the transition to democracy in several Islamic nations, including Iran, Kuwait, and Saudi Arabia.

Regional instability hinders promoting pluralism, to say nothing of a functioning democracy. The discontent of the disadvantaged, particularly among youth suffering few opportunities, mobilized the pro-democracy protests of the Arab Spring. Although initially promising, study of the determinants and consequences of democratic transitions advise caution. Historically, violent uprisings struggle to institutionalize durable democratic change. Moreover, weak property rights thwart democratic ideals.[89] Productive economies in the oil-rich Persian Gulf also stall the spread of democracy as it appears that democracy is not a prerequisite of prosperity.[90] Moderate Arab leaders contend that the transition from totalitarianism to democracy is, at best, "a slow process." Hardliners, meanwhile, vilify individualism.[91]

The reluctance of some Islamic states to adopt democracy animates the "clash of civilizations" scenario. Irreconcilable religious differences between Islam and the West, goes this reasoning, fuel backlash against Western ideals and their crystallization in the ideologically interventionist Washington Consensus.[92] Some speculate that the epic clash between oppositional civilizations will usher in a new political ideology.

What's Next? Managers Ask

Managers study the direction that political ideologies might track. Will liberal democracy *à la* the Washington Consensus regain the commanding heights? Ongoing developments worldwide, led by a growing middle class linked into expanding social networks, support that forecast.[93] Will the one-party trademark of the Beijing Consensus set political standards? China's growing involvement in receptive countries worldwide endorses that projection. To that end, when recently asked, "How satisfied are you with the country's direction?" 83 percent of Chinese reported satisfaction; in contrast, 31 percent in the United States, 19 percent in France, 15 percent in Britain, and 7 percent in Japan did so.[94] Or, if countries bypass the American Way or the Chinese Path, might a clash of civilizations give rise to new ideas of freedom?[95]

Whatever the scenario, history reminds us that it matters. The first and second waves of democratization (1828–1926 and 1943–1962, respectively) were followed by periods of freedom backlash, democracy retreat, and backslides into authoritarianism. Hence, the question arises: Are we once again facing a cycle of transition and consolidation?[96] Suffice to say, it's risky to underestimate political change. If the Washington Consensus proves resilient, managers must adjust operations to the growing pains of countries that champion freedom, advocate human rights, and adopt the rule of law. Prosperity will come with difficulty, but there will be prosperity for many. If the Beijing Consensus predominates, managers must rethink business in a world where governments regulate growth in order to legitimate state control and secure social stability. Prosperity may come more easily, but its price will include individual freedoms. If ideologies transform as civilizations clash, the resulting religious orders will reset systems. Prosperity may prove a wild card as oppositional ideologies battle for the commanding heights. ■

POLITICAL RISK

Political risk refers to the threat that decisions or events in a country will negatively affect the profitability and sustainability of an investment.

Map 3.1 profiles the scale and scope of political risk that MNEs face operating in countries throughout the world. No matter whether it operates in Canada, Cambodia, Cameroon, or Chad, for instance, an MNE faces the risk that the political events in the host country will adversely affect its operational objectives, strategic goals, and profitability. Technically, **political risk** is the risk that political decisions, events, or conditions change a country's business environment in ways that force investors to accept lower rates of return, cost them some or all of the value of their investment, or threaten the sustainability of their operation.

Various trends increase political risk worldwide (See Figure 3.3). First, many emerging markets are rife with flashpoints. Arbitrary laws, fragile institutions, volatile societies, and corrupt regimes fuel uncertainty. Often, foreign investors must compete with state-run rivals whose political orientations complicate economic situations. Aggravating matters is the fact that political risks differ from market to market. In Venezuela, managers face economic nationalism; in Brazil, a manager must understand Congress's multiparty alliances; in China, the task is interpreting the power and play of the CCP; in Saudi Arabia, a manager must decipher the internal dealings of the ruling family. Hence, operating in many emerging markets differs significantly from the comparatively predictable politics in Western democracies. Analytics that work in one country often travel poorly to others.

Second, declining political freedom increases political risks. The Third Wave of Democratization began stabilizing the play of politics across markets. As countries developed democracies, often in the context of the Washington Consensus, managers could reasonably assume that the principles of Western-style political economy, not authoritarian outlooks, would shape national affairs. Flagging political freedom, by boosting the uncertainty of local politics, increases political risks.

The primary types of political risk, from least to most disruptive, are

- systemic,
- procedural,
- distributive,
- catastrophic.

CLASSIFYING POLITICAL RISK

The evaluation of political risk often applies a macro-micro criterion.[97] Macro risks affect all companies, both domestic and foreign alike, in a given country. Micro risks are agent-specific actions that affect individual, usually foreign-owned, companies. Figure 3.4, besides identifying leading causes of political risk, applies this approach. It qualifies the macro-micro division with the characteristics of the type of risk.

FIGURE 3.3   Freedom in the World: Gains and Declines by Country

The momentum of political freedom has changed over the past decades, as early gains have given way to increasing decline.

Source: "Freedom in the World 2015: The Return of the Iron Fist," www.freedomhouse.org. Used by permission of Freedom House.[98]

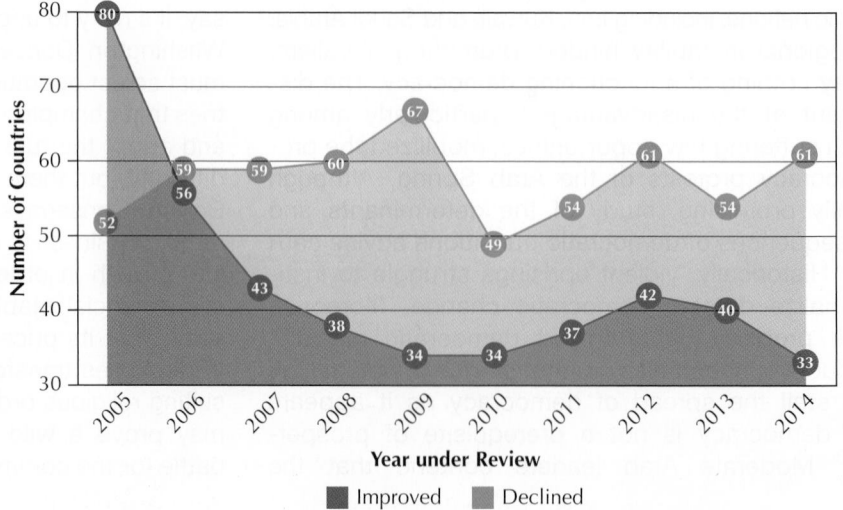

FIGURE 3.4 Classes and Characteristics of Political Risk

Political risks have telltale characteristics in terms of types, techniques, and outcomes.

Scale	Class	Type	Outcome
Micro		Financial Anomalies	Regulatory policies that make it difficult for the company to get credit or arrange overseas loans.
	Systemic	Competing Perspectives	The host government's policies on, for instance, human rights, labor conditions, or environmental sustainability, create public relations problems for a foreign company at home.
		Unilateral Breach of Contract	The host government repudiates a contract negotiated with a foreign company or approves a local firm's doing the same.
	Procedural	Tax Discrimination	A foreign company is saddled with a higher tax burden than a local competitor.
		Restrictions on Profit Repatriation	The host government arbitrarily limits the amount of profit that a foreign company can remit from its local operations to the home office.
	Distributive	Destructive Government Actions	Unilateral trade barriers, often via local-content requirements, interfere with the distribution of products to local consumers.
		Harmful Action Against People	Local employees of a foreign company are threatened by kidnapping, extortion, or terrorist actions.
	Catastrophic	Expropriation/Nationalization	The host government or a political faction seizes a company's local assets. Compensation, if any, is usually trivial. Resurgent totalitarianism and resource nationalism increase this risk.
Macro		Civil Strife, Insurrection, War	Military action damages or destroys a company's local operations.

Systemic political risks, by influencing the macro business environment, affect the operation of all firms.

Systemic Political Risk A country's political processes aim not to punish companies arbitrarily. Few would hazard the investment otherwise. Rather, investors commonly face political risk that follows from shifting public policy. Newly elected officials, for instance, adopt policies that differ from their predecessors—say, increasing individual tax rates to improve collective welfare. Similarly, a government may target a sector that it sees dominated by foreign interests, such as Venezuela's program to nationalize energy companies.[99] In both situations, politically motivated polices alter the macro environment, thereby creating systemic political risks that affect all firms.

Systemic political risks do not necessarily reduce potential profits. Policy shifts also create opportunities. Newly elected governments in Vietnam, Malawi, Estonia, and Guinea, for instance, deregulated previously state-controlled economies. Investors who accepted the risk of a policy reversal prospered as freer markets emerged. Our opening case traces similar patterns in China, showing how political trends encouraged pro-market reforms that, by changing the risk–return relationship, created opportunities for enterprising MNEs.

Procedural political risk institutes impediments that constrain the flexibility of local operations.

Procedural Political Risk People, products, and resources ceaselessly travel through the global market. Each move creates a procedural transaction between individuals, subsidiaries, companies, institutions, or countries. Political policies sometimes impose frictions that slow or stop these transactions. Corrupt officials, for instance, might pressure a firm to pay additional monies to clear goods through customs or obtain a permit to open a factory.[100] Political interference escalates expenses, thereby lowering returns. Procedural political risk is a micro risk—that is, it affects some but not all companies. Monitoring industry developments, minding the relative contribution of their firms to the local economy, and promoting solid citizenship help MNEs manage it.

Distributive political risks gradually eliminate the local property rights of foreign companies.

Distributive Political Risk Countries see successful foreign investors as agents of innovation and sources of prosperity. Often, as MNEs generate greater profits in the local economy, the host government questions its share of the rewards. Many conclude they should receive a larger cut and impose policies to reset the distribution. Sometimes, changes happen quickly; for example, rising silver prices led the Bolivian government to quickly "dismantle the privatization model" governing its mining industry and expropriate assets owned by foreign-owned mining companies.[101] More often, governments apply *creeping expropriation,* whereby the gradual reduction of the MNE's local property rights (via legislation, regulation, and taxation) captures a bigger share of its profits.[102]

Vigilance helps MNEs reduce exposure. Many take preemptive steps, configuring activities to diversify operations. Chrysler deterred creeping expropriation in Peru by restricting its local factory to make about half the parts needed to assemble a car; importing the rest meant the local facility was useless if the government expropriated it. Likewise, Japan's escalating tension with China (notably, consumer boycotts of Japanese products, anti-Japanese riots, and foreboding military confrontations) pushes Japanese MNEs to hedge their political risk. Some apply a "China-plus" approach whereby they backstop their supply chains, once anchored in China, with a shadow hub in another Asian market such as Thailand, Vietnam, or the Philippines. Although inefficient, alternative locations safeguard the Japanese firms' Asian operations in the event that hostilities escalate.[103]

Sometimes the importance of the market leaves MNEs few options. The United States, for instance, is not generally considered a hotbed of distributive political risk. If you're in the cigarette business, however, the United States is a hazardous market.[104] Its government battles cigarette makers (both domestic, like Philip Morris, and foreign, like British American Tobacco) on matters of taxation, regulation, business practice, and liability. Preserving market access requires adeptly managing escalating political risks.

| Catastrophic political risk devastates the business environment for all companies. | **Catastrophic Political Risk**   Political developments that adversely affect the operations of every firm in a country arise from macro flashpoints—for instance, ethnic discord, illegitimate regime change, civil disorder, or insurrection. No matter the cause, these sorts of threats fundamentally disrupt society. Antistate activities in Egypt, for example, paralyzed its economy. Foreign commerce and domestic business halted, markets seized, and supplies of all sorts vanished. Auspiciously, Egypt pulled back from the brink. In other situations, such as in failed states like Chad, Libya, or Zimbabwe, spiraling disruptions trigger conflicts that devastate the business environment for all firms.[105] |

Point

Proactive Political Risk Management: The Superior Approach

Point   **Yes** Companies take politics seriously, aware that host governments regulate the business environment and, hence, their performance. Consequently, MNEs face threats that demand political risk management strategies. All have a choice: apply either a proactive or a passive approach. Those who advocate active political risk management reason that the best defense is a good offense. In my opinion, they're right. Taking charge, predicting problems, and controlling risks, besides the basis of good management, is the path to reduce risk.

WHAT TO DO Executives use battle-tested tactics. First, they apply state-of-the-art statistical modeling to quantify political risks. Second, they stress-test their models, consulting experts on the political drama in a country. This two-pronged approach integrates hard-nosed analysis with insightful interpretation. It begins with the thesis that

neither positive nor negative political events are independent or chance events. Civil strife, creeping expropriation, regime change, ethnic tension, terrorism, and the like do not happen randomly. They unfold in observable patterns that bright folks applying sharp analytics can measure to estimate the odds of future outcomes. Applying rigorous models that detect, measure, and frame scenarios moves an MNE ahead of the curve, proactively managing its political risk exposure.

WHAT TO WATCH Measuring the right set of discrete events is the key to modeling political risk—one identifies valid indicators that one can reliably track. Research isolates useful candidates such as the number of military officers holding political office, pace of urbanization, frequency of government crises, pervasiveness of corruption, extent of crony capitalism, scope of counterfeiting, ethno-lingual fractionalization, and so on. Evolving methods fortify analyses.

For example, sentiment analysis, opinion mining, and computational linguistics track emotionally charged words and phrases used in online communications. Comparing the relative frequency of positive and negative words used in millions of exchanges, feeds, and posts on the Internet produces a national as well as a global heat map of how people "feel." Sentiment analysis, for example, indicated that people's resentment of autocratic rule crossed critical thresholds in Egypt and Libya weeks before violence exploded.[106] Moreover, sentiment analysis confirms that the challenge is not identifying individual measures, but rather identifying the right mix. Once done, skillful statistical modeling can objectively estimate risk exposure.

WHAT TO ADD Yes, the proactive approach faces limits. Spreadsheet estimation, no matter how rigorous, carries analysis only so far. Reaching this bound need not halt risk management. One complements quantitative measures with in-depth, country-specific qualitative indicators. Surveying country experts taps interpretation of a country's political drama in ways that numbers struggle to represent. Specialists make sense of subtle intricacies, enhancing quantitative analyses with their expertise on subjective conditions. Then, what appear to be idiosyncratic circumstances become, in their eyes, systematic political patterns.

Integrating expert assessments into a political risk strategy is straightforward. Begin by running standardized interviews with experts to assess a country's political environment. If stuck, a useful starting point is the Internet; searching "political risk management" generates resources. Collectively, they support projecting realistic scenarios and logically assigning probabilities to reasonable outcomes—the hallmarks of proactive political risk management.

Proactive Political Risk Management: The Superior Approach

Counterpoint

No Unquestionably, a proactive approach exhibits the hallmark of good management—enterprising, confident, and controlling. However, it fails to explain why many MNEs do the exact opposite, choosing to manage political risk passively by treating it as an unpredictable hazard. These companies reason that no model, regardless of how brilliantly it has been conceptualized, how systematically it has been specified, and how precisely it has been administered, can consistently predict political risk. Granted, shrewd models extrapolate meaningful insights from economic, political, and social reports about who may take office, what policies may pass, and how these sorts of political events may affect markets. Unquestionably, these insights make the political system and its risks understandable. They do not, however, make it predictable.

WHAT TO HEDGE Insights do not qualify as predictions precisely because of the impracticality of reliably measuring messy, ill-structured situations. The political world is complex, its inalienable feature is ambiguity, and its tendency to change is absurdly high. Complicating matters are the innumerable variables and their interaction that shape a political system—think of the 60 indicators that the EIU evaluates to assess the texture of democracy in a nation. This situation becomes more difficult as MNEs venture into emerging markets, each with its own political peculiarities. Going from the United States to Mexico may be a stretch, but that pales in comparison to expanding from the United States to, say, Saudi Arabia, Kazakhstan, or Zimbabwe. No matter how powerful the spreadsheet or insightful the expert, the

Counterpoint

dimensions and dynamics of a political environment defy precise specification. Yes, developing broad frameworks that anticipate unpredictable hazards is good business sense. However, prudently managing political risk starts by rejecting the delusion that one can. The objective is protection, not prediction—or, put differently, the best offense is a good defense.

HOW TO HEDGE This, of course, raises the question: How does one hedge exposure? Typically, an MNE purchases political risk insurance. Policies provide single-country coverage or broad, multi-country, regional, or global coverage for a number of risks, including expropriation, political violence, currency inconvertibility, nonpayment, and contract frustration. A range of public agencies, international organizations, and private companies offer coverage options.

- Multilateral development banks (MDBs) are international financial institutions funded and owned by member governments that promote growth in member countries by providing financial incentives to potential investors. Reducing the capital at risk encourages firms to expand into otherwise unacceptably risky environments. Examples are the African Development Bank, the Asian Development Bank, and the World Bank Group.

- The Overseas Private Investment Corporation (OPIC) encourages U.S. investment projects overseas by protecting ventures against various forms of risk, including civil strife, expropriation, and currency inconvertibility. Increasingly, OPIC promotes investments in emerging markets that support U.S. foreign policy priorities.

• Private insurance companies underwrite political risk protection. Many cover "routine" distributive and procedural risks that involve property and income, such as contract repudiation and currency inconvertibility. Private insurers are reluctant to cover catastrophic risks that result from civil strife, insurrection, or war.

WHAT TO REALIZE Ultimately, we have no quarrel with the notion that prediction and control are touchstones of professional management. Still, politics are anything but predictable and controllable. Few, if any, predicted the political turmoil of the Arab Spring and the swift collapse of the Mubarak regime in Egypt. Likewise, Britain's vote to depart the European Union surprised many. Moreover, few forecast democracy's retreat a decade ago, especially when leading analysts were celebrating the "end of history." Not to put too sharp a point on it, but if one cannot predict these mega-events, then exactly what can one predict? Therefore, it just makes more sense—and, we might add, more cents—to resist the delusion of proactive management and opt for the practicality of passively managing political risk.

THE LEGAL ENVIRONMENT

Just as political ideologies differ among countries, so also do legal systems. Thus, a key aspect of the IB environment is how a country develops, interprets, and enforces its laws. Businesspeople champion consistency in laws from country to country. Uniform, transparent laws make it easier to plan where to invest and, once there, how to compete on competencies, not connections. In theory, legitimate rules that apply without prejudice to individual or company conduct, regardless of political, cultural, or economic status, anchor a just and fair legal environment. Done judiciously, individuals and companies can make lawful decisions that support peace and prosperity. Done arbitrarily, all suffer because, Honoré de Balzac warned, "To distrust the judiciary marks the beginning of the end of society."

The **legal system** specifies the rules that regulate behavior, the processes that enforce laws, and the procedures that resolve grievances. Legal systems differ across countries due to variations in tradition, precedent, usage, custom, or religious precepts. Moreover, with the exception of the members of the European Union, countries rarely recognize the legitimacy of legal practices or court judgments from other nations; "Products move very easily across borders. Legal judgments, not so much."[107]

All things being equal, every legal system institutes rules that support business formation, regulate transactions, and stabilize relationships. Doing so ensures that a society can pursue economic development and, when disagreements arise, resolve them without resorting to lawlessness. Modern legal systems share three components: (1) **constitutional law**, which translates the country's constitution into an open and just legal system, setting the framework for government and defining the authority and procedure of political bodies to establish laws; (2) **criminal law**, which safeguards society by specifying what conduct is criminal, and prescribing punishment to those who breach those standards; and (3) **civil and commercial laws**, which ensure fairness and efficiency in business transactions by stipulating private rights and specific remedies in order to regulate conduct between individuals and/or organizations. No single legal component in and of itself guarantees a functioning legal system. Success depends on the collective effectiveness of all components to set and sustain philosophical integrity, procedural justice, and personal security.

Aspects of each type of law influence MNEs' actions in a host country.[108] Our opening case profiled how China's legal traditions and practices attract, retain, as well as deter investment. Whereas Western investors are accustomed to transparent bankruptcy laws that protect creditors, Chinese law presently protects debtors. Likewise, one in six business practitioners in Russia has been prosecuted for alleged economic crime over the past decade; most cases have no plaintiff, acquittals are rare, and company assets are often expropriated by the state.[109] Russian law, contends critics, "is the property of those who enforce it, and written exclusively for them."[110]

> The legal system is the mechanism for conceiving, stipulating, interpreting, and enforcing the laws in a formal jurisdiction.

> Modern legal systems evidence three components:
> • Constitutional Law
> • Criminal Law
> • Civil and Commercial Law

MAP 3.4   The Wide World of Legal Systems

Managers operating internationally face legal environments anchored in a variety of philosophies and principles. Here we see the world organized by predominant types.

Source: University of Ottawa, "World Legal Systems," retrieved February 15, 2016, from http://www.juriglobe.ca/eng/index.php. Used by permission.

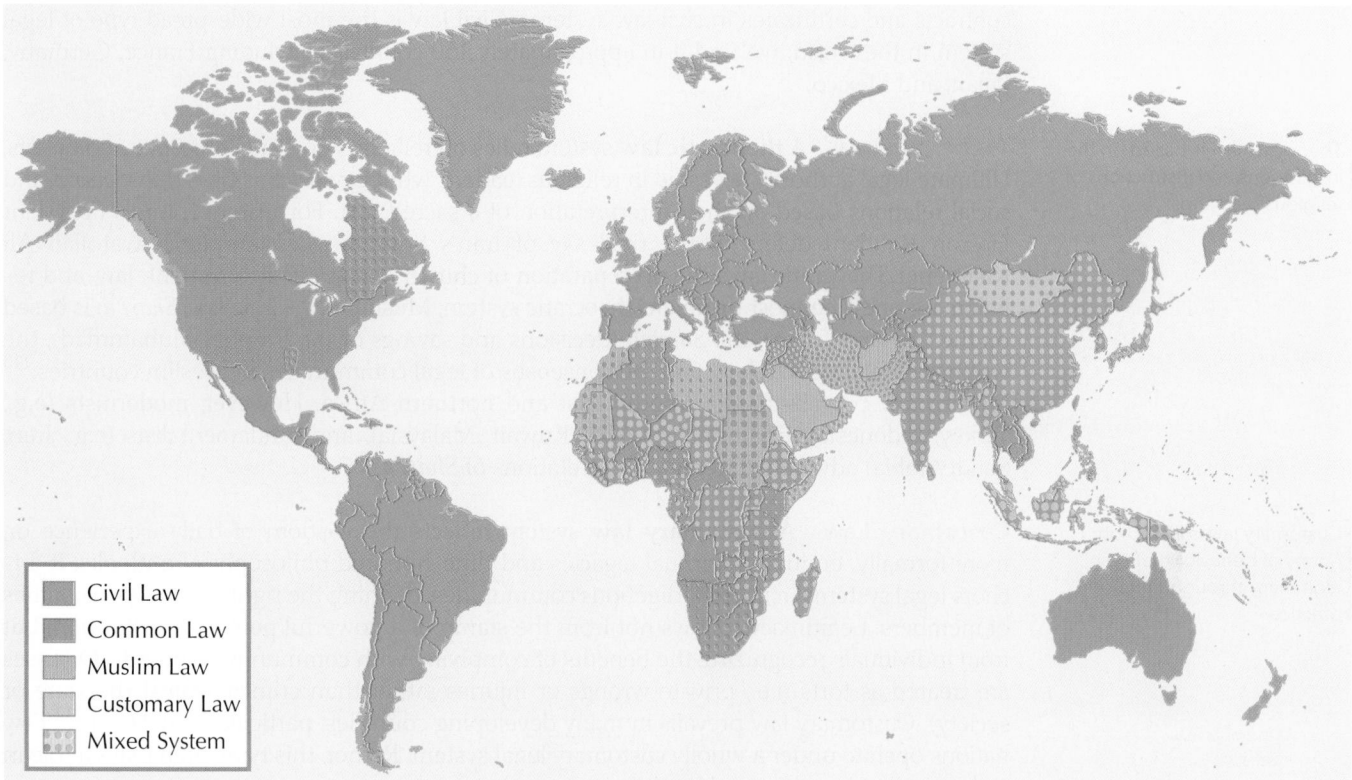

- Civil Law
- Common Law
- Muslim Law
- Customary Law
- Mixed System

TYPES OF LEGAL SYSTEMS

A country's legal system officially regulates the conduct of business transactions, the rights and obligations of those doing business, and the legal redress open to those who believe they have been wronged. Understanding its nuances pushes executives to assess a variety of issues: Are laws based on abstractions or practicality? Do judges or juries pass judgment? Is justice based on objective principle or seen as the province of divinity? Do personal connections trump case facts? Peculiar as these questions sound, IB puts managers into different situations wherein different interpretations of these issues result in different standards that regulate the legality of their actions.

The globalization of business drives the standardization of laws across countries. Still, enduring philosophical outlooks and practical orientations result in different types of legal systems around the world. Map 3.4 identifies the primary types that prevail today, namely *common law, civil law, theocratic law, customary law,* and *mixed systems.*[111]

> Managers face five types of legal systems in the world today:
>
> - Common law
> - Civil law
> - Theocratic law
> - Customary law
> - Mixed

Common Law   A **common law** system relies on tradition, judge-made precedent, and usage. It respects established case law in resolving disputes. Judicial officials refer to statutory codes and legislation, but only after considering the rules of the court, custom, judicial reasoning, prior court decisions, and principles of equity. The doctrine of *stare decisis* is a distinguishing feature—it obliges judges to respect the precedent established by prior court rulings.[112] Common law has Anglo-American legacies; it prevails in, among others, Australia, Canada, England, Hong Kong, India, New Zealand, and the United States.

> Common law is developed by judges through the decisions of courts.

Civil Law   A **civil law** system relies on the systematic codification of accessible, detailed laws. It assigns political officials, rather than government-employed judges, the responsibility to translate legal principles into a compendium of regulatory statutes. Rather than create

> Civil law is based on strict application of statutory laws.

law, as they do in the common law system, judges apply the relevant statutes to resolve disputes. In contrast to *stare decisis*, judicial officers in a civil law system are not bound by precedent. Statutory codes, however, constrain their authority. Similarly, notaries public play minor roles in common law countries, but are important gatekeepers as well as regulators of contracts and certificates in civil law systems. Civil law is the most widespread type of legal system in the world; we find it in approximately 150 countries, including France, Germany, Japan, and Mexico.

| Theocratic law is based on the inspirations and instructions of religious teachings.

Theocratic Law   A **theocratic law** system relies on religious doctrine, precepts, and beliefs. Ultimate legal authority is vested in religious leaders, who regulate business transactions and social relations based on their interpretation of a sacred text. For instance, Iran's President Hassan Rouhani defers to the final say of Iran's Supreme Leader, cleric Ayatollah Ali Khamenei. Theocratic laws see no separation of church and state; government, law, and religion are one. The most prevalent theocratic system, Muslim or Islamic law, *Shari'a*, is based on the Qur'an (Koran), the *Sunnah* (decisions and sayings of the Prophet Muhammad), the writings of Islamic scholars, and the consensus of legal communities in Muslim countries.[113] Muslim law prevails in the Middle East and northern Africa. However, modernists (e.g., Turkey, Indonesia), traditionalists (e.g., Kuwait, Malaysia), and fundamentalists (e.g., Iran, Saudi Arabia) advocate different interpretations of *Shari'a*.

| Customary law is based on norms of behavior that gain legitimacy through ongoing practice.

Customary Law   A **customary law** system reflects the wisdom of daily experience or, more formally, enduring spiritual legacies and time-honored philosophical outlooks. It anchors legal systems in many indigenous communities, defining the rights and responsibilities of members. Legitimacy follows not from the stamp of a powerful person or institution, but from individuals recognizing the benefits of complying with community standards. Offenses are treated as torts (i.e., private wrongs or injuries rather than crimes against the state or society). Customary law prevails in many developing countries, particularly in Africa.[114] Few nations operate under a wholly customary legal system. Rather, this type often plays a role in countries that have a mixed legal system.

Mixed System   A **mixed legal system** results when a nation uses two or more of the preceding types. Map 3.4 shows that one finds most mixed legal systems in Africa and Asia. The Philippines, South Africa, and Guyana, for instance, follow a blend of civil and common law. Nigeria, Malaysia, and Kenya mix common, theocratic, and customary law. Bangladesh, Singapore, and Pakistan blend common and theocratic law. Indonesia, Djibouti, and Oman, conversely, blend theocratic law with civil codes.[115]

THE FOUNDATION OF LEGALITY

CONCEPT CHECKS

As we saw in Chapter 1, national business environments vary. Granted, there are points of convergence, but conducting international business means recognizing the existence of fundamental differences across countries. Here, we stress legal systems differ on a variety of principles and practices.

The Third Wave of Democratization supplanted the philosophy of collectivism with individualism. This change endorsed individuals' inalienable legal rights and instituted due process to protect them. In many countries, the law grew more transparent, the courts more impartial, and officials more accountable. Presently, democracy's retreat, by signaling the rise of single-party governments advocating state-sponsored collectivism, pushes managers to pinpoint likely changes in legal systems. Given that authoritarian governments use the legal system to regulate business activity in order to support and sustain the state, there is little separation of law and the state. Bluntly put, justice is not blind, but arbitrary, oppressive, and state-serving.

Recall earlier observations on legal affairs in China. Doing business there, said an observer, means dealing with "a society that had…plenty of rules, but they were seldom enforced. China appeared to be run by masterful showmen: appearances mattered more than substance, the rules were there to be distorted."[116] Moreover, the CCP's official status above the law further complicates determining what is right and what is wrong. China is not the exception. The ambiguities that permeate Russia's legal code means businesses "cannot even keep track of the law, let alone decide whether to follow it."[117] Besides confusion, ambiguity renders the law less about protecting citizens and more a tool of arbitrary state power.

CONCEPT CHECKS

As developed in Chapter 2, a country's cultural orientation toward standards of account- ability, equity, and fairness influ- ences the principles that anchor its legal environment.

The rule of man holds that the ruler, in whatever form, com- mands authority that is above the law.

The rule of man anchors the legal system in totalitarian states.

The rule of law holds that no individual is above laws that are clearly specified, com- monly understood, and fairly enforced.

The Basis of Rule Once relegated to the periphery of the global economy, emerging mar- kets steadily command center stage. Their expanding economies increasingly frame interpre- tation of legal trends. Managers assess the prevailing philosophical basis of law in order to understand how local officials will regulate their activities. Specifically, the rise of emerging economies, along with their dissimilar conceptions of legality, requires managers ask, "What is the *basis of rule* in a given country?" This question inevitably directs attention to the rule of man versus the rule of law.

The **rule of man** holds that ultimate authority resides in a person whose word and whim, no matter how unfair or unjust, is law. For much of history, rulers and law were one and the same—the law was the will of the ruler, whether that ruler was called king, lord, empress, shogun, czar, raj, chief, caliph, etc.[118] Today, these titles have given way to others, such as chairman, comandante, generalissimo, dictator, or supreme leader. In whatever form and with whatever title, the rule of man defines a legal system in which the sovereign leader's actions are not restricted by a constitution, regulated by criminal codes, or open to opposi- tion. For example, Saddam Hussein, former president of Iraq, imperiously declared the "law is anything I write on a scrap of paper."[119] In China, top-ranked party members accused of wrongdoing answer to the CCP first, not to the law of the land, precisely because "the Party sits outside, and above the law."[120] In effect, the sovereign leader creates the law, officials are the followers of the law, and the citizens its subjects. The law is an apparatus of the state, used to suppress threats to, and reward support for, its authority. Constitutional issues are discretionary, criminal law is arbitrary, and opportunism taints commercial and civil matters. Hence, the rule of man is an instrumental device of authoritarianism.

The **rule of law** holds that no one, whether a public official or private citizen, is above the law. The U.S. Declaration of Independence's decree, for instance, that "all men are cre- ated equal" holds that everyone, from kings to peasants, is subject to the same laws.[121] More symbolically, in front of courthouses worldwide stands a statue of a woman, carrying a sword and measuring balances, sometimes wearing a blindfold, sometimes with eyes closed. Her sword stands for the power of the court; her scales for the competing claims of the petition- ers; and her blindfold signifies that justice is meted out objectively, without fear or favor, regardless of identity, power, or weakness. Justice is blind so that justice is impartial.

The rule of law holds that governmental authority is legitimately exercised in accordance with written, publicly disclosed laws. Citizens regard constitutional principles as legitimate, criminal codes as fair, and commercial/civil matters as just. Laws are clear, publicized, and protective of fundamental rights; they are developed, administered, and enforced transpar- ently; all citizens have access to a competent, independent, and ethical judiciary; and all of- ficials are accountable to the law of the land.[122] Democracy, fortified by the rule of law, works precisely because it has the legal tools to constrain state power in safeguarding lives, liberty, and property.[123]

MAPPING THE BASIS OF LAW

Originating in the Magna Carta of 1215, the concept of the rule of law anchored the legal evolution of many developed economies, most notably Great Britain, the United States, France, and Germany. Besides instituting a just political environment, the rule of law guar- antees the enforceability of commercial contracts and business transactions while safe- guarding property rights. Investors and companies rely on it to validate the laws, codes, and statutes that support investment and enterprise.

For example, in the West, property rights—namely, the authority to determine how one controls, benefits from, and transfers one's property—are so taken for granted that they rarely cross our minds. We cannot say the same for many countries in Asia, Africa, the Middle East, and South America. There, the historic centrality of the rule of man makes the principles and practices of the rule of law remote abstractions. At best, the rule of law has a negligible legacy in the legal traditions of many long-developing, now-emerging countries. As a result, ambiguous property rights in countries like Russia, China, Venezuela, Malaysia,

The rule of man anchors the legal systems of many of today's emerging countries.

Ukraine, Saudi Arabia, and Vietnam are an enduring concern.[124] In countries where the rule of man is the basis of law, acceptable marketplace behavior is unpredictable. Managers stay alert to trumped-up charges, solicitation of bribes, and favoritism of local rivals.

Map 3.5 indicates that the rule of law prevails in wealthier, westernized countries (i.e., the United States, Canada, Japan, New Zealand, Australia, and most of Europe).[125] In contrast, the countries that fall in the long crescent that starts in northern Russia, cuts southward through China, circles down to South East Asia, moves on toward the Middle East, and extends through Africa over to South America show the far greater pervasiveness of the rule of man. Conclusion? The rule of man anchors the legal systems of many of today's emerging countries. Managers, eyeing these fast-growing markets, realize that where there is no formal law officially in place, society typically defaults to the rule of man.

WHICH RULE WHEN?

Some hypothesize that developing countries, especially fast-growing emerging economies like China, Nigeria, Peru, Thailand, and Malaysia, will follow the precedent of developed countries and gradually accept the legitimacy of the rule of law. History shows that as the developed, wealthier countries moved from agrarian to industrial economies, individuals called

MAP 3.5   The Worldwide Practice of the Rule of Law

The coding of this map reflects the degree that a government exercised its authority according to written laws and established enforcement procedures. The United States' classification at the 90th percentile indicates the pervasiveness of the rule of law in that nation. Conversely, Venezuela's classification below the 10th percentile indicates the pervasiveness of the rule of man in that nation.[126]

Source: Kaufmann D., A. Kraay, and M. Mastruzzi (2010). The Worldwide Governance Indicators: Methodology and Analytical Issues. The Worldwide Governance Indicators are available at: www.govindicators.org. © 2015 The World Bank Group. All Rights Reserved.

Lady Justice, here seen in the Römer Square in Frankfurt, Germany, is an allegorical personification of the moral force of the rule of law.[127]

Source: klickable/Fotolia.

CONCEPT CHECKS

Chapter 1 suggests that democratic political systems grant MNEs the freedom to engage in their preferred modes of international business. Democracy's retreat creates uncertainty about operating in particular countries given that all use their legal system to encourage, regulate, or prohibit business activity.

The growing confidence of emerging economies increasingly calls into question the long-running presumption that "the West knows best."

for laws to protect property rights. Sustaining economic development, as well as protecting growing wealth, required a legal system that no longer looked to the "man" for guidance and resolution, but to just, fair, and transparent laws. Therefore, extrapolating from western history, the shift from agrarianism to industrialism in developing countries should progressively support the institution of the rule of law.

Recent circumstances, however, complicate the projected progression. Democracy's ongoing decline has slowed progress precisely because the rule of law is antithetical to totalitarianism—one cannot be the "man" if one must answer to the law. More practically, China's economic performance tests the thesis that a positive relationship exists between the rule of law, economic growth, and prosperity.[128] China's status as the world's largest recipient of foreign investment over the past few decades, notwithstanding troublesome crony capitalism and persistent corruption, questions the necessity of the rule of law. Similar situations in Russia, Venezuela, Saudi Arabia, Belarus, and Turkmenistan, among others, highlight foreign investors' capacity to prosper in markets run by the "man."

Along these lines, some point to the powerful influence of national legacies. The forecast of the rule of law as the inevitable end-state for all nations presumes that the legal philosophies of the West apply to all. Instead, some counter that the "West does not know best," arguing that the efficiency and stability of a progressive, autocratic ruler are often more important than the liberty and freedom of a messy democracy. Explained a prominent Western U.S. commentator, "One-party autocracy certainly has its drawbacks. But when it is led by a reasonably enlightened group of people, as China is today, it can also have great advantages."[129] Indeed, throughout its storied 5000-year history, Chinese civilization has never practiced democratic governance based on the rule of law. Instead, as dynasties came and went, each followed its mandate of heaven in instituting authoritarian governance and applying the rule of man. Consequently, managers watch and learn as changing economic environments influence the basis of law. That is, growing demand from increasingly wealthy citizens for stronger property rights, by forcing the accountability of public officials, may gradually legitimate the institution of the rule of law.[130]

IMPLICATIONS TO MANAGERS

Rising authoritarianism in many developing countries complicates legal circumstances. Again, look at Maps 3.2 and 3.3. Every country that Freedom House rates as "Partly Free" or "Not Free," or, for that matter, the EIU classifies as a "hybrid regime" or "authoritarian regime," lies within the "rule of man crescent." Uncertainty about the basis of law and the goals of government throughout much of the world creates risky environments. Operating in markets regulated by the rule of law sees consistent application of legitimate laws. Operating in markets regulated by the rule of man sees arbitrary, self-serving regulation.

In Germany, for example, action taken by foreign firms against local companies that counterfeit their products consistently proves decisive. Violators are restrained and punished. In Belarus or Kazakhstan, however, the same sorts of legal actions often prove pointless. There, as in other rule-of-man systems, writs, injunctions, and lawsuits are trapped in a slow-grinding legal machine that answers to the leader, not to impartial legal standards.[131] Violators in the good graces of the "man," whether Alexander Lukashenko of Belarus or Nursultan Nazarbayev of Kazakhstan, flourish.[132]

Certainly, as had long been the case, MNEs could avoid risky markets. Until 2000 or so, the basis of law was perhaps interesting, but largely extraneous. Western markets provided many opportunities for productive, profitable activity. Developing markets were the periphery of the global economy, providing raw materials or low-cost labor. The occasional dispute between the adventurous Western company and the locals was typically resolved in the favor of the former. Today, slow growth in the West moves the fast-growing emerging economies to the center of the global market. Abundant supply of inexpensive, productive resources along with accelerating local demand is a siren call few MNEs can resist. As GE's CEO explained, "We've globalized around markets... Today we go to Brazil, we go to China, we go to India because that's where the customers are."[133] Looking forward, 400 midsize emerging-market cities (many unfamiliar in the West, such as Sanaa, Ibadan, Ouagadougou, Chittagong, Kinshasa, and Bamako), will generate nearly 40 percent of global growth over the next 15 years.[134] Consequently MNEs long accustomed to the rule of law in markets like Germany and Japan, increasingly operate in markets anchored in the rule of man, like China and Russia.

LEGAL ISSUES FACING INTERNATIONAL COMPANIES

The globalization of markets progressively standardizes legal systems. Countries intent on attracting foreign investors develop positive reputations, transparent regulation, and consistent politics. Similarly, officials design business regulations that are easily accessible and objectively administered. Straightforward, well-designed rules discourage corruption, improve accountability, and boost economic growth. Joining transnational organizations accelerate these trends. For instance, the European Union requires that all member countries satisfy standards of the rule of law; the World Bank requires borrowers to agree to legal reforms; the WTO imposes a raft of legal standards that supersede national statutes.

Despite convergence, different countries regulate business activity differently. Besides the operating problems posed by differing political ideologies, countries' application of diverse legal principles complicates matters. Moreover, new forms of business activity along with changing patterns of trade and investment put MNEs in uncertain legal situations. Aspects of day-to-day decision-making in the MNE adjust to obey local laws on starting, running, and closing a business. Likewise, how MNEs hire workers, obtain credit, pay taxes, and enforce contracts must comply with applicable, often differing, laws.[135]

Uncertainty about the basis of law in a particular country complicates decision-making in the MNE.

CONCEPT CHECKS

A theme of the text is the expanding linkages among individuals, companies, countries, and institutions. Here, we emphasize the importance of relationships between ideas and ideals, namely the interplay among its type of political system, its organizing legal philosophy, and its prevailing doctrine of law. Making these connections helps managers assess the systemic nature of the country's business environment.

TABLE 3.4 The Rules of the Game

The World Bank tracks micro-level characteristics of the regulatory frameworks in 185 economies. Comparative information on the rules of the game encourages officials to streamline their legal systems, thereby improving the efficiency of national business environments. Here we highlight data for a subsample of countries in terms of opening, running, and closing a business.

Economy	GNI Per Capita (US$)	Starting a Business			Enforcing Contracts			Closing a Business		
		Number of Procedures	Time (Days)	Cost (% of income per capita)	Quality of judicial process	Time	Cost* (% of Claim)	Recovery rate (C on the $)	Time (Years)	Cost (% of Estate)
Australia	64,680	3	2.5	0.7	15.5	395	21.8	82.18	1	8
Brazil	11,760	11	102	3.7	12.5	731	20.7	22.4	4	12
Canada	51,690	2	1.5	0.4	10.5	570	22.3	87.3	0.8	7
Chad	1,010	9	60	150.4	6.5	743	45.7	0	4	60
China	7,380	11	30	0.6	14.5	406	15.1	36.2	1.7	22
France	43,080	5	4	0.8	12	395	17.4	77.5	1.9	9
Germany	47,640	9	10.5	1.8	12	429	14.4	83.7	1.2	8
Guatemala	3,440	6	18.5	25	6	1402	26.5	27.5	3	14.5
India	1,610	14	29	17	7.5	1420	39.6	25.7	4.3	9
Japan	42,000	8	10.5	7.5	7.5	360	23.4	92.9	0.6	3.5
Korea, Rep.	27,090	3	For	14.5	13.5	230	10.3	83.6	1.5	3.5
Russia Fed.	13,210	5	12	1.2	12.5	310	15	41.3	2	9
Singapore	55,150	3	2.5	0.6	15.5	150	25.8	89.7	0.8	3
United States	55,200	6	4	1.3	15	370	22.9	81.5	1.5	7
United Kingdom	42,690	4	4.5	0.1	15	437	43.9	80.6	1	6

Source: Compiled from "Doing Business 2012" The World Bank.

OPERATIONAL CONCERNS

Operational concerns that managers face worldwide include

- starting a business,
- entering and enforcing contracts,
- hiring and firing workers,
- closing a business.

A fundamental thesis holds that productive business activity requires fair, just, and transparent rules that (1) set and sustain property rights, (2) minimize the costs and complications of resolving disputes, (3) specify rules that reduce the riskiness of business transactions, and (4) organize rules to protect contractual partners against abuse. Annually, the World Bank assesses how well countries meet these standards, evaluating the influence of local laws on the day-to-day operations of private companies. Specifically, the World Bank looks at the costs, requirements, and procedures a business faces, at last count, in 185 countries in terms of starting a business, dealing with construction permits, employing workers, registering property, getting credit, protecting investors, taxes, trading across borders, enforcing contracts, getting an electricity connection, and closing a business. Table 3.4 provides a snapshot of cross-country variation in starting, running, and closing a business. Let's take a closer look at each.

One quick note: We focus on the first-order effects of day-to-day operations for a small to medium-size enterprise. Keep in mind that the same sorts of activities challenge large MNEs. For instance, when entering India, multi-brand foreign chains, such as Walmart, Carrefour, IKEA, and Tesco, face a battery of regulations. They must operate as joint ventures, have no higher than a 51 percent ownership share, direct at least half of their capital investments into processing infrastructure, and open outlets only in cities that have at least 1 million residents.[136]

Getting Started Starting a business involves activities such as registering its name, adopting the appropriate tax structure, obtaining licenses and permits, arranging credit, and securing insurance. Some countries expedite this process, others complicate it. A Brazilian entrepreneur recalled his experience starting his company in his home country; obtaining authorizations, licenses, and permits from seven different ministries took about 150 days. Subsequently, he launched a U.S.-based business and noted that "within a week I had formed an LLC (limited liability corporation), incorporated in Delaware, and set up bank accounts."[137] Similarly, start-up is a straightforward process in Canada, requiring two registration procedures that cover tax, labor, and administrative declarations. Conversely, India imposes 14 procedural requirements, including regulations for bank deposits, court registration, health benefits, and so on. The upshot: it takes about a day and a half to start a business in Canada but about two weeks in India.

| The type of legal system in the country directly influences the standards of acceptable contracts.

Making and Enforcing Contracts   Once up and running, companies enter contracts with buyers and sellers.[138] The sanctity of a contract is vital to business transactions. The United Nations Convention on Contracts for the International Sale of Goods sets guidelines for negotiating and enforcing contracts. Still, standards vary across legal systems. Countries using a common law system, for instance, encourage precise, detailed contracts, whereas those with a civil law system sanction less exact agreements. Similar tendencies show up in contract-enforcement policies. Australia, Norway, and the United Kingdom impose the fewest number of enforcement procedures. Burundi, Angola, Bolivia, Cameroon, El Salvador, Mexico, and Panama require many. Singapore needs 150 days to enforce a contract, the United States about 370 days, and Timor-Leste some 1,800 days.

Hiring and Firing   No matter where a firm operates, it must hire and, when necessary, fire workers. Worldwide, workplace regulation and employment law speak to how workers are hired, what they are paid, how many hours they can work, and how they are fired. Singapore, New Zealand, and the United States have flexible labor-regulation statutes. China provides the greatest flexibility in hiring, firing, and setting employment conditions (work hours, minimum wages, and benefits). In contrast, Angola, Belarus, and Paraguay strictly regulate how companies terminate employees as well as require generous severance payments.

Slow-moving bureaucracies often complicate workplace regulation. Mexico, for instance, last overhauled its labor law in the 1970s; today, sacking a worker after a year of employment costs three times as much as in Chile, and eight times more than in Brazil. Mexico's higher severance costs also constrain firms' flexibility.[139] Regarding bureaucracy, India's national government imposes nearly 60 labor laws while its various states add another 150 or so. India's Industrial Disputes Act, for example, requires any company employing 100 or more workers to obtain state permission before firing anyone, even if it has hit hard times.[140]

Getting Out or Going Under   Closing a business involves more than padlocking the doors and walking away. In Western markets, the bankruptcy process is anchored in the English bankruptcy law of 1732, the first modern law to address this issue, and its progressive revision, beginning in 1800, by the United States. Ireland, Japan, Canada, and Hong Kong, for instance, make shutting down fast (between four to eight months) and cheap (between 1 and 10 percent of the estate).[141] The situation differs in developing countries. India's lack of a comprehensive bankruptcy code complicates dealing with creditors, officials, and courts, which in turn discourages bankruptcy. Consequently, only 4 of every 10,000 firms go bankrupt in India, compared with 350 per 10,000 firms in the United States.[142] Bankruptcy in Indonesia, Vietnam, and Ecuador is slow (between five to eight years) and expensive (between 10 and 30 percent of the estate). Several countries, including Burundi, Cambodia, Guinea-Bissau, and Dominica, stipulate no standards to govern dissolution.

| Strategic concerns that managers face worldwide include

- product origin and local content,
- marketplace behavior,
- legal jurisdiction,
- product safety and liability,
- intellectual property protection.

STRATEGIC CONCERNS

Operational concerns focus managers' attention on the day-to-day demands of opening, running, and closing a business. Strategic concerns direct their attention to long-term issues that shape the competitiveness, profitability, and sustainability of the firm. A country's legal environment influences each aspect. Let's see how it shapes an MNE's strategic decisions on making a product, marketing it, and safeguarding its proprietary features.

Product Regulation National laws affect the flow of products across borders. Host governments set laws that regulate access based on the product's **country of origin**—the country where it was grown, produced, or manufactured. Some countries apply this policy to product labels, under the title COOL (country-of-origin labeling), to inform consumers and support local producers. National security concerns also shape country-of-origin regulations. Suspicion about the espionage capabilities of their communication products dog Huawei and ZTE. Both Chinese MNEs are marked by opaque governance and tight linkages with the Communist Party of China. National security concerns have led Australia, Canada, and U.S. authorities to exclude their network equipment products from public contracts.[143]

Politicians also enact regulations to protect jobs, appease voters, placate special interests, and preserve tax revenue. Host governments prefer that MNEs make the greatest possible portion of their product(s) locally. Besides boosting local enterprise, technology transfers and knowledge spillovers support domestic innovation. To spur reluctant companies, governments enforce **local content** regulations, thereby requiring that a certain percentage of intermediate goods used in the production processes come from domestic suppliers. Brazil, for instance, levies a 30 percent tax increase on imported cars with less than 65 percent local content.[144]

| Product safety regulations set by the European Union shape standards worldwide.

Product Safety and Liability Regulation Countries impose product-safety and liability laws that require an MNE to adapt a product or else forsake market access. As a rule, wealthier countries impose stringent standards, whereas poorer countries, reflecting developing legal codes and rule-of-man legacies, inconsistently apply broader regulations. Presently, the European Union's product-liability directive shapes global standards.[145] It outlines the legal responsibility of manufacturers and stipulates the process of product-liability compensation claims. Then again, some MNEs proactively preempt the risk. The Danish toy maker Lego, for instance, noted consumers' fear of the possible toxicity of plastic toys made in China and did not open a factory there. Instead, Lego opted for factories in comparatively more expensive, but less worrisome Mexico and Eastern Europe.[146]

| The addition of a choice-of-law clause to contracts between different parties in different countries is an effective legal safeguard.

Legal Jurisdiction Determining which country's legal system will adjudicate a dispute is the matter of legal jurisdiction. Typically, in a cross-national dispute, each company claims jurisdiction in the belief that it will likely receive favorable treatment from its home court. This situation is especially pressing when an MNE from a rule-of-law system, say Canada, has legal difficulties in a rule-of-man environment, say Venezuela. Complicated ownership patterns coupled with interdependent operations spanning multiple countries often make it difficult to determine legal jurisdiction. Hence, MNEs commonly specify a **choice-of-law clause** in contracts that stipulates whose laws, when necessary, govern dispute resolution. Similarly, companies initiating contracts commonly add an arbitration provision, agreeing in advance to resolve potential disputes outside of court through agencies such as the International Court of Arbitration.

| Intellectual property is the general term for creative ideas, expertise, or intangible insights that grant its owner a competitive advantage.

| Intellectual property rights refer to the right to control and derive the benefits from writing (copyright), inventions (patents), processes (trade secrets), and identifiers (trademarks).

Intellectual Property In Adam Smith's time, countries drew strength from their agricultural prowess. Later, smokestack industries defined a nation's prosperity and power. Now, countries look to their brainpower to create might, prestige, and wealth. We call this output **intellectual property (IP)**—the creative ideas, innovative expertise, or intangible insights that create a competitive advantage for an individual, company, or country. The rising power of ideas in the global economy has made protecting intellectual property a growing concern.

Mainstream thought holds that the right to claim ownership of intellectual property stimulates innovation.[147] Transnational institutions—notably, the World Intellectual Property Organization (WIPO), along with governments and industry associations—push for stronger protection. The primary safeguard is an **intellectual property right (IPR)** that grants the

CONCEPT CHECKS ●

Chapters 1 and 2 note that income and wealth influence the actions that countries, both rich and poor, take to develop their business environments. Correspondingly, these factors also influence countries' approach to regulating MNEs local operations.

Richer countries typically regulate business activities less. Poorer countries typically regulate more.

registered owners of inventions, literary and artistic works, and symbols, names, images, or designs the right to determine the legal authority to decide who may use the property and under what circumstances. Essentially, an IPR constitutes a legally enforceable, but limited monopoly granted by a country to the innovator.[148]

Matters of jurisdiction complicate IP protection. A U.S. patent, for example, establishes an IPR only in the United States and its territories and possessions; it does not extend to foreign markets. There's no shortcut to worldwide protection—a company cannot register a "global" patent, trademark, or copyright. Although an IPR sounds secure, enforcing it often proves difficult. For example, in the United States, companies can go after the makers and sellers, not users, of counterfeit goods.[149] Worldwide, governments claim to abide by these agreements and enforce IPRs. However, piracy threatens popular, pricey, and vital products.

MNEs invest great effort to safeguard their intellectual property. The pervasiveness of piracy worldwide testifies to the challenge. Our closing case, "It's a Knockoff World," profiles this situation. Weak enforcement in some countries, particularly those marked by a rule of man bias and authoritarian politics, imposes obstacles. Other problems arise because not all countries support the various agreements that protect IPRs—primarily, the Paris Convention for the Protection of Industrial Property and the Berne Convention for the Protection of Literary and Artistic Works. Both emerged in the 1880s and are periodically updated. The WTO's Trade-Related Aspects of Intellectual Property Rights (TRIPS) broadens IP protection while, more recently, the EU is moving toward a "unitary patent" recognized automatically in all member countries.

POLITICS, LAW, AND THE BUSINESS ENVIRONMENT

CONCEPT CHECKS ●

Chapter 1 notes that some interest groups fear globalization fatally weakens national sovereignty—that is, growing external control reduces a nation's right to act in its own interests. Here, we observe that this attitude often intensifies political risk. Foreign investors face higher risks when a host government becomes increasingly sensitive to threats to its sovereignty.

Table 3.5 identifies the top-ranked and bottom-ranked countries whose political and legal policies enact, respectively, the most or least supportive business environments. In terms of the former, Singapore has developed a comprehensive legal code that fosters the most favorable business environment in the world. Conversely, the Central African Republic's political risks create the world's least favorable business environment. The rankings highlight a key relationship: most of the top-ranked countries have a democratic political system and a common or civil law legal system anchored in the rule of law. In contrast, most bottom-ranked countries exhibit authoritarian politics and a mixed legal system anchored in the rule of man.

TABLE 3.5   Easy Here, Hard There: Doing Business In Various Countries

The World Bank ranks 185 countries on their respective ease of doing business—the higher the score, the more favorable the business environment. Technically, the ease of business index averages the country's percentile rankings on ten dimensions: starting a business, dealing with construction permits, employing workers, registering property, getting credit, protecting investors, paying taxes, trading across borders, and enforcing contracts. Here we see the best and worst performers.

Country	Ranking	Country	Ranking
Singapore	1	Niger	176
Hong Kong SAR, China	2	Côte d'Ivoire	177
New Zealand	3	Guinea	178
United States	4	Guinea-Bissau	179
Denmark	5	Venezuela	180
Norway	6	Congo, Dem. Rep.	181
United Kingdom	7	Eritrea	182
South Korea	8	Congo, Republic	183
Georgia	9	Chad	184
Australia	10	Central African Republic	185

Source: Doing Business 2016. The World Bank. Retrieved May 15, 2016.

Countries that observe the rule of law, as opposed to the rule of man, more aggressively protect intellectual property rights. Hence, the predominant share of counterfeit products is made in countries in which the rule of man prevails.

Table 3.5, along with Table 3.4, highlights an inverse relationship between nation's general income levels and its scope of regulation—generally, richer countries regulate less and poorer countries regulate more. In high-income countries (e.g., the United States, France, Japan), starting a business requires an average of 6.28 procedures, spans 18 days, and costs 7 percent of per capita income. Doing the same in middle-income countries (e.g., Mexico, Poland, Malaysia, China, India, South Africa), requires an average of 7.8 procedures, spans 36 days, and costs 28 percent of per capita income. Lastly, in low-income countries (e.g., Bangladesh, Ethiopia, Nepal), one is facing 7.5 procedures, a 90-day span, and 37 percent of per capita income. Furthermore, legal systems in wealthier nations tend to regulate operational activities more consistently than do those in poorer countries—as one would expect, given the prevalence of the rule of law in the former and the rule of man in the latter.[150]

CASE   It's a Knockoff World

Companies are dogged by piracy—the illegal imitation, copying, or counterfeiting of their registered products. It's a tense issue given that it cuts to issues of innovation, history, culture, politics, and prosperity. Making matters worse is that pirates, besides being everywhere, come in every form: individuals making unauthorized copies at work, imitators laboring in dingy sweatshops, and hardened criminals running global networks.

The problem, basically, is straightforward: intellectual property (IP) in the form of books, music, product designs, brand names, process innovations, software, film, and the like is tough to conceive but ridiculously easy to copy.[151] Moreover, notwithstanding moral shortcomings, pirates do not lack initiative or imagination. In our knockoff world, if it's being made, it's being faked. Fair game includes virtually everything—from the humble aspirin to the flashy Ferrari.[152] And, for the kicker, knockoffs sell for a fraction of the price of the real thing to eager buyers worldwide.

Big Money, Big Risks

IP theft is big business. Globalization and the Internet fuel the perfect storm, the former moving much of the world's manufacturing to countries with poor IP protection, the latter providing cheap, easily accessible marketing platforms and distribution channels. The costs of counterfeit IP, from lost sales, eroded consumer confidence, diminished brand reputation, dangerous products, enforcement expenses, and legal costs, is staggering. The International Anti-Counterfeiting Coalition (IACC) estimates that international trade in illegitimate goods runs more than US$1.75 trillion a year—

approximately 7 percent of world merchandise trade. To top it off, piracy has grown more than 10,000 percent in the past three decades—it was a paltry $5.5 billion in 1982.[153]

Piracy grows because counterfeiting is astoundingly profitable; gross margins of 500 to 5,000 percent are common.[154] Counterfeit medicines are more profitable than heroin, copywatches may run a couple of bucks to make but sell for $20 in Beijing's Silk Market and $250 on Internet sites, and sales of high-end counterfeit software rival the return from cocaine trafficking.[155]

The lucrative rewards of piracy entice even notorious drug cartels to diversify. Mexico's La Familia and Los Zetas, for example, generate hundreds of millions of dollars selling counterfeit DVDs. Their expanding operations have made Mexico the piracy capital of Latin America. The cartels export so many bootleg movies to Central America, for example, that some studios have stopped shipping their products there. Also, whether buying it in Cancun, Cozumel, Monterrey, or Tijuana, the bootleg DVD more than likely bears a stamp indicating it was distributed by La Familia (a butterfly) or Zetas (a stallion).[156] Similarly, the cartels pirate software. La Familia sells counterfeit Microsoft software through kiosks, markets, and stores in the Michoacán region. Adding insult to injury, it stamps counterfeit Office discs with its "FMM" logo.[157]

Microsoft's predicament in China highlights common problems. Copies of its Office and Windows programs are peddled in market stalls for a few dollars, a fraction of their retail price. Rampant software piracy means Microsoft's revenue in China is a small fraction of its U.S. sales—even though personal-computer sales are higher in China. Early on, explained its former CEO, Microsoft's total revenue in China, with its population of 1.34 billion, was less than what it collects in the Netherlands, a country of fewer than 17 million.[158] This situation is not Microsoft's particular problem; thousands of companies in dozens of countries struggle with the same challenge.

Nothing Is Off-Limits

Many think piracy is the problem of snobbish, expensive brands. Certainly, counterfeits target high-end brands—the top 10 brands counterfeited include Microsoft, Nike, Adidas, Burberry, Louis Vuitton, and Sony. Luxury fakes, however, account for about 5 percent of the problem. The remaining 95 percent include copies of everyday products. Nothing is off-limits; "If it's making money over here in the U.S., it's going to be reverse-engineered or made overseas."[159]

The pharmaceutical supply chain is a pirate's paradise and counterfeiting threatens global health and safety; counterfeit medicines annually kill tens of thousands and it's anyone's guess how much fake medicine is floating around the world today. The Food and Drug Administration estimates that counterfeits account for 10 percent of all drugs sold in the United States. Studies of anti-infective treatments in Africa and Southeast Asia *peg* up to 70 percent as fake.[160] The United Nations estimates that half of the anti-malarial drugs sold in Africa are counterfeits. Imitations of Pfizer's best-selling drugs show up in legitimate supply chains in more than 50 countries.[161]

Waging a Multifront War

Companies, industry associations, and governments use a battery of weapons to wage war on pirates. An enduring approach relies on dispatching squads of lawyers on search-and-destroy missions. Big companies lawyer-up to lobby officials, monitor the web, prod Internet providers to take down copycat sites, and file injunctions against illegal sellers. UGG Australia began enforcing its IP upon realizing the prevalence of counterfeit boots. It has shut down thousands of websites selling fake UGGs and blocked many thousands more online listings. Liz Claiborne, owner of the Juicy Couture and Kate Spade brands, fights legions of websites selling counterfeits; it removed 27,000 auction listings of counterfeits in just a few months.

Some companies prefer high-tech assault. One approach embeds radio frequency identification (RFID) chips in the product packaging to allow precise tracking; IBM, 3M, and Abbot Laboratories are pacesetters. Others provide software programs that track products from factories to consumers. In Ghana, mPedigree lets consumers use their mobile phones to confirm the product is genuine; buyers call in a special code embossed inside the package to the vendor, who then verifies its authenticity.[162] Moving forward, some anticipate weaving microscopic markers into a product's packaging.

Governments, fearful of losing tax revenues and pressed by legitimate businesses, devise aggressive protection programs. The European Union ranks IP theft as a high priority.[163] The United States has elevated software piracy from a misdemeanor to a felony and boosted enforcement efforts by threatening to sanction notorious pirates with records of "onerous and egregious" IPR violations (including countries such as China, Russia, Argentina, India, Thailand, Turkey, and Ukraine). Likewise, its Federal Drug Administration has opened offices in China, India, South Africa, and Mexico, among others, in effect taking the fight to the frontier. On other fronts, rhetoric escalates. The U.S. Trade Representative, for instance, declared, "We must defend ideas, inventions, and creativity from rip-off artists and thieves."[164]

MNEs, officials, and trade associations lobby transnational institutions to apply stronger tools. Industry associations, like the IACC, spearhead efforts to toughen laws. Governments worldwide provide global services in public policy, business development, and consumer education. The World Intellectual Property Organization (WIPO) fortifies IP treaties and spurs members to bolster antipiracy programs. Likewise, the WTO applies the Trade-Related Aspects of Intellectual Property Rights (TRIPS) program to regulate enforcement, which requires member nations to protect and enforce IPRs according to global, not local, standards.

A barrage of legal assaults, novel technologies, smarter investigations, diplomatic efforts, industry initiatives, consumer education, stronger IP policies, aggressive law enforcement, and concerted political, commercial, and institutional action, one would think, should prove more than sufficient. Then, to make things a bit more interesting, add in the firepower of the global reach of vigilant MNEs, high-profile legal proceedings, increased government cooperation, criminalization of piracy, and tougher trade agreements. Such a shock-and-awe campaign should devastate the pirates, right? Surprise, surprise: Piracy continues to grow at an increasing rate. For instance, in 2009, Pfizer found counterfeit versions of 20 of its medicines in 81 countries. In 2012, Pfizer found 60 fakes in 106 countries. In 2015, Pfizer found 78 fakes in 109 countries.[165]

"The Bandits Are Everywhere"

The global cat-and-mouse game between MNEs and pirates, far from winding down, escalates. Booming piracy in big, fast-growing emerging markets like China and India spells big, fast-growing trouble. As more people enter the global market, many of them are eager to consume Western brands despite income constraints. Experts warn that the resulting quest for low prices turbocharges piracy.

In addition, crafty pirates quickly overcome IP defenses. They crack licensing codes, duplicate holograms, falsify e-mail headers, and utilize crypto-currencies. Staying one step ahead of the IP police is a widespread competency. "Like drug trafficking, the counterfeiting problem is so massive

[that] you don't know how to get a handle on it. The bandits are everywhere."[166] Worrisomely, successful pirates evolve into sophisticated entrepreneurs. "When you are dealing with high-end counterfeits, you are talking about organizations that have a full supply chain, a full distribution chain, a full set of manufacturing tools all in place and it is all based on profits."[167] Lamented one analyst, "Counterfeiting is like a balloon filled with water. You push it on one side, but when you remove your hand, it bounces back even stronger."[168]

Piracy gets a huge boost from the increasing availability of counterfeit goods through Internet channels, such as P2P file-sharing sites, mail order sites, or auction sites. Outgunned and outfoxed, some companies surrender. Foley & Corinna, a high-end handbag maker, explained that as it saw more Internet fakes, it stopped looking altogether. "It's just too frustrating. You can try to do something, but it's so big and so fast."[169] Then again, there are those who treat IPR as the price of doing business. Despite everyday piracy of his products in the Chinese market, an executive reasoned that the profitability of his legal sales more than offset the losses due to counterfeits.[170]

Is Piracy Inevitable?

The pervasiveness of piracy, in the face of aggressive lawyering, sophisticated tracking and tagging technologies, database software, and security controls, poses profound questions for protecting IPRs. Some worry that different legal legacies and political ideologies among countries complicate basic issues. TRIPS, by standardizing codes and norms, should have settled such troublesome issues. Legal and operational boundaries have limited its impact.

Others fear that the antipiracy war may already be lost. Evidently, a not-too-small number of consumers and businesses around the world have few ethical qualms about using counterfeits. Take software, for instance. Global software piracy is rampant. In 2013, the worldwide PC software piracy rate hit 43 percent. Put differently, of all the packaged software installed on PCs worldwide, 43 percent was obtained illegally, at a cost of US$62.7 billion in lost revenue (up from losses of $29 billion in 2003). For many nations, such as Armenia, China, Indonesia, Nigeria, Thailand, Ukraine, Venezuela, and Vietnam, software piracy rates top 70 percent. Even the best-behaved nations, like France, Japan, and the United States, report software piracy rates north of 18 percent.[171] Consequently, Microsoft's biggest rival is not another software company—it is counterfeiters.

Ultimately, the quest to live prosperous lives on tight budgets pushes people to seek counterfeits. Similarly, some in collectivist cultures reason that IP holders should honor society by abandoning their profit-maximizing business models. Sharing knowledge to benefit all, not protecting it for personal gain, is the moral imperative. But, counter others, without protection, ultimately there will be no IP to share or, for that matter, steal.

QUESTIONS

3-3. Would you expect piracy to thrive in a democracy or authoritarian state? Why?

3-4. Can you envision a scenario where developers and consumers of IP develop a relationship that eliminates the profitability of piracy?

3-5. Put yourself in the place of a poor individual in a poor country struggling to improve the quality of your life. What thoughts might shape how you interpret the legality of IPRs?

MyLab Managment

Go to **mymanagementlab.com** for the following Assisted-graded writing questions:

3-6 Can MNEs stop piracy without government help? Why would they prefer greater government assistance? Why would they oppose it?

3-7 Do you think consumers in wealthier countries versus those in poorer countries justify piracy with similar rationalizations? Why?

Endnotes

Scan for Endnotes or go to www.pearsonglobaleditions.com/Daniels

CHAPTER 4
Economic Systems and Market Methods

OBJECTIVES

After studying this chapter, you should be able to

4-1 Explain the value of economic analysis

4-2 Differentiate the types of economic environments

4-3 Explain the idea of economic freedom

4-4 Differentiate the types of economic systems

4-5 Interpret indicators of economic development, performance, and potential

4-6 Profile elements of economic analysis

MyLab Management®
Improve Your Performance!
When you see this icon ⭐, visit **www.mymanagementlab.com** for activities that are applied, personalized, and offer immediate feedback.

A man is rich who owes nothing.

—French proverb

Globalization Concept ▶

Source: ArtisticPhoto. Shutterstock

CASE

Emerging Economies: Comeback or Collapse?[1]

An epochal shift in the center of gravity of the global economy is underway. By 2050, four of the six largest economies in the world—China, India, Japan, and Russia—will be in greater Asia. Their growth will create a second tier of robust economies among their Asian neighbors, such as Singapore, the Philippines, South Korea, Indonesia, Taiwan, Kyrgyzstan, Vietnam, and Thailand. Countries in other, once sluggish parts of the world, like Africa and South America, will develop along with their Asian counterparts. Although the pace varies, all are moving from the periphery to the center of the global economy.[2]

Extrapolating from 2017 to 2050 is, undeniably, more speculation than specification. Still, many emerging economies are applying potent pro-growth policies. Hard data confirm their success so far. In 1980, their combined output accounted for 36 percent of global GDP. They crossed a milestone in 2009, accounting for more than half of total world GDP.[3] Similarly, emerging economies' share of world exports exceeds more than 50 percent, versus 20 percent in 1970. The IMF reports that the 10 fastest-growing markets in the years ahead are in emerging economies. Others suggest that 400 midsize emerging-market cities, many unfamiliar in the West, such as Abidjan, Chittagong, Khartoum, Kinshasa, Luanda, and Ouagadougou, will produce about 40 percent of global growth over the next 15 years.[4] Institutionally, the G-7, long a U.S.-Europe stronghold, has expanded into the G-20, thereby giving members like China, India, Brazil, Mexico, and South Korea greater say in global governance. These new stakeholders advocate different views of trade promotion and investment regulation. Moreover, emerging economies build institutions, such as the Asian Infrastructure Investment Bank, to champion their agenda. Collectively, the accelerating rise of emerging economies signaled that the wealthier countries of the twentieth century would not dominate the global economy in the twenty-first century.[5]

The past generation of progress and prosperity in emerging markets suggests the revolution has only begun. The ambition to improve infrastructure, increase productivity, create jobs, and alleviate poverty has put into motion what will likely be the biggest stimulus in history. The last transformation of similar magnitude—the Industrial Revolution—involved far fewer people in far fewer nations, but still powered a century-and-a-half expansion that altered lives everywhere. Today's revolution spans the globe, includes far more people in far more countries, and represents the biggest opportunity in the history of capitalism.[6] The transfer of the leadership baton from wealthy countries to emerging markets, for better and for worse, revolutionizes our interpretation of economic environments.

PRECEDENTS AND PREDICTIONS

Tracking the past millennium puts the current drama into perspective. Before the steam engine and the power loom drove the transfer of

FIGURE 4.1 Emerging Markets Make a Comeback

Throughout much of the past millennium, today's emerging economies, notably China and India, accounted for about 70 percent of global economic output. By the twentieth century, today's developed economies, such as the United States, Germany, and Japan, generated nearly three-quarters of global economic output. Trends suggest that by 2050, if not sooner, emerging economies will again account for more than 70 percent of global economic output, thereby culminating in their comeback.

Source: Based on Development Centre Studies, *The World Economy: A Millennial Perspective,* OECD Publishing, 2006. *Looking to 2060: A Global Vision of Long-Term Growth,* OECD Economic Policy Papers, November 2012.

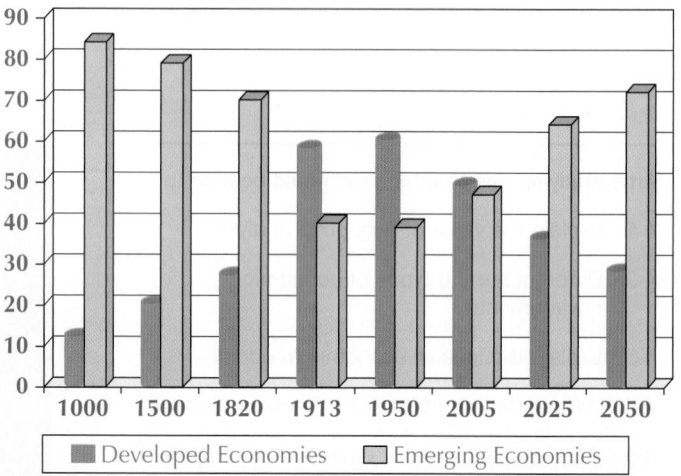

economic might from Asia to the West, today's emerging economies dominated world output. From 1000 to the mid-1880s, they produced, on average, 70 to 80 percent of world output (see Figure 4.1). Over this span, China and India were the world's two biggest economies; China alone generated one-third of global gross domestic product in 1820. In 1850, China produced the highest percent of all the goods consumed in the world. Britain, riding the Industrial Revolution, soon claimed this title before ceding the top spot to the United States around the beginning of the twentieth century. By 1950, emerging economies' share of global output had fallen to 40 percent, China's to 5 percent. Many floundered as internal political failure, aggravated by colonialism and dubious trade agreements, spurred isolationism and xenophobia. Consequently, the Industrial Revolution benefited the West while bypassing today's emerging markets.

Presently, the ambition of emerging economies is straightforward: Restore their historic stature as the engine of the global economy. This goal will culminate in their comeback, where, once again, they account for more than 70 percent of global output.[7] Symbolizing this change, in 2009 China reclaimed the top spot it last held in 1850—producing about 20 percent of all the goods consumed in the world; the United States, leader for the previous 110 years, fell to second.[8] Likewise, the IMF reported that China has become the central trading power in the world—it is the biggest or second-biggest trading partner for 78 countries.[9]

PROBLEMS IN PARADISE

Notwithstanding the spectacular performance and potential of emerging economies, by mid-2016 a steady stream of foreboding developments sounded alarms. A startling collapse in many commodity prices, from coffee to oil to cement to iron, has dampened prospects for many. Brazil, besides experiencing a severe recession, faced tough political times as corruption and cronyism triggered an impeachment crisis. Russia resorted to fanning nationalism to neutralize its declining prospects given the collapse in energy prices. South Africa appeared overwhelmed by the worldwide decline in commodity prices, waning demand from China, its biggest trading partner, and the worst drought in 50 years; it teeters on the edge of an economic cliff as credit agencies threaten to cut its sovereign debt to junk status. Saudi Arabia, struggling with the dramatic drop in oil prices and record budget deficit in 2015, cut social services for the first time in decades and faced an "economic time bomb." Bleak financial situations pushed emerging economies toward debt to finance budget shortfalls and balance-of-payment problems. In 2007, China had $7.4 trillion in debt; by 2015 it had risen to over $30 trillion. Increasingly, China's growing debt mountain casts a worrisome shadow over its prospects, especially as its growth in 2015 was the slowest in 25 years, continued a multiyear slowdown, showed little sign of abating, and fanned social unrest.[10]

Skeptics suggested that the overhyped comeback had morphed into an inevitable collapse. Limiting economic freedom, others added, had finally caught up with emerging economies. Now, with markets crumbling, state authorities, once omnipotent, looked impotent. Anemic economic performance, for instance, eroded confidence in Thailand's ruling junta, Venezuela's dominant party system, and Zimbabwe's long-running dictatorship.[11] The customary policy solutions, namely market reforms, deregulation, and privatization, directly opposed the state capitalist systems that prevailed in many emerging economies. Those cures, by reducing state authority, threatened the sustainability of the single-party government that is the institutional core of many emerging economies.

MAKING SENSE TO MAKE CENTS

Megatrends such as the comeback are millennial events. And, unquestionably, trends can go dramatically awry. Consequently, the global economic environment was caught in challenging times—one way or another, policymakers, executives, workers, and investors wrestled with the unfolding revolution powered by the comeback, or, as the case may be, the fallout of the collapse. Making investments, positioning assets, and running operations for either outcome pushed managers to make sense of the possibly good, possibly bad, brave new global business environment. ■

QUESTIONS

4-1. Transformations such as the comeback of the emerging economies happen quite rarely. Their infrequency amplifies their impact on our lives. Identify from the case how your life has changed, or will likely change, given the comeback.[12]

4-2. Now, flip analysis and consider the implications of the possible collapse of emerging economies to your life. How might it change?

INTERNATIONAL ECONOMIC ANALYSIS

Studying an economic environment helps managers make better investment choices and operating decisions.

In the IB realm, cultural, political, and legal systems influence a company's decision on where, when, and how to do business. This chapter completes our profile of the environmental domains of IB, evaluating how economic systems shape a market. Throughout it, we spotlight the relevance of economics to citizens, executives, companies, officials, and institutions. And, with that in mind, apply the idea that a broad understanding of its dimensions and dynamics helps all make better consumption, investment, operating, and policy decisions. This chapter presents the general perspectives and specific tools that assess economic environments. It also profiles the ideas and frameworks that integrate interpretation.[13]

Resource constraints require managers to identify which countries in the world warrant investment as well as those they must avoid.

Developing an understanding of the global business environment is a fascinating challenge. Think about the scale and scope of the task. The World Bank identifies 214 discrete economic environments in the world today—188 countries and 26 economies with populations of more than 30,000. The former include countries that most are quite familiar with, such as Australia, China, France, Indonesia, and Singapore. The set of 26 includes some that many have likely heard of, but also others that many have not, such as the Isle of Man, Macao, San Marino, and Vanuatu.[14] Mapping these markets, from the biggest (China) to the smallest (Tuvalu), is an essential aspect of IB. In this chapter, we profile how managers do so, highlighting principles and tools that make sense of the remarkable diversity of markets.

Managers study a country's economic environment to assess its development, explain its performance, and estimate its potential.

Few, if any, MNEs can fund and run operations in all 214 economic environments. Resource constraints require managers prioritize options, targeting markets that offer the greatest return with the least risk. Improving the odds of success depends on assessing the development, performance, and potential of an economy. Economics identifies a range of rigorous tools that help systematize evaluation. Familiar metrics, such as gross domestic product, interest rates, inflation, and unemployment, estimate important features. Integrating analysis taps scientific principles, like production functions, marginal analysis, and the general equilibrium model, as well as behavioral assumptions, like rationality and incentives. Both perspectives clarify consumer choice, firm conduct, industry structure, and market activity.[15] The combined mix of objective and subjective analytics support insightful interpretations. Still, challenges emerge on several fronts.

CONCEPT CHECK

A principle of globalization is the broadening network of relationships among people, companies, countries, and institutions. Philosophically, the same principle applies to the emergence and evolution of economies.

Various principles help managers better assess economic environments, including

- system complexity,
- market dynamism,
- market interdependence.

Complexity   Economic environments are dynamic systems. The intricacy of the simplest economic system defies straightforward specification. Stipulating models that definitively represent a country's economic performance and potential as well as work reliably in all types of economic environments is difficult. Hence, managers wrestle with identifying valid measures for developed, developing, and emerging economies, then modeling their relationships, mapping them onto a particular market, and monitoring their reliability. Confounding matters is the fact that managers are inundated with more raw knowledge, accessible information, and clever insights than ever before. Rather than improving analysis, expanding data streams often make a hard task harder.[16]

Dynamism   Market changes can make today's valid measures dubious tomorrow. Evolving circumstances, compounded by disruptive situations and puzzling trends, generate anomalies and exceptions that convert comebacks into collapses. For instance, analytics anchored in the politically free markets commonly found in the West poorly translate to the state-sponsored capitalism at play in the East. Likewise, product development strategies in affluent developed countries struggle to fit the profound poverty often found in developing economies. In the former, customers prefer robust product functionality, whereas inexpensive simplicity matters more in the latter. Managers' economic instincts, tried and tested for the past decades in developed economies, adapt to the changing, often contradictory circumstances in emerging markets. The characteristics of an economic environment determine which, where, and when each approach makes sense.

Interdependence   Just as no one is an island, no country is isolated. The consequence of cross-national connections means actions here influence outcomes there. For instance, growing political control of economic processes improves efficiencies in developing economies, but lessens them in their developed counterparts; recycling foreign-exchange reserves means capital is too cheap here, but too expensive there; greater competition for scarce resources raises the prices of commodities, but lowers the costs of manufactured goods; and poverty falls in developing economies, but rises in their developed counterparts.[17] Cross-national interdependencies moderate the forces of supply, demand, and their pricing signals. Adjusting analysis for actions and reactions across an expanding scope of markets complicates interpretation.

NAVIGATING CHALLENGES

Figure 4.2 shows how managers navigate these challenges. It holds that economic conditions shape a country's development, performance, and potential. It highlights the elements that guide assessment and emphasizes that change in one causes change in others. Clarifying interactions among these features, no matter if the context is a developed, developing, or **emerging economy**, assists with mapping development paths and estimating

FIGURE 4.2   Economic Factors Affecting International Business Operations

Although economic environments vary from country to country, they share telltale principles and practices. Managers focus on these, as well as their interactions, to organize analysis.

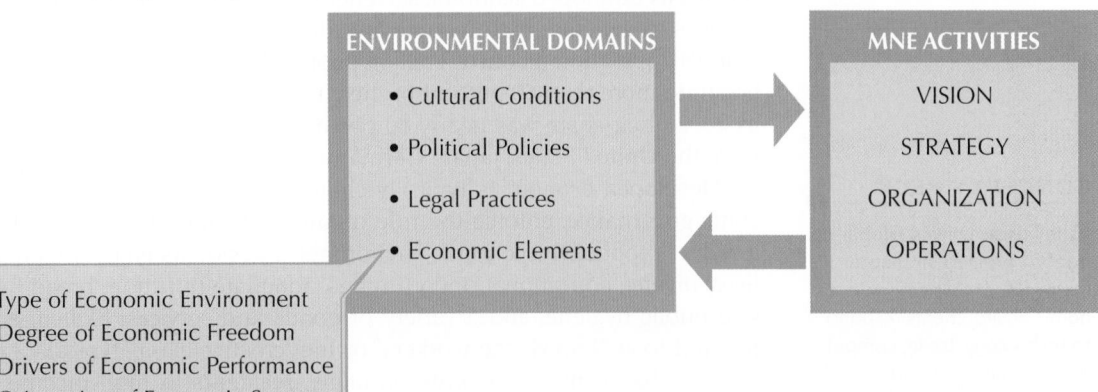

CONCEPT CHECK

Chapter 1 notes changing environmental conditions that promote and constrain globalization, Chapter 2 notes changing cultural identities, and Chapter 3 notes changing political philosophies and legal outlooks. The same perspective applies here as well—namely, the changing economic environments of IB create opportunities and impose constraints.

potentials. Hence, Figure 4.2 endorses a systems perspective that qualifies interpretation in terms of:

1. The type of economic environment in terms of its state of development.
2. The economic freedom managers have to make investments and run operations.
3. The orientation of the economic system that shapes its path of development, performance, and potential.
4. The drivers of economic change, particularly the moderators of productivity, innovation, and competitiveness.[18]

Collectively, engaging these issues pinpoints where investments should go and, more importantly, where they should not.

WHO'S WHO IN THE GLOBAL BUSINESS ENVIRONMENT

Broad classes of countries include
- developed countries,
- emerging economies,
- developing countries.

Managers track economies, evaluating events and trends to spot opportunities and preempt risks. The scale and scope of economics spanning 214 markets quickly muddle assessment. Getting one's bearing often begins by determining general characteristics—essentially, assessing who's who and then aggregating the data in order to compare consumers, companies, and countries. In IB, the development level of a country is the single most important indicator of who's who. It influences nearly every aspect of business, including the nature of consumer demand, organization of productive activity, attitudes toward foreign investors, regulatory transparency, sophistication of market systems, and the freedom one has to make effective and efficient business decisions. Hence, estimating the attractiveness of a country as a place to do business and, once there, making smart investment and operational decisions depends on how well managers understand its economic environment. We follow the lead of the United Nations (UN) to identify who's who. Based on a wide range of dimensions, it classifies a nation as a **developed economy**, developing economy, or an **economy in transition**.[19]

DEVELOPED ECONOMIES

Developed economies generally have high income levels, extensive industrialization, advanced technological infrastructure, and high standard of living.

A developed economy has a robust economic environment marked by wide-ranging activities, efficient capital movement, stable institutions, extensive infrastructure, international trade and investments, advanced technologies, and higher economic freedom. Developed countries cluster in a few regions of the world; the UN classifies Australia, Canada, Japan, New Zealand, Norway, Switzerland, United States, members of the European Union, and the like as developed economies. Generally, each relies on a broad mix of manufacturing and services to generate high income and deep wealth. Today, approximately 16 percent of the world's population (about 1.2 billion people) lives in developed economies. Collectively, they generate more than 60 percent of the current gross world product of $78 trillion; as recently as 2002, their share was nearly 80 percent.[20] In 2016, the five largest developed economies were the United States, Japan, Germany, the United Kingdom, and France.

Developed economies typically champion political freedom, practice multiparty democratic governance, enforce the rule of law, and support free markets. In turn, these anchor a stable, productive economic environment. Residents enjoy a high standard of living, long lives, diverse educational opportunities, adequate nutrition, broad health care, comprehensive public hygiene, and a variety of goods and services. Skilled, educated workers, often referred to as "knowledge workers" or the "creative class," typically earn high salaries working in urban centers.[21] Correspondingly, residents in high-income developed economies, such as Austria, Norway, South Korea, Switzerland, and the United States, averaged nearly $45,000 in annual income in 2015.

Still, many people struggle with poor quality jobs in developed countries. One of four jobs in the United States, for instance, qualify as low-paying positions with an approximate annual income of $23,000.[22] Likewise, an individual must work 55 hours per week at the minimum wage to move a four-person family above the relative poverty line in the United States.[23] In comparison, one must work 85, 66, 64, 52, and 40 hours per week in a minimum wage job in the Czech Republic, Israel, South Korea, Canada, and France, respectively, to lift a four-person family out of poverty.[24] Consequently, many developing countries experience rising income inequality, whereby the rich grow richer while the poor grow poorer.[25]

Developed economies steadily shift to diversified, service-oriented activities that rely on information and technology to support product and process innovation. Manufacturers in developed economies have outsourced many activities to low-cost factories in the emerging economies. Robotics, 3-D printing, and the like spur new manufacturing methods that may reshore some outsourced activities (i.e., returning outsourced personnel and services to developed economies). Still, the dominant trend in developed economies for the past generation has been migrating manufacturing to lower cost, higher productivity factories in developing economies.

Movement from manufacturing to service as the basis of economic activity prompts referring to developed countries as high-income economies, advanced markets, advanced industrial economies, or postindustrial economies. In the future, we may see the term "established market economies," given their high per capita income, high standard of living, and sophisticated institutional framework but slower growth relative to developing economies.

DEVELOPING ECONOMIES

Generally, a developing economy has an uneven economic environment that is marked by narrow market activities, inefficient capital movement, resistance to foreign ownership, trade restrictions, imperfect competition, unstable institutions, limited infrastructure, sketchy technologies, and lower economic freedom.[26] Corruption, cronyism, and crime complicate efforts to regulate society consistently or adopt prudent economic policies. Workers, often lacking formal education or practical training, earn low annual incomes. Certainly, a few developing economies are rapidly industrializing; these are commonly called emerging economies. Many are not, and remain extensively agrarian. Typically, a small share, say 2 to 4 percent, of workers in developed economies work on a farm. In some developing economies, such as Angola, Ethiopia, Indonesia, and Pakistan, 30 to 90 percent do. The UN classifies approximately 150 countries as developing; they span Africa, Asia, Eastern Europe, Latin America, the Middle East, and South America. Today, roughly 85 percent of the world's population resides in developed economies. Collectively, they generate about 40 percent of

CONCEPT CHECK

"The Forces Driving Globalization" profiled in Chapter 1 (page 50), explained how economic environments respond to technology, trade, competition, consumer attitudes, and cross-border relationships. The scope of the connections among these conditions differs given the level of development in the particular economic systems.

Developed economies are also referred to as

- high-income economies,
- advanced markets,
- advanced industrial economies,
- postindustrial economies.

Developing economies generally have low income levels, slight industrialization, incomplete infrastructure, and lower standards of living.

gross world product.[27] In 2016, the five largest developing economies were China, India, Russia, Brazil, and Indonesia.

Developing economies, as a rule, have a low gross national income per capita. At the lower range, one sees average annual incomes in the mid to high hundreds (US$) in countries such as Afghanistan, Chad, Liberia, Malawi, and Togo. In others, like Cameroon, Nicaragua, Nigeria, Uzbekistan, and Yemen, average annual incomes run in the low thousands (US$).[28] Finally, some, such as Azerbaijan, China, Indonesia, Mexico, and Turkey, see per capita income in the high thousands. Developing economies often have pockets of great wealth; in 2015, for instance, China reported more billionaires than the United States, with 596 versus 537.[29] Still, many of the approximately 6 billion residents of developing economies endure abject poverty, low living standards, scarce opportunities, and limited access to few goods and services.

Life differs on innumerable aspects between developed and developing economies. Some argue that developing countries have strong communities and social ties, extraordinary self-sufficiency, and admirable work ethics. Alternatively, one regularly finds higher infant mortality, shorter life expectancy, lower literacy levels, poorer public hygiene, insufficient health care, and inadequate nutrition in developing countries relative to their developed counterparts. Harsh conditions largely follow from the poverty that prevails throughout developing economies. Certainly, poverty shapes economic environments of all countries, from the wealthiest developed to the poorest **developing country**. However, poverty profoundly influences life and markets in developing economies. Approximately 2.1 billion people in the developing world live on less than US$3.10 a day.[30] Poverty forces many to struggle for food, shelter, clothing, clean water, and health services, to say nothing of safety, education, and opportunity. Deprivation contributes to malnutrition, mental illness, epidemics, famine, conflict, and humanitarian crises. Governments struggle to provide social services, health care, education, and civil stability. Markets are prone to corruption, cronyism, and political risk. The grinding struggle for survival deters enterprise, stymies entrepreneurs, and slows productivity, thereby recharging a brutal cycle of persistent poverty. Ultimately, however, economic progress and IB expansion ultimately depend on developing the means to alleviate poverty.

Markets experiencing widespread, oftentimes extreme, poverty require MNEs reassess many taken-for-granted aspects of an economy. For instance, advertisers in developed

Significant gaps exist in economic and social characteristics between developed and developing economies.

Poverty is the state of having little or no money, few or no material possessions, and limited access to education, health, and community.

Morocco, Marrakech, View over roofs with satellite dishes towards Atlas mountains

Once unusual, satellite dishes are now ubiquitous throughout developing countries. Here, we see a view over roofs in Marrakech, Morocco, many tagged with satellite dishes, each expanding cross-national linkages that promote economic development.

Source: Westend61 Premium/ Shutterstock

The worldwide growth of business activity and economic progress ultimately depends on alleviating poverty.

economies assume high rates of literacy; in South Korea, France, and New Zealand, for instance, virtually everyone can read. However, in Chad, Ethiopia, and Mali, fewer than half can. Hence, managers must fine-tune analytics anchored in the wealthy developed economies for the radically different market circumstances routinely found in developing economies.

ECONOMIES IN TRANSITION

The term emerging economies is often used in place of economies in transition. One also sees terms such as frontier markets and newly industrializing countries.

Great range marks the economic performance among developing economies precisely because different economies experience different levels of development at different rates. At the low end, countries marred by fragile political institutions, heavy indebtedness, poorly performing markets, and ongoing conflict (e.g., Afghanistan, Democratic Republic of Congo, or Timor Leste) average per capita incomes in the low hundreds (US$). Besides poverty, these sorts of economies contend with governments overcome by sovereign responsibilities. In contrast, at the high end of developing economies, we find faster-growing, quickly industrializing countries such as China, Mexico, Indonesia, and the Philippines. Increasingly, these countries are referred to as economies in transition, emerging markets, frontier markets, or newly industrializing countries; generally, description defaults to emerging economies.

There are approximately 30 or so emerging economies in the world (see Map 4.1).[31] These nations are experiencing accelerating growth in productivity, manufacturing, exporting, and per capita income, resulting in material improvements achieved in years, rather than decades. Their financial systems, political institutions, and market infrastructure steadily modernize. Market liberalization promotes foreign investments and growing exports, deregulation and privatization improve business efficiency, and expanding economic freedoms encourage entrepreneurialism. Prosperity and progress support a growing middle class whose economic aspirations fuel a revolution of rising expectations, thereby spurring society and the state to improve living standards.

When one speaks of the emerging economies, many point to Brazil, Russia, India, and China (referred to as the **BRIC**s); officially, emerging economies are developing countries, but the pace of their performance leads to distinguishing them. Table 4.1 identifies other groupings. Although much larger in scale and scope than other emerging economies, many see the

MAP 4.1   Emerging Economies of the World

Various designations organize economic environments. Here we highlight markets commonly referred to as emerging economies, namely those given their accelerating economic development.

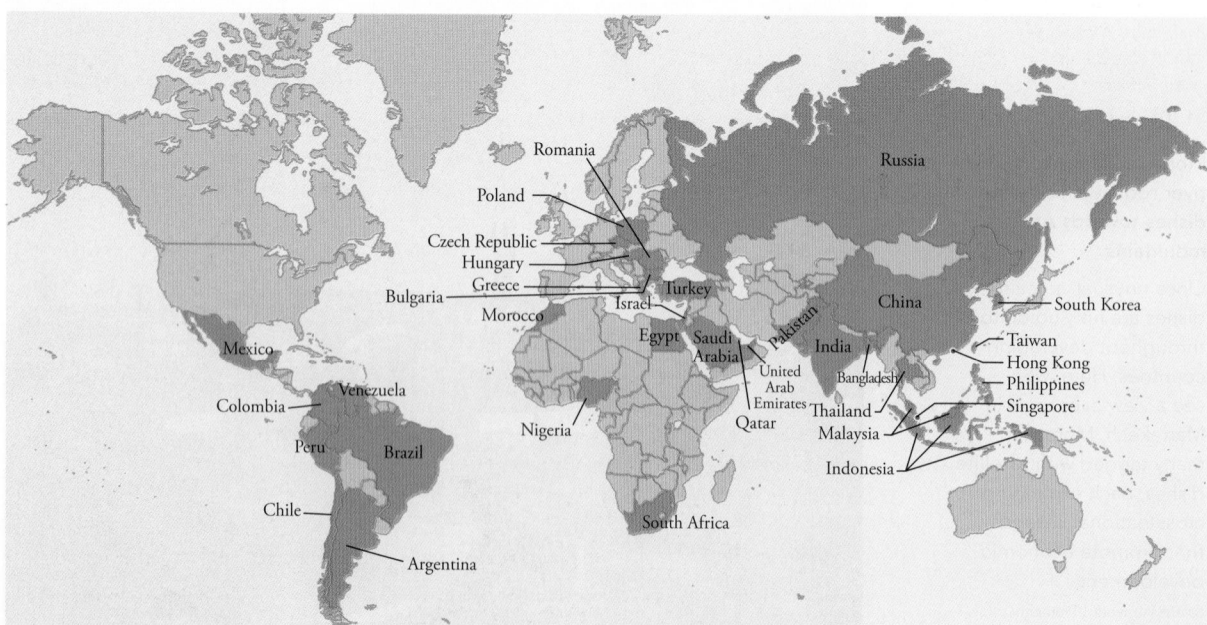

TABLE 4.1 The Alphabet of Emerging Economies

A range of acronyms classify various sets of emerging economies. As different countries develop, observers have coined a variety of shorthand codes.

Acronym	Specification
BRIC	B for Brazil, R for Russia, I for India, C for China
BASIC	Add AS for South Africa, Removes R for Russia
BIC	Remove R for Russia
BRICA	Add A for Arab countries—Saudi Arabia, Qatar, Kuwait, Bahrain, Oman, and the United Arab Emirates
BRICET	Add E for Eastern Europe, T for Turkey
BRICIT	Add I for Indonesia, T for Turkey
BRICK	Add K for South Korea
BRICS	Add S for South Africa
BRIIC	Add I for Indonesia
BRIMC	Add M for Mexico
CARBS	Canada, Australia, Russia, Brazil, South Africa
CIVETS	Colombia, Indonesia, Vietnam, Egypt, Turkey, South Africa
MIST	Mexico, Indonesia, South Korea, Turkey
N-11 (*The Next 11*)	Bangladesh, Egypt, Indonesia, Iran, Mexico, Nigeria, Pakistan, Philippines, South Korea, Turkey, Vietnam
PPICS	Peru, Philippines, Indonesia, Colombia, Sri Lanka

Emerging economies exhibit improving productivity, rising income, and growing prosperity, particularly relative to slower growing developing economies.

CONCEPT CHECK

Although developing countries are attractive in terms of economic potential, managers heed the discussions of Chapters 2 and 3 concerning the different cultural, political, and legal environments found in developing countries. Still, Chapter 1 notes the drivers of globalization steadily narrow the gap between developed and developing countries.

BRICs as the vanguard of the comeback or collapse, presuming that where the BRICs go, both good and bad, others will follow. Currently one sees improving productivity and prosperity in an expanding range of countries, often referred to as frontier markets, such as Oman, Kenya, Nigeria, Romania, Rwanda, and Vietnam. Their performance echoes policies and programs commonly seen in the BRICs rather than in poor, slower growing developed economies.

Estimates see more than 70 percent of the world's growth over the next few years in emerging markets and, to a lesser degree, secondary developing economies.[32] Some 400 midsize emerging-market cities will generate about 40 percent of global growth over the next 15 years. Many of these, such as Chittagong, Bamako, Kampala, Kano, Kinshasa, and Sanaa, are strategic centers in, respectively, Bangladesh, Mali, Uganda, Nigeria, Democratic Republic of Congo, and Yemen.[33] Low-cost resources, productive labor, expanding consumption, pro-business policies, and enterprising conglomerates power their emergence. Indeed, companies in emerging economies are cleverly reinventing systems of production and distribution and experimenting with new business models. From mobile money in Kenya to frugal innovation in India, pioneering companies like Safari.com and Goonj improve the performance and potential of developing countries. Figure 4.3 highlights the consequence of these trends, showing the shifting center of economic gravity in our world. Since the mid-1980s, the pace of change—from the nations of the West toward those in the East—is moving faster than ever before in human history.[34]

THE ISSUE OF DIFFERENT DEGREES OF DEVELOPMENT

Gross world output increased nearly sixfold between 1970 and 2015, growing from $12 trillion to $78 trillion. In absolute terms, globalization expanded the economy for all. In relative terms, though, many countries prospered, some more than others, and a few not at all. Different reasons explain different levels of economic development in different countries. Analysis directs attention to the economic, political/legal, and cultural moderators of development (see Table 4.2). Various models, for instance structural change theory, linear stages of growth, international dependence theory, and neoclassical theory, propose integrative

FIGURE 4.3   Mapping the Earth's Economic Center of Gravity: 1 CE to 2025

The world's center of economic gravity has shifted over the past centuries. One sees here the jump from Asia to Europe in the 1800s due to the Industrial Revolution, and then onward to the United States in the nineteenth century. Since the mid-1980s, however, the direction and pace of the shift have changed. Now, for a host of reasons, the center of economic gravity is increasingly returning to Asia. Presently, it's shifting approximately 140 kilometers/85 miles eastward per year.

Source: Dobbs, R, Jaana Remes, James Manyika, Charles Roxburgh, Sven Smit, and Fabian Schaer. *Urban world: Cities and the rise of the consuming class.* McKinsey Global Institute, 2012.[35]

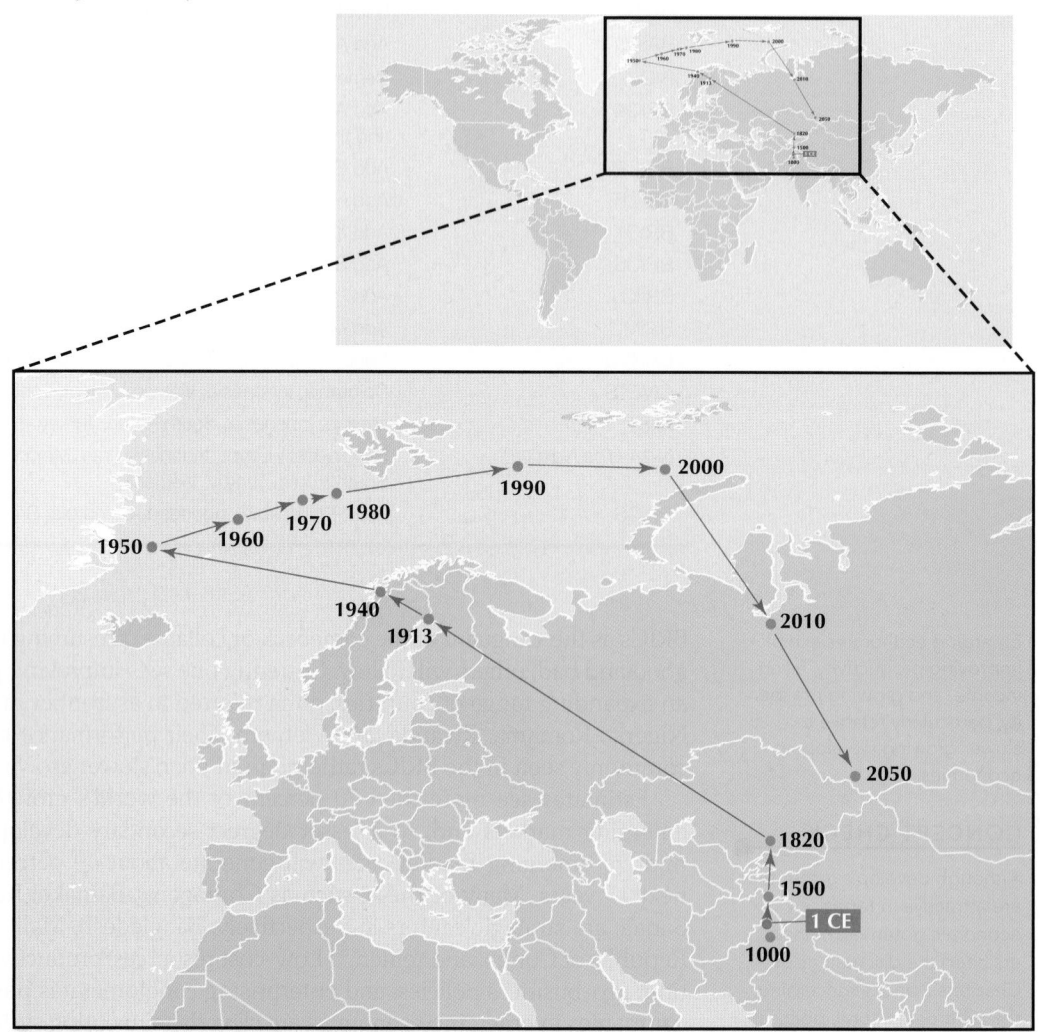

> The Base of the Pyramid is the largest, but poorest, socioeconomic group in the world.

interpretations of progress and prosperity.[36] Findings indicate market situations and economic circumstances often overlap among countries, but, just as well, they differ among others. And, as we just saw, differences are often extreme. For example, annual income per person in, for instance, Singapore versus the Central African Republic, finds a gap of $80,000 to $600 per person. Observed one analyst, "That's absolutely astounding, to be on the same planet and to have that extreme variation in material well-being."[37] As such, the mysteries of capitalism and their implication to the different levels of economic development endure.

Recent trends refine interpretations of economic development. One, the **Base of the Pyramid** spotlights the some four billion people who earn a few dollars per day and live primarily in developing economies. Though long seen as inaccessible and unprofitable, the Base represents a tremendous volume of consumption, and is the next frontier of the global economy.[38] Likewise, accelerating income growth in developing economies moves many of today's poor up the income ladder.[39] Middle-class consumer spending in the developed economies of North America and Europe, for example, is approximately $15 trillion; it will grow to $17 trillion by 2030.[40] Meanwhile, middle-class consumer spending in Asia–Pacific, home to many emerging and developing economies, is presently $4.9 trillion. It will

TABLE 4.2 Moderators of Economic Development

Research reports that various economic, political/legal, and cultural conditions moderate growth, progress, and prosperity.

Economic Factors	• Advocacy of Economic Freedom • Agrarian, Industrial, or Service Based Activity • Business Efficiency • Degree of Literacy • Educational Opportunity • Entrepreneurial and Executive Expertise • Equality of Income Distribution • Land, Labor, Capital, and Technology Factors • Poverty and Productivity • Scale and Scope of Market Systems • Sophistication of Infrastructure • Sound Macroeconomic Policies
Political/Legal Factors	• Advocacy of Political Freedom • Basis of Law • Extent of Criminality, Corruption, and Cronyism • Extent of Government Bureaucracy • Membership in Regional/Global Trade Groups • Openness to Foreign Trade and Investment • Political Risk and Sovereign Fragility • Prevalence of Privatization and Deregulation • Sanctity of Property Rights • Stability of Public Policy • State of Social Services, Health Care, and Hygiene • Tariff Policies, Subsidies, and Investment Regulations
Cultural Factors	• Expectation of Fairness, Equality, and Justice • Interplay of Individualism and Collectivism • Legitimacy of Free Enterprise • Measures of Achievement • Meritocratic, Aristocratic, or Militaristic Elites • Religious vs. Secular Schooling • Size and Stability of the Middle Class • Technological Aptitude and Orientation • Tolerance for Counterfeiting and Piracy • Transparency Standard

expand nearly 600 percent to roughly $33 trillion by the year 2030. Some see it powering an economic surge unlike any we have ever seen.[41]

ECONOMIC FREEDOM

The scale and scope of the differences among developed, developing, and emerging economies challenge analysis. A key idea, namely that of economic freedom, bolsters interpretation. Think back for a moment to Chapter 3's use of political freedom to anchor evaluation of the political environment. Political freedom is the central concept in political thought and the pivotal dynamic of a political environment. Any dialogue on politics, no matter the terminology, dimensions, or dynamics, ultimately addresses the issue of what one is free to do and, arguably more importantly, what one is prohibited from doing. We apply the same logic here, focusing on the degree of economic freedom an individual has to use initiative, effort, and competencies to pursue one's ambitions.

Economic freedom reflects the liberty managers have to decide endless aspects of everyday business operations. For example, what investments they make, how they allocate resources, what property rights they claim, how they compete, whom they hire and fire, and what forms of operations they engage in. In many countries, primarily developed economies, aspects of economic freedom are so taken for granted that they rarely cross managers' minds. In many others, primarily developing economies, they are so restricted that they serve as topics of ongoing fascination and, often, flashpoints.

Economic freedom holds that one has the right to work, produce, consume, save, and invest in the way that one prefers.

Formally, **economic freedom** is the "absolute right of property ownership, fully realized freedoms of movement for labor, capital, and goods, and an absolute absence of coercion or constraint of economic liberty beyond the extent necessary for citizens to protect and maintain liberty itself."[42] The greater the degree of economic freedom in an economic environment, the greater the freedom an individual has to decide how to work, produce, consume, save, invest, and innovate. Furthermore, the greater the degree of economic freedom, the greater an individual's confidence in the legitimacy of property rights, liberty to use factors of production, flexibility to organize goods and services, and protection from undue political interference. Economic freedom creates opportunities and boosts productivity, functioning as the critical link between ambition and actions.[43] Economically free countries support activities that create income and generate wealth. Successful entrepreneurs map paths that others follow to build better lives.

Economic freedom measures the absence of government coercion or constraint on the production, distribution, or consumption of goods and services beyond the extent necessary for citizens to protect and maintain liberty.

Economic freedom does not signify the absence of government. Ultimately, freedom requires protection. Think of, for example, the police force that protects property rights, market regulators that ensure fair competition, monetary authorities that monitor a sound currency, or an impartial judiciary that enforces business contracts. Each, as an agent of the state, safeguards economic freedom. Hence, protecting economic freedom requires government regulation, but, ideally, only to the degree needed to transparently protect and legitimately sustain it. Excessive regulation, by substituting political judgment in place of individual choice, constrains entrepreneurialism and reduces market efficiency.

The **Economic Freedom Index** estimates economic freedom in a particular nation. In principle, this index measures the degree that a nation accepts Adam Smith's thesis that "basic institutions that protect the liberty of individuals to pursue their own economic interests result in greater prosperity for the larger society."[44] In practice, it sets 4 key categories and disaggregates those into 10 dimensions that then organize 50 measures (see Table 4.3).[45] The ultimate score ranges from zero (no freedom) to 100 (full freedom); hence, the higher the index for a particular nation, the higher its degree of economic freedom.

TABLE 4.3   Dimensions of the Economic Freedom Index

Category	Component	Measure
Rule Of Law	Property Rights	Ability of individuals to accumulate private property, secured by clear laws that are fully enforced by the state.
	Freedom from Corruption	Degree that corruption introduces insecurity and uncertainty into economic relationships.
Limited Government	Fiscal Freedom	Tax burden imposed by government on its citizens.
	Government Spending	Government expenditures as a percentage of GDP.
Regulatory Efficiency	Labor Freedom	Aspects of the legal and policy framework that regulates the country's labor market.
	Business Freedom	The ability to start, operate, and close a business that represents the overall burden of regulation as well as the efficiency of government in the regulatory process.
	Monetary Freedom	The degree of price stability and the extent of price controls.
Open Markets	Trade Freedom	The absence of tariff and nontariff barriers that affect imports and exports of goods and services.
	Investment Freedom	Ability of individuals and firms to move resources, without restriction, into and out of activities both internally and across the country's borders.
	Financial Freedom	Efficiency of banking as well as the independence of the financial sector from government control and interference.

Adapted from information reported in "Methodology," *2015 Index of Economic Freedom*, The Heritage Foundation, in partnership with the Wall Street Journal, retrieved February 6, 2016, from www.heritage.org/index/book/methodology.

CONCEPT CHECK ●

Chapter 1 suggests that income inequality and poverty should diminish as IB improves the efficiency of resource allocation. Chapter 3 highlighted the importance of people's freedom to do so. Here we add to the mix ideas of economic freedom and its thesis that productive use of liberated capital creates progress and prosperity.

THE VALUE OF ECONOMIC FREEDOM

Economic Freedom delivers ongoing dividends, supporting higher growth in the short- (5 years), medium- (10 years), and long-term (20 years). Today, the average income in economically free countries is more than double the worldwide average and four times higher than that found in mostly unfree and repressed economies (see Figure 4.4). Freedom lets managers better balance risk and return over economic cycles, particularly given confidence in efficient capital markets and prudent monetary policy. Economic freedom fortifies macroeconomic stability;

FIGURE 4.4 Economic Freedom and the Standard of Living

Economic freedom has significant relationships with a variety of market, social, and political measures. Here we see the relationship between economic freedom and a broad indicator of the standard of living, GDP per capita.

Source: Adapted from Terry Miller and Anthony Kim, "Why Economic Freedom Matters | 2015 Index of Economic Freedom Book." 2016. Accessed April 15. http://www.heritage.org/index/book/chapter-2. Used by permission.

Note: GDP is adjusted for PPP.

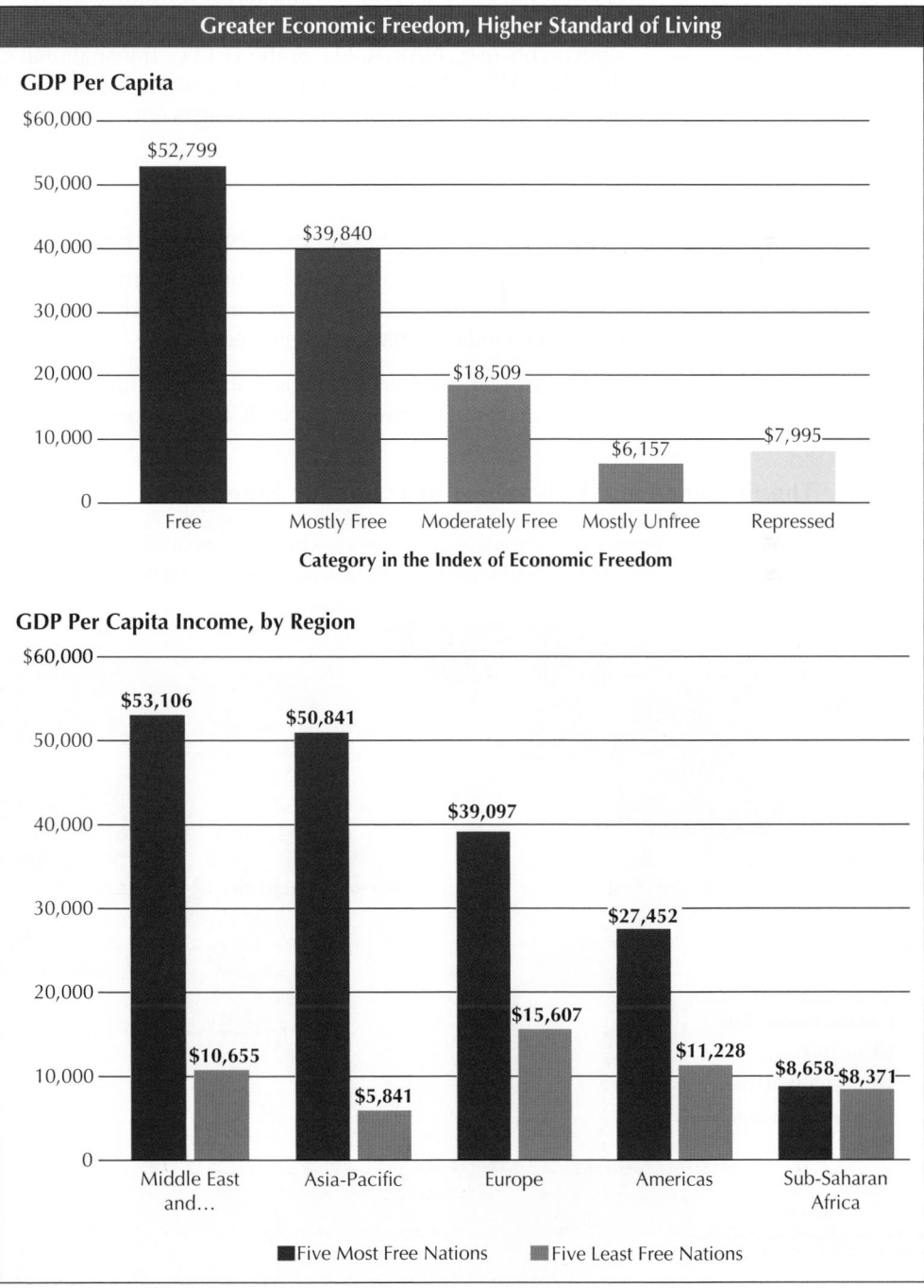

The track record of free markets around the world indicates that economic freedom is positively related to financial prosperity, economic stability, and standards of living.

Economic freedom, by expanding international trade across open borders, promotes globalization.

inflation and unemployment rates, for example, are significantly lower in freer countries. Higher economic freedom supports business efficiency, a key moderator of productivity and catalyst of new business development. The World Competitiveness Yearbook, for instance, concludes that the freedom of private firms to choose how to operate innovatively, profitably, and responsibly is the key feature shared by the world's most competitive nations.[46]

Standards of living and human development thrive in economically free markets. Improving prosperity expands access to education, promotes literacy, boosts health care, and supports sustainability. Poverty rates are lower in economically free countries; they run about a quarter of that found in less free nations. Growing prosperity in economically free nations, by improving the quality of life, supports social stability and diminishes the frequency and severity of humanitarian crises.[47]

Economic freedom promotes the globalization of markets. Fortifying property rights, limiting the scale and scope of government, streamlining regulations, and liberalizing markets opens a nation to investment and trade. Countries intent on improving economic freedom generally endorse WTO initiatives to boost trade as well as enter into regional free trade agreements (e.g., NAFTA, EU, or the TPP) or transnational capital market mechanisms (e.g., the AIIB, IMF, or World Bank). Trade promotion institutionalizes elements of economic freedom into market structures and encourages entrepreneurs as well as established companies to pursue international opportunities.

THE PREVALENCE OF ECONOMIC FREEDOM

Map 4.2 displays the Economic Freedom Index for 178 developed, developing, and emerging economies.[48] Collectively, these represent nearly all global market activity. Recent performance data indicate that economic freedom:

- Improved in 97 countries, most commonly among developing and emerging economies, such as Benin, Botswana, Burundi, Israel, Morocco, Senegal, and Tonga.

MAP 4.2   The Presence and Prevalence of Economic Freedom

The Economic Freedom Index classifies a country as either *free, mostly free, moderately free, mostly unfree,* or *repressed* given the degree to which its government regulates individual economic choices. The greater the regulation, as indicated by a lower score, the less choice an individual commands.[49]

Source: Terry Miller and Kim Holmes, *2016 Index of Economic Freedom,* (Washington, DC: The Heritage Foundation and Dow Jones & Co., Inc., 2016).

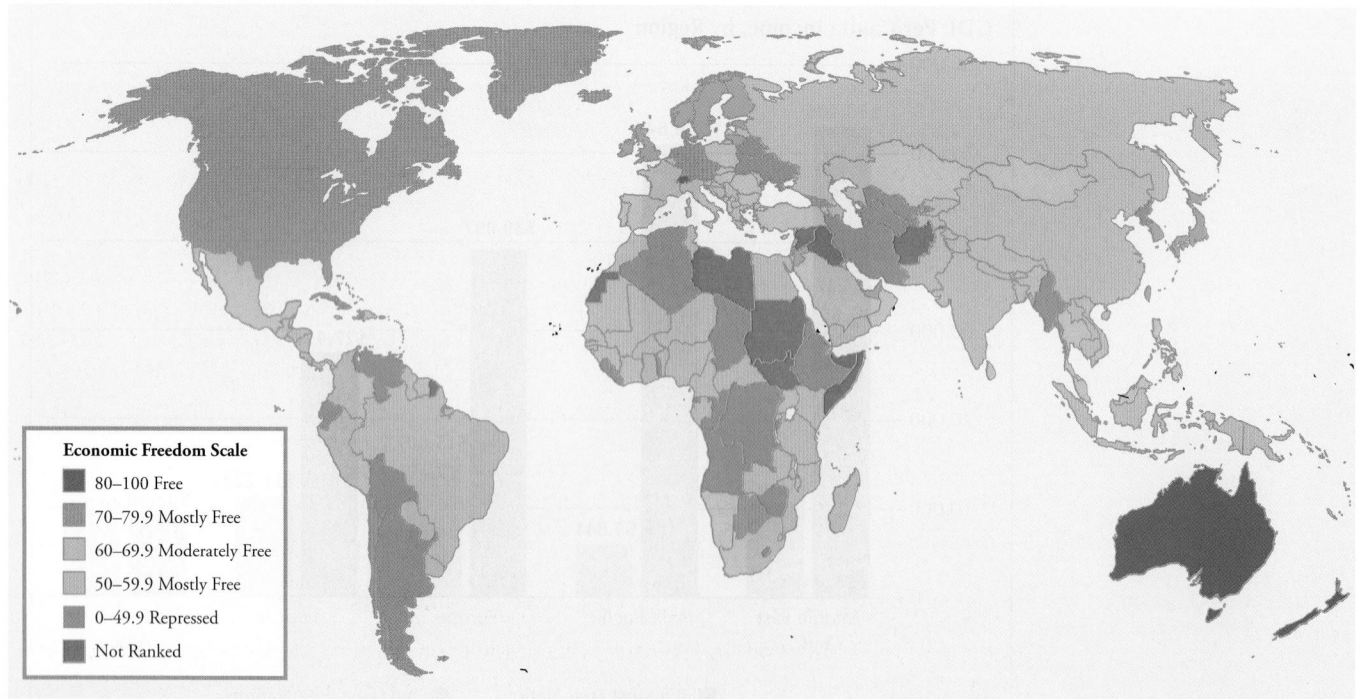

Economic Freedom Scale
- 80–100 Free
- 70–79.9 Mostly Free
- 60–69.9 Moderately Free
- 50–59.9 Mostly Free
- 0–49.9 Repressed
- Not Ranked

- Achieved the highest ever scores in 32 countries, including Burma, Germany, India, Israel, Lithuania, the Philippines, Poland, and Vietnam.
- Declined in 74 countries, most commonly among developed markets such as Austria, Australia, Canada, Hong Kong, New Zealand, Singapore, Switzerland, and the United States.
- Fell to the lowest level ever in 11 countries, notably Venezuela, Argentina, Bolivia, Algeria, Greece, and El Salvador.

National and regional developments amplify these trends.

- The freest economies are Hong Kong, Singapore, New Zealand, Australia, and Switzerland; the least free are Eritrea, Zimbabwe, Venezuela, Cuba, and North Korea.
- Regionally, on average, economic freedom has advanced the most for countries in sub-Saharan Africa and Asia–Pacific, changed little for those in the Middle East/North Africa, South and Central America/Caribbean region, and declined for those in Europe and North America.
- Prominent emerging economies, notably Brazil, India, China, and Russia, showed little improvement; these, like many other emerging economies, rate as mostly unfree.
- The United States is currently rated a "mostly free" economy. In 2007, prior to the great financial crisis, it ranked as a "free" economy. Decreasing labor, business, and fiscal freedoms dropped the United States to 75.4 percent in 2015, matching its lowest score in Index history.

| Worldwide, economic freedom dropped in the aftermath of global financial crisis. It has steadily regained ground.

Recently, economic freedom has benefited from expanding international trade, improving capital market stability, and decreasing corruption. In global terms, the average economic freedom score across the 178 sampled countries set a record in 2016, reaching 60.7 percent.[50] The world average has now regained the ground lost in the aftermath of the great financial crisis and subsequent recession. Over time, economic freedom performance changes for nations, regions, and the world—and as we see in Table 4.4, variation in the degree of economic freedom modifies, from a little to a lot, the marketplace. Certainly, the pace of change varies from country to country, as governments relax or impose controls that promote or restrict individual choice. Consequently, executives monitor economic environments, studying policies and practices to determine government intentions and the implications for economic freedom.[51]

ECONOMIC FREEDOM AND TYPE OF ECONOMIC ENVIRONMENT

Table 4.5 reports the average freedom score by type of economic environment. It also reports the average score per the 10 components of economic freedom. The different characteristics of different levels of economic development are apparent in terms of the corresponding degree of freedom across market types. Consistently, developed countries devise policies that promote and protect individual choice—hence, their average economic freedom score runs higher. Notably, property rights and freedom from corruption differ by type of economic environment. As discussed in Chapter 3, gaps largely follow from the prevalence of the rule of law in developed economies versus the rule of man in developing economies. Similarly, developing countries regulate investment and financial freedoms more strictly. Collectively, the development status of an economic environment influences managers' freedom to make investments, build operations, and run businesses.

| Paradoxically, despite the documented benefits of economic freedom, just 5 countries, out of 178, have policies that maximize it.

THE PARADOX OF PROMISE VERSUS PREVALENCE

The fall of the Berlin Wall in 1989 symbolized the triumph of capitalism over **communism**. More pointedly, it signified the supremacy of economic freedom over state regulation

TABLE 4.4   Economic Freedom: Classification and Characteristics[52]

Economic Freedom Score	Class	General Characteristics	Representative Nations[53]
80–100	Free	• Companies, both domestic and foreign, face none to few restrictions making or selling products. • Government advocates openness to international trade and investment. • Negligible to nominal government interference in the economy. • Slight corruption or risk of expropriation. • Government guarantees property rights. • Regulation is minimal and centers on improving transparency, fairness, and firm conduct.	Australia, Hong Kong, New Zealand, Singapore, Switzerland
70–79.9	Mostly Free	• Corruption is possible, but rare, and the risk of expropriation is low. • Foreign companies are subject to few restrictions. • Judicial system is subject to delays and may arbitrarily enforce contracts. • Limited state interference in the movement of labor, capital, and goods. • Sizable government ownership of companies in key sectors.	Canada, Chile, Colombia, Estonia, Ireland, Israel, Lithuania, South Korea, St. Lucia, Sweden, Taiwan, United States
60–69.9	Moderately Free	• Inflexible, often rigid, labor regulations. • Inward and outward capital movements face some restrictions. • Moderate government interference in economic affairs. • Regulations are somewhat burdensome and costly. • The government exercises ownership and control of significant economic sectors. • The judiciary may be unduly influenced by other governmental agents.	Azerbaijan, Belgium, Botswana, Ghana, Italy, Jamaica, Kazakhstan, Kuwait, Mexico, Morocco, Oman, Peru, Philippines, Rwanda, Saudi Arabia
50–59.9	Mostly Unfree	• Considerable state action interferes with individual choice. • Foreign companies are subject to significant constraints. • Government owns or controls some to all of many companies. • Limited repatriation of profits; some transactions require state approval. • Private allocation of capital faces significant barriers. • Some laws are opaque or arbitrarily applied. • The court system is inefficient and subject to delays. • The State hinders the free flow of foreign commerce.	Bangladesh, Brazil, Cambodia, Cameroon, China, Ethiopia, Fiji, Greece, India, Lebanon, Nepal, Nicaragua, Pakistan, Russia, Sri Lanka, Swaziland, Tunisia, Vietnam
0–49.9	Repressed	• Burdensome regulations administered by an oppressive bureaucracy. • Corruption is pervasive and endemic. • Foreign companies, if permitted, are heavily restricted and face barriers to entry and mobility. • Private property ownership is at best, weakly protected, at worst, outlawed. • Supervision and regulation are designed to restrict, if not eliminate, private enterprise. • The State owns some to all property and directly produces goods and services. • Coercion and constraint pervade an unfair market.	Angola, Argentina, Belarus, Burma, Bolivia, Chad, Ecuador, Iran, North Korea, Turkmenistan, Venezuela, Zimbabwe

Source: Adapted from "Methodology | 2015 Index of Economic Freedom Book." Accessed December 8, 2015. http://www.heritage.org/index/book/methodology.

to promote development, improve performance, and boost potential. Since then, more and more folks worldwide saw greater personal choice improving their livelihood; and, as we see in Figure 4.4, economically free nations consistently outperform all others.[54] Correspondingly, countries progressively abandoned the policies of state control and adopted the hallmarks of economic freedom: stronger property rights, improving governmental transparency, and fairer competition. Worldwide, governments deferred to the laws of supply and demand—the invisible hand of the marketplace rather than the visible hand of politicians—to anchor the principles and regulate the practices of their economic environments.

TABLE 4.5 Average Freedom Scores by Type of Economic Environment (in %)[55]

The higher the percent per category, the greater the freedom an individual commands in that domain.

Dimension		Developed Countries	Emerging Economies	Developing Countries
Overall Economic Freedom		75	65	58
Rule Of Law	Property Rights	88	49	33
	Freedom from Corruption	80	47	36
Limited Government	Fiscal Freedom	64	79	80
	Government Spending	40	67	65
Regulatory Efficiency	Labor Freedom	69	62	58
	Business Freedom	85	71	60
	Monetary Freedom	82	77	74
Open Markets	Trade Freedom	87	80	73
	Investment Freedom	83	59	51
	Financial Freedom	74	58	42

Note: Scores range from zero (no freedom) to 100 (full freedom).

Managers watch key events to gauge the contest between economic freedom and state control. These include how the government

- regulates the economy,
- protects property rights,
- sets fiscal and monetary policies,
- promotes transparent policies.

The surge in state capitalism helps explain why many emerging and developing economies deemphasize economic freedom.

Notwithstanding progress, today we see a paradoxical gap between the promise and the prevalence of economic freedom. Specifically, given the documented benefits of economic freedom, why do so few countries maximize it? Take a quick look at Map 4.2. As you see, presently Hong Kong, Singapore, New Zealand, Australia, and Switzerland are the only "free" economies in the world; they are home to about 50 million people. Some 33 countries are rated mostly free, including Canada, the United States, Germany, Sweden, South Korea, and Malaysia; they are home to another 950 million or so. In contrast, 54 countries are moderately free, 62 are mostly unfree, and 24 are repressed; they are home to approximately 6.3 billion people. Put differently, 38 of 178 countries—about 22 percent—grant their residents considerable to extensive economic freedom. The rest do not.[56]

Managers study this irony, gauging its implications to property rights, government regulation, and market systems. Increasingly, as countries in the West struggle with economic shortfalls, managers wonder if free markets will prevail. Or, will governments claim the commanding heights of the economy, controlling markets in order to supervise development, regulate performance, and, ultimately, determine potential? Performance data complicates interpretation, raising the question of whether optimizing economic freedom is still necessary to anchor a productive economic system.[57] The record of various countries, such as China, Russia, South Africa, Mexico, and Rwanda, indicate that economic freedom is not necessarily a requirement. Since 2008, real cumulative growth in prominent developed economies, historically advocates of economic freedom, has amounted to about 6 percent. In comparison, China, technically a mostly unfree economy, has seen its GDP increase more than 70 percent. Similarly, for the past decade, Rwanda, one of the developing world's shining stars and a moderately free economy, has cranked out average growth of 7.5 percent and doubled its income per capita.[58] China and Rwanda's success is due not to maximizing economic freedom, but rather central direction by an authoritarian government. Furthermore, they are not isolated cases. Analysts note that many fast-growing emerging and developing economies deemphasize economic freedom. Instead, they advocate an alternative relationship between individuals, markets, and governments. This outlook, as we profile in our *Looking to the Future* insert, spotlights the idea of **state capitalism**.

Looking to the Future
State Capitalism: Detour or Destination?

An epic philosophical contest is underway. In one corner, we have the ideals of economic freedom, anchored in notions popularized by Adam Smith and implemented via free markets. In the other, we have models of state power, loosely tied to notions popularized by Karl Marx and Vladimir Lenin, and implemented via state capitalism. A generation ago, the state-controlled economy was seen as a way station on the path to a capitalist system. Now, impressive performance in many countries with emerging and developing economies suggests that free market economics is no longer the only viable route to modernization. Worldwide, managers watch and wait as the contest between free markets and state power determines the sort of economy that works best in the modern world.

State capitalism is an economic system whereby political officials shape how assets are valued and when and where they are used.[59] The state nurtures national champions, manages trade relations and exchange rates to promote exports and discourage imports, mediates the financial system to provide low-cost capital to domestic industries, and runs nationalist legal systems. State capitalism, unlike market capitalism or communism, does not stipulate an ideological component. The government manages markets for long-term political survival and power projection, not to enforce an abstract ideal or promote a personality cult. Instead of politicized revolutionaries promising a brave, new future, state capitalism relies on pragmatic technocrats who, applying sophisticated management ideas, develop a prosperous, productive economy.

The government manipulates market outcomes for political purposes. It aims to stabilize market cycles, equalize income distribution, and preempt self-interests that threaten social harmony. Allowed to run free, market economies can encourage the psychology that greed is good. Only a strong state, goes the reasoning, stops it from devolving into psychosis.[60] Hence, the state uses the market to promote stability and growth, thereby creating the prosperity that maximizes state power and legitimates its ongoing rule. The payoff is plain: subverting political freedom with economic prosperity fortifies the authority of the state. Unburdened of an ideological agenda, the state prefers anonymity. As long as a growing economy supports stability, it stays in the shadows, influencing activities and shaping outcomes. In the event that plans go awry, the veiled hand quickly turns visible. The state steps in, revises policies, resets funding, and redirects activities.

Who Owns Whom

State capitalism calls for the government to own, either directly or indirectly, its national champions, using them to influence market activity as well as consolidate its authority. For instance, the CCP of China is the majority owner of many of the largest publicly listed Chinese companies, including major banks, energy producers, telecom carriers, and media firms. Collectively, huge conglomerates in finance, media, mining, metals, transportation, communication, and so on answer to the CCP.[61] Furthermore, party officials in China's provinces and cities own and run thousands of medium-sized and smaller ones. State officials, while discreet, are not shy. At all levels, "the tentacles of state-owned enterprises extend into every nook where profits can be made."[62] Similar situations in Brazil, Rwanda, Russia, Saudi Arabia, and South Africa, for instance, highlight the state's expanding economic clout.

Telltale Marks

State capitalist economies, whether in the Middle East, Asia, Eastern Europe, or South America, have telltale marks. Public investment, public wealth, and public enterprise prevail. Officials fan economic nationalism. State capitalism promotes the growth of particular industrial sectors and companies in order to speed development. The state promotes domestic markets as sanctuaries for national champions, aspiring to nurture them into global leaders.[63] The state games the system, capturing competitive advantages through whatever means necessary. Officials install trade and FDI barriers in order to spur local development. Often, the state attracts innovative foreign companies, using state-owned banks to provide cheap loans, favorable regulations, and stable industry settings. Regulators may then require that foreign investors create joint ventures with local companies when entering strategic industries. Moreover, if push comes to shove, foreign companies receive scant protection and even weaker legal defense. State capitalism has little need for an independent judiciary; the legal system legitimates state policies as needed. Similarly, the state uses the tax code as a tool for economic, not social, engineering.

Gaining Momentum

Presently, some 70 or so strategically important countries worldwide are at a crossroads in determining their political and economic futures.[64] Whether they adopt free markets or state capitalism remains to be seen. Many see China as the bellwether; it has used state capitalism to develop and direct the world's fastest-growing economy that, in turn, has powered the swiftest, most extensive rise out of poverty any nation has ever seen. Its success—not just surviving, but also prospering during the great financial crisis—convinced "Chinese leadership that state control of much of the country's economic development is

the steadiest path toward prosperity—and, therefore, domestic tranquility."[65] Some dismiss state capitalism as inevitably unacceptable. Keep in mind that in 2002, asked whether the country's economic situation is good or bad, some 52 percent of Chinese versus 46 percent of Americans respondents affirmed it as good. In 2015, asked the same, 90 percent of Chinese while 40 percent of Americans saw good times.[66]

Given the economic circumstances in the world today, one should not be surprised if others, particularly authoritarian one-party political systems, find state capitalism attractive. Throughout Asia, the Middle East, Africa, and Latin America, authoritarian governments emulate China's model.[67] Their state-backed companies grow and expand, steadily generating progress and prosperity. The surging success of state capitalism, besides clarifying surging single-state authoritarianism, helps explain why many countries, collectively home to several billion people, restrict economic freedom. ■

TYPES OF ECONOMIC SYSTEMS

An economic system organizes the production, distribution, and consumption of goods and services.

Wherever they go, managers question how the host government might regulate the market, authorize property rights, implement fiscal and monetary policies, and interpret the standards of economic freedom. Evaluating the particular type of **economic system** in a country enhances analysis. This perspective spotlights drivers of supply and demand, their implication to resource allocation, and the consequence to managers' economic freedom. Presently, we see variations of three types of economic systems, namely, the market, mixed, and command economies (see Figure 4.5).

THE MARKET ECONOMY

Capitalism and its advocacy of the private ownership of factors of production anchors a market economy.

An economic system whereby individuals, rather than the government, make most decisions is a **market economy**. It is anchored in the doctrine of **capitalism** and its thesis that private ownership confers inalienable property rights that legitimize the profits earned by one's initiative, investment, and risk. Optimal resource allocation follows from consumers exercising their freedom of choice and producers responding accordingly. Market economies are commonly found in developed economies, such as Australia, Canada, Hong Kong, Singapore, Switzerland, and the United States. Each grants its citizens wide-ranging freedom to decide where to work, what to do and for how long, how to spend or save money, and whether to consume now or later.[68]

CONCEPT CHECK

Chapter 3 notes that the individual voter is the cornerstone of a democracy. Here we add that the individual, as a consumer, is the key factor in a free market. Whereas democracy recognizes the supremacy of voter sovereignty, the market economy recognizes the supremacy of consumer sovereignty.

The market economy champions the "invisible hand" of economically free, self-interested consumers as the driver of productive efficiency. Consumers, through their interactions with producers, shape aggregate growth, thereby optimally determining the relationships among price, quantity, supply, and demand. A market economy pushes producers, spurred by the profit motive, to make products that consumers, spurred by their quest to maximize utility, buy. Consequently, by virtue of what they buy—and, for that matter, do not—consumers direct the efficient allocation of resources and the optimal valuation of assets.

FIGURE 4.5   Types of Economic Systems

The three predominant types of economic systems endorse different philosophies, advocate different principles, and apply different approaches.

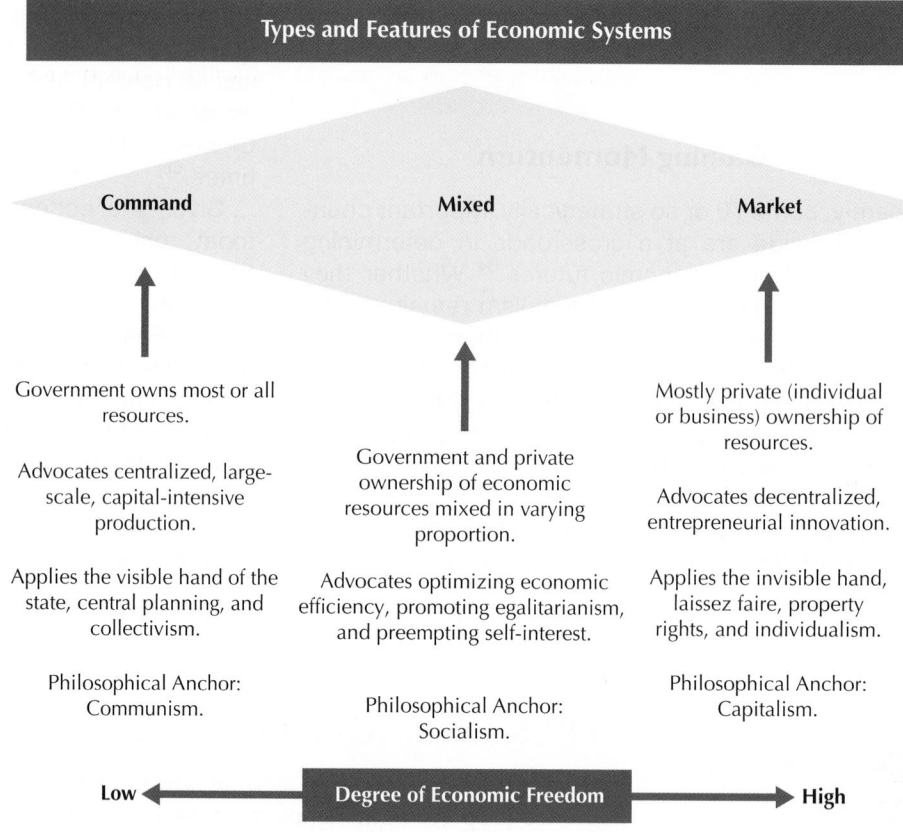

Types and Features of Economic Systems

Command	Mixed	Market
Government owns most or all resources.		Mostly private (individual or business) ownership of resources.
Advocates centralized, large-scale, capital-intensive production.	Government and private ownership of economic resources mixed in varying proportion.	Advocates decentralized, entrepreneurial innovation.
Applies the visible hand of the state, central planning, and collectivism.	Advocates optimizing economic efficiency, promoting egalitarianism, and preempting self-interest.	Applies the invisible hand, laissez faire, property rights, and individualism.
Philosophical Anchor: Communism.	Philosophical Anchor: Socialism.	Philosophical Anchor: Capitalism.

Low ◄———— **Degree of Economic Freedom** ————► High

> A market economy endorses the doctrine of capitalism, its principles of the invisible hand and laissez-faire, and the goal of maximizing economic freedom.

An enduring bias toward minimal government intervention anchors market economies. The less visible the "hand" is due to government intervention, the more efficient is the market. Fundamentally, a market economy endorses the ideal of ***laissez-faire***, which can be literally translated as "Let do," and more broadly advises "Let it be" or "Leave it alone." *Laissez-faire* opposes governmental interference in economic affairs beyond the minimum necessary to maintain property rights, safety, and peace. The consequence, as Adam Smith reasoned, is a market whereby "Every man, as long as he does not violate the laws of justice, is left perfectly free to pursue his own interest his own way, and to bring both his industry and capital into competition with those of any other man or order of men."[69] Still, the need for public goods (e.g., traffic lights, clean air, national defense) and regulatory protections (e.g., minimum wage, product safeguards, and environmental standards) requires governmental involvement. Therefore, a market economy looks to the state to enforce contracts, protect property rights, ensure fair and free competition, regulate certain activities, and provide general safety and security.

> The need for government to provide public goods and protect society makes visible the otherwise invisible hand in a market economy.

THE COMMAND ECONOMY

> In a command economy, the visible hand of the state supersedes the invisible hand of the market.

In theory, communism champions state ownership of resources and control of economic activity. Nominally a political ideology, communism calls for an egalitarian, classless, and ultimately stateless society based on the government's command of the economy (the instrumentality of attaining the Marxian mandate, "From each according to his ability, to each according to his need").[70] Implementing this system requires the state adopt a **command economy** in which it owns and controls the factors of production (namely, land, labor, capital, and entrepreneurship). Public officials, not private agents, decide what products to make, in what quantity, at what price, and in what way. For example, in a market economy, if the government needs automobiles, it collects taxes and buys cars at market prices from privately held carmakers. In a command economy, the visible hand of the government, with little regard for price, orders state-owned carmakers to produce them.[71]

Making the invisible hand explicitly visible means that government officials, not private consumers, determine the prices of goods and services and, hence, the allocation of resources. Consequently, product quality is often erratic and, absent profit-maximizing incentives, typically deteriorates. Products are usually in short supply and there are few substitutes. State-owned enterprises, typically large-scale, inefficient, and unprofitable, have few resources to upgrade or incentives to innovate.

Command economies can outperform free markets for short periods. Controlling everyone and everything lets the state mobilize idle resources, usually labor, to generate high-growth spurts. High productivity continues as long as the state competently manages the supply of slack, low-cost resources. Improving performance often moves state officials to proclaim that the command economy is superior to a free market. History, however, shows otherwise. Central planning commonly proves counterproductive, given that officials, no matter how astute, cannot consistently predict consumers' preferences, craft incentives for entrepreneurs, or efficiently allocate resources. Far more typically, command economies struggle in the face of diminishing productivity, along with growing inefficiency, inequality, cronyism, corruption, and, ultimately, failure to meet rising expectations. Command economies have included the Soviet Union (which, at its peak, was the world's second-largest economy), China during its Great Leap Forward era beginning in 1958, India prior to its economic reforms in 1991, and Afghanistan during the rule by Soviet occupation and the Taliban. Today, we see few pure examples, most notably North Korea and, to a diminishing degree, Cuba.

A command economy and state capitalism, while overlapping on some elements, differ on others. Surveying the economic environments of various countries, such as China, Iran, Rwanda, Russia, Saudi Arabia, and Vietnam, finds the visible hand of a single-party authoritarian state directing resource allocation, controlling some to many companies, and regulating individual autonomy. Correspondingly, many developing economies fall in the "mostly unfree" and "repressed" categories of the Economic Freedom Index. Hence, state capitalism exhibits hallmarks of state control that are suggestive of a command economy. Fundamentally, they ultimately differ. As noted in the *Looking to the Future* profile, instead of organizing a command economy anchored in some version of communism, governments practice state capitalism. In that model, the state manipulates the economic environment, not in line with a grand ideological agenda, but with the goal of improving individual prosperity in order to legitimate and sustain its authority.

MIXED ECONOMY

Most economies, broadly labeled **mixed economies**, fall between the market and command types. A mixed economy is a system in which economic decisions are principally market driven and ownership is largely private, but the government intervenes, from a little to a lot, in valuing assets, allocating resources, regulating activities, and organizing markets. Put simply, the state reasons that it is the government's responsibility to make strategic decisions about strategic industries.

The mixed economy blends elements of the command and market systems. On one hand, the state intermingles ownership of some resources, centralizes certain planning functions, and regulates market systems. On the other hand, the state authorizes a range of economic freedoms to individuals and companies. Fundamentally, the interaction of supply and demand, signaled to producers through the choices that consumers make, rather than public dictate, organizes production.[72] For example, in a mixed economy the government may partially own a carmaker. Rather than instructing it on the

CONCEPT CHECK

Totalitarianism subordinates people's day-to-day lives—including their market behavior and economic outlook—to the state. Government command of the economy supports this policy, enabling it to determine asset valuation, direct resource allocation, and regulate productivity.

Despite points of overlap, state capitalism is not a form of a command economy; the former promotes state wealth whereas the latter promotes state ideology.

A mixed economic system combines elements of the market and command economic systems; both government and private enterprise influence production, consumption, investment, and savings.

A market economy is anchored in capitalism, a command economy is anchored in communism, and a mixed economy is anchored in socialism.

type, quantity, and style of cars to make, the government authorizes the firm to decide. Generally, a mixed economic system falls short of the productivity of a market economy, but outperforms a command economy. Presently, countries classified as mixed economies include South Africa, Japan, South Korea, Sweden, Austria, France, Brazil, Germany, and India. They typically fall in the "mostly" and "moderately" free categories of the Economic Freedom Index.

Democracy promotes a market economy. Communism promotes a command economy. Similarly, **socialism** promotes a mixed economy. The notion of "mix" follows from the state letting the market allocate resources, as does capitalism, but directly channeling their use given political goals, as does communism. Philosophically, socialism holds that a fair and just economy, besides optimizing productivity, promotes common cause by supporting low unemployment, prevents the consolidation of wealth and privilege, helps the impoverished by fairly redistributing income, stabilizes society by mediating market failures, and protects the public by limiting abuses of market power. Advocates of socialism, and by extension a mixed economy, reason that governments more conscientiously promote an egalitarian ethos that deters the opportunistic individualism found in a market economy as well as prevents the oppressive collectivism found in a command economy.[73]

Like many features of IB, the extent of state intervention in a mixed economy varies from country to country. Political leadership, societal agendas, and market circumstances distinctively shape how a government interprets economic freedom and state intervention.[74] In Sweden, like fellow Nordic countries, the state applies the idea of *lagom* ("just the right amount") to promote work-life balance, income equality, and collaborative social relations. Implementation calls on the state to set a broad range of employment, social, welfare, environmental, and market standards. Alternatively, France champions the notion of *dirigisme* ("to direct"), whereby the state shapes market conduct, often taking control of key sectors, but refrains from regulating social standards. The extent of the French government's economic direction falls short of that seen in Sweden.[75]

ASSESSING ECONOMIC DEVELOPMENT, PERFORMANCE, AND POTENTIAL

Managers tap a broad portfolio of macro and micro measures to assess a country's development, performance, and potential. Some measures may be informal or idiosyncratic, such as the number of wireless subscriptions, Internet searches for telltale terms, scale of family-owned conglomerates, or prevalence of military officers controlling companies.[76] Typically, convention dominates practice and managers use monetary metrics to estimate productivity, income, and wealth. Improving their understanding leads them to augment analyses with measures of sustainability and stability.

MONETARY MEASURES

Among monetary aggregates, GNI provides the broadest measure of economic performance.

Comprehensive, single-item monetary measures are incisive indicators of whether an economy (1) is expanding or contracting, (2) needs a boost or should be constrained, and (3) is threatened by inflation or recession. Taking the temperature of a patient is a simple procedure, for instance, but it quickly highlights the performance of vital activities that are essential to life. The same holds true for single-item monetary measures. Standards, notably gross national income, gross domestic product, or gross national product, efficiently summarize the economic activity of households, businesses, and governments in terms of their consumption, investment, spending, and trading. Furthermore, tracking real change in an aggregate measure, like GDP, models overall production, maps the direction of the market, and indicates the health of the country's economy. Some see, for instance, the GDP statistic as "truly among the great inventions of the 20th century, a beacon that helps policymakers steer the economy toward key economic objectives."[77]

Gross National Income (GNI) is the broadest measure of a country's economic performance. It has four components: personal consumption, business investments, government spending, and net exports of goods and services. It measures the value of all production in the domestic economy together with the income that the country receives from other countries (in the forms of profits, interest, and dividends), less the same sorts of payments that it has made to other countries. For example, the value of a Samsung TV built in South Korea as well as the value of a Samsung TV made in Japan using Samsung's resources is counted in South Korea's GNI. Similarly, the value of a Sony TV built in South Korea using Sony's resources counts in the GNI of Japan. Too, if Samsung's Japanese subsidiary repatriates profits to headquarters in Seoul, it increases South Korea's GNI.

For most countries, incomes received by the country versus payments made to the rest of the world typically offset each other; hence, there is little difference between GNI and other macro estimators, like GDP. For instance, GNI for the United States in 2014 was only about a percent higher than its GDP. For some countries, MNEs play an outsized role and, consequently, flows are uneven.[78] Large-scale repatriation of profits from a country's MNEs' foreign subsidiaries, for instance, can drop GDP well below GNI, thereby understating a nation's economic performance. In 2014, for instance, Japan's GDP was $4.61 trillion while its GNI hit $5.34 trillion.[79]

> GDP is the total market value of goods and services produced by workers and capital within a nation's borders; it provides the truest measure of national economic activity.

Gross Domestic Product (GDP) is the total market value of all output produced within a nation's borders, no matter whether it is generated by a domestic or foreign-owned enterprise, over a fixed period of time.[80] It estimates the output from a sample of businesses in every part of a nation's economy, from agriculture to social media. Each sector's weight reflects its relative importance in the national economy. As such, GDP measures the total value of finished goods and services that have been produced for consumers, business, and government in that nation. Measuring the flow of economic activity in terms of producing goods and services, not simply its stock of productive assets, indicates if an economy is expanding or contracting. Presently, GDP is the most commonly used estimator of economic performance, serving as a universal benchmark of productivity and prosperity. Table 4.6 lists the largest economies by GDP.

Technically, GDP plus the income generated from exports, imports, and the international activities of a nation's companies equal its GNI. For instance, a smartphone made by Samsung and Sony in South Korea contributes to South Korea's GDP. A computer made in Japan by Samsung, a South Korean MNE, does not. Instead, it contributes to Japan's GNI. Therefore, GDP better estimates performance in those markets, such as South Korea, Ireland, or China, where foreign MNEs' local output is a significant share of total activity.[81]

> GNP is the total value of all final goods and services produced within a nation in a particular year.

Gross National Product (GNP) begins by estimating the market value of goods and services produced in a given year by the labor, assets, and capital supplied by the resident

TABLE 4.6   The 10 Largest Economies by GDP, 2014[a]

Rank	Country	Type of Economy	GDP ($, billions)	% of World Total
1	United States	Developed	17,419	22.4
2	China	Emerging	10,345	13.3
3	Japan	Developed	4,601	5.9
4	Germany	Developed	3,868	5.0
5	United Kingdom	Developed	2,988	3.8
6	France	Developed	2,829	3.6
7	Brazil	Emerging	2,346	3.0
8	Italy	Developed	2,141	2.8
9	India	Emerging	2,048	2.6
10	Russian Federation	Emerging	1,860	2.4
**	World		$77,845	

Source: World Bank Development Indicators 2014.[82]

of a country. It then adds the income that its citizens earned working abroad, but removes the income earned by foreigners working domestically (the latter counts toward their home nation's GNP). Effectively, GNP estimates economic performance in terms of the location of ownership, including production done locally as well as when the country's capital or labor produces value outside of its borders.[83] As such, GNP counts the production by citizens and companies of a nation–even if this production occurs in another country. In contrast, GDP centers on the geographical location of production, namely that done by any and all workers within a country's borders.[84] GDP, by tracking only national production, supports short-term monitoring and analysis as well as facilitates cross national comparisons. Countries began emphasizing GDP in the 1960s, and by 1990, it had eclipsed GNP as the superior estimator of productivity and performance.[85]

IMPROVING ECONOMIC ANALYTICS

GNI, GDP, and GNP estimate an economy's absolute performance. Despite strengths, they can distort country comparisons. For example, economic powers like the United States, Japan, and Germany consistently claim the top rankings in the league tables for GNI, GDP, and GNP. Some may mistakenly conclude that they are also more productive and faster growing than lower-ranked countries. Often, the opposite is true. Therefore, we improve the usefulness of macro estimators by adjusting for the (1) rate of economic growth, (2) size of the population, and (3) purchasing power of the local currency.

> Managers improve the economic indicators by adjusting for the
> - growth rate of the economy,
> - number of people in a country,
> - local cost of living.

Rate of Economic Growth   Monetary aggregates take a static snapshot of an economy at a point in time. Hence, they do not capture its rate of change. Interpreting present and forecasting future performance prompts considering an economy's growth rate. In the short term, an expanding economy, indicated by positive growth in, say, GDP, means that business, jobs, and personal income are growing. Longer term, GDP's growth rate estimates a country's economic potential: If it is growing faster (or *slower*) than the growth rate of its population, then the country's standards of living are rising (or *falling*).[86]

The growth rate of aggregate measures helps managers identify promising business opportunities. Looking at the 214 countries that compose the global business environment, one finds, as expected, a wide range of growth rate. For instance, GDP in many developing economies is rising at two to five times the rate of per capita growth in the world's richest countries. China has been one of the fastest-growing economies over the past three decades; it has expanded by 9.8 percent on average since 1995. Commensurately, its GDP has gone from about $600 billion then (with a population of 1.2 billion) to $10.35 trillion in 2014 (with a population of 1.34 billion).[87] Its expanding market has created many jobs, boosted workers' income, increased aggregate demand, attracted foreign investors, and raised living standards.

> Purchasing power parity provides a method of measuring the relative purchasing power of different countries' currencies for the same basket of goods and services.

Population Size   Managers routinely adjust indicators by the number of people who live in a country.[88] This conversion is sensible given how unevenly the world's population of 7,514,656 is distributed (e.g., from a high of 1.383 billion in China to a low of 56 in the Pitcairn Islands).[89] Adjusting GNI by population, therefore, lets managers qualify a country's performance for its demographics. For instance, China is the world's second-largest economy when ranked by aggregate GNI. Adjusting its performance for its population of 1.34 billion people, however, moves it to the lower-middle income tier. Similarly, in 2014, Norway's GNI hit $336 billion, versus the $17,419 billion reported by the United States. However, given its population of 5.1 million residents, Norway ranked first by GNI per capita at $103,630.[90] By comparison, the United States, with its 320 million citizens, reported GNI per capita of $55,200, ranking seventh.[91]

> Adjusting for PPP controls for differences in the relative cost of living between countries.

Purchasing Power Parity   The prices of goods and services vary from country to country due to, among other things, differing factor endowments, productivity rates, and regulations. Some prices vary little, say from one developed economy to another developed economy. Some vary a lot, say from a developed country to a developing country. One can buy a liter of gasoline, for instance, in Kuwait for $.23 or in Malaysia for $.39; the same liter of gas costs $.59, $1.49, and $1.73 in the United States, the United Kingdom, and Norway, respectively.[92] As such, simple comparisons cannot tell how many goods and services one can buy with a unit of income in one country (e.g., India) versus how much one can buy with an equivalent unit of income in another country (e.g., the United States). Likewise, measures like GNP per capita presume that a dollar of income in Mumbai has the same purchasing power as a dollar of income in Miami, even though the cost of living differs dramatically between India and the United States. Overlooked, price differences distort the usefulness of macro estimators.

Analysts overcome this problem by adjusting for the relative purchasing power parity (PPP) between countries. Technically, one applies the rate at which the currency of one country converts into that of another country in order to buy an equivalent basket of goods and services. The "basket" commonly includes items such as a liter of cooking oil, cell-phone plan, a liter of gasoline, or even a McDonald's Big Mac. Setting equivalent baskets and then calculating their local price given the relative costs of living and currency effects between countries, say India and the United States, makes the purchasing power of a dollar in Mumbai equivalent to that in Miami.[93] Commonly, the PPP conversion rate is set in terms of the number of units of a country's currency needed to buy a basket of goods and services with an equivalent basket in the United States.

Table 4.7 shows the effect of adjusting national economic performance by PPP. Notably, the rankings by GDP reported in Table 4.6 change considerably. For instance, China displaces the United States as the largest economy in the world—its GDP of $10,069 billion, adjusted for PPP, converts to $17,918 billion. Similarly, PPP adjustments boost India and Russia, drop Japan, Germany, the United Kingdom, and France, and replace Italy with Indonesia. Relatedly, PPP reduces some of the otherwise extreme variability in many country-to-country per capita comparisons. Norway's GDP per capita falls from $97,363 to $65,970 when adjusted for the reduced purchasing power that a unit of its currency commands in its relatively expensive market. The opposite occurs in the case of countries with less expensive standards of living, such as India; its GDP per capita of $1,530 rises to $5,640 when adjusted for PPP.[94] These sorts of adjustments help explain the appeal of the Base of the Pyramid, highlighting the real economic potential of billions of poorer people spanning the globe. Map 4.3 profiles countries in terms of GNI per capita adjusted for PPP.

TABLE 4.7 The 10 Largest Economies, GDP Adjusted for Purchasing Power Parity, 2014

Rank	Country	Population (millions)	GDP by PPP (US$ trillions)	% of Total World Economy
1	China	1,341	$18,017	16.5
2	United States	322	$17,419	16.0
3	India	1,267	$7,384	6.8
4	Japan	127	$4,630	4.3
5	Russian Federation	142	$3,745	3.4
6	Germany	83	$3,704	3.4
7	Brazil	203	$3,263	3.0
8	Indonesia	252	$2,676	2.5
9	France	64	$2,571	2.4
10	United Kingdom	63	$2,560	2.4
	World	7,386	$108,596	

Source: World Bank Development Indicators 2015.[95]

MAP 4.3   GDP per Capita, 2015, Adjusted for Purchasing Parity

Source: Based on World Bank Indicators, Data; Map access link: http://data.worldbank.org/indicator/NY.GDP.PCAP.PP.CD/countries?display=map

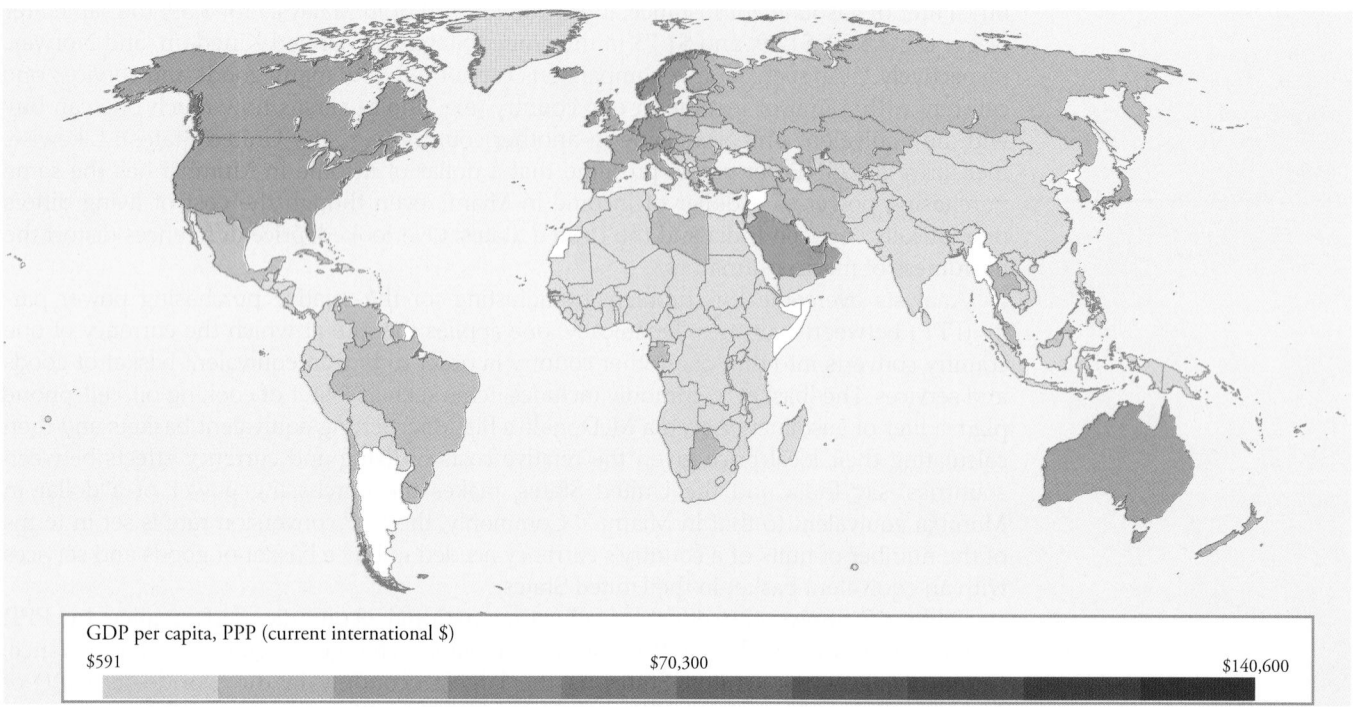

GDP per capita, PPP (current international $)

| $591 | $70,300 | $140,600 |

THE WILDCARD: THE SHADOW ECONOMY

All countries experience the effects of the shadow economy; they are particularly influential in developing economies.

Estimating and adjusting GNI, GDP, and GNP, as well as a host of similar indicators, requires good statistics. Throughout the world, governments ably collect data. Their efforts are complicated by the shadow economy (sometimes called the black, gray, or parallel market, or the informal economy). Found anywhere and everywhere, the shadow economy includes the extra-legal activities (e.g., driving an unlicensed taxi, street trading, or unregistered day care center) as well as well as illegal doings (e.g., prostitution, drug-slinging, illicit gambling, cigarette and alcohol smuggling, product piracy) that fall beyond official statistics. Besides conducting business in hard-to-track cash, shadow players typically go to great lengths to hide illicit transactions or dodge taxes. The off-the-books activities of the shadow economy evade and, therefore, confound official performance estimates.[96]

Developed economies, such as Canada, Germany, and the United States, tend to have a smaller shadow economy than developing economies, such as Greece, India, and Mexico. In the former, the shadow economy commonly runs up to 15 percent of GDP. In developing economies, particularly in Latin America and sub-Saharan Africa, it typically runs much higher—recent reports estimate that in Georgia, Bolivia, Azerbaijan, Peru, Tanzania, Zimbabwe, Thailand, Uruguay, and Guatemala, the shadow economy ran from 55 to 73 percent of GDP.[97] Worldwide, the shadow economy accounts for 23 percent of global GDP—more than $16 trillion, which is almost as large as the U.S. economy.[98]

Growing pressure to keep a nation's debt and deficits, relative to the size of its reported GDP, within the EU's prescribed targets spurs some European countries to increase the size of their economy. As such, the scale and scope of shadow economies lead governments to rethink how they tally GDP. Ireland, Italy, and the United Kingdom, among others are moving to include shadow activities when measuring production in their economy. The United Kingdom, for example, estimated that including the value of illicit drug trade (about $7.5 billion) and prostitution activity (about $9 billion) would boost its GDP by 0.7 percent.[99] Including all extra-legal and illegal activities that presently go uncounted would lift British GDP by 3 to 4 percent.[100]

CONCEPT CHECK

Chapter 1 notes that some groups oppose globalization, Chapter 2 discussed cultural objections, and Chapter 3 identified political reasons that inspire opposition. Here, we add that critics charge that overly emphasizing monetary measures misrepresents the economic benefits of globalization.

Green measures gauge economic performance in terms of the effect of current choices on long-term sustainability.

Estimators of economic progress toward improving happiness include

• Net National Product,
• Genuine Progress Indicators,
• Human Development Index.

Sustainability and stability perspectives hold that the objective of economic activity is to create an environment for people to enjoy long, healthy, and happy lives.

SUSTAINABILITY AND STABILITY

GNI, GDP, and GNP, even after adjusting for growth rates, population size, and purchasing power, partially profile a country's economic performance and potential. Besides the complication posed by the shadow economy, misestimating the costs and consequences of growth distorts analysis. At the least, the term "gross," rather than "net," signifies that the value lost through the wear and tear of the resources used in production is not deducted from the value of total output. Moreover, as we'll see below, monetary aggregates miss other costs, so-called externalities like air, water, or noise pollution, which are the by-products of economic activity. Representing the performance of an economy beyond the information provided by monetary aggregates directs our attention to estimating its sustainability and stability.

SUSTAINABILITY

Green economics holds that an economy is a component of, and dependent on, the natural world. Measuring the monetary quantity of market activity through GNI, GNP, and GDP, without accounting for the associated social and ecological costs that result from the activity that generated the growth, misestimates performance and misrepresents potential. **Sustainability** endorses a broader accounting of the gains and costs of growth that fall beyond monetary metrics but help gauge an economic environment. For instance, many countries have seen startling growth result in worrisome imbalances among economic, social, and environmental objectives. Sustainability advocates complementing monetary metrics by assessing economic performance in terms of "meeting the needs of the present without compromising the ability of future generations to meet their own needs."[101] Presently Sweden, Switzerland, Norway, the United Kingdom, and New Zealand top the world rankings for sustainability; at the other extreme, Nigeria, Venezuela, Egypt, Thailand, and China face the greatest challenge.[102] Several proposals outline paths to 'greenify' GNI, GNP, or GDP. Current candidates include the following:

• **Net National Product (NNP)** measures the depletion of natural resources and degradation of the environment that result from making and consuming products. Just as a company depreciates its tangible and intangible assets when making a product, so too should countries. NNP does so by depreciating the country's assets commensurate with their wear and tear in generating growth.[103]

• **Genuine Progress Indicators (GPI)** begin by applying the same accounting framework used to calculate GDP. It then adjusts for the corresponding costs of reduced environmental quality, health and hygiene, livelihood security, equity, free time, and educational attainment. For example, unlike GDP, GPI values voluntary and unpaid household work as paid labor and subtracts the costs of crime, pollution, and family stress. Effectively, GDP versus GPI is analogous to gross profits versus net profits—accounting for all costs converts gross to net. Accordingly, GPI will equal zero if the costs of pollution, crime, and family troubles, holding all other factors constant, equal the monetary gains from the production of goods and services.

• **Human Development Index (HDI)** Matters of human development do not show up immediately in income or growth measures. Ultimately, the reasoning goes, they will, given that improving the human condition through better nutrition, education, health care, and hygiene improves economic performance. So, estimating a country's degree of human development, in terms of the physical, intellectual, and social standards that shape its overall quality of life, helps managers measure market potential.[104] The UN translates this view into the HDI and its components: *Longevity*, measured by life expectancy at birth; *Knowledge*, measured by the adult literacy rate and the combined primary, secondary, and tertiary gross enrollment ratio; and *Standard of Living*, measured by GNI per capita (PPP). Nations scoring high on the HDI include Norway, Australia, Switzerland, Denmark, and the Netherlands. Laggards include Benin, Uganda, Rwanda, Haiti, and Togo.[105]

STABILITY

Universal affluence, despite its appeal, is presently impossible: the earth lacks sufficient resources to support and sustain high consumption for 7.4 billion people, to say nothing of earth's projected population of 9.7 billion by 2050. Indeed, warns the WorldWatch Institute, if all countries were to consume resources and produce pollution at the current per-capita level in the United States, an affluent country, we would require five planet Earths to meet demand and sustain the system. Rather than assessing an economy's potential for increasing affluence, perspectives like **happynomics** or welfare economics encourage incorporating elements of psychology, health, security, and sociology. More fundamentally, they advocate redefining the traditional performance standards of wealth, income, or profit to reflect principles of well-being, quality of life, and life satisfaction.[106] As the UN declares, "Happiness is increasingly considered a proper measure of social progress and a goal of public policy."[107]

Happynomics encourages moving "from the concept of financial prosperity to the idea of emotional prosperity."[108] The constitution of Bhutan, for instance, advocates making its citizens happier, not richer, every year; goals include the happiness of society, people's satisfaction with their lives, and national well-being independent of monetary achievement. Rethinking the goal of economic activity in terms of happiness, the argument goes, promotes the sustainability and stability that better represents performance and potential. For instance, happynomics reports that nearly 70 percent of personal satisfaction is determined by the quantity and quality of interpersonal relationships, not by economic output, income flow, or wealth creation.[109] The United States, when rated on monetary metrics, leads Australia, the Netherlands, and Sweden. Re-sorting performance in terms of life expectancy, leisure time, income equality, freedom to make life choices, generosity, and trust, however, moves Australia, the Netherlands, and Sweden ahead of the United States.[110]

Estimating stability, happiness, and the like, is difficult. For instance, happiness, like beauty, is often in the eye of the beholder. Potential indicators such as enjoyment, altruism, engagement, or, conversely, depression, sadness, and stress, are notoriously difficult to pin down. In addition, how does one meaningfully assign a monetary value to reasonable goals, like safe streets and clean air, which can be measured? Some contend that mapping happiness unnecessarily confuses economic analysis. However, an unhappy citizenry may be a leading indicator of a secular shift in consumption or social instability that increases economic risk.[111] Too, measuring subjective well-being positions policymakers to improve the design of public spaces and the delivery of public services, thereby fortifying economic performance and potential.

The intricacies of happiness capture increasing attention; insight promises to clarify measurement. The UN, for instance, is progressively operationalizing its resolution, *Happiness and Well-Being: Defining a New Economic Paradigm*.[112] In the meantime, managers tap the following estimators:

- **Your Better Life Index (YBLI)**: Developed by the Organization for Economic Cooperation and Development (OECD), the YBLI advocates evaluating economic performance in terms of matters that people worldwide believe are important (e.g., housing, jobs, social relationships, health, security, work–family balance, education) but that fall beyond the narrow scope of monetary measures. Doing so directly measures people's well-being and perceptions of living conditions. Explained the OECD, YBLI pushes the "boundaries of knowledge and understanding in a pioneering and innovative manner.... It has extraordinary potential to help us deliver better policies for better lives."[113]

- **Gross National Wellness Index (GNWI)**: Others contend that material and spiritual development occur side by side; one reinforces the other or both suffer. GNWI measures a country's capacity to promote individual well-being in terms of mental, health, work, income, social relations, economic, retirement, political, and environmental standards. The GNWI is purposely secular, unlike its complementary counterpart, the Bhutan gross national happiness index. The latter, reflective of Bhutan's Buddhist orientation, emphasizes equitable and sustainable socioeconomic development, elevating spirituality, preserving cultural values, conserving the natural environment, and championing fair, just governance.

Fully understanding growth, progress, and prosperity calls for assessing the consequences of economic choice on sustainability and stability.

Estimators of economic progress toward improving happiness include

- Your Better Life Index,
- Gross National Happiness,
- Happy Planet Index.

CONCEPT CHECK

As we saw in Chapter 1, critics of globalization often point to the inefficient use of resources to promote economic activity. Hence, many advocate considering sustainability in evaluating the benefits and costs of globalization.

• **Happy Planet Index (HPI)**: A utilitarian view holds that people aspire to live long, healthy, ecologically sensitive lives. How well a country helps its citizens to do so, while not infringing on the opportunity of future generations and people in other countries to do the same, fully represents its economic performance and potential. The HPI holds that the fundamental logic of monetary metrics are misaligned, overly emphasizing growth at all costs while downplaying its costly, destabilizing, and often destructive externalities. In the realm of the HPI, progress is defined not in terms of economic development, but through success in achieving a sustainable well-being for all.[114] Presently, the HPI ranks 151 countries.[115] Costa Rica leads the world table; it is followed by Vietnam, Colombia, Belize, and El Salvador. At the other end, Botswana, Chad, Qatar, Central African Republic, and Mali face the greatest challenge.

Point

Growth: Positive and Productive?

Point   **Yes** Growth is not only good, it is an absolute necessity. Growth is life, actualizing the productive potential of individuals, communities, institutions, and countries. Growth creates benefits for everyone, anywhere and everywhere. It morally stabilizes society. It liberates those trapped in poverty. It reduces violent conflict. It raises living standards. It funds safety nets and government backstops. It creates material improvements that comfort life. It creates jobs, income, wealth, and prosperity for individuals and society. Let's take a closer look at each.

Civil Stability Growth rallies social attitudes and fortifies political institutions, key anchors of civil stability. People experiencing rising incomes are commensurately tolerant of and benevolent toward each other. In a word, wealth engenders humanity. Growth creates the resources that promote transparency of authority, openness of opportunity, tolerance of diversity, pathways of social mobility, fair and just laws, and virtues of democracy.

Poverty Reduction Notwithstanding the kindness of strangers, growth is the only means to alleviate poverty for the billions struggling to sustain life. Growth has reduced the number of people living in abject poverty. Some 1.94 billion people, or 43 percent of the world population, lived below the extreme poverty line of $1.25 a day in 1981. Today, as freer markets fuel growth, it has dropped to 15 percent of the world—about 1.3 billion people.[116] Without growth, humanity loses the war against poverty and countless millions will suffer physically and psychologically.

Business Dividend Growth stimulates higher employment, capital investment, and productivity. Rising asset valuations, stabilizing wealth effects, and confidence in surviving tough times supports the prosperity of individuals and companies. Amidst the panic of the recent global crisis, for instance, people endorsed the virtue of growth. Some 76 percent of Americans agreed that U.S. strength is "mostly based on

the success of American business" and 90 percent stated that they respect people who "get rich by working hard."[117]

Fiscal Dividend Government finances are ultimately at the mercy of growth. A thriving economy boosts tax revenues, thereby providing local, state, regional, and national governments the monies to finance spending projects that support, enrich, and sustain society. Although appealing, history shows cheap government does not translate into good government.

Peace Dividend Growth creates more opportunities for more people in more places. People who see the potential for prosperity behave peacefully. Poor people who move into the middle class, for example, think and behave differently. Free from the tyranny of ceaselessly seeking sustenance, shelter, and security, they become more open-minded, more concerned about their children's future, more influenced by abstract values than traditional norms, more inclined to settle conflicts peacefully, more supportive of free markets and democracy, and more inclined to have faith in the future.

Environmental Benefits Growth encourages innovation. People specialize in what they do best and, courtesy of pro-growth policies, outsource the rest. Collectively, insightful paths promote the efficient allocation of resources. The falling ratio of energy consumption per unit of GDP, in the face of the growing abundance of goods and services, testifies to the benefits of growth. By making resources valuable, growth spurs us to consume them wisely.

Quest to Excel Growth incents people to bring to bear their ingenuity, their imagination, and their industriousness to find a better way, every day, to make a productive difference. Pushing back the frontier of human experience—whether it involves the trivial (e.g., forms of social media) or the substantive (e.g., alternative energy)—is powered by the quest to grow. Eliminating the pursuit of progress, by diminishing the quest to excel, saps society's vibrancy.

Life Growth supports longer lives. In 1900, life expectancy at birth was 47 years in the United States. In 2015, after a century marked by an epic burst in growth, it was 78 years. Moreover, people now need to work just half the time they once had to, relying on new tools to boost productivity, finding comfort in rising quality-of-life standards, taking solace in improving health care, and seeing inspiration and a brighter future.

Progress or Decline Unquestionably, as the Counterpoint argues, growth imposes costs on individuals, humanity, and the planet. We agree that these costs are striking. Still, our position is unequivocal: No matter the costs of growth, they pale in comparison to the unacceptable, if not indefensible, price of not growing. Bluntly put, when growth stops, decay starts.

Growth: Positive and Productive?

Counterpoint

No We accept the premise that growth supports life, fostering morality, transparency, tolerance, mobility, justice, and liberty. However, ignoring or, worse, denying the costs of these benefits, costs that seem to grow faster than growth itself, imperils civil society and, ultimately, the stability of humanity and sustainability of the planet. Once you untangle the strands of half-truths, falsehoods, and self-interests that lace deceptive pro-growth arguments, the promise of endless milk and honey for all devolves into a bitter delusion. The problems of growth span the immediate and the future; where one stops and the other starts is tough to pinpoint. Still, as we contend, each hits society hard.

Growth Privileges Few The quintessential promise of growth is "a rising tide lifts all boats." In theory, as an economy grows, it generates higher wages, income, and wealth for all. In reality, the benefits of growth are unevenly distributed, creating extreme inequalities of income, wealth, and power. We agree that over the long run, increasing growth has lifted the tide for millions around the world. However, a share of the global population has seen their patchwork-rafts capsize, many struggle to keep their leaky boats afloat, and a tiny fraction upgraded to even more ostentatious yachts.

Growth Is Misleading Despite the hype and hoopla, growth does not deliver the benefits it promises. It rewards the financially strong, but punishes the economically weak. It liberates people from old routines, but enslaves them to new habits. It creates free time to spend with family and community, but then demands mobility and migration that cut connections. It promises newer, cooler products to enable self-fulfillment, and then insidiously traps consumers in a never-ending cycle of hope and deception. Put simply, growth oversells and underdelivers, condemning people to "spiritual despair scarcely concealed by the frantic pace of life."[118] People, trapped on hedonic treadmills, endlessly searching for newer, shinier, better, bigger, faster, or fancier, confuse consumption of the latest and greatest as the path toward of actualization (i.e., 'I shop, therefore I am'). Instead, the destination is alienation.

Counterpoint

Growth Threatens Life Polluted air, poisoned water, and toxic land—let alone global warming, biodiversity collapse, and resource depletion—are the inevitable by-products of growth. Indisputably, we need some production and consumption. Overproduction and overconsumption, however, destabilize the basis of life. Ironically, when we measure the value created by an economy—say, in GNP—no costs are tallied. Rather, they are labeled "externalities," mysteriously understood to affect society, but conveniently excluded while we praise the wondrous "benefits" of growth in the church of conspicuous consumption. Effectively, since "nobody" is responsible for the costs of externalities, "nobody" pays for them, and the growth engine chugs merrily along. Ultimately, "everybody" pays with a despoiled environment, warped values, and financial servitude.

Growth Destroys Individuality Growth's mandate to maximize efficiency requires massification—mass production, mass consumption, mass distribution, mass markets, mass media, and so on. Maximizing massification delivers tremendous economic benefits, but at extreme social cost. One analyst notes that "a part of the price that people in the West pay for this unending procession of shiny assembly-line products is the concomitant loss of those now rarer things that once imparted zest and gratification—the loss of individuality, uniqueness and flavor; the loss of craftsmanship, local variety and richness; the loss of intimacy and atmosphere, of eccentricity and character."[119]

Current Growth Is Unsustainable Humanity plunders the earth at an unprecedented rate. Presently, human consumption is 30 percent greater than nature's capacity to regenerate. By 2050, at current trends, humanity will require three to five planets of natural resources just to keep the game going. "For more than 20 years we have exceeded the Earth's ability to support a consumptive lifestyle that is unsustainable and we cannot afford to continue down this path," warns the Worldwatch Institute.[120] Barring black-swan innovations in mining, agriculture, manufacturing, and recycling, no matter how hard we wish otherwise, Mother

Earth is going to stop current growth patterns sooner rather than later.

Change the Game Our position is straightforward. Epic poverty for billions, slow-motion death spiral of ecosystems, false hope of actualization through consumption, binge-buying alienation, and the deterioration of nominal democracies into shadow plutocracies puts the world at the proverbial fork in the road. We can remain blissfully ignorant of the price of growth, lost in the endless rush of apparent gains, but continually surprised by inevitable and underestimated externalities. Or, alternatively, we can face the issue full on, applying the standards of sustainability and radically resetting the equation so that growth "meets the needs of the present without compromising the ability of future generations to meet their own needs."[121]

ELEMENTS OF ECONOMIC ANALYSIS

Economics is rich with metrics to measure performance and potential.

Narrow (e.g., GNI, GDP, and GNP) and broad (e.g., HDI, HPI, and NPP) estimators profile absolute and relative economic conditions in developed, developing, and emerging economies. Partial equilibrium analysis, for instance, encourages assessing a restricted range of discrete indicators in order to refine analyses and elaborate interpretation. For instance, central bankers' monetary policies directly influence interest and inflation rates; hence, managers keen to the performance of capital markets concentrate on those indicators. Table 4.8 profiles key indicators including the balance of payments, income distribution, inflation, poverty, public debt, and unemployment. Besides specifying measurement, it highlights market implications.

INTEGRATING ECONOMIC ANALYSIS

The complexity of modern market systems, both absolute and relative, prevents fully representing the properties of economic environment by evaluating a snapshot of disaggregated components. Studying the connections among micro elements of a macro system refines analysis of economic performance and potential. Let's take a look at various meta-models.

TABLE 4.8   Key Components of Economic Analysis

Dimension	Specification	Implication
Balance of Payments (BOP)	Summary of an economy's trade and financial transactions, as conducted by individuals, businesses, and government agencies, with the rest of the world.	Indicates if a country has sufficient savings to pay for its imports as well as if it produces enough income to finance growth.
Deflation	General decline in prices, often caused by a reduction in the supply of money or credit or declining aggregate demand.	Slows economic growth; anticipating lower prices, consumers defer purchases, thereby risking a deflationary spiral. Increases the real value of debt.
Foreign Direct Investment	Controlling ownership in a business enterprise in one country by an entity based in another country.	Promotes development, job expansion, industrialization, and exports. Transfers skills and technologies.
Income Distribution	The distribution of income among a nation's population; estimated by the Gini coefficient.[122]	Equality opens opportunities whereas inequality promotes debt, stress, and risks.
Inflation	The sustained rise in consumer prices measured against a standard level of purchasing power.	Influences interest rates, living costs, consumer confidence, and, ultimately, political stability.
Misery Index	The sum of a country's inflation and unemployment rates. The higher the sum, the greater the economic misery.	Higher misery discourages spending and investment in the face of growing austerity.
Poverty	Multidimensional condition whereby a person or community lacks the essentials for a minimum standard of well-being and life.	Persistent poverty destabilizes performance and constrains potential. Creates stress points that challenge civil society.
Public Debt	The total of a state's financial obligations; measures what the government borrows from its citizens, foreign organizations, foreign governments, and international institutions.	Decreasing debt opens growth opportunities. Growing debt signals increasing austerity, rising taxes, and, if uncontrolled, debt crises that impose political, economic, and social costs.
Unemployment	The share of out-of-work citizens actively seeking employment for pay relative to the total civilian labor force.	People gainfully employed testify to the competency of policymakers to sustain a productive economy. Persistent unemployment spotlights government ineptitude.

Managers often consider meta-models to improve their understanding of the absolute and relative potential of an economic environment. Popular indices include

- Global Competitiveness Index,
- Global Innovation Index,
- Where-To-Be-Born Index,
- World Competitiveness Index.

CONCEPT CHECK

Making sense of the different domains in a big world, as we saw in Chapters 1, 2, and 3, encourages the integration of various indicators into a comprehensive, coherent index. Indices of the sort we see here help managers develop a holistic profile of particular markets in terms of productivity, competitiveness, innovation, and the quality of life.

The Global Competitiveness Index (GCI)   The World Economic Forum holds that providing increasing prosperity hinges on how well a country develops institutions, regulates activity, and uses resources to improve productivity. A country's proficiency managing these domains determines its international competitiveness.[123] The GCI summarizes the performance and relationship among 110 variables that compose 12 so-called "pillars of competitiveness" within a nation. These pillars tap dimensions like financial market development, macroeconomic environment, technological readiness, market efficiency, and innovation. The impact of each pillar on competitiveness varies across countries, given the stage of economic development, as indicated by GDP per capita. Whereas productivity in developed economies like Sweden or Taiwan is largely innovation driven, for instance, it's determined by factor endowments of labor and natural resources in developing economies like Ghana, Nigeria, or Cambodia. Ultimately, the GCI links a broad set of economic indicators, effectively integrating macroeconomic and microbusiness aspects of competitiveness into a single, summary index.

Today's top 10 competitive economies are a diverse bunch. Switzerland, annually ranked first since 2010, continues to set the standard. It is followed by Singapore and the United States. Rounding out the top 10 are Germany, the Netherlands, Japan, Hong Kong, Finland, Sweden, and the United Kingdom. Of the big emerging economies, China and India steadily move up the rankings. Smaller markets, notably Qatar, Malaysia, and the United Arab Emirates, are rising quickly.[124]

The Global Innovation Index (GII)   Countries increasingly look to brainpower for innovations that boost productivity, fortify competitiveness, and increase prosperity. The growing power of ideas and insights in the global market makes a country's capacity for innovation a key determinant of its economic performance and potential. Rather than focus on the scale of research and development, the GII estimates a nation's capacity to imagine ideas, leverage them into pioneering products, and, in the process, generate knowledge, competitiveness, and wealth. The GII anchors analysis in terms of inputs and outputs. Inputs, which promote and enable innovation, include institutions and policies, human capacity, infrastructure, technological sophistication, business markets, and capital. Outputs include knowledge, competitiveness, and wealth. Collectively, these indicators measure a country's competency in promoting technologies, expanding human capacities, streamlining organizational capabilities, and improving institutional responsiveness. The GCI indicates that those who do well consistently transform neat ideas into real innovations.[125]

Presently, developed countries claim the top spots in the GII standings: Switzerland is the global leader, followed by Sweden, Singapore, Finland, the United Kingdom, the Netherlands, Denmark, Hong Kong, Ireland, and the United States. Accelerating innovation in Asia sees India, Turkey, and China rising in rank. Collectively, the data show more Asian countries shifting from practices that had optimized industrial efficiency to policies that improve the environment for innovation.[126]

An economy's productivity, namely its efficiency in converting inputs into useful outputs, is a key determinant of its competitiveness.

The World Competitiveness Index (WCI)   The World Competitiveness Project assesses a nation's ability to set and sustain a business environment that enables enterprises to compete, prosper, and create wealth. Four factors determine a nation's competitiveness: economic performance, government efficiency, business efficiency, and infrastructure. Each category has sub-measures that tap dimensions such as international trade, employment, prices, business legislation, productivity, and management practices. Ultimately, the WCI evaluates more than 300 criteria to summarize a nation's performance.

In 2015, the United States, on the strength of its business efficiency, financial sector, innovation, and infrastructure, topped the WCI scoreboard. Hong Kong and Singapore moved up, overtaking Switzerland, which dropped to fourth place. Canada, Luxembourg, Norway, Denmark, Sweden, and Germany, in sequence, completed the top 10.[127] Cross-national commonalities highlight the decisive importance of business productivity. Country movement, both up and down the rankings, follows performance moving into higher value-added activities, improving business efficiency, and promoting international connectivity.

In general, smaller economies score higher in the lottery of life.

The Where-To-Be-Born Index (WTBBI)   Finally, looking a bit further into the future, the WTBBI holds that how well a country provides opportunities for a healthy, safe, and prosperous life helps explain both its current and future economic environment.[128] The WTBBI evaluates 11 indicators, such as geography, demography, quality of life, per capita income, and life expectancy. Presently, the "lucky baby" league table, comprising 80 countries, is topped by Switzerland, followed by Australia, Norway, Sweden, and Denmark. Smaller nations dominate the top performers, accounting for the top 15 countries in the lottery of life. Large, wealthy countries—notably the United States, Japan, France, and Great Britain—populate the next tier. Emerging and developing economies run from the middle down to the bottom of the ranking.

Economic freedom has a strong relationship with a country's relative competitiveness and innovation performance.

ECONOMIC FREEDOM, INNOVATION, AND COMPETITIVENESS

We close by highlighting the connection of the conceptual anchor of this chapter, economic freedom, to meta-measures of the vitality of developed, developing, and emerging economies. Specifically, Table 4.9 reports the economic freedom score for various countries as well as their ranking on the preceding measures of competitiveness and innovation. Countries with higher degrees of economic freedom consistently show higher degrees of competitiveness and innovation. Singapore and Switzerland stand out; each has high economic freedom and ranks highly in terms of competitiveness, innovation, and, incidentally, as a great place to be born. The data indicate that countries that emphasize economic freedom, aiming to improve the efficiency of business activity and flexibility of individual choice, are more likely to develop environments that install systems that support productivity. In turn, they reap the rewards of world-class innovation and competitiveness.

TABLE 4.9   Integrating Economic Freedom, Innovation, and Competitiveness

Nation	Economic Freedom Score	Type of Economy[129]	Rank, Global Competitiveness Index	Rank, World Competitiveness Index	Rank, Global Innovation Index	Rank, Where-To-Be-Born Index
Singapore	89.4	Developed	2	3	8	6
Australia	81.4	Developed	22	18	19	2
Switzerland	80.5	Developed	1	4	1	1
Canada	79.1	Developed	15	5	11	9
China	78.5	Emerging	28	23	35	49
United States	76.2	Developed	3	1	5	16
Germany	73.8	Developed	5	10	15	16
Japan	73.3	Developed	6	27	22	25
Sweden	72.7	Developed	10	9	2	4
Colombia	71.7	Emerging	66	51	60	42
South Korea	71.5	Developed	26	25	13	19
Malaysia	70.8	Emerging	20	14	32	36
Poland	68.6	Emerging	43	33	49	33
Mexico	66.4	Emerging	61	39	63	39
South Africa	62.6	Emerging	56	53	58	53
Philippines	62.2	Developing	52	41	90	63
Saudi Arabia	62.1	Developing	24	*	42	38
Indonesia	58.1	Emerging	34	42	85	71
Brazil	56.6	Emerging	57	56	64	37
Kenya	55.6	Developing	90	*	99	79
Nigeria	55.6	Developing	127	*	120	80
India	54.6	Emerging	71	44	7	66
Russia	52.1	Emerging	53	45	62	72

The BRICs: Vanguard of the Revolution[130]

Improving performance showcases the accelerating success of emerging economies. The focus of attention is now squarely on the vanguard of emerging economies, the so-called BRICs: Brazil, Russia, India, and China. Together, they are home to nearly 2.8 billion people (40 percent of the planet's population) and cover a quarter of the area of the world, spanning three continents. Combined, they presently account for about 18 percent of global GDP. That share will head to 25 percent over the next 10 years and about one-third by 2030. Adjusting for PPP pushes this performance forward: the BRIC countries currently generate about 30 percent of the world's GDP, with a projected 38 percent by 2020 and nearly 45 percent by 2030.

Unquestionably, the BRIC countries are much larger in scale and scope than other emerging markets. Still, they are leading indicators of consumption patterns, investment policies, and social trends that are gaining momentum worldwide. Many see the BRIC countries as vanguards of the revolution: where they go, both good and bad, others will follow. The following sections look at the emergence of BRICs, highlighting its implications to the global marketplace and closing by analyzing the future prospects.

Changing of the Guard

First off, remind yourself where the BRICs were just 30 or so years ago. Brazil was an economic basket case suffering hyperinflation, Russia was in lockdown behind the Iron Curtain, India's aggressive socialism had led it to expel IBM and Coca-Cola, and China was recovering from the bedlam of the Cultural Revolution and struggling with the legacies of Mao Zedong. Today, conditions and circumstances have radically changed. At current trends and with reasonable projections, over the next few decades the four of them will become premier, powerful economies.

Originally, some thought it would take until 2050 before the BRICs bypassed today's rich countries. The global financial crisis, however, has accelerated the schedule. While the BRICs are growing, Germany, Japan, England, Italy, France, and the United States, among others in the West, continue to struggle. Wealthy countries also face many other constraints: their aging workforces, overwhelming debt, and slowing productivity suggest growth will be hardfought. Moreover, it will fall short of the growth in emerging markets. In the meantime, the speed of the BRICs' recovery paints the global financial crisis as a pivot point in the redistribution of economic power.

So, again, thinking of where the BRICs were around 30 years ago, mapping their accomplishments, and projecting trend lines 30 years from today makes for an astonishing or worrisome outcome, depending on your perspective. Current circumstances make any timeline for the changing of the guard speculative. It does not, however, change secular trends that will culminate in the BRICs' converting demographic dividends, rising productivity, improving innovation, and increasing capital efficiency into the comeback of the emerging economies.

Changing Markets

The BRICs, like many fellow emerging markets, report rapidly growing economies. Historically, consumer demand takes off when GNI per capita is between US$3,000 and $10,000. Russia hit those levels first; China, India, and Brazil are steadily heading there. When adjusted for purchasing power, all have crossed the threshold.

The BRICs, save Russia, have growing middle classes. Forecasts see them expanding from 50 million to almost 600 million by 2025. More immediately, between 2005 and 2015, over 800 million people in the BRICs will cross the annual income threshold of US$3,000. By 2025, approximately 200 million people in the BRICs will have annual incomes above $15,000. Escape from poverty is a game changer; besides permitting more consumption, it often allows people to move from consuming generic necessities to preferring branded goods.

As income grows, so does demand for what once were unreachable luxuries. For example, estimates of 2014–16 indicate that, for every 1,000 people, there are 167 motor vehicles in India and 154 in China. In comparison, for every 1,000 people in the United States and in Germany there are 797 and 572 motor vehicles respectively. By 2030, India and China's car ownership will likely increase 5- to 25-fold. The total number of cars in the two countries combined could rise from around 150 million today to north of a billion by 2030, thereby accounting for more than half of all cars on the world's roads. Other countries show similar vehicle per capita rates: the Philippines' is 3.3 percent, Indonesia's 7 percent, and Turkey's 14 percent. Introduction of low-price automobiles like the Tata Nano, which was initially launched at ₹100,000 (US$1,600) but has increased with time, expand the global auto market. Similar trends in virtually every product class, many anchored in economical innovation programs targeting the lower socio-economic groups, indicate market potentials last seen at the start of the Industrial Revolution.

Big Plans but Big Problems

Notwithstanding the spectacular performance and potential of the BRICs, there are skeptics. First, there is the problem of recency bias, which is the delusion that current trends will continue indefinitely and uninterrupted. History shows great mistakes made by many who extrapolated the present into the future. Invariably, economic growth rates slow as the base of activity expands. Moreover, advantages such as cheap labor or low-cost capital wane as growing demand increases marginal price pressures. And always on the horizon is a blackswan event—a large-impact, hard-to-predict, but rare event beyond the realm of normal expectations that resets the game, such as the collapse of the Soviet Union, the emergence of the Internet, or the global financial crisis.

Despite high-octane growth, the BRICs face futures of persistent poverty and distorted income distributions. By 2025, the income per capita in today's richer countries will exceed $35,000 for more than a billion people. In contrast, only 10 to 20 percent of the nearly 3 billion population in the BRIC economies will hit that threshold. For the long run, income per capita in the United States is projected to reach $80,000 by 2050, while China will likely be just over $31,000, Brazil about $26,600, and India just $17,400. With the possible exception of Russia, hundreds of millions of people in the BRICs will be far poorer on average than individuals in Germany, France, Japan, Italy, Canada, and the United States. Consequently, for the first time in history, the largest economies in the world will no longer be the richest when measured by GNI per capita.

National Challenges

Each of the BRICs struggles with its particular problems. Russia is particularly vulnerable. It depends on various energy and mineral exports for revenue. Erratic swings in commodity prices complicate setting budgets and planning programs. Additionally, Russia is considered riskier because of long-simmering tensions with the West and a legal and political infrastructure that imposes the rule of man. Going forward, besides its aging and declining population, Russia's oligarchic government and crumbling infrastructure confound growth projections. Hence, some advise replacing the BRIC notion with that of "BICs."

Brazil's economic potential has been anticipated for decades, but it has struggled to achieve expectations. Difficulties in income equality, productivity, and education have often snatched defeat from the jaws of victory. India, in addition to pressing economic and political challenges, has immense infrastructure shortfalls and hundreds of millions of poor people. Meeting current demands while building for the future poses immense resource demands. China's particular interpretation of the rule of law, rights of citizens, environmental sustainability, and principles of governance poses problems. China also faces a steadily closing window of opportunity; by 2020, it will have the largest number of old and very old people on earth. The IMF forecasted in 2013 that China's demographic dividend would end by 2020; its working age population would then go into precipitous decline. By 2030, China will face a labor shortage of almost 140 million workers, arguably the greatest jobs crunch in history.

Green Constraints

Wish as we might, the sad fact that there are only so many resources to go around shadows the bright futures of all. The emergence of the BRICs sorely challenges the sustainability of the global environment. Global warming, diminishing raw materials, and escalating pollution suggest that there is a limit to how much the BRICs, to say nothing of the 150 or so countries who seem intent on following in their footsteps, can develop before exceeding the capacity of the global economy to supply the necessary resources and of the environment to support them. More worrisomely, notes the Worldwatch Institute, if China and India were to consume resources and produce pollution at the current U.S. per capita level, we would need the resources of two additional Earths. Throwing everyone else into the mix ratchets up the pressure—estimates are that we are short approximately five planets of resources if the living standards found in today's wealthy countries prevailed worldwide.

Adding Mortar

BRIC leaders have not been idly sitting by, watching these threats thwart their future. Overlapping ambitions and agendas have led them to develop bilateral and multilateral agreements. India and China, the world's two most populous countries, formed a strategic partnership to end border disputes and boost trade. The agreement eased decades of mutual distrust between the two following a 1962 border war. At a ceremony for ex-Chinese Premier, Wen Jiabao, the former Prime Minister of India, Manmohan Singh had stated that India and China can reshape the world order.[131]

There have also been indications of a strengthening relationship between Russia and China. In the first quarter of 2017, bilateral trade between China and Russia amounted to $18.1 billion and is expected to $80 billion by the end of 2017. Spearheading these efforts, with a goal to build a new world economic architecture is the Prime Minister of Russia, Vladimir Putin. This reflects the rising power of emerging economies alongside existing heavyweights like the United States, Japan, and Europe.[132]

The Road Ahead

Inevitably, some speculate that the BRICs might turn into bricks in their march to miracle economies. Granted, their governments have developed economically sensible policies, opened trade and domestic markets, and begun building institutions that support economic freedom. The global financial crisis, however, brutally illustrated that economics can quickly move out of sync.

Despite the ever-present gloom, reasonable optimism prevails. Research identifies four preconditions of consistent macro growth: sound macroeconomic policies; political institutions committed to transparency, fairness, and the rule of law; openness to trade and capital; and strong education systems. By and large, the BRICs, along with other emerging markets, steadily meet the general spirit of some of these standards. None, however, presently meets all. That said, the success of the BRICs questions whether, in fact, one needs to meet all. Their improving performance as their wealthier counterparts struggle suggests that a conventional understanding of markets possibly underestimates the dynamics of economic environments.

No matter what the future holds, the growth of the BRIC countries signals that the next phase of the global economy is also developing. And even if the BRICs fall short of their potential, their successes will redefine the structure of economic environments, patterns of growth, and dynamics of economic activity.

QUESTIONS

4-3. Estimate the likely market evolution of the BRICs over the next decade. What economic indicators might companies monitor to best guide their investments and actions?

4-4. Identify three implications of the emergence of the BRICs for careers and companies in your country.

4-5. Do you think recency bias has led to overestimating the potential of the BRICs? How would you, as a manager for a company assessing these markets, try to control this bias?

4-6. How might managers interpret the potential for their product in a market that is, in absolute economic terms, large but, on a per capita basis, characterized by a majority of poor consumers?

4-7. In the event that the BRICs fail to meet projected performance, what would be some of the implications for the international business environment?

MyLab Management

Go to **mymanagementlab.com** for the following Assisted-graded writing questions:

4-8   Identify the three most important factors that you believe drive the comeback of emerging economies. Explain why you think they would have the greatest impact on the development, performance, and potential of the economic environment in a developed country such as Germany, Japan, or the United States.

4-9   Identify three implications of the emergence of BRICs for careers and companies in a developed country.

Endnotes

Scan for Endnotes or go to www.pearsonglobaleditions.com/Daniels

CHAPTER 5
Trade and Factor Mobility Theory

OBJECTIVES

After studying this chapter, you should be able to

5-1   Understand why policymakers rely on international trade and factor mobility theories to help achieve economic objectives

5-2   Illustrate the historical and current rationale for interventionist and free trade theories

5-3   Describe theories that explain national trade patterns

5-4   Explain why a country's export capabilities are dynamic

5-5   Summarize the reasons for and major effects of international factor movements

5-6   Assess the relationship between foreign trade and international factor mobility

MyLab Management®

Improve Your Performance

When you see this icon ✪, visit **www.mymanagementlab.com** for activities that are applied, personalized, and offer immediate feedback.

A market is not held for the sake of one person.

—African (Fulani) proverb

The Han River, Korea. ▼

Source: Hans Kim. Shutterstock

South Korea's Success Story in the Post-WWII International Economy[1]

—Stefania Paladini

By looking at South Korea's complex story and challenges since the mid-20th century, nobody would have imagined it would achieve such an importance in the world economy. A snapshot of its economy in the 1960s would have shown a GDP per capita at about the same level of some of the poorest African and Asian countries; forty years later, in 2004, South Korea joined the trillion-dollar club of world economies.

With a land area of 99,720 square kilometers, the size of South Korea's area ranks only 109th among countries (roughly a quarter the size of Japan and overall about the size of England). However, with 51 million people, it ranks higher (28th) in population. When looking at GDP things change substantially, with South Korea ranking 14th in the world with US$1.929 trillion (estimates for 2016), just after Italy and before countries such as Canada, Spain, and Australia.

Korea is an old country that has been independent for most of its long existence even though being influenced greatly by China. This came to a sudden stop with the Japanese occupation in 1905, in the aftermath of the Russo-Japanese War. Japan occupied Korea until 1945, when the peninsula regained its independent status. The Korean woes, however, didn't end with World War II (WWII) because Korea split after the 1950–53 Korean War when a demilitarized zone was established at the 38th parallel and an authoritarian government led South Korea.

THE ECONOMIC POLICY POST-WWII: FIVE-YEAR PLANS AND EXPORT EXPANSION

Post WWII, South Korea's economic policy can be roughly divided into three phases. The first one (1954–1960) was known as the *import substitution* phase. Government strictly controlled imports and gave production subsidies to many sectors so that domestic consumers would buy domestically-produced goods rather than imported ones. This was followed by the second phase (1961–1979), when South Korea looked outward and started its remarkable growth; and the final one (from 1980s onward), which saw a stabilization and a more mature economic outlook. For each one of these phases it is possible to identify a clear set of policy instruments and target sectors for development and, if it's true that import substitution just after the Korean War resulted in a low growth, it also dealt with the fundamental task of post-war reconstruction, and put in place the economic pillars to the successive phases.

Import substitution ceased when General Park Chung-hee rose to power. He first enacted a national Five-Year Plan (1962–1966), which was an important factor for the country's development by focusing on expanding both agriculture and heavy industries, such as coal and electric power. It was under Park Chung-hee's controversial

regime between 1961 and 1979 that South Korea started a model of export-led growth that achieved rapid economic development. In recent years, GDP comparison between North and South Korea has been somewhere around 36 to 40. In a development strategy also adopted by other countries in the region (often referred to as the Asian Tigers), South Korea opted for producing labor-intensive products enjoying competitive price advantages over Western companies, starting with light industry and then switching to electronic goods. Since then South Korea became a major producer of telecommunication and computer parts, a specialization that has remained until the present day.

Among the contributing factors for the success of export-led growth, government support was historically one of the key factors. Starting in the 1960s, the government created a full set of incentives to encourage exports by providing direct and indirect support in the forms of tax reduction, import tax exemptions on goods to create exports, import financing and tax rebates, reserve funds and even foreign currency loans. This form of government aid served the country's growth well and even today is firmly in place in the form of public agencies—like KOTRA and KORES—that support FDI acquisition in target markets.

TRANSITIONING TO A DEMOCRATIC REGIME

The country's stunning progression continued with the successive regimes, including the country's transition to a democratic government in the 1980s.

In what is called the Miracle on the Han River, South Korea transformed itself from a developing country to an advanced economy, growing its GDP until 1994 at a rate of 10 percent annually. The achievements are even more startling when considering that in the same period exports grew at a yearly 20 percent. Events like the 1988 Summer Olympics and the 2002 FIFA World Cup offered evidence abroad of the country's achievements.

However, this economic model also generated vulnerabilities, illustrated by the issues faced by the country during the recent world economic crises. In the 1990s it became clear that South Korea looked over-stretched and with some longstanding weaknesses, such as non-performing loans in its banks, high debt/equity ratios by Korean companies and, more troubling, a massive amount of short-term foreign borrowing. These issues surfaced in full during the Asian financial crisis of 1997–98, which saw the country's GDP plunging by 7 percent in 1998 and recovering over several years through intelligent reforms in terms of debt restructuring and increased market openness. This new market configuration translated into a sustained growth about 4 percent annually between 2003 and 2007.

MAP 5.1   South Korea

Estimates for 2016 indicate that South Korea is a mature economy, with its foreign trade value (exports and imports) amounting to about US$912 billion.

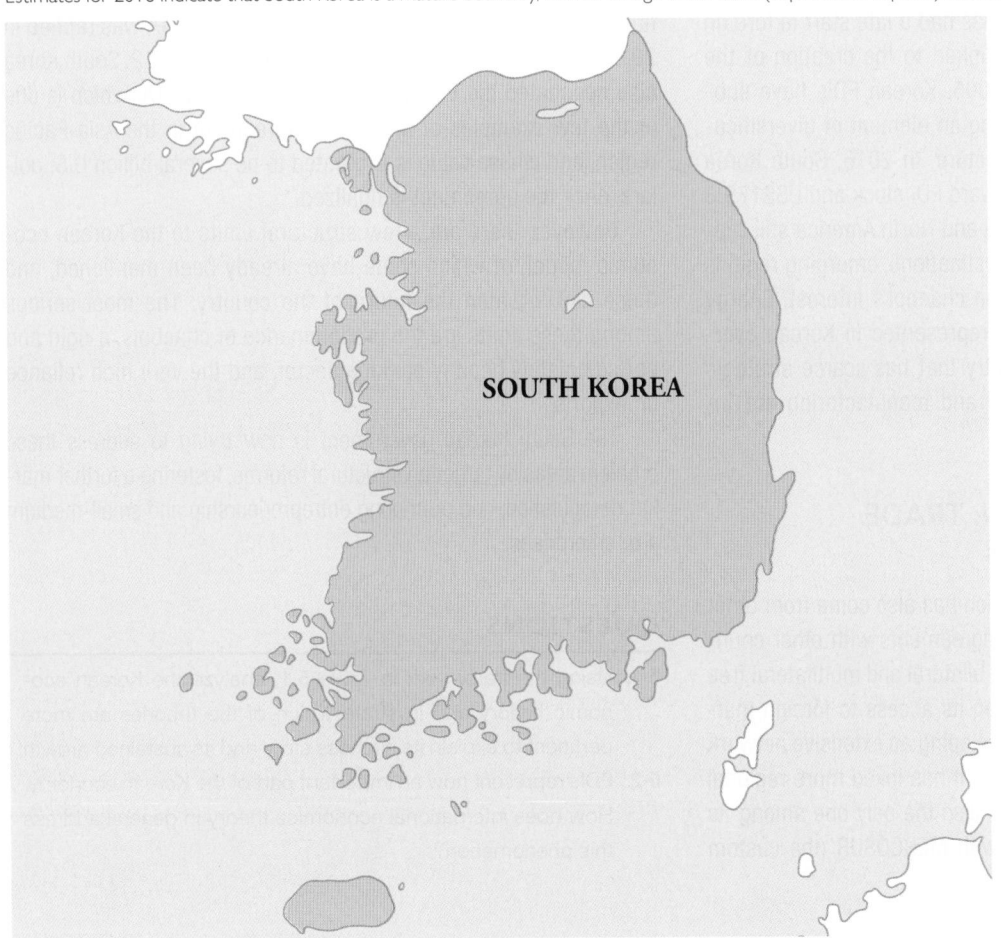

SOUTH KOREA

In 2008–09, another financial crisis, this time a global one, hit South Korea's exports; however, the country was better equipped this time to deal with the global upheaval and was able to recover reasonably fast.

The most recent years (2012–2015) were characterized by a slow growth—about 2 to 3 percent—due to depressed global trade and sluggish domestic consumption.

CHAEBOLS AND CONTINUOUS EXPORT EXPANSION

Today, South Korea is a mature economy, with its foreign trade value (i.e., exports plus imports) amounting to about US$912 billion in 2016. It has maintained a positive trade balance over the last few years despite the global economic crisis. It is the world's 5th-largest exporter, while it ranks 10th in imports. In terms of sectors, South Korea's top export products include electronic goods, integrated circuits, refined petroleum, automotive products, and ships. Its main imports are essentially energy resources (e.g., crude oil and gas,

refined petroleum, and coal) and integrated circuits. China, the United States, Japan, Vietnam, and Germany represent the most important commercial partners.

Korea's economic openness translates into a comparative its having a lower import market protection than, for example, China or Japan, even though Korea, like Japan, has a highly concentrated corporate sector, with a few big conglomerates (chaebols). Chaebols are very important and relevant to the country's development. They are the Korean version of Japanese keiretsus—global multinationals with their operations sprawling over different sectors and markets, generally controlled by only one family. Famous Korean companies, such as Hyundai, Daiwoo, Samsung, and LG, are all important examples. Chaebols played a fundamental role in the development of the post-war Korean economy, and their cooperation with the government was one of the reasons of the success of the export-led growth strategy. This also meant an involvement of chaebols in Korean politics, with Hyundai featuring prominently in the national assembly and even playing a role in the Sunshine policy (the thawing of North-South Korea relations).

Chaebols have also been significant in Korean outbound FDIs, which have surged since 2002. Compared to other countries in the region, such as Japan, South Korea has had a late start in foreign direct investment, which has been linked to the creation of the Korean Investment Corporation in 2005. Korean FDIs have substantially increased since then, adding an element of diversification to the country's productive structure. In 2016, South Korea had U.S. $318 billion in terms of outward FDI stock and US$179.6 billion in inward FDI stock. While Asia and North America still represent Korea's favorite investment destinations, emerging regions like Latin America have attracted the chaebol's interest. Energy and raw materials sectors are well represented in Korean overseas investment—normal in a country that has scarce strategic materials and energy—but industry and manufacturing are increasingly represented.

INTERNATIONALIZATION: TRADE AGREEMENTS AND FTAs

Internationalization and trade promotion has also come from other routes—for example, through trade agreements with other countries. Not only has South Korea signed bilateral and multilateral free trade agreements (FTAs) to strengthen its access to foreign markets, it has led Asian countries in developing an extensive network of partnerships. With 33 deals in 2015, it has inked more regional trade deals than China or Japan. It is also the only one among its competitors to have an agreement with MERCOSUR (the custom union in the Southern Cone of Latin America). South Korea signed an important agreement with the United States after lengthy negotiations over sensitive products. The U.S.–Korea FTA was ratified in 2011 by both countries and was put into force in 2012. South Korea also negotiated the European Union (EU)–Korea FTA, which is one of the few examples of an EU FTA agreement in the Asia-Pacific region, and whose value is estimated to be several billion U.S. dollars, once the agreement is finalized.

However, there are a few structural limits to the Korean economic model, of which some have already been mentioned, and these can threaten the future of the country. The most serious among these limits are the predominance of chaebols, a rigid and not completely healthy banking sector, and the very high reliance on exports.

The South Korean government is now trying to address these problem areas by targeting structural reforms, fostering a further market deregulation, and promoting entrepreneurship and small-medium size enterprises.

QUESTIONS

5-1. Using the framework in Table 5.1, analyze the Korean economic history and illustrate which of the theories are more pertinent to explain its success story and its sustained growth

5-2. FDIs represent now an important part of the Korean economy. How does international economics theory in general address this phenomenon?

INTRODUCTION: WHY DO POLICYMAKERS RELY ON INTERNATIONAL TRADE AND FACTOR MOBILITY THEORIES?

Trade theory helps managers and government policymakers focus on these questions:

- What products should we import and export?
- How much should we trade?
- With whom should we trade?

Some trade theories prescribe that governments should influence trade patterns; others propose a laissez-faire treatment of trade.

Figure 5.1 shows countries' international links through trade and factor mobility (movement of capital, technology, and people). The opening case illustrates South Korea's use of certain links to help achieve its economic objectives. Not only are trade and factor mobility important in growing portions of the global economy, the theories to explain them help all governments wrestle with the decisions of what, how much, and with whom to trade. These questions are intertwined with considerations of what they can produce competitively by boosting the quality and quantity of capital, technical competence, and worker skills.

This chapter will first examine theories that endorse great governmental intervention in trade movements (*mercantilism* and *neomercantilism*) versus a laissez-faire approach of no governmental intervention (*free-trade theories of absolute advantage and comparative advantage*). It will then look at theories to explain trade patterns (how much countries depend on trade, in what products, and with whom), including theories of *country size, factor proportions,* and *country similarity*. It will subsequently consider theories dealing with the dynamics of

FIGURE 5.1   International Operations and Economic Connections

To meet its international objectives, a company must gear its strategy to trading and transferring its means of operation across borders—say, from (Home) Country A to (Host) Country B. Once either of these processes has taken place, the two countries are connected economically.

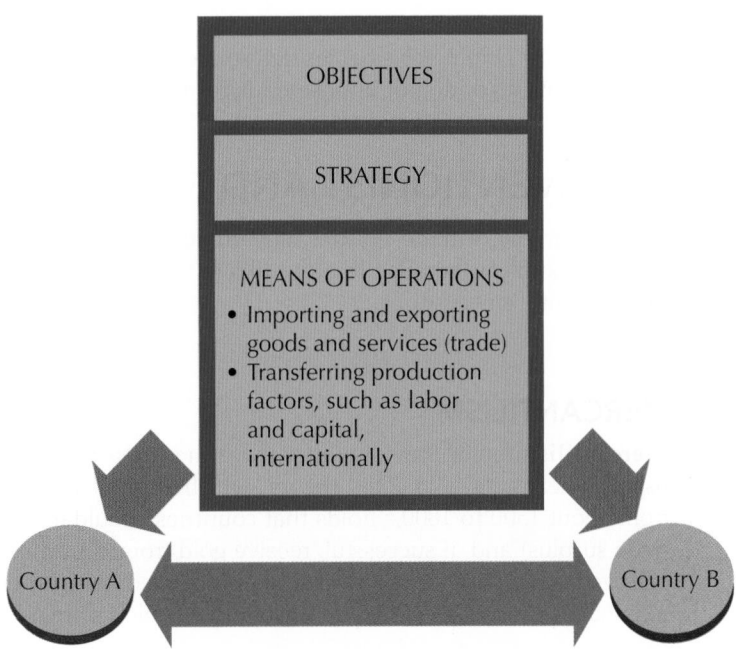

countries' trade competitiveness for particular products, which include the *product life cycle theory* and the *diamond of national competitive advantage theory.* Because the stability and dynamics of countries' competitive positions depend largely on the quantity and quality of their production factors (land, labor, capital, technology), we'll conclude this chapter with an overview of factor mobility, mainly emphasizing the mobility of human resources. Whether taking a laissez-faire or interventionist approach, countries rely on trade and factor mobility theories to guide policy development. In turn, companies respond by basing their location decisions on these policy developments.

Table 5.1 summarizes the major trade theories and their emphases. These different theories expand our understanding of how government trade policies might affect business

TABLE 5.1   What Major Trade Theories Do and Don't Discuss: A Checklist

A check mark indicates that a theory of trade concerns itself with the question asked at the head of the column; if there's a dash, it doesn't. In the last four columns, you can see how each theory responds to the specific question; again, a dash indicates that the theory does not address the question.

Theories	Description of Natural Trade			Prescription of Trade Relationships			
	How Much Is Traded?	What Products Are Traded?	With Whom Does Trade Take Place?	Should Government Control Trade?	How Much Should Be Traded?	What Products Should Be Traded?	With Whom Should Trade Take Place?
Interventionist & free trade							
Mercantilism	—	—	—	yes	✓	✓	✓
Neomercantilism	—	—	—	yes	✓	—	—
Absolute advantage	—	✓	—	no	—	✓	—
Comparative advantage	—	✓	—	no	—	✓	—
National trade patterns							
Country size	✓	✓	—	—	—	—	—
Factor proportions	—	✓	✓	—	—	—	—
Country similarity	—	✓	✓	—	—	—	—
Export dynamics							
Product life cycle (PLC)	—	✓	✓	—	—	—	—
Diamond of national competitive advantage	—	✓	—	—	—	—	—

competitiveness. For instance, they provide insights on favorable locales and products for exports, thereby helping companies determine where to locate their production facilities when governments do or do not impose trade restrictions.

INTERVENTIONIST AND FREE TRADE THEORIES

At one extreme of trade policies, governments intervene a great deal in trade. Let's begin with mercantilism because it is the oldest trade theory, out of which neomercantilism has more recently emerged.

MERCANTILISM

Mercantilism holds that a country's wealth is measured by its holdings of "treasure," which usually means its gold. This theory, which formed the foundation of economic thought from about 1500 to 1800,[2] holds that countries should export more than they import (run a trade surplus) and, if successful, receive gold from countries that run deficits. Nation-states emerged during this period, and gold empowered governments to raise armies and invest in national institutions that helped to solidify people's primary allegiance to the new nations.

According to mercantilism, countries should export more than they import.

Governmental Policies   To run a trade surplus, governments restricted imports and subsidized noncompetitive production. Countries with colonies imported commodities from them that they would otherwise have to purchase from elsewhere. They monopolized colonial trade in order to force the colonies to export less highly valued raw materials to them and import more highly valued manufactured products from them. This way, the colonies ran deficits that they paid off with gold.

As mercantilist policies weakened after about 1800, governments seldom directly limited their colonies' development of industrial capabilities. However, their home-based companies had technological leadership, ownership of raw material production abroad, and usually some degree of protection from foreign competition—a combination that continued to make colonies dependent on raw material production and tie their trade to their industrialized mother countries. We still see vestiges of these relationships, which we discuss in the next chapter.

The Concept of Balance of Trade   Some mercantilist terminology has endured. For example, a **favorable balance of trade** (also called a **trade surplus**) still indicates that a country is exporting more than it imports. An **unfavorable balance of trade** (also known as a **trade deficit**) indicates the opposite. These terms are misnomers because the word *favorable* implies "benefit," and the word *unfavorable* suggests "impairment." In fact, running a trade surplus is not necessarily beneficial, nor is running a trade deficit necessarily detrimental. A country with a favorable balance of trade is supplying people in foreign countries with more than it receives from them.[3] In the mercantilist period, the deficit was paid by a gold transfer. Today, the surplus country, say China, grants credit to the deficit country, say the United States, by holding its currency (U.S. dollars) or investments denominated in U.S. dollars. If that credit cannot eventually buy sufficient goods and services, the so-called favorable trade balance actually may turn out to be disadvantageous for the country with the surplus.

Running a favorable balance of trade is not necessarily beneficial.

NEOMERCANTILISM

Neomercantilism is the running of a favorable balance of trade to achieve some social or political objective. For example, a country may reduce unemployment by encouraging its companies to produce in excess of the home demand and send the surplus abroad. Or it may attempt to maintain political influence in an area by sending more merchandise there than it receives, such as a government granting merchandise aid or loans to a foreign government.

A country that practices neomercantilism attempts to run an export surplus to achieve a social or political objective.

FREE TRADE THEORIES

Why do countries need to trade at all? Why can't Taiwan (or any other country) be content with the goods and services it produces? To begin with, no nation has all the natural resources, geographic conditions, and technology necessary to produce everything we consume today. In addition, two free trade theories further help answer this question: *absolute advantage* and *comparative advantage*.

Both theories hold that nations should let the market determine producers' survival based on what consumers choose to buy.[4] Both theories also imply *specialization*. Just as individuals and families produce an excess of specialized goods and services and exchange them for others' excess specialized goods and services, nations export their specialized surpluses and pay for imports with their export earnings.

THEORY OF ABSOLUTE ADVANTAGE

In 1776, Adam Smith declared that a country's well-being is its citizens' access to goods and services rather than the mercantilists' concept of its ownership of gold. His theory of **absolute advantage** holds that different countries produce different things more efficiently than others and that consumers should not have to buy domestically produced goods when they can buy them more cheaply from abroad. Smith reasoned that unrestricted trade would lead a country to specialize in those products that gave it a competitive advantage. Its resources would shift to the efficient industries because it could not compete in the inefficient ones. Through specialization, it could increase its efficiency for three reasons:

1. Labor could become more skilled by repeating the same tasks.
2. Labor would not lose time in switching production from one kind of product to another.
3. Larger amounts of production would provide incentives for developing more effective working methods.

In what products should a country specialize? Although Smith believed the marketplace would make the determination, he thought that a country's advantage would be either *natural* or *acquired.*

Natural Advantage   A country's **natural advantage** in production comes from climatic conditions, access to certain natural resources, or availability of certain labor forces. A country like Taiwan exports tea, which it has advantages in producing because its high elevations give its oolong tea a unique taste. Taiwan imports wheat. If it were to increase its wheat production, for which its climate and terrain are less suited, it would have to use land now devoted to tea as well as workers in some of its high-tech industries, thus reducing those earnings.

Conversely, the United States produces a small quantity of tea. To become self-sufficient in tea production would require diverting resources away from products such as wheat, for which its climate and terrain are naturally suited. Trading tea for wheat achieves more efficiency than if these two countries were to try to become self-sufficient in the production of both. The more the two countries' natural advantages differ, the more likely they will favor trade with one another.

Variations among countries in natural advantages also help explain where certain manufactured or processed items might best be produced, particularly if a company can reduce transportation costs by processing an agricultural commodity or natural resource prior to exporting. Processing tea leaves reduces bulk and is likely to reduce transport costs on tea exports; producing bottles of a prepared tea drink would add weight, lessening the industry's internationally competitive edge.

Acquired Advantage   Most of today's world trade is in manufactured goods that compete through an **acquired advantage**, usually in either product or process technology. A *product*

CONCEPT CHECK

In Chapter 1 (page 52), we observe that nations have been reducing barriers to the movement of trade and production factors because competition spurs efficiency and consumers want a greater variety of goods and services at lower prices.

According to Adam Smith, a country's wealth is based on available goods and services for its residents rather than on gold.

Specialization increases efficiency because
- labor skills improve,
- less time is lost by not switching production,
- it incentivizes better working methods.

Natural advantage considers climate, natural resources, and labor force availability.

Acquired advantage occurs through either product or process technology.

technology enables a country to produce a unique product or one that is easily distinguished from those of competitors. For example, Denmark exports silver tableware, not because there are rich Danish silver mines but because Danish companies have developed distinctive products. A *process technology* enables a country to efficiently produce a homogeneous product (one not easily distinguished from that of competitors). Iceland now exports tomatoes grown near the Arctic Circle, while Brazil exports quality wine produced near the equator—both of which were impossible until the countries developed fairly recent process technology.[5] Countries that develop product or process technologies have acquired advantages, but only until producers in another country emulate or surpass them successfully. Such dynamics are commonplace as new products replace old ones, as new uses develop for old products, and as different ways of production come into play.

Free trade will bring
• specialization,
• higher global output.

How Does Specialization Increase Output?   We can demonstrate absolute trade advantage by examining two countries and two commodities. Because we are not yet considering the concepts of money and exchange rates, we define the cost of production in terms of the resources needed to produce either commodity. This example is realistic because real income depends on the output of goods compared to the resources used to produce them.

Say that Taiwan and the United States are the only two countries and each has the same amount of resources (land, labor, and capital) to produce either tea or wheat. Using Figure 5.2, let's say that 100 units of resources are available in each country. In Taiwan, assume that it takes 4 units to produce a ton of tea and 10 units per ton of wheat. The purple Taiwanese production possibility line shows that Taiwan can produce 25 tons of tea and no wheat, 10 tons of wheat and no tea, or some combination of the two.

In the United States, it takes 20 units per ton of tea and 5 units per ton of wheat. The green U.S. production possibility line indicates that the country can produce 5 tons of tea and no wheat, 20 tons of wheat and no tea, or some combination of the two. Taiwan is more efficient in tea production (that is, requires fewer resources to produce tea), while the United States is more efficient in wheat production.

How can production be increased through specialization and trade? Let's say the two countries have no foreign trade. We could start from any place on each production possibility line; for convenience, let's assume that if each country devotes half of its 100 resources to production of each product, Taiwan can produce 12.5 tons of tea (divide 50 by 4) and 5 tons of wheat (divide 50 by 10), shown as point A in Figure 5.2, while the United States

FIGURE 5.2   Production Possibilities under Conditions of Absolute Advantage

In short, specialization increases potential output.

ASSUMPTIONS
for Taiwan

1. 100 units of resources available
2. 10 units to produce a ton of wheat
3. 4 units to produce a ton of tea
4. Uses half of total resources per product when there is no foreign trade

ASSUMPTIONS
for United States

1. 100 units of resources available
2. 5 units to produce a ton of wheat
3. 20 units to produce a ton of tea
4. Uses half of total resources per product when there is no foreign trade

PRODUCTION	Tea (tons)	Wheat (tons)
Without Trade:		
Taiwan (point A)	12½	5
United States (point B)	2½	10
Total	15	15
With Trade:		
Taiwan (point C)	25	0
United States (point D)	0	20
Total	25	20

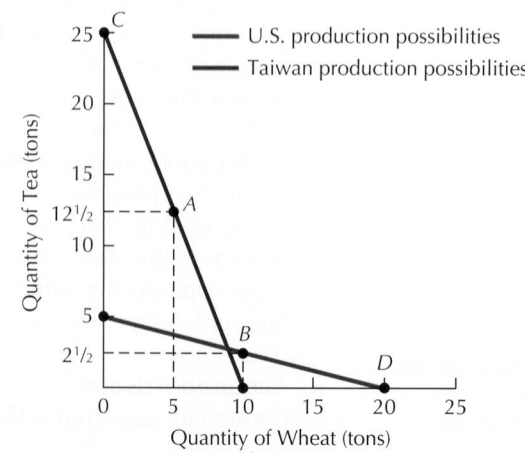

can produce 2.5 tons of tea (divide 50 by 20) and 10 tons of wheat (divide 50 by 5), shown as point B in Figure 5.2.

Because each country has only 100 units of resources, neither can increase wheat production without decreasing tea production, or vice versa. Without trade, the combined production is 15 tons of tea (12.5 + 2.5) and 15 tons of wheat (5 + 10). If each country specialized in the commodity for which it had an absolute advantage, Taiwan could then produce 25 tons of tea and the United States 20 tons of wheat (points C and D in the figure).

You can see that specialization increases the production of both products. By trading, global efficiency is optimized, and the two countries can have more tea and more wheat than they would without trade.

THEORY OF COMPARATIVE ADVANTAGE

We have just described absolute advantage, which is often confused with *comparative advantage.* In 1817, David Ricardo examined the question, "What happens when one country can produce all products at an absolute advantage?" His resulting theory of **comparative advantage** says that global efficiency gains may still result from trade if a country specializes in what it can produce most efficiently—regardless of other countries' absolute advantage.

Comparative Advantage by Analogy   Although this theory may seem initially incongruous, an analogy should clarify its logic. Imagine that the best physician in town also happens to be the best medical administrator. It would not make economic sense for the physician to handle all the office's administrative duties because the physician can earn more money by concentrating on medical duties, even though that means having to hire a less-skilled office administrator. In the same manner, a country gains if it concentrates its resources on the commodities it can produce most efficiently. It then trades some of those for commodities produced abroad. The following discussion clarifies this theory.

Production Possibility   Assume the United States is more efficient in producing tea and wheat than Taiwan is, thus having an absolute advantage in the production of both.[6] Take a look at Figure 5.3. As in our earlier example, it assumes that there are only two countries, each with a total of 100 units of resources available, and half of each used in each product.

> Gains from trade will occur even in a country that has absolute advantage in all products, because the country must give up less efficient output to produce more efficient output.

FIGURE 5.3   Production Possibilities under Conditions of Comparative Advantage

There are advantages to trade even if one country enjoys an absolute advantage in the production of all products.

ASSUMPTIONS
for Taiwan

1. 100 units of resources available
2. 10 units to produce a ton of wheat
3. 10 units to produce a ton of tea
4. Uses half of total resources per product when there is no foreign trade

ASSUMPTIONS
for United States

1. 100 units of resources available
2. 4 units to produce a ton of wheat
3. 5 units to produce a ton of tea
4. Uses half of total resources per product when there is no foreign trade

PRODUCTION	Tea (tons)	Wheat (tons)
Without Trade:		
Taiwan (point A)	5	5
United States (point B)	10	12½
Total	15	17½
With Trade (increasing coffee production):		
Taiwan (point C)	10	0
United States (point D)	6	17½
Total	16	17½
With Trade (increasing wheat production):		
Taiwan (point C)	10	0
United States (point E)	5	18¾
Total	15	18¾

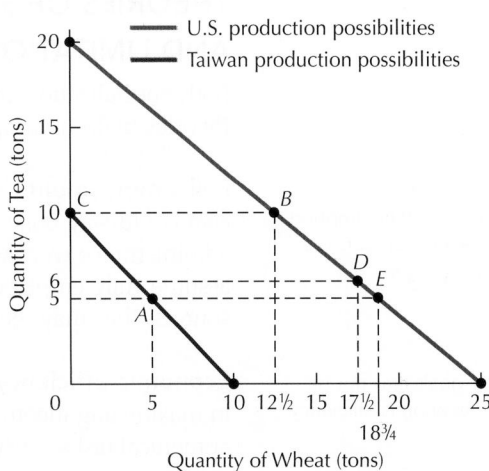

Quantity of Tea (tons)

Quantity of Wheat (tons)

It takes Taiwan 10 units of resources to produce either a ton of tea or a ton of wheat, whereas it takes the United States only 5 units to produce a ton of tea and 4 for a ton of wheat. Taiwan can produce 5 tons of tea and 5 tons of wheat (point A on the purple line), and the United States can produce 10 tons of tea and 12.5 tons of wheat (point B on the green line). Without trade, neither country can increase its tea production without sacrificing some wheat production, or vice versa.

Although the United States has an absolute advantage in producing both commodities, its comparative advantage is only in wheat. This is because its wheat production is 2.5 times that of Taiwan, whereas its tea production is only twice as much. Although Taiwan has an absolute disadvantage in the production of both products, it has a comparative advantage (or less of a comparative disadvantage) in tea. Why? Because its production is half as efficient in tea and only 40 percent as efficient in wheat.

Without trade, the combined production is 15 tons of tea (5 in Taiwan plus 10 in the United States) and 17.5 tons of wheat (5 plus 12.5). Through trading, the combined production of the commodities within the two countries can be increased. For example, if the combined wheat production is unchanged from when there was no trade, the United States could produce all 17.5 tons by using 70 units of resources (17.5 tons times 4 units per ton). The remaining 30 resource units could be used for producing 6 tons of tea (30 units divided by 5 units per ton), shown by point D in Figure 5.3. Taiwan would use all its resources to produce 10 tons of tea (point C). The combined wheat production has stayed at 17.5 tons, but the tea production has increased from 15 to 16 tons.

If the combined tea production is unchanged from the time before trade, Taiwan could use all its resources to produce tea, yielding 10 tons (point C in Figure 5.3). The United States could produce the remaining 5 tons of tea by using 25 units, with its remaining 75 units being used to produce 18.75 tons of wheat (75 divided by 4). This production possibility is point E. Without sacrificing any of the tea available before trade, wheat production has increased from 17.5 to 18.75 tons.

If the United States were to produce somewhere between points D and E, both tea and wheat production would increase over what is possible without trade. Whether the production target is a rise in tea or wheat or a combination of the two, both countries can gain by having Taiwan trade some of its tea production to the United States for some U.S. wheat output.

Don't Confuse Comparative and Absolute Advantage   Most economists accept the comparative advantage theory, which influences them to promote policies for freer trade. Nevertheless, many so-called knowledgeable people confuse comparative advantage with absolute advantage and do not understand how a country can simultaneously have a comparative *advantage* and absolute *disadvantage* in the production of a given product.

THEORIES OF SPECIALIZATION: SOME ASSUMPTIONS AND LIMITATIONS

Both specialization theories claim an increased production through trade. However, these theories make assumptions, some of which are not always completely valid.

| Full employment is not necessarily a valid assumption of absolute and comparative advantage.

Full Employment   Our earlier physician/administrator analogy assumed that the physician could stay busy full time practicing medicine. If not, the physician might perform the administrative work without sacrificing earnings from medical duties. The free trade theories assume fully employed resources. When countries have many unemployed or unused resources, they may seek to restrict imports to employ or use idle resources.

| Countries' goals may not be limited to economic efficiency.

Economic Efficiency   Our analogy also assumes that the physician is interested primarily in maximizing income. Yet there are a number of reasons for choosing not to work full time at medical tasks, such as finding administrative work relaxing and self-fulfilling, fearing that a hired administrator would be unreliable, or wishing to maintain administrative skills in the somewhat unlikely event that administrators will command higher wages than physicians in the future. Often, countries also pursue objectives other than output efficiency. They may avoid overspecialization because of the vulnerability created by changes in technology and by price fluctuations or because they do not trust foreign countries to always supply them with essential goods.

CONCEPT CHECK

Recall from Chapter 1 (page 56) that individuals evaluate their well-being on both an absolute and a comparative basis. In Chapter 2 (page 83) we noted national differences in preference for "live to work" versus "work to live."

Division of Gains   Although specialization brings potential economic benefits to all trading countries, the earlier discussion did not indicate how countries will divide increased output. In the case of our wheat and tea example, if both the United States and Taiwan receive some share, they will both be better off in an absolute sense. However, people and nations are concerned with relative as well as absolute economic gains. If they perceive that a trading partner is gaining too large a share of benefits, they may prefer to forgo absolute gains for themselves so as to prevent others from gaining a relative economic advantage.[7]

Transport Costs   If it costs more to transport the goods than is saved through specialization, the advantages of trade are negated. In other words, in our two-country scenario, some workers would need to forgo producing tea or wheat in order to work in transporting the tea and wheat abroad. However, as long as the diversion reduces output by less than what the two countries gain from specialization, there are still gains from trade.

Insufficient Demand   If trade increases production by more than normally acceptable tea and wheat consumption, is there still an advantage? Yes. The consumers in the two countries can gain access to sufficient output by working fewer hours, thus giving them more leisure time.

Countries' absolute and comparative advantages can change.

Statics and Dynamics   The theories of absolute and comparative advantage address countries statically—by looking at them at one point in time. However, countries' abilities change. Recall the earlier two-product example (see p. 159) where the resources needed to produce tea or wheat in either Taiwan or the United States could change, such as because of advancements in mechanized tea harvesting and acceptance of genetically modified crops.[8] Thus, we should not assume that future absolute or comparative advantages will remain as they are today. We return to this theme later in the chapter as we examine theories to explain the dynamics of competitive production locations.

Free trade advantages apply to services as well as physical products.

Services   The theories of absolute and comparative advantage deal with products rather than services. However, with a growing portion of world trade made up of services, the theories apply because resources must also go into service production. For instance, the United States sells an excess of such services as education to foreign countries (many foreign students attend U.S. universities). At the same time, it buys an excess of foreign shipping services. To become more self-sufficient in international shipping, the United States might have to divert resources from its more efficient use of them in higher education or in the production of other competitive products.

CONCEPT CHECK

Chapter 1 (page 49) explained that many products are partially made in different countries. Nevertheless, the concepts of absolute and comparative advantage hold in these instances.

Production Networks   Although portions of products increasingly may come from different countries, this development fits well with the concept of advantages through specialization. In other words having portions of products produced in those countries where there is an absolute or comparative advantage saves costs.

Neither domestic labor mobility nor international labor immobility is as great as implied by the free trade theories.

Mobility   These theories assume that resources can move domestically from the production of one good to another—and at no cost. But this assumption is not completely valid. For example, wheat farmers might not easily become tea harvesters because of different skill needs and having to move to new locations. Even if they do, they may be less productive than before.[9]

The theories also assume that resources are immobile internationally. Increasingly, they are mobile, thus affecting countries' production capabilities. For instance, nearly half a million contract workers are in Taiwan, mainly because of better job opportunities there.[10] Further, foreign companies have moved both managers and capital to support their investments there, which has contributed to changing Taiwanese capabilities. Such movement is clearly an alternative to trade, a topic discussed later in the chapter. However, it is safe to say that resources are more mobile domestically than they are internationally.

THEORIES TO EXPLAIN NATIONAL TRADE PATTERNS

The free trade theories demonstrate how output growth occurs through specialization and free trade; however, they do not deal with trade patterns such as how much a country trades, what products it trades, or who will be its trading partners. In this section, we discuss the theories that help explain these patterns.

HOW MUCH DOES A COUNTRY TRADE?

Free-trade theories of specialization neither propose nor imply that only one country should or will produce a given product or service. **Non-tradable goods**—products and services (haircuts, retail grocery distribution, etc.) that are seldom practical to export because of high transportation costs—are produced in every country. However, among tradable goods, we'll now discuss theories to explain why some countries depend on imports and exports more than others.

Theory of Country Size   The **theory of country size** holds that countries with larger land masses usually depend less on trade than smaller ones. They are apt to have more varied climates and an assortment of natural resources that make them more self-sufficient. Most large countries (such as Brazil, China, India, the United States, and Russia) import less of their consumption and export less of their production output than do small nations (such as Uruguay, Belgium, and Sri Lanka).

Furthermore, distance to foreign markets affects large and small countries differently. Normally, the farther the distance, the higher the transport costs, the longer the inventory carrying time, and the greater the uncertainty and unreliability of timely product delivery. The following example illustrates why distance is more pronounced for a large country than for a small one.

Assume that the normal maximum distance for transporting a product is 100 miles because costs rise too much at greater distances. Although almost any location in Belgium is within 100 miles of a foreign country, the same isn't true for its two largest neighbors, France and Germany. This shorter distance to foreign markets for Belgium additionally helps to explain its higher dependence on trade as a percentage of its production and consumption.

Size of the Economy   While land area helps explain the *relative* dependence on trade, countries' economic size helps explain *absolute* differences in the amount of trade. The world's largest five economies in 2014 were also the top five exporting countries. Simply put, the largest economies produce so much that they have more to sell, both domestically and internationally. At the same time, most of developing countries' trade is with developed countries. There has, however, been a recent upsurge of trade among developing countries, mainly because the economic growth in China and India has increased their demand for raw materials found mainly in developing countries.[11]

Related to levels of economic development is landlocked countries' disadvantage in trade. With few exceptions, these countries lag maritime countries in both trade and GDP per capita. They must depend on other countries to build infrastructure to gain their access to the

[margin note] Bigger countries (in terms of land mass) differ in several ways from smaller countries. They

- tend to export a smaller portion of output and import a smaller part of consumption,
- have higher average transport costs for foreign trade.

[margin note] Larger economies are the biggest traders because they produce and consume more.

sea, and there is little incentive for them to do this. At the same time, landlocked countries generally have higher transport costs for exporting. Further, potential trading partners view suppliers from landlocked countries as less reliable because conditions in transit countries can impede trade. Those exceptional landlocked countries' success hinges on forgoing transit problems by depending on service exports (e.g., Switzerland with financial services) or on goods exported by air (e.g., Botswana with diamonds).[12]

The United States offers a good example of the difference between relative and absolute dependence on trade because it is the third-largest country in area and the largest economically. Although its dependence on either imports or exports is comparatively low as a percentage of either production or consumption, it is the world's largest trader (imports + exports). In fact, the output of each U.S. state is so high that states have plenty of opportunity to buy and sell with each other. Map 5.2 illustrates the large U.S. economic size by showing how each of its states compares economically with countries.

MAP 5.2 U.S. States' Economies Compared to National Economies

The U.S. size, both geographically and economically, results in its being one of the world's largest trader while also depending relatively less than most countries on imports and exports.

GDP figures for the U.S. states are based on https://en.wikipedia.org/wiki/List_of_U.S._states_by_GDP#2015_data and U.S. Department of Commerce, Bureau of Economic Activity, retrieved December 14, 2015. Country GDP figures came from http://knoema.com/nwnfkne/world-gdp-ranking-2015-data-and-charts and IMF World Economic Outlook (WEO), October 2015.

WHAT TYPES OF PRODUCTS DOES A COUNTRY TRADE?

We won't delve again into those factors we've already discussed (climate and natural resources) that give a country a natural advantage; instead, we will examine the factor endowment theory of trade and the importance of production and product technology.

According to the factor proportions theory, countries have their best trade advantage when depending on their relatively abundant production factors.

Factor Proportions Theory   Eli Heckscher and Bertil Ohlin developed the **factor proportions theory**, maintaining that differences in countries' proportional endowments of labor, land, and capital explain differences in these endowments' costs. For instance, if labor were abundant in comparison to land and capital, labor costs would be low relative to land and capital costs; if scarce, the costs would be high. These relative factor costs would lead countries to excel in the production and export of products that used their abundant—and therefore cheaper—production factors.[13]

General Observation   Factor proportions theory appears logical, and a general observation gives many examples that conform to the theory. For instance, densely populated Hong Kong uses little land for agriculture and produces manufactured products not requiring large amounts of land. Canada is the opposite. Hong Kong does best in manufacturing operations that use a minimum of land per worker (e.g., printing, clothing, watches) by locating these in multistory buildings. Canada produces agricultural and manufactured products that require lots of land per worker, such as wheat and automobiles. On the one hand, Germany, a country with a vast amount of capital relative to its population excels at chemical production, which requires capital intensity. On the other hand, Bangladesh, a country with abundant labor relative to capital, excels at apparel production, which is labor intensive.

Production factors, such as land and labor, are not homogeneous.

A Closer Observation   However, because the factor proportions theory assumes production factors to be homogeneous, tests to substantiate the theory have been mixed.[14] Neither land nor labor is homogeneous. Land varies, for example, in its arability and productivity. Labor varies by skill level because of training and education differences that require capital expenditures. These expenditures do not show up in traditional capital measurements, which include only plant and equipment values. When the factor proportions theory accounts for capital invested to train people, the factor endowment theory explains many trade patterns.[15] For example, because high-income countries employ a higher proportion of highly educated employees (e.g., scientists and engineers) than do developing economies, they depend on an abundance of highly trained human resources in the production that they export. Low-income countries, though, show a high dependence on less-skilled labor in their exports.[16]

Companies may substitute capital for labor, depending on the cost of each.

Process Technology   Factor proportions analysis becomes more complicated when the same product can be created by different methods, such as with labor versus capital intensity. The following photos show rice harvesting in Indonesia, where many manual laborers are employed, versus Italy, where mechanized methods require few workers. In the final analysis, the optimum location of production depends on comparing the cost in each locale based on the type of production that minimizes costs there.

Countries with bigger markets depend more on producing products requiring larger production runs.

Not all products lend themselves to such trade-offs in production methods. Some require huge amounts of fixed capital and long production runs to spread the fixed capital costs over more output units. These usually are located in countries with large markets.[17] However, companies may locate long production runs in small countries if they are able to export from them.[18] In industries where long production runs reduce unit costs substantially, companies tend to locate production in only a few countries, using these locations to export. Where long production runs are less important, we find a greater prevalence of multiple production units scattered around the world in different countries so as to minimize transportation costs.

In addition, high R&D expenditures create high up-front fixed costs. Therefore, a technologically intensive company from a nation with a small market may need to sell more abroad

Source: Roberto Caucino/Shutterstock

▲

The rice harvesting is capital intensive in Italy (left), where labor rates are high. It is labor intensive in Indonesia (right), where labor rates are low.

Source: mosista/Shutterstock

| Most new products originate in developed countries.

than a company in a large domestic market. It may, in turn, pull resources from other domestic industries and companies, which leads to more national specialization than one finds in a larger country.[19]

Product Technology   Manufacturing is the largest sector in world trade, with commercial services the fastest-growing sector. Manufacturing competitiveness depends largely on technology to develop new products and processes, which, in turn, depends on a large number of highly educated people and a large amount of capital to invest in R&D. Because developed countries have an abundance of these features, they originate most new products and account for most manufacturing output and trade. Developing countries depend much more on the production of primary products; thus, they depend more on natural advantage.

WITH WHOM DO COUNTRIES TRADE?

Below, we discuss the roles that country similarity and distance play in determining trading partners.

Developed countries trade primarily with each other because they

- produce and consume more,
- emphasize technical breakthroughs in different industrial sectors.

Country-Similarity Theory   The **country-similarity theory** says that companies create new products in response to market conditions in their home market. They then turn to markets they see as most similar to what they are accustomed, especially those markets where consumers have comparable levels of per capita income.[20]

Specialization and Acquired Advantage   In order to export, a company must provide consumers abroad with an advantage over what they could buy from their domestic producers. Trade occurs because companies in a given country spend more on R&D in some sectors than in others, thus leading to countries' specialization and acquired advantage. Germany, for instance, is traditionally strong in machinery and equipment, Switzerland in pharmaceutical products, and Denmark in food products.[21] Even developing countries gain advantages through specialization in very narrow product segments. Bangladesh has succeeded in exporting shirts, trousers, and hats, but not bed linens or footballs, which Pakistan has successfully exported.[22]

| Product differentiation causes countries to conduct two-way trade in seemingly similar products.

Product Differentiation   Trade also occurs because *companies* differentiate products, thus creating two-way trade in seemingly similar products. The United States is both a major exporter and a major importer of tourist services, vehicles, and passenger aircraft because different firms from different countries have developed product variations with different appeals. For instance, both Boeing from the United States and Airbus from Europe produce large passenger jets that will fly from point A to point B, but airlines buy both companies' aircraft because their models differ in such features as capacity, flying range, fuel consumption, and perceived reliability.[23] As a result, Boeing and Airbus sell within their own and each other's home markets as well as within countries that produce no aircraft.

Trading partners are affected by

- cultural similarity,
- political relations between countries,
- distance.

CONCEPT CHECK

In Chapter 2 (page 90), we showed that a company should expect fewer adjustments when moving to a country whose culture is close to that of its home base.

The Effects of Cultural Similarity   Importers and exporters perceive greater ease in doing business in countries that are culturally similar to their home country, such as those that speak a common language. Likewise, historic colonial relationships explain much of the trade between specific developed and developing economies. For instance, France's colonial history in Africa has given Air France an edge in serving the continent's international air passenger markets.[24] Importers and exporters find it easier to continue business ties than to develop new distribution arrangements in countries where they are less experienced.

The Effects of Political Relationships and Economic Agreements   Political relationships and economic agreements among countries may discourage or encourage trade between them. Witness the political animosity between Israel and most other Middle Eastern countries that has diminished their mutual trade for about six decades. An example of trade encouragement is the agreement among many European countries to remove all trade barriers with each other, thereby causing a greater share of the countries' total trade to be conducted with each other.

The Effects of Distance   Although no single factor fully explains specific pairs of trading partners, the geographic distance between two countries is important in as much as transport costs increase with distance. However, distance is more important for homogeneous products than for differentiated products inasmuch as the former compete more on the basis of price.[25] In addition, analysis of cost differences must take into account the available transportation modes. Wine exports from Australia can reach the United Kingdom (UK) by container ship for about the same transport cost as wine exports to the UK from southern France because the latter have substantial overland and expensive transport.[26]

THE DYNAMICS OF EXPORT CAPABILITIES

We've alluded to the fact that trading patterns change due to such factors as political and economic relations among countries and the development of new product and process capabilities. We now discuss two theories—the product life cycle theory and the diamond of national advantage—that help explain how countries develop, maintain, and lose their competitive advantages.

According to the PLC theory of trade, the production location for many products moves from one country to another depending on the stage in the product's life cycle.

The introduction stage is marked by

- innovation in response to observed need,
- exporting by the innovative country,
- evolving product characteristics.

PRODUCT LIFE CYCLE (PLC) THEORY

The international **product life cycle (PLC) theory** of trade states that the production location of certain manufactured products shifts as they go through their life cycle. The cycle consists of four stages: *introduction, growth, maturity,* and *decline.*[27]

Product Introduction   Most new products and process technologies originate in developed countries in response to companies' observation of nearby needs for them.[28] Once a company creates a new product, theoretically it can manufacture it anywhere in the world. In practice, however, during this *product introductory stage,* it generally produces domestically to obtain rapid market feedback and save on transport costs to its predominantly domestic market. Production is apt to be more labor-intensive than in later PLC stages because more labor-saving machinery may be introduced only when sales begin to expand rapidly and the product becomes highly standardized. At this point the highly skilled and educated labor in high-income countries is usually cost efficient despite its high compensation because of its adeptness on nonstandardized production. Even if its cost is somewhat higher than production in a developing country, many consumers are willing to pay a high price for new products rather than wait for future price reductions.

Growth is characterized by
- increases in exports by the innovating country,
- more competition,
- increased capital intensity,
- some foreign production.

Growth   Sales growth attracts competitors to the market, particularly in other developed countries where firms have technology to replicate the innovating company's product. Let's say the innovator is in the United States, and a competitor is in Japan. The Japanese production is sold mainly in Japan because:

1. The growing Japanese demand does not allow for much attention to other markets.
2. Japanese producers stay occupied in developing product variations for Japanese consumers.
3. Japanese costs may still be high because of production start-up problems.

Global sales growth creates an incentive for companies to develop labor-saving process technology, but this incentive is partly offset because competitors are differentiating their products, especially to fit the needs of different countries' consumers. Thus the capital intensity, though growing, is less than will come later. The original producing country will increase its exports, especially to developing countries, but will lose certain key export markets where local production commences.

Maturity is characterized by
- a decline in exports from the innovating country,
- more product standardization,
- more capital intensity,
- increased competitiveness of price,
- production start-ups in emerging economies.

Maturity   In the *maturity stage,* worldwide demand begins to level off, although growing perhaps in some countries and declining in others. Typically, there is a shakeout of producers, more standardized production, and increased importance of price as a competitive weapon. Increased capital-intensive production reduces per-unit cost, thus creating even more demand in developing economies. Because markets and technologies are widespread, the innovating country no longer commands a production advantage, thus its exports decrease as foreign production replaces it. Shifting production to developing countries is advantageous because firms can employ less skilled and less expensive labor efficiently for standardized (capital-intensive) production.

Decline is characterized by
- a concentration of production in developing countries,
- an innovating country becoming a net importer.

Decline   As a product moves into the *decline stage,* those factors occurring during the maturity stage continue to evolve. The markets in developed countries decline more rapidly than those in developing economies as demand among affluent customers becomes saturated and because those customers want ever newer products. By this time, market and cost factors dictate that almost all production is in developing economies. They export to the declining or small-niche markets in the developed world. In other words, the country in which the innovation first emerged—and was exported from—then becomes the importer.

Verification and Limitations of PLC Theory   Empirical evidence verifies the PLC theory for many products, such as ballpoint pens and hand calculators. They were first produced in a single developed country and sold at a high price; then, production shifted to multiple developed country locations to serve those local markets. Today, most production is in developing countries, and prices have declined.

Not all products conform to the dynamics of the PLC.

However, types of products abound for which production locations usually do not shift. Such exceptions include the following:

- Products with high transport costs (non-tradable goods) that may have to be produced close to the market, thus never becoming significant exports.
- Products that, because of very rapid innovation, have extremely short life cycles, making it impossible to reduce costs by moving production from one country to another. Some fashion items fit this category.
- Luxury products for which cost is of little concern to the consumer. In fact, production in a developing country may cause consumers to perceive the product as less luxurious.
- Products for which a company can use a differentiation strategy, perhaps through advertising, to maintain consumer demand without competing on the basis of price.

- Products that require specialized technical personnel to locate near production so as to continually move the products into their next generation of models. This seems to explain the long-term U.S. dominance of medical equipment production and German dominance in rotary printing presses.

Regardless of product, the current trend is for international companies to introduce new products at home and abroad almost simultaneously. In other words, instead of merely observing needs within their domestic markets, companies develop products and services for observable worldwide market segments. In so doing, they choose an initial production location (which may or may not be in the innovating company's home market) that will minimize costs for serving markets in multiple countries.

THE DIAMOND OF NATIONAL COMPETITIVE ADVANTAGE

According to the diamond of national competitive advantage theory, companies' development and maintenance of internationally competitive products depends on favorable

- demand conditions,
- factor conditions,
- related and supporting industries,
- firm strategy, structure, and rivalry.

Why have countries developed and sustained different competitive advantages? The **diamond of national competitive advantage** is a theory showing four features as important for competitive superiority: demand conditions; factor conditions; related and supporting industries; and firm strategy, structure, and rivalry[29] (see Figure 5.4).

We have discussed these conditions in the context of other trade theories, but how they combine affects the development and continued existence of competitive advantages. The framework of the theory, therefore, is a useful tool for understanding how and where globally competitive companies develop and sustain themselves.

Facets of the Diamond   Usually, all four conditions need to be favorable for an industry within a country to attain and maintain global supremacy.

Demand Conditions   Both PLC theory and country-similarity theory show that new products (or industries) usually arise from companies' observation of need or demand, which has traditionally been in their home countries, where they start production. This was the case for the Italian ceramic tile industry after World War II: In a postwar housing boom, consumers wanted cool floors (which tile would provide) because of the hot Italian climate.

Factor Conditions   Recall natural advantage within the absolute advantage and factor proportions theories. Wood was expensive, and most production factors (skilled labor, capital, technology, and equipment) for producing tile were available within Italy on favorable terms.

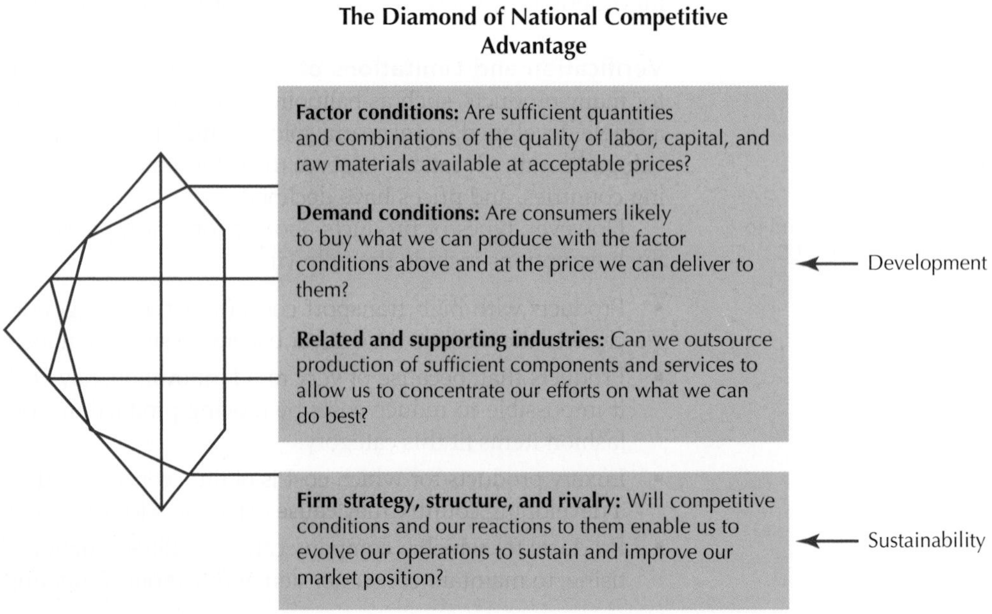

FIGURE 5.4   The Diamond of National Competitive Advantage

The interaction of these conditions must usually be favorable if an industry in a country is to develop and sustain itself. The theory was developed with domestic conditions in mind, but globalization results in favorable conditions that may come from anywhere.

Source: Based on Michael E. Porter, "The Competitive Advantage of Nations," *Harvard Business Review,* 68:2 (March–April 1990).

The Diamond of National Competitive Advantage

Factor conditions: Are sufficient quantities and combinations of the quality of labor, capital, and raw materials available at acceptable prices?

Demand conditions: Are consumers likely to buy what we can produce with the factor conditions above and at the price we can deliver to them?

Related and supporting industries: Can we outsource production of sufficient components and services to allow us to concentrate our efforts on what we can do best?

← Development

Firm strategy, structure, and rivalry: Will competitive conditions and our reactions to them enable us to evolve our operations to sustain and improve our market position?

← Sustainability

Related and Supporting Industries   Tile production needed enamels and glazes. Had these not been available nearby, as they were in the case of Italy, costs would have increased too much. Recall, for instance, the importance of transport costs in our discussions of the theory of country size, assumptions of specialization, and factors limiting the PLC theory.

Firm Strategy, Structure, and Rivalry   The combination of three features—demand, factor conditions, and related and supporting industries—influenced companies' ability to successfully initiate ceramic tile production in postwar Italy. The ability of the companies to sustain a competitive advantage required favorable circumstances for the fourth feature: *firm strategy, structure,* and *rivalry.*

Barriers to market entry were low in the tile industry (some companies started up with as few as three employees), and hundreds of companies initiated production. Rivalry became intense as companies tried to serve increasingly sophisticated Italian consumers. These circumstances forced breakthroughs in both product and process technologies, which gave the Italian producers advantages over foreign firms and enabled them to gain the largest global share of tile exports.

Limitations of the Diamond of National Advantage Theory   The existence of the four favorable national conditions does not guarantee that a flourishing industry will develop. Entrepreneurs may face favorable conditions for many different lines of business. In fact, comparative advantage theory holds that resource limitations may cause a country's firms to avoid competing in some industries despite having an absolute advantage. For instance, Swiss conditions would seem to have favored success if companies in Switzerland had become players in the personal computer industry. However, doing so might have lessened protection of Swiss global positions in such product lines as watches and scientific instruments as companies downsized innovation in those industries by moving their highly skilled people into developing a new industry.

A second limitation concerns the growth of globalization. The industries on which this theory is premised grew when companies' access to competitive capabilities was much more domestically focused. We can see how globalization affects each of the four conditions:

> Domestic existence of all conditions
> - does not guarantee an industry will develop,
> - is not necessary with globalization.

1. Observations of foreign or foreign-plus-domestic demand conditions have spurred much of the recent Asian export growth. In fact, such Japanese companies as Uniden and Fujitech target their sales almost entirely to foreign markets.[30]
2. Companies and countries do not depend entirely on domestic factor conditions. For example, capital and managers are now internationally mobile, and companies may depend on foreign locations for portions of their production.
3. If related and supporting industries are not available locally, materials and components are now more easily brought in from abroad because of transportation advancements and relaxed import restrictions. In fact, many MNEs now assemble products with parts supplied from a variety of countries.
4. Companies react not only to domestic rivals but also to foreign-based rivals at home and abroad. Thus the prior domestic absence of any of the four conditions from the diamond may not inhibit companies and industries from gaining these conditions and becoming globally competitive.

Using the Diamond for Transformation   By expanding the diamond of national advantage theory to include changes brought about by globalization, we can see its validity for countries' economic policies. In our opening case, South Korea diversified its economy from agriculture and light industries to modern high-tech products by satisfying the market entry conditions of the diamond of national competitive advantage. This transformation could not have occurred had South Korean authorities looked only at what was available within their own borders. In South Korea itself, there was insufficient demand for the high-tech products, which it now produces; good transportation systems, however, makes efficient export possible. Similarly, the country initially lacked some of the factor conditions necessary for producing high-tech products, like FDI. Eventually, though, it altered its agreements and trade relations so that the agreements made fit the production needs. It also allowed companies to bring in foreign managers and technicians to fill personnel gaps. Finally, it developed local factors and competition, through chaebols, to ensure a vibrant competitive environment. Thus, understanding and having the necessary conditions to be globally competitive is important, but these conditions are neither static nor purely domestic.

THE THEORY AND MAJOR EFFECTS OF FACTOR MOBILITY

As both the quantity and quality of countries' factor conditions change, their relative capabilities change as well. The change may be due to internal circumstances. For instance, if savings rates increase, countries have more capital relative to their factors of land and labor. If they spend relatively more on education, they improve the quality of the labor factor. The change may also be due to international mobility as people, capital, and technology move across borders.

Point

Point

A **strategic trade policy**, or **industrial policy**, is one in which a government identifies target industries to develop to be internationally competitive.

Yes If you're a country that wants to compete in today's globalized business environment (and you have to), you must develop and maintain some industries that will be internationally competitive. Those industries must grow and earn sufficient revenues to keep your domestic economy growing at least as well as other countries are performing.

A government's role is rarely neutral. The government may claim that its economic policies don't affect the performance of specific domestic industries on the world stage, but a lot of those policies are bound to have precisely that effect. Who will argue that U.S. efforts to "improve agricultural productivity" and "enhance defense capabilities" have nothing to do with the fact that the United States does a healthy business in the export of farm and aerospace products?

Moreover, just about every government policy designed to help one industry will have a negative effect on another. European airlines complain (with some justification) that European government support for high-speed rail traffic deprives them of the revenue they need to compete with U.S. overseas carriers, which don't have much to worry about from railroad passenger traffic at home. In other words, national policymakers everywhere face trade-offs. So if every government policy will help one party while hurting another, why shouldn't a country's practices call for taking special care of the industries that will likely give it its best competitive advantage?

Executing such a plan can be pretty simple. First, target a growth industry and figure out what factors make it potentially competitive. Next, identify your country's likely competitive advantages (and make sure you know why you have

Should Nations Use Strategic Trade Policies?

them). Finally, develop a little synergy between the strong points you've uncovered during both processes: Target the resources needed to support the industries that fit best with your country's advantages.

A strategic trade policy is particularly effective if you're a developing country. Why? Because you've probably already decided that (1) you need to integrate yourself into the global economy and (2) you need to figure out the best way to excel in the international game. If other countries support high-potential start-ups and you don't, your new industries will be disadvantaged.[31] But you need to remember that simply opening up your borders to foreign competition doesn't necessarily mean that domestic producers will have an easier time competing either abroad or at home.

When you do this, foreign competitors may have considerable advantages over homegrown companies you're trying to foster. They've had a head start that's allowed them to develop not only certain efficiencies but cozy relations with everybody in the international distribution channel. Moreover, no matter how promising your targeted industries may be, or how carefully you've tried to match up your industries with your competitive advantages, as a developing country your businesses probably lack the technology and marketing skills they'll need to compete. So, why not help them?[32]

This brings us back to why strategic trade policy is your optimal choice. Your government must protect your local industries—say, by helping them get the skills and technology they'll need. You could also focus your efforts on attracting foreign investment by companies that have the marketing and technical skills you need; that's one good way to bring in the kind of production you need. It also wouldn't hurt to extend incentives within the industries you're counting on.

Want some evidence that strategic trade policy is effective in helping developing nations go global? Look at South

Korea, which not only managed to attract companies with experience in consumer-electronics production but eventually emerged as a global competitor by building on imported technologies and targeting technical education to become both a competitive and technical leader.[33] By the same token, we have ample evidence that laissez-faire often doesn't work in developing countries. In sub-Saharan Africa, for example, government institutions are so deeply rooted that it's almost impossible for anyone—either individuals or multinationals—to make a move without getting entangled in the bureaucratic undergrowth.[34]

Moreover, because no single political institution in developing countries has much in the way of resources, all are better off focusing their collective efforts on specific industries that have some potential for international competitiveness; otherwise, what you have is a bunch of under-resourced agencies and ministries aiming at markets scattered all over the economic landscape.[35]

Should Nations Use Strategic Trade Policies?

Counterpoint

No Of course, countries should try to become most competitive in the industries that promise the best returns and have the most potential for going global. Obviously, they're the ones most likely to add value to the national economy. However, strategic trade policy is not the best way to achieve this goal.

I'll make a concession: Under limited circumstances a targeting program will work, particularly for small countries such as Taiwan. Because Taiwan's GDP amounts to just a little more than the value of Walmart's annual sales, parties involved can manageably work together to reach mutually beneficial agreements with minimal frustration. But in a large economy? Impossible.

However, it's debatable just how much Taiwan's economic success is due to strategic trade policy and how much goes back to conditions that existed before the government began involving itself in foreign trade. During the era of Japanese occupation, Taiwan's infrastructure, literacy, and school attendance improved markedly so that its environment for becoming internationally competitive was well established. Further, when it instituted its import substitution policies, these policies were not really targeting industries to be internationally competitive.

An alternative is for a country to focus on conditions affecting its attractiveness as a competitive location in *general* instead of targeting *specific* industries. In other words, a government can alter conditions affecting, say, factor proportions, efficiency, and innovation by upgrading production factors—cultivating human skills, moving to new levels of infrastructure, encouraging consumers to demand higher-quality products, and promoting an overall competitive environment—for any industry interested in doing business within its borders.

Let's turn to your comments about sub-Saharan Africa. I'll even make another concession: Inefficiency from political bureaucracy is indeed a way of life in much of the area, and there's no reason to expect that it will go away any time soon.[36] But what if we looked at things from another perspective? Rather than trying to focus on a specific industry in, say, the global high-tech universe, wouldn't all these bureaucratic agencies and ministries find it more constructive

Counterpoint

to review (and enforce) their own laws; take steps to stabilize their populations; rectify their most glaring economic, social, and gender inequities; and support entrepreneurial activity in the informal sectors of their economies? Wouldn't they find it more positive to foster an environment of trust—one in which, say, the government helps cut transaction costs so local firms will be willing to work with other companies, domestic and foreign, to acquire a little of the knowledge and a few of the resources they need to compete?[37] Again, instead of picking and haggling over special industries, wouldn't they be better advised to improve the investment environment in which, after all, everybody will ultimately have to operate anyway?

At this point, I might as well take the offensive in this debate. Strategic trade policies typically result in no more than small payoffs—primarily because most governments find difficulty in identifying and targeting the right industries.[38] What if a country targets an industry in which global demand never quite lives up to expectations? That's what happened to the United Kingdom and France when they got together to underwrite supersonic passenger planes. Or what if the domestic companies in a targeted industry simply fall short of being competitive? That's what happened when Thailand decided to support the steel business.[39]

What if too many nations target the same global industries, thereby committing themselves to excessive competition and inadequate returns?[40] What if two countries compete to support the same industry, as happened when both Brazil and Canada decided to produce regional jets in the same hemisphere?[41] Finally, what if a country successfully targets an industry only to find unexpected conditions? Should it stay the course by reacting to various pressures, such as the pressure to support employment in a distressed industry?[42]

Finally, even if a government can identify a future growth industry in which a domestic firm is likely to succeed—a very big if—it doesn't follow that a company deserves public assistance. History recommends that nations permit their entrepreneurs to do what they do best: take risks that don't jeopardize whole sectors of the economy. The upshot will probably be the same as always: Some will fail, but the successful ones will survive and thrive competitively.

Currently, one of the biggest changes underway concerns relative population numbers. Presently, 46 percent of the world's population lives in countries, mainly developed ones, where the fertility rates are below the population replacement rate.[43] These countries are also encountering a higher portion of people at a postretirement age along with a higher portion who are entering the workforce at a later age because of engaging in extended education. This leaves a smaller percentage of residents in their workforces. Further, the aging of the population is expected to require more workers in order to care for illnesses, such as dementia.[44] Even with increases in productivity, these countries will need more immigrants to help provide for their nonemployed populations. Concomitantly, nine countries are expected to account for half of the world's population increase, with India, Pakistan, and Nigeria leading the pack.[45]

These changes, of course, are important in understanding and predicting changes in export production and import market locations. At the same time, the mobility of capital, technology, and people affect trade and relative competitive positions. Here we address the **factor mobility theory**, which focuses on why production factors move, the effects of that movement on transforming factor endowments, and the impact of international factor mobility (especially people) on world trade.

WHY PRODUCTION FACTORS MOVE

Capital and labor move internationally to

- gain more income,
- flee adverse political situations.

Capital

Capital, especially short-term capital, is the most internationally mobile production factor. Companies and private individuals primarily transfer capital because of differences in expected return (accounting for risk) that is caused by their outlooks of economic and political conditions. They find information on interest-rate differences readily available, and they can transfer capital by wire instantaneously at a low cost. Short-term capital is more mobile than long-term capital, such as direct investment, because there are more active markets to buy foreign holdings and sell them if investors want to transfer capital back home or to another country.

At the same time, companies invest abroad for the long term to tap markets, improve quality, and lower operating costs. However, businesses do not make all the international capital movements. Governments give foreign aid and loans. Not-for-profit organizations donate money abroad to relieve worrisome conditions, and individuals remit funds to help their families and friends in foreign countries. Regardless of the donor or motive, the result affects factor endowments.

People

People are less mobile than capital. Some, of course, travel to other countries as tourists, students, and retirees; however, this does not affect factor endowments because these travelers do not work in the destination countries. Unlike funds that can be cheaply transferred by wire, people usually must incur high transportation costs to work abroad. Also, if they move legally, they must get immigration papers, which most countries provide sparingly. Finally, they may have to learn another language and adjust to a different culture away from their customary support groups. Despite such barriers, people do endure hardships and risks to move to other countries.

Migration was the major engine of globalization during the late nineteenth and early twentieth centuries, and at present it is important again. About 3.3 percent of the world's population (about 244 million people) has migrated to another country. Because this movement is spread unevenly, the percentage is much greater in some countries than in others (e.g., 27 percent of the population in Australia and less than 1 percent in Mexico).[46]

Of the people who go abroad to work, some move permanently, some temporarily. On the one hand, some people immigrate to another country, become citizens, and plan to reside there for the rest of their lives. On the other hand, some enter a country on temporary work permits, usually for short periods. For instance, most workers in the United Arab Emirates are there on temporary work permits.[47] In addition, MNEs may assign employees to work abroad for periods ranging from a few days to several years (usually to a place where they also transfer capital). In many cases, workers leave their families behind in the hopes of returning home after saving enough money while working in the foreign country. Some move legally, others illegally (undocumented)—that is to say they lack government permission to enter or work.

Motives   People move to another country largely for economic reasons, such as Indonesian laborers working in Malaysia to earn more than at home. People also move for political reasons—for example, because of persecution or war dangers, in which case they are known as refugees and usually become part of the labor pool where they live. It is not surprising that most refugees emanate from war-torn countries—recently many from Syria, Afghanistan, South Sudan, The Democratic Republic of the Congo—and mainly go to nearby countries. Recently, the largest recipients have been Turkey, Pakistan, and Iran.[48] In addition, there are about 10 million people who have no citizenship, most of whom are seeking some country to give them rights as citizens.[49]

Sometimes it is difficult to distinguish between economic and political motives for international mobility because poor economic conditions often parallel poor political conditions. In recent years, hundreds of thousands of Syrians fled the civil war in their country; however, the fact that many have returned after not finding work may indicate that their motive was economic.

EFFECTS OF FACTOR MOVEMENTS

| Factor movements alter factor endowments.

Neither international capital nor population mobility is a new occurrence. For example, had it not been for historical mass immigration, Australia, Canada, and the United States would have greatly reduced populations today. Further, many immigrants brought human capital with them, thus adding to the base of skills that enabled those countries to be newly competitive in an array of products they might otherwise have imported. Finally, these same countries received foreign capital to develop infrastructure and natural resources, which further altered their competitive structures and international trade.

What Happens When People Move?   Recent evidence is largely anecdotal. Nevertheless, we have indicated that immigration is substantial for many countries and insignificant for others.[50]

The United States is currently an example of a country whose recent immigration is largely concentrated at the high and low ends of human skills. Over a third of all people with doctoral degrees in the United States are foreign-born. At the other extreme, much recent U.S. immigration has been made up of low-skilled workers. At both extremes, the United States has had shortages of native-born workers, which has been partially alleviated through immigration.

A controversial issue is the effect of outward migration on countries. On the one hand, countries lose potentially productive resources when educated people leave—a situation known as a **brain drain**. On the other hand, many of these people are now sending remittances back. For example, remittances account for 29 percent of Nepal's GDP.[51]

There is also evidence that the outward movement and remittances of people leads to an increase in start-up companies and capital in their home countries. Further, the emigrants learn abroad, transfer ideas back home, use remitted capital to start businesses in their native lands, and export to companies with which they have developed connections abroad.[52]

Finally, countries receiving productive human resources also incur costs by providing social services and acculturating people to a new language and society. Thus, on the one hand there is an employment need for the immigrants; on the other hand, there have been backlashes concerning the costs and the possible infiltration of terrorists. The unskilled workers who take jobs native-born workers don't want—dishwashing, maintaining grounds, picking agricultural produce—often have children who eventually enter the workforce. If these children are also unskilled, the country is perpetuating a long-term class of "have-nots." If the children attain skills, then there is a need to bring in even more unskilled workers from abroad.

THE RELATIONSHIP BETWEEN TRADE AND FACTOR MOBILITY

Factor movement is an alternative to trade that may or may not be a more efficient use of resources.[53] Let's see how international factor mobility can affect trade.

SUBSTITUTION

There are pressures for the most abundant factors to move to areas of scarcity.

When the factor proportions vary widely among countries, pressures exist for the most abundant factors to move to countries with greater scarcity, where they can command a better return. If permitted, many in the labor pool where workers are unemployed or poorly paid, go to countries that have full employment and higher wages. They receive higher wages not only because of the greater scarcity, but also because more capital-rich countries have invested in machinery and infrastructure that make the imported laborers more productive than in their home countries.

Of course, as we discussed in the section on factor endowment theory, the ratio of land (an immobile factor) to people also influences the movement of labor. Russia has a low population density and the most unfarmed arable land of any country. Next door is China with the highest population and little available unfarmed land. About 400,000 Chinese are now working on Russian farms, and much of the output is shipped to China.[54]

Similarly, capital tends to move away from countries in which it is abundant to those in which it is scarce (e.g., Mexico getting capital from the United States, which gets labor from Mexico).[55] If finished goods and production factors were both free to move internationally, the comparative costs of transferring goods versus factors would determine production location. Let's look at a hypothetical example of supplying the United States with tomatoes. Because U.S. labor to cultivate and pick tomatoes is costly, U.S. capital might move to Mexico to set up tomato production, which is then exported to the United States. Or Mexican labor might move to the United States to work in tomato production. The comparative cost of moving either workers or tomatoes will determine whether trade or factor mobility is used to minimize costs.

In some cases, the inability to gain sufficient access to foreign production factors may stimulate efficient methods of substitution, such as the development of alternatives for traditional production methods.[56] For example, at one time U.S. tomato growers in California depended almost entirely on Mexican temporary workers under what was known as the *bracero program*. Since the termination of this program, the California tomato harvests have quadrupled, while mechanization has replaced 72 percent of the number of workers.

However, not all harvesting jobs can reasonably be mechanized at present. Because cantaloupes ripen at different times, pickers go through a cantaloupe field about 10 times. A robot would have to be able to distinguish colors so as to leave green cantaloupes behind.[57] However, advancement of robots using cameras that distinguish ripeness foretell the diminished need for future agricultural laborers.[58] At the same time, many other jobs that defy mechanization—such as bussing tables at restaurants and changing beds in hotels—are largely filled by unskilled immigrants in developed countries.

COMPLEMENTARITY

Factor mobility through foreign investment often stimulates trade because of

- the need for components,
- the parent company's ability to sell complementary products,
- the need for equipment for subsidiaries.

In our tomato example for the United States and Mexico, we showed that factor movements may substitute for or stimulate trade. Companies' investments abroad often stimulate exports from their home countries. In fact, MNEs account for 80 percent of global exports, such as among their parents and subsidiaries or to independent companies.[59]

Many of the exports would not occur without foreign investments, partly because a company may export equipment as part of its foreign investment. Or, domestic operating units may export materials and components to their foreign facilities for use in a finished product, such as Coca-Cola's exports of concentrate to its bottling facilities abroad. Finally, a company's foreign facility may produce part of the product line while serving as sales agent for exports of its parent's other products.

Finally, immigration enhances trade by creating ethnic enclaves of networks that link immigrants with their native countries. The enclaves serve as niche markets for imports from their native countries (e.g., early U.S. soy sauce imports sold mainly to Asian-Americans). The ethnic networks also embody product and country-specific knowledge that aids in exporting to immigrants' birth-countries. This is more important when a network is from a low-trust culture, especially one that also values family ties strongly. Most people from such a culture have more trust for people they know better, which leads them first to prefer business within the family, next with close friends, etc. Conducting business with people from another country is well down the list of trusted people. But the ethnic network offers an alternative, allowing people from low-trust cultures to deal abroad with others whose language and responses are similar to their home-country experiences. Without this network, they need more time to overcome the perceived risk brought about by lack of knowledge and low trust of potential business partners. Thus potential importers and exporters are more willing to trade when they are part of the ethnic network.[60]

CONCEPT CHECK

In Chapter 2 (page 85), we emphasized societal differences in trust along with strength in family ties, especially as it affects trust. We also discussed that higher trust reduces the cost of business transactions.

Looking to the Future
Scenarios That May Change Trade Patterns

When countries have few restrictions on foreign trade and factor mobility, companies have greater latitude in reducing operating costs. For example, fewer trade restrictions give them opportunities to gain economies of scale by servicing markets in more than one country from a single base of production. Fewer factor movement restrictions allow them to combine factors for more efficient production. However, government trade and immigration restrictions vary among countries, over time, and under different circumstances.

Nevertheless, it's probably safe to say that trade restrictions have been diminishing, primarily because of the economic gains that countries foresee through freer trade. Further, restrictions on the movement of capital and technology have become freer, but whether restrictions on the movement of people are freer is questionable.

There are uncertainties as to whether the trend toward the freer movement of trade and production factors will continue. Groups worldwide question whether the economic benefits of more open economies outweigh some of the costs, both economic and noneconomic. Although the next chapter discusses government influence on trade in detail, it is useful at this point to understand the overall evolution of protectionist sentiment.

One key issue is the trade between developed and developing economies. As trade barriers are being lowered, some developing economies with very low wage rates are growing economically more rapidly than developed countries. Concomitantly, as companies shift production to developing economies, they displace jobs at home. These displaced workers need to find new jobs. But it is uncertain how quickly new jobs will replace old ones and how much developed countries will tolerate employment displacement and job shifts. If they become intolerant, they may enact protectionist measures that would stifle trade.

Another key issue is the future of factor endowments. If present trends continue, relationships among land, labor, and capital will continue to evolve. For example, the population growth rate is expected to be much higher in developing economies than in developed ones, which could result in continued shifts of labor-intensive production to developing economies and pressures on the developed countries to accept more immigrants.

Urbanization will likely grow faster in developing than in developed countries, which are already heavily urbanized. Considerable evidence indicates that productivity rises with urbanization because firms can more likely find people with the exact skills they need, because there are economies in moving supplies and finished products, and because knowledge flows more easily from one company and industry to another. Thus we might expect higher growth in some developing countries due to their pace of urbanization. Such growth should also help them account for a larger share of world trade.

At the same time, on the one hand the finite supply of natural resources may lead to price increases for these resources, even though oversupplies have often depressed prices. The limited supply may work to the advantage of developing economies because their supplies have been less fully exploited. On the other hand, technology to find and extract natural resources, such as fracking to secure natural gas from shale, may shift supply locations and lessen price rises.

We will probably see the continued trend toward a more finely tuned specialization of production among countries to take advantage of specific conditions. Although part of this will be due to wage and skill differences, other factors are important as well. For instance, country differences in property right protection may influence businesses to locate more of their technologically intensive activities within countries that offer more protection. Or they may disperse portions of production to different countries in order to hinder potential competitors from gaining the full picture needed to pirate their products and processes.

Four interrelated factors are worth monitoring because they could cause product trade to become relatively less significant in the future:

1. As economies grow, efficiencies of multiple production locations also grow because they can all gain sufficient economies of scale. This may allow country-by-country production to replace trade in many cases. For example, most automobile producers have moved into China and Thailand—or plan to do so—as a result of those countries' growing market size.

2. Flexible, small-scale production methods, especially those using robotics and digital technologies, may enable even small countries to produce many goods efficiently for their own consumption, thus eliminating the need to import them. For example, before the development of efficient mini-mills that can produce steel on a small scale, steel production took larger capital outlays that needed enormous markets. Similarly, consumers' demand for evermore differentiated products largely negates the cost advantages of long production runs, thus making smaller scale manufacturing close to markets more advantageous.[61]

3. Output from and research on 3-D printers are increasing expeditiously. We already see production of such final products as medical implants, jewelry, lampshades, car parts, and mobile phones. Now there is research using 3-D printers for making molds, tools, and dyes. There have been notable breakthroughs, such as the printing of a footbridge, prefabricated sections of buildings, and the replica of an automobile.[62] As this technology develops, products can be fabricated efficiently where they are used rather than traded from one country to another. However, there will still be a need to trade production-grade materials as inputs to the printers.

4. Services are growing more rapidly than products as a global portion of production and consumption. Part of this change involves technology, such as substituting digitalized products like music and reading material for traditionally manufactured products. Thus, one buys the right to copy (a service sale) from anywhere in the world with no need to ship products. Consequently, product trade may become a less important part of countries' total trade. ■

CASE
LUKOIL: Foreign Trade and Investment

To keep an economy growing, we also have to keep putting oil into energy expansion. A major oil and energy player is LUKOIL, which with 2012 sales of $139 billion, produces and distributes a wide range of petroleum and energy products such as gasoline, heating oil, crude petroleum, jet fuel, lubricants, natural gas, and petrochemicals. It is listed in both Fortune's and Forbes' world's 100 largest companies; in the former by sales, and the latter by valuation. It is not only Russia's second largest company, but also its largest privately-owned company. Many of the world's largest oil companies are government-owned, such as in Saudi Arabia, Iran, and Venezuela. Among privately owned oil firms, LUKOIL is the world's fourth largest, accounting for 17 percent of Russian crude oil production and refining.

The Russian Economy

LUKOIL's position is inexorably tied to conditions in Russia. Before the knocking down of the Berlin Wall in 1989 and the collapse of the Soviet Union, the Russian oil industry was government owned within a command economy. In addition, the Soviet Union followed an inward-looking economic policy that depended minimally on foreign trade. In fact, a government monopoly handled all foreign trade and did not always relate prices to production costs. Russia privatized most industries in the 1990s; however, it has only partially privatized the energy sector because of its essentiality to national well-being.

Russia faced abundant economic problems during most of the 1990s when it was transitioning to a market economy. Among other factors, many newly privatized companies lacked sufficient management and marketing skills, especially for selling abroad. However, during the 10-year period from 1999 to 2008, Russia enjoyed significant GDP growth, led by the export of commodities. During this period, Russia became the world's largest natural gas and second largest oil exporter. The Russian economy was one of the hardest hit by the global economic crisis that began in 2008. Its GDP fell 8 percent in 2009, but it has since recovered largely due to high oil prices, in 2010, and grew 4 percent. Russia's oil and gas sector accounts for about 25 percent of its GDP and a third of all its exports. Russia consumes about 55 percent of its oil production and exports the rest. On the downside, its dependence on petroleum exports makes Russia vulnerable to fluctuations in global petroleum markets, such as that caused by the 2009 economic downturn when global demand and prices for energy plummeted.

Further, when the yearly average price per barrel of oil shifts by as much as $1, Russian revenues shift by about $2 billion in the same direction.

In recent years, Russia has discovered so much oil that the country now has the world's eighth highest level of proven reserves. In addition, Russia also controls petroleum exports from the former Central Asian Soviet republics of Azerbaijan and Kazakhstan, both of which, like Russia itself, are oil rich. Although some oil producing countries, especially members of the Organization of Petroleum Exporting Countries (OPEC), cut back production to maintain higher prices, Russia, which is not an OPEC member, is content to sell all the oil it can produce. This helps to explain the disparity between Russia's rank in exports versus proven reserves. However, its prices depend, of course, on the world petroleum prices. Because of fierce competition in the global oil industry, even control of such vast supplies is no guarantee that Russia can sell its output at an acceptable margin. In addition,

Russia depends on oil exports to pay for imports, primarily machinery needed to sustain the present pace of economic development. In recent years, more than half of Russian imports have been of machinery and transportation equipment, which is a top priority for the Russian government for three primary reasons:

1. At a purchasing price parity of $15,900 in 2010, Russian GDP per capita is still well below that of any other G8 country.

▲ Oil and gas industry, Russia.

Source: George Spade. Shutterstock

2. The oil sector—which is a capital- rather than labor-intensive industry—employs less than 1 percent of the country's population.
3. Natural disasters, such as the 2010 drought and fires, wreak havoc directly on the agricultural sector and indirectly on other economic sectors.

A Little History of LUKOIL

LUKOIL was formed in 1991 as a government-owned enterprise through a merger of three state-run companies in Siberia. LUK is an acronym for the names of the home cities of the three preexisting companies. At the time, the former Soviet deputy minister of oil production, Vagit Alekperov, believed the only way Russian oil companies could successfully compete against Western companies would be to vertically integrate the three main components of their business—exploration, refining, and distribution. In the old Soviet system, these components were strictly separate.

After its founding, LUKOIL moved quickly to establish this integration. In 1993, the government approved LUKOIL's privatization plan, and a little more than 9 percent of the ownership went private, mainly by giving shares to its employees. The following year LUKOIL sold its first private shares through an auction, which reduced government ownership to 80.59 percent. Government ownership fell to 33 percent by 1996, 20 percent by 2000, and finally to 0 in 2004 when ConocoPhillips bought the last 7.59 percent of the company from the government. In the interim, LUKOIL began selling shares (depository receipts) over the counter in New York and through several German exchanges in 1996. In 2002, LUKOIL became the first Russian company listed on the London Stock Exchange. The decrease in government ownership occurred partially by selling government shares and partially by issuing additional shares that diluted the government's ownership. Subsequent to being fully privatized, ConocoPhillips upped its ownership to 20 percent, but in 2011, it withdrew fully from LUKOIL by selling all its shares on the open market.

Although the Russian government is no longer a shareholder, it maintains close ties with LUKOIL because of its significance to the Russian economy—LUKOIL controls about 19 percent of all Russian production and refining—and its political importance as a symbol of Russian prestige in foreign markets. An illustration of the latter was President Vladimir Putin's attendance to open a LUKOIL filling station in New York City.

LUKOIL began its first foreign project in 1994, when it took a stake in an Azerbaijan oilfield. It has since expanded so that it now does business in 37 foreign countries through a combination of exploration (10 countries), refining (5 countries), and distribution/transshipment (27 countries). Note that most of these countries are close to Russia.

As of 2015, LUKOIL host a diversified distribution network and has 5,556 filling stations worldwide across 22 countries.

One of the locations farthest away from Russia is the United States, where the company's expansion has occurred mainly through acquisitions of Getty Petroleum in 2000 and of a string of gasoline stations owned by ConocoPhillips in 2004. Despite, LUKOIL's foray into international business, it depends mainly on the Russian market for its sales and oil reserves.

LUKOIL sells its petroleum products on the retail market. In this respect, in 2015 the total retail sales of petroleum products made 19.4 million tons, which is a 3.1% decline vs. 2014. The decline is conditioned by a reduction in purchasing power and the decrease in the number of gas stations as part of optimizing the marketing assets that are not integrated into the common business model.

Why Export?

As we've already seen, Russia and LUKOIL have a lot of oil reserves. When countries or companies have an abundant storable commodity, which is not easily spoiled, a number of factors may influence the quantity they try to sell in the short term, especially to export markets. One is the expectation of future prices compared with present ones (i.e., if future prices are expected to be higher than the net present value of investment earnings from immediate sale), one may be better off by limiting current sales. However, in the case of oil exports, projecting future prices is particularly problematic because they depend so much on derived demand, which in turn depends on uncertainties about industrial output, climatic and natural disaster conditions (Think, for example, of the future uncertainty of energy sources brought about by concern after a 2011 tsunami damaged a Japanese nuclear facility), and technological changes (for example, think that the United States displaced Russia as the largest oil and gas producer in 2013 because of innovations in fracking technology). Likewise, prices depend on competition, and competitors never know what other producing countries and companies will do.

At any rate, we have discussed reasons for the Russian policy of expanding current export oil sales, thus the decision is a "given" from the country standpoint. We should point out that, since the beginning of the twenty-first century, the global price of oil has fluctuated substantially even though there has been a trend toward higher prices. For instance the average monthly prices in 2008 were 42 percent higher than in 2007. Then they fell 41.5 percent in 2009. (If the highs and lows within particular years are compared rather than the yearly averages, the fluctuations are even greater.) Some of the factors influencing both price changes and price trends have been uncertainty following 9/11, Chinese economic expansion, production cutbacks by OPEC, unsettlement in and trade embargoes with various oil-producing countries (e.g., Libya, Venezuela, and Iran), seasonal abnormal temperatures, and the global economic crisis that began in 2008. Nevertheless, Russia's export position has been generally quite good throughout the twenty-first century's first decade, with favorable balances of trade each year that have helped to pay for both imports and a high level of external credit.

Although the foregoing deals with Russia's desire to export, what about LUKOIL's? Despite a growing domestic market, Russian demand is insufficient to absorb all of LUKOIL's capacity. Overall, it has been able to sell more oil at higher prices outside Russia than it could just a few years previously. Further, if LUKOIL were to curtail exporting, it might incur a political backlash of the Russian government as a result of economic policies deemed favorable for the entire economy.

In addition to its increase in sales through exporting, the practice has enabled LUKOIL to amass a substantial store of capital that it has been able to channel into foreign investment.

Why LUKOIL Went the Foreign Investment Route

LUKOIL's management has long seen foreign expansion as a means both of earning bigger margins and of ensuring more reliable, full, on-time payment than it can get in Russia. The question, however, still remains: Why doesn't LUKOIL simply export rather than risk foreign investment? The answer lies in a combination of factors.

Fluctuating World Markets

We have discussed how supply and demand changes have influenced prices, but they also affect the ability to sell. In the late 1990s, when a global oil glut impaired foreign sales, LUKOIL decided to emulate its larger Western competitors through a strategy of forward integration into the ownership of foreign distribution outlets. (Nevertheless, its plan for the 2012–2021 period is for over 80 percent of investment to be spent on exploration and production.) LUKOIL made its first foreign distribution investments not far from home in former Soviet satellite countries by buying longtime retail customers in Bulgaria and Romania that were state-owned operations being privatized.

Since then, LUKOIL has ventured farther afield, almost exclusively by means of purchasing existing operations. It's a sound strategy. When oil producers invest in distribution, they strengthen their ties to markets where they may be better able to sell crude oil in times of global oversupply. Moreover, integrating into distribution can potentially reduce operating costs, primarily because a producer doesn't have to rely on negotiating and enforcing a network of agreements by which it sells oil to intermediaries in other countries. Further, this vertical integration enables LUKOIL to smooth its profits by operating in the ever-changing portion going to production versus distribution.

Concomitantly, LUKOIL has rebranded its acquisitions to gain uniformity in its image, which also helps to promote sales better.

Political Uncertainty

LUKOIL has been well aware of the fact that export sales are always subject to political disruptions. What if an importing country decides to reduce its purchases of Russian oil to protest some internal Russian political policy (or simply to diversify its own supply sources)? In turn, this risk has been a factor in LUKOIL's decision to expand into exploration and refining outside

Russia. Or consider another problem that's more or less unique to LUKOIL's situation. As it turns out, the Russian government owns the pipeline system through which virtually all Russian oil exports must pass, allocating access to the system by means of quotas among domestic oil companies. What if a competitor manages to gain sufficient influence with certain political decision makers to siphon off part of LUKOIL's quota? Further, LUKOIL can never forget that, although it has itself been almost completely privatized, the Russian government still owns some of its domestic competitors and has often given its own firms preferential treatment in various matters. That is just one reason why LUKOIL is trying to increase foreign oil supplies to 20 percent of its total. However, moving internationally creates other political risks, such as ownership of assets in volatile environments, such as Egypt and Venezuela. International sanctions caused LUKOIL to cease operating in Iraq when Saddam Hussein was in power, but it has since returned. Some U.S. Congressmen have made scathing attacks against LUKOIL because some oil it shipped to China was then shipped to Iran despite a contract clause saying "not for supplies to the territory of Iran."

Efficiency Imperatives

To be a major global competitor, LUKOIL must become as efficient as its major Western competitors. Toward that end, it must not only achieve operating efficiencies but also acquire state-of-the-industry technology and marketing skills. For instance, it must adhere to ever-changing national product requirements, such as on gasoline octane and cleanliness. In the past, LUKOIL's administrative expenses and cost of capital were high compared with those of Western competitors. At home, such inefficiencies resulted in only minor problems because the competition consisted solely of other Russian oil companies hampered by the same operational inefficiencies inherited from the former state-owned oil monopoly. Even in Russia, however, new competitive threats are starting to emerge as Western oil firms have bought interests in Russian oil companies.

LUKOIL, however, sees foreign oil companies as something more than stiffer domestic competition: They're also potentially valuable sources of the technology and knowledge that it needs to compete not only at home but abroad as well. With this strategy in mind, it has placed independent directors from Western oil companies on its board, used

ConocoPhillips's management expertise when it owned 20 percent of the company, and has established several partnerships abroad, such as with Norway's Statoil. Meanwhile, foreign acquisitions, such as Getty in the United States, present another source of experienced personnel, technology, and competitive know-how. ■

QUESTIONS

5-3. What theories of trade help explain Russia's position as an oil exporter? Why? Which ones don't? Why not?

5-4. How do global political and economic conditions affect global oil markets and prices?

5-5. Discuss the following statement as it applies to Russia and LUKOIL: Regardless of the advantages a country may gain by trading, international trade will begin only if companies within that country have competitive advantages that enable them to be viable traders—and they must foresee profits in exporting and importing.

5-6. In LUKOIL's situation, what is the relationship between factor mobility and exports?

MyLab Management

Go to **mymanagementlab.com** for the following Assisted-graded writing questions:

5-7 Why do you think LUKOIL's first foreign direct investments were in countries nearby to Russia (e.g. former Soviet republics and satellite countries)?

5-8 Discuss each of the trade theories that help explain LUKOIL's competitive position in exporting oil.

Endnotes

Scan for Endnotes or go to www.pearsonglobaleditions.com/Daniels

CHAPTER 6
Trade Protectionism

OBJECTIVES

After studying this chapter, you should be able to

6-1 Recognize the conflicting outcomes of trade protectionism

6-2 Assess governments' economic rationales and outcome uncertainties with international trade intervention

6-3 Assess governments' noneconomic rationales and outcome uncertainties with international trade intervention

6-4 Describe the major instruments of trade control

6-5 Classify how companies deal with governmental trade influences

MyLab **Management**®
Improve Your Performance!
When you see this icon ✪, visit
www.mymanagementlab.com for
activities that are applied, personalized,
and offer immediate feedback.

Charity begins at home.

—***English proverb***

Mining work in Chile ▶

Source: FXEGS Javier Espuny. Shutterstock

CASE

The Case of REEs: Trade Disputes and Protectionist Measures for Strategic Materials[1]

—Stefania Paladini

China's rapid rise as a political and economic power has caught the attention of many countries across the world, especially with regard to natural resources. Rare earth elements (REEs), important strategic materials for many countries in terms of production of advanced technologies globally, are almost exclusively mined by Chinese firms due to the low costs of production there. As it has a large REE mining industry, both state-owned and private, the Chinese government has a massive political and economic influence in the REE market.

The REEs are the 17 elements scandium, yttrium, and the 15 elements in the lanthanide series. The term REE comes from the fact that these elements have only been discovered quite recently, the first one at the end of 18th century in Sweden, the other blocks in the course of the 19th century. In addition, the extraction is usually complicated, expensive, and often environmentally taxing because of their low concentration in the minerals that contain them. The use and relative importance of REEs has been increasing due to the special properties that characterize them; they are essential components in magnets and indispensable for hybrid vehicles, computer screens, smart phones, and turbines for wind farms.

THE CHINESE MARKET DOMINANCE AND PROTECTIONISM

The recent case of the REEs is in many ways emblematic of the way protectionist measures can lead to disputes (and in extreme cases may even result in trade wars), and offers an example of the recourses that states can expect from the World Trade Organization (WTO).

Mostly unknown to a majority of the world, REEs suddenly came into the spotlight when, in 2009, the world industry realized that 97 percent of the production was primarily in China, creating a situation of virtual monopoly. From 2005, China had started imposing an export quota to maintain a substantial part of the product in the domestic market, causing a spike in the spot and future prices of the minerals. These economic policies imposed by the Chinese government, restricting trade between it and other countries to promote domestically produced goods, are indicators of China's protectionism. The forms of protectionism include exchange rate controls, tariffs, direct subsidies, and administrative barriers of various kinds.

The reasons for China's quotas are generally two-fold. The first is linked to economic reasons. China's industries require huge amounts of raw materials that generally they are forced to import, with the exceptions of a few, like rare earths, which, however, need to be secured for domestic producers, especially now that the extraction is concentrated in China. The second reason is the high environmental costs involved in the extraction of REEs, which China has become sensitive to in the last decade. The quotas have had the effect of a sharp rise in prices, which had previously fallen in the 1990s as a result of the overproduction in China. Therefore, they represent an environmental tax that China imposes on the rest of the world.

TRADE DISPUTE SETTLEMENT: THE OPPOSITION

China's approach to the exports of REEs caused concern in the global market. It's attempt to acquire the Mountain Pass mine in California, which had been at the center of REE world production before China, and the Australian Lynas Corporation, reflected a need for regulated trade at a global level. In 2012, Japan, the United States, and the European Union (EU) filed a complaint to the WTO Dispute Settlement Board (DSB), stating that free trade was being undermined by the imposition of such regulations. In 2015, after the DSB examined the issue, China lost the case and had to remove the export quotas. The procedure that had been followed for this REE case is an example of how trade disputes are often tackled.

Various countries—like Brazil, Canada, India, Korea, Norway, and Australia—registered as co-complainants, while the United States, the EU, and Japan requested and obtained from the WTO the right to constitute an inquiring panel. It was found that tungsten and molybdenum—two other raw materials not listed as part of the REE 17—were also under the restriction. While China did lift the restrictions, the government did not lift similar export quotas and duties that applied to materials like tungsten and molybdenum. The WTO stated that China's sovereign rights pertaining to its natural resources do not give it the right to control global markets or the distribution of raw materials. The investigating panel was given time to issue its final report by November 2013, in accordance with the timetable adopted after consultations with all the countries that had filed their interest in this case.

In March 2014, the panel issued a report presenting its conclusions and recognizing the allegations as valid. Regarding the trade quotas and restrictions, the WTO decided that that China's export quotas were not designed to preserve China's natural resources and environment, but there were directed instead to meet precise industrial policy goals. As a result, the restrictive measures were removed.

In a 2015 paper by Schlinkert and Boogaart, an economic model was proposed to explain China's behavior as an REE supplier. According to the model, how the world REE market develops can be divided into four stages

1. **Market penetration.** Due to lower costs of production, China enters the REE market.

2. **Market exploitation.** China enjoys monopoly status and restricts the export of REEs in order to maximize profit and gain political influence.

MAP 6.1 The People's Republic of China (PRC)

The People's Republic of China has a large REE mining industry that incur low costs of production, the Chinese government has a massive political and economic influence in the REE market.

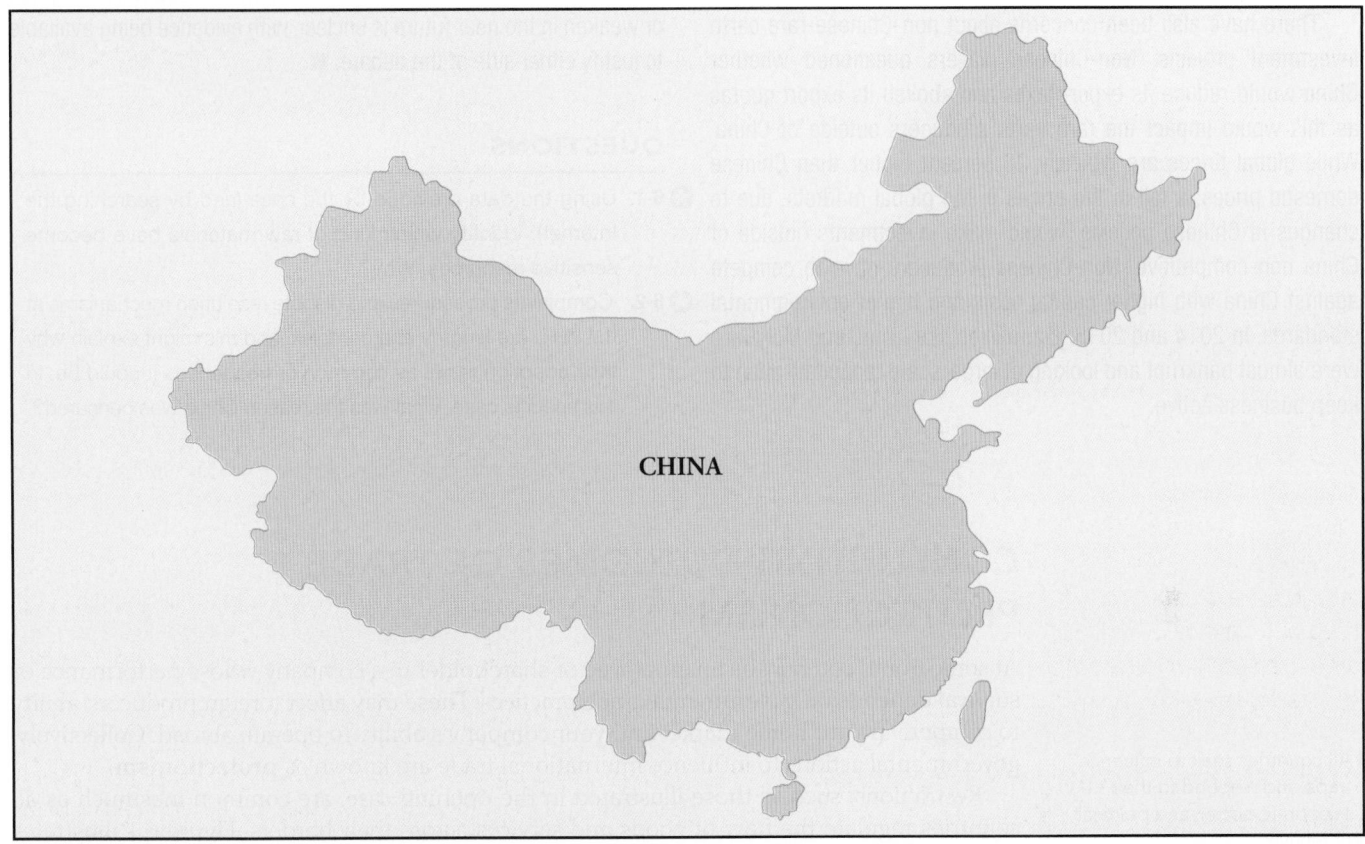

3. **Declining market.** China begins to lose its monopoly as production costs increase and foreign mining operations restart.

4. **Moving from monopoly to oligopoly.** With external competitors increasing their share in the industry, Chinese producers and global producers reach a state of equilibrium.

GLOBAL REE SUPPLY AND OTHER ALTERNATIVES

While many did state that China created a monopoly by increasing export prices, some experts felt that the bubble created by the high prices made it economically possible for global business like the Mountain Pass mine and Lynas Corporation to invest in the production of other rare earth mines. In 2011, Lynas commenced its production activities at its rare earth mine in Mount Weld. It also has a refining facility built in Malaysia where it processes REE products. In 2015, Mountain Pass began full production.

China's trade quotas also forced foreign companies and governments to consider other options to ease the supply tension. Alternative options, while they require a significant investment, do exist. Created as byproducts of various mining activities, REEs are often present in other countries, but are rarely used. Potential sources of REEs, while not very economical, include sifting through

the fly ash residue from the production of minerals like alumina and zirconium.

Kazakhstan, the leader of global uranium production, is considering entering the REE market as both heavy and light elements are commonly found in uranium mines. In 2012, Japanese corporation Sumitomo invested in Kazatomprom, a state-owned nuclear company in Kazakhstan, and laid plans to create a factory with a production capacity of 1,500 tons of rare earth oxides per year.

Another alternative has been found in recycling REEs from discarded consumer goods and hardware. Countries like Japan, Europe, and the United States are researching this area.

THE FUTURE

The immediate concern for China was the environmental impact of REE mining in the country and that the alternatives created a declining global demand for China's REE, which hurt job prospects in domestic markets.

We should, however, understand that China's behavior is not in isolation. Its market is not the first to have had a near monopoly on strategic materials and definitely not the first (or last) to have considered using it to its advantage. This economic outlook also indicates that protectionism may lead to trade retaliation, which in turn would raise prices, detrimentally affect living standards, leave business in a worsened fiscal position, and counteract the effects of any positive initiatives that may have been taken for domestic and global growth.

There have also been concerns about non-Chinese rare earth investment projects. Non-Chinese players questioned whether China would reduce its export taxes and abolish its export quotas as this would impact the rare earth producers outside of China. While global prices are typically 20 percent higher than Chinese domestic prices, a fall in the prices in the global markets, due to changes in Chinese policies, would make investments outside of China non-competitive. Non-Chinese producers have to compete against China with higher capital costs and higher environmental standards. In 2014 and 2015, companies like Lynas and MolyCorp were almost bankrupt and looking at large-scale recapitalization to keep business active.

The technological importance of rare earth elements and China's near monopoly makes the REE industry full of political and economic uncertainty. Whether the country's monopoly on REEs will strengthen or weaken in the near future is unclear, with evidence being available to justify either side of the debate. ∎

QUESTIONS

⭐ **6-1.** Using the data provided by the case (and by searching the Internet), identify which kind of raw materials have become sensitive resources. Why?

⭐ **6-2.** Complaints procedures and dispute resolution mechanisms at the WTO are lengthy and complex, and this might explain why their adoption is not as common or frequent as it could be. In this specific case, what was the reason China was censured?

CONFLICTING OUTCOMES OF TRADE PROTECTIONISM

> All countries seek to influence trade and respond to their economic, social, and political objectives.

CONCEPT CHECK

Chapter 5 (pages 180–182) demonstrates how specialization and free trade can increase output, but here we point out that protectionist policies, although sometimes warranted, can lead to conflicting outcomes.

At some point, you may be an employee or shareholder in a company whose performance or survival depends on governmental trade practices. These may affect foreign producers' ability to compete in your home market and your company's ability to operate abroad. Collectively, governmental actions to influence international trade are known as **protectionism**.

Restrictions, such as those illustrated in the opening case, are common inasmuch as all countries regulate the flow of goods and services across their borders. Figure 6.1 illustrates the institutions that pressure governments to regulate trade and the subsequent effect on business competitiveness. This chapter reviews the economic and noneconomic rationales for trade protectionism, the major forms of trade controls, and trade control's effects on companies' operating decisions.

Despite free-trade benefits, governments intervene in trade to attain economic, social, or political objectives. Officials enact trade policies that they reason will have the best chance to benefit their nation and its citizens—and, in some cases, their personal political longevity. Their decisions are complicated because outcomes are uncertain and affect groups of their citizens differently.

FIGURE 6.1   Institutional Factors Affecting the Flow of Goods and Service

In response to a variety of institutional factors (i.e., cultural, political/legal, and economic), governments enact measures designed to either enhance or restrict international trade flows. These measures invariably affect the competitive environment in which companies operate internationally. To an extent, of course, the converse is also true: Companies influence government trade policies that affect their institutions.

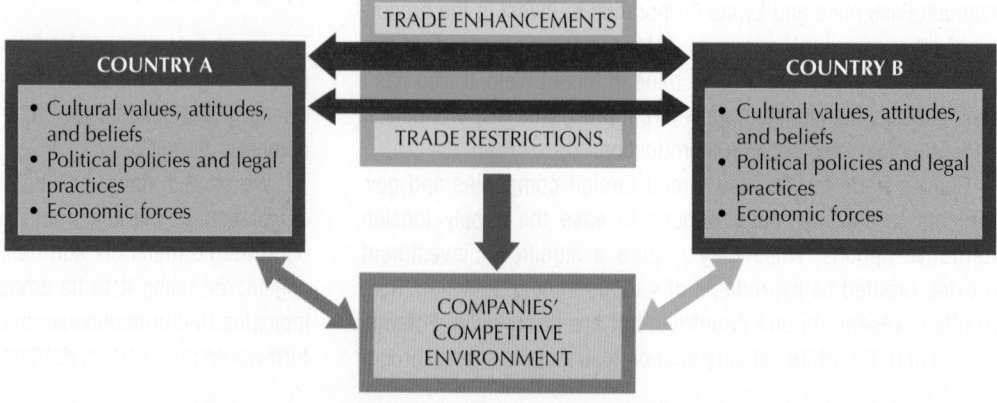

THE ROLE OF STAKEHOLDERS

Those stakeholders most affected by trade regulations push hardest for trade rules favorable to them.

Proposals on trade regulations often spark fierce debate among people who believe they will be affected—the so-called *stakeholders.* Of course, those most directly affected are most apt to speak out, such as workers, owners, suppliers, and local politicians whose livelihoods depend on the actions taken. Displaced workers may see themselves as unemployed for the long term or forced to take new jobs in new industries, perhaps even in new towns at lower wages. People threatened in this way tend to voice their views often and loudly.

In contrast, consumer stakeholders typically buy the best product they can find for the lowest price, often without knowing or caring about its origin. They frequently don't realize how much retail prices rise in aggregate because of import restrictions. Nor do they take much notice, since the retail price rises are typically spread out among many people over time and entail a small increase for individual purchases. For example, even if U.S. consumers realized that import restrictions cause them to pay more for catfish at restaurants and supermarkets, they would not likely band together to lobby for removal of the restrictions. In effect, their potential gains would be too low in comparison with their efforts.

ECONOMIC RATIONALES FOR GOVERNMENTAL TRADE INTERVENTION AND OUTCOME UNCERTAINTIES

Governments intervene in international trade for either economic or noneconomic reasons, as shown in Table 6.1. Let's begin by analyzing some leading *economic rationales.*

FIGHTING UNEMPLOYMENT

The unemployed can form an effective pressure group for import restrictions.

Probably no pressure group is more effective than the unemployed; no other group has more time and incentive to protest publicly and contact government representatives. Import-displaced workers are often the least able to find alternative work, especially if large numbers are concentrated in small company towns where there are virtually few alternative employment opportunities.[2] When they do, they generally earn less than before.[3] Moreover, they often need to spend their unemployment benefits to survive in the short term, and they put off retraining because they hope to be recalled to their old jobs. Further, many workers, especially older ones, lack the needed educational background to gain required skills. Or they train for jobs that do not materialize.

What's Wrong with Full Employment as an Economic Objective?   Nothing! However, gaining jobs by limiting imports may not fully work as expected. Even if jobs are gained, the costs may be high and must be borne by someone.

Import restrictions to create domestic employment

- may lead to retaliation by other countries,
- affect large and small economies differently,
- reduce import handling jobs,
- may decrease jobs in another industry,
- may decrease export jobs because of lower incomes abroad.

The Prospect of Retaliation   When imposing trade restrictions used to protect or promote domestic industries at the expense of foreign players, the foreign players will retaliate. The opening case addressed concerns about how China retaliated the WTO decision by lifting restrictions on REE trade, but retaining those on other strategic materials like tungsten. Thus, the restrictions would merely move from one industry to another.

TABLE 6.1   Why Governments Intervene in Trade

Economic Rationales	Noneconomic Rationales
Fighting unemployment	Maintaining essential industries
Protecting infant industries	Promoting acceptable practices abroad
Promoting industrialization	Maintaining or extending spheres of influence
Improving comparative position	Preserving national culture

Large trading countries are more important in the retaliation process. For instance, China would have more power to retaliate than, say, Mauritius, to U.S. limits on clothing imports. And the United States is less apt to retaliate against Mauritian than Chinese trade restrictions because of the lesser effect on the U.S. economy.

Other Limits on Employment   In addition to retaliation, gaining jobs by limiting imports has the following limitations:

1. Fewer imports mean fewer import-handling jobs, such as those in the container-shipping industry, the clearance of goods through customs, and the distribution of the imports.
2. Given the global complexity of production, import restrictions on one industry cause higher input costs for other industries, thus making them less competitive.[4] For example, U.S. import restrictions on steel raise input costs in the U.S. automobile and farm equipment industries.
3. Imports stimulate exports, though less directly, by increasing foreign income, which foreign consumers then spend partially on new imports. Thus, restricting earnings abroad has some negative effect on domestic earnings and employment.

Analyzing Trade-Offs   Analysis of net changes in employment cannot capture the price of distress suffered by people who lose their jobs through import competition. Nor is it easy for working people to understand that their economic gains through lower prices from freer trade may exceed their higher taxes to support unemployment or welfare benefits for those who lose jobs.

In summary, many groups call for protectionism to increase or protect employment. However, evidence suggests that employment is better dealt with through fiscal and monetary policies.

PROTECTING "INFANT INDUSTRIES"

The infant-industry argument says that production becomes more competitive over time because of

• increased economies of scale,
• greater worker efficiency.

The **infant-industry argument** holds that a government should shield an emerging industry from foreign competition by guaranteeing it a large share of the domestic market until it can compete on its own.

Underlying Assumptions   The infant-industry argument presumes that early operating costs within a newly producing country may be too high to compete in world markets and that sufficient cost reductions will occur over time. Therefore, protection for fledgling companies enables them to gain economies of scale and higher productivity through worker experience.

CONCEPT CHECK

In Chapter 5 (pages 192–193 in the Point-Counterpoint section), we discuss governmental problems to determine what industries to support in a strategic trade policy and the difficulty of removing the support if the industries do not become globally competitive.

Risks in Designating Industries   However, production costs may never fall enough to create internationally competitive products. Inherently, there are problems.

Determining Probability of Success   First, governments must identify those industries that have a high probability of success, and this is hard. For example, governmental protection worked for the Brazilian automobile industry, but not for the Malaysian one. Second, the security of government import protection may deter managers from adopting the cost and quality measures needed to compete. Third, if a protected industry fails to become globally competitive, its affected stakeholders may successfully prevent the imports that benefit consumers.

Possible costs of import restrictions include higher prices and higher taxes. Such costs should be compared with those of unemployment.

Who Should Bear the Cost?   Even if policymakers choose the right industries, some economic segment must absorb the high early cost before domestic production becomes internationally viable. This burden may fall on consumers who pay higher prices for the protected products or on taxpayers who pay for subsidies. When taxes go for subsidies, governments may be less able to spend to improve overall competitiveness, such as on education and infrastructure. Finally, why rely on governmental assistance? Many entrepreneurs have endured early losses to achieve future competitiveness.

DEVELOPING AN INDUSTRIAL BASE

Since the industrial revolution, countries increasing their industrial bases grew their employment and economies more rapidly. This observation led to protectionist arguments to spur local industrialization. These arguments have been based on the following assumptions:

1. Surplus workers can increase manufacturing output more easily than agricultural output.
2. Import restrictions lead to foreign investment inflows, which provide jobs in manufacturing.
3. Prices and sales of agricultural products and raw materials fluctuate widely, which is a detriment to economies that depend heavily on them, especially if the dependence is on just one or a few commodities.
4. Markets for industrial products grow faster than markets for both agricultural and raw material commodities.

In the sections that follow, we review each of these assumptions.

Surplus Workers Disguised unemployment is high in rural areas of many developing countries, where many people effectively contribute little, if anything, to the agricultural output. Consequently, they can move into the industrial sector without significantly reducing agricultural output. This **industrialization argument** presumes that, although a country may develop an inefficient and non-globally competitive industrial sector, it will achieve economic growth by enabling the unemployed and underemployed to work in industry.[5]

Shifting people out of agriculture, however, can create problems:

1. The underemployed in rural areas may lose the safety net of their extended families, while many migrating to urban areas cannot find enough suitable jobs, housing, and social services. For example, although millions of Chinese have moved to cities to find jobs, many have not prospered through the move.[6]
2. Improved agricultural practices may be a better means of achieving economic success than a drastic shift to industry. Many developed countries continue to profit from exports of agricultural products and maintain high per capita income with a mix of industry and efficient agricultural production.
3. Most past manufacturing was performed by relatively unskilled workers and at a time when this output's proportion of global output and growth exceeded those in other sectors (e.g., agriculture, raw materials, and services). Thus, there were ample opportunities in factories for the unskilled labor force who were "fresh off the farm." However, this situation has changed and is known as *premature industrialization*. Manufacturing employment has been falling as a portion of total global employment because technology is replacing the need for as many workers, especially unskilled ones. Although there are growing employment opportunities in the service sector, people lacking much education are forced into low-paying service jobs.[7]

Investment Inflows Import restrictions, applied to spur industrialization, also may increase FDI, which provides capital, technology, and jobs. Barred from exporting to an attractive foreign market, foreign companies may transfer manufacturing to that country to avoid the loss of a lucrative or potential market.

Diversification Export prices of many commodities, such as oil and coffee, fluctuate markedly because of weather and technology affecting supply or business cycles affecting demand, thus wreaking havoc on economies that depend on their export. Because many developing countries rely on only one or a few commodities, they are caught in a feast-or-famine cycle, as it were: able to afford foreign luxuries one year but unable to find the funds for essential equipment's replacement parts the next. However, a greater dependence on manufacturing does not guarantee diversification of export earnings. The population of many developing economies is small; a move to manufacturing may shift dependence from

---

Margin notes:

Countries seek protection to promote industrialization because that type of production

- can use surplus agricultural workers more easily,
- brings in investment funds,
- diversifies the economy,
- brings faster growth than primary products do.

When a country shifts from agriculture to industry

- output may increase if the agricultural workers produced little before,
- demands on social and political services in cities may increase,
- development possibilities in the agricultural sector may be overlooked,
- industrial jobs may not be forthcoming.

If import restrictions keep out foreign-made goods, foreign companies may invest to produce in the restricted area.

Although demand and prices for commodities fluctuate markedly, a shift to production of manufactures creates competitive risk.

one or two agricultural commodities to one or two manufactured products, which face competitive risks and potential obsolescence.

Growth in Manufactured Goods   The quantity of imports that a given quantity of a country's exports can buy—say, how many bananas Country A must sell to Country B to purchase one refrigerator from Country B—is the **terms of trade**. Historically, except for short periods, the prices of commodities have not risen as fast as those of finished products.[8] Over time, therefore, it takes more low-priced primary products to buy the same amount of high-priced manufactured goods.

Why? First, the quantity of primary products demanded does not rise as rapidly as manufactured products and services, due partly to consumers' spending a lower percentage of income on food as their incomes rise and partly to raw-material-saving technologies. Second, because commodities are hard to differentiate, they usually must compete on price, whereas the prices of manufactured products can stay high because competition is based more on differentiation.

Import Substitution and Export-Led Development   Traditionally, developing countries fostered industrialization by promoting **import substitution**—restricting imports to boost local production of products they would otherwise import. In contrast, some countries, such as Taiwan and South Korea, have achieved rapid economic growth by promoting the development of industries with export potential, an approach known as **export-led development**. In reality, it's not easy to distinguish between import substitution and export-led development. Industrialization may result initially in import substitution, yet export development of the same products may be feasible later.

ECONOMIC RELATIONSHIPS WITH OTHER COUNTRIES

Nations monitor their absolute economic situations and compare their performance to other countries. Among their many practices to improve their relative positions, four stand out: making balance-of-trade adjustments, gaining comparable access to foreign markets, using restrictions as a bargaining tool, and controlling prices.

Balance-of-Trade Adjustments   A trade deficit influences reductions in a nation's exchange reserves—the funds that help purchase priority foreign goods and maintain the trustworthiness of its currency. So balance-of-trade deficits may cause a government to act to reduce imports or encourage exports. Two options that can affect its competitive position broadly are:

1. Depreciating or devaluing its currency, which makes basically all of its products cheaper in relation to foreign products
2. Relying on fiscal and monetary policy to bring about lower price increases in general than those in other countries

Both of these options take time. Furthermore, they aren't selective; for instance, they make both foreign essentials and foreign luxury products more expensive. Thus, a country may use protection instead to affect only certain products. Doing so is really a stopgap measure to gain time to address the fundamental competitive situation—the perceived quality, quantity, characteristics, and prices of products—that is causing its residents to buy more abroad than they are selling.

Comparable Access or "Fairness"   The **comparable access argument** holds that industries are entitled to the same access to foreign markets as foreign industries have to theirs. Economic theory supports this idea when substantial production cost decreases result from economies of scale. Companies that lack equal access to a competitor's market will be relatively disadvantaged in gaining enough sales to be cost-competitive.[9]

Terms of trade may deteriorate because

- demand for primary products grows more slowly than manufactured ones,
- production cost savings for primary products will be passed on to consumers.

Industrialization emphasizes either

- products to sell domestically or
- products to export.

If domestic producers have less access to foreign markets than foreign producers' have to their market,

- they may be disadvantaged,
- restricting foreign entry may disadvantage domestic consumers,
- negotiating equal market access for each product is impractical.

Comparable access is also presented from a fairness perspective. For instance, the U.S. government permits foreign financial service firms to operate in the United States, but only if their home governments allow U.S. financial service firms equivalent market access. There are, however, at least two practical reasons for rejecting the idea of fairness:

1. Tit-for-tat market access can lead to restrictions that may deny one's own consumers lower prices.
2. Governmental negotiation and monitoring of separate agreements for each of the thousands of different products and services that might be traded would simply be impractical.

Import Restrictions as a Bargaining Tool   The threat or imposition of import restrictions may persuade other countries to lower their import barriers or not raise them. The danger is that each country then escalates its restrictions instead, creating, in effect, a trade war that negatively impacts all their economies. Using restrictions successfully as a bargaining tool requires very careful product targeting by considering the following criteria:

> Successful countries' threats to levy trade restrictions to coerce other countries to change their policies
> - must be believable,
> - involve products important to the other countries.

- *Believability:* Either the country has access to alternative sources for the product or its consumers are willing to do without it. The EU successfully retaliated against U.S. import restrictions on clothing by threatening to impose trade restrictions on U.S.-grown soybeans when Brazil had a surplus.
- *Importance:* Exports of the restricted product must be significant to influential parties in the producer country. This consideration was emphasized when the United States placed restrictions on imported steel. The EU threatened to restrict apple and orange imports, which would hurt producers in Washington and Florida. Given the importance of these two states in a close presidential election, apple and orange stakeholders quickly convinced the United States to remove the steel import restrictions.

Export Restrictions   Countries that hold a near-monopoly of certain resources sometimes limit their international sale in an effort to raise prices abroad. However, this policy often encourages smuggling (such as occurs with emeralds and diamonds), the development of technology (such as synthetic rubber in place of natural rubber), or different means to produce the same product (such as caviar from farm-grown rather than wild sturgeons).[10] Export controls are especially ineffective for digital products because they are so easily copied abroad.

> Export restrictions may
> - raise world prices,
> - require more controls to prevent smuggling,
> - be ineffective for digital products,
> - lead to product substitution or new ways to produce the product,
> - keep domestic prices down by increasing domestic supply,
> - give producers less incentive to increase output.

A country may also limit exports of a product that is in short supply worldwide to favor domestic consumers. Typically, a greater supply drops domestic prices beneath foreign ones. Russia and Argentina have pursued this strategy by limiting exports of food products; India has limited cotton exports to increase supplies for its textile industry, and the United States has curtailed crude-oil exports.[11] However, favoring domestic consumers disfavors domestic producers, so they have less incentive to maintain production when prices are low.

Affecting Exporters' Prices   Import restrictions may aim either to raise or lower exporters' prices.

Prevention of Foreign Monopolies   There is fear that foreign producers will price their exports so artificially low that they will drive producers out of business in the importing country. If they succeed, there are two potential adverse consequences for the importing economy:

CONCEPT CHECK

Discussion of neomercantilism in Chapter 5 (page 178–179) explained that countries may attempt to shift their economic and social problems abroad.

1. The foreign country may be shifting its unemployment abroad by subsidizing the sales.
2. If there are high entry barriers, surviving foreign producers may be able to charge exorbitant prices. However, for most products competition is so widespread that no country or company can reach such a dominant position. For example, low import prices have eliminated most U.S. production of consumer electronics; still, the United States has some of the world's lowest consumer electronics prices because so many companies make them in so many countries.

Prevention of Dumping   Exporting below cost or below home-country price is **dumping**. Most countries restrict imports of dumped products, but enforcement usually occurs only if

Dumping

- may be used to introduce a new product,
- may cause higher prices or subsidies in the exporting country,
- is hard to prove.

the imported product disrupts domestic production; otherwise host-country consumers get the benefit of lower prices and don't complain. While exporting countries may encourage dumping to improve employment, companies may dump products to introduce them and build a market abroad. Essentially, a low entry price encourages consumers to sample the foreign brand—after which they can charge a high enough price to make a profit.

Companies can afford to dump products if they are subsidized or if they can charge high prices in their home market. Ironically, exporting-country consumers or taxpayers seldom realize that they are paying for foreign consumers' lower prices. An industry that believes it's competing against dumped products may appeal to its government to restrict the imports. However, determining a foreign company's cost or even its domestic price to middlemen is difficult because of limited access to its accounting records, fluctuations in exchange rates, and the passage of products through layers of distribution before reaching the end consumer. Nevertheless, industries do manage to succeed, (e.g., U.S. steelmakers' curtailment of Korean steel pipes).[12] However, critics claim that governments allegedly limit imports arbitrarily through antidumping restrictions and are slow to dispose of the restrictions if pricing situations change. Companies caught by antidumping restrictions often lose the export market they labored to build.

An optimum tariff's success

- shifts revenue to an importing country,
- is difficult to predict,
- may cause lower worker income in developing countries.

Invoking the Optimum-Tariff An **optimum-tariff theory** is one by which a foreign producer lowers its export prices when an importing country places a tax on its products. If this occurs, benefits shift to the importing country because the producer lowers its profits on the export sales.

Let's examine a hypothetical situation. Assume an exporter has costs of $500 per unit and is selling abroad for $700 per unit. With the imposition of a 10 percent tax on the imported price, the exporter may choose to lower its price to $636.36 per unit, which, with a 10 percent tax of $63.64, would keep the price at $700 in the foreign market. The exporter may feel that a foreign market price higher than $700 would result in lost sales and that a profit of $136.36 per unit instead of the previous $200 is better than no profit at all. Consequently, an amount of $63.64 per unit has shifted to the importing country.

As long as the foreign producer lowers its price by any amount, some shift in revenue goes to the importing country and the tariff is deemed an optimum one. There are many examples of products whose prices did not rise as much as the amount of the imposed tariff. For instance, purveyors of luxury producers have narrowed profit margins in Brazil to help offset import levies and sales taxes.[13] However, predicting when, where, and which exporters will voluntarily reduce their profit margins is imprecise. Further, a criticism of the optimum tariff is that developing country exporters reduce payment to their workers rather than absorbing the full impact through a lower profit margin, thus sometimes causing severe hardships.[14]

GOVERNMENTS' NONECONOMIC RATIONALES AND OUTCOME FOR TRADE INTERVENTION

Although noneconomic arguments are used to influence trade, many of these also have economic undertones and consequences. However, let's look at the major noneconomic rationales:

- Maintaining essential industries (especially defense)
- Promoting acceptable practices abroad
- Maintaining or extending spheres of influence
- Preserving national culture

In protecting essential industries, countries must

- determine which ones are essential,
- consider costs and alternatives,
- consider political and economic consequences.

MAINTAINING ESSENTIAL INDUSTRIES

Under the **essential-industry argument** nations apply trade restrictions to protect crucial domestic industries so that they are not dependent on foreign supplies during hostile political periods. For example, the United States subsidizes domestic silicon production so that its computer-chip makers need not depend on foreign suppliers. (In some cases, countries also prevent foreign companies from acquiring domestic companies needed for national security; the United States does this through the Committee on Foreign Investment in the United States [CFIUS].) Because of nationalism, defense needs have much appeal in rallying support for import barriers. However, in times of real (or perceived) crisis or military emergency, almost any product could be deemed essential.

The essential-industry argument should not be (but frequently is) accepted without a careful evaluation of costs, real needs, and alternatives. Once given, protection is hard to remove, even when the rationale for protection no longer exists. For instance, the United States subsidized mohair producers for more than 20 years after mohair was no longer essential for military uniforms.[15]

In addition, governments buy and stockpile supplies of essential raw materials that might be in future short supply. For example, the United States stockpiles rare-earth elements because China controls most output and because the military needs them for weapons, jet engines, high-powered magnets, and other gear.[16]

PROMOTING ACCEPTABLE PRACTICES ABROAD

Trade limitations may be used to compel a foreign country to amend an objectionable practice.

Governments limit exports, even to friendly countries, of strategic goods that might fall into the hands of potential enemies. They also limit exports and imports to compel a foreign country to change some objectionable policy or capability. The rationale is to weaken the foreign country's economy by decreasing its foreign sales and by limiting its access to needed products, thus coercing it to amend its practices on some issue such as human rights, environmental protection, military activities, and production of harmful products. Trade limitations are often combined with other economic pressures and incentives such as restricting access to bank accounts and cutting off or increasing foreign aid.

The effectiveness of trade sanctions depends on the sanctioned country's inability to retaliate effectively, secure alternative markets and supplies, and develop a production capability of its own. Our Point-Counterpoint section discusses the pros and cons of sanctions.

Point

Should Governments Impose Trade Sanctions?

Point **Yes** Let's face it: We're now living in a global society where actions in one country can spill over and affect people all over the world. For instance, the development of a nuclear arsenal in one nation can escalate the damage that terrorists can do elsewhere. The failure of a country to protect endangered species can have long-term effects on the whole world's environment. We simply can't sit back and let things happen elsewhere that will come back to haunt us.

At the same time, some pretty dastardly things occur in some countries that most of the world community would like to see stopped: human trafficking for forced prostitution, child slaves to harvest crops, political prisoners given near-starvation diets, to name a few. Even if we can't stop such occurrences, we have a moral responsibility not to participate even if it costs us. I may get some economic benefits by buying from criminals, and I may not stop their activity by withholding my business; however, I refuse to deal with them because, in effect, that makes me a criminal's associate.

Although not all trade sanctions have been successful, many have at least been influential in achieving their objectives. These included UN sanctions against Rhodesia

(now Zimbabwe), U.K. and U.S. sanctions against the Amin government of Uganda, and Indian sanctions against Nepal.[17] Sanctions against Myanmar helped bring the country to such economic disaster that its military leaders decided democracy was a better route to take.[18] Sanctions against Iran helped terminate Iran's nuclear program, and pressure on Brazil led to greatly reduced cutting of Amazon forests.[19] Further, even if sanctions do not completely change behavior, they may force countries not to escalate their unacceptable practices.[20]

Finally, when a nation breaks international agreements or acts in unpopular ways, what courses of action can other nations take? Between 1827 and World War I, nations mounted 21 blockades, but these are now considered too dangerous. Military force has also been used, for example, during the overthrow of the Saddam regime in Iraq, but such measures have little global support. Thus, nations may take such punitive actions as withholding diplomatic recognition, boycotting athletic and cultural events, seizing the other country's foreign property, and eliminating foreign aid and loans. These may be ineffective in and of themselves without the addition of trade sanctions.

Should Governments Impose Trade Sanctions?

Counterpoint

Counterpoint **No** Every time I turn around, I see governments imposing a new sanction. Some of these cause law-abiding companies to lose revenue that took years to develop. For one, there is a chance of retaliation. Trade sanctions on Russia after its annexation of Crimea were costly to Norwegian fish exporters because Russia turned to Chile.[21] Thus, the trade sanctions aimed at hurting the Russian government ended up hurting non-Russian companies even though they'd never engaged in any objectionable behavior.

Besides, I really question whether these sanctions even work. When the United States was maintaining its 20-year trade embargo on Vietnam, Vietnamese consumers could still buy U.S. products such as Coca-Cola, Kodak film, and Apple computers through other countries that did not enforce the sanctions.[22] The more than 50-year trade embargo with Cuba weakened over time and became ineffective as countries ceased their trade suppression. Oil embargoes against South Africa, because of its racial policies, merely spurred South African companies to become leaders in converting coal to oil.[23]

Even if trade sanctions succeed at weakening the targeted countries' economies, who really suffers? You can bet that the political leaders will still get whatever they need, so innocent people bear the costs of sanctions. This occurred in Iran, where there were widespread reports of deaths because of sanction-induced shortages

Counterpoint

of medicine.[24] Moreover, the people adversely affected usually blame their suffering not on their internal regime but on the countries carrying on the sanctions. Despots are very good at manipulating public opinion.[25]

In addition, critics of sanctioning point to import restrictions that are not fully effective because they aim too much at curtailing supply rather than demand (e.g., U.S. actions aiming to curtail the production of opiates abroad rather than efforts to restrain U.S. demand). In another example, many countries restrict ivory imports so that countries (mainly African) will limit ivory supplies by protecting elephants.[26] However, although restrictions may have slowed elephant slaughter, poaching still continues (in the five years between 2010 and 2015, Tanzania and Mozambique lost 60 and 48 percent of their elephants respectively) because of high demand for ivory.[27] The below photo shows part of 1.5 tons of imported ivory products seized and destroyed by the Belgian government.

Finally, governments sometimes seem to impose trade sanctions based on one issue rather than on a country's overall record. For instance, some critics have suggested using trade policies to press Brazil to restrict the cutting of Amazon forests, even though its overall environmental record—particularly its limitation of adverse exhaust emissions by converting automobile engines to use methanol instead of gasoline—is quite good.

▶ Photo shows seized ivories and ivory products prior to their destruction in Belgium.

Source: Gong Bing/Xinhua/Alamy Stock Photo

MAINTAINING OR EXTENDING SPHERES OF INFLUENCE

Governments use trade to support their spheres of influence—giving aid and credits to, and encouraging imports from, countries that join a political alliance or vote a preferred way within international bodies. For example, the EU and 78 states from Africa, the Caribbean, and the Pacific participate in the Cotonou Agreement that formalizes an array of economic and political ties and economic issues.

PRESERVING NATIONAL CULTURE

CONCEPT CHECK

We observe in Chapter 2 (pages 73–74) that a primary function of culture is that it supports a nation's sense of its uniqueness and integrity.

To help sustain a collective identity that sets their citizens apart from other nationalities, governments prohibit exports of art and historical items deemed to be part of their national heritage. In addition, they limit imports that may either conflict with or replace their dominant values. The relevance of culture has been confirmed through several UNESCO conventions aimed at preserving cultural diversity, and the concern has been largely focused, but not entirely, on media (print, visual, and audio).[28] For instance, many countries, such as Canada and Australia, require levels of national content in media.[29] In addition to media, Japan, South Korea, and China maintained for many years an almost total ban on rice imports, largely because rice farming has been a historically cohesive force in each nation.[30]

MAJOR INSTRUMENTS OF TRADE CONTROL

In seeking to influence exports or imports, governments' choice of trade-control instrument is crucial because each may incite different responses from domestic and foreign groups. One way to understand these instruments is by distinguishing between those that directly influence export or import *prices* and those that directly limit the *amount* of a good that can be traded. Let's review these instruments.

TARIFFS: DIRECT PRICE INFLUENCES

Tariffs may be levied

- on goods entering, leaving, or passing through a country;
- for protection or revenue;
- on a per-unit basis, a value basis, or both.

Tariff barriers directly affect prices, and *nontariff barriers* may directly affect either price or quantity. A **tariff** (also called a **duty**) is a tax levied on a good shipped internationally. That is, governments charge a tariff on a good when it crosses an official boundary—whether it be that of a nation or a group of nations that have agreed to impose a common tariff on goods crossing the boundary of their bloc. A tariff assessed on a per-unit basis is a **specific duty**, on a percentage of the item's value an **ad valorem duty**, and on both a **compound duty**.

Tariffs collected by the exporting country are called **export tariffs**; if they're collected by a country through which the goods pass, they're **transit tariffs**; if they're collected by importing countries, they're **import tariffs**. Because import tariffs are by far the most common, we discuss them in some detail.

Import Tariffs   Unless they're *optimum tariffs* (discussed earlier in the chapter), import tariffs raise the price of imported goods by taxing them, thereby giving domestically produced goods a relative price advantage. Although consumers are often unaware of the cost increase from tariffs on imports, they learn very quickly when encountering duty-free shops in international airports and at cruise ship stopovers. (See the following photo.)

Tariffs as Sources of Revenue   Tariffs also generate governmental revenue, but revenue is of little importance to developed countries because collection costs usually exceed the yield.[31] In many developing countries, though, they are a major source of revenue because they are often more easily collected than income taxes. Although revenue tariffs are most commonly

Tourists shopping for duty-free items in St. John's, Antigua and Barbuda.

Source: M.Sobreira/Alamy Stock Photo

collected on imports, some countries charge export tariffs on raw materials. Transit tariffs were once a major source of countries' revenue, but governmental agreements have nearly abolished them.

Developing countries argue that their processed portion of commodities have higher tariffs than the published rates.

The Effective Tariff Controversy   Raw materials (say, coffee beans) from developing countries frequently enter developed countries free of duty; however, if they are processed (say, instant coffee), developed countries then assign an import tariff. Because an ad valorem tariff is based on the total value of the product (say, 10 percent on a $5 jar of instant coffee), the raw materials and the processing combined (say, $2.50 for the coffee beans and $2.50 for the processing) pays $.50. Developing countries have argued that the **effective tariff** on the manufactured portion turns out to be higher than the published tariff rate because the manufactured portion is effectively charged 20 percent. This anomaly further challenges developing countries to find export markets for products that use their raw materials.

NONTARIFF BARRIERS: DIRECT PRICE INFLUENCES

Now that we've shown how tariffs raise prices, let's discuss other ways that governments alter product prices to affect their trade.

Governmental subsidies may help companies be competitive,

- but there is little agreement on what a subsidy is,
- but agricultural subsidies are difficult to dismantle,
- especially to overcome market imperfections because they are least controversial.

Subsidies   **Subsidies** offer direct assistance to companies to boost their competitiveness. Although this definition is straightforward, disagreement on what constitutes a subsidy causes trade frictions. In essence, not everyone agrees that companies are being subsidized just because they lose money, nor that all types of government loans or grants are subsidies. One long-running controversy involves commercial aircraft. Airbus Industrie and the EU claim that the U.S. national and state governments subsidize Boeing through R&D contracts for military aircraft that also have commercial applications and through the granting of incentives to influence their location decisions. Further, because the U.S. Ex-Im Bank offers loan guarantees to foreign buyers, Delta Air Lines has argued that this gives non-U.S. airlines an advantage not available to U.S. airlines.[32] Meanwhile, Boeing and the U.S. government claim that the EU subsidizes Airbus Industrie through low-interest government loans.[33]

An area that may well raise future questions about subsidies is governmental support to shore up floundering companies and industries, especially during global recessions. For instance, governments have bailed out banks, granted generous consumer loans to support their auto companies, eliminated taxes on their companies' export earnings, and invested in an ownership share of key companies. In turn, these actions alter international competitiveness.[34]

Agricultural Subsidies   The one area in which everyone agrees that subsidies exist is agriculture, especially in developed countries. The official reason is that food supplies are too critical to be left to chance. Although subsidies lead to surplus production, they are argued to be preferable to the risk of food shortages. Further, to counter overproduction, the United States pays additional subsidies to farmers so that they do not produce as much.[35] However, this official reason does not explain agricultural subsidies for nonfood products, such as U.S. cotton subsidies that Brazil claims to disadvantage its competitiveness.[36]

The strength of agricultural interests is also important. Within Japan, the United States, and the EU, rural areas have a disproportionately high representation in government decision-making. For instance, Japanese rural interests have been able to force a 778 percent tariff on rice.[37] In the United States, there is one senator per 300,000 people in Vermont (a state with a 68 percent rural population) and one senator per 19 million in California (which is 93 percent urban). Agriculture accounts for 38 percent of the EU budget even though it composes only 7 percent of GDP.[38] The result is that internal politics effectively prevent the dismantling of such instruments as price supports for farmers, government agencies to improve agricultural productivity, and low-interest loans to farmers.

What is the effect? Although some developing countries, such as India, are also major agricultural subsidizers, many are deprived from fully serving the developed markets with competitive agricultural products. Further, much surplus production from developed countries is exported at very low prices, thus distorting trade and further disadvantaging developing countries' production.[39]

Overcoming Market Imperfections   Most countries offer potential exporters many business development services, such as market information, trade expositions, and foreign contacts. This type of subsidization is less contentious than tariffs because the actions seek to overcome, rather than create, market imperfections. Further, collecting and disseminating information widely is less costly than if each potential exporter were to work individually.

Aid and Loans   When governments require foreign aid and loan recipients to spend the funds in the donor country, a situation known as *tied aid* or *tied loans,* some otherwise noncompetitive output can compete abroad. For instance, tied aid helps win large contracts for infrastructure, such as telecommunications, railways, and electric power projects.

However, tied aid and loans sometimes require the recipient to use output and suppliers that may not be the best. They may also slow the advancement of local suppliers in developing countries. These concerns led OECD members to untie financial aid to developing countries.[40] However, China is using tied aid for nearly all its foreign infrastructure projects.[41]

Customs Valuation   Import tariff assessments depend on the product, price, and origin—which tempts exporters and importers to declare these wrongly to pay a lower duty and tempts governments to declare wrongly as a protectionist measure.

What Is the Import Worth?   Most countries have agreed to use import invoice information unless customs doubt its authenticity. Agents must then appraise on the basis of the value of identical or similar goods arriving at about the same time.[42] Customs must appraise similarly when goods enter for lease rather than purchase because there is no invoice. Critics,

Because it is difficult for customs officials to determine the honesty of import invoices,

- valuation procedures have been developed,
- they may restate the value,
- they may question the origin of and product-classification of imports.

especially companies and governmental authorities from exporting countries, complain that agents in importing countries too often use discretionary power to levy higher duties, such as on Philippine cigarettes imported into Thailand.[43]

What Is the Product?   Misclassifying a product (by accident or intentionally) is an easy way to change its corresponding tariff. Administering more than 13,000 categories of products (with new products coming onto the market all the time) means a customs agent must use discretion to determine, say, if silicon chips should be considered "integrated circuits for computers" or "a form of chemical silicon." In our opening case, we saw the controversy over whether China lifted restrictions over REEs and whether they lifted the restrictions on other strategic materials like Tungsten. The differences between the elements in terms of production use are also minute. For example, the U.S. tariffs on athletic footwear are different from those on sports footwear, and these are subcategorized by whether the sole overlaps the upper part of the shoe or not. Each type of accessory and reinforcement of the shoes' uppers is a different category.

Although classification differences may seem trivial, the disparity in duties may cost or save companies millions of dollars. Some contentious examples include whether the French company Agatec's laser leveling device would be used primarily indoors or outdoors,[44] whether Marvel's X-Men Wolverines were toys or dolls, and whether sport utility vehicles—such as the Suzuki Samurai and the Land Rover—were cars or trucks.

Where Does the Product Originate?   Because of different trade agreements, customs must determine products' origins. For example, red meat products may involve animals born in one country, raised in a second, and slaughtered in a third. U.S. Customs requires traders to provide details on these stages of production, thus adding documentation costs above those for meat products of a 100 percent U.S. origin.[45] Officials have also uncovered many instances of product transshipment and document falsification to avoid or lessen restrictions. For instance, U.S. Customs fined Staples, OfficeMax, and Target for mislabeling the country of origin of pencils in order to avoid paying antidumping duties assessed on Chinese imports.[46]

Other Direct-Price Influences   Countries use other practices to affect import prices, including special fees (such as for consular and customs clearance and documentation), requirements that customs deposits be placed in advance of shipment, and minimum price levels at which goods can be sold after they have cleared customs.

NONTARIFF BARRIERS: QUANTITY CONTROLS

Governments' regulations and practices affect the quantity of imports and exports directly. Let's take a look at the various forms these typically take.

A quota may

- be on imports or exports,
- set the total amount to be traded,
- allocate amounts by country,
- be negotiated as a voluntary export restraint (VER),
- prohibit all trade when it is an embargo.

Quotas   A **quota** limits the quantity of a product that can be imported or exported in a given time frame, typically per year. *Import quotas* normally raise prices because they (1) limit supplies and (2) provide little incentive to use price competition to increase sales. A notable difference between tariffs and quotas is their effect on revenues. Tariffs generate revenue for the government. Quotas generate revenue only for those companies that obtain and sell a portion of the intentionally limited supply of the product at prices higher than what competitive prices would be. (Sometimes governments allocate quotas among countries based on political or market conditions.)

To circumvent quotas, companies sometimes convert the product into one for which there is no quota. For instance, the United States maintains sugar import quotas that result in its sugar prices averaging more than the world market price. As a result, some U.S. candy producers have moved plants to Mexico and Canada where they can buy lower-cost sugar and import the candy duty-free to the United States.[47]

A country may establish *export quotas* to provide domestic consumers a sufficient supply of goods at a low price, to prevent depletion of natural resources, or to attempt to raise prices abroad by restricting foreign supply.

Voluntary Export Restraints A **voluntary export restraint (VER)** is a quota variation whereby, essentially, Country A asks Country B to voluntarily reduce its companies' exports to Country A. For instance, the United States and Mexico agreed on a VER dealing with Mexican tomato exports.[48] The term *voluntarily* is misleading; typically, either Country B agrees to reduce its exports or else Country A may impose tougher trade restrictions. Procedurally, VERs have unique advantages. They are much easier to switch off than an import quota, and the appearance of a "voluntary" choice by a particular country to constrain its shipments can do less damage to political relations than an import quota.

Embargoes A specific type of quota that prohibits all trade is an **embargo**. As with quotas, a country or group of countries may place embargoes on either imports or exports, on particular products regardless of origin or destination, on specific products with certain countries, or on all products with given countries. Governments impose embargoes in an effort to use economic means to achieve political goals, thus they are a type of trade sanction which we discuss in our Point-Counterpoint section.

> Through "buy local" rules
> - government purchases give preference to domestically made goods,
> - governments sometimes legislate a percentage of domestic content.

"Buy Local" Legislation *Buy local legislation* sets rules whereby governments give preference to domestic production in their purchases. Given the enormity of government sectors in most economies, this preference can be substantial. Sometimes governments, such as the U.S. government, specify a domestic content restriction—that is, a certain percentage of the product must be of domestic origin.[49] Sometimes governments favor domestic producers through price mechanisms, such as permitting an agency to buy a foreign-made product only if the price is a predetermined margin below that of a domestic competitor. Sometimes governments favor domestic purchases indirectly, such as the U.S. prohibition of foreign Medicare payments for elderly Americans except in emergency situations—a regulation that limits U.S. foreign purchases in the fast-growing area of medical tourism.

> Other types of trade barriers include
> - arbitrary standards;
> - importing, exporting, and currency licensing;
> - administrative delays;
> - reciprocal requirements;
> - service restrictions.

Standards and Labels Countries can devise classification, labeling, and testing standards to allow the sale of domestic products while obstructing foreign-made ones. Consider product labels. The requirement that companies indicate products' origins informs consumers who may prefer buying domestic products. In our opening case, we saw that the U.S. catfish industry sought country-of-origin labeling on fish. Countries also may dictate that companies place content information on their packaging, which differs from what is required elsewhere. These technicalities may seem trivial, but they add to a firm's costs, particularly if the labels must be translated for different export markets. In addition, raw materials, components, design, and labor increasingly come from many countries, so most products today are of such mixed origin that they are difficult to sort out.

The professed purpose of standards is to protect safety or health, but some companies argue they are just a means to protect domestic producers. For example, some U.S. and Canadian producers have contended that EU regulations and labeling requirements on genetically engineered corn and canola oil are merely means to keep out the products until their own technology catches up.[50] In another case, following U.S. publicity about contaminated Chinese foods, China retaliated by upping its rejection of foodstuffs from the United States, citing contamination with drugs and salmonella.[51]

In reality, there's no way of knowing to what extent products are kept out of countries for legitimate safety and health reasons versus arbitrarily protecting domestic production. Rejecting shipments for health and safety reasons, particularly those from developing countries, may cause a negative image for the exporting countries' other products, causing them to lose sales and lower their export prices.[52]

Specific Permission Requirements Countries may require that importers or exporters secure governmental permission (an **import or export license**) before transacting trade. A company may have to submit samples to government authorities to obtain such a license. The procedure can restrict imports or exports directly by denying permission or indirectly because of the cost, time, and uncertainty involved.

A **foreign exchange control** requires an importer to apply to a government agency to secure the foreign currency to pay for the product. As with an import license, failure to grant the exchange, not to mention the time and expense of completing forms and awaiting replies, obstructs foreign trade.

Administrative Delays   Closely akin to specific permission requirements are administrative customs delays that may be caused by intention or inefficiency. In either case, they create uncertainty and raise the cost of carrying inventory. Intentional delays may occur not only to protect domestic producers, but also for political reasons. Japanese companies reported such delays in China after Japan and China clashed over ownership of islands in the East China Sea.[53]

Reciprocal Requirements   Importing countries sometimes require that whole or partial payment be made to exporters in merchandise rather than fully in currency, a transaction known as barter trade. The World Trade Organization estimates that 15 percent of world trade involves some type of barter.[54]

Countertrade   In **countertrade** or **offsets**, a government in the importing country requires the exporter to provide it with additional economic benefits such as jobs or technology as part of the transaction. Critics in exporting countries contend that large defense contractors, by participating in these arrangements, shift purchases from smaller domestic contractors to those in foreign countries, thus weakening these domestic suppliers and the exporting country's future defense capabilities.[55]

Problems for Exporters   Reciprocal requirements necessitate that exporters assess the value and find markets for goods outside their expertise, engage in complicated operating arrangements, and undertake activities outside their proficiency. Raytheon, which makes such products as missiles and radar systems, had to undertake shrimp farming to gain a Saudi Arabian contract.[56] All things being equal, companies avoid these transactions. However, some have developed competencies in these types of arrangements in order to gain competitive advantages. Others rely on specialized companies that handle barter transactions.

Restrictions on Services   Service is the fastest-growing sector in international trade. In deciding whether to restrict service trade, countries typically consider four factors: *essentiality, not-for-profit preference, standards,* and *immigration.*

Four main reasons why trade in services is restricted are

- essentiality,
- preference for not-for-profit operations,
- different professional standards,
- immigration.

Essentiality   Governments sometimes prohibit private companies, foreign or domestic, from operating in some sectors because they feel the services are essential and provide social stability. In other cases, they set price controls or subsidize government-owned service organizations that create disincentives for foreign private participation. Some essential services in which foreign firms might be excluded are media, communications, banking, utilities, and domestic transport.

Not-for-Profit Services   Mail, education, and hospital health services are often not-for-profit sectors in which few foreign firms compete. When a government privatizes these industries, it customarily prefers local ownership and control.

Standards   Some services require face-to-face interaction between professionals and clients, and governments limit entry into many of them to ensure practice by qualified personnel. The licensing requirements include such professionals as accountants, actuaries, architects, electricians, engineers, gemologists, hairstylists, lawyers, medical personnel, real estate brokers, and teachers.

At present, there is little reciprocal recognition in licensing because countries' occupational standards and requirements differ substantially. Thus an accounting or legal firm from one country faces obstacles in another, even to serve its domestic clients' needs. The firm must hire professionals within each foreign country or else have its domestic professionals earn certification abroad. The latter option is problematic because of having to take examinations and learn new materials, sometimes in a foreign language. There also may be lengthy prerequisites for taking an examination, such as internships, time in residency, and coursework at a local university.

CONCEPT CHECK

In discussing "Factor Mobility" in Chapter 5 (pages 194–195), we explain the increasing reliance on people as an internationally mobile production factor and that countries hand out immigration papers only sparingly.

When facing import competition, companies can

- move abroad or find foreign supplies,
- seek other market niches,
- make domestic output competitive,
- try to get protection.

Immigration   Satisfying the standards of a particular country is no guarantee that a foreigner can then work there. In addition, governmental regulations often require an organization—domestic or foreign—to search extensively for qualified personnel locally before it can even apply for work permits for personnel it would like to bring in from abroad.

HOW COMPANIES DEAL WITH GOVERNMENTAL TRADE INFLUENCES

When companies are threatened by import competition, they have several options, four of which stand out:

1. Move operations to another country.
2. Concentrate on market niches that attract less international competition.
3. Adopt internal innovations, such as greater efficiency or superior products.
4. Try to get governmental protection.

   Each option entails costs and risks; therefore, different companies make different choices. For example, competition from Japanese imports spurred the U.S. automobile industry to move some production abroad (such as subcontracting with foreign suppliers for parts), develop niche markets through the sale of minivan and sport utility vehicles (SUVs) that initially had less international competition, and adopt innovations such as lean production techniques to improve efficiency and product quality. They also successfully sought VERs from Japan, and General Motors and Chrysler eventually received substantial government funding to survive.

TACTICS FOR DEALING WITH IMPORT COMPETITION

Granted, these methods are not realistic for every industry or company. Companies may lack the resources to shift their own production or find suppliers abroad. They may not be able to identify more innovative or profitable product niches. Even if they do, foreign competitors may quickly emulate them. In such situations, companies often ask their governments to restrict imports or open export markets.

CONVINCING DECISION-MAKERS

Governments cannot try to help every company that faces tough international competition. Likewise, helping one industry may hurt another. Thus, as a manager, you may propose or oppose a particular protectionist measure. Inevitably, the burden falls on you and your company to convince officials that your situation warrants particular policies. You must identify the key decision-makers and convince them by using the economic and noneconomic arguments presented in this chapter. You must also put forward the types of restrictive mechanisms most likely to help your situation and convey to public officials that voters and stakeholders support your position.[57]

INVOLVING THE INDUSTRY AND STAKEHOLDERS

A company improves the odds of success if it can ally most, if not all, domestic companies in its industry. Otherwise, officials may feel that its problems are due to its specific inefficiencies rather than the general trade challenges. Similarly, involving stakeholders, such as taxpayers and local merchants, can help. Finally, it can lobby decision-makers and endorse the political candidates who are sympathetic to its situation.

PREPARING FOR CHANGES IN THE COMPETITIVE ENVIRONMENT

Companies take different approaches to deal with changes in the international competitive environment. Frequently, their attitudes toward protectionism are a function of the investments they have made to implement their international strategy. Those that depend on freer trade and/or have integrated their production and supply chains among countries tend to oppose protectionism. In contrast, those with single or multi-domestic production facilities, such as a plant in Japan to serve the Japanese market and a plant in Taiwan to serve the Taiwanese market, tend to support protectionism.

Companies also differ in their confidence to compete against imports. Thus when companies recommend protection for their industries, typically one or more companies in that industry oppose it. The opposition usually comes from companies with commanding competitive advantages in terms of scale economies, supplier relationships, or differentiated products. Thus, they reason that not only can they successfully battle international rivals, they also stand to gain even more as their weaker domestic competitors fail to do so.[58]

Looking to the Future
Dynamics and Complexity of Future World Trade

When trade restrictions change, there are winners and losers among countries, companies, and workers. So it's probably safe to say that we'll see mixtures of pushes for freer trade and greater protection.

In addition, consumers' gains from freer trade may be at the expense of some companies and workers—people who see themselves as big losers. They are not apt to lose without a struggle; they'll garner as much support for protection as they can, and they may win. The support may well come from alliances that cross national borders, such as clothing companies in various developing nations uniting to push importing countries to enact quota agreements to protect their export markets against Chinese and Indian competition. Thus, if you are a manager in an industry that may be affected by changes in governmental protection, you must watch closely to predict how the evolving politics may affect your own situation.

Finally, the international regulatory situation is becoming more, rather than less, complex—a situation that challenges companies to find the best locations in which to produce. These complexities include new products that challenge the task of tariff classification, Internet services that create new channels of foreign competition, and heightened concerns about terrorism and product safety that compound considerations of what can be traded and with whom. ■

CASE Doing Business in Singapore[59]

The Government of Singapore offers a pro-business environment and Singapore is placed 1st in the World Bank's global ranking index for "Ease of Doing Business" and "Trading Across Borders." To achieve this, the Singapore government has created a robust ecosystem to promote international trade and investments through its various ministries and agencies or statutory boards. For instance, the mission of the Ministry Of Trade and Industry (MTI) of Singapore is to promote economic growth and create jobs, so as to achieve higher standards of living for its citizens, protecting Singapore's international trade interests, in particular, with a view to enhance access to global markets for goods, services and investments; and providing a good understanding of the current state of and outlook, for policy formulation and refinement.

These strategies are derived from Singapore's general philosophy of economic management—strong adherence to a free market economic system, and active pursuit of outward-oriented economic policies. Its vision is to develop a globalized, entrepreneurial and diversified economy to turn Singapore into a leading global city. MTI oversees ten statutory boards including the Singapore Economic Development Board (EDB). The EDB is the lead government agency that plans and executes strategies to enhance Singapore's position as a global business center and grow its economy. Its "Host to Home" strategy aims to move Singapore from being a host to companies to becoming a home where global business, innovation, and talent are nurtured. EDB's consistently result-oriented initiatives are testament to Singapore's governmental influence on trade. The following are examples of some global companies that leveraged good government policy to expand their Asia wide presence in Singapore.

Siemens Medical Instruments

As one of the world's leading manufacturers of digital hearing instruments utilizing the latest microelectronic technology, Siemens established the operations of Siemens Medical Instruments (SMI) in Singapore in 1974. Ever since, their research department has grown into a full-fledged R&D center taking advantage of the robust growth and market opportunities in Asia that now homes a fast rising ageing population (estimated to cross 850 million by 2050) and middle class. These factors prompted Siemens to boost its investments in research and development by 10 percent in 2013. Siemens' long term investment in and dedication to the region is testament to the Singapore government's growing role as a strategic partner with leading companies, to achieve visionary growth.

Trina Solar

Similarly in 2011, Trina Solar, one of the world's leading photovoltaic (PV) companies, established its Asia Pacific operating headquarters in Singapore to strengthen its growing presence and customer base in Asia after it sealed a research agreement with the Solar Energy Research Institute of Singapore to develop high efficiency solar cells using Trina Solar's mono-crystalline wafers.

The Singapore government through its energy agency Energy Innovation Programme Office (EIPO) created an investment environment that fostered the development of a skilled talent base and strong logistics infrastructures. These made it strategically advantageous for Trina Solar's regional R&D center as it developed new solar technologies and applications to meet the demands for clean energy expected to be fueled by Asian markets.

Rolls-Royce

Since its entry into the country in the 1950s, Rolls-Royce has become a major player in Singapore's aerospace industry, accounting for over 15 percent of Singapore's aerospace output. A world leader of power systems and services, Rolls-Royce is anticipating strong growth in its operations in Asia achieved through joint ventures with key local industry partners including Singapore Airlines Engineering, and activities in the energy and marine sector. The Singapore government has been a strong partner of growth for Rolls-Royce and the country is a leader in aerospace maintenance, repair and overhaul, aviation manufacturing and R&D in Asia. According to Jonathan Asherson, Regional Director, Rolls-Royce, the company has also benefited from the valuable business opportunities, excellent talent pool, and solid infrastructure that Singapore offers.

Procter & Gamble

Procter & Gamble or P&G's market capitalization is more than the GDP of many countries and it markets its products in over 180 countries. It is the largest household and personal care company in the world, and its brands include some of the world's best-known names such as Gillette, Pampers, Pantene, Oral-B, and SK-II. The Asia Pacific headquarters for P&G's operations in Singapore carries out brand and business management activities like manufacturing, marketing, supply chain management, research and development, finance and talent development across the region. Singapore is also home to P&G's Asia Leadership Development Center

P&G leveraged on the strong research capabilities in Singapore through an agreement with Singapore's government Agency for Science, Technology and Research (A*STAR). In 2011, P&G invested US$192 million to build a mega innovation center in Singapore. Deborah Henretta, Group President, Asia, P&G remarked that Singapore embodies the essence of what successful companies look for: commitment to innovation, world-class infrastructure, business- friendly environment, excellent local talent and an ability to work as partners in progress.

Unilever

Another leading global supplier of fast moving consumer goods (FMCG) with a presence in more than 150 countries is Unilever. Parent to the world's best-known brands such as Lipton, Wall's, and Dove, Unilever deals products in nutrition, hygiene and personal care reaching out to a wide range of consumers. Established in Singapore over 50 years ago, Unilever Singapore has since emerged as a strategic global hub for Unilever, and is home to several key members of its senior leadership team. Through Four Acres Singapore, its new global leadership development center, Unilever will access the Singapore EDB's LINK (Leadership Initiatives, Networks and Knowledge) ecosystem to provide executive talent development and leadership programs with business schools and corporate partners. Paul Polman, CEO of Unilever, recognizes that Singapore's evolved business infrastructure, excellent human capital, connectivity, and strong base for supporting industries combined with the support provided by the Singapore Government make it an ideal regional business hub.

Dell

Since 1984, Dell has pioneered technologies and innovations as the front-runner in the computer industry that sells custom-built computers directly to customers. Dell currently operates its Asia Pacific headquarters in Singapore using this cosmopolitan market and strategic location as a test bed for its services and solutions in Asia. Dell opened its first design center in Singapore in 2005 to boost the company's R&D capabilities in display and imaging products. It further added its Dell Singapore Solution Center (DSC) in 2011, tapping into the country's large pool of infocomm industry professionals and highly proactive government agency, the Infocomm Development Authority of Singapore (IDA). Amit Midha, President of Dell Asia Pacific and Japan, points to the fact that Singapore's robust ecosystem, pro-business environment, geo-political landscape and high-technology infrastructure enables Dell to bring the benefits of technology solutions to customers in the Asia Pacific region.

Mitsui Chemicals

Mitsui Chemicals (MCI) is one of the largest chemical companies in Japan. In Singapore, its business includes manufacturing plants, R&D facilities, and sales offices. MCI subsidiaries in Singapore are Mitsui Chemicals Asia Pacific Ltd, Mitsui Phenols Singapore Pte Ltd, and Mitsui Elastomers Singapore Pte Ltd. The company has invested over US$600 million to expand its operations in Singapore since the 1980s including phenol, bisphenol and Tafmer plants. MCI's Asia Pacific Headquarters in Singapore also provides support in sales and marketing, technical, logistics, and business planning functions. In 2011, it opened its R&D Center (MS-R&D) working closely with its Singapore government agency partner A*STAR and research institutes. Mr Yasushi Nawa, Managing Director of Mitsui Chemicals Asia Pacific, commented that Singapore's pro-business government policies, talented and hardworking workforce and top infrastructures have enabled Mitsui Chemicals to look to the country as a launch pad for its growth strategies in the Asia Pacific region.

China-Singapore Cooperation Initiatives

As part of an ongoing effort by Singapore's government to influence and facilitate international trade, the Monetary Authority of Singapore (MAS) has developed new initiatives to influence and support trade. Singapore and China have agreed on new initiatives to strengthen cooperation on financial sector development and regulation. The new initiatives will further promote the international use of the Renminbi (RMB) through Singapore.

China will extend its Renminbi Qualified Foreign Institutional Investor (RQFII) program to Singapore, with an aggregate quota of RMB 50 billion. This will allow qualified Singapore-based institutional investors to channel offshore RMB from Singapore into China's securities markets. RQFII license holders may also issue RMB investment products to the broad pool of investors in Singapore, using the RQFII quota. The RQFII program will help to diversify the base of investors in China's capital markets and promote adoption of the RMB for investment.

Singapore will be given consideration as one of the investment destinations under the new Renminbi Qualified Domestic Institutional Investor (RQDII) scheme. This will allow qualified Chinese institutional investors to use RMB to invest in Singapore's capital markets. The measure will help to broaden the universe of assets available to Chinese investors as well as the investor base for Singapore's capital markets.

China and Singapore will introduce direct currency trading between the Chinese Yuan and Singapore Dollar. New measures will allow cross-border flows of RMB between Singapore and Suzhou Industrial Park (SIP) as well as Tianjin Eco-City (TEC). In addition, Singapore and China have agreed on and announced measures to strengthen regulatory cooperation. Relevant agencies are in discussions to facilitate

China-incorporated companies which have received regulatory approval to list directly in Singapore, instead of through entities incorporated outside China.

Furthermore, the Singapore Exchange and Shanghai Futures Exchange have signed an MOU to strengthen collaboration in the joint development of commodity derivatives.

The Singapore and Chinese governments have also agreed to strengthen cooperation in banking regulatory issues, through exchanges and dialogs on topics of shared interest, and enhanced coordination on international regulatory issues. These new initiatives build on agreements concluded earlier this year, including the signing of the MOU on RMB Business Cooperation between the Monetary Authority of Singapore (MAS) and the People's Bank of China (PBC), and the enhancement of the bilateral swap agreement between the two central banks, which paved the way for the launch of RMB clearing functions in Singapore in May this year (2013).

Ravi Menon, the Managing Director of MAS, already declared that 2013 had been the productive year with lots of cooperation initiatives between Singapore and China. The excellent relations between MAS and the central bank and their regulatory counterparts in China only cemented ties between the two countries, putting Singapore in a position to promote RMB for long-term trade and investment in the future.

QUESTIONS

6-3. Discuss why and how the Singapore government promotes the international trade process.

6-4. Why is free trade so vital to Singapore's survival and growth?

6-5. Singapore has a highly developed trade-oriented market economy and its economy has been ranked as the most open in the world. What has been the government's role in achieving this feat?

MyLab Management

Go to **mymanagementlab.com** for the following Assisted-graded writing questions:

6-6 Why do multinational corporations (MNCs) find Singapore an attractive place to do business?

6-7 Discuss the advantages and disadvantages of protectionist policies to domestic industry.

Endnotes

Scan for Endnotes or go to www.pearsonglobaleditions.com/Daniels

CHAPTER 7
Economic Integration and Cooperation

OBJECTIVES

After studying this chapter, you should be able to

7-1 Define the three major types of international economic integration

7-2 Explain what the World Trade Organization is and how it is working to reduce trade barriers on a global basis

7-3 Summarize the major benefits of regional economic integration

7-4 Compare and contrast different regional trading groups

7-5 Describe the forces that affect the prices of commodities and their impact on commodity agreements

MyLab Management®

Improve Your Performance!

When you see this icon ⭐, visit **www.mymanagementlab.com** for activities that are applied, personalized, and offer immediate feedback.

Marrying is easy, but housekeeping is hard.

—German proverb

Brexit concept ▶

Source: Delpixel/Shutterstock

CASE

Regional Integration and the Different Modalities of a Custom Union Divorce

—Stefania Paladini

One of the major events that will always be associated with 2017 is the Brexit—the divorce of the United Kingdom from the most developed and comprehensive example of regional integration, the European Union (EU). While those relations have been trouble for many years, some say since the very beginning of the union, the dissolution appears problematic in terms of what is coming next for the United Kingdom, and also for the EU up to a certain extent. The case itself offers an excellent opportunity to evaluate the different kinds of regional integrations, together with their challenges and opportunities.

Almost everyone, even the staunchest supporters of Brexit, were expecting some sort of preferential trade agreements (PTA) between the remaining 27 countries of the EU and the United Kingdom; however, the specific form of this PTA or free-trade agreement (FTA) is not something simple enough to agree upon.

It is unlikely that the United Kingdom will remain a part of the Common Market, even though in that particular kind of access that previews paying the access, like in the case of Norway. The reason for this is that the access to Common Markets, the EU or others in kind, requires agreeing to the free movement of the productive factors (goods, services, capitals, and people) and applying all the rules, which was exactly what the United Kingdom was unhappy about. It is also the case to notice that this solution would not avoid per se the reintroduction of lengthy custom procedures which were, historically, one of the main gains of the EU in terms of costs and complexity of trade, especially for small and medium-sized enterprises (SMEs). This is because custom borders are only lifted when countries also enter into a custom union, which is the case of the EU member states but not, for example, of the ones who only pay their access to the Common Market, like Norway, which, in fact, maintains its own custom borders, procedures, and tariff.

A possible solution of compromise would be a custom union, similarly to what the EU maintains with Turkey; and, while in this case there are those clear advantages mentioned before, it will also prevent the United Kingdom to sign custom union agreements with countries that don't share the same conditions with the United Kingdom. Considering that one of the announced United Kingdom initiatives is to sign preferential trade agreements with these countries, this rules out a custom union.

There are, of course, alternatives to these scenarios that allows more freedom of the signing partners, and in many have mentioned the case of Switzerland. Switzerland is not formally part of the single market; it enjoys only a limited access, so it can effectively restrict factors movement from the EU (like people) and signs its own trade agreements. But it is also the case to notice that there's no such thing like a "Swiss solution" as it has been often dubbed by the press. More than a solution, it is a patchwork of several agreements negotiated over a period of twenty years or more, and which now amounts at about 120 bilateral deals in continuous amendment and renegotiation.

All considered, the outcome that seems more likely at the moment is a trade agreement similar to the one that the EU has negotiated with Canada and that is going to enter into force in 2017 once the EU parliament ratified it—the Comprehensive Economic and Trade Agreement (CETA). The CETA is a typical FTA model of agreement, which will (among other provisions) eliminate about 98 percent of the tariffs between Canada and the EU and will, even more importantly, maintain the freedom of negotiation and independence of trade policy both parties do require. The signing of a similar kind of treaty between the EU and the United Kingdom is not going to be either quick or even simple, though. Canada and the EU have finally agreed to the treaty charter after seven years (2007–2014) of long negotiations. Moreover, difficulties and the lengthy ratification process CETA has going under are telling. Since CETA and the prospective U.K.–EU treaty are considered mixed agreements, they have to be ratified by each EU member state and together must also receive the European Parliament's consent. In the case of CETA, the latest ratification, the one from Belgium, only came in October 2016, after long discussions in the Belgian parliament.

There is also a final, but fundamental point, which both the United Kingdom and the EU—and in general, any country in a similar scenario is going to face—and it is the WTO status of both trading partners. This is something that has been often overlooked in the discussions over Brexit but that has been recently reminded by the WTO DG Roberto Azevedo himself. As Azevedo allegedly warned, it will be likely that both parts, the United Kingdom and the EU itself, will have to renegotiate their terms of their WTO status with the rest of the WTO members.

This might prove especially cumbersome for the United Kingdom, which will at the same time be pressed to negotiate a deal with the EU before 2019. While the United Kingdom is a full member of the WTO, the terms of British WTO membership are "bundled" with the EU, and they will need to be separately agreed upon.

While nobody can tell at the moment when the Article 50 will be actually triggered and the terms of the Brexit itself, it is likely that the United Kingdom will have to renegotiate treaties with its most important trade partners. In an adage well known in international trade, "free trade doesn't just happen" and any free trade deals has to pass under a series of difficult negotiations. The United Kingdom will, therefore, not only exit from the EU trade-wise but also will renounce all the trade measures the EU has in place with the rest of the world. (To date, the EU has 34 bilateral and regional trade agreements in place, which cover in total 60 partners.) This is likely to translate in higher transaction costs for companies, in terms of custom procedures and treaty access, including customs checks for rules of origin and custom declaration procedure, which, according to some estimates offered by the magazine *The Economist* in September 2016, could add between 4 percent and 15 percent to the overall costs of exports. ∎

QUESTIONS

7-1. What are the most likely resultant scenarios of a Brexit scenario? What are the main issues that may prevent them from occurring?

7-2. What are the issues related to the WTO status of both the United Kingdom and the European Union?

FORMS OF ECONOMIC INTEGRATION

CONCEPT CHECK

Recall from Chapter 5 (page 197) our discussion of the ways in which the mobility of capital, technology, and people affects a country's trade and the relative competitive positions of domestic firms and industries. Imbalances in the mobility of factors of production are often addressed in strategies for cross-national integration.

Approaches to economic integration—political and economic agreements among countries in which preference is given to member countries— may be

• bilateral,
• regional,
• global.

In the mid- to late 1940s, many nations decided that if they were going to emerge from the wreckage of World War II and promote economic growth and stability within their borders, they would have to assist—and get assistance from—nearby countries. How do nations and regions combine forces to give and gain the assistance they need to prosper together?

Economic integration is a term used to describe the political and monetary agreements among nations and world regions in which preference is given to member countries. There are three major ways to approach such agreements:

• **Global integration**—Countries from all over the world decide to cooperate through the World Trade Organization (WTO)
• **Bilateral integration**—Two countries decide to cooperate more closely together, usually in the form of tariff reductions
• **Regional integration**—A group of countries located in the same geographic proximity decide to cooperate, as with the European Union

Trade groups, whether global, bilateral, or regional, are an important influence on MNE strategies. They can define the size of the regional market and the rules under which a company must operate. In fact, an increase in market size is their single most important reason for existing.[2] A company, or a region, in the initial stages of foreign expansion must be aware of how the groups encompass countries with good trade locations or market opportunities. Recall from our opening case how the United Kingdom is likely to face higher transaction costs for companies and an increase in the overall costs of exports as a result of Brexit and WTO terms bundled with the EU. In the ending case we'll see how NAFTA affected Walmart's expansion into Mexico and Central America. Thus, as a company expands internationally, it must change its operating strategies to continually benefit from these alliances. Similarly, in the ending case we'll see how NAFTA affected Walmart's expansion into Mexico and Central America. Thus, as a company expands internationally, it must change its operating strategies to continually benefit from these alliances.

MNEs are interested in regional trade groups because they tend to be regional as well. Although MNEs operate worldwide, they usually generate a large percentage of their revenues in their home regions.[3] Additional research has shown that a 1 percent increase in physical distance results in a 1 percent decrease in trade and that a common border between two countries is likely to increase trade flows by 80 percent. This provides further evidence that firms are likely to generate a reasonably high percent of revenues from their home regions.[4] However, companies that sell in their own region are also interested in trade agreements with other regions.

THE WORLD TRADE ORGANIZATION—GLOBAL INTEGRATION

GATT: PREDECESSOR TO THE WTO

CONCEPT CHECK

In Chapter 6 (page 206), we explain that, in principle, no country allows an unregulated flow of goods and services across its borders; rather, governments routinely influence the flow of imports and exports. We also observe that governments directly or indirectly subsidize domestic industries to help them compete with foreign producers, whether at home or abroad. (In Chapter 1, we list the motivations for governments to engage in cross-national agreements—indeed, to cooperate at all.)

CONCEPT CHECK

In Chapter 6 (page 215), we define a tariff as the most common type of trade control and describe it as a "tax" that governments levy on goods shipped internationally. Here we emphasize the fact that tariff barriers affect the prices of goods that cross national borders.

CONCEPT CHECK

In discussing "Nontariff Barriers" as instruments of trade control in Chapter 6 (page 216), we include subsidies, which we describe as direct government payments made to domestic companies, either to compensate them for losses incurred from selling abroad or to make it more profitable for them to sell overseas.

The World Trade Organization is the major body for

- reciprocal trade negotiations,
- enforcement of trade agreements.

In 1947, 23 countries formed the General Agreement on Tariffs and Trade (GATT) under the auspices of the United Nations to abolish quotas and reduce tariffs. By the time the WTO replaced GATT in 1995, 125 nations had become members. Many believe that GATT's contribution to trade liberalization enabled the expansion of world trade in the second half of the twentieth century.

Trade Without Discrimination   The fundamental principle of GATT was that each member nation must open its markets equally to every other member nation. This principle of "trade without discrimination" was embodied in GATT's **most-favored-nation (MFN) clause**—once a country and its trading partners had agreed to reduce a tariff, that tariff cut was automatically extended to every other member country, irrespective of whether the country was a signatory to the agreement.

Over time, GATT grappled with the issue of nontariff barriers in terms of industrial standards, government procurement, subsidies and countervailing duties (duties in response to another country's protectionist measures), licensing, and customs valuation. In each area, GATT members agreed to apply the same product standards for imports as for domestically produced goods, treat bids by foreign companies on a nondiscriminatory basis for most large contracts, prohibit export subsidies except on agricultural products, simplify licensing procedures that permit the importation of foreign-made goods, and use a uniform procedure to value imports when assessing duties on them.

Then GATT slowly ran into problems. Its success led some governments to devise craftier methods of trade protection. World trade grew more complex, and trade in services—not covered by GATT rules—grew more important. Procedurally, GATT's institutional structure and its dispute-settlement system seemed increasingly overextended. Moreover, it could not enforce compliance with agreements. These market trends and organizational challenges made trade agreements harder to work out. Restoring an effective means for trade liberalization led officials to create the **World Trade Organization (WTO)** in 1995.

WHAT DOES THE WTO DO?

The WTO adopted the principles and trade agreements reached under the auspices of GATT but expanded its mission to include trade in services, investment, intellectual property, sanitary measures, plant health, agriculture, and textiles, as well as technical barriers to trade. Its 162 members collectively account for most of the world trade. The entire membership makes significant decisions by consensus. However, there are provisions for a majority vote in the event of a nondecision by member countries. Agreements then must be ratified by the governments of the member nations, which can be politically challenging in the member countries.

Most Favored Nation   The WTO continued the MFN clause of GATT, which implies that member countries should trade without discrimination, basically giving foreign products "national treatment." Although the WTO restricts this privilege to official members, some exceptions are allowed, especially for developing countries or countries that are part of a regional or bilateral trading group.

Dispute Settlement   One function of the WTO that is garnering growing attention is the organization's dispute settlement mechanism, in which countries may bring charges of unfair trade practices to a WTO panel, and accused countries may appeal. There are time limits on all stages of deliberations, and the WTO's rulings are binding. If an offending country fails

CONCEPT CHECK

In Chapter 6 (page 206), we show how the imposition of import restrictions can be used as a means of persuading other countries to lower import barriers. Here we point out that the same practice can also be used to punish nations whose policies fail to comply with provisions of the WTO or other agreements.

Bilateral agreements can be between two individual countries or may involve one country dealing with a group of other countries.

Regional trade agreements—integration confined to a region and involving more than two countries.

CONCEPT CHECK

In discussing geographic distance in Chapter 5 (page 188), we observe that because greater distances ordinarily mean higher transportation costs, geographic proximity usually encourages trade cooperation. In the same chapter, we explain country similarity theory by showing that once a company has developed a new product in response to conditions in its home market, it will probably try to export it to those markets that it regards as most similar to its own.

Geographic proximity is an important reason for economic integration.

Major types of economic integration:

- Free trade area—no internal tariffs.
- Customs union—no internal tariffs plus common external tariffs.
- Common market—customs union plus factor mobility.

to comply with the panel's judgment, its trading partners have the right to compensation. If this penalty is ineffective, then the offending country's trading partners have the right to impose countervailing sanctions. However, the effectiveness of this system is under serious debate, given the ambiguity and time-consuming nature of certain cases.

REGIONAL ECONOMIC INTEGRATION

BILATERAL AGREEMENTS

Even though bilateral trade agreements are simpler than trying to forge a deal with the WTO, no trade agreement is easy. An example of a bilateral agreement is the U.S.–Colombia Trade Promotion Agreement, which is a free trade agreement and not a customs union. It also includes provisions for gaining better access for U.S. investors and service providers as well as commitments to protect labor rights and the environment in Colombia, two key provisions to gain political support in the United States to sign the agreement.

Regional trade agreements are reciprocal pacts between two or more partners that lie somewhat between bilateral treaties and the WTO. Some of the best known RTAs are the European Union, the North American Free Trade Agreement (NAFTA), and the ASEAN (Association of Southeast Asian Nations) Free Trade Area (AFTA).

GEOGRAPHY MATTERS

It's logical that most trade groups contain countries in the same area of the world. Neighboring nations tend to ally for several reasons:

- The distances that goods need to travel are short.
- Consumers' tastes are likely to be similar, and distribution channels can easily be established.

Neighboring countries may have common histories and interests, and they may be more willing to coordinate their policies than non-neighbors.[5] Even though geographic proximity is a major factor leading to RTAs, this is not the case for all agreements. India has a number of trade agreements with most of the countries in its region, but also with Finland, Japan and Korea; Germany exports and imports about 58 percent of its merchandise to other EU members; Switzerland, which is not a member of the EU but which has a trade agreement with it, shares more than half its exports and imports with EU countries; and NAFTA includes Canada and Mexico, both of which share a common border with the United States. The Canada–Israel RTA, on the other hand, is certainly not based on geographic proximity, nor is the U.S.–Korea FTA.

Geography matters for a number of reasons in the case of RTAs. Neighboring countries often share a common history, language, culture, and currency. Unless the countries are at war with each other, they have usually developed trading ties already. Close proximity reduces transportation costs, thereby making traded products cheaper in general. In fact, as physical distance between two countries increases by 1 percent, international trade drops by 1.1 percent. On the other hand, trade is likely to rise by 80 percent between countries with a common border, 200 percent with a common language (such as English between Canada and the United States), and 340 percent with a common currency (such as the euro for countries in the EU that have adopted it). Another strong incentive for geographically close countries to establish an RTA is that trade among bloc members is likely to rise by 330 percent once an agreement is established.[6]

As noted earlier, the major reason to establish a regional trade group is to increase market size. There are two basic types of RTAs from the standpoint of tariff policies; however, many agreements (especially agreements involving the United States) go beyond the liberalization of tariffs to include such issues as intellectual property, foreign direct investment, and services. From the standpoint of tariff reduction, the two main types of agreements are free trade agreements and customs unions.

- *Free Trade Agreement (FTA)* The goal of an FTA is to abolish all tariffs between member countries. It usually begins modestly by eliminating them on goods that already have low tariffs, and there is usually an implementation period during which all tariffs are eliminated on all products included in the agreement. Moreover, each member country maintains its own external tariffs against non-FTA countries. About 90 percent of the RTAs identified by the WTO are free trade agreements.

- *Customs Union* In addition to eliminating internal tariffs, member countries levy a common external tariff on goods being imported from nonmembers in order to establish a customs union. For example, when the EU was organized in 1957, it began to remove internal tariffs among member states, but in 1967 it eliminated the remaining internal tariffs and established a common external tariff, meaning that goods shipped into one member country from abroad are free from tariffs in the rest of the member countries. Now the EU negotiates as one region in the WTO and other regional and bilateral agreements rather than as separate countries.

Common Market   Beyond the reduction of tariffs and nontariff barriers, countries can enhance their cooperation in a variety of other ways. The EU also allows free mobility of production factors such as labor and capital. This means that labor, for example, is generally free to work in any country in the common market without restriction. Adding free mobility of production factors to a customs union results in a **common market**. In addition, the EU has harmonized its monetary policies through the creation of a common currency, complete with a central bank. This level of cooperation creates a degree of political integration among member countries, which means they lose a bit of their sovereignty.

THE EFFECTS OF INTEGRATION

Regional economic integration can affect member countries in social, cultural, political, and economic ways. Initially, however, our focus is on its economic rationale. As we noted in Chapter 5, the imposition of tariff and nontariff barriers disrupts the free flow of goods, affecting resource allocation.

Static and Dynamic Effects   Regional economic integration reduces or eliminates those barriers for member countries, producing both *static* and *dynamic effects*. **Static effects** are the shifting of resources from inefficient to efficient companies as trade barriers fall. **Dynamic effects** are the overall growth in the market and the impact on a company caused by expanding production and by its ability to achieve greater economies of scale. Figure 7.1 shows how RTAs result in static and dynamic effects on trade and investment flows.

Static effects may develop when either of two conditions occurs:

1. *Trade Creation:* Production shifts to more efficient producers for reasons of comparative advantage, allowing consumers access to more goods at lower prices than would have been possible without integration. Companies protected in their domestic markets face real problems when the barriers are eliminated and they attempt to compete with more efficient producers. The strategic implication is that companies that were unable to export to another country—even though they might be more efficient than producers there—are now able to export when the barriers come down, creating more demand for their products and less for the protected ones. Investment also might shift to countries that are more efficient or that have a comparative advantage in one or more factors of production.

2. *Trade Diversion:* Trade shifts to countries in the group at the expense of trade with other countries, even though the nonmember companies might be more efficient in the absence of trade barriers.

Sidebar notes (left margin):

Regional integration has social, cultural, political, and economic effects.

Static effects of integration—the shifting of resources from inefficient to efficient companies as trade barriers fall.

Dynamic effects of integration—the overall growth in the market and the impact on a company caused by expanding production and by the company's ability to achieve greater economies of scale.

CONCEPT CHECK

In Chapter 5 (page 181), we define comparative advantage as the theory that global efficiency gains may result from trade if a country specializes in those products it can produce more efficiently than other products (regardless of whether other countries can produce the same products even more efficiently).

Trade creation—production shifts to more efficient producers for reasons of comparative advantage.

Trade diversion—trade shifts to countries in the group at the expense of trade with countries not in the group.

FIGURE 7.1 Impact of Free Trade Agreements

When economic integration reduces or eliminates trade barriers, the effects on the nations involved may be either *static* or *dynamic*. *Static effects* apply primarily to trade barriers themselves—for member countries they go down, and for nonmembers they go up. *Dynamic effects*, on the other hand, apply to economic changes affecting the newly structured market—not only does the market expand, but so do local companies, which take advantage of the larger market.

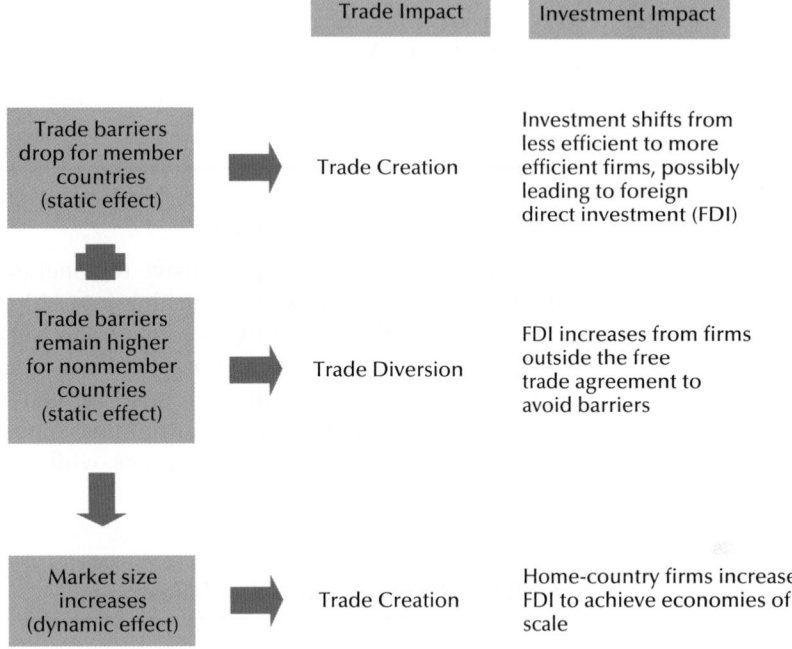

Economies of scale—the average cost per unit falls as the number of units produced rises; occurs in regional integration because of the growth in the market size.

Economies of Scale Dynamic effects of integration occur when trade barriers come down and markets grow. Because of that growth, companies can increase their production, which will result in lower costs per unit—a phenomenon we call **economies of scale**. Companies can produce more cheaply, which is good because they must become more efficient to survive. This could result in more trade between the member countries (trade creation) or an increase in investment in the region by local or foreign companies as the market grows.

Increased Competition Another important effect of an RTA is greater efficiency due to increased competition. Many MNEs in Europe have attempted to grow through mergers and acquisitions to achieve the size necessary to compete in the larger market. Companies in Mexico were forced to become more competitive with the passage of NAFTA due to competition from Canadian and U.S. companies. This could result in investment shifting from less efficient to more efficient companies, or it could result in existing companies becoming more efficient.

MAJOR REGIONAL TRADING GROUPS

MNEs are interested in regional trading groups for their markets, sources of raw materials, and production locations. The larger and richer the new market, the more likely it is to attract the attention of the major investor countries and companies. In addition, it is important to understand how the reduction of tariffs and other barriers improves access to countries in the region. Table 7.1 compares the GDP, population, and per capita GNI of three regional trade groups to give you an idea of how different they are in size. Pick just one country in each group, such as Ireland in the EU, Mexico in NAFTA, and Vietnam in ASEAN, and notice how small their national market would be compared with how big their market opportunities are in their regional trade group.

TABLE 7.1   Comparative Statistics by Trade Group

	Population in Millions (2014)	GDP Trillions of $ (2014)	Per Capita GNI in $ (2014)
European Union (EU)	508.3	18.5	35,718
North American Free Trade Agreement (NAFTA)	479.84	20.5	42,723
ASEAN Free Trade Area (AFTA)	622	14.3	4,136

Source: Based on information from http://data.worldbank.org/ (accessed on March 5, 2016); http://www.asean.org/ (accessed on March 5, 2016).
The data for the EU includes the United Kingdom, which voted to leave the EU in 2016.

The European Union:

- Changed from the European Economic Community to the European Community to the European Union
- The largest and most successful regional trade group
- Free trade of goods, services, capital, and people
- Common external tariff
- Common currency

THE EUROPEAN UNION

The largest and most comprehensive regional economic group is the **European Union (EU)**. It began by gradually abolishing internal tariffs but eventually established an external tariff while integrating in other ways such as facilitating the free movement of workers, establishing a common agricultural policy, and agreeing on a value-added tax system. The formation of the European Parliament and the establishment of a common currency, the euro, make the EU the most ambitious of all the regional trade groups.[7] Table 7.2 summarizes its key milestones, while Map 7.1 identifies its members and other key European groups.

TABLE 7.2   European Union Milestones

From its inception in 1957, the EU has been moving toward complete economic integration. The initial six members were Belgium, Germany, France, Italy, Luxembourg, and the Netherlands.

1959	The first steps are taken in the progressive abolition of customs duties and quotas within the EEC (European Economic Community). The European Coal and Steel Community established in 1951 gave way to a broader vision of economic integration.
1960	The Stockholm Convention establishes the European Free Trade Association (EFTA) as a free trade alternative to the EU. Now, only four countries remain: Iceland, Norway, Liechtenstein, and Switzerland.
1961	The first regulation on free movement of workers within the EEC comes into force.
1962	The Common Agricultural Policy is adopted.
1966	Agreement is reached on a value-added tax (VAT) system; a treaty merging the Executives of the European Communities comes into force; and the EEC changes its name to European Community (EC).
1967	All remaining internal tariffs are eliminated, and a common external tariff is imposed.
1973	Denmark, Ireland, and the United Kingdom become members 7, 8, and 9 of the EC.
1981	Greece becomes the 10th member of the EC.
1986	Spain and Portugal become the 11th and the 12th members of the EC.
1990	East and West Germany unite.
1992	Agreement to change the EC to the European Union is adopted in 1992 and implemented in 1993.
1995	Austria, Finland, and Sweden become the 13th, 14th, and 15th members of the EU.
1996	An EU summit names the 11 countries that will join the European single currency with all EU countries joining except Britain, Sweden, Denmark (by their choice), and Greece (not ready).
1999	The euro, the single European currency, comes into effect (January 1, 1999). Coins and notes enter circulation on January 1, 2002.
2001	Greece becomes the 12th country to adopt the euro.
2004–2016	Admission of 10 new member countries. Bulgaria and Romania join in 2007, and Croatia joins in 2013, raising the membership to 28. Candidate countries as of 2016 are Croatia, Former Yugoslav Republic of Macedonia, and Turkey. The UK voted to exit the EU in 2016, but it will take two years to finalize the exit strategy.

Source: Europa, "The History of the European Union," at http://europa.eu/about-eu/index_en.htm (accessed March 5, 2016)

MAP 7.1 European Trade and Economic Integration

Although the 28-member EU is easily the dominant trading bloc in Europe, it's not the only one. Founded in 1960, the four-member European Free Trade Association (EFTA) also maintains joint free trade agreements with several other countries. The European Economic Area (EEA) includes three members of the EFTA and all members of the EU.

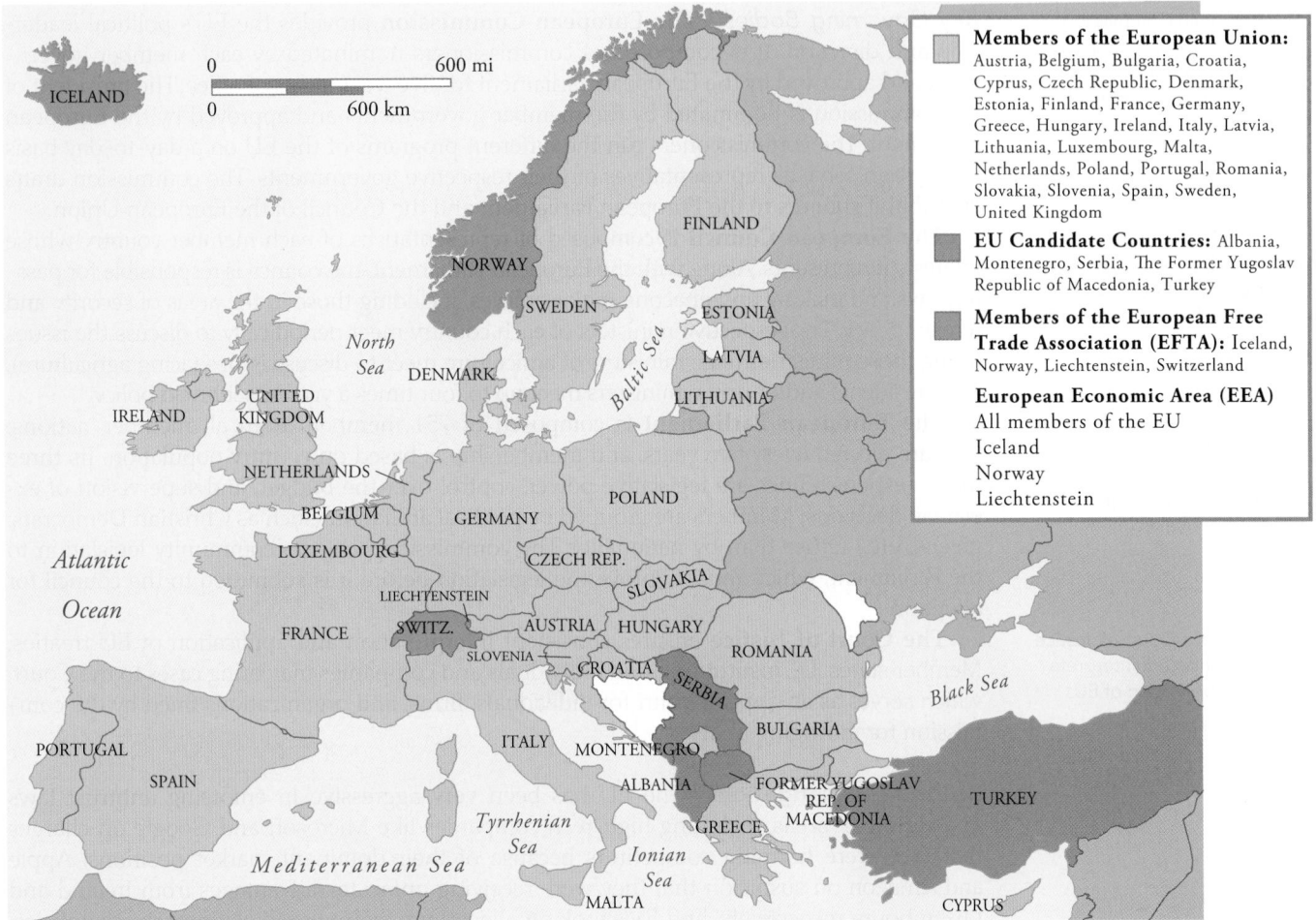

Members of the European Union: Austria, Belgium, Bulgaria, Croatia, Cyprus, Czech Republic, Denmark, Estonia, Finland, France, Germany, Greece, Hungary, Ireland, Italy, Latvia, Lithuania, Luxembourg, Malta, Netherlands, Poland, Portugal, Romania, Slovakia, Slovenia, Spain, Sweden, United Kingdom

EU Candidate Countries: Albania, Montenegro, Serbia, The Former Yugoslav Republic of Macedonia, Turkey

Members of the European Free Trade Association (EFTA): Iceland, Norway, Liechtenstein, Switzerland

European Economic Area (EEA)
All members of the EU
Iceland
Norway
Liechtenstein

CONCEPT CHECK

In Chapter 5 (page 184), we discuss the theory of country size, which holds that large countries usually depend less on trade than small countries. The same principle tends to be true of economic blocs, and here we point out that regional integration is one way to achieve the size necessary to reduce members' dependence on trade.

European Free Trade Association—FTA involving Iceland, Liechtenstein, Norway, and Switzerland, with close ties to the EU.

Predecessors Because of the economic and human destruction left by World War II, European political leaders realized that greater cooperation among their countries would help speed up recovery. Many organizations were formed, including the European Economic Community (EEC), which eventually emerged as the organization that would bring together the countries of Europe into the most powerful trading bloc in the world. Several other countries, including the United Kingdom, formed the European Free Trade Association (EFTA) with the limited goal of eliminating internal tariffs. But most of those countries eventually became part of the EU. Those that have decided not to leave EFTA (Iceland, Liechtenstein, Norway, and Switzerland) still have a free trade agreement with each other. All but Switzerland are part of the European Economic Area, which provides them access to the "four freedoms" of the EU: the free movement of goods, services, persons, and capital. However, it does not include other areas of cooperation, such as a customs union and monetary union.[8]

Organizational Structure The EU encompasses many governing bodies, among which are the European Commission, European Council, European Parliament, European Court of Justice, and European Central Bank.[9]

To be successful in Europe, MNEs need to understand the EU's governance process, just as they need to understand the governance process of each individual European country in which they invest or do business. These institutions set parameters within which companies must operate, so management needs to understand the institutions and how they make decisions that could affect corporate strategy. This is because even though all of the countries are a part of the same trade agreement, there are still individual differences that need to be understood and planned for.

Key Governing Bodies   **The European Commission** provides the EU's political leadership and direction. It is composed of commissioners nominated by each member government and approved by the European Parliament for five-year terms of office. The president of the commission is nominated by the member governments and approved by the European Parliament. The commissioners run the different programs of the EU on a day-to-day basis rather than serve as representatives of their respective governments. The commission drafts laws that it submits to the European Parliament and the Council of the European Union.

The European Council is composed of representatives of each member country whose interests it represents. Along with the European Parliament, the council is responsible for passing laws and making and enacting major policies, including those in the areas of security and foreign policy. The respective ministers of each country meet periodically to discuss the issues facing those ministries (e.g., ministers of agriculture meet to discuss issues facing agriculture). The presidents and/or prime ministers meet up to four times a year to set broad policy.

The European Parliament is composed of 751 members from all member nations; they are elected every five years, and membership is based on country population. Its three major responsibilities are legislative power, control over the budget, and supervision of executive decisions. Members are grouped by political affiliation (such as Christian Democrats, greens, etc.) rather than by nationality. The commission presents community legislation to the Parliament, which must approve the legislation before it is submitted to the council for adoption.[10]

The Court of Justice ensures consistent interpretation and application of EU treaties. Member states, EC institutions, and individuals and companies may bring cases to the Court, which serves as an appeals court for individuals, firms, and organizations fined by the commission for infringing treaty law.[11]

Antitrust Investigations   The EU has been very aggressive in enforcing antitrust laws in a variety of areas, including high-tech companies like Microsoft and Google on charges that they were harming competitors because of their dominant market positions, Apple and Amazon on suspicion that they were receiving unfair tax advantages from Ireland and Luxembourg respectively, and Facebook on allegations that it was violating privacy policies. Although most cases are still in process, the non-tax cases are always complicated because of the ever-changing landscape of technology, consumer behavior, and market demand.[12] It is interesting to note that the EU is far more aggressive than the Fair Trade Commission in the United States, but it is also understandable that the EU would be more aggressive against foreign companies.

Monetary Union: The Euro   In 1992, the members of the EU signed the Treaty of Maastricht in part to establish a monetary union. The decision to move to a common currency, the **euro**, in Europe has eliminated currency as a trade barrier for its adopters. As of 2016, 19 of the 28 EU members had adopted the euro. Others are preparing to do so as well, while only Denmark and the United Kingdom have opted out of the common currency. Other European countries also use the euro, even though they are not EU members. We'll discuss the euro in more detail in Chapter 9 as well as the debt crisis that began with Ireland and then spread to Greece, Spain, Portugal, Italy, and Cyprus. The inability of these countries to meet their external debt obligations has threatened the banking system and forced other European countries to come to the rescue. As possibly the EU's single biggest challenge, this threatens the future of the euro.

The Schengen Area   In order to facilitate the free flow of people from country to country within the EU, the Schengen Agreement was signed in 1990 with gradual implementation allowing citizens to cross internal borders without having to go through border checks. Not

The European Commission provides political leadership, drafts laws, and runs the various daily programs of the EU.

The Council of the European Union, or European Summit, is composed of the heads of state of each member country.

The three major responsibilities of the European Parliament are legislative power, control over the budget, and supervision of executive decisions.

The European Court of Justice ensures consistent interpretation and application of EU treaties.

The Treaty of Maastricht sought to foster political union and monetary union.

The euro

• is a common currency in Europe,
• is administered by the European Central Bank,
• was established on January 1, 1999,
• resulted in new banknotes in 2002.

all members of the EU, including the UK and Ireland, have opted to be in the Schengen Area, whereas some non-EU states, such as the EFTA countries, are part of it.

Migration: A Threat to Schengen   Two things have hindered the free flow of people across national borders in Europe in recent years: terrorism and migration. Terrorist attacks in France and the fear that migrants would cross the border from France to Belgium forced Belgium to partly suspend passport-free travel to Belgium from France; large numbers of migrants from Syria and other countries who were living in camps close to the Belgium border were trying to move into Belgium.[13] The fear is that although Europe has always been open to refugees, especially political refugees, the crisis in Syria resulted in a massive flow of people to Europe in greater numbers than any time since World War II. It happened so fast that the EU was not prepared. Refugees streamed from Syria to Turkey to Greece and then elsewhere in Europe. The EU worked with Turkey to convince them to keep the Syrian refugees there and even promised financial support and help in completing their entrance into the EU if they would harbor more of the refugees. However, the refugees continued to flow into Greece where an economy with over 20 percent unemployment and a financial crisis was hard pressed to accept and keep all of the Syrian refugees.[14] As world leaders tried to figure out a way to solve the political crisis in Syria, Europe was trying to solve the refugee crisis. Solutions ranging from making borders more difficult to cross to actually sealing borders are among the options being considered. Clearly solving the migration crisis is important; otherwise, the idea of open borders in Europe will be a major casualty, not only causing irreparable damage to the idea of open borders but also slowing and harming cross-border commerce. And simply closing the borders could result in a serious humanitarian crisis.[15]

Expansion   One of the EU's major challenges is expansion. Official candidates for future membership currently include Turkey, Montenegro, Serbia, and the former Yugoslav Republic of Macedonia. Turkey is an interesting candidate since it straddles Europe and Asia, is 99.8 percent Muslim (mostly Sunni), and has a large population of 75.9 million people, second only to Germany with 80.89 million people. It has a strong manufacturing base and strong trade ties with Europe. As noted above, it may also be a key to help the EU come to grips with the humanitarian crisis with the Syrian refugees. Given its close proximity to the Syrian border, Turkey is in a unique position to help assimilate Syrian refugees with temporary work visas and then facilitate their return to Syria if and when political conditions stabilize there.

Bilateral Agreements   In addition to reducing trade barriers for member countries, the EU has signed numerous bilateral free trade agreements with other countries outside the region. Since the EU negotiates with other countries as one entity, its trade talks are considered bilateral, even though all member states benefit from the results of the talks. The benefit to the other party to the agreement is that they get access to 28 countries when they sign the agreement.

The Transatlantic Trade and Investment Partnership (T-TIP)   One of the more intriguing potential agreements involves the United States and the EU. Even though tariffs between the two superpowers are already low (the United States and the EU have the world's largest trading relationship and account for nearly half of the world's economic output), the new agreement would eliminate the remaining tariffs, boost trade between the regions, and aid in harmonizing product standards between them. U.S. labor unions would be more willing to support such an agreement because of the region's similar labor and environmental standards and because an agreement could result in billions of dollars in yearly growth and thousands of jobs.[16]

   As the United States and the EU began negotiations in 2013, however, a number of challenges began to arise. The French, backed by the European Parliament, want to continue providing subsidies and quotas to support its film and music industries and thus exclude the cultural industries from any future trade talks. On the other side, U.S. farmers are very upset about European agricultural safety standards and view them as protectionist. Obviously, any agreement will be difficult to reach, in spite of the hope for expanding economic growth in the regions.[17]

Sidebar notes (left margin):

Migration and terrorism are threatening the open borders that are at the heart of the Schengen Agreement.

The EU expanded from 15 to 25 countries in 2004 with countries from mostly Central and Eastern Europe. Romania and Bulgaria were admitted in 2007 and Croatia in 2013, bringing the number to 28.

CONCEPT CHECK

In Chapter 5 (page 194), we point out that in countries where labor is abundant compared to capital, many workers (not surprisingly) tend to be either unemployed or poorly paid. If permitted, they will migrate to countries that enjoy full employment and higher wages—a form of factor mobility that governments in the latter group of countries often restrict.

How to Do Business with the EU: Implications for Corporate Strategy   The EU is a tremendous market in terms of both population and income—one that companies cannot ignore. It is also a good example of how geographic proximity and the removal of trade barriers can influence trade. More than half the merchandise exports and imports of EU countries are considered to be intrazonal trade. That is far better than other regional or even bilateral trade agreements. Again, geographic proximity, a common currency for most of the member countries, and the length of time the EU has been in existence are key reasons why the intrazonal trade is so high.

Doing business in the EU can influence corporate strategy, especially for outside MNEs, in three ways:

1. *Determining where to produce.* One strategy is to produce in a central location in Europe to minimize transportation costs and the time it takes to move products from one country to another. However, the highest costs are in central Europe. As we saw in our opening case, for instance, manufacturing wages in the German auto industry were much higher than the lower wages among Eastern European members.

2. *Determining whether to grow through new investments, through expanding existing investments, or through joint ventures and mergers.* As the United Kingdom enters into a decision-making phase and companies reassess the set up of the manufacturing platforms in Europe, the prospective U.K.–EU treaty is being determined (along the lines of CETA) and WTO terms are being looked at, small and medium-sized companies are looking to exploit the trading opportunities offered by the United Kingdom's withdrawal from a competition-stifling EU. Rentokil International, a pest control company, is a big gainer from the plunging pound. Since 90 percent of its revenue is from outside the United Kingdom and if pound rates stay the same, it will make up to £15m more than its usual revenue. On the other hand the International Airlines Group, which owns British Airways, stated that its annual profit would be lower because of weak trading, a result of the referendum.

3. *Balancing "common" denominators with national differences.* There are wider national differences in the EU due to language and history. But there are also widely different growth rates, although that varies from year to year. Also, slow economic growth since 2008 means that nobody is growing very fast. In recent years, for example, economic growth in Southern Europe, especially Greece, Cyprus, Italy, and Spain, has been in negative territory, Germany and France have been positive but relatively flat, and Ireland has been relatively robust.

A good example of adapting business strategies to Europe is the Associated British Foods (ABF). In 2016, the organization stated that Primark, the clothes retailer owned by ABF, the gap would be made up by a substantial increase in profits in its sugar business. Since it is an international business, profits earned outside the United Kingdom will continue to grow because of the weak pound. As part of this strategy and by improving its performance in the sugar business using the weak pound, ABF saw its revenue rise 22 percent following Britain's vote to leave the EU.

Companies will always struggle with the degree to which they develop a European strategy versus different national strategies inside Europe. In spite of the challenges, there are many opportunities for companies to expand their markets and sources of supply as the EU grows and encompasses more of Europe.

THE NORTH AMERICAN FREE TRADE AGREEMENT (NAFTA)

Various forms of mutual economic cooperation have historically existed between the United States and Canada, such as the Canada–U.S. Free Trade Agreement of 1989, which eliminated all tariffs on bilateral trade. In February 1991, Mexico approached the United States to establish a free trade agreement. Canada was included in the formal negotiations and the resulting **North American Free Trade Agreement (NAFTA)** became effective on January 1, 1994.

Why NAFTA?   NAFTA has a logical rationale in terms of both geographic location and trading importance. Although Canadian–Mexican trade was not significant when the agreement was signed, the United States had key trade relationships with each of them. In fact,

NAFTA rationale:

- U.S.–Canadian trade is the largest bilateral trade in the world.
- The United States is Mexico's and Canada's largest trading partner.

the one between the United States and Canada is the largest in the world, not including the 28-member EU. As Table 7.1 indicates, NAFTA is a powerful trading bloc with a combined population and GDP slightly less than the 28-member EU. What is significant, especially when compared with the EU, is the tremendous size of the U.S. economy compared to those of its neighbors, whereas there is no such dominant country in the EU. In addition, Canada generates a slightly higher GDP than does Mexico ($1.785 trillion vs. $1.295 trillion). However, Mexico has a larger population (125.4 million vs. 35.54) that is growing faster than that of Canada. But with roughly equal total GDP and the wide disparity in population, Canada has a higher per capita income than does Mexico.

NAFTA is a free trade agreement in goods and services rather than a customs union or a common market, and there is no common currency. However, its cooperation extends far beyond reductions in tariff and nontariff barriers to include provisions for services, investment, and intellectual property.

Mexico made significant strides in tariff reduction after joining GATT in 1986, when its tariffs averaged 100 percent. Since January 1, 2008, all tariffs and quotas were eliminated on U.S. exports to Canada and Mexico.

NAFTA calls for the elimination of tariff and nontariff barriers, the harmonization of trade rules, the liberalization of restrictions on services and foreign investment, the enforcement of intellectual property rights, and a dispute settlement process.

Static and Dynamic Effects NAFTA provides the static and dynamic effects of economic integration. For example, Canadian and U.S. consumers benefit from lower-cost agricultural products from Mexico, a *static* effect of economic liberalization. U.S. producers also benefit from the large and growing Mexican market, which has a huge appetite for U.S. products—a *dynamic* effect.

Trade Diversion NAFTA is also a good example of trade diversion. Prior to the agreement, many U.S. and Canadian companies had established manufacturing facilities in Asia to take advantage of low-cost labor. IBM, for example, was making computer parts in Singapore. After NAFTA, Mexico became a good option for those companies, and in five years IBM boosted exports from Mexico to the United States from $350 million to $2 billion.

Non-NAFTA companies are also investing in Mexico to take advantage of NAFTA.

NAFTA is a good example of trade diversion; some U.S. trade with and investment in Asia has been diverted to Mexico.

Rules of Origin and Regional Content

An important component of NAFTA is the concept of rules of origin and regional content. Because it is a free trade agreement and not a customs union, each country sets its own tariffs to the rest of the world. That's why a product entering the United States from Canada must have a commercial or customs invoice that identifies the product's ultimate origin. Otherwise, an exporter from a third country could always ship the product to the NAFTA country with the lowest tariff and then re-export it to the other two countries duty-free. A major criticism of RTAs like NAFTA is that the rules of origin are complex and detract from the spirit of multilateral tariff reductions in the WTO.

Rules of origin—goods and services must originate in North America to get access to lower tariffs.

Rules of Origin "Rules of origin" ensure that only goods that have been the subject of substantial economic activity within the free trade area are eligible for the more liberal tariff conditions created by NAFTA. This is a major contrast with the EU, which is a customs union rather than just an FTA. When a product enters France, for example, it can be shipped anywhere in the EU without worrying about rules of origin because tariffs are the same for all member countries. If NAFTA were a customs union instead of a free trade agreement, a product entering Mexico from, say, Japan and shipped to the United States would enter the United States duty-free because both countries would have the same duty on imports.

Regional Value Content Requirement One aspect of rules of origin in NAFTA refers to the Regional Value Content requirement. According to regional content rules, at least 50 percent of the net cost of components, raw materials, and labor of most products must come from the NAFTA region to qualify for the FTA. As long as a company meets the standard— and the regional content rules may vary depending on the nature of the product—a company may manufacture or assemble products in the NAFTA region and ship the goods to other members duty-free.

Regional content:

- The percentage of value that must be from North America for the product to be considered North American in terms of country of origin.
- 50 percent for most products, 62.5 percent for autos.

The Impact of NAFTA   There are pros and cons to any trade agreement, and NAFTA is no exception. It is obvious that trade and investment have increased significantly since the agreement was signed in 1994. U.S. goods and services trade with NAFTA totaled $1.6 trillion in 2009 (according to the latest data available). U.S. goods trade with the two partners totaled $918 billion in 2010, with the United States recording a trade deficit in goods.[18] Canada is the largest export market for U.S. goods, and Mexico is number two. And Canada and Mexico are the second- and third-largest suppliers of goods to the United States.

Because of its size, the United States is very important to Canada and Mexico for both exports and imports. Canada exports 76.7 percent of its merchandise to the United States and receives 54.3 percent of its imports from the United States. Mexico exports 80.2 percent of its merchandise and imports 49 percent of its merchandise from the United States. Mexico's trade with Canada is less than 5 percent for both exports and imports. Canada is the number one export market for U.S. merchandise and is the third-largest supplier of merchandise imports to the United States just above Mexico.[19]

> A major challenge to NAFTA is illegal immigration.

Immigration   A major challenge to NAFTA is immigration. As trade in agriculture increased with the advent of NAFTA, more than a million farm jobs disappeared in Mexico due to U.S. competition. Many of these farmers ended up as undocumented workers in the United States, sending home more money in wire transfers (see the opening case in Chapter 8) than Mexico receives in FDI. Rapid economic growth in the United States compared with Mexico in the 1990s also resulted in a rise in migration from Mexico to the United States. However, that has now changed due to smaller families and a stronger economy in Mexico. During the period 2009–2014, more Mexicans returned to Mexico from the United States than migrated to the United States from Mexico. A major factor in their decision to return was reunification with their families.[20] In spite of that, immigration still remains a hot issue on both sides of the border.

CONCEPT CHECK

As you'll recall from Chapter 6, page 221, trade restrictions may diminish export capabilities and induce companies to locate some production in countries imposing the restrictions; the absence of trade barriers gives them more flexibility not only in deciding where to locate production but also in determining how to service different markets.

How to Do Business with NAFTA: Implications for Corporate Strategy   Although NAFTA has not expanded beyond the original three countries due to political obstacles, each member has entered into bilateral agreements with other countries. However, when U.S. companies invest in Mexico, for example, they have an opportunity to penetrate markets in countries where Mexico has FTAs, as we will see in the case on Walmart at the end of the chapter. That allows them to add additional scale as the market broadens, even though Mexico's other trading partners are not members of NAFTA.

Rationalization of Production   One of the predictions made when NAFTA was signed was that companies would look at it as one big regional market, allowing them to rationalize production, products, financing, and the like. That has largely happened in a number of industries, especially in automotive products and electronics. Each NAFTA member ships more automotive products, based on specialized production, to the other two countries than any other manufactured goods. Rationalization of automotive production has taken place for years in the United States and Canada, but Mexico is a recent entrant, attracting auto manufacturing from all over the world, not just the United States. NAFTA's rules of origin have forced European and Asian automakers to bring in parts suppliers and set up assembly operations in Mexico. U.S. auto companies are shifting more of their production from the United States to Mexico, and the same is true for non-NAFTA companies, such as VW and Toyota. The Mexican Automobile Association trade group estimates that 70 percent of Mexican auto production will be exported to the United States.[21]

An interesting development in recent years is the decision by Chinese firms to invest more in Mexico as a platform for manufacturing electronics to ship into Canada and the United States. Hisense, a Chinese electronics company, purchased a factory in Mexico from Japanese company Sharp Corp. to manufacture TVs, with a goal of increasing its shipment of TVs to North America from 1.5 million (currently) to over 4 million. Higher wages and operating costs in China make Mexico an attractive alternative and allow Hisense to establish a regional manufacturing base in Mexico.

Mexico as a Consumer Market An additional benefit is that Canadian and U.S. companies have realized that Mexico is a consumer market rather than just a production location. Initially, the excitement over the country for U.S. and Canadian firms was the low-wage environment. However, as Mexican income continues to rise—which it must do as more investment enters and more of its companies export production—demand is rising for foreign products.

REGIONAL ECONOMIC INTEGRATION IN THE AMERICAS

If you look at Maps 7.2 and 7.3, you'll see six major regional economic groups in the Americas, divided into Central American and South American. Central America (excluding Mexico) has the Caribbean Community (CARICOM), the Central American Common Market (CACM), and the Central American Free Trade Agreement (CAFTA-DR)—which includes the members of CACM but also Honduras and the Dominican Republic, along with the United States. The two major groups in South America are the Andean Community (CAN) and the Southern Common Market (Mercosur). The Andean Community is a customs union, whereas Mercosur is set up to be a common market.

The major reason for these different collaborative groups was market size. The post–World War II strategy of import substitution to resolve balance-of-payments problems in much of Latin America was doomed because of the region's small national markets. Therefore, some form of economic cooperation was needed to enlarge the potential market size so that Latin American companies could achieve economies of scale and be more competitive worldwide.

CARICOM The **Caribbean Community (CARICOM)** is working hard to establish an EU-style form of collaboration, complete with full movement of goods and services, the right of establishment, a common external tariff, free movement of capital and labor, a common trade policy, and so on. It is officially classified by the WTO as an Economic Integration Agreement. Many of these initiatives have come about through an initiative called the CARICOM Single Market and Economy (CSME).

MAP 7.2 Economic Integration in Central America and the Caribbean

Throughout Central America and the Caribbean, the focus on economic integration has shifted from the concept of the *free trade agreement* (whose goal is the abolition of trade barriers among members) to that of the *common market* (which calls for internal factor mobility as well as the abolition of internal trade barriers). The proposed structure of the Caribbean Community and Common Market (CARICOM) is modeled on that of the EU.

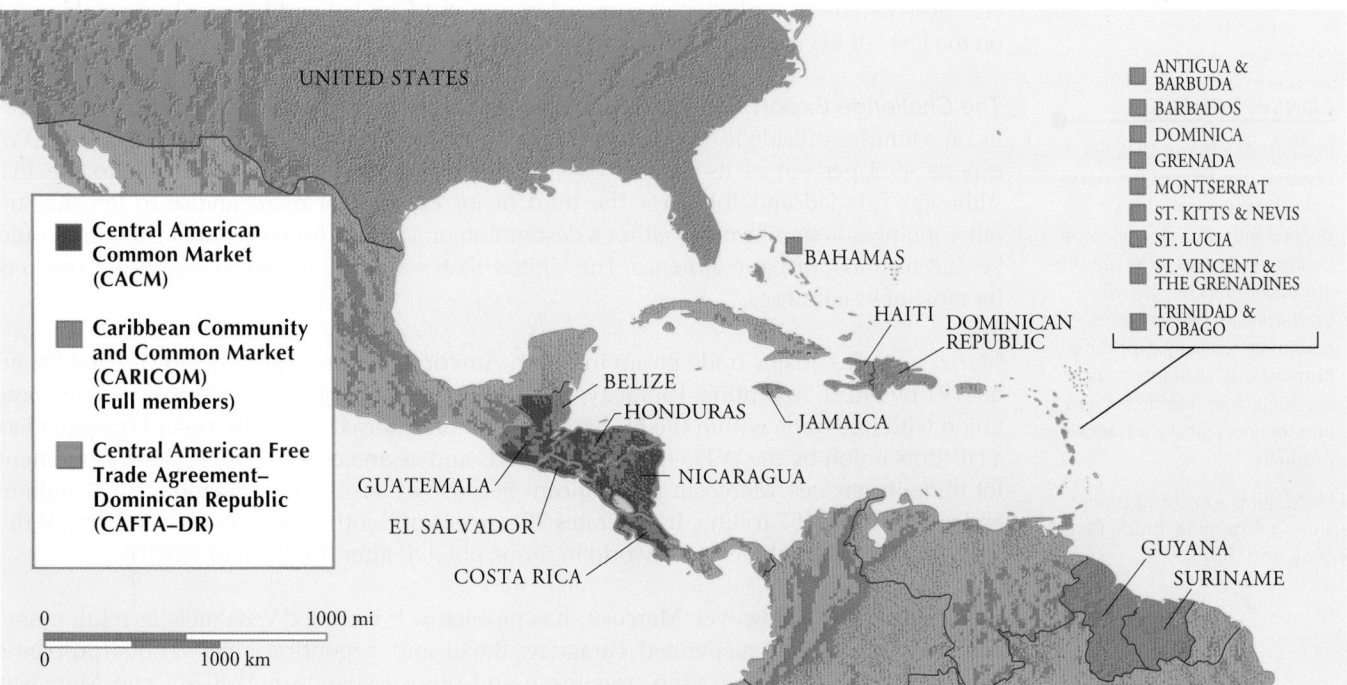

MAP 7.3   Latin American Economic Integration

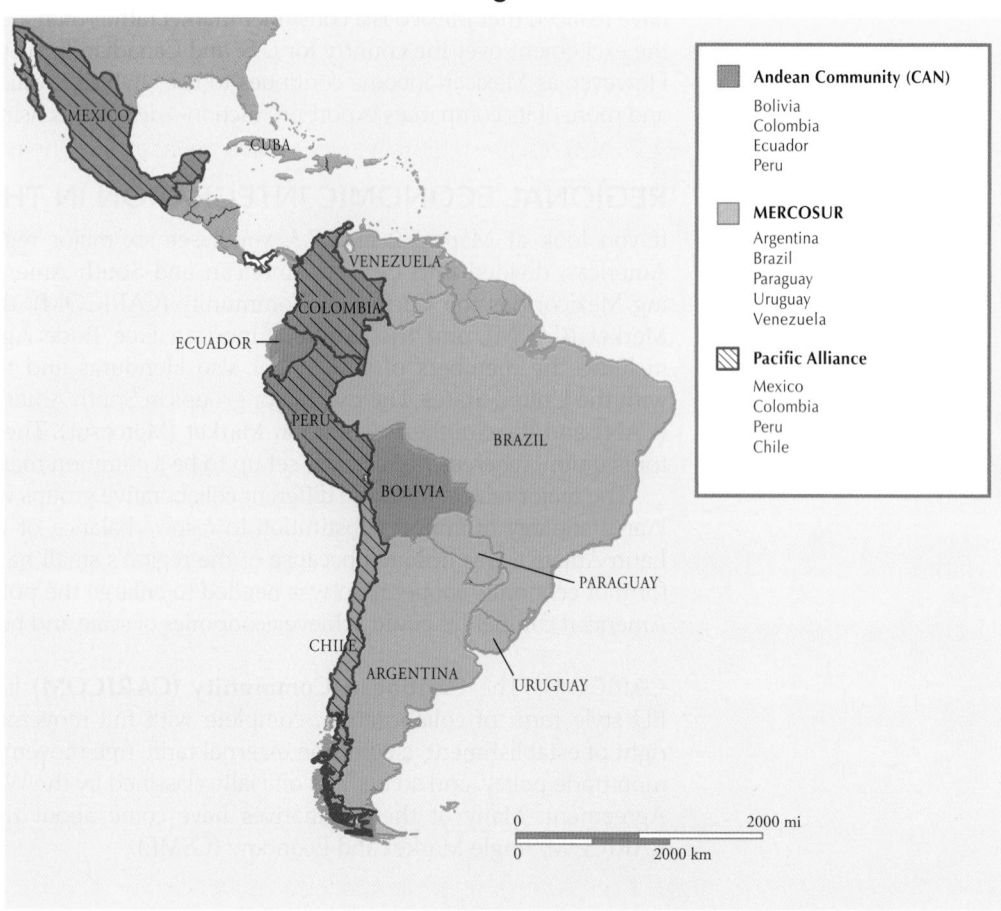

In some ways, the changes in the Caribbean Community mirror what has happened in the EU, though on a smaller scale. The entire population is only 6.5 million people, 60 percent of whom live in only two countries: Jamaica and Trinidad and Tobago. That would put it on the level of EU member Bulgaria in terms of population.

The Challenge Export Reliance   Countries in Latin America and the Caribbean rely heavily on countries outside the region for trade. For example, Jamaica, a member of CARICOM, exports 49.3 percent of its merchandise to the United States and 18 percent to the EU. Although Trinidad and Tobago is the third major exporter of merchandise to Jamaica, no other member is significant as either a destination or a source for its exports. The same could be said for most of Latin America. The United States and EU represent significant markets for most of its countries.

Mercosur   The major trade group in South America is **Mercosur**, which was established in 1991 by Brazil, Argentina, Paraguay, and Uruguay. Its major goal is to become a customs union with free trade within the bloc and a common external tariff. Mercosur is classified as a customs union by the WTO for trade in goods and as an economic integration agreement for trade in services. Mercosur is significant because of its size: a population of 251 million and a GDP of $2.457 trillion. It generates 75 percent of South America's GDP, making it the third-largest trading bloc in the world in terms of GDP after the EU and NAFTA.

Pacific Alliance   However, Mercosur has problems. It included Venezuela as a full member, and temporarily suspended Paraguay. Brazil and Argentina have serious problems with protectionism. Frustration over these and other issues in both CAN and Mercosur

CONCEPT CHECK

In Chapter 5 (page 184), we observe that little of the trade of low-income countries is conducted with other low-income countries. By and large, emerging economies rely heavily on trade with high-income countries, typically exporting primary and labor-intensive products in exchange for new and technologically advanced products.

Mercosur is a customs union among Argentina, Brazil, Paraguay, and Uruguay.

led to the creation in 2012 of the **Pacific Alliance**, comprising Mexico, Colombia, Peru, and Chile. These countries refer to themselves as more hospitable to trade and investment due to their adherence to democracy and the rule of law rather than the more populist and protectionist philosophies of other countries in CAN and Mercosur.[22] Having borders with the Pacific also means that they are trying to be a bridge between Latin America and the Asia–Pacific region, which makes sense given their dynamic and market-oriented economies.[23]

Andean Community (CAN)   Although the **Andean Community (CAN)** is not as significant economically as Mercosur, it is the second most important official regional group in South America. CAN has been around since 1969. However, its focus has shifted from one of isolationism and statism (placing economic control in the hands of the state—the central government) to being open to foreign trade and investment. Colombia and Peru, two of the founding members of CAN, have changed significantly in recent years and entered into bilateral trade agreements with the United States, solidifying their move to greater openness in comparison with other members of CAN. As noted above, they also have decided to join the Pacific Alliance.

> The Andean Community is one of the original regional economic groups but has not been successful in achieving its original goals.

REGIONAL ECONOMIC INTEGRATION IN ASIA

There are several RTAs in Asia as recognized by the WTO and a few significant trade initiatives in process. Of the officially approved RTAs, the most important is the Association of Southeast Asian Nations/ASEAN Free Trade Area. As is the case in Latin America, regional integration in Asia has not been as successful as in Europe or North America because most of the countries in the region have relied on U.S. and EU markets for as much as 20 to 30 percent of their exports—not as extensive as in Latin America but still significant. In addition, China and Japan, which are not members of ASEAN/AFTA, are significant players in the region in terms of trade and investment.

Association of Southeast Asian Nations (ASEAN)   Organized in 1967, **ASEAN** is a comprehensive association that includes preferential trade as one of its many goals. This preferential trade agreement comprises Brunei Darussalam, Cambodia, Indonesia, Laos, Malaysia, Myanmar, the Philippines, Singapore, Thailand, and Vietnam (see Map 7.4). With a combined GDP of $2.249 trillion and an estimated population of 634.8 million people,[24] it is a significant organization.

ASEAN Free Trade Area   On January 1, 1993, ASEAN officially formed the ASEAN Free Trade Area (AFTA) with the goal of cutting tariffs on all intrazonal trade to a maximum of 5 percent by January 1, 2008. The weaker ASEAN countries would be allowed to phase in their tariff reductions over a longer period. By 2005, most products traded among the AFTA countries were subject to duties from 0 to 5 percent, so AFTA has been successful in its objectives. Free trade is crucial to the member countries because their ratio of exports to GDP is almost 70 percent. The best achievement of AFTA is that is has reduced tariffs, attracted FDI, and turned the region into a huge network of production, leading to what some call "factory Asia."[25]

> The ASEAN Free Trade Area is a successful trade agreement among countries in Southeast Asia.

Although China is not a part of ASEAN, it is essential to ASEAN's future. China's working-age population is 795.4 million people, compared with 298 million for the ASEAN countries. Although the average monthly wage for manufacturing workers is much higher in Singapore and Malaysia than in China, it is much lower in the other ASEAN countries. As wages continue to rise in China, there are opportunities for ASEAN countries to attract more FDI, but those countries need to work hard to improve their infrastructure, especially supply chain and manufacturing infrastructure.[26] These opportunities combined with China's competitive position are forcing ASEAN to work harder to strengthen the ties among member countries. In addition to the FTA, ASEAN finalized the establishment of

MAP 7.4   The Association of Southeast Asian Nations

Although the total population of ASEAN countries is larger than that of either the EU or NAFTA, per capita GDP is considerably lower. Economic growth rates among ASEAN members, however, are among the highest in the world.

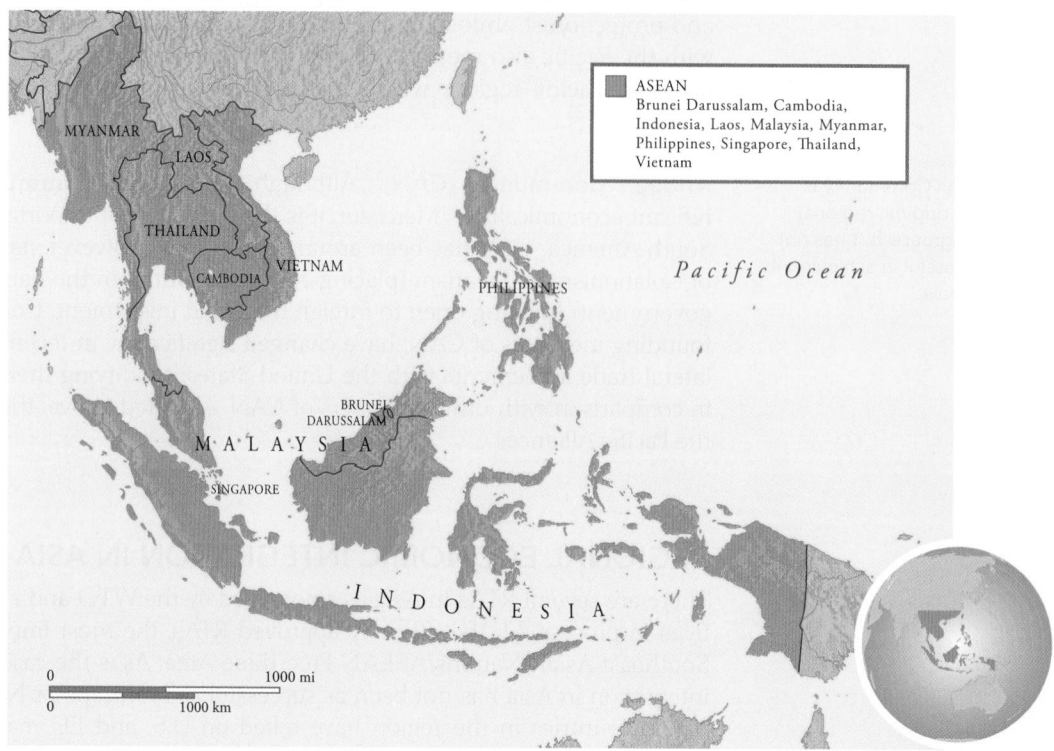

the ASEAN Economic Community (AEC) in 2015, which the member countries hope will go beyond trade liberalization and help establish the region as a single market and production base.

> APEC comprises 21 countries that border the Pacific Rim; progress toward free trade is hampered by size and geographic distance between member countries and by the lack of a treaty.

Asia Pacific Economic Cooperation (APEC)   Formed in November 1989 to promote multilateral economic cooperation in trade and investment in the Pacific Rim,[27] **Asia Pacific Economic Cooperation (APEC)** is composed of 21 countries that border both Asia and the Americas. All but three members of AFTA are members of APEC, plus Canada, the United States, Mexico, Peru, and Chile in the Americas; Australia and New Zealand; and China, Japan, Korea, Russia, and Chinese Taipei. It is a large and powerful organization that is focused on a wide range of activities related to trade and investment, security, energy, sustainability, anticorruption, and transparency, among other things. However, it is not an RTA as defined by the WTO and does not show up on that list of RTAs. The sheer size of APEC is what sets it apart: 55 percent of global GDP and 43 percent of world trade.

Trans-Pacific Partnership (TPP)   The TPP was initiated by the United States to spur economic growth and create jobs, and it involves Australia, Brunei, Canada, Chile, Japan, Malaysia, Mexico, New Zealand, Peru, Singapore, the United States, and Vietnam. The formation of the initiative was announced in 2011, the agreement was concluded in October 2015 and signed by the trade ministers in February 2016. However, the TPP will not actually come into effect until it is approved by the government of each member, which is a difficult political task, especially during a contentious election year in the United States. It is interesting to note that that the signatories to the agreement include the members of NAFTA, many but not all of ASEAN, and the Pacific Alliance. Other countries may eventually join if the TPP continues forward. A main goal of the TPP is to enhance trade and investment, although it also is concerned with labor and environmental standards. Its comprehensiveness will make it more difficult to approve and enforce.

REGIONAL ECONOMIC INTEGRATION IN AFRICA

There are several African trade groups, but they rely more on their former colonial powers and other developed markets for trade than they do on each other.

Africa is truly the new frontier. The UN keeps revising its estimates of population growth in Africa, but the latest estimates are that South Africa's population will double to 2.5 billion in 2050, up from 1.2 billion people in 2015, with Nigeria having a population of 400 million. In 2015, only China and India had more than 400 million people. Not only is Africa's population large, but it is growing faster than most regions of the world as life expectancy has gone up from 37 years in 1955 to 60 years in 2015. Families are still large as fertility rates are among the highest in the world and infant mortality has dropped.[28] Africa has the fastest-expanding labor force in the world with more than 500 million people of working age (15–64), and is expected to surpass China and India in working-age population by 2040.[29]

From the standpoint of regional integration, however, Africa is complicated because of the large number of countries on the continent and the fact that there are 3 regional monetary unions and 17 trade blocs. On Map 7.5, we have selected only four of the trade blocs

MAP 7.5 Regional Integration in Africa

Although most African nations are members of more than one regional trade group, the total amount of trade among members remains relatively small. African nations tend to rely heavily on trading relationships with countries elsewhere in the world—notably with former colonial and other industrialized nations.

to illustrate the situation in Africa. The problem is that African countries have been struggling to establish a political identity, and the different trade groups have political as well as economic underpinnings. The key to continued growth in Africa is the reduction of risk as conflicts drop and peace improves. Nearly all of the 54 countries in Africa belong to more than one trade agreement.

To illustrate the challenges of economic integration in Africa, ECOWAS is a customs union, but there are lots of exceptions and there has not been a lot of progress on free movement of people, goods and transportation. The lack of intrazonal trade is generally because most countries rely on export of commodities to developed countries, especially former colonial powers, and they have little else to trade with each other. As a result, they resort to protecting local industry rather than increasing intrazonal trade. The markets, with the notable exception of South Africa, are relatively small and undeveloped, making trade liberalization a relatively minor contributor to economic growth in the region. The East African Community is successful because it only includes five neighboring countries so it is easier to resolve trade differences. A relatively new agreement was signed in 2015 creating the Tripartite Free Trade Area which covers 26 African countries, but that is pretty ambitious, and most members are already part of other trade agreements that don't work very well.[30]

Point

Point   **Yes** A regional free trade agreement among a small group of

countries is easy to establish and monitor, unlike the broader agreements of the WTO. It provides a larger market area which will increase economies of scale and open up investment opportunities. An example is NAFTA which only involves three countries, with the United States having a common border with both. Since NAFTA is not a customs union, each country is free to set up bilateral trade agreements with other countries. The other extreme, however, is the European Union. From a trade perspective, the EU includes both a free trade agreement and a customs union.

The EU, unlike NAFTA and most other regional groups, has gone far beyond trade by establishing a common currency, a European Central Bank, a European parliament, and a fairly extensive bureaucracy that is trying its best to bring the region ever closer together. In essence, countries are willing to give up sovereignty in order to receive the economic benefits of being part of a larger community. The advantage of this more extensive approach is that large and small nations in Europe can work together to solve common problems, including migration, security, and economic turmoil. Because of its longevity, the EU has seen its intrazonal trade rise to nearly 50 percent, which is much higher than other regional groups.

Is Regional Economic Integration a Good Idea?

Another good example of the positive benefits of regional economic groups is the Dominican Republic-Central American Free Trade Agreement which links the United States together with six other countries—Costa Rica, Dominican Republic, El Salvador, Guatemala, Honduras, and Nicaragua. The FTA holds enormous benefits for its signatories: opening the door for increased trade between the United States and the region; stimulating economic growth in the region by encouraging FDI and offering shorter international supply chains; and encouraging economic and political reform in an area historically plagued by Marxism, dictatorships, and civil wars.

The United States has free trade agreements in force with 20 countries, including the members of CAFTA-DR and NAFTA. One of the biggest benefits for the United States is reciprocal tariff treatment from the other nations. Due to temporary trade-preference programs and other regional agreements, 80 percent of the products from at least five Central American nations already enter the United States duty-free. Prior to signing the agreement, U.S. manufactured exports were subject to tariffs that averaged 30 to 100 percent higher than those faced by Central American exports when entering the United States.[31] CAFTA-DR allows the Central American nations to maintain these favorable gains, but it also leaves the playing field open for the United States to benefit similarly by reducing restrictions on 80 percent of U.S. consumer and industrial exports to the region.

Is Regional Economic Integration a Good Idea?

Counterpoint **No** The proponents of regional integration are governments, and they invest so much political capital in negotiating and signing agreements that they get trapped and can never get out. Also, a dominant economic power, such as the United States can impose its will on smaller trade partners such as those in CAFTA-DR. As free trade agreements progress to a customs union to more extensive integration, national sovereignty becomes gradually more compromised. It is not uncommon to overstate the benefits and understate the shortcomings. The British found that out in 2016 as the UK was faced with "Brexit"—a national referendum on whether or not to exit the EU.[32] Those in favor of staying in were the Labour Party, the Liberal Democrats, and business and trade unions, which is ironic in comparison with the United States, where labor unions tend to be against any trade agreement. The main fear the Brits had was the unknown. There didn't seem to be a good alternative to membership in the EU, so why leave? They were worried that if the UK left the EU, they would have to renegotiate all of their trade and investment relationships with EU countries and who knows what they would have ended up with. In addition, there were fears that London might lose its status as the financial center in Europe, even though the UK continued to use the British pound as their currency rather than join the Eurozone and adopt the euro. There was also a fear that if they left the EU, Scottish nationalists, who were not euro skeptics, might resurrect their desire to break away from the UK and join the EU on their own.

There were lots of reasons to support Brexit. The UK was not one of the original six members of the EU, and it never did want to join the common Eurozone. The free flow of labor and open borders are critical to the EU. This seems like a good idea for aging countries that need younger workers, but the increase of migrants from war-torn Syria caused serious political tensions in the UK. Should they continue to have open borders and the risk of escalating social costs? It is hard to reject the EU mandate of the free flow of labor and still be a member of the EU.

Counterpoint

A major problem of the EU is the broad diversity of political, cultural, and language forces. Of course, all countries have to deal with these differences in normal trading relationships, but the problem with the EU and other regional trade groups is that these factors become more complicated with expansion, and it is harder to find a common ground to solve problems.

A major argument for Brexit is the loss of sovereignty. Although there is bureaucracy and a loss of sovereignty in the simplest of free trade agreements, the growth of the bureaucracy in the EU is pretty extreme. If the goal of the EU is to keep bringing countries closer together, it is obvious that there will be an increasing loss of sovereignty. But Brexit forces in the UK are particularly concerned about the centralization of power in Brussels which has affected many aspects of life. Thus any member of a regional group has to decide if the benefits of free trade outweigh the potential loss of sovereignty. The forces that are leading to Brexit are extreme since they could lead to a powerful country leaving a powerful regional economic alliance, but they are the same forces at the heart of the negotiations of any potential regional economic alliance. As a result of these arguments for and against Brexit, 51.9 percent of the British people voted on June 23, 2016 to leave the EU, even though the people in Scotland, Northern Ireland, and London voted to remain. Stock markets plunged around the world, the pound dropped, and the yen went up in value as uncertainty plagued markets. In order for the UK to leave the EU, it has to officially notify the other member countries, which then initiates a complex process that could take up to two years, or possibly longer, to work out the details for the UK's exit. There are even rumblings that Scotland might try to leave the UK and become a sovereign member of the EU, and Northern Ireland might also leave the UK and become part of Ireland, resulting in Brexit leaving England and Wales as the remaining two countries in the EU. Clearly, there is a tremendous amount of uncertainty over the next few years, just as predicted in the run-up to the June referendum.

THE UNITED NATIONS AND OTHER NGOS

The UN was established in 1945 following World War II to promote international peace and security. It deals with economic development, antiterrorism, and humanitarian movements.

The United Nations The first form of cooperation worth exploring is the United Nations, which was established in 1945 in response to the devastation of World War II to promote international peace and security and to help solve global problems in such diverse areas as economic development, antiterrorism, and humanitarian actions. If the UN performs its responsibilities, it should improve the environment in which MNEs operate around the world, reducing risk and providing greater opportunities.

The historic "yes" vote for Brexit will change the face of the EU forever.

Source: Marian Weyo/Shutterstock

Organization and Membership   The UN family of organizations is too large to list, but it includes the WTO, the International Monetary Fund, and the World Bank (the latter two discussed in subsequent chapters). These organizations are all part of the Economic and Social Council, one of six principal organs of the UN System, which also includes the General Assembly, the Security Council, and the International Court of Justice.

The UN has 193 member states represented in the General Assembly, including 15 that compose the Security Council. There are 5 permanent members of the Security Council—China, France, the Russian Federation, the United Kingdom, and the United States—and 10 other members elected by the General Assembly to serve 2-year terms.[33]

UNCTAD was established to help developing countries participate in international trade.

UNCTAD   The UN Conference on Trade and Development, or **UNCTAD**, was established in 1964 to integrate developing countries into the global economy. UNCTAD's main activities include globalization and development strategies, trade in goods and services, commodities, investment and enterprise development, and trade logistics and human resource development. In particular, UNCTAD has been active in contributing to the debate on issues related to developing countries and the global economy.[34]

NGOs—private nonprofit institutions that are independent of the government.

Nongovernmental Organizations (NGOs)   Nongovernmental, nonprofit voluntary organizations are all lumped under the category of NGOs: private institutions that are independent of any government. The UN is an intergovernmental organization and thus not an NGO. Some NGOs operate only within the confines of a specific country, whereas others are international in scope. An example of the latter is the International Red Cross, which is concerned with humanitarian issues around the world, not just in one country. One of the functions of UNCTAD is to work with NGOs in helping shape policies and activities related to concerns of developing countries. NGOs perform an important role in bringing potential abuses to light and tend to be very narrowly focused, usually on a specific issue (e.g., Transparency International discussed in Chapter 11).

COMMODITY AGREEMENTS

The attempts of countries to stabilize commodity prices through producer alliances and commodity agreements have been largely unsuccessful.

Commodities refer to raw materials or primary products that enter into trade, such as metals or agricultural products. Primary commodity exports—such as crude petroleum, natural gas, copper, iron ore, tobacco, coffee, cocoa, tea, and sugar—are still important to developing countries. Out of 135 developing countries tracked by the UN Conference on Trade and Development, 94 generated at least 60 percent of the exports from commodities, up from 88 countries in 2009–2010. It is clear from the UN Report that dependence on commodity exports by developing countries has risen in recent years, even as commodity prices have fallen due to the weak global economy.[35]

COMMODITIES AND THE WORLD ECONOMY

Both long-term trends and short-term fluctuations in commodity prices have important consequences for the world economy. On the demand side, commodity markets play an important role in industrial countries, transmitting business cycle disturbances to the rest of the economy and affecting the growth rate of prices. On the supply side, as noted above, primary products account for a significant portion of the GDP and exports of many commodity-producing countries.

CONSUMERS AND PRODUCERS

CONCEPT CHECK

Commodities often represent natural advantages, which we define in Chapter 5 (page 179) as advantages in production resulting from climatic conditions, access to certain natural resources, or availability of certain labor forces.

CONCEPT CHECK

Remember from Chapter 5 (pages 184–186) the fact that lower-income countries depend much more on the production of primary products than do wealthier nations; consequently, they depend more heavily on natural advantage as opposed to the kinds of acquired advantage that involve more advanced technologies and processes.

Many commodity agreements now exist for the purpose of

- discussing issues,
- disseminating information,
- improving product safety.

For many years, countries tried to band together as producer alliances or joint producer/consumer alliances to try to stabilize commodity prices. However, these efforts—with the exception of OPEC, which we discuss below—have not been very successful. UNCTAD established a Special Unit on Commodities to attempt to deal with the issues facing developing countries because of high dependence on commodities, especially agricultural commodities, for export revenues. Given such reliance, UNCTAD is concerned that it will be impossible to resolve poverty issues, especially in Africa, without dealing with fluctuating commodity prices.

The most important international commodity organizations and bodies, such as the International Cocoa Organization and the International Copper Study Group, take part in UN-led discussions to help commodity-dependent countries establish effective policies and strategies. However, each one, such as the International Coffee Organization (ICO), has its own organizational structure independent of the UN. The ICO is composed of 42 coffee-exporting nations—all of them developing countries—and 8 importing nations, most of which are developed countries, although the entire EU is considered one country. ICO members are responsible for over 98 percent of the world's coffee exports and 83 percent of the world's coffee consumption.[36]

Whereas many of the original commodity agreements were designed to influence price through a variety of market-interfering mechanisms, most of the existing ones have been established to discuss issues, disseminate information, improve product safety, and so on. Very little can be done outside of market forces to influence price. The ICO, for example, helps fund projects for coffee growing nations to combat pests and diseases and to expand coffee consumption through promotion efforts. Coffee consumption varies a lot from country to country, so the promotion efforts supported by ICO are designed to increase per capita consumption in low-consuming countries.

For many years, commodity prices fluctuated but did not increase dramatically. In the decade of the 2000s, however, global economic growth pulled them up. China, in particular, was growing so fast that it was pulling most commodity prices up, leading to trade agreements between China and many commodity-producing countries, as well as substantial foreign investment. The global economic crisis, however, caused a significant contraction in commodity prices of nearly 17 percent in 2009, which had a very negative impact on the economies of the commodity-producing countries. The prices increased by 23 percent from January 2010 to January 2011 as the global economy began to recover.[37] However, as the Chinese economy and the rest of the global economy began to contract in 2013, commodity prices dropped again through 2015. But as economic growth recovers, so too will commodity prices.

THE ORGANIZATION OF THE PETROLEUM EXPORTING COUNTRIES (OPEC)

OPEC is a producers' alliance in oil that has been successful in using quotas to keep oil prices high.

Although OPEC supplies oil and natural gas, it's important to understand that the world is dependent on the following main sources of energy: oil (31.1 percent), coal (28.9 percent), natural gas (21.4 percent), and everything else (18.6 percent). In terms of crude oil, OPEC is an important player.

The **Organization of the Petroleum Exporting Countries (OPEC)** is an example of a producer cartel that relies on quotas to influence prices. It is a group of 13 oil-producing countries that have significant control over supply and band together to control output and price. Its members include Algeria, Angola, Ecuador, Indonesia, Iran, Iraq, Kuwait, Libya, Nigeria, Qatar, Saudi Arabia, the United Arab Emirates, and Venezuela. Several of the largest oil-exporting countries, including Russia, Norway, Canada, the United States, and Mexico, are not members of OPEC. Saudi Arabia is the largest producer of oil, closely followed by Russia and the United States. Saudi Arabia is also the largest net exporter of oil, followed by Russia and the United Arab Emirates.

Price Controls and Politics   OPEC controls prices by establishing production quotas on member countries. Saudi Arabia has historically performed the role of the dominant supplier in influencing supply and price. Periodically OPEC oil ministers gather together to determine the quota for each country based on estimates of supply and demand. Politics is also an important dimension of the deliberations. OPEC member countries with large populations need large oil revenues to fund government programs. As a result, they are tempted to exceed their export quotas to generate more revenues.

Output and Exports   OPEC member countries produce about 33.6 percent of the world's crude oil and 19 percent of its natural gas. However, its oil exports represent about 60.4 percent of the oil traded internationally.[38] In addition, OPEC has 81 percent of the world's crude oil reserves, with the Middle East containing 66.4 percent of OPEC's total reserves. Therefore, OPEC can have a strong influence on the oil market, especially if it decides to reduce or increase its level of production.

Sometimes OPEC policies work; sometimes they don't. In addition, events beyond its control can influence prices. The rapidly escalating price of crude oil prior to the global economic crisis was a mixture of rising demand worldwide (especially in China), political instability in the Middle East, and a shortage of refining capacity, caused in part by environmental rules in some countries that preclude the building of new refineries.

The downside of high oil prices for OPEC:

• Producers investing in countries outside of OPEC
• Complication of balancing social, political, and economic objectives

The Downside of High Prices   Keeping oil prices high has some downside for OPEC. Competition from non-OPEC countries rises because the revenues accruing to the competitors are higher. Because some OPEC countries are putting up roadblocks to production, major producers like BP, ExxonMobil, and Shell are investing heavily in areas like the Caspian Basin, the Gulf of Mexico, and Angola and are trying to enter areas like the Russian Federation. Production in these areas is expected to grow significantly.

High prices also attract competition to conventional oil, including nonconventional oil (such as oil shale, oil sands, and biofuels) and nuclear energy, although the damage to the nuclear reactors in Japan as a result of the earthquake and tsunami in 2011 had a chilling effect on nuclear energy.

Political and social forces also affect oil prices. The civil war in Libya impacted oil markets in 2011, causing oil prices to spike due to the fear that the unrest could spread to other big Middle East oil producers. The same was true when Russia invaded the Ukraine and annexed Crimea, resulting in sanctions against Russia. Companies that had hoped to cash in on Russian oil were forced to pull back until political relations between Russia and the West could be normalized, if ever.

Looking to the Future
Will the WTO Overcome Bilateral and Regional Integration Efforts?

Will regional integration be the wave of the future, or will the World Trade Organization become the focus of global economic integration? The WTO's objective is to reduce barriers to trade in goods, services, and investment. Regional groups attempt to do that and more. Although the EU has introduced a common currency and is increasing the degree of cooperation in areas such as security and foreign policy, the WTO will likely never engage in those issues. Regional integration deals with the specific problems facing member countries, whereas the WTO needs to be concerned about all countries in the world.

However, regional integration might actually help the WTO achieve its objectives in three major ways:

1. Regionalism can lead to liberalization of issues not covered by the WTO.
2. Regionalism is more flexible, given that it typically involves fewer countries with similar conditions and objectives.
3. Regional deals lock in liberalization, especially in developing countries.

As we have seen in this chapter, no trade agreement is easy or perfect. The WTO has serious challenges due to its size. Regional agreements like NAFTA, the EU, Mercosur, and others have many different challenges as well. In cases of NAFTA and Mercosur, one dominant country in each (the United States and Brazil, respectively) implies that the balance of power among the member countries is not equal.

The EU has its own challenges due to enlargement; the debt crises of several member countries, especially Greece; inward migration from Syria and other countries and Brexit.

Regional integration in Africa will continue at a slow pace due to the vast size of the continent and that fact that so many countries have common borders with countries that are involved in different regional economic groups. However, Africa is flush with natural resources and will be a favorite trading partner of resource-hungry China as the Chinese and global economies recover. In addition, greater peace and stability in Africa and the rise in working-age population will make the continent an interesting place in which to invest and a potential source for consumer growth.

Asian integration, primarily in AFTA, APEC, and possibly the Trans-Pacific Partnership, will pick up steam as the economies of East and Southeast Asia continue to open up and as they collaborate to meet the challenge of China. Japan, which is not a member of AFTA, has signed a number of bilateral agreements with other countries in Asia, including an FTA with the members of ASEAN. It became a member of the Trans-Pacific Partnership in 2013 and is in the process of implementing new agreements with Australia, the Gulf Cooperation Council, India, and Korea. However, the key to the growth of most countries in Southeast Asia may be China and its rapidly growing influence in Asia and the rest of the world. ■

CASE   Unilever Goes East[39]

—Stefania Paladini

The five main economies of Southeast Asia—Thailand, Malaysia, Singapore, Philippines, and Indonesia—signed an association agreement. The other five members (Myanmar, Laos, Cambodia, Vietnam, and Brunei) have aggregated over time, until the last one, Cambodia, joined in 1999. The importance of ASEAN has been growing over time, linked to the progressive growth of the economies of Southeast Asia since the early 80s, and only temporarily slowed down by the Asian crisis in the 90s. Increasingly, a number of multinationals with a steady interest in Asia Pacific have been selecting the region as their manufacturing base, also serving as a hub for their operations. The list of reasons for this choice is long and substantial.

The area is currently a market of 617 million people (about 10 percent of the world population), with a global GDP projected to reach US$4.7 trillion in 2020 (approximately Japan's level of today) and a share of world trade of about 7 percent. ASEAN has been working towards creating an East Asian Community (EAC) by the end of 2015, by integrating into a single and coherent market the 10 economies that up to now have been functioning at different speeds.

While there are still a lot of differences among member states, the main economies of the region share a long tradition in manufacturing, and some of them enjoy excellent facilities in terms of infrastructure, ports, and technology (Singapore is the best example, but not the only one), which makes them an excellent choice for offshoring.

Unilever and the ASEAN countries: a success story

The world's third largest FMCG company, with 173,000 employees in 190 countries and an established presence in food and personal care, Unilever features in its vast portfolio some of the world's most famous food and household products, including Dove, Lipton, Rexona, Vaseline, Magnum, Omo, Cif, Ponds, P&G, and Knorr. Founded in 1930—even though some of the companies that later on joined forces to create it were already existing since 1885—the Anglo-Dutch giant was one of the first to enter Southeast Asian markets and has certainly been one of the most successful worldwide.

In 2011, Paul Polman, the newly appointed CEO, decided to make the corporation more dynamic and even further oriented to emerging markets. At the same time, he created the post of COO, with the directive of concentrating on these new regions and elaborating a unique strategy for them. This meant instead of replicating what Unilever was doing in first-world markets—where food represents half their business—the Asian subsidiaries were going to heavily invest in personal and health care, allotting food products a more marginal space in their business plans. This winning strategy has yielded remarkable results.

Even with the global slowdown and problems in some of its core markets (namely Europe), Unilever's 2012 operative results were remarkably good, with an increase in turnover of

Unilever, comprised of some of the world's best known brands in FMCG including Vaseline, Dove, and Lipton, floods markets in the East.

Source: joephoto. 123rf.com

10.5 percent which brought it to € 51.3 billion overall. During the 2012 World Economic Forum, Davos, Harish Manwani, the COO of Unilever, allegedly declared that the company's diversified portfolio and its presence in Asia has helped it offset its weakness in Europe. Unlike competitors P&G and Nestle, who were more focused on mature markets, Unilever, whose business comprises 56 percent emerging markets, has been less affected by challenging global economic conditions than some of its rivals because of its extensive portfolio of brands and its emphasis on emerging markets. Preliminary results for 2013 confirmed this trend of a shifting importance towards extra- Europe markets, still growing in contrast with the slowing sales in the EU. The company has an established presence in Southeast Asia, going back to the end of World War II, and has been steadily growing since.

From the regional HQ in Kuala Lampur, Unilever has been active in Malaysia since 1947. As recently as 2013, Unilever Malaysia, also responsible for Singapore, has opened up Four Acres Singapore, a huge training facility of 2.3 hectares for its management, the only center of its kind outside the United Kingdom—a clear indication of the importance the Anglo-Dutch multinational attaches to the region. Unilever Thailand is another rapidly expanding subsidiary. Currently Thailand's largest FMCG firm, the corporation is going to spend B$2.8 billion (US$ 90 million) on building additional facilities to support its growth. Among them is the projected manufacturing plant for homecare products due for completion by the end of 2013.

Indonesia is one of the largest emerging markets for Unilever, where it had invested more than US $625.9 million over the period 2007-2012. Unilever Indonesia's turnover had reached US$ 2.3 billion in 2011 (around 5 percent of Unilever's global turnover for that year), and registered an internal growth of almost twice the worldwide equivalent.

Unilever Vietnam has achieved a strong and sustained growth over the last 14 years, with an astounding average of over 30 percent making it one of the fastest growing companies within Unilever Asia, as well as in Vietnam's FMCG sector. In 2008, the company's total sales represented around 1 percent of Vietnam's GDP, with a network of about 200 distributors and over 400,000 retail outlets. A case study conducted by the Central Institute for Economic Management (CIEM), a think tank under the Vietnamese Ministry of Planning & Investment with an advisory role, has investigated the reasons for its exceptional performance. According to its findings, a substantial part of its success was due to the fact that the company is a long-term investor, representing a model of constructive partnership and efficient collaboration between an MNC and local business. Also, its positive spillover is not only linked to capacity building and technology transfer, but also involves a global socioeconomic development for the country.

Unilever Philippines aims to source all of its peanut, tamarind, and tuber supplies from local farmers as part of its strategy to support indigenous business growth in the regions it operates. The Unilever Sustainable Living Plan, in fact, targets to halve the environmental footprint of the multinational's products and source 100 percent of the agricultural raw materials by local farmers in a sustainable fashion.

Future developments

More is to come from Unilever in the near future, as the company enlarges its operations, reaching out to countries outside its area of recent interest. Investments into China are going to keep their pace, even if moving inward, in the so-called fourth pole of China's socio-economic development after the Yangtze River Delta, the Pearl River Delta and the Beijing-Tianjin-Hebei region. This is the Sichuan Province, geographically and logistically connected to Yunnan and the Mekong area, and therefore nearer to the ASEAN countries.

Other bases are being developed as well. The most remarkable case in point being Myanmar, where Unilever was present since the 1960s and then left when the junta seized power to institute a dictatorship. Following news of the country's reopening and its democratic elections, the company returned in 2010 as one of the first to invest. Furthermore, to strengthen the relevance and standing of Unilever in Myanmar and the whole region on 30th May 2012, Aung San Suu Kyi, General Secretary of Myanmar's National League for Democracy, paid a visit to Unilever Thailand's Minburi factory, during her first overseas visit in over 24 years.

What lies ahead?

Unilever represents the clear success story of a multinational that has been able to diversify its portfolios of countries and products, showing no sign of slowing down. Its focus on emerging markets, primarily ASEAN, seems to have reaped good dividends. More companies are going to follow this approach, especially at the completion of the EAC in 2015.

The future will most likely witness additional foreign investments pouring into the regions both as M&A and as greenfield investments, especially since even more multinationals will aim at cutting their operation costs and pursuing a more aggressive integration with China and India's consumer markets. Furthermore, consumer spending in Asia-Pacific will keep rising, making the whole region even more attractive to investors. Corporations will certainly profit from Singapore's centrality as a hub its highly sophisticated facilities, technology infrastructures and deep-sea container port. Unsurprisingly, 75 percent of the companies also run their regional operations from there, followed by a 10 percent in the nearby Kuala Lumpur (Malaysia).

It is no mystery that China's labor costs have been steadily rising over the years, becoming almost aligned with U.S. costs (even if, by hourly measure, China's is still substantially lower. The difference here is clearly in productivity). ASEAN is therefore becoming increasingly popular as a manufacturing center and a constant presence in the global supply chain of multinationals, using countries like

Indonesia and Vietnam—with a labor cost only 37 percent of the U.S. level—as favorite production bases. Analysts observed that this offshoring process toward the region is only beginning.

However, challenges do loom ahead. Southeast Asia faces a series of obstacles on its road to achieving full economic integration, comparable to the EU—which nonetheless remains, since the beginning the model ASEAN is constantly striving towards. Protectionism in the region keeps running high, even in the framework of free-trade areas, which yet allow for sensitivity lists for particular products, without even mentioning non-tariff barriers like industrial standards and red tape.

Other problematic issues include the implementation of AFTA (ASEAN Free Trade Area). While AFTA has been a success, together with the one-to-one preferential trade agreements linking each one of the ASEAN countries to the rest of East Asia, a more cautious evaluation has to be done of the complex regional trade agreements of the Asia Pacific region. More often than not, its hurdles have outweighed its advantages, and it has been reported that its implementation is sometimes costly and complex, making it impossible for Small and Medium Enterprises (SMEs) to benefit from this. An abundance of academic literature on this aspect, together with some firm surveys, seems to confirm this problematic point.

Another issue is the lack of infrastructure. Transportation costs can represent a formidable obstacle in some of the most promising countries for offshoring. For example, for Unilever Indonesia the cost of transportation, warehousing, and logistics was about 4 percent of the total sales revenue.

Finally, diversity in the countries of the region constitute a threat as well as an opportunity. Consumer purchasing power is a good example, since the ten states present a whole range of cases, between Singapore, with almost US$ 50,000 GDP per capita and Myanmar, the poorest member of ASEAN, with only US$ 896 GDP per capita. Furthermore, there are huge differences in terms of political systems, religions and languages, making agreements difficult to reach. For this reason, it's often impossible for multinationals to adopt a single market approach and they are often obliged to resort to a variety of strategies. The coming years and the implementation of the EAC, will probably make or break the region as one of the new powerhouses of global growth, and significantly affect market results of Unilever and the other MNEs in the region.

QUESTIONS

7-3. Why is Unilever investing so much in emerging markets, especially Southeast Asia?

7-4. Myanmar is a country opening up after decades of having been closed to business due to political issues. Based on further data collection, explain Unilever's investment strategy in the country.

MyLab Management

Go to **mymanagementlab.com** for the following Assisted-graded writing questions:

7-5 Why does ASEAN represent an area of growing interest for multinationals, to the point that some of them use it as an operations management hub? Cite clearly reasons that make the region an attractive place for manufacturers to set up their bases.

7-6 What are the challenges for a real regional integration among ASEAN countries? Mention some of the main issues that make it a difficult and lengthy process and their impact on companies like Unilever.

Endnotes

Scan for Endnotes or go to www.pearsonglobaleditions.com/Daniels

CHAPTER 8
Markets for Foreign Exchange

OBJECTIVES

After studying this chapter, you should be able to

8-1 Define what foreign exchange is and who the major players are in the foreign-exchange market

8-2 Summarize the major characteristics of the foreign-exchange market

8-3 Compare and contrast spot, forward, options, and futures markets

8-4 Explain some of the major aspects of the foreign-exchange markets

8-5 Show how companies use foreign exchange to facilitate international trade

MyLab Management®
Improve Your Performance!
When you see this icon ⭐, visit **www.mymanagementlab.com** for activities that are applied, personalized, and offer immediate feedback.

Another man's trade costs money.

— **Portuguese proverb**

Currencies and foreign exchange. ▶

Source: Tupungato. Shutterstock

Going Down to the Wire in the Money-Transfer Market

Long known as "the fastest way to send money," U.S.-based Western Union is the world leader of retail wire transfers—the electronic transfers of funds from one financial institution to another.[1] However, it is facing stiff competition from a variety of sources and is also struggling with a complex economic and political environment.

Western Union was started in 1851 when a group of businessmen in Rochester, New York, formed the New York and Mississippi Valley Printing Telegraph Company. The name was changed to Western Union in 1861 when the first transcontinental telegraph line was completed. Western Union introduced its money-transfer service in 1871, and in 1989 it began offering it outside North America. Today, more than 500,000 Western Union agent locations are found in over 200 countries and territories around the world, in addition to more than 100,000 ATMs and kiosks. Because of their global reach, they execute transactions in more than 130 currencies. Western Union operates C2C, B2C, and B2B, although 80 percent of its revenues are C2C (consumer to consumer).

Consumers have many different options when sending money through Western Union: in person, at an agent location, over the phone, or online; via cash, debit cards, or credit cards. And they can use the service at a variety of locations: an actual Western Union office, a grocery store, a post office—just about anywhere people go to transact business. To send money to, say, India or Mexico using a Western Union agent location, the customer fills out a "Send Money" form and gets a receipt, which includes a Money Transfer Control number to give to the person receiving the funds. To retrieve the funds, the receiver then fills out a "Receive Money" form and presents the Money Transfer Control number along with valid identification at a Western Union agent location.

CONVERTING CURRENCY

Transfer funds are converted into the foreign currency using an exchange rate set by Western Union. The fees for sending money are determined based on how much is sent, in what form (cash or debit/credit card), and where it is going. For example, sending $500 to Mexico from a grocery store in Utah costs $8.00 (down from $12 only four years ago). In this case, payment must be made in cash, the $8.00 fee is subtracted, and the recipient on the other end receives 8,644 Mexican pesos, which is about 1.8 percent less than the going spot exchange rate. Part of Western Union's attractiveness is its speed and anonymity—it can move cash from one location of the world to another in just minutes. Money can be sent through an agent by cash (as in the case above), debit card, credit card, or a Western Union Gold Card, and senders are required to fill out a form and show a proper ID.

HOW MIGRATION DRIVES WESTERN UNION'S BUSINESS

From a business standpoint, it is interesting to think of corridors, such as the U.S.–Mexico corridor, or the India–United Arab Emirates (primarily Dubai) corridor. The larger and more stable the corridor, the more important it is to have the availability of Western Union services on both ends. Migration is based on supply and demand. People generally migrate to other countries because of better economic opportunities, although the flow of immigrants from Syria to Europe is also a function of political unrest and security. The World Bank estimates that the top recipients of officially recorded remittances in this $600 billion annual market are India, China, the Philippines, Mexico, Nigeria, and Egypt. Each of these countries has large numbers of people working abroad who are sending money home to their families.

Most of the migrant workers in the United States come from North America (which includes Canada and Mexico), Latin America, and the Caribbean. Most of Western Union's wire transfer business in the United States comes from Mexican immigrants who send part of their paychecks home to support their families. Mexico has historically ranked as the largest host country in Latin America for remittances, followed by Brazil. Remittances often exceed foreign direct investment and overseas aid as sources of foreign exchange. Before the drop in oil prices, annual remittance income passed tourism to become the second-largest source of foreign-exchange income in Mexico, after oil revenues.

COMPETITIVE FORCES

Financial institutions such as banks have pressured Western Union to use better exchange rates. Profit margins in the money-transfer business can reach 30 percent, and many banks have started to offer their own money-transfer services in an attempt to take advantage of the continued expected growth of the foreign money-transfer industry.

This new onslaught of competition by banks has forced Western Union to cut its fees and offer new services, including a home-delivery service, where money is delivered directly to the recipient's door. Western Union is also moving into countries such as China and India to boost its market share. The increased competition has driven down remittance fees around the world. Western Union has also developed other delivery mechanisms, including online and mobile delivery.

In addition, Western Union is affected by currency forces since it is a dollar-based company and earns revenues in other currencies. When the dollar strengthens, its revenues from foreign earnings fall. A slowdown in economic growth worldwide means that some countries are not attractive for immigration due to the lack of good jobs. Terrorism has also forced countries to implement stronger immigration policies and tighten up controls on the movement of money that could be used to finance terrorism.

EXAMPLES FROM MEXICO AND DUBAI

Immigrant workers may complain about the high transfer fees and exchange-rate spread associated with Western Union, but many continue to use this service instead of the lower-cost method of remitting money through banks. For example, Mexico has a history of unstable currencies and widespread inflation, resulting in a traditional mistrust of banks. Other immigrants base their choice of how to remit money on word of mouth or convenience and location.

A major advantage of Western Union is its worldwide availability. For thousands of tiny villages, Western Union is the main link to the outside world. Coatetelco, a small village south of Mexico City, has no bank. Remittances—mostly from agricultural or construction workers in Georgia and the Carolinas—account for 90 percent of the villagers' incomes. Patricio, 49, says that at the end of each month he gets a call from his two sons, who are working in Georgia. They give him a code number, and he drives or rides his horse four miles to the nearest Western Union office, located in a government telegraph office, to pick up the $600 they spent $40 to wire to him. Less expensive remittance services are available at the nearby Banamex branch in Mazatepec, but so far Patricio and his neighbors are not willing to travel the eight miles to get there. Besides, he says, "we do not trust the banks, and they make everything more difficult." Fortunately costs have dropped dramatically since Patricio first started receiving money from his sons in Georgia.

Dubai, one of the seven states in the United Arab Emirates (UAE), is an interesting point of comparison with Mexico. Although workers from India and Pakistan go to Dubai to work because of higher wages, they are actually recruited by companies in Dubai. Because of Dubai's relatively small local Emirati population (only 19 percent of the total population), there is no way the country could develop without foreign workers—skilled, semiskilled, and unskilled. India is the natural source of workers, with Mumbai only about 1,200 miles (1,900 km) away. Employees must have a permit to work in Dubai, typically for three years at a time. Workers can be sent home whenever their employers decide they are no longer needed. But these workers are critical for the growth of the local economies. They have increased the speed of urbanization, fast-tracked infrastructure and economic development, helped the GCC countries diversify from oil by helping construct hotels and tourist attractions, and contributed to solid economic growth.

Western Union, with a deep understanding of the remittance markets, its ethnic marketing expertise, diversified presence and resulting closeness to customers, and its rapid growth in Dubai, has developed high and growing brand awareness there and has worked hard to develop products and messages that appeal to the customers. Dubai and the United States are different in terms of size and the demand for labor, while India and Mexico are different in terms of how and why they supply labor, but there is one constant: people need to move money, and that is where Western Union comes in. ■

QUESTIONS

8-1. The United Emirates, of which Dubai is a member, is one of the Gulf Cooperation Council members. How does it compare with the other GCC countries in terms of total population and the nonimmigrant population as a percentage of total population? How important do you think migration and therefore capital remittances are for each of the countries in the GCC?

8-2. What forces are likely to have the greatest influence on Western Union's business in the future?

CONCEPT CHECK

When we introduced the idea of a **multinational enterprise (MNE)** on p. 60 in Chapter 1, we emphasized that MNEs are firms that take a global approach to production and markets. Here we add that the need to deal with **foreign exchange** is one of the important factors in the environment in which MNEs must conduct business.

WHAT IS FOREIGN EXCHANGE AND WHO ARE THE MAJOR PLAYERS IN THE MARKET?

Foreign exchange is money denominated in the currency of another nation or group of nations.[2] The market in which such transactions take place is the **foreign-exchange market**. Foreign exchange can be in the form of cash, funds available on credit and debit cards, traveler's checks, bank deposits, or other short-term claims.[3] As an example, our opening case illustrates how Mexican immigrant workers in the United States often use Western Union to convert dollars to pesos and then wire the pesos to offices in Mexico where relatives can retrieve the cash.

Foreign exchange—money denominated in the currency of another nation or group of nations; an exchange rate is the price of a currency.

An **exchange rate** is the price of a currency—specifically, the number of units of one currency that buy one unit of another currency. The number can change daily. On March 25, 2016, €1 could purchase US$1.3181 (or $1 could purchase €0.7587).

The foreign-exchange market is made up of many different players. The **Bank for International Settlements (BIS)**, a financial organization centered in Basel, Switzerland, owned and controlled by 60 member central banks, divides the market into three major categories: *reporting dealers,* other *financial institutions,* and *nonfinancial institutions.*[4]

The Bank for International Settlements divides the foreign-exchange market into reporting dealers (also known as dealer banks or money center banks), other financial institutions, and nonfinancial institutions.

Reporting dealers, also known as *money center banks,* are large financial institutions that actively participate in local and global foreign-exchange and **derivative** markets. They are widely assumed to include the largest banks and financial institutions in terms of overall market share in foreign-exchange trading, such as Deutsche Bank, Citi, Barclays Capital, UBS, JP Morgan, HSBC, RBS, Credit Suisse, and Goldman Sachs. Because of the volume of transactions that the money center banks engage in, reporting dealers influence price-setting and are the market makers.

The other financial institutions are not classified as reporting dealers. They include smaller local and regional commercial banks, investment banks and securities houses, **hedge funds**, pension funds, money market funds, currency funds, mutual funds, specialized foreign-exchange trading companies, and so forth. Western Union is a nonbanking financial institution that deals in foreign exchange. Nonfinancial customers comprise any counterparty other than those described above and include any nonfinancial end user, such as governments and companies. In the 2013 BIS Triennial Central Bank Survey of foreign-exchange and derivatives market activity, 39 percent of the daily turnover of forex was by reporting dealers, whereas 53 percent was by other financial institutions, and only 9 percent by nonfinancial customers.[5]

SOME ASPECTS OF THE FOREIGN-EXCHANGE MARKET

HOW TO TRADE FOREIGN EXCHANGE

Dealers can trade foreign exchange

- directly with customers,
- through voice brokers,
- through electronic brokerage systems,
- directly through interbanks.

Foreign exchange is traded using electronic methods (eTrading), customer direct, interbank direct, or voice broker. Recently, more than 50 percent of foreign-exchange trading volume was being executed by electronic means. Although connection by voice with a broker is still important for some types of transactions, high touch trades by voice (where the broker provides research and advice) is giving way to low touch voice (which involves a voice transaction combined with eTrading).[6] Different kinds of electronic methods are involved. One is an electronic broking system in which trades are matched up for foreign-exchange dealers using electronic systems such as EBS, Thomson Reuters, and Bloomberg. Another is an electronic trading system that is executed on a single-bank proprietary system or a multibank dealing system. Interbank direct refers to trades between dealer banks via telephone or direct electronic trading.

The electronic services provided for customers by EBS, Thomson Reuters, and Bloomberg also furnish a great deal of market data, news, quotes, and statistics about different markets around the world. It is not uncommon for a trading room to have more than one electronic service and for traders to have different preferences within the same office. Bloomberg and Reuters provide market quotes from a large number of banks, so their quotes are close to the market consensus.

Foreign-exchange market:

- Over-the-counter (OTC) commercial and investment banks
- Securities exchanges

The foreign-exchange market has two major segments: the over-the-counter market (OTC) and the exchange-traded market. The OTC market is composed of commercial banks as just described, investment banks, and other financial institutions. The exchange-traded market comprises securities exchanges, such as the CME Group, NASDAQ OMX, and Intercontinental Exchange (ICE), where certain types of foreign-exchange instruments, such as futures and options, are traded.

GLOBAL OTC FOREIGN-EXCHANGE INSTRUMENTS

The phrase "global OTC foreign-exchange instruments" refers to *spot transactions, outright forwards, FX swaps, currency swaps, currency options,* and other foreign-exchange products. These instruments are all traded in the markets mentioned above.

> The spot rate is the exchange rate quoted for transactions that require delivery within two days.

> Outright forwards involve the exchange of currency beyond three days at a fixed exchange rate, known as the forward rate.

> An FX swap is a simultaneous spot and forward transaction.

- **Spot transactions** involve the exchange of currency for delivery in two business days after the day the transaction was made. For example, a bank would quote an exchange rate for a transaction on Monday, but delivery would take place on Thursday.[7] The rate at which the transaction is settled is the **spot rate**.

- **Outright forward transactions** involve the exchange of currency on a future date beyond two business days. It is the single purchase or sale of a currency for future delivery. The rate at which the transaction is settled is the forward rate and is a contract rate between the two parties. The forward transaction will be settled at the forward rate no matter what the actual spot rate is at the time of settlement.

- In an **FX swap**, one currency is traded for another on one date and then swapped back later. Most often, the first or short leg of an FX swap is a spot transaction and the second or long leg a forward transaction. Let's say IBM receives a dividend in British pounds from its subsidiary in the United Kingdom but has no use for British pounds until it has to pay a UK supplier in 30 days. It would rather have dollars now than hold on to the pounds for a month. IBM could enter into an FX swap in which it sells the pounds for dollars to a dealer in the spot market at the spot rate and agrees to buy pounds for dollars from the dealer in 30 days at the forward rate.

> Currency swaps, options, and futures contracts are other forms of transactions in foreign exchange.

- **Currency swaps** deal more with interest-bearing financial instruments (such as a bond) and involve the exchange of principal and interest payments.

- **Options** are the right, but not the obligation, to trade foreign currency in the future.

- A **futures contract** is an agreement between two parties to buy or sell a particular currency at a particular price on a particular future date, as specified in a standardized contract to all participants in a currency futures exchange rather than in the over-the-counter market.

Outright forwards (13 percent) and FX swaps (42 percent) remain the dominant category of instruments, closely followed by spot transactions (38 percent). Options and other transactions are only 6.3 percent of the market.[8]

SIZE, COMPOSITION, AND LOCATION OF THE FOREIGN-EXCHANGE MARKET

Before we examine the market instruments in more detail, let's look at the size, composition, and geographic location of the market. The BIS estimated in its 2013 survey of global foreign-exchange activity that daily foreign-exchange turnover was $5.3 trillion, an increase of 32.5 percent over the 2010 survey. However, the rise in activity was much smaller than the 71 percent increase from 2004 to 2007 due to the global economic crisis that began in 2008. Current daily turnover (mid-2016) is estimated to be closer to $7 trillion.

CONCEPT CHECK

The most widely traded currencies in the world are those issued by countries that enjoy high levels of political freedom (Chapter 3, page 111) and economic freedom (Chapter 4, page 150).

Using the U.S. Dollar on the Foreign-Exchange Market   The U.S. dollar is the most important currency on the foreign-exchange market; in the latest BIS Survey, it was one side (buy or sell) of 87 percent of all foreign currency transactions worldwide, as Table 8.1 shows. (Numbers in the table are percentages and add up to 200 percent because there are two sides to each transaction.) Although the dollar, euro, yen, and pound sterling are the most widely traded currencies, the Chinese yuan is steadily growing in importance. In 2014, nearly 25 percent of China's trade took place in yuan, as compared with only 2 percent in 2009.[9]

The City of London is one of the leading financial centers of global finance and handles 40.9 percent of the foreign exchange trading in the world.

Source: QQ7/Shutterstock

There are five major reasons why the dollar is so widely traded:[10]

1. It's an investment currency in many capital markets.
2. It's a reserve currency held by many central banks.
3. It's a transaction currency in many international commodity markets.
4. It's an invoice currency in many contracts.
5. It's an intervention currency employed by monetary authorities in market operations to influence their own exchange rates.

The U.S. dollar is an important vehicle for foreign-exchange transactions between any two countries. Let's say a Mexican company importing products from a Korean exporter

TABLE 8.1   Global Foreign Exchange: Currency Distribution

The U.S. dollar is involved in 87 percent of all worldwide foreign-exchange transactions.

Currency	April 2001	April 2004	April 2007	April 2010	April 2013
U.S. dollar	89.9	88.0	85.6	84.9	87.0
Euro	37.9	37.4	37.0	39.1	33.4
Japanese yen	23.5	20.8	17.2	19.0	23.0
Pound sterling	13.0	16.5	14.9	12.9	11.8
Australian dollar	4.3	6.0	6.6	7.6	8.6
Swiss franc	6.0	6.0	6.8	6.4	5.2
All others	25.4	25.3	31.9	30.1	31.0

Source: Based on Bank for International Settlements, *Central Bank Survey Report on Foreign Exchange Turnover in April 2013* (Basel, Switzerland: BIS, September 2013): 10.

converts Mexican pesos into dollars and sends them to the Korean exporter, who converts them into Korean won. Thus, the dollar has one leg on both sides of the transaction—in Mexico and in Korea. Why? One reason is that the Korean exporter might have no need for pesos but can use dollars for a variety of reasons. Or the Mexican importer might have trouble getting won at a good exchange rate if the Mexican banks are not carrying won balances. However, the banks undoubtedly carry dollar balances, so the importer might have easy access to the dollars. Thus, the dollar greatly simplifies life for a foreign bank because the bank doesn't have to carry balances in many different currencies.

> The dollar, the most traded currency in the world, is part of four of the top seven currency pairs: the dollar/euro and the dollar/yen are the top two.

Frequently Traded Currency Pairs   Another way to consider foreign currency trades is to look at the most frequently traded currency pairs. The top seven pairs in the 2013 BIS Survey involved the U.S. dollar, with the top two being euro/dollar (EUR/USD)—24.1 percent of the total—and dollar/yen (USD/JPY).[11] Because of the importance of the U.S. dollar in foreign-exchange trade, the exchange rate between two currencies other than the dollar—for example, the exchange rate between the euro and the Brazilian real—is known as a **cross rate**.

> The biggest market for foreign exchange is London, followed by New York, Tokyo, and Singapore.

The Euro   The euro is also in four of the top ten currency pairs. The top three currency pairs involving the euro are the dollar, the yen, and the British pound. However, the euro is also important for other currencies in the EU that are not part of the monetary union as well as non-EU countries in Europe, such as Turkey.

Given that the dollar is clearly the most widely traded currency in the world, you'd expect the biggest market for foreign-exchange trading to be in the United States. As Figure 8.1 illustrates, however, the biggest by far is in the United Kingdom. The four largest centers for foreign-exchange trading (the United Kingdom, the United States, Japan, and Singapore) account for 71.1 percent of the total average daily turnover. The U.K. market is so dominant that more dollars are traded in London than in New York.[12]

FOREIGN-EXCHANGE TRADES AND TIME ZONES

If the U.S. dollar is the most widely traded currency in the world, why is London so important as a trading center? There are two major reasons. First, London, which is close to the major capital markets in Europe, is a strong international financial center where many domestic and foreign financial institutions operate. Thus, its geographic location relative to significant global economic activity is key.

FIGURE 8.1   **Foreign-Exchange Markets: Geographical Distribution, September 2013**

The United Kingdom handles 40.9 percent of all world foreign-exchange activity (compared to just 18.9 percent by the United States). Location is a big factor in the United Kingdom's popularity: London is close to all the capital markets of Europe, and its time zone makes it convenient for making trades in both the U.S. and Asian markets.

Source: Based on Bank for International Settlements, *Central Bank Survey Report on Foreign Exchange Turnover in April 2013: Preliminary Global Results* (Basel, Switzerland: BIS, September 2013: 14): 1.

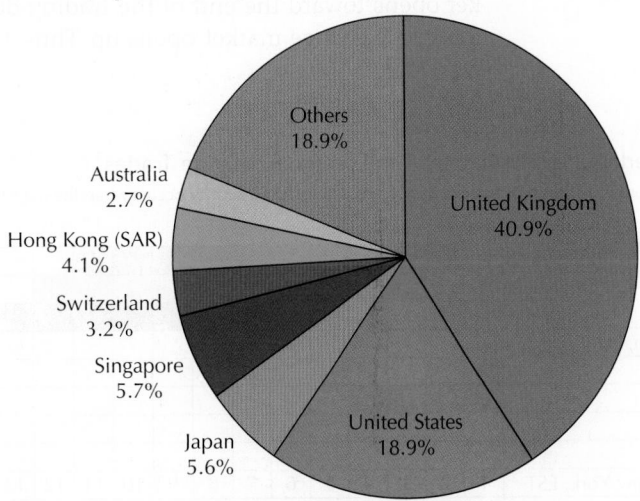

MAP 8.1   International Trade Zones and The Single World Market

The world's communication networks are now so good that we can talk of a single world market. It starts in a small way in New Zealand at around 9:00 A.M., just in time to catch the tail end of the previous night's market in New York. Two or three hours later, Tokyo opens, followed an hour later by Hong Kong and Manila, then half an hour later by Singapore. By now, with the Far East market in full swing, the focus moves to the Near and Middle East. Mumbai opens two hours after Singapore, followed after an hour and a half by Abu Dhabi and Athens. At this stage, trading in the Far and Middle East is usually thin as dealers wait to see how Europe will trade. Paris and Frankfurt open an hour ahead of London, and by this time Tokyo is starting to close down, so the European market can judge the Japanese market. By lunchtime in London, New York is starting to open up, and as Europe closes down, positions can be passed westward. Midday in New York, trading tends to be quiet because there is nowhere to pass a position to. The San Francisco market, three hours behind New York, is effectively a satellite of the New York market, although very small positions can be passed on to New Zealand banks.

Source: Based on Julian Walmsley, *The Foreign Exchange Handbook* (New York: John Wiley, 1983): 7–8. Reprinted by permission of John Wiley & Sons, Inc. Some information taken from David Crystal, ed., *The Cambridge Factfinders*, 3rd ed., (New York: Cambridge University Press, 1998): 440.

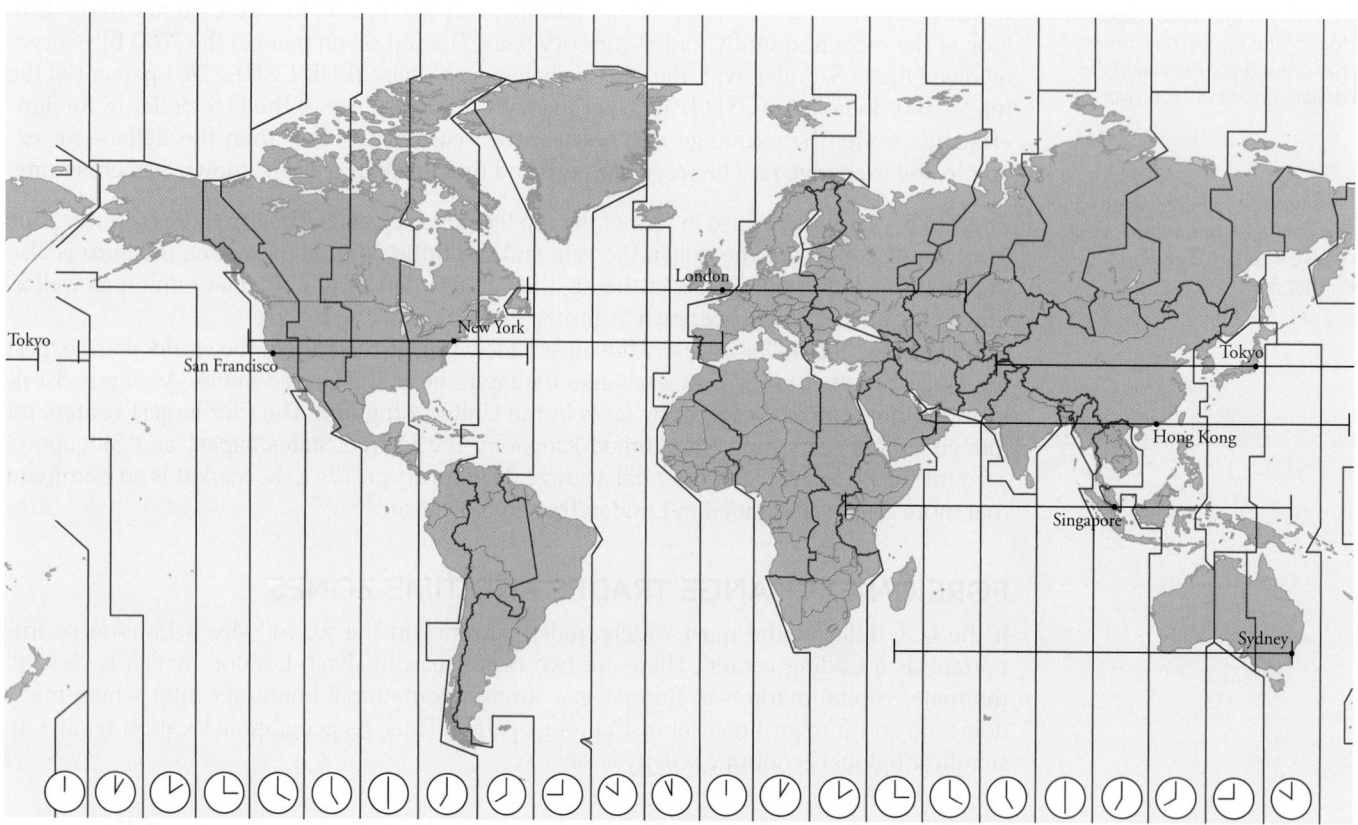

Second, London is positioned in a unique way because of its time zone. As Map 8.1 shows, noon in London is 7:00 A.M. in New York and evening in Asia. The London market opens toward the end of the trading day in Asia and is going strong as the New York foreign-exchange market opens up. Thus, the city straddles both of the other major world markets.

FIGURE 8.2   Overlapping Time Zones and Foreign Exchange Trades

Although foreign exchange is traded 24 hours a day, most of the trading activity occurs when the major foreign-exchange markets, especially London and New York, are open.

Frankfurt																								
London																								
New York																								
Wellington, NZ																								
Sydney																								
Tokyo																								
Singapore																								
Time in New York, EST	1	2	3	4	5	6	7	8	9	10	11	12	13	14	15	16	17	18	19	20	21	22	23	24

Because of overlapping time zones, the times of greatest foreign-exchange activity are when Tokyo and London are both open, a period of about two hours. The next period of greatest foreign-exchange activity is when New York opens and London is still in full swing, from 8:00 A.M. until noon New York time. However, London has already been open and active for four hours before New York opens, so New York foreign-exchange traders usually start early so as not to miss the activity in London.

MAJOR FOREIGN-EXCHANGE MARKETS

THE SPOT MARKET

Rates are quoted by foreign-exchange dealers. The **bid (buy) rate** is the price at which the dealer is willing to buy foreign currency; the **offer (sell)** is the price at which the dealer is willing to sell foreign currency. The difference between the bid and offer rates is the dealer's profit margin.

> Key foreign-exchange terms:
> - Bid—the rate at which traders buy foreign exchange.
> - Offer—the rate at which traders sell foreign exchange.
> - Spread—the difference between bid and offer rates.
> - American terms, or direct quote—the number of dollars per unit of foreign currency.
> - European terms, or indirect quote—the number of units of foreign currency per dollar.

Direct and Indirect Quotes Let's look at an example of how a bid and offer might work. For example, the rate a U.S.-based dealer quoted for the British pound on April 1, 2016, was $1.4228/30. This means the dealer is willing to buy pounds at $1.4228 each and sell them for $1.4230 each (i.e., buying low and selling high). In this example, the dealer quotes the foreign currency as the number of U.S. dollars for one unit of that currency. This method of quoting exchange rates is called the **direct quote**, which is the number of units of the domestic currency (the U.S. dollar in this case) for one unit of the foreign currency. It is also known as **American terms**.

The other convention for quoting foreign exchange is known as the **indirect quote**, or **European terms**. It is the number of units of the foreign currency for one unit of the domestic currency. On April 1, 2016, the indirect quote for the U.K. pound was £0.7028, which is the number of British pounds per U.S. dollar.[13]

Base and Term Currencies When dealers quote currencies to their customers, they always quote the **base currency** (the denominator) first, followed by the **terms currency** (the numerator). A quote for USD/JPY (also shown as USDJPY = X) means the dollar is the base currency and the yen is the terms currency (the number of Japanese yen for one U.S. dollar). If you know the dollar/yen quote, you can divide that rate into 1 to get the yen/dollar quote. In other words, the exchange rate in American terms (the direct quote) is the reciprocal or inverse of the exchange rate in European terms (the indirect quote). For example, on April 1, 2016, the indirect quote for Japanese yen (USD/JPY) was ¥111.72 for one dollar. The reciprocal would be 1/¥11.72 = $0.00895.[14]

In a dollar/yen quote, the dollar is the denominator, the yen the numerator. By tracking changes in the exchange rate, managers can determine whether the base currency is strengthening or weakening. For example, on April 1, 2015, the dollar/yen rate was ¥119.75/$1.00, compared with ¥111.72/$1.00. As the numerator decreases, the base currency (the dollar) is weakening. Conversely, the terms currency (the yen) is strengthening.

There are many ways to get exchange rate quotes, including online and print media. Because most currencies constantly fluctuate in value, it is possible to get up-to-the-second quotes from providers like Reuters or Bloomberg. Quotes are also available from online and printed media such as *The Wall Street Journal* or *Financial Times.*

Interbank Transactions The spot rates provided by *The Wall Street Journal* are the selling rates for **interbank transactions** of $1 million and more. Retail transactions—those between banks and companies or individuals—provide fewer foreign currency units per dollar than interbank transactions.

THE FORWARD MARKET

As noted earlier, the spot market is for foreign-exchange transactions that occur within two business days. But in some transactions, a seller extends credit to the buyer for a period longer than that. For example, a Japanese exporter of consumer electronics might sell television sets to a U.S. importer with immediate delivery but payment due in 30 days. The U.S. importer is obligated to pay in yen in 30 days and may enter into a contract with a currency dealer to deliver the yen at a forward rate—the rate quoted today for future delivery.

In addition to the spot rates for each currency, foreign-exchange traders can provide forward rates for most currencies. The most widely traded are the euro, the Japanese yen, the Swiss franc, and the British pound due to their market liquidity. Although forward rates are available for different dates in the future, the more exotic the currency, the more difficult it is to get a forward quote out too far in the future, and the greater the difference is likely to be between the forward rate and the spot rate.

Forward Discounts and Premiums   Building on what we said earlier, we now can say that the difference between the spot and forward rates is either the **forward discount** or the **forward premium**. In order to explain how to compute and interpret the premium or discount, let's use the direct rate between the U.S. dollar and the Swiss franc from the perspective of a U.S. trader—in this case, the number of dollars per franc. If the forward rate for the Swiss franc is greater than the spot rate, the franc would get more dollars in the future, so it would be trading at a premium. If the forward rate is less than the spot rate, the franc would be selling at a discount since it would get you less dollars in the future. Assume the spot rate for the Swiss franc is $1.0784 and the six-month forward rate is $1.0808. The premium or discount would be computed as follows:

$$\frac{\$\,1.0808 - 1.0784}{1.0784} \times \frac{12}{6} = .00445 \times 100 \text{ or } 0.45\%$$

The premium is annualized by multiplying the difference between the spot and forward rates by 12 months divided by the number of months forward—6 months, in this example. Then you multiply the results by 100 to put them in percentage terms. Because the forward rate is greater than the spot rate, the Swiss franc is selling at a premium in the forward market by 0.45 percent above the spot rate. During this particular period of time, interest rates in the major economies were quite low because of the global economic slowdown and the desire to keep interest rates low in order to speed up economic growth. Thus the premium is also quite low. During periods of greater divergence in interest rates, the premium or discount could be much larger. In 2007, for example, the franc was selling at a 2.5 percent premium in the six-month forward market.

OPTIONS

An option is the *right*, but not the *obligation*, to buy or sell a foreign currency within a certain time period or on a specific date at a specific exchange rate. It can be purchased OTC from a commercial or investment bank or on an exchange. For example, a U.S. company purchases an OTC option from a commercial or investment bank to buy 1,000,000 Japanese yen at ¥85 per US$ ($0.011765 per yen)—or $11,765. The writer of the option will charge the company a fee for writing it. The more likely the option is to benefit the company, the higher the fee. The rate of ¥85 is called the *strike price* for the option; the fee or cost is called the *premium*. On the date when the option is set to expire, the company can look at the spot rate and compare it with the strike price to see what the better exchange rate is. If the spot rate were ¥90 per US$ ($0.01111 per yen)—or $11,000—it would not exercise the option because buying yen at the spot rate would cost less than buying them at the option rate. However, if the spot rate at that time were ¥80 per US$ ($0.0125 per yen)—or $12,500—the company would exercise the option because buying at the option rate would cost less than at the spot rate. The option gives the company flexibility because it can walk away from the option if the strike price is

The forward rate is the rate quoted for transactions that call for delivery after two business days.

A forward discount exists when the forward rate is weaker than the spot rate.

A premium exists when the forward rate is stronger than the spot rate.

An option is the right, but not the obligation, to trade a foreign currency at a specific exchange rate.

not a good price. In the case of a forward contract, the cost is usually cheaper than the cost for an option, but the company cannot walk away from the contract. So a forward contract is cheaper but less flexible.

The above example is for a simple, or *vanilla,* option. However, exotic or structured options are used more widely to hedge exposure, especially by European companies. The idea behind them is to provide an option product that meets a company's risk profile and tolerance and results in a premium that is as close to zero as possible. The writer of the option can still make money on the structured option, but if the option is set up effectively, the company buying it won't have to write out a big check for the premium.

FUTURES

A futures contract specifies an exchange rate in advance of the actual exchange of currency, but it is not as flexible as a forward contract.

A foreign currency futures contract resembles a forward contract insofar as it specifies an exchange rate some time in advance of the actual exchange of currency. However, a future is traded on an exchange, not OTC. Instead of working with a bank or other financial institution, companies work with exchange brokers when purchasing futures contracts. A forward contract is tailored to the amount and time frame the company needs, whereas a futures contract is for a specific amount and maturity date. It is less valuable to a company than a forward contract. However, it may be useful to speculators and small companies that cannot enter into the latter.

THE FOREIGN-EXCHANGE TRADING PROCESS

When a company sells goods or services to a foreign customer and receives foreign currency, it needs to convert it into the domestic currency. When importing, the company needs to convert domestic to foreign currency to pay the foreign supplier. This conversion usually takes place between the company and its bank.

Sometimes foreign-exchange services are provided by the large money center banks, such as Citi or HSBS, to corporate clients. For mid-market and smaller local companies, services are provided by the local banks who establish correspondent relationships with the larger money center banks. The left side of Figure 8.3 shows what happens when U.S. Company A needs to sell euros for dollars. This situation could arise when A receives payment in euros from a German importer. The right side of the figure shows what happens when B needs to buy euros with dollars, which could happen when a company has to pay euros to a German supplier. In either case, the U.S. company would contact its bank for help in converting the currency. If it is a large MNE, such as a *Fortune 500* firm in the United States or a Global *Fortune 500* company, it will probably deal directly with a money center bank (as shown on the top arrow in Figure 8.3) and not worry about another financial institution. Smaller companies would probably work through Financial Institution A or B (a local or regional bank), which operates through a money center bank to make the trade. Assume that U.S. Company B is going to receive euros in the future. Because it cannot convert in the spot market until it receives the euros, it can consider a forward, swap, options, or futures contract to protect itself until the currency is finally delivered. Financial Institution B can do a forward, swap, or options contract for Company B. However, Company B can also consider an options or futures contract on one of the exchanges, such as the CME Group. The same is true for Company A, which will need euros in the future.

BANKS AND EXCHANGES

At one time, only the big money center banks could deal directly in foreign exchange. Regional banks had to rely on them to execute trades on behalf of their clients. The emergence of electronic trading has changed that. Now even the regional banks can hook up to

FIGURE 8.3   The Foreign-Exchange Trading Process

Let's say that you're U.S. Company A, that you've received euros in payment for goods, and that you want to sell your euros in return for dollars. To make the exchange, you may contact your local bank or go directly to a money center bank.

On the other hand, perhaps you're U.S. Company B and you expect to receive euros as a future payment. To protect yourself against fluctuations in the exchange rate, you want to buy euros that you can subsequently trade back for dollars. You could choose, say, a forward or a swap, and your path would be essentially a mirror image of Company A's. Finally, either Company A or Company B could choose to convert by such means as an option or a futures contract—in which case the trade could be made by an options and/or futures exchange, either directly or through a broker.

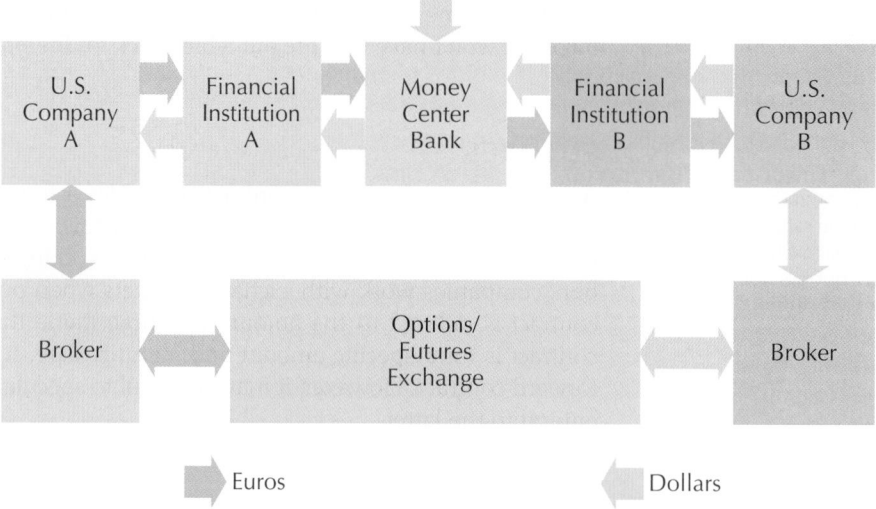

Bloomberg, Thomson Reuters, or EBS and deal directly in the interbank market or through brokers. Despite this, the greatest volume of foreign-exchange activity takes place with the big money center banks. Because of their reach and volume, they are the ones that set the prices in global trading of foreign exchange.

Top Foreign-Exchange Dealers   There is more to servicing customers in the foreign-exchange market than size alone. Each year, *Euromoney* magazine surveys treasurers, traders, and investors worldwide to identify their favorite banks and the leading dealers in the interbank market. The criteria include transaction volumes and quality of services, their location, the capability of handling major and exotic currencies, their offering of derivatives, and their research and consulting capabilities.[15]

Given the differing capabilities, large companies may use several banks to deal in foreign exchange, selecting those that specialize in specific geographic areas, instruments, or currencies. At one time, for example, AT&T used Citi for its broad geographic spread and wide coverage of different currencies, Deutsche Bank for euros, Swiss Bank Corporation (now the Union Bank of Switzerland) for Swiss francs, NatWest Bank for British pounds, and Goldman Sachs for derivatives. Based on the criteria mentioned above, the major banks that deal in foreign exchange worldwide in a recent *Euromoney* survey are Citicorp, Deutsche Bank, Barclays, JP Morgan, UBS, BAML (Bank of America Merrill Lynch), and HSBC.[16]

TOP EXCHANGES FOR TRADING FOREIGN EXCHANGE

In addition to the OTC market, foreign-exchange instruments, mostly options and futures, are traded on commodities exchanges. In the OTC market, companies work directly with their banks to enter into forward and options contracts. On the commodities exchanges, buyers and sellers enter into contracts with each other without going through banks. Three of the best-known exchanges are the **CME Group**, **NASDAQ OMX**, and **NYSE:ICE (Intercontinental Exchange)**.

The top banks in the interbank market are chosen because of their location, expertise in major and specific currencies, and ability to deal in different financial instruments.

CONCEPT CHECK

In Chapter 12, starting on p. 358, we explain why companies establish and maintain effective value chains—frameworks for dividing value-creating activities into separate processes. A reliable value chain permits a firm to focus on its core competencies—the unique skills or knowledge that make it better at something than its competitors. Because managing currencies and cross-trades is typically not among a firm's core competencies, its bankers are key components of its value chain.

Major exchanges that deal in foreign currency derivatives are the CME Group, NASDAQ, and NYSE:ICE.

CME Group   The CME Group was formed on July 9, 2007, as a merger between the Chicago Mercantile Exchange and the Chicago Board of Trade. The CME operates according to so-called open outcry: Traders stand in a pit and call out prices and quantities. The platform is also linked to an electronic trading platform, which is growing rapidly. The CME Group handles 3 billion contracts worth $1 quadrillion annual on average across a wide range of commodities, including foreign-exchange futures and options.[17] Contracts are available for the dollar against a variety of currencies as well as cross-trades, such as the euro against the Australian dollar. CME uses three electronic trading platforms to trade different commodities, including currencies: CME Globex, DME Direct, and CME Clearport.

NASDAQ   Prior to 2008, the Philadelphia Stock Exchange was one of the pioneers in trading currency options. In July 2008, PHLX merged with NASDAQ OMX, and in 2014, the name was changed to NASDAQ. NASDAQ trades options in seven currencies—the Australian dollar, the British pound, the Canadian dollar, the euro, the Swiss franc, the New Zealand dollar, and the Japanese yen.

NYSE:ICE   In 2013, Intercontinental Exchange (ICE) purchased NYSE Euronext, forming NYSE:ICE. The combined company is a giant in futures and options. ICE Futures US offers cross-trades in a number of currencies through ICE's futures contracts on key currency pairs traded in the interbank market through an electronic trading platform.[18]

HOW COMPANIES USE FOREIGN EXCHANGE

Companies enter the foreign-exchange market to facilitate their regular business transactions and/or to speculate. Their treasury departments are responsible for establishing policies for trading currency and for managing banking relationships to make the trades. From a business standpoint, a company, first of all, trades foreign exchange for exports/imports and the buying or selling of goods and services.

When Boeing sells the new 787 Dreamliner commercial airplane to LAN, the largest airline in South America, it has to be concerned about the currency in which it will be paid and how it will receive payment. In this case, the sale is probably denominated in dollars, so Boeing will not have to worry about the foreign-exchange market (nor, in theory, will its employees). However, LAN will have to worry about the market. Where will it come up with the dollars, and how will it pay Boeing?

CASH FLOW ASPECTS OF IMPORTS AND EXPORTS

When a company must move money to pay for purchases, or receives money from sales, it has options as to the documents it can use, the currency of denomination, and the degree of protection it can ask for. Although transactions can be settled with cash in advance, it is more common to use a commercial bill of exchange or letter of credit.

With a draft or commercial bill of exchange, one party directs another party to make payment.

Commercial Bill of Exchange   An individual or a company that pays a bill in a domestic setting can pay cash, but checks are typically used—often electronically transmitted. The check is also known as a **draft** or a **commercial bill of exchange**. A draft is an instrument in which one party (the *drawer*) directs another party (the *drawee*) to make a payment. The drawee can be either a company, like the importer, or a bank. In the latter case, the draft would be considered a bank draft.

A sight draft requires payment to be made when it is presented. A time draft permits payment to be made after the date when it is presented.

Documentary drafts and documentary letters of credit are used to protect both the buyer and the seller. They require that payment be made based on the presentation of documents conveying the title, and they leave an audit trail identifying the parties to the transactions. If the exporter requests payment to be made immediately, the draft is called a **sight draft**. If the payment is to be made later—say, 30 days after delivery—the instrument is called a **time draft**.

A letter of credit obligates the buyer's bank to honor a draft presented to it and assume payment; a credit relationship exists between the importer and the importer's bank.

Letters of Credit   With a bill of exchange, it is always possible that the importer will not be able to make payment to the exporter at the agreed-upon time. A **letter of credit (L/C)**, however, obligates the buyer's bank in the importing country to honor a draft presented to it, provided the draft is accompanied by the prescribed documents. Of course, the exporter still needs to be sure the bank's credit is valid as well, since the L/C could be a forgery issued by a nonexistent bank. Even with the bank's added security, the exporter still needs to rely on the importer's credit because of possible discrepancies that could arise in the transaction. The L/C could be denominated in the currency of either party. If it is in the importer's currency, the exporter will still have to convert the foreign exchange into its currency through its commercial bank.

Although a letter of credit is more secure than a documentary draft alone, there are still risks. For the L/C to be valid, all of the conditions described in the documents must be adhered to. For example, if the L/C states that the goods will be shipped in five packages, it will not be valid if they are shipped in four or six packages. It is important to understand the conditions of the documents, as well as counterparty risk. Although a forged L/C is an obvious danger, the global financial crisis has exposed counterparty risk when banks did not have sufficient capital to stand behind their L/Cs. In addition, letters of credit are irrevocable, which means they cannot be canceled or changed in any way without the consent of all parties to the transaction.

In addition, the L/C needs to specify the currency of the contract. If the L/C is not in the exporter's currency, the exporter will have to convert the foreign exchange into that currency as soon as it is received.

Confirmed Letter of Credit   A letter of credit transaction may include a confirming bank in addition to the parties mentioned previously. With a **confirmed letter of credit**, the exporter has the guarantee of an additional bank—sometimes in the exporter's home country, sometimes in a third country. It rarely happens that the exporter establishes the confirming relationship. Usually, the opening bank seeks the confirmation of the L/C with a bank with which it already has a credit relationship.[19]

OTHER FINANCIAL FLOWS

Companies may have to deal in foreign exchange for other reasons. For example, if a U.S. company has a subsidiary in the United Kingdom that sends a dividend to the parent company in British pounds, the parent company has to enter into the foreign-exchange market to convert pounds to dollars. If it lends dollars to the British subsidiary, the subsidiary has to convert them into pounds. When paying principal and interest back to the parent company, it has to convert pounds into dollars.

Speculators take positions in foreign-exchange markets and other capital markets to earn a profit.

Speculation   Companies sometimes deal in foreign exchange for profit. This is especially true for some banks and all hedge funds. But sometimes corporate treasury departments see their foreign-exchange operations as profit centers and also buy and sell foreign exchange with the objective of earning profits.

Investors can use foreign-exchange transactions to speculate for profit or to protect against risk. Speculation is the buying or selling of a commodity—in this case, foreign currency—that has both an element of risk and a chance of great profit. Assume that a hedge fund buys euros in anticipation that the euro will strengthen against other currencies. If it does, the investor earns a profit; if it weakens, the investor incurs a loss. Speculators are important in the foreign-exchange market because they spot trends and try to take advantage of them. They can create demand for a currency by purchasing it in the market, or they can create a supply by selling. However, speculation is also a very risky business. In recent years, the advent of eTrading has attracted a lot of day traders in foreign exchange. The problem is that day traders rarely make money speculating in exchange rates. Forecasting currency movements is a risky business.

Arbitrage is the buying and selling of foreign currencies at a profit due to price discrepancies.

Arbitrage   One type of profit-seeking activity is **arbitrage**, which is the purchase of foreign currency on one market for immediate resale on another market (in a different country) to profit from a price discrepancy. For example, a dealer might sell U.S. dollars for Swiss francs in the United States, then Swiss francs for British pounds in Switzerland, then the British pounds for U.S. dollars back in the United States, with the goal of ending up with more dollars.

Here's how the process might work: Assume the dealer converts 100 dollars into 150 Swiss francs when the exchange rate is 1.2 francs per dollar. The dealer then converts the 150 francs into 70 British pounds at an exchange rate of 0.467 pounds per franc and finally converts the pounds into 125 dollars at an exchange rate of 0.56 pounds per dollar. In this case, arbitrage yields $125 from the initial sale of $100. Given the transparency of exchange rate quotes globally, it is difficult to make a lot of money on arbitrage, but it is possible for an investor who has a lot of money and can move quickly.

Interest arbitrage involves investing in interest-bearing instruments in foreign exchange in an effort to earn a profit due to interest rate differentials.

Interest arbitrage is the investing in debt instruments, such as bonds, in different countries. A dealer might invest $1,000 in the United States for 90 days, or convert $1,000 into British pounds, invest the money in the United Kingdom for 90 days, then convert the pounds back into dollars. The investor would try to pick the alternative that would yield the highest return at the end of 90 days.

Point

Is It OK to Speculate on Currency?

Point   **Yes** People trade in foreign exchange for a number of reasons, and one of them is speculation, which is not illegal or necessarily bad. Just as stockbrokers invest people's money to try to earn a return higher than the market average; foreign currency traders invest people's money in foreign exchange to make a profit for the investors. Speculation is merely taking a position on a currency in order to profit from market trends.

Electronic trading has made it easier for a variety of investors to speculate in foreign exchange. Hedge funds are an important source of this foreign-exchange speculation. However, the transparency in trading has driven the smaller players out of the market and allowed the large institutions and traders to earn profits on small margins that require large volumes of transactions. Hedge funds generally deal in minimum investments that are quite large, so the hedge fund managers that trade in foreign exchange trade in very large volumes. They might make long-term bets on a currency based on macroeconomic conditions, or they might try to balance off buy-and-sell strategies in currencies so that one side offers protection against the other. In either case, the hedge fund manager is betting on the future position of a currency to earn money for the investors in the fund.

Political and economic conditions outside the speculators' control can quickly turn profits to losses. Currencies are inherently unstable. Consider the problems of the U.S. dollar in 2007 and 2008, when it was quite weak against the euro and the yen. What should hedge fund managers do? They might expect the dollar to continue to weaken. But what if

it strengthens? Or they might think the dollar has reached its floor and is ready for a rise, which would argue that the managers should buy dollars. But when will it rise and by how much? By mid-March 2008, the dollar had declined by 15 percent in the prior 12 months; 2 months later, many experts felt it had reached a low point and expected it to rise. This was based on the market expectations that interest cuts by the Fed were expected to stop and that the credit crisis was beginning to soften. Now the speculators had to decide what to do with those expectations. Sometimes speculators can buy a currency on the basis of good economic fundamentals, or they can buy or sell currency because they feel that governments are following poor economic policies. In late 2012, the Japanese economy was very weak, but the yen was strong. As the new Japanese government announced that it was considering policies to weaken the yen, many hedge funds jumped into the market and sold yen, helping to push down the value. At what point do they feel that the yen has fallen enough and that it will rise again? As long as markets are free and information is available, traders ought to be able to make some money on their predictions of the future. There is even a good argument that speculators help keep governments honest by betting in directions they feel reflect political and economic fundamentals.

The key is that currency speculation is a different way to invest money and allows investors to diversify their portfolios from traditional stocks and bonds. Just as foreign exchange can be traded for speculative purposes, trading in shares is also speculation. Even though we call such trades "investments," they are just another form of speculation.

Is It OK to Speculate on Currency?

Counterpoint

No It depends on whose money you are using to speculate, whether the speculation is supposed to benefit the institution or the trader, and if positions and gains and losses are accurately reported. There are plenty of opportunities for a trader, whether in foreign exchange or securities, to make money illegally or contrary to company policy. The culture of individual traders trying to make money off trading foreign exchange or other securities, combined with lax controls in financial institutions, contributes greatly to these scandals.

One of the most publicized events in the derivatives markets in recent years involved 28-year-old Nicholas Leeson and the 233-year-old British bank Barings PLC. Leeson, a dealer for Barings, went to Singapore in the early 1990s to help resolve some of the bank's problems. Within a year, he was promoted to chief dealer, with responsibility for trading securities and booking the settlements. This meant that there were no checks and balances on his trading actions, thus opening the door to fraud.

In 1994, Leeson bought stock index futures on the Singapore International Monetary Exchange, or SIMEX, on the assumption that the Tokyo stock market would rise. Most dealers watching his feverish trading activity assumed Barings had a large client that he was trading for. It turns out, however, that he was using the bank's money to speculate. Because the Japanese economy was recovering, it made sense to assume the market would continue to rise, thus generating more profits for Leeson and Barings. Unfortunately, something happened that nobody could predict—the January 17, 1995, earthquake that hit the port city of Kobe.

As a result of the devastation and uncertainty, the market fell, and Leeson had to come up with cash to cover the margin call on the futures contract. A margin is a deposit made as security for a financial transaction that is otherwise financed on

Counterpoint

credit. When the price of an instrument changes and the margin rises, the exchange "calls" the increased margin from the other party—in this case, Leeson.[20]

However, Leeson soon ran out of cash from Barings and had to come up with more. One approach he used was to write options contracts and use the premium he collected on the contracts to cover his margin call. Unfortunately, he was using Barings' funds to cover positions he was taking for himself, not for clients, and he also forged documents to cover his transactions.

As the Tokyo stock market continued to plunge, Leeson fell further and further behind and eventually fled the country, later to be caught and returned to Singapore for trial and prison. Barings estimated that Leeson generated losses in excess of $1 billion, and the bank eventually was purchased by Dutch bank ING.[21]

In 2012, Bruno Iksil, nicknamed the London Whale because of the large positions he was taking in derivatives trades, engaged in a trading strategy that cost JP Morgan Chase $6.2 billion in losses, far exceeding Leeson's losses. Iksil, a French citizen, was working for an investment unit of JP Morgan Chase in London, and he executed a trading strategy that he claimed was "initiated, approved, mandated, and monitored" by his supervisors. Although four regulators in two countries investigated the case, it was decided to drop charges against him. He supposedly alerted everyone internally about the concerns with the trading strategy and increasing exposure, someone had to shoulder the blame. Iksil, his boss, and his subordinate were all fired, and JP Morgan Chase paid over $6 billion in fines for fraudulently hiding the amount of the losses and using improper valuation procedures. Speculation is the name of the game, but the key is to make sure regulatory oversight is followed carefully. It's one thing to lose money, and it's another thing to hide the losses.[22]

Looking to the Future
Where Are Foreign-Exchange Markets Headed?

Significant strides have been made and will continue to be made in the development of foreign-exchange markets. The speed at which transactions are processed and information transmitted globally will certainly lead to greater efficiencies and more opportunities for foreign-exchange trading. The impact on companies is that trading costs should come down and companies should have faster access to more currencies.

Although the dollar will continue to be the major player in the foreign-exchange market in terms of the total transactions as well as the top currency pairs, the euro and yen will continue to be strong. However, the big change in the future will be the increasing usage of the yuan in global transactions, especially for countries that trade with China. The yuan can only be successful as a major player in the global foreign-exchange market as it becomes more accepted as a reserve currency that countries have confidence in. The sheer size of the Chinese economy and the efforts of the Chinese government to move the yuan closer to becoming a reserve currency will help the yuan become more accepted as a major player in the foreign-exchange market.

Presently, London and New York are the major financial centers for trading currencies. As the yuan increases in importance, it will be interesting to see how much Singapore and Hong Kong will increase in importance, and whether or not Shanghai will increase in importance. Currencies from emerging markets are in deep trouble and will continue to be so until the global economy begins to grow again. Many of these currencies, such as the Brazilian real, are tied to the strength of the Chinese economy. However, Brazil is also suffering from a collapse in confidence in the government due to corruption, so that will be a drag for the foreseeable future.

Technological Developments

Technological developments may not cause the foreign-exchange broker to disappear entirely, but they will certainly cause foreign-exchange trades to be executed more quickly and cheaply. The advent of technology clearly has caused the market to shift from phone trades to electronic trades.[23]

Cryptocurrency

In 2009, the Bitcoin was launched, ushering in the world of cryptocurrencies, also known as virtual or digital currencies. Although other virtual currencies, such as Ethereum, have been launched, Bitcoin is still the number one virtual currency—but Ethereum is gaining ground. These digital currencies are based on a blockchain in which every transaction is recorded publicly. Programmers write the software behind the currencies, and "miners" use computers to mint the digital currency. It is estimated that there are around $6 billion of Bitcoin outstanding, compared with $1 billion in Ether, and both systems are supported by thousands of computers or nodes. Both are small compared with foreign-exchange markets, but the blockchain concept is being strongly considered by banks and corporations for certain types of transactions. Bitcoin and Ethereum, therefore, are looking at different ways to use their digital currencies for legitimate transactions while at the same time working to get regulatory approval and protect their blockchains from illegal activities, including financing terrorism.[24] ■

Do Yuan to Buy Some
Renminbi?

On November 30, 2015, the International Monetary Fund announced that the Chinese yuan, also known as the renminbi (RMB or "people's currency"), would finally join the U.S. dollar, the euro, the British pound, and the yen in the basket of reserve currencies also known as SDRs or Special Drawing Rights. Although this will not become effective until October 2016, the recognition of the yuan is due to China's increasing dominance in the global economy and its moves in recent years to liberalize its financial markets. However, what does all of this mean to China and the rest of the world, and will China continue down the road to liberalization of its currency and other financial markets?

A Little History

In the currency markets, the sign for the yuan is ¥ (the same symbol used for the Japanese yen) and the code is CNY. On January 7, 1994, the Chinese government, after debating what to do with its currency, decided to fix the value to the U.S. dollar at a rate of ¥8.690 per dollar.[25] This was easy to do, given that currency trading was controlled by the Chinese government and not allowed offshore. In 2004, Hong Kong residents were allowed to exchange local Hong Kong dollars for yuan in a first move to allow some limited trading offshore. By early 2005, the yuan was trading at a fixed rate of ¥8.2665 per dollar. But pressure began to build in 2005 as both the European Union and the United States faced strong competition from imports from China as well as from Chinese exports to developing markets.

When China fixed the value of its currency in 1994, the country was not considered a major economic powerhouse. Then things began to change. By 1999, China was the largest country in the world in population, and in 2003 it was the seventh-largest in the world in GNI, exceeded only by the United States, Japan, Germany, the United Kingdom, France, and Italy. It was also growing faster than any of the top six countries. In the decade of the 1990s, China grew by an annual average of 9.5 percent and was above 8 percent every year in the first half of the 2000s.

Because of China's low manufacturing wages, it was exporting far more to the United States than it was importing. In 2004, it had a trade surplus of $155 billion with the United States, compared with a surplus of only $86 billion with the EU. However, between 2002 and 2004, China's surplus with the EU doubled, while growing by a little over one-half with the United States. Also during that time, there were capital controls on the flow of yuan in and out of China, so there was a tremendous inflow of yuan into the banking sector in China with no real way to move the money offshore. That meant that banks could lend money at very low interest rates, fueling a

real estate boom. Also, China had to do something with its building reserves. Initially it invested huge sums of money in U.S. treasury bills, helping to fund the growing U.S. budget deficit. Then it began encouraging foreign direct investment, especially in natural resources around the world.

However, the competitive pressure of China in Asia was not the same. Because most Asian currencies were also locked onto the dollar, the yuan traded in a narrow range against those currencies. Most of the Asian countries were using China as a new market for their products, and they were not anxious to have anything upset the Chinese economy and reduce demand for their products.

Critics from the United States and EU argued that the yuan was undervalued by 15 to 40 percent and the Chinese government needed to free the currency and allow it to seek a market level. The pressures for and against change were both political and economic. The U.S. government had been working with the Chinese for an extended period of time to get them to revalue their currency, but the Chinese government had found plenty of excuses not to do that.

Political Pressures in China

China had its own political pressures. For one thing, a lot of people had been moving currency there in anticipation of a revaluation of the yuan, which was creating inflationary pressures. The Chinese government was forced to buy the dollars and issue yuan-denominated bonds as a way of "sterilizing" the currency—taking it off the market to reduce the pressures. The government was not very excited about revaluing the yuan and rewarding the speculators, so it kept saying it would not announce if, when, or how much the revaluation would be. It also did not want to revalue under pressure from foreign governments lest it appear to be bowing under pressure from abroad.

Finally, China has serious problems with employment. Even though its billion-plus population grows at only 1 percent annually, it adds the equivalent of a new country the size of Ecuador or Guatemala every year. China needs to add enough jobs to keep up with its population growth and displaced workers from its agricultural sector and state-owned firms. That means adding 15 to 20 million new jobs per year, or about 1.25 million per month.

The Advent of the Currency Basket

Given these pressures, China took an historic step on July 21, 2005, and de-linked the yuan from its decade-old peg to the U.S. dollar in favor of a currency basket. Although the dollar has been the dominant currency in determining the value of the yuan, there are periods of time when some Asian currencies have also shown themselves to be influential. So the currency basket was largely denominated by the dollar, the euro, the yen, and the South Korean won—currencies that were selected because of their impact on China's foreign trade, investment, and foreign debt. Even when the basket grew to 11 currencies, these 4 dominated.

The People's Bank of China (PBOC, the country's central bank) decides a central parity rate daily and then allows a trading band on either side of the decided point. The move to the currency basket increased the yuan-to-dollar rate by 2.1 percent. Before the peg was de-linked, the yuan was kept around ¥8.2665; immediately afterward, it rose to ¥8.1011, an increase of 2 percent. The PBOC responded to the pressures by the international community to strengthen the yuan by widening the trading band on May 18, 2007, from 0.3 percent to 0.5 percent on either side of the fixed rate. Obviously, that small difference allowed little room for traders.

Playing it Safe

Until the yuan began its ascent against the U.S. dollar, it was very easy to deal in foreign exchange in China because the rate was fixed against the dollar. It doesn't take a lot of judgment for a trader to operate in a fixed-rate world. The exchange rate is managed by the State Administration of Foreign Exchange (SAFE), which is closely linked to the PBOC. SAFE is responsible for establishing the new foreign-exchange trading guidelines as well as for managing China's foreign-exchange reserves. A major concern of the PBOC is that China's financial infrastructure might be capable of trading foreign exchange in a free market.

SAFE was moving to change that. When the PBOC made the decision to loosen up the value of the yuan in 2005, it opted to allow banks in Shanghai to trade and quote prices in eight currency pairs, including the dollar-sterling and euro-yen. Prior to that, licensed banks were only allowed to trade the yuan against four currencies: the U.S. dollar, the Hong Kong dollar, the euro, and the yen. Shanghai was being positioned as the financial center of China, hopefully by 2020. However, all the trades were at fixed rates, and they did not involve trades in non-yuan currency pairs. SAFE also decided to open up trading to seven international banks (HSBC, Citigroup, Deutsche Bank, ABN AMRO, ING, Royal Bank of Scotland, and Bank of Montreal) and two domestic banks (Bank of China and CITIC Industrial Bank).

Fast-Forward

However, the global financial crisis forced the Chinese government to return the yuan to a peg against the U.S. dollar from July 2008 until June 2010, during which time the United States and China were embroiled in a war of words over the value of the currency. The United States wanted the Chinese to allow their currency to continue to rise to help solve the trade imbalance, and the Chinese wanted the United States to get its economy under control and stabilize the value of the dollar, which had been falling in value against most other currencies. China was even calling for the creation of a new reserve asset to take the place of the dollar in the global economy. Why was China so worried about the dollar's value? Because most of its reserves—the largest in the world at more than $3 trillion, fed largely by its huge trade surplus—are in U.S. dollars. The last thing China wanted was to have all of its dollar reserves losing value in the global economy.

China's Economic Challenges

By the end of 2010, not only had China replaced Japan as the second-largest country in the world in terms of GDP, it was closing fast on the United States. In addition, China surpassed Germany and the United States as the largest exporter in the world, which meant that it was continuing to generate large foreign-exchange assets that were exposed to losses in value as the dollar fell against other world currencies.

China, however, had its own set of problems, irrespective of what was going on in the West. When it decided to let the yuan gradually rise against the dollar in June 2010, the result was a 3.6 percent rise in the yuan's value against the dollar by the end of 2010. However, inflation was rising in China faster than in the United States, so Chinese exports were becoming increasingly expensive. The rise in the currency compounded the loss in competitive position brought on by the rise in inflation. Powerful Chinese exporters were very upset with the idea that the government might free up the currency and speed up their competitive challenges. Because of inflation, Chinese workers were increasingly unhappy with their working conditions, and they began to demonstrate, sometimes violently. As workers pushed for higher wages, manufacturers faced even greater cost pressures. With general inflation, higher wages, and the possibility of an even more expensive yuan, manufacturers were being forced to move further inland to find cheaper labor, or even move abroad. Many U.S. manufacturers began moving manufacturing back to the United States or to cheaper Asian countries.

Improvement of the Trading Infrastructure

In the meantime, the PBOC announced in 2009 that it was going to allow companies in Shanghai and four other major cities to settle foreign trade in yuan instead of dollars. If Chinese companies can get more exporters and importers to settle their obligations in yuan instead of dollars, they can save a lot of transaction fees and the yuan will gradually increase in importance.

Even though China wants to make Shanghai its future financial center, a lot of yuan transactions occur in Hong Kong. For a while, it was the only place outside of mainland China allowed to set up yuan bank accounts. Hong Kong is China's testing ground for the liberalization of currency

The Shanghai World Financial Center is located in the Pudong district of Shanghai, a global financial center and the largest city in China.

Source: Sean Pavone/Shutterstock

trading. However, Singapore is also being considered as a place for yuan transactions, and it also trades about the same as Hong Kong in foreign exchange.

The PBOC permitted HSBC and the Bank of East Asia to issue yuan-denominated bonds in Hong Kong in 2007, allowing Hong Kong to increase in importance as an offshore financial center for yuan trading. As banks and companies issue bonds and securities in yuan, the amount of yuan in circulation outside China will steadily grow. In October 2010, ICAP PLC and Thomson Reuters began to trade yuan on their electronic-trading platforms and announced that they were working with banks in the United States and Europe to use their platforms to trade yuan. Before this, banks in Hong Kong were trading yuan with each other OTC or through brokers. The use of the electronic platform promises to increase transparency and traffic. In spite of these moves, the onshore market in mainland China still dwarfs the offshore trading, and the fixed exchange rate set by SAFE will be the most important rate. The onshore market in mainland China is far more tightly controlled. Even though major money center banks such as HSBC are allowed to trade currency in China, their volume dwarfs that of the large Chinese banks. As those banks gain greater expertise in global trades, they will become even more significant outside of China. And as China and Singapore explore the possibility of Singapore joining Hong Kong as another location for yuan trades, the international banks will ramp up their yuan trading competencies in both locations. As capital controls in China are loosened, the international banks will also have to ramp up their presence there to compete with the huge Chinese banks that are now starting to get involved in the global foreign-exchange trading game.

What's Next?

As China moved closer to the yuan being accepted as a global currency in late 2015, it allowed the yuan to appreciate against a basket of currencies by more than 30 percent, and by 10 percent alone from mid-2014 to mid-2015. The IMF finally said that the yuan changed from being undervalued to "roughly appropriate," although that is disputed by the United States. The government is also moving to allow foreign investors greater access to Chinese securities and made it easier for Chinese to invest abroad. The yuan is still not freely convertible, but a number of central banks are using yuan as reserve assets. However, in August 2015, the PBOC allowed the biggest devaluation of the yuan in two decades in order to rekindle economic growth. The PBOC said it was doing this to show that the yuan was more flexible and that it could move both up and down. Every morning, the PBOC sets the value of the yuan, and the feeling is that the devaluation gives the market more freedom in setting rates. However, the devaluation resulted in many Chinese companies paying off foreign debts for fear that more devaluations would occur, and investors switched out of yuan to dollars and other currencies. This forced the bank to spend over $100 billion in August 2015 to support the yuan.

In addition, 2015 saw more non-Chinese banks start using yuan. More than 1000 banks in 100 countries were using yuan for payments with China and Hong Kong, up more than 20 percent compared with 2013. Although Hong Kong is still the major clearing center for yuan transactions, other clearing centers are being set up around the world. In addition, several central banks have entered into swap agreements with China, including the Bank of England and the European Central Bank.

In spite of the current moves, the yuan is still not widely accepted, especially by consumers. In London, for example, the yuan represents only 1.8 percent of daily currency turnover. Chinese tourists can't use yuan for daily transactions, whereas the U.S. dollar and euro are freely accepted. London is trying to attract more yuan deposits, but banks there trail Hong Kong and Singapore by a significant margin. Even though Canada and the U.K. have set up yuan-clearing hubs in Toronto and London, the United States is still lagging behind. Part of that is because U.S. companies can still use dollars to settle transactions with Chinese companies, so they don't see a big demand to use yuan. But the United States will have to take the yuan seriously.

As China moves closer to being a global currency, it will achieve greater control over global decisions that used to be made by the global reserve currencies. On the other hand, China will lose control over its ability to manage its economy and control its capital flows. It will also have to be more transparent in its financial dealings. Also, to be accepted as a global currency, it will need legal, political, and institutional reforms that will inspire confidence of foreign investors. Is it ready to do that?

QUESTIONS

8-3. Why is it important for the Chinese yuan to become a major world currency? What are the risks for China?

8-4. What role do foreign banks like HSBC and electronic platforms like Thomson Reuters and ICAP play in helping the yuan move closer to becoming a global currency?

8-5. Why is the yuan being used more widely in global business transactions? Do you think it will ever replace the dollar or the euro? Why or why not?

MyLab Management

Go to **mymanagementlab.com** for the following Assisted-graded writing questions:

8-6 What needs to take place for the yuan to be listed right along with the U.S. dollar and the euro as global currencies?

8-7 Why is the Chinese government so hesitant to open up the yuan to market forces to determine its value inside and outside of China?

Endnotes

Scan for Endnotes or go to www.pearsonglobaleditions.com/Daniels

CHAPTER 9
Factors that Influence Exchange Rates

OBJECTIVES

After studying this chapter, you should be able to

9-1 Describe the International Monetary Fund and its role in determining exchange rates

9-2 Discuss the major exchange-rate arrangements that countries use

9-3 Identify the major determinants of exchange rates

9-4 Show how managers try to forecast exchange-rate movements

9-5 Examine how exchange-rate movements influence business decisions

MyLab Management®

Improve Your Performance!

When you see this icon ⭐, visit **www.mymanagementlab.com** for activities that are applied, personalized, and offer immediate feedback.

He that has no money has no friends.

—Arabian proverb

Plaza Francia, Caracas, Venezuela. ▶

Source: Alexander Chaikin. Shutterstock

Venezuela's Rapidly Changing Currency[1]

Angel Falls is the world's highest uninterrupted waterfall. The 807 meter drop (2,648 feet) is symbolic of the steep fall of the Venezuelan bolívar in the past few years. Just as the mist rises from the floor of the falls, inflation is rising as well. In 2015 when inflation in the developing countries was 5.7 percent, inflation in Venezuela was 159.1 percent, the highest in the world by far. And the IMF expected inflation in 2016 to rise 720 percent. That may not be quite the record of Zimbabwe which hit 80 billion percent in November 2008, but Zimbabwe figured it out got inflation under control, at least for a few years.

The rapid rise in inflation resulted in the precipitous drop of the Venezuelan bolívar fuerte (known at the VEF), which ironically means the strong Venezuelan bolívar. The bolívar, named after Simón Bolívar, a Venezuelan military leader who was instrumental in South America's revolutions against the Spanish empire in the early 1800s, wasn't always so weak. In 1934, the bolívar (then known as the VEB) was fixed at 3.914 per U.S. dollar, and three years later, it strengthened to 3.18 per dollar. For the next 40 years, the VEB was one of the strongest and most internationally recognized currencies in the region. However, in 1983, the VEB was devalued, partially because of the drop in oil prices in the early to mid-1970s. The currency continued to slide, and oil prices took a big hit in the early 2000s as the terrorist attacks on September 11, 2001, led to a slowdown in the global economy. Then strikes in 2002 at PdVSA, the Venezuelan state oil company, cut production. The drop in production and softening of oil prices forced the government to devalue the VEB to 1600 VEB per dollar in 2003, and foreign-exchange controls were instituted to limit capital flight.

THE IMPORTANCE OF OIL

The key to the Venezuelan economy is oil. Venezuela, a founding member of OPEC, is the world's fifth-largest oil-exporting country, and it has the world's largest oil reserves. It relies on the shipment of crude oil for 95 percent of its export revenues and ½ of its government's revenue. However, massive budget deficits are pushing Venezuela closer to default on its sovereign debt. RBC Capital Markets estimates that oil prices have to reach $121.06 per barrel for Venezuela to balance its budget, the second highest breakeven price after Libya. But that seems impossible. On June 20, 2014, oil prices reached $114.81 per barrel. An oversupply of oil, the development of shale oil and other alternatives to conventional oil, combined with a slowdown in the global economy, especially China, began a precipitous drop in oil prices. By January 1, 2015, oil prices were $50.17 per barrel. After a brief recovery, they fell again to $28.94 per barrel in mid-January 2016. Prices began to climb, but who knows high they will go and how long the recovery will last.

SHORTAGES AND CONTROLS

Hugo Chavez, the president of Venezuela from 1999–2013, implemented a program of nationalism, a centralized economy, a strong military, and a focus on social programs for the poor, the basis of his political support. His programs, known as *chavismo*, resulted in huge budget deficits that led to extensive external borrowing as well as a reliance on high oil prices to fund government programs. On March 7, 2007, Chavez announced that the currency would have three zeros dropped from the value so that the rate would be 1:1000, and the currency would be renamed the bolívar fuerte or VEF on January 1, 2008. Along with the devaluation of the currency, Chavez instituted foreign-exchange controls. On January 8, 2010, he devalued the currency from 2.15 VEV/$ to 2.60 VEF/$ for some imports and 4.30 for other imports. On April 11, 2011, he changed the VEF to 4.30 per dollar for all imports. The VEF was locked onto the U.S. dollar at a fixed rate known as a conventional peg, and it was not allowed to freely float. However, Chavez retained the right to devalue the VEF if he wanted to.

After Chavez died in 2013, his successor, Nicolás Maduro, continued with *chavismo*. However, that was just before the plunge in oil prices. Shortages began to mount in Venezuela. Russia went through a similar transformation when *perestroika* was instituted in mid-1980s: prices were controlled and shortages were the norm. The joke in Russia was that if you saw a line, you waited in it; when you got to the front of the line, you bought whatever was available; if you didn't need it, someone in your family did. Subsidies on everything from rice to gas to rural homes may seem to make life easier, but it's making things worse. Shortages in everything from pharmaceuticals and medical supplies to toilet paper to diapers have led to the creation of a thriving black market. One woman described how she bought a bag of washing powder for 400 VEF (when the controlled price was actually VEF 32), and she sold it for 600 VEF. Even though this is illegal, it is the norm. Sometimes companies get around the price controls by changing the nature of the product. For example, if they add garlic to rice, they sell it as garlic rice and avoid the price controls on rice. This happens all over the world where there are price controls. You change the ingredients or you change the size of the package.

In February 2015, the VEF was devalued to 6.3 per dollar for most essential imports. Some imports, such as auto parts, could convert currency at an intermediate rate of 12 VEF per dollar, and a free rate which was about 50 VEF per dollar. The free rate replaced the third tier exchange rate that existed before. In 2016, President Maduro adjusted the VEF again. Whereas the devaluation of the VEF in 2013 resulted in 6.3 VEF per dollar, on February 18, 2016, the VEF was changed to 10.0 per dollar. However, the government adopted a second rate which allowed it to float against the dollar but was managed by the government and not freely floating. Unfortunately, this also resulted in black market for the currency. Instead of the fixed rate of 10 VEF per dollar, the black market rate at times was as high as 1,150 VEF per dollar.

IS DOLLARIZATION THE SOLUTION?

Obviously, many of Venezuela's problems could be solved with very high oil prices. However, that will take too long to solve the serious pain being inflicted on the Venezuelan economy. Riots at the end of April 2016 due to power and water cuts and shortages in food and medical imports led to petitions to recall President Maduro. In addition, Venezuela runs the risk of not having enough bills to circulate in the economy. It doesn't print its own bills but has them printed by companies in France, Britain, and Canada, among others. In 2015, it ordered more than 10 billion banknotes, more than the United States ordered. Now, the companies that printed the bills are finding out that they aren't receiving payment for the deliveries. Even the supply of printed money could dry up.

Even though Chavez said that he would never dollarize the economy, meaning that he would never replace his currency with the U.S. dollar, he pegged the value of the VEF to the U.S. dollar. That is mostly because oil is priced in dollars. And while the VEF is pegged to the dollar, Venezuela has the flexibility to devalue against the dollar if it chooses to do so. That allows it to inflate the currency at will. But there are countries that have successfully replaced their currency with the dollar as their legal tender. As mentioned earlier, Zimbabwe dropped its currency and replaced it with the U.S. dollar, and after some economic pain, inflation dropped to 0.1 percent in 2015. But then it began to rise again in 2016 as the government started to print money.

In Latin America, both El Salvador and Ecuador dropped their currencies in favor of the dollar. In 1994, the government of El Salvador decided to peg its currency, the colón, to the U.S. dollar. In 2001, it did away with the peg and the colón altogether and adopted the dollar as the national currency, thus completing the transition to dollarization. El Salvador is now one of 13 countries that have entered into an exchange arrangement in which they do not have their own currency; 8 of the 13 use the U.S. dollar. By switching to the dollar, Salvadoran companies and the government gained access to cheaper interest rates because the move eliminated, or at least reduced, the risk of devaluation, thereby infusing more confidence in foreign banks to lend to the country. Corporate borrowing rates in El Salvador are among the lowest in Latin America, and consumer credit rose as the lower rates made it more attractive to borrow.

Two other countries in Latin America have adopted the dollar as their currency: Panama did so when it gained independence from Colombia over a century ago. Ecuador tied its currency to the dollar in 2000. When Ecuador decided to dollarize its economy, the president was in the midst of a political crisis and the announcement was totally unexpected. In 1999, the country's consumer price inflation was 52.2 percent, the highest in Latin America at the time. Until February 1999, the central bank had maintained a crawling peg exchange-rate system. However, pressure on the currency forced the central bank to leave the peg and allow the currency to float freely, upon which it promptly devalued by 65 percent. Finally, the president of Ecuador realized that the best thing to do was dollarize the exchange-rate system. Initially, Ecuador continued to use the sucre, but within a year, it decided to drop the sucre and use the dollar as its currency.

A World Bank official, discussing the rationale for Ecuador's decision, noted that "most countries have a large amount of their debt in dollars, maintain a large percent of their reserves abroad in dollars, and write contracts indexed to the dollar." Moreover, Ecuador, a member of OPEC, generates most of its foreign-exchange earnings from oil, which is also priced in dollars. In some respects, Venezuela is similar to Ecuador in its reliance on oil.

QUESTIONS

9-1. Do you think Venezuela should drop its currency, the VEF, and adopt the U.S. dollar? Why or why not?

9-2. If Venezuela does not replace the VEF with the dollar, what do you think will happen to the Venezuelan economy, inflation, and the exchange rate?

CONCEPT CHECK

Recall that we devote Chapter 8 to discussions of the **foreign-exchange market**, the ways in which currencies are quoted and traded, and the various instruments through which foreign exchange may be traded. In this chapter, we shift our focus to the ways in which currency values are determined, considering especially the roles of governments and the vagaries of the market.

INTRODUCTION

As we learned in Chapter 8, an exchange rate represents the number of units of one currency needed to acquire one unit of another. Although this definition seems simple, managers must understand how governments set an exchange rate and what causes it to change. Such understanding can help them anticipate exchange-rate changes and make decisions about business factors that are sensitive to those changes, such as the sourcing of raw materials and components, the placement of manufacturing and assembly, and the choice of final markets.

THE INTERNATIONAL MONETARY FUND

In 1944, toward the close of World War II, the major Allied governments met in Bretton Woods, New Hampshire, to determine what was needed to bring economic stability and growth to the postwar world. As a result of those meetings, the **International Monetary Fund (IMF)** came into official existence on December 27, 1945, with the goal of promoting exchange-rate stability and facilitating the international flow of currencies. The IMF began financial operations on March 1, 1947.[2]

ORIGIN AND OBJECTIVES

CONCEPT CHECK

In Chapter 7, we report on the establishment of the United Nations and the subsequent creation of a number of UN satellite organizations, including the **IMF**. Today, the IMF is in a position to influence economic policy among UN-member nations.

Twenty-nine countries initially signed the IMF agreement; there were 189 member countries as of April 28, 2016.[3] The fundamental mission of the IMF is to:

- Foster global monetary cooperation,
- Secure financial stability,
- Facilitate international trade,
- Promote high employment and sustainable economic growth, and
- Reduce poverty around the world.[4]

Through a process of surveillance, the IMF monitors the global economy as well as the economies of individual countries and advises on needed policy adjustments. In addition to surveillance, it provides technical assistance—mainly to low- and middle-income countries—and makes loans to countries with balance-of-payments problems.

Bretton Woods and the Principle of Par Value   The **Bretton Woods Agreement** established a system of fixed exchange rates under which each IMF member country set a **par value** for its currency based on gold and the U.S. dollar. Because the value of the dollar was fixed at $35 per ounce of gold, the par value would be the same whether gold or the dollar was used as the basis. This par value became a benchmark by which each country's currency was valued against others. Currencies were allowed to vary within 1 percent of their par value (extended to 2.25 percent in December 1971), depending on supply and demand. Additional moves from, and formal changes in, par value were possible with IMF approval. As we see later, par values were done away with when the IMF moved to greater exchange-rate flexibility.

The Bretton Woods Agreement established a par value, or benchmark value, for each currency initially quoted in terms of gold and the U.S. dollar.

Because of the U.S. dollar's strength during the 1940s and 1950s and its large reserves in monetary gold, currencies of IMF member countries were denominated in terms of gold and U.S. dollars. By 1947, the United States held 70 percent of the world's official gold reserves, so governments bought and sold dollars rather than gold. The understanding, though not set in stone, was that the United States would redeem dollars for gold. The dollar became the world benchmark for trading currency and has remained so, in spite of the move away from fixed rates to flexible exchange rates.

THE IMF TODAY

The IMF quota—the sum of the total assessment to each country—becomes a pool of money that the IMF can draw on to lend to other countries. It forms the basis for the voting power of each country—the higher its individual quota, the more votes a country has.

The Quota System   When a country joins the IMF, it contributes a certain sum of money, called a **quota**, broadly based on its relative size in the global economy. The IMF can draw on this pool of money to lend to countries, and it uses the quota as the basis of how much a country can borrow from the Fund. It is also the basis on which the IMF allocates special drawing rights (SDRs). Moreover, the quota determines the voting rights of the individual members. The largest quotas are held by the United States (16.67 percent), Japan (6.21 percent), China (6.14 percent), and Germany (5.37). Moreover, the quota determines the voting rights of the individual members. On December 15, 2010, the Board of

Governors of the IMF approved a package of reforms that would double the total quotas to SDR 476.8 (about $750 billion at current exchange rates at the time) and shift more of the quota shares to dynamic emerging market and developing countries (EMDCs). According to the realignment, the United States would still have the largest quota, but China would be number three, and the four BRIC countries would be among the 10 largest shareholders in the Fund.[5]

Special Drawing Rights (SDRs)   To help increase international reserves, the IMF created the **special drawing right (SDR)** in 1969 to help reinforce the fixed exchange-rate system that existed at that time. To support its currency in foreign-exchange markets, a country could use only U.S. dollars or gold to buy currency. However, the collapse of the Bretton Woods system, the move to floating exchange rates by most of the major currencies, and the growth of global capital markets as a source of funds for governments lessened the need for SDRs. Thus, the SDR is an international reserve asset created to supplement members' official holdings of gold, foreign exchange, and IMF reserve positions. In addition, the SDR serves as the IMF's *unit of account*—the unit in which the IMF keeps its records—and can be used for IMF transactions and operations.

On January 1, 1981, the IMF began to use a simplified basket of four currencies for determining valuation, the U.S. dollar, the euro, the British pound, and the Japanese yen. In 2016, however, the Chinese renminbi (or yuan) will be added to the basket. The new weights will be 42 percent for the dollar, 31 percent for the euro, 11 percent for the renminbi, 8 percent for the yen, and 8 percent for the pound. The weight of the dollar remained the same, but the weights of the other three currencies fell to make room for the renminbi.[6]

THE ROLE OF THE IMF IN GLOBAL FINANCIAL CRISES

An important responsibility of the IMF is to monitor and assess vulnerabilities of the economic and financial policies of member countries in relation to domestic and global stability. Where necessary, the IMF can provide precautionary credit lines to countries that are in distress. These loans are short-term emergency assistance loans, and in order to receive a loan, a country has to ensure that it will follow sound fiscal and monetary policies as determined jointly with the IMF staff.[7] Mozambique has major economic problems, and it was relying on medium- and long-term loans from commercial banks and the World Bank, a multi-lateral UN-based lending organization that is close to but separate from the IMF. The IMF had also been working with Mozambique on short-term relief on the assumption that they were accurately disclosing their external debt position. When it was revealed that the government had borrowed far more money than had been disclosed to the IMF, the World Bank and others scaled back their support until after the IMF could complete a study on Mozambique's risk and vulnerability. This is important because donors and other lenders rely on IMF information when determining where and how much to give to emerging markets.[8]

EVOLUTION TO FLOATING EXCHANGE RATES

The IMF's system was initially one of fixed exchange rates. Because the U.S. dollar was the cornerstone of the international monetary system, its value remained constant with respect to the value of gold. Other countries could change the value of their currency against gold and the dollar, but the value of the dollar remained fixed.

On August 15, 1971, as the U.S. balance-of-trade deficit continued to worsen, U.S. President Richard Nixon announced that the United States would no longer trade dollars for gold unless other industrial countries agreed to support a restructuring of the international monetary system. That resulted in the Smithsonian Agreement in December 1971.

The SDR is

- an international reserve asset given to each country to help increase its reserves,
- the unit of account in which the IMF keeps its financial records.

Currencies making up the SDR basket are the U.S. dollar, the euro, the Chinese renminbi, the Japanese yen, and the British pound. The Chinese renminbi (yuan) was added in 2016.

Exchange-rate flexibility was widened in 1971 from 1 percent to 2.25 percent from par value.

The Smithsonian Agreement   The agreement resulted in:

- An 8 percent devaluation of the dollar (an official drop in the value of the dollar against gold)
- A revaluation of some other currencies (an official increase in the value of each currency against gold)
- A widening of exchange-rate flexibility (from 1 to 2.25 percent on either side of par value)

This effort did not last, however. World currency markets remained unsteady during 1972, and the dollar was devalued again by 10 percent in early 1973 (the year of the Arab oil embargo and the start of fast-rising oil prices and global inflation). Major currencies began to float against each other, relying on the market to determine their value. The period from 1972–1981 led to the end of the Bretton Woods system and the move to flexible exchange rates.

The Jamaica Agreement of 1976 resulted in greater exchange-rate flexibility and eliminated the use of par values.

The Jamaica Agreement   Because the Bretton Woods Agreement was based on a system of fixed exchange rates and par values, the IMF had to change its rules to accommodate floating exchange rates. The **Jamaica Agreement** of 1976 amended the original rules to eliminate the concept of par values and permit greater exchange-rate flexibility.

EXCHANGE-RATE ARRANGEMENTS

The IMF surveillance and consultation programs are designed to monitor exchange-rate policies of countries and to see if they are acting openly and responsibly in exchange-rate policies.

The IMF requires countries to identify how they base their exchange-rate policy—hard peg, soft peg, or flexible.

As part of this move to greater flexibility, the IMF permitted countries to select and maintain an exchange-rate arrangement of their choice, provided they communicated their decision to the IMF. The formal decision of a country to adopt a particular exchange-rate mechanism is called a *de jure* system. In addition, the IMF surveillance program determines the *de facto* or actual exchange-rate system that a country uses.

The IMF consults annually with countries to see if they are acting openly and responsibly in their exchange-rate policies. Each year, each country notifies the IMF of the arrangement it will use, and the IMF uses information provided by the country and evidence of how the country acts in the market to place it in a specific category. Table 9.1 identifies the different exchange-rate arrangements that countries have adopted. The arrangements are ranked primarily on their degree of flexibility, from least to most.

THREE CHOICES: HARD PEG, SOFT PEG, OR FLOATING ARRANGEMENT

The IMF classifies currencies into one of three broad categories, moving from the least to the most flexible. Each category is subdivided into other categories as described below. If they have adopted a hard peg (13.1 percent of the total), they lock their value onto something and don't change. If they have adopted a soft peg (43.5 percent), they are pretty rigid but not as rigid as the hard peg. If they have adopted a floating arrangement (34.0 percent), their value is based on supply and demand. Some countries are not classified.[9]

TABLE 9.1   Exchange Rate Arrangements, October 2014

	Percent*	Number
Hard Peg	13.1	25
Soft Peg	43.5	83
Floating	34.0	65
Residual	9.4	18
Total	100.0	191

*includes 188 member countries plus 3 territories

Source: Based on International Monetary Fund, *Annual Report on Exchange Arrangements and Exchange Restrictions*, 2014 (Washington, DC, IMF, October 2014, p. 4–8).

HARD PEG

Countries can adopt another currency in place of their own, as is the case with Zimbabwe or Ecuador.

There are two possibilities for countries that adopt a hard peg. The first, called *dollarization*, can occur when a country like Zimbabwe or Ecuador does not have its own currency but has adopted the U.S. dollar as its currency.

Another form of a hard peg is a currency board.

The second example of the hard peg is a *currency board*, which is separate from a country's central bank. It is responsible for issuing domestic currency, typically anchored to a foreign currency. If it does not have deposits on hand in the foreign currency, it cannot issue more domestic currency. Twelve countries now have currency boards, of which eight are anchored to the U.S. dollar.[10] Hong Kong is a good example. Even though the HK dollar is locked onto the U.S. dollar, it moves up and down against other currencies since the U.S. dollar is a freely floating currency.

SOFT PEG

There are many different kinds of soft pegs but the most common is a conventional fixed-peg arrangement.

There are several different types of soft pegs, but most countries in this category (44 out of 83) have adopted a *conventional fixed-peg arrangement,* whereby a country pegs its currency to another currency or basket of currencies and allows the exchange rate to vary plus or minus 1 percent from that value.[11] Most countries use the U.S. dollar and the euro to anchor their pegs. In the other soft peg categories, the degree of flexibility increases, but the IMF determines that the currencies are not floating.

FLOATING ARRANGEMENT

Floating exchange-rate regimes include floating and freely floating.

Currencies considered to be in a floating arrangement are either floating (36 countries) or free floating (29 countries). Floating currencies are those that generally change according to market forces but may be subject to market intervention with no predetermined direction in which the currency should move. Free floating currencies are subject to intervention only in exceptional circumstances. The major trading currencies, including the U.S. dollar, the Japanese yen, the British pound, and the euro, are freely floating currencies. Brazil and India, two of the BRIC countries, are considered to have floating currencies.

THE EURO

CONCEPT CHECK ●

Each of these commitments to greater economic cooperation represents a step in the direction of regional integration, a form of economic integration that we defined on p. 229 in Chapter 7 as the elimination of economic discrimination among geographically related nations. Here we emphasize that the EU has introduced a common currency to its already-existing internal free trade agreement and common external tariff policy.

The criteria that are part of the Stability and Growth Pact include measures of deficits, debt, inflation, interest rates, and exchange-rate stability.

One of the most ambitious examples of a freely floating arrangement that resulted in countries giving up their own currency to create a new one is the euro. Not content with the economic integration envisaged in the Single European Act, the EU nations signed the Treaty of Maastricht in 1992, which set steps to accomplish two goals: political union and monetary union. To replace each national currency with a single European currency, the countries first had to converge their economic policies.

The European Monetary System and the European Monetary Union   Monetary unity in Europe did not occur overnight. The roots of the system began in 1979, when the **European Monetary System (EMS)** was set up as a means of creating exchange-rate stability within the European Community (EC). A series of exchange-rate relationships linked the currencies of most members through a parity grid. As the countries narrowed the fluctuations in their exchange rates, the stage was set for replacing the EMS with the Exchange Rate Mechanism (ERM) and full monetary union.

According to the Treaty of Maastricht, countries had to meet certain criteria to comply with the ERM and be part of the **European Monetary Union (EMU)**. Termed the "Stability and Growth Pact," the criteria outlined in the treaty are:

- Annual government deficit must not exceed 3 percent of GDP,
- Total outstanding government debt must not exceed 60 percent of GDP,

CONCEPT CHECK

When we get to Chapter 12, page 358, we'll point out that when a country initiates a comprehensive policy change over which businesses (whether domestic or foreign) have no control, they should reexamine each link in their value chains—the collective activities required to move products from materials purchasing through operations to final distribution. Here we observe that a change in a nation's exchange-rate regime is just one of the changes in economic conditions that foreign firms can't control.

19 of 28 members of the EU are members of the Eurozone. The UK and Denmark have opted out of the Eurozone, and the other members are working to qualify for the Eurozone.

The European Central Bank sets monetary policy for the adopters of the euro.

- Rate of inflation must remain within 1.5 percent of the three best-performing EU countries,
- Average nominal long-term interest rate must be within 2 percent of the average rate in the three countries with the lowest inflation rates,
- Exchange-rate stability must be maintained, meaning that for at least two years the country concerned has kept within the "normal" fluctuation margins of the European Exchange Rate Mechanism.[12]

As of May 1, 2016, 19 members of the EU were officially in the Eurozone, two had opted out (Denmark and the U.K.), and 7 were still preparing to join the Eurozone. The ERM requires countries to have a budget deficit of 3 percent of GDP and public debt 60 percent of GDP. However, the economic crisis of 2008 created problems for countries. For example, Greece's public debt is 182 percent of GDP, Italy's is 135.8 percent, and France's is 98.2 percent. Rather than levy major sanctions against these and other members of the Eurozone, there is an attempt to work with them to get them back into compliance.

The euro is administered by the **European Central Bank (ECB)**. The ECB has been responsible for setting monetary policy and managing the exchange-rate system for all of Europe since January 1, 1999. Because the ECB is independent of the political process, it can focus on its mandate of controlling inflation. Of course, different economies are growing at different rates in Europe, and it is difficult to have one monetary policy that fits all. Because of slow economic growth in the EU, the ECB recently adopted a policy of negative interest rates and quantitative easing (printing euros to purchase government debt). Although a popular strategy among the southern European countries that were struggling with high unemployment and budget problems, it was less popular in countries like Germany and the Netherlands where the population was getting very low returns on their savings. But the president of the ECB could see no reason to raise interest rates when economic growth was so slow.[13]

The Euro and the Global Financial Crisis   During the financial crisis of 2008, the euro fell because investors were pulling money out of stocks and putting it into safe-haven currencies such as the Japanese yen and the U.S. dollar. When the stock markets recovered, the dollar fell in value and the euro rose. At the time, interest rates were higher in Europe than in the United States, so the euro was perceived to be an investment asset whose value was greater than the dollar. As interest rates fell in the major industrial countries to help stimulate their economies, the interest rate differential disappeared, and currency values began to reflect other factors, such as the perceived strength in their relative economies. This was not helpful to the euro since the European economies were in serious financial trouble.

The role of the European Central Bank is to protect the euro against inflation. However, the weakness in European economies, especially countries like Greece, Italy, and Spain, forced the ECB to use monetary stimulus to attempt to boost economic growth. The hardest hit has been Greece. Because of Greece's large sovereign debt and weak economic growth, it has been difficult for Greece to make debt payments to external creditors. As a result, the European Central Bank teamed up with the IMF and the European Commission, nicknamed the "troika," to help increase financial liquidity and to pressure Greece to solve its budget problems. The ECB's main mandate to control inflation expanded to include increasing liquidity when they approved a European stability mechanism that would enable them to lend to struggling countries that met certain conditions. The idea was to allow the fund to buy bonds from troubled Eurozone governments to keep interest rates low. However, the concern in Europe is that if the ECB purchases bonds that default, the individual governments would be stuck with the bill, which means that taxpayers from the entire EU, especially powerful Germany, could be the ones to pay for Greek debt. Obviously, that is not a politically popular situation.

Point

Point   **Yes** So far, we've looked at the success of the EU in initiating a common currency. But what about Africa, the continent of some of the world's fastest-growing frontier economies? The success of the euro and the deep economic and political problems in Africa have caused many experts to wonder whether the continent should attempt to develop one common currency with a central bank to set monetary policy.[14] In 2003, the Association of African Central Bank Governors of the African Union (AU) announced it would work to create a common currency by 2021. This would benefit Africa by hastening economic integration in a continent that desperately needs to increase market size to achieve more trade and greater economies of scale. A common currency would lower transaction costs and make it easier to engage in intra-country trade.

Africa has several degrees of economic cooperation already, including two forms of currency cooperation that are classified by the IMF as conventional pegs tied to the euro:

1. The Economic and Monetary Community for Central Africa (CAEMC), including Cameroon, Central African Republic, Chad, Republic of Congo, Equatorial Guinea, and Gabon
2. The West African Economic and Monetary Union (WAEMU), including Benin, Burkina Faso, Côte d'Ivoire, Guinea-Bissau, Mali, Niger, Senegal, and Togo

Should Africa Develop a Common Currency?

Both monetary unions are part of the CFA franc zone. Their respective currencies are the Central African CFA franc and the West African CFA franc. The French treasury guarantees the full convertibility of both currencies.[15]

In addition to the two regional monetary unions, Africa has five existing regional economic communities: Arab Monetary Union, Common Market for Eastern and Southern Africa, Economic Community of Central African States, Economic Community of West African States, and Southern African Development Community. These groups are working hard to reduce trade barriers and increase trade among member countries, so all they would have to do is combine into one large African economic union, form a central bank, and establish a common monetary policy like the EU has.

A major advantage of establishing a central bank and common currency is that institutions in each African nation will have to improve, and the central bank may be able to insulate the monetary policy from political pressures, which often create inflationary pressures and subsequent devaluations. The East African Council of Ministers announced in 2013 that it planned to establish an East African Bank to facilitate the development of a common currency within 10 years, but that assumes the countries can resolve issues of differences in GDP, currencies, and institutions.[16]

Should Africa Develop a Common Currency?

Counterpoint   **No** There is no way the countries of Africa will ever establish a common currency, even though the African Union hopes to do so by 2021 and the East African Council even sooner. The institutional framework in the individual African nations is simply not ready. Few of the individual central banks are independent of the political process, so they often have to stimulate the economy to respond to political pressures. If the process is not managed properly and the currency is subject to frequent devaluation, there will be no pride in the region or clout on the international stage. The only two regional economic groups that are successful at this point have adopted the euro as their reference point, and the French treasury is backing up their currencies, so they are acting as if they were the central bank.

Further, each country will have to give up monetary sovereignty and rely on other measures—such as labor mobility,

Counterpoint

wage and price flexibility, and fiscal transfers—to weather the shocks. Even though there is good labor mobility in Africa, it is difficult to imagine that the African countries will be able to transfer tax revenues from country to country to help stimulate growth. In addition, it is difficult to transfer goods among the different countries in Africa because of transportation problems.

The establishment of the euro in the EU was a monumental task that took years, following a successful customs union and a gradual tightening of the ERM in Europe. For Africa to establish a common currency, there must first be closer economic integration. Thus, it is important to be patient and give Africa a chance to move forward. Maybe one way to move to a common currency is to strengthen the existing regional monetary unions, then gradually open them up to neighboring countries until there are a few huge monetary unions. These can then discuss ways to link together into a common African currency.

DETERMINING EXCHANGE RATES

A lot of different factors cause exchange rates to adjust. The exchange-rate regimes described earlier in the chapter are either fixed (hard peg or soft peg) or floating, with fixed rates varying in terms of how fixed they are and floating rates varying in terms of how much they actually float. However, currencies change in different ways depending on the type of regime.

NONINTERVENTION: CURRENCY IN A FLOATING-RATE WORLD

Demand for a country's currency is a function of the demand for that country's goods and services and financial assets.

Currencies that float free respond to supply and demand conditions. This concept can be illustrated using a two-country model involving the United States and Japan. Figure 9.1 shows the equilibrium exchange rate in the market and then a movement to a new equilibrium level as the market changes. The demand for yen in this example is a function of U.S. demand for Japanese goods and services, such as automobiles, and yen-denominated financial assets, such as securities.

The supply of yen is a function of Japanese demand for U.S. goods and services and dollar-denominated financial assets. Initially, this supply of and demand for yen meet at the equilibrium exchange rate e_0 (for example, 0.00926 dollar per yen, or 108 yen per dollar) and the quantity of yen Q_1.

Assume that Japanese consumers' demand for U.S. goods and services drops because of, say, high U.S. inflation. This lessening demand would result in a reduced supply of yen in the foreign-exchange market, causing the supply curve to shift to S'. Simultaneously, the rising prices of U.S. goods might lead to an increase in American consumers' demand for Japanese goods and services, which in turn would lead to an increase in demand for yen in the market, causing the demand curve to shift to D', and finally to an increase in the quantity of yen and in the exchange rate.

The new equilibrium exchange rate would be at e_1 (for example, 0.00943 dollar per yen, or 106 yen per dollar). From a dollar standpoint, the higher demand for Japanese goods would increase the supply of dollars as more consumers tried to trade their dollars for yen, and the reduced demand for U.S. goods would result in a drop in demand for dollars, causing a reduction in the dollar's value against the yen.

FIGURE 9.1   The Equilibrium Exchange Rate and How It Moves

Let's say that inflation in the United States is comparatively higher than in Japan. In that case (and assuming that Japanese consumers are buying U.S. goods and services), the demand for the Japanese yen will go up, but the supply will go down. What if Japan wants to keep the dollar-to-yen exchange rate at e_0? It can increase the supply of yen in the market—and therefore lower the exchange rate—by selling yen for dollars.

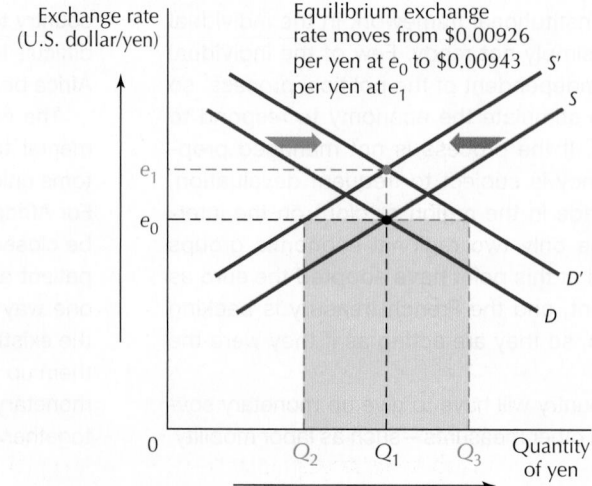

INTERVENTION: CURRENCY IN A FIXED-RATE OR MANAGED FLOATING-RATE WORLD

In the preceding example, Japanese and U.S. authorities allowed supply and demand to determine the values of the yen and dollar. However, assume that the United States and Japan decide to manage their exchange rates. Although both currencies are independently floating, their respective governments could intervene in the market. The U.S. government might not want its currency to weaken because its companies and consumers would have to pay more for Japanese products, which would lead to more inflationary pressure in the United States. Or the Japanese government might not want the yen to strengthen because it would mean unemployment in its export industries. Let's examine the role of central banks in this process.

| Central banks control policies that affect the value of currencies; the Federal Reserve Bank of New York is the central bank in the United States.

The Role of Central Banks   Each country has a central bank responsible for the policies affecting the value of its currency, although countries with independent currency boards use them to control the currency value. In the United States, the New York Federal Reserve Bank, in close coordination with and representing the Federal Reserve System of 12 regional banks and the U.S. Treasury, is responsible for intervening in foreign-exchange markets to achieve dollar exchange-rate policy objectives and counter disorderly conditions in foreign-exchange markets. The U.S. Treasury is responsible for setting exchange-rate policy, whereas the Fed is the central bank and is responsible for executing foreign-exchange intervention. Further, the New York Fed serves as a fiscal agent in the United States for foreign central banks and official international financial organizations.[17]

In the European Union, the European Central Bank coordinates the activities of each member country's central bank, such as the Bundesbank in Germany, to establish a common monetary policy in Europe, much as the Fed does in the United States.

| Central bank reserve assets are kept in three major forms: gold, foreign-exchange reserves, and IMF-related assets. Foreign exchange is 90 percent of reserve assets worldwide.

Central Bank Reserve Assets   Central bank reserve assets are kept in three major forms: foreign-exchange reserves, IMF-related assets (including SDRs), and gold. Foreign exchange composes over 90 percent of total reserves worldwide. In fourth quarter 2015, the U.S. dollar represented 64 percent of total foreign-exchange reserves, followed by the euro at 19.9 percent, the British pound at 4.88 percent, and the Japanese yen at 4.08 percent. The IMF will begin to identify the Chinese renminbi in its official foreign-exchange reserves database and will publish the data in March 2017.[18] The countries with the most foreign-exchange reserves are China, Japan, Europe (the Eurozone), Switzerland, and Saudi Arabia.

Having strong central bank reserve assets is essential to a country's fiscal strength. When the financial crises in Asia, Russia, and South America hit in the late 1990s, very few countries had strong central bank reserve assets. As a result, they had to borrow a lot of U.S. dollars, which turned out to be devastating when they finally had to devalue their currencies. Since 2000, however, the picture has changed. Due to strong commodity prices, expanding exports, and restraint in incurring dollar debt, many of those same countries have strengthened their financial position by increasing their reserves.

| Central banks intervene in currency markets by buying and selling currency to affect its price.

How Central Banks Intervene in the Market   A central bank can intervene in currency markets in several ways. The U.S. Fed, for example, can use foreign currencies to buy dollars when the dollar is weak, or sell dollars for foreign currency when the dollar is strong. Central banks may coordinate actions with other central banks, make policy statements to influence markets, and intervene to reverse, resist, or support a market trend.

Different Attitudes Toward Intervention   Government policies change over time, depending on economic conditions and the attitude of the prevailing administration in power, irrespective of whether the currency is considered to be freely floating.

The global financial crisis has roiled foreign-exchange markets and forced many central banks to intervene to support their currencies. During the crisis, Switzerland was forced to place a cap on its rate against the euro, and it kept it in place for 3 ½ years. However, in January 2015, the Swiss Central Bank was concerned about stability of the euro, coupled with falling energy prices and a rising dollar, so it eliminated the cap on the exchange rate against the euro, causing a rapid rise in the SwF against the euro.[19] On the other hand, although the United States has intervened in markets in the past, sometimes in conjunction with other countries, it did not intervene at all during the fourth quarter of 2015 when the dollar was strong against other currencies.

Challenges with Intervention   In general, it is very difficult, if not impossible, for intervention to have a lasting effect on the value of a currency. Given the daily volume of foreign-exchange transactions, no one government can move the market unless its movements can change market psychology. Intervention may temporarily halt a slide, but the country cannot force the market to move in a direction it doesn't want to go, at least for the long run.

BLACK MARKETS

A black market closely approximates a price based on supply and demand for a currency instead of a government-controlled price.

In many of the countries that do not allow their currencies to float according to market forces, a **black market** can parallel the official market and yet be aligned more closely with the forces of supply and demand. The less flexible a country's exchange-rate arrangement, the more likely there will be a thriving black (or parallel) market, which exists when people are willing to pay more than the official rate for hard currencies, such as dollars and euros. In order for such a market to work, the government must control access to foreign exchange so it can control the price of its currency. The opening case on Venezuela demonstrated how the black market in currency existed because of an artificial exchange rate set by the government.

In 2009 when Zimbabwe was in a financial crisis, the government issued a $100 trillion banknote that was worth about US$5 on the black market. Prices were doubling every day, and food and fuel were in short supply. The currency was so worthless that most trades in Zimbabwe were in U.S. dollars or the South African rand. That led to the country converting to the use of dollars in place of their currency.[20]

FOREIGN-EXCHANGE CONVERTIBILITY AND CONTROLS

Some countries with fixed exchange rates control access to their currencies. *Fully convertible currencies* are those that the government allows both residents and nonresidents to purchase in unlimited amounts.

Rampant inflation in Zimbabwe drove down the value of the currency so much that the Central Bank had to issue a 100 trillion Zimbabwe dollar banknote. It finally adopted the U.S. dollar as its currency.

Source: Catchlight Lens/Shutterstock

A hard currency is a currency that is usually fully convertible and strong or relatively stable in value in comparison with other currencies.

A soft currency is one that is usually not fully convertible and is also called a weak currency.

In a multiple exchange-rate system, a government sets different exchange rates for different types of transactions.

Hard and Soft Currencies   **Hard currencies**—such as the U.S. dollar, euro, British pound, and Japanese yen—are those that are fully convertible. Highly liquid and relatively stable in value over a short period of time, they are generally accepted worldwide as payment for goods and services. They are also desirable assets. Currencies that are not fully convertible, or **soft currencies**, have just the opposite characteristics: they are very unstable in value, not very liquid, and not widely accepted as payment for goods and services. A major reason why countries restrict convertibility of their currencies is that they are short on foreign-exchange reserves and try to use them for essential transactions.

Most countries today have *nonresident* (or *external*) *convertibility,* meaning that foreigners can convert their currency into the local currency and back into theirs as well. Tourists generally have no problems doing this, although sometimes countries put restrictions or conditions on trade from the local currency back to the hard currency when tourists leave the country.

Controlling Convertibility   To conserve scarce foreign exchange, some governments impose exchange restrictions on companies or individuals who want to exchange money.

Licenses   Government licenses fix the exchange rate by requiring all recipients, exporters, and others who receive foreign currency to sell it to its central bank at the official buying rate. The bank then rations the foreign currency it acquires by selling it at fixed rates to those needing to make payment abroad for essential goods. An importer may purchase foreign exchange only if it has obtained an import license for the goods in question.

Multiple Exchange Rates   Another way governments control foreign-exchange convertibility is by establishing more than one exchange rate. This restrictive measure is called a **multiple exchange-rate system**. The government determines which kinds of transactions are to be conducted at which exchange rates. Countries with multiple rates often have a floating rate for luxury goods and financial flows, such as dividends, and a fixed, usually lower rate for other trade transactions such as imports of essential commodities and semi-manufactured goods. The opening case on Venezuela illustrated how the government used multiple exchange rates. The IMF reported that out of 188 countries, only 16 use dual exchange rates and 6 use multiple rates.[21]

Import Deposits   Another form of foreign-exchange convertibility control is the **advance import deposit**. In this case, the government tightens the issue of import licenses and requires importers to make a deposit with the central bank—often for as long as one year and interest-free—covering the full price of manufactured goods they would purchase from abroad.

Quantity Controls   Governments may also limit the amount of exchange through quantity controls, which often apply to tourism. A quantity control limits the amount of currency a local resident can purchase from the bank for foreign travel.

EXCHANGE RATES AND PURCHASING POWER PARITY

The next two sections examine the relationship between inflation and exchange rates and the relationship between interest rates and exchange rates. These relationships are important in helping to forecast exchange rates.

Purchasing Power Parity (PPP)   The PPP exchange rate is the rate at which the currency of one country would have to be converted into that of another country to buy the same amount of goods and services in each country.[22] Examining the difference between the PPP exchange rate and the market exchange rate helps us understand how trade relations might be affected.

The "Big Mac Index"   An illustration of the PPP theory is the "Big Mac index" of currencies used by *The Economist* each year. Since 1986, the British periodical *The Economist* has used the price of a Big Mac to estimate the exchange rate between the dollar and another currency (see Table 9.2 for a sample of countries). Because the Big Mac is sold in more than 36,000 McDonald's restaurants in more than 100 countries every day, it is easy to use it to compare prices. PPP would suggest that the exchange rate should leave hamburgers costing the same in the United States as abroad. However, the Big Mac sometimes costs more and sometimes less, demonstrating how far currencies are under- or overvalued against the dollar.

The Big Mac price in U.S. dollars is found by converting the price in the local currency into dollars at the current exchange rate. For example, in Table 9.2, the dollar equivalent of a Big Mac in China is US$2.68 which is the price of the Big Mac in China (¥17.6) converted into dollars at the actual exchange rate (which was CNY6.56). Column 3, the implied PPP of the dollar, shows what the exchange rate should be if the price in dollars equals the price in the local currency. Continuing with China as the example, if you divide ¥17.6 by US$4.93 (the prices of the Big Mac in China and in the United States), you get ¥3.57 per dollar, which is what the exchange rate should be for a Big Mac to cost the same in the two countries. Column 4 shows the actual exchange rate, and Column 5 shows how much the currency is under- or overvalued. For the Chinese yuan, you take $(3.57 - 6.56)/6.56 = -.04558$, which shows that the yuan is undervalued against the dollar by 45.6 percent.

As you can see from Table 9.2, most currencies were undervalued against the dollar, so it was harder for U.S. companies to export during this period of the strong dollar. Conversely, it was easier for companies outside of the United States to export to the United States. However, these relationships change as the dollar weakens against other currencies.[23]

The Big Mac index, also known as "McParity," has both supporters and detractors. Although it is an easy way to see how PPP works, the index only includes one product, the Big Mac, rather than a basket of commodities. The IMF goes to great lengths to identify a basket of goods that makes sense when determining its PPP index.[24]

> If the domestic inflation rate is lower than that in a particular foreign country, the domestic currency should be stronger than the foreign currency.

The value of the Big Mac index is in understanding that price differences are not sustainable in the long run. Exchange rates will eventually have to equalize price differences more closely, or the law of supply and demand will take over. Of course, nobody is going to import Big Macs from China to the United States because they are so cheap. Nor will people fly to Venezuela just to buy a Big Mac. But if Big Macs are cheap, so are other products, and trade

TABLE 9.2   The Big Mac Index

Country	Big Mac Prices		Implied PPP of the Dollar	Actual Exchange Rate: Jan 30, 2013	Under (−)/Over (+) Valuation Against the Dollar, %
	In Local Currency	In Dollars			
United States	4.93	4.93	−	1.00	0.00
Argentina	33.0	2.39	6.69	13.81	−51.5
Brazil	13.5	3.35	2.74	4.02	−32.0
China	17.6	2.68	3.57	6.56	−45.6
Euro area	3.72	4.0	0.75	0.93	−18.9
Hong Kong	19.2	2.48	3.89	7.75	−49.80
India	127	1.90	25.76	68.80	−61.4
Japan	370	3.12	75.05	118.65	−36.7
Mexico	49	2.81	9.94	17.44	−43.0
Russia	114	1.53	23.12	74.66	69.0
Switzerland	6.50	6.44	1.32	1.01	+30.7
Venezuela	132	.664	26.77	198.7	−86.58

Source: Based on The Big Mac Index, http://www.economist.com/bigmac (accessed January 7, 2016).

flows could be influenced by price differences. For example, during the financial crisis in Venezuela, people were traveling from Brazil to Venezuela for plastic surgery because it was so much cheaper than it was in Brazil.

EXCHANGE RATES AND INTEREST RATES

Although inflation is the most important medium-term influence on exchange rates, interest rates are also important. Interest rate differentials, however, have both short-term and long-term components to them. In the short term, exchange rates are strongly influenced by interest rates. When the U.S. Federal Reserve Bank raised interest rates on December 16, 2015, the first time in nearly a decade, the result was hot money flowing into the United States to take advantage of the slightly higher interest rate. In early 2015, even before the rise in U.S. interest rates, money was flowing out of Europe at a rapid pace because of differences in interest rate policies, which also pushed down the euro against the dollar by 22 percent in less than a year. Investors were moving cash based on future expectations.[25]

In the long term, however, there is a strong relationship between inflation, interest rates, and exchange rates. To understand this, we need to examine two key finance theories: the *Fisher Effect* and the *International Fisher Effect*. The first links inflation and interest rates, while the second links interest rates and exchange rates.

| The nominal interest rate is the real interest rate plus inflation. Because the real interest rate should be the same in every country, the country with the higher interest rate should have higher inflation.

The Fisher Effect   The **Fisher Effect** is the theory that the nominal interest rate in a country (r, the actual monetary interest rate earned on an investment) is determined by the real interest rate (R, the nominal rate less inflation) and the inflation rate (i) as follows:

$$(1 + r) = (1 + R)(1 + i) \text{ or } r = (1 + R)(1 + i) - 1$$

According to this theory, if the real interest rate is 5 percent, the U.S. inflation rate 2.9 percent, and the Japanese inflation rate 1.5 percent, then the nominal interest rates for the United States and Japan are computed as follows:

$$r_{US} = (1.05)(1.029) - 1 = 0.08045, \text{ or } 8.045\%$$

$$r_j = (1.05)(1.015) - 1 = 0.06575, \text{ or } 6.575\%$$

Thus, the difference between U.S. and Japanese interest rates is a function of the difference between their inflation rates. If inflation rates were the same (zero differential) but interest rates were 10 percent in the United States and 6.575 percent in Japan, investors would place their money in the United States, where they could get the higher real return.

| The IFE implies that the currency of the country with the lower interest rate will strengthen in the future.

The International Fisher Effect   The bridge from interest rates to exchange rates can be explained by the **International Fisher Effect (IFE)**, the theory that the interest-rate differential is an unbiased predictor of future changes in the spot exchange rate. For example, if the IFE predicts that nominal interest rates in the United States are higher than those in Japan, the dollar's value should fall in the future by that interest-rate differential, which would be an indication of a weakening, or depreciation, of the dollar. That is because the interest-rate differential is based on differences in inflation rates, as we discussed earlier. The previous discussion on PPP also demonstrates that the country with the higher inflation should have the weaker currency. Thus, the country with the higher interest rate (and the higher inflation) should have the weaker currency.

Of course, these issues cover the long run, but anything can happen in the short run. During periods of general price stability, a country that raises its interest rates is likely to attract capital and see its currency rise in value due to the increased demand. However, if the reason for the increase in interest rates is that inflation is higher than that of its major trading partners, and if the country's central bank is trying to reduce inflation, the currency will eventually weaken until inflation cools down.

OTHER FACTORS IN EXCHANGE-RATE DETERMINATION

Exchange-rate movements are also influenced by investors' appetite for risk versus their appetite for safety.

Confidence: Flight to Risk Versus Flight to Safety   Various other factors can affect currency values. One not to be dismissed lightly is confidence: In times of turmoil, people prefer to hold currencies that are considered safe. When the banking crisis in Cyprus unfolded in March of 2013, investors moved money out of euros and invested in U.S. dollars (a flight to safety) because of concerns over the effect of the crisis on the rest of Europe, which was already very fragile in the banking sector.

On the other hand, sometimes the appetite for risk (which implies greater returns) is more important than safety. In early 2016, the dollar began to fall as oil prices stabilized and increased, and investors began to look at investments in emerging markets like Brazil which caused their exchange rates to rise against the dollar. Clearly, the flight to risk outweighed the flight to safety.

FORECASTING EXCHANGE-RATE MOVEMENTS

FUNDAMENTAL AND TECHNICAL FORECASTING

Fundamental forecasting uses trends in economic variables to predict future exchange rates.

Technical forecasting uses past trends in exchange-rate movements to spot future trends.

Managers can forecast exchange rates by using either of two approaches: fundamental or technical. **Fundamental forecasting** uses trends in economic variables to predict future rates. The data can be plugged into an econometric model or evaluated on a more subjective basis.

Technical forecasting uses past trends in exchange rates themselves to spot future rate trends. Technical forecasters, or *chartists,* assume that if current exchange rates reflect all facts in the market, then under similar circumstances future rates will follow the same patterns.[26] However, research has shown that, except in the very short run, past exchange rates are not an accurate predictor of future ones. According to this theory, then, exchange-rate movements are a random walk, implying they cannot be predicted.[27]

Dealing with Biases   Some biases exist that can skew forecasts:

- Overreaction to unexpected and dramatic news events;
- Illusory correlation—that is, the tendency to see correlations or associations in data that are not statistically present but are expected to occur on the basis of prior beliefs;
- Focusing on a particular subset of information at the expense of the overall set of information;
- Insufficient adjustment for subjective matters, such as market volatility;
- The inability to learn from one's past mistakes, such as poor trading decisions;
- Overconfidence in one's ability to forecast currencies accurately.[28]

Good treasurers develop their own forecasts of what will happen to a particular currency and use fundamental or technical predictions of outside forecasters to corroborate them. Doing this helps them determine whether they are considering important factors and whether they need to revise their forecasts in light of outside analysis.

Managers need to be concerned with the timing, magnitude, and direction of an exchange-rate movement.

Timing, Direction, and Magnitude   Forecasting includes predicting the timing, direction, and magnitude of an exchange-rate change or movement. For countries whose currencies are not freely floating, the timing is often a political decision and not easy to predict. And though the direction of a change can probably be predicted, the magnitude is difficult to forecast. So, not only is it difficult to predict what will happen to currencies, it is equally difficult to use those predictions to forecast profits and establish operating strategies.

FUNDAMENTAL FACTORS TO MONITOR

Key factors to monitor—the institutional setting, fundamental analysis, confidence factors, events, and technical analysis.

For freely fluctuating currencies, the law of supply and demand determines market value. Your ability to forecast exchange rates depends on your time horizon. In general, the best predictors of future exchange rates are interest rates for short-term movements, inflation for medium-term movements, and current account balances for long-term movements.[29] Given that even those countries whose currencies are freely floating are concerned about the value of their currencies, managers can monitor the same factors the governments follow to try to make a prediction:

- *Institutional Setting*
  - Does the currency float, or is it managed—and if so, is it pegged to another currency, to a basket, or to some other standard?
  - What are the intervention practices? Are they credible? Sustainable?

- *Fundamental Analyses*
  - Does the currency appear undervalued or overvalued in terms of PPP, balance of payments, foreign-exchange reserves, or other factors?
  - What is the cyclical situation in terms of employment, growth, savings, investment, and inflation?
  - What are the prospects for government monetary, fiscal, and debt policy?

- *Confidence Factors*
  - What are market views and expectations with respect to the political environment, as well as to the credibility of the government and central bank?

- *Circumstances*
  - Are there national or international incidents in the news, the possibility of crises or emergencies, or governmental or other important meetings coming up?

- *Technical Analyses*
  - What trends do the charts show? Are there signs of trend reversals?
  - At what rates do there appear to be important buy and sell orders? Are they balanced? Is the market overbought? Oversold?
  - What is the thinking and what are the expectations of other market players and analysts?[30]

We have already discussed interest rates and inflation, but what about current account balances? A current account surplus means that a country exports more than it imports and is building foreign-exchange reserves from the countries that are buying its goods and services. For the long term, the expectation is that the currency of that country will strengthen vis-à-vis its trading partners. Conversely, a current account deficit means that a country imports more than it exports and is building up debt abroad as it struggles to find the foreign exchange to pay for its imports. In that case, the long-term expectation is that the currency will weaken vis-à-vis its trading partners.

BUSINESS IMPLICATIONS OF EXCHANGE-RATE CHANGES

As we will see in the closing case, exchange-rate changes can dramatically affect operating strategies as well as translated overseas profits.

MARKETING DECISIONS

Marketing managers watch exchange rates because they can affect demand for a company's products at home and abroad. For example, in 2013, as the Indian rupee plunged in value against the U.S. dollar, Indian small importers were in trouble because they didn't have the financial strength to deal with the currency fluctuations. In most cases, they had to pay their suppliers in U.S. dollars; when the rupee fell, they had to come up with more rupees to convert into dollars to pay the suppliers, and they were struggling to do so.[31] On the other side, U.S. exporters struggled with a strong dollar as the prices in local currencies rose during a time when economic growth abroad was weak in the first place.

PRODUCTION DECISIONS

Companies might locate production in a weak-currency country because

- initial investment there is relatively cheap,
- such a country is a good base for inexpensive exportation.

Exchange-rate changes can also affect the location of production, although it will be only one of many variables companies consider. A manufacturer in a country where wages and operating expenses are high might be tempted to relocate production to a country with a currency that is rapidly losing value. The company's home currency would buy lots of the weak currency, making the company's initial investment cheap. Further, goods manufactured in that country would be relatively low-cost in world markets.

FINANCIAL DECISIONS

Exchange rates can influence the sourcing of financial resources, the cross-border remittance of funds, and the reporting of financial results.

Exchange rates can affect financial decisions primarily in sourcing financial resources, remitting funds across national borders, and reporting financial results. In the first area, a company might be tempted to borrow money in places where interest rates are lowest. However, recall that interest-rate differentials often are compensated for in money markets through exchange-rate changes.

In deciding about cross-border financial flows, a company would want to convert local currency into its own home-country currency when exchange rates are most favorable so it can maximize its return. However, countries with weak currencies often have currency controls, making it difficult for MNEs to do so.

CONCEPT CHECK

In Chapter 19, pages 571–572 and 580, we'll explain how companies factor in foreign exchange in preparing financial statements, we'll show how exchange rates influence financial flows, and describe some of the strategies that companies enlist to protect themselves against exchange-rate risk.

Finally, exchange-rate changes can influence the reporting of financial results. Procter & Gamble generates 65 percent of its revenues from outside of the United States. Because of the strong dollar in 2015, P&G found that its revenues and earnings generated in weaker currencies were lower than if the dollar were stable or a little weaker. On the other hand, sales and earnings in a strong currency result in higher profits when translated back into dollars; when they are generated in a weaker currency, they are lower when translated back into dollars.[32]

Looking to the Future
Changes in the Relative Strength of Global Currencies

The international monetary system has undergone considerable change since the early 1970s, when the dollar was devalued the first time. New countries have been born with the breakup of the Soviet empire, and with them have come new currencies. In addition, China has come of age.

The world has come out of the global financial crisis, but it is still weak. Inflation is relatively low, and so are interest rates. In some cases, rates are below zero, which was unthinkable not too many years ago. Deflation is a greater concern than inflaton. Oil prices are low, which adds to low levels of inflation and is a result of slow economic growth. Estimated global growth in GDP was only 3 percent in 2015, and it was only 6.8 percent in China, the third consecutive year that GDP has fallen. Because of the slow economic growth, many countries, including Greece, are having budget crises that are affecting their ability to service debt.

Although the U.S. dollar is the main reserve asset used by central banks, the Chinese RMB is gaining steam. However, the three key determinants of the reserve status of a currency are size, stability, and liquidity.[33] Will the RMB ever replace the dollar as the chief reserve asset, or will they share power? Or will there be three reserve assets—the dollar, the RMB, and the euro? And will the yen be part of that picture?

The RMB suffers in all three areas: size (although the Chinese economy is formidable), stability, and liquidity. The financial institutions in China are still very weak, even though they are improving. Although the RMB became part of the SDR basket in 2016 and thus eligible to be a reserve asset, it has been struggling. It has the largest foreign-exchange reserves in the world, exceeding $4 trillion in mid-2014. However, the RMB is not a freely floating currency. In spite of that, there has been a large outflow of RMB from China for several reasons. One is that the People's Bank of China has been trying to support the RMB by using its foreign-exchange reserves. In January 2016 alone, it used $100 billion in reserves to defend the RMB, pushing its reserves to about $3.23 trillion.[34] Although that is still a large amount of reserves, it is clear that the outflow of money from China by private investors as well as the government is draining the reserves. Will the government have to continue to support the RMB and further drain its foreign currency reserves?

The euro is a strong currency and represents the second-largest amount of allocated reserves behind the dollar. The major challenge of the euro is that its member countries are fragmented with numerous internal problems, such as Greek debt. In addition, Britain, one of the strongest countries in the EU, never adopted the Euro, and in 2016 it voted to leave the EU. ∎

CASE   Welcome to the World of Sony— Unless the Falling Yen Rises (or Falls) Again[35]

For five consecutive years, the yen was falling against the U.S. dollar, which actually was a good deal. The reason is because stronger revenues and earnings from abroad were translated into more yen. In addition, the weaker yen helped Sony in export markets. However, in early 2016, the yen began to strengthen against the dollar from ¥123 in November 2015 to ¥120 at the end of 2015, to ¥112.4 on March 31, 2016, the close of Sony's fiscal year. Whereas Toyota disclosed in August 2015 that the weaker yen was fueling its profits, in the first quarter of 2016 it changed its tune and noted that the stronger yen was going to hurt sales and profits. What will the future bring for Sony and other Japanese companies?

The Past

Before attacking the future, let's look at the past, especially from the perspective of the Japanese yen. In the post–World War II years, the yen was extremely weak against the dollar, trading at ¥357.65 in 1970. At that time, in 1946, the Tokyo Tsushin Kogyo Corporation was founded, officially becoming known as Sony Corporation in 1958, the year its stock was first listed on the Tokyo Stock Exchange. It also became the first Japanese company to list American Depositary Receipts (ADRs) on the New York Stock Exchange in 1961, finally listing its own shares in September 1970.

In those early years of operation, Sony had the luxury of operating in a currency that was not only weak against the dollar, but also highly controlled by the government. Japanese foreign-exchange policies favored companies and industries that the government wanted to succeed, especially in export markets. With a cheap yen, it was easy for companies to expand exports rapidly.

The First Endaka

From its 1970 high, the yen steadily strengthened until 1985, when it *really* shot up in value. Due to economic problems in the United States, the dollar began to fall during the latter part of 1985, and the yen ended the year at ¥200 per dollar (as the number of yen per dollar falls, the dollar gets weaker and the yen gets stronger). By the latter part of 1986, it was trading at ¥150, a steep rise from its historical highs. The Japanese called this strengthening of the yen *endaka*, which literally translates "high yen." *Endaka* resulted in serious problems for Japanese exporters and potential pain for the entire Japanese economy, which depended heavily on international trade. However, one advantage of *endaka* was that imports were cheaper, and Japan relied heavily on imports of virtually all commodities. Thus its input costs fell, even as it found its export prices rising.

The strong yen was due primarily to a strong Japanese economy, large trade surpluses, and the largest foreign-exchange reserves in the world. In addition, Japan had low unemployment, low interest rates, and low inflation. But cracks began to show in its economy. A combination of a drop in the stock market, a rise in inflation, and a real estate bubble hurt

Tokyo Tower, modeled after Paris' Eiffel Tower, is the world's tallest self-supported steel tower. Located in Tokyo, home of the corporate headquarters of both Sony and the Bank of Japan (which serves as the Central Bank of Japan), the Tokyo Tower dominates the Tokyo skyline and offers a view of Mt. Fuji on a clear day.

Source: Sean Pavone/Shutterstock

the economy and confidence in the yen. Since the interest rates in the United States were higher, investors pulled money out of Japan and put it into U.S. dollars to take advantage of higher returns. This drop in demand for yen and rise in demand for dollars pushed up the value of the dollar against the yen, and the yen closed out 1989 at ¥143.45, from ¥125.85 only a year earlier.

Both the United States and Japan were worried about inflation in the early 1990s, and they tried to coordinate exchange-rate policies, but the United States didn't want to push down the value of the dollar too much and lose its own fight against inflation. The two nations tried to get the central banks of Germany, the United Kingdom, and other countries to intervene in the markets and sell their currencies for yen in order to strengthen it. But there wasn't much they could do to move the market given that interest rates were driving market psychology.

In the ensuing years, many factors influenced the yen/dollar exchange rate, including a weak U.S. economy (favoring a drop in interest rates), the Persian Gulf War (which favored the dollar as a safe-haven currency), a rise in Japanese interest rates relative to U.S. interest rates, and a lack of agreement among G8 countries in 1993 about whether the yen was too weak or about right.

A Second Endaka

As if one *endaka* were not enough, a second one hit in 1995, when the yen rose to ¥80.63 per dollar. As they did with the first *endaka,* Japanese companies looked for ways to cut costs and remain competitive. During that period, the Japanese economy was in a recession, so the Bank of Japan cut interest rates to stimulate demand, and the yen fell against the dollar, favoring exporters once again.

Competitive Pressures

During these decades of currency swings, Sony kept moving along as one of the premier companies in the world in consumer electronics, games, music, and movies. Its wide array of product innovations earned it a premium in the market; then competition began to step in. Korean companies like Samsung began to produce cheaper products that rose in quality as each year went by, and Samsung began to develop its own reputation for innovation in electronics. In addition, Samsung and other foreign competitors began setting up plants offshore, especially in China, to improve their cost advantage even more. Some of Sony's Japanese competitors, including Toshiba and Panasonic, reduced their exposure to a strong yen by moving plants overseas to countries like Indonesia and the Philippines and by increasing the dollar-based imports of parts.

From the beginning of 2003 until the end of 2004, the dollar continued to weaken against both the euro and the yen. In an attempt to strengthen the dollar, the Japanese central bank spent a record 20 trillion yen in 2003 and 10 trillion yen in the first two months of 2004. Despite such efforts, the yen rose 11 percent against the dollar in 2003 and continued to strengthen through 2004. The Japanese finance ministry stopped its foreign-exchange intervention in March 2004, but the dollar's continued weakening against both the euro and the yen at the end of 2004 sparked new threats of intervention by the Japanese and Europeans.

Fast-Forward to 2008

The collapse in the housing market in the United States and the ensuing credit crisis in 2007, followed by the bankruptcy of Lehman Brothers and the U.S. government takeover of global insurer AIG in September 2008, had a devastating effect on the global economy. The U.S. stock market crashed, followed by similar crashes around the world, and investors pulled funds out of risky emerging markets and placed them in safe-haven assets. As a result, the euro dropped against the U.S. dollar and the Japanese yen.

Why did this happen? In the case of the U.S. dollar, the market reaction was a standard flight to safety—which often happens when global events get scary—even though the U.S. markets started the collapse. Political stability and the size of the economy tend to make the United States an attractive place for investment. Thus, the fear factor seemed to be a critical vote for the dollar during the crisis. This was a short-term phenomenon, however, and was eventually replaced by economic fundamentals.

During the crisis, the dollar vacillated depending on what news was most important. When the crisis was the news, the dollar was strong. When the news favored a recovery of the U.S. economy, money flowed into equity markets in the United States and abroad, seeking higher returns and causing the dollar to drop in value. With the slowdown in the U.S. economy, export-dominated countries, especially emerging markets, were expected to suffer. Also, the credit crisis the United States was going through was expected to expand to other countries. One interesting effect of the crisis was that the euro tended to be very sensitive to the U.S. stock market. When the market was falling, so was the euro. When the market began to recover, so did the euro. The euro is obviously a strong and important currency, but it lacks a strong central government that can coordinate a response to economic crisis. The European Central Bank can influence interest rates, but that's about all.

What about the yen? Interestingly enough, the yen also became a safe-haven currency during the crisis, along with the dollar. At the time, the yen was Asia's most important currency because Japan had the second-highest foreign-exchange reserves in the region and the world (just after China) and because it is a freely convertible currency with high market liquidity, as well as an important trading currency. Also, with Japanese interest rates so low, many investors were borrowing in yen and investing their proceeds abroad to get access to higher returns. When the crisis hit, the money quickly left the emerging markets and returned to Japan, a practice called *carry trade*. Whenever volatility in currency markets goes up, investors unwind (reverse) their trades; this gave strength to the yen.

The markets also demonstrated that the yen and U.S. stock market were inversely related. When markets are less risk-averse, stocks gain in value and the yen drops in value. When markets are more risk-averse, stock prices fall and the yen trades higher.

2011: The Year of Tragedy

The earthquake and tsunami that struck Japan on March 11, 2011, were devastating in terms of lives lost and overall human tragedy. In addition, there was a great deal of uncertainty over damage to nuclear reactors and disruption to the global supply chain. (Consider that Japanese factories produce about 25 percent of the world's semiconductors and 40 percent of electronic components.) Plants in affected areas were shut down due to property damage, power outages, and a transportation infrastructure that ground to a halt.

What happened to the Japanese yen during this crisis? Conventional wisdom would say that the yen fell against the dollar, but it actually rose in value. After the quake, there was a massive inflow of capital from the Japanese as they liquidated investments made with cheap Japanese money which were invested in emerging markets where returns are high (another example of carry trade). In addition, many Japanese companies brought money back to the country at the end of the fiscal year (March 31), so the need for capital resulted in a tremendous inflow of it, causing the yen to rise in value.

What Does All This Mean to Sony?

Now we are in 2016 where the yen reversed years of weakness against the dollar and started an upward climb. In FY 2015, Sony generated 27.2 percent of its sales in Japan, 18.6 percent in the United States, 23.5 percent in Europe, 12.8 percent in Asia/Pacific, 6.7 percent in China, and 11.2 percent elsewhere. Thus, the company was well diversified geographically.

Sony's production of electronics products was done 60 percent in-house and 40 percent outsourced. Of the in-house production, 35 percent was done in Japan, of which 75 percent was exported; 40 percent was manufactured in China, of which 75 percent was exported; 5 percent was manufactured in the United States and Europe for local consumption; and the rest was manufactured in other parts of Asia, of which 65 percent was exported to the Americas, Japan, Europe, and China, and the rest was sold in local markets. What is interesting about the location of sales and manufacturing is that are multiple kinds of exposure. For example, products manufactured in Japan and exported to other markets are affected by the value of the yen: When the yen is weak, exports benefit. When the yen is strong, exports suffer.

One major effect of the strong yen and the global slowdown was the sharp drop in exports from Japan. In January 2009, for example, exports dropped 49 percent compared to a year earlier. As exporters found their sales falling, they cut orders from their suppliers, so there was a ripple effect in the Japanese economy, affecting both production and employment. These events caused a sharp contraction in Japan as GDP fell 12.1 percent in the fourth quarter of 2008 compared to a year earlier, and many experts felt that Japan was going through its worst recession since World War II. Deflation was also affecting the Japanese economy again, and consumers were delaying purchases hoping that prices would continue to fall, while companies were hesitant to invest more. Is it possible that the opposite took place when the yen weakened in the past few years? Now that the yen is getting stronger, will Japan repeat its experience of 2009?

The strong yen was also hurting Sony's financial statements. As Sony translates U.S. dollar or euro financial statements into yen, net assets and earnings are worth less in yen, dragging down Sony's consolidated results. The only way to offset this drop is to sell more and improve profit margins, both of which are hard to do in a slow global economy. From a cash-flow point of view, Sony's operations abroad are remitting dividends back to Japan, but they are worth less yen as the dollar and euro weaken against it. One silver lining is that the purchasing power of the yen rises as it strengthens compared to other currencies, so everything Sony imports into Japan for its manufacturing is cheaper. The same would be true for anything manufactured outside Japan, thus reducing costs and hopefully increasing margins. As long as Sony is invoicing its exports in dollars to customers worldwide, it needs to match the dollar revenues with dollar expenses through investing more in the United States or in other countries in Asia, like Taiwan, where components are cheaper and where Sony can invoice its purchases in dollars.

A Reversal of Fortunes—Abenomics   Just when things looked bleak due to the strong yen and weak demand in Europe and China, Japan elected a new prime minister in November 2012, Shinzo Abe, who decided to fight deflation at home and a weak domestic economy through loose monetary, fiscal, and structural policies. For most of 2012, the yen had been trading below ¥80/US$, but by the end of 2012 it was trading at 85.96; by May 6, 2013, it was at 99.10 and falling. At the end of the first quarter of 2013, Sony doubled its annual profit estimates due partly to the falling yen.

If the strong yen made it difficult for exporters to sell abroad and weakened foreign earnings, the weak yen was just the opposite. Exporters like Sony, Toyota, and Panasonic were ecstatic about the weaker yen (which had fallen by more than 20 percent since Abe took office) and the opportunity to expand their sales abroad. The full extent of their ability to take advantage of the weaker yen still depended on economic recovery in the United States, Europe, and China, but at least the currency wasn't an additional weight on their competitive position.

QUESTIONS

9-3. Why do you think it is important for Sony to manufacture more products in the United States and Europe and to also buy more from suppliers in other countries in Asia?

9-4. What are the major forces that affected the Japanese yen over the years? What factors do you think are important to monitor as you try to forecast what will happen to the value of the yen in the future?

MyLab Management

Go to **mymanagementlab.com** for the following Assisted-graded writing questions:

9-5   What were the major factors that led to the drop in Sony's exports from Japan?

9-6   In what other ways has the strong yen affected Sony's bottom line? What would be the effect of a weak yen?

Endnotes

Scan for Endnotes or go to www.pearsonglobaleditions.com/Daniels

CHAPTER 10
Global Debt and Equity Markets

OBJECTIVES

After studying this chapter, you should be able to

10-1 Describe the finance function of an MNE in a global context

10-2 Define leverage and how it affects the choice of capital structure

10-3 Explain the different ways to access debt internationally

10-4 Summarize how foreign source income is taxed

10-5 Analyze how offshore financial centers provide financing opportunities for MNEs

MyLab Management®

Improve Your Grade!

When you see this icon ⭐, visit **www.mymanagementlab.com** for activities that are applied, personalized, and offer immediate feedback.

To have money is a good thing; to have a say over the money is even better.

—Yiddish proverb

A man passing a currency board. ▶

Source: Mr Doomits. Shutterstock

Tax Wars: Pfizer Versus the U.S. Government[1]

In 2014, Pfizer, the U.S.-based pharmaceutical company, began looking at Allergan, the pharma headquartered in Ireland, for a possible merger. From one perspective, the deal made sense. Pfizer needed to expand its portfolio of new drugs, and Allergan had some high-profile drugs, like Botox. From another perspective, Allergan's headquarters were located in Ireland, where the corporate tax rate is 12.5 percent, compared with the 35 percent U.S. corporate tax rate (39 percent for combined federal and local tax rate), the highest in the world. If the merger went though and Pfizer was able to move its corporate headquarters to Ireland, it stood to significantly reduce its corporate tax liability and therefore free up more cash for its equity shareholders and for reinvestment into the development of new drugs.

TAX INVERSIONS

Pfizer and Allergan were caught in a war of words and phrases, like serial inverters, earnings-stripping, stuffing, cherry-picking, and the best of them all, skinny down. But let's go back a few years to when tax inversions really took hold because of high U.S. corporate tax rates and the inability of Congress to make any progress on comprehensive tax reform. It's easy to see the difference in corporate tax rates between the United States and Ireland, but the rates are 30.18 percent in Germany, 20 percent in the U.K., 25 percent in the Netherlands, 21.5 percent in Switzerland, and 26.7 percent in Canada. However, tax loopholes in the U.S. tax code allow the 50 biggest MNCs to reduce their effective tax rate to 24 percent compared to 35 percent for their European counterparts. In order to reduce the U.S. corporate tax rate to be comparable with their European counterparts, comprehensive tax reform also needs to take place.

Burger King, a U.S.-based company that was owned by 3G Capital Partners LP, a Brazilian private equity firm, was part of one of the first high-profile tax inversions that created tensions on both sides of the Canadian border, but for different reasons. In 2014, Burger King decided to merge with Tim Hortons, a coffee-and-doughnuts chain started in Canada. Burger King's goal was to complete the merger with Tim Hortons, move the corporate headquarters to Canada, and change the name to Restaurant Brands International. In the process, it would save $117 million dollars in U.S. taxes since it would never have to pay U.S. taxes on foreign profits it holds offshore. Of course, Burger King announced that it was driven by growth opportunities, not tax savings, by completing the inversion. On the Canadian side, the concern was that Canada was losing another one of its corporate icons, Canada's largest coffee-shop chain with a market cap about the same size as Burger King. In spite of Burger King being called "unpatriotic" by the U.S. government for completing the tax inversion, it has since proven its prediction that growth, not just taxes, was the foundation of the merger. 3G Partners is now expanding its new Tim Hortons business in the United States, creating more American jobs as well as creating more wealth for Tim Hortons.

In the absence of tax reform, enterprising U.S. companies discovered tax inversion as a way to reduce their tax liability. Using Pfizer as an example, Pfizer would merge with Allergan and adopt Ireland as its tax domicile. Since the new firm would not be a U.S. company, it would not be subject to U.S. corporate income taxes. It could then use its tax savings to pay dividends to shareholders and use the excess cash for global expansion. It is estimated that since 2012, there have been at least 20 such tax inversions, including Burger King and Tim Hortons, and many others were moving in that direction.

THE FIGHT AGAINST TAX INVERSIONS

The fight against inversions was taken up by the U.S. Treasury, not Congress. The problem with Congress is that the Democrats and Republicans couldn't agree on comprehensive tax reform, so there wasn't much incentive to take on one isolated issue. However, the Treasury was looking for money anywhere it could find it to fund government programs. In addition, there was a broader concern that U.S. companies wanted to have all the benefits of the United States without paying the taxes. As noted by the U.S. Treasury Secretary leading the fight against tax inversions, "These firms involved in these transactions still expect to benefit from their business location in the United States, with our protection of intellectual property rights, our support of research and development, our investment climate and our infrastructure, as funded by various levels of government. But these firms are attempting to avoid paying taxes here, notwithstanding the benefits they gain from being located in the United States."

In September 2014, the Treasury Department announced its first set of rules to try to discourage tax inversions. The rules would prohibit companies from using offshore profits to finance the inversion deals. While President Obama said there is no substitute for Congressional action, and Senator Hatch who is on the Senate Finance Committee said that "any solution that permanently addresses inversions must be legislated by Congress," it was clear that Congress would not be part of the solution and that the Treasury Department would make the rules.

THE FINAL BATTLE

In spite of the rules announced in 2014, Pfizer and Allergan moved ahead in their plans to merge and for Pfizer to move its corporate headquarters to Dublin. If successful, it would have been the largest inversion yet. The $151 billion would also have been the largest merger in 15 years, as well as the largest corporate inversion. Pfizer's CEO maintained that the reason for the inversion wasn't just to save taxes. He maintained that some of Pfizer's biggest global rivals, GlaxoSmithKline and AstraZeneca of Britain and Novartis of Switzerland are at a distinct advantage because of their lower tax rates which puts them at an advantage over Pfizer in acquiring other companies. The merger would give each company access to new technologies and would allow Pfizer the size and product diversity it needs to split the company into two parts—one emphasizing faster-growing, innovative drugs and the other for more mature products that have to compete with generics. However, tax issues are not insignificant. Not only was Pfizer interested in the tax benefits from the inversion, but it also had over $74 billion in profits kept overseas that would be subject to U.S. tax if brought back to the United States. If Pfizer became an Irish company, it would no longer have to worry about that. A merger between Pfizer and Allergan would probably not have been an issue for U.S. regulators from a competitive standpoint. However, the Treasury Department has a different mandate than the Federal Trade Commission. The issue for them is not a loss of competition; it's a loss of tax revenues. The real question was, if the U.S. government eliminated the possibility of a tax inversion, would the merger still go through?

In 2016, the Treasury Department slammed the door shut on certain tax inversions, or at least made it more difficult for them, in a series of regulations aimed directly at Pfizer. The 300-page ruling included as its centerpiece the acquisitions of "serial inverters," when determining whether a company is a foreign company. In the case of Pfizer and Allergan, Pfizer would have to own between 50 and 60 percent of the combined company in order to obtain full benefits from the inversion. When the last three years of Allergan's acquisitions were eliminated, Allergan shareholders

would have held only 20 percent of the shares, with Pfizer owning 80 percent. That meant that the merged company would be subject to U.S. tax and would not be a foreign company. A second change was the elimination of "earnings stripping" where the inversion company would lend money to its U.S. subsidiaries, allowing the subsidiaries to claim the interest paid as a tax deduction, thus lowering U.S. taxes. The interest earned by the inverted company would be considered taxable income but at the lower rate in the inversion country.

What about the merger? After the new regulations were announced in April 2016, Pfizer and Allergan followed up with their own announcement that the merger would no longer make sense. Who won the war? Obviously the U.S. government felt like it won since it eliminated another case of tax inversion. Congress didn't win, because it wasn't part of the decision, and nothing was done to reform the tax code. However, the United States now has another 300 pages of regulations developed to solve one problem – tax inversions. ∎

QUESTIONS

11-1. In the case of Allergan and Pfizer, there are two sovereign powers in play – Ireland and the United States. Why was Ireland interested in letting the inversion take place, and why was the U.S. government against the inversion? Is the decision by the United States a direct affront to the sovereignty of Ireland?

11-2. In what ways are tax inversions beneficial to both the United States and the host country of the inversion?

CONCEPT CHECK

In Chapter 19, page 564, we will discuss how the corporate controller reports to the CFO and is responsible for accounting and managing foreign-exchange exposure. In Chapter 15, page 451, we will show how the expansion of the MNE through FDI and other entry strategies requires financial resources that must be managed by the CFO.

The corporate finance function acquires and allocates financial resources among the company's activities. The key functions are

- making financing decisions,
- making investment decisions,
- managing short-term capital needs.

THE FINANCE FUNCTION

The role of the chief financial officer (CFO) and the financial management is to maintain and create economic value or wealth by maximizing shareholder wealth—the market value of existing shareholders' common stock.[2] The management activities related to cash flows can be divided into three major areas:

- Make financing decisions—especially regarding capital structure (the proper mix of debt and equity) and long-term financing (selecting, issuing, and managing long-term debt and equity capital, including location—home country or elsewhere—and currency—home or foreign)
- Make investment decisions—typically in the context of capital budgeting
- Manage short-term capital needs managing the MNE's currency assets and liabilities (cash, receivables, marketable securities, inventory, trade receivables and payables, and short-term bank debt)

THE ROLE OF THE CFO

The CFO acquires financial resources—that is, the CFO is responsible for generating funds either internally or from external sources at the lowest possible cost—and allocates them among the company's activities and projects. Allocating resources (investing) means increasing stockholders' wealth through the allocation of funds to different projects and investment opportunities.

CONCEPT CHECK •

The *treasurer* is responsible for controlling the company's cash payments and the related financial functions, both domestic and foreign. The treasurer's functions fall under the overall responsibility of the chief financial officer (or the VP of finance), as we'll describe in Chapter 19, page 564.

The CFO's Global Perspective   The CFO's job is more complex in a global environment than in the domestic setting because of such forces as foreign-exchange risk, currency flows and restrictions, political risk, different tax rates and laws determining taxable income, and regulations on access to capital in different markets. The rest of this chapter examines the following areas:

1. Overall capital structure
2. Global capital markets
3. Taxation of foreign-source income and influence on capital markets
4. Offshore financing, offshore financial centers, and tax havens

CAPITAL STRUCTURE

A CFO must determine the company's proper mix between long-term debt and equity—in other words, its *capital structure*. Many companies start off with an initial investment and then grow through internally generated funds. However, when those sources are inadequate to fund continued growth into new markets, the CFO's office must decide the proper debt/equity mix.

LEVERAGING DEBT FINANCING

Leverage—the degree to which a firm funds the growth of business by debt.

The degree to which a firm funds the growth of business by debt is known as **leverage**. The degree to which companies use leverage instead of *equity capital*—known as stocks or shares—varies throughout the world. Country-specific factors are a more essential determinant of a firm's capital structure than any others because a firm tends to follow the financing trends in its own country and within its particular industry there. Leveraging is often perceived as the most cost-effective route to capitalization because the interest that companies pay on debt is a tax-deductible expense in most countries, whereas the dividends paid to investors are not.

When Is Leveraging *Not* the Best Option?   Leveraging is not always the best approach in all countries, for two major reasons. First, excessive reliance on long-term debt raises financial risk and thus requires a higher return for investors. This was very evident in Europe during the global financial crisis as companies and governments tried to raise capital through bond issues, and they either had to offer high interest rates to attract investors or they had difficulty getting any investors at all. Second, foreign subsidiaries of an MNE may have limited access to local capital markets, making it difficult for the MNE to rely on debt to fund asset acquisition.[3]

FACTORS AFFECTING THE CHOICE OF CAPITAL STRUCTURE

Choice of capital structure depends on tax rates, degree of development of local equity markets, and creditor rights.

In a recent and extensive study on leverage of 36,767 firms in 39 countries over a 15-year period, it was shown that the financing choices available to a company depend on many factors, both unique to the firm itself as well as the environment in which they operate.[4] The authors found that the most important determinants in capital structure are a country's legal and taxation system, the level of corruption, and the preferences of capital suppliers (banks and pension funds). Where tax differences are critical, firms tend to use more debt since they can deduct interest expense and therefore lower their tax liability. However, that is not as significant as other factors. Firms in corrupt countries tend to use more debt, especially short-term debt, to fund operations. Firms in common law countries, such as the United States, the United Kingdom, Canada, etc., use less leverage and more long-term debt, and firms in countries with an explicit bankruptcy code have higher leverage and more long-term debt. When examining the median leverage ratio (in this case being defined as total debt over the market value of the firm), firms in developing countries tend to have the highest amount of leverage. The top most highly leveraged countries are Korea, Indonesia, Brazil, Portugal, and Pakistan. Firms in developed countries tend to be in the lower end of the leverage spectrum. The five countries with the lowest leverage are Australia, South Africa, Canada, the United States, Turkey (an outlier), and the United Kingdom.[5] Firms that rely excessively on leverage often are in countries with less active securities markets, as opposed to those that rely less on debt which are often in countries with large, active, and liquid stock markets.

A separate study of the capital structure of U.S.-based MNEs' foreign affiliates found that local tax rates strongly influenced the debt-to-equity ratios. Although the firm as a whole might have a debt-to-equity ratio based on U.S. capital-market expectations, its foreign affiliates have to be sensitive to local conditions. The study noted:

> Ten percent higher local tax rates are associated with 2.8 percent higher debt/asset ratios, with internal borrowing particularly sensitive to taxes. Multinational affiliates are financed with less external debt in countries with underdeveloped capital markets or weak creditor rights, reflecting significantly higher local borrowing costs. Instrumental variable analysis indicates that greater borrowing from parent companies substitutes for three-quarters of reduced external borrowing induced by capital market conditions. Multinational firms appear to employ internal capital markets opportunistically to overcome imperfections in external capital markets.[6]

Debt and Exchange Rates   The global financial crisis of 2007–2009 highlighted foreign-exchange risk. Leading up to the crisis, many Asian companies borrowed in dollars at relatively low interest rates. But when the dollar rose in value, the companies couldn't generate enough cash to convert into dollars to pay off their debts.

A similar phenomenon occurred in Iceland, a country with its own currency (the krona). The Central Bank of Iceland kept interest rates high, attracting lots of foreign investment and keeping the krona strong. People's standards of living, among the highest in the world, were supported by the strong currency and the ability to import products. They sustained their high consumption by financing houses and other purchases through borrowing in euros when interest rates were low. When the global crisis hit in 2007–2009, however, the krona plunged in value, the banks failed, and firms as well as consumers could not afford to service their debts. Sourcing debt in a currency with a lower interest seemed like a good idea, but the lower foreign interest rates were replaced by exchange-rate risk.[7]

Regulatory Risk   A second factor that affects local borrowing is regulatory risk. Regulatory reform has complicated access to debt financing. As noted below, bonds are a great way for companies to raise capital for operations. However, companies also rely heavily on bank financing, and the failure of banks during the global financial crisis and resulting impact on the global economy has made countries very nervous about the financial stability of banks. The Basel Committee on Global Banking Supervision, which is a part of the Bank for International Settlements and comprises some of the world's top regulators and central bankers, has worked hard to put together rules to ensure that banks will be able to withstand future economic crises. The basic idea is to set standards for stronger capital positions and increased liquidity. The most recent agreement is called Basel III; it is designed to strengthen regulation, supervision, and risk management of the banking sector.[8] On the one hand, the world should be better off as banks comply with Basel III and increase their capital positions, but on the other hand, higher capital requirements also mean lower funds available to lend to companies that might not be able to raise capital through an IPO (discussed below) or by issuing bonds.

MNEs tend to use debt in countries with relatively high tax rates and a high degree of corruption. Also, capital structure of foreign subsidiaries tends to be more sensitive to local conditions.

GLOBAL DEBT MARKETS

Two major sources of funds external to the MNE's normal operations are debt markets and equity markets.

Companies have many ways of raising capital to fund operations, including debt and equity sources as well as domestic and international sources. Initially, we'll examine sources of debt financing. As an example, NuSkin Enterprises, a company that specializes in personal care products and nutritional supplements, sells products in more than 50 international markets, and Japan was initially their most important international market. Recently NuSkin entered into a Japanese yen denominated credit term loan facility for 6.6 billion yen at 2.3 percent variable interest rate. NuSkin pays its bank installments over a five-year period beginning in 2014. It hopes to use revenues in Japanese yen to pay off the debt in yen which helps eliminate the foreign-exchange risk. In addition to the long-term debt in yen, NuSkin also has a revolving line of credit in yen which is classified as short-term since it pays off the funds over a relatively short time. Many firms like NuSkin use banks in the local markets as an important source of financing.

EUROCURRENCIES AND THE EUROCURRENCY MARKET

A Eurocurrency is any currency outside its country of origin, but it is primarily dollars banked outside the United States.

The **Eurocurrency market** is an important source of debt financing to complement what MNEs can find in their domestic markets. A **Eurocurrency** or *offshore currency*, is any currency banked outside its country of origin.

The Eurodollar market is the most significant eurocurrency market. A **Eurodollar** is a certificate of deposit in U.S. dollars in a bank outside the United States. Most Eurodollar CDs are held in London, but they could be held anywhere outside the United States, such as the Bahamas, the Cayman Islands, etc. A major advantage of the Eurodollar market is that it is outside of the control of national banking regulators. The Eurodollar market started with the deposit of U.S. dollars in London banks during the Cold War by the Soviet Union to avoid the possibility that their accounts could be frozen in the United States. As other currencies entered the offshore market, the broader "Eurocurrency" name was adopted for market use, although the market tends to use the name of the specific currency, such as *Euroyen* or *Eurosterling*. Eurodollars constitute a majority of the Eurocurrency market. Dollars held by foreigners on deposit in the United States are not Eurodollars, but dollars held at branches of U.S. or other banks outside the United States are.

There are several sources of eurocurrencies, including governments, banks, and companies that have excess amounts of cash that they want to deposit in offshore locations.

Major Sources of Eurocurrencies   There are four major sources of Eurocurrencies:

- Foreign governments or individuals who want to hold dollars outside the United States
- Multinational enterprises that have cash in excess of current needs
- European banks with foreign currency in excess of current needs
- Countries such as China, that have large foreign-exchange reserves

Characteristics of the Eurocurrency Market   Because the Eurocurrency market is a wholesale (companies and other institutions) rather than a retail market (individuals), transactions are very large. Public borrowers such as governments, central banks, and public-sector corporations are the major players. Since the late 1990s, however, London banks have shifted to using nonbank customers for Eurodollar transactions, partly because of the introduction of the euro and consolidation in the banking sector.[9]

Eurocredits are loans with a maturity of one to five years. Syndicated loans involve several banks.

The Eurocurrency market is both short- and medium-term. Short-term borrowing is composed of maturities of less than one year. Anything from one to five years is considered a **Eurocredit**, which may be a loan, a line of credit, or another form of medium- and long-term credit. This would include **syndication**, in which several banks pool resources to extend credit to a borrower and spread the risk. Short-term borrowings, called euro commercial paper, are unsecured loans issued by a bank or corporation in the offshore money market and typically in the currency that is different from the corporation's domestic currency. For example, a German company can issue eurocommercial paper in London, denominated in U.S. dollars. Maturities are less than one year.

Interest Rates in the Eurocurrency Market   A major attraction of the Eurocurrency market is the difference in interest rates compared to those in domestic markets. Domestic rates are a function of the monetary policies adopted by the central banks of each country. The rate a company must pay to get loans or issue bonds depends not only on benchmark rates but also its creditworthiness. The better the creditworthiness, the lower the rate compared to other borrowers.

London Interbank Offered Rate   Because of the large transactions and the lack of controls and their attendant costs, Eurocurrency deposits tend to yield more than domestic deposits do, and loans tend to be cheaper than in domestic markets. Traditionally, loans are made at a certain percentage above the **London Interbank Offered Rate (Libor)**, which is a short-term interest rate for loans priced in London. Until recently, the British Bankers' Association published Libor rates in 10 currencies and 15 different maturities based on rates submitted by 18 different banks, reflecting the rate at which banks can borrow from each other.[10]

> ICE LIBOR is an interest rate on five different currencies for seven different maturities, the most common of which is the three-month Eurodollar rate.

However, in 2012, a scandal broke out in London over how Libor was set. There were rumors that bankers were collaborating to fix the rates, and since then, tens of billions of dollars in fines have been levied against the worst offenders. In 2014, the responsibility for setting Libor shifted to the Intercontinental Exchange or ICE. Now the ICE Benchmark Administration is responsible for setting interest rates for five currencies in seven different maturities. The most common ICE Libor rate is the three-month U.S. dollar rate. ICE Libor is the benchmark interest rate for a variety of debt instruments, including corporate bonds, mortgages, credit cards, etc.[11] The Libor benchmark three-month rate is a reference rate for $160 trillion of loans in the United States and $350 trillion in global credit when Asia and Europe are included.[12] More recently, a group of global banks has been working with U.S. regulators to come up with a replacement for Libor. Until then, ICE Libor is still the standard.

INTERNATIONAL BONDS

Many countries have active bond markets available to domestic and foreign investors. The United States is the largest market in the world for domestic bonds, with $39.5 trillion outstanding in mid-2015, 1 ½ times the size of the U.S. stock market.[13] Bonds are used by governments, financial institutions, and corporations, with corporate issues being the smallest segment.[14] Seventy percent of the global bond market is composed of domestic bonds, and 30 percent are international bonds. Also, the global bond market in 2012 was almost twice the size of the global equity market as defined by **market capitalization**.

> The United States has the largest domestic bond market in the world, and the bond market exceeds the stock market in size.

One reason the bond (and stock) markets in the United States are so influential is because the companies of continental Europe have traditionally relied on banks for finance. However, that began to change due to the economic crisis in Europe and the drop in available bank funding. Emerging markets are increasingly turning to the bond market for funding and now constitute about 10 percent of the market worldwide.[15] MNEs can use their domestic bond market to raise capital in the local currency, and the bonds can be sold to both domestic and foreign buyers. The bond market in Europe is interesting. Since the countries in the Eurozone use the same currency, a German firm could issue a bond denominated in euros and have it be a domestic bond and a Eurobond. If it's listed in Germany, it would be considered a domestic bond. If it's listed in London, it would be a Eurobond. When the European Central Bank announced that it would start buying corporate bonds of European companies as part of its quantitative easing strategy, bonds suddenly became cheaper for European companies to issue, thus opening up more possibilities for European firms to issue bonds.[16]

There are also three types of international bonds: foreign bonds, Eurobonds, and global bonds. The international bond market is primarily a wholesale market in which bond holders are usually institutional investors while issuers are large companies, governments, and international organizations.

A foreign bond is one sold outside the country of the borrower but denominated in the currency of the country of issue.

A Eurobond is a bond issue sold in a currency other than that of the country of issue.

A global bond is a Eurobond which is issued in several locations at the same time.

Foreign Bonds   **Foreign bonds** are sold outside the borrower's country but denominated in the currency of the country of issue. A French company floating a bond issue in London in pounds sterling would be issuing a foreign bond.

Eurobonds   A **Eurobond** is usually underwritten (placed in the market for the borrower) by a syndicate of banks from different countries and sold in a currency other than that of the country of issue. A French company issuing a bond in London, denominated in U.S. dollars, is an example of a Eurobond.

Global Bond   A global bond is issued outside of the country where the currency is denominated, such a U.S. dollar bond issued outside of the United States in multiple locations. For example, it could be a U.S. dollar bond issued by a U.S. company in London, Paris, Frankfurt, and Hong Kong. The goal is to get access to investors in multiple locations, sometimes in countries where the MNE is doing business or considering doing business.

Rising in importance are "dim sum" bonds, which are offshore bonds denominated in Chinese yuan. Although Chinese companies are issuing bonds in China that are available to foreign investors, capital outflow restrictions by the Chinese government are increasing the risk of raising capital in China.[17] However, the bonds' popularity rises as China looks for a way to capitalize on its immense foreign-exchange reserves. Foreign investors who want to buy debt denominated in Chinese yuan can purchase dim sum bonds, which are typically issued in Hong Kong.[18]

What's So Attractive About the International Bond Market?   The international bond market is a desirable place to borrow money. For one thing, it allows a company to diversify its funding sources from the local banks and the domestic bond market and borrow in maturities that might not be available in the domestic markets. It also tends to be less expensive than local bond markets and attracts investors from around the world.

U.S. firms first issued Eurobonds in 1963 as a means of avoiding U.S. tax and disclosure regulations. They're typically issued in denominations of $5,000 or $10,000, pay interest annually, are held in bearer form, and are traded over the counter (OTC), most frequently in London.[19] Any investor who holds a bearer bond is entitled to receive the principal and interest payments. In contrast, for a registered bond, which is more typical in the United States, the investor is required to be registered as the bond's owner to receive payments. The secrecy of a bearer bond also makes the Eurobonds more attractive.

For example, Gazprom, Russia's largest company, uses the Eurobond market extensively. In 2016, it issued a 500 million Swiss franc Eurobond maturing in November 2018 at a yield of 4.625 percent. The main purchasers of these Eurobonds were private banks managing the savings of wealthy individuals, whereas Eurodollar bonds are typically acquired by institutional investors. Approximately 39.4 percent of the bonds were bought by Swiss investors, 34.1 percent by Russian investors, and the rest by other European investors. Private banks and wealth management firms bought 58.6 percent of the bonds.[20] In 2015, U.S. companies accounted for about 22 percent of all corporate Eurobond issues, taking advantage of low interest rates in Europe resulting from the ECB's easy-money policies. Apple Inc. floated two Euro-denominated Eurobond issues in 2015, for a total of €2 billion. Apple planned on using the proceeds for a variety of issues, including share buybacks, higher dividends (both directly benefitting shareholders), capital expenditures, investments, debt repayment, and working capital.[21]

GLOBAL EQUITY MARKETS

Another source of financing is *equity securities,* whereby an investor takes an ownership position in return for shares of stock in the company and the promises of capital gains and dividends. A company that wants to raise equity capital to fund operations may work with private investors who want to take an equity interest in the company rather than just loan money to the company. Or it might raise equity capital through an Initial Public Offering where it goes directly to a stock market. If the company wants to issue an IPO, it has to decide if it wants to raise capital in its domestic market or abroad.

Sovereign wealth funds (SWFs) are also an important source of capital. An SWF is a state-owned investment fund that generates its resources from a variety of places, including revenues from the exports of natural resources such as oil.[22] The top five SWFs in terms of assets are Government Pension Fund (Norway), the Abu Dhabi Investment Authority, the China Investment Corporation, SAMA Foreign Holdings (Saudi Arabia), and the Kuwait Investment Corporation. Five of the top 10 funds are based on oil revenues.[23] The funds, which are professionally managed, can invest in specific projects or stock markets. For example, Invest AD (the Abu Dhabi Investment Company) is one of the SWFs in the UAE, with a primary role of investing in the Middle East and Emerging Africa and providing investment opportunities to third-party clients. Its officers scour the capital markets in the region to find stocks to invest in, and it has developed several funds, including the Emerging Africa Fund and the GCC (Gulf Cooperation Council) Focus Fund. When SWFs invest in specific projects, they operate more like a venture capital firm. When they invest in stock markets, one of the strategies of Invest AD, they are not providing new capital but are taking advantage of shares already listed on stock markets.

MNEs can raise new capital in the equity capital market through an Initial Public Offering, or IPO, by listing their shares on a stock exchange, either in their home country or in another country. An example of the former is the 2012 IPO by U.S.-based Facebook when it raised $16 billion in the United States. However that was topped on September 14, 2014, when e-commerce giant Alibaba Group of China raised $21.8 billion in an IPO issued in the United States through American Depositary Receipts. An ADR is a negotiable certificate of deposit issued by a U.S. bank which represents a specific number of shares of the underlying stock. Although Alibaba could have issued the IPO in China or Hong Kong, it decided to go after funds in the U.S. market instead.[24]

THE SIZE OF GLOBAL STOCK MARKETS

Map 10.1 identifies the 10 largest stock markets in the high-income countries and top-10 largest stock markets in emerging countries in terms of domestic market capitalization in January 2016. Stock market capitalization worldwide dropped by 10 percent in January 2016 compared with the prior year, with Brazil's market falling 45.4 percent and the Ukraine falling 57.4 percent.[25] The numbers in Map 10.1 represent each specific stock market rather than all of the markets in the country. The three largest stock markets in the world are the New York Stock Exchange, the Tokyo Stock Exchange, and the London Stock Exchange, closely followed by the Shanghai Stock Exchange.

Political and Economic Forces and Trends in Global Stock Market   During the past few years, global markets have been in turmoil, and that will continue to be the case. There are several factors that are affecting markets, although the forces change from year to year and aren't always consistent. In the first place, when oil prices began dropping in 2014, so did the stock markets. When oil prices began to rise, so did the markets. One possible explanation is that rising prices resulted from increased demand and possibly a recovery in economic growth.[26] Second, weakness in the global economy hurt markets in general and caused money to flee to safety rather than gamble on returns from risk.[27] Third, China has been a huge force. When the Chinese economy dropped, the impact was felt all over the world, from the drop in demand in commodities to the resulting drop in commodity prices. When China devalued the yuan, the ripple effect was felt worldwide and equity markets fell.[28] Fourth, uncertainly in interest rates created uncertainty in markets. When the U.S. economy was weak, interest rates were low, but when it looked like economic activity was heating up, interest rates were predicted to rise. This caused a drop in the U.S. stock market, the largest in the world. On the other hand, as emerging markets reduced interest rates, investment money began to flood into the emerging markets on the bet that their economies would grow and provide higher returns than in the weaker industrial markets.

A Sovereign Wealth Fund is a state-owned investment fund that generates its resources from a variety of sources, with oil being the main source for many SWFs.

An IPO is the first sale of stock by a company to the public. It may be in the issuer's home country or in another country.

The three largest stock markets in the world are in New York, Tokyo, and London, with the U.S. markets controlling nearly half of the world's stock market capitalization.

Major sources of influence on global stock markets are oil prices, weakness in the global economy, weakness in the Chinese economy, and interest rates.

MAP 10.1   Global Markets: Domestic Market Capitalization, January 2016

Data reflects domestic market capitalization of the top 10 high-income countries and the top 10 emerging markets—total number of shares of stock listed multiplied by market price per share.

Source: Based on World Federation of Exchanges, Statistics, www.world-exchanges.org/statistics/monthly-reports, (accessed May 7, 2016).

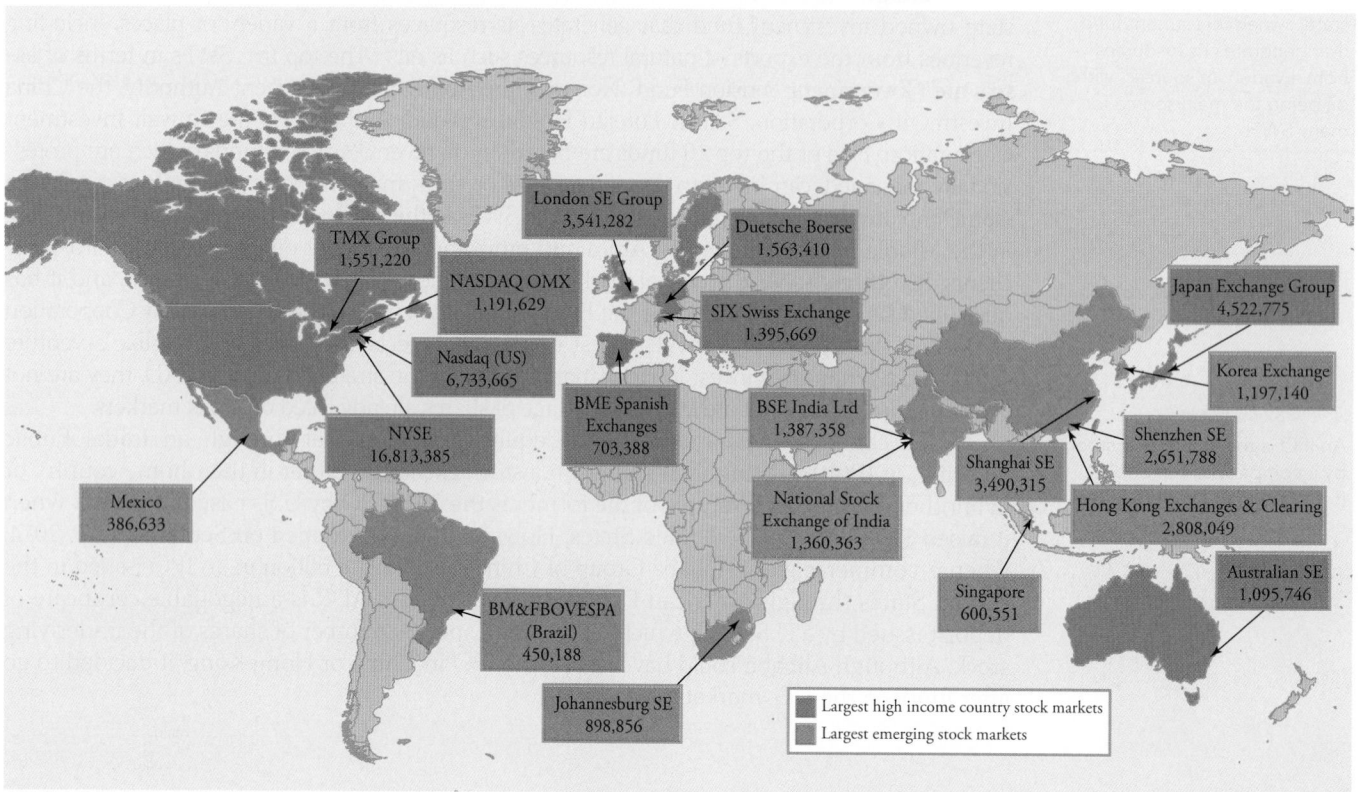

An interesting example is Europe. In 2016, investors were pulling money out of Europe at a rapid rate. This was due largely to concerns about an unstable political situation in Europe, low interest rates (thus low returns on many investments), weak banks, and a broader European economy that continued to be weak. That was in sharp contrast to 2015 when it looked like Europe had recovered from the debt crisis of 2010–2012.[29] It is clear that to understand trends in stock markets, it is important to understand trends in political and economic forces worldwide and that forces in countries or regions often vary.

The Rise of the Euroequity Market   Besides domestic markets, there is also the **euroequity market**, the market for shares sold outside the boundaries of the issuing firm's home country. A euroequity IPO occurs simultaneously in two countries different from the one where the company is based.[30] Another way to look at euroequity is when a company's shares are made available internationally rather than just in the country where the company is based.[31] The Alibaba IPO mentioned above is an example of a euroequity IPO even though it was issued in the United States rather than in Europe. Another way to look at an IPO like Alibaba is to consider it an offshore IPO, or an IPO anywhere outside of its home country. Sometimes, an MNE will list its existing shares on multiple stock markets. For example, Ford lists its shares in the United States, Belgium, and France, but its shares are listed in euros in Belgium and France.[32]

The Trend Toward Delisting   The trend of listing on more than one exchange began to reverse somewhat as more and more companies reduced the number of exchanges on which their stocks were listed. In 2013, Tata Communications, an Indian company, announced that it was going to delist from the NYSE due to low trading volumes and liquidity.[33] Investors are finding that the best price for stocks is usually in the home market of the company in which they are investing.

Euroequities are shares listed on stock exchanges in countries other than the home country of the issuing company.

Furthermore, companies pay annual fees to list on exchanges, so if trading is light on a certain exchange, as was the case with Tata Communications, they can save money by listing on an exchange with heavier trading volume. Other reasons for delisting shares include weak market returns (fewer investors are putting their money into stocks) and increased regulation (such as the U.S. Sarbanes–Oxley Act).

American Depositary Receipt   In 2016, 513 foreign companies or 21.3 percent of the total listings on the NYSE[34] were made through an **American Depositary Receipt (ADR)**. As noted earlier in the chapter, an ADR is a negotiable certificate issued by a U.S. bank in the United States to represent the underlying shares of a foreign corporation's stock held in trust at a custodian bank in the foreign country. ADRs are traded like stock shares, with each one representing some number of shares of the underlying stock. For example, Toyota has listed ADRs on the NYSE since 1999 at a rate of two per common Toyota share. They issue through a sponsored ADR facility operated by the Bank of New York. In addition to the NYSE and the Tokyo Stock Exchange, Toyota also lists its ADRs on the London Stock Exchange.

> Most foreign companies that list on the U.S. stock exchanges do so through American Depositary Receipts, which are financial documents that represent a share or part of a share of stock in the foreign company.

TAXATION OF FOREIGN-SOURCE INCOME

Gaining access to capital is about more than interest rates and stock exchange listing requirements. Tax planning is a crucial responsibility for a CFO because taxes can profoundly affect profitability and cash flow. This is especially true in international business. As complex as domestic taxation seems, it is child's play compared to the intricacies of international taxation. The international tax specialist must be familiar with both the home country's tax policy on foreign operations and the tax laws of each country in which the MNE operates.

Taxation has a strong impact on several choices:

- Location of operations
- Choice of operating form, such as export or import, licensing agreement, or overseas investment
- Legal form of the new enterprise, such as branch or subsidiary
- Possible facilities in tax-haven countries to raise capital and manage cash
- Method of financing, such as internal or external sourcing, and debt or equity
- Capital budgeting decisions
- Method of setting transfer prices

INTERNATIONAL TAX PRACTICES

Differences in tax practices around the world often cause headaches for MNEs. Lack of familiarity with laws and customs can create confusion. In some countries, tax laws are loosely enforced. In others, taxes may generally be negotiated between the tax collector and the taxpayer—if they are ever paid at all. In still others, they must be rigidly followed.

> With a value-added tax, each company pays a percentage of the value added to a product at each stage of the business process.

Differences in Types of Taxes   Countries differ in terms of the types of taxes they have (income versus excise), the tax rates applied to income, the determination of taxable income, and the treatment of foreign-source income. Although we focus in this section on corporate income taxes, excise taxes are another important source of income to governments. The **value-added tax (VAT)** is an example of an excise tax used in Europe as well as other parts of the world, including China. It is a percentage levied on products at the point of sale in every stage of the value chain, and is included in the final price of the product rather than added to the price at the final point of sale, as is the case with the sales tax in the United States. There are many other excise taxes, and the large number of taxes in some countries, like Brazil, is very confusing to both local and foreign investors.

Differences in Generally Accepted Accounting Principles (GAAP)   Variations among countries in GAAP can lead to differences in determining taxable income. In countries where tax laws allow firms to depreciate assets faster than accounting standards allow but where the firms must use the same standards for tax and book accounting, higher depreciation expenses result in lower income and therefore lower taxes. Revenue recognition is also an important issue. Some countries tax income from worldwide revenues of MNEs, whereas others only recognize income from revenues generated in the domestic environment.

Differences in Tax Rates   Corporate tax rates also vary from country to country. As noted in the opening case, corporate tax rates vary from 12.5 percent in Ireland to 35 percent in the United States, when considering the issue of tax inversion. However, tax rates vary depending on whether the rate includes a combined central government and sub-central government (such as federal and state taxes in the United States).[35]

| In the separate entity approach, governments tax each taxable entity when it earns income.

Two Approaches to Corporate Taxation   Taxation of corporate income is accomplished through one of two approaches in most countries: the *separate entity approach* (also known as the *classical approach*) or the *integrated system approach.*

Separate Entity Approach   In the separate entity approach, which the United States uses, each separate unit—company or individual—is taxed when it earns income. For example, a corporation is taxed on its earnings, while stockholders are taxed on the distribution of earnings (dividends). The result can be double taxation.

| An integrated system tries to avoid double taxation of corporate income through split tax rates or tax credits.

Integrated System Approach   Many other developed countries use an integrated system to eliminate double taxation. Australia and New Zealand, for example, give a dividend credit to shareholders to shelter them from double taxation. This means that when shareholders report the dividends in their taxable income, they also get a credit for taxes paid on that income by the company that issued the dividend. That keeps the shareholders from paying tax on the dividend because the company has already done so.

Germany used to have a split-rate system with two different tax rates on corporate earnings: one on retained earnings and one on distributed earnings. However, they abolished it in 2001 and adopted a classical system with an overall lower corporate tax rate on earnings of 15 percent (15.285 percent including the solidarity surcharge to help with the reunification with East Germany) plus a municipal trade tax ranging from 14 to 17 percent, resulting in an effective tax rate of 30 and 33 percent.[36] Taxation of foreign-source income depends on the country where the parent company is domiciled. It is common for most developed countries to tax MNEs on their worldwide income and give them a credit for foreign corporate income taxes paid. That is not true everywhere, however. Hong Kong companies, for example, pay tax only on Hong Kong-source income, even if remitted to Hong Kong, and their corporate tax rate is only 16.5 percent.[37]

TAXING BRANCHES AND SUBSIDIARIES

In order to innovate and expand, companies need to gain access to capital, both debt and equity, from home-country capital markets or markets abroad. However, companies can also raise capital through minimizing their tax liability worldwide so that they can use internally generated cash to expand. To illustrate how this is done, let's look at how U.S.-based companies tax earnings from a *foreign branch* and a *foreign subsidiary.*

| Foreign branch income (or loss) is directly included in the parent's taxable income.

The Foreign Branch   A foreign branch is an extension of the parent company rather than an enterprise incorporated in a foreign country. Any income the branch generates is taxable immediately to the parent, whether or not cash is remitted by the branch to the parent as a distribution of earnings. However, if the branch suffers a loss, the parent is allowed to deduct that loss from its taxable income, reducing its overall tax liability.

The Foreign Subsidiary   Whereas a branch is a legal extension of a parent company, a foreign corporation is an independent legal entity set up in a country (incorporated) according to that country's laws of incorporation. When an MNE purchases a foreign corporation or sets up a new one in a foreign country, it is called a *subsidiary* of the parent. Income earned by the subsidiary is either reinvested in the subsidiary or remitted as a dividend to the parent company.

Subsidiary income is either taxable to the parent or tax-deferred—that is, it is not taxed until it is remitted as a dividend to the parent. Which tax status applies depends on whether the foreign subsidiary is a *controlled foreign corporation (CFC)*—a technical term in the U.S. tax code—and whether the income is active or passive. This is a relatively unique concept for U.S. companies since most countries only tax income earned in their countries and do not tax foreign source income.

> Tax deferral means that income is not taxed until it is remitted to the parent company as a dividend.

The Controlled Foreign Corporation

A **controlled foreign corporation (CFC)**, from the standpoint of the U.S. tax code, is any foreign company in which more than 50 percent of its voting stock is held by "U.S. shareholders," which are U.S. citizens or companies that each hold 10 percent or more of the CFC's voting stock. Any foreign subsidiary of an MNE would automatically be considered a CFC from the standpoint of the tax code. However, a joint venture company abroad that is partly owned by the U.S.-based MNE and partly by local investors might not be a CFC if the U.S. MNE does not own more than 50 percent of the JV's stock.

> In a CFC, U.S. shareholders hold more than 50 percent of the voting stock.

To qualify as a *controlled foreign corporation (CFC),* more than 50 percent of a company's voting shares must be held by U.S. shareholders. A *U.S. shareholder* must be a U.S. person or company holding at least 10 percent of the corporation's voting shares. Assume three scenarios: foreign corporation A has one U.S. shareholder who owns 100 percent of the shares. Foreign Corporation B has 4 shareholders. One owns 45 percent of the shares, one owns 10 percent, one owns 20 percent, and one owns 25 percent. Foreign corporation C has 4 shareholders. One owns 30 percent, one owns 10 percent, two each own 8 percent, and one, a non-U.S. person, owns 44 percent. Which of these are CFCs? A definitely is. B is because all of the shareholders are U.S. persons who own at least 10 percent of the shares. C is not, because two U.S. persons own at least 10 percent of the shares, and they only own a total of 40 percent.

When former U.S.-based company Enron set up its shell companies in tax-haven countries, it was careful not to own more than 50 percent of the stock so that it could avoid having to include the debt in those operations in its consolidated income.[38]

Active Versus Passive Income

If a foreign subsidiary qualifies as a CFC, the U.S. tax law requires the U.S. investor to classify the foreign-source income as *active* or *Subpart F (passive) income.* **Active income** is derived from the direct conduct of a trade or business, such as from sales of products manufactured in the foreign country. **Subpart F or passive income**, which is specifically defined in Subpart F of the U.S. Internal Revenue Code, comes from sources other than those connected with the direct conduct of a trade or business, generally in tax-haven countries, and includes the following:

> Active income is derived from the direct conduct of a trade or business. Passive income (also called Subpart F income) is usually derived from operations in a tax-haven country.

- *Holding company income*—income primarily from dividends, interest, rents, royalties, and gains on sale of stocks.
- *Sales income*—income from foreign sales corporations that are separately incorporated from their manufacturing operations. The product of such entities is manufactured and sold for use outside the CFC's country of incorporation, and the CFC has not performed significant operations on the product.
- *Service income*—income from the performance of technical, managerial, or similar services for a company in the same corporate family as the CFC and outside the country in which the CFC resides.

Subpart F income usually derives from the activities of subsidiaries in tax-haven countries such as the Bahamas, the Netherlands Antilles, Panama, and Switzerland. The tax-haven subsidiary may act as an investment company, a sales agent or distributor, an agent for the parent in licensing agreements, or a holding company of stock in other foreign subsidiaries that are called *grandchild—*or *second-tier—subsidiaries.* This setup is illustrated in Figure 10.1. In the role of a holding company, its purpose is to concentrate cash from the parent's foreign operations into the low-tax country and use the cash for global expansion.

FIGURE 10.1   The Tax-Haven Subsidiary as Holding Company

A U.S. company has established a *tax-haven subsidiary* as a *holding company* in an offshore location. As such, the offshore subsidiary owns shares in three foreign subsidiaries called *grandchild subsidiaries*. The offshore holding company generates *holding company income*, which is recorded by the U.S. parent company as *Subpart F income*.

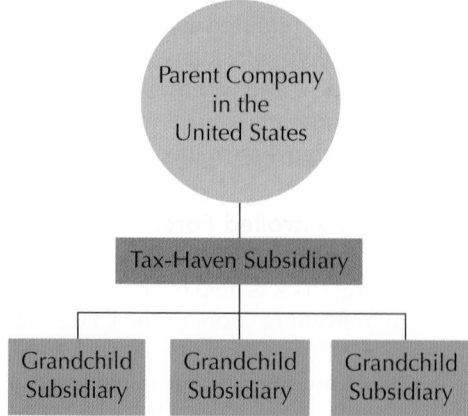

Determining a Subsidiary's Income   Figure 10.2 illustrates how the tax status of a subsidiary's income is determined. All non-CFC income—active and Subpart F—earned by the foreign corporation is deferred until remitted as a dividend to the U.S. shareholder (the parent company, in this example). In contrast, a CFC's active income is tax-deferred to the parent, but its Subpart F income is taxable immediately to the parent as soon as the CFC earns it, subject to some limitations and exceptions. If a foreign branch earns income, it is immediately taxable to the parent company, whether it is active or Subpart F income.

TRANSFER PRICES

| A transfer price is a price on goods and services one member of a corporate family sells to another. |

A major tax challenge as well as an impediment to performance evaluation is the extensive use of transfer pricing in international operations. Because the price is between related entities, it is not necessarily an **arm's-length price**—that is, a price between two companies that do not have an ownership interest in each other. The assumption is that an arm's-length price is more likely than a transfer price to reflect the market accurately.

Transfer Prices and Taxation   Companies establish arbitrary transfer prices primarily because of differences in taxation between countries. For example, if the corporate tax rate is higher in the parent company's country than in the subsidiary's country, the parent could

FIGURE 10.2   The Tax Status of U.S.-Owned Foreign Subsidiaries

Both CFC and Subpart F provisions are designed to prevent U.S. firms from establishing tax-haven subsidiaries for the purpose of investing *passive income* indefinitely, thus earning tax-free income. Basically, these provisions treat tax income just as if it had been remitted to the U.S. parent at the time when it was earned.

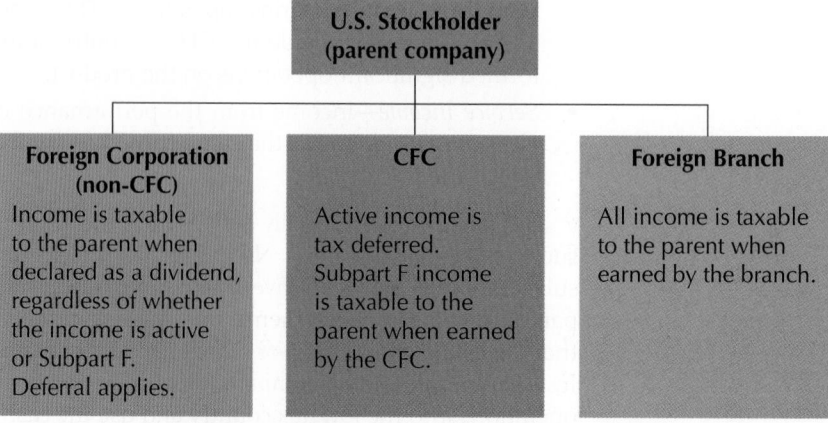

set a low transfer price on products it sells to the subsidiary to keep taxable profits low in its country and high in the subsidiary's country. The parent could also set a high transfer price on products sold to it by the subsidiary.

The OECD is very concerned about the ways in which companies manipulate transfer prices to minimize their tax liability worldwide. For this reason, the OECD Centre for Tax Policy and Administration meets periodically to discuss the adoption of sound transfer pricing policies (along with a wide range of other tax issues). The OECD issued guidelines on transfer pricing in 1979 and updated the policies in 1995 to provide guidance on different transfer methods that could be used and how to tell if a transfer between independent firms is similar to a transfer within a group. To avoid transfer-price manipulation, it recommends determining the tax liability in each country by applying an arm's-length price, and it has issued guidelines on the matter. Additional OECD policy revisions have been published since 1995 and continue to be published periodically.[39]

Companies can get into disputes with different tax jurisdictions over transfer pricing policies. GlaxoSmithKline (GSK), the British pharmaceutical company, settled a transfer pricing dispute with the U.S. Internal Revenue Service in 2006 by paying $3.1 billion in federal, state, and local taxes and interest—slightly less than the $5 billion the IRS was seeking and nearly half of GSK's operating cash flow. The IRS contends that GSK charged its U.S. affiliate too little for marketing services provided by the affiliate, which meant that U.S. earnings were low, resulting in lower taxes collected in the United States. The dispute arose over whether GSK should have paid for the marketing services at cost or at the price it would have paid an independent third party. These are complex issues that leave companies open to significant financial risks if they don't price services or products correctly.[40]

DOUBLE TAXATION AND TAX CREDIT

Every country has a sovereign right to levy taxes on all income, which could result in double taxation if both the home and host country tax the income.

In U.S. tax law, a U.S. MNE gets a credit for income taxes paid to a foreign government. For example, when a U.S. parent recognizes foreign-source income (such as a dividend from a foreign subsidiary) in its taxable income, it must pay U.S. tax on that income. However, the IRS allows the parent company to reduce its tax liability by the amount of foreign income tax already paid. It is limited by the amount it would have had to pay in the United States on that income.

Assume, for example, that U.S. Company A earns $100,000 of foreign-source income and that it paid $40,000 (40 percent tax rate) on that income in the foreign jurisdiction. If that income is considered taxable in the United States, Company A would have to pay $35,000 in income taxes (35 percent tax rate). In the absence of a tax credit, Company A would have paid a total of $75,000 in income tax on the $100,000 of income, a 75 percent tax rate.

The IRS, however, allows Company A to reduce its U.S. tax liability by a maximum of $35,000—what it would have paid in the United States if the income had been earned there. If Company A's subsidiary had paid $20,000 in foreign income tax (a 20 percent tax rate), it would be able to claim the entire $20,000 as a credit because it was less than the U.S. liability of $35,000. Company A will pay a total of $35,000 in corporate income tax on its foreign-source income—$20,000 to the foreign government and $15,000 to the U.S. government.

Tax Treaties: Eliminating Double Taxation The primary purpose of tax treaties is to prevent international double taxation or to provide remedies when it occurs. The United States is an active participant in 75 different tax treaties involving 58 different countries.[41] The general pattern between two treaty countries is to grant reciprocal deductions on dividend withholding and to exempt royalties—and sometimes interest payments—from any withholding tax.

The United States has a domestic withholding tax of 30 percent for dividends, interest, and royalties for owners of U.S. securities issued in countries with which it has no tax treaty. When a tax treaty is in effect, the U.S. rate on dividends is generally reduced to 5 to 15 percent, and the tax on interest and royalties is either eliminated or reduced to 5 to 10 percent. The rate varies by country, however.

The IRS allows a tax credit for corporate income tax that U.S. companies pay to another country. A tax credit is a dollar-for-dollar reduction of tax liability and must coincide with the recognition of income.

The purpose of tax treaties is to prevent double taxation or to provide remedies when it occurs.

DODGING TAXES

Two things will always be true: governments will always try to figure out how to collect as much in taxes as they can and companies (and individuals) will try to avoid paying as much in taxes as they can. The challenge is that some countries provide tax incentives to attract investment, and these incentives can help MNEs lower their overall tax liability. Take Google, for example, a U.S.-based company that operates worldwide. Google established its European headquarters in Ireland where the corporate tax rate is 12.5 percent, as mentioned elsewhere in the chapter, and has its customers who buy advertising on Google's search engine sign contracts with its Irish subsidiary rather than in the country where they reside. Thus Google generates revenues across Europe but pays taxes in Ireland rather than in the other countries whose tax rates are substantially higher. To reduce their tax liability even more, Google runs some of its royalty payments through a subsidiary in Bermuda, where there are no corporate income or withholding taxes.[42] The EU is now forcing MNEs to pay tax in the countries where their sales are generated rather than in low-tax countries like Ireland.

There are many reasons why companies locate in Ireland, such as cheap workers and a business friendly environment, but the low corporate tax rate is not insignificant. To attract more knowledge-based firms, Ireland announced a 6.25 percent tax rate on revenue generated from patents and other intellectual property developed in Ireland.[43] In some ways, this avoids the criticism that MNEs develop their R&D outside of Ireland but collect royalties in low-tax Ireland.

One advantage that MNEs have is that it may be hard for a country to figure out its own tax policy, but it is almost impossible for countries to come up with one global tax policy that everyone can agree on. As a result, companies do the best they can to exploit the differences. The EU is even fighting over differences in tax policies from country to country. Luxembourg and the Netherlands, in addition to Ireland, are criticized by the European Commission, which is trying to eliminate different tax policies as tools to attract investments from MNEs. And the United States is also getting involved in the criticism of the EU because U.S. tax treaties are made with individual countries, not the EU as a whole. They worry that the European Commission is bullying individual countries that have set their own tax policies.

OFFSHORE FINANCING AND OFFSHORE FINANCIAL CENTERS

| Offshore financing—the provision for financial services by banks and other agents to nonresidents.

Companies are partly able to be successful in reducing their tax liabilities because of tax-haven countries and the ability to use them for a variety of offshore activities. **Offshore financing** is the provision of financial services by banks and other agents to nonresidents. In its simplest form, this involves borrowing money from and lending to the nonresidents.[44] A good example of legitimate offshore financing is the use of the Eurodollar market. A U.S. company can raise Eurodollars in London by working with a bank to issue bonds or syndicate a loan. Or it could float Eurobonds in Bermuda where there are no withholding taxes on interest, which is more beneficial to the investor.

WHAT IS AN OFC?

Offshore financial centers (OFCs) are cities or countries that provide large amounts of funds in currencies other than their own and are used as locations in which to raise and accumulate cash. Usually, the financial transactions are conducted in currencies other than that of the country and are thus the centers for the Eurocurrency market. An OFC could be defined as any financial center where offshore activity takes place, but a more practical definition is a center where the bulk of financial activity is offshore on both sides of the balance sheet, the transactions are initiated elsewhere, and the majority of the institutions involved are controlled by nonresidents.[45]

Characteristics of OFCs   The markets in these centers tend to be regulated differently—and usually more flexibly—than domestic markets. The centers provide an alternative, (usually) cheaper source of funding for MNEs so the latter don't have to rely strictly on their own national markets. Offshore financial centers have one or more of the following characteristics:

CONCEPT CHECK

We introduced the OECD in discussing the OECD Anti-Bribery Convention on p. 333 in Chapter 5. In addition, the OECD is concerned about a broader range of activities that involve cross-border operations. We also mention the OECD's earlier Guidelines for MNEs, which came out in 1976 and includes a code of conduct for MNEs engaged in cross-border operations. Here we observe that, because **offshore financing** has proved conducive to such misbehavior as tax avoidance, the OECD and several other multilateral organizations have made efforts to strengthen ethical practices in offshore transactions.

Offshore financial centers (OFCs)—cities or countries that provide large amounts of funds in currencies other than their own.

- A large foreign-currency (Eurocurrency) market for deposits and loans (in London, say)
- A market that functions as a large net supplier of funds to the world financial markets (such as in Switzerland)
- A market that functions as an intermediary or pass-through for international loan funds (e.g., the Bahamas and the Cayman Islands)
- Economic and political stability
- An efficient and experienced financial community
- Good communications and support services
- An official regulatory climate favorable to the financial industry, in the sense that it protects investors without unduly restricting financial institutions[46]

However, the OECD prefers to differentiate between well and poorly regulated financial centers rather than offshore and onshore.[47]

Operational Versus Booking Centers   *Operational centers* have extensive banking activities involving short-term financial transactions; *booking centers* have little actual banking activity taking place but transactions are recorded to take advantage of secrecy and low (or no) tax rates. In the latter case, individuals may deposit money offshore to hide it from their home-country tax authorities, either because the money is earned and/or to be used illegally—such as in the drug trade or to finance terrorist activities—or because the individual or company does not want to pay tax. London is an example of an operational center; the Cayman Islands is an example of a booking center.

OFCs as "Tax Havens"   A major concern with OFCs is the tax avoidance dimension of their activities. The OECD has been working closely with the major OFCs to ensure that they are engaged in legal activity. It uses the following key factors in identifying tax havens: (1) no or only nominal taxes, (2) lack of effective exchange of information (especially bank secrecy), (3) lack of transparency, and (4) no substantial activities.[48] Although not trying to tell the sovereign countries what their tax rates should be, the OECD is trying to eliminate harmful tax practices in these four areas:

OFCs offer low or zero taxation, moderate or light financial regulation, and banking secrecy and anonymity.

1. The regime imposes low or no taxes on the relevant income (from geographically mobile financial and other service activities).
2. The regime is ring fenced (i.e., separated) from the domestic economy.

Most tax haven countries are ▶ synonymous with beaches and easy living.

Source: JFs Pic Factory/Shutterstock

3. The regime lacks transparency; for example, the details of it or its application are not apparent, or there is inadequate regulatory supervision or financial disclosure.
4. There is no effective exchange of information with respect to the regime.[49]

Obviously, there is a lot of overlap in these definitions. In a 2009 report, the OECD identified 28 tax-haven countries and 10 other financial centers that were moving to adopt their standards for good tax behavior, while no national jurisdictions were reported that had not committed to the internationally accepted tax standard. That is pretty significant progress.[50] The OECD is trying to reduce harmful tax practices through improved translation and disclosure. Putting the spotlight on countries seems to be the best approach.

Point

Should Offshore Financial Centers and Aggressive Tax Practices Be Eliminated?

Point

Yes The problem with OFCs is that they operate in a shroud of secrecy that allows companies to establish operations there for illegal and unethical purposes. In 2016, the so-called Panama Papers, a treasure trove of an estimated 11.5 million internal documents of a firm in Panama called Mossack Fonseca, were obtained by German newspapers and shared with others worldwide, including the *New York Times*. The papers showed how Mossack Fonseca helped wealthy clients evade U.S. tax laws in very creative ways. Mossack Fonseca set up over 2,800 companies for at least 2,400 U.S. clients in the British Virgin Islands, Panama, and the Seychelles, among other tax-haven countries. However, this scandal was worldwide. The prime minister of Iceland, who was named in the papers, even resigned because of the appearance of impropriety. Not all of the transactions were considered illegal, and no charges have been filed yet. But it's probably just a matter of time.[51]

As another example, Italian company Parmalat set up three shell companies based in the Caribbean to capture cash. The companies allegedly sold Parmalat products, and Parmalat sent them fake invoices and charged costs and fees to make the sales look legitimate. It would then write out a credit note for the amount the subsidiaries supposedly owed and take

that to banks to raise money. Given the location of the subsidiaries, you would think the banks would have been suspicious, but Parmalat got away with these activities.

Off-balance-sheet financing was also used to hide debts. The company transferred over half of its liabilities to the books of small subsidiaries based in offshore tax havens such as the Cayman Islands. This allowed it to present a healthy balance sheet and a profitable income statement to investors and creditors by hiding large amounts of debt, understating interest expenses (thus overstating income), and overstating revenues for false bookings. Parmalat's actual debt was nearly double the amount disclosed to outsiders.

Terrorists and drug dealers also use OFCs to launder money. When the U.S. government went after the money of Osama bin Laden, it went after OFCs notorious for their secrecy. When a bank in the Bahamas refused to open its books to U.S. government investigators, the United States cut the bank off from the world's wire transfer systems. Within two hours, the bank changed policies.[52] Standard Chartered plc, a British bank, was fined $340 million for violating U.S. money-laundering laws involving an illegal scheme to hide more than 60,000 transactions worth $250 billion for Iranian clients.[53] These kinds of activities must stop.

Should Offshore Financial Centers and Aggressive Tax Practices Be Eliminated?

Counterpoint

Counterpoint

No OFCs are an efficient way for companies to use their financial resources more effectively. They are good locations for establishing finance subsidiaries that can raise capital for the parent company or its subsidiaries. And they allow the finance subsidiaries to take advantage of lower borrowing costs and tax rates.

Not all types of tax-minimization activities are illegal because the companies are still subject to home- and host-country laws and tax regulations. It is true that some transactions may be illegal, but most are not. The key to policing truly illegal activities, such as hiding drug money or engaging in corporate fraud

like the Parmalat case, is to improve transparency and reporting.

Why shouldn't countries have the opportunity to attract business by offering tax-haven status to MNEs? Many don't have other visible means of generating resources. They are too small to set up manufacturing operations, have too small a population base to offer low-cost labor, and don't have natural resources they can sell. So what can they do? Companies and individuals need places to bank their wealth or raise capital, so the OFCs have decided to use the theory of factor proportions (discussed in Chapter 5) and develop the banking and financial infrastructure necessary to attract wealth. As long as they establish banking, privacy, and taxation laws that attract money, they should be allowed to do so. The Cayman Islands attract a lot of tourism, but the territory is also one of the world's biggest financial centers, and one of the most secretive as well. It has worked hard to crack down on money laundering so it can use its financial expertise in legal ways to help companies and individuals.[54]

OFCs don't rely on taxation to fund huge government expenditures because they don't have a large military budget or significant welfare costs. Is there anything wrong with not collecting large amounts of taxes? Some countries are upset that OFC's offer a tax-free environment for revenues generated offshore, but that's their business. Nobody should force them to collect higher taxes just because the high-tax countries are at a disadvantage in attracting banking and finance. If

countries want to charge high taxes on financial transactions, let them do so, but don't force the OFCs to play their game.

Even the chairwoman of the British Public Accounts Committee, in complaining about the tax policies of MNEs like Google, Amazon, and Starbucks, admitted that they are probably not doing anything illegal; she was accusing them of being immoral.[55]

QUESTION

1. You can order a book from Amazon in the UK using a British website (amazon.co.uk) and receive it from a British warehouse through the British Royal Mail. However, you will be paying an Amazon subsidiary set up in Luxembourg, which offers more favorable tax conditions than the UK. Is Amazon illegal, immoral, both, or neither for having a subsidiary in Luxembourg to minimize its tax bill?

Looking to the Future
The Growth of Capital Markets and the Drive by Governments to Capture More Tax Revenues by MNEs

Global capital markets are in disarray largely because of unstable macroeconomic forces—weak economic growth, low interest rates, low prices on commodities, and political instability. Stock markets are very volatile as they rise and fall with changing economic news. With low oil prices, many of the sovereign wealth funds don't have the resources to invest in companies or take advantage of IPOs. In spite of this, companies are scouring the world in search of cheap capital. Because of low interest rates in Europe, there will be continued interest by corporate and sovereign buyers to issue bonds as a way to capture investment capital. The stock and bond markets will be increasingly important as banks deal with their own financial problems and increased regulations to protect against default.

Emerging markets can be great places to invest if their economies begin to recover. However, investments in emerging markets will continue to be a flight to risk, assuming that the unstable global economy doesn't favor the flight to safety in places like Japan, the United States, and Switzerland. China is in deep trouble and will continue to be so for several years because of mountains of debt and weak economic growth.

The competition for global capital will be fierce as companies are forced to shift funding from banks that are under great financial stress to issuing stocks and bonds as a way to grow and expand. In addition, stock markets will continue to compete with each other to attract companies that are looking for a place to raise capital. Mergers of stock markets to reduce costs and

expand their market potential will continue to be the wave of the future, barring regulatory concerns.

Another source of cash to MNEs will continue to be tax minimization schemes. However, the OECD countries are working hard to close tax loopholes used by MNEs as they expand abroad. As seen by the tax inversion scheme employed largely by U.S.-based MNEs, governments will continue to look at the economic rationale for expansion abroad and do whatever they can to go after companies that structure transactions to take advantage of low tax rates. On the other hand, there will be tension between those countries trying to close the loopholes and countries using loopholes to attract investment. It is safe to say that governments will continue to push for ways to increase their tax base, and companies will continue to react to the changing tax environment to find new ways to reduce their tax burden.

The OECD, the IMF, and the EU are three institutions that will help countries narrow their tax differences and crack down on the transfer of money for illegal purposes. Although illegal financial transfers have occurred for years, drug trafficking and the financing of terrorist activities have created a more urgent need to reform the global financial system. As governments attempt to institute tax reform to collect more tax revenues from companies, they will have to perform a delicate balancing act of increasing revenues without stifling innovation and forcing companies to search for the next best tax-haven country. ■

CASE   Does the Devil Really Wear Prada?

Probably not, but the Italian Prada Group, clearly one of the top luxury businesses in the world, is designing, producing, and distributing luxury handbags, leather goods, footwear, ready-to-wear apparel, accessories, eyewear, and fragrances all over the world.[56] It operates in 70 countries through 618 directly operated stores and selected, high-end multi-brand stores and luxury department stores.

Prada is a closely held firm in which the Prada family—led by Miuccia Prada, president and head designer, and her husband, CEO Patrizio Bertelli—holds 80 percent of the shares, with Italian bank Intesa Sanpaolo holding the rest. When Bertelli and Prada realized that the future of luxury consumption would be in Asia, they had to decide how they were going to fund their expansion. Due to a string of debt-financed acquisitions in the early 2000s, Prada ran into liquidity problems and had to turn to Intesa for funding. Intesa purchased the 5 percent interest in the company in 2006 for €100 million, which put a valuation on Prada of €2 billion at the time. They had considered an IPO in 2001 and 2008, but the collapse in global stock markets both times forced them to pull back. However, 2011 seemed like a good time. Issuing stock to outside investors would bring in new money, but it would also force Prada to deal with nonfamily shareholders and the financial discipline of the market. Also, they had to figure out where to issue the IPO and how much of the company they should sell. Should they list on the Milan Stock Exchange, as they were being advised by nearly everyone in Italy? Or should they become the first Italian company to list in Hong Kong, where they could be closer to the future growth markets in China?

Who Is Prada?

Prada began in 1913 when Mario Prada opened a luxury store in the Galleria Vittorio Emanuele II in Milan. Prada quickly built a strong reputation in luxury goods due to its exclusive designs, superior manufacturing techniques, and high-quality materials. By 1919, Prada had become an official supplier to the Italian Royal Family and a benchmark for fashion throughout Europe.

At the end of the 1970s, Mario's great-granddaughter, Miuccia Prada, entered into a partnership with Patrizio Bertelli, a Tuscan businessman who was involved in high-quality leather goods. Initially, Bertelli's company, I.P.I. SpA, had an exclusive license to produce and distribute leather goods using the Prada name, but in 2003 I.P.I. SpA and Prada merged into Prada SpA. (SpA—Società per Anzioni—is the same as "corporation" in the United States or plc in the U.K.)

In the 1990s and early 2000s, Prada began to expand by launching new brands (such as Miu Miu), acquiring new businesses (such as Church's Group and Car Shoe), and entering into licensing and joint venture agreements with Italian eyewear manufacturer Luxottica and Spanish cosmetic manufacturer PUIG Beauty & Fashion Group. With these acquisitions, Prada expanded its product lines and opened new stores. It even launched a new phone by LG of South Korea.

In 2010, Prada was basically a European company, generating nearly half of its revenues from Europe, including 19.5 percent from Italy. However, the importance of Asia was expanding. By 2012, European revenues were 22.7 percent, including 16.2 percent from Italy, but Asia–Pacific (excluding Japan) rose to 35.6 of total revenues. In spite of its acquisitions, the Prada brand still counted for nearly 80 percent of the company's global revenues. The Asia–Pacific area had the highest growth rate of all geographic areas in which Prada was operating, benefitting from organic growth rather than acquisitions. Prada opened 17 new stores in the region and did a lot of work upgrading existing stores.

Why China?

The luxury goods market, of which Prada is a member, is hard to define. It is typically composed of goods that are high-priced, high-quality, and high-status. Some of the other largest luxury goods firms in the world are French-based LVMH, Christian Dior (which holds 42 percent of LVMH), PPR (which includes Gucci and Yves Saint Laurent), and Richemont (which includes Cartier, Chloé, and Alfred Dunhil, and has a JV with Polo Ralph Lauren). Of course, there are also luxury goods firms in many industries, such as fashion, automobiles, watches and jewelry, and drinks. It is clear, however, that Asia, especially China, is rapidly becoming the future of the luxury goods industry.

In addition to having the largest population in the world, China is now the world's second-largest economy and growing at a faster rate than any of the advanced countries and the rest of the BRICs. There are several reasons why China is becoming the target of the luxury goods markets. The country is expected to be the largest luxury market in the world by 2020, catering to both men and women. Until recently, the market in China was driven by men, but women are becoming increasingly important. Maserati SpA and Bulgari SpA have been successful in China because they have positioned themselves as the ultimate male status symbols. Much of the luxury goods purchases were by men for women, but now women are starting to assert themselves as consumers. In 2009, for example, 30 percent of Maserati's sales were to women, up from 7 percent in 2005. In the broader luxury market sales, women accounted for over half of the $15 billion in sales, compared with 45 percent in 2008. Also, the average female luxury consumer spent 22 percent more in 2010 than in 2008.

◀ Prada is moving aggressively in Asia to take advantage of the strong demand for luxury goods, as illustrated in this poster in Aberdeen Harbor in Hong Kong.
Source: Lou Linwei/Alamy Stock Photo

The upshot of the emerging female luxury goods consumer is that brands that have catered more to women are putting even greater emphasis on China. Female luxury consumers in China are a result of more women achieving success in business.

This is not lost on Prada, but it is interested in China for other reasons as well. As the head designer for the company, Ms. Prada is especially drawn to Chinese influences on fashion, which she feels are more contemporary than conservative Europe. Her company has a design team of 60 designers that she feels are curious, excited, fresh, and innovative. To take advantage of this talent, Prada is opening a design center in Hong Kong and hopes to expand its stores by 10–12 per year from only 14 stores in 2011. Not only is China its market of the future, as it is for many other luxury goods companies, but it is also the location of ideas. It makes sense that Prada would need to set up a team to design products for the Chinese market, as well as get innovative ideas that it can use for its products worldwide.

Where to Issue the IPO?

As Prada considered how to expand, it looked at several options. It could borrow from banks, issue bonds in the domestic and international bond markets, or bring in outside investors. In 2010, 51 percent of Prada's assets were funded by equity and 49 percent by debt; compare that to a sample of Italian companies, whose average debt/asset ratio in 2009–2010 was much higher at 57.4 percent. Of the debt, 57 percent was in current liabilities and 43 percent in long-term debt. Prada's long-term debt is primarily bank debt, sometimes to a syndicate of banks. Although its largest exposure in long-term debt is in euros, it also has long-term debt in U.S. dollars, Chinese renminbi, Japanese yen, and British pounds. Apparently, Prada's strategy in debt markets has been to work with banks instead of relying on the Eurobond or Foreign Bond markets.

The decision to raise capital in the form of equity is complicated. As noted earlier, Prada is a closely held family company, so raising capital through an IPO is a major departure from the past. Would the Prada family be willing to give up a say in the future of the company? If so, where would be the best place to list the IPO? As an Italian company based in Milan, it would seem logical to list on the Milan Stock Exchange. But being the rebel she is, Ms. Prada had other ideas. Her feeling was that Hong Kong would be a better choice for several reasons. First, brand-name companies feel that having an important presence in the region is the best way to get your brand out to the consumer. Road shows attract a lot of press and attention from consumers as well as the financial community. Given the projected growth of China, Hong Kong makes sense. Second, Hong Kong was the world's biggest IPO market in 2010, with US$57.7 billion raised from 87 listings.

Timing is everything, of course. Prada has tried to raise capital before, but the timing just wasn't right, mostly due to factors out of their control. After the Japanese earthquake on March 11, 2011, there was a lull in market activity, but sales began to pick up again once markets quieted down. For instance, Glencore International plc raised more than $10 billion in a London-Hong Kong listing—the largest in 2011—which made the IPO market in general seem promising. And the rapid influx of capital into Hong Kong from China coincided with Prada's decision to go to the markets.

The IPO

Finally, Prada decided to move forward with the IPO in Hong Kong, not Milan. The feeling was that since the proceeds would be used to fund expansion in China, why not bring in investors from Hong Kong, the gateway to China? Prada decided to sell a 20 percent stake in the company, significantly changing its ownership structure. But Ms. Prada knew it was the right move. Friends and advisors convinced her that in some respects the stock market and the discipline it imposes would help ensure the future of Prada and help with the succession. Prada hoped to raise 20 billion HK$ in the offering (about US$2.6 billion), a significant amount of money. The goal was to sell about 423 million shares at HK$36.50 to HK$48.00. If the demand were strong, Prada could sell an additional 63 million shares, or 15 percent of the offer on an over-allotment option. That goal was to list on the stock exchange on June 24, 2011, after beginning the process with institutional investors and then the wider investing public. As Prada got closer to the listing date, prices began to move down a little due to uncertainty in global markets from the European debt crisis, the U.S. debt crisis, and inflation in China. Prada adjusted its target price to consumers to a range of HK$39.50 to HK$42.25 per share (US$5.07 to US$5.42). This would put its value at 22.8 to 24.4 times 2011 expected earnings, which is still higher than LVMH, which trades at 20.1 times earnings. Pricing is clearly better in Hong Kong than elsewhere.

When the stock finally hit the exchange, retail investors didn't come into the market as much as anticipated, and Prada wasn't able to sell all of the shares allotted to investors. In addition, prices didn't really jump all that much initially. Within about two weeks, however, prices were up 13 percent over their HK$39.50 IPO price, or HK$44.64.

As we moved into 2016, Prada has suffered for a variety of reasons. Persistent weakness in Hong Kong has really hurt Prada sales. Tighter visa restrictions on Chinese shoppers who looked to Hong Kong as the place to shop pushed a lot of Chinese shoppers to Europe. However, the terrorist attacks in Paris dramatically reduced the flow of Chinese tourists to Europe. The economic slowdown in China coupled with a rise in the Hong Kong dollar which is pegged to the United States also hurt the sales of Prada and other luxury brands. Will China ever come back to the point that Prada will be as successful as it anticipated when it offered its IPO in Hong Kong?

QUESTIONS

⭐ **11-3.** Do you agree with the decision to list an IPO, or should Prada have borrowed more money, possibly floating a dim sum bond or a Eurobond in London or elsewhere?

11-4. What do you feel are the best justifications for Prada to issue the IPO in Hong Kong? Are there any downsides to their decision to list in Hong Kong?

⭐ **11-5.** Many of the other luxury fashion companies are also largely family owned. What is the impact to Prada of diluting the family ownership, and is this a model that other companies can be expected to follow?

11-6. Given the downturn in the economy in Hong Kong and China, what do you think Prada's future is in the region?

MyLab Management

Go to **mymanagementlab.com** for the following Assisted-graded writing questions:

11-7   Why did Prada need to raise additional funds?

11-8   What types of foreign-exchange risk does Prada face, and what advice would you give them to hedge against their risks?

Endnotes

Scan for Endnotes or go to www.pearsonglobaleditions.com/daniels

CHAPTER 11
Ethics and Social Responsibility

OBJECTIVES

After studying this chapter, you should be able to

11-1 Describe the trade-offs among different stake-holders in MNE activities

11-2 Evaluate the major economic effects of MNEs on home and host countries

11-3 Explain the broad foundations of ethical behavior

11-4 Identify the cultural foundations of ethical behavior

11-5 Illustrate how ethical behavior is affected by different legal attitudes

11-6 Show how corruption and bribery affect and are affected by cultural, legal, and political forces

11-7 Summarize what the roles are of governments and companies in resolving environmental issues

11-8 Demonstrate how global labor issues need to be addressed by MNEs to their stakeholders

11-9 Restate how codes of conduct can help MNEs respond to concerns by stakeholders over responsible corporate behavior

MyLab Management®
Improve Your Performance!

When you see this icon ⊙, visit **www.mymanagementlab.com** for activities that are applied, personalized, and offer immediate feedback.

When the last tree has been cut down, the last river has been polluted and the last fish has been caught—only then do you realize that money can't buy everything.

—Native American proverb

▼ Solar electricity plants like this one will help the transition to sustainable energy.

Source: 1224. Shutterstock

Ecomagination and the Global Greening of GE

As noted on Map 11.1, a recent TV ad invites viewers to "accompany" a small green frog as it does a little globe hopping from one exotic location to another.[1] The frog, however, doesn't seem intent on hitting the usual tourist spots, instead preferring stopovers at such places as a solar farm in South Korea, a water-purification plant in Kuwait, and a wind farm in Germany. To begin the second leg of his tour, he hops on a GE90 aircraft engine flying over China and takes viewers to a "clean" coal-powered facility somewhere in Florida. Then he boards a GE Evolution locomotive in the Canadian Rockies as a voiceover explains the point of all this seemingly ordinary sightseeing: "At GE, we're combining imagination with advanced technology around the world to make it a better place to live for everyone." The journey's end finds our frog in the midst of a lush, green tropical rain forest.

"GREEN IS GREEN"

The ad is part of a major promotional campaign by General Electric Company (GE) for its Ecomagination Initiative. Announced in 2005 by CEO Jeffrey Immelt, Ecomagination is an ambitious strategy designed to demonstrate that an ecologically conscious conglomerate can cultivate the bottom line while doing its duty toward the global environment—hence, the campaign motto "Green Is Green."

The world's eighth-largest corporation (in terms of market capitalization), U.S.-based GE sells products in more than 175 countries through its industry business and GE capital. Industry is further divided into oil and gas, energy management, health care, transportation, and appliances and lighting. It sells, among other things, appliances, aircraft engines, consumer electronics, energy-related products such as solar panels and wind generators, and locomotive engines. It also operates research centers in the United States, Brazil, India, China, Germany, and Israel. In early 2016, GE announced that it was selling its appliance business to Chinese company, Haier.

When the company announced its plan to launch an internal green revolution, GE surprised both investors and industrial customers who had long seen the firm as an ally in the struggle against environmental activists and lobbyists. But as more and more evidence piles up to support the claim that carbon dioxide emitted from human-made sources is heating up average global temperatures, GE has decided to take a more conciliatory stance, allying itself with a growing number of companies that regard investor and environmental interests as intrinsically interlocked, rather than diametrically opposed.

COMMITMENTS AND GOALS

GE's new initiative represents five basic commitments on its part: (1) to reduce greenhouse emissions and improve the energy efficiency of operations; (2) to double investment in the research and development of "clean" technologies; (3) to increase revenues from those same technologies; (4) to reduce its global water use by 20 percent; and (5) to keep the public informed. It now evaluates business unit managers not only on profitability and return on capital but also on success in reducing carbon dioxide emissions, the chief greenhouse gas (GHG) attributed to global warming. Energy-intensive divisions, such as those catering to the power and industrial sectors, are responsible for the largest cuts.

The company's overall target was a 1 percent reduction from 2004 levels by 2012. At first glance, the goal doesn't seem to have been overly ambitious, but that number represents a significant improvement if you account for the fact that, given GE's projected growth, levels would otherwise soar to 40 percent above 2004 levels. Immelt also committed the company to reducing the intensity of GHG emissions—its level of emissions in relation to the company's economic activity—30 percent by 2008 and to improving energy efficiency 30 percent by 2012. To ensure that these goals were met, Immelt assembled a cross-business, cross-functional team to oversee planning and monitor progress. By 2014, the company had reduced GHG emissions by 31 percent from its 2004 baseline, more than the 25 percent it had forecast. It also had improved energy intensity by 32 percent from 2004 levels.

A LITTLE CONSENSUS SEEKING

In addition to instituting the internal changes necessary to curb GHG emissions, Immelt considered GE's global political environment. He enlisted the Belgian and Japanese governments in the global ecological discussion and allied GE with other green-minded corporations to lobby American lawmakers on such matters as mandatory GHG reductions. Working with the Environmental and Natural Resources Defense Council and the Pew Center on Global Climate Change, GE also joined other companies to form the U.S. Climate Action Partnership to help shape the international political debate over global warming.

GE and its allies want to be known for developing forward-looking strategies and making long-term investments in an increasingly fragmented regulatory environment. With half of its markets located outside the United States, GE is already under the jurisdiction of foreign governments that are more active than the United States in addressing environmental issues.

TECHNOLOGICAL TACTICS AND ECO-FRIENDLY PRODUCTS

Under Immelt's direction, GE has also been gearing up to double R&D investment in clean technologies, including renewable-energy, water-purification processes, and fuel-efficient products from which it expects significant revenue growth. GE had already spent $10 billion on R&D investment between 2010 and 2014.

MAP 11.1   Global Travels of GE's "Green Frog," Its Symbol of Commitment to the Environment

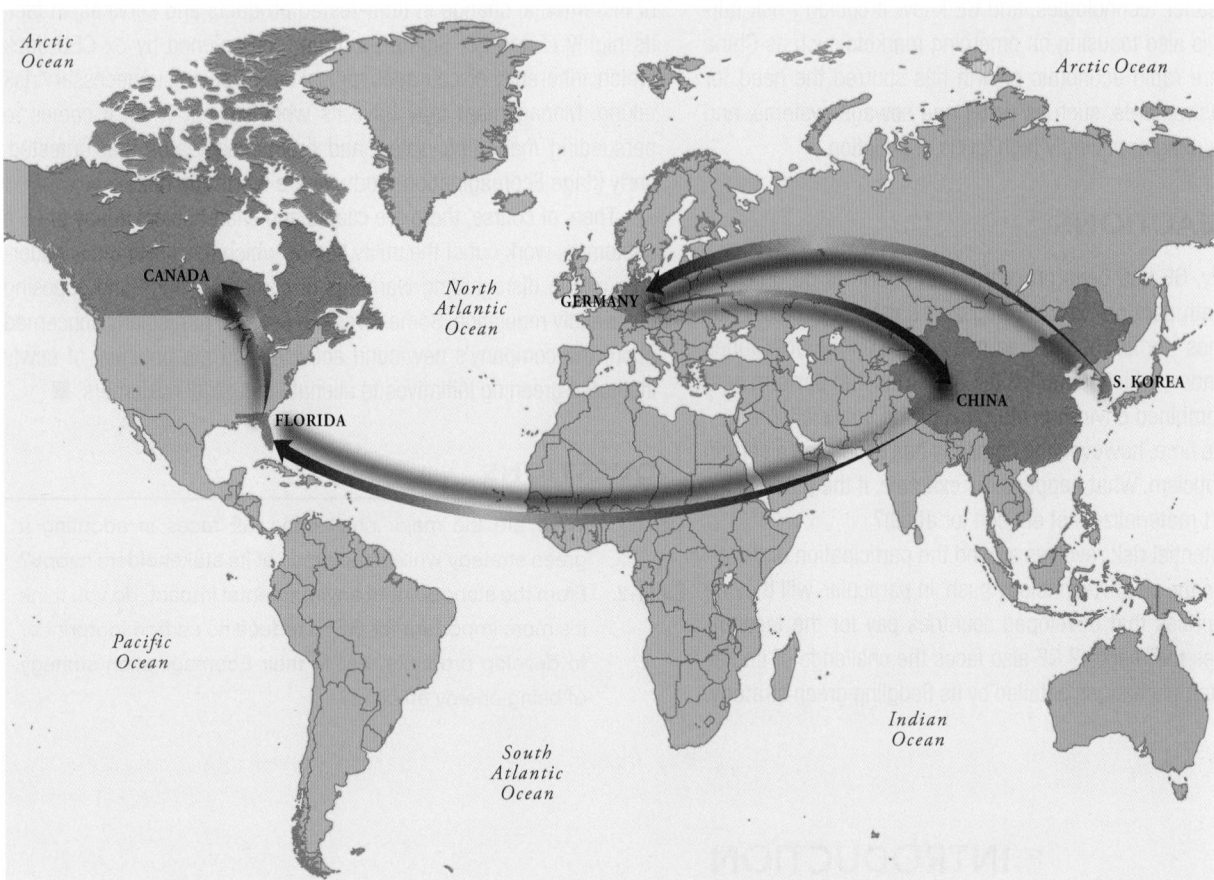

In 2006, GE announced that it would reduce water usage by 25 percent from its 2006 baseline, and it achieved a 42 percent reduction by 2014.

When the Ecomagination initiative was first launched, GE marketed only 17 products that met its own Ecomagination criteria; by 2009, there were 90 such products, and by 2011, there were 140 products and solutions generating $105 billion in revenues. By 2014, revenues over the 2010–2014 period had increased to $200 billion. GE wind was generating $30 billion in revenues, and there were over 30,000 wind turbines in operation. In 2016, GE purchased the energy business of French-based Alstom, giving GE access to Alstom's giant offshore wind turbine technology.

In addition to making other products, such as appliances and light bulbs, energy efficient, GE intends to establish itself as an "energy-services" consultant and to bid on contracts for maintaining water-purification plants and wind farms, a venture that could be five times as lucrative as simply manufacturing the products needed for such projects. The use of its website to communicate information about its green products and the efforts to improve its own GHG emissions reduction is an example of commitment #5, listed above:

to keep the public informed. In addition, it communicates information through social media such as Twitter and Facebook.

"SOLVING ENVIRONMENTAL PROBLEMS IS GOOD BUSINESS"

GE insists that the markets for such products and services are both growing and profitable, and Immelt is convinced that taking advantage of them not only helps the environment but also strengthens the company's strategic position with major profit opportunities.

GE also regards its Ecomagination strategy as a necessary response to customer demand. Before embarking on this initiative, GE spent 18 months working with industrial customers, inviting managers to two-day "dreaming sessions" to imagine life in 2015 and to discuss the kinds of products they'd need in such an environment. The result? Management came out of the talks with the indelible impression that both GE's customers and the social and political environments in which it conducted business would be demanding more environmentally "clean" products.

Many of GE's Asian and European competitors had already begun investing in cleaner technologies, and GE knew it couldn't risk falling behind. GE is also focusing on emerging markets such as China and India, where rapid economic growth has spurred the need for expanded infrastructures, such as water and sewage systems, and for means of curbing appallingly high levels of pollution.

MIXED REACTIONS

Not surprisingly, GE has been praised for its efforts to go green. It reached the ninth spot on *Fortune* magazine's list of the "Most Admired Companies" for 2015, and it earned a place on the Dow Jones Sustainability Index, which identifies the 300 firms that perform best according to combined environmental, social, and financial criteria.

At the same time, however, the company has generated a certain amount of skepticism. What happens, for example, if the markets it's betting on don't materialize fast enough (or at all)?

Another potential risk revolves around the participation of developing nations in the clean-technology push. In particular, will they be willing to pay prices that developed countries pay for the technology that reaches the market? GE also faces the challenge of implementing the internal changes entailed by its fledgling green strategy.

Traditionally, the firm's culture has been accustomed to strategies of incremental change in time-tested products and services. In fact, its highly touted Six Sigma program, championed by ex-CEO Jack Welch, inherently discourages radical deviation and unnecessary risk taking. Management may have its work cut out when it comes to persuading marketing, sales, and production teams that untested, early stage Ecomagination products are worth the risk.

Then, of course, there are clients and shareholders. Many of GE's customers work out of the utility sector, which has assumed a leadership role in disregarding warnings of climatic change and opposing ecofriendly regulation. Some investors seemed particularly concerned about the company's newfound activism and the potential of newly instituted greening initiatives to alienate industrial customers. ∎

QUESTIONS

11-1. What are the major challenges GE faces in adopting a green strategy while keeping all of its stakeholders happy?

11-2. From the standpoint of environmental impact, do you think it's more important for GE to reduce its carbon footprint or to develop products that fit their Ecomagination strategy of being energy efficient?

INTRODUCTION

In this chapter, we'll examine how globalization affects society and managers' judgments as they interact with different laws and cultures and try to be socially responsible. Doing business abroad is not easy. The greater the "distance" from one's home country, the more complicated it is to do business. Distance can be described in many different ways, but one way to identify it is the acronym CAGE: cultural (also known as psychic distance), administrative (such as political and institutional policies), geographic, and economic.[2] Given the criticisms of globalization and the challenge of companies and individuals doing business in areas of the world that are quite distant, as defined above, how can companies and individuals be successful, or at least not create serious mistakes?

STAKEHOLDER TRADE-OFFS

Companies must satisfy the demands of

- shareholders,
- employees,
- customers,
- suppliers
- society.

To prosper—indeed, to survive—a company must satisfy different groups of **stakeholders**, including shareholders, employees, customers, suppliers, and society at large. Obviously, this juggling act can be quite tricky. The shareholder (or stockholder)-versus-stakeholder dilemma pits the demands of one stakeholder against all the others. There is a debate on the idea of shared value, which implies that companies can increase profits while at the same time addressing critical social problems. It is tricky to do both successfully, but many MNEs feel it is worth the effort.[3] The basic idea of focusing on stakeholders more broadly is that companies can consider various socially important groups when making decisions.[4] In the short term, for example, group aims often conflict. *Shareholders* want additional sales and increased productivity (which result in higher profits and returns). *Employees* want safer workplaces and higher compensation. *Customers* want higher-quality products at lower prices. *Society* would like to see more jobs, increased corporate taxes, more corporate support for social services, and more trustworthy behavior on the part of corporate executives.

In the *long* term, all of these aims must be adequately met. If they aren't, there's a good chance that none of them will be, especially if each stakeholder group is powerful enough to bring operations to a standstill. In addition, pressure groups—which may reflect the interests of any stakeholder group—lobby governments to regulate MNE activities both at home and abroad.

As we noted in our opening case, for example, GE's Ecomagination initiative has generated pressure from various constituencies, including clients and shareholders concerned about profitability, various governments concerned with drafting regulations, employees wondering about changes in the company's strategies and goals, and environmental lobbyists, NGOs, and fellow businesses trying to preserve the environment. Each group has a powerful influence on how GE does business and on how successful it is in the marketplace. However, GE has to satisfy a variety of stakeholders with different concerns. For that reason, it has many different initiatives working with different stakeholders, not just those interested in climate change.

THE ECONOMIC IMPACT OF THE MNE

As we examine globalization and society, let's begin with a discussion of the impact of MNEs on the countries where they operate. As discussed in Chapter 1, there are many ways a company can do business abroad, and its success or failure can be strongly affected by the operating environment, including physical, social, and competitive factors as illustrated in Figure 1.1. In addition, the MNE's activities can also affect the operating environment, such as through corruption and bribery, environmental impact (i.e., air and water pollution), and labor policies.

Although not all companies engage in foreign production, the dynamics involved in this decision raise lots of interesting issues. According to the eclectic paradigm of international production, there are three conditions that help explain the foreign production decision: ownership-advantages of MNEs that give them an advantage over companies in the host countries, location-specific advantages of the host country that make them attractive locations for FDI, and internalization advantages for the MNEs to utilize their specific ownership advantages rather than sell or license them to outsiders to exploit.[5] Figure 11.1 identifies some of the ownership-specific advantages of the MNE, focusing on what the MNE has to offer.

Measuring the impact of the MNE on home and host societies depends on its stakeholders, the ability to understand cause-and-effect relationships, and individual versus aggregate effects.

It is hard to determine whether or not the actions of MNEs affect societal conditions.

Cause-and-effect relationships refer to the true impact of an MNE on a host country. Opponents of FDI persist in trying to link MNE activities to such problems in host countries as inequitable income distribution, political corruption, environmental debasement, and social deprivation.[6] In contrast, proponents of MNE activities tend to assume a positive

FIGURE 11.1 What MNEs Have to Offer

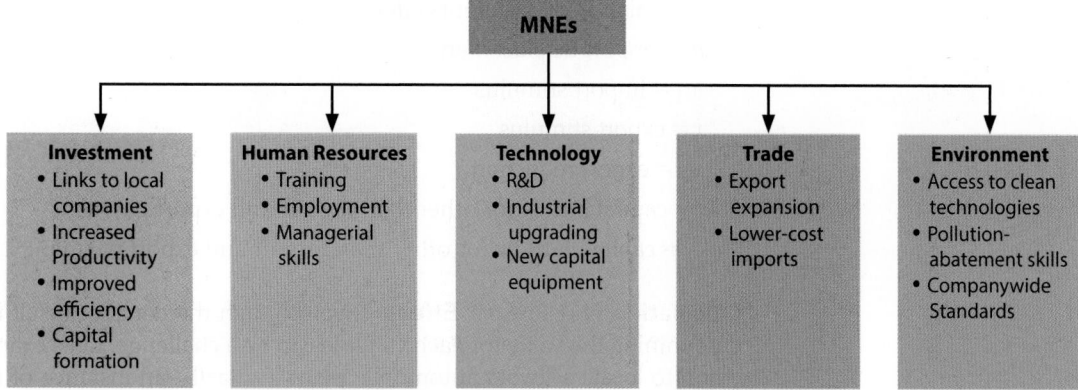

link between their activities and such effects in recipient countries as higher tax revenues, increased levels of employment and exports, and greater innovation. There may or may not be a link, but each side needs to provide evidence to back up their position.

In terms of individual versus aggregate effects, some countries evaluate MNEs and their activities on individual or case-by-case bases. Other countries prefer to apply the same policies and control mechanisms to all MNEs, even though this approach risks missing some good opportunities while steering clear of dubious ones. Moreover, it's hard to choose between these two approaches because the governments that have applied one or the other have been far from perfect in predicting the future impact of FDI activities in their jurisdictions.

The philosophy, goals, and actions of each MNE are unique.

BALANCE-OF-PAYMENTS EFFECTS

The effect of an individual MNE may be positive or negative.

This refers to trade and capital flows that result from FDI. Under different conditions, these effects may be positive or negative, either for the host country or the home country.

Host countries want capital inflows because they provide the foreign exchange needed to import goods and services and to pay off foreign debt. Remember, however, that FDI results in both capital inflows and capital outflows. Many countries, therefore, are concerned about the net balance-of-payments effect and about the possibility that, when the books are ultimately balanced, the effect of FDI on their net balance of payments may be negative.

CONCEPT CHECK

On page 167 of Chapter 4, we mention how the balance-of-payments is a key feature of a country's economy.

Effect of Individual FDI To appreciate better why countries must evaluate the effect of each investment on their balance of payments, we can examine two extreme hypothetical scenarios reflecting the effects of FDI on a nation's balance of payments:

- *Scenario 1:* Assume that a Mexican MNE makes an FDI when purchasing a Haitian-owned company as a portfolio investment. If the MNE makes no changes in management, capitalization, or operations, profitability remains the same for the Haitian company. Dividends, however, now go to the Mexican owners rather than remaining in Haiti. This results in a drain on Haiti's foreign exchange and a corresponding inflow to Mexico.
- *Scenario 2:* A Mexican MNE purchases idle resources (land, labor, materials, equipment) in Haiti and converts them to the production of formerly imported goods. Rising consumer demand leads the MNE to reinvest its profits in Haiti, where import substitution increases the host country's foreign-exchange reserves.

Most FDI falls somewhere between these two extreme examples. That's why they're hard to evaluate, particularly when policymakers try to apply regulations to all in-bound investments.

There is, however, a basic equation for analyzing the effect of FDI on a host country's balance of payments:

The formula to determine the balance-of-payments effect is simple but the data used must be estimated and are subject to assumptions.

$$B = (m - m_1) + (x - x_1) + (c - c_1)$$

where

> B = balance-of-payments effect
> m = import displacement
> m_1 = import stimulus
> x = export stimulus
> x_1 = export reduction
> c = capital inflow for other than import and export payment
> c_1 = capital outflow for other than import and export payment

Calculating Net Import Effect Even though the equation itself is pretty straightforward, determining the value for each variable can be a challenge. Let's examine the effect of the decision to locate a Toyota automobile plant in Brazil—an instance of FDI by a Japanese MNE.

First, to calculate the net import effect ($m - m_1$), we need to know how much Brazil would import if the Toyota plant were not built.

We must, of course, consider the amount that Toyota makes and sells in Brazil, but that would be only a rough indication of how much Brazil would import. Why? Because the selling price and product characteristics of the Brazilian-made cars may differ from those of the cars that Brazil would otherwise import from Japan. Moreover, sales of the Brazilian-made Toyota cars may come at the expense either of cars from other plants in Brazil or of imported foreign cars other than Toyotas. Note, too, that by definition, the value of m_1 should include the equipment, components, and materials brought by Toyota into Brazil. Remember, for example, that Toyota buys a lot of parts from suppliers that may be made locally or imported from other countries.

Finally, the value of m_1 should also include estimates of the increase in Brazilian imports due to increases in national income caused by the capital inflow from Japan. Assume, for instance, that, because of the Toyota investment, Brazilian national income rises R$50 million (50 million reais). At this point, we have to consult the marginal propensity to import, which is the fraction of a change in imports due to a change in income and assumes that the recipients of that income will spend some portion of it on imports. If we calculate this portion as 10 percent, imports should rise by R$5 million (that is, 10 percent of R$50 million).

The net export effect is the *export stimulus* minus the *export reduction* ($x - x_1$), but bear in mind that this figure is particularly controversial, because different evaluators, starting out with different assumptions, regularly arrive at widely varying conclusions. Let's go back to our Toyota example. In this case, we can make the assumption that the Brazilian plant merely substitutes for imports from and production in Japan. If in fact we proceed on this assumption, we get no net export effect for Brazil. For Japan, we arrive at a negative net export effect because of Toyota's export reduction (it's now selling cars made in Brazil to Brazilian consumers instead of exporting Japanese-made cars to Brazil). Toyota, however, might well defend itself on the grounds that its moves abroad are (largely) defensive. How so? Under this assumption, Toyota can argue that it is capturing sales that would otherwise go to non-Japanese carmakers in Brazil. In that case, Toyota's export reduction from Japan amounts only to the export replacement (loss) resulting from the decision to build a production plant in Brazil.

In some cases, MNEs have argued that their overseas investments stimulate home-country exports of complementary products (say, in Toyota's case, auto parts) that they can sell in host countries through foreign-owned facilities.

Calculating Net Capital Flow   *Net capital flow* ($c - c_1$) is the easiest figure to calculate because of controls maintained by most central banks. There are, however, a few sticking points. Basing your evaluation on a given year is problematic because there's a time lag between a company's outward flow of investment funds and the inward flow of remitted earnings. Because companies eventually plan to take out more capital than they originally put in, what appears at a given time to be a favorable (or unfavorable) capital flow may prove, over a longer period, to be the opposite. The time it takes Toyota to recoup its capital outflow to Brazil depends on such factors as the need to reinvest funds in the host country, the ability to borrow locally, estimates of future exchange rates, and rules on the repatriation of capital.

As a rule, MNE investments are initially favorable to the host country and unfavorable to the home country in the short run. After some time, however, the situation usually reverses.[7] Why? Because nearly all foreign investors eventually plan to have their subsidiaries remit dividends back to the parent company in excess of the amount they sent abroad. If the net value of the FDI continues to grow through retained earnings, dividend payments for a given year may ultimately exceed the total amount of capital transfers composing the initial investment.

GROWTH AND EMPLOYMENT EFFECTS

In contrast to balance-of-payments effects, MNE effects on growth and employment don't necessarily amount to *zero-sum games* (where gains must equal losses) between home and host countries. Classical economists assumed that production factors were always at full

On the import side, the balance-of-payments is positive if the FDI results in a substitution for imports and negative if it results in an increase in imports.

The balance-of-payments effects in terms of capital flows for FDI are usually

- positive for the host country initially and negative for the home country,
- negative for host country and positive for the home country later.

employment; consequently, any movement of any of these factors from home to abroad would result in an increase in foreign output abroad and a decrease in domestic output. Even if this assumption were realistic, it's still possible that gains in the host country will be greater or less than the losses in the home country.

The argument that both home and host countries may gain from FDI rests on two assumptions: 1) resources aren't necessarily being fully employed and 2) capital and technology can't be easily transferred from one industry to another. Let's say, for example, that a soft-drink maker is producing at maximum capacity for the domestic market but is limited (say, by high transportation costs) in generating export sales. In addition, moving into other product lines or using its financial resources to increase domestic productivity aren't viable options.

> Growth and employment effects are not a zero-sum game because MNEs may use resources that were unemployed or underemployed.

Setting up a foreign production facility is appealing because it would allow the company to develop foreign sales without reducing resource employment in its home market. In fact, it may wind up hiring additional domestic managers to oversee international operations; perhaps it will also end up earning dividends and royalties from the foreign use of its capital, brand, and technology.

In recent years, many U.S. and European garment manufacturers have moved production operations to low-wage countries to realize cost advantages. In the process, they've shut down—or at least declined to expand—home-country operations. Thus overseas FDI in the garment-making industry has resulted in a loss of jobs in home countries while creating jobs abroad. The situation may be unfortunate, but the fact that it did come about may mean it was inevitable. In the absence of serious protection, argue some experts, home-country operations would have closed down because of competition from abroad, and jobs would have been lost anyway. Conversely, of course, host countries gain through the transfer of capital and technology. If that capital is used to acquire host-country operations that are going out of business, then the foreign investor may very well save host-country jobs and, through the import of technology and managerial ability, even create new jobs.

Critics, however, contend that MNEs often make investments that domestic companies could otherwise make, thereby locking out local entrepreneurs. Likewise, they say, foreign investors often bid up prices when competing with local companies for labor and other resources. Critics also claim that FDI destroys local entrepreneurship in ways that affect national development. Because entrepreneurs are inspired by the reasonable expectation of success, the collapse in several countries of small cottage industries, especially in the face of MNE efforts to consolidate local operations, may have played a role in undermining the competitive confidence of local businesspeople.

THE FOUNDATIONS OF ETHICAL BEHAVIOR

Companies and those who work for them must act *responsibly* wherever they go. However, a look at ethical behavior tends to focus on individuals—those who finally make the decision of how to behave. But top management can determine the values a company espouses and to which employees must adhere. Such values are generally included in a Code of Conduct (discussed at the end of the chapter) and in the behavior of other individuals in the organization, especially peers and superiors. In order to ensure adherence to those values, management will try to hire individuals who are willing to work in the type of ethical environment it is trying to create. However, people still must make the decision about how they are going to act in any given situation.

> Many actions elicit universal agreement on what is right or wrong, but other situations are less clear.

The sections below will examine the cultural and legal dimensions of ethical behavior in a global context. First, though, let's briefly examine the broad foundations of ethical behavior. There are three levels of moral development:[8]

> There are three levels of moral development:
> • Preconventional
> • Conventional
> • Postconventional, autonomous, or principled

- Level 1, the *preconventional* level, where children learn what is right and wrong but don't necessarily understand *why* their behavior is right or wrong.

- Level 2, the *conventional* level, where we learn role conformity, first from our peers (including parents), then from societal laws. One could argue that company codes of conduct are also part of the *conventional* level of behavior in the narrow context of a company rather than a society. However, behavior espoused by companies likely reflects the values of the company's home country.

- Level 3, the *postconventional, autonomous, or principled* level, where individuals internalize moral behavior, not because they are afraid of sanctions, but because they truly believe such behavior is right.

It is possible that behaviors under Level 2 and Level 3 are the same as long as individuals accept the laws where they live, or the codes of conduct of the companies they work for.[9]

When individuals confronted with ethical decisions enter the realm of moral reasoning, they examine their moral values, especially as related to Levels 2 and 3 above, and decide what to do. One method of doing so, the **teleological approach**, holds to the idea that decisions are based on the consequences of the action. **Utilitarianism**, a consequences-based theory of moral reasoning, means that "an action is right if it produces, or if it tends to produce, the greatest amount of good for the greatest number of people affected by the action. Otherwise, the action is wrong."[10] A second method, the **deontological approach**, asserts that we make moral judgments or engage in moral reasoning independent of consequences. It implies that actions are right or wrong *per se*.[11] In other words, ethics teaches that "people have a responsibility to do what is right and to avoid doing what is wrong."[12] When individuals engage in moral reasoning, they use one or the other of these methods, or possibly some mixture of the two.

When an individual moves abroad, moral reasoning becomes very complicated. Consequences may vary due to legal differences, and what is right or wrong may depend to an extent on local values. People need to figure out how make moral decisions—and so do the companies they work for. Two questions arise here: Why should companies and individuals care about ethical behavior? And what are the cultural and legal foundations of ethical behavior when it comes to adapting to a foreign environment?

> Teleological Approach: Decisions are based on the consequences of the action.
>
> Utilitarianism: An action is right if it produces the greatest amount of good.
>
> Deontological Approach: Moral judgments are made and moral reasoning occurs independent of consequences.

WHY DO COMPANIES CARE ABOUT ETHICAL BEHAVIOR?

Why should companies worry about ethical behavior at all? From a business standpoint, ethical behavior can be instrumental in achieving one or both of two possible objectives:

1. To develop competitive advantage
2. To avoid being perceived as irresponsible

First, some argue that responsible behavior contributes to strategic and financial success because it fosters trust, which in turn encourages commitment.[13] For instance, GE's Ecomagination program reflects top managers' belief that by actively responding to social concerns about global warming, GE can gain a strategic advantage over competitors, perhaps developing an edge in emerging markets that are facing severe environmental problems.

Second, companies are aware that more and more NGOs and other groups and individuals are becoming active in monitoring—and publicizing—international corporate practices. Governments also want to ensure that individual and corporate behavior is consistent with the best interests of the broader community and that laws are being duly followed. Even worse than perception is reality. Unethical behavior can result in serious sanctions against companies and legal action against individuals.

> NGOs are active in prodding companies to comply with certain standards of ethical behavior.

THE CULTURAL FOUNDATIONS OF ETHICAL BEHAVIOR

RELATIVISM VERSUS NORMATIVISM

Despite the cultural differences found among countries, as discussed in Chapter 2, it is tempting to assume that there is almost universal agreement on what's right and what's wrong when it comes to ethical and socially responsible behavior in business. In the real

> Values differ from country to country and between employees and companies.

CONCEPT CHECK

Recall from Chapter 2, pages 73–74, our discussion of "Cultural Awareness" and the various ways in which social and cultural distinctions can characterize a country's population. We also observed that companies doing business overseas need to be sensitive to internal diversity: They should remember that people in most nations are often members of multiple cultures and in some cases have more in common with certain foreign groups than with domestic groups.

Relativism: Ethical truths depend on the groups holding them.

CONCEPT CHECK

In discussing "guidelines for cultural adjustment" on page 89 in Chapter 2, we demonstrate that successful accommodation to a host country's culture depends not only on that culture's willingness to accept anything foreign but also on the extent to which foreign firms and their employees are able to adjust to the culture in which they find themselves.

Normativism: There are universal standards of behavior that all cultures should follow.

Managers need to exhibit ordinary decency—principles of honesty and fairness.

Social responsibility requires human judgment, which is subjective and ambiguous.

CONCEPT CHECK

Note that on page 122 in Chapter 3 we define a country's legal system as the fundamental institution that creates a comprehensive legal network to regulate social interaction; its purpose is to stabilize political and social environments as well as to ensure a fair, safe, and efficient business environment.

world, however, managers face situations in which the whys and hows of applying cultural values are less than crystal clear. Everything that complicates dilemmas in the domestic business environment tends to complicate them even further in the international arena. So, does ethical behavior vary by country, or are there uniform values that everyone should share?

Relativism   One point of view is to accept that there are significant differences from country to country that might affect our behavior. "When in Rome, do as the Romans do" is an oft-quoted expression that dates to the fourth century AD which implies that in different environments, one must adapt to local customs out of respect for them.[14]

Applying this expression in an international environment may depend on whether we assume that decisions are based on the consequences of our actions or on a strongly held view of right and wrong. **Relativism** holds that ethical truths depend on the values of a particular society and may vary from one society or country to another.[15] The implication is that it would not be appropriate to inject or enforce one's ethical values on another, or that a foreigner must adopt local values or morals whether or not they are consistent with the foreigner's own home values and beliefs.

Normativism   In contrast, **normativism** holds that there are indeed universal standards of behavior that, although influenced by different cultural values, should be accepted by people everywhere. Even a pluralistic society such as the United States has a large core of commonly held values and norms.[16] However, people may adopt other values and norms as their own. The key is to distinguish between what is common to all and what is unique to the individual.

Walking the Fine Line Between Relative and Normative   Companies and their employees struggle with the problem of how to implement their own ethical principles in foreign business environments: Do those principles reflect universally valid "truths" (the normative approach)? Or must they adapt to local conditions on the assumption that every place has its own "truths" and needs to be treated differently (the relative approach)?

Many individuals and organizations have laid out minimum levels of business practices that they say a company (domestic or foreign) must follow regardless of the legal requirements or ethical norms prevalent where it operates.[17] One could consider this as behavior based on principles of honesty and fairness, or "ordinary decency."[18]

THE LEGAL FOUNDATIONS OF ETHICAL BEHAVIOR

Dealing with *ethical dilemmas* is often a balancing act between *means* (the actions we take, which may be right or wrong) and *ends* (the consequences of our actions, which may also be right or wrong). Legal foundations for ethical behavior can provide guidance here, but legal justification is more rooted in the teleological approach to moral reasoning and moral behavior (consequences) than in the deontological approach (right vs. wrong behavior). However, there are good reasons to consider the law as a foundation of ethical behavior, just as there are limitations to using the law. Another concern is whose laws take precedence? Should the MNE only worry about local laws, or do they have to worry about the laws of the country where their headquarters are located? If there is a conflict between home country and host country laws, which laws take precedence?

LEGAL JUSTIFICATION: PRO AND CON

According to the legal argument, an individual or company can do anything that isn't illegal. However, there are five good reasons why this is inadequate:

1. Some things that are *unethical* are not *illegal*. Some forms of interpersonal behavior, for example, can clearly be wrong even if they're not against the law.

2. The law is slow to develop in emerging areas, and it takes time to pass and test laws in the courts. Moreover, because laws essentially respond to issues that have already surfaced, they can't always anticipate dilemmas that will arise in the future.

3. The law is often based on imprecisely defined moral concepts that can't be separated from the legal concepts they underpin.

4. The law often needs to undergo scrutiny by the courts. This is especially true of case law, in which the courts create law by establishing precedent.

5. The law simply isn't very efficient. "Efficiency" in this case implies achieving ethical behavior at a very low cost, and it would be impossible to solve every ethical behavioral problem with an applicable law.[19]

In contrast, there are also several good reasons for using the law to justify ethical behavior:

1. The law embodies many of a country's moral principles, making it an adequate guide for proper conduct.

2. The law provides a clearly defined set of rules, and following it at least establishes a good precedent for acceptable behavior.

3. The law contains enforceable rules that apply to everyone.

4. Because the law represents a consensus derived from widely shared experience and deliberation, it reflects careful and wide-ranging discussions.[20]

> Legal justification for ethical behavior may not be sufficient because not everything that is unethical is illegal.

> The law is a good basis for ethical behavior because it embodies local cultural values.

CORRUPTION AND BRIBERY

Bribery is one facet of *corruption*. The determinants of corruption include cultural, legal, and political forces.[21] As defined by NGO Transparency International, corruption is "the abuse of entrusted power for private gain. When government officials are involved, bribes can be paid to obtain government contracts, or they can be as minor as trying to get government officials to do what they should be doing anyway. It can be grand, petty, and political depending on

> Bribery of public officials takes place to obtain government contracts or to get officials to do what they should be doing anyway.

Rejecting the temptation to ▶ receive bribes comes from principled behavior reinforced by corporate standards of conduct that prohibit bribes.

Source: Maryna Pleshkun/Shutterstock

FIGURE 11.2 Where Bribes Are (and Are Not) Business as Usual

Transparency International asked country experts, nonresidents, and residents about the overall extent of corruption (frequency and/or size of bribes) in the public and private sectors. The scale runs from 0 to 100, where 0 means that a country is perceived as highly corrupt and 100 means it is perceived as very clean. The figures include a sample of countries.

Source: Based on Transparency International, "TI Corruption Perceptions Index" (2015), transparency.org/cpi2015 (accessed February 15, 2016).

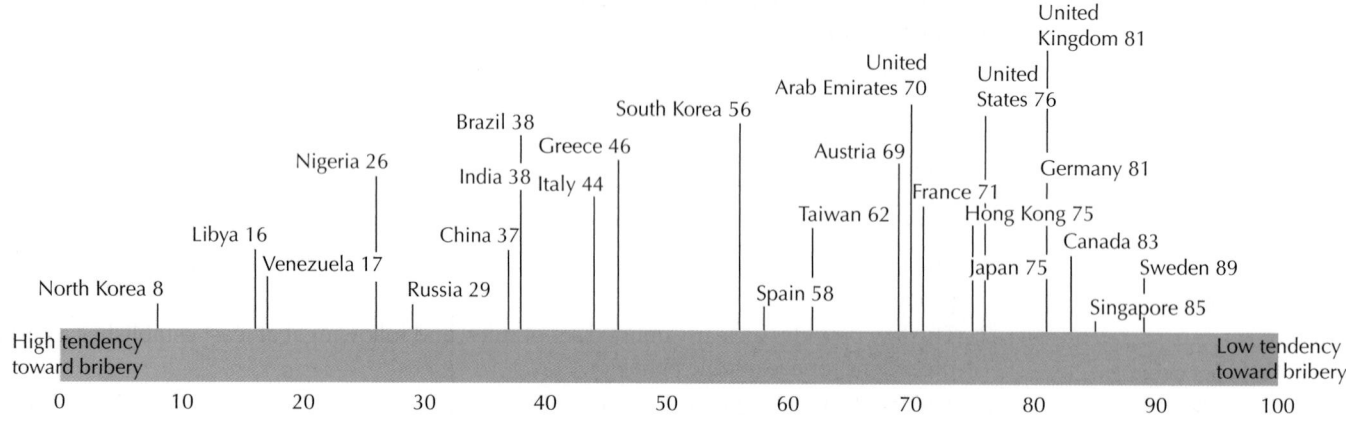

the amounts of money and the sector where it operates."[22] Bribes are payments or promises to pay cash or anything of value.

Figure 11.2 provides information on the Corruption Perceptions Index for 2015 by identifying the perceived levels of public-sector corruption for a small sample of countries. Although no country is free of corruption, it is depressing to note that the most corrupt countries tend to be in high-conflict regions, especially in Africa. Clearly poverty is an issue, although corruption and bribery occur at all income levels. Higher levels of corruption and bribery can also lead to or result from destabilized political environments, which can create problems for foreign investors as well as local companies. Transparency International not only publishes a Corruption Perceptions Index but also a Bribe Payers Index, which identifies which of the top 28 countries in the world are likely to have companies that pay bribes to do business abroad. In a recent survey, they reported that companies from Russia, China, Mexico, Indonesia, and the United Arab Emirates were most likely to pay bribes, either to foreign government officials or to other private sector companies.[23]

| Bribes are payments or promises to pay cash or anything of value.

PETROBRAS: CORRUPTION IN BRAZIL WITH A GLOBAL TWIST

Corruption is a widespread phenomenon. Sometimes it occurs within a country involving local politicians and companies or between companies and individuals outside of the political system. But corruption can also involve foreign actors. A good example involves Petrobras, the Brazilian national oil company, which has resulted in the disclosure of at least $2 billion in bribes, kickbacks, and money laundering, involving payments to company executives, the ruling Brazilian Worker's Party, and more than 50 sitting politicians and numerous companies trying to secure lucrative contracts with Petrobras. The speaker of Brazil's lower house of Congress and a powerful senator close to Brazil's president are also being implicated. On the international side, British Engineering group Rolls-Royce was also accused of paying bribes to secure contracts.[24] Other foreign engineering companies are also being investigated for overinflating services and funneling bribes to Petrobras officials and political parties. The Petrobras corruption scandal is one of nine such scandals targeted by Transparency International for a campaign called "Unmask the Corrupt."

THE CONSEQUENCES OF CORRUPTION

Corruption affects company performance and local economies. Higher levels of corruption, for instance, correlate strongly with lower national growth rates and lower levels of per capita income.[25] Corruption can also erode the authority of governments that condone it, as is being seen in Brazil because of the Petrobras scandal. Over the years, bribery-based scandals have led to the downfall of numerous heads of state, with many government officials and business executives being imprisoned, fined, or forced to resign. President Dilma of Brazil was impeached in 2016 over the bribery scandals. Moreover, disclosures of corruption not only damage the reputations of companies and whole countries, they also compromise the legitimacy of MNEs in the eyes of local and global communities when they become involved in the scandals.[26] Finally, corruption is expensive, inflating a company's costs and bloating its prices. Nevertheless, it persists as one of the most challenging concerns in international business and politics in the world today.

WHAT'S BEING DONE ABOUT CORRUPTION?

Many efforts are underway to slow the pace of bribery as an international business practice at international and national levels. International efforts to combat bribery include those established by the OECD (Organization for Economic Cooperation and Development), the ICC (International Chamber of Commerce), and the United Nations through UNCAC (United Nations Convention against Corruption). The problem is that none of the conventions have the force of law behind them. They can identify key issues in corruption and shine the spotlight on offenders, but legal action under the control of national governments must be taken for the fight against corruption to be effective.

The OECD comprises 34 mostly high-income countries from around the world. Its Anti-Bribery Convention, signed in 1997 by the 34 member countries plus six nonmember countries (Argentina, Brazil, Bulgaria, Colombia, Russia, and South Africa), establishes legally binding standards to criminalize bribery of foreign public officials in international business transactions and provides recommendations to the 40 signatory countries, which adopted the 2009 Anti-Bribery Recommendation. As shown in the case of Brazil, it's clear that the Convention isn't working as anticipated. Prior to the signing of the convention, only one country had made foreign bribery a crime, and most others treated foreign bribe payments as legitimate tax-deductible expenses. Of course, the member countries have to implement the recommendations into national law in order for them to have any weight. In addition, the countries have to do a better job of enforcement.[27] For example, a 2015 study by Transparency International found active enforcement in only 4 of the signatory countries, moderate enforcement in 6, and limited, little, or no enforcement in 29 countries.[28]

The European Union   The European Commission confirmed its support for strong anticorruption measures within the EU in a 2007 communication to the European Council, Parliament, and Economic and Social Committee. This included the adoption of the UN's official definition of corruption and support for many of the policies contained within international agreements. The communication also sanctions the work of the Commission's office of antifraud (OLAF), which conducts the affairs of the EU relevant to corporate and individual corruption, as well as an internal auditing service that monitors the activities of all of the Commission's departments. The EU does not have specific anticorruption legislation, but it encourages member nations to adopt high standards and follow them. In its most recent Anti-Corruption Report, the EU noted that corruption costs the EU 120 billion euro per year, and that efforts to combat corruption are very uneven across the EU[29]—thus the importance of national legislation.

National Initiative: The United States   There are several ways the United States has gotten involved in foreign corruption. For example, the **Foreign Corrupt Practices Act (FCPA)** outlaws bribery payments by U.S. firms to foreign officials, political parties, party officials, and political candidates. The coverage of the FCPA was extended in 1998 to include bribery by foreign firms operating in any U.S. territory. The FCPA applies not only to companies registered in the United States but also to any foreign company quoted on any U.S. stock exchange.

> The Foreign Corrupt Practices Act is U.S. legislation that makes bribery illegal. It applies to domestic or foreign operations and to company employees as well as their agents overseas.

Although it is legal to make payments to officials to expedite otherwise legitimate transactions (officially called *facilitating payments* but sometimes referred to as *speed money* or *grease money*), payments can't be made to officials who aren't directly responsible for the transactions in question. In 1988, an amendment to the FCPA actually excluded facilitating payments from the definition of *bribery.* Now, for example, payment to a customs official to clear legitimate merchandise is legal, whereas paying a government minister to influence a customs official is not.

The Justice Department can also fight against global corruption even when it doesn't affect government officials. For example, an estimated $150 million bribery scandal involving FIFA, the Swiss-based governing body of football (or soccer in the United States), was brought to light by the U.S. Justice Department because of income tax evasion in the United States by some of the parties, and because of the use of the U.S. financial system to facilitate the flow of funds. Even U.S.-based Nike was brought into the picture because of possible bribes paid to the Brazilian soccer federation. However, the allegations against Nike would not be prosecuted under the FCPA since it didn't involve a foreign government. The scandal became truly global, and the powerful head of FIFA was forced to resign.[30]

Another major legislative effort in the United States is the Sarbanes–Oxley Act (SOX), which was passed in 2002 as a response to an epidemic of well-known corporate scandals. SOX toughened standards with regard to corporate governance, financial disclosure, and oversight of accounting and auditing practices. With its passage, the Justice Department began to use the FCPA more aggressively to combat bribery.

Sarbanes–Oxley legislation in the United States is helpful in combating corruption through more effective corporate governance, financial disclosure, and public accounting oversight.

ETHICS AND THE ENVIRONMENT

Companies that extract natural resources, generate air or water waste, or manufacture products such as autos that generate pollution need to be concerned with their environmental impact.

In this section, we refer to the environment more narrowly in the context of pollution, both air and water, and global warming. Although global warming is the dominant concern from a global perspective, pollution is important as well. Companies can create water pollution through disposal of industrial waste into water systems as well as the inefficient use of water, which results more in water shortage than in water pollution. There is a link between air pollution and global warming, but the dominant greenhouse gas (GHG) that causes global warming is carbon dioxide, whereas air pollution is more affected by ozone (also a GHG), sulphur dioxide, nitrogen oxide, and particulates. In modern times, China and India are famous for poor air quality. Even though the advanced industrial countries have seen a reduction in air pollution due to industrial decline and clean air policies, there are still major issues. The European Union estimates that more than 400,000 Europeans die prematurely each year due to air pollution and that health-related issues from air pollution cost 3–7 percent of GDP.[31] Even as the world struggles with global warming, they still have to fight against air pollution.

As we saw in our opening case, GE has come to see eco-responsibility as a matter of protecting not only the future of the environment but also its own future. Like GE, companies contribute to environmental damage in a variety of ways. Some, for example, contaminate the air, soil, or water during manufacturing, or make products such as automobiles or electricity that release fossil-fuel contaminants into the atmosphere.

In extracting natural resources, other companies also have a direct and unmistakable effect on the environment. But even in these cases the issue isn't necessarily clear-cut. Granted, although some resources (such as minerals, gas, and oil) may not be renewable, others (such as timber) are, and some observers even suggest that resources can never really become scarce. Why? Because as they become less available, prices go up and technology or substitutes compensate.

WHAT IS "SUSTAINABILITY"?

Sustainability involves meeting the needs of the present without compromising the ability of future generations to meet their own needs while taking into account what is best for the people and the environment.

Sustainability means meeting the needs of the present without compromising the ability of future generations to meet their own needs. In this section, we use sustainability from the perspective of environmental sustainability. Proponents of the concept argue that sustainability considers what's best for both people and the environment. It is important that companies that affect the environment establish policies for responsible behavior toward the earth—a responsibility that has both cultural and legal ramifications.

But is it possible that sustainability is not only a good business practice, but also good business? GE has demonstrated that it makes good business sense to adopt a strong policy of sustainability, but it also has vast resources at its disposal. However, even born-global companies can adopt a sustainable strategy and generate export revenues at the same time.

Sustainability is no longer just good business practice. New businesses are emerging that are combining the idea of environmental responsibility and profitability.

GLOBAL WARMING AND THE PARIS AGREEMENT ON CLIMATE CHANGE

Global warming results from the release of greenhouse gases that trap heat in the atmosphere rather than allowing it to escape.

At the core of the United Nations Climate talks held in Paris in December 2015 is the concept that global climate change results from an increase in carbon dioxide and other gases that act like the roof of a greenhouse, trapping heat that would normally radiate into space, and thereby warming the planet. If carbon dioxide emissions aren't reduced and controlled, rising temperatures could have catastrophic consequences, including melting the polar ice cap, flooding coastal regions, shifting storm patterns, reducing farm output, causing drought, and even killing off plant and animal species.[32] The UN Framework Convention on Climate Change (UNFCCC) dates back to 1992 at the Rio Earth Summit. The **Kyoto Protocol**, which was signed in 1997, committed signatory countries to reducing the emissions to 5.2 percent below 1990 levels between 2008 and 2012. However, the Protocol did not include rapidly growing emerging economies like India and China who were two of the biggest polluters, the United States withdrew its support in 2001, and Canada withdrew from the Protocol in 2011.

The Paris Climate Agreement involving 187 countries targeted policies to reduce GHG emissions in order to keep the global average temperature to 2°C above pre-industrial levels.

However, the Paris Agreement changed everything. One hundred eighty-seven countries agreed to keep the increase in the global average temperature to 2°C above pre-industrial levels and try to achieve 1.5°. The countries also agreed to try to shoot for a target of zero net GHG emissions by the second half of the century.[33] That would involve moving away from fossil fuels for electricity and transportation, the two primary creators of GHG emissions, and moving more toward sustainable energy, such as solar and wind. To achieve this ambitious and improbable goal, all countries, including the emerging markets, intended to set national goals called "intended nationally determined contributions or INDCs." In addition, the developed countries agreed to provide $100 billion per year by 2020 to developing countries to help them adapt to climate change. The Paris Agreement discussed how to not only stabilize atmospheric concentration of GHG emissions, but also to avoid dangerous anthropogenic (human) interference with the climate. A big target of the latter concern is reducing deforestation and forest degradation in countries like Indonesia and Brazil. The problem is that shrinking forests contribute to GHG emissions, and their disappearance also eliminates a major natural way to sop up and store carbon dioxide.[34]

The success of the Paris Agreement to slow global warming has to come from two sources—the public sector and the private sector. The problem with the public sector is that countries still rely heavily on fossil fuels. India, for example, is the world's third-largest producer of coal, behind China with 46.1 percent and the United States with 11.6 percent. However, India generates 71 percent of its electricity from coal. Even though it invests heavily in alternative energy, especially solar, it will take a while to replace coal. Given the drop in oil prices since mid-2015, the shift to solar and wind energy will require a significant amount of government subsidies. The second source is the private sector. Most large MNEs, as demonstrated by GE in the opening case, are responding to global concerns about the environment by setting their own goals and reporting progress to their stakeholders. Most annual reports are replete with information about the efforts of the companies to reduce their carbon footprint and respond to other environmental concerns. However, a major challenge will be enticing companies to invest heavily in the development of alternative sources of energy without government subsidies to fund growth and money from outside investors. If investors don't see a viable return from investing in alternative energy, they decide not to invest in the energy sector.

Finally, bear in mind that many MNEs, based in the United States or elsewhere, also have the task of adapting to different standards in different countries. A European-based MNE with operations in, say, the United States, Germany, and China, and a U.S.-based MNE with plants in the same countries are faced with a smorgasbord of regulatory environments. On the one hand, the *legal* approach to responsible corporate behavior says an MNE can settle for operating in accord with local laws. The *ethical* approach, on the other hand, urges companies to go beyond the law to do whatever is necessary and economically feasible to reduce GHG emissions, given that they still have multiple stakeholders to satisfy.

ETHICAL DILEMMAS OF LABOR CONDITIONS

A major challenge facing MNEs today is the labor conditions of foreign workers, whether in their own offshore operations or their outsourced supply chains. They're especially critical in retail, clothing, footwear, electronics, and agriculture—industries in which MNEs typically outsource huge portions of production to independent companies abroad.

Point

Should MNEs Accept Full Responsibility for the Unethical Behavior of Their Employees?

Point **Yes** However, it is hard to know where the corruption begins and who knows what. On September 18, 2015, the U.S. Environmental Protection Agency announced that it was going to order German auto company, Volkswagen AG, one of the world's leading auto manufacturers and the largest in Europe, to recall over 500,000 vehicles in the United States because they were equipped with software that allowed them to evade emissions standards for reducing smog during testing. The software would recognize when a car was being tested and turn up emissions controls. Then when the car wasn't being tested, the software turned down the emissions controls, which resulted in better driving performance and fuel economy. It was estimated that in normal driving conditions, cars would emit up to 40 times the amount of pollutants allowed by U.S. government regulations. VW announced that the software designed to trick or "defeat" the emissions tests had been installed in millions of vehicles.[35] Eventually, this spread to certain models in Audi and Porsche, two other VW brands. How could this have happened? There were several very interesting dimensions to the case—different regulatory environments in Europe and the United States; VW's desire to increase its market share in the United States, especially in diesel cars; and the efforts of the regulators and VW itself to find out who knew what was going on.

One of the real ironies is that in its 2014 Sustainability Report, VW claimed that it was selling environmentally friendly products and meeting the guidelines for emissions of carbon dioxide, nitrogen oxide, and other pollutants. It also said it was in compliance with the Global Reporting Initiative (G4),

the UN Global Compact, and the German Sustainability Code. PricewaterhouseCoopers, one of the leading global public accounting firms, certified that the Sustainability Report was accurate. Not only did VW claim that it was operating according to high standards, but it also had a program to make sure its employees understood what the company stood for.

Different legal and regulatory systems also contributed to differences between U.S. and German stakeholders. Given that VW is a German Company and therefore under the regulatory environment of the European Union, it claimed that even though it was violating U.S. regulatory guidelines, it was not violating European regulatory guidelines. Is it possible that the software was not illegal in Europe, even though it was in the United States? There are not only different standards in the United States and EU, but there are also different testing procedures. In the United States, California has a stringent antipollution regulatory environment, and VW realized it had to find a way to be successful there if it wanted to increase the sale of its diesel engines. Also, U.S. regulators conduct their own tests to see if auto manufacturers' claims are accurate, whereas European regulators leave the testing and verification to the manufacturers themselves.[36] In order to keep from losing its U.S. customers, VW offered payments to customers who had bought cars with the diesel engines that had the "defeat" software installed. Of course, the legal environment in the United States that allows for class-action suits probably had something to do with that. Class-action lawsuits are relatively unknown in Europe, and payments were not offered to European customers, especially since VW didn't feel it was violating any law in Europe.

Should MNEs Accept Full Responsibility for the Unethical Behavior of Their Employees?

Counterpoint **No** VW obviously must take responsibility for installing the "defeat" software into some of the diesel models it is selling worldwide, but who is responsible for this happening? Wolfgang Hatz, the head of engines and transmissions for VW, is one of the key people in this scandal. He was also one of the first employees suspended by VW when the crisis broke in September 2015. One of his first concerns at VW was to figure out how to develop a diesel engine that would meet the stringent antipollution requirements set by the State of California. He was hired from the same position at Audi, one of VW's brands as well as Porsche. Hatz loved his cars, and he realized that to meet emission requirements VW would have to introduce more diesels into the United States. But how could they develop a car that would still be alluring and peppy, something that American drivers wanted? Diesels have better fuel economy and lower GHG emissions, but they also have higher smog-forming pollutants. One strategy being considered at VW was to build an alliance with Mercedes-Benz and BMW to develop new technologies, but Mr. Hatz and others at VW decided they wanted to develop a less expensive alternative. However, it was clear that this would not meet the emissions requirements. Rather than scale back their strategy to increase the sales of diesels in the U.S. market, someone decided to cheat.

But who was behind the scheme to introduce the "defeat" software? Was it Hatz? Was it Martin Winterkorn, the CEO who hired Mr. Hatz and who retired from VW just before the scandal hit? Or was it Matthias Muller, the current CEO of VW who has denied any knowledge of the software? An internal whistle-blower at VW was responsible for uncovering exaggerated carbon-dioxide and fuel economy claims, but

Counterpoint

the U.S. EPA uncovered the "defeat" software strategy for pollutants in the United States. VW decided to offer amnesty to anyone at VW who could shed any light on this subject. So far, a number of employees have stepped forward with some information, but we still don't know who is holding the smoking gun. Offering amnesty for information is relatively rare in these cases, but a similar thing happened in 2008 when the Siemens bribery scandal broke. In this case, it was determined that Siemens diverted funds filed under bogus consulting contracts into a network of "black accounts" for bribing officials in countries like Italy, Greece, Argentina, and Saudi Arabia. One thing that came out of the investigation is that Siemens had created a culture of corruption. Although the VW example doesn't involve bribery, it obviously involved corrupt behavior in the sense that somebody felt comfortable breaking regulatory guidelines in the United States and probably Europe in order to enhance sales. As noted by Hans-Dieter Potsch, VW's chairman, "There was a tolerance for breaking the rules. It proves not to have been a onetime error, but rather a chain of errors that were allowed to happen."[37]

Given what we know about VW's supposed commitment to a high level of corporate behavior, why didn't someone step forward and say "no!"

QUESTION

1. If you were an engineer working on the project to develop the software that would allow VW to avoid providing regulators and consumers accurate data about GHG and pollution emissions, would you have said "no"? Explain why or why not.

Major labor issues that MNEs get involved in through FDI or purchasing from independent manufacturers in developing countries are fair wages, child labor, working conditions, working hours, and freedom of association.

Figure 11.3 highlights the multiple pressures external stakeholders place on companies to encourage them to adopt responsible worker-related practices in their overseas operations. A more specific listing of worker issues was developed by the Ethical Trading Initiative (ETI), a British-based organization that focuses on MNEs' employment practices and whose standards are consistent with those adopted by the UN-based International Labor Organization. Its members include representatives from GAP Inc., Inditex, H&M, Marks & Spencer, The Body Shop International, and other companies, as well as from trade union organizations, NGOs, and governments. The objective of ETI is to get companies to adopt ethical employment policies and then monitor compliance with their overseas suppliers. ETI's trading initiative base code identifies the following issues:

1. Employment is freely chosen.
2. Freedom of association and the right to collective bargaining are respected.
3. Working conditions are safe and hygienic.
4. Child labor shall not be used.
5. Living wages are paid.
6. Working hours are not excessive.

FIGURE 11.3   Sources of Worker-Related Pressures in the Global Supply Chain

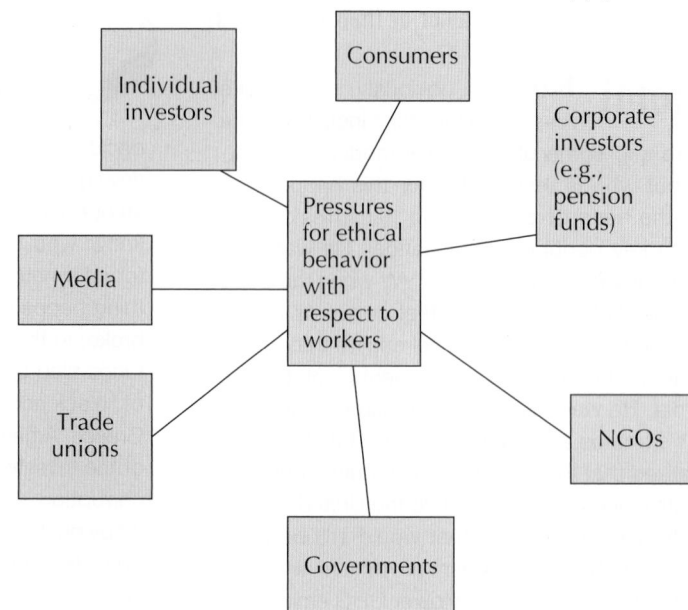

7. No discrimination is practiced.
8. Regular employment is provided.
9. No harsh or inhumane treatment is allowed.[38]

Although all issues identified by ETI are important, we focus on the one that, for a variety of good reasons, receives significant attention: *child labor.*

THE PROBLEM OF CHILD LABOR

Let's start by considering a couple of very brief cases:

- There are two arguments for the use of children in the Indian carpet industry: (1) they're better suited than adults to perform certain tasks, and (2) if they weren't employed, they'd be even worse off. In fact, children in India are often put to work because parents don't earn enough to support families; if parents can't pay off debts, their children are often *indentured* to creditors.

- In the 1990s, the impoverished Asian nation of Bangladesh was pressured to stop employing thousands of child workers or face U.S. trade sanctions. In this case, the plight of the children did in fact go from bad to worse. Between 5,000 and 7,000 young girls, for example, went from factory work to prostitution.[39]

According to the International Labor Organization (ILO), a UN institution, 168 million children between the ages of 5 and 17 are not legally working worldwide.[40] The challenge is that much of this data is not current or is difficult to get. However, the ILO has very specific guidelines describing what it considers child labor to be and what the worst forms of child labor are. In particular, the worst forms involve slavery and prostitution—illicit activities that are a danger to the health, safety, and morals of a child. ILO guidelines state that children who are at least 12–14 years old may be employed in "light" work that's not harmful to their health, is less than 14 hours a week, and doesn't interfere with school. All children under the age of 18 should be protected against the most abusive labor conditions.[41]

For MNEs, the basic challenge is negotiating a global labyrinth of business environments with different cultural, legal, and political rules than those they're used to at home. In addition, they typically rely on local suppliers who are subject to specifically local pressures.

WHAT MNES CAN AND CAN'T DO

In spite of these difficulties, MNEs are not powerless when it comes to labor-related matters in overseas facilities. When the Swedish retailer IKEA ran into trouble in India for buying carpets from local companies that relied heavily on extensive child labor, it identified and tackled two different problems rather than try to force suppliers to stop exploiting the children. First, it helped working mothers increase family earning power so they could escape the clutches of the loan sharks to whom they were putting up their children as collateral. Second, it set up "bridge schools" to enable working children to enter mainstream education channels within a year.[42]

Frequently, MNEs operating in countries with very different labor policies succumb to the pressure to simply leave the market. Usually, this turns out to be a shortsighted decision. Research shows, for instance, that companies like IKEA have substantially improved the conditions of workers in overseas facilities. Granted, MNEs are in no position to revolutionize the employment practices of the countries in which they operate, but they can improve conditions at subcontract facilities and even influence the guidelines set by other foreign investors.[43]

CORPORATE CODES OF ETHICS: HOW SHOULD A COMPANY BEHAVE?

MOTIVATIONS FOR CORPORATE RESPONSIBILITY

Companies generally experience four strong motivations for acting responsibly:

1. Unethical and irresponsible behavior can result in *legal headaches,* especially in such areas as financial mismanagement, bribery, and product safety.
2. Such behavior could also result in *consumer action* such as a boycott.
3. Unethical behavior can affect *employee morale.* Conversely, responsible behavior can have a positive influence on a workforce, both at corporate headquarters and in overseas facilities.
4. You never know when *bad publicity* is going to cost you sales. Perhaps this concern is one reason why many global apparel and clothing companies responded so quickly to criticism about unfair employment practices in developing countries.

DEVELOPING A CODE OF CONDUCT

A code of conduct is a major component of most companies' strategies for ethical and socially responsible behavior. In the context of international operations, it can take the form of two perspectives: external and internal. Codes of conduct are useful insofar as they give companies some general guidance on how to operate. The practical challenge for the company is familiarizing itself with the codes of many different organizations and using them to fashion its own *internal code of conduct.*

What makes a good internal code of conduct? Here are four criteria:

1. *It sets global policies with which everyone working anywhere for the company must comply.* A good example is the code promulgated by the Finnish cell-phone company Nokia, which discusses how its code was set, who approved it, how it is communicated to its employees, and what its foundation values are.
2. *It communicates company policies not only to all employees but to all suppliers and subcontractors as well.*
3. *It ensures that the policies laid out in the code are carried out.* This usually occurs through training programs where employees sign off on their compliance and sometimes through internal audits.

Margin notes:

Some companies avoid operating in countries where child labor is employed, whereas others try to establish responsible policies in those same countries.

Companies need to act responsibly because unethical and irresponsible behavior

- could result in legal sanctions,
- could result in consumer boycotts,
- could lower employee morale,
- could cost sales because of bad publicity.

A major component in a company's strategy for ethical and socially responsible behavior is a code of conduct.

Codes of conduct involve four dimensions:

- Setting a global policy that must be complied with wherever the company operates
- Communicating the code to employees, suppliers, and subcontractors
- Ensuring that policies are carried out
- Reporting results to external stakeholders

4. *It reports the results to external stakeholders.* This usually occurs in a company's annual report to shareholders, but GE uses social media to communicate with external stakeholders, a common practice of most MNEs. In addition, a major contributor to enhanced transparency is the Global Reporting Initiative (or GRI) which has issued G4 sustainability reporting guidelines that identify several different areas related to the environment, society, and the economy. GRI is an independent international organization that links the interests of governments, companies, and various stakeholders to encourage responsible behavior by companies. The reports are broad and comprehensive and pull together many of the issues discussed in the chapter.[44]

Looking to the Future
Dealing with Ethical Dilemmas in the Global Economy

This chapter has continued the discussion from Chapter 1 on the effects of globalization, but with more focus on the ethical issues and how companies can be more responsible as they operate abroad. Chapter 1 identified three scenarios on the future of globalization:

- Further globalization is inevitable.
- International business will grow primarily along regional rather than global lines.
- Forces working against further globalization and international business will slow down the growth of both.

Regardless of what happens, the more companies expand abroad, the greater the likelihood they will have hard decisions to make on how they should operate in a socially responsible manner. As discussed by Bartlett and Beamish[45], MNEs can operate in one four major ways. They can be exploitative, which is the model of the past. However, some MNEs still operate exploitatively in poorer countries that do not have the strength to stand up for what they think is best. Second, they can operate on a transactional basis where they engage in doing deals and respecting the law. The challenge is that they may have to choose between local law and the law of the country where their corporate headquarters is domiciled. Third, they can be responsive in the sense of trying to make a difference in the countries where they operate. This is clearly the direction that most large MNEs find themselves. Many of them have signed on to the UN Global compact and try to make a difference in human rights, labor standards, the environment, and anticorruption. Finally, they can be transformative in terms of taking the lead in generating broad change. This is far more difficult and requires a joint partnership with NGOs and local governments, often responding to the wishes of their stakeholders.

It is clear that social media will have a greater impact on socially responsible behavior in the future. Historically, we have always thought that one of the keys to transparency is an independent press willing to investigate and report on wrongdoings. But now social media such as Facebook, Twitter, YouTube, and so on have added an important new dimension to transparency. Neither companies nor governments can hide in the shadows, so it is critical for socially responsible companies to be transparent, and a solid social media strategy is an important dimension of their transparency. ■

Anglo American PLC in South Africa: What Do You Do When Costs Reach Epidemic Proportions?

By now it should be obvious that, regardless of where it chooses to do business, an MNE is going to face quite a variety of threats and disruptions to its plans and operations, ranging from bureaucratic corruption and political instability to terrorism and war. In 2007, Anglo American PLC, at that time one of the world's largest gold miners, found itself facing a threat that defies most traditional categories of things that complicate business overseas—an HIV/AIDS epidemic in South Africa.[46]

In 2002, Anglo American made a landmark decision to provide free antiretroviral therapy (ART) to HIV-infected employees there. Surprisingly, however, this commitment met with mixed reactions from various stakeholders and achieved only controversial results. Now the U.K.-based company is asking itself, "Where do we go from here?"

AIDS in South Africa

How bad must a disease be to be accorded the status of an "epidemic"? When Anglo American was first confronted with the issues of HIV/AIDS, sub-Saharan Africa was home to just over 10 percent of the world's population and 60 percent of all people infected with HIV, the virus that causes AIDS. South Africa had the highest number of people living with HIV/AIDS and one of the world's highest rates of HIV infection and mortality from AIDS-related diseases.

Thus, over the past decade the spread of HIV/AIDS has had a profound impact on the people of South Africa and their economy. Life expectancy is 56.1 years compared to, say, 76.8 years in Poland, a country with a similar population size and per capita GDP. AIDS has also devastated the country's economy. Between 1992 and 2002, South Africa lost $7 billion annually—around 2 percent of GDP—as a result of AIDS-related worker deaths. Experts were predicting that, if AIDS continued to spread throughout sub-Saharan Africa at the same pace, it would continue to reduce per capita growth by 1 to 2 percent per year and, in the worst-affected countries, cut annual GDP growth by as much as 0.6 percent by 2010. The consequences include both diminishing populations and shrinking economies, with GDPs deflating anywhere from 20 to 40 percent of the sizes they would have reached in the absence of AIDS.

Anglo American Operations in South Africa

Anglo American PLC is a diversified mining conglomerate operating worldwide in 45 countries and employing 133,900 employees to produce diamonds, precious metals (platinum), base metals (copper, nickel, zinc, and phosphates), and bulk metals (for ferrous metals and coal). Founded in 1917 as the Anglo American Corporation of South Africa, it

HIV awareness in Capetown, South ▶ Africa, is an important part of the effort to control HIV/AIDS.

Source: Monkey Business Images/Shutterstock

was South Africa's first home-based public limited company, but now it is a multinational firm headquartered in London.

In spite of its global spread, the company dominates South Africa's domestic economy through direct employment, contractors, and its supply chain.

Anglo American and ART

With such a huge investment in South Africa, Anglo American has been hit hard by the HIV/AIDS epidemic. Having recognized the threat as far back as the early 1990s, Anglo was one of the first corporations to develop a comprehensive, proactive strategy to combat the ravages of the disease on its workforce and the repercussions for its operations.

Originally, the program consisted of prevention initiatives aimed at education and awareness, the distribution of condoms, financial and skill-related training to alleviate poverty, and a survey system to monitor the prevalence of the infection. Eventually, these policies were expanded to include voluntary counseling, testing, and care-and-wellness programs, and the services of all programs were extended to cover not only the families of employees but also the populations of surrounding communities. Anglo also became a member of the Global Business Council on HIV/AIDS, an organization of multinational companies that focuses on alleviating the effects of AIDS throughout the world and on protecting the rights of infected workers.

By adopting these strategies so early, Anglo American became a de facto leader in the private-sector fight against HIV/AIDS in Africa. Many other MNEs—including Coca-Cola, Ford, Colgate-Palmolive, and Chevron Texaco—soon followed Anglo's example and initiated prevention, education, and wellness programs of their own. Even then, however, the majority of companies operating in South Africa still hesitated, which is why Anglo's 2002 announcement that it would provide ART to its South African workforce (at company expense) was met with a good deal of excited approval from such interested parties as the WHO, the Global Business Council on HIV/AIDS, and a host of other NGOs.

The Costs of Operating in an Epidemic

The incentive for Anglo American's ART program largely came from the failure of its AIDS-prevention efforts to make much headway in stemming the spread of the disease. By 2001, the prevalence of HIV-positive workers had risen to an average of 21 percent across all operations—a figure that was climbing steadily at a rate of 2 percent annually. It was estimated that HIV/AIDS was adding as much as $5 to the cost of producing one ounce of gold, thereby tacking on $11 million a year to the company's production costs. Then there was the $7 million it was spending annually to combat such AIDS-related illnesses as tuberculosis (which was five times as prevalent as it had been just a decade earlier).

Finally, in addition to losses in productivity, the company had to bear the costs entailed by high levels of absenteeism, the constant retraining of replacement workers, and burgeoning payouts in health, hospitalization, and death benefits. Studies conducted at the time indicated not only that the costs of AIDS could reach as much as 7.2 percent of the company's total wage bill but also that the costs of leaving employees untreated would be even higher than the cost of providing ART.

Nine years after it rolled out its ART program, Anglo now finds itself struggling to please various stakeholders and determine whether all of its efforts are making a difference in the underlying problem or merely masking its effects. By the end of 2009, for instance, although 27 percent of the HIV-infected workforce were receiving ART, the company still struggled with high rates of non-adherence and dropout from treatment regimens.

Anglo also faces the problem of spiraling costs for the program itself. Even though the prices of most of the necessary drugs have been decreasing, the cost of distributing them remains high, and the treatment regimen costs the company an estimated $4,000 per year per employee—quite expensive, especially compared to the wages and benefits that Anglo typically offers mineworkers. (Average monthly wages in the South African mining industry are about 5,100 rand, or US$830.) Meanwhile, as Anglo officials continue to remind investors that treating workers ultimately serves the bottom line, recent estimates project a total cost to the company of $1 billion or more over 10 years.

On the upside, cost per patient should decrease as the number of workers participating in the program increases. Unfortunately, one of the biggest challenges facing Anglo is encouraging participation among a migrant and largely uneducated workforce laboring under harsh conditions in an unstable environment. In South Africa, HIV/AIDS still carries a severe stigma, and many South Africans refuse to be tested or to admit they've been infected for fear of discrimination by managers, fellow employees, and even society at large. Moreover, many of those who agreed to participate have been confused by rumors and misinformation, leading them to assume that they could stop using condoms once they were on the drugs—a situation, of course, that only exacerbated the prevalence of unsafe behavior.

In addition, harsh working conditions often make it hard for workers to take medications on time or to deal with certain side effects. Finally, migrant workers—about four-fifths of the total workforce—who come from isolated villages hundreds of miles away are 2.5 times more likely to contract the disease, which they take with them back to their villages.

Constituencies and Critics

Anglo American also faces the problem of pressure from various stakeholders. The National Union of Mineworkers has been hesitant to voice its support, citing the company's limitations on health-insurance benefits and lack of cooperation with national agencies. The union has also accused the company of helping to foster working conditions that exacerbate the problem. Even Brian Gilbertson, former CEO of BHP Billiton, another large mining concern operating in South Africa, charged Anglo with merely trying to contain the problem instead of attacking its underlying causes, saying, "You don't approach the problem by just throwing drugs at it."

Anglo has countered many of these criticisms, insisting that it's beyond the resources and capacity of a single company to combat the overall problem, and it has called for more involvement on the part of the South African government. Instead of cooperation, however, the company initially encountered outright opposition from political leaders.

In addition, dealing with pharmaceutical companies has proved a tricky proposition. On the one hand, Anglo has a deal with GlaxoSmithKline allowing it to purchase ART drugs at a tenth of the market price in the industrialized world (the same that GSK charges not-for-profit organizations). At the same time, however, other pharmaceutical companies have been hesitant and unreliable at best, promising price cuts and then reneging over fears of violating intellectual property rights. As a matter of fact, several of these companies, complaining that cheap generic drugs made available in Africa will eventually be resold by profiteers on higher-priced Western markets, have put their energies into suing the South African government for what they claim to be generally poor enforcement of their patent rights.

Given the many challenges Anglo has faced, not to mention the opposition from unexpected quarters, some observers have gone so far as to suggest that the company would be better off simply pulling back on its HIV/AIDS treatment program rather than pouring more resources into the effort to make it work. In the long run, however, Anglo must consider the continued pressure it will get from ethically minded shareholders as well as its own sense of moral responsibility.

There are also indications that the future may not be as bleak as it initially appeared. Due to an aggressive global campaign to deal with HIV/AIDs, new HIV infections dropped by 41 percent between 2000 and 2014. AIDS related deaths also fell by 48 percent. For its part, Anglo American extended its treatment program to the dependents of its employees in 2008, and by 2014, 86 percent of its employees and dependents received free ART therapy, testing, and treatment.

Anglo American's strategy for HIV/AIDS intervention has in some ways become a model closely followed by other companies with operations in regions heavily affected by the disease. Perhaps the criticism for such interventions is waning as companies continue to adopt responsible and effective initiatives for HIV/AIDS treatment.

QUESTIONS

11-3. Because such a large percentage of its workforce consists of migrant workers who are more likely to acquire and spread HIV/AIDS, should Anglo adopt the policy of not hiring migrant workers? Should the South African government close the doors to migrant workers?

11-4. What role do pharmaceutical companies play in responding to the HIV/AIDS epidemic in South Africa? Given that HIV/AIDS drugs can be exported from India at a lower cost than from the pharmaceutical companies themselves, should Anglo just import the drugs to be used for their employees?

MyLab Management

Go to **mymanagementlab.com** for the following Assisted-graded writing questions:

11-5   Who are the various stakeholders that Anglo American needs to consider as it adopts an effective HIV/AIDS strategy?

11-6   What are the pros and cons of Anglo's adoption of an aggressive strategy in combating HIV/AIDS among its South African workforce? What recommendations would you give the company concerning its HIV/AIDS policy?

Endnotes

Scan for Endnotes or go to www.pearsonglobaleditions.com/Daniels

CHAPTER 12
Strategies for International Business

OBJECTIVES

After studying this chapter, you should be able to

12-1   Explain the idea of strategy in the MNE

12-2   Profile how executives make strategy

12-3   Differentiate resources, capabilities, and core competencies

12-4   Assess approaches to create value

12-5   Diagram the features and functions of the value chain

12-6   Compare global integration and local responsiveness

12-7   Differentiate the types of strategies used by MNEs

MyLab Management®
Improve Your Performance!
When you see this icon ✪, visit **www.mymanagementlab.com** for activities that are applied, personalized, and offer immediate feedback.

Vision without action is a daydream. Action without vision is a nightmare.

—Japanese proverb

Source: aastock. Shutterstock

Zara's Disruptive Vision: Data-Driven Fast-Fashion[1]

Apparel and textile is one of the largest industries in the world. It employs approximately 75 million people and generates more than US$3 trillion in transactions.[2] Its activities are global in scale and scope; design, branding, fiber production, fabric cutting, assembly, finishing work, logistics, merchandising, and marketing functions circle the world. Traditionally, big retailers drive the market, determining what to make, where to make it, how to distribute it, and then, how to sell it. Operationally, global apparel companies and national retailers outsource apparel production via global brokers, such as Li & Fung. The latter, for instance, supplies billions of pieces of apparel to department stores, hypermarkets, specialty stores, and e-commerce sites worldwide. It owns no fabric mills, no sewing machines, and no clothing factories. Rather, Li & Fung oversees a network of 15,000 suppliers spanning 60 countries that can make virtually any clothing article.[3]

Historically, the typical garment maker is a small-scale, labor-intensive operation, usually located in a low-wage country that employs a few to a few dozen workers. There, workers make specific pieces of apparel, often in a narrow range of sizes and colors, which global brokers then integrate with the output of hundreds of other such companies that span dozens of countries. As more companies in more countries make more specialized products (i.e., one factory makes zippers, one makes linings, one makes buttons, and so on), global brokers perform as cross-border intermediaries and supervise the logistics and assembly of components into finished goods. Ultimately, these goods are distributed to apparel retailers worldwide.

Responding to ever-changing fashion, markets relentlessly pressure apparel retailers to have the right style in the right sizes in the right quantities at the right time for the right price. In turn, they press global brokers to improve coordination among the many different players. By planning collections closer to the selling season, testing the market, placing smaller initial orders, and reordering more frequently, retailers can reduce forecasting errors and avoid the dreaded "death by inventory."[4]

Industry wisdom and historic practice spurred apparel firms, no matter how big or small, to choose a "sliver" of a particular activity (i.e., make zippers, manage logistics, focus on retail operations) instead of creating value across multiple slivers. Effectively, the global apparel industry pressed firms to see strategy in terms of 'doing what you do best and outsourcing the rest.'

CHANGING MARKETS, CHANGING OPPORTUNITIES

Steadily, globalization resets the global apparel industry. Fewer barriers, better logistics, and improving technologies create paths to disrupt industry standards. That is, rather than accepting the deter-minism of industry structure, some managers bet on revolutionary visions and radical missions.[5] A compelling example is the compression of cycle times in the apparel-buyer chain. Traditionally, moving a garment from designer to brokers to factories to shops takes approximately six months—three to design a new collection and another three to make and ship it. Now, a few companies, notably H&M, have cut the cycle to three to five months. One, Zara, has slashed the cycle to a phenomenal two weeks. Zara's vision of data-driven fast-fashion, by outright rejection of sacred rules about strategy and success, has disrupted long-running principles and practices in the apparel industry.[6] For instance, unlike its rivals, Zara makes most of what it sells, shuns advertising, avoids sales, and directs distribution and delivery. These choices, once seen as heresies, have propelled Zara to the world's leading apparel company and made its founder, Amancio Ortega, the world's second-wealthiest person with a fortune of nearly $70 billion.[7]

THE VISION OF FAST FASHION

In 1975, Señor Ortega opened a small clothing shop, 'Zara,' in La Coruña, a small, shipbuilding town found in a remote section of Spain, far away from the fashion capitals of New York, London, Paris, Milan, and Tokyo.[8] Now, in 2016, from its humble beginnings, there are more than 2,000 Zara storefronts strategically located in leading cities spanning 88 countries.[9] In the beginning, Ortega had a straightforward vision: "Give customers what they want, and get it to them faster than anyone else."[10] Over the years, Zara's founding vision has held true, and today anchors its mission: "satisfying the desires of our customers...we plan to continuously innovate our business to improve your experience. We promise to provide new designs for quality materials that are affordable."[11] Others offer clever spins, characterizing Zara's vision as "Armani at moderate prices," or "Banana Republic priced like Old Navy."[12] No matter the nuance, Zara's vision of data-driven fast-fashion anchors its strategy to integrate cutting-edge systems; state-of-the-art information technology; efficient, scale-driven production; astonishing logistics; and alluring distribution that designs, makes, moves, and sells sophisticated, yet affordable, apparel.

BUILDING A STRATEGY OF FAST FASHION

Effectively disrupting a global industry requires radically rethinking what customers want, how you make and market it, and how you make money doing so. Zara, in starting and sustaining the data-driven fast-fashion revolution, translates its vision into a practical strategy through a range of ingenious choices in acquiring resources, developing capabilities, and creating competencies. Separately and collectively, these anchor Zara's competitiveness.

Resources

Making and selling fast fashion calls for an exquisitely tuned set of technological expertise, designers, manufacturing systems, logistic know-how, and retail locations. Progressively, Zara has developed world-class resources in these functions.

Manufacturing   Zara, as does virtually every other apparel firm, sources finished garments, like generic t-shirts, slips, and the like, from suppliers in Europe, North Africa, and Asia. Unlike its rivals, Zara employs more than 20,000 people, distributed across 23 factories circling La Coruña, to make more than half of its fashion garments. Zara's production prowess stems from Ortega's insight that exploiting short-lived fashion trends requires speedy designs and decision—which, operationally, means making items close to home. Hence, Zara makes millions of its most time- and fashion-sensitive products in its own state-of-the-art factories on its own schedule based on its own market data that are then fed into its own logistic system to quickly deliver them to its own storefronts.

Logistics   Garments flow through Zara's distribution center in La Coruña—about the size of 90 football fields—or smaller satellite centers in Brazil and Mexico. In La Coruña, garments travel along 125 miles of underground rails that link its factories. Along the way, they are sorted in carousels capable of processing 45,000 folded garments per hour. Zara ships more than 2.5 million items per week to its stores worldwide. Custom orders reach its stores in Europe, the Middle East, and much of the United States in 24 hours, and 48 hours for Asia and Latin America.

Retail Sites   If there is marketing at Zara, it's done via high-profile real estate. "We invest in prime locations. We place great care in the presentation of our storefronts. That is how we project our image" explained Director Luis Blanc. Zara's stores command high-profile slots in premier shopping venues such as the Champs-Elysées in Paris, Regent Street in London, Fifth Avenue in New York, and Nanjing Road in Shanghai. The opening photo, for example, showcases Zara's flagship storefront in Barcelona. Its location strategy has created interesting tensions. Noted a consultant, "Prada wants to be next to Gucci, Gucci wants to be next to Prada. The retail strategy for luxury brands is to try to keep as far away from the likes of Zara. Zara's strategy is to get as close to them as possible."[13]

Capabilities

Building factories and opening shops set the firm's resources. Managers' insight in how best to bundle them to complete an activity in a way that is integrative, consistent, and productive creates capabilities. Expectedly, Zara shines in translating ordinary aspects of a firm, such as factories and shops, into formidable capabilities.

Design   Zara's designers gather data from store managers, industry publications, TV, Internet, and films. Its trend spotters focus on university campuses and nightclubs. Its slaves-to-fashion staff snaps photos at couture shows and posts them to headquarters. There, designers sift the data, quickly converting the latest, greatest looks into affordable, hot fashion for the masses. Zara often translates a fashion trend from a catwalk in Paris to a blouse or ensemble ready for sale in Shanghai in as little as two weeks; its rivals, notably Gap and H&M, take months to do the same. For example, when Madonna played a series of concerts in Spain, teenage girls arrived at her final show sporting a Zara knockoff of the outfit that she had worn during her first show. Zara's real-time sense of what people want to wear lets it tap the convergence of fashion and taste across national boundaries. It does not adapt products to a particular country's preferences, but looks to standardize its designs for the global market. Executives reason that offering customers an affordable, quality garment with an edgy vibe, in effect a hard-to-resist value proposition, globalizes fashion trends.[14]

Scenery and Scarcity   Attractive stores, both inside and out, are vital to Zara's mystique. Explains Luis Blanc, "We want our clients to enter a beautiful store where they are offered the latest fashions. We want our customers to understand that if they like something, they must buy it now because it won't be in the shops the following week. It is all about creating a climate of scarcity and opportunity."[15] Fitting in with fancy neighbors, like Prada and Gucci, requires that Zara put its best face forward. Retail specialists roam the globe, adjusting window displays, testing store ambience, and rethinking presentation schemes. Just as layouts are always changing, so too is the look of the inventory mix. Zara rejects the idea of conventional spring and fall clothing collections in favor of "live collections" that are designed, manufactured, and sold almost as quickly as customers' fleeting tastes—no style lasts more than four weeks.[16]

Promotion   Zara's product policy emphasizes reasonable quality, affordability, and high fashion. It has little use for advertising or promotion. Amancio Ortega saw advertising as a "pointless distraction"; he himself has never given an interview and rarely allows his picture to be taken.[17] Zara spends just 0.3 percent of sales on advertising, compared with 3 to 4 percent for most fashion retailers. It avoids flashy campaigns, relying instead on word-of mouth among loyal shoppers. Like its founder, it does not promote itself; it leaves that to thrilled customers.

Core Competencies

Just as bright managers combine resources into capabilities, they also transform capabilities into core competencies. Somewhat difficult to pinpoint, one can think of a core competency as the special outlook, skill, or technology that, by synthesizing links between resources and capabilities, sets and sustains the firm's ability to create superior value for its customers.

Flexibility   Zara has quick turnaround on fashion trends—many items you see in its stores didn't exist a few weeks earlier. Explains Director Marcos Lopez, "The key driver in our stores is the right fashion. Price is important, but it comes second."[18] Zara aggressively prices its products, and adjusts pricing for the international market, making customers in foreign markets bear the costs of shipping products from Spain.[19] Likewise, if the product line fails to excite customers, Zara can "scrap an entire production line if it is not selling. We can dye collections in new colors, and we can create a new fashion line in days."[20] Integrating new ideas and new designs into reasonably priced, high-fashion garments that are available worldwide within two weeks is an awfully hard task. Zara's capacity to blend its resources and capabilities successfully develops a value-creating, hard-to-copy competency—perhaps best seen in its rivals' struggles to do so.

Fashion-Tech   Zara's stores, besides presenting its face to the world, function as grassroots marketing agents. Networked stores feed sales data and customer requests (the latter helping to localize otherwise globally standardized products) to headquarters in La Coruña. At the center of the Zara-web, physically and symbolically, is "The Cube," the gleaming central command of the company. Here, designers, operations folks, and strategic planners bundle and blend resources and capabilities, experimenting with ways to leverage real-time data into real-time fashions. Designers, for instance, simulate product presentation and positioning (even testing the acoustics of the in-store soundtrack) on its "Fashion Street," a Potemkinesque strip of mock storefronts that mimic the layout of its strategically significant storefronts around the world. Constant and continual refinement of resources and capabilities fortifies Zara's competencies.

Clothes Shopping as an Exciting Adventure   Zara's timeliness of its offerings, aura of exclusiveness, captivating in-store ambience, and positive word of mouth, fed by rapid product turnover, leverages various resources and capabilities. Loyal shoppers learn which days of the week the latest, greatest fashions are delivered—so-called "Z-days"—and shop accordingly. Zara fuels the frenzy with small shipments—say, three or four dresses in a particular style—to a store. Small shipments make for sparsely stocked shelves. Moreover, products have a display limit of one month. Rapid turnover does the rest: even though consumers visit Zara frequently, when they return, things look different. The CEO of the National Retail Federation, reflecting on Z-days, rapid turnover, and sparse inventory, marveled, "It's like you walk into a new store every two weeks."[21]

MOVING ONWARD

The first Zara shop opened its doors in 1975 in La Coruña. Today, there are more than 2,000 outlets and, on average, a new one opens every day. The elegant clarity of Zara's vision, mission, and strategy, translated into a compelling set of resources, capabilities, and competencies, supports its stunning success. Impressive in its own right, Zara's choice to be great rejected the contrary imperatives of long-established strategic standards in the global apparel industry.[22] Presently, no other apparel company comes close to designing, making, moving, and selling fashion as speedily as Zara. Its success leaves rivals with less time to figure out how to better configure and coordinate their operations. Some stay in the game, such as H&M, while others fall further behind, notably Gap. Ultimately, struggling rivals must follow Zara's strategic lead—if they don't, warns a leading retail analyst, they "won't be in business in 10 years."[23] ∎

QUESTIONS[24]

✪ **12-1.** Which element of Zara's strategy do you believe best explains its success?

✪ **12-2.** Assess the difficulty a competitor, such as Gap, faces trying to re-create the resources, capabilities, and core competencies that define Zara.

STRATEGY IN THE MNE

Evolving customer preferences, innovative competitors, changing market structures, and shifting institutional contexts create opportunities and threats. The job of the strategist is identifying the implications of these situations to which products to make, where to make them, where to sell them, how to compete, and, all the while, earn a profit. Doing so, as we'll see in this and subsequent chapters, centers on how managers assess and enter foreign markets, make investments, form alliances, and organize activities. Then, given these configuration choices, we profile how managers implement marketing, manufacturing, supply, accounting, finance, and human resource programs.[25]

For the strategist in the MNE, the global marketplace is often too much of a good thing. The World Bank identifies 214 discrete economic environments in the world today—188 countries and 26 economies with populations of more than 30,000. The former include

Superior performance requires managers to plan for the opportunities and threats in the global business environment.

countries that most are familiar with, such as Australia, China, France, Indonesia, and so on. The set of 26 includes some that many have likely heard of, such as Bermuda or Macau, but also others that many have not, such as the Isle of Man or Vanuatu.[26] No matter the designation, managers scan these markets, evaluating events and trends in mapping the ideal path to formulate and implement a value-creating strategy.

The scale and scope of opportunities and, inevitably, threats spanning 214 markets can overwhelm analysis. Complicating matters is ever-present resource scarcity. The reality of never enough time, talent, and capital means managers, at some point, must make choices: which opportunities to pursue, which to pass, and then, based on the targeted products and markets, what actions to take to do so. These tasks focus our attention on the idea of strategy. In principle, **strategy** is an integrated set of choices and commitments that supports and sustains an MNE's competitiveness. It defines and communicates an MNE's plan on how it will use its resources, capabilities, and competencies to compete in different countries (see Figure 12.1). Strategy maps an MNE's plan to create value, both for itself and its stakeholders. Importantly, strategy specifies what an MNE will do and what it will not do. Strategy calls on managers to deal with the questions and complexities that follow from cross-checking opportunities with competencies, assessing competitive threats, and setting and sustaining superior performance. As tough as that sounds, the performance track record of MNEs consistently confirms that managers make it happen, formulating strategies that build endlessly clever new ways to build productive and profitable enterprises.[27]

> Strategy is an integrated and coordinated set of commitments and actions that reflects the company's present situation, identifies the direction it should go, and determines how it will get there.

GETTING STARTED: VISION AND MISSION

Strategy starts with a vision and a mission. The MNE's **vision**, a future-oriented declaration of its purpose and aspirations, outlines its broad ambitions. It communicates to stakeholders, namely employees, stockholders, governments, partners, suppliers, customers, and society, what the MNE is, where it is going, and the values that will guide its efforts. The MNE's **mission** complements its vision. Whereas the vision statement inspires people to dream, the mission statement inspires them to action. It communicates what the MNE is going to do, why it's going to do that, and the general approach to doing so. Put differently, the vision outlines the goals to pursue, while the mission specifies the objectives to attain. Combined, an MNE's vision and mission define its purpose, values, goals, and direction.[28]

> Vision is the idealization of what an MNE firm wants to be. It expresses, in broad terms, its ultimate goal.

> The MNE's mission defines its business, its objectives, and its approach to achieve them.

FIGURE 12.1   The Role of Strategy in IB

Chapter 1 showed that that the MNE's operating environment includes physical, cultural, market, monetary, and competitive factors. Chapters 2 through 11 developed key features of each. This chapter discusses these features in relation to an MNE's strategy. It highlights how managers configure operations to respond to opportunities and threats. These ideas anchor our discussions in Chapter 12 through 20.

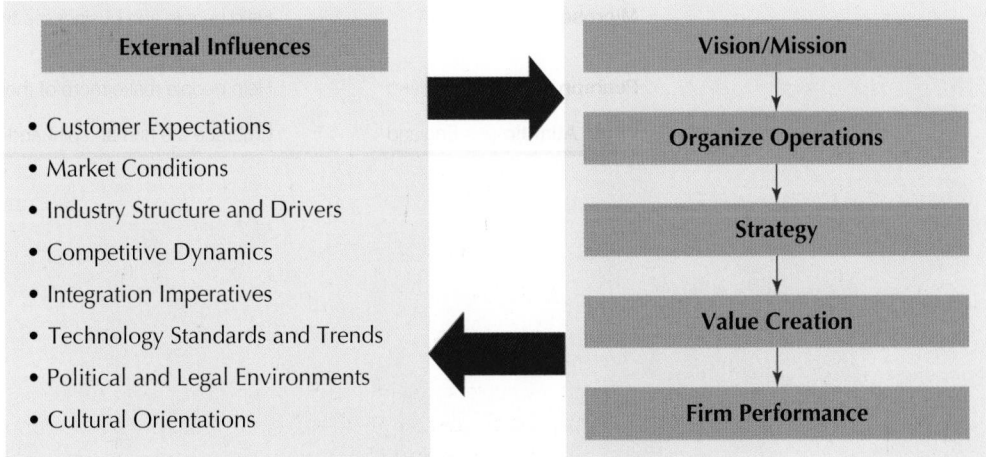

Table 12.1 profiles the vision and mission statements of various MNEs. This set shows how executives worldwide use these tools. Some look to communicate a message in clear, simple, and precise language—for instance, Google's declaration "to organize the world's information and make it universally accessible and useful." Others, like Microsoft, Pearson, and Virgin Atlantic, take a more aspirational approach, appealing to the boundless spirit of humanity to set goals, identify direction, and inspire performance. Finally, others like Areva, Pearson, and Vale anchor the company with modest declarations of purpose and performance. No matter the scale or scope, the vision and mission statements guide management's thinking on strategic issues, promote buy-in, outline performance standards, and guide employee action. They also serve an external purpose, improving communication with customers, suppliers, and partners as well as courting public support. Likewise, they give analysts a perspective to interpret an MNE's choices. Most importantly, MNEs with easily understood, plainly communicated, and collectively shared vision and mission outperform those without them.[29]

Rhetoric to Reality   Translating the lofty rhetoric of an MNE's vision and mission into relevant programs and realistic performance standards, one can imagine, is tough. Increasing the challenge for the typical MNE is the fact that its vision and mission statements must work in many businesses run by many different people operating in many different environments. Nestlé, for instance, has operations in 197 countries, relies on 442 factories in 86 countries, directs more than 2,000 brands, and has 339,000 employees. Likewise, the 338,787 employees of Toyota make vehicles in 70 factories spanning 29 countries and then sell them in more than 170 countries. Lastly, Vodafone's 101,443 employees direct telecom networks in 26 countries and work with partners in 50 more to provide telecom and IT services to clients in more than 150 countries. For Nestlé, Toyota, and Vodafone, like other MNEs, the vision and mission statements help everyone, from headquarters to the front lines, work purposefully toward common goals.

TABLE 12.1   Vision and Mission Statements, Leading MNEs

Company	Home	Vision/Mission Statement[30]
Adidas	Germany	Creating the "new" by focusing on speed, cities and open source
BMW	Germany	World's leading provider of premium products and premium services for individual mobility.
Google	USA	Organize the world's information and make it universally accessible and useful.
Infosys	India	Provides best-of-breed business solutions, leveraging technology, delivered by best-in-class people.
Microsoft	USA	Help people and businesses throughout the world realize their full potential.
Pearson	England	Help people make more of their lives through learning.
Virgin Atlantic	England	Embrace the human spirit and let it fly.

MOVING ONWARD: STRATEGIC PLANNING

Ensuring the consistency of interpretation and action spurs an MNE to systematize the ideals that anchor its vision and mission. Strategic planning does so, converting them into reasonable intellectual challenges, testable propositions, action programs, and measurable outcomes. Done well, strategic planning promotes a common understanding about how the world works and how the MNE will navigate it.[31] Toyota, for instance, anchors strategic planning in its so-called "Toyota Way," and its specification of how managers define issues, solve problems, and make decisions.[32]

Operationally, the discipline of strategic planning sets a rigorous decision-making framework. Its goal—formalizing the actions that an MNE will take to achieve its vision and mission—has several benefits. Strategic planning organizes how managers deal with the routine as well as the unusual so that they can resolve situations consistent with the company's vision and mission. It promotes consensus on intended outcomes and results, harmonizes standards of interpretation, socializes managers to think longer-term, sets success standards, and increases confidence in the business's direction. Each and all are fundamental facets of an effective, high-performance strategy.

Managers use various frameworks to organize strategic planning. No absolute standard prevails. Most frameworks follow a similar logic and share common steps, typically cycling through some variation of the following sequence: (1) identify potential product markets and assess each for opportunities and threats; (2) assess the preferences of targeted customer segments; (3) analyze internal strengths and weaknesses relative to customers' expectations and competitors' competencies; (4) formulate a strategy; (5) set clear and compelling objectives; (6) formalize programs, policies, and tactics; (7) acquire resources, create capabilities, and develop competencies; and (8) monitor thresholds and adjust standards given change in performance, rivals, or markets.

> Planning is a comprehensive process that determines how the firm can best achieve its goals.

MAKING SENSE TO MAKE STRATEGY

The complexity of the global business environment can easily overtax strategic planning; think of, for a moment, the sorts of planning challenges regularly facing Nestlé, Toyota, or Vodafone. A common problem, in the face of the vast scale and scope of global operations, is overanalyzing a situation to the point that a decision or action is never taken, in effect, "analysis paralysis." Consider, for instance, the typical sorts of question that face strategic planners in the MNE: How should we set global standards? When does local responsiveness make sense? Where do we find design ideas? Should we make products here, there, or everywhere? How might host governments respond? Can our suppliers support our mission? What are our most effective marketing tools? What kind of people should we hire to run operations? Answering these, along with many similar questions, is tough for one market. It's challenging, to say the least, for planners evaluating say, 2, 20, or even 200 markets.

Preempting analysis paralysis spurs managers to integrate sensemaking perspectives into strategic planning. Sensemaking involves studying shifting markets, competitors' initiatives, and changing consumer behaviors in order to determine how economics, politics, culture, trade, and industry influence the company's plans. Sensemaking transforms the complexities of the world into a "situation that is comprehended explicitly in words and that serves as a springboard into action."[33] These insights help strategic planners determine the correlates of success and the catalysts of failure in the global business environment. Managers apply a range of sensemaking perspectives. No standard governs which perspective is used in which situation. One commonly sees variations of the Industrial Organization and the Great by Choice outlooks.

CONCEPT CHECK

In Chapter 3, we used the dichotomy between democracy and totalitarianism to build a framework to assess political freedom. In Chapter 4, the differences among market, mixed, and command economies built a similar framework that assessed resource allocation. A key framework in this chapter is the different ways managers make sense of strategy.

> Sensemaking is collaborative process to promote a shared understanding.

Industrial Organization (IO) The IO outlook sets the external environment as the primary determinant of an MNE's strategic plan. It emphasizes the determinism of industry

The idea of industry structure represents the interdependent relationships among

- suppliers of inputs,
- buyers of outputs,
- substitute products,
- potential new entrants,
- rivalry among competing firms.

structure given the thesis that its characteristics (for instance, the threat of new entrants, scale of entry barriers, or power of buyers and supplies) directly influence the potential profitability of an MNE's strategy. The IO model holds that markets tend toward perfect competition (e.g., many firms with small market shares are all price takers, sell identical products, and freely enter and exit the industry; buyers understand product features and competitors' prices; and risk-adjusted rates of return are constant). Consequently, in situations of high profits, new companies enter and compete on the basis of superior products or processes that lower industry profits. In situations of declining profits, more firms exit, fewer firms enter.

Over time, a market's tendency toward perfect competition means that no firm or industry consistently outperforms others, no matter the innovativeness of a particular company or the imperfections within a particular industry (e.g., government subsidies to local rivals).[34] Strategic planning processes anchored in the IO sensemaking perspective assess how an industry's structural characteristics shape competitive dynamics that, in turn, determine the profitability of different choices.[35] As a rule, an unattractive industry is one in which perfect competition drives down overall profitability. An attractive industry is one in which short-term imperfect competition lets companies earn above-average, risk-adjusted returns.

Great by Choice Outlook   In reality, some industries are, and persistently remain, far-from-perfectly competitive. In these settings, proprietary advantages, high entry barriers, or oligopolistic dynamics, for instance, produce market imperfections. Consequently, some MNEs earn above-average, risk-adjusted returns, while others in the same industry underperform. In this context, industry structure shapes, but does not determine, a firm's strategic performance.[36]

Firm conduct refers to the choices a company makes regarding research, manufacturing, marketing, distribution, and the like that influence its profitability.

These sorts of situations spotlight an alternative sensemaking perspective. That is, managers' insight in terms of acquiring resources, organizing capabilities, and developing competencies, rather than the structure of the industry, fundamentally shapes strategic success. This view, generally referred to as Great by Choice, highlights the power of bright managers and their keen sense of devising a strategy that is difficult, if not impossible, to copy. In contrast to the industry determinism of the IO model, this view holds that "Greatness is not a function of circumstance. Greatness, it turns out, is largely a matter of conscious choice."[37] Think of, for example, the genius of Amazon's e-commerce platform, LVMH's luxury goods portfolio, Zara's vision of affordable fast fashion, Tata's industrial scope, or Google's search expertise.[38] Rather than emphasizing elements of industry structure, managers anchor strategic planning process in a sensemaking perspective that engages tools such as BHAGs (Big Hairy Audacious Goals), Tyranny of the 'OR,' Genius of the 'AND,' Level 5 Leadership, or the Hedgehog Concept. Certainly, industry structure matters, but some MNEs thrive because of their executives' choice to be great—and their keen ability to ingeniously bundle resources, capabilities, and competencies to make it happen.[39]

Some firms find ways to exploit market imperfections to sustain success in spite of industry conditions.

THE ROLE OF RESOURCES, CAPABILITIES, AND COMPETENCIES

An MNE's strategy organizes its resource accumulation, capability development, and core competencies development.

The IO Model focuses sensemaking in terms of an MNE's external environment. The Great by Choice outlook centers on the MNE's internal setup. Each perspective, along with its variations, focuses strategic planning on articulating where the MNE is going and the actions it must take to get there. Granted, each represents a different dimension of the MNE's competitive advantage. Still, each speaks to the importance of resources, capabilities, and competencies in supporting a strategy that creates competitive advantages.

TABLE 12.2   Resources of the Firm: Specification and Profile

Resources are available factors that are owned or controlled by the MNE. Here we see types of tangible and intangible resources.

Type	Example
Tangible: Physical resources that are observable and measurable.	• Creditworthiness in terms of Selling Equity or Debt • Employees Skills • Property Portfolio • Retail Network • Scale of Distribution Network • Scale of Manufacturing Facilities • Scope of Service System • Sophistication of Technology Systems
Intangible: Resources that lack physical form.	• Brand Recognition • Corporate Goodwill • Decision-Making Process • Foreign Exchange Risk Management • Intellectual Property • Managerial Skills • Public Affairs Management

Resources are inputs into an MNE production process. A capability is the capacity for resources to perform an activity in an integrated manner.

Resources drive the production of goods and services that are sold to customers. Resources of the sort seen in Table 12.2 develop the firm's productive capacity. Resources are controlled by the MNE and are largely inaccessible to customers; these include manufacturing systems, technological expertise, and information systems. For example, Zara's manufacturing and logistics operations represent some of its resources. Its retail units are resources as well and, yes, they are accessible to customers, but only partially and on a regulated basis. Collectively, resources represent the stocks of available factors that managers bundle together into **capabilities**. Managers' insight in organizing resources to engage an activity or complete an action in a way that is integrative, consistent, and productive creates firm-specific capabilities. As such, capabilities reflect how well an MNE productively bundles its resources. Although not directly used in the production process, capabilities directly support productive operations. Capabilities are found throughout the firm, as suggested in Table 12.3. Again, Zara developed powerful capabilities by ingeniously bundling its resources in market intelligence, design creativity, manufacturing flexibility, and logistics efficiency to sense, design, make, move, and sell affordable, cutting-edge fashion.

Managers bundle resources and capabilities to create a core competency.

Just as bright managers combine resources into capabilities, they also transform resources and capabilities into **core competencies**. Difficult to define precisely, most see a core competency as the special outlook, skill, or technology that, by synthesizing links between resources and capabilities, sets and sustains the firm's capacity to create superior value. Think of, for example, Zara's blend of high-tech and high-fashion or, for that matter, Apple's eye for design and delivery, the elegance of Google's search algorithm, Walmart's sophisticated information-management and product-distribution systems, Honda's mastery of engine mechanics, or Nestlé's marketing finesse.[40] Core competencies emerge over time—managers accumulate resources, combine them into capabilities, and convert them into core competencies. The challenge of accumulation, combination, and conversion makes core competencies the 'crown jewels' of a company. With them, the MNE outperforms rivals. Without them, the MNE struggles. Furthermore, the fact that rivals find it difficult, if not impossible, to copy an MNE's core competencies makes them the basis for superior, sustainable competitive advantage.

TABLE 12.3   Capabilities of the Firm: Specification and Profile

Capabilities are the nontransferable, firm-specific bundles of an MNE's resource. Here we see leading types.

Functional Orientation	Capability
Decision-Making	Envisioning strategic choices and consequences.
Design	Capacity to translate insights into products and processes.
Distribution	Mastering global logistics to support JIT design and delivery.
Management Information Systems	Operationalizing platforms that translate big data analytics into planning tools.
Manufacturing	Devising assembly line layouts that maximize efficiency.
Marketing	Promoting brand recognition that inspires customer loyalty.
Product Technology	Developing a product portfolio that leverages proprietary technology.
Research & Development	Creation of cool, clever, functional designs.
Strategic Visioning	Willingness to question current vision, mission, and strategy.

THE QUEST TO CREATE VALUE

Value is the measure of a firm's capability of selling what it makes for more than the costs incurred in making it.

Fundamentally, strategy is doing what others are doing, but doing it more efficiently, or doing something no one else can do and doing it effectively. Successfully done, an MNE creates superior value by then selling products that competitors cannot duplicate or find too costly to imitate.[41] In either scenario, one company successfully creates value while others scramble for solutions. Now, regarding the idea of value, one can define it in various ways, including economic, market, pro forma, social, book, insurance, use, par, or replacement. One can also define value from different perspectives, such as that of customers, employees, stakeholders, or shareholders. We follow convention and define **value** in economic terms, specifying it as the difference between the cost of making a product and the price that customers are willing to pay for it. If an MNE can sell its product for more than the costs incurred to make it, it generates profits, and hence, creates value.[42] The greater its ability to make and sell products that exceed customers' value expectations, the higher the price it can charge, and the more value it creates. Consider, for instance, the popular iPhone 6. Technically, each unit costs approximately $200 in parts and labor. Apple also adds value through a strategy of cool design, ingenious features, and neat marketing. Ultimately, Apple sells the iPhone 6 for $549, thereby generating $350 in gross value.[43]

MNEs create value by developing a compelling value proposition (why a customer should buy its goods or use its services) that specifies its targeted markets (those customers for whom it creates goods or services). This analysis, whether done on a nation-by-nation, region-by-region, or worldwide basis, requires managers make and sell products that exceed customers' value expectations. In broad terms, an MNE can create value by perfecting processes and products in order to do things more efficiently than others, thereby making products for lower costs than can competitors (the strategy of *cost leadership*). Alternatively, an MNE can create value by doing something no one else can do, and doing it effectively, thereby making products for which consumers pay a premium price (the strategy of *differentiation*).[44] In some situations, an MNE insightfully combines the two approaches (the strategy of *integrated cost leadership/differentiation*).

THE COST LEADERSHIP STRATEGY

The cost leadership strategy aims to make a product at a given level of quality for a cost below those of competitors.

An MNE implementing a cost leadership strategy aims to make a product at the lowest cost, relative to those offered by rivals, which appeals to the largest number of potential customers. Minimizing cost inevitably requires maximizing efficiency, a quest that

CONCEPT CHECK ●

Chapter 4 discusses features of emerging markets, notably the appearance of new companies looking to expand internationally, the influence of the tens of millions of consumers who are experiencing rising incomes, and the emergence of the Base of the Pyramid. All indicate changing customer needs. These developments spur MNEs to rethink cost imperatives.

compels exploiting scale, learning, and location economies. As a rule, the greater the quantity of a good produced, the lower its per-unit fixed cost, given that the firm allocates fixed costs over more units of output. Consequently, the cost leadership strategy spurs selling standardized goods or services to the broadest customer segment. Singular focus on cost reduction leads executives to acquire resources and develop capabilities that reduce its costs relative to rivals. Common methods include product innovations, such as frugal designs or enhanced materials, or process innovations, such as lean production or Six Sigma.

One routinely sees the cost leadership strategy in scale-sensitive industries, such as the airline, steel, mortgage, white goods, consumer credit, and package delivery markets. MNEs such as Southwest Airlines, UPS, Haier, Thai Union Frozen, Citigroup, ArcelorMittal, Cemex, Ranbaxy Laboratories, Virgin Mobile, and Foxconn apply it. Many emerging market companies apply the cost leadership strategy, outperforming rivals by combining state support, growing scientific and technological sophistication, efficient manufacturing, inexpensive labor, and expanding distribution.[45]

The cost leadership strategy has several risks, including

- disruptive technologies change efficiency standards;
- customer's needs change;
- cheaper, better products from rivals.

Risk of the Cost Leadership Strategy The cost leadership strategy requires a single-minded commitment to standardizing processes and products. Disruptions, incremental or transformational, can change customers' expectations or bolster competitors' competencies, thereby obsolescing the MNE's otherwise efficiently configured resources and capabilities. The relentless quest to lower costs may blind managers to evolving markets. For instance, a classic example is Henry Ford's mission to make the lowest cost car, the Model A, and its translation into the strategy that "Any customer can have a car painted any color that he wants so long as it is black." General Motors successfully exploited this fixation, making a comparably priced car that was available in different colors.

Disruptive innovations trigger secular shifts that displace established market leaders' precisely engineered systems. For example, Walmart's core competency of offering everyday low prices depends on the finely honed integration of its retail network resources and global supply chain capabilities. Increasingly, online retailers such as Amazon, by disrupting the traditional dynamic of the shopping experience, challenge Walmart's low-cost leadership. Amazon's improving capability to offer competing, if not the same, products at an equivalent, if not lower, price, threatens the sustainability of Walmart's cost leadership. Similarly, success inspires emulation, and rivals invariably study market leaders, assessing their innovative ways and then tweaking their operations.

THE DIFFERENTIATION STRATEGY

The differentiation strategy champions developing products that customers value and that rivals find hard, if not impossible, to match or copy.

An MNE implements a differentiation strategy when it aims to do something no other firm can do, and, besides doing it, doing it effectively. Just like cost leadership, a differentiation strategy is an integrated set of choices to make a good or provide a service. Unlike the cost leadership strategy, the differentiation strategy requires designing and delivering products that customers see as different in ways that are important to them—and thus are willing to pay a premium price. Differentiation pushes managers to fixate on continuous innovation, not relentlessly reducing costs, as the basis for sustainable value creation. It compels developing resources, capabilities, and competencies that rivals find hard, if not impossible, to match. For instance, think of the sleek design of an Apple iPhone, the engineering sophistication of a Lexus sedan, the customer service at Ritz-Carlton, or the appeal of Coca-Cola's secret formula.

Products are differentiated on a variety of tangible and intangible dimensions.

Approaches to differentiation are many, including speedy product innovations, responsive customer service, prestige and status, and design and performance standards. The differentiation strategy is customary with high-profile products in high-margin markets. Still, differentiation dynamics play elsewhere. MNEs try to differentiate commodities, such as milk, aspirin, DRAM chips, cellphone plans, or debit cards, based on features some customers value more than just low price.[46] In either case, selling a product at a price that exceeds the cost of creating its unique attributes helps the MNE outperform its rivals. Interestingly, the effort to reduce costs ultimately hits hard boundaries, such as the price of inputs, physics of materials, or capacity for service. In contrast, anything a firm can do to produce value that no one else can do quite as effectively creates a virtually infinite basis for differentiation. Think of, for example, the powerful appeal of prominent brands, like Apple or Zara, to loyal fans.

The differentiation strategy has several risks, including
- customers' expectations change;
- customers no longer see sufficient value to justify the price premium;
- a rival introduces a newer, cooler, higher-performing alternative;
- counterfeits that offer a cheaper imitation.

Risks of the Differentiation Strategy   The ever-present threat to the differentiation strategy is shifting customer preference that provokes objection to the higher price of a product, particularly if a rival offers an alternative that provides more value, real or perceived, for the same or lower price. This threat is salient in poorer markets, where cost-conscious customers are particularly value sensitive. For example, Apple has adjusted its premium pricing strategy in emerging markets, notably India, to compete with far cheaper, full-function smartphones. Still, the perceived price-performance gap persists, resulting in Apple's 1 percent share of India's booming smartphone market versus its 44 percent market share in the United States.[47]

An ongoing threat to the differentiation strategy is the risk that today's innovation is tomorrow's relic. The presence of aggressive rivals worldwide makes sustaining the basis of differentiation a never-ending challenge. Innovations conceived in Germany quickly diffuse to rivals in Brazil, the United States, and China. Companies that battle on product features must, as the former CEO of IBM notes, tirelessly determine "what will cause work to move to me? On what basis will I differentiate and compete?"[48]

THE INTEGRATED COST LEADERSHIP/DIFFERENTIATION STRATEGY

The differentiation strategy calls for continual innovation, whereas cost leadership champions sustainable efficiency. The integrated cost leadership/differentiation strategy aims to do both.

In principle, the asymmetric demands of cost leadership and differentiation make it difficult to pursue both simultaneously. In practice, some MNEs do, successfully blending standards of efficiency and effectiveness to offer low-cost, high-performance products. Zara, for instance, implementing a vision of "Armani at moderate prices," turns cool ideas into competitively priced, hot fashions. Lexus, likewise, delivers high-performance cars, replete with impressive features that customers see offering greater value, relative to price, than alternatives from other luxury carmakers. Lastly, Target, targeting higher-income, fashion-conscious yet price-sensitive customers, implements its integrated strategy of "Expect More. Pay Less" that "delivers greater convenience, increased savings and a more personalized shopping experience."[49] Zara, Lexus, and Target use an integrated cost leadership/differentiation strategy to design products and processes with differentiated features, make them efficiently, and sell them effectively. Successfully implementing the integrated cost leadership/differentiation strategy requires an MNE adapt quickly to change, particularly when disruptive innovations call for new capabilities. Production must optimize efficiency in order to generate the funds that support differentiation.

The integrated cost leadership/differentiation strategy provides customers with relatively lower-cost products that also have differentiated features.

The key threat to the integrated cost leadership/differentiation strategy is getting "caught in the middle."

Risks of the Integrated Cost Leadership/Differentiation Strategy   Making inexpensive, unique products for which customers willingly pay a premium price is awfully difficult. Implementing it requires that an MNE manage a symbiosis of resources, capabilities, and competencies in developing mutually beneficial relationships that reconcile the asymmetric standards of efficiency and effectiveness. Some MNEs get "caught in the middle," falling short of optimizing production or sufficiently differentiating. Trapped between competing goals, their cost structure neither supports suitably low prices nor delivers appealing prestige or performance.

Point

Point **Yes** Strategic planning was once similar to playing chess. The board, the players, and the moves were fairly well-defined, the pace of play permitted deliberative movement, and surprises were few and far between. Indeed, one needs only recall the infamous "3-6-3" rule in banking a generation or two ago: bankers gave 3 percent interest on depositors' accounts, lent depositors money at 6 percent interest, and then planned to hit the golf links at 3 P.M.[50] Today, the global business environment, turbocharged by innumerable causes and effects, makes for a far more complex game. Technology, both routine and disruptive, resets efficiency frontiers and market boundaries. Competitors, both established and emerging, reinvent systems of production and distribution as well as experiment with entirely new business models. Governments, both democratic and authoritarian, change the rules of the game. Making sense of the situation and then acquiring resources, developing capabilities, and creating competencies is tough. Strategic planning makes it possible.

Strategic planning pushes managers to break free of day-to-day routines, look toward the horizon, and ask and answer big questions. Determining goals and mapping optimal paths pinpoints the potential of a business and directly links objectives to actions and required resources. Setting systematic criteria and imposing rigorous analytics, by organizing the complexity of the global business environment, helps managers formalize goals, formulate strategies, determine programs, and define standards. Besides that, the planning process frames and facilitates coordination, communication, and learning. Promoting conversations among decision-makers about the future of the MNE and the resources, capabilities, and competencies required to reach it fortifies decision-making.

Strategic planning improves the flexibility to change as markets change. Few contest the importance of proactive executives, but, still, passivity often prevails. Planning pushes managers to get on with it, asking big as well as small questions. Purposeful debate helps reposition resources to new courses of action as well as estimate the urgency to reset or reverse commitments. Instituting strategic planning with an eye toward improving flexibility prior to the change, rather than after, sensitizes managers to alternative options.

Is Strategic Planning Productive?

Not surprisingly, strategic planning supports higher performance and improved competitiveness. The interplay of formal planning processes, greater flexibility, and improved innovativeness across multiple industries in multiple countries shows that planning pays off. Performance effects do not vary significantly between different industry groups. Some empirical evidence indicates a positive and direct relationship—the more one plans, the better the firm performs.[51]

Unquestionably, the intrinsic complexity of mapping markets means that strategic planning often hits difficulties. Ironically, its shortcomings follow from its strengths. Planning imposes an analytical discipline that frames how managers assess markets. Acceptable for similar markets (say, moving from the United States to Canada), this perspective may struggle to adjust analytics for dissimilar markets (say, moving from Australia to Venezuela). In theory, anchoring analysis in terms of the orderly progression of systematic planning procedures helps managers formulate optimal strategies. Still, as with any objective model, the template might encourage linear thinking that misinterprets markets and misdirects decision-making.

Enterprising executives, recognizing the messiness of internal conditions and external circumstances, stress-test their planning process. High-power brainstorming procedures identify "what-if" situations that help managers challenge their planning model before committing to a course of action. In particular, managers incorporate elements of scenario analysis and contingency planning. In the former they assess alternative futures, interpreting likely outcomes of a variety of operating strategies and industry conditions. Alternatively, contingency planning helps managers estimate the effect of market disruptions and devise preemptive strategies.

Ultimately, performance records of leading MNEs worldwide show that tried-and-true strategic planning processes productively equip managers to deal with what the processes are best suited to deal with: the messy, ill-structured realities of IB. Strategic planning, by enforcing rigorous, disciplined, systematic decision-making, makes expanding into familiar markets or venturing into different territories manageable.

Is Strategic Planning Productive?

Counterpoint

No The productivity of strategic planning rests on an appealing, yet ultimately dubious, thesis: strategy is a science with immutable laws that, by reliably guiding decision-making toward optimal outcomes, lets bright strategists imagine bright plans that build bright futures. In actuality, the shifting dynamics of the global marketplace present overwhelming challenges that suggest strategic planning is arguably ineffective. Correspondingly, after more than 40 years of empirical study, the data suggest an equivocal relationship between strategic planning and firm performance.[52]

Notwithstanding managers' best intentions to map the future, many continually run into the problem that the future famously does not cooperate with pre-set visions, missions, and plans. Consider the less-than-inspiring record of firms that consistently invest great effort into strategic planning, namely the Standard & Poor's 500 Index (S&P 500).[53] The average time a company spends in the S&P 500 index has declined from 61 years in 1958 to about 18 years today; removal typically follows strategic shortfall. An average of 22 companies are replaced annually.[54] Nearly 50 percent of the companies included in the S&P 500 index in 2000 no longer exist. Similarly, up to 90 percent of ventures fail shortly after start-up; venture-capital firms see more than 80 percent of their investments fail; more than 80 percent of equity mutual funds consistently underperform the S&P 500; the average business model life span has fallen from about 15 years to less than 5 over the past 50 years; and more than 75 percent of mergers and acquisitions never pay off.[55] Many companies committed to rigorous, objective, systematic planning processes, rather than reaping great success, struggle to survive.

Skeptics point to planning's fundamental limit: the deception that a comprehensive strategic planning process, anchored in countless hours of assessing strengths, weaknesses, opportunities, and threats, fundamentally influences short-term competitiveness and long-term sustainability. Notwithstanding best intentions, strategic plan-

Counterpoint

ning falls prey to deficiencies and delusions. It confuses the superficial trappings of rigor and discipline with grand storytelling. It muddles managers' ability to think critically about the nature of success in business—including vastly underestimating the power of plain old good luck.[56] Inevitably, planning devolves into glorified soothsaying that undermines the effectiveness of decision-making.[57] Then, in the off chance that planning generates a genuine insight, it often runs into implementation problems—plans poorly connected to vague action steps that are just as likely to be a day late and a dollar short.

Scarcely tolerable under stable conditions, these tendencies prove damaging given the extreme sorts of changes that mark the global business environment. Significant trends and innovations reconfigure the global marketplace. Expansion in once peripheral, but now core markets (such as China, India, Indonesia) resets performance standards. Some 400 midsize emerging-market cities, many unfamiliar in the West (e.g., Sanaa, Ouagadougou, Chittagong, Kinshasa), will produce about 40 percent of global growth over the next 15 years.[58] Today's market revolution spans the globe, includes far more people in far more countries, and represents the biggest change in the history of capitalism. The Internet further turbocharges change. Already, it is the most powerful force for globalization, economic growth, and education in history. Indeed, say some, whatever the Internet touches, it transforms in ways that reset analytics and defy prediction.

The upshot is that no matter how sensitive their strategic compass, executives' struggle to plan in the face of minor as well as momentous dynamism.[59] Ultimately, managers intent on overlaying logical rules of cause and effect on markets delude themselves that strategic planning is an effective decision-making process. Beset by intractable decision biases—from generalizing halo effects, confusing correlation and causality, and connecting only the winning dots—strategic planning inevitably proves unproductive.[60] Then, as before, impressive plans fall short of performance targets.

ORGANIZING VALUE CREATION: THE VALUE CHAIN

An MNE sets and sustains its competitive advantage when the value it creates, whether through cost leadership, differentiation, or a combination, is greater than the costs it incurs in doing so. In practical terms, an MNE faces issues, opportunities, and constraints in designing, making, moving, selling, and servicing products; each activity imposes costs that influence value creation. Just as strategic planning helps managers develop their strategy, value chain analysis helps them assess how activities create value.

Value chain analysis frames the evaluation of an MNE's strengths and weaknesses. Doing so guides managers' breakdown of the components and determinants of the internal cost

Value-chain analysis helps managers understand the potential and performance of resources and capabilities, thereby clarifying cost structures and value creation.

FIGURE 12.2   Visualizing the Value Chain

The value chain is made up of primary activities that reflect classical business functions and managerial orientations. The value chain also specifies support activities, representing day-to-day tasks, which help implement the primary activities. Support activities apply to primary activities, as we see in their run along the breadth of the value chain.

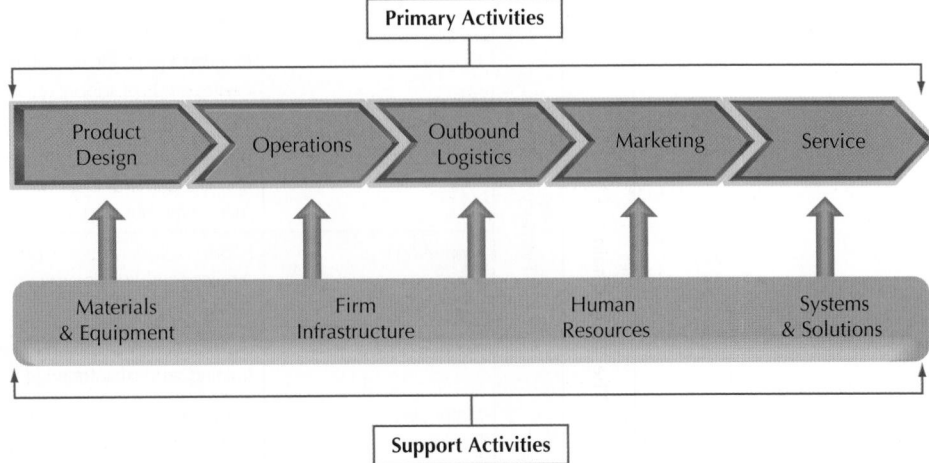

structure. Value chain analysis neatly represents resources and capabilities, emphasizing their linkage to the cost leadership, differentiation, or integrated strategy. In the case of cost leadership, it identifies the potential of resources and capabilities to streamline value activities. In the case of differentiation, it highlights activities that support outperforming rivals in providing the latest, greatest products. In the case of the integrated mix, it helps reconcile the efficiency–effectiveness dialectic. Lastly, value chain analysis guides estimating rivals' cost structures and, thus, their relative competitiveness.

> The value chain is the set of linked activities the company performs to design, make, market, distribute, and support a product.

Procedurally, the systemic perspective of value chain analysis deconstructs the abstraction of creating value into a step-by-step model. This sequence specifies the value that is created as a product moves from conception in R&D through sourcing materials, organizing manufacturing, supervising logistics, applying marketing, and servicing.[61] Put differently, value chain analysis maps the productivity of each functional activity, pinpointing how resources and capabilities improve efficiency or boost effectiveness. Figure 12.2 maps the discrete activities that define the value chain. Figure 12.3 profiles the characteristic of each.

Primary activities represent the core business functions that make and move products. Its organization follows from that of designing a product and building the operations that make it onward through the tasks of logistics, marketing, distribution, and service. Primary activities reflect classic business activities and managerial orientations. Thus, they carry functional labels such as operations or marketing. Figure 12.2 also identifies secondary processes called **support activities**. These represent the infrastructure of the firm, identifying the activities that support the work done in carrying out primary activities. Human resources, for example, are needed for each primary activity, from supervising warehousing materials, to directing production, to shipping products, to serving customers.

> A value chain disaggregates a firm into
>
> - primary activities that design, make, sell, and deliver the product;
> - support activities that implement the primary activities.

CONFIGURING THE VALUE CHAIN

> Value-chain analysis helps managers evaluate their cost structure and identify the activities through which they can create value.

An MNE's option to go anywhere in the world to perform a primary or support activity gives it tremendous choice of location. How an MNE distributes value activities around the world is the matter of **configuration**—essentially, the task of deciding which activity to do where. Besides the option to sell in the 214 markets that compose the global business environment, the MNE has the option to install operations in each. For example, Nestlé operates 442 factories in 86 countries whereas Toyota runs 70 factories in 29 countries.[62] Rather than happenstance, the decision to open a factory here, but not there, reflects their strategic planners' interpretation of the opportunities and constraints of a location.

FIGURE 12.3   Specifying the Value Chain

The primary and support activities of the value chain identify the steps an MNE takes to create value. By disaggregating activities into discrete responsibilities, as we see here, the value chain provides managers a powerful tool to plan strategically.

The Value Chain	**Primary Activities**	Product Design	Design the functions, features, and aesthetics of the product or process.
		Operations	Convert inputs into a finished product in terms of sourcing components, arrange supply chains, configure plant location, and optimize manufacturing processes.
		Outbound Logistics	Move finished product from operations to wholesalers, retailers, or end-consumers. Deal with distribution channels, inventory management, warehousing, and transportation logistics.
		Marketing	Inform buyers and consumers about products and services, develop a sales force, devise packaging schemes, define the brand, and devise promotions.
		Service	Service customers with installation support, after-sales assistance, training, and maintenance.
	Support Activities	Materials & Equipment	Manage the procurement, transportation, storage, and distribution of materials and equipment necessary to conduct the primary activities.
		Human Resource Management	Recruit, develop, motivate, compensate, and retain workers.
		Systems & Solutions	Manage information processing, oversee information systems, and integrate technology platforms.
		Infrastructure	Classic overhead functions, like accounting, finance, legal, safety and security, and quality control.

Managers can either concentrate or disperse value activities.

In theory, configuration ranges from **concentrated** (the MNE performs all value-chain activities in one location) to **dispersed** (the MNE performs different value-chain activities in different locations).[63] The tension between which activities to concentrate and which to disperse follows from the fact that different activities impose different costs in different locations. Say a single market provides the lowest-cost, highest-productivity environment for all activities. An MNE would then concentrate its value chain there and serve its global market through exports. Conversely, a dispersed value chain makes sense when some activities cost less in country X, others cost less in country Y, and still others less in country Z. So, if the best industrial designers are in Taiwan, the company bases R&D there. If the most productive labor force for assembly is in Vietnam, that's where it builds its plants. If the most creative minds are in Denmark, it develops its advertising campaign there.[64]

Location economics influence an MNE's decision to concentrate or disperse value activities.

Location Advantages   Differing environmental conditions, given differing political, legal, and market features, means costs differ from country to country. The option to go anywhere to do anything pushes MNEs to exploit **location advantages**. Labor, capital, and resources costs are traditional determinants of location advantages. Increasingly, the matters of digitization and cluster effects moderate configuration choices (see Table 12.4). The MNE pursuing a low-cost leadership strategy with a labor-intensive production process, for instance, is sensitive to the supply, cost, and productivity of workers. Locating primary and support activities operations in productive places optimizes the MNE's operational efficiency and strategic effectiveness.

Increasingly, MNEs target international locations to exploit opportunities to create knowledge, boost innovation, and improve customer responsiveness. For instance, Halliburton, a U.S.-based oil field services MNE, opened a second headquarters in Dubai to better serve its Middle East customers. Likewise, IBM relies on workers in Shanghai to process accounts receivable, specialists in Manila to oversee human resources, accountants in Kuala Lumpur to keep the books, buyers in Shenzhen to procure components, and tech

CONCEPT CHECK

3-D printing, introduces revolutionary production technologies. Besides resetting the economics of manufacturing, these sorts of innovations also change the IB domain. Similarly, the profile of "Scenarios That May Change Trade Patterns" in Chapter 5 (page 197) notes technological innovations can diminish world trade due to the efficiency and ease of manufacturing goods nearer to customers.

TABLE 12.4 Locating Value Activities: Key Moderators

The MNE assessing "where to go to do what" considers a variety of moderators.

Dimension	Influence
Business Environment Quality	MNEs configure value chains to enter, or avoid, a country given its business environment. Countries improve their location economics by reducing capital requirements for start-ups, streamlining property registration, expediting regulatory review, and liberalizing labor regulations. Opportunistic governments recruit foreign investors, promising business-friendly markets that offer flexible operating requirements, lower tax rates, cheap financing, and responsive public policies.[65]
Cluster Effects	Competing, complementary, interdependent firms and industries that do business with each other and share overlapping needs for talent, technology, and infrastructure increasingly operate in close geographic proximity, namely clusters (e.g., New York City for global finance). Vibrant clusters attract related vendors, service providers, investors, analysts, skilled workers, trade association members, and consultants.[66]
Innovation Context	Host governments build knowledge-intensive, technology-enabled business environments. Promoting technologies, expanding human capacities, streamlining organizational capabilities, and improving institutional responsiveness develops locations that leverage knowledge into innovations.
Labor Costs	Differences in wage rates, worker productivity, and workplace regulations mean that the labor cost of doing the same thing varies from country to country. MNEs configure value chains to exploit these differentials.
Logistics	Logistics, namely procuring, transporting, transshipment, and storing products, enables transactions among value-chain activities. Depending on the industry, logistics adds 5 percent to 50 percent to a product's total landed cost.[67] Hence, MNEs configure the location of value activities to minimize logistics expenses.
Political Risk	Distributing value activities across nations exposes an MNE to political risk, namely that local decisions, events, or conditions will cause it to lose some or all of the value of its investment or accept a lower than the projected rate of return. Political risks differ from market to market; some countries are less risky than others, given fair legal systems, stable institutions, and the rule of law.

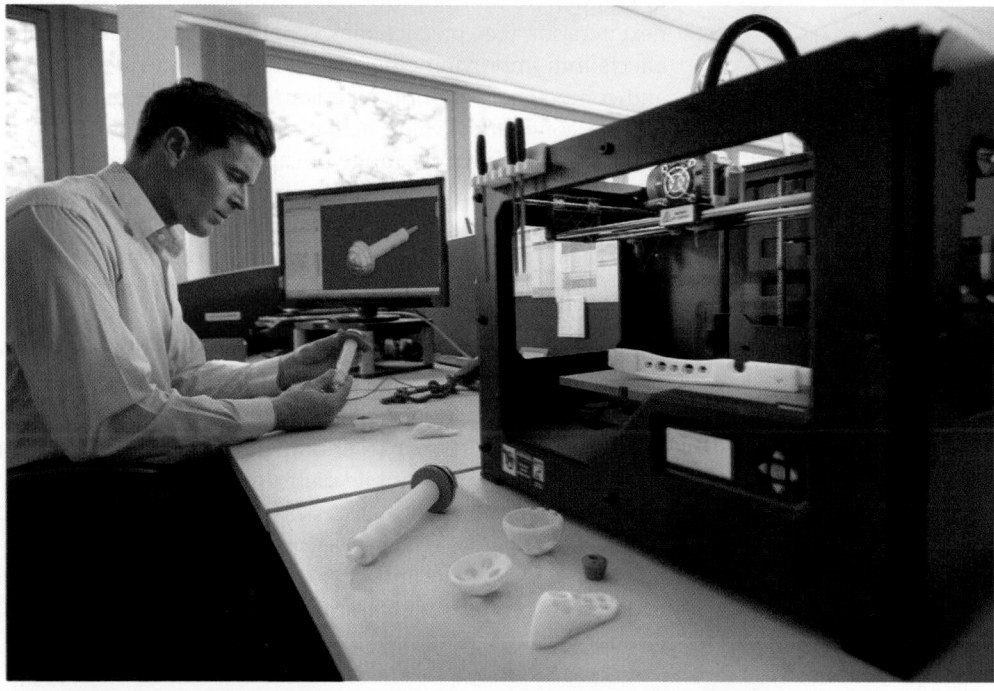

The improving functionality ▶ of 3-D printing foreshadows a radical reset in our idea of of the scale and location of "factories" in the future.

Source: Cultura Creative/Alamy Stock Photo

analysts in Brisbane to run its help desk. Current trends in robotic technologies, as we see in our *Looking to the Future* profile, signal a brave new world that may radically reset our understanding of location advantages.

CONCEPT CHECK

In discussing "Elements of Economic Analysis" in Chapter 4 (page 167), we note labor costs and productivity are key elements of an MNE's strategy. In Chapter 5 (page 184), we discuss theories to explain the relative trade performance of different countries. Here, we reiterate that location economics directly moderate how MNEs configure value activities.

Economies of Scale   The degree that an MNE concentrates or disperses its value-chain activities reflects the importance of efficiency to its quest to create value. In the case of the MNE implementing a cost leadership strategy, efficiency is the foundation of its competitiveness. This concern is less pressing for an MNE implementing a differentiation or integrated strategy. Still, overcoming the **liability of foreignness**—namely, the additional costs that an MNE operating outside its home country incurs above those experienced by a local firm—requires achieving some offsetting efficiencies, no matter which strategy an MNE chooses.[68]

Technically, an MNE captures **economies of scale** in terms of size, output, or scale of operation. Increasing output lets it distribute fixed costs across a higher number of units, thereby systematically decreasing per-unit cost. Technically, steep up-front capital costs create high potential for scale economies. Long production runs lower per-unit costs as marginal production cost decreases while cumulative output increases. Exploiting scale effects is a powerful driver of productivity and profitability. It's an enduring explanation of value chain configurations.

An MNE implementing the cost leadership strategy concentrates its value activities among large-scale plants to capture available scale economies. A minimum efficient-sized factory for making integrated circuits, for instance, costs several billion dollars. As a result, Intel, the world's largest semiconductor chipmaker, supplies customers from eight fabrication plants located in four countries—five in the United States, and one each in Ireland, Israel, and China. Certainly, Intel could opt for smaller plants in more countries. The reduced productivity of dispersed, small-scale manufacturing activities would suboptimize scale efficiencies, thereby inflating its operating costs and diminishing its capacity to create value.

Factors that influence the configuration of a value-chain include

- business environment,
- digitization,
- economies of scale,
- innovation context,
- logistics,
- resource costs,
- robotics.

Experience and Learning Effects   Industry and firm conduct confirms that low costs create strategic advantage.[69] Hence, MNEs look to capitalize on the scale and scope of their operations to exploit potential cost minimization via experience and learning effects. Technically, as a worker, through repetition, progressively masters the intricacies of a job, improving mastery predictably lowers costs. On the factory floor, costs characteristically decline by 20–30 percent in real terms each time accumulated experience doubles. Experience and learning effects also extend to professional sectors. The more times that managers perform a task, the more they improve their mastery of that task, meaning less time is required for the next iteration (i.e., practice makes perfect). Continual learning translates ongoing experience effects into improving efficiencies. Hence, strategic planners bundle resources, capabilities, and competencies to optimize learning and leverage experience effect. Common methods include configuring value activities to arrange long-term contracts for inputs, developing know-how of a broader range of capital instruments in a wider range of countries, and distributing marketing expertise over more markets.

Mangers rely on scenario planning to anticipate reconfiguring the value chain to changes in customers, industries, institutions, and environments.

The Risks of Configuration Choices   Configuration decisions face the risks of unpredictable market change. Disruptions, such as a regime change, material shortages, labor unrest, or currency instability, can quickly convert an efficient location into a costly one. Civil unrest in Egypt in 2011, for example, paralyzed its economy. Foreign commerce and domestic business all but halted, markets seized, and supplies of all sorts vanished. Recurring disruptions complicate configuration choices. Following yet another gyration in the business environment, Jack Welch, former chair and CEO of General Electric (GE), thought the best location for GE factories was a mobile platform, explaining, "Ideally, you'd have every plant you own on a barge, to move with currencies and changes in the economy."[70] The impracticality of an armada of barges ferrying factories through the seven seas requires that managers monitor how markets shift and environments evolve. Strategic planning tools, such as scenario analysis and contingency assessments, help managers estimate the implication of shifting location advantages to configuration choices.

Looking to the Future
Digits, Widgets, and Changing Location Advantages

Since business began, location advantages have influenced how MNEs configure value activities. Searching for raw materials, seeking productive, low-cost labor, arbitraging tax and tariff incentives, and the like have led MNEs to travel the world seeking optimal locations. Often, they had to operate in faraway locations marked by instability, uncertainty, and risk. Moreover, making products there yet moving products here required an ever-expanding, often expensive transportation matrix. Today, in a bit of understatement, 'the times they are a changin.' Revolutionary developments in digitalization, robots, and 3-D printers spur radically rethinking the implication of location advantages to configuring value activities.

Digitization

The representation of an object, image, sound, document, or signal into a series of numbers digitizes it. Increasingly, MNEs digitize products like software, music, and books, as well as services like application processing, financial consolidation, and legal assistance. Jacked into the network, MNEs move goods and provide services anywhere in the world at negligible cost and complication. The flexibility to locate digital activities virtually anywhere, particularly as the Internet expands, influences how and where MNEs do what. Options unavailable a generation ago—say, X-rays taken in Boston, but read in Bangkok—are now commonplace. Distance, historically represented in terms of geographic space, is now measured in terms of electronic time in the ether of cloud computing.

Ongoing improvements in digitization signal continuing disruption. Once, many activities could be done in a few specialized places. For instance, due diligence processes in mergers and acquisitions largely took place in New York City or London given the corresponding concentration of value activities such as regulatory registration or evaluation. Digitization disperses these activities. Indeed, it has created a new global model for financial services, unleashing disruptive innovations that change the rules of the game. One analyst maintains that "there has never been an economic discontinuity of this magnitude in the history of the world.... These powerful forces are allowing companies to rethink their sourcing strategies across the entire value chain."[71] Some see digitization

"creating a second economy that's vast, automatic, and invisible—thereby bringing the biggest change since the Industrial Revolution."[72]

Similar trends disrupt location effects in the legal field. India's legal outsourcing industry is growing from an experimental enterprise to a mainstream part of the global business of law. At Pangea3 and Lexadigm, Indian lawyers do the routine work traditionally assigned to enterprising junior lawyers in the United States, but at a fraction of the cost. Moreover, amendments to the U.S. Federal Rules of Civil Procedure have expanded discovery to include electronic documents, such as e-mails, instant messages, and voice mails. E-discovery further incents offshoring legal work to productive providers, if not moving into the cloud itself. Add it all up, and legal outsourcing "is not a blip...it is a big historical movement."[73]

Going forward, the narrowing **digital divide**—the gap between those with regular access to digital technologies and those without—plugs more people into the network. Accordingly, location economics change and MNE's configuration choices evolve. The diffusion of lower-priced technology to people worldwide means that fewer spots remain off the grid. As newly wired folks connect with counterparts worldwide, they develop proficiencies with various technology platforms. Consequently, MNEs rethink configuration options in order to tap emerging sources of capabilities.[74]

The Rise of Robots

Widgets, technically small, mechanical devices, sound benign. In the context of the rise of robots and the expansion of 3-D printing, the idea of widgets takes on an entirely new meaning. The rise of robots threatens to disrupt much of what we know about configuring activities. These decisions, originally made based on hand labor, later based on factory assembly lines manned by humans, increasingly follow the promise of robots getting the job done. In your daily life, think of the implications of ATMs, self-checkout tills, remotely guided trains, and the soon-to-arrive driverless cars. More pointedly, consider that the Philips Electronics factory in Zhuhai, China, employs hundreds of workers who work old-school, using hand tools to assemble electric shavers.

One wonders, considering the rise of robots in workplaces worldwide, how unfolding tech trends will reset our understanding of strategy in the global business environment.

Source: Echo/Getty Images

Meanwhile, 128 robots do the same work making the same product at a sister factory in the Netherlands. The Dutch factory has several dozen workers per shift, about a tenth as many as the Zhuhai plant. Still, it out-produces its Chinese counterpart.[75] Elsewhere, fear of rising wages drives others to do the same. Foxconn, the maker of "all things Apple," has factories filled with tens of thousands of workers, but looks to install more than a million robots.

Change is not limited to manufacturing. In distribution warehouses, robots store, retrieve, and pack goods far more adeptly than people. In journalism, robot writers generate hundreds of millions of news reports annually—more than all human journalists in the world—at an increasingly diminishing cost.[76] In accountancy, forecasters see computer systems replacing 99 percent of tax preparers, 97 percent of bookkeepers, 93 percent of budget analysts, and 93 percent of accountants and auditors.[77] Machines' ability to do things faster, cheaper, and more capably anywhere in the world at any time makes them more productive than humans in an increasing number of applications.[78] Says the founder of robot builder Industrial Perception, "We're on the cusp of completely changing manufacturing and distribution. I think it's not as singular an event, but it will ultimately have as big an impact as the Internet."[79]

Robots in the form of 3-D printing add fascinating angles to future location decisions. Building big factories in low-cost labor markets to mass-produce standardized goods, long a determinant of plant location, slowly becomes secondary to smaller-scale, 3-D printer-equipped facilities that enable 'mass customization.' The capacity of 3-D printers to efficiently make smaller batches of a wider variety of goods supports scenarios where products are made on-site, in real time, and tailored to a customer's precise specification. Increasingly, 3-D printing, powered by progressive software and ingenious materials, supports small-scale factories "manned" by maker-bots located anywhere and everywhere in the world. And, given the advantages of proximity to customers, likely down the street, and, one day, likely in your home rather than in factories across the world.

Implications

Digits and widgets push managers to increasingly question long-sacred strategic principles, such as "Exploit location advantages," "Maximize production runs," "Go big or go home," or "Minimize unit-labor costs."[80] Locating value activities, based not on the availability of land, labor, or materials, but on network connectivity, robotics, and 3-D printers, lets MNEs radically rethink how they configure operations.[81] We already see production activities that had been moved to low-cost labor locations now reshoring to developed countries, and in the process expanding the notions of locations (see Table 12.5). Nearly half of U.S.-based manufacturing executives at companies with sales greater than $10 billion are planning to or are actively considering bringing production back to the United States from China.[82] Further, a third of the goods that the United States imports from China in transport, computer fabricated metals, and machinery industries could be made with robots and 3-D printers, in the United States by 2020. These trends, unfolding worldwide, herald a widget-led, digitally fueled revolution that likely resets our ideas and interpretation of location advantages.[83] ■

TABLE 12.5   The Expanding Lexicon of Locations

Options for configuring value activities expand in scale and scope. Once, discussion revolved around the issue of offshoring. Now, trends in digitization and automation, shifting location effects, intellectual property protection, and customer responsiveness expand interpretation. Consequently, the interpretation of "shoring" evolves.

Form of Shoring	Characteristic
Homeshoring	Home-based staff handle activities that had previously been offshored to foreign locations.
Nearshoring	A less aggressive form of offshoring whereby an MNE transfers an activity to a neighboring or nearby country.
Offshoring	Relocating a value activity to a different country that either remains within or moves outside the MNE.
Onshoring	Relocating a business process or work unit to a more productive, lower-cost location in the home country.
Reshoring	Returning an activity from the foreign location to the country where the work had originally been done.

GLOBAL INTEGRATION VERSUS LOCAL RESPONSIVENESS

Global integration standardizes worldwide activities to maximize efficiency, whereas national responsiveness adapts local activities to optimize effectiveness.

Competing in the global marketplace puts an MNE on the horns of a dilemma: should it single-mindedly standardize products and processes and resolutely exploit location effects in order to maximize the efficiency gains of **global integration**? Or, should it adapt products and processes to the unique situations in each market in order to maximize the effectiveness benefits of **local responsiveness**? As we see in Table 12.6, significant motivations endorse each imperative. The perpetual tug-of-war between global integration and local responsiveness fuels ongoing debate about the ideal bundle of resources, capabilities, and competencies that maximizes value creation. Few MNEs operate in an industry where either globalization or localization pressure indisputably predominate. Rather, most MNEs, given their vision, mission, and strategy, navigate the competing demands of the dual imperative of IB.[84]

For instance, consider Nestlé's situation. Its vision, "Good Food, Good Life," anchors its mission to provide food that is a source of nourishment and satisfaction, but also pleasure, health, happiness, and peace of mind. These ideals, although universal in theory, differ in practice given that local habits, cultural traditions, and social norms shape the standards of preferred, palatable food from market to market. Moreover, food inputs are generally commodities, production has limited scale potential, widespread distribution faces high costs given low value-to-weight ratios, and promotion is best done locally given differentiated tastes, regulations, rivals, and retail channels. Hence, Nestlé's designers, regulatory specialists, and consumer care representatives apply a local outlook to customize its activities so that they respond effectively to situations in the 197 markets in which Nestlé sells its products.

Global integration combines differentiated parts into a standardized whole. Local responsiveness disaggregates the standardized whole into differentiated parts.

Offsetting its liability of foreignness, however, requires that Nestlé standardize some activities, such as information systems, brand names, advertising message, and packaging processes, which overlap across countries. To that end, Nestlé looks to its 5,000-plus scientists,

TABLE 12.6 Motivations of Global Integration and Local Responsiveness

Motivations for Global Integration	Motivations for Local Responsiveness
• Standardize products and processes to maximize scale, experience, and learning effects	• Customize products and process to local customer preferences to optimize scale, experience, and learning effects
• Maximize productivity of resources, capabilities, and competencies	• Satisfy host government requirements and regulations
• Exploit location effects	• Tap local resources, capabilities, and competencies
• Capitalize on converging consumer preferences and universal needs	• Promote a local profile to placate national stakeholders
• Provide uniform service to all customers	• Directly engage local competitors
• Accelerate consumers' quest to maximize purchasing power parity	• Adjust to local political, economic, and cultural circumstances
• Source materials and inputs globally	• Increase sensitivity to new product and process options
• Directly engage global competitors	• Tailor marketing message to local ideals
• Build global image with universal message	• Build local goodwill by supporting national agenda
• Exploit integration efforts of transnational institutions	• Accommodate differences in distribution channels and service systems
• Leverage expanding cross-national technological connectivity	• Respond to historical or geographic imperatives
• Respond to the progressive, ongoing globalization of markets	• Adjust products and processes to the digital divide

CONCEPT CHECK

As seen in Chapter 4, fast-growing emerging economies spur big changes in global strategies. Here, we observe that one of these shifts moves companies to assess operating in different environments with a keen eye toward leveraging innovations across subsidiaries.

engineers, and nutritionists who staff its worldwide network of 34 R&D facilities to set global standards for safe products of the highest quality that support its vision of 'Good Food, Good Life.' Granted, the executive leadership of Nestlé would prefer to do the same thing, the same way, everywhere—strategic planning would be far easier, operations would run far smoother, and complications would be far fewer. However, they cannot. Consequently, Nestlé, like many MNEs, manages the conflicting pressures of global integration and local responsiveness by standardizing some activities worldwide but adapting others to local situations.

Reconciling the competing imperatives of integration and responsiveness calls on managers to navigate a range of issues, constraints, and concerns. Strategic planning, in framing analysis and developing scenarios, helps managers assess resources, capabilities, and competencies relative to opportunities and threats. As a rule, planners monitor multiple aspects of the environment. Key concerns center on interpreting the potential for standardization along with understanding the characteristics of consumer preferences and the influence of institutional agents.

THE POTENTIAL FOR STANDARDIZATION

The greater the potential to standardize value activities, the greater the importance of global integration to an MNE's competitiveness. Presently, some see standardization offering immense potential, given the growing degree to which the "experience of everyday life is becoming standardized around the world."[85] So put, people worldwide consume an increasing number of products increasingly in the same way. The stronger this tendency, the greater the imperative for MNEs to produce low-cost, high-quality products that differ little, if any, in features and functionality, in order to develop the most compelling value proposition.

The logic of standardization is straightforward. Repeatedly doing the same task the same way, by maximizing scale and learning effects, creates efficiencies that reduce costs without sacrificing quality. Efficiencies emerge across the value chain. An MNE, for example, can streamline product designs in order to rationalize assembly, negotiate quantity discounts on material purchases, rationalize materials management, and optimize outbound logistics. The MNE also realizes efficiencies in other value activities: R&D benefits by leveraging a common design platform, advertising benefits by communicating a universal message, and distribution benefits by streamlining channels.[86]

Our opening case profiles the power of standardization to create compelling competitive advantage in the global apparel industry. Zara saw that standardizing its product offerings supported longer production runs that translated into lower costs. This, in turn, enables Zara to offer attractive fashion at reasonable prices that neutralize stubborn local preferences. Relatedly, its global network, supported by its state-of-the-art logistics, gave customers worldwide real-time access to the newest, coolest fashion trends. Manufacturing standardized products for global markets, therefore, lets Zara leverage its investment in design, manufacturing, distribution, and retail activities. The resulting efficiencies, in turn, support making high-quality, competitively priced products that, in offering compelling value to customers worldwide, repowered the cycle.[87]

The convergence of national markets, standardization of business, and efficiency imperatives push MNEs to integrate activities.

THE CHARACTERISTICS OF CONSUMER PREFERENCES

Responding to local customers' preferences requires customizing products and processes. Adaptation reduces the efficiencies of standardization, thereby aggravating the liability of foreignness, inflating operational costs, and reducing value creation. Hence, MNEs oppose adapting operations unnecessarily. Still, local imperatives often compel them to do so. Differing cultural, political, legal, and economic circumstances shape unique business environments that press for commensurate customization of products and processes. Some differences surrender to the allure of higher-quality, lower-cost products—think of worldwide demand for an Apple iPod, Starbucks latte, or Facebook wall. In these sorts of situations, the appeal of the standardized products trumps local consumer preferences.

Others differences, however, press MNEs to tailor products and processes. *Ceteris paribus*, consumers prefer products that are sensitive to their particular lifestyle. Examples include designing and making products that local customers prefer (e.g., large cars in the United States, smaller cars in Europe, still smaller cars in emerging markets), tailoring channel structures to buyer preferences (e.g., web-based and 4G-driven content in South Korea, print and media promotion in France, personal selling in Brazil), modifying product features for local tastes (e.g., light coffee roasts in Germany and Scandinavia; dark coffee roasts in Italy and Spain; coffee flavored with spices, like cinnamon, cardamom, or cloves, in Ethiopia), and adapting marketing practices to consumption patterns (e.g., large package sizes in Australia, smaller sizes in Japan, single-unit sizes in poorer countries). In these sorts of situations, local preferences often trump global standards.

Standardization advocates counter that expanding connections across borders steadily converges consumer preferences. Ultimately, they infer, we will consume the same brands in the same way. As Steve Jobs noted during his travels to Turkey, "All day I had looked at young people in Istanbul. They were all drinking what every other kid in the world drinks, and they were wearing clothes that look like they were bought at the Gap, and they were all using cell phones like kids everywhere else. It hit me that, for young people, the whole world is the same now."[88] Skeptics quickly reject this argument. They point out that about 1 percent of the world's physical mail crosses borders, less than 2 percent of calling minutes are international, and a quarter of Internet traffic crosses national borders.[89] Likewise, just 329 brands are recognized by consumers in 8 or more countries; only 16 percent of all brands are recognized in 2 or more countries.[90] Furthermore, most people live their entire lives within one country, supporting local production and consumption of goods and sustaining local politics, history, culture, and identity. Localism, not globalism, is the lifestyle of many people in many countries.

MNEs facing stubborn variation in consumer preferences across countries, therefore, adapt products and processes to local circumstances.[91] Certainly, expanding connectivity encourages consumer behaviors that trump nationalism. Nevertheless, differences endure due to cultural predisposition, historical legacy, and latent nationalism (i.e., buy-local campaigns).[92] Responding to cross-national differences presses MNEs to adapt products and processes to local consumer preferences; optimizing, rather than maximizing, standardization creates competitive advantage.

CONCEPT CHECK

In Chapter 2, we explain how globalization spurs a variety of managerial approaches. Similarly, in Chapters 3 and 4, we emphasize how companies operating internationally encounter a variety of political, legal, and economic environments. Likewise, here we highlight how globalization imperatives and local constraints shape planning processes in the MNE.

Differences in local consumers' preferences endure due to cultural predisposition, historical legacy, and latent nationalism.

THE EFFECT OF INSTITUTIONAL AGENTS

Aspects of standardization endorses global integration whereas the issue of divergent consumer behaviors endorses local responsiveness. A third factor, institutional agents and their policy agendas, can, at different times, support either scenario. Various transnational institutions, such as the IMF, WTO, and World Bank, build an increasingly seamless global business environment. Systematically opening national borders to trade and investment creates greater potential for MNEs to build, expand, and integrate global operations. Presently, for instance, 162 nations are members of the WTO, the regulator of the rules of world trade.[93] Membership requires replacing differentiated national regulations with global standards that liberalize trade and investment. Standardizing the rules of the globalization game, so to speak, supports standardizing the methods of play. Progressive liberalization permits MNEs to configure value activities in optimal locations without forsaking access to markets worldwide. Hence, business-process outsourcing firms in India, robot builders in Germany, solar-panel makers in China, or chip architects in Taiwan can design value chains that maximize efficiency without sacrificing access to consumers in other countries.

On the other hand, institutional agents, particularly host governments, often strongly encourage, if not compel, local responsiveness. In general, different countries take different paths to develop fiscal, monetary, and business regulations. Some champion economic freedom, others constrain it. Some recommend openness, others advocate insularity. Facing constraints and insularity, MNEs respond by localizing value activities or else forsake sales, if not market access.[94] Routine pressures for local responsiveness, for example, require pharmaceutical MNEs to disperse value activities to meet a host government's mandate that clinical testing, certification procedures, pricing policies, and marketing practices comply with local regulations. An MNE trades global efficiency for local access, and correspondingly adapts resources, capabilities, and competencies.

MNEs often face extraordinary pressures for local responsiveness. Brazil, for instance levies a 30 percent tax increase on imported cars with less than 65 percent local content. Likewise, it requires foreign energy firms to spend 1 percent of gross revenue on local R&D. Thailand's Alien Occupation Act reserves many architecture and engineering services jobs for Thai nationals. Uber's international expansion has hit speed bumps; in Paris and Madrid, protests mobilize public opposition while in Frankfurt and London, regulators mull stricter regulations to spur responsiveness.[95] Consequently, host-country policies on, say, local content standards, buy-national policies, trade protectionism, hiring regulations, and currency repatriation, often require the MNE to localize value activities or else forsake market access.

CONCEPT CHECK

Chapter 7 (page 231) profiles movements in national markets toward regional trade agreements while Chapter 9 (page 280) highlights the cross-national integration of capital markets. These trends, by standardizing key aspects of the global market, support the standardization of products and processes. Increasing standardization, in turn, supports concentrating value chains.

GLOBAL INTEGRATION AND LOCAL RESPONSIVENESS: MAPPING THEIR INTERACTION

Operating internationally calls for configuring and coordinating operations in ways that reconcile the competing demands of global integration and local responsiveness. The **Integration-Responsiveness (IR) Grid** provides a straightforward framework to organize analysis (see Figure 12.4). Procedurally, it positions an industry in the quadrant that represents its sensitivity to the dual imperatives. As such, it provides executives a framework to interpret the challenge.

Strong pressures to respond locally, but low pressures to integrate globally—the lower-right quadrant of the IR Grid—encourage adapting value activities to host-country conditions. In this context, MNEs that operate in industries with strong cultural sensitivities see higher returns from local responsiveness and fewer benefits from global integration. Alternatively, high pressure to integrate globally along with slight pressure for local responsiveness—the upper-left quadrant of the IR Grid—encourages standardization to support the low cost leadership strategy. MNEs in this context exploit location effects and

The IR Grid relates the global and local pressures that influence an MNE's strategy.

FIGURE 12.4 The Integration-Responsiveness Grid

Each strategy archetype embodies a unique concept of value creation that reflects its resolution of the asymmetric pressure for global integration versus local responsiveness. The Integration-Responsiveness Grid maps this response, highlighting the interaction between each pressure that confronts an MNE in a particular industry. As such, it helps managers reconcile the competing imperatives of standardization and adaptation.

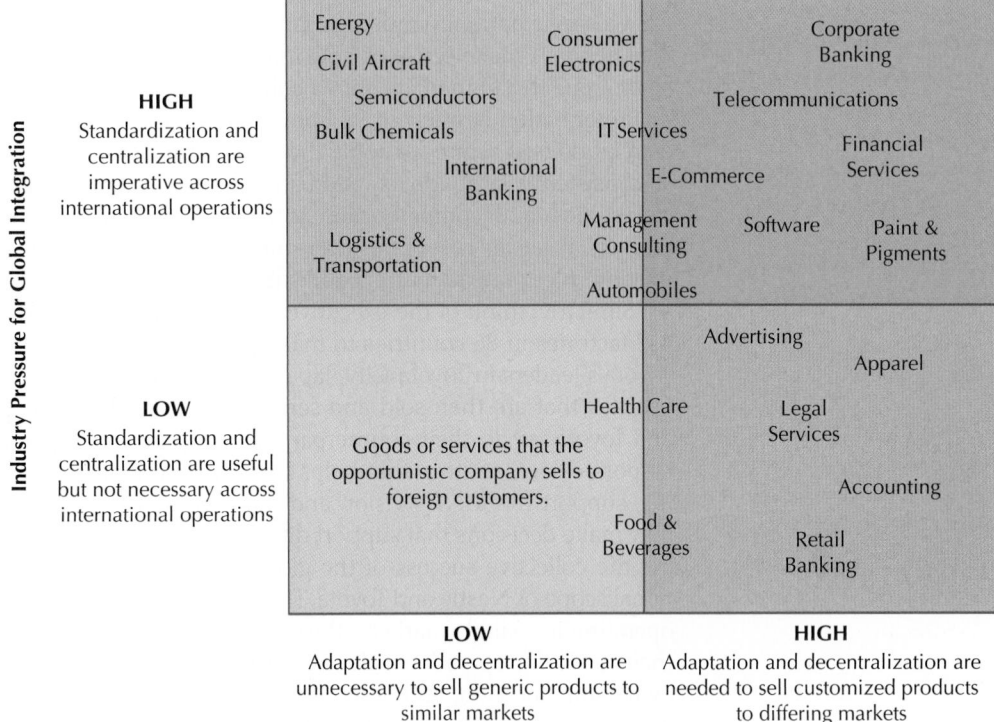

Industry Pressure for Local Responsiveness

maximize scale economies in order to provide consumers worldwide competitively priced, acceptably standardized products that meet universal needs. Flat-panel displays, for instance, are vital components for a range of products; few consumers care where they are made, as long as they are competitively priced. Thus, manufacturers like LG Philips, Chi Mie Optoelectronics, and Samsung respond to competitive pressures by concentrating value activities in economically superior locations.

A third class of MNEs compete in industries that simultaneously impose powerful demands for local responsiveness and strong pressures for global integration; we find these industries in the center zone of the IR Grid. MNEs operating in salient national sectors, such as telecommunications, information technology, automobiles, pharmaceuticals, and financial services, face differing customer preferences, market structures, regulatory codes, and institutional settings. Still, investment requirements, scale economies, and learning effects set high productivity thresholds. Configuring and coordinating value activities to resolve this dilemma poses enduring challenges. MNEs like Dentsu, China Mobile, Vodaphone, or Infosys must develop complex configuration formats that support an intricate integrated-differentiation strategy.

In summary, the IR Grid helps managers map their strategic options given prevailing pressures for standardization and adaptation in their particular industry.[96] It proves useful in making sense of competitive situations, helping to frame analytics as well as providing tools to track rivals' moves in terms of the underlying cost structure in an industry, evolving institutional dynamics, and shifting consumer preferences. It maps how **industry structure** sets the context, strategy specifies the end, and managers configure operations to mediate the two.

CONCEPT CHECK

Globalization, though a powerful force, is not inevitable. Chapters 3 and 4 developed this thesis by noting that political and economic freedoms are in flux. Similarly, both consumer preferences and host-government pressures prompt companies to adapt their value chains to local conditions.

INTERNATIONAL CORPORATE-LEVEL STRATEGIES

Earlier, we profiled business-level strategies—namely, the cost leadership, differentiation, and the integrated cost leadership/differentiation strategy. These ideas explain how a company competes in a given market. Going international, by diversifying an MNE's operation from a single nation to multiple nations, introduces the idea of corporate-level strategy. This idea helps us make sense of how managers unite the individual parts of the MNE, whether spanning 2 to 214 markets, into a cohesive, coherent whole. For example, Apple implements a differentiation strategy in its home market, the United States. As Apple expands into foreign markets, it aspires to apply the same business strategy in each additional market. Doing so consistently supports its vision and mission and productively uses its bundle of resources, capabilities, and competencies. As Apple expands strategic planning from one to many markets, it sets its corporate-level strategy to manage issues, such as the respective decision-making roles of headquarters and subsidiaries, which span multiple markets.

Similarly, think of the executives at Nestlé headquarters in Vevey, Switzerland, directing 442 factories in 86 countries to make products that are then sold in 197 countries. Or, also, Toyota's leaders in Toyota City, Japan, overseeing 70 factories spanning 29 countries making vehicles that are then sold and serviced in more than 170 countries. The leaders of Nestlé and Toyota, as do their counterparts at other MNEs, organize worldwide operation with a corporate-level strategy that helps everyone, no matter where they are or what they are doing, support the MNE's vision and mission. Absent this unifying logic, workers worldwide may make decisions that support different, even contradictory, strategies, thereby undermining the collective success of the global enterprise.[97] In addition, think again of the operational scope of Nestlé and Toyota. Their global span imposes costs and complications beyond operating in a single market—the so-called liability of foreignness. HQ executives, surveying their far-flung operations, develop a corporate strategy to specify how they will leverage ownership, location, and asset advantages to generate the value that offsets the additional expenses of international operations.

Therefore, a corporate-level strategy (1) articulates how managers plan to reconcile global integration and local responsiveness in ways that support the MNE's vision and mission, (2) stipulates how managers will integrate the MNE's various parts into a strategic whole, and (3) specifies the decision-making role the headquarters and subsidiaries take doing so. The international, localization, global standardization, and transnational strategies anchor contemporary interpretation. Table 12.7 profiles the principles and practices of each archetype.

> **Corporate-level strategy** determines the actions an MNE takes to gain a competitive advantage by selecting and managing its business across a group of nations.

THE INTERNATIONAL STRATEGY

MNEs competing in markets marked by low pressures for global integration and local responsiveness (the lower-left quadrant of the IR Grid) have the flexibility to sell products designed for their home market, with minimal, if any, customization for foreign markets. Moreover, they often face few, if any, rivals that offer a competitive product. In addition, their superior competitiveness creates the flexibility to arbitrage location effects. Given this scenario, managers position the MNE to implement the **international strategy**.

The international strategy transfers home-country-based competencies, such as production expertise, design skills, or brand power, to foreign markets. Ultimate control resides with headquarters, since senior executives understand the optimal bundling of the company's resources and capabilities. The testing ground of new ideas is the home market, not foreign countries. Headquarters-based strategic planners regulate foreign units' market moves and operating choices, directing local managers to leverage home-country competencies. This outlook gives local managers limited authority to adapt plans, processes, or products. MNEs implementing an international strategy include Airbus, Apple, and Google.

Google, for example, develops the core architecture of its web products and platforms at the Googleplex, its headquarters complex in Mountain View, California. It allows national

> **The international strategy** transfers a company's resources, capabilities, and core competencies into foreign markets where they do not exist, or do exist but are less efficiently made or less effectively delivered.

TABLE 12.7   Characteristics of the Strategy Types Used by MNEs

The strategy gamut of "international-localization-global-transnational" anchors IB theory. Each archetype speaks directly and differently to how an MNE reconciles the tension of global integration versus local responsiveness as well as the respective decision-making authority of headquarters and subsidiaries. Managers, mindful of industry structure and drivers of value creation, trade-off the characteristics of the four archetypes in making their strategic choice.

	International Strategy	**Localization Strategy**	**Global Strategy**	**Transnational Strategy**
Orientation	Leverage core competencies and home-country innovations into superior competitive positions abroad.	Differentiate products to respond to national differences in customer preferences, industry characteristics, or government regulation.	Target universal needs or wants that support selling standardized products worldwide. Emphasize volume, cost minimization, and efficiency.	Simultaneously manages the tensions of global integration and local differentiation in ways that leverage specialized knowledge and promote worldwide learning.
Value Chain Configuration	Concentrated; value activities are set and directed by headquarters.	Dispersed; subsidiaries command discretion to adapt value activities.	Concentrated; value activities exploit location economics.	Concentrated to tap location economies. Dispersed, subject to minimum efficiency standards, to meet local preferences.
Decision-Making Outlook	Centralization as HQ retains control of resources and capabilities to apply, regulate, and protect core competencies.	Decentralization as subsidiaries operate quasi-independently, tailoring activities to local circumstances.	Centralization as HQ directs activity to maximize standardization, enforce consistency, regulate the global matrix of inputs and outputs, and contain costs.	Simultaneous goals of integration and responsiveness calls for sharing decision-making between headquarters or subsidiaries.
Key Advantage	Directly transfers expertise from headquarters to international units.	Reduced need for central support to manage local activities. Sensitivity to local preferences.	Make low-cost, high-quality, standardized products that differ little, but appeal to consumers worldwide.	Supports efficiency, compels effectiveness, and leverages learning that drives innovations through units worldwide.
Key Disadvantage	Centralizing decision-making in the home country can misread local innovations.	Encourages "mini-me" phenomenon that replicates value activities across subsidiaries. Fuels accountability and allegiance conflicts.	Reduced learning opportunities given the dominance of the global standard.	Elaborate decision-making mechanisms integrate dispersed operations. Difficult to configure, tough to coordinate, and prone to performance shortfalls.
IR Grid Positioning	High pressure for global integration. Low to mid-pressure for national responsiveness.	Low pressure for global integration. High pressure for national responsiveness.	High-pressure for global integration. Low to mid- pressure for national responsiveness.	High pressure for global integration. High pressure for national responsiveness.
Examples	Google, P&G, Nucor, Harley Davidson, Baidu, Apple, Tesco, Facebook, Carrefour.	Unilever, Nestlé, McDonald's, Johnson & Johnson, Pfizer, Embraer, Ranbaxy.	Toyota, Canon, Haier, Caterpillar, Cemex, Infosys, Walmart, Huawei, Haier, American Express, Cisco.	GE, Tata, Zara, IBM, SAP.

subsidiaries to customize aspects of its web pages to deal with local differences in language and alphabet. Executives in the Googleplex safeguard the search algorithms and platform systems that build its competitive advantage. Planners in the Googleplex direct product development and set business processes for overseas operations. Hence, headquarters transfers principles, practices, and processes to foreign operations. It does not, however, transfer control.

Advantages   The international strategy works well when an MNE's products or processes speak to a universal customer preference. Again, think of Apple or Google operating overseas; no matter the market, each offers an appealing option that transcends product preference or price elasticity. Each MNE's products, by setting the global standard, benefits from few rivals (the result of superior competitiveness), moderate operational costs (the efficiency of direct product transfer), and high profits (the yield of international leverage).

Limitations   Headquarters' confidence in the superior competitiveness of its competencies discourages local adaptation. Initially, this outlook does not carry high risks. But, as an

MNE expands its global operations, a one-way view of the world may miss opportunities or misread threats in foreign markets. Moreover, the international strategy sustains strong performance as long as foreign rivals scramble futilely. Companies in many foreign markets, especially those in emerging economies, are reinventing systems of production and distribution, experimenting with new business models, and resetting the standards of innovation. An unexpectedly enterprising competitor may disrupt industry structure or market dynamics. Google, for example, faces increasingly adept local rivals in South Korea and China, Naver and Baidu, respectively, whose native sensitivities to local search tendencies strongly position them in fast-growing Asian markets.[98] The centralization ethos of the international strategy, consequently, can struggle reconciling local responsiveness pressures.

THE LOCALIZATION STRATEGY

Some MNE faces higher pressure for local responsiveness, but lower pressure to reduce costs via global integration (the lower-right quadrant of the IR Grid). Cultural, political, legal, and economic conditions in foreign markets require MNEs, like J&J, McDonald's, Nestlé, or HSBC, adapt products and processes to local circumstances. Cost pressures shape, but do not determine, local competitiveness. Still, offsetting the liability of foreignness as well as providing a reasonably priced alternative to local products requires an MNE to optimize productivity. Efficiently customizing products and process from market to market, if headquarters aims to direct activity despite high responsiveness pressures, is costly and complicated. Instead, an MNE adopts a **localization strategy**, orienting its vision, mission, and plans to provide customers products that fit their distinctive preferences.

> The localization strategy encourages decentralized decision-making so that local subsidiaries can adjust value activities to local circumstances.

The localization strategy decentralizes strategic planning. National subsidiaries, not global headquarters, organize the resources and capabilities needed to design, make, and sell products that respond to preferences, practices, and the mélange of politics, law, and culture in the local marketplace.[99] At J&J, for example, headquarters' recognizes that health-care regulations and patient care standards vary across countries. The scale and scope of differences preclude universal planning from headquarters. Optimizing global performance requires J&J let its 275 business units worldwide behave like innovative, entrepreneurial firms, directing strategic planning and organizing value activities to fit local circumstances.[100]

Advantages　The localization strategy superbly speaks to the unique features of consumer preferences, market situations, and environmental context found in a national market. It drives MNEs to customize products and processes. Starbucks, which began internationalizing operations in 1996 and now has nearly 23,000 outlets in 65 countries, expands by locally adapting its blend of coffee, aesthetics, and aura. Boosting performance in Europe, for example, relies on edgy architecture, including chandeliers and stages for poetry readings, in order to lure customers socialized to a high-touch café culture. In contrast, Starbucks runs its 75 outlets in India through a 50/50 joint venture with Tata Global Beverages. These outlets sell coffee from beans grown and roasted in-country, brewing a distinct Indian blend. Too, it alters its menus to Indian tastes, offering a unique dish in each city that hosts a franchise.[101] Likewise, Starbucks taps the expertise of its joint venture partner to design outlets that, besides respecting historical architecture and ideals, incorporate the local culture.

The localization strategy gives the MNE's local units a distinctive advantage against in-country competitors who lack the benefits provided by the parent company. Industries of the sort found in the lower-right corner of the IR Grid, such as apparel, food, health care, and retail banking, historically had local companies that operated nationally. Although competitive, many cannot match the pools of resources, capabilities, and competencies found in successful MNEs. For example, J&J's headquarters configures and coordinates global activities that support local units that leverage its world-class research, executive, financial, marketing, and logistics competencies. Hence, the localization strategy helps subsidiaries build superior competitive positions in local markets on the strength of the parent's global advantages.[102]

CONCEPT CHECK

Chapter 4 (page 154) profiles the idea of state capitalism, Chapter 4 (page 207) discussed the economic rationales for governmental trade intervention, and Chapter 7 (page 231) notes how trade agreements shape markets. In these and similar cases, state intervention into the market reduces the freedom MNEs have to pursue the efficiencies of global integration. On the other hand, state intervention also benefits those MNEs that stress local responsiveness.

The localization strategy, by encouraging operational overlap, increases overhead expenses.

Limitations   The customer centricity of localization requires replicating value activities from subsidiary to subsidiary. Essentially, an MNE implementing localization builds "mini-me" units around the world. Customizing products or processes requires different resource and capabilities, thereby increasing costs along the value chain. Different product designs necessitate different materials, smaller markets make for shorter production runs, different channel structures call for dissimilar distribution formats, and divergent technology platforms complicate information exchange. Hence, the localization strategy is practical for the MNE competing in largely price inelastic markets.[103]

Likewise, localization promotes management styles and value chains that differ from unit to unit. Allocating authority to local decision-makers can, over time, develop powerful subsidiaries. Eventually, some may opt to ignore headquarters' lead, instead maintaining that the unique features of their situation warrants a different, even contradictory, vision and mission. Left to their own devices, they may design programs that, by nullifying potential scale effects of cross-national integration, escalate costs. If a subsidiary evolves into a virtual stand-alone operation, resource and power dynamics may neutralize headquarters' authority. Ensuing contests over visions, mission, and plans blunt competitiveness.[104]

GLOBAL STRATEGY

MNEs competing in industries of the sort found in the upper-left quadrant of the IR Grid face high pressures for global integration yet low pressures for local responsiveness. Industry effects press these firms to adopt a **global strategy** that is keenly sensitive to the economics of efficiency, advantages of standardization, and the imperative of integration. Productivity pressures push an MNE to, ideally, be the cost leader or, minimally, be competitive with the industry pacesetter. Either objective compels it to exploit potential scale economies, learning effects, and location advantages. Operationally, an MNE concentrates value activities in a few, ideal locations; standardizes products to simplify design and support long production runs; and rationalizes marketing to back aggressive pricing and direct distribution.

A global strategy champions worldwide standardization of value activities.

The global strategy has stark implications to value-chain design. Units operate in favorable locations that maximize productivity (e.g., a shoe factory in Vietnam, an auto-parts maker in China, a service call center in the Philippines). Value activities need not take place in the same location; a fully optimized global value chain locates an activity in the most efficient locale. IBM, for instance, supports its Asian value chain with HR specialists in Manila, accounts receivable experts in Shanghai, accountants in Kuala Lumpur, and procurement officers in Shenzhen.[105] Headquarters directs decision-making by standardizing the practices and processes used in overseas units. Relentless cost pressures from rivals require headquarters to continually raise productivity thresholds.[106]

For some products, notably commodities, the global strategy is essentially the only profitable option. Commodities serve a universal need (think of gasoline, steel, aspirin, memory chips, debit cards, sugar, and so on). Consumer preferences in different countries, if not identical, are similar. Choosing between basically identical products (i.e., Company X's gasoline versus Company Y's gasoline) makes price a key point of competitiveness. The global strategy is not restricted to commodity markets. The globalization of markets encourages MNEs like Zara in apparel, IKEA in home furnishings, or LVMH in luxury goods to standardize features of historically differentiated products, manufacture them on a global scale, market them with a global brand, and sell them through focused distribution channels. Unquestionably, cross-national differences in consumer preferences exist, but they necessitate minor, if any, customization.

Money has three inalienable features: It is

- difficult to acquire,
- transient,
- scarce.

Some MNEs, such as Caterpillar or Tesla, reason that even if there are significant differences, target customers will sacrifice their preference to buy local and switch to a higher-quality, competitively priced, substitute—even if it's foreign made. Anchoring this view is the outlook that no matter the society, money exhibits three inalienable features: it is hard to acquire (one typically must work for it), transient (it is quickly used), and scarce in supply (no matter the amount, it inevitably seems too little). Consequently, consumers worldwide pursue a common quest: maximize utility by buying the highest-quality product for the lowest possible price.[107] Ultimately, economically rational consumers disregard a product's national origin, buying a foreign-made product rather than a local substitute, as long as it delivers superior value. The sweep and scope of technology intensifies this tendency. Consumer preferences converge as connections proliferate across countries. The shrinking digital divide exposes more people to common media, thereby promoting universal consumption ideals, and, in turn, standardizing consumer behaviors. Ultimately, consumers' disposition to discount nationalism in the quest for a product offering superior value girds the global strategy.

Advantages   The global strategy exploits economies of scale, learning effects, and location economies in order to translate the MNE's resources and capabilities into core competences that support cost leadership worldwide. Efficiently configuring value activities competes with like-minded rivals as well as persuades consumers, given the product's superior value proposition, to switch from a local to a global brand. The global strategy benefits from the ongoing integration of national markets; emerging global standards fan demand for universal goods and services. Institutional developments progressively reduce the trade frictions and investment restrictions that had historically constrained **location economics**. MNEs increasingly move anything anywhere in the pursuit of maximizing efficiency. The globalization of markets, quite simply, expands opportunities for cross-national integration. Lastly, the global strategy clarifies sensemaking and decision-making. Single-minded focus on improving efficiency imposes an absolute logic on strategic planning.

Limitations   The cost sensitivity of the global strategy leaves MNEs little latitude to customize processes or products to local conditions; each change reduces efficiency. Hence, an MNE's success is a function of the validity of the 'one type product fits all customers' needs worldwide' thesis. A single bet on a single approach for a single global market is risky. Disruptive change can turn the laser focus of a globally tuned value chain into a maladapted delusion. The fallout of the global financial crisis, for example, saw big banks such as Citibank, Royal Bank of Scotland, and Fortis foiled by their previously high-performance global strategies. Despite leadership in global capital markets, the crisis and ensuing demand for local responsiveness turned many of their strengths into liabilities. Finally, concentrating value activities in a few productivity-maximizing locations exposes the MNE to a host of risks, such as political change, legal manipulations, trade conflicts, and exchange-rate instability.

TRANSNATIONAL STRATEGY

The asymmetric demands of maximizing efficiencies through cost leadership and effectiveness via differentiation make it difficult to pursue both simultaneously. Still, some companies successfully adopt an integrated cost leadership/differentiation business-level strategy. The corporate-level analogue, the **transnational strategy**, takes this idea globally.

The MNEs operating in the sort of industries we see in the upper-right quadrant of the IR Grid, notably, airlines or e-commerce, must simultaneously integrate globally in order to reduce costs as well as adapt to national circumstances to appease local stakeholders. Resolution requires managers standardize some activities while differentiating others. Choosing to optimize both objectives, rather than maximize one, reduces efficiency and caps effectiveness. Offsetting high costs, given the ever-present liability of foreignness, requires that an MNE develop firm-specific capabilities and competencies that create difficult-to-copy points of competitive advantage. Hence, the transnational strategy

CONCEPT CHECK ●

Several points in previous chapters profile the growing potential and performance of emerging economies, such as China, India, and the Philippines. Fast-rising MNEs in these countries develop product and process innovations to frugally engineer goods and services that respond to the Base of the Pyramid phenomenon. These innovations push Western MNEs to rethink the economics of value creation.

Standardization drives improving the efficiency of effort, which, in turn, supports charging lower prices while still earning profits.

The transnational strategy targets the efficiency of global integration, the effectiveness of local responsiveness, and the systematic diffusion of innovations.

champions interactive "global learning," leveraging local insights developed in meeting "particularizing tendencies" to upgrade resources and improve capabilities and then diffusing them worldwide to respond to "universalizing tendencies."[108] Systematically diffusing local insights earned via adaptation in one locale to others enables the transnational strategy to optimize location economics and scale efficiencies.

The transnational strategy does not centralize authority in headquarters or decentralize it to local units. Instead, its advocates communication and collaboration between idea generators and idea adopters, no matter where each resides. Implementing the transnational strategy requires a sophisticated value chain that simultaneously supports integration, responsiveness, and learning. Managers configure value activities, ideally satisfying minimum efficiency standards, on a country-to-country basis given prevailing cultural, political, legal, and economic conditions. Location choices are neither biased toward concentration nor dispersal. Rather, they balance the universalizing tendencies that endorse global integration with the particularizing tendencies that push local responsiveness, effectively shifting the MNE toward a 'glocal' orientation.[109] Successfully implementing the transnational strategy opens tremendous opportunities to optimize productivity, create value, and sustain competitiveness 'glocally.' Hence, for MNEs in the upper-right quadrant of the IR Grid, this strategy is obligatory. For those facing similar trends in technology, competition, and globalization, it's crucial.

> The transnational strategy reconciles global integration and local responsiveness in ways that leverage the MNE's core competency throughout worldwide operations.

Advantages Some see the transnational strategy, in contrast to the international, localization, or global strategy, better suited to optimally respond to the emerging requirements of the global business environment. Charging strategic planners to gain location economies and experience effects without sacrificing the flexibility to customize processes and products pushes for an innovative integration of vision, mission, resources, capabilities, and competencies. The transnational strategy recognizes the payoff of multidirectional knowledge exchange between units to develop this mix. Essentially, as we saw in the opening profile of Zara, strategic planning presumes that neither headquarters nor local subsidiaries know best, but collectively they develop 'glocal' innovations that help each reconcile the dual imperative. Validating the vitality of learning throughout the MNE's global network helps managers make sense of optimizing headquarters' resources and local subsidiaries' capabilities given particularizing and universalizing tendencies.

> The transnational strategy is difficult to implement in practice, given the challenges of complicated agendas, high costs, and cognitive limits.

Limitations The transnational strategy is tough to direct, difficult to configure, and prone to shortfalls. Reconciling integration and responsiveness pressures, further complicated by the necessity to generate knowledge locally but diffuse it worldwide, can overwhelm the best-intentioned MNEs. Simultaneously developing integration and differentiation advantages requires converting resources and capabilities into competencies that support a broad cross-section of value activities. Developing a network mindset among employees, installing the requisite communication network, and navigating the ambiguity of multi-criteria decision makes strategic planning challenging. The complexity of the transnational strategy means the MNE may fall short of sufficiently integrating global activities and/or differentiating local operations—essentially, getting caught in the dreaded middle zone where costs run too high and responsiveness runs too low.

The Multinational Enterprise of the Future: Leading Scenarios

Evolving workflows, technology platforms, and market dynamics intensify globalization trends. MNEs respond in kind, rethinking visions, clarifying missions, adjusting strategies, and reconfiguring value chains to compete in the brave new world.[110] Forecasts of accelerating change due to digitization, frugal innovations, robotic cells, and activist transnational institutions, among others, spur MNEs to assess the best path to bundling resources, capabilities, and competencies. Let's take a look at some high-concept visions of the MNE of the future.

The Globally Integrated Enterprise

The evolutionary perspective sees MNEs responding systematically to the steadily unfolding imperatives of globalization. As policies and practices progressively connect countries, MNEs similarly respond, progressively integrating their cross-national operations. Sam Palmisano, the past CEO of IBM, has a provocative take. Reflecting on IBM's evolution, he contends that it has passed through three strategic phases, each fitting the prevailing circumstances and collectively foreshadowing the MNE of the future.

First, there was the nineteenth-century "international model, whereby the company was headquartered both physically and mentally in its home country; it sold goods, when it was so inclined, through a scattering of overseas sales offices."[111] Headquarters focused on business activities in its home country and configured international operations with little input from overseas units. As such, it used an international strategy to engage a world composed of unevenly connected countries.

Phase two of the evolution ushered in the classic multinational firm of the late twentieth century. Echoing the localization strategy, this phase saw HQ build smaller versions of itself abroad. Steadily, the expanding connection among countries, by supporting concentrated value chains geared toward exploiting location economics and scale economies, highlighted the inefficient economics of the "mini-me" option.[112] The cost of redundancy—each country essentially ran a stand-alone operation—grew unacceptable in the face of intensifying competition.

The third phase, the "globally integrated enterprise," speaks to the dawn of globality in which "business flows in every direction. Companies have no centers. The idea of foreignness is foreign. Commerce swirls and market dominance shifts."[113] Competing with everyone from everywhere for everything requires putting investments, people, and work anywhere in the world "based on the right cost, the right skills and the right business environment [with] work flow[ing] to the places where it will be done...most efficient-

ly and to the highest quality."[114] Earlier models saw configuration and coordination barriers constrain knowledge flows, production opportunities, and organizational options. Now, like the Internet, the globally integrated enterprise designs its strategy, configures its activities, and coordinates its processes to connect everything, everywhere, 24/7.

The Metanational

In the future, goes this scenario, world-class operational efficiency will no longer determine an MNE's competitive advantage. Nor will an MNE build superior competitiveness from unique features of its home country or, for that matter, from a set of national subsidiaries. Rather, victory will go to those who move from designing multinational operations to synthesizing metanational competencies. The metanational seeks unique ideas, activities, and insights that complement its existing operations as well as create new leverage points. It expands its mission from selling stuff worldwide to mining the treasure trove of ideas, resources, and capabilities that emerge anywhere and everywhere. Its managers scan the world, identifying and interpreting the untapped potential of the specialized knowledge that lays latent in unique market situations. Exploiting these opportunities positions managers to "build a new kind of competitive advantage by discovering, accessing, mobilizing, and leveraging knowledge from many locations around the world."[115]

Metanationals, goes the theory, orient strategic planning to:

- *Prospect* for and access untapped technologies and unidentified consumer trends.
- *Leverage* globally the specialized knowledge scattered throughout local subsidiaries.
- *Mobilize* fragmented knowledge to generate innovations that produce, market, and deliver value on a global scale.
- *Apply* superior project management skills across teams to foster a strong collaborative culture and to engage a robust array of communications tools.[116]

MNEs like Shiseido, ARM, McDonald's, STMicroelectronics, Acer, Procter & Gamble, SAP, Tata, and PolyGram are emergent metanationals, able to turn underused knowledge into global-dominant innovations. Consider the experiences of McDonald's in its fast-growing market—Russia. It has more than 500 outlets and plans to add hundreds more, given that Russia is one of its fastest-growing and most-profitable markets.[117] Successfully building its Russian operations required McDonald's to rethink its value chain. In the West, it buys ingredients from third parties, rather than producing its own. Upon entering Russia, the lack of local suppliers required opening the *McComplex*, a full-scale production system outside of Moscow. Making virtually every ingredient from scratch at the McComplex required rethinking how to reconfigure activities to tap Russia's unique market.[118] Besides building better burgers, McDonald's leveraged its Russian experiences worldwide to develop new competencies. In metanational style, McDonald's began its worldwide pushback against coffee chains by tapping knowledge it developed with test runs in Russia. It opened McCafés there in 2003, fine-tuned its espresso-style drinks, and then successfully moved the concept to the United States in 2009 and, from there, to the world.[119]

Which sorts of MNEs aspire to be a metanational? Generally, those facing pressures for global integration and local responsiveness yet seeing opportunities in prospecting, leveraging, and mobilizing knowledge that is fragmented across countries. Until recently, the metanational option attracted few companies. Communication and collaboration barriers complicated sharing knowledge. Moreover, significant national differences, although shrinking, posed problems. Today, environmental conditions, institutional agendas, and technology trends, by easing sensing, mobilizing, and operationalizing knowledge, steadily support the metanational's emergence.[120]

The Micro-Multinational

The future frontier for the MNE is set by the matter of size, say others.[121] Historically, MNEs were colossi that straddled the globe. Today, the number of MNEs grows worldwide, but the average size is falling—many of the 80,000 plus firms that operate internationally employ fewer than 250 people.[122] This anomaly signals the era of so-called "micro-multinationals": nimble, small firms that are born global, operating internationally from day one.[123] Unlike their bigger counterparts that expanded internationally by gradually entering new markets, micro-multinationals go global immediately. They go where they wish, typically following the circuit paths of the Internet, but always targeting markets with plentiful customers and innovative environments. The born-global does not see international markets as a refuge when sales slow at home. Rather, it begins with the belief that the domestic market is just one of the many opportunities in the world.[124]

The micro-multinational's distinctive break from the past follows from its global focus at start-up. Folks who found born-global firms often have a strong international orientation gained from living or studying abroad. Logitech, the Swiss-based maker of computer devices like mice, keyboards, and speakers, was founded by a Swiss and an Italian who met while studying at Stanford University in the United States. Soon after start-up, Logitech was selling its products worldwide and now does business in more than 100 countries.[125] Often, too, we see a seasoned executive,

motivated by an entrepreneurial vision, leaving a large MNE and launching a firm that goes global from the get-go.[126]

The micro-multinational moves from theory to practice precisely because circumstances let it do so. The ongoing globalization of markets, marked by falling trade barriers, expanding demand for specialized products, and improving technologies, enables born-globals to implement their vision cheaply and quickly. Micro-multinationals exploit these circumstances, building powerful platforms to develop and deliver innovations in niche markets that span the world.

The Glorecalizized MNE

Advocates of regionalization endorse the awkward term "Glorecalization" as the next logical step of global strategy.[127] Glorecalization, a portmanteau of **Glo**balization-**Re**gionalization-Lo**calization**, champions a global vision and customized local tactics through a value chain configured to exploit location economies within a regional market. The glorecalized MNE leverages its regional network to gain the necessary operational efficiencies without forsaking local flexibility. Various conditions support the glorecalized MNE. First and foremost, regional trade blocs (e.g., AU, ASEAN, CARICOM, EU, NAFTA, and TPP) create ample location effects in terms of institutional structure, regulatory framework, and market integration. The European Union, for example, unites 28 countries and creates a common "home" for more than 500 million who share similar outlooks, overlapping national interests, and convergent consumption preferences. Efficient flows of people, capital, information, products, and processes throughout the EU streamline how an MNE acquires resources, develops capabilities, and crafts competencies. Similarly, regionalizing production exploits location effects and scale economies, but without sacrificing the flexibility to adapt goods and services.

The Cybercorp

The cybercorp, a form unimaginable a generation ago, is increasingly a reality today.[128] The cybercorp does not organize products, consumers, or markets to reflect or respect the physical geography of lines on a map. Instead, the connectivity network of the Internet, not national borders, defines its operational boundaries. Facebook, for instance, exists physically in its California headquarters, but its workforce of about 13,000 run a company that serves more than 1.5 billion "customers" in more than 150 nations through a website interface translated into more than 100 languages.[129]

Cybercorps develop competencies that help them react in real time to changes in customers, markets, and environments. They engage perspectives and strategies that bias value chains toward virtuality in order to link capabilities and competencies within dynamic networks. For instance, Reebok owns no plants, instead relying on contract manufacturers to make and distribute its products. Similarly, Nike, Apple, Cisco, and Qualcomm outsource production to manufacturers in low-cost labor locations in order to do what each does best: maximizing value creation through R&D and marketing. Though nominally independent, communications and collaboration systems integrate agents into the network, thereby creating virtual capabilities. Nike, for example, focuses on increasing value creation by leveraging its competencies in design and marketing, confident in manufacturers' expertise to adjust product mixes as consumer preferences evolve.

The cybercorp builds on crowdsourcing, swarm intelligence, and artificial intelligence to tap the collective insight developed in self-organizing systems that are remotely executing, global, always on, and endlessly configurable. It, in collaboration with partners, operates here, there, and everywhere. Many of these agents were, just a decade earlier, far off the global grid. Now, innovations enact a techno-utopia that connects everyone to the "evolving nervous system of civilization."[130] The cybercorp, built to engage strategies that learn, evolve, and transform, moves business toward the emerging standards of the Singularity Principle.[131]

Make the Call

Yes, the ideal MNE of the future is more speculation than stipulation. No matter the standard that ultimately emerges, we expect it will showcase the historic markers of companies that are built to last: a down-to-earth, pragmatic, committed-to-excellence framework run by bright people who articulate an insightful vision, practical mission, and clever strategy that change the game.[132] Still, we watch, tracking the emergence of the contenders, waiting to see which form sets the standard.

QUESTIONS

12-3. You have a choice to work for a globally integrated enterprise, a metanational, a glorecalized MNE, a micro-multinational, or a cybercorp. Which would you choose? Why?

12-4. Looking out over the next decade, estimate the likely standards of how an MNE will create value. In your opinion, which form of MNE is best designed for this scenario? Why?

12-5. The MNE of the future, in whatever form it takes, will face pressures for global integration along with those clamoring for local responsiveness. In your opinion, which form will best reconcile that challenge?

MyLab Management

Go to **mymanagementlab.com** for the following Assisted-graded writing questions:

12-6 What environmental conditions, institutional agendas, and technology trends support the emergence of the cybercorp? Do the same apply to a metanational?

12-7 What sort of management skills and executive perspectives make someone an attractive candidate for a micro-multinational?

Endnotes

Scan for Endnotes or go to www.pearsonglobaleditions.com/Daniels

CHAPTER 13

Evaluation of Countries for Operations

OBJECTIVES

After studying this chapter, you should be able to

13-1   Elaborate on the significance of location in IB operations

13-2   Illustrate why comparing countries through scanning is important and how it connects to final location choices

13-3   Discern major opportunity and risk variables and how to prioritize and relate them when deciding whether and where to expand abroad

13-4   Summarize the sources and shortcomings of comparative country information

13-5   Explain alternative considerations and means for companies to allocate resources among countries

13-6   Recognize why companies make noncomparative decisions when choosing where to operate abroad

MyLab Management®
Improve Your Performance!
When you see this icon ⭐, visit
www.mymanagementlab.com for activities that are applied, personalized, and offer immediate feedback.

The place to get top speed out of a horse is not the place where you can get top speed out of a canoe.

—African (Hausa) proverb

▼ An international business group considering global business expansion.

Source: wavebreakmedia. Shutterstock

CASE Burger King®

In 2016 Burger King Worldwide (referred to hereafter as Burger King) was the world's largest flame-broiled fast-food hamburger chain. Figure 13.1 shows Burger King's four geographic divisions in terms of the number of restaurants and amount of sales.[1] The chapter's opening photo shows a Burger King in Tokyo, Japan.

A BIT OF HISTORY

Starting out as Insta-Burger King in 1954, the company grew to five restaurants in the next five years. In 1959, with its name shortened to Burger King, it began domestic franchising. Beginning in the early 1960s the company expanded internationally to the Bahamas and Puerto Rico. Then it entered Europe, Asia, and Latin America in the 1970s.

Since 1967, Burger King has at times been publicly owned, a division of other companies, a holding company owned by private equity firms, and a privately owned company. In fact, over a 20-year period it had seven different parents and corporate structures. The years of transformed ownership caused changes in its emphasis, and its interests have sometimes been secondary to those of its parent company. Nevertheless, some of its international moves turned out to be highly successful, and a few did not. It entered and then retreated from operations in such countries as Colombia, France, Israel, Japan, and Oman. (It has reentered some of these.) Much of Burger King's early international forays came about either because someone in another country approached it or because a corporate manager was familiar with a particular country and thought it would offer opportunities. Its retreats have occurred because of not receiving adequate payments and

because of having entered markets too small to support the necessary infrastructure, such as slaughterhouse and beef-grinding facilities.

Over time, Burger King has taken a more systematic approach toward restaurant expansion. It still sees substantial U.S. growth opportunities but considers it to be a more mature market than other countries. In seeking new places to enter, Burger King looks most favorably at countries with large populations (especially young people), high consumption of beef, availability of capital to franchisees for growth, a safe pro-business environment, growth in shopping centers, and availability of a potential franchisee with experience and resources. Recently its model has been to grant franchise rights by pairing a private equity firm with an experienced restaurant operator in a joint venture (JV). In some cases, Burger King has become the third party in the JV without committing capital to it.

Overall, Burger King has expanded abroad later than its primary rival, McDonald's. On the one hand, later entry is a drawback in very small markets due to an inadequate number of suppliers, such as only one slaughterhouse whose owners may be unwilling to work with more than one customer. On the other hand, its later entry into larger markets allows Burger King to benefit from earlier entrants' creation of product demand and a supply infrastructure. In Latin America and the Caribbean, McDonald's and Burger King compete in almost all countries and territories, with Burger King currently leading in the number of restaurants in about half of those markets.

Burger King's Latin America and Caribbean group has many sparsely populated countries (e.g., the Cayman Islands, Aruba, and Saint Lucia) in which Burger King developed a presence long before

FIGURE 13.1 Regional Emphasis of Burger King
Based on data from *2015 Burger King 10K Report*. The sales figures are for 2013, and the restaurant figures are for 2014.

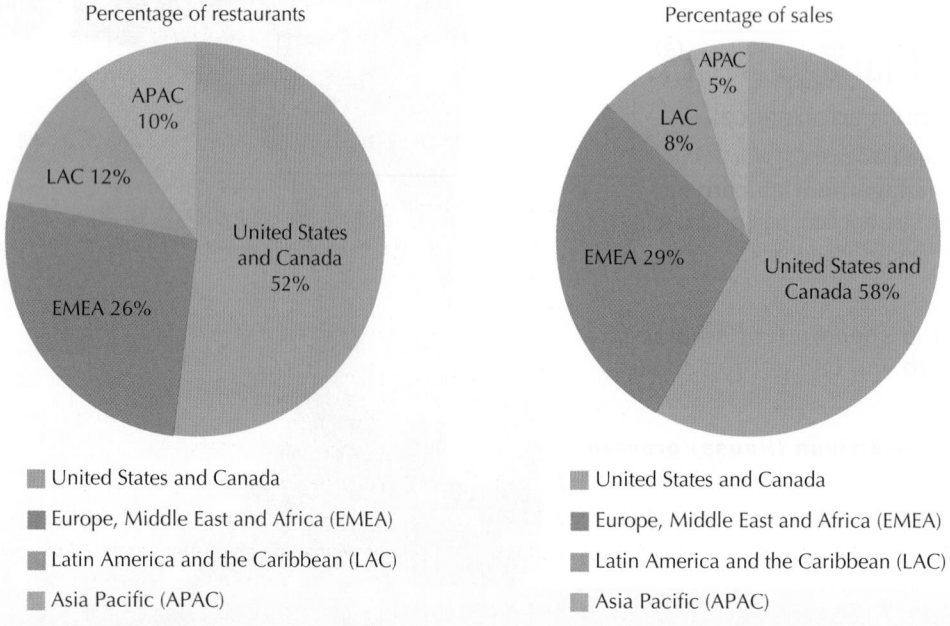

entering more abundantly populated countries such as China, Russia, and South Africa. The reason is largely due to its headquarters location in Miami, which is often called "the capital of Latin America." Because so many people from that region go to or through Miami, the Burger King reputation spilled over there early on, which simplified gaining brand recognition and acceptance. Further, Miami's nearness to Latin America and the Caribbean enhances the ability of Burger King's executives and franchisees to visit each other.

REENTERING COLOMBIA AND FRANCE

Colombia

Burger King entered Colombia in the early 1980s but departed because of Colombian royalty expatriation restrictions and prolonged economic and political turmoil. By the time Burger King reentered the country in 2008, the cities were safe for people to go out to eat, the peso was strong, families had disposable income to eat out, and all the major cities had large new shopping centers with food courts. Although incomes were unevenly distributed, the richest 20 percent of the population (almost 9 million people) had a per capita expenditure in 2007 of over US$17,000. In addition, Burger King was able to sign franchise rights with two well-established and experienced companies.

France

Burger King entered France in 1979, departed in 2001, and reentered in 2013. When entering, Quick (a Belgian fast-food operator) and McDonald's were already well established there. Burger King's British parent, Grand Metropolitan, also owned Wimpy, a chain of U.K. hamburger restaurants, and required Burger King to absorb the chain. This sapped resources needed for French expansion. When Burger King left the French market, it had grown to only 16 restaurants there, whereas McDonald's had about 450.

When reentering France, Burger King was determined to put in enough effort to compete. By 2015, it grew to 50 restaurants there, and it then acquired Quick, which had about 500 restaurants. Those in France will be re-branded as Burger King; whereas those in Belgium and Luxembourg will maintain the Quick brand.

THE BRICS

The possibilities in the BRIC countries are too great to ignore. Burger King opened its first Brazilian and Chinese restaurants in 2004. While Burger King has had success in both these countries, it has been able to expand much faster in the former due largely to its recognition advantage in Brazil. A half million Brazilians fly into Florida each year, where Burger King's restaurants abound. In addition, about 300,000 Brazilians live in South Florida, most of whom maintain contact with relatives and friends back home.

In China, Burger King encountered laws requiring it either to form a JV with a Chinese firm or own and operate two or more stores for at least a year before starting franchise operations. The company chose the latter alternative, which delayed its start of franchising. After doing so, finding potential franchisees with sufficient financial and restaurant capabilities was difficult, particularly since the franchise concept was rather new to China. (Some of its competitors, mainly Yum! Brands and McDonald's, made joint venture investments and expanded with owned stores.) In 2012 Burger King entered a three-partner JV to serve the Chinese market. One partner, the Carpesian Capital Group, is a global private equity company specializing in developing country investments. The other is the Korduglu family from Turkey, which is Burger King's largest non-U.S. franchisee.

In 2010 Burger King entered Russia, an attractive country not only because of its large population and growth potential, but also because of integration possibilities with operations in Eastern Europe. Indeed, Burger King entered Slovenia in 2011 and now depends on supplies from the Russian operation. In addition, concluding the essentiality of finding the right franchisee, Burger King's managers spent over a year getting to know the eventual franchisee, who owns a chain of about 200 Russian coffee shops. Although the franchise has resulted in growth in Moscow and St. Petersburg, the franchise formed a JV with Russia's VTB Capital in 2013 to gain resources needed to expand outside those cities.

In 2014 India became Burger King's 100th operating country. It partnered with Everstone Capital, a private equity firm that also holds controlling interest in India's largest restaurant group. India's fast-food segment has recently been growing at 26 percent per annum. Because of the large number of vegetarians in India, Burger King has delegated much of the menu selection to its partner. At the same time, it has done extensive market research to develop a vegetarian menu to accompany its nonvegetarian one.

THE FUTURE

Burger King's recent growth in its U.S. and Canada region has lagged its growth elsewhere. To counter McDonald's faster growth in breakfast sales, Burger King merged in 2014 with Tim Hortons, a Canadian coffee and doughnuts chain with about 4500 (almost all franchised) restaurants.

At the same time, Burger King is planning unprecedented expansion. The fact that some of its competitors have expanded abroad much more than Burger King may indicate that it has untapped international potential. However, Burger King's management faces a number of questions regarding location priorities; such questions of location priorities dog managers in any company with international operations. ■

QUESTIONS

✪ **13-1.** Discuss the risks that an international restaurant company such as Burger King would have by operating abroad rather than just domestically.

✪ **13-2.** How has Burger King's headquarters location influenced its international expansion? Has this location strengthened or weakened its global competitive position?

THE IMPORTANCE OF LOCATION

Companies lack resources to take advantage of all international opportunities.

The adage that "location, location, and location" are the three most important factors for business success rings true for IB. The world has a bit more than 200 countries, each offering distinct opportunities and risks. Thus some fit companies' capabilities and strategies better than others. By comparing the external environment with a company's objectives and capabilities, managers might ask: Where can we best leverage our existing competencies? And where can we best sustain, improve, or extend our competencies? Because companies have limited resources, they must be careful in choosing among countries when making the following decisions:

1. The location of sales, production, and administrative and auxiliary services, such as R&D
2. The sequence for entering different countries
3. The portion of resources and efforts to allocate to each country where they operate

Companies need to
- determine the order of country entry,
- allocate resources among countries.

Committing human, technical, and financial resources to one locale may mean forgoing or delaying projects elsewhere. In actuality, a company may first set a strategy of domestic versus international emphasis, such as General Electric's objective of making 60 percent of its sales internationally.[2] Afterward, a company may sequence its entry by country or region. Once operating in multiple countries, it must allocate efforts among them. This chapter emphasizes the country decision process.[3] Taking time to pick and emphasize the more outstanding locations affects firms' ability to gain and sustain competitive advantage.[4]

The choice of country sales may or may not coincide with the choice of country to produce. On the one hand, they may be the same, particularly if transport costs or government regulations require production in the countries where you sell. Many service industries, such as restaurants (like Burger King), construction, and retailing, must locate most production facilities near their foreign customers.

In choosing geographic sites, a company must decide
- where to sell,
- where to produce.

On the other hand, large-scale capital-intensive production technology favors producing in only a few countries and exporting to others, such as with automobiles and steel. Further, production locations are complex, such as sourcing raw materials and components from different countries and dividing operating functions among countries (e.g., headquarters in one, a call center in another, an R&D facility in still another, and so on).

Location flexibility is essential because conditions change. A company must respond to new opportunities and withdraw from less profitable ones. There is no one-size-fits-all theory for picking operating locations because product lines, competitive positions, resources, and strategies make each company unique.[5] Moreover, hiring the right people to analyze country differences and implement company operations is critical. Highly skilled managers can sometimes compensate for location deficiencies, and poor managers can sometimes cause poor performance in the best locations. However, having skilled management in the most appropriate locations is the best possible combination. Figure 13.2 shows the major steps IB managers should take in making location decisions. The following discussion examines those steps in depth.

COMPARING COUNTRIES THROUGH SCANNING

Managers use scanning techniques to examine and compare countries on broad indicators of opportunities and risks.[6]

WHY IS SCANNING IMPORTANT?

Without scanning, a company may
- examine too many or too few possibilities.

Scanning is like seeding widely and then weeding out; it is useful insofar as a company might otherwise consider too few or too many possibilities. However, comparison among countries is not always practical. We discuss later in the chapter when noncomparative decisions are appropriate.

FIGURE 13.2 The Location Decision Process

Location, location, location: Committing resources to a foreign location may entail risky trade-offs—say, forgoing or abandoning projects elsewhere. The start of the decision-making process is essentially twofold: examining the external environments of proposed locations and comparing each of them with the company's objectives and capabilities.

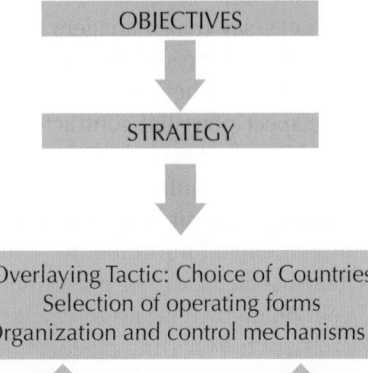

OBJECTIVES

STRATEGY

Overlaying Tactic: Choice of Countries
Selection of operating forms
Organization and control mechanisms

Choosing new locations
- Scan for alternatives
- Choose and weight variables
- Collect and analyze data for variables
- Use tools to compare variables and narrow alternatives

Allocating among locations
- Analyze effects of reinvestment versus harvesting in existing operating locations
- Appraise interdependence of locations on performance
- Examine needs for diversification versus concentration of foreign operations

Making final decisions
- Conduct detailed feasibility study for new locations
- Estimate expected outcome for reinvestments
- Make location and allocation decisions based on company's financial decision-making tools

SCANNING VERSUS DETAILED ANALYSIS

 Scanning answers questions through "yes" or "no," direct statistics, indirect indicators, and qualitative assessment.

Step 1: Scanning In **scanning**, managers examine many countries broadly—using information that is readily available, inexpensive, and fairly comparable—to narrow detailed analysis and travel to only the most promising ones. They analyze publicly available information and communicate with experienced people on conditions that could significantly affect the success and fit for their business. Because of using fairly easy-to-find information, they may consider a large group of countries, such as all those within a global region.

Keep in mind, though, that information gathered at this point may be of four types:

1. *Yes or no* For a question like, "Does the country allow 100 percent ownership of foreign direct investments?" the answer is "yes" or "no."

2. *Direct statistics* For a question such as, "What is the highest marginal tax rate on corporate earnings?" direct information is available from tax schedules.

3. *Indirect indicators* For a question such as, "What are the potential sales for my product?" estimates must use indirect indicators, such as those based on per capita GDP and population size.

4. *Qualitative assessment* For a question akin to, "What will be the future political leaders' philosophy about IB?" a qualitative assessment is necessary based on different opinions and indirect indicators.

On-site visits follow scanning and are part of the final location decision process.

Step 2: Detailed Analysis　Once narrowing the number of countries, managers need to compare them in greater detail. Unless they are satisfied to outsource all their production and sales, they almost always need to go on location to collect and evaluate more specific information.

Let's say that managers need to decide where best to emphasize sales. They will likely need to visit the shortlisted countries to observe the market and visit with distributors. Or let's say managers need to decide where best to locate production. If outsourcing, they may want to inspect potential contractors' facilities. If planning to own facilities themselves, they will need to collect such specific on-site information as availability and cost of land and supplies.

Intel's manufacturing expansion into Latin America illustrates this process. Intel used scanning to limit visits to a few Latin American countries. The follow-up visits sought much more detailed information—even the availability of suitable housing, medical services, and food products for the personnel Intel would need to transfer. The visitors were also able to gain qualitative information, such as impressions of the welcome they might get from government officials and business leaders.

The more time and money companies invest in examining an alternative, the more likely they are to accept it, regardless of its merits—a situation known as an **escalation of commitment**. A feasibility study should have clear-cut decision points, whereby managers can discontinue the commitment before they invest too much.

OPPORTUNITY AND RISK VARIABLES

Companies may simplify scanning research by first eliminating countries with conditions unacceptable to them.

Managers should first identify country conditions they will not accept. Companies differ in what these conditions are, such as prohibitions of 100 percent foreign ownership or the common use of child labor in hazardous jobs. By eliminating countries with unacceptable conditions, they simplify the task of scanning. Companies then need to consider opportunity and risk indicators that could significantly affect their success or failure. Keep in mind that some conditions may be viewed by one company as an opportunity, but by another as a risk. We discuss a sample of these below.

OPPORTUNITIES: SALES EXPANSION

Expectation of a large market and sales growth are probably a potential location's major attractions.

Sales expansion is probably companies' most motivating factor for IB engagement because managers assume that more sales will lead to more profits.

Managers would like to have country sales figures for what they want to sell, but such information may be unavailable, especially if they want to introduce a new product. In such instances, they can estimate sales potential roughly by examining what has happened to sales for a similar or complementary product, such as projecting potential 3-D television sales based on past sales for HD units. They can also use economic and demographic data to project sales potential, the most common of which are a combination of income and population size.

Of course, you should examine indicators related directly to your products. If you're trying to sell, say, luxury products, GDP per capita may tell you very little. Instead, you need to know how many people have income above a certain level. If you are trying to reach a youth market or an elderly market, total population figures will not help you as much figures on the number of people by age category. Moreover, although your product or service may not appeal to the average customer, you may seek out niches. Guatemalan-based Pollo Campero identified countries and then cities with large Central American populations, which led it to enter the United States by going first to Los Angeles.[7]

Companies must consider variables other than income and population when estimating potential demand for their products in different countries.

Examining Economic and Demographic Variables　Some primary considerations when examining economic and demographic variables are listed below:

- *Obsolescence and leapfrogging of products.* Demand estimation in one country based on occurrence in others, should take into account that emerging economy consumers do not necessarily follow the same patterns as those in higher-income countries. Chinese consumers have largely leapfrogged landline telephones by going from phoneless to cell phones.[8]

- *Demand for necessities versus discretionary products.* People buy necessities, such as food, before making discretionary purchases, thus the cost of necessities influences the demand for optional ones. For example, expenditures on food in Japan are high because food is expensive and work habits promote eating out, thus food purchases displace some discretionary purchases.

- *Substitution.* Consumers may substitute certain products or services differently in one country than in other countries. In India, increased gasoline prices relative to diesel prices forced companies such as Suzuki, Toyota, and General Motors to alter their mix of vehicle production to include a higher portion of diesel-powered cars.[9] In Venezuela, an economic downturn caused a huge switch from traditionally popular expensive Scotch whisky to rum, which was less expensive.[10]

- *Income inequality.* Where income inequality is high, the per capita GDP figures are less meaningful. Many people have little to spend, while many others have substantial spending money. For example, high income inequality has resulted in a very small middle class in most sub-Saharan African countries.[11]

- *Cultural factors and taste.* Although cultural factors affect overall country sales for certain products, such as Hindu restrictions on meat in India, one needs to examine cultural sub-segments. There is a large market for Indian meat sales among people who are neither Hindu nor vegetarian.

- *Existence of trading blocs.* A country's small population and GDP obscure its potential if it is in a regional trading bloc.[12] For instance Uruguay has a small domestic market, but its production has duty-free access to other countries in Mercosur unless countries leave the bloc.

CONCEPT CHECK

In Chapter 7 (page 239), we explain that when trade barriers come down within a regional bloc, the size of the market available to small member nations typically increases quite dramatically.

Although managers cannot project potential demand perfectly, they can make workable estimates that help them narrow detailed studies to a reasonable number.

OPPORTUNITIES: RESOURCE ACQUISITION

When undertaking IB to secure resources (e.g., labor, raw materials, knowledge), companies are limited to those locales that likely have what they want, such as securing petroleum only where there are prospective reserves. Even among these countries, some offer better opportunities than others (e.g., petroleum cost variations from extraction, transportation, and taxes). When considering cost differences, a particular resource may be overriding for specific industries or companies, such as sugar for candy companies or low-cost water power for aluminum companies.

Cost Considerations   A company's total cost is made up of numerous sub-costs, many of which are industry- or company-specific. Nevertheless, several of the factors affecting these sub-costs—*labor, infrastructure, external connections,* and *government incentives*—apply to a large cross-section of companies.

Costs—especially labor costs—are an important factor in companies' production-location decisions.

Labor   Although capital intensity, especially through the use of robotics, is growing in most industries, labor cost remains important for most companies. Scanning allows companies to examine such factors as labor market size, minimum and ongoing wages, required and customary fringe benefits, education levels, and unemployment rates. These help in comparing labor cost, skills, and availability. Analyses should also include likely changes, such as cost increases in China that have been making such countries as Myanmar and Mexico more attractive.[13]

Neither labor nor companies' needs are homogeneous. Take call centers. U.S. and French companies have different language needs (English and French respectively), which have led

Source: Femi Ipaye Xinhua News Agency/Newscom

CONCEPT CHECK

We show in Chapter 5 that, in applying factor proportions theory to locate production, a company needs to consider that factors of production are not homogeneous. We also show (page 198) that new technologies can change optimal production locations.

many U.S. companies to the Philippines and French companies to Senegal. Or, take the desire to acquire R&D personnel as opposed to inexpensive manufacturing labor. Figures on the number of science and engineering graduates have given a rough idea of where needed skills are available and have influenced companies to set up R&D facilities in China, Hungary, India, and Israel.[14]

Entering a country with a shortage of required labor skills will require MNEs to train, redesign production, or add supervision—all of which are expensive. Keep in mind also that a country's wage rates (and education) may differ by sector and region and may change because of emigration and health conditions.

Note also that when companies move into emerging economies because of low labor-wages, their advantages may be short-lived for one or more of three reasons:

- Competitors follow leaders into low-wage areas.
- There is little first-mover advantage for this type of production migration.
- The costs may rise quickly as a result of pressure on wage or exchange rates.

| Infrastructure problems add to operating costs.

Infrastructure   Poor internal infrastructure escalates costs. Consider Nigeria where employees spend extra hours commuting for work on congested roads, which decreases their productivity. Many companies, such as Cadbury and Nestlé, use their own costly power generators because of erratic publicly provided power so as to prevent assembly line stoppages and spoilage of food products. Because phone reception is often unreliable, they must send people out to visit customers and suppliers. Delivery of goods must again face the congestion on inferior roads.[15] The photo below shows traffic on a Nigerian highway.

| The need to integrate operations among countries influences location decisions.

External Connections   IB requires diverse levels of cross-national integration, all of which incur time and costs. At a minimum, headquarters personnel visit foreign locations to support control efforts. Further, companies need a smooth flow of shipments as they import and export among their facilities in different countries. Because distance roughly correlates with time and cost, a geographically isolated country like New Zealand does not fit as easily into a company's global integration strategy as one located near the headquarters or various suppliers.[16] Relatedly, countries with few trade restrictions and efficient customs offer advantages of reduced tariff costs and shorter clearance times.[17]

▲ A congested highway in Nigeria.

Government practices may increase or decrease companies' costs.

Governmental Incentives and Disincentives Governments promote inward foreign investment to create jobs, enhance competitiveness, and improve trade balances. They do so through ads, investment missions, and foreign consular activities. In addition, many provide incentives that cut investors' costs, such as lower taxes, employee training, loan guarantees, low-interest loans, exemption of import duties, and subsidized energy and transportation. For example, the European Structural Funds program has helped finance projects for such companies as Coca-Cola, Fiat, and GlaxoSmithKline.[18] However, incentives and entry conditions often depend on company–government negotiations (i.e., how much each needs and offers the other). When a company wants limited resources, such as prime areas for building beach resorts, governments are in a strong bargaining position when ceding rights to a foreign firm.[19] When companies have hard-to-duplicate assets, such as unique technology, access to foreign markets, and well-known global brands, they are in a strong position.

Companies prefer operating in countries where red tape and corruption are minimal and where legal transparency and law enforcement are high.[20] In contrast, when managers must spend excessive time to satisfy government agencies on taxes, labor conditions, environmental compliance, and other matters because of uncertainty about the legal consequences of their actions, they take time away from their primary responsibility of overseeing production and sales.[21]

Poor protection of intellectual property rights is a double-edged sword. On the one hand, international companies might relinquish technology to competitors where protection is poor. On the other hand, these locations may enable international companies to more easily gain access to competitors' technologies.[22]

RISKS

CONCEPT CHECK

In Chapter 6 (pages 205-206), we detail country differences in red tape (i.e., the time and steps necessary to start-up, operate, and close down businesses).

Company decisions should weigh opportunity against risk. For example, a company may forgo the country with the highest sales potential or the cheapest assets because decision-makers perceive that risks are too high. In this section we examine four types of risks: political, foreign exchange, natural disaster, and competitive.

Factors to Consider in Analyzing Risk Keep in mind several factors as we discuss specific types of risk:

Estimation of risk varies because of different perceptions, company situations, product lines, and operating forms.

1. *Companies and their managers differ in their perceptions of what is risky,* how tolerant they are of taking risk, the returns they expect, and the portion of their assets they are willing to put at risk.[23]
2. *One company's risk may be another's opportunity.* For example, companies offering security solutions (e.g., alarm systems, guard services, insurance, and armaments) may find their biggest sales opportunities where other companies find only risks. Companies offering risk-assessment services do better when the perception of risk increases.[24]
3. *Companies may reduce their risks by means other than avoiding locations,* such as by insuring. But all these options incur costs.
4. *There are trade-offs among risks.* Avoiding a country where, say, political risk is high may leave a company more vulnerable to competitive risk if another company earns good profits there.
5. *Risks may occur for suppliers and within suppliers' supply chains,* thus companies need to examine the complex external dependencies and vulnerabilities of its suppliers.[25]

CONCEPT CHECK

Recall from Chapter 3 (pages 118–119) that political risk is the possibility that political decisions, events, or conditions will reduce investors' value or force them to accept lower-than-projected profits.

Political Risk Changes in political leaders' opinions and policies, civil disorder, and animosity between the host and other countries, particularly the firm's home country, may lead to a company's loss of or damage to property, disruption of operations, and adjustment to changes in operating rules. For example, Unilever encountered foreign executives' refusal to work in Pakistan because of security concerns; Chiquita Brands had to pay Colombian revolutionaries to protect its employees there; Owens-Illinois's investments were nationalized in Venezuela; Marriott's Indonesian hotel was bombed; and Coca-Cola's Angolan services required police to protect its trucks and telephone services.

Managers use three approaches to predict political risk: *analyzing past patterns, evaluating opinions,* and *examining potentially risky social and economic conditions.*

Analyzing Past Patterns   Predicting political risk based on past patterns is problematic because situations may change. Moreover, a country's overall political situation masks differences within countries and for different firms. For example, unrest may be limited geographically, such as Slovenia's avoidance of damage during Yugoslavia's civil war. Nationalizations have generally been highly selective, primarily affecting only operations with a visibly widespread effect on the country because of their size or monopoly position. Further, state-owned MNEs from countries with strong ties to the host country appear to be less subject to expropriation risk.[26]

Property damage or asset takeover does not necessarily cause investors a full loss. First, insurance may cover damage. Second, most nationalizations have begun with formal declarations of intent and have followed with legal processes to determine the foreign investor's compensation, such as the settlement between Venezuela and Holcim.[27] (Past settlements serve as indicators of likely compensation.) In addition to the settlement value, there may be side agreements that affect the adequacy (or not) of compensation. For example, the former investor may continue to manage an operation for a fee and receive output at a favorable price.

Evaluating Opinions   Because influential people may sway future political events, managers should evaluate statements by political spearheads to determine their philosophies on private business, foreign business relations, means of effecting economic changes, and feelings toward given foreign countries. They should also access polls showing different leaders' likelihood of gaining political office. Opinions from a cross-section of embassy officials, foreign and local businesspeople, journalists, academicians, middle-level local government authorities, and labor leaders often reveal their attitudes, which often reflect current and future political conditions. These opinions may be gathered through publications and conversations or, if the firm is already operating within a country, through reports from its managers working therein.

Examining Social and Economic Conditions   Unrest may occur if population segments have unmet social and economic aspirations. Frustrated groups may disrupt business by calling general strikes, destroying property and supply lines, and causing the downfall of government leaders. And political leaders sometimes harness support by blaming problems on foreigners and foreign companies, which could lead to boycotts, property damage, expropriation, or changes in operating rules. Thus, the examination of social and economic conditions in relation to aspirations helps companies foresee deteriorating political situations.

Foreign-Exchange Risk   Let's examine two types of risk: exchange-rate changes and immobility of funds. In both, companies should consider current situations along with conditions that can lead to changes.

Exchange-Rate Changes   The change in foreign currency value is a two-edged sword, depending on whether you are going abroad to seek sales or resources. Let's say a U.S. company exports to India; deterioration in the Indian rupee's value makes the exports less competitive because it takes more rupees to buy them. If it produces within India to serve the Indian market, its competitiveness within India will likely change insignificantly, but its rupee profits will buy fewer U.S. dollars to bring back to the United States. If, however, it is seeking resources from India, such as Indian personnel to staff a call center, a fall in the rupee value lowers the dollar cost.

Immobility of Funds   When a company exports to or invests in a foreign country, it prefers international mobility of its sales receipts, earnings, and capital there. Without the mobility, many firms either forgo operations or expect a higher rate of return there than elsewhere. Simply, their liquidity preference results from their needs or desires to make near-term

---

To predict political risk, companies can

- examine views of government decision-makers,
- get a cross-section of opinions,
- use expert analysts,
- examine unsatisfactory social and economic conditions.

CONCEPT CHECK

In Chapter 9 (page 286), we discuss some of the causes of exchange-rate changes and explain methods of forecasting exchange-rate movements.

Companies may accept a lower return in order to move their financial resources more easily.

payments, such as for dividends, unexpected contingencies (such as stockpiling materials before a threatened strike), and shifting of funds to possibly more profitable opportunities.[28]

A greater facility to access funds is affected by active capital markets and an absence of governmental exchange controls. An active capital market, particularly a stock market, helps a company sell its assets, especially if it wishes to sell a portion of ownership on a local exchange or dispose of its operations. An absence of exchange controls enables companies to convert their local currencies. Thus, it's not surprising that companies prefer operations in countries with strong and convertible currencies.

Natural Disaster Risk   Adverse "mother nature" catastrophes and widespread debilitating diseases have existed throughout history, but their relationship to choosing optimal IB locations has emerged only recently as comparative data have become more obtainable.

"Mother Nature" Catastrophes   Each year, hundreds of millions of people are exposed to risks from earthquakes, cyclones, flooding, drought, volcanic eruptions, rising ocean levels, mudslides, and tornados. These disasters upset markets, infrastructure, and production while damaging companies' property, injuring their personnel, and increasing their insurance costs. They also play havoc with global supplies; the Japanese earthquake-induced tsunami in 2011 disrupted the world auto industry's production by creating auto parts shortages.[29]

These events are spread unevenly. Parts of Asia are heavily exposed to earthquakes; some African countries are most vulnerable to drought. However, exposure must be examined alongside countries' abilities to cope. Although only 11 percent of people exposed to such disasters are in the world's poorest nations, those nations account for 55 percent of the deaths because so much of their population live in poor housing and lack adequate medical assistance. Likewise, their rural-to-urban migration is largely to dangerous mountainsides, ravines, and low-elevation areas ill-equipped to deal with earthquakes, mudslides, and cyclones. Map 13.1 shows the most and least vulnerable countries, taking into account both their potential exposure and their coping abilities.

Debilitating Diseases   The World Health Organization has developed global atlases of infectious diseases,[30] many of which occur where medical facilities are weakest because of the diseases' association with poverty. They are also associated with catastrophic events, such as cholera and malaria outbreaks after flooding, and tend to follow geographic patterns. For example, malaria kills about 2 million people a year, mainly in Africa.

The incapacitating effects of disease have an impact on several facets of business operations. For example, during the West African Ebola outbreak, the financial performance of many Sierra Leone firms declined in tandem with economic deterioration from the reduced workforce. In turn, international firms with Sierra Leone clients, such as KPMG, saw weakened sales.[31] During the Zika crisis in Latin America and the Caribbean, many companies, such as Kimberly-Clark, set up costly education programs for employees in affected areas to educate them regarding how to protect against the virus.[32] At the same time, companies faced new ethical and legal decisions, such as whether to advise employees about dangers of pregnancies. Further, because of both Ebola and Zika, companies decreased business travel to distressed areas, thus hindering their buying programs and oversight of subsidiaries there.[33]

Competitive Risk   We now examine four factors affecting companies' competitive positions through location decisions: *compatibility for companies' operations, diversification of locations, following competitors or customers,* and *heading off competitors.*

Compatibility for Companies' Operations   Because companies encounter less familiar environments abroad than at home, their operating risks are normally higher abroad. Thus, managers initially prefer to operate where they perceive conditions to be more similar to their home country—provided, of course, that the location also offers sufficient opportunities.[34] In

CONCEPT CHECK

On page 289 of Chapter 9, we review the methods countries use to control currency convertibility in order to conserve scarce foreign exchange.

Natural disasters and debilitating diseases upset operations and are spread unevenly around the world.

Companies are highly attracted to countries that

- share the same language,
- have institutions similar to those in their home countries,
- are located nearby.

MAP 13.1   The 20 Countries at Highest and Lowest Risk from Natural Disasters

The calculations are based on a combination of exposure (number of people exposed or threatened by earthquakes, storms, floods, droughts, and sea level rise), susceptibility (infrastructure, housing conditions, nutrition, poverty and dependencies, and economic capacity and distribution), and coping and adaptive capacities.

Source: Based on data from United Nations University Institute for Environmental and Human Society, *World Risk Report 2013,* 46–67.

CONCEPT CHECK

In Chapter 2 (page 90), we observe that a company usually expects fewer differences— and must make fewer adjustments— when moving to culturally similar countries. In Chapter 5 (pages 187–188), we explain that country similarity helps support patterns of trading partners.

CONCEPT CHECK

Recall from Chapter 5 (page 198) that a positive historical relationship, especially between a former colonizer with its former colonies, helps explain trade patterns.

fact, MNEs have a lower survival rate than local companies for many years after they begin operations, a situation known as the *liability of foreignness*.[35]

This perception of similarity helps explain why more U.S. companies put earlier and greater emphasis on Canada and the United Kingdom than is indicated by the opportunity and risk variables discussed so far. In short, managers feel more comfortable doing business where the per capita GDP is comparable and where there is a similar language, culture, and legal system.[36] Following early entries, companies also find usefulness in creating an expansion pattern that allows a portfolio of countries to work interdependently.[37]

Similarity also occurs among adjacent nations because of the ease of travel and communications among them. For example, marketing programs in one country often result in product awareness elsewhere, particularly in an adjacent country, an occurrence known as a **spillover effect**. For example, U.S. television ads regularly reach Canadians, making it easier for U.S. firms to do business there.

Positive historical home and host countries' ties also help explain companies' location preferences because companies perceive lower risk therein.[38] A company may also reduce risk by choosing countries where it can employ products, plant sizes, and practices familiar to its managers and which are crucial for its competitive advantage. For instance, Blockbuster failed in Germany partially because of laws preventing store-openings in evenings and on Sundays and holidays—popular times for last-minute impulse video rentals.[39]

Diversification of Locations   Operating in economically diverse countries whose business cycles are not highly interrelated may enable companies to smooth their sales and profits,

In terms of location strategies, some options are to go

- first to a few versus many foreign countries,
- to similar versus dissimilar countries,
- to places to prevent competitors from gaining advantages,
- into markets that competitors have not entered versus where there are clusters of competitors.

CONCEPT CHECK

In Chapter 5 (page 187), we explain how countries' traditional specialization has led to long-term production advantages over other countries.

which, in turn, is an advantage in raising funds.[40] They may further guard against the effects of currency value changes by locating in countries whose exchange rates are not closely correlated with each other.[41] These diversifications are in many ways opposite to what we just discussed about advantages of operating in countries similar to the home country. Thus management must weigh the importance of one type of risk reduction versus the other.

Given the growth in product complexity, technology content, and companies' product specialization, there is a need to tap knowledge emanating from multiple companies. At the same time, such knowledge may be country-specific because of long-term country dominance in some industries. Thus, there is a need to tap knowledge in different countries. Although knowledge flows internationally and from one organization to another, MNEs enhance their speed of access to it by having foreign subsidiaries that serve as information access points in source countries.[42]

Following Competitors or Customers   Managers may purposely crowd a market to prevent competitors from gaining advantages there that they can use to improve their positions elsewhere—a situation known as **oligopolistic reaction**.[43] In other words, a company's location decision is made on the basis of a competitor's action rather than on location-based characteristics such as the cost of labor or market size and growth. It looks at performance *relative* to that of competitors rather than on its *absolute* performance.

At the same time, companies may gain absolute performance advantages by locating where competitors are. First, they may follow competitors that have performed the costly task of evaluating locations and building market acceptance for a particular type of product, thus getting a so-called free ride. Second, clusters of competitors (known as agglomeration) attract multiple suppliers, personnel with specialized skills, and buyers who want to compare a number of product and service options in a single trip. In agglomeration, a company also gains better access to information about new developments because it has frequent contact with its competitors' personnel, customers, and suppliers.[44] The photo below shows a portion of the diamond district in Antwerp, Belgium, where numerous diamond cutters, wholesalers, and retailers locate in close proximity to each other.

Agglomeration by nationality occurs when firms from the same home country, regardless of industry, cluster in a location. The cluster provides expatriate employees with a

Source: Bart Nedobre/Alamy Stock Photo

Part of the diamond business agglomeration in Antwerp, Belgium.

more familiar environment to live and work. However, this gathering may shield MNEs from the interactions with competitors from elsewhere, thus delaying their ability to innovate and adapt.[45]

Following customers into a foreign market may secure sales with them and help secure relationships in their home market. For example, Bridgestone Tires followed one of its Japanese customers, Toyota, into the United States. First, its track record with Toyota gave it an advantage over other tire companies in the U.S. market. Second, if another tire manufacturer were to develop a strong U.S. relationship with Toyota, it might use this to undermine Bridgestone's sales to Toyota in Japan.

Heading Off or Avoiding Competition   Companies may seek competitive advantage by (1) being first into a foreign country, (2) avoiding country entry where competition is strong, and (3) moving quickly by whatever operating mode into as many markets as possible. We now discuss each of these.

First, being first into a country enables a firm to more easily gain the best partners, best locations, and best suppliers—a strategy known as a **first-mover advantage**. This strategy may also support attaining strong relations with the government, such as Volkswagen did in China and Lockheed in Russia.[46]

Second, a company may try to avoid significant competition, especially if competitors are much larger. PriceSmart, a U.S.-based discount operator, has all its warehouse stores outside the United States and has succeeded by targeting locations in Central America, the Caribbean, and Asia that seemed too small to attract early entry of competitors like Walmart, Carrefour, and Tesco.[47] However, its Central American success has drawn Walmart into that market.

Third, moving as quickly as possible by whatever operating mode into many markets is advantageous within an industry with very rapidly changing technology. In other words, waiting to enter a country increases the risk of competitors' superseding one's technology and securing markets with it. However, as we discuss later in the section, "Geographic Diversification Versus Concentration," there are other considerations for entering markets quickly or slowly.

ANALYZING AND RELATING THE OPPORTUNITY AND RISK VARIABLES

Teams comprising people from different functional areas are useful in choosing and rating indicators of countries' opportunity and risk.

After companies have completed the data collection for their scanning process, they must scrutinize that data to prioritize among countries. Using a team of people from different functions—marketing, finance, etc.—will more likely uncover the best fits with companies' resources and objectives. Dividing data collection based on team-members' functional expertise (e.g., having the finance member examine all the countries' foreign exchange situations, having the accounting member examine tax rates, etc.) allows for more uniform analysis of data across the spectrum of countries. (If responsibility is divided, instead, by having each member examine a subsection of countries in their entirety, there is a risk that optimistic members will rate their countries more favorably than pessimistic members, thus diminishing the equivalence of the assignment.)

Obviously, the team will consider some conditions as more important than others, say that political risk is more important than natural disaster risk. Thus some variables need to be weighted more heavily than others. Two common tools to help at this stage are *grids* and *matrices*. We now illustrate each of these with abbreviated and simple examples.

Grids are tools that

- may depict acceptable or unacceptable country conditions,
- rank countries by important variables.

Grids   Table 13.1 is a simplified example of a grid with information placed into three categories: (1) acceptable/unacceptable conditions, (2) opportunity indicators, and (3) risk indicators. Note in this example that country I can be immediately eliminated because the company will go only where it can take 100 percent ownership. Although, in this example,

TABLE 13.1   Simplified Country Comparison Grid

This table is merely an example. In reality, a company chooses the variables and countries to consider (usually many more than this table demonstrates) and weights some variables as more important than others. Here managers eliminate Country I because the company will go only where 100 percent foreign ownership is allowed. Country II is the most attractive because it's regarded as having high opportunity and low risk. (With a larger number of scanned countries, several should end up with these characteristics and become the ones for detailed analysis.) Country III offers low opportunity and risk, and Country IV has high opportunity and risk. (One of these may be chosen for further analysis, depending on the company's tolerance for risk.) Country V is eliminated because of having low opportunity and high risk.

Country Variable	Weight	I	II	III	IV	V
1. Acceptable (A), Unacceptable (U)						
a. Allows 100% foreign ownership	–	U	A	A	A	A
2. Opportunity						
a. Sales potential	0–5	–	4	3	3	3
b. Labor conditions	0–3	–	3	1	2	2
c. Infrastructure	0–2	–	2	1	2	2
d. Ease of external integration	0–4	–	3	2	4	1
e. Possibility of governmental incentives	0–3	–	2	1	3	1
f. Tax rate	0–2	–	2	1	2	0
Total	–	–	16	9	16	9
3. Risk (lower number = preferred rating)						
a. Political	0–4	–	2	1	3	2
b. Foreign exchange	0–3	–	1	0	3	3
c. Natural disaster	0–4	–	0	0	4	3
d. Competitive	0–2	–	0	1	2	2
Total	–	–	3	2	12	10

sales potential is given more weight than infrastructure as an opportunity indicator and political is given more weight than competitive as a risk indicator, different companies will choose indicators and weight them differently. Table 13.1's description shows how this exercise helps managers choose countries for a more detailed analysis.

Matrices   To more clearly show the opportunity/risk relationship, managers can plot values on a matrix such as the one shown as Figure 13.3. The plotting of this type matrix also allows a company to make a more precise distinction in weighting and comparing variables.

But how can managers plot values on such a matrix? As in the case of grids, they must determine unacceptable factors so as to eliminate countries from consideration and choose indicators for their companies' risk and opportunity. Then, they weight them to reflect their importance. For instance, using the same risk factors as we used for the grid explanation, they might give 35 percent (0.35) of the weight to political risk, 30 percent (0.30) to foreign-exchange risk, 20 percent (0.2) to natural disaster risk, and 15 percent (0.15) to competitive risk, for a total allocation of 100 percent. They would then rate each country on a scale, such as from 1 to 10 for each variable, with 10 indicating the best score (note that more than one country may have the same score), and multiply each variable by the weight they allocate to it. If they rate Country A as 8 on the political risk variable, they would multiply 8 by 0.35 (the weight they assign to expropriation) for a score of 2.8. They would then sum all of Country A's risk-variable scores to place it on the risk axis, and similarly plot the location of Country A on the opportunity axis.

But how might managers come up with a score of 8 for a country's political risk? They would likely divide the maximum score of 10 into subcategories, such as expropriation, civil unrest, relationship with the company's home government, and likelihood of negative regulatory changes. They might even weight these subcategories before totaling them to secure the score for political risk. They would do similarly for each of their variables.

With an opportunity–risk matrix, a company can

• decide on factors to consider and compare them.

FIGURE 13.3 Opportunity–Risk Matrix

Countries E and F are the most desirable because they boast a combination of a high level of opportunity and a low level of risk. But what if the decision came down to Countries A and B? The level of opportunity in Country A may not be as high as a company would like, but the low level of risk may be attractive. Country B, however, promises a high level of opportunities but also threatens a high level of risk. A decision between Countries A and B will probably take the firm's risk tolerance into consideration.

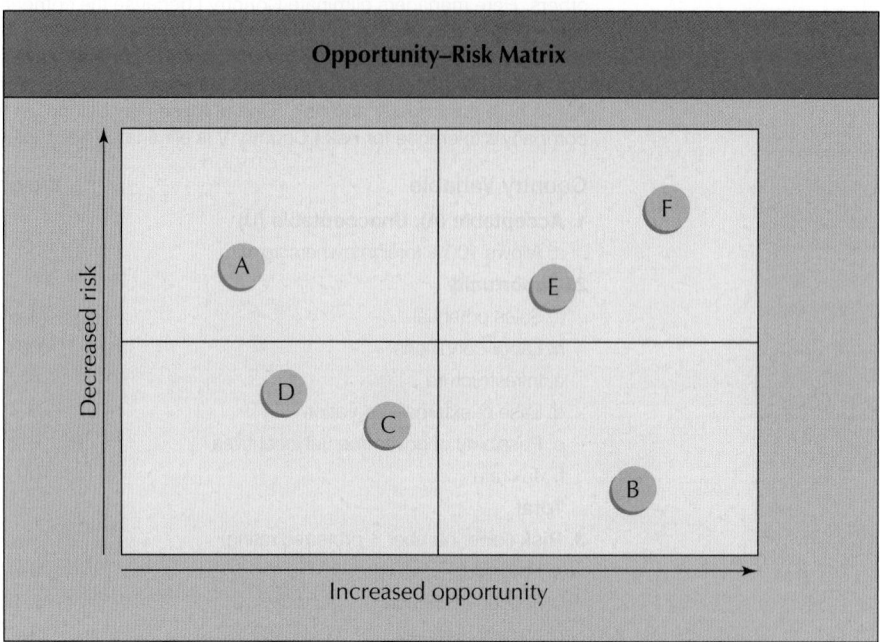

Once managers plot each country's values on the matrix, they may sometimes have to choose between a country with high risk and high opportunity and another with low risk and low opportunity, thus making a decision based on their tolerance for risk. Further, although A, B, C, and D are less appealing than E and F in Figure 13.3 the company may nevertheless find opportunities in A, B, C, and D—perhaps licensing or shared-ownership arrangements—without necessarily making a large commitment.

A key element of this kind of matrix, and one that managers do not always include in practice, is the projection of where countries will be in the future, or at least the *direction* in which they are expected to move. Such a projection is obviously useful, but the farther one forecasts into the future, the less certain the projection.

SOURCES AND SHORTCOMINGS OF COMPARATIVE COUNTRY INFORMATION

Companies undertake business research to reduce uncertainties and to assess performance. Our emphasis here is on information to aid in choosing the location decision. Because managers can seldom get all the information they want, they should compare information costs with the probable payoff it will generate in revenue gains or cost savings.

SOME PROBLEMS WITH RESEARCH RESULTS AND DATA

Because of the lack, obsolescence, and inaccuracy of data on many countries, research can be problematic. Let's discuss the two basic problems: inaccuracy and noncomparability.

Inaccuracy   We list six basic reasons why reported information may be inaccurate:

1. *Governmental resources* may limit accurate data collection. Countries' resources may limit budgets for data collection, the latest computer hardware, software, and training

---

Information is needed at all levels of control.

- Companies should compare the cost of information with its value.

Information inaccuracies result from

- difficulty in collecting and analyzing data,
- purposefully misleading data,
- exclusion of nonmarket and illegal activity.

programs (e.g., they may give priority, for example, to spending on health and literacy programs rather than on measuring health and literacy rates).

2. *Governments must depend on estimates and revisions.* Although both are important, there is a trade-off between accuracy and timeliness of data. Estimates, for example of countries' GDP growth, are initially made without the full range of sample returns so as to honor timeliness. But then revisions (sometimes several) are necessary to improve accuracy as more sample information is available. For example, the United States revised its GDP downward by an amount about the size of Sri Lanka's total output.[48]

3. *Governments may omit or purposely publish misleading information.* Government researchers sometimes publish false or purposely deceptive information designed to mislead their superiors, the country's rank and file, or companies and institutions abroad. For instance, Venezuela suspended release of data on mosquito-borne diseases, GDP, and balance of payments to prevent the public from receiving bad news.[49]

CONCEPT CHECK

In Chapter 2 (pages 75–76), we discussed that false responses hinder accuracy when comparing cultures.

4. *Respondents may give false information to data collectors.* Mistrust of data usage may lead respondents to answer questions falsely, particularly if questions probe financial details or anything else that respondents either consider private or to be used by government authorities against them.

5. *Official data may include only legal and reported market activities.* Nationally reported income figures seldom include illegal income from such activities as the drug trade or cash transactions to avoid tax payments. EU countries have begun estimating these within their GDPs, but they admit that the math can be fuzzy.[50]

6. *Questionable methodology may be used.* Inaccuracies may occur because of methods use to collect and analyze information. For instance, by using two different methods (both generally acceptable) to estimate Chinese consumption in 2012, there was a difference of more than the entire GDP of Australia.[51]

Noncomparability   Countries do not necessarily publish reports for the same length of time periods or at the same time as each other. So a company must extrapolate in order to estimate how countries compare. Countries also differ in accounting rules and how they define items, such as family income, literacy, and FDI. Activities taking place outside the market economy, such as within the home, do not show up in income figures. Because people in developing countries are more prone to produce for their own consumption (growing vegetables, preparing meals at home, sewing clothes, cutting hair, and so on), developing countries' official income figures tend to understate economic levels.

Further, exchange rates must be used to convert countries' financial data to some common currency, usually U.S. dollars. Although 10 percent appreciation of the Japanese yen in relation to the U.S. dollar results in a 10 percent increase in the dollar value of Japanese per capita GDP, it does not mean the Japanese are suddenly 10 percent richer. Because Japanese use about 85 percent of their income to make purchases in yen within Japan, they have little additional purchasing power for 85 percent of what they buy.

Problems in information comparability arise from

- differences in definitions and base years,
- distortions in currency values.

EXTERNAL SOURCES OF INFORMATION

Information sources differ by cost and detail.

Companies need information for making good location decisions. Chances are, at least for scanning purposes, the Internet will be the source for most of the information. Some of the information there is free, and some requires payment. Apart from the Internet, the most costly sources are marketing research and consulting companies, but the advantage is that they can target more closely what companies want. Some of the major Internet sources are prepared by service companies (e.g., banks, transportation agencies, accounting firms), government agencies (e.g., the U.S. Department of Commerce, CIA), international organizations (e.g., the UN, the WTO, the IMF, the OECD, and the EU), and trade associations. In any case, it is wise to know how sources generate their information and, in the case of those offering advice (e.g., a risk-assessment company), what their past success rates have been.

INTERNALLY GENERATED DATA

MNEs may have to collect much information themselves, sometimes simply by observing keenly and asking many questions. During visits to countries, investigators can see, for example, what kind of merchandise is available, determine who is buying and where, and uncover hidden competition—such as seamstress-made clothes in homes versus ready-made clothing in stores. They might also discover that surreptitiously sold contraband is a competitive factor in the market.

Companies may also seek out information from companies already experienced in the country. Limited Brands, for example, met with Apple's managers in China to ascertain experiences they encountered during entry.[52]

Point

Should Companies Operate in and Send Employees to Violent Areas?

Point   **Yes** Where there's risk, there are usually rewards. Companies should not shun areas with violence. Businesspeople have always taken risks, and employees have always gone to dangerous areas. As far back as the seventeenth century, immigrants to what are now the United States, India, and Australia encountered disease and hostile native populations. Had companies and immigrants not taken chances, the world would be far less developed today.

Violence is only one type of risk. Although we lack historical data, most locations are probably safer today. Disease is still a bigger danger than violence, but medical advances against a number of historic killers (polio, measles, smallpox, tuberculosis, etc.) have reduced that risk, while evacuation in case of a *real* emergency is much faster.

But let's assume that we decide to avoid countries with the potential for violence against our facilities and employees. Is there any such place? To answer this question, you need to consider an array of indicators that include overall crime and murder rates, terrorism, kidnapping, and political violence. Because so many occurrences go unreported, sta-

tistics are unreliable. Further, situations change quickly, such as the sudden outbreak of violence in Syria. Opinions from so-called risk experts are conflicting. Finally, countries that we think of as safe—France, Belgium, the United States—have had recent fatal violence.

Some industries don't have the luxury of avoiding violent countries. Take the petroleum industry. Oil companies have to go where there is a high likelihood of finding oil. Most of the credible alternatives have had recent bombings, kidnappings, or organized crime—the Middle East, West Africa, the Central Asian former Soviet republics, and Colombia. If companies didn't go to these places, they'd be out of business.

In effect, we'll keep operating anywhere there are opportunities. If a place seems physically risky, we'll take whatever precautions we can. We'll share intelligence reports, put people through safety training courses (there are plenty of these available now), and take security actions abroad. And perhaps we won't transfer spouses and children to the "risky" areas so we don't have to be on top of what is happening with as many people.

Counterpoint

Should Companies Operate in and Send Employees to Violent Areas?

Counterpoint   **No** We're no longer concerned simply with being caught in the crossfire between opposing factions. Antiglobalization groups want international publicity, and they also target MNEs' personnel and facilities so that they'll leave or pay ransoms. Still others are against foreigners or people of another religion, regardless of their aims. Such groups have killed staff members from Médecins sans Frontières and the Red Cross who were abroad to treat sick and injured people.[53]

At the same time, getting caught in the crossfire has become a bigger risk. Arms trafficking has risen and has lowered

prices not only to revolutionaries but also to drug and alien smugglers and money launderers.[54] MNEs can't help being visible, and thus vulnerable.

In essence, if MNEs operate where risk of violence is great, they put their personnel in danger. Even if no violence comes to them, they endure stress that negatively affects their performance.[55] Although local personnel may be at a lesser risk of, say, kidnapping, experience shows that they too are not immune. Further, MNEs must send personnel to areas where they operate. Some go as managers or technicians on long assignments; others go short-term to audit books, ensure control, and offer staff support. The dangers are not inconsequential. There are thousands of reported kidnappings per year as well as countless unreported ones. Many of these target foreign workers and their families.

It's simply unethical to put employees in such situations. Of course, they are not forced to go to dangerous places, and firms can get enough people to work there. However, experience shows there are three types of people who want or are willing to work in such areas, and none are ideal. First are those who simply want the high compensation and big insurance policies, some of whom are experienced in military or undercover activities. They tend to be highly independent and hard to control. Second are the naïve who don't understand the danger and are difficult to safeguard through training and security activities. Third are the thrill seekers who find that adrenaline is like an addictive drug; they are most at risk because of the thrill of danger and their reluctance to leave when situations worsen.[56]

High risk to individuals is indicative of a political situation out of control—a harbinger of additional risks that may occur through governmental changes, falls in consumer confidence, and a general malaise that damages revenues and operating regulations. This is not the kind of country in which to conduct operations.

ALTERNATIVES FOR ALLOCATING RESOURCES AMONG LOCATIONS

We now examine three complementary strategies for international expansion: alternative gradual commitments, geographic diversification versus concentration, and reinvestment versus harvesting.

ALTERNATIVE GRADUAL COMMITMENTS

Companies may reduce risks from the liability of foreignness by

- going first to countries with characteristics similar to those of their home countries,
- having experienced intermediaries handle operations for them,
- operating in formats requiring commitment of fewer resources abroad,
- moving initially to one or a few, rather than many, foreign countries.

As we've discussed, liability of foreignness influences companies to minimize risk by favoring operations in countries similar to their own. Nevertheless, Figure 13.4 illustrates alternative expansion patterns for minimizing this risk. As you examine this figure, note that the farther a company moves from the center on any axis, the deeper its international commitment. However, a company does not necessarily move at the same speed along each axis. In fact, it may jump over some of the steps. A slow movement along one axis may free up resources and lower risk that allows faster expansion along another.

Let's examine Figure 13.4 more closely. Axis A shows that companies may move gradually from a purely domestic focus to one encompassing operations in countries similar and then dissimilar to one's own country. However, an alternative when moving quickly along the A axis (and even jumping the intermediate step) is to move slowly along the B axis.

The B axis shows that a company may use intermediaries—especially ones that already know how to operate in a dissimilar foreign market—to handle operations abroad during early stages of international expansion. Doing so minimizes the resources the company puts at risk abroad and, thus, its degree of liability of foreignness. A related example is the international expansion of some high-tech companies from emerging economies. Rather than first targeting nearby countries with characteristics similar to their home markets, they have gone to high-income countries while relying heavily on intermediaries and foreign acquisitions to utilize personnel who know the markets they are targeting. However, over time the company may want to move farther out on the B axis by handling the operations with its own staff. This is because, by learning more about foreign operations, it perceives them as less risky than at the onset, and it realizes that its growth in business may justify the inclusion of internal capabilities, such as a department to handle foreign sales or purchases.

Axis C illustrates companies' beginning IB by importing or exporting, forms that require the placement of few company resources abroad. Again, as the company gains experience it might commit capital, personnel, and technology abroad by making a direct investment.

Axis D shows that companies can move internationally one country at a time, which keeps them from being overwhelmed by learning about many countries all at once. However,

FIGURE 13.4   The Usual Pattern of Internationalization

The farther a company moves outward along any of the axes (A, B, C, D), the deeper its international commitment. Most companies move at different speeds along different axes.

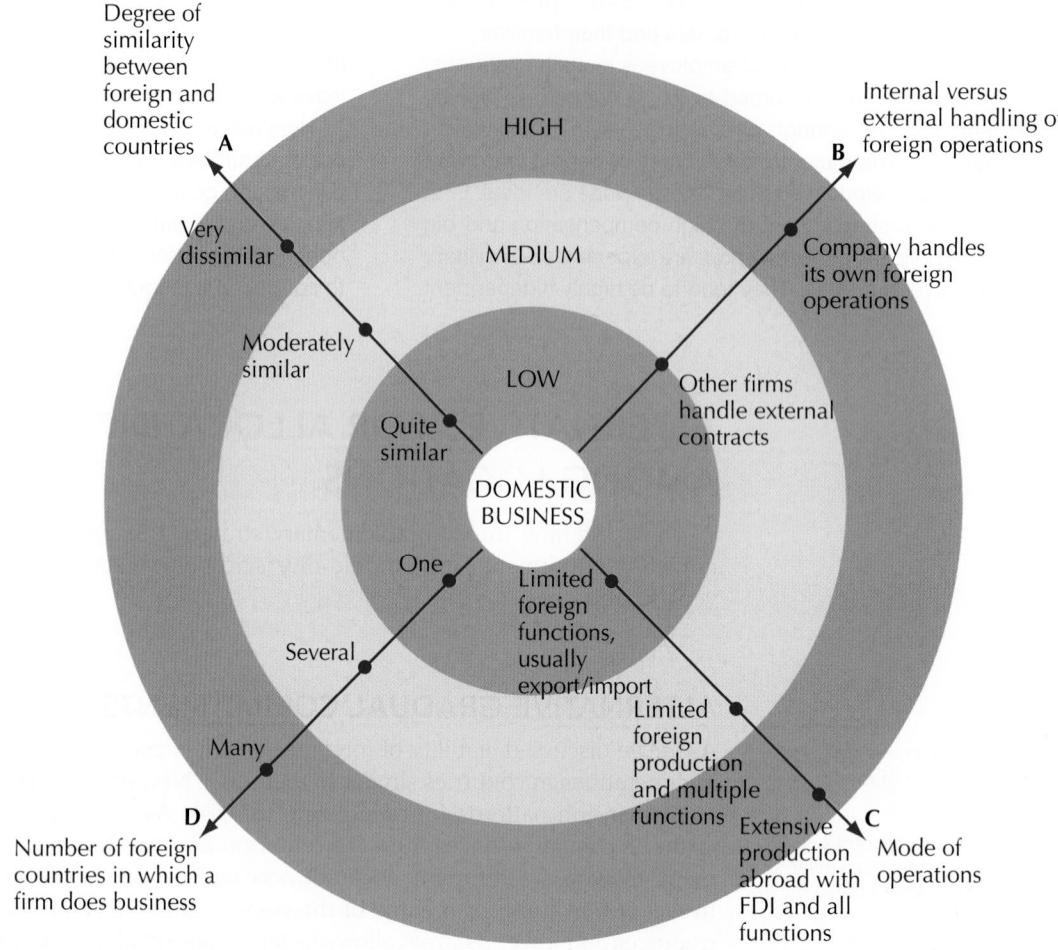

as we discuss in the next section, there may be operational reasons to move to a number of countries almost simultaneously.

GEOGRAPHIC DIVERSIFICATION VERSUS CONCENTRATION

Ultimately, a company may gain a sizable presence in most countries; however, there are different paths to that position. Although any move abroad means some geographic diversification, the term **diversification strategy** in the context of IB location describes a company's rapid movement into many foreign markets, gradually increasing its commitment within each one. A company can do this, say, through an initial liberal licensing policy that enables widespread expansion, followed by increasing involvement that takes on activities it first contracted to other companies.

At the other extreme, with a **concentration strategy**, the company will first move to only one or a few foreign countries, not going elsewhere until it develops a very strong involvement and competitive position. There are, of course, hybrids of the two strategies—for example, moving rapidly to most markets but increasing commitment in only a few.[57] We now outline reasons for using one strategy versus the other.

1. *Need for Rapid Growth in Country* Within industries requiring a high entry cost because of capital intensive technology or mass marketing, companies may lack resources enabling

---

> Strategies for ultimately reaching a high level of commitment in many countries are
>
> - diversification—go to many fast and then build up slowly in each,
> - concentration—go to one or a few and build up fast before going to others,
> - a hybrid of the two.

them to enter many countries simultaneously, thus a concentration strategy is usually preferred. Similarly, if country markets are all growing rapidly, companies may need to invest heavily in each to build and maintain a threshold market share, thus straining resources if simultaneously entering a large number of countries.[58]

2. *Competitive Lead Time* We have discussed that in cases where technology obsolesces rapidly, companies need to enter many markets quickly before competitors usurp their advantages, thus being in situations that favor a diversification strategy. Born-global companies are particularly prone to follow diversification strategies because so many of them depend on new and quickly obsolescing technologies that require fast market penetration.[59]

3. *Need for Product, Communication, and Distribution Adaptation* When companies must tailor their products and operating methods for each country they enter, they incur additional costs. They may need to follow a concentration strategy to minimize the costs of entering multiple countries simultaneously.

4. *Program Control Requirements* The more a company wants to control its operations in a foreign country, such as because of fear that a partner will become a competitor, the more favorable a concentration strategy is. This is because the company will need to use more of its resources to maintain that control, such as by taking a larger percentage of ownership in the operation.

REINVESTMENT AND HARVESTING

So far, we've discussed the sequencing of country entry. Then, once operating abroad, a company must evaluate how much effort to allocate to each location. With successful FDI, the company earns money that it may remit back to headquarters or reinvest to increase the investment value. However, if the investment returns are inadequate, the company may consider transferring capital and diverting efforts elsewhere.

> A company may have to make new commitments in a locale to maintain its competitiveness.

Reinvestment Decisions Once committed to a given locale, a company may need to reinvest its earnings there. The failure to expand might result in not attaining its target growth objectives. Moreover, headquarters management may delegate certain investment decisions to experienced foreign subsidiary managers because they believe that subsidiary management is the best judge of what the operation needs.

> Companies must decide how to get out of operations if
> - they no longer fit their overall strategy,
> - there are better alternative opportunities.

Harvesting Companies commonly reduce commitments in some countries because they have poorer performance prospects than do others—a process known as **harvesting (or divesting)**. Burger King, for example, sold off underperforming operations in Korea and Slovakia so as to have funds for more promising ventures in the Chinese and Russian markets. There are other reasons as well. Dana sold its U.K. facility to use funds to concentrate on developing different automotive technologies.[60] Goodyear sold its Indonesian rubber plantation because of its decision to stop producing rubber.[61]

Evidence suggests that companies might benefit by planning divestments better and by developing divestment specialists. Companies have tended to wait too long before divesting, instead trying expensive means, usually suggested by subsidiary managers, to improve performance. After all, these managers' performance evaluations typically depend heavily on growth in their areas of responsibility, but they have no such incentive to propose divestments.[62]

A company may divest by a sale or closure of facilities, usually preferring a sale because it receives some compensation. If it considers divesting because of a country's well-publicized political or economic situation, it may find few potential buyers except at very low prices. In such situations, it may try to delay divestment, hoping that the situation will improve.

A company cannot always simply abandon an investment either, and leaving may take years. Governments frequently require performance contracts, such as substantial severance packages to employees that make a loss from divestment greater than the direct investment's net value. Further, many MNEs fear adverse international publicity as well as difficulty in re-entering a market if they do not sever relations with a foreign government on amicable terms.

NONCOMPARATIVE LOCATION DECISIONS

Most companies examine proposals one at a time

• and accept them if they meet minimum-threshold criteria,

• because unforeseen opportunities give little time to make decisions,

• because of difficulty in incorporating global performance into single country analyses.

One might expect companies to maintain a storehouse of ranked foreign operating proposals, undertaking the best, second best, etc. until they could make no further commitments, but this is usually not the case. They make **go-no-go decisions** by examining one opportunity at a time and pursuing it if it meets some threshold criteria.

To begin with, companies sometimes need to respond quickly to prospects they had not anticipated, such as unsolicited proposals to sell abroad, to enter a joint venture, or sign a licensing contract. In fact, many companies initiate export activity passively—that is, foreign companies approach them to be suppliers. Similarly, undertakings may be onetime opportunities because a government or another company solicits bids, requests collaboration, or changes rules to encourage competition and foreign acquisitions, such as Mexico did for telecommunications.[63] Moving fast enables a company to acquire the best assets. Further, there may be a chance to buy properties that another company divests.

Another factor inhibiting country operating comparison is their interdependence. Profit figures from individual operations may obscure the real impact on overall company performance. For example, placing a production facility abroad may either increase or reduce exports from the home country. Moreover, headquarters may have to incur additional costs to oversee the foreign facility, particularly if it coordinates the movement of components between the home and foreign countries. These costs are difficult to estimate and to allocate among the different countries. Further, a supplier's dealings with a global customer may cause it to suboptimize profits in one country in order to satisfy the customer in a second country. Finally, interdependence occurs because much of the sales and purchases of foreign subsidiaries are among units of the same parent company. The prices the company charges on these transactions will affect the relative profitability of one country's unit compared to another's.

Clearly, companies cannot afford to conduct very many feasibility studies simultaneously. Even if they can, the studies are apt to be in various stages of completion at any given time. Can the company afford to hold off on making a decision about a study that has been completed? Probably not. Waiting would likely invalidate much of the completed data, thus necessitating added expense and further delays to update it. In sum, three factors inhibit companies from comparing investment opportunities: cost, time, and the interrelation of operations on global performance.

Looking to the Future
Conditions That May Cause Prime Locations to Change

Will Prime Locations Change?

Future sales- and resource-seeking opportunities and risks may shift among countries because of a variety of demographic, sociocultural, political-legal, technological, and economic occurrences. We will concentrate here on population changes and where people can and will prefer to work.

Comparative Market Growth In Chapter 5, we discussed how demographers expect a slowing in the growth of global population through 2050, with some countries experiencing declining populations

and the most robust growth in developing economies, particularly those in sub-Saharan Africa. The projection is that the percentage of people living in currently developed countries is expected to fall to 13.7 percent from a 2000 figure of 19.7 percent. Given the importance of population size for sales potential, these changes, if they materialize, will be profound.

Further, because the world's population will continue to age and people will pursue education for more years, the share of what we now consider the working-age population should fall for developed countries and increase in many developing ones. Because there is a positive relationship between the proportional size of the working-age population and per capita GDP, the growth in per capita GDP should be higher in today's developing economies than in today's developed countries unless we redefine working age.[64] If these demographic changes occur, they will affect the location of both markets and labor forces.

Where Will People Work? An intriguing possibility is the near-officeless headquarters for international companies. Technology may permit more people to work from anywhere as they e-mail and teleconference with their colleagues, customers, and suppliers. In fact, they can live anywhere in the world and work from their homes, as is already occurring at least part-time within some professions. However, if people can work from home, they may situate their homes where they want to live rather than living near their employers. Highly creative, innovative, self-motivated people can usually get permission to live in almost any country of the world.

A leading researcher on urbanization and planning has shown that beginning at least as early as the Roman Empire these types of people have been drawn to certain cities that were innovation centers. This attraction is due to people's desire to improve through interchange with others like themselves—like "a very bright class in a school or a college. They all try to score off each other and do better." Thus, if he's correct, the brightest minds may work more at home but still need the face-to-face interaction with their colleagues.[65] The continued attraction of young technical people to places like Silicon Valley seems to confirm this viewpoint.[66] The researcher further suggests that these people will be drawn to the same places that attract tourists.

These arguments are provocative, particularly because we now have technology to allow people to communicate without traveling as much. Yet the continued increase in business travel shows that there is still a need for face-to-face interaction.

Concomitantly, another view is that in leading Western societies the elite, made up of intellectuals and highly educated people, is increasingly using its capability to delay and block new technologies. If successful, their efforts will result in the emergence of different countries at the forefront of technological development and acceptance.[67] ■

CASE The Lego Group Case

LEGO® Group is a family business that started in 1932 making wooden toys in the city of Billund, Denmark. In 1958, Godtfred Kirk Christiansen, son of the company founder Ole Kirk Christiansen, created the LEGO© brick, later praised "Toy of the Century," by both Fortune Magazine and the British Association of Toy Retailers (LEGO, Annual Report, 2011). Today LEGO is the 4th largest toy manufacturer in the world in terms of sales volume, after Mattel, Bandai-Namco and Hasbro, with a turnover of €2,511 million in 2012 and employing more than 9,000 worldwide. LEGO's sales during the first-half of 2013 increased by 13 percent with the strongest growth in Asia, with stagnating markets in North America and Europe. Besides toys, the company has a diverse portfolio of products and services including games, video games, apparel, and theme parks.

The diversification was a direct response to developments and challenges in the industry. In the 1990s the segment for construction toys was shrinking. The competition for kids' time and their parents' money was getting sharper. LEGO is part of the market called "edutainment," including products with ability to entertain and educate at the same time. First of all, computer games "stole" a lot of the potential LEGO users. For those who enjoyed constructing little worlds with the LEGO bricks games like "SimCity" and "Civilization" computers could now satisfy the curiosity and the natural creative urge a lot faster than LEGO. Computer games became in a sense the "fast food" of edutainment.

In a parallel development, the power of the retailers grew. Especially in the United States the buyers of the LEGO products were reduced to only a few companies like

Toys' R'Us, Walmart, and Kmart. LEGO's business model was very dependent on retailers, who now started demanding larger discounts and special adjusted products. LEGO' dilemma was whether to become more flexible. To protect the strong brand of the company, LEGO wanted that people could buy the same products at almost the same price everywhere. If the customers knew that there was only one price and only one quality level for a LEGO product, they would see the company as a lot more trustworthy as opposed to the situation where they could buy low-cost and, possibly, low-quality products at some retailers. The overall reliability is better with only one quality and one price. The image of LEGO might be damaged by the flexibility.

Building Blocks of Independence

To become more independent the company slowly began to look for new ways of selling the product. The Internet gave that opportunity. In early 2000s, LEGO launched LEGO Direct, which was the successor of the not so successful LEGO World Shop. With LEGO Direct it became possible for the customers to virtually invent their own LEGO construction in front of the personal computer. When finished, they could order the exact LEGO products needed for their construction. This option gave the company some valuable advantages: they became more independent of the retailers and they had a direct communication channel to their customers. Thereby, they could quickly realize new demands from the consumers. LEGO.com has been very successful in the way that it has had millions of visitors per month, with the average visitor staying for 8–9 minutes.

The global toy industry has been growing at CAGR of 2.9 percent from 2008 to 2012, while the global economy has grown only 2.6 percent over the same period. The industry growth is not equally divided neither by region, neither by country. While some countries, especially emerging markets, are experiencing relevant growth, such as France, Germany, Australia, Brazil, and China, others are experiencing negative growth in their market shares, like the USA and Canada. To reach its global customer base, LEGO currently has offices in 29 countries (LEGO website). Because its products don't need local adaptation the company has over time reduced its office base. The company simply needs to accommodate the products to local laws, which can be done initially for each product line in a centralized setting. From the production viewpoint, LEGO moved several production sites to international locations, in search for lower costs. This was the case of the Czech Republic and Mexico plants, as well the production outsourcing of Flextronics to Poland.

In October 2013, LEGO announced it is building manufacturing facilities in Jiaxing, China. China is among the fastest growing markets in this industry. As Euromonitor International reports, sales growth in China's toy market increasing by 18 percent, to nearly $9 billion, in 2011 from a

year earlier. The new facility will be a complete factory, a replica of LEGO's four existing factories in Denmark, Mexico, Hungary, and the Czech Republic. It will consist of all production processes, from molding the bricks, processing them and packaging the Lego boxes. LEGO expects construction to begin in 2014 and be completed by 2017, at which time the factory will have about 2,000 employees. The choice of the location is based on its proximity to LEGO's regional distribution centre and the city having all the facilities and infrastructure needed. In addition to these, the company believes the location is perfect in regards to securing the best environment for future LEGO employees. The city is the strongest possible match with core LEGO values, and the plans for a sustainable city development are well under way. Jiaxing has been named "National Health City," "National Model City for Greening," "National Garden City."

Major Location Decisions

Over the past two decades LEGO has made several production location decisions, with the underlying purpose being cost savings. However, this time seems to be different. Growing demand and an effort to reduce times between order and delivery are the main drivers behind the company's decision to invest hundreds of millions of euros in the new factory. According to global research firm Companies and Markets, by 2016, the Asian-Pacific region is expected to become the world's largest toy market. In the words of Lego's spokesman Roar Rude Trangbaek "...this is not a cost-cutting exercise. It is a direct result of our strategy to have production close to the core markets. This factory will not supply Europe or North America." He also ads that the Lego factory in China will be able to supply 70 percent to 80 percent of the Lego bricks sold in Asia in 2017. While Asia is still the smallest region for Lego, with the region contributing less than 10 percent of LEGO's revenue, sales there in recent years have soared by more than 50 percent annually as Asia's hundreds of millions of children are increasingly picking up educational toys amid improved wage and living standards. Lego Chief Executive Jørgen Vig Knudstorp has pinned much of the closely held company's hopes on Asia, forecasting growth rates in coming years at about twice the speed of its North American market. Over the long term, LEGO wants the Europe, Africa, and Middle East region, Asia and the Americas to contribute equally to sales, paving the way for further expansions to other regions.

The choice of China as the country of setting up the production facility might raise some eyebrows. Previously, toy makers have faced continuous struggles in China, where parents would rather have their children reading books than playing. In fact, playing has, often, even been considered a dirty word in a culture where education is prioritized. However, many toy companies are already figuring out that they can win over China's parents by positioning their toys as educational items. In this respect, LEGO has struck a chord with increasingly affluent Chinese parents with toys that are presented as helping children with developing dexterity and creativity. In its attempts to make itself visible to Chinese public, LEGO foundation, independent but affiliated with LEGO corporation, is already working with Chinese students. For instance, a group of students from Tsinghua University built a low-cost atomic force microscope using LEGO's, 3D-printed parts and off-the-shelf electronics.

The Future

A challenging issue for LEGO in China, similar to other manufacturers in the past, is that popularity increases the pressure from manufacturers who build identically looking Lego bricks, commonly known as "Logo clones." LEGO has a long history of court battles to protect its copyright. Currently, it is entangled in a legal fight with Hong Kong-based Best-Lock Construction Toys, which stands accused of ripping LEGO off its signature "mini-figures." Although LEGO has been relatively successful in its copyright battles so far, there are many copies and clones on the market that either claim to be Lego products or state that they are compatible with the leading building bricks.

For instance, blocks marketed from Chinese companies Ligao and Banbao are often direct copies of LEGO deigns. One potential strategy to keep these pirates at bay is to increase LEGO's already high manufacturing standards as most Chinese toy factories are focused on producing and exporting low-cost products rather than high-quality ones for domestic consumption. Further, LEGO may also want to invest in creating customized products for Chinese and/or Asian markets. This is a risky strategy, with the resulting products having the same fate as the now-defunct "Orient Expedition" set.

QUESTIONS

13-3. LEGO has placed an emerging country such as China ahead of developed economies of Japan and South Korea in its location decision. Discuss the pros and cons of this strategy.

13-4. LEGO's product portfolio is quite large. What are the advantages and disadvantages of product concentration versus diversification?

13-5. LEGO is a late comer in the Chinese market. Discuss how it can overcome this barrier.

MyLab Management

Go to **mymanagementlab.com** for the following Assisted-graded writing questions:

13-6 LEGO is heavily investing in the Chinese consumer before it entered the country. Discuss the pros and cons of this strategy.

13-7 China is considered the land of knock-offs and imitation products. Should major multinationals then bypass China in their location decisions?

Endnotes

Scan for Endnotes or go to www.pearsonglobaleditions.com/Daniels

CHAPTER 14
Modes of Trading Internationally

OBJECTIVES

After studying this chapter, you should be able to:

14-1   Explain the principles and practices of exporting

14-2   Articulate the motivations and methods of exporting

14-3   Understand export startup and expansion

14-4   Explain the principles and practices of importing

14-5   Articulate the motivations and methods of importing

14-6   Describe the problems and pitfalls that challenge international traders

14-7   Differentiate the resources and assistance that help international traders

14-8   Define the standards of an export plan

14-9   Distinguish the principles and practices of countertrade

MyLab Management®
Improve Your Performance!
When you see this icon ⭐, visit
www.mymanagementlab.com for
activities that are applied, personalized,
and offer immediate feedback.

When one is prepared, difficulties do not come.

—Ethiopian proverb

Source: MAGNIFIER.Shutterstock

CASE

SpinCent: The Decision to Export[1]

More than 300,000 U.S. companies export goods. Some 7,000 of these, such as Caterpillar, Boeing, General Electric, and Intel, generate about 65 percent of total exports.[2] Their smallest shipments are typically larger than the largest shipments of smaller companies. Still, some 297,000 small and medium-size enterprises (SMEs)—specifically, companies with fewer than 500 workers—account for nearly 98 percent of all U.S. exporters.[3] One such SME is SpinCent of Pennsylvania.

SpinCent manufactures laboratory and industrial centrifuges. Companies in chemical, pharmaceutical, food, environmental, and mining industries use them to spin a substance into high-speed rotation around a fixed axis, thereby moving heavy elements to the bottom, lighter objects toward the top, and liquid in between. SpinCent's 56 employees—43 workers, 8 product and process engineers, and 5 managers—operate out of its 90,000-square-foot facility in suburban Philadelphia. SpinCent began operations in 2010 with one goal in mind: create high-performance centrifuges that inspire absolute confidence. Its patented technology anchors a full line of automatic and manual centrifuges recognized for quality and value. To this day, management believes it builds "centrifuges for which there simply are no equals."

TO EXPORT OR NOT TO EXPORT: THAT IS THE QUESTION

From inception, SpinCent approached export passively. Its international sales often resulted from other U.S. firms' orders that were set for export, occasional sale leads received at trade shows, or an unsolicited order from a foreign buyer. Export sales generated high gross margins; occasionally, unexpected complications, such as customs or credit problems, increased administrative costs. Still, SpinCent's net margins on export sales ran about 15 percent higher than domestic sales.

Paul Knepper, CEO and founder, explained that recurring problems had dampened his interest in exporting. First, he and his colleagues were skeptical about the likelihood of international success. Previous efforts, they felt, had spent more time on unfocused searching or solving situations than on purposefully growing export activity. Moreover, serving customers in the domestic market had kept them quite busy. As a result, developing exports stretched their already thin management structure. Going international, they feared, would pose tough challenges, especially heading into direct competition with seasoned exporters from Germany and Japan.

Still, as time passed, market pressures raised concerns about SpinCent's ongoing productivity and profitability. The struggling U.S. manufacturing sector had slowed SpinCent's growth and pushed some of its customers to import cheaper, lower-end centrifuges

from foreign suppliers. Increasing price competition was inevitable. Knepper knew the day of reckoning was at hand: SpinCent must (1) focus on the domestic market and exploit every possible efficiency to sustain productivity or (2) expand aggressively into export, looking to fast-growing overseas markets. Ultimately, Knepper conceded, market trends forced his hand. The slow-moving deindustrialization of the United States, forecast to continue for years, would steadily reduce domestic demand. Meanwhile, quickly industrializing emerging economies, particularly in Asia, signaled rich opportunities. Hence, Knepper accepted, somewhat grudgingly, that SpinCent must export to promising markets.

ASIA CALLS

Big market trends signaled big opportunities in Asia. "Industries were coming online everywhere and seemingly overnight," observed Knepper. Pro-market reform, improving economic freedom, and accelerating economic development spurred industrialization throughout Asia. Moreover, the types of goods moving through Asia's seaports signaled budding industries that used SpinCent's sorts of centrifuges. And, unlike the United States, which was in the mature part of the product life cycle, emerging economies looked set to grow for years.

GETTING STARTED

New to the idea of the Asian market, SpinCent sought help on how best to access the large, diverse region. Knepper feared wasting resources flying solo. Moreover, he was not looking to generate a single-shot export burst, but aimed to build relationships that would support long-term growth. Hence, the primary challenge was finding competent and trustworthy distributors who would develop, make, and service local sales. "We were looking for a long-term partner and not a quick export sale," said Knepper. "The right partner for SpinCent needed to be as confident and competent about the product as we are, and able to promote, educate, and serve consumers in the respective territories." The key, he added, was partnering with respected firms. On the flip side, SpinCent had to convince potential agents that partnering with it made long-term sense.

Knepper began by seeking information on potential distributors, confirming their reputation and resources. A few of the company's earlier export transactions, for instance, had run into problems with agents who struggled financially. As Knepper warned, "Getting paid is a huge part of running a business, and unless a company has the right payment policies in place with the right partners, it will get scammed."

Mindful of these issues, Knepper attended a trade seminar sponsored by the U.S. Commercial Service's Export Assistance Center of

Philadelphia. On the agenda were market analysis and trade reports on the emerging economies of Asia. Taking his seat, he couldn't help but wonder about the opportunities. Sure, he conceded, they sounded great. However, he had seen hype like this come back to bite, not to mention the horror stories he'd heard of the problems and pitfalls of exporting. Indeed, he reflected, a key reason for attending was reconciling his sense of the opportunities and threats.

GETTING HELP

Since exports promote economic growth, government agencies offer extensive assistance, such as trade seminars, market research, training programs, and financial planning. Trade officials encourage SMEs like SpinCent, seeing them as the primary beneficiaries of initiatives to initiate and accelerate international trade activity. Given that 60 percent or so of all SME exporters posted sales to only one foreign market, many could boost performance by entering just one or two others. Expanding SMEs' market horizons through trade seminars, official reasoned, bolstered their confidence to do so.

After a full morning of profiles and presentations, Knepper believed Asian markets held far more opportunities than risk. He had learned quite a bit about Asia, as well as some technicalities of exporting. Still, his unfamiliarity of local business practicalities, compounded by the lack of local sales representatives, bothered him. Filling in these blanks, he concluded, called for some on-the-ground research. So, before leaving, he spoke to Commercial Service agents and arranged to join a 12-day trade mission that was heading to Hong Kong, the Philippines, Vietnam, and Taiwan the following month.

GOAL SETTING

Knepper's trip had straightforward goals: assess market potential, identify competitors, get a sense of reasonable price points, and recruit local sales representatives and distributors. Although he had never visited Asia, he believed he had prepared well. His time with the trade representatives in Philadelphia gave him a good sense of the general characteristics and industry conditions in Asian markets. Also, in the past, SpinCent had received inquiries from Asian distributors ordering centrifuges; some had inquired about representing the company locally. Depending on how busy it was with domestic customers, SpinCent tried to respond yet nothing substantial had ever come of it. Still, these contacts had been saved, thereby giving Knepper a start on potential distributors and likely customers.

Knepper also tapped the Commercial Services' Gold Key program to prescreen potential distributors. This program helps SMEs enlist Commercial Services agents overseas to scan local markets for qualified agents, distributors, and representatives. Gold Key agents will prescreen and prequalify potential partners, conduct background checks, and customize local market research. Exporters report that the Gold Key program ensures that when a firm adds a partner to its network, it is a respected company in the target country.

Thinking back to his days as a Boy Scout, Knepper believed that he met the sacred command: "Be prepared." With a briefcase full of brochures, a laptop loaded with profiles of his product line, and the sense of doing something potentially great, he headed to Asia. Over the next two weeks, he interviewed potential agents, chatted with likely customers, scouted competitors' offerings, test called their service support, spoke to freight forwarders and logistics companies, and visited local government officials and customs agencies.

ASIA CALLS, SPINCENT ANSWERS

On the flight home, tired but charged, Knepper realized that his misgivings about exporting had been unfounded. There were risks, but the opportunities outweighed them. Exporting was no longer an option for SpinCent—it was an imperative. Besides a new sense of commitment, Knepper had a bit more confidence, given the newly signed distributors in the Philippines and Taiwan as well as promising sales leads there and in Hong Kong.

Back in Philadelphia, Knepper tested the Asian market a bit more, advertising in trade publications as well as running banner ads on trade sites in tandem with his newly signed distributors (he handled the English ads, they, the Mandarin versions). In addition, he began working with an agent from Commercial Services on an export plan. This work helped SpinCent secure its largest overseas partner to date, a distributor in Hong Kong who served the fast-growing Chinese market. Commercial Services arranged meetings with others, eventually signing a distributor in Singapore and generating leads in Australia.

Allied with strong partners, SpinCent continues tapping the support provided by government agencies. The more he has dealt with them, the more Knepper appreciates a friend's advice: "Let the government do what it can for you. This is their niche and they're the best at it." Now, with an export plan in hand, Knepper has begun working with the Export-Import Bank to secure financing options for overseas distributors and customers.[4] And, with a gleam in his eye, he's set to attend a U.S. Commercial Service's profile of the emerging markets of sub-Saharan Africa.

GOING FORWARD

Steadily, as SpinCent gains experience in Taiwan, the Philippines, Hong Kong, and Singapore, it looks onward and upward. Although exporting creates challenges, it helps SpinCent boost productivity and profitability. Indeed, overseas sales provided the firm with a growing stream of business during the economic downturn in the United States, while rivals who had not diversified via exports struggled. More important, exporting taps a low-cost, high-return opportunity to leverage SpinCent's centrifuge technology.

This experience, reflects Knepper, has straightforward lessons: "If you are thinking about exporting internationally, do it. Get going, do your homework, utilize low-cost resources, participate in trade missions, learn about business cultures, and build relationships.

Always verify your potential business partners. Gather as much information as you can. Stress-test your assumptions; the wrong guess costs you time and money. Above all, no matter the problems that you'll run into, stay committed. All of these seem tough, but they only cost pennies on the dollar and the returns can be substantial." ■

QUESTIONS

★ **14-1.** Analyze two challenges that SpinCent overcame in developing its export activity. Describe how it overcame them.

★ **14-2.** Based on its Asian experiences, map a sequence to guide SpinCent's export expansion to sub-Saharan Africa.

INTRODUCTION

Exporting and importing are among the fastest-growing economic activities in the world.

Exports and imports have always been an important facet of the global economy. Expanding consumer demand, cross-national linkages, and free trade agreements progressively open more markets, thereby increasing the ease of international trade. Figure 14.1 shows that the value of trade as a share of world GDP has steadily risen over the past 50-plus years. This trend, while hitting air pockets now and then, has been relentless. Even the recent drop in world trade, the consequence of the global financial crisis in 2008, has already faded.[5]

Earlier chapters report that companies engage in international business through several modes. The choice a company makes, say, choosing exporting rather than licensing, joint ventures, or FDI, follows from its analysis of market factors as well as its resources, capabilities, and competencies (see Figure 14.2). Export and import are, by far, the most common modes of international business. The scale and scope of firms that trade steadily increases.[6] Exports and imports are a major part of the global economy, a critical driver of nations' economic performance, and a strategic choice for companies of all sizes in countries worldwide.

FIGURE 14.1   World Trade as a Percent of World GDP, 1960–2013

Here we see the sum of exports and imports of goods and services measured as a share of gross domestic product on a global basis over the past 55 years. Despite periodic ups and downs, the dominant trend in international trade, as a share of global business activity, has been steady expansion. By the way, these trade data combine imports and exports (i.e., a bit of double counting). Still, the upward trend powers on.

Source: Assembled from data reported in the World Bank's World Development Indicators, particularly Trade (percent of GDP), Series NE_TRD_GNFS_ZS, retrieved June 16, 2016, from http://data.worldbank.org/data-catalog/world-development-indicators.

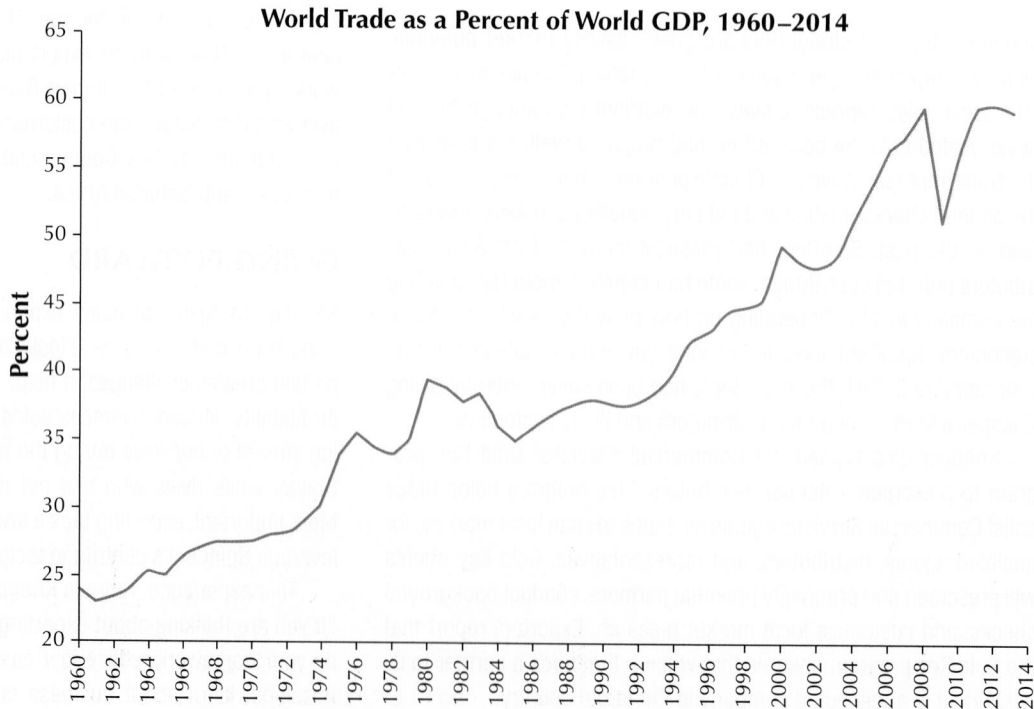

World Trade as a Percent of World GDP, 1960–2014

FIGURE 14.2 Factors Influencing Export and Import Operations

Assessing export and import highlight the environmental and operational factors that influence practice and performance.

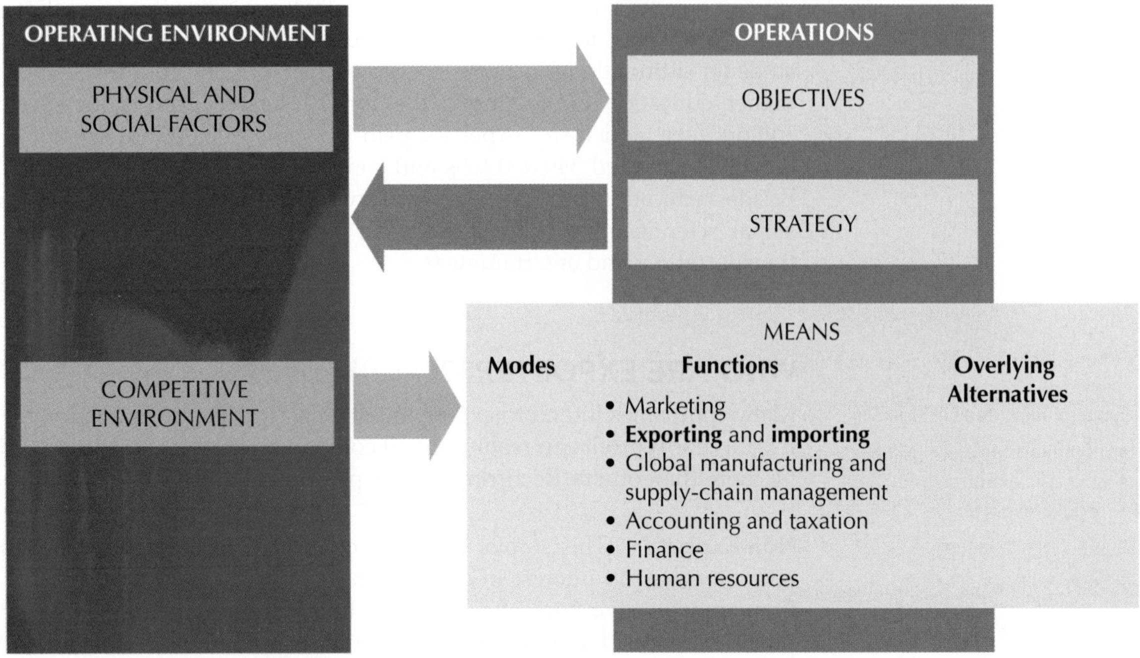

OPERATING ENVIRONMENT		OPERATIONS
PHYSICAL AND SOCIAL FACTORS	→	OBJECTIVES
	←	STRATEGY
COMPETITIVE ENVIRONMENT	→	MEANS

MEANS

Modes	Functions	Overlying Alternatives
	• Marketing	
	• **Exporting** and **importing**	
	• Global manufacturing and supply-chain management	
	• Accounting and taxation	
	• Finance	
	• Human resources	

Exporting sends products to another country; importing brings products in from another country.

The popularity of export and import follows from their key advantages. Both are straightforward, low-cost, and quick means to engage foreign markets. Both impose minimum business risk and require relatively low resource commitment. Moreover, whether large or small, international trade helps companies improve productivity, increase profits, and diversify risk. Finally, trade effectively deals with the fact that most people live elsewhere in the world than in any one country. In the case of Germany, an export powerhouse, nearly 99 percent of potential consumers live outside it and, by the way, they command more than 95 percent of the world's purchasing power. Therefore, a German company selling domestically can reach a maximum of some 81 million consumers; selling internationally reaches 7.3 billion more.

In sum, international trade presents opportunities to enterprising companies. It also exposes them to threats. Still, as this chapter shows, there are useful approaches to interpret options and tried-and-true methods to overcome challenges.

EXPORTING: PRINCIPLES AND PRACTICES

CONCEPT CHECK

As we saw in Chapter 1 (page 58), "Why Companies Engage in IB" emphasized three operating objectives: expanding sales, acquiring resources, and minimizing risk. To achieve one or more of these objectives, companies choose from various "IB Operating Modes." Among these modes, **exporting** and **importing** are the most prevalent, especially among small and medium-sized enterprises (SMEs).

Exporting is the sale of goods or services produced by a firm based in one country to customers that reside in another country. The idea of exporting manufactured goods presents a clear situation, as in the case of Indian carmaker Tata Motors shipping (exporting) automobiles made in Pune to customers (importers) in Bangladesh. Hence, exports involve any good or service that is traded from sellers in one country to buyers in another country.

Service exports occur across a range of industry sectors. However, the sometimes hazy standards of a service make it a bit tougher to define what qualifies as an export. For instance, engineering contractors—such as Bechtel, Skanska AB, or Kajima—export services when they construct buildings, roads, utilities, airports, or seaports in a foreign country. Management consultants, such as McKinsey & Company, export when they perform advisory services for foreign clients. Investment banks, such as Goldman Sachs and UBS, export when they help a foreign client to arrange financing or navigate capital markets. Similarly, services are exported indirectly when the Japanese advertising firm Dentsu, the world's largest single-brand agency, creates a marketing campaign for Sony that is then used outside of Japan. Hydraulx Visual Effects, designers of digital monsters, exports its services when it helps overseas clients add visual effects to feature films, commercials, and music videos. In these examples, the seller is the exporter while the buyer is the importer.[7]

Technically, a service need not physically leave a country to qualify as an export. Rather, it need only earn foreign currency. For example, you may not think of the foreign national students sitting alongside you in class as part of your country's export strategy. However, higher education ranks among the top 10 service exports for several Western nations. Tuition, fees, and living expenses paid by some 900,000 international students and their families supported 340,000 jobs and contributed $27 billion to the U.S. economy in 2014.[8] Besides education, leading types of service exports include financial, information, professional, scientific, and technical services; telecommunication; travel and tourism; insurance; transportation; and entertainment.

WHO ARE EXPORTERS?

Many companies intend to export, anticipating it will accelerate growth, improve productivity, and boost profits. In reality, not all companies export, and among those that do, a few do far more than others. Recurring market patterns identify the following types.

Non-Exporter This sort of company commands little to no knowledge about exporting and often has no interest in international trade. This is not necessarily a deficiency. Many firms grow in their domestic market without exporting simply because they make goods or provide services that do not travel well to foreign markets. Some firms, even though making products that customers elsewhere demand, disregard exporting for various reasons, including general disinterest or insufficient resources.

Sporadic Exporter This type of company takes a passive approach to assessing international trade options.[9] It fills an unsolicited order from the occasional foreign buyer, but prefers to focus on the domestic market. Think of SpinCent's international activities prior to Knepper's realization of the imperative to export. It filled export orders as they arrived, but generally, though, saw them as anomalies. Sporadic exporters understand the basics of the export process, but assign it low priority.

Regular Exporter The company that aggressively pursues export sales as a productive, profitable, strategic activity is a regular exporter. It's experienced with the technicalities of international trade. Regular exporters look to international markets for growth, invest resources to expand export operations, and proactively respond to export signals.[10] Again, think of SpinCent's evolution following Knepper's realization—corroborated by his chats with Commercial Service agents and travels to Asia—of the importance of exporting. Each step demystified aspects of the experience, steadily supporting Knepper's progression from a sporadic to regular exporter.

THE MATTER OF ADVANTAGES

The question of who is likely to start and sustain exporting directs us toward a broader profile of a company's choice of how best to go international. Earlier materials identified several options that firms consider, most notably licensing, joint venture, alliances, or FDI. They also profiled the influence of ownership, location, and internalization advantages on a firm's preferred entry mode into foreign markets.[11] Here, we apply these discussions to the export decision.

Ownership Advantages Managers bundle resources and capabilities to develop core competencies that, in defining the firm's competitive advantage, influence if and how it enters foreign markets. For instance, SpinCent capitalized on its ownership advantages by

Margin notes:

Types of exporters include
- non-exporter,
- sporadic exporter,
- regular exporter.

Ownership advantages of the company, location advantages of the market, and internalization advantages from controlling transactions shape how firms enter foreign markets.

leveraging its core competency in designing, manufacturing, and servicing centrifugal equipment. These advantages, "owned" by SpinCent due to its proprietary technology and expertise, guided its export expansion. Companies that command weak ownership advantages, anticipating fierce struggles with foreign rivals, typically disregard export.

Resource-constrained or risk-averse companies that have strong ownership advantages often enter foreign markets through export.

Location Advantages   The combination of high sales opportunity and low investment risk in foreign markets creates favorable export locations. Stable markets with many consumers increase the odds that someone wants your product. Favorable business environments such as Canada, Japan, or Germany attract exporters, though high-potential markets throughout the world interest aspiring and experienced traders. Again, SpinCent saw the industrialization of emerging economies creating favorable locations marked by strong demand and pro-business policies.

Internalization Advantages   Companies often respond to uncertainties caused by market imperfections by internalizing market processes—that is, conducting a transaction within the controlled confines of the company rather than in the open, imperfect market. Migrating market activities into the company reduces the risks as well as exploits gaps resulting from say, incomplete information, arbitrary regulation, or unfair competition. Internalizing activities, for instance, enables executives to safeguard their core competency within the company rather than licensing it in markets that poorly protect intellectual property.

Again, SpinCent could have bypassed exporting, instead opting to license its proprietary centrifuge technology to Asian manufacturers. While cheap in the short term, this choice would likely prove costly over the long haul as SpinCent inadvertently helped local licensees evolve into rivals. Chapter 3's profile of the rule of man as the basis of law, such as that prevailing in several Asian markets, highlighted the corresponding poor protection of intellectual property. This sort of market imperfection leads companies to retain control of their core competencies by internalizing manufacturing and relying on export.

CHARACTERISTICS OF EXPORTERS

CONCEPT CHECK

The complexity posed by differing cultural, political, legal, and economic environments imposes a so-called "liability of foreignness." This idea holds that foreign companies, by virtue of their spotty familiarity, incur additional economic and social costs of doing business overseas. Companies offset this liability by capitalizing on their advantages as well as selecting the mode of international business that best reflects their resource profile and risk tolerance.

The largest companies are the biggest exporters. SMEs, however, are steadily expanding export activity.

The quest to promote international trade spurs officials to identify the characteristics of successful exporters. Pinpointing important attributes helps officials improve support programs that, in turn, help companies develop the necessary competencies. Identifying the correlates of export success often starts by examining the influence of firm size, comparing and contrasting the trading activities of big and small companies.

Company size has interesting relationships with export activity. Large MNEs like Samsung, Boeing, and Hon Hai are big exporters. Their ownership, location, and internalization advantages help them identify markets, leverage organizational capabilities, and manage market risks. The difficulty of these tasks leads many to presume that export is an option best left to large companies. This inference does have face validity. The largest companies routinely account for the lion's share of exporting throughout countries worldwide. In the United States, the 500 biggest firms accounted for nearly 60 percent of total export value, the 250 biggest accounted for more than half, and the 100 biggest contributed just under one-third.[12]

Nevertheless, many see export potential in **small and medium-sized enterprises (SMEs)**—those firms that, by definition, have fewer than 500 employees. In the United States, SMEs account for 97.8 percent of all exporters and 97.2 percent of all importers. Too, SMEs claim 33.7 percent and 31.6 percent of the total value of export and import, respectively.[13] This situation is not unique to the United States. Worldwide, more than two-thirds of exporters have fewer than 20 employees. More than 98 percent of companies in the Asia–Pacific region are SMEs. China registered SMEs account for about 99 percent of all companies, exceeded 4.3 million in number, and contributed 59 percent of GDP, 50 percent of tax revenues, 68 percent of exports, and 75 percent of new jobs.[14] Likewise, Pakistan has more than 3.2 million SMEs; they contribute almost 30 percent to

GDP, employ over 70 percent of the nonagricultural workforce, and generate 25 percent of export earnings.[15] As do others, Pakistan sees SME as a catalyst to generate jobs, boost exports, and reduce poverty.

Unquestionably, firm size helps explain who exports. It does not, however, determine who exports. SpinCent, a typical SME, marshaled resources and made export a part of its strategy. Its size guided its decision to seek assistance from federal and state agencies, but it did not determine its decision to export. Rather than size, research finds that characteristics such as core competencies, competitive prices, efficient production, executive leadership, and effective marketing better predict export activity than does firm size.[16] For instance, production efficiency was the best predictor of Swedish companies' export activity; those firms with higher productivity targeted foreign markets while those with lower productivity focused on domestic customers.[17] Chinese SMEs' labor costs, R&D advantages, and state ownership better predicted their export activity than did their size.[18] Likewise, high-performing Taiwanese firms, no matter how large or small, were more likely to become exporters than low-performing firms.[19] Similarly, firm competencies, not size, better explained Canadian companies' export propensity, the number of countries they exported to, and their export intensity (the ratio of a firm's revenue from its export sales to its total revenue). Finally, top management's favorable perception of exports, based on its anticipated contribution to growth and profits, powered exporting in British companies.[20]

In summary, firm size influences a company's inclination to initiate or escalate exporting. Oftentimes, however, other features matter far more than firm size. For example, Texas-based Coffee & More, a small company selling premium coffee and related products, looked to boost growth through export. Its CEO's reasoning captures many common themes: "People thought we were cutting our throats by exporting, and I admit we had our own doubts. However, we knew the customer base for our product outside the United States was large, and so was the potential for success. Perseverance and commitment paid off. Now international exporting has become an integral part of the company."[21]

| A firm's characteristics moderate its export activity. Size matters, but often management commitment, efficiency, and cost structure matter more.

EXPORTING: MOTIVATION AND METHODS

Why companies export has received extensive study. Analysis studies the influence of external (e.g., unsolicited orders, profit potential, large market size, physical proximity of the foreign market) and internal (e.g., diversification, excess capacity, growth prospects) motivators. Companies that are capital and research intensive, such as those making pharmaceuticals or avionics equipment, export products to amortize the steep costs of development and production. Others in less capital-intensive enterprise, such as advertisers, lawyers, and consultants, export their services to meet clients' overseas needs; they follow clients abroad or risk losing them to rivals. Relative size matters as well, as smaller firms in their domestic markets may export to counter the production advantage commanded by the industry leader. Finally, some companies export rather than invest abroad because the latter, done via licensing, joint ventures, or FDI, strikes them as too risky. Furthermore, serving foreign markets via export imposes fewer operational requirements than these modes.

| Exporting helps companies
| • increase profitability,
| • improve productivity,
| • diversify activities.

Study of export scenarios identifies many motivators. Ultimately, the export decision centers on improving profitability, boosting productivity, and achieving diversification.

PROFITABILITY

Exporting opens opportunities to increase profits. Often, companies sell their products for higher prices abroad than at home. Foreign markets may lack competitive alternatives. Or, they may be in different stages of the product's life cycle. Mature products at home often face price competition, whereas growth stages in foreign markets tolerate premium prices.

Also, exports enable a firm to expand its sales frontier efficiently. Though not quite decisive for firms in large markets, such as the United States, accessing bigger markets is a make-or-break factor for those in small markets, such as Belgium or Switzerland. "By not exporting, we were not tapping our full sales potential—sort of like leaving money on the table," said the Director of Business Development for Certified Worldwide.[22] Too, the Office of International Trade for the U.S. Small Business Administration found that "companies that export are more resilient, and they are more likely to stay in business."[23] Beside growing sales, creating more jobs, and paying employees higher wages, U.S. exporters are less likely to go out of business than non-exporters.[24]

PRODUCTIVITY

CONCEPT CHECK

The attraction of **trade** as a means of internationalization has been enhanced by the improving efficiencies of import and export. Chapter 6 (page 207) and Chapter 7 (page 229) note how the liberalization of the cross-border movement of resources and the development of services that support trade make these modes more attractive to a broader range of companies.

Exporting helps companies improve productivity, creating options to use scarce resources, such as capital and labor, more efficiently. Productivity is often linked to increasing economies of scale; exploiting capacity or spreading costs over more customers improves efficiency. Hence, selling more products to more people in more markets drives productivity gains. The U.S. International Trade Commission reports that despite facing trade barriers and other impediments, SMEs that export outperform those that do not. Besides more than doubling the total revenue of their non-exporting counterparts, their revenue per employee, a rough measure of labor productivity, was more than 70 percent higher than that of the non-exporters.[25]

Exporting improves productivity by inspiring innovation. Research reports a "dynamic virtuous cycle" between export and innovation in which each positively reinforces the other.[26] Exporters often run into ideas and practices that are absent in their domestic market. New, different knowledge promotes learning, thereby helping managers develop higher-quality products. Ingenious products and processes, in turn, open more export markets, thereby boosting productivity. For instance, when Mississippi-based Domes International, maker of inexpensive housing, decided to expand internationally, it headed to India. Early experiences spurred innovations that improved its productivity and fortified its competitiveness. Its CEO explained, "There's no doubt that Domes International is a better company as a result of our experience in India. We are much more flexible and innovative. The client wanted a less expensive structure, so we went back to our labs and came up with an insulation solution that met their needs. Now we use these discoveries to improve core products and to offer more variations. We are much more confident going into new situations—listening, adapting, and finding the best solution."[27]

DIVERSIFICATION

Exporting diversifies activities, thereby fortifying a firm's adaptability to business cycles and disruptive innovations. Serving customers in different markets reduces a firm's vulnerability to the loss of a local buyer while safeguarding its bargaining power with suppliers. Different growth rates in different markets enable an exporter to use strong sales in one country to offset weak sales in another. SpinCent, for example, saw export markets in faster growing Asia as a means to reduce its overdependence on the slowing U.S. economy.[28]

The shift in economic power from the West to the East is often portrayed as a threat to developed countries. Alternatively, it likely signals export opportunities. The industrial and infrastructure ambitions of emerging economies push them to import tools and technologies from wealthier, developed countries. In fact, imports into emerging economies have grown twice as fast as those into richer nations over the past decade.[29] The United States, for instance, saw 30 percent of its export go to emerging markets in 1990; by 2015, nearly 60 percent did. Western companies from, for instance, the United States and Germany, diversify sales by exporting to faster-growing, increasingly prosperous emerging countries.[30]

EXPORT: START-UP AND EXPANSION

Two views of export shape interpretation: the deliberate, sequential dynamic of incremental internationalization and the instant internationalization of the born global.

Research studies how, when, and why a company initiates and develops exporting. Reports cover a lot of territory, evaluating the influence of managerial attitudes, product features, organizational resources, firm strategy, competitive circumstances, market trends, technology platforms, public policy, and so on. Although there is some consensus, wide-ranging interpretations persist. Indeed, as far back as 1991, research identified more than 700 variables as credible drivers of export initiation and expansion.[31] Presently, making sense of this situation relies on two perspectives: "incremental internationalization" and the "born-global phenomenon."

INCREMENTAL INTERNATIONALIZATION

This view, developed in the 1980s and 1990s, sees physical distance, cultural ties, and market circumstances fundamentally shaping how a company approaches and engages export.[32] Specifically, export activity follows a sequential process that leads a company to sell initially from its home market to geographically and psychologically proximate countries. From there, it methodically expands, systematically exporting to more dissimilar and distant countries. So, for example, a U.S. company would initiate export by looking first toward Canada and, if successful, then onward to the United Kingdom, and then into Europe.

Initially, companies find it easier and less risky to trade with customers in countries that share geographic, cultural, linguistic, political, and legal commonalities. As one would expect, trading with folks in similar markets—such as the United States and Canada—who speak the same or similar languages and share historical legacies puts less stress on managers' competencies. Trade data confirm these effects: two countries will engage in 42 percent more trade with each other if they share a common language than if they do not, 47 percent more if both countries belong to a trading bloc such as the European Union or NAFTA, 114 percent more if they share a common currency, and 188 percent more if they have a common colonial past.[33]

Progressively gaining experience in successfully dealing with dissimilar markets encourages managers to expand their international horizon to include increasingly different markets.

The dynamic of incremental internationalization is straightforward: Initial success trading with similar foreign customers, by developing managers' confidence and competencies, encourages export activity. Practically, the firm's country-by-country export expansion follows a learning process through which managers' growing experience with and knowledge of increasingly dissimilar foreign markets develop the self-assurance to export to countries that share fewer commonalities and are farther afield. Essentially, as the company exports more, managers' perception of the severity of challenges declines and their sense of opportunities expands. Rising confidence leads them to assess increasingly distant and dissimilar markets.

Consider the experiences of Analytical Graphics of Pennsylvania, a manufacturer of software applications that support cost-effective development and deployment of space, defense, and intelligence missions. It began exporting in the late 1990s, targeting opportunities in Europe. Gradually, success there encouraged management to pursue export opportunities in Japan and South Korea. Its growing experience with the various business cultures in the Asian region, particularly regarding language customization and local training requirements, led it to open an office in Singapore to coordinate its increasing Asian sales.[34]

The interaction of managers' experiential learning and the market features of various countries results in common export expansion scenarios. SMEs in the United States, for example, typically export first to Canada or the United Kingdom, then move on to Europe, Mexico, and eventually countries in South America, Asia, Africa, and the Middle East.[35] Conversely, an SME in Vietnam, Thailand, or Malaysia would follow a different path, exporting first to countries in Southeast Asia, moving on to greater Asia, and then, as business practices improved based on lessons learned, looking to the United States, Europe, and Africa.

THE BORN-GLOBAL PHENOMENON

The international entrepreneurship literature reports that that some firms initiate exporting as a **born global** (also known as an "instant international," micronational, or "international new venture"). Rather than methodically engaging a sequence of increasingly dissimilar foreign markets, born globals step onto the world stage immediately upon their founding or soon after. They regard their home as just one of many opportunities in the world.[36]

We find born globals worldwide, in markets big and small, looking beyond their borders from the get-go. A key characteristic is their executives' international focus. Logitech, the Swiss-based maker of such computer devices as mice, keyboards, and speakers, was founded by a Swiss and an Italian who met while studying at Stanford University in the United States. It began exporting products worldwide soon after start-up.[37] Similar examples indicate that folks who start born globals have a strong international orientation owing to insights gained from living or studying abroad. Often, too, we see a seasoned executive leave an MNE and launch a born global.[38]

The born-global phenomenon largely follows the ongoing globalization of markets, falling trade barriers, growing demand for specialized products, and, perhaps most decisively, improving communication and logistics technologies—essentially, changing times change the game. Managers of born globals internationalize quickly because environmental circumstances let them. Technological advances along with expanding, cross-national linkages enable managers to implement global visions, quickly and cheaply delivering innovations in markets spanning the world.

Consider the moves of Zady, a New York–based online retailer of clothing, accessories, and household goods that prides itself as a provider of high-quality products that had been manufactured mindful of environmental and labor standards. Launched in August 2013, by 2014, 20 percent of its website sales traffic came from Canada, France, Japan, and the United Kingdom. Then in summer 2015, Zady enlisted Borderfree, the global e-commerce subsidiary of Pitney Bowes, to manage its international shopping experience, including site localization, multicurrency pricing, payment processing, fraud management, customs clearance, and global logistics. Supported by Borderfree, Zady's products are available, via its website, to shoppers in 220 countries and territories who use 74 currencies.[39] Our closing case profiles the performance and potential of Borderfree.

Likewise, Evertek Computer, a U.S. SME started in 1990, quickly began exporting. By 2009, it was exporting to customers in 105 countries, 30 percent of which were in South America, 20 percent in Europe, and 20 percent in the Middle East and North Africa. Its success comes from selling refurbished computers and parts, for which worldwide demand is booming because buyers, particularly poorer ones, don't need the latest, greatest tech. "They want cheap," says Evertek's international sales manager, John Ortley. "The firm's business model," he adds, "matches these folks with those who want to sell their used personal computer equipment."[40]

At first glance, liquidating obsolete pieces and parts seems an unlikely basis for successful exporting. Also, Evertek does not command the intimidating ownership advantages that usually supports exporting. However, the international orientation of its top management creates a powerful driver. Mr. Oxley's enthusiasm for international business, for example, fortifies the firm's belief that a big part of its business is found abroad: "For me," he says, "it started with being curious about the world. I enjoy learning about other cultures and respecting people who have a different background than mine."[41] Then, speaking like a true born global, he adds, "We're thriving. The world is shrinking, and it's getting easier and less expensive to do business on a global basis."[42]

THE INFLUENCE OF TIME AND PLACE

Neither the incremental-international nor born-global perspective definitively represent how companies initiate and increase exporting. Company practices confirm that each credibly interprets elements of the export process. For instance, U.S. companies' exports travel

Born globals, owing to their executives' international orientation and improving technological options, begin trading internationally at inception.

CONCEPT CHECK

Change in the structure and dynamics of world business endorses new and novel standards. A flat world, billions of new capitalists, emerging economies, the global financial crisis, and so on, challenge many conventional theories. Consequently, scholars study trends, such as those dealing with incremental internationalization and the born-global phenomenon, to assess the direction and momentum of change.

to 233 countries and territories around the world.[43] Many paths reflect long-running trade relationships, such as that between the United States and Canada. Others reflect newer links, such as the United States and Kyrgyzstan. The scale and scope of this export universe support scenarios in which companies have developed the competencies to service more markets (the incremental-internationalization perspective) and can reach faraway markets with greater ease and immediacy (the born-global view).

Going forward, we anticipate stronger interaction effects between the incremental-internationalization and born-global perspectives. First, e-commerce continues turbocharging the latter. A generation ago, going global involved slow-acting trade officials directing slow-moving flows between tough-to-understand markets that differed on countless regulations and routines. Hence, incremental, market-by-market export expansion was not only feasible, it was arguably the only practical option.[44] Now, e-commerce tools and platforms, fortified by social media and supply-chain networks, immediately give small start-ups global reach, providing a platform that efficiently overcomes historic barriers to internationalization. Second, exporters inclined toward incremental expansion find the Internet enables cheap, easy, and effective means to analyze and access dissimilar markets. Hence, their progressive expansion to dissimilar markets fits the incremental view, whereas the acceleration of this process fits the born-global perspective.

> Trade data suggest an increasing interaction between the incremental-international and born-global perspectives.

THE WILDCARD OF SERENDIPITY

It's appealing to depict export initiation and development, whether done incrementally or immediately, as a purposeful strategy designed and delivered by proactive executives. However, reports tell of accidental exporters who, responding to happenstance or odd circumstances, unexpectedly but successfully enter foreign markets. Essentially, some companies start exporting because of fortuitous events rather than purposeful intent. Perhaps the most common trigger is the arrival of an unsolicited order from a foreign buyer. Others include a new hire that has connections to foreign markets, an international contact made at an industry conference, or personal travel abroad that alerts one to opportunities. Thus, **serendipity**—making fortunate discoveries by accident—is not an uncommon export trigger.

Edward Cutler is such a case. He is the owner and founder of Pennsylvania-based Squigle, a unique brand of toothpaste for people who cannot tolerate mass-produced varieties.[45] Upon launching Squigle, Mr. Cutler exclusively focused on the U.S. market. Internet posters spread news of his product, and Squigle soon received inquiries from Canada, France, Turkey, and elsewhere. One customer, a canker-sore sufferer in England, was so enthusiastic about it that he began importing Squigle into England for local sale. That was good news for Mr. Cutler because it lets him expand abroad at little cost and low risk. Now he is eager to export more, explaining, "We're looking to sell overseas for the same reason the big companies do: Most of the world's population lies outside the United States."[46]

Similarly, Vellus is a small Ohio-based company that makes a line of high-end pet grooming products. It began its export odyssey when a Taiwanese businessperson, after trying its customized shampoos, bought $25,000 worth of the company's products to sell in Taiwan. Soon, word spread from show to show on the global canine circuit. Recounted Vellus's CEO, "I started receiving calls from people around the world who would hear of our products at dog shows and ask organizers how they could get in touch with me to buy our products."[47] Today, Vellus exports its products to more than 30 countries.

> Exporters are often proactive decision-makers. Sometimes, however, serendipity—making fortunate discoveries by accident—initiates export activity.

APPROACHES TO EXPORTING

Granted, export sounds straightforward—'make it, sell it, pack it, ship it.'[48] This holds true for many trades. Others, though, impose stiffer requirements. Generally, the ease of exporting reflects how a company chooses to serve foreign customers. As we now see, there are several options.

> **CONCEPT CHECK**
>
> The Internet influences political change, improves the operations of **foreign-exchange markets**, and changes the location economies that drive **value chain** configurations. Similarly, the Internet reshapes export and import activity by opening new markets, supporting new strategies, and providing new tools.

Exporting directly involves independent representatives, distributors, or retailers outside of the exporter's home country.

Direct Exporting   In this scenario, the company directly sells its products to an independent intermediary, such as an agent, distributor, or retailer outside its home country. The intermediary then sells the product to the local consumer. **Direct exporting** requires a company manage the export process, minding all aspects of making and marketing the product. Likewise, it supervises the exporting process from market research to foreign distribution and collections. Done well, direct exporting maximizes a company's sales growth and profits. Direct exporting requires executive commitment and company resources to get the show started and then to sustain activity.[49]

Indirect exports are products sold to an intermediary in the home market, which then exports those products to other countries.

Indirect Exporting   Some companies prefer to do what they do best and outsource the rest. In this situation, they enlist independent distributors, agents, or export management companies to ship, market, and sell their goods abroad. Operationally, the company sells its products to an independent intermediary in the domestic market, which then exports the product to its foreign agents, who then sell it to the end consumer. This process results in **indirect exporting** whereby an exporter makes its product, but relies on an intermediary to supervise marketing, terms of sale, packaging, distribution, and credit and collection procedures. This approach is relatively stress-free. Explained Edward Cutler, maker of Squigle toothpaste, "It is just easier to deal with distributors. We prefer to deal in master shippers of 144 tubes. We don't have to do anything then but slap a label on it."[50] However, unlike direct exporting, where the company handles all the work and retains all the profits, indirect exporting lowers margins and reduces returns. Moreover, indirect exporting constrains developing customer relationships.

The intersection of retail and globalization trends makes indirect selling increasingly practical, especially for SMEs. Global retail chains such as Walmart, Carrefour, and Ahold easily move products from exporters to storefronts. Think of, for example, a DVD manufacturer in Vietnam who supplies Walmart International with a product that Walmart then sells in its retail locations worldwide. Though not as lucrative as direct exporting, indirect exporting imposes fewer demands. Too, it is often a transition phase whereby the neophyte can gain familiarity with foreign consumers and competitors.

Service companies often export their product indirectly rather than directly. Technically, an indirect service export results when a non-exporting firm provides services to another company that ultimately exports its products abroad. An indirect service export on the part of, say, a Swedish accounting firm occurs when it prepares the books of a Swedish company that exports to foreign markets. We commonly see indirect services exports with professional and business services such as accounting, advertising, consulting, and legal services. But, they occur in many industries, including audiovisual providers to film and television studios whose media are viewed overseas, or a hedge fund that sells shares to foreign investors through a wealth management advisory firm.

Passively Filling Orders from Domestic Buyers Who Then Export the Product   In this mode, a company supplies inputs to other firms who then use that as a component in making a product that they then export. Essentially, a buyer contacts Firm A, submits an order, takes delivery, uses that good as an input into its product, which it then exports. From the perspective of Firm A, these sorts of international sales are indistinguishable from domestic sales. The supplier may be unaware that its product has been exported.[51]

WHICH APPROACH WHEN?

Several factors shape an SME's preferred approach to export, notably its mix of ownership, location, and internalization advantages.

No export approach is intrinsically superior. At the broadest level, a company's particular ownership, location, and internalization advantages determine the optimal approach. Generally, large MNEs serve foreign customers directly through their foreign affiliates, while SMEs may export directly or indirectly.[52] There is no hard-and-fast rule that one option is superior—approximately half of SMEs' exports are direct (i.e., produced by the exporting SME immediately before export) while the other half are indirect (i.e., supplied by the SME to other companies that then ultimately export it).[53]

Several factors shape an SME's preferred approach. Protecting ownership advantages endorses exporting directly. SpinCent, for example, saw direct selling as the best means to retain control of its core competency. Similarly, top management experience as well as company resources endorse some choices while discouraging others. A regular exporter is more likely to export directly. Firms new to exporting or those that lack sufficient resources generally prefer indirect methods.

> Internet marketing helps companies—large and small—engage in international trade quickly, easily, and cheaply.

The Influence of Technology   Technology influences the relative merits of the various export approaches. The Internet makes direct exporting increasingly efficient and effective by providing immediate, low-cost means that lets regular exporters, particularly born globals, easily access more markets.[54] Too, e-commerce helps companies, both big and small, overcome capital and infrastructure limitations.[55] For example, exporters in Chile use extranets to communicate with importers around the world, while exporters in Costa Rica use online shops to export directly.[56] Likewise, tapping Borderfree's global platform made Zady's products quickly available to international shoppers in 220 countries and territories. Electronic magic at innumerable sites, from Alibaba to Amazon, helps SMEs easily, efficiently, and effectively engage buyers and sellers worldwide. Twenty years ago, firm resources, communication channels, and trade logistics mattered immensely if you were an SME in Patagonia trying to reach markets in Europe. Today, Internet tools and platforms make them matter far less.

> The four approaches to exporting are not mutually exclusive; company and market circumstances moderate whether managers opt to apply one or a mix.

Mix-and-Match   Export approaches are not mutually exclusive. A firm can engage different methods to trade different products to serve different markets. A Canadian company may export directly to similar markets such as the United States, Australia, and Britain, while using indirect methods to handle exports to dissimilar markets in Asia or Africa. For example, Analytical Graphics, which began exporting in the late 1990s, had expanded sales into 13 countries, serving them through a mix of methods. It uses direct exporting in Canada and the United Kingdom, and indirect exporting via reseller partners in Japan, South Korea, India, Russia, and Brazil.[57] Hence, the optimal choice(s) fits the firm's competencies, its executives' outlook, and the market characteristics of the targeted countries.

Point

Exporting E-waste: A Fair Solution?

Point   **Yes** Exporting is always and everywhere a win-win situation: The more companies and countries export, the more they improve market efficiency. Exporting enables companies to increase sales, improve productivity, and diversify activities. Likewise, exporting helps countries generate jobs, accelerate innovation, and improve living standards. In broader terms, it promotes connections among countries that improve foreign relations and stabilize international affairs.

Despite these virtues, some contend there is a dark side of exporting, namely the trade of hazardous waste in the form of obsolete tech equipment. E-waste—trash composed of computers, monitors, electronics, game consoles, hard drives, television, smartphones, and other items—inexorably increases as the Information Age rolls on. In 2006, nearly 66 million used electronic components were collected for reuse or recycling in the United States; most were exported. By 2016, e-waste was pushing several hundred million pieces,

representing more than 4 million tons.[58] Ongoing trends crank out newer, cooler, faster, smaller, fancier devices that, in replacing their predecessors and then eventually being replaced themselves, will increase e-waste nearly 500 percent over the next decade.

Where Should E-waste Go?   Where to put all this e-trash is a tough question. Many countries and municipalities in the United States, for example, ban outright dumping of e-waste in local landfills. This legislation means that disposing of e-waste products, when possible, in any given industrialized country costs from $2,500 to $4,000 a ton. In contrast, untreated waste can be sold to countries in Africa and Asia—where it will be recycled, reused, or dumped—for reportedly as little as $50 a ton.[59] Low costs are a result of cheap labor, different environmental regulations, and growing processing capacity. Plus, the absence of public opposition reduces processing expenses and desperate folks seeking work dampens public objections. As might be expected, major e-waste shipping routes show that the industrial nations export the bulk of their e-waste to developing countries, notably China, Malaysia, India, Mexico, Nigeria, and Bangladesh (see Map 14.1).[60]

Benefits for All Exporting e-waste to recycling centers throughout the world is an efficient solution to an escalating problem. First and foremost, recycling sustains our resources and helps us protect the environment. In developing countries, industries have sprung up to recycle old computers, monitors, circuit boards, scanners, printers, routers, cell phones, and network cards. While rudimentary, these industries create jobs in places where jobs are hard to find and difficult to sustain. To their credit, developing countries have converted their superior location economics into vital jobs, income, and markets. There are more than 6,000 businesses employing 100,000 workers at ground zero of the e-waste trade: Guiyu, China. Previously subsistence farmers and fishermen, they now process an endless stream of truckloads of e-waste that arrive daily.[61] Mexico has similar spots, many waiting for the 18-wheelers full of spent batteries from cars, phones, computer, solar appliances, and tools that cross the U.S.–Mexican border each day. Again, the locals benefit. Despite the dangerous,

dirty work of recycling spent batteries, people living near the Acumuladores de Jalisco plant find opportunity. As the wife of one worker said, "There are not many other jobs around here."[62]

Similarly, exporting e-waste helps entrepreneurs in developing countries create value by recovering, recycling, and reusing scarce resources. Copper, a valuable commodity, can represent nearly 20 percent of a mobile phone's total weight. Rising commodity prices have made these activities quite profitable. Atul Maheshwar, owner of a recycling depot in India, says of U.S. exports, "If your country keeps sending us the material, our business will be good."[63] In addition, some of the equipment shipped to Asia helps improve the local standard of living. Graham Wollaston of Scrap Computers, a recycler in Phoenix, claims that virtually every component of old electronic devices is reusable. Old televisions turn into fish tanks in Malaysia, while silicon shortage creates demand for old monitors elsewhere. "There's no such thing as a third-world landfill," Mr. Wollaston explains. "If you were to put an old computer on the street, it would be taken apart for the parts."[64] Similarly, Luc Lateille of the Canadian firm BMP Recycling says, "We don't send junk—we only send the materials that they are looking for."[65]

Exporting hazardous waste also helps MNEs improve their social responsibility. Samsung, Mitsubishi, and Nokia,

MAP 14.1   The Patterns of Trade of Electronic Waste

When computers, cell phones, and other electronic equipment become obsolete, they are no longer worth much in rich countries. E-waste, however, has some value in developing countries. That is exactly where, as exports, it usually ends up. Proponents note it promotes productive recycling as well as local economic development. Critics charge it is viciously hazardous and callously exploits cheap labor and lax regulations.

Source: Data from Basel Action Network; Silicon Valley Toxics Condition, www.ban.org/about/.

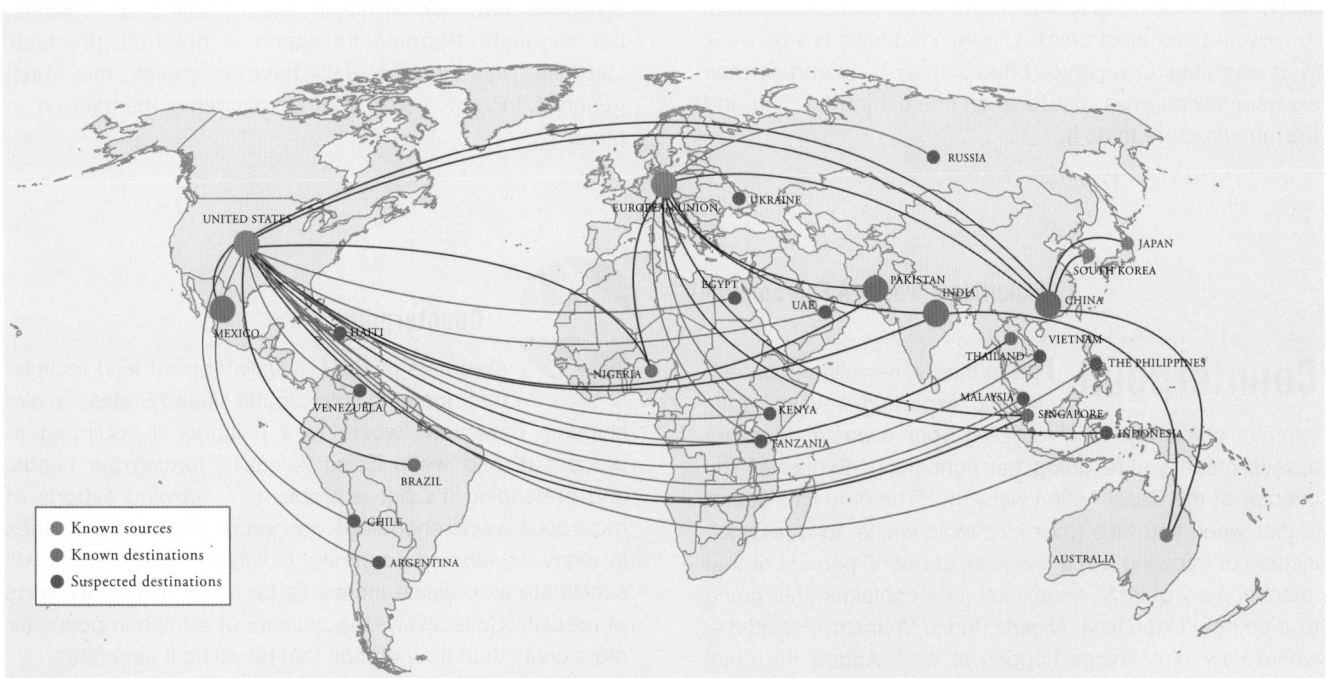

Here we see an enterprising ▶ Nigerian child running a grassroots e-recycling facility. Although junk to many, scavenging and selling useful parts creates value for him, his community, and the world.

Source: Enrique Soriano-Silverlens/ ZUMA Press/Newscom

among others, increasingly take a cradle-to-grave responsibility for their products. The eCycling Leadership Initiative, launched in 2010, commits makers of consumer electronics to recycle a billion pounds of e-waste responsibly by 2016; in 2011, members spent more than $100 million to recycle about 500 million pounds of old electronics. Elsewhere, state regulation spurs laggards to support green recycling. Since 2004, more than 20 U.S. states have required manufacturers to recycle used electronics. Like-minded laws are on deck in other states. Companies often comply by exporting their e-waste to countries that have an interest in recycling and the infrastructure to do it.

A Tough Solution   Certainly, callous companies dump useless, toxic e-waste around the world. And, yes, some of it pollutes landfills, poisons waterways, and fouls the air. Overall, though, exporting e-waste works for citizens, consumers, companies, and countries. Ultimately, nations really don't have a choice. The U.S. Environmental Protection Agency, for example, concedes inappropriate practices have occurred in the recycling of e-waste, but suggests stopping its export is not truly practical. Likewise, poor nations really have no choice; they must generate income some way or condemn themselves to poverty.

Exporting E-waste: A Fair Solution?

Counterpoint   **No** In theory, recycling is beneficial and exporting e-waste does improve efficiency. Still, recycling your e-waste does not always mean you're doing the right thing. Explained the director of the Basel Action Network, "The dirty little secret is that when you take [your electronic waste] to a recycler, instead of throwing it in a trashcan, about 80 percent of that material, very quickly, finds itself on a container ship going to a country like China, Nigeria, India, Vietnam, Pakistan— where very dirty things happen to it."[66] Added the chief

Counterpoint

executive of RSR, a Dallas-based lead recycler that operates solely in the United States, "We're shipping hazardous waste to a neighbor ill-equipped to process it, and we're doing it legally, turning our heads, and pretending it's not a problem."[67] Growing exports of hazardous waste encourage dangerous recycling industries in many developing countries. Going forward, exports will accelerate as e-waste increases far faster than other sorts of rubbish. Collectively, the tsunami of e-trash imposes far more costs than the pittance that recycling it generates.

A Witch's Brew Most developing countries lack the regulatory codes or disposal infrastructure to safeguard against such dangers. Locals often use crude methods that, besides being illegal in the United States, expose workers and residents to a witch's brew of toxins. For example, some e-waste contains trace amounts of precious metals like copper and silver. Extracting them encourages cash-strapped, loosely regulated recyclers to use unsafe, antiquated open-air incineration methods. Burning electronic parts to separate copper, solder, or other metals from plastic coatings releases dioxins and other hazardous chemicals. Indeed, snagging that sliver of silver unleashes a mixture of more than a thousand chemicals, including toxic metals (e.g., lead, barium, and mercury), flame-retardants, cadmium, acids, plastics, and chlorinated and brominated compounds. Local air quality suffers as "circuit boards are burned after acid washing, spewing deadly smoke and exposing workers and people living around these facilities."[68] Once local scrap shops finish disassembling equipment, the trash goes into public landfills, the acid runoff flows into groundwater, and the noxious fumes follow air currents—all mercilessly contaminating the environment.

Casual Inhumanity Madhumita Dutta of Toxics-Link Delhi argues that these problems are less disturbing than the "appalling" working conditions in recycling facilities: "Everything from dismantling the computer to pulling out parts of the circuit boards to acid-washing boards to recover copper is done with bare hands without any protective gear or face protection." Rare is the worksite that uses proper

disposal practices. Workers and society, to say nothing of environmental sustainability, suffer.

What, then, of the premise of charity—that is, sending computer equipment from countries where it has little use to countries where it can make a difference? Critics shred this straw man, asserting that wealthier countries and powerful companies conveniently donate obsolete equipment to dodge high recycling expenses. "Too often, justifications of 'building bridges over the digital divide' are used as excuses to obscure and ignore the fact that these bridges double as toxic waste pipelines," said one critic.[69] Moreover, most of the computer equipment sent is worthless trash—waste that can be neither repaired nor resold.[70]

Institutional Gaps Some argue that manufacturers need to step up and take full responsibility for the hazardous materials they used to build products that had earned them profits.[71] Companies have moved in this direction, sponsoring green campaigns to recycle e-waste. Substantive progress has been slow, however. Environmentalists recommend that countries set tougher standards to monitor, control, and certify cross-border shipments of e-waste. That has proven disappointing. Inspections of e-waste cargo headed from European seaports to developing countries, for example, found that nearly half was illegal.[72]

Then again, presumed solutions can lead to unintended problems. The fact that many U.S. states require companies to take responsibility for recycling electronic equipment has curtailed the export of e-waste to developing countries—but only of the more valuable components. Processors cherry-pick parts

Here we see a frightful wasteland near Lagos, Nigeria. Notwithstanding the toxic threats of this witch's brew, desperation spurs people to scavenge for anything of value.

Source: n86/ZUMA Press/Newscom

that can be refurbished for reuse. The remainder is disassembled, with urban miners targeting silver, gold, and palladium. The final batch of trash, the worst of the worst, has no reuse market and is shipped to developing countries for disposal.[73]

Who to Turn To?   Others endorse stronger enforcement of the Basel Convention on the Transboundary Movement of Hazardous Wastes and their Disposal, a United Nations treaty that regulates the generation, management, movements, and disposal of hazardous waste. It proposes aggressive measures, including an international ban on the export of all toxic waste, no matter whether for recovery, recycling, reuse, or final disposal. As of 2015, 182 states and the European Union are parties to the Convention. Haiti and the United States have signed the Convention but not ratified it.[74]

IMPORTING: PRINCIPLES AND PRACTICES

Together, imports and exports are the foundation of international trade.

Together, importing and exporting is the foundation of international trade. **Importing** is the purchase of a good or service by a buyer in Country X—the importer—from a seller in Country Y—the exporter. Effectively, importing is the reverse of exporting. Practically, Samsung's shipment of a smartphone made in Seoul to a buyer in Montreal registers as an import for Canada and an export for South Korea. Service imports, given their intangibility, take various forms. Financial services provided by foreign banks to U.S. customers qualify as service imports. Similarly, when Lloyd's of London writes an insurance policy for a client in Brazil, trade authorities in Brazil record an import. The import of services has subtle characteristics. For example, the installation of nuclear power equipment in Sweden by French firm Areva, even though it is tangible, qualifies as a service import for Sweden. The standard to keep in mind is that the import of a service consists of any transaction that (1) does not result in ownership and (2) is rendered by nonresidents to residents.

CHARACTERISTICS OF IMPORTERS

A service import is a service transaction that does not result in ownership and is rendered by nonresidents to local residents.

Wide-ranging research has assessed the characteristics of exporters; for various reasons, however, importers receive less attention. Still, data indicate that importers are also likely to be exporters, and that these firms account for the bulk of the world's exports and imports.[75] In the United States, for instance, 405,000 U.S. companies traded goods internationally and, of those, 83,199 both exported and imported merchandise.[76] On fundamental points, then, the characteristics of exporters apply to importers. For instance, as do exporters, importers tailor international activities to reflect their ownership, localization, and internalization advantages. Similarly, importers exhibit incremental and born-global characteristics, and firm size, efficiency, innovation, and management commitment moderate their trading activity.

The scale and scope of goods and services imported steadily expands.

Several points qualify the degree of overlap. Historically, importers traded relatively few products with relatively few developing countries.[77] Essentially, the bulk of imports tended toward opportunism or arbitrage (i.e., cheap oil in Saudi Arabia became expensive oil in the United States). Fast-growing economies, such as the Philippines, Peru, Nigeria, and Indonesia, accelerate and alter this relationship. These countries produce more goods and services that outperform, in price and function, local choices in developed markets. They also provide higher-end products that once were the exclusive province of advanced markets—for example, think of Western companies now importing business process services from Indian MNEs like Infosys and Cognizant. Finally, globalization supports differentiated supply chains that are longer, have more links, and cross more markets. Their growth commensurately increases the import of inputs among an increasing number of nations.

IMPORTING: MOTIVATION AND METHODS

Several reasons motivate importing:

• Specialization of labor
• Global rivalry
• Local unavailability
• Diversification
• Top management's outlook

Various factors spur a firm to start and sustain importing. Research emphasizes the importance of high-quality products, lower prices, reliable logistics, and local market imperfections. These factors, singly and collectively, push importers to scan foreign markets in search of lower-priced, higher-quality, or locally unavailable products. This situation inevitably raises the question: Why do these anomalies exist? Absent these gaps, there is little need to import or, for that matter, export. Other parts of our text, particularly materials in Chapters 5 and 12, speak to this issue. For our purposes, the following conditions clarify key import motivations.

IMPORT DRIVERS

The specialization of labor is a powerful force to improve productivity. It benefits the import potential and performance of SMEs and large firms.

Specialization of Labor   Managers usually divide a production process into a sequence of separate yet interdependent steps and assign workers to particular steps so that one worker does one task, another does another task, and so on. The specialization of labor organizes production to achieve economies of scale (i.e., the inverse relationship between the quantity produced and per-unit fixed costs) as well as exploit location economics (i.e., different wage rates and material costs across countries). The resulting efficiencies reduce costs, thereby enabling a company to offer higher quality products at lower costs to consumers locally and abroad. Sales to the latter, naturally, lead to imports. For instance, Nike buys shoes manufactured by companies in several Asian countries, where local companies make higher quality shoes for lower cost. Nike finds it impossible to manufacture the same products in its home market, sell them for a reasonable price, and still make a profit. As a result, it profitably imports shoes made in Asian factories into markets worldwide.

Input Optimization   Companies import goods from foreign suppliers in order to lower costs. This is imperative in industries where competitive rivalry imposes persistent cost pressures, such as we see in telecommunications and business services. Many industrial and consumer goods, such as aircraft or cars, rely on thousands of parts produced in factories around the world. Likewise, many services, such as finance, information, and customer, hire back-office support or call-centers in foreign markets. Importing lets companies efficiently tap lower-cost inputs.

Local Unavailability   The WTO identifies the expanded scope of choice as the chief benefit of import. Importing lets local markets improve the variety of their offerings, providing consumers with products that are either unavailable locally or that can serve as competitive substitutes to local options. Practically, think of the seasonal consequence of geography to trade flows; Canada imports bananas from tropical climates because of its unsuitable climate; absent imports, Canadians would not enjoy fresh bananas. The same goes for eating seasonal fruits and vegetables out of season (e.g., grapes from Chile grace Christmas dinner in Denmark).

Diversification   Importers, like exporters, diversify by tapping international markets to develop options. Diversification through importing lets companies find higher-quality, lower-cost products and services, thereby making it less vulnerable to the dictates of a local supplier or business cycle. For example, customers of U.S. steelmakers, such as automobile companies, diversified their purchases to include Chinese, European, Indian, and South Korean suppliers. Developing alternative suppliers reduces the consequence of local supply shortages or unilateral price hikes by U.S. steelmakers.

WHO ARE IMPORTERS?

There are three general types of importers:

- Input optimizers
- Opportunistic
- Arbitrageurs

Importers process a wide range of goods and services. Moreover, importers operate in mass markets, such as apparel or food, and niche markets, such as medical devices or legal discovery. No matter the product or business, one commonly sees three broad types.

Input Optimizers   This type of importer uses foreign sourcing to optimize, in terms of price or quality, the inputs fed into its supply chain. Essentially, a company scours the globe for optimal inputs, then directs them to its various production points that it has configured worldwide. Its various factories then assemble them into finished goods that are then imported by markets worldwide. Logically, the flow of inputs and finished goods from country to country, besides representing imports, also qualifies as exports.

Opportunistic   This type of importer looks for products around the world that it can import and profitably sell to local citizens. It identifies imperfections in the local marketplace, whether real (customers prefer higher-quality or lower-cost options) or perceived (the presumption that foreign products are superior to local substitutes). It then opportunistically exploits a gap by finding, buying, transporting, and distributing those products from foreign suppliers to local customers. To a large degree, the specific product is secondary; rather, the game is using import channels to fill gaps in the local marketplace profitably. For instance, Utah-based SME ForEveryBody began making bath and body products locally. It began importing upon discovering low-cost home decorations from Asian manufacturers that were competitive with premium products in the United States.

In principle, arbitrage is the simultaneous buying and selling of the same product in different markets in order to exploit differences in price.

Arbitrageurs   In theory, a good sold in one market should sell for the same price in another. In practice, prices vary due to gaps resulting from market regulations, trade inefficiencies, political risks, and other factors. These imperfections, by creating supply gaps, create the basis for import arbitrage. Effectively, an enterprising firm in one country looks to others for locally unavailable products, and then imports and sells them. For example, the release of the latest, greatest iPhone typically triggers a consumer frenzy, including scalpers aiming to exploit a temporary market gap given that it is only available in the United States for the first several weeks. Demand in other countries creates compelling opportunities. Buyers in China, for instance, hire shoppers in Los Angeles, Chicago, and New York to buy as many iPhones as they can and overnight them to Beijing, Chengdu, or Shanghai, where they are then marked up twice or thrice more.[78] Eventually, once Apple sells the 'latest, greatest' iPhone directly in China, through its local retail outlets and licensed resellers, the gap closes.

IMPORTING AND EXPORTING: PROBLEMS AND PITFALLS

CONCEPT CHECK

As straightforward as the concept of **exporting** may seem on the surface, whether you are a born-global entrepreneur or an established **MNE**, it is fraught with challenges. *Behavioral barriers* complicate international operations. Political and legal codes pose pitfalls, *government regulation* impacts trade relationships, and *foreign-exchange instruments* necessitate financial sophistication.

Companies identify many problems that complicate international trade. The types, characteristics, and impact of trade barriers vary considerably. The United States International Trade Commission polled more than 8,400 U.S. firms—both big companies and SMEs from the manufacturing and service sectors—about the influence of 19 potential barriers to trade.[79] The data confirm that international traders deal with a battery of impediments (see Table 14.1).

As SMEs export more, their perception of the severity of barriers declines—much as one would expect, given the earlier discussion of the role of managerial confidence in the internationalization process.[80] Likewise, SMEs that export sporadically to fewer markets see barriers as far more burdensome than do regular exporters. However, trade experience is not a panacea. Regular, as well as sporadic, exporters struggle with various barriers. Let's take a look at persistent concerns.

FINANCIAL RISKS

SMEs regularly rate financial constraints as the most daunting barrier to trading internationally.

Financial constraints pose tough impediments to international traders. A survey of 978 SMEs asked their perceptions of trade barriers—the greatest problem was the shortage of working capital to finance export.[81] Financial concerns, such as payments and taxation, consistently affect companies, big and small, in both manufacturing and services. Some traders reason that export or import offers low profitability given higher costs and financial risks, both of which are aggravated by fluctuating exchange rates. Managing these problems involves currency and credit processes that call for sophisticated expertise. Furthermore, completing international sales often requires helping foreign customers obtain credit, whether in the form of trade credits, government-financed support, or bank guarantees.[82] Firms accustomed to offering financing in terms of the traditional 30- or 60-day trade-credit cycle at home understandably dislike developing alternative arrangements, particularly when involving different currencies.[83]

CUSTOMER MANAGEMENT

An enduring barrier to exporting is misunderstanding the difficulty of profitably serving consumers in foreign markets.

Historically, exports and imports were arm's-length, ship-it-and-forget-it transactions. Contact with customers relied on documents either faxed or posted overnight. This situation created useful time lags with which to deal with questions and complaints. Now,

TABLE 14.1   The Relative Influence of Common Barriers to Export[84]

International trade presents a range of difficulties. Here we see how managers of SMEs and large companies, either making a good or providing a service, rate the challenge of common barriers.

Note: The higher the percentage, the greater the perceived severity of the impediment.

Barrier to Export	Manufacturing		Service	
	SME	Large Firm	SME	Large Firm
Transportation/shipping costs	88.5	93.6	53.6	35.1
Language/cultural barriers	82.2	86.8	53.4	42.2
Difficulty locating sales prospects	79.1	83.2	55.8	45.2
Foreign regulations	78.0	90.0	51.1	48.3
U.S. regulations	73.4	86.8	45.4	37.8
Foreign sales not sufficiently profitable	72.5	84.4	58.7	46.2
Customs procedures	71.9	87.4	44.6	35.5
Difficulty receiving or processing payments	67.9	87.9	39.3	41.1
U.S. taxation issues	62.8	80.7	37.4	39.2
Lack of trained staff	62.6	85.7	36.7	46.5
Insufficient intellectual property protection	61.8	71.6	43.6	27.3
Foreign taxation issues	60.4	80.5	36.1	40.6
Preference for local goods/services in foreign market	57.4	81.7	37.8	35.8
Difficulty establishing affiliates in foreign markets	57.2	76.9	29.8	33.8
High tariffs	56.6	81.6	36.8	28.8
Lack of government support programs	56.4	70.3	29.2	29.4
Obtaining financing	51.6	63.8	38.5	31.9
Unable to find foreign partners	50.5	66.6	33.0	36.0
Visa issues	30.1	67.8	34.9	33.5

Source: "Small and Medium-Sized Enterprises: Characteristics and Performance," United States International Trade Commission, Investigation No. 332–510, November 2010.

contacting vendors via e-mail or voice-over-Internet-protocol (VoIP) gives customers, no matter how far away, real-time access. The resulting rise in customers' service expectations diminishes the appeal of international trade to some. "The new notch in the bar for us is the requests from our customers for additional services beyond the port of delivery," said the materials manager of Seco/Warwick, a manufacturer of heat-treating equipment. "In previous years, I would be responsible for cost, insurance, and freight (CIF) to the port of import, but now I'm often tasked with all aspects of delivery to the customer's plant location. Now we're often involved in the installation and start-up of the equipment, so we have service engineers and cranes waiting for the on-time delivery."[85] Customer management concerns particularly challenge SMEs. Their orientation toward specialized opportunities and narrow market segments often prompts them to apply niche strategies. Increasing expectations push them to customize services and marketing support to fit overseas segments in ways that can exceed those offered in the home market.[86]

INTERNATIONAL BUSINESS EXPERTISE

The problems and pitfalls of international trade consistently frustrate the sporadic and regular exporter.

International traders, like most managers dealing with foreign markets, must understand local business practices. Ordinary as well as idiosyncratic problems include limited knowledge of local rivals, unfamiliarity with local regulations, uncertainty about the prevailing price-to-quality standards, difficulty optimizing transportation and insurance options, and questions about market channels, promotion tactics, and consumer behavior. Firms that struggle to interpret export markets typically exit international trade. Still, as evident in the steady expansion of trade, enterprising managers find solutions. Think back, for example, to our opening profile of SpinCent. Fear of misunderstanding export markets led its CEO to hire local agents and distributors as well as consult with trade officials, both at home and overseas.

MARKETING CHALLENGES

Traders regularly complain about high shipment costs and logistic demands, weak foreign market connections, difficulties in matching foreign rivals' prices, effectively promoting products and establishing distribution networks, and tailoring after-sales service programs. Non-exporters express greater anxiety about these marketing uncertainties, particularly when they benchmark them against the comparatively easier demands in their home markets. In addition, shifting economics opens markets in places where different market structures and consumer behaviors pose new challenges. Going from the United States to Canada is one thing; going from the United States to Turkmenistan, Zambia, or Kosovo, for example, is entirely another.

TOP MANAGEMENT COMMITMENT

Persevering in the face of problems and pitfalls requires executives committed to internationalization.

Management characteristics, especially executives' international outlook and risk orientation, influence export and import activity. For many reasons, companies, particularly SMEs, focus on domestic rather than foreign markets. In the United States, for instance, SMEs compose 97 percent of all exporters, yet less than 1 percent of all SMEs export. Of those that do, nearly two-thirds export to just one foreign market.[87] Asked why, managers' preference for the predictable familiarity of the home market diminishes their overseas interest. Even when they concede the benefits of trade, the riskiness and resource demands of internationalization dissuade many.

Exporting and importing put tough demands on management. Rare is the firm that eagerly adjusts its customary practices for foreign business standards. As a result, top management often emphasize domestic sales, duly noting the intention to export down the road. Recall Paul Knepper's original export outlook at SpinCent; at best, he was a sporadic exporter who saw risks outweighing rewards. Eventually, productivity, profitability, and diversification concerns forced him to reconsider. From then on, ownership advantages, support from public agencies, and trustworthy distributors fortified his export commitment.

GOVERNMENT REGULATION

Export and import inefficiencies persist due to delays, documents, and administrative fees. The rules and regulations governing trade, notwithstanding the success of the WTO, endure. New Jersey–based Spectra Colors, manufacturer and distributor of high-quality, customized dyes and colorants, runs into problems because import regulations differ from one country to the next. "In Europe, REACH regulations (Registration, Evaluation, and Authorization of Chemicals) have caused us lengthy delays and expense," said Spectra's business manager.[88] Occasionally, shipments to various markets require government clearance. Refusals come easily to officials facing product constraints at home or political tension abroad. REACH disproportionately affects SME exporters, given staff and resource constraints to ensure compliance. Worse still, Canada, China, Japan, Switzerland, Taiwan, and Turkey are developing regulations like those of REACH.[89]

Similar regulatory situations emerge elsewhere. Exporters of medical devices face complex regulations and lengthy approval times that require extensive test data. Many countries, including Australia, Canada, China, certain EU member states, Japan, and the United States, impose approval procedures that require firms to implement an ISO-certified production quality management system. Firms must pay various fees to obtain and maintain certification. Many exporters, particularly SMEs, struggle to fund such efforts.

Table 14.1 shows that service exporters run into other problems. Professional service providers, such as the sort found in engineering, legal, finance, and entertainment sectors, regularly send employees abroad to perform contracted services. In Malaysia, however, foreign engineers cannot work on building projects unless the hiring company convinces the Malaysian Board of Engineers that a Malaysian engineer cannot do the job.[90] It's harsher in Thailand—its Alien Occupation Act reserves architecture and engineering services jobs for Thai nationals.[91] Morocco prohibits foreign architects from registering with its National Association of Architects, then mandates that only Association members can legally practice architecture. The Philippines goes even further, reserving the practice of most licensed professions to Filipino citizens.[92] Finally, India restricts the right to practice law to persons who are both Indian citizens and on the advocates' roll in the particular Indian state where legal services will be provided. Furthermore, to qualify as an advocate, candidates must be either an Indian citizen or a citizen of a country that allows Indian nationals to practice law on a reciprocal basis, hold a degree from a university recognized by the Bar Council of India, and be at least 21 years of age.[93] Similar situations in Brazil, Bahrain, and Hong Kong, to name just a few, challenge the legal firm with international ambitions.

E-commerce, while a powerful trading platform, does not let companies circumvent barriers. Government regulations may lag company actions, given the speed by which e-commerce evolves, but they eventually regain their authority. For example, Chinese law holds that an enterprise seeking to operate in its national digital publishing field must obtain at least one of the four licenses for publishing, copying, distributing, or importing e-books. Within a day of Amazon announcing its Kindle store launch in China, for instance, the Chinese authorities challenged its legality, claiming its licensing agreement with its Chinese partner, Chineseall.com, was insufficient.[94]

In the United States, security issues constrain international trade. Ensuring a homeland that is safe, secure, and resilient against terrorism and other hazards inevitably limits business freedom. The logistics manager at Schott North America, for example, explained that the real danger

CONCEPT CHECK

"Legal Issues Facing International Companies," profiled in Chapter 3 (page 128), notes how a country's legal system influences operating decisions. Chapter 6 (page 215) shows how governments influence import flows with instruments of trade control. Here, we add revenue collection and homeland security to the list of moderators.

to international trade these days is not tariffs; rather, it's "that your containers are stuck down at the terminal in New York [harbor] waiting for inspection" by radiation detection instruments before being allowed to enter the United States.[95] Likewise, moving goods across borders takes far longer today given expanding security procedures: processing a truckload of goods across the Canadian–American border, for instance, takes three times as long as it did pre–September 11, 2001.[96] The United Kingdom, likewise, replaced its "account consignor scheme" that had allowed logistics groups to accept goods for cargo planes from self-certified businesses in order to improve its air cargo safety. As a result, importers and exporters must have all shipments scanned by the freight firms, such as FedEx, TNT, and UPS, or establish high-security sites.[97]

Governments work toward common standards, adopting similar screening methods, and harmonizing security measures. For example, concern for views like that expressed by the logistics manager at Schott North America led the U.S. Customs and Border Patrol to implement the Container Security Initiative (CSI). This program negotiates bilateral cargo security agreements with trading partners to set procedures for inspecting high-risk maritime cargo containers before they are loaded aboard vessels bound for the United States. Presently, CSI is operational at nearly 60 ports in North America, Europe, Asia, Africa, the Middle East, and Latin and Central America.[98]

TRADE DOCUMENTATION

Governments require international traders to thoroughly document trade transactions.

A battery of documents regulates international trade; Table 14.2 profiles a few. Keep in mind that customs regulations, though overlapping, invariably differ across countries. Tariff classifications, value declarations, and duty management create questions and boost costs. Furthermore, homeland security adds other regulations in the belief that protecting territory, sovereignty, citizens, and infrastructure requires more, not less, information.[99] Navigating

TABLE 14.2   Types of Export Documents

Many concerns motivate a government to monitor export activities, ranging from tracking transactions to safeguarding national security. The burden of reporting trade flows largely falls upon the trader. Here we see a small subset of the forms that exporters complete to comply with U.S. Customs and Border Protection and Homeland Security.

Type	Specification
Bill of Lading	A receipt for goods delivered to the common carrier for transportation, a contract for services rendered by the carrier, and a document of title. The customer usually needs the original as proof of ownership before assuming title.
Certificate of Origin	Indicates the product's origination and is usually validated by locally designated agency, such as a Chamber of Commerce. It helps customs officials determine the appropriate tariff schedule.
Commercial Invoice	A bill for the goods from the buyer to seller describing the goods, buyer/seller addresses, and delivery and payment terms. Governments use it to determine the value of goods when assessing customs duties.
Consular Invoice	Sometimes required by countries to monitor imports; it's used by governments to track trade flows.
Electronic Export Information (EEI)	The most common export document whereby an exporter declares key elements of the transaction, such as the involved parties, dates, ultimate consignee, forwarding agent, ultimate destination, and loading pier. Provides export statistics and enables export control.[100]
Export-Packing List	Itemizes the material in each individual package, indicates the type of package, and is attached to the outside of the package. Used by the shipper and customs officials to verify the cargo.
Pro Forma Invoice	A document from the exporter to the importer that outlines the selling terms, price, and delivery as if the goods had actually shipped. If the importer accepts the terms and conditions, it sends a purchase order and arranges for payment. At that point, the exporter issues a commercial invoice.

these obstacles requires that traders manage the paper trail that documents, certifies, and legalizes transactions.

The fact that paperwork tracks international trades means that missing or inaccurate documents boost costs, disrupt schedules, or halt the transaction. Many loss-and-damage challenges follow from incorrect use of International Commercial Terms, or Incoterms.[101] Sometimes, exporters fail to classify their products accurately in terms of the tariff schedule of the country of destination. Goods that arrive with commercial invoice descriptions that do not match those of the importing country's tariff classification are registered under a catchall description, such as "machinery, other." Besides slowing the transaction, imprecise descriptions often incur higher duty charges.

Importers face similar, yet also different, difficulties. Some importers receive products prior to purchasing them—that is, they take the title of ownership without laying out any money, waiting to see if the shipment actually arrives and is as contracted. Its arrival in-country requires the importer deal with various offices and agencies to settle accounts, take title, settle duty charges, and arrange delivery. Required documents vary by country. Typically, customs agencies require an importer to provide an entry manifest, bill of lading, commercial invoice, valuation statement, and packing list.

IMPORTING AND EXPORTING: RESOURCES AND ASSISTANCE

CONCEPT CHECK

In Parts I and II of the text, we note that **international business** creates jobs, generates income, and raises living standards. Parts II and III show how governments shape trade relationships through trade policies and regulations. Here, we observe that governments provide a variety of programs to improve the ease and efficiency of **exporting** and **importing**.

Globalization spurs companies to expand their market frontiers. Liberalizing markets and opening borders increases the potential for trade. Generally, big companies outperform their smaller counterparts pursuing these opportunities. Their ownership and internalization advantages as well as superior resources expedite expansion. Many SMEs lack the competencies and connections to pursue trade opportunities straightforwardly.[102] These constraints might not matter greatly in some places, but in others, they are decisive. Quite simply, there is wide variability in the ease of exporting and importing among countries (see Table 14.3).

In some countries, trading is easy. For example, several of the top 10 countries on the ease-of-trading list are European. Trading across Europe has become progressively seamless due to the ongoing integration efforts of the European Union. Free trade pacts in other parts

TABLE 14.3   Where the Trading Is Easy—and Where It's Not

Here, we see those countries that lead and lag the world in increasing the ease of export and import. These rankings reflect a country's performance in terms of the time and cost (excluding tariffs) involved in exporting and importing a standardized cargo of goods by sea transport. Key indicators include the number of documents customs requires traders to complete and the length of time and overall cost required to complete a transaction.

Easiest	Rank	Hardest	Rank
Singapore	1	Haiti	180
New Zealand	2	Angola	181
Hong Kong SAR, China	3	Venezuela	182
Denmark	4	Afghanistan	183
South Korea	5	Congo, Democratic Republic	184
Norway	6	Chad	185
United States	7	South Sudan	186
United Kingdom	8	Central African Republic	187
Finland	9	Libya	188
Australia	10	Eritrea	189

Source: Doing Business in 2015: Going Beyond Efficiency, 2014 International Bank for Reconstruction and Development/The World Bank.

of the world have similar effects, such as NAFTA expediting trade among Canada, Mexico, and the United States. In contrast, trading is hard elsewhere. For example, irregular customs practices in African and South Asian markets routinely hamper exports and imports. Moving from port to port in these markets finds a hodgepodge of hazy regulations that can veer toward illegality. One Zambian trader noted, "My cargo of copper wire was held up in Durban, South Africa, for a week. The port authorities required proof that the wooden pallets on which the wire was loaded were free of pests. After some days, the Ministry of Agriculture's inspector checked that the wood was fumigated—for a $100 fee."[103] No matter the locale, importing requires understanding relevant customs regulations and policies, knowing how to clear goods through customs, assigning the appropriate customs duties, and complying with special procedures.

Many firms find themselves in situations where assistance can meaningfully influence the productivity and profitability of their international activities. They can enlist aid from various public or private agents.

PUBLIC AGENCIES

Public officials champion export given its macroeconomic and microeconomic benefits. Exporting helps countries generate jobs, build foreign-exchange reserves, improve the balance of trade, develop foreign relationships, and raise living standards. In the United States, for example, exports support more than 10 million jobs. Notably, export-related jobs accounted for 22 percent or more of total employment in 10 U.S. manufacturing industries. Overall, manufacturing exports support more than one of every five jobs in the United States.[104] From a microeconomic perspective, exporting helps firms leverage core competencies, improve financial performance, diversify risk, and fortify competitive positioning. New markets open paths to higher productivity and profitability. Consequently, governments assist potential and active exporters, offering trade counseling, market intelligence, business matchmaking, and commercial diplomacy. To a lesser degree, given regulations set by cross-national trade agreements, they protect the interests of their struggling importers.[105]

In the United States, as in most countries, public agencies help firms initiate and develop exports and imports.

Agents and Services   In the United States, SMEs can start at the nearest Commercial Service office, the trade promotion arm of the U.S. Department of Commerce's International Trade Administration. In Japan, one contacts JETRO, while in the United Kingdom, UKTI. Like similar organizations worldwide, they are government-related units that promote trade and investment, particularly helping SMEs exploit export potential. In terms of the U.S Commercial Services, its representatives in more than 100 U.S. cities and 70 countries help U.S. companies tap export opportunities. Its global network helps SMEs target markets, organize operations, and overcome barriers.[106]

Companies look to the International Trade Administration (ITA) for negotiation expertise and commercial diplomacy in order to resolve trade complications. Remember, imports replace local production; labor pressures often spur public officials to install import barriers. Garmine Marine, for example, asked the ITA to help clear its navigational GPS through Turkish customs, asking the ITA to advise Turkish government officials that the units can be self-certified by an accredited independent lab, in compliance with the relevant EU standard.[107] The ITA, here and elsewhere, works with government officials and, as needed, the WTO Technical Barriers to Trade Committee to promote fair trade.

U.S. government agencies provide information and share advice on the practicalities and technicalities of exporting. Its official gateway, www.export.gov, offers many services. SMEs also tap personal help at export centers run by various branches of the Commerce Department, ITA, and the Small Business Administration. These agencies promote trade and investment, help U.S. companies compete at home and abroad, and ensure fair trade through the rigorous enforcement of trade laws and agreements.[108] Similarly, local government offices run export financing programs, including pre- and post-shipment working-capital loans and guarantees, accounts receivable financing, and export insurance. The limited reserves of some agencies requires proof of adequate safeguards from the exporter. For instance, authorities usually require a letter of credit or confirmed credit insurance. In return, they stipulate that the exporter then transact part of the funded activity within their jurisdiction.

PRIVATE AGENTS

CONCEPT CHECK

In Chapter 1, we suggest that **international business** is challenging for people who like to operate solo. Collecting information about foreign markets, navigating export regulations, mastering foreign-exchange procedures, or complying with homeland security policies can prove overwhelming. Consequently, some companies prefer help in finding information about potential markers. International trade intermediaries often command sophisticated knowledge of international trade.

| Trade intermediaries are third parties that provide exporters a variety of services.

| Many EMCs are entrepreneurial ventures that specialize by product, function, or market area.

| The United States exempts ETCs from antitrust provisions, thereby permitting competitors to combine forces in foreign markets.

| ETCs operate based on demand rather than supply. They identify suppliers who can fill orders in overseas markets.

Companies routinely enlist private agents to help navigate international trade. Prominent types include export intermediaries, freight forwarders, customs brokers, World Trade Centers, and international banks. These agents offer an operationally easier and less risky approach to export than going alone.[109] Their expertise provides skills and advantages that companies, especially SMEs, typically lack. Likewise, their experience with regulations, duties, insurance, and transportation preempts common problems.

Export Management Company (EMC) An EMC, by acting as the international trade arm of a company, helps firms establish overseas markets. An EMC helps SMEs enter foreign markets, overcoming otherwise daunting start-up barriers. It often acts as an unofficial marketing department, generating orders, organizing distribution channels, and developing promotions. Likewise, it verifies credit information, clarifies foreign accounts and payment terms, and even uses the firm's letterhead in communicating with foreign sales representatives. An EMC oversees trade documents, schedules transportation, and arranges patent and trademark protection.[110] Finally, it can expedite resolutions and, if needed, represent its client in customs investigations.

EMCs operate on a contractual basis, providing exclusive representation in a formally defined market. Their contract with a company specifies pricing, credit, and financial policies, promotional services, and method of payment. An EMC might operate on a commission basis (unless it takes title to the merchandise) and charge fees for other services. It usually concentrates on complementary and noncompetitive products from various companies in order to market a full product line.

In the United States, most EMCs specialize by product, function, or market area. Some are large concerns, handling lines from many manufacturers that cut across several industries. Others are smaller and work with fewer clients. Some specialize in certain products or focus on particular places, while others are generalists. The Federation of International Trade Associations (FITA) estimates that more than 1,000 EMCs operate in the United States, each representing, on average, about 10 companies. Although few U.S. companies use them, FITA reasons that many would benefit.[111] Still, though versatile, EMCs are not a panacea. Some EMCs have limited resources and may struggle to warehouse a company's product or develop financing options.

Export Trading Company (ETC) In 1982, the United States instituted the Export Trading Company Act, thereby permitting U.S. firms to collaborate with each other to reduce their export costs, improve export efficiency, and, in turn, compete more effectively in export markets.[112] Exemption from U.S. antitrust laws let's exporters coordinate overseas activities with rivals. They often collaborate to share expertise, reduce shipping costs, boost negotiating power, and fill larger orders. An ETC differs from an EMC in that it operates based on demand rather than supply. Operationally, an ETC brings buyers and sellers together, functioning as a trade matchmaker. It creates value by determining foreign customers' preferences, identifying domestic suppliers, and facilitating transactions. Rather than representing a single manufacturer, an ETC works with many. Operating as independent distributors, they avoid carrying inventory in their own name or performing post-sales service.

Freight Forwarders Popularly known as the "travel agent of cargo," freight forwarders are the largest export/import intermediary in terms of the value and weight of products shipped internationally.[113] Operationally, upon finalizing a foreign sale, an exporter hires a freight

The Pack Mules of Globalization
Container ships, of the sort seen here lined up in the Port of Hamburg, are the patient, sure-sailing, hardy and long-lasting movers of imports and exports. Pound for pound, they are the most efficient means of transporting goods between countries.
Source B Christopher / Alamy Stock Photo,

forwarder to arrange the fastest, cheapest transportation method. More often than not, freight forwarders look to the pack mules of globalization. Container ships, like those seen in the above photo transport nearly 90 percent of non-bulk cargo worldwide. Balancing the constraints of space, speed, and cost, a freight forwarder identifies the optimal path to move the shipment from the manufacturer to an air, land, or ocean terminal, supervises clearing customs, and schedules delivery to the foreign buyer. A freight forwarder also arranges pre-shipping storage, verifies credit-worthiness, obtains export licenses, pays consular fees, processes documentation, and prepares manifests. It may also advise on packing and labeling, transportation insurance, repacking of shipments damaged en route, and warehousing products. It does not take ownership title or act as a sales representative— those tasks fall in the realm of an EMC or ETC. As a rule, freight forwarders offer fewer services than those agents.

> A freight forwarder specializes in moving goods from sellers to buyers.

Freight forwarders are particularly important when the cost or timing of freight can make or break a deal. One straightforward solution, advises the director of business development of Certified Worldwide, is "seek out your local Commercial Service office and find a freight forwarder, interview different freight forwarders, and remember that the company chosen will be responsible for shipping your product."[114] A freight forwarder usually charges the exporter a percentage of the shipment value, plus a minimum charge depending on the number of services provided. It also receives a brokerage fee from the carrier. Most companies, especially SMEs, find international logistics costly and complex. Freight forwarders' expertise enables them to secure shipping space at better rates and efficiently organize shipments.

> A 3PL is a trade intermediary that applies sophisticated technologies and systems to supervise trade logistics.

Third-Party Logistics (3PLs) This agent is a fast-growing force in international trade. Like freight forwarders, 3PLs move cargo across global markets. Unlike freight forwarders, 3PLs collaborate with manufacturers, shippers, and retailers to relieve them of the logistics responsibilities of transportation, warehousing, cross-docking, inventory management, packaging, and freight forwarding. 3PLs, such as Mohawk Global Logistics, UPS, or FedEx, simplify the complexities of international logistics through seamless, end-to-end solutions in transportation, customs brokerage, cargo insurance, and most everything else needed to move cargo across the globe on time, cheaply, and worry-free. Think of, on a very small scale, your last UPS experience; just as you did, an SME relies on UPS to track and transport the product, all the while providing access to real-time information to chart its progress. 3PLs also consolidate billing inclusive of all transportation, customs brokerage, duties, taxes, and package delivery services. Finally, they handle product returns, warranty claims, parts exchanges, and reverse logistics.

Expanding globalization and trade liberalization accelerate the growth of 3PLs.[115] They are particularly helpful to the born-global company. Rather than building its own logistics operation, it need only tap the services of a 3PL. Big companies also benefit: nearly 80 percent of *Fortune 500* companies use 3PLs to manage logistics and supply chains. Procter & Gamble, Walmart, PepsiCo, and Ford, for example, use them. Overall, 3PLs have been growing their business at the expense of freight forwarders. In response, the latter expands its historical role as the travel agents of cargo to provide logistics support.

| A customs broker helps an importer navigate the regulations imposed by customs agencies. It helps importers in matters of
- valuation,
- qualification,
- deferment,
- liability.

Customs Brokers Trading internationally requires understanding relevant customs regulations and policies, knowing how to clear goods through customs, assigning the appropriate customs duties, and complying with special procedures. The United States has nearly 10,000 classifications in its Harmonized Tariff Schedule. Approximately 60 percent of these are open to interpretation—that is, a particular product fits more than one classification. Often, it is an art form to determine the tariff classification that minimizes duty assessment. Importing requires considerable expertise to manage this and other processes. Trade paperwork is extensive, involving document preparation and/or electronic submissions; calculating and paying taxes, duties, and excises; and overseeing communications between government authorities and traders. Not every company commands these proficiencies, especially SMEs. Consequently, some hire a customs broker to navigate customs regulations.[116]

The Costs and Constraints of Private Agents Expectedly, private intermediaries charge for their services. Many variables influence fees. For freight forwarders, the mode of transport, distance/destination, weight and volume, value, contract type, handling requirements, and security needs influence charges. Changing the degree of collaboration and interdependence, as is the case with hiring a 3PL or an EMC, changes the fee structure. 3PLs often charge upfront costs based on the complexity of the service. This cost reflects the planning and development of material handling, operational and information systems required for distribution, and implementation of the proposed system. Similarly, ETCs and EMCs operate on (1) a commission rate ranging from 10 percent for consumer goods to 15 percent or more for industrial products, (2) a buy-sell basis that asks for a firm's best home-country discount plus an extra discount for a product that is marked up when sold abroad, and/or (3) contributions for special events such as exhibiting products in a foreign trade show or an advance payment for advertising and promotion.

| Enlisting the support of a trade intermediary requires the trader surrender some degree of operational control.

Besides payments, hiring a trade intermediary requires an exporter relinquish some, or even considerable, decision-making control regarding shipping, buyer segments, price policies, quality of promotion materials, delivery schedules, or customer service. Depending on the contract, the intermediary oversees some to all of these matters. The intent to retain control leads some traders to use intermediaries less comprehensively. But, as in any make-versus-buy situation, companies balance their control preference relative to the demands of managing the activity.[117]

Longer terms, supportive governments, fading language barriers, improving communications and connections, harmonizing finance practices, and efficient electronic exchange steadily diminish the appeal of fee-based trade agents. In response, private intermediaries innovate and upgrade their services. Some focus on exporting high-value products within the context of a single industry to select markets, rather than exporting bulk and commodity products. Others improve industry expertise in order to boosts effectiveness, whereas others offer multiple product lines to optimize efficiency. These sorts of innovations, by moving SMEs into foreign markets faster, help justify their fees.

RECONCILING OPPORTUNITY AND CHALLENGE: AN EXPORT PLAN

Beginning with identifying attractive markets, and moving onward through negotiating an international sale to shipping and receiving products, an exporter/importer manages an array of marketing, financial, logistic, and regulatory responsibilities. At times, some activities press more than others, such as financial concerns prior to shipment, delivery concerns post-shipment, and so on. The decision to engage or escalate these activities, given their implication to profitability, is one that few companies take lightly. It is one thing to consider exporting and quite another to take the first steps in doing so. Going international imposes many demands that, collectively, influence resource allocation, executive effectiveness, operational flexibility, and financial stability. Successful exporters, citing the notion that "companies don't plan to fail, they fail to plan," indicate that developing an **export plan** manages these demands.

An export plan prioritizes markets, formalizes top management buy-in, organizes trade activities, and forecasts market scenarios. The process of defining objectives, sequencing tactics, and setting timelines pushes the firm to assess resources, develop competencies, assign responsibilities, and stipulate controls. A rigorous export plan helps executives track performance in the face of the ongoing, if not seemingly endless, decisions. At first glance, compiling an export plan may appear daunting. Remember, though, it need only be just a few pages to start. It steadily expands as it evolves.

Managers report that developing an export plan in a transparent, collaborative process improves its effectiveness.[118] By no means does that guarantee success. Strategic planning in any context is challenging, especially when one must abandon the familiarity of domestic routines for the contingencies of international trade. External validation goes a long way toward preempting blind spots as well as potential delusions about the likely success of export ventures. More practically, a well-specified plan is a precondition for export financing assistance from public agencies.

Successful exporters note that consulting government agencies and third-party intermediates helps clarify opportunities and preempt problems. Noted the CEO of Coffee & More, "My advice to other companies considering exporting is to go for it, but be smart and do your homework first. Educate yourself and use your local U.S. Commercial Service office."[119] Added the Manager of International Operations at Analytical Graphics, "Don't just strike out on your own; take advantage of the U.S. Commercial Service. They are familiar with the ways of doing business in your market destination and know how U.S. companies can succeed there. It's saved us valuable time and resources."[120]

> An export plan defines a company's intent to leverage resources and manage constraints in initiating and developing export activity.

> Traders stress-test an export plan by consulting trade specialists along with public and private agents.

TABLE 14.4   Improving the Effectiveness of the Export Planning Process

Strategic planning is a challenging but rewarding process. Considering the following questions throughout the process improves the quality of analysis:

- Is exporting consistent with our vision and mission?
- Do we see ourselves as sporadic or regular exporters?
- Would our resources be better utilized in developing our domestic businesses?
- Will exporting put undue demands on management, production, finance, and marketing?
- Does exporting leverage our ownership advantages?
- Do our internalization advantages support export activity?
- Do targeted export markets provide location advantages?
- Does exporting fit our current mix of resources, capabilities, and competencies?
- What is the relative price performance of competitive products?
- How much will it cost to get the product to the foreign market?
- Do the financial and strategic benefits of exporting exceed its direct and indirect costs?
- What is the best mix of public and private assistance?

The element of an export plan that routinely stymies companies, particularly SMEs, is selecting the "right" foreign market. SMEs are often discouraged when their first foray fails. Instead of applying the standards of sound strategy that made them successful in the first place, many follow hunches about foreign markets (i.e., "China is growing so fast that there must be many people there who want my product"). Likewise, it is tough to try to conquer customers from Bonn to Beijing to Benares in a day. A useful rule is to look at a few markets where the odds favor success rather than trying to sell to the world.[121] Table 14.4 identifies productive questions to frame the planning process. Last, like yin and yang, import and export are complementary opposites within the greater whole of international trade. Strategic and practical aspects of the import process mirror those of the export process. Changing the terminology from "export" to "import" does not require changing the contents of the plan. Rather, companies adjust their analytics, interpreting events from a particular perspective.

Looking to the Future
Technology Transforms International Trade

The transaction costs of international trade steadily decrease. Advances in transportation and communications systems, by making it easier and cheaper to trade, expedite exporting and importing. The Internet helps individuals engage each other easily and quickly. Online filing of cargo manifests, customs documents, and transit forms expedites shipments. Customs software that works in Hamburg or Sydney is used in Hong Kong and Long Beach. More parties, from the originating shipper, transit depots, and customs agents, along with the buyer and seller, easily monitor trade flows. All in all, greater flexibility and improving efficiency let companies engage an expanding range of export and import options.

Synchronizing import or export activities redefine how companies, both big and small, connect with foreign buyers and sellers. Historically, big companies reaped the biggest rewards. Their superior resources, capabilities, and competencies enabled them to directly move goods, funds, and information. Now, the technology of trade seems to offer bigger benefits to smaller companies. Improving technologies create online, software, and logistics platforms that blur the distinction between the big, global giant and the small, neighborhood start-up. In fact, it has become harder to tell the difference between an SME operating on a shoestring budget and its larger, richer counterpart.

Online Platforms

Companies look to online technologies to start or expand exporting. They rely on the Internet to get information, source products, find suppliers, market products, and tap new markets. Some companies build virtual value chains, running export transactions from start to finish without ever leaving their hometown. The inexorable expansion of the Internet gives potential and practicing international traders nearly infinite resources. They browse government trade data, online catalogs, business-to-business exchanges, electronic trade boards, consumer surveys, trade journals archives, and virtual trade shows to find a product to import or a market for their export.

The emergence of country-specific portals and web exchanges accelerates this trend. Replicating the dynamics of consumer-to-consumer e-commerce, several sites offer online bazaars for international traders. Here, exporters can lay out their wares on the digital carpet and haggle with potential buyers from the far corners of the world. For instance, potential importers looking for products from South Korea can access www.koreatradeworld.com; those targeting India can check out www.trade-india.com; those focusing on Europe need only visit www.bizeurope.com to tap into high-quality trade boards. One can also shop the world at www.tradekey.com or www.alibaba.com.

These and similar sites promote the commercial potential of a country or region. They provide services to large and small international traders, such as export training, cyber-trade infrastructures, international special exhibitions, virtual trade shows, and trade strategies. Conceptually, their mission is direct: connect sellers here to buyers there. Operationally, they provide powerful business-to-business tools that improve the mechanics of trade, creating flexible and dynamic platforms that let buyers and sellers of everything from bamboo toothpicks to crawler bulldozers find each other, negotiate the terms of trade, and seal the deal.

Increasingly, as SMEs worldwide gain Internet access, they use online platforms to build their export businesses. Besides introducing mom-and-pop shops throughout the world to each other, websites open a vast and largely uncharted small-business hinterland. Long the unseen production sites for many pieces of the global economy, these small companies had to trade within the context of global supply chains directed by large MNEs. Now, going online plugs them into the matrix, letting them go straight to buyers.

Software Platforms

A burst of business software in the past few years has "created a total revolution in what small businesses are able to accomplish overseas."[122] Collaborative software lets entrepreneurial exporters with single-digit headcounts track foreign vendors without traveling the world. For example, Edgar Blazona of True Modern used to log 100,000 miles annually visiting factories in the Far East. Now he uses two factories—one in Thailand and one in India—to manufacture his modernist furniture designs that he then imports into the United States. A meeting and document-sharing program lets him work in real time with his overseas factories. At a price of less than $100 per month, this software coordinates workflows, expedites exchanges, and eases communications.

Similarly, Evertek Computer Corporation, a U.S. SME, has capitalized on software innovations to build e-commerce websites and portals that expand its market frontier. In 1990, Evertek began selling new and refurbished computers and parts; by 2008, it had become the world's largest close-out computer wholesaler, clearance computer supplier, and closeout electronics wholesaler. Within a year of purchasing BuyUSA.com, an Internet-based program from the U.S. Commerce Department that identifies buyers around the world, Evertek began selling in 10 new countries, with single purchases reaching up to $75,000. By 2010, it reported exports to 105 countries. Today, Evertek serves customers, principally via the web, in over 200 countries.

Companies use innovative programs to manage overseas factories with tools that once were reserved for big MNEs. Global Manufacturing Network, for instance, relies on its 10-person staff in California to coordinate production of industrial devices among more than 100 independent factories in China, Malaysia, and Singapore. It uses on-demand, scalable enterprise software to track activity orders, monitor build rates, and manage inventory across its manufacturing network.

Logistics Platforms

Improving logistics help SMEs move products more cheaply and easily to more places. High-tech, low-cost shipping services rob big firms of a long-running advantage. Now, the no-name, one-person exporter down the street from you, because of its big-name shipping partners spanning the globe, has many of the same logistics capabilities commanded by a large MNE, but at a fraction of the cost. In fact, SMEs increasingly have as much, if not a bit more, logistic flexibility. Unlike big companies that rely on their in-house systems, SMEs arbitrage solutions from freight forwarders to 3PLs—think of the ease of using FedEx or UPS, for example. The small international trader can hire any of these sorts of intermediaries to warehouse, truck, ship, fly, and deliver goods from factories in Asia to customers in Europe—all the while never taking physical possession of the goods.

South West Trading in Arizona, a family-owned start-up, imports yarns made from bamboo, corn, and soy fibers by fabric plants in China. South West Trading's recurring problems importing products from China led it to consult UPS. The latter organized its Shanghai facility to consolidate orders from various Chinese factories into one container which other units then supervised, shipped, and trucked to South West Trading's warehouse. South West Trading's bottom line immediately benefited. Where it once paid $9,400 to run four China-to-Arizona shipments per month, its once-a-month UPS shipment costs about $3,600 and reliably takes 21 days to travel.

The Great Leveling

Improving online, software, market, and logistics platforms, by improving the technology of buying and selling, levels the playing field of international trade.[123] The combination of ubiquitous Internet connections and cheap cloud-based computing makes it easier to export and import. Big and small companies respond, confident that technology creates tools that let them jump hurdles and capture opportunities. SMEs, in particular, prosper from the improving technology of trade. Perhaps most significantly, technology decouples the issues of size and capability. Observed the CEO of China Manufacturing, "Our customers can't really tell how big we are. In a way, it's irrelevant. What matters is that we can get the job done."[124] ■

COUNTERTRADE

Companies and countries often use countertrade to build mutually beneficial relationships.

Currency or credit—easy, fast, and direct—are the preferred payment options for export or import transactions. Sometimes, though, companies face the harsh reality that a buyer cannot pay in cash because the home country's currency is nonconvertible or the nation holds scant reserves, has insufficient credit, or imposes strict currency controls. Consequently, if they wish to trade, they must resort to other means.

Consider the following transactions. Coca-Cola has traded its syrup for cheese from the Soviet Union, oranges from Egypt, tomato paste from Turkey, beer from Poland, and soft drink bottles from Hungary. Malaysia swapped palm oil for fertilizer and machinery with North Korea, Cuba, and Russia and negotiated similar deals with Morocco, Jordan, Syria, and Iran. Thailand, the world's largest exporter of rice, uses rice-for-oil deals with Middle Eastern countries. Boeing exchanged ten 747s for 34 million barrels of Saudi Arabian oil. Chinese companies agreed to build a coal mine, a power station, and a dam in Zimbabwe, with revenue from the mine being used to repay the loan.[125] These sorts of trades fall under the umbrella term **countertrade**. Any one of several different arrangements that parties use to trade products via transactions that use limited or no currency or credit qualify as a countertrade. Table 14.5 identifies its principal forms.[126]

Inconsistent disclosure hinders estimating the volume of countertrade. Secretive government-to-government deals and disguised transactions are not unusual. Roughly, more than 80 countries nowadays use or require countertrade. These transactions compose anywhere between 5 to 15 percent of the world trade.[127] Countertrade generally increases as countries experience economic difficulties. Boom-bust market dynamics, particularly in commodity markets, makes countertrade an enduring feature of international trade.

Companies and countries often use countertrade to build mutually beneficial relationships.

Countertrade is an umbrella term for several sorts of trade, such as barter or offset, in which the seller accepts goods or services, rather than currency or credit, as payment.

Countertrade has several disadvantages:
- *Inefficiency*
- *Risk*
- *Complicated*

COSTS

Countertrade is an inefficient way of doing business. Companies prefer straightforward cash or credit to settle a transaction. That sort of deal only requires consulting foreign-exchange tables to set exchange rates. Countertrade, instead, requires buyers and sellers rely on non-market factors to set the value of the trade, negotiating some standards such as how many tons of rice for how many farm tractors. Negotiating "payment" is not the only hurdle. Goods may be of poor quality, packaged unattractively, or difficult to sell and service. Consequently, countertrade deals are prone to price, financing, and quality problems. Ultimately, countertrade and its variations threaten free market forces with indirect protectionism and price-fixing.

TABLE 14.5   Common Forms of Countertrade

Barter	Products are exchanged directly for products of equal value without the use of cash or credit.
Buyback	A supplier of capital or equipment agrees to accept future output generated by the investment as payment. For example: The exporter of equipment to a chemical plant may be repaid with output from the factory to whose owner it "sold" the equipment.
Offset	An exporter sells products for cash and then helps the importer find opportunities to earn hard currency for payment. One often sees offsets with big-ticket (e.g., military equipment) deals.
Switch or Swap Trading	One company sells to another its obligation to purchase something in a foreign country. Typically, the arrangement involves switching the documentation and destination of merchandise while it's in transit.
Counter-purchase	A company sells products to a foreign country, promising to make a future purchase of a specific product made in that country.

CONCEPT CHECK

Recall our discussions of poverty in Chapters 4 and 11. Here, we point out that shortages of resources impoverish nations as well as individuals. Some countries struggle to acquire the foreign reserves they need to purchase goods from other nations. If unsuccessful, they may resort to countertrade.

BENEFITS

Countertrade is often unavoidable for companies that want to do business with buyers who have limited or no access to cash or credit. Companies and countries in tough binds use it to generate jobs, preserve foreign-exchange holdings, and develop trade relationships. Countertrade helps countries reduce their need to borrow working capital and gives them access to companies' technological skills and marketing expertise. Companies also benefit; they can resolve bad debts, repatriate blocked funds, or develop customer relationships. Accepting countertrade signals a seller's good faith and flexibility, often positioning it to gain preferential market access in the future.

CASE [128]   The Borderfree Option: Going Global—Simplified

E-commerce, by changing the way companies around the world do business, makes international trade easier and cheaper. Before the Internet, tracking down a product to import, or finding foreign customers to export to, overwhelmed the typical SME. Some relied on occasional trade shows and expensive, time-consuming foreign travel to identify possible products or assess potential suppliers. Certainly, traders could tap local embassies or consulates to support export promotion or provide import assistance. Although sounding straightforward, in practice these sorts of options typically proved expensive and cumbersome. Consequently, international trade was largely limited to big companies that could afford to attend trade shows, translate marketing materials, travel internationally, hire intermediaries, and supervise the many activities that make up international trade.

Today, the Internet gives SMEs cost-effective means to manage these demands. It makes information on any conceivable product from virtually any market readily and inexpensively accessible. Falling trade barriers (due to expanding cross-national trade agreements) along with improving logistics options (courtesy of enterprising freight forwarders and 3PLs), offer an array of trade possibilities.

The Internet, simply put, transforms whatever it touches. It's already the most powerful force for globalization, democratization, economic growth, and education in history. The same, we see, applies to the game of international trade. As such, e-commerce is now inherently global—just as the Internet knows no physical boundaries,

so too with Internet sales. Consumers' growing disposable income and interest in global brands, especially in a screen-saturated world, highlights the potential of global e-commerce.

Still, national markets differ in different sorts of ways—ranging from market structure and growth dynamics to consumer preferences and media consumption practices. Staying ahead of trends, both national and global, is no small task. It calls for companies to study the demographics, psychographics, preferences, and behaviors of the global consumer landscape, identify how to manage payments and collections, and organize supply chains that reflect when, where, what, and how consumers buy. Tough in just one market, the task can grow stunningly complex when looking at the 200-plus national markets or territories that compose the global business environment.

Launch a Website, Go Global

Capturing those sales, along with riding expanding technologies, has led many retailers to open websites with an eye to opening export markets far and wide. Now, opening a website, whether you like it or not, means you are global. Consumers from anywhere and everywhere can go to your website and, when there, do business. Done well, enterprising companies can leverage cross-border e-commerce into powerful international expansion. Done poorly, a retailer wastes energy, effort, and equity. Despite best intentions, the challenges of international inexperience, currency ills, payment problems, logistics challenges, and cultural contingencies can prove daunting.

E-commerce's growing potential spurs vendors to make going global as simple as linking your current website with their behind-the-scenes, back-office expertise. They develop end-to-end solutions that break down barriers and borders, thereby enabling a company to sell its products worldwide with reduced effort.

These companies are not your typical e-commerce, business-to-consumer model retailer, like Amazon, eBay, or Alibaba. Moreover, they are unlike traditional logistics companies, such as FedEx, DHL, UPS, and their core business of delivering packages. Rather, these companies, such as BorderJump, Venda, International Checkout, and Borderfree, provide proprietary technology that enables retailers to transact with customers in virtually every country and territory worldwide.

Borderfree: Fine-Tuning the Global Game

Founded in 1999, Borderfree is headquartered in New York City. It has offices in Dublin, London, Tel Aviv, Toronto, and Shanghai. From these, Borderfree helps more than 200 retailers—such as Neiman Marcus, Lands' End, and Harrods—conduct cross-border online sales in more than 220 countries that are transacted in 74 currencies.

Borderfree manages a retailers' international shopping experience, suggesting real-time merchandising insights and marketing strategies to help it target international consumers, whether through web, mobile, or in-store channels. Then, Borderfree's systems seals the deal, administering multicurrency pricing and payment processing, tending to fraud and tax management, calculating landed costs, arranging customs clearance and brokerage, and supervising logistics.

Borderfree's mission, declared its CEO, "is to make it as simple as possible for online retailers to reach new consumers and sell their products around the world globally." Added its chief technology officer, the rise in global consumerism means that "There's a lot of growth still out there for companies in the industry. Growth from a revenue perspective, growth from a coverage perspective."

Capturing that growth requires companies, both large and small, overcome the barriers to buying and selling internationally. Borderfree, by linking customers and companies through tap-web and mobile platforms, helps consumers worldwide shop across geographies and devices while enabling companies to leverage their brand, inventory, and expertise.

Arranging the Pieces

Borderfree's turnkey installation system integrates with the retailer's e-commerce infrastructure. Moreover, its plug-in modules connect a retailer's existing e-commerce infrastructure and international operations. The end result is that customers enter international markets quickly after system rollout. Moreover, Borderfree's software helps its clients localize the website experience, supporting country-specific marketing messages, pricing strategies, international checkouts with translation, local payment options, and fully landed delivery quotes.

Operationally, a retailer can add plug-ins that track what people are buying, where and when they are buying it, and adjust promotions in real time. On the service side, Borderfree also manages international fraud, customs clearance, and all global logistics. Collectively, Borderfree enables the internationally ambitious retailer to quickly move from domestic today to global tomorrow.

Borderfree works with retailers to optimize international site experience based on local preferences, best practices, and marketing customization. It provides targeted marketing campaigns, data analysis and insight into prospective markets, website localization, duty and tax compliance, pricing in different currencies, customs clearance, and customer care. Harrods' e-commerce director, for instance, explained, "We were drawn to Borderfree's ability to further enhance our capacity to serve our customers seamlessly across geographies. We also were particularly interested in partnering with Borderfree to extend our reach into China and Russia, two markets that hold great consumer promise for us."

The director of e-commerce at The Dune Group, a fashion footwear and accessories company that has over 300 stores and concessions in 24 countries, said that Borderfree provides "potential growth opportunities in markets such as South America, Africa, and Asia." Likewise, head of digital at Trunci planned to use Borderfree's platform to further its growth in India, Japan, Ireland, Mexico, Pakistan, South America, and South Korea.

Promising Solutions

In 2014, Borderfree generated more than $125 million in revenue. It is paid by its clients based on a percentage of sales, generally up to 12 percent, that take place on Borderfree's platform. It generates additional revenue from fulfillment services, foreign exchange, and other transaction-related fees. Looking to the future, as more countries champion international trade, as more executives target international sales, as more consumers develop global brand awareness, and as more technologies improve connectivity, shoppers worldwide will make more purchases on the Internet.

Capturing these opportunities pushes some companies to go alone in the world of import and export. Others, managing a differing mix of ownership, location, and internalization advantages, see that the growing competencies of companies such as Borderfree make going global with the help of an intermediary the superior choice.[129]

QUESTIONS

14-3. Explain what Borderfree does. Why would an SME find that appealing?

14-4. What mix of ownership, location, and internalization advantages would encourage a company to hire Borderfree?

14-5. Borderfree's clients expect it to be knowledgeable about the key markets in which they operate and to be able to advise on how to prioritize, budget, and compete. How does Borderfree make that happen?

14-6. Borderfree promises to help its partners drive international growth. What sorts of marketing and sales techniques help it do so?

14-7. Do you think most international trade might eventually take place through intermediaries like Borderfree.com? Does that influence your interest in importing and exporting?

MyLab Management

Go to **mymanagementlab.com** for the following Assisted-graded writing questions:

14-8   Provide two recommendations that you would offer an SME, based on the opportunities and constraints of electronic websites like Borderfree, as it considers engaging in exporting or importing.

14-9   Visit www.alibaba.com and www.europages.com. Compare and contrast these websites.

Endnotes

Scan for Endnotes or go to www.pearsonglobaleditions.com/Daniels

CHAPTER 15

Forms and Ownership of Foreign Production

OBJECTIVES

After studying this chapter, you should be able to

15-1 Comprehend why export and import may not suffice for companies' achievement of IB objectives

15-2 Explain why and how companies make wholly owned foreign direct investments

15-3 Ascertain why companies collaborate in international markets

15-4 Compare and contrast forms of and considerations for selecting an international collaborative arrangement

15-5 Grasp why IB collaborative arrangements fail or succeed

> ### MyLab Management®
> **Improve Your Performance!**
> When you see this icon ⭐, visit **www.mymanagementlab.com** for activities that are applied, personalized, and offer immediate feedback.

If you can't beat them, join them.

—American proverb

ME By Meliá Hotel in Madrid, Spain. ▶

Source: StockOption/Shutterstock

CASE Meliá Hotels International[1]

—Fidel León-Darder and Cristina Villar[2]

God bless the inventor of sleep.
(Miguel de Cervantes Saavedra, *Don Quijote de la Mancha*)

Li Feng arrived in London after a 13-hour flight from Beijing, her first company trip since completing her MBA and her first time outside China. Upon entering her room at the Meliá White House, she felt too exhausted to do much more than shower and enjoy the comfort and amenities in her room. (The quote from Don Quijote was certainly applicable.) However, her excitement kept her from sleeping right away. So she perused the attractive hotel directory on her bedside table and was surprised to read that her hotel belonged to a Spanish company with more than 300 hotels all over the world. The photos showed an array of attractive hotels, ranging from those in big cities (primarily to serve businesspeople) to others on pristine beaches (primarily to serve vacationers).

She was also intrigued by a small picture of Gabriel Escarré, who founded the chain in 1956. At only 21, he leased his first hotel in Majorca (Mallorca), Spain, with only his savings and the expertise gained from his job at a travel agency. Li Feng fell asleep and dreamt of holidaying in a Meliá beach resort, but she awoke curious as to how Mr. Escarré had built Meliá's position in the global hospitality industry. For the next five days, she worked long hours, squeezed in a little sightseeing, and then returned to Beijing. Despite jet-lag, she worked the next day and began catching up with the accumulated papers on her desk. In her spare time she did some research on Meliá. What she learned is described below. (The chapter's opening photo shows the tower of a Meliá Hotel in Madrid.)

GROWTH IN SPAIN

That Gabriel Escarré's first hotel was in Majorca is not surprising because most entrepreneurs begin in familiar surroundings. His timing was good—European incomes were rising and package tours for sun-loving tourists were gaining popularity. Most important, Escarré exhibited both a knack for hotel management and a motivation to expand. He grew by acquiring other properties in Spain's Balearic and Canary Islands, branding them first as Hoteles Mallorquines, later as Hoteles Sol, still later to Sol-Meliá, which many people still call it, and finally to Meliá Hotels International in 2011. The early hotels aimed sales at beach-seeking tourists. In 1982, three years before its first foreign entry, the company began diversifying with urban hotels targeted to business travelers.

In 1984, the company rebranded hotels as Sol and bought 32 hotel properties of a Spanish chain, Hotasa, which expanded the company into more Spanish cities. Three years later, Sol acquired

Meliá from Paretti, an Italian group, which led to further client-based diversification—most Sol Hotels were three- and four-star beach properties, whereas most Meliá's were four- or five-star urban hotels. In 2000, Meliá merged with another Spanish hotel chain, TRYP, thus adding 45 hotels in Spain. Meliá is now the largest hotel operator in Spain, and Spain is the largest location for Meliá.

INTERNATIONAL EXPANSION

Despite the importance of Spain to Meliá, where it still concentrates 49 percent of its hotels, 75 percent of its current income is from international operations. Some international expansion came from the acquisitions. The TRYP agreement included eight leased arrangements in Tunisia and three management contracts in Cuba. Meliá has used its 1999 purchase of the White House in London and the 2007 acquisition of the Innside Inns in Germany to bolster its European urban presence. (Map 15.1 shows the regional breakdown of Meliá's hotels.)

Having acquired experience and expertise within Spain, the firm's first start-up abroad was a joint venture for the Meliá Bali in Indonesia. This start-up was long and complicated, involving difficulty in finding local suppliers. There were also logistics and import problems in sending materials from Majorca. Soon after, the company focused on Latin America and eventually on other areas. Let's examine some major international forays that demonstrate different modes of operations.

Cuba In terms of the number of hotels, Cuba's 28 composed Meliá's largest foreign presence until its recent growth in Germany. Yet the company has no ownership in hotels there because Cuba's centralized economy disallows full ownership by foreign hotel groups. Thus, Meliá had to establish an agreement with a public agency, which usually owns the properties. Meliá has a contract to manage properties owned by Cubanacán.

Operating in Cuba slowed Meliá's access to the U.S. market because the U.S. government maintained restrictions on companies doing business with Cuba, such as on those managing expropriated assets once owned by U.S. citizens. Meliá had to prove that the hotels it managed were not expropriated from U.S. citizens before it could enter the U.S. market, where it currently operates.

China Despite more than 25 years of international expansion, Meliá's Asian expansion has been slow. In 2009, Meliá signed a 10-year contract renewable for 10 more to manage The Gran Meliá Shanghai. This became the first Spanish-branded hotel in China,

MAP 15.1 Regional Breakdown of Meliá Hotels

The numbers refer to the number of hotels within each region at the end of 2014.

Source: The regional breakdown is taken from *Meliá Hotels International Annual Report 2014,* page 6, http://www.meliahotelsinternational.com/sites/default/files/informes-financieros/Informe_anual_RSC_14_completa_en.pdf, (accessed December 4, 2015).

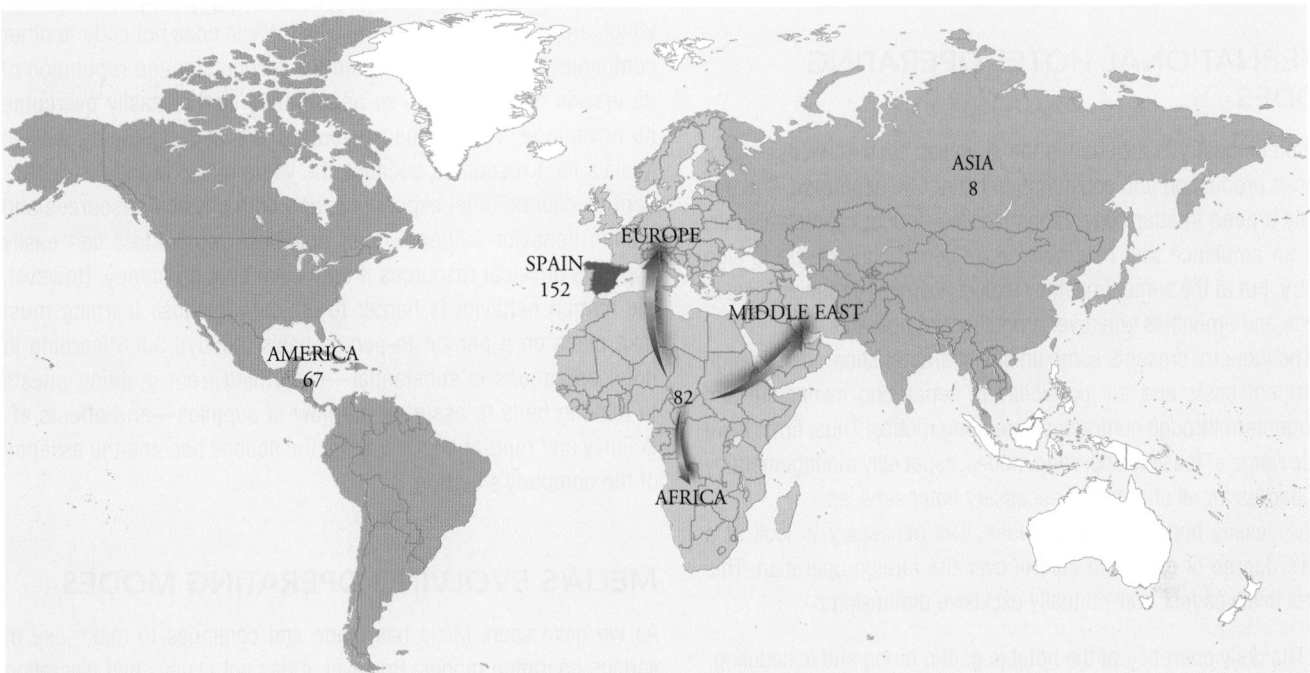

even though the country had long been an important growth market for many international hotel chains, such as Hyatt, Marriott, Radisson, and China's largest hotel chain, Jin Jiang. This anomaly is not due to Spanish hotel chains' unawareness of the Chinese market potential; indeed, many projects were developed to conquer the market as much as 10 years earlier. However, the unsuccessful experience of Spain's Barceló Hotels discouraged other Spanish hotel chains from carrying out Chinese operations.

Barceló, one of Meliá's main competitors, reached an agreement in 2000 with a Chinese state-owned company to manage the Shanghai International Convention Center & Hotel. Surprisingly, after operating eight months and bringing the hotel back into the black within six, the owners unilaterally terminated the contract by stating that the results were inadequate. Although Barceló won a two-year court battle on breach of contract and received some compensation, the affair left Spanish hoteliers with a bitter aftertaste and the suspicion that Chinese government partners would break agreements once they learned enough from their foreign partners.

Meliá's entry into China was facilitated by its favorable 20-year relationship with Cubanacán, which shares the Shanghai hotel ownership with the Chinese company Xintian (Suntime). Still, getting the deal was not easy; it took more than five years from the time talks began to the hotel's opening. Further, from almost the beginning, there was friction between Meliá and the hotel's owners, which led to cancellation of the agreement in 2013. The hotel is now operated by the Swiss chain, Kempinski.

During the period of friction, Meliá began seeking other means of growth in China. In 2011 it opened a representative office in Shanghai in order to boost its brand image and broaden its alliances within China. Subsequently, Meliá announced comanagement plans with Jin Jiang and Greenland, a Chinese real estate company. The plans provide for management sharing in six hotels, of which each partner had previously managed three. This allows the Chinese partners to extend their operations into three hotels—one each in Germany, Spain, and France—in exchange for Meliá's comanagement of hotels in three Chinese cities. The partners share knowledge and best practices as well as integrate and develop training, information, and booking systems.

Relationship with Wyndham Meliá's motivation for a 2010 agreement with Wyndham was largely to facilitate North American expansion by using Wyndham's knowledge of that market and reputation with developers who are potential hotel investors. (Wyndham is one of the world's largest hospitality companies and hotel franchisors, with 7700 hotels and 15 brands in 75 countries.) Through the agreement, Meliá sold its TRYP brand to Wyndham, but sold no real estate. The hotels in the transaction were re-branded as TRYP by Wyndham. Meliá became the franchisee for all the hotels using the TRYP by Wyndham brand for a 20-year period. Wyndham gained by increasing its reservations offerings for a mid-market brand in Europe and Latin America, even though the same hotels are also included in Meliá's reservation system. Of the hotels in the 2010 agreement,

Meliá maintains ownership of 6, leases 49, has management contracts in 24, and re-franchises 12 to other parties. Subsequently, TRYP by Wyndham has opened hotels in 21 countries.

INTERNATIONAL HOTEL OPERATING MODES

The hotel industry is included in the so-called "soft services" sector because production and consumption cannot be separated. There is usually a need to adapt operations locally—tourist clientele usually want an ambiance that resembles their perceptions of the foreign country, but at the same time, they expect a similar threshold level of service and amenities wherever a hotel brand operates.

The industry presents some unique characteristics, such as high investment costs and the possibility of separating ownership and management through contractual operating modes. Thus, firms have a wide range of feasible operating modes, especially management by third parties for all or a part of necessary hotel services.

To classify hotel operating modes, it is necessary to look at a chain's degree of exercised control over the foreign operation. This control involves four non-mutually exclusive dimensions:

1. The daily operation of the hotel (e.g., the hiring and scheduling of personnel and the securement of supplies).
2. Physical assets (primarily property ownership and the maintenance thereof).
3. Organizational routines and tacit elements of the company, such as the culture and systems to gain both efficiency and effectiveness.
4. Codified assets, such as the brand and reservations system.

The responsibility for controlling these elements may lie with the international hotel chain or with contractual parties, depending on the operation mode used. The capital contribution for each of the above four dimensions may be categorized as controlling ownership (usually direct investment), shared ownership (usually equity joint ventures, though non-equity joint ventures also exist, such as the one between Meliá and Jin Jiang to comanage hotels in Europe and China), and no ownership (licensing, management contracts, turnkey operations, franchising, and leasing).

Operating modes can be combined. For instance, for the TRYP by Wyndham brand, Meliá owns some hotels, pays a franchise fee to Wyndham for using the brand name, and depends both on its own and Wyndham's reservation systems. In some other cases, it has no property ownership and is paid for managing the operation. The former Gran Meliá Shanghai is a joint venture between Chinese and Cuban organizations that, in turn, granted a management contract to Meliá (and subsequently to Kempinski) for day-to-day operations and signed a franchise contract to use its name and reservations services.

In partnering with other companies, regardless of operating mode, one increases the chance of developing competitors because partners may gain access to critical and core resources, especially knowledge. Thus, Meliá, like other companies, seeks ways to prevent partners' opportunistic behavior. Meliá's main control is over its codified resources, especially brands and reservations system, which are protected legally and which Meliá does not cede to other companies. Meliá has developed the recognition and reputation of its brands over decades, so new brands cannot easily overcome its advantage. The codified resources are tied closely as well to Meliá's tacit resources because the value of the brands is dependent on clients' hotel experience, and both physical resources and human behavior influence their opinions. Competitors can easily copy the physical resources if they have enough money. However, the human behavior is harder to emulate because learning must take place on a person-to-person basis (tacitly). Such learning in hotel operations is substantial—everything from greeting guests to making beds to assuring the flow of supplies—and affects efficiency and reputation. Over time, the actions become the essence of the company's culture.

MELIÁ'S EVOLVING OPERATING MODES

As we have seen, Meliá has made and continues to make use of various operating modes. However, it has not always had discretion in choosing a mode. When Gabriel Escarré established his first hotels, he had no track record to entice other hotel owners to pay him to manage their facilities or use his brand name and reservations system. He developed a positive reputation through his successful expansion over nearly 30 years in Spain before moving internationally.

Nevertheless, most of Meliá's early international growth resulted from acquisitions, such as its purchase of the Spanish chain TRYP that already had foreign operations and of Innside Inns in Germany. The success of these ventures built Meliá's reputation as a quality hotel operator, allowing it to keep expanding its hotel portfolio with shared or no capital investment, including growth in countries that place restrictions on foreign ownership.

Why grow? There are economies in handling larger hotel portfolios because of the clout and logistics in dealing with suppliers and the spreading of reservation and training system costs over more properties. There are also marketing advantages because potential customers are more familiar with the larger chains.

MELIÁ NOW AND IN THE FUTURE

Currently, Meliá Hotels International comprises strong brands such as Meliá, Gran Meliá, ME by Meliá, Paradisus, Innside by Meliá, TRYP by Wyndham, Sol Hotels, and Club Meliá. The maintenance of different brands is important because of existing brand recognition and value when Meliá made acquisitions. Nevertheless, Meliá is linking that recognition with its name (hence Innside by Meliá and Meliá White House). In fact, the company includes "Meliá" in almost all its brands because the name has long been associated with luxury hotels and thus brings a certain cachet to its hotels. Additional brand linkage comes from handling all of them in the same reservations system (currently 37 percent of its beds are sold directly to customers through the corporate website). Further, the different brands are aimed at different market niches.

Meliá suffered the effects of the global crisis of 2007. Growth based on acquisitions had increased Meliá's debt to more than €1 billion. In turn, it sold some of its flagship hotels, such as the Meliá Mexico Reforma to help reduce the debt. The company resumed its growth with 120 new hotels from 2012 to 2015.

In recent expansion, such as in Africa and the Middle East, Meliá has used alliances with local or international partners. Typically, the partners develop and own the properties while Meliá participates in the design and the subsequent management of the new hotels. In the United States, Meliá has signed long-term lease agreements with property owners that guarantee a source of income to the owners. In these agreements the developer assumes the risk associated with the ownership while Meliá assumes the operational risks.

In Venezuela, where Meliá has owned the Gran Meliá Caracas since 1997, the company announced a management contract agreement for five new hotels starting from 2016. Foreign companies in Venezuela face high inflation rates and frequent currency depreciations and devaluations (e.g., a devaluation of 88 percent in 2014). Currency conversion and repatriation is sometimes authorized only after strong devaluations. However, Meliá's international reservation system allows it to receive payments in hard currency. Meliá expects more international growth by entering additional countries and adding hotels in those where it now operates. It has also indicated an interest in linking with brands held by other companies, such as the Hard Rock Café and Flintstones. Its ambitions seem too great to do everything alone. And it might not want to, even if it

has the capital resources. For instance, it has so far been reluctant to make big commitments in countries, such as those in Southeast Asia, where it perceives the operating environment to be too different from its European (especially Spanish) experience. Thus, the use of non-equity operations is the crux of Meliá's future.

As part of its growth strategy in high-potential markets, Meliá has recently entered several African and Middle Eastern countries and has indicated an interest in others by focusing on both the leisure and business traveler. In Asia, it has doubled its presence in recent years and has announced agreements in new countries such as Mongolia and Myanmar. In Latin America, recent growth has been carried out through the TRYP by Wyndham brand in Brazil, which has wide experience in that market.

Its strategic plan for 2015–2017 calls for 99 percent of new projects outside Spain, 65 percent of which will be in emerging countries. However, so far, Meliá has no presence in Russia and India, nor do any other Spanish chains.

Fast-forwarding to nearly a year since Li Feng returned to Beijing, we find that she has worked almost nonstop and has taken no more trips. Contractually, physically, and emotionally she is ready for a vacation. She looks back at the hotel directory she brought from London and focuses on a picture showing a hotel half hidden among the foliage in front of a white sand beach and turquoise waters. "Who knows," she thought, "maybe I should forget my laptop and spend some time in such a beautiful place." ■

QUESTIONS

✪ **15-1.** After reading the chapter, explain the advantages for Meliá to own its hotels versus managing them for other organizations.

✪ **15-2.** After reading the chapter, discuss the advantages and risks for Meliá in its non-equity joint venture with Jin Jiang.

INTRODUCTION

To tap foreign market opportunities, firms may

- not be able to depend entirely on home-country production,
- rely on most types of operating modes,
- combine different operating modes for their foreign production.

As Figure 15.1 shows, companies must choose an international operating mode/form to fulfill their objectives and carry out their strategies. These are sometimes referred to as *entry strategies*, however, we prefer to refer to them as operating modes because companies frequently enter with one and change to another later on.[3] The preceding chapter examined exporting and importing—the preferred and most common modes of IB. Nevertheless, compelling factors can make these choices impractical. When companies depend, instead, on foreign production, they may own it in whole or in part, develop or acquire it, and/or use some type of collaborative agreement with another company.

Figure 15.2 shows the types of operating modes associated with each of these options, categorized by whether the company's IB activity involves foreign production and, if so, whether the company owns equity in the foreign production or depends on a collaborating company to own the equity. Experienced MNEs with a global orientation commonly use most of the operational modes, selecting them according to company capabilities, specific product, and foreign operating characteristics. The modes may also be combined, as with

FIGURE 15.1   Factors Affecting Operating Modes in IB

Companies may conduct IB operations independently or in collaboration with other companies. The choice will be determined both by external factors in the firm's operating environment and by internal factors that include its objectives, strategies, and means of operation (e.g., such modes of IB as exporting, franchising, etc.).

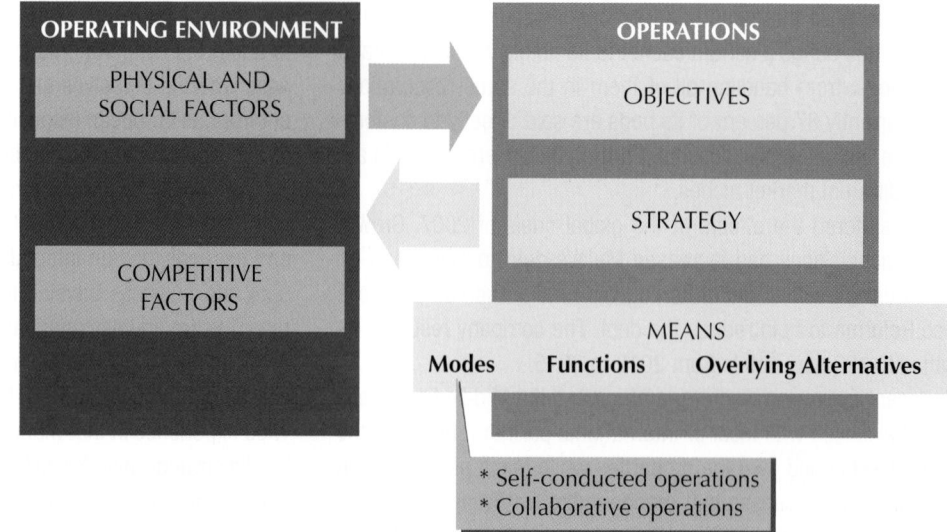

Meliá's contract to manage the Shanghai hotel owned by a joint venture between Chinese and Cuban organizations. This chapter first examines why exporting/importing may not suffice, thus leading to foreign production.

WHY EXPORT AND IMPORT MAY NOT SUFFICE

Companies may find more advantages to locate production in foreign countries than export to them. The advantages occur under six conditions:

1. When production abroad is cheaper than at home
2. When transportation costs are too high for moving goods or services internationally
3. When companies lack domestic capacity
4. When products and services need to be altered substantially to gain sufficient consumer demand abroad
5. When governments inhibit the import of foreign products
6. When buyers prefer products originating from a particular country

FIGURE 15.2   Foreign Expansions: Alternative Operating Modes

A firm may choose to operate globally either through equity arrangements (e.g., joint venture) or through non-equity arrangements (e.g., licensing). Exporting operations are conducted in the home country, while all other modes entail production in foreign locations. The modes listed in the shaded area are collaborative arrangements. Note that, in any given location, a firm can conduct operations in multiple modes.

*Joint ventures may also be non-equity, but equity joint ventures are by far the more common.

PRODUCTION OWNERSHIP	PRODUCTION LOCATION Home country	Foreign country
Equity arrangements	a. Exporting	a. Wholly owned operations b. Partially owned with remainder widely held c. Joint ventures* d. Equity alliances
Non-equity arrangements		a. Licensing b. Franchising c. Management contracts d. Turnkey operations

WHEN IT'S CHEAPER TO PRODUCE ABROAD

Although companies may offer products or services desired by consumers abroad, producing them in their home markets may be too expensive. For example, Turkey has been a growing market for automobiles. However, it is generally less expensive to produce the vehicles in Turkey than to export them there because the country's skilled laborers and sophisticated engineers cost less and are willing to work more days per year and longer hours per day than workers in the home countries. Thus, automakers (e.g., Toyota, Renault, Fiat Chrysler, Ford) and many of their parts suppliers have established Turkish production to serve that market.[4]

WHEN TRANSPORTATION COSTS TOO MUCH

CONCEPT CHECK

In Chapter 5 (page 184), we explain the concept of non-tradable goods—products and services that are seldom practical to export because of high transportation costs.

The cost of transportation added to production costs makes some products and services impractical to export. Generally, the more distant the market, the higher the transportation costs; the higher those are relative to production costs, the harder it is for companies to develop viable export markets. For instance, the international transportation cost for a soft drink is a high percentage of the manufacturing cost, so a sales price that includes both would be so high due to exporting that soft-drink companies would sell very little of the product.

However, products such as watches have low transportation costs relative to production costs, so watch manufacturers lose few sales through exporting. The result is that companies such as Universal Genève and Seiko export watches from Switzerland and Japan, respectively, into the markets where they sell them.

WHEN DOMESTIC CAPACITY ISN'T ENOUGH

Excess home-country capacity

- usually leads to exporting rather than direct investment,
- may lead to competitive exports because of declining unit costs.

A company with excess capacity may export effectively as long as the excess exists. In fact, its average cost of production per unit usually falls as it uses more of its capacity, such as by selling abroad, because of spreading fixed costs over more sales units. But this decrease continues only as long as there is unused capacity. Volkswagen, for instance, located its first plant to build the new Beetle at its Mexican facilities, which served global markets. When demand pushed that plant toward capacity, Volkswagen built a second plant in Europe to serve the markets there, thus freeing Mexican capacity to serve nearby markets while reducing transport costs for European sales.[5]

WHEN PRODUCTS AND SERVICES NEED ALTERING

Product alterations for foreign markets

- require additional investment,
- may lead to foreign production of the products.

Altering products to gain sufficient sales in a foreign market affects production costs by requiring firms to make an additional investment, such as adding an assembly line to put automobile steering wheels on the right as well as on the left. As long as they must make an investment to run an added assembly line, they may place it near the market they wish to serve.

The more a product must be altered for foreign markets, the more likely some production will shift abroad. Whirlpool finds that most U.S. washing machine demand is for top-loading, large-capacity washing machines using 110 electrical voltage, whereas most European demand is for front-loaders with less capacity using 220 volts.[6] Given the differences in preference, Whirlpool produces in both the United States and Europe.

WHEN TRADE RESTRICTIONS HINDER IMPORTS

CONCEPT CHECK

In Chapter 7 (pages 232–233), we explain why governments are reciprocally reducing trade restrictions. Nevertheless, exporters still face regulatory restrictions, of which some encourage them to produce abroad.

Despite worldwide reduction in overall import barriers, there are still many import restrictions. As a result, companies may find that they must produce in a foreign country if they are to sell there. This has been the case with many auto companies, which manufacture, or at least assemble, in India because it charges a high duty on fully built imported cars.[7]

Managers must view import barriers along with other factors, such as the market size of the country imposing the barriers and the scale of production technology. For example, import trade restrictions have been highly influential in enticing automobile producers to locate in Brazil's large market. Similar restrictions by Central American countries have been ineffective because of their small markets. However, Central American import barriers on products requiring lower amounts of capital investment for production, such as pharmaceuticals, have successfully enticed direct investment because these industries can be efficient with smaller-scale technologies and markets.

Regional or bilateral trade agreements may also attract direct investment because they create expanded markets that may justify scale economies.

WHEN COUNTRY OF ORIGIN BECOMES AN ISSUE

Consumers sometimes prefer goods produced in certain countries because of

- nationalism,
- a belief that these products are better,
- a fear that foreign-made goods may not be delivered on time.

Exporting to countries where consumers prefer to buy goods from certain countries (perhaps preferring domestic products because of nationalism) is difficult.[8] These consumers may push for country-of-origin labels, such as those for many Australian- and U.S.-made products.[9] Consumers may also believe goods from certain countries are superior, like German cars and Italian fashion.[10] They may also fear that service and replacement parts for imported products will be more difficult to obtain. Finally, companies using just-in-time manufacturing systems favor nearby suppliers who can deliver quickly and reliably. In any of these cases, companies may find advantages in placing production where their output will best be accepted.

WHY AND HOW DO COMPANIES MAKE WHOLLY OWNED FDI

In situations where exporting is not feasible, a company may choose to "go it alone" or contract another company to produce or provide services on its behalf. In this section, we discuss the reasons and methods for making FDI for the two arrangements in Figure 15.2 that do not require collaboration: wholly owned operations and partially owned with the remainder widely held.

REASONS FOR WHOLLY OWNED FOREIGN DIRECT INVESTMENT

Generally, the more ownership a company has, the greater its control over decisions. However, if equity shares are widely held, a company may be able to effectively control with even a minority interest. Nevertheless, governments often protect minority owners so that majority owners do not act against their interests; thus, companies may opt for 100 percent ownership if they want control. There are four primary explanations for companies to make a wholly owned FDI: *market failure, internalization theory, appropriability theory,* and *freedom to pursue global objectives.*

Market Failure   Collaboration is appealing as an entry strategy because it is a means whereby a firm may reduce its liability of foreignness. But this works only if management can find an associate knowledgeable about the host country at acceptable terms, which may be impossible since such companies may be inadequately equipped to deal efficiently with the entry company's technology.[11] Or, they may know too little about the entering company to entice them to consign sufficient resources to a collaboration. In these instances, companies must control foreign activities within their own management structures (internal hierarchies) rather than depending on the external market to do it for them.[12] Of course, the failure of the market to connect firms as collaborators will entice a company to enter with wholly owned operations only if it perceives having operating advantages to overcome its liability of foreignness.

Internalization   **Internalization** is control through self-handling of operations.[13] The concept comes from *transactions cost theory,* which holds that companies should seek the lower cost between self-handling of operations and contracting another party to do so for them. Self-handling may reduce costs for the following four reasons:

1. *Different operating units within the same company are likely to share a common corporate culture, which expedites communications.* Executives have concluded that a lack of trust, common terminology, and knowledge are major obstacles to successful collaboration.[14]

2. *The company can use its own managers, who understand and are committed to carrying out its objectives.* When GE acquired a controlling interest in the Hungarian company Tungsram, it was able to expedite control and changes because it put GE managers in key positions.[15]

3. *The company can avoid protracted negotiations with another company on such matters as partner responsibilities and how each will be compensated for contributions.* Negotiations for establishing a collaboration may go on for years, with no guarantee that an agreement will be reached.[16]

4. *The company can avoid possible enforcement problems.* Such companies as L'Occitane and Burberry's have had to fight licensed manufacturers from selling production overruns to non-prestige distributors, which cheapens their brand image.[17]

Appropriability   The idea of denying rivals access to resources is called the **appropriability theory**.[18] Companies are reluctant to transfer vital resources—capital, patents, trademarks, and management know-how—to another organization for fear of their competitive position being undermined. In fact, Chinese automakers that have collaborative arrangements with major global auto competitors make no secret of their desire to learn from their partners so as to become global competitors.[19] The fear of turning over know-how has led Germany's Faber-Castell to manufacture abroad only where it can own its factories.[20] This does not imply that the transfer of know-how to firms abroad is unnecessary. In fact, such transfer improves suppliers' efficiency, and companies use formal and informal mechanisms to speed and improve the comprehension of transferred knowledge.[21] Nevertheless, companies are less concerned about appropriability of non-strategic than of strategic resources. For instance, Coca-Cola collaborates with partners all over the world, but it steadfastly refuses to collaborate in concentrate production because its formula is too critical to the company's competitive viability.

> Companies may want control through FDI to lessen the chance of improving competitors' capabilities.

Freedom to Pursue a Global Strategy   A wholly owned foreign operation permits a company to more easily participate in a global strategy. For instance, a U.S. company owning 100 percent of its Brazilian operation might be able to take actions that, although suboptimizing Brazilian performance, could deal more effectively with competitors and customers globally, such as by decreasing prices to an industrial customer in Brazil to gain that customer's business in Germany. Or it might standardize its product to gain global cost savings even though this loses some sales in Brazil. But if the company shared ownership in Brazil, its partners would balk at such practices.

> **CONCEPT CHECK**
>
> In Chapter 12 (pages 365–367), we explain the difference between a global and a local responsiveness strategy.

ACQUISITION VERSUS GREENFIELD

Companies acquire FDI by transferring abroad financial and/or other tangible or intangible assets. They can either acquire an interest in an existing operation or make a greenfield (start-up) investment. The reasons for each are discussed below.

Acquisition   One reason for a company to invest abroad via acquisition is to obtain some vital resource that may otherwise be slow or difficult to secure.[22] Let's say a company acquires knowledgeable personnel that it cannot easily hire at a good price on its own[23]—or perhaps it could hire them, but lacks experience in managing them effectively. For instance, many Russian companies with good scientific inventions and innovative products have recently expanded internationally to acquire management with experience in transforming innovation to successful

> The advantages of acquiring an existing operation include
>
> - gaining vital resources that are otherwise hard to develop,
> - making financing easier at times,
> - adding no further capacity to the market,
> - avoiding start-up problems.

product sales.[24] Acquisitions allow a company to get not only labor and management, but also an existing organization with experience in coordinating functions such as product development and the subsequent marketing of the developed products.

In addition, a company may gain goodwill, brand identification, and access to distribution. Recently, much Chinese investment in the United States has been by acquisition, seemingly because of Chinese companies' desire to secure well-known brand names that will help them sell.[25]

There are also financial considerations. First, a company depending substantially on local financing rather than on transferring capital may find local capital suppliers more willing to put money into a known ongoing operation than to invest in a new facility owned by a less familiar foreign enterprise. Second, a company may be able to buy facilities, particularly those of a poorly performing operation, for less than the cost of new operations. For example, Brazil's José Batista Sobrinho (JBS), the world's largest meat company, bought U.S. companies Swift and Pilgrim's Pride at opportunistically low prices because they were in financial trouble.[26] Third, if a market does not justify added capacity, acquisition enables a firm to avoid the risk of depressed prices through overcapacity. Finally, by buying a company, an investor avoids start-up inefficiencies and gets an immediate cash flow rather than tying up funds during construction.

Making Greenfield Investments   Foreign companies may face local roadblocks to acquisitions. For example, local governments may want more competitors in the market because of fearing market dominance. In addition, a foreign company may find that development banks prefer to finance new operations because they create new jobs.

Acquisitions often don't succeed.[27] First, turning around a poorly performing operation is difficult because of potential personnel and labor relations problems, ill will toward its products and brands, and inefficient or poorly located facilities. Second, managers in the acquiring and acquired companies may not work well together because of different management styles and organizational cultures or because of conflicts over decision-making authority.[28] For instance, after acquiring IBM's PC division, Lenovo had to overcome cultural differences between its Chinese and U.S. managers (e.g., the former thought the Americans talked even when having nothing to say, and the latter disapproved of publicly shaming latecomers to meetings).[29] Intuition tells us that acquisitions in more culturally distant countries, such as in the Lenovo example, would perform less well than those in more culturally similar countries; however, some evidence shows the contrary. Evidently, there are performance gains from added diversity. In addition, acquiring companies take greater care in culturally distant countries to get a better match between organizational cultures, thus easing their integration into the corporate culture.[30]

Leasing   We saw in our opening case that Meliá operates extensively by leasing hotels. This mode is much like an acquisition, but one that forgoes the need to invest. While common in the hospitality industry, it is not common in others. Although companies in other industries might lease certain assets abroad—computers, vehicles, buildings—such arrangements are quite different from leasing an entire operating facility.

> **Companies may choose greenfield expansion if**
> - host governments discourage acquisitions,
> - it is easier to finance,
> - available acquisitions are performing poorly,
> - personnel in acquiring and acquired firms may not work well together.

WHY COMPANIES COLLABORATE

Companies collaborate (use alliances that are often called *strategic alliances*) abroad for much of the same reasons they do so domestically. However, there are some reasons specific to international operations. Figure 15.3 shows both the general and internationally specific reasons for collaborative arrangements.

GENERAL MOTIVES FOR COLLABORATIVE ARRANGEMENTS

Both domestically and internationally, companies collaborate to spread and reduce costs, enable them to specialize in their competencies, avoid competition, secure vertical and horizontal links, and gain knowledge.

FIGURE 15.3   Collaborative Arrangements and International Objectives

A company may enter into an international collaborative arrangement for the same reasons that it does so domestically (e.g., to spread costs). In other cases, it may enter into a collaborative arrangement to meet objectives that are specific to its foreign-expansion strategies (e.g., to diversify geographically).

OBJECTIVES OF INTERNATIONAL BUSINESS
- Sales expansion
- Resource acquisition
- Risk reduction

MOTIVES FOR COLLABORATIVE ARRANGEMENTS
General
- Spread and reduce costs
- Specialize in competencies
- Avoid or counter competition
- Secure vertical and horizontal links
- Learn from other companies

MOTIVES FOR COLLABORATIVE ARRANGEMENTS
Specific to International Business
- Gain location-specific assets
- Overcome legal constraints
- Diversify geographically
- Minimize exposure in risky environments

Sometimes it's cheaper to get another company to handle work, especially

- at small volume,
- when the other company has excess capacity.

To Spread and Reduce Costs   Producing and selling incur fixed costs. At a small volume of business, contracting to a specialist rather than self-handling may be cheaper because a specialist can spread the fixed costs to more than one company. If business increases enough, the contracting company may then be able to handle the business more cheaply itself.

A company can use excess production or sales capacity to handle the activities for a client company. This may lower average costs by covering fixed costs more fully, and it can prevent the client from having to incur fixed costs and longer delays for start-up and receipt of cash flows.

Companies may lack resources to "go it alone"—especially small and young ones.[31] By pooling efforts, they may be able to undertake activities that otherwise would be beyond their means. But large companies may also benefit when the cost of development and/or investment is very high. Disney's theme park in Hong Kong cost so much to develop that Disney and the Hong Kong government share ownership and expenses.[32]

One of the fastest collaborative growth areas has been for projects too large, both in capital and technical-resource needs, for any single firm to handle, such as new aircraft and communication systems. From such an arrangement's inception, different firms (sometimes from different countries) take on the cost and risk of developing different components. Then a lead company buys the components from the companies. A good example is the Boeing 787 aircraft, which involves companies from around the globe.

Granting asset rights to another company can yield income when the asset does not fit the yielding company's strategic priority based on its competencies.

To Specialize in Competencies   The **resource-based view** of the firm holds that each company has a unique combination of competencies. A company may improve its performance by concentrating on those activities that best fit its competencies, depending on other firms to supply it with products, services, or support activities in which it is less competent. However, a collaborative arrangement has a limited time frame, which may allow a company to exploit a particular product, asset, or technology at a later date if its core competencies change.

By banding together, companies may move faster, raise profits, and fight larger competitors.

To Avoid or Counter Competition   When markets are too small to accommodate many competitors, companies may band together so as not to compete. Companies may also combine resources to combat competitors (e.g., Sony and Samsung combined resources to move faster in the development of LCD technology).[33] Or they may simply collude to raise everyone's profits. For example, Canpotex, a group of Canadian companies accounting for more than a quarter of the world's potash market, joined together so as not to compete on export sales.[34] Only a few countries take substantial actions against the collusion of competitors.[35]

| Allying to gain vertical and horizontal links may enable companies to fill competency gaps, reduce costs, and deal more effectively with customers and suppliers.

To Secure Vertical and Horizontal Links   Vertical integration provides potential cost savings and supply assurances. However, companies may lack competences or resources necessary to own and manage the full value chain of activities, thus they ally themselves closely with other companies to handle their gaps. Horizontal links may provide economies of scope in distribution, such as by offering a full line of products, thereby increasing the sales per fixed cost of customer visits. For example, in many parts of the world Avon representatives market such products as books and crayons in addition to the company's cosmetics fare. An example of gains from both vertical and horizontal links involves a group of small and medium-sized Argentine furniture manufacturers. By allying horizontally, they pool resources to gain manufacturing efficiencies. In turn, their vertical alliance enables them to deal more effectively to sell abroad and to gain supplies.[36]

| A company can improve its competence by learning from partners.

To Gain Knowledge   Many companies pursue collaborative arrangements to learn about a partner's technology, operating methods, or home market so as to improve their competitiveness.[37] Sometimes each partner can learn from the other, a motive driving joint ventures between U.S. and European winemakers—such as the Opus One Winery owned by Constellation Brands' Robert Mondavi from the United States and Baron Philippe de Rothschild from France.[38]

INTERNATIONAL MOTIVES FOR COLLABORATIVE ARRANGEMENTS

In this section, we continue discussing why companies enter into collaborative arrangements, covering those reasons that apply only to international operations. Reasons include gaining location-specific assets, overcoming legal constraints, diversifying geographically, and minimizing risk exposure.

| Local companies may more easily access competitively important country-specific knowledge than foreign companies can.

To Gain Location-Specific Assets   Cultural, political, competitive, and economic differences among countries create barriers for firms operating abroad. Those ill-equipped to handle the differences may seek help through collaboration with local firms. When Walmart first entered the Japanese market on its own, it gave up after having disappointing sales. It has since returned with a Japanese partner, Seiyu, which is more familiar with Japanese tastes and rules for opening new stores.[39] In fact, most foreign companies in Japan need to collaborate with Japanese firms that can help in securing distribution and a competent workforce—two assets that are difficult for MNEs to gain on their own there.

Collaborations may also facilitate companies' learning about markets they enter. However, there is some danger that they assume wrongly that they can apply this learning effectively when entering subsequent countries—even those that appear to be similar to their previous entries.[40]

| Legal factors may
| • prohibit certain operating forms, such as wholly owned foreign facilities,
| • favor locally owned firms.

To Overcome Governmental Constraints   Recall that in centrally planned economies (e.g., China and Cuba) Meliá cannot own its hotels, so it must collaborate with local organizations. In addition, virtually all countries limit foreign ownership in some sectors. India, for example, sets maximum foreign percentage ownership in an array of industries.[41]

Government procurement policies also sometimes lead to collaboration because they favor bids that include national companies. Taiwan does this with purchases by the state enterprise monopoly, Taiwan Power (Tai Power).[42]

| Collaboration may hinder nonassociated companies from pirating an asset.

Protecting Assets   Many countries provide little protection for intellectual property rights such as trademarks, patents, and copyrights unless authorities are prodded consistently.

To prevent pirating of these proprietary assets, companies sometimes collaborate with local companies, which can more effectively monitor the local market and deal with authorities.

In addition, some countries provide protection only if the internationally registered asset is exploited locally within a specified period. If not, then whatever entity first does so gains the right to it. In some cases, local citizens, known as *trademark squatters*, register rights to the not-yet-exploited trademarks, then negotiate sales to the original owners when they do try to enter the market. One Russian company registered over 300 foreign trademarks, including Starbucks's trademark. Foreign companies then have to pay to regain their rights or go through lengthy and expensive court proceedings.[43] Or they enter under a different name. Burger King sells under the Hungry Jack brand in Australia for this reason.[44]

CONCEPT CHECK

In Chapter 13 (pages 398–399), we explained the differences between and reasons for pursuit of a geographic diversification versus concentration strategy.

Collaborative arrangements reduce risk by allowing for greater asset-spreading among countries.

To Diversify Geographically   For a company wishing to pursue a geographic diversification strategy, collaborative arrangements offer a faster initial means of entering multiple markets because other companies contribute resources. Arrangements will be less appealing for companies that have ample resources for such extension.

To Minimize Risk Exposure   One way to lessen a company's international political and economic risk is to minimize its assets located abroad, which may be possible through collaboration. Further, if the company's foreign assets are spread among countries, there is less chance that they will all encounter political adversity or economic downturns at the same time.

Local partners may also be effective at thwarting governmental takeover of assets. Further, partnerships with other foreign companies, especially from different countries, may inhibit host governments' takeovers because each can elicit support from its home government.

FORMS OF AND CHOICE OF COLLABORATIVE ARRANGEMENTS

CONCEPT CHECK

In Chapter 1 (page 60), we defined the different forms of collaborative arrangements.

Each operating mode brings both advantages and disadvantages.

Companies have a wider choice of operating mode when they hold unique and needed capabilities.

Terms differ for alliances depending on their purposes, whether they extend cooperation vertically or horizontally, and whether they involve competitors.

Now that we have discussed reasons for collaborating in IB, we shall first discuss some factors to consider when choosing among collaborative forms, also known as alliances. Then we shall describe each of the forms.

SOME CONSIDERATIONS IN CHOOSING A FORM

Trade-offs and Limitations   Recall from Figure 15.2 that operating modes for foreign operations differ in the amount of resources a company commits and the proportion of the resources it locates abroad. In this respect, keep in mind that there are *trade-offs*. A decision, let's say, to take no ownership abroad, such as by licensing another company to handle foreign production, may reduce exposure to political risk. However, learning about that environment will be slow, delaying (perhaps permanently) the ability to reap the full profits from producing and selling the product abroad.

Furthermore, a company may be limited in entering a market with its preferred operating mode. Governmental actions and potential partners have a great deal to say. However, if a company has a desired, unique, difficult-to-duplicate resource, it is in a much better position to choose its preferred operating form and to increase its compensation therein.

What's the Purpose?: Alliance Types   Alliances vary by objective and by place in the value chain. These variances have led to terms that describe different types. *Scale alliances* aim to provide efficiency for partners by pooling similar operations, such as airlines have done by combining their lounges. In a *link alliance,* firms use their partners' complementary resources to expand into a new business.[45] Nokia did this to develop and market cellular phones.[46] A *vertical alliance* connects firms in different links of their value chains, such as a food franchiser with a franchisee. A *horizontal alliance,* such as the Mexican joint venture between Mercedes and Infiniti, enables each partner to extend its product offerings (in this case, a new compact car) on the same level of the value chain.[47] **Coopetition**, such as the Mercedes-Infiniti example, refers to collaboration while competing (i.e., although these partners closely collaborate at every development stage, their end products are different and competitive with each other).[48]

Companies' experience and assets in a foreign country influence their choices of operating mode when introducing new products or businesses.	**Prior Company Expansion** Each time a company adds products or businesses that it wishes to internationalize, it must decide on an operating form. If it already has operations (especially wholly owned ones) in a foreign country, some of the advantages of collaboration are no longer as important. It knows how to operate within that country and may have excess plant or human resource capacity it can use for new production or sales. However, much depends on the compatibility between existing foreign operations and the new ones the company is planning abroad. The less similarity between them, the more that collaboration may be advantageous.
Collaboration in foreign operations implies less control and a sharing of profits.	**Compensation** Collaboration also implies sharing revenues and knowledge—an important consideration when profit potentials are high. How to divide revenue is not clear-cut because many variables influence the outcome. Certainly, the bargaining power of the collaborative partners is important in any agreement, but such factors as government mandates, partners' perception of risk, and competitive constraints are all important.[49] Further, the mode of collaboration guides normal practices. As we discuss the different modes, we will introduce some of these practices.

Point

Should Countries Limit Foreign Control of Key Industries?

Point   **Yes** I believe they should, because a key industry affects a very large segment of the economy by virtue of its size or influence on other sectors. I'm not talking about either foreign control of small investments or noncontrolling interest in large investments. If countries need foreign firms' resources—technology, capital, export markets, branded products, and so on—they can get them by requiring collaborations without ceding control to foreigners. In turn, the foreign companies can still achieve their objectives, such as gaining access to markets.

Of course each country should and does define key industries. For instance, the United States prohibits foreign control of television and radio stations and domestic transportation because of security concerns. Canada limits foreign control of sectors that are sensitive to maintenance of its culture. Chile prohibits foreign investment in its economically dominant copper industry because of negative experiences with past foreign control therein.

The rationale for protecting key industries is supported by history, which shows that home governments have used powerful companies to influence policies in the foreign countries where they operate. During colonial periods, firms such as Levant and the British East India Company often acted as the political arm of their home governments.

More recently, governments, especially the United States, have pressured their companies to leave certain areas and to prohibit their subsidiaries from doing business with certain countries, even though the prohibition is counter to the interests of the countries where the subsidiaries were located.[50]

At the same time, some companies are so powerful that they can influence their home-country governments to intercede on their behalf. Probably the most notorious example was United Fruit Company (UFC) in so-called banana republics, which persuaded the United States to overthrow governments to protect its investments. Miguel Angel Asturias, a Nobel laureate in literature, referred to UFC's head as the "Green Pope" who "lifts a finger and a ship starts or stops. He says a word and a republic is bought. He sneezes and a president ... falls.... He rubs his behind on a chair and a revolution breaks out."[51]

Whenever a company is controlled from abroad, its decisions can be made there. Such control means that corporate management abroad can decide such factors as personnel staffing, export prices, and the retention and payout of profits. These decisions might cause different rates of expansion in different countries as well as possible plant closings, sometimes with subsequent employment disruption.

Finally, by withholding resources or allowing strikes, MNEs may affect other local industries adversely. In essence, the MNE looks after its global interests, which may not coincide with what is best for an operation in a given country.

Should Countries Limit Foreign Control of Key Industries?

Counterpoint

No The passionate arguments against foreign control of key industries don't convince me that such control leads to corporate decisions that are any different from those local companies would make. Nor do they convince me that limits on foreign ownership are in the best interests of people in host countries.

Certainly, companies make strategic global decisions at headquarters, but typically they depend on a good deal of local advice beforehand. Further, MNEs staff their foreign subsidiaries mainly with nationals of the countries where they operate, and these nationals make most routine decisions.

Regardless of the decision-makers' or companies' nationalities, managers decide based on what they think is best for their firms' business, rather than based on some home-country or local socioeconomic agenda. At the same time, their decisions have to adhere to local laws and consider the views of their local stakeholders. Of course, MNEs sometimes make locally unpopular decisions, but so do local companies. In the meantime, governments can and do enact laws that apply to both local and international companies, and these laws can ensure that companies act in the so-called local interest.

Although preventing foreign control of key industries may be well intentioned, the resultant local control may lead to the protection of inefficient performance. Further, the key-industry argument appeals to emotions rather than reason. That's why arguments in the United States for security make little sense on close examination. Although foreign propaganda through foreign ownership of radio and television stations is the rationale

Counterpoint

for ownership restrictions, there are no such restrictions on foreign ownership of U.S. newspapers or on material appearing on the Internet. (Is this because people who read the news are presumed to be less swayed by propaganda?) The protection of U.S. domestic transportation for security reasons is a sham, just to protect the shipbuilding industry and maritime employees. For instance, U.S. merchant flagships must employ only U.S. citizens as crews because of ships' vulnerability to bombs in U.S. waters, but foreign flag carriers regularly use U.S. ports, while foreigners can join the U.S. Navy.

The banana-republic arguments are outdated and go back to **dependencia theory**, which holds that emerging economies have practically no power in their dealings with MNEs.[52] More recent **bargaining school theory** states that the terms of a foreign investor's operations depend on how much the investor and host country need each other.[53] In effect, companies need countries because of their markets and resources, while countries need MNEs because of their technology, capital, access to foreign markets, and expertise. Through a bargaining process, they come to an agreement or contract that stipulates what the MNE can and cannot do.

I completely disagree that either countries or companies can necessarily gain the same through collaborative agreements as through FDI. Although collaborative agreements are often preferable, there are company and country advantages from foreign-controlled operations. For example, with wholly owned operations, companies are less concerned about developing competitors, so they are more willing to transfer essential and valuable technology abroad.

LICENSING

> Licensing agreements may be
> - exclusive or nonexclusive,
> - used for patents, copyrights, trademarks, and other intangible property.

The rights for use of intangible property may be for an *exclusive license* (the licensor can give rights to no other company for the specified geographic area for a specified period of time) or a nonexclusive one.

The U.S. Internal Revenue Service classifies intangible property into five categories:

1. Patents, inventions, formulas, processes, designs, patterns
2. Copyrights for literary, musical, or artistic compositions
3. Trademarks, trade names, brand names
4. Franchises, licenses, contracts
5. Methods, programs, procedures, systems

Usually, the licensor is obliged to furnish sufficient information and assistance, and the licensee is obliged to exploit the rights effectively and pay compensation to the licensor.

Major Motives for Licensing A product or process may affect only part of a company's total business, and then only for a limited time. In such a situation, the company may foresee

> Licensing often has an economic motive, such as to gain faster start-up, lower costs, or access to additional resources.

insufficient sales to warrant establishing or continuing its own manufacturing and sales facilities. Meanwhile, a licensee may be able to produce and sell at a low cost and within a short start-up time. In turn, the licensee's cost may be less than if it developed the product or process on its own.

For industries in which technological changes are frequent and affect many products, companies in various countries often exchange technology or other intangible property rather than compete with each other on every product in every market—an arrangement known as **cross-licensing**. An example is Google (U.S.) and Samsung (Korea) entering a cross-licensing agreement for access to each other's current and future patents.[54]

Payment Considerations   The amount and type of payment for licensing arrangements vary, as each contract is negotiated on its own merits. For instance, the value to the licensee will be greater if potential sales are high. Potential sales depend, in turn, on such factors as the size of the sales territory and the longevity of the asset's market value.

Putting a Price on Intangible Assets   Valuing partners' contributions and rewards is complex and negotiable. Companies commonly agree on a "front-end" payment to cover technology transfer costs. Licensors of technology do this because there is usually more involved than simply transferring *explicit* knowledge, such as through publications and reports. The move requires the transfer of *tacit* knowledge, such as through engineering, consultation, and adaptation. To understand the difference between the two, think of giving a novice cook only a recipe for a chicken pot pie (explicit knowledge) versus going with the novice cook to choose a chicken, feel and smell produce in the market, and work together on the manual chores, such as chopping ingredients and rolling out dough (tacit knowledge). Of course, the license of some assets, such as copyrights or brand names, has much lower transfer costs.

Intangible assets may be old or new, obsolete or still in use in the home market when a company licenses them. Many companies transfer rights to assets at an early or even a developmental stage so products hit different markets simultaneously. This is important when selling to the same industrial customers in different countries and when global advertising campaigns can be effective. On one hand, a licensee may be willing to pay more for a new intangible asset because it may have a longer useful life. On the other hand, a licensee may be willing to pay less for a newer one because of its untested market value.

> Licensing to subsidiaries is common because of parent and subsidiary legal separation and the potential effect on taxes.

Licensing to Subsidiaries   Although we think of licensing among unassociated companies, it is also common between parents and their foreign-owned companies. One reason is that operations in a foreign country, even if 100 percent owned by the parent, are usually subsidiaries, which are legally separate companies. As such, taxes may differ depending on whether funds transferred to the parent are in the form of dividends or royalties. When a company owns less than 100 percent, a separate licensing arrangement also helps compensate the licensor for contributions beyond the mere investment in capital and managerial resources.

FRANCHISING

In franchising, a specialized form of licensing, the parties act almost as a vertically integrated company because they are interdependent and each creates part of the product or service that ultimately reaches the consumer.

> Franchising includes providing an intangible asset (usually a trademark) and a continual infusion of necessary assets.

Today, franchising is mostly associated with U.S. fast-food operations, although many international franchisors are from other countries and in many other sectors, such as Meliá's hotel franchises discussed in the opening case. To illustrate how diverse franchising can be, consider the Danish company Cryos International, which franchises sperm banks in about 40 countries.[55]

> Many types of products, companies, and countries participate in franchising.

Franchisors once depended on trade shows and costly visits to foreign countries to promote their expansion. While such trade shows are still important, especially for young franchising operations that are not well-known, the Internet has given companies another channel to exchange information.

Franchise Organization A franchisor may deal directly with individual franchisees abroad or set up a *master franchise* that has rights to open outlets on its own or to develop subfranchisees in the country or region. Subfranchisees pay royalties to the master franchisee, which then remits some predetermined percentage to the franchisor. Companies are most apt to use a master franchise system when they are not confident about evaluating potential individual franchisees and when overseeing and controlling them directly would be too expensive.[56] Picking good franchisees is, of course, essential for success.[57]

Operational Modifications Franchising success generally depends as well on product and service standardization, high identification through promotion, and effective cost controls. The latter two are pretty straightforward, but transferring the home country's product and service, especially for food franchising, is often difficult, first, because of local supplies. McDonald's, for instance, had to build a plant to make hamburger buns in the United Kingdom, while in Thailand it had to help farmers develop potato production.[58] Second, foreign country taste preferences may differ from those in the home country—even within regions of large countries. In China, for example, Yum! Brands offers regionally different food in its KFC and Pizza Hut outlets.[59] However, the more adjustments made for the host consumers' different tastes, the less a franchisor has to offer a potential franchisee.

> Franchisors face a dilemma:
> - Inadequacy of local supplies may hamper global product uniformity.
> - The more global standardization, the less acceptance in the foreign country.
> - The more adjustment to the foreign country, the less the franchisor is needed.

MANAGEMENT CONTRACTS

An organization may pay for managerial assistance under a management contract when it believes another can manage its operation more efficiently than it can, usually because the contractor has industry-specific capabilities. British Airport Authority (BAA) has these for airport administration, and it manages some airports in the United States, Italy, and Australia.[60]

Such contracts are common when host governments want foreign expertise, but do not want foreign ownership. In turn, the management company receives income without having to make a capital investment. Contracts are also popular in the hotel industry. (Recall the Meliá case.) In essence, host-country real estate owners may have good hotel locations, but know little about running a hotel. At the same time, many hotel chains have been shying away from property ownership abroad because of the perceived risk.[61]

> Foreign management contracts are used primarily when the foreign company can manage better than the owners.

TURNKEY OPERATIONS

Companies handling turnkey operations are usually industrial-equipment manufacturers, construction companies, or consulting firms. Manufacturers also sometimes provide turnkey services when they are disallowed to invest. The customer for a turnkey operation is often a governmental agency. Recently, most large projects have been in those developing countries that are moving rapidly toward infrastructure development and industrialization.

Contracting to Scale One characteristic setting turnkey business apart from most other IB operations is the size of most contracts, frequently for billions of dollars. This means that a few very large companies—such as Vinci (France), Bechtel (U.S.), and Hochtief (Germany)—account for a significant market share. Recently, several Chinese firms have become major players[62] Some projects are so large that they are handled by a consortium of turnkey operators, such as the additional wider channel for the Panama Canal, led by Spain's Sacyr Vallehermoso. (The following photo shows that channel's construction.) Often, smaller firms serve either as subcontractors for primary turnkey suppliers or specialize in a particular sector, such as the handling of hazardous waste.

> Turnkey operations are
> - most commonly performed by industrial-equipment, construction, and consulting companies,
> - often performed for a governmental agency.

> Turnkey operations generally differ from other IB collaborations because they
> - may be so large,
> - depend on top-level governmental contacts,
> - are often in very remote areas.

Making Contacts The nature of these contracts places importance on hiring executives with top-level governmental contacts abroad, as well as on ceremony and building goodwill, such as opening a facility on a country's national holiday or getting a head of state to inaugurate a facility. Although public relations is important to gain contracts, other factors—price,

Construction on Panama's wider canal channel. ▶

Source: Alejandro Bolivar/EPA/Newscom

export financing, managerial and technological quality, experience, reputation, and so on—are necessary to sell contracts of such magnitude.

Marshaling Resources   Many turnkey contracts are in remote areas, necessitating massive housing construction and importation of personnel. Projects may involve building an entire infrastructure under the most adverse conditions, such as Bechtel's complex for Minera Escondida high in the Andes, so turnkey operators must have expertise in hiring people willing to work in remote areas for extended periods and in transporting and using supplies under very difficult conditions.

If a company has a unique capability, such as the latest refining technology, it will have little competition. As the production process becomes known, however, competition increases. Companies from developed countries have moved largely toward projects involving high technology, whereas those from such countries as China, India, Korea, and Turkey can compete better for conventional projects requiring low labor costs. The Chinese companies, China State Construction Engineering and Shanghai Construction Group, have worked on subway systems in Iran and Saudi Arabia, a railway line in Nigeria, a tourist complex in the Bahamas, an oil pipeline in Sudan, and office buildings in the United States.

JOINT VENTURES (JVs)

Although usually thought of as 50/50 companies, JVs may nonetheless involve more than two companies and ones in which a partner owns more than 50 percent. For example, Flagship Ventures (U.S.), AstraZeneca (U.K.-Sweden), Nestlé Health Science (Switzerland), and Bayer CropScience (Germany) have joined together to develop health-care innovations.[63] When more than two organizations participate, the venture is sometimes called a **consortium**. JVs may also involve a partner owning over 50 percent, such as ANA's ownership of 67 percent in AirAsia Japan.[64]

Joint venture ownership may vary by type of participants and the portion of ownership they hold.

Possible Combinations   Examples of the many combinations of JV partnerships include:

- Two companies from the same country joining together in a foreign market (e.g., NEC and Mitsubishi [Japan] in the United Kingdom)
- A foreign company joining with a local company (e.g., Barrick [Canada] and Zijin Mining Group in China)
- Companies from two or more countries establishing a joint venture in a third country (e.g., Mercedes-Benz [Germany] and Nissan [Japan] in Mexico)

FIGURE 15.4 Collaborative Strategy and Complexity of Control

The more equity a firm puts into a collaborative arrangement, coupled with the fewer partners it takes on, the more control it will have over the foreign operations conducted under the arrangement. Note that non-equity arrangements typically entail at least one and often several partners.

Source: Based on Shaker Zahra and Galal Elhagrasey, "Strategic Management of International Joint Ventures," *European Management Journal* 12:1 (March 1994): 83–93. Reprinted with permission of Elsevier.

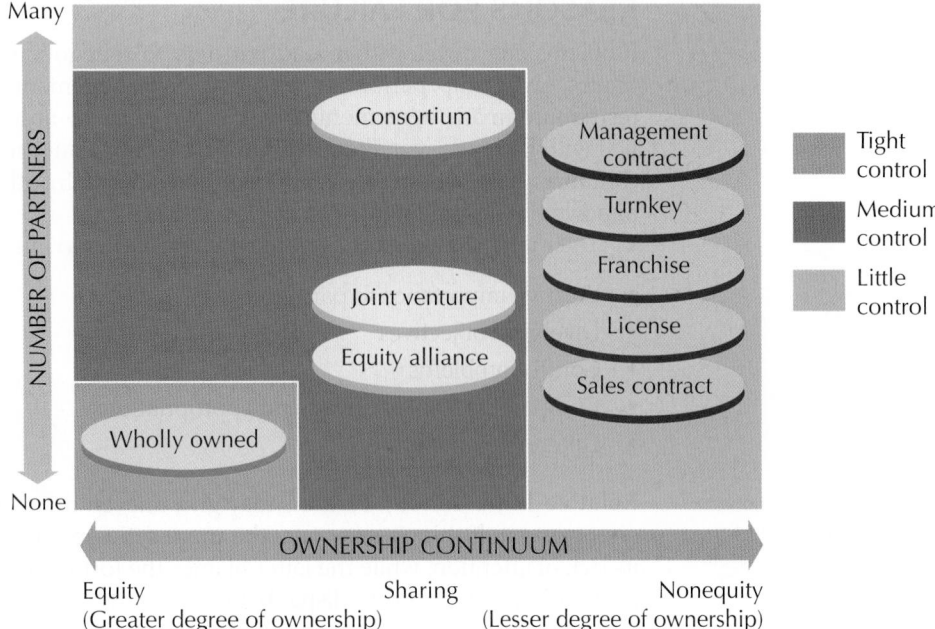

- A private company and a local government forming a joint venture, or *mixed venture* (e.g., Mitsubishi [Japan] with the government-owned Exportadora de Sal in Mexico)
- A private company joining a government-owned company in a third country (e.g., BP Amoco [private British-U.S.] and Eni [government-owned Italian] in Egypt)

The more companies in the JV or any alliance, the more complex its management becomes. Development of the Boeing 787 (the Dreamliner) and the Airbus A380 were joint efforts among numerous companies from several countries.[65] The projects were difficult to control, and a delay or performance hitch by any participating company delayed the others and caused project problems. Figure 15.4 shows that as a company increases the number of partners and decreases its portion of equity in a foreign operation, its ability to control that operation decreases.

EQUITY ALLIANCES

Equity alliances help solidify collaboration.

An **equity alliance** is a collaborative arrangement in which at least one of the companies takes an ownership position (almost always minority) in the other(s). For instance, the Port of Antwerp (Belgium) took a minority position in Essar Ports (India) when the two signed a long-term alliance to mutually improve quality and productivity.[66] In some cases, each party takes an ownership in the other, such as occurred with Panama-based Copa and Colombia-based AeroRepublic (airlines).[67]

The purpose of the equity ownership is to solidify a collaborating contract, such as a supplier–buyer contract, so that it is more difficult to break—particularly if the ownership is large enough for the investing company to secure a board membership.

WHY COLLABORATIVE ARRANGEMENTS FAIL OR SUCCEED

All collaborative arrangement parties must be satisfied with performance; otherwise, the arrangement may fail.

REASONS FOR FAILURE

Problems can develop that lead partners to renegotiate in terms of objectives, responsibilities, ownership, performance criteria, or management structure. Despite renegotiation to restructure, many agreements break down because at least one partner becomes dissatisfied with the endeavor. Frequently, a partner buys out the other's interest and the operation continues as a wholly owned foreign subsidiary. In other breakups, companies agree to dissolve the arrangement.

The major strains on the arrangements are due to five factors:

- Relative importance to partners
- Divergent objectives
- Control problems
- Comparative contributions and appropriations
- Differences in culture

Partners' uneven attention to a collaborative arrangement is often due to their disparate sizes.

Relative Importance   Partners may give uneven management attention to a collaborative arrangement. If things go wrong, the more active partner blames the less active partner for its lack of attention, while the latter blames the former for making poor decisions. Difference in attention may be due to disparity in the partners' sizes. For example, a smaller partner may take more interest in the venture because it is using a larger portion of its resources therein.

Further, the smaller firm may be disadvantaged in fighting its bigger partner legally. For example, Igen, a small U.S. firm, licensed its technology to Boehringer Mannheim of Germany, whose sales were more than 100 times greater. When the two companies disagreed over royalty payments, Igen fought four years and spent the equivalent of one year's sales on legal fees before winning a settlement.[68] This example is unusual, however, because few small firms can or will fight a much larger company so effectively.

As partners' capabilities and strategies evolve, their collaborative objectives may change.

Divergent Objectives   Partners' initial complementary objectives may evolve differently as a result of competitive forces and product dynamics. Thus, a partner may no longer perceive collaboration to be in its best interest. For instance, IBM partnered with Toshiba, but later it shifted its product line. At that point, it required a type of monitor with which Toshiba lacked expertise.[69] Further, one partner may want to reinvest earnings for growth while the other wants to receive dividends. Or one partner may want to expand the product line and sales territory while the other may see this as competition with its wholly owned operations (a point of disagreement between BP and its Russian partner, TNK.)[70] If one partner wants to sell or buy from the venture, the other may disagree with the price.

"Who's in charge?" plagues collaboration despite all parties being held responsible.

Questions of Control   Sharing assets with another company may generate confusion over control. Such confusion is rife with gray areas and may cause anxiety among employees. In a proposed JV between Merrill Lynch and UFJ, a Japanese senior manager queried, "Who is going to be in charge—a Japanese, an American, or both?"[71] Moreover, when companies license their logos and trademarks for use on products they do not make, they may lack the ability to discern and control quality. Pierre Cardin's licensing of its label for hundreds of products—from clothing to clocks to toilets—led to some poor-quality goods that hurt the image of the high-quality ones.[72]

In collaborative arrangements, even though control is ceded to one of the partners, both may be held responsible for problems. In a joint venture to make baby formula between the Israeli company Remedia and the German firm Humana Milchunion, Humana Milchunion's removal of Vitamin B1 from the formula concentrate led to the deaths of three infants.[73] Remedia was jointly responsible even though it had not been notified of the removal.

If one partner perceives that the other is contributing too little or taking out too much, the collaboration may weaken.

Comparative Contributions and Appropriations   Partners' relative capabilities may change, thus one partner may no longer contribute as much as the other or as much as was expected initially. In addition, one partner may suspect that the other is taking more from the operation than it is (particularly knowledge-based assets or key JV personnel).

To counteract this appropriability, the suspicious firm may withhold information, eventually weakening the operation. In fact, there are many examples of companies "going it alone" after they no longer needed their partners—particularly if the purpose of the collaboration was to gain knowledge.

Culture Clashes   Both national and company cultural differences can affect the relationship between partners.

Differences in Country Cultures   Managers and companies are affected by their national cultures, and collaborative arrangements bring them directly together. For instance, preferences may vary in the method, timing, and frequency with which they report on performance and whether they evaluate primarily on the operations' effect on shareholders or on stakeholders in general.[74] These differences may mean that one partner is satisfied while the other is not. Such a clash led to the dissolution of a joint venture between Danone and its Chinese government-owned partner because the latter put employment maximization ahead of efficiencies and profits.[75]

Trust is another factor. There are national differences that influence interactions with foreign partners. In fact, some companies don't like to collaborate with those of very different cultures.[76] Nevertheless, JVs from culturally distant countries can thrive when partners learn to deal with each other's differences.[77]

Differences in Company Cultures   Similar company cultures aid companies' ability to communicate and transfer knowledge to each other, whereas collaborations can experience problems when these cultures differ.[78] For example, the joint venture between Japan's ANA and Malaysia's AirAsia broke up as the former wished to emphasize its culture of "meticulous service," whereas the latter had a culture of cutting costs.[79] One partner may be accustomed to internal managerial promotions while the other opens its searches to outsiders. One may use a participatory management style and the other an authoritarian style. One may be entrepreneurial, the other risk-averse. This is why many companies delay JV collaboration until they have had long-term positive experiences with each other, such as through distributorship or licensing arrangements which involve lower levels of commitment. In fact, there is evidence that a gradual increase in commitment, such as developing an alliance with a company before acquiring it, is a means of improving performance.[80] Of course, as with marriage, a good prior relationship between two companies does not guarantee a good match in a joint venture.[81]

HELPING COLLABORATIVE OPERATIONS SUCCEED

Despite our discussion on problems and failures of collaborative operations, we do not mean to imply that there are no success stories. There are. The JV between Xerox (U.S.) and Rank (U.K.) is a case in point: not only has it performed well for a long period, it even has a JV in Japan with Fuji Photo, which has also performed well.

Aside from awareness of and adjustment to the pitfalls we have discussed, the following considerations help assure success when choosing among and managing operating forms:

- Fitting modes to country differences
- Finding and evaluating partners
- Negotiating agreements: The question of secrecy
- Controlling through contracts and trust
- Evaluating continually
- Adjusting the internal organization

Fitting Modes to Country Differences   Country conditions influence the operating forms that best suit companies' IB operations. To begin with, regulations (such as prohibitions on 100 percent foreign-owned FDI) and national conditions (such as political risk)

Margin notes:

Differences in country and company cultures may cause one partner to be satisfied and the other dissatisfied.

CONCEPT CHECK

In Chapter 2 (page 85), we discussed differences in trust among cultures and explained that in high trust cultures, the cost of doing business tends to be lower.

Companies should make their highest commitments in terms of operating modes where markets are most attractive and best fit their competences and strategies.

influence what companies can't and won't do in a foreign country. Concomitantly, countries offer different opportunities that mesh differently with companies' capabilities and strategies. Thus, choosing the best operating form for each country helps companies succeed.

A company should ordinarily commit more of its IB resources to those markets that are most attractive and fit best with its strategies and competence. The choice of operating mode directly affects this resource allocation inasmuch as different modes commit different levels of resources and different portions of those resources abroad. Figure 15.5 illustrates a matrix relating country attractiveness, a company's competitive strength per country, and operating forms. Step one for a company is to evaluate countries' general attractiveness (high, medium, or low) irrespective of the company's fit with that country. Step 2 is to assess the company's competitive strength to fulfill its objectives (high, medium, or low) for each of the countries. By using results from the two steps to plot each country within the six sectors of the matrix, one has a visual description of preferred mode per country.

Although such a matrix may serve to guide decision-making, managers must use it with caution. First, separating the attractiveness of a country from a company's position is often difficult; the country may seem attractive because it fits with the company. Second, some of the recommended actions take a defeatist attitude toward competitive capability. Many companies have built competitive strength in markets where they initially were weak competitively.

Finding and Evaluating Potential Partners   Contracting with a satisfactory partner is significant for success in collaborative agreements. Managers can identify potential partners by monitoring journals, attending technical conferences, developing links with academic institutions—even through social acquaintances.[82]

Whether seeking a partner or reacting to a partnership request, a company must evaluate the potential partner's resources, motivation, and compatibility. The potential partner's proven ability to handle similar types of collaboration is a key professional qualification. A good track record may indicate trustworthiness that could negate the need for expensive control mechanisms to carry out interests.

CONCEPT CHECK

In Chapter 13 (pages 392–394), we discussed how risk and opportunity differ among countries and how (pages 397–398) the choice of operating mode may reduce a company's risk.

Partner pairing should depend on mutual assessment of each other's resources, motivation, and compatibility.

FIGURE 15.5   Country Attractiveness/Company Strength Matrix

In a given scenario, a country in the upper left-hand corner may be the most attractive place for a company to locate operations. Why? Because its market is well suited to the company's greatest competitive strength and thus to its highest level of commitment (e.g., establishing a wholly owned subsidiary). A country in the upper right-hand corner also boasts an attractive market but poses a problem for a company whose competitive strengths don't quite match the opportunity (perhaps it has no experience in this particular market). It needn't forgo the opportunity, but it will probably prefer a joint venture or some other form of collaborative operation. Finally, note that because everything is subject to change—both a company's capabilities and the features of a country's market—firms try to be dynamic in their approach to potential operating modes.

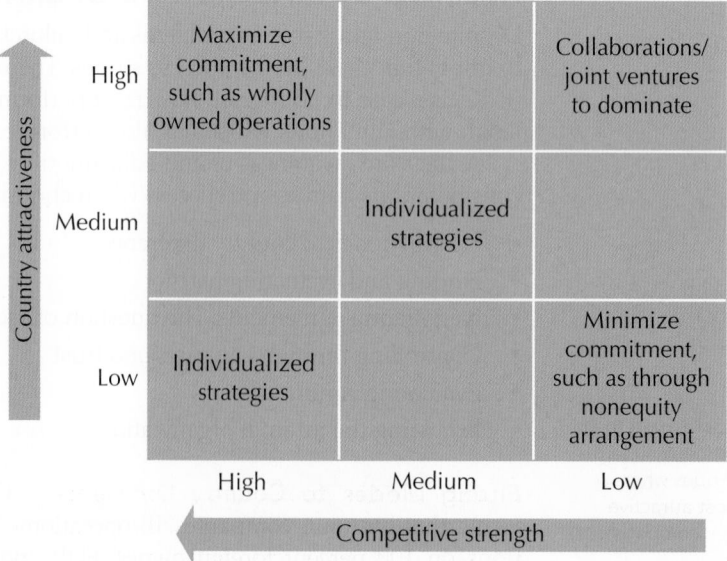

At the same time that you are looking for and evaluating potential partners, those potential partners are doing the same. You can boost your visibility and partnership potential through trade fair attendance, brochures, websites, and contacts in the potential collaboration locale. If you are new to foreign operations and to collaboration, you have no track record and you may have to negotiate harder and make more concessions.

Negotiating the Arrangement: The Question of Secrecy Numerous collaborative arrangements involve technology transfers. Because the value of many technologies would diminish if they were widely used or understood, technology owners have historically insisted on including contract provisions whereby recipients will not divulge such information. Some have also held onto the ownership and production of specific components so recipients would not have full knowledge of the product or the capability to produce an exact copy.

Often companies want to sell techniques they have not yet completed, much less commercialized. A buyer is reluctant to buy what it has not seen, but a seller that shows the work in process to the potential buyer risks divulging the technology. For these and other reasons, it is common to set up pre-arrangement agreements that protect all parties.

A controversial negotiation area is the secrecy surrounding the financial terms of arrangements. In some countries, for example, licensing contracts must be approved by governmental agencies, which consult their counterparts in other countries about similar agreements in order to improve their negotiating position. Many MNEs object, believing that contract terms between two companies are proprietary information with competitive importance, and market conditions usually dictate the need for very different terms in different countries.

Controlling Through Contracts and Trust Contracts with other companies entail some loss of control over the asset transferred. This creates two concerns—the partner's performance competency and the partner's integrity so as not to act opportunistically.[83] A host of potential problems must be settled as well as possible by setting mutual goals and spelling out all expectations in the contract, but not everything can be included in a contract. The parties need to develop sufficient rapport so that common sense also plays a part in running the operation.[84] Once operating, partners can also build trust through actions.[85] At the same time, national culture influences how much a partner wants to cover in a contract. Thus, if parties from cultures with similar levels of trust come together, they can more likely agree on what must be incorporated in detailed contractual arrangements and what must be left to trust.[86]

Partnering with a firm that highly values its reputation is probably a plus as well, inasmuch as it may prefer to settle differences quietly rather than having them exposed in the press. Frank communications may help determine potential partners' underlying expectations, which may otherwise come as a surprise. One study of local firms in China and Russia discovered that they had expected their foreign partners to deal much more with the Chinese and Russian governments (such as to alleviate bribery payments) than the foreign partners realized or actually did.[87]

Although contracts cannot cover everything, their provisions should at least address the following issues:

- Will the agreement be terminated if the parties don't adhere to the directives?
- What methods will be used to test for quality?
- What geographic limitations should be placed on an asset's use?
- Which company will manage which parts of the operation outlined in the agreement?
- What will be each company's future commitments?
- How will each company buy from, sell to, or otherwise use assets that result from the collaborative arrangement?
- How will revenues be divided?

Evaluating Continually Contracting with a capable and compatible partner is necessary but insufficient to ensure success. An agreement, once operational, must be run effectively. Management should estimate potential sales and costs, determine whether the arrangement

---

Margin notes (left column):

In technology agreements,

- sellers do not want to give information before assuring an agreement can be reached,
- buyers want to evaluate information before committing to an agreement,
- the contract terms may be considered proprietary.

Although both trust and contracts have control limitations, there are provisions that should be included in any collaborative agreement.

When collaborating with another company, managers must

- continue to monitor performance,
- assess whether to change the form of operations,
- develop competency in managing a portfolio of collaborations.

is meeting quality standards, and assess servicing requirements to check whether goals are being met and whether one's partners are doing an adequate job. In this respect, the relationship among partners may evolve positively or negatively, thus necessitating operational changes or even the termination of an agreement.

In addition to continually assessing partners' performance, a company must periodically assess the need for change in the type of collaboration, such as whether to replace a licensing agreement with a joint venture. Such modifications may be warranted because of companies' changes in resources and strategies and because of external conditions such as host-country political and economic conditions.

Adjusting Within the Internal Organization   As companies enter into and grow their international collaborative arrangements, they gain competencies. As they change operating modes, they encounter pressures necessitating organizational adjustments. These include organizational application of what they have learned and the need to alter group and individual evaluations as operating forms change.

The evolution to a different operating mode may
- *be the result of experience,*
- *create organizational tensions.*

Learning and Its Applications   Evidence suggests that companies' collaborative performance improves with experience. However, improvement is most associated with similar types of collaborations, such as applying what a firm has learned from JV operations in one country to JVs in another country.[88] With experience, companies learn to choose partners better and to improve synergies with them. Thus, as a company's number of collaborations grows, it should work toward developing competency in managing the portfolio of arrangements so that it applies what it learns in one situation to others.[89] Nevertheless, companies should take into consideration that effective alliance management has been undergoing significant changes, thus they may not necessarily replicate their past successes.[90]

Pressures from Switching Collaborative Modes   Changes in operating mode, such as from exporting to foreign production to serve a market, cause some individuals to gain and others to lose responsibilities. For example, the size of domestic marketing and manufacturing divisions may contract, thus disadvantaging people who lost responsibilities if bonuses and promotions are based largely on their sales or profits. Given that lower performance is due to decisions outside their control, companies will need to revise performance evaluations.

Looking to the Future
Growth in Project Size and Complexity

More than a half century ago, John Kenneth Galbraith wrote that the era of cheap invention was over "because development is costly, it follows that it can be carried out only by a firm that has the resources associated with considerable size."[91] The statement seems prophetic in terms of the estimated dollars needed to bring a new commercial aircraft to market, eliminate death from diseases, develop defenses against unfriendly countries and terrorists, guard against cyberspace intrusions, and develop means to counteract adverse effects of climate change. However, Galbraith's conclusion overlooks several factors.

First, can firms reach the "considerable size" to solve the problems just mentioned? This is doubtful. Some of the largest companies in the world are in the

auto industry, but they are finding that they have to work with each other (e.g., Toyota with BMW, to meet ever-stricter rules on carbon-dioxide emissions).[92] Further, governments constrain mergers and acquisitions because of antitrust concerns, thus inhibiting companies' growth.

Second, can companies internalize the breadth of technology necessary to solve these big problems? This is also doubtful. The recent mantra in strategy is to do what you do best and outsource the rest. Thus large companies' breadth of technology has been receding rather than growing. Consequently, we are apt to see more horizontal and vertical linkages among firms from many industries in many countries. On the downside, some evidence indicates that collaborations slow the speed of innovation because firms consider internalization and appropriation factors.[93]

If we see greater horizontal and vertical linkages, will these linkages be traditional? Some will probably not be. For instance, in recent years, some of the fastest-growing start-ups, such as Uber and Airbnb, have been companies that link with outsiders who provide most of the investment. Thus, collaboration will probably increase, but it will involve new forms and may not attack the big developments that Galbraith envisioned.

At the same time, most product development is much more modest than required to unravel the gigantic projects. Concomitantly, although business strategists have advised companies for some time to specialize on what they do best (which fosters collaboration), there is growing evidence that many customers prefer to deal with one rather than multiple suppliers. The result, especially in emerging economies, may be the return in popularity of conglomerates.[94] Thus smaller companies may be able to handle much development for their domestic markets alone, even if they are conglomerates. Nevertheless, they lack all the product- and market-specific resources to go it alone everywhere

outside their home markets, especially if national differences dictate operating changes on a country-to-country basis. Thus we may see them embracing more collaboration as they move internationally.

Collaborative arrangements will bring both opportunities and problems as MNEs move simultaneously to new countries and to contractual arrangements with new companies. Differences must be overcome in a number of areas:

- Country cultures that may cause partners to obtain and evaluate information differently
- National disparities in governmental policies, institutions, and industry structures that constrain companies from using operating forms they would prefer
- Distinct underlying ideologies and values affecting corporate cultures and practices that strain relationships
- Different strategic directions resulting from partners' interests that cause disagreement over objectives and contributions
- Diverse management styles and organizational structures that cause partners to interact ineffectively[95] ■

CASE   The oneworld Airline Alliance[96]

The airline industry is almost unique in that its need to form collaborative arrangements has been important almost from the start of international air travel because of cost, regulatory, and competitive factors. In recent years, this need has accelerated because of airlines' difficult profit performance.

In effect, the airlines have been squeezed. First, costs have become uncertain, particularly due to fluctuations in oil prices. Second, there is a need for greater security. In addition to airport passenger-security checks, airlines must provide advanced passenger information to governmental agencies and work with freight forwarders and supply-chain operators to ensure the safety of cargo shipments on passenger aircraft. Third, a long-term trend toward greater

price competition has hindered airlines' ability to pass on increased costs to passengers—a situation exacerbated by discount airlines and customers' ability to search for lower fares on the Internet.

Although growth in international passenger travel has largely spurred globalization, no airline has sufficient finances or aircraft to serve the whole world. Yet passengers are traveling the whole world and want airline connections that will minimize both distances and connecting times at airports while offering reasonable assurance of reaching destinations with checked luggage more or less on schedule. Thus, airlines have increasingly worked together to provide more seamless experiences for passengers and to cut costs.

This discussion, however, should not imply that all cost cuts necessitate collaboration. Airlines have implemented cost-saving changes that cover the gamut from ticket purchase to arrival at destination. Online purchases of electronic tickets have largely replaced airlines' need to pay travel agency commissions and to issue and maintain costly inventories of paper tickets. Self-service check-in at airports reduces the need for agents. On board, especially on short flights, less is included in the price of a basic ticket, such as generous leg space between rows of seats, food, pillows, and headphones.

A Bit of History: Changing Government Regulations

Historically, governments played a major role in airline ownership. Many government-owned airlines were monopolies within their domestic markets, money losers, and recipients of government subsidies. However, although some airlines remain subsidized, there has been a subsequent move toward privatization.

What Governments Can Regulate

Despite the move toward privatization, governments still regulate airlines and agree on restrictions and rights largely through reciprocal agreements. Specifically, they control:

- Which foreign carriers have landing rights
- Which airports and aircraft the carriers can use
- The frequency of flights
- Whether foreign carriers can fly beyond the country (for instance, whether Iberia, after flying from Spain to the United States, can then fly from the United States to Panama)
- Overflight privileges
- Fares airlines can charge

Several notable regulatory changes have occurred in recent years. First, the U.S. domestic market has been deregulated, which means that any approved U.S. carrier can fly any U.S. domestic route in any frequency while charging what the market will bear. Once deregulation was instituted, many U.S. airlines were competitively forced out of business. Second, similar deregulation within Europe influenced the demise of some airlines. Third, several open-skies agreements permit any airline from countries in an agreement to fly from any city in one signatory area to any city in the other signatory area. Further, these flights have no restrictions on capacity, frequency, or type of aircraft. For instance, an open-skies agreement between the United States and Japan spurred American Airlines (AA) to begin previously unapproved service between New York and Haneda International Airport. Fourth, European countries have permitted cross-national acquisitions, such as German Lufthansa's acquisition of Swissair.

Why Governments Protect Airlines

Three factors influence governments' protection of their airlines:

1. Countries believe they can save money by maintaining small air forces and relying on domestic airlines in times of unusual air transport needs (e.g., the U.S. government using U.S. commercial carriers to help carry troops to and from Iraq and Afghanistan).
2. Public opinion favors spending at home. The public sees, for example, the requirement that government employees fly on national airlines as foreign-exchange savings.
3. Airlines are a source of national pride, and aircraft (sporting their national flags) symbolize a country's sovereignty and technical competence. This national identification has become less important, but it still persuades some developing countries.

Regulatory Obstacles to Expansion

Even if airlines had the financial capacity to expand everywhere in the world, national regulations would limit this expansion. With few exceptions, airlines cannot fly on lucrative domestic routes in foreign countries. For example, Japan Airlines (JAL) cannot compete on the New York to Los Angeles route, nor can AA fly between Tokyo and Nagoya. These restrictions prevent airlines from developing domestic routes abroad to feed into their international routes (e.g., JAL has no U.S. flights into Chicago to connect to its Chicago–Tokyo flights, but AA does). Further, the U.S. government limits foreign ownership in a U.S. airline to 25 percent of voting stock.

Finally, airlines usually cannot service pairs of foreign countries. AA cannot fly between Brazil and South Africa because those governments give landing rights on such routes only to Brazilian and South African airlines. To avoid these restrictions, airlines must ally themselves with carriers from other countries.

Collaboration Examples Related to Motives

Cost Factors

Certain airlines have always dominated certain international airports, thereby amassing critical capabilities in them, such as baggage handlers and aircraft-handling equipment. Sharing these capabilities with other airlines may spread costs. For example, British Airways (BA) has long handled passenger check-in, baggage loading, and maintenance for a number of other airlines at London's Heathrow Airport.

The high cost of maintenance and reservations systems has led to JVs involving multiple airlines from multiple countries, such as ownership in the Apollo and Galileo reservation systems. Actually, the reservations systems are motivated by more than cost savings, inasmuch as the pooling of resources provides customers with better service.

Connecting Flights

Given that governments restrict routes, airlines have long had agreements whereby passengers can transfer from one to another with a through ticket. However, people tend to select from among the first routings that show up on computer screens, and routings from one airline to another often appear on screens after those involving only one airline. Further, when passengers see that they must change airlines, they worry more about making those connections across great distances within ever-larger airports. To help avoid this worry, airlines have agreed to code sharing—a procedure whereby the same flight may have a designation for more than one carrier. For instance, the same flight operated by Iberia from Miami to Madrid is listed as AA 8636, Finnair 5642, and Iberia 6118. Hence, AA passengers originating in, say, Tampa and connecting at Miami may worry less about the connection because they see themselves on the same airline all the way. However, they may still need to go from one departure section to another to make the plane-change. In such a situation, airlines must adhere to a longer minimum connecting time when showing a through/connecting flight.

The oneworld Alliance

The oneworld Alliance comprises 15 airlines: airberlin, American Airlines, British Airways, Cathay Pacific, Finnair, Iberia, Japan Airlines, LAN Airlines, Malaysia Airlines, Qantas, Qatar, Royal Jordanian, S7 Airlines, SriLankan Airlines, and TAM. At this writing, Aer Lingus is negotiating to become the 16th member, and Qatar has indicated it may leave the alliance. oneworld competes largely with two other alliances: Star and SkyTeam. Airlines in these alliances cooperate on various programs, such as allowing passengers to earn credits for free or upgraded travel on any one of them. In the case of oneworld, all members flying into Narita Airport in Tokyo have moved into terminal 2, which shortens legal connecting times among them. They also advertise their affiliation; you may have seen aircraft painted with the airline's name and logo along with the oneworld name. These alliances allow for considerable cooperation, such as code-sharing; however, antitrust regulations (unless given immunity) prohibit their members from coordinating routes, schedules, and prices.

Antitrust Immunity

AA has received antitrust immunity that allows it to cooperate more in both a joint venture across the Atlantic and one across the Pacific. In both cases, the agreements allow representatives from each airline to jointly manage capacity, sell and promote space on flights operated by each other, divide revenues, and schedule connecting flights. The major thrusts for these ventures are to cut operating costs by better controlling capacity, to avoid disruptive price competition, and to improve scheduling so that there are more and better departure times and connections for passengers.

Source: TRISTAR PHOTOS / Alamy Stock Photo

▲ The adjacent photo shows an aircraft bearing both the oneworld and British Airways identifications.

The Transatlantic Joint Venture

Three airlines—AA, BA, and Iberia—have a combined network of over 400 destinations in over 100 countries and account for more than 6,000 daily departures. When their JV and antitrust immunity were approved, they collectively had 48 different routes between Europe and North America that included 22 North American and 13 European cities. Of these 48 routes, they competed directly on only 9.

Since these airlines entered this JV, they have been able to coordinate schedules better for the convenience of passengers. For instance, whereas AA and BA used to have flights leaving between New York-JKF and London-Heathrow within minutes of each other, they now operate 16 flights per day between those two airports and have been able to coordinate departure times so that the flights leave approximately one hour apart. This gives passengers more options in finding a departure time convenient to them and allows for more connecting flight alternatives in either direction. Further, the participating airlines can now designate their own flight numbers on domestic connections when they connect to transatlantic destinations. For instance, Iberia shows one of its routes as San Diego to Madrid, even though both the San Diego–Chicago and Chicago–Madrid flights are operated by AA.

Because of dual or multiple designations and the sharing of revenue, more than one airline's sales force is trying to fill seats on the same route. The result is boosted sales, which allows the JV members to offer new routes—nonstop service between Chicago and Helsinki and between New York and Budapest have come about since the JV's formation.

The AA–JAL Joint Venture

JAL is also a large airline, serving 85 cities in 20 countries and territories. Its joint venture with AA has the same advantages and objectives as the JV across the Atlantic. Some changes since inaugurating the JV are notable. By altering each company's flight times between Chicago O'Hare and Tokyo Narita and tweaking schedules of connecting flights in both cities, many more passengers can make connections within two hours. For instance, 22 more flights from 20 more departure cities can make such connections for travel from O'Hare to Narita. Map 15.2 shows the joint AA–JAL routes and illustrates that flights between Honolulu and Japan are not included in the agreement.

JAL moved its O'Hare flights from the international terminal to be adjacent to AA. Meanwhile, AA moved its Japanese offices to JAL's headquarters building, a move that eases communications between the two airlines. Both are helping each other with cultural questions, such as JAL aiding AA with public address announcements in Japanese to make them more meaningful to Japanese passengers. Meanwhile, the airlines have greatly increased code sharing between

MAP 15.2   American Airlines and Japan Airlines: Transpacific Routes

Note that the joint activity involves only flights from mainland North America into East Asia.

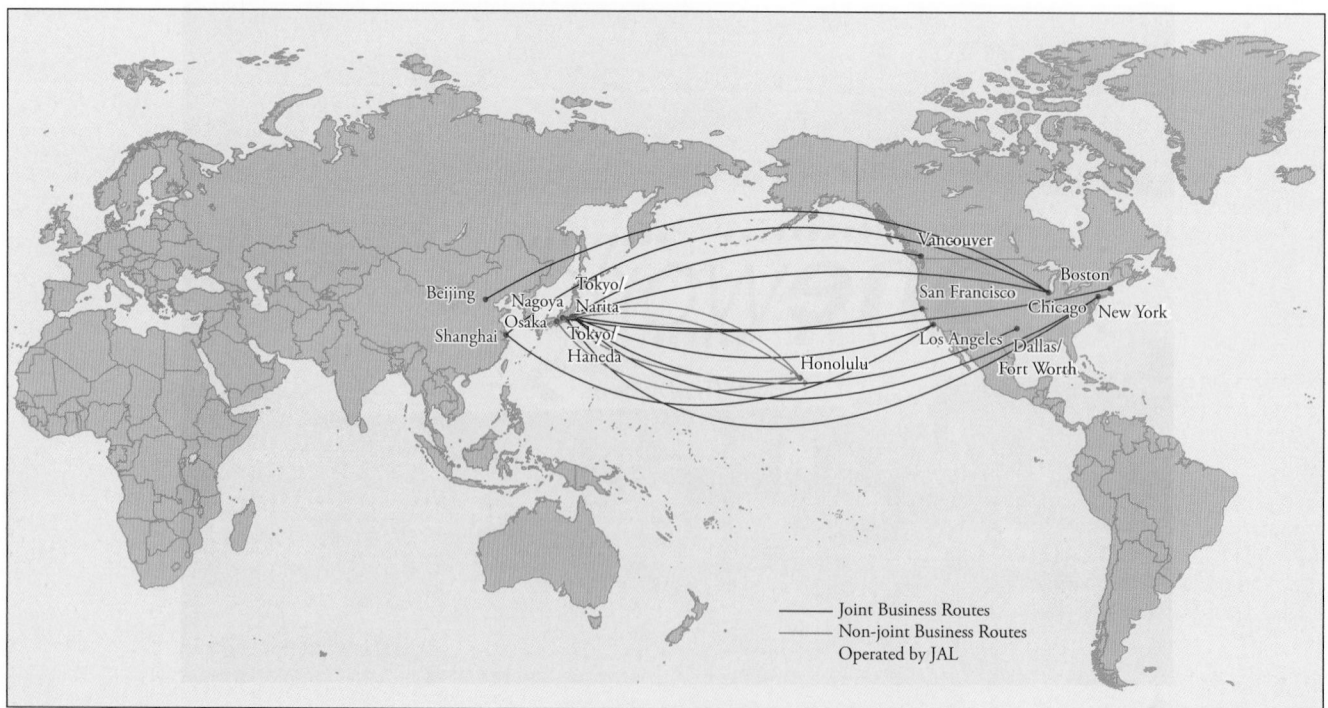

them, especially to points beyond gateway cities, such as showing a JAL flight as Tokyo–Salt Lake City and as an AA flight beyond Tokyo to JAL-served cities such as Hanoi.

Why Not a Merger or an Acquisition?

To begin with, government regulations such as ownership requirements would prevent a merger or acquisition between U.S. and non-U.S. carriers. Even if they didn't, fusing companies together creates daunting problems, even for domestic mergers and acquisitions. To complete the merger between AA and US Airways, the companies had to merge different operating and compensation systems between their respective pilots' unions. US Airways transatlantic routes had to interface with AA's agreements with BA and Iberia. US Airways had to sever its membership in the Star Alliance, and AA and US Airways had to combine their accrued frequent flyer passenger points.

The Advantages of JVs

In the JVs, each company keeps its own identity and operates independently except for the coordination of the transoceanic routes. In addition, each airline in the JVs and within oneworld has developed its own culture and brand to appeal to its own nationality. BA is still strongest with British passengers, JAL with Japanese passengers, etc. By keeping separate identities, despite sharing flights, the member airlines can capitalize on the differences. Nevertheless, natural extensions

are possible by strengthening collaboration, such as having check-in counters worldwide that handle all oneworld passengers and combining more airport lounges as a cost-saving measure. It is probably safe to say that future cooperation will strengthen rather than weaken among oneworld members.

QUESTIONS

✪ **15-3.** Companies within the oneworld, Star, and Sky Team alliances have also engaged in major mergers and acquisitions (M&A): American and US Air (oneworld), Delta and Northwest (Sky Team), and Continental and United (Star). What are the advantages and disadvantages of M&A versus non-equity alliances in this industry?

15-4. Some airlines, such as Southwest, have survived as niche players without extensive international connections. Can they continue this strategy?

15-5. Why should an airline not be able to establish service anywhere in the world simply by demonstrating that it can and will comply with the local labor and business laws of the host country?

✪ **15-6.** The U.S. law limiting foreign ownership of U.S. airlines to no more than 25 percent of voting shares was enacted in 1938. Is this law an anachronism, or are there valid reasons for having it today?

15-7. Many airlines have sometimes been no more than marginally profitable. Is this such a vital industry that governments should intervene to guarantee survival? If so, how?

MyLab Management

Go to **mymanagementlab.com** for the following Assisted-graded writing questions:

15-8 What will be the consequences if a few large airlines or networks dominate global air service?

15-9 What methods could JAL and AA use to divide revenue and expenses on code-shared routes?

Endnotes

Scan for Endnotes or go to www.pearsonglobaleditions.com/Daniels

CHAPTER 16

The Organization and Governance of Foreign Operations

OBJECTIVES

After studying this chapter, you should be able to

16-1 Profile the evolving idea of organization in the MNE

16-2 Interpret classical organization structures

16-3 Interpret neoclassical organization structures

16-4 Differentiate the systems used to coordinate international activities

16-5 Differentiate the systems used to control international activities

16-6 Explain the purpose and characteristics of organizational culture

MyLab Management®

Improve Your Performance!

When you see this icon ⭐, visit **www.mymanagementlab.com** for activities that are applied, personalized, and offer immediate feedback.

Words have no wings but they can fly many thousands of miles.

—South Korean proverb

Source: Cheuk-king Lo. Pearson Education Asia Ltd

Organizing Global Operations: The "Gore Way"

Since 1958, W. L. Gore & Associates have found ways to convert the versatile polymer polytetrafluoroethylene (PTFE) and related fluoropolymers into pioneering materials and products that are used in all sorts of ways by all sorts of people to do all sorts of jobs.[1] Best known for its waterproof, breathable, high-performance GORE-TEX® fabric, the company's portfolio includes medical devices, pharmaceutical processing, consumer products, cables and cable assemblies, fibers, sealants, industrial components, and aerospace electronics. Its ingenuity and imagination has earned it more than 2,000 patents worldwide. Analysts often point to Gore as the "the world's most innovative company."[2]

Notwithstanding its discoveries, many contend that Gore's supreme invention is setting and sustaining a stunningly effective global organization. Report after report confirmed something special goes on. In 2016, Gore ranked 12th on the "Fortune 100 Best Companies to Work For"; it has appeared on every *Fortune* list since the rankings began in 1984. Gore's locations in China, France, Germany, Italy, Korea, Sweden, and the UK have been named one of the respective nation's best workplaces. Globally, Gore gains accolades. For instance, nearly 3,000 MNEs worldwide participated in the 2015 Great Place to Work® review. Assessment centered on issues of mutual trust, esprit de corps and camaraderie, and supportiveness of the work environment. From the global pool, the review identified the 25 World's Best Multinational Workplaces—Gore ranked third.[3]

START-UP

Gore and its subsidiaries employ more than 10,000 Associates, based at research labs, manufacturing facilities, and sales offices in the United States, Germany, the United Kingdom, Japan, China, and elsewhere. Gore, headquartered in Newark, Delaware, is one of the 200 largest privately held companies in the United States; it had more than $3 billion in sales in 2016. The Gore family, along with its Associates (the official designation of its employees), owns the company. Private ownership, Associates profess, helps them to "take a long-term view."

In 1958, Bill Gore quit DuPont, a U.S. chemical MNE, and started a business to explore new uses for PTFE. Beyond that, he aspired to create a company that puts into play then, and still today, far-reaching management ideas on organization, enterprise, accountability, and authority. Or, in company shorthand, the "Gore Way."

SETTING THE GORE WAY

Philosophically opposed to the customary chain of command found in a top-down organization, Bill Gore rejected any sort of classical hierarchy. He shunned an organization that ranked people or groups above others according to status or authority. He installed a flat organization whereby everyone could freely talk with anyone else, no matter their role or rank. Making this happen, he figured, meant eliminating obstacles to communication: hence, no one in the company, not even Bill himself, had an authoritarian title like boss, supervisor, manager, director, controller, etc.[4] Everyone was and, to this day, is an "Associate." As an aside, Gore's opposition to boxing in, either an individual or an idea, anchors the symbolism of its corporate logo. The obtuse triangle has three vertices; the one toward the furthest left represents the past, the one midway represents the present, and the one that has broken through the box represents the future.

In 1976, Bill Gore set forth his manifesto, "*The Lattice Organization—A Philosophy of Enterprise.*" It articulates the Gore Way, beginning with a flat, network-like structure that rejects the standard that one person (the boss) should specify who others (workers) may talk to.[5] In addition, it models a team-based, non-hierarchical organization that promotes personal initiative by rejecting conventional structural formats, replaces an authoritarian chain of command with connections and collaborations, and lets channels of communication emerge naturally. Gore's lattice organization enacts an interlaced system of relationships among Associates. Operationally, leaders attract team members based on their effectiveness in getting things done, and Associates, based on their read of opportunities and colleagues, self-organize into multifunctional teams. Associates play a role in choosing what they work on, aligning their talents and interests with business needs. Associates create value that supports business goals—and their fellow Associates, by directly assessing each other, corroborate their performance.[6]

Liberated from a rigid bureaucracy, Associates make decisions based on knowledge and initiative rather than seniority and titles. Success translates into credibility to define and drive projects. Gore's lattice organization frees the flow of information and spurs the sorts of personal communications that drive productive collaboration—and, as report after report indicates, makes for a great workplace. No matter where in the world, no matter what an Associates works on, the Gore Way champions entrepreneurial innovation. Notwithstanding considerable personal autonomy, Associates stay mindful of Bill Gore's four basic guiding principles: (1) Fairness to each other and everyone with whom we come in contact; (2) Freedom to encourage, help, and allow other Associates to grow in knowledge, skill, and scope of responsibility; (3) The ability to make one's own commitments and keep them; and (4) Consulting other Associates before undertaking actions that could impact the reputation of the company.[7]

SUSTAINING THE GORE WAY

A vibrant element of the Gore Way is its organizational culture. Intentionally humanistic, its foundational belief holds that the innate motivation of each Associate, given the opportunity, drives one and all to stretch toward their full potential. To that end, Associates collectively commit to foster a safe and healthy work environment in which they develop their talents, enjoy their work, and responsibly direct their activities—as founder Bill Gore once noted, "The objective of the Enterprise is to make money and have fun doing so."[8] Gore continues championing that cause—and, the results suggest, it pays off. Associates find ingenious ways to meet the needs of customers through innovative products. They aim to improve the communities in which they work and live, all the while sustaining the company's legacy of taking a long-term perspective.

Shared norms and values help facilitate coordination and collaboration between Associates as well as support informal integrative mechanisms. Explained CEO Terri Kelly, who joined Gore as an engineer more than 30 years ago, "At Gore, we take great pride in our culture and recognize the very important role it plays in driving business success. By fostering an environment where people feel motivated, engaged, and passionate about the work they do, we are better able to tap into our potential and create innovative products that truly make a difference in the world."[9] Added Marcie Lee, leader of a company-wide culture initiative, "Our global teams bring together the best knowledge by collaborating across the enterprise to take on opportunities where we can make the biggest impact. Our strongly embedded values, passionate Associates, and winning teams are instrumental to creating a rewarding environment and great experiences for our customers. This is our culture in action."[10]

CHANGING FOR CHANGING TIMES

Continuing growth, fueled by expanding internationalization, has led Gore to formalize some elements of its organization. Today, it has a CEO, several product divisions, numerous product-focused business units, and the usual business support functions. Each has a recognized leader. Coordinating far-flung global operations mean Associates use e-mail, phone and video conferencing, and the like. Still, teams regularly convene, physically and virtually, to plan, assess gaps, and fortify the relationships that anchor the Gore Way.[11] Too, at its core, Gore is a flat organization, with no traditional management layers and no official organization chart. Multidisciplinary teams, freed from layers of supervisory "management," protect the innovative spirit of individuals that power the company's entrepreneurialism.

Certainly, one wonders how these principles and practices can organize the work of 10,000 employees running 50 facilities spanning 30 countries. Gore prefers opening new subsidiaries, rather than acquiring an existing enterprise. It reasons that it's easier to set and sustain its unique vision and values in a new enterprise than transforming workers' legacy mindsets. Gore's commitment to keeping units small and informal plays a vital role. Gore generally prefers that a unit, whether research, manufacturing, or sales, grow to no more than 200 Associates. Crossing that threshold, whether in the United States, Germany, or China, insidiously turns decision-making from "we decided" to "they decided," and sets a company on the path to hierarchy, bureaucracy, control, and coercion. Likewise, Gore mobilizes its plants into clusters, like the dozen plants located in Arizona or the multiple plants interspersed throughout the Delaware Valley. Then, within a cluster, Gore maximizes opportunities for cross-functional collaboration by having R&D specialists, engineers, marketers, chemists, and machinists work in the same plant or on the same campus. Even Gore's headquarters has remained simple and intimate: several low-rise buildings built not far from Bill's house in the Delaware countryside, each housing small, autonomous teams. And, outside of many, one finds a volleyball court, picnic areas, horseshoe pits, and other areas that promote teamwork, fun, and camaraderie. Unofficially the company's official sport, volleyball has the unique feature whereby every player plays every position, unlike, say, in baseball or football, where players specialize in a particular slot.

MELDING THE LATTICE AND THE NET

Going forward, Associates look to meld the Gore Way with the transformational connection, communication, and collaboration technologies unleashed by the Internet. Explained Brad Jones, an enterprise leader, "Twenty or thirty years ago, markets in different parts of the world were still somewhat distinct and isolated from one another. At that time, we could have pretty much the entire global business team for a particular market niche located in a building. Today, as our markets become more global in nature, we are increasingly seeing the need to support our customers with global virtual teams. How do our paradigms and practices have to change to accommodate those changing realities?"[12] Answering these questions inevitably had big implications. Still, Gore' 50-year record of insight and adaptation signaled that, come what may, its Associates would develop ingenious solutions that leveraged the ideals of the Gore Way. ∎

QUESTIONS

✪ **16-1.** Identify three advantages of working for Gore. Do you find them appealing?

✪ **16-2.** What mix of knowledge, skills, and abilities would make you a high-performing Associate at Gore?[13]

INTRODUCTION

Designing an organization that adeptly runs global activities is an enduring concern of multinational firms. Managers must decide how employees get work done, minding how they coordinate activities spanning many markets, apply controls when situations go awry, and sponsor values that support a common cause. Overhanging these issues are the contingencies of international operations: How does it balance global standards with local circumstances? How should workers communicate with colleagues? How does it promote a universal outlook among different units doing different jobs in different countries? Worldwide, executives engage these sorts of questions, determining how to configure subsidiaries, coordinate and control activities, and develop a unifying esprit de corps. These tasks, the crux of organizing an MNE, require managers specify the structure that arranges the workflow, install the systems that get and keep it moving, and promote the culture that sustains it (see Figure 16.1). Effectively done, managers convert strategic ambitions into performance outcomes.[14]

CHANGING TIMES, CHANGING ORGANIZATIONS

In the early twentieth century, companies responded to the emerging technologies of railroads, telephone, and telegraph by engaging then unusual organizational ideas.[15] The global titans of the day, such as General Motors, Ford, DuPont, and Sears, developed hierarchical structures, reasoning that this then-novel organizational format would best implement their novel strategies that had been made possible by emerging technologies. Succeeding generations of managers refined these designs, better determining who did what job, who made which decision, who worked in which unit, who reported to whom, and who told whom what to do. The output of these analyses, codified in the "lines and boxes" that represent an MNE's structure, instituted a hierarchical system of command, control, constraint, and contract. It directed the efforts and ensured the compliance of workers worldwide.[16]

The hierarchical model has routinely organized MNEs' operations. For many, it defines work life in the modern-day corporation. Now, market trends, design revolutions, and workplace resets pose both opportunities and challenges.

Environmental differences, technology trends, executive practices, and labor markets challenge how managers organize an MNE.

FIGURE 16.1 Factors Affecting Organizing Operations

The idea of an organization refers to the activities through which managers build the structure, systems, and culture needed to implement their strategy. The resulting organization, by arranging roles, responsibilities, and relationships, directs an MNE's operations.

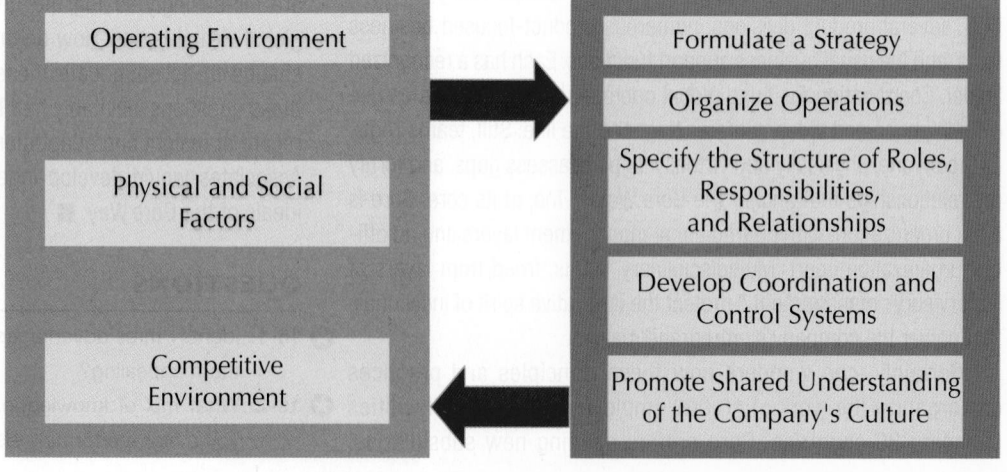

EXPANDING SCOPE OF IB

The growth of global business changes MNEs' opportunity sets and efficiency frontiers. Markets once predominant, like the United States, Japan, and Germany, transition to new positions. Markets once on the periphery, such as China, Indonesia, and Rwanda, move toward center stage. For instance, 400 midsized emerging-market cities, many unfamiliar in the West, such as Ghaziabad, Chittagong, Sanaa, Kano, and Bamako, will generate about 40 percent of global growth over the next 15 years.[17] MNEs respond by redeploying operations and engaging strategies that impose intricate workflow patterns. Implementation requires new approaches to coordination, collaboration, and control. These choices demand far more sophisticated organizations than MNEs have traditionally used.

IBM's transition into its third organizational phase illustrates this process. It's read of market conditions and corresponding organizational requirements spurs it to build a "globally integrated enterprise" that puts investments, people, and work anywhere in the world based on the optimal mix of costs, skills, and location effects. Explained IBM's vice president of global strategy, "Instead of taking people to where the work is, you take work to where the people are."[18] Resetting workflows within the context of transforming technologies pushes IBM to rethink how to reboot its organization to run the new show. Managing increasingly sophisticated strategies, made possible by transforming technologies, calls for managing increasingly sophisticated organizations.

> Implementing increasingly sophisticated strategies requires increasingly sophisticated organizations.

THE INTERNET AS A DESIGN STANDARD

The invention of the telephone and telegraph, by expanding connections and improving communication, reset the standards of workflow in the early twentieth century. At the time, corporations responded with formats that reflected the organizing logic of these technologies. We see the same processes in play today. The Internet, by efficiently and effectively organizing knowledge and resources, pushes managers to rethink their assumptions of how they arrange work, roles, and responsibilities. Incongruously, the Internet has no formal structure, no board of directors, and no official administrator. Its self-organizing and self-regulating capabilities prompt rethinking conventional notions of design, coordination, and control. Consider, for example, that contemporary global juggernauts like Facebook, Red Hat, Yandex, Alibaba PayPal, Naver, and Baidu could not have existed a generation ago. Therefore, just as novel strategies called for innovative structures in the early 1900s, so too do we see similar circumstances today. Managing new workplace arrangements calls for managing new structural formats.

> The Internet, in developing new workplace arrangements, calls for managing new structural formats.

MANAGERIAL STANDARDS

The evolving nature of work changes the conduct and context of employees' jobs, whether done at the biggest headquarters or the smallest subsidiary. Change in the nature of work changes the nature of management. Historically, the higher one's level in the hierarchy, the more one knew about the various jobs in the company. Hence, a generation ago, MNEs could rely on an elite set of executives making the big decisions. Today that thesis is increasingly debatable–and, at MNEs like Gore and Johnson & Johnson (J&J), invalid. Similarly, at one time frontline employees were the masters of their local marketplace, yet far removed from the global drama. That, too, no longer holds. Real-time access to information, facilitated by cheap, powerful telecommunications, closes the global–local gap. Consequently, there are far fewer jobs that senior executives can script or that subsidiary managers cannot do. The intrinsic dynamism of

> Managing new workplace standards calls for managing new forms of coordination and control.

the global market along with evolving workplace standards calls for a finer distribution of authority between headquarters and subsidiaries. Therefore, managing new workplace standards calls for managing novel coordination and control systems.

SOCIAL CONTRACT

Competitive changes and performance expectations alter the social contract between high-performance workers and MNEs. Traditional concerns for security, pay, and benefits have expanded to expectations of participating in decision-making, devising solutions to unique problems, and receiving challenging assignments.[19] Furthermore, employees working with information technologies create value of astonishing variety, problem solving, and intellectual content. "Controlling" workers charged with reasoning or problem-solving tasks is problematic; the bright, self-motivating, self-organizing people who staff these sorts of slots generally oppose direct supervision. Whether "knowledge workers" or the "creative class," these individuals aim to behave as if they are the CEO.[20] Moreover, social contracts increasingly rely on the fit between worker's outlook and the norms and values that anchor a company's organizational culture. Google's worries about brain drain to rivals, for instance, led it to identify why people quit; it found that executives left when they no longer felt connected to the company's mission.[21] Managing new expectations calls for managing the social dynamic of the organization's culture. Consequently, MNEs develop organizational cultures that people do not want to merely work for, but aspire to belong to.

CHANGE AND CHALLENGE: MNES RESPOND

These trends push MNEs to test the best mix of structure, systems, and values when building, as we'll see in our closing case, what J&J calls a "magical" organization. Different MNEs apply different approaches to create magic. Some, like Nestlé in Switzerland, Cemex in Mexico, Toyota in Japan, Infosys in India, and Walmart in the United States, apply and refine classical hierarchical formats. Walmart, for example, relies upon a tried-and-true international division, based in Arkansas, to oversee operations in 27 countries that collectively generate nearly $150 billion in sales. Walmart, as does Nestlé, Infosys, Toyota, and Cemex, fine-tunes its classical organization, process-mapping activities to rationalize the work environment and improve system standards. Reengineering workflows, streamlining information technology, tightening planning sequences, and minimizing duplication are key tools of organization design.

Others, like Oticon in Sweden, Gore in the United States, Belcorp of Peru, Grupo Empresarial Antioqueño of Colombia, Mitsui of Japan, and Li & Fung in Hong Kong, engage neoclassical heterarchial formats. Li & Fung, the world's largest sourcing and logistics company, supplies billions of pieces of apparel to department stores, hypermarkets, specialty stores, and e-commerce sites worldwide. However, it owns no fabric mills, no sewing machines, and no clothing factories. Rather, Li & Fung oversees a network of 15,000 suppliers spanning 60 countries that make virtually any clothing article.[22] Li & Fung, like Oticon, Gore, and Mitsu, replaces the command-and-control ethos of the classical hierarchy with the goals of coordinating and collaborating in the context of the neoclassical heterarchy. Cross-functional task forces, knowledge networks, flat structures, virtual formats, and social networking methods are key tools of organization design.

Subject to its vision, mission, and strategy, the classical or neoclassical approach effectively organizes an MNE's workflow. This chapter examines the intricacies of each approach. We study how an MNE builds an **organization** in terms of the (1) structure it specifies to arrange its workplace, (2) the systems it installs to coordinate and control what it does, and (3) the culture it promotes to shape and sustain its collective effort.

Changes in the market environment and nature of work push managers to evaluate the effectiveness of their organization.

CONCEPT CHECK

Designing an organization's structure requires fitting it to conditions in the external environment. These conditions involve, among many others, legal regulations on ownership structures, degree of economic freedom, location economics, and expectations of alliance partners.

Organizing is the process of building the structure, systems, and culture that implement the MNE's strategy.

The MNE specifies its organization to arrange its domestic and international units and activities, and the relationships among units.

CLASSICAL ORGANIZATION STRUCTURES

Structure is the formal arrangement of jobs that specifies roles, responsibilities, and relationships.

The formal arrangement of roles, responsibilities, and relationships in the MNE represents its **organization structure**. Managers configure the elements of the company's workflow to stipulate the lines of authority and communication, assign rights and duties, and set connections between units. These decisions often spell the difference between success and failure.[23] Executives of J&J, for example, see its decentralized structure as the bedrock of its "magical" organization. Similarly, Zara's CEO says the company's structure anchors its competitiveness. Innovatively combining vertical integration, tech-choreographed coordination, just-in-time manufacturing, finely tuned logistics, and state-of-the-art merchandising poses tough challenges. Zara's structure, by arranging jobs, roles, rules, and responsibilities, organizes its workflows to implement its strategy.

Designing an organization typically begins by determining the ideal structure for arranging individuals and units to implement the MNE's strategy—indeed, a long-running thesis in management theory holds that "structure follows strategy." Does the MNE's vision, for instance, champion global integration or local adaptation? In the former, centralization is crucial, while, in the latter, decentralization is decisive. Operationally, has its mission led it to concentrate value activities in a few nations or disperse them across many countries? Concentration requires precise controls, whereas dispersal calls for robust coordination systems. Moreover, organizing domestically lets one reasonably set technology level, cultural orientation, and workplace practices as constants. Organizing internationally requires treating them as variables. Collectively, these sorts of circumstances endorse the usefulness of some, while rejecting other, forms of structure.

Making sense of the strategy-structure situation forces a cascade of decisions. Many managers begin by resolving (1) the degree of **vertical differentiation** (deciding who has what authority to make which decision) and (2) the degree of **horizontal differentiation** (the task of specifying which people in which units do which jobs).

VERTICAL DIFFERENTIATION

CONCEPT CHECK

International business is marked by recurring dialectics; for example, global versus local, pro- versus anti-globalization, democracy versus totalitarianism, economic freedom versus state capitalism, standardization versus adaptation. Here we add another, namely, centralization versus decentralization.

No matter the mix of markets, products, or ambitions, MNEs face competing calls for global integration and local responsiveness. The questions run the gamut: Who should decide to close a factory in Switzerland or open one in Malaysia? Does only headquarters decide whom to hire and whom to fire, both at home and overseas? How often and in what format do foreign subsidiaries report to headquarters? In classical terms, the company's structure reconciles these sorts of questions by specifying who has the authority to make what decision. If the plan is to make those issues headquarters' call, then managers must build an organization that supports that outlook. Conversely, if the plan is to have those calls made by local subsidiaries, then, again, managers must build an organization to support that outlook. More formally, managers reconcile this tension by vertically differentiating the company's structure in terms of the **centralization** (how high up) versus the **decentralization** (how low down) of decision-making.

Generally, decisions made above the subsidiary level signify centralization, whereas those made at or below that level signify decentralization. Operationally, a centralized structure concentrates decision-making authority among the executives staffing the top levels of the MNE. A decentralized structure pushes decision-making authority down to the folks on the front lines, namely those running local subsidiaries. Resolving the tension between centralization versus decentralization, as seen in Table 16.1, endorses different principles, advocates different practices, and emphasizes different objectives.

Differentiation means that the company is composed of different units that work on different kinds of tasks with different degrees of authority.

Structure Follows Strategy The choice of centralization versus decentralization is not an either-or proposition. Some activities spur centralized decision-making, such as

Centralization is the degree to which high-level managers, usually above the country level, make strategic decisions and delegate them to lower levels for implementation.

configuring value activities worldwide to exploit location economies or rationalize production systems. Likewise, other activities encourage decentralized decision-making, such as adapting products or negotiating with local officials. Again, in the context of the "structure follows strategy" thesis, the requirements of the MNE's strategy determine its ideal structure and, by extension, how managers balance centralization and decentralization.[24]

An MNE implementing an international strategy, for instance, centralizes most decision-making. Headquarters, in its role as overseer of global operations, retains control of the firm's resources, capabilities, and core competencies, and makes the decisions that the troops running the local subsidiaries then implement.[25] For example, Google, given its international strategy, centralizes strategic planning at the Googleplex in Mountain View, California, but decentralizes some elements of the marketing mix to local subsidiaries. Alternatively, the MNE implementing a multi-domestic strategy decentralizes extensive authority to the troops in the field, reasoning that those closest to the customer have a superior understanding of the situation than do far-removed generals.

Decentralization is the degree to which lower-level managers, usually at or below the country level, make and implement strategic decisions.

Technology, Balance, and Globality   Technology increasingly alters the calculus of who should have the authority to make which decision. The Internet, for example, progressively makes it easier for executives at headquarters as well as subsidiaries to track global conditions and local performance in real time. Not long ago, each relied upon

TABLE 16.1   The Principles and Practices of Centralization and Decentralization

Centralization	Decentralization
Premise	**Premise**
• Decisions should be made by senior managers who have superior expertise and broader experiences.	• Decisions should be made by managers closest to customers.
• Effective configuration and coordination of the value chain requires headquarters direct local activities.	• Effective configuration and coordination of the value chain requires adaptation by local managers.
• Centralized decision-making ensures local operations support the MNE's vision and mission.	• Success achieving local objectives anchors global performance.
Advantages	**Advantages**
• Ensures decisions support objectives.	• Managers that directly deal with customers, competitors, officials, and markets make decisions.
• Retain authority with HQ to regulate change.	• Encourages lower-level managers to behave entrepreneurially.
• Preempts duplicating activities.	• Improves the allegiance and accountability of frontline employees.
• Reduces the risk lower-level managers make strategic errors.	• Links subsidiary managers' choices directly to performance.
• Simplifies coordinating activities	
• Promotes consistent relationships with stakeholders.	
Disadvantages	**Disadvantages**
• Requires top executives monitor and manage multiple activities.	• Risks subunits making counterproductive decisions.
• Discourages initiative among lower-level employees.	• Subsidiaries champion local interests at the expense of global performance.
• Demoralizes lower-level employees who must wait to be told what to do.	• Slows the company's response to global innovations.
• Information flows 'top-down,' thereby preempting bottom-up innovations.	• Information flows 'bottom-up,' thereby obstructing top-down innovations.
Factors Encouraging Centralization	**Factors Encouraging Decentralization**
• Environment and industry conditions push for worldwide uniformity of products, methods, and policies.	• Environment and industry conditions require adapting products and policies.
• Interdependent subsidiaries share activities, segments, and rivals.	• Local production fully exploits location affects.
• Strategy calls for exploiting location economics globally.	• Lower-level managers are effective decision-makers.
• Lower-level managers are less experienced decision-makers than upper-level executives.	• Speed and flexibility drive performance.
• Decisions are important and downside risk is great.	• Little need to develop managers for positions elsewhere in the world.
	• Supports rapid expansion into new markets.
	• Goal to develop executive talent at the local level.

slow-moving reports provided by counterparts. Now, ERP, e-mail, VoIP, teleconferencing, social networks, and the like eliminate the lag. Economical, off-the-shelf platforms, such as Microsoft's Skype, Google's Hangout, Polycom's RealPresence, or Cisco's TelePresence, make the magic of being in many places simultaneously happen effortlessly. The click of a mouse lets one "meet" anyone, anywhere, anytime. Consequently, MNEs fine-tune decision-making for growing **globality** in which "business flows in every direction. Companies have no centers. The idea of foreignness is foreign. Commerce swirls and market dominance shifts."[26] Competing with everyone from everywhere for everything makes historically blunt decisions to centralize this activity or decentralize that responsibility far more intricate issues.

HORIZONTAL DIFFERENTIATION

> In principle, decision-making should occur at the level of those who (1) are most directly affected by its outcome and (2) have the most direct knowledge of the situation.

Vertically speaking, MNEs run from top (the CEO) to the bottom (the entry-level worker). Horizontally speaking, MNEs run sideways from function to function, such as research to production to marketing to finance. Horizontal differentiation involves assigning specific tasks to specific people in specific functions. Disaggregating tasks makes manageable the scale and scope of international operations. Technically, an MNE horizontally differentiates its structure to (1) specify the set of tasks that must be done; (2) specify who does what by dividing those tasks among a mix of business units, divisions, subsidiaries, departments, committees, teams, jobs, and individuals; and (3) stipulates superior and subordinate relationships within a unit.

> Vertical differentiation deals with the chain of command that runs from the "top to the bottom" of the organization. Horizontal differentiation deals with the separate tasks or skills that run "sideways" in the organization.

In theory, managers can horizontally differentiate a structure in terms of function, process, product, service, location, or client. For an MNE, the standards of function, product, area, or some combination have traditionally dominated. Horizontally differentiating on the basis of business activity anchors the *functional* structure; doing so on the basis of product or geography installs a *divisional* structure; and doing so on the basis of a combination results in a *matrix* or *mixed* structure. The long-running use of these formats by MNEs designates them as **classical structures**. By no means does that characterization suggests they are an anachronism. Rather, it signifies the use of traditional design tools to specify the roles, responsibilities, and relationships in the MNE. As had many 50 years ago, many MNEs today rely on classical structures.[27]

> A classical structure uses explicit vertical and horizontal differentiation to organize the workplace.

THE FUNCTIONAL STRUCTURE

> Functional structures
> - group people based on common expertise and resources,
> - fit the organizational demands of MNEs that have narrow product lines.

The **functional structure**, as depicted in Figure 16.2, arranges the workplace by business functions (i.e., production people work with production people, marketing people work with marketing people, finance people work with finance people). MNEs with a narrow range of products, particularly those whose capital-intensive operations create steep scale effects, find functional structures appealing. Efficiently arranging responsibilities and relationships streamlines decision-making. Energy and extraction MNEs, such as ExxonMobil, Vale, or Rio Tinto, as well as aircraft manufacturers such as Airbus, Boeing, or Bombardier commonly use it. They, like others who install a functional structure, see global integration (and its demands to leverage core competencies, capture experience economies, and exploit location effects) trumping local responsiveness (and its demands to adapt products and processes to national circumstances).

Limits   Horizontally differentiating people and processes by business function constrains the development of cross-functional knowledge-generating and decision-making relationships. Consequently, coordinating different functional units, in response to a market disruption or strategic change, is difficult. The often-extreme vertical differentiation found in the functional structure, represented by a multi-layered chain of command, bureaucratizes decision-making. Finally, classical structures, such as the functional format, fuel zero-sum battles for

FIGURE 16.2   The Functional Structure

Rationale: Structure is set by business functions that reflect the firm's value-chain activities. Organizing workflow according to common tasks captures scale and location effects. Centralized decision-making usually prevails.

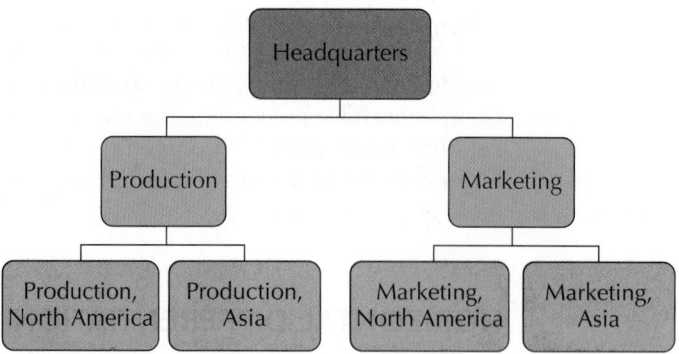

control among divisions, groups, and people. The goal of maximizing organizational power, to say nothing of the all-too-often imperative of organizational survival in a compartmentalized hierarchy, hinders collaboration.

DIVISIONAL STRUCTURES

Divisional structures

- divide employees based on the product type, customer segment, or geographical location,
- duplicate functions and resources across divisions,
- fit the organizational demands of the MNE that manages conventionally differentiated activities.

Whereas executives specify roles and relationships in a functional structure in terms of inputs (e.g., oil, natural gas, solar, and coal for an energy producer), they use a **divisional structure** to specify them according to product (e.g., soap, toothpaste, and cosmetics for a consumer products firm) or markets (e.g., North America, Europe, Africa, and Asia). Each division is responsible for its assigned products or markets. The MNE's strategy determines if it adopts an international, a global product, or a worldwide area divisional structure.

International Division   An MNE prefers this format when its international activities represent a small share of its total activity. It charges a separate, stand-alone operating unit with responsibility for overseas activities (see Figure 16.3). Domestic units supervise the home market, while the international division takes responsibility for the less strategic foreign sector. Consolidating international personnel within a single unit, by promoting knowledge-generating and decision-making relationships, improves decision-making effectiveness.

FIGURE 16.3   The International Division Structure

Rationale: Structure is set by organizing the various activities related to the firm's international operations into a self-contained, relatively autonomous unit. The international division is charged with directing value activities outside of the home market.

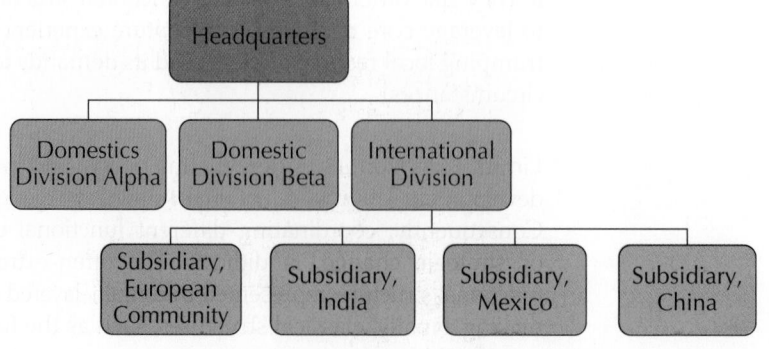

An international division

- creates a critical mass of international expertise,
- competes with powerful domestic divisions for resources,
- fits the demands of the MNE that generates most sales in a single nation.

Limits Disaggregating an MNE into domestic-international divisions can fan "us versus them" tensions, thereby blocking cross-division connections. Conflict between domestic and international units obstructs sharing competencies, leveraging best practices, and exploiting experience effects. Domestic managers, evaluated based on their home market performance, may withhold resources from the international division in order to boost their relative performance. Likewise, performance suffers when domestic and international counterparts see little incentive to collaborate. Historically, U.S. MNEs found the international division appealing, given that the scale of their home market often exceeds their overseas activity. This format finds less use among European MNEs, given the small size of their domestic markets relative to their international activity.

The worldwide product divisional structure centralizes decision-making authority.

Worldwide Product Division The product division format is the most widely used structure among MNEs. Its usefulness follows from the fact that many MNEs make and sell a broad portfolio of similar products based on overlapping competencies in multiple markets.[28] For example, Gore's structure sets four product divisions: electronics, fabrics, industrial, and medical. Each division serves different industries, but each makes and sells products based on Gore's proprietary PTFE expertise. The electronics product division, for example, makes PTFE-based high-performance cables and assemblies. Alternatively, the fabrics division makes PFTE-based materials for the outdoor clothing, military, law-enforcement, and fire protection markets.[29] The worldwide product division structure provides MNEs the flexibility to support differentiated product groups that share resources, capabilities, and competencies.[30] In turn, each division's global mandate orients managers toward consolidating and coordinating activities to tap location and experience economies (see Figure 16.4).

Limits The autonomy of each product division means that different subsidiaries from different product divisions within the same foreign country often report to different executives at headquarters. Unless safeguarded, coordination problems create inefficiencies.[31] At one point, Nestlé's various product divisions had configured more than 500 factories in nearly 90 countries to produce some 8,000 brands. Headquarters in Switzerland struggled to determine the costs of the raw materials its factories purchased from suppliers. In an extreme case, Nestlé's 40 U.S. factories procured raw materials independently. Lack of cross-division coordination, compounded by the fact that Nestlé product divisions used five different e-mail systems, meant that its U.S. factories, affiliated with different product divisions, unwittingly paid more than 20 different prices for vanilla extract to the same supplier.[32] Improving communication systems, by supporting better exchange, steadily reduced cross-divisional barriers.

Worldwide Area Division An MNE uses geographic divisions, as depicted in Figure 16.5, when its sales are not dominated by a single country or region (including the home

FIGURE 16.4 The Worldwide Product Division Structure

Rationale: Structure is set by organizing the various activities related to a product within a self-contained, relatively autonomous unit. Each product division is charged with configuring and coordinating value activities in its assigned product area.

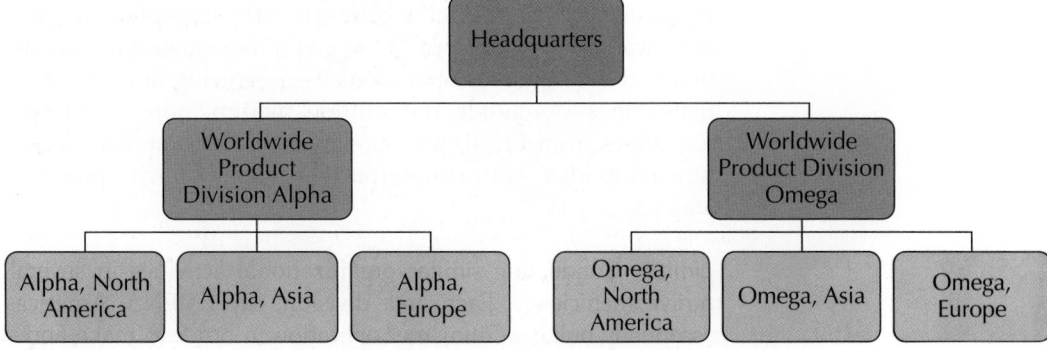

FIGURE 16.5   The Worldwide Area Division Structure

Rationale: Structure is set by organizing the various activities related to a product within a set geographic area. Each area division is charged with configuring and coordinating value activities in its assigned territory.

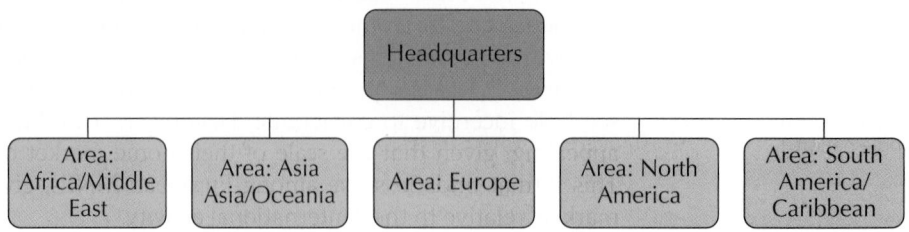

country). Typically, its activities are evenly distributed across multiple markets. In this scenario, an MNE horizontally differentiates activities by geography, whereby Division Alpha is responsible for region/country A, Division Beta takes region/country B, and so on. Historically, European MNEs preferred the area structure. Based in small countries, they expanded into bigger markets worldwide. Then, the size of one market, such as the United States, or proximity of several smaller markets, such as the Middle East/North Africa, supported a self-contained area division. For example, Swiss-based Nestlé organizes most of its food and beverage business geographies by disaggregating the globe into Zones EMENA (Europe, Middle East and North Africa), Americas, and Asia/Oceania/Africa. England-based Diageo similarly organizes in terms of North America, Europe, Africa, Latin America and the Caribbean, and Asia–Pacific territories.

> Geographic divisions fit the demands of MNEs who have extensive international operations that are distributed across many countries.

Emerging markets push MNEs to tweak the worldwide area structure. Once small in scale and scope, markets in Asia, Africa, and South America command greater attention. For example, the rising strategic importance of China and Eastern Europe led Nike to reset its four-region structure into six areas: North America, Western Europe, Eastern/Central Europe, Japan, Greater China, and Emerging Markets. Nike also announced that China and Eastern Europe would operate separately from the other divisions. Their growing share of the company's total sales, comparatively faster growth rates, and superior long-term potential called for different degrees of vertical and horizontal differentiation.

The geographic division structure is commonly used by MNEs pursuing multi-domestic strategies—as seen in Nike's reorganization to better respond to Eastern Europe and China. The decentralization of the area structure—North America tends to North America, Europe tends to Europe, and so on—gives local managers more authority to adapt value activities. As Nike explained, "We are confident these changes will best position us for future growth.... This model allows our global categories to connect directly with consumers at the local level."[33] Boosting local subsidiaries' responsiveness spurs headquarters to decentralize decision-making authority. Typically, headquarters retains strategic and financial controls.

> The worldwide product divisional structure decentralizes decision-making authority.

Similar moves by other MNEs highlight a key trend afoot. Historically West-centric companies rethink the horizontal differentiation of their structures given the emergence of larger, faster-growing markets. For example, Panasonic adjusted its worldwide area structure given sales trends in its emerging versus developed markets. Historically, Panasonic had maintained a conventional geographic format organized in terms of North America, Europe, and Asia. Now, given the equatorial proximity of many emerging economies, it differentiates operations by organizing in terms of temperature and tropical climate zones—longitude, not latitude, matters more in setting its structure. Operationally, executives from Brazil, who previously collaborated with colleagues in South America, now swap ideas with counterparts in Malaysia, who previously had conferred with colleagues in Asia.[34]

Limits   Conducting similar organizational activities in several places increases administrative inefficiency. Each area division, say EMENA, Americas, and Asia/Oceania/Africa, essentially builds a "mini-me" operation in order to make and sell products in its assigned territory. Replication, besides expensive, complicates integration and coordination. Some MNEs accept this inefficiency as the cost of a locally responsive organization. Rather than a structural deficiency, the requirements of its strategy necessitate replicating business operations across markets.

GLOBAL MATRIX STRUCTURE

A matrix organization

- institutes overlap among functional and divisional forms,
- gives functional, product, and geographic groups a common focus,
- has dual-reporting relationships rather than a single line of command,
- fits the demands of MNEs that cannot easily reconcile competing market pressures.

The worldwide product division structure centralizes decision-making to improve operational efficiencies. Alternatively, the worldwide area structure decentralizes decision-making to improve local responsiveness. The MNE implementing a global strategy, given its emphasis of integration and standardization, would opt for the former, while an MNE implementing a multi-domestic strategy, given its emphasis of adaptation and responsiveness, would opt for the latter. As we saw in Chapter 12, some MNEs implement the transnational strategy, aiming to ingeniously reconcile global integration and local responsiveness. Organizing workflows to implement this strategy directs management's attention to the **global matrix structure** (see Figure 16.6).

A global matrix structure horizontally differentiates the MNE along two dimensions; in Figure 16.6, those dimensions are geography and product. Interlacing different types of divisions integrates units that are sensitive to competing pressures. Requiring managers from both divisions to negotiate mutually agreeable plans, goes the reasoning, infuses both perspectives into decision-making, thereby more effectively reconciling integration and responsiveness pressures. Operationally, the matrix format means that a manager running a subsidiary now has two bosses: one represents the product side, the other represents the geographic domain. Since the matrix structure assigns equal authority to the product and area managers, both must work together to set relationships, coordinate resources, and share rewards.[35]

Limits In principle, the global matrix structure promotes cross-divisional communication and multifunctional collaboration. In practice, organizational politics fans competition for resources and rewards. Unchecked, gamesmanship threatens collaboration, thereby short-circuiting the knowledge-generating and decision-making relationships that were the original promise of the matrix. A matrix structure also institutes a dual hierarchy that runs afoul

FIGURE 16.6   The Matrix Structure

Rationale: Structure is set by organizing a dual relationship among different divisions in order to integrate complementary activities. Product divisions direct value activities in mutually beneficial collaboration with the choices made by area divisions.

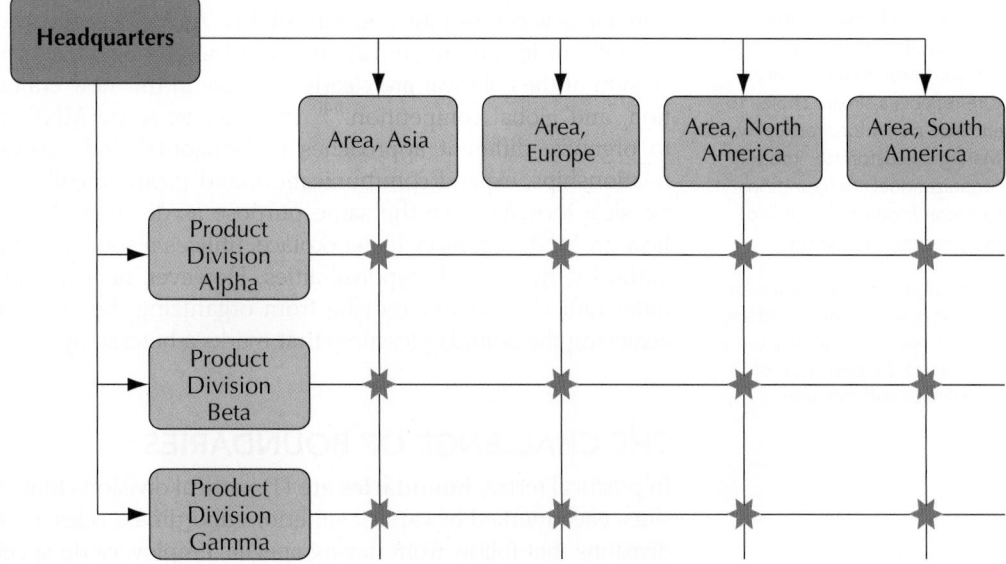

of the **unity-of-command principle**. This notion holds that an unbroken chain of command should flow through the levels of the hierarchy, beginning with the CEO down to the entry-level employee. Giving one worker two bosses, by blurring lines of responsibility, creates conflicting lines of command and nebulous accountability.[36] The CEO of Dow Chemical, an early adopter of the matrix structure, explained, "We were an organization that was matrixed and depended on teamwork, but there was no one in charge. When things went well, we didn't know whom to reward; and when things went poorly, we didn't know whom to blame."[37] Persistent problems coordinating responsibilities and resources have led MNEs to question its practical usefulness.

MIXED STRUCTURE

Each MNE's structure reflects its particular

• market circumstances,
• strategic choice,
• value chain configuration,
• administrative legacy,
• executive preferences.

Few MNEs set a structure that neatly applies the precise characteristics of a functional, divisional, or matrix format. Most face situations where different market conditions prevent instituting a single format—recall, for example, Nike's dilemma organizing its regional operations given their different performance prospects. Thus, some MNEs combine features of the functional, geographic, and product structures into a **mixed structure**. This format does not signify indecisiveness. Rather, some MNEs see no superior single organizational model given changing industry conditions, market trends, strategic capabilities, and company legacies (e.g., some conditions support a geographic format in Area A but fit a functional structure for business activity in Area B). Again, Nike installed vertical and horizontal arrangements in China and Eastern Europe that were unsuitable for organizing its activities in North America, Western Europe, and Japan. Likewise, Dell Computers horizontally differentiated its Asian headquarters in Singapore by business function, aiming to improve its regional financial, operational, and tax efficiency. Nestlé organizes most of its food and beverage business in terms of geographies (Areas EMENA, Americas, and Asia/Oceania/Africa) but runs some businesses globally (e.g., Nestlé Waters, Nestlé Nutrition, Nespresso). Although executives prefer structural consistency, organizing for differing market conditions often results in mixed structures.[38]

NEOCLASSICAL STRUCTURES

CONCEPT CHECK

Discussion of the "Types of Economic Systems" in Chapter 4 (page 155), noted that a mixed economy combines some of the characteristics of a free market with certain features of command systems. A mixed organizational structure reflects a similar choice to sacrifice purity for practicality. Managers customize "model" organizational configurations to accommodate their mix of businesses and countries.

MNEs, looking to implement increasingly sophisticated strategies, look for commensurately sophisticated structures that support the emerging communication and collaboration patterns.[39] Some find the hierarchical architecture of classical structures, designed to maximize command, control, coercion, and compliance, more commonly promotes complexity, bureaucracy, conformity, and inflexibility. As some argue, the "models and frameworks that shaped our leading organizations from the end of the second world war through the conclusion of the cold war are clearly obsolete in this new era of e-business, perpetual innovation, and global competition."[40] In recourse, some MNEs adopt **neoclassical structures** to organize different approaches to horizontal and vertical differentiation that broaden relationships, expand communication, and promote collaboration. In absolute terms, neoclassical formats serve the same purpose as do their classical counterparts. They stipulate how an MNE organizes its workplace, utilizes resources, administers systems, and specifies authority, rights, and responsibilities. However, neoclassical structures do so in ways that differ radically, notably moving from organizing the boundaries that define a hierarchy to achieving the boundarylessness that marks a heterarchy.

Classical structures emphasize the principles of command and control. Neoclassical structures emphasize the principles of coordinate and cultivate.

THE CHALLENGE OF BOUNDARIES

In practical terms, **boundaries** are (1) vertical divisions that separate employees into specific slots, each marked by explicit superior-subordinate roles, in the hierarchy and (2) horizontal divisions that follow from having specific employees do specific jobs in specific units.[41] In a

CONCEPT CHECK

"The Forces Driving Global-ization and IB," profiled in Chapter 1 (page 50), explains that market drivers such as expanded technology, liberal-ized trade, and increased cross-national cooperation reset the external environment of international business. Recog-nizing changes as opportunities moves MNEs to experiment with neoclassical structures that reset degrees of vertical and horizontal differentiation.

classical structure, vertically and horizontally differentiating the workflow leads to specify-ing precise rules, responsibilities, and relationships—each, in turn, institutes a boundary. Think of, for example, the schematic of boxes and lines shown in Figures 16.2 through 16.6; each demarcate the boundaries that hierarchically segregate the people who run the various functions, markets, and businesses. The boundaries that establish the command-and-control format of classical structures, by instituting divisions between people, pose organizational challenges. Divisions typically slow communication, discourage collaboration, create rigidi-ties, and bureaucratize decision-making.

Sony's CEO, for example, blames his company's poor performance not on the wrong strategy, but the reality that rivalry and conflict between its differentiated businesses obstructs individual effort and collective effectiveness.[42] Removing the boundaries that block communication, coordination, and collaboration among divisions, he added, would position Sony to engage its expanding diversity of markets, customers, and rivals. In recourse, Sony, like other MNEs, looks to a heterarchial structure whose fewer boundaries speed coordina-tion and spur collaboration.

THE GOAL OF BOUNDARYLESSNESS

Increasingly sophisticated strategies require minimizing the internal structural, systemic, and interpersonal boundaries that constrain collaboration in the MNE.

A neoclassical structure directs MNEs to the issue of boundaries and, more importantly, how to dismantle as well as avoid them. It urges busting boundaries between vertical ranks and roles; between horizontal units in different functions, products, and areas; and between the firm and its suppliers, distributors, JV partners, strategic allies, and customers. General Electric's performance highlights the process. Directing GE's far-flung global operations led former CEO Jack Welch to experiment with progressively flatter organizational formats. He aimed to build a heterarchial organization that eliminated the vertical and horizontal boundaries that put barriers between company, managers, customers, suppliers, and stake-holders. As Welch explained, "The simplest definition of what we are trying to create—what our objective is—is a **boundaryless** company, a company where the artificial barriers and walls people are forever building around themselves or each other—for status, security, or to keep change away—are demolished and everyone has access to the same information, everyone pulls in the same direction, and everyone shares in the rewards of winning—in the soul as well as in the wallet."[43] Radical then, less so today, moves by Welch and Gore, as we saw in our opening profile, pioneer the transformation of 'Organization Man' into 'Network Person.'[44]

Boundarylessness refers to eliminating vertical, horizontal, and external boundaries that hinder the flow of information and formation of relationships.

Gore's lattice structure and its egalitarian workplace philosophy exemplify boundaryless-ness practices. The Gore Way sees the hierarchy suppressing creativity and innovation and hence avoids organizational charts, chains of command, predetermined communication channels, and job titles. Rather, Associates share information, as opposed to controlling it. Instead of a few telling the many what to do, multifunctional teams self-organize around opportunities. Collaboration compels communication, and high-performance validates lead-ers. "We work hard at maximizing individual potential, maintaining an emphasis on product integrity, and cultivating an environment where creativity can flourish," says CEO Terri Kelly. She added, "A fundamental belief in our people and their abilities continues to be the key to our success, even as we expand globally."[45]

Loosely connected networks of self-organizing and self-governing agents are key features of neoclassical structures. Likewise, the flexibility of these formats promotes fewer rules and regulations. Employees act as entrepreneurial owners rather than as risk-averse bureaucrats. At Gore, for example, every Associate is a shareholder after one year. Unlike classical structures, in which the formal attributes of managers (i.e., title, location, number of direct reports) matter most, neoclassical formats make the managers' relationships with other agents in the network matter more. Again, at Gore, team members evaluate one another. In summary, the boundarylessness of a neoclassical structure spurs people to share rather than control informa-tion; collaborate rather than compete on projects; promote rather than suppress innovation; cultivate rather than command relationships; and engage rather than resist change.

THE NETWORK STRUCTURE

A network structure anchors a dynamic organization that outsources value activities to firms whose core competency supports greater innovation at lower cost.

The **network structure,** a leading neoclassical format, arranges roles, relationships, and responsibilities in a patterned flow of activity that allocates people and resources to decentralized projects (see Figure 16.7).[46] It is anchored by a core unit that outsources activities in which it has no core competency to firms that do—or, put differently, "do what you do best and outsource the rest."[47] For example, MNEs like Nike, Apple, Qualcomm, and Cisco concentrate on value creation in R&D, product design, or marketing. They then contract external suppliers and independent manufacturers, like Pegatron, Foxconn, Kyocera, or Yue Yuen Industrial, to make their products. Operationally, cross-partner arrangements share production, distribution, and service resources. The latest and greatest communication systems, leveraging the Internet, e-mail, file sharing, social media, and teleconferencing tools, support coordination and expedite collaboration. Admittedly, its difficult to visualize the ever-expanding connections in a network organization. The adjacent photo provides one view of the scope of connectivity created by an expanding set of links.

The network structure minimizes rules and regulations processes in order to preempt potential boundaries. Cross-partner linkages emphasize transactional efficiency, but also advocate developing specialized decision-making relationships based on long-term common interests. Units link self-organizing and self-regulating teams into loosely connected networks. They act as entrepreneurial owners rather than as risk-averse bureaucrats. Unlike classical hierarchical structures, in which the formal attributes of managers matter most, in the heterarchial network structure, relationships with other agents matter more.

Networks Aren't New   The network structure is not unprecedented. Japanese MNEs have long used the so-called *keiretsu* format, an integrated collective of nominally independent companies in which each owns a share of the others.[48] *Keiretsus* rely on long-term personal relationships among the companies' executives. Sometimes they are vertical, such as the *seisan keiretsu,* a manufacturing network in which managers connect the factors of production of a certain product (e.g., Toyota and its parts suppliers), or the *ryūtsū keiretsu,* a

CONCEPT CHECK

The notion of a network shapes discussions of IB: Chapter 1, for instance, notes the idea of connectography and the expanding cross-national infrastructure links, Chapter 6 describes the trade networks formalized by the WTO, Chapter 8 discusses financial networks composed of global capital markets, and Chapter 14 analyzes the effort of MNEs to network with partners through collaborative alliances.

FIGURE 16.7   A Network Structure

A network structure connects people, products, and processes into a coherent, collaborative system. At its center is a core unit that aims to "do what it does best and outsource the rest." Similarly, network partners focus on their core competencies. A network structure uses extensive communication channels to maximize the connections that energize collaboration. Dynamic coordination and control methods set, regulate, and integrate the interactions among members, the latter motivated by common goals and specific objectives.

Differentiated units to which headquarters delegates decision-making authority. These units, whether a local marketing subsidiary, international production center, or suppliers, are the front line of the network. They have responsibility for sensing, processing, and acting upon specialized as well as generalized information in entrepreneurial fashion.

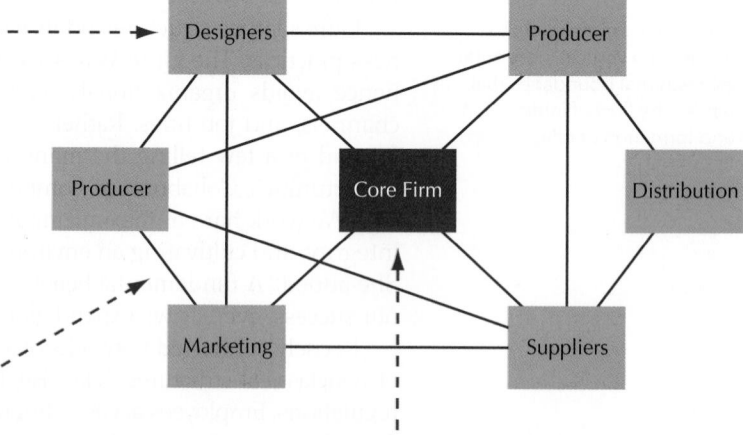

The channels of exchange that facilitate and fine-tune the volume, content, and flow of hard data and soft information. These linkages animate the network by setting paths of interaction, coordination, collaboration, and integration among the differentiating yet interdependent functional, area, and product units.

The formal center of the network that coordinates and controls strategic objectives and operational policies across the differentiated units. This unit ensures the efficient flow of resources, supplies, components, and funds throughout the network. It creates value by effectively collecting, sorting, and brokering the network's accumulated wisdom, knowledge, and experiences.

One View of Network Connectivity.

It's difficult to pinpoint the ever-expanding connections in a network organization. Here, though, we see a take on the likely configuration of links. This network, set by major air routes among key geographic nodes in Africa, Europe, the Middle East, and Asia, depicts the principles of connectivity.

Source: Anton Balazh/Shutterstock

A network organization emphasizes lateral decision processes, horizontal linkages, and extensive collaboration.

distribution network. Or they can be horizontal, like a *kigyō shūdan*, essentially a diversified business group that links companies across related and different industries; at its center is a *sogo shosha* (trading company), like Mitsubishi, or a financial institution, like Sumitomo. In both vertical and horizontal *keiretsu*s, the network center coordinates marketing and controls financing among the allied units.

MNEs worldwide use various forms of the neoclassical network structure.

Worldwide, MNEs exhibiting elements of the *keiretsu* form include IKEA, Scania, Virgin Group, Cisco, and Grupo Empresarial Antioqueño.[49] South Korean companies like Samsung, LG, or Hyundai share some of the characteristics of the *keiretsu* in their *chaebol* format; the ten main *chaebols* list nearly 600 affiliated companies.[50] German firms, such as Deutsche Bank, are similarly intertwined, but no formal term describes the format.[51] Like their Japanese counterparts, these groups have extensive, self-sustaining connections. Unlike the Japanese, they formalize central control.

VIRTUAL ORGANIZATION

A virtual organization arranges roles, responsibilities, and relationships to deemphasize boundaries.

A **virtual organization** uses technologies to connect otherwise detached entities (from employees to entire enterprises). The neoclassical arrangement between independent companies, suppliers, customers, and even rivals enables them to "work across space, time, and organizational boundaries with links strengthened by webs of communication technologies."[52] Instead of command and control, a virtual organization uses associations, agreements, and alliances.[53]

Deemphasizing formal rules, responsibilities, and procedures promotes informal communication that disregards hierarchical boundaries. Improving technologies support coordination among people working from different locations, making it easier to cultivate relationships, acquire resources, and develop capabilities.[54] Market mechanisms, such as contracts, formalize relationships. Strong performers replace poor performers.[55] Analysts point to MNEs like British Telecom, Reuters Holdings, and Aventis as virtual organizations. The film industry provides an extreme model. "Employees" are free agents who move from project to project, applying their skills (i.e., directing, acting, talent search, animation, costuming, and set design) as contracted. Temporary arrangements let them organize, disband, and reorganize as projects emerge.[56]

NEOCLASSICAL STRUCTURES IN ACTION

A virtual organization is a dynamic arrangement among partners that efficiently adapts to market change.

Some 400 midsized emerging-market cities, many unfamiliar in the West, will generate nearly 40 percent of global growth over the next 15 years. MNEs respond in kind, opening high-profile corporate centers in places that, although far from home, are close to the action. Company history, CEO preference, or legal constraints make some prefer less dramatic change, opting instead to create a global virtual headquarters from which to locate key functions in high-priority markets: finance and tax may go to Singapore, as Dell did, while global procurement goes to Shenzhen, as Walmart chose.[57] Similarly, P&G moved the headquarters of its global skin, cosmetics, and personal-care unit from its Cincinnati headquarters to Singapore while Philips Electronics moved the headquarters of its domestic appliances business from Eindhoven to Shanghai. Finally, IBM relies on its workers in Shanghai to process accounts receivable, specialists in Manila to oversee human resources, accountants in Kuala Lumpur to keep the books, buyers in Shenzhen to procure components, and customer specialists in Brisbane to run its help desk. Each unit, responding to IBM's quest to move work to places where it will be done most efficiently and to the highest quality, manages projects that arise throughout the global market. Nearly half of its employees worldwide are "mobile," meaning that they do not report daily to an IBM site.[58]

Customers, meanwhile, care less where work is done provided the results satisfy contract specifications. Within this context, IBM's decision to reset its structure to reflect its changing workflow, in turn, reflects the fact that markets and technologies meant it now could build a globally integrated enterprise. Instead of a classical hierarchy, IBM organizes a conglomeration of loosely connected, cloud-based, dynamic suppliers of IT services. Implementing this vision—intensified by competitors such as SAP, Infosys, Wipro, Cognizant, and others traveling the same path—spurs IBM to champion the coordination, collaboration, and control ethos of a neoclassical structure. Redesigning its organization to suit its changing workflow fortifies its ability to manage its strategy, costs, people, and risk on a global basis.[59]

The flexibility of virtual organizations expedites the replacement of poor performers.

Likewise, consider the choices made by Cisco. Changing markets and enterprising rivals put it at a structural crossroads. Rather than give a classical divisional hierarchy another go, Cisco developed an elaborate system of cross-functional, cross-market, and cross-business committees, some of which go without a formal leader in order to promote a culture of collaboration. Cisco relies on cross-national teams to bust the structural, cultural, and procedural boundaries that separated colleagues. Social-network analyses map the frequency and effectiveness of communications, thereby clarifying the flow of information among personnel. These results connect different functional roles, across multiple countries, through multiple languages, and in dozens of areas of domain knowledge. Asked why he led Cisco into uncharted organizational territory, its CEO replied that he had no choice. He needed a structure that would react quickly to new opportunities, develop entire solutions rather than stand-alone products, and help Cisco "become a globally integrated company by making it easier for executives from all around the world to weigh in."[60] Going forward, he expects increasingly cheaper, easier communication technology will move more MNEs from the classical standards of command and control to the neoclassical ideals of coordinate and cultivate.

PITFALLS OF NEOCLASSICAL STRUCTURES

Neoclassical structures, like their classical counterparts, run into operational problems.

Like its classical counterparts, neoclassical structures have limits. Networks are intrinsically dynamic structures, spurring adaptive reconfiguration, responsive coordination, and real-time control.[61] Organizing something that continually evolves poses problems. Gore worries that the internal workings of its many management committees may prove too socially complex as well as physically tiring. Cisco struggles to manage teams amid its ongoing acquisitions and divestures. Nokia's consensus-seeking leaders promoted esprit de corps among its loosely bounded units; that, though, did not stop the company's gradual collapse.

Similarly, the egalitarianism of network formats works well organizing small firms, but struggles doing the same for larger ones. Some firms devise means to preempt these threats. Srijan, an Indian software company, lets employees monitor coworkers' compensation. Others, such as SumAll or Zappos, institute a corporate constitution that formalizes the rights of employees to participate in decision-making. The jury is still out on their effectiveness. Boundary-busting could prove detrimental in knowledge-intensive firms, like McKinsey or Google, that already struggle to measure individual productivity.[62]

Lastly, some executives champion self-organization to the troops but still regulate decision-making. When push comes to shove, they pull rank, intervening in workers' independence. Recurring gaps between policy and practice fans motivation problems. Hidden hierarchies can arise as workers forsake management's rhetoric and organize around the reality of rules, rewards, and punishments.[63] Said one observer, "I've been inside a lot of companies that espouse flat organizational structures and self-management. But when you really start looking at how things actually work, you find that there is in fact a hierarchy—just one that is not explicit."[64]

Point

Point

Yes The hierarchy is the enduring foundation for how MNEs optimally arrange the roles, responsibilities, and relationships of its structure for a simple reason—it is the superior format for doing so. It sets a clear chain of command, functional span of control, effective allocation of authority, and precise assignment of tasks. It specifies the ideal degree of rules, routines, policies, and procedures. Its vertical and horizontal differentiation spells out, as we see in Figure 16.8, who's who in the organization. It effectively organizes planning, coordination, and control systems.

An advocate of the hierarchy, Harold Geneen of ITT, argued correctly that it "makes people as predictable and controllable as the capital resources that they're responsible for."[65] The hierarchy's strengths rightly made it the *sine qua non* of the professional management model since the early twentieth century. Given the strong preference for hierarchical organizations in countries such as India and China, it will flourish through the twenty-first century. While neoclassical structures emerge here or there in the West, the East has many companies whose lofty leader, many rungs removed from the factory floor, uses a hierarchical structure to command and control activity.

Ongoing Refinements Contemporary technological, regulatory, and competitive trends, we agree, have interesting implications for organizing a company. We concede that as environments change, so too must companies' strategies and structures. However, the Counterpoint's call to discard the classical principles of the hierarchy strikes us as reckless. Yes, gaps emerge in the hierarchy, but managers need only reengineer processes to fill them. Powerful programs, like Total Quality Control, Six Sigma, and the Balanced

The Hierarchical Structure: The Superior Format

Scorecard, effectively modernize the hierarchy. Fine-tuning workplace arrangements through these and similar methods equips the organization to meet the challenge of changing markets.[66]

What then, you ask, do we think of the neoclassical alternative of a heterarchy that the Counterpoint champions? We see radical tinkering with the day-to-day reality of organizing international operations exhibiting commendable courage but questionable judgment. Avoiding failure requires thoughtful adjustment to the way organizations run, not the wistfulness of a brave new cyberworld powered by newfangled social networking tools.

Leading Indicator Google, we submit, foreshadows the approach to designing a classical hierarchy that respects the past but engages the future. Google organizes its senior executives and work groups by business function, with the largest functions represented by engineering, product management, and marketing divisions. Despite the founders' description of Google as engineering-centric, they see virtue in chaos by design. Insiders' tales of orderly disorder, purposeful disarray, and certain uncertainty signal its plans to thrive on the edge of controlled chaos, all the while firmly anchored in the functional order of a classical hierarchy.

Rather than retreat to the hierarchical conventions commonly found in engineering-centric companies, such as DuPont and General Motors in earlier times, Google stretches its hierarchy as much as possible. Asked why, Larry Page (Google's co-founder, CEO, and unofficial thought leader) explained, "I want to run a company where we are moving too quickly and doing too much, not being too cautious and doing too little. If we don't have any of these mistakes, we're just not taking enough risk."[67]

FIGURE 16.8   A Classical Hierarchy

Although quite simple, this depiction effectively communicates the organizing logic of a hierarchy—different people of different rank at different levels do different jobs. As such, the various shades of folks speak to the matter of horizontal differentiation while the top-down flow highlights the idea of vertical differentiation.

Source: Paperboat/Shutterstock

The Hierarchical Structure: The Superior Format

Counterpoint **No** Although imperfect, history is often a useful interpreter of the present and predictor of the future. So, think back to the early 1900s, when emerging technologies signaled to some the superiority of the then-heretical hierarchy. One sees the same today, as emerging technologies endorse new structural heresies. Expanding digital infrastructures allows MNEs to organize their activities in new ways, letting them efficiently diffuse information and effectively integrate its flows. Today, just as a century earlier, astute executives break free of the shackles of the status quo, building organizations that leverage the expanding waves of information flowing in, though, and out of the MNE.

The Crux of Change   Unquestionably, the tried-and-true classical hierarchy has virtues. Nevertheless, market trends spotlight its increasing limits. It organizes workplace activities and information flows in ways that thwart integration. Even when turbocharged with matrix overlays and mixed adjustments, the hierarchy slows relationships, confuses accountability, and complicates collaboration.[68] McKinsey & Company, for example, report that struggling MNEs' reliance on traditional organization formats imposes a steep penalty. By leashing the intrinsic motivation of employees, stifling adaptation, and squelching entrepreneurialism, hierarchies impede common cause, discourage innovation, and erode relationships.[69]

The Heterarchy   Looking around today one sees examples of networks, virtual organizations, lattice structures, flat formats,

Counterpoint

or peer-to-peer formats. These neoclassical forms exhibit the general properties of a heterarchy: namely, "a large-scale, self-organizing community that sets free unusually high degrees of energy and engagement—despite the lack of clear or direct economic payoff for participants."[70] The heterarchy is a constellation of actors and relationships that follow from the interactions of technology, knowledge, social relations, administrative routines, and legal ties. Figure 16.9 conveys these properties. A heterarchy is "infinitely large, never balanced, never optimal and has unique perspectives for all members."[71] Agents connect to others through direct and indirect channels. "Information flows along multiple and intermediate paths; this allows for multiple and overlapping points at which information can be sorted and interpreted. It makes it possible to process an abundance of information effectively."[72] By remedying the bias toward instituting bureaucratic boundaries, the heterarchy provides the framework to build a truly integrated enterprise.

A notable heterarchy is the open-source model, a software movement in which program source code is given to volunteers who fix bugs and design new features with no compensation. Operationally, it applies basic rules to increase transparency, coordinate efforts, and control performance. Programmers' ability to monitor peer production encourages collaboration. Similar situations unfold with the ecosystems that power the Apple and Android "app" phenomena. Others point to Technology, Entertainment, Design (TED), a nonprofit devoted to "Ideas Worth Spreading," which hosts conferences that are then distributed in video format via the Internet. Absent central direction, an informal, loosely coupled network of several thousand volunteers has translated subtitles for thousands of videos into more than 90 languages.[73]

The Test   The standards of organization are fundamentally shifting. The precision of vertical and horizontal differentiation gives way to loosely coupled, less-bounded neoclassical formats.[74] Moreover, it's over-optimistic to think that one need merely apply organizational band-aids, such as Six Sigma or the Balanced Scorecard, to update an increasingly anachronistic, command-and-control classical structure. Quite simply, "today's big companies do very little to enhance the productivity of their professionals. In fact,

their vertically oriented organizational structures, retrofitted with ad hoc and matrix overlays, nearly always make professional work more complex and inefficient."[75]

Andy Grove, once CEO of Intel, foreshadows how the apparent chaos of the heterarchy will reset the presumed order of the hierarchy. A structure must encourage and energize constructive confrontation in ways that let workers agree and disagree, but, ultimately, commit to the same goals. The challenge, he advises, is developing a structure that will "let chaos reign and then rein in chaos."[76] In our view, the neoclassical heterarchy, not the classical hierarchy, meets the challenge of changing market situations, shifting technological frontiers, and radical workflow resets.[77]

FIGURE 16.9   A Neoclassical Heterarchy

This depiction of a heterarchy, again quite simplified, highlights key features. Dynamic patterns of relationships, in place of the ranks and divisions found in a classical hierarchy, mark a heterarchy. Communication, coordination, and collaboration links, aided and abetted by technology, integrate equivalent "blue" managers.

Source: Paperboat/Shutterstock

COORDINATION SYSTEMS

Configuring resources, capabilities, and competencies arranges the strategic architecture of the firm. Making it perform requires, as we saw earlier, setting a structure, and as we see now, coordinating how people and processes work. One way to engage this idea is to think of the configuration process as the MNE placing its pieces atop the global game board. An MNE moves its R&D piece to Sweden, factory piece to Vietnam, logistics piece to the United States, marketing piece to Italy, and the service piece to Malaysia. Once configured, executives specify how these pieces link to and relate with each other. In other words, MNEs develop **coordination systems** to link the people and processes that run its various 'pieces.' Coordination ranges from nonexistent (each piece is independent) to comprehensive (all pieces are interdependent).

The shifting pressures of global integration and local responsiveness, fueled by dynamic industry structures and evolving market conditions, push MNEs to devise sophisticated strategies.[78] Pioneering plans to reset value activities require commensurately innovative coordination methods. Coordinating activities requires adeptly moving ideas, materials,

The MNE uses coordination and control systems to synchronize, integrate, and regulate value activities across the units of its organization.

people, and capital. For example, IBM, GE, Microsoft, and Accenture opened R&D facilities in India, reasoning that the productivity of the local scientific community coupled with its unique outlook of frugal innovation offered promising points of value creation. Breakthroughs at GE's Technology Center in Bengaluru, owing to adroit coordination processes, spread to GE's operations in Hungary, Brazil, China, the United States, and onward. In one instance, GE's Indian technology center developed a low-cost electrocardiograph machine for doctors and hospitals in rural communities. Coordination links diffused it elsewhere, and soon GE's German and U.S. subsidiaries began selling it in their home markets.[79]

Improving communications systems, made faster by cheaper voice, video, and data options, help link people and processes. Still, MNEs run into problems due to time zones, differing languages, and ambiguous interactions. Picture a company whose resources, capabilities, and competencies span the globe. Parts and products flow from South Africa and Chile to their ultimate destination in Malaysia, Germany, Canada, the United States, and China. Each transfer, from mines to depots to plants to ships to warehouses to storefronts, creates links that require coordination. Toss into the mix multiple time zones and multiple languages, and the potential for misalignment escalates. Coordination systems maximize alignment by synchronizing rules, responsibilities, and relationships. Therefore, organizing activities, whether the structural format is classical or neoclassical, requires managers develop the requisite coordination methods. Today, prevalent coordination frameworks revolve around the ideas of standardization, planning, or mutual adjustment.

CONCEPT CHECK

Earlier discussion of the "Rise in and Application of Technology" in Chapter 1 (page 51) notes that technology fosters new ways of communicating among worldwide operations. New technologies enable MNEs to experiment with options, many of them unprecedented, to coordinate dispersed value activities.

Coordination by standardization

- sets universal rules and procedures that apply to units worldwide,
- enforces consistency of activities among dispersed units.

COORDINATION BY STANDARDIZATION

Standardizing rules and routines to compel operational consistency has a straightforward mandate: do the same thing, the same way, everywhere. **Coordination by standardization** attains this goal by specifying the way employees do their jobs, work with one another, and deal with customers. Aspects range from the mundane (i.e., dress and decorum requirements stipulated in employee manuals) to the strategic (i.e., decision-making heuristics, protocols for entering new markets). Asked why it standardizes its processes and procedures worldwide, Starbucks notes the need to replicate the aesthetics, aura, and performance of its coffee shop concept in the thousands of Starbucks spanning the globe—Starbucks in Seattle is interchangeable with Starbucks in Sydney.[80] Coordination by standardization, by precisely specifying workplace standards and workflow scripts, achieves this goal.

Coordination by standardization is ideally suited for the MNE implementing an international or global strategy. Each strategy's imperative for worldwide consistency advocates a universal approach. For an international strategy, transferring, applying, and protecting core competencies promotes unswerving rules and regulations. For the global strategy, running densely linked, interdependent activities leaves little slack for deviations. Clear lines of accountability, centralized decision-making, and codified knowledge prescribes who, when, why, and how one does a job. Resources and components, for instance, are needed at specific plants at specific times. Standardizing coordination methods—such as the format for processing information and supervising logistics—preempts disruptive irregularities.

Standardizing coordination processes reduces the influence of national cultures in the workplace. The performance of an integrated value chain depends on links between interconnected activities satisfying precise schedules. A unit office in a monochronic culture likely sees deadlines as hard promises while its counterpart in a polychronic culture likely sees them as guidelines. Coordination by standardization synchronizes how both interpret time in the workplace. Similarly, an MNE might have factories in Japan and Mexico that manufacture the same product, but, because of cultural legacies and location economics, each applies a different production model. The Mexican factory uses a traditional assembly-line operation because of inexpensive local labor, patchy transportation infrastructure, and a high marginal cost of technology. The Japanese factory, in contrast, uses a lean production system due to local labor competency, manufacturing expertise, efficient logistics, and high warehouse expense. Coordination by standardization, in synchronizing their activities, enables the MNE to harmonize different manufacturing orientations.

Challenges   Differences in industry conduct and host-government attitudes complicate coordination by standardization. Market circumstances, strategic goals, or workflow patterns often prevent specifying universal policies and procedures. Too, often they do not fit every situation in every unit in every country. Some MNEs, especially those implementing a multi-domestic strategy, decentralize authority to let subsidiaries adapt activities to local conditions. Ongoing calls to adjust this rule or change that procedure undermine the authority of standardization.

COORDINATION BY PLAN

Coordination by plan requires that interdependent units meet common deadlines and objectives.

Applying general objectives, extensive guidelines, and sequences and schedules to link people and processes implements **coordination by plan**. Generally, plans set success factors, specify expectations, assign accountability, and formalize deadlines. They regulate how units accept, adopt, and, where legitimate, adjust tactics. Plans identify participating managers and programs, establish timing and format, and set communication schedules. Unlike coordination by standardization, managers of interdependent units have the latitude to mutually adjust goals and schedules—provided they still hit targets. In a sense, then, coordination by standardization helps the MNE maximize operational efficiency while coordination by plan helps it optimize organizational effectiveness.

Coordination by plan requires synchronizing people and processes across countries.[81] Red Hat's Global Support Services, for example, solves technical problems facing users of its intricate software products. Red Hat's support engineers and account managers work from 16 countries, support 3,600 coworkers in 65 offices distributed across 35 countries, and provide round-the-clock customer service in 9 languages. Improving technologies fortify the practicality of coordination by plan by improving the ease of analyzing, exchanging, and synthesizing information. Faster travel, expanding exchange options, and teleconferencing technologies overcome long-running barriers to multinational planning. Teleconferencing, for instance, lets those who prefer dealing with counterparts through face-to-face contact do so in ways that let them capture the nonverbal nuances of body language. The historic bane of IB has been the necessity of visiting faraway colleagues, partners, and customers, often at a moment's notice, high expense, and considerable effort. Now, teleconferencing creates the magical ability to be many places at once, thereby boosting the practicality of coordination by plan.

Innovative management methods bolster coordination by plan. Six Sigma, a rigorous and disciplined planning process, uses data and statistical analysis to coordinate practices and systems. Credit Suisse, Siemens, GE, Korea Telecom, Wipro, Nortel Networks, Air Canada, and DuPont have all used it to improve their planning processes. The analytics of similar programs, such as the Balanced Scorecard or Total Quality Management, are used worldwide. Likewise, MNEs apply other methods. Some locate international and domestic personnel in proximity to each other—say, by placing the international division in the same building as product divisions—to promote networks that facilitate communication and collaboration. Others build cross-national teams of people with different responsibilities to debate objectives and bridge gaps.[82]

CONCEPT CHECK

No matter the coordination approach adopted by an MNE, none are immune to the complications posed by national cultures. Different national cultures differently influence the social, workplace, political, legal, and economic contexts. Differences in cultural conditions, first introduced in our profile of "Major Behavioral Practices Affecting Business" Chapter 2 (page 79) also influence a company's strategic options, shaping its choices regarding coordination by standardization, planning, or adjustment.

Challenges   Notwithstanding a plan's brilliance, the unexpected is ever-present; recall, for example, the aphorism, "the best-laid plans of mice and men often go awry." Market disruptions, government regulations, mergers and acquisitions, to name just a few, cause big changes. Adjusting objectives and schedules requires communication among different groups spanning multiple borders. Cultural differences routinely pose complications. Coworkers differ in their orientations toward trust, exchange, accountability, and allegiance.[83] Units anchored in individualistic cultures may disagree over information sharing or task responsibilities with their collectivist counterparts; ensuing uncertainty muddles coordination. Absent rules regulating relationships, cultural divergence increases the time, expense, and errors in cross-national exchange.

COORDINATION BY MUTUAL ADJUSTMENT

Coordination by mutual adjustment depends on managers interacting extensively with counterparts.

Some MNEs coordinate people and processes with a personal touch, socially engineering their systems to cultivate relationships among workers that, in turn, promote coordination. Rather than rules and routines in the context of standardization, or objectives and schedules in the context of planning, **coordination by mutual adjustment** relies on social networking outlooks and methods. Promoting collaboration among coworkers, goes the reasoning, builds systems that support sophisticated strategies.

Consider 3M's technology experts in its 100-plus laboratories worldwide. 3M links its innovativeness to developing systems that help its lab workers form robust knowledge-generating and decision-making relationships. The system then supports exchanging ideas, coordinating programs, and integrating activities. The abstraction of the scientific process along with the complexity of product development are intrinsically challenging. 3M realizes that productive communication among bright, independent-minded knowledge workers, distributed across more than 100 laboratories worldwide, requires robust, personal, and frequent interactions to set the trust that sustains collaboration. Hence, 3M uses coordination by mutual adjustment.

Key tools include a Technical Council, which comprises the heads of the major labs, meets monthly, and has a three-day annual retreat to boost exchanges across units. A broader-based Technical Forum, composed of scientists and technical experts chosen as representatives of various units, extends the social network.[84] Both methods cultivate the personal exchange of ideas, a key precondition of coordinating activities by mutual adjustment. Similarly, Gore relies on coordination by mutual adjustment. And, as does 3M, Associates conduct monthly technical meetings during which scientists and engineers from different divisions share ideas with fellow Associates. Reflecting on the process, Jack Kramer, an enterprise leader, explained "we put a lot of effort into trying to make sure that we connect informally and formally across a lot of boundaries."[85]

The personalized dynamic of coordination by mutual adjustment resets the official trappings set by formal roles, status, and power. Adjustment processes blur positional relationships among superiors, colleagues, and subordinates. Coordination by standardization or plan, in contrast, explicitly recognizes and reinforces vertical and horizontal differentiation. Coordination by mutual adjustment puts big demands on senior executives. Collaboration requires resetting executives' roles from telling people what to do to facilitating their success. Hence, coordination by adjustment is philosophically and practically compatible with neo-classical structures.[86]

Coordination by mutual adjustment taps various methods. Commonly, MNEs assess opportunities or check threats by building cross-national, cross-functional, and cross-business teams. Assembled and explicitly charged with collaborating, these teams share viewpoints and champion cooperative efforts while establishing liaisons among subsidiaries. Similarly, MNEs rotate managers among various slots in the company, reasoning that personal familiarity cultivates productive relationships. In addition, rotation across divisional, business, or functional lines promotes relationships that weaken insular thinking and reinforce idea sharing.[87]

Challenges   Coordination by mutual adjustment imposes tough demands, especially as globalizing markets press companies to support customers through traditional methods as well as virtual formats. The MNE opting for coordination via mutual adjustment must facilitate collaboration among associates in different parts of the world. The scale and scope of the typical MNE, naturally, pose logistical obstacles. Leading-edge social networking technologies provide only a partial solution. Ordinary geographic constraints, for example, require teams alternate meetings between early morning and late evening to accommodate various time zones. It is not unusual, over the course of the day, for a manager in the United States to teleconference with folks in Asia at 2 a.m., colleagues in Western Europe at 9 a.m., and coworkers and South America at 3 p.m.. Senior executives working on three to five coordination groups, and often many more, may have teleconferencing meetings around the clock. Often, decision-making slows as views adjust and readjust. Managers' commitment may waver as some tire of ongoing negotiations.

CONTROL SYSTEMS

CONCEPT CHECK

"Guidelines for Cultural Adjustment," profiled in Chapter 2 (page 89), notes that managers deal with differences in the ways in which colleagues and subordinates, especially those with different cultural outlooks, respond when it comes to issues like task motivation, relationship preferences, and workplace behavior. Here we observe that, to accommodate these differences, MNEs mind cultural orientations when setting coordination systems.

A key function of management is making sure workers are doing what must be done. If not, and productivity is sliding, schedules are slipping, and resources are wasting, then managers step in and correct problems. **Control systems**, the methods and means of problem correction, are part of a well-designed organization.[88] Managers apply them to compare performance to plans, identify differences, and, where found, analyze the gap and impose adjustments. Control systems regulate executive efforts, resource allocation, and self-interest. They directly complement coordination processes and structural designs. Prominent control systems include bureaucratic, market, and clan.

> Control system are policies and procedures that command, direct, or regulate workplace behavior.

BUREAUCRATIC CONTROL

> Bureaucratic control emphasizes organizational authority and relies on rules and regulations.

Explicit rules and routines that govern activities install **bureaucratic control**. This control system supports operations that lend themselves to universal rules and exact scripts and, importantly, fits workplaces where rules regiment behaviors. It effectively supports organizations using programs like Six Sigma or Total Quality Management to specify procedures. Bureaucratic controls also partition authority and accountability, thereby stipulating connections among relevant workers. The scale and scope of global operations, executives consistently report, means rules and regulations can vary unintentionally across cultures and countries; bureaucratic controls reduce this problem.[89] Bureaucratic control shares organizing principles with coordination by standardization and supports classical structures.

MARKET CONTROL

> Market control uses external market mechanisms to set standards that regulate performance.

Establishing performance benchmarks with external market mechanisms, such as profitability or market share, installs **market controls**. Objective standards, not subjective interpretations, control activities. Control systems escalate when a unit deviates from independent benchmarks—say, a market share drop or productivity decrease. Relying on market standards creates universal metrics that work in all countries (e.g., we measure market share the same way, everywhere). The objective indicators of market control help executives track a subsidiary's performance. This is particularly useful when executives decentralize decision-making. For instance, MNEs such as Gore, Nestlé, and Nike decentralize considerable authority to local subsidiaries. The home office supports subsidiaries with technological, financial, administrative, and legal resources, and waits for superior results. If not forthcoming, control systems activate and senior executives step in. Market control metrics simplify tracking performance across different units in different countries. The principles of market control overlap with those of coordination by plan and fit the principles of the classical and neoclassical structures.

CLAN CONTROL

Clan control uses shared values and ideals to moderate employee behavior.

Clan control relies on values, beliefs, shared norms, and informal relationships to regulate employee behaviors. Its goal is socializing employees to personally identify with the MNE's vision and mission as they go about their day-to-day routines, thereby necessitating minimal control.[90] Clan control is especially difficult in an MNE. A unifying vision that regulates a dispersed, diverse global workforce inevitably conflicts with some employees' values and norms. Certainly, there are notable successes, like the social aspects of renowned clan control systems, such as J&J's Credo, the Toyota Way, Matsushita's Seven Spiritual Values, or the Gore Way. Clan control shares organizing principles with coordination by mutual adjustment and supports neoclassical structures.

CONTROL MECHANISMS

Effective control requires objective mechanisms. A generation ago, the costs of travel, data exchange, and communication technologies endorsed certain control mechanisms. Improving economics, courtesy of expanding infrastructures and revolutionary technologies, make control cheaper, faster, and easier. This process has reduced the productivity of some tools, boosted the usefulness of others, and created the possibility for new mechanisms. Presently, MNEs support their control system with the following sorts of tools.

Timely reports allow managers improve the speed and insight of decision-making.

Reports   The intricacies of IB make reports a vital control method. Frequent, accurate, and real-time reports help managers allocate resources and monitor performance. Reports function as early warning systems, alerting managers to deviations from plan or market standards. Often, MNEs use report formats for foreign operations that resemble those used domestically, reasoning that they have worked here so they should work there. International operations, by expanding the volume of performance data, call for sophisticated information technologies to support control processes. The global diffusion of standardized software packages, often in the form of enterprise resource planning platforms, from SAP, Oracle, IBM, Microsoft, and Red Hat, organize many report systems. Standardizing the format worldwide, by leveraging corporate management's familiarity, improves the real-time performance of reporting controls. Also, reports that share the same format ease comparing the performance of different units.

Visiting Subsidiaries   Intrinsic boundaries limit the usefulness of reports. Senior executives, especially those applying coordination by adjustment and clan control, amplify control by visiting subsidiaries. Face-to-face meetings, formal budget reviews, and planning seminars fortify responsibility and accountability. Old-school subsidiary visits, awash with strategizing and socializing, promote communication between headquarters and local managers.[91] Increasingly, technologies expand managers' options. Teleconference innovations, supported by wikis, social networking, and web-based collaboration services, help MNEs reduce travel, save time, boost productivity, and tighten controls. Cisco, for instance, averages several thousand teleconferences a week. Besides cutting its annual travel budget by more than half, teleconferencing significantly increased "face time" among managers.[92]

CONCEPT CHECK

In discussing measures for "Degrees of Cultural Differences" in Chapter 2 (page 89), we explain how different attitudes toward cultural distance and different responses to culture shock frustrate the efforts of managers to coordinate value activities that span different cultural environments. Here, we add that they can create problems beyond the corrective capacity of a coordination system. In such cases, managers use control measures to impose order.

Information Systems   Technology platforms, by expediting information exchange, provide useful control tools. MNEs use enterprise resource planning to monitor activities, such as product planning, parts purchasing, maintaining inventories, customer service, and order fulfillment.[93] Most MNEs apply browser-based communication tools to coordinate data flows. Electronic transactions boost efficiency by streamlining exchanges among links in the chain. In larger markets, this interface is prevalent among manufacturers and their first-tier suppliers, such as the relationship between Costco and Procter & Gamble. Many MNEs set the open-source language protocol of the Internet—specifically, hypertext markup language (HTML) or XML—as the global standard. So far, though, there is evolving consensus on interface standards, as evidenced in the proliferation of web service composition standards.[94]

However, the increasing simplicity, generality, and usability of information exchange over the Internet spurs global standards. Still, MNEs face constraints in acquiring information, notably the cost of that information compared to its value and the difficulty of identifying redundancies and excluding the irrelevant.[95]

WHICH CONTROL SYSTEM WHEN?

A system that relies on a combination of control policies and systems is more reliable than one that does not.

Like most operational decisions in IB, there are few hard and fast rules about which control system when. Generally, as structure follows strategy, so too does control. MNEs following a global strategy prefer market controls, given that they can apply standard, objective benchmarks to evaluate performance in any market. Alternatively, transnational companies find value in clan control; the necessity of open exchange among geographically diffuse workers encourages control based on common values and norms. In any scenario, managers adjust their control system for the contingencies posed by the competing pressures of global integration and local responsiveness.

Likewise, implementing sophisticated strategies requires managers craft commensurately sophisticated control methods that reflect the different operating circumstances of different units. Consequently, few MNEs rely on a single control method. J&J and Gore, for instance, uses market and clan control to regulate performance. Certainly, both would prefer the efficiency of a universal system. But, both adjust to the contingencies imposed by the formal structure, coordination approaches, and, as we now see, organizational culture.

ORGANIZATIONAL CULTURE

Organizational culture refers to the ideologies, symbols, and core values that employees, no matter their location in the MNE's worldwide operations, regard as legitimate.

Having profiled the roles played by structure and systems in organizing an MNE, we turn to the final design element: organizational culture. In theory, one could profile it from an applied perspective, specifying it as the way things are done in an MNE and evaluating how workers organize around rules, rewards, and punishments.[96] Alternatively, we could adopt a philosophical view and assess how organizational culture, as an embedded set of shared values and normative principles, guides actions and sanctions behaviors within the MNE. We opt to integrate these perspectives and define **organizational culture** as the coherent, consistent system of workplace norms and idealized values that describe the goals and endorse the practice shared by employees. This system legitimates standards, endorses common beliefs about how the world works, and frames how workers make decisions, take actions, and sustain a common cause.

A KEY PIECE OF THE PERFORMANCE PUZZLE

Everywhere and always, organization culture influences how employees do their job.

Analyses and anecdotes of corporate performance indicate that building a resourceful organization is a challenging balancing act: an MNE must find ways to inspire employees worldwide to develop and apply new ideas but ensure that they implement them in ways that fit the MNE's vision and mission. Few MNEs strike and sustain this balance solely by designing the structure, coordination, and control systems. They also look to their organizational culture to complete the trick. On this point, Jack Welch, former CEO of GE, advised that "In real life, strategy is actually very straightforward. You pick a general direction and implement like hell…. But objectives don't get you there. Values do."[97]

Assessment of strategic successes and failures spotlights the performance implications of organizational culture. Executives apply a progressively expansive view, seeing it as a powerful tool to shape the workplace, integrate decision-making, and implement strategy. Recognition follows from a series of studies confirming a significant link between an MNE's organizational culture and its strategic success. Facets of its culture, such as the values and principles of management, nature of the work climate and atmosphere, and traditions and ethical standards, always and everywhere influence a firm's performance.[98]

An organization's culture, by endorsing workplace values, shapes the behavior patterns of current workers as well as new hires.

CONCEPT CHECK

The accelerating comeback of emerging economies indicates an "inflection point" at which old strategic patterns of thought give way to new. Our discussion of different national perspectives on *value creation* in Chapter 12 argues that such problems challenge coordinating increasingly sophisticated value chains. Evidence indicates that developing a supportive organizational culture provides a powerful tool.

Sophisticated Strategy, Sophisticated Culture   The importance of organizational culture grows as the rise of emerging economies and maturing growth in the West push managers to rethink strategies and reset operations. Expanding to increasingly diverse markets with increasingly diverse workplace norms calls for boosting the flexibility and versatility of an organization. For example, GE has reconfigured its value chain to reflect market trends. Notably, these changes have required adjusting its historic West-centric orientation for the accelerating rise in emerging economies. Asked about GE's future, CEO Jeffery Immelt replied, "We've globalized around markets, not cheap labor. The era of globalization around cheap labor is over. Today we go to Brazil, we go to China, and we go to India because that's where the customers are."[99] On a related front, emerging rivals from fast-growing economies devise strategies to navigate bustling markets that run the gamut from the billions of poor people who populate the Base of the Pyramid to the millions enjoying surging affluence. Companies from both the East and the West pursue new, often astounding opportunities. Capturing them involves reinventing systems of production and distribution as well as experimenting with new business models.

Managing sophisticated resources, capabilities, and competencies escalate demands on MNEs' structure and systems. There are low odds of successfully meeting those demands without a supportive organizational culture. Poorly understood, partially shared cultural values impose boundaries that distort the communication and collaboration that gird coordination and control systems. Certainly, MNEs could opt to develop elaborate constraints, controls, and contracts in order to compel employees to do their job. And, granted, the notion that "beatings will continue until morale improves" may boost short-term performance. But improving compatibility between an MNE's culture and its strategy has proven a far more powerful driver of superior performance.

THE POWER OF COMMON CAUSE

Successful MNEs develop a culture that instills in their employees the engagement and enthusiasm beyond that justified solely by economic rewards. Certainly, pay motivates performance. An effective organizational culture, however, stimulates people to identify with the company's vision, do their jobs well, and collaborate with others while lessening the need to regulate their behaviors with elaborate structures and systems. Its capacity to power individual performance beyond that motivated by monetary incentives puts the onus on executives to build a company that people do not want to merely work for, but aspire to belong to. Employees no longer check in to get a check, but become vision-led and principle-driven. Google's worries about brain drain to rivals, for instance, led it to identify why people quit; it found that executives left for another company not for higher pay, but when they identified with its vision and mission.[100]

The shared values that enact an organization's culture, goes the reasoning, influence what employees perceive, how they interpret, and how they respond to their world. Convergent cultural values ease the exchange of ideas, thereby improving communication, coordination, and collaboration. J&J, for example, anchors its vision of value creation in the principles of its Credo. This manifesto unequivocally champions the values that embody J&J's responsibilities to its stakeholders worldwide. When employees are confronted with opportunities or threats in the world, the Credo helps them define, analyze, and resolve them in ways that respect and reinforce J&J's culture and, by extension, its strategy.[101]

A vibrant organizational culture helps explain why some companies make the leap from good to great and, likewise, why others do not.[102] Unquestionably, product development, marketing ingenuity, and financial stewardship moderate progress. Attaining greatness, however, depends on a culture of unwavering faith and passion; rigorous discipline and focus; clearly communicated and practiced core values and timeless principles; strong work ethics; and finding and promoting people with the right outlook.[103] Great companies purposefully promote an integrated system of overarching values, perspectives, and practices—much as J&J does with its Credo, Toyota with its Toyota Way, and Gore with the

The shared meaning and beliefs that shape how employees interpret information, make decisions, and implement actions define an organization's culture.

Gore Way—in order to give employees a consistent way to relate to their jobs, to each other, to customers, to shareholders, and to stakeholders. Perhaps most decisively, it legitimates the company's vision and mission in the eyes of employees worldwide.

DEVELOPING AN ORGANIZATIONAL CULTURE

MNEs proactively develop their organizational culture, just as they purposefully design their structure and systems.

Historically, uncertainty about the dynamic of social engineering led managers to adopt a benign perspective, letting the organization's culture naturally emerge and evolve. Information and advice on "how things work around here" spread by word of mouth on factory floors or coffee-break chats. Today, MNEs proactively manage culture's emergence and evolution.[104] Organizing a globally integrated enterprise requires extensive coordination and collaboration among workers. The importance and intricacies of setting and sustaining common values among employees worldwide turn our attention to how an MNE develops, diffuses, and sustains its organizational culture.[105] The overlapping practices of cultural exemplars, notably Gore, J&J, Google, Infosys, and Toyota, highlight the importance of hiring, rewarding, and promoting people who support the MNE's vision and then, "walk the talk" implementing its mission. Leading through example, they promote socialization processes and communication practices that diffuse as well as fortify the idealized values and norms.

Key features of a company's organization culture include

- values and principles of management,
- work climate and atmosphere,
- patterns of "how we do things around here,"
- traditions,
- ethical standards.

Tools and Techniques   In reality, the values and norms of managers, especially those from culturally dissimilar countries, often differ.[106] Furthermore, many workers, especially those in markets far removed from the home office, have slight, if any, exposure to the behaviors of senior managers. Even on the standards of the MNE's strategy, a far more objective concept than the values and norms of its culture, executives struggle to unify interpretations across boundaries. Barely half of the managers in a cross-section of MNEs believed that they communicated their strategy clearly to their workers worldwide.[107] Rather than relying on chance encounters among employees to develop common cause, MNEs proactively set and sustain their idealized organizational culture with fascinating methods.

Setting the System   Overcoming hurdles calls for arranging closer contact among managers from different countries to unify values. Cross-national teams are a prevalent tool.[108] Consensus depends on coworkers sharing common values, rather than coerced compliance through coordination routines or control systems. Executives also advocate interpersonal approaches, notably rotating high-performing executives from headquarters and subsidiaries throughout global units. Wipro, an Indian technology company, employs 54,000 people in 35 countries, more than 11,000 of whom work for units outside of India and more than 90 percent of whom are Indian. Explained the chief executive of global programs, "We sprinkle Indians in new markets to help seed and set up the culture and intensity."[109] Others endorse focused methods. GE's Leadership Development Center thrusts managers from different businesses and different parts of the world into a classroom; there, they challenge and clarify the principles of the company's culture.

CONCEPT CHECK

Chapter 12 explains that MNEs face various obstacles building communication channels among the links in their value chains. Not long ago, inefficient transportation and expensive communications hindered efforts to coordinate global activities. Today, improving social networking tools make clan control an increasingly practical option.

Sustaining the System   Ad hoc approaches effectively set the standards of an organization's culture. Sustaining that calls for instituting outlooks and systems. Instead of letting the organization's culture emerge naturally, many managers do as they do with structure and systems: purposefully and proactively develop the system of shared values that supports the MNE's vision and mission. Reflected Gore CEO Terri Kelly, "we take great pride in our culture and recognize the very important role it plays in driving business success. By fostering an environment where people feel motivated, engaged, and passionate about the work they do, we are better able to tap into our potential and create innovative products that truly make a difference in the world."[110]

Toyota relies on its Technical Skills Academy, its corporate university, to fortify its culture as well as firmly anchor its next generation of leadership in it. Some sessions teach factory controls and assembly procedures, others develop management skills, but all inculcate the principles of the esteemed "Toyota Way."[111] Directly familiarizing employees with its renowned methods, top management believes, helps them base decisions on a "philosophical sense of purpose, to think long term, to have a process for solving problems, to add value to the organization by developing its people, and to recognize that continuously solving root problems drives organizational learning."[112] Toyota posts graduates to its offices worldwide, acting as missionaries who spread the Toyota Way. Long a fundamental feature of the company, the Toyota Way steadily plays a bigger part in developing the organizational culture. Expanding international operations, particularly into emerging economies, fueled concern among senior management that the key principles of its organizational culture were weakening.[113] Now, the company relies on the Toyota Way to socialize workers worldwide with its core values, thereby harmonizing its organizational culture throughout its global operations.

An organization's culture shapes the success of its strategic moves.

Executives apply a variety of methods to set and sustain the organizational culture. An intriguing development is the rise of the corporate university as a key change agent. Within the bounds of a university setting, both physical as well as virtual, managers lead training efforts, facilitate learning, and upgrade competencies with an eye toward setting and sustaining the philosophical ideals that anchor the organization's culture. Our *Looking to the Future* profiles their rising prominence.

Looking to the Future
The Rise of Corporate Universities

Worldwide, more than a thousand companies have opened universities over the past decade. By region, they are steadily expanding in the United States, thriving in Europe, and accelerating in Asia. The number of U.S. corporate universities grew from around 400 in 1993, to 2,000 in 2001, to nearly 4,000 today. Prominent MNEs with corporate universities include Apple, Walt Disney, Infosys, General Electric, J.P. Morgan Chase, and SAP.[114]

The first big one, McDonald's Hamburger University, began operating in 1961 in the basement of a McDonald's restaurant in Elk Grove, Illinois. Hamburger University now consists of a 130,000-square foot facility on an 80-acre campus located at McDonald's Corporate Offices in Oak Brook, Illinois. It has trained more than 80,000 restaurant managers and owner/operators in 28 languages from 119 countries in "hamburgerology." Now, McDonald's runs Hamburger Universities in Sydney, Munich, London, Tokyo, São Paulo, and Shanghai. Elsewhere, like-minded MNEs develop similar setups. ArcelorMittal, a steelmaker, has six corporate university campuses, including sites in Ukraine and South Africa, and is opening others in Kazakhstan and Brazil. Infosys's 337-acre campus houses the world's largest corporate university in Mysore, India. Its 400-plus faculty annually socialize thousands of new hires to the ways of Infosys as well as align

employees with its evolving strategy. To date, it has trained more than 125,000 "Infoscians."

Whereas some MNEs attach their university to headquarters, others sprinkle them worldwide. Unisys, for example, has campuses in its key market regions. Increasingly, MNEs break free of geography, running virtual online universities where employees e-learn via live webcasts, online discussion groups, webinars, video-conferences, and interactive sessions. Going forward, the issue of who teaches what and where will test unprecedented platforms and pedagogies. The potential disruptive innovation of online education will likely reset our understanding of corporate universities. Presently, we see players, such as Coursera and Instructure, offering services to students, institutions, and, increasingly, companies.[115] Vendors offer courses, designed by or tailored to the company's situation, through their proprietary learning management system.[116]

An Expanding Mission

Unlike customary universities, corporate universities emphasize practical skills and workplace systems rather than grand theories. Too, they rarely confer degrees. The founding goal of McDonald's Hamburger University, for instance, was preparing people to run the day-to-day operations of a franchise. Today, reports the American Society for Training and Development, "training isn't just a nice thing to do anymore. Companies are now thinking of training as a strategic imperative."[117] Mattel, for instance, runs executive development programs via a global e-learning system that puts its people and its principles into play. Improving managers' understanding at both headquarters and subsidiaries means its "global management is more closely aligned with the corporate strategies and goals."[118]

The challenges of changing global markets require continually upgrading managers' competencies with a curriculum that fits the MNE's strategy. Some look to their universities to give new hires a big-picture view of global operations and to reenergize current workers' commitment to its vision and mission. Others amplify this theme, declaring that their corporate university "inculcates everyone, from the clerical assistant to the top executive, in the culture that makes the organization unique and special and defines behaviors that enable employees to 'live the values.'"[119]

The Crucible of Change

Corporate universities target several goals, including maximizing return on educational investments, tailoring training to its workplace systems, and upgrading employees' skill sets. On a larger stage, they look to start and support strategic change, inspiring executives to develop the insights and cultivate the personal relationships that energize the globally integrated enterprise. Its rise as the forum of the MNE's future increasingly makes it the crucible of company strategy. Some foresee it becoming the MNE's thought center that sets, rather than follows, its strategy.[120]

Linking executive learning with the company's strategy drives the recent and projected growth of corporate universities. The CEO of Unipart, a British auto parts maker, notes that his center "is at the very heart of the business" and a "key enabler for future growth of the business."[121] Like many other CEOs, he runs a monthly course on his company's philosophy and practices. On this measure Jack Welch set the standard. Over his 20-year run as GE's CEO, he appeared more than 300 times at the company's training center at Croton-on-Hudson. Holding forth in "the Pit," he socialized some 20,000 GE managers to the ways of the company.[122]

Senior executives who take on the hat of teacher generate great benefits. The director of LVMH's university believes that putting top people into the pit "gives them access to people they would never get access to.... It is the role of our top senior executives to get a feel for what is going on."[123] Benefits accrue to attendees too. Activities, seminars, and training sessions fortify skills, build networks, and improve analytics. Attendees return home with new ideas and a better sense of how their professional development stacks up to counterparts. Indirect benefits emerge. For instance, less than a fifth of ArcelorMittal workers use English as a first language; hence, coworkers require training in local tongues. Improving local managers' skills, ArcelorMittal found, reduces the necessity of posting expensive expatriates to support those units.

Sophisticated strategies push MNEs to involve more employees, both those staying home and those heading abroad, in general international development. Few question the need to generate, transfer, and adopt ideas from wherever they originate to wherever they add value. Still, this goal calls for preparing employees to do so. Growing globalization spurs MNEs to help employees, both national and international, to understand worldwide operations, opportunities, and constraints. IB content once reserved for international executives is shared with all workers. Examples include Procter & Gamble's training on globalization issues, programs at Honda of America to improve cultural awareness, and Mattel's and Infosys's regional training centers, where managers from several countries convene to study specific topics.

Integrating Diversity

A rising mandate for corporate universities is integrating diverse workforces. Hiring people from around the world expands the mix of nationalities and ethnicities. Organizing engineers in Mumbai or Sophia to collaborate with folks in Redmond makes compelling economic sense. Preempting a Tower of Babel requires socializing the mix of people to the sensitivities and skills needed to navigate multifunctional, multicultural, multinational teams. Tempting as it is to rely upon happenstance to manage the process, benign neglect is risky.[124] Executives turn to corporate universities, seeing in them a robust platform for integrating diversity in a purposeful setting. The vice president of Unisys University explains that getting people into the classroom aligns employee development with the company's strategy and fortifies their identification with the organization's culture.[125]

Expanding operations into dissimilar emerging markets challenges sustaining common values.

Toyota, for example, saw the globalization of its business steadily diluting the principles of the Toyota Way. When the firm was primarily Japan-centric, it relied upon spontaneous chats on the factory floor and informal networking in the executive suite to sustain its organizational culture. Explained the director of the Toyota Institute, "Before, when everyone was Japanese, we didn't have to make these things explicit," "Now we have to set the Toyota Way down on paper and teach it."[126] To that end, it relies on its Toyota Institute in Toyota City, Japan, along with satellite centers in Thailand and the United States. ■

CASE  Hyundai Motor Company: Expanding through Organizational Excellence[127]

The automobile has shaped not only the global economy but also the way billions of people live. In Europe, the automotive industry accounts for almost 12 million jobs; more than 8 million in the United States; and more than 5 million in Japan. Since the first modern car was built in 1885, this industry, dominated by firms such as Toyota and GM, has seen considerable changes. Instead of the initial manufacture of automobiles for the local market, firms today have been expanding their operations to span the globe through export and international production factories in key regional markets. This expansion has forced companies to come to grips with unique structural, cultural and control issues. One firm that has risen from obscurity to preeminence by successfully overcoming these challenges is Hyundai Motor Company.

Hyundai Overview

Based in Seoul, South Korea, the Hyundai Motor Company (HMC) was created in 1968 and initially served as a complete knock down assembler for Ford Motors. Growing from its humble beginnings, the HMC, with its sister company, Kia Motors, has become the largest automaker in South Korea and the fifth largest automaker in the world based on 2012 car sales totaling 1.26 million units. The South Korean auto giant owns and operates not only its automotive division, but also possesses a 32.8 percent stake in Kia Motors and a full spectrum of vertically oriented subsidiaries that supply Hyundai with goods and services ranging from raw materials and parts to logistics and financing. As of 2013, the company employs over 104,731 people worldwide.

Establishment and Growing Pains

Founded in 1968 by the Hyundai business group, one of Korea's largest chaebols or family-owned conglomerates, HMC initially served as an automotive assembler for Ford Motor Company. However, Chung Ju-yung, the founder of Hyundai had big plans for the future direction and growth of the firm in hopes that it would help the chaebol to both diversify and to maximize its economies of scale and scope. In 1974, HMC took the next step and began producing and selling its first wholly designed model, the Pony. The following year, Chung firmly set his company's future in motion by beginning the export of the Pony to Ecuador and the Benelux countries and eventually exported worldwide utilizing a low cost strategy. Despite the growing international sales of the Pony and subsequent models, these times were not without their issues. Some of Hyundai's early models gave rise to ridicule due to "shoddy construction, underpowered engines and boring designs." Recognizing the barriers before them, HMC went on to expand its range of market offerings and especially worked on improving vehicle quality, which, over time, began to bear fruit by greatly improving sales.

Perhaps the greatest impact on Hyundai was felt when Chung Mong-koo, the founder's eldest son, was given the position of chief executive office. "The Chairman" contributed his relentless drive to push HMC into world class status by adopting flashier designs and driving quality improvements necessary to stand behind a US product warranty that was dubbed "America's Best Warranty" for its extensive coverage and other manifestations of its quality aspirations.

Global Growth

Another major contributor to Hyundai's spectacular growth is their efforts to expand overseas through both export and the push to produce vehicles in key foreign markets. Although its first attempt at an international assembly plant built in Canada failed, HMC internalized and implemented the new knowledge they gained in the form of new ventures. Today, the company runs three domestic assembly plants in South Korea and other facilities in Brazil, Czech Republic, China, India, Turkey, and the United States. Foreign annual vehicle production has far outstripped domestic capabilities, producing 57 percent of its 4.4 million vehicles outside of Korea. This growth is expected to continue for the foreseeable future as Hyundai continues to add additional overseas facilities as well as refine its approach to the global market and its quality capabilities.

Organizational Success Factors

There are several organizational pillars that have proven to be sources of Hyundai's ability to continue to adapt to and overcome often adverse market conditions. However, in some cases, these same success factors have also created issues when applied to foreign operations. These factors refer to Hyundai's unique yet locally-responsive centralized organizational structure, the control methods used both domestically and especially in its expansive overseas production facilities, and HMC's highly developed and strong corporate culture.

Hyundai: Centralized yet Locally Responsive

Although HMC assembly plants and subsidiaries are spread out across the world, the organizational structure and approach remains similar throughout the company footprint. Like many Korean firms, Hyundai is a top-down, hierarchical company which employs a very hands-on authoritative management style. CEO Chung was widely known for his "Bulldozer" leadership style, could often be seen at surprise, on-site visits to Hyundai plants, pulling executives from their offices to directly show them issues. "He held monthly meetings, he pounded on tables, and people were afraid to disappoint him," reported one country manager. Furthermore, the decision making style of the Hyundai CEOs can also be characterized as quick and decisive. Se-young Chung, the second CEO of the company, made a snap decision on an aggressive, new warranty policy during a car ride that would fundamentally revolutionize the commitment that HMC had towards quality. Regarding the quickness of the decision, it was commented that, "The Koreans are cowboys and very different from the Japanese. At Toyota, it would have taken 18 months to get the idea through the consensus process."

Beyond the direct control of the president, Hyundai's Seoul executives maintain full control over all of their operations, which has implications regarding the ability for local country executives to autonomously operate. Reports from many of HMC's foreign operations, such as Russia, India, and the US, report similar situations.

However, despite the high degree of centralization, Hyundai has learned the necessity of relying on their international non-Korean teams to pick up on local market needs and opportunities and rapidly turn them into tangible products. The firm goes as far as encouraging the local teams to take risks in the form of ambitious schedules, designs and unconventional solutions. This reliance and trust can be seen especially in HMC's older and more established assembly plants. In India, one of Hyundai's oldest international operations, headquarters realized the need for host country official's authority and has made commitments for all management staff to be Indian nationals by 2014. Despite this practice in India, however, it appears that HMC management does not lightly award trust. As of 2012, their Russian operations were still stratified into "...Koreans representing management..., while Russians get positions of manual workers and clerks."

Control Systems

HMC's competition-based and bureaucratic control systems make up the second organizational success factor. Hyundai is well known for their competitive, team-based approach to the marketplace. Different teams regularly vie against each other to determine product or feature designs or even technology to identify the most effective or innovative solutions to the firm's challenges. The output of these internal competitions are said to often produce some of Hyundai's most spectacular results. However, they often engender mistrust and disunity amongst the personnel.

HMC's bureaucratic controls can be equally beneficial and disruptive. Working alongside the managers in Hyundai's international plants are Korean coordinators. These coordinators are typically young, western-educated Korean workers whose job is to bridge the language and cultural gaps with the international managers and help them operate with their Korean counterparts. Decisions made in the Korean headquarters are relayed through these coordinators to be followed without exception. It has been noted that coordinators often possess even more decision making power than the foreign executive that they serve. This degree of hands-on, long distance supervision has often been a serious issue between home and local offices.

Culture

HMC is well known for its vibrant corporate culture that heavily focuses on traditional Korean cultural attitudes such as collectivism and paternalism. Due to its history of Confucianism, Korea possesses a culture still highly aligned with collectivism which is embedded in the core of HMC beliefs. This belief has imbued HMC with a very strong work ethic and intolerance for deviation from the group. Workers at

Hyundai facilities around the globe are known for the frantic pace and long hours, often without extra compensation, that are expected from employees of the HMC family. Like Hyundai's collective approach, the firm's paternalistic focus has also both benefited and hurt the company. Decisions by management, and especially the chairman, are "often carried out with unquestioning reverence, without hesitation or argument," and achieved with breakneck speed. The term "Hyundai Speed" became part of HMC culture when the chairman stressed the importance of reaching operational status during the 2002 setup of the first operation plant in China. Only after herculean efforts by the Korean and Chinese workers was the plant able to begin manufacturing.

One area of constant contention in HMC's global organization that is contrary to the cultural approach management has tried to install regards the creation of independent employee unions. Most of the firm's global operations are periodically affected by labor talks and strikes. Labor strikes in Korea alone in 2012 resulted in $1.5 billion in lost production and have affected domestic production in 23 of the last 27 years. International facilities show similar patterns as workers strike in protest of practices like obligatory overtime, management harassment and intimidation, and poor working conditions.

The Road Ahead

The future of Hyundai is far from determined. Although sales are fairly constant and well distributed worldwide and the orga-nization appears to be well-prepared for most contingencies, many factors are yet unknown. Some believe that the company is overreaching itself by continuing to develop its luxury brands and others see that Japanese car firms are learning by following HMC's examples. However, through the firm's focus on quality, innovation and the growth and maintenance of its strong structural, cultural and organizational strengths, Hyundai Motor Company hopes to maintain its continued growth and profitability in the world market.

QUESTIONS

16-3. Is it possible for Hyundai to retain its core culture and structure as it continues to expand? Is it desirable for HMC to try?

16-4. Would it have been possible to resolve Hyundai's initial quality issues without the use of a strong, central figure making the decisions?

16-5. Evaluate the dangers of HMC's centralized approach versus a more decentralized path?

16-6. Identify the issues with using a competition-based control mechanism. Is there an alternative?

16-7. The Korean culture often doesn't lend itself to being easily understood by others. What could Hyundai do to better communicate its core beliefs?

MyLab Management

Go to **mymanagementlab.com** for the following Assisted-graded writing questions:

16-8 Hyundai management always possesses issues with unions. What could be done to promote a more cooperative and mutually beneficial working environment?

16-9 Which organizational shortcomings do you feel are the most necessary for Hyundai to address? How would you address the issues?

Endnotes

Scan for Endnotes or go to www.pearsonglobaleditions.com/Daniels

CHAPTER 17
Global Marketing

OBJECTIVES

After studying this chapter, you should be able to

17-1 Classify international marketing strategies in terms of marketing orientations, segmentation, and targeting

17-2 Discuss the pros and cons of adaptation versus global standardization of products

17-3 Describe pricing complexities when selling in foreign markets

17-4 Recognize the advantages and problems of using uniform promotional marketing practices among countries

17-5 Explain the different branding strategies companies may employ internationally

17-6 Discern major practices and complications of international distribution

17-7 Illustrate how gap analysis can help in managing the international marketing mix

MyLab Management®
Improve Your Performance!
When you see this icon ★, visit
www.mymanagementlab.com for
activities that are applied, personalized,
and offer immediate feedback.

Markets have customs and communes have traditions.

—Vietnamese proverb

People on escalators at a modern shopping mall, Asia. ▼

Source: hxdbzxy. Shutterstock

CASE

Tommy Hilfiger

For it's Tommy this, an' Tommy that

—"Tommy" from Department Duties:
Barrack Room Ballads (1890),
United States Book Company, New York.

Mark Twain said, "The finest clothing is a person's skin, but, of course, society demands more than this."[1] Tommy Hilfiger, a notable international clothing brand, now owned by Phillips-Van Heusen (PVH), exemplifies efforts to respond to these demands. Its 2015 retail sales exceeded $8 billion, with over half coming from abroad. Europe, to which it began its push in 1997, accounts for the largest portion of international sales, and China is the fastest-growing area. (The opening photo shows one of its stores in Manchester, England.) As the company moved internationally, it learned that applying every U.S. marketing strategy abroad did not work because country markets are very different. Our discussion centers on contrasting Hilfiger's U.S. and foreign (mainly European) operations.

PRODUCT

The Hilfiger brand's early success was largely due to two men: U.S. designer Tommy Hilfiger and Indian clothing magnate Mohan Murjani. Murjani sought Hilfiger as a designer for a new brand of clothing by offering a line of slightly less preppy and less expensive clothes than those offered by Ralph Lauren to attract a young mass-appeal audience. From the start, Hilfiger clothes have been casual, of good quality, and distinctive enough in color and shape (along with their little red, white, and blue logos) that the public can usually distinguish them from those of competitors. Nevertheless, this is an industry in which product lines must evolve. Maintaining that "Fashion brands have to reinvent themselves, just like Madonna does," Hilfiger has gone from preppy to urban and back again.

In addition, Hilfiger has encountered some different national preferences. To accommodate European tastes, Hilfiger has added wool sweaters, adjusted to the European partiality for slimmer-looking jeans and smaller shirt logos, and created a line of added-luxury items, such as leather jackets and cashmere sweaters for the Italian market. It has also developed brighter colors for Italy, tartans and plaids for Japan, and sleeker designs for Chile.

During the late twentieth and early twenty-first century, Hilfiger's U.S. sales fell each year, apparently because its product lines had become faddish (e.g., baggy jeans and large logos on clothing) and no longer compatible with its established image. This led to discounting, compromising on quality, and a resultant lower brand image. Meanwhile, the autonomously operated European division refused to go along with the U.S.'s faddish moves, and its sales grew in tandem with U.S. decreases.

In response, Hilfiger set up a European design staff that has led to more harmonization in its U.S. and European products, a move more up-market, and a turnaround of its U.S. performance.

PRICING

Whereas the early U.S. pricing strategy was to sell a shirt for $79 that looks like an $89 shirt, Hilfiger learned that its brand cachet warranted selling a shirt in Europe for $99 that looks like a $150 shirt. For instance, in Germany, its largest European market, men don't mind paying $50 more than the highest-priced Hilfiger shirts in the United States, but they want them in a higher-quality cotton. In addition, European department store margins can be 50 percent to 100 percent higher than those in the United States, thus impacting price differences.

PROMOTION AND BRANDING

Hilfiger's promotion and branding have been so intertwined that separating them is almost impossible. At the company's inception, there were two primary needs: to convince stores to stock a new brand and to convince customers to want it. Although the first year's (1985) ad budget was US$1.4 million, quite small for an unknown brand in a mass consumer market, the ads were aimed strictly at getting Tommy Hilfiger's name known. These ads were in leading magazines and newspapers, along with a billboard in New York's Times Square. They showed no clothes or models. Instead, they included Hilfiger's face, the logo for the clothes, and words describing Hilfiger as being on a par with such well-known designers as Ralph Lauren, Perry Ellis, and Calvin Klein.

The bizarre ads resulted in free publicity through newspapers around the world and quips on popular late-night TV shows. The publicity showed an eclectic group of celebrities—Bill Clinton, the Prince of Wales, Michael Jackson, Elton John, and Snoop Dogg—wearing Hilfiger clothes. This fed into the image that Hilfiger clothes had cachet; thus the company's brand was quickly known nationally and internationally. Soon, New York surveys revealed that the public thought of Hilfiger as one of the four or five most important U.S. designers. And the logo-loving public rushed to buy the brand, especially young managers who were eager to be seen in upscale sportswear during the newly popular "casual Friday" workdays.

Despite Hilfiger's early publicity in Europe, its acceptance was not as quick as it expected. Because Europeans tend to see France and Italy as the upscale fashion centers and the United States as a trendsetter in jeans, Hilfiger initially encountered some negative reactions to being a U.S. upscale brand. However, Hilfiger has since played up its Americanism, and the perception that the brand and price are a step below the pure luxury brands has successfully helped its European sales find a niche.

Hilfiger has used celebrity advertising, such as Sheryl Crow, Jewel, Beyoncé, Rafael Nadal, and the husband and wife team of the late David Bowie and supermodel Iman. The company has used "delebs" (dead celebrities), such as Grace Kelly and James Dean. To help advertise its children's clothes, Disney artists have drawn Pluto and other Disney characters wearing the line. However, aside from celebrities, Hilfiger learned that the type of models it uses to sell successfully in the United States may not work well in Europe. For example, its models for men's underwear in Europe, including those on point-of-purchase package displays, must be thinner and less muscular than those in the United States. Hilfiger also found that its average European consumer was older than that in the United States, so it dropped the Tommy Jeans name because it sounded too much like a teen product.

Advertising has been a cornerstone of Hilfiger's success, depending on multimedia campaigns that include indoor and outdoor print placements, digital and social media promotions, and webisodes.

DISTRIBUTION

Early on, Hilfiger relied mainly on wholesaling to about 1,800 U.S. department stores, many of which contained stand-alone Hilfiger departments. It has avoided chains considered more low-end, such as JCPenney and Sears, though it does sell its outdated stock to discount chains T.J. Maxx and Marshalls. However, in 2007, Hilfiger gave Macy's exclusive rights to sell its sportswear lines. Although Macy's has about 800 stores, the move required Hilfiger to pull sales from other department stores, such as Dillard's.

Distribution is perhaps the biggest difference Hilfiger found when entering Europe. Because of the company's U.S. department stores success, it put an early European emphasis on such department stores as Galeries Lafayette in France and El Corte Inglés in Spain. However, Hilfiger found the European market to be one of fragmentation (sending small amounts to small stores that carry select pieces) as opposed to the U.S. market's concentration (sending a lot to department stores). European operational costs are about three times those in the United States because of this more fragmented retail and wholesale system.

Hilfiger has inaugurated large flagship stores in prime locations within large markets, such as in New York City, Paris, and Tokyo. These stores not only make sales, but also demonstrate the variety of Hilfiger merchandise. Non-U.S. stores are decorated to emphasize an American image, while simultaneously connecting the United States to the host country, such as including a poster of a U.S. magazine with the Eiffel Tower on the cover in the Paris store. By locating in prestige areas, Hilfiger promotes an aura of having high-end products, yet its aim is to be a high-margin brand with prices a notch lower than luxury brands. Nevertheless, this concept did not work in London, where Hilfiger closed its Bond Street store a year later. In effect, Hilfiger over-promoted to retailers and under-promoted to final consumers. Thus, too much merchandise was in stores, which forced them to get rid of excess inventory. Further, a cheap lookalike brand called Tommy Sport confused consumers, tarnished Hilfiger's image, and forced the company to buy it out.

There is an old adage that clothes make the man. Hilfiger, while making and selling clothes, has succeeded in convincing customers that its merchandise will help boost (or make) their positions. ■

QUESTIONS

17-1. The chapter explains five international marketing orientations. Which one most applies to Tommy Hilfiger? Explain why.

17-2. The chapter explains five elements in the marketing mix (product, price, promotion, brand, and distribution). In which of these have Tommy Hilfiger's operating practices been the most standardized globally? Explain why this has been possible and desirable.

INTERNATIONAL MARKETING STRATEGIES: ORIENTATIONS, SEGMENTATION, AND TARGETING

Although marketing principles are global, companies need to apply them differently abroad.

Marketing brings revenue, without which a firm cannot survive. Similar principles apply globally (i.e., a company must have desirable products and services, tell people about them, and offer them at appropriate prices at consumers' favored locations). However, companies may apply these principles differently abroad, such as by customizing products to correspond with local preferences. Hilfiger's experience in the opening case emphasizes the need to find the right balance between the benefits of local responsiveness and the efficiency gains of standardization.

CONCEPT CHECK

In Chapter 12 (pages 365–367), we describe the strategies of global integration versus local responsiveness and explain how a company can save money by standardizing many of its policies and practices.

Although international marketing approaches should be compatible with companies' overall aims and strategies, they need not standardize every practice for every product where they sell. For instance, market differences may call for pursuing cost leadership through standardization in some countries and more costly differentiation in others. A mass-market orientation may be appropriate in one country and a focused strategy in another. Finally, the degree of global standardization versus national responsiveness may vary within the marketing mix, such as standardizing the product as much as possible while promoting it differently among countries.

Figure 17.1 shows marketing's place in IB.

As we first discuss the orientations that commonly describe companies' marketing strategies, keep in mind that they are not entirely mutually exclusive. We emphasize product policy in our discussion because it is central to a firm's strategy, whereas the other elements in the marketing mix are supportive to it.[2]

Under certain circumstances, the assumptions that consumers simply want lower prices or higher quality are valid.

CONCEPT CHECK

In Chapter 6 (page 210), we explain that commodity prices rise less than manufacturers' prices, partially because of differentiation difficulty. Here, we demonstrate success in differentiation.

MARKETING ORIENTATIONS

Five common marketing orientations can be applied around the world: *production, sales, customer, strategic marketing,* and *social marketing.* Each is discussed below.

Production Orientation   Rather than analyzing foreign consumer needs to a high degree, managers concentrate on production by assuming that customers simply want products with lower prices, higher quality, or whatever they sell domestically. Although this approach has largely gone out of vogue, it is used internationally for certain cases (as described in the following sections).

Commodity Sales   Companies sell many undifferentiated commodities primarily on the basis of price because of universal demand. However, even for commodities, companies

FIGURE 17.1   Marketing as a Means of Pursuing an International Strategy

Recall that we used Figure 15.1 to introduce the various modes and means by which a company can pursue its international objectives and strategy. Among those means we included functions, and here we focus on one of the most important of those functions: *marketing.*

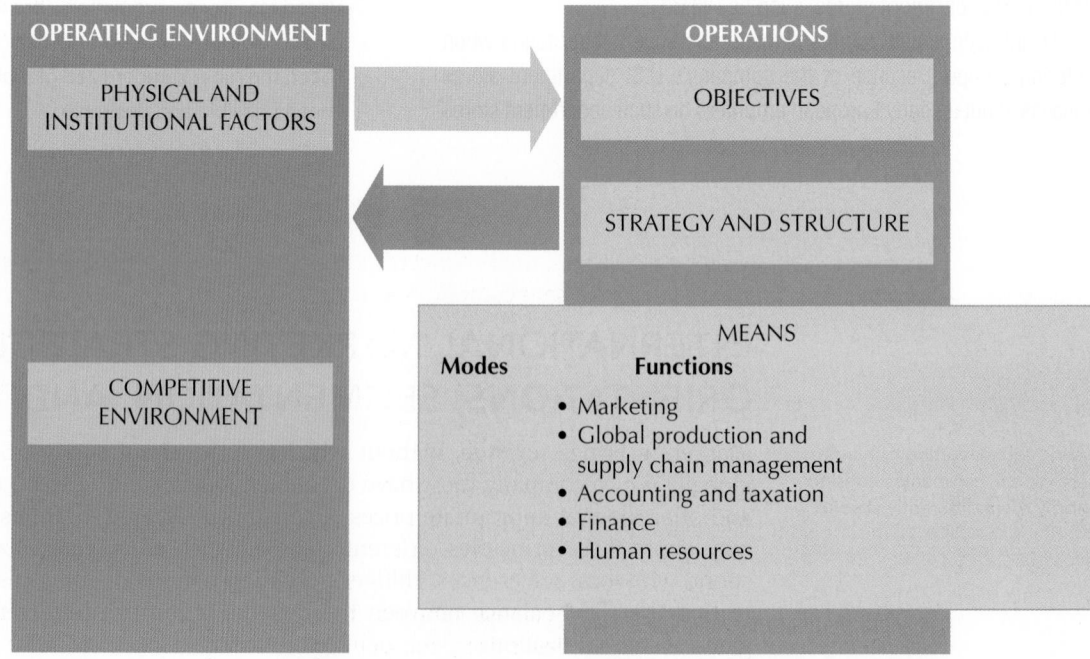

have sometimes had positive international sales results through differentiation that builds favorable consumer perceptions such as with the Chiquita brand on bananas. In addition, oil producers, such as Venezuela's PdVSA have bought branded gasoline-distributors, such as CITGO, to extend operations in their value chains and help them sell an otherwise undifferentiated product. Commodity producers also put effort into business-to-business marketing by providing innovative financing and ensuring timely, high-quality supplies.

Passive Exports   Many companies export passively by filling unsolicited foreign requests and adapting their products very little, if at all. This suffices for companies that view foreign sales simply as a means to dispose of excess inventory they can't reasonably sell domestically. In fact, if they cover fixed costs through domestic sales, they can quote lower export prices to liquidate inventories without disrupting their domestic markets.

Foreign-Market Segments or Niches   A company may aim a product at a large share of its domestic market and then find a few consumers abroad who will also buy it. Inca Kola, a major soft drink brand in Peru, has only niche markets abroad, primarily among people who consumed it in Peru. However, a niche market abroad may become a mass market, as is the case with Mexico's Corona beer.

Similarly, a company may sell in countries with minimal market potential and little competition from firms that adapt to local market preferences, particularly in small developing nations. In effect, the market size does not justify the alteration expense—for instance, not even changing plugs on electrical products to fit local sockets, which local purchasers must convert.

Sales Orientation   In a sales orientation, a company sells abroad what it sells domestically by assuming that consumers are sufficiently similar. Hilfiger launches much of its children's collection simultaneously in multiple countries this way.[3] Similarly, some products need no international adaptation, such as razor blades, aircraft, and cat food. For others, however, a company may succeed best with a sales orientation by selling to culturally similar countries with a great deal of spillover in product information, such as between the United States and Canada.[4]

This orientation differs from the production orientation because of its active rather than passive approach to promoting sales. However, there is much evidence of failures because of a mismatch between managers' perception and the reality of what will be accepted abroad.[5] To help alleviate this mismatch, product development teams composed of different nationalities can create customer solutions that apply globally from the start.[6] Additionally, a strong information exchange between foreign subsidiaries and headquarters can help develop products that can be sufficiently standardized and still fit the needs of consumers in different countries.[7]

Customer Orientation   In a *sales orientation*, management is usually guided by answers to such questions as: Should the company send some exports abroad? Where can it sell more of product X? That is, the product is held constant and the sales location is varied.

In contrast, management in a *customer orientation* asks: What and how can the company sell in country A or to a particular type of consumer? In this case, the country or type of consumer is held constant and the product and marketing method vary. An MNE may most likely take this approach because the country's size and growth potential or the consumer type is attractive. In an extreme case, it would move to completely different products—an uncommon strategy that some MNEs nonetheless have adopted. Compañía Chilena de Fósforos, a Chilean match producer, wanted to tap the Japanese market because of its growth and size. However, because its matches were too expensive in Japan, it successfully entered the market by making chopsticks, a product that would use its forest resources and wood-processing capabilities.[8]

Business-to-business suppliers may be concerned primarily with promoting their production capabilities, prices, and delivery reliability rather than determining what will sell in

---

Passive sales occur when foreign buyers seek new products.

Serving niche markets abroad may forgo the need to be nationally responsive.

The unaltered product may have appeal at home and abroad because of
- globally similar demand,
- spillover in product information from its home country,
- foreign and domestic input in development.

CONCEPT CHECK

In Chapter 2 (page 74), we discuss that companies may gain competitive advantages by nurturing cultural diversity, such as within teams.

A customer orientation takes geographic areas as given and seeks products to sell there.

foreign markets. Instead, they depend on other companies to give them product specifications. For example, Hong Kong's Yue Yuen Industrial is the world's largest branded-footwear manufacturer, making athletic shoes to the specifications of companies such as Nike, New Balance, and Adidas.

The most common product strategy is to adapt by degree.

Strategic Marketing Orientation   Companies committed to continual rather than sporadic foreign sales usually adopt a strategy that combines production, sales, and customer orientations. They customize to accommodate foreign customers so as not to lose too many sales to aggressive competitors while, at the same time, considering their own competencies so as not to deviate too much from what they do well. Thus, they rely on product variations. Hermès, known for its luxury silk products, has introduced limited edition luxury silk saris for the Indian market.[9] Thus, Hermès uses its competency in prestige design clothing to produce something that fits the unique Indian market. Such personal care firms as Procter & Gamble and Henkel have altered their cosmetics' content by eliminating pork derivatives and alcohol on sales to the Islamic (Halal) market.[10]

Companies consider the effects on all stakeholders when producing and selling their products.

Social Marketing Orientation   Companies with social marketing orientations pay close attention to the potential environmental, health, social, and work-related problems that may arise when selling or making their products. Such groups as consumer associations, political parties, labor unions, and NGOs are becoming more globally aware—and vocal. Because they can quell demand when they believe a product somehow violates their concept of social responsibility, companies must consider how a product is made, purchased, used, and discarded. Such considerations led Coca-Cola to use returnable glass containers for Argentina and Brazil.[11]

CONCEPT CHECK

Chapter 11 (pages 326–327) illustrated the problem in trading off the interests of diverse stakeholders.

SEGMENTING AND TARGETING MARKETS

Seldom can a company convince virtually an entire population to consume its product. Thus, based on the orientations just discussed, companies must segment markets for their products and services and then decide which to target and how. The most common way to do this is through demographics, such as income, age, gender, ethnicity, religion, or a combination of factors. Companies may further refine these segments by adding psychographics (attitudes, values, lifestyles). Internationally, segmentation and targeting may take place at a global or country level.[12]

Companies must decide on their target markets, which may include segments that exist in more than one country.

By Global Segment   An MNE may identify some global segments that transcend countries.[13] For instance, Red Bull targets a global, athletically minded, young-adult market.[14] Ferrari targets high-net-worth individuals who want the exclusivity of having a product whose demand exceeds supply.[15] Thus, each country may have some people within the same segment, but the proportional and actual size of the segment will vary by country.

By Country   Let's say a company decides to go to the Canadian market. It may modify its global segmentation to fit Canadian nuances, for example by including regional ethnic differences such as Quebec's and British Columbia's French and Chinese speakers, respectively. It must decide whether to target one or multiple segments there, whether to use the same marketing mix to sell to all segments, whether to tailor the products separately to each segment, and whether to vary the promotion and distribution separately as well. The company may also compare these Canadian segments with those in other countries in order to gain possible economies through standardization that serves market segments that cut across countries.

CONCEPT CHECK

Chapter 13 (pages 384–385) describes the importance of demographics in selecting countries for operations, and much of these data are valid in marketing decisions.

Mixing the Marketing Mix   A company may hold one or more elements of its marketing functions—prices, promotion, branding, and distribution— constant while altering the others. For instance, Chanel aims its cosmetics sales at a segment that transcends national boundaries. It uses branding, promotion, pricing, and distribution globally, but adapts the cosmetics to local ethnic and climatic norms.[16]

Mass Markets Versus Niche Markets   At the same time, most companies have multiple products and product variations that appeal to different segments; thus, they must decide which to introduce abroad and whether to target them to mass markets or niche segments. For example, General Motors aims at most income levels in the United States with models ranging in price from its Chevrolet Spark through its Cadillac Escalade SUV, but it entered China by aiming only at a high-income segment—first with Buicks and later with Cadillacs.

Because the percentage of people who fall into any segment varies among countries, a niche market in one country may be a mass market in another. An MNE may be content to accept a combination of mass and niche markets; however, if it wishes to appeal to mass markets everywhere, it may need to change elements in its marketing program.

PRODUCT POLICIES: COUNTRY ADAPTATION VERSUS GLOBAL STANDARDIZATION

Although cost is a compelling reason to globally standardize any part of a company's marketing mix, product standardization generally gains the biggest savings.[17] Nevertheless, product adaptations are common.

WHY FIRMS ADAPT PRODUCTS

Companies have legal, cultural, and economic reasons for adapting their products to fit the customers' needs in different countries.

Direct and indirect legal factors are usually related to safety, health, and environmental protection.

Legal Considerations   Obviously, explicit legal requirements, usually meant to protect consumers, cause companies to customize products for foreign markets. If they don't comply with the law, they won't be allowed to sell. Pharmaceuticals and foods are particularly subject to regulations concerning purity, testing, and labeling, while automobiles must conform to diverse safety, pollution, and fuel-economy standards.

When standards (such as for safety) differ among countries, firms may either conform to the minimum standards of each country or make and sell products fabricated to the highest country standard everywhere. Managers must consider cost along with public opinion by having lower standards in some countries. Critics have complained, for example, about companies' sales—especially in developing countries—of such products as toys, automobiles, contraceptives, and pharmaceuticals that did not meet safety or quality standards elsewhere.

Labeling Requirements   One of the more cumbersome product alterations concerns laws on labeling, such as for origin, ingredients, and warnings. Labeling differences on food products include their bioengineered content and whether they are organic or fairly traded. Countries have varying requirements for warnings on cigarette packages; Australia requires all companies to use the same drab dark brown packages and standardized type for their brand names.[18]

Environmental-Protection Regulations   Another problem concerns laws that protect the environment, such as Denmark's onetime ban on aluminum cans and a current requirement for a refundable deposit on them. Other countries restrict the volume of packaging materials to save resources and decrease trash. There are also differences in national requirements as to whether containers are reusable and whether packaging materials must be recycled, incinerated, or composted.

Indirect Legal Considerations   Indirect legal requirements also affect product content or demand. In some nations, companies cannot easily import certain raw materials or components, forcing them to construct a product with local substitutes that may modify the final result. Laws, such as high taxes on heavy automobiles, also shift companies' sales to smaller models, thus indirectly altering demand for tire sizes and grades of gasoline.

Issues of Standardization   Countries' legal differences require firms to incur costly product adjustments. Although governments have reached agreements to standardize some product aspects (technical standards on mobile phones, bar codes to identify products), other products (railroad gauges, power supplies) continue to vary. A global standard has usually resulted from companies wanting to emulate a dominant producer, such as making blades to fit Gillette razors.

In reality, there is both consumer and economic resistance to uniformity—such as the U.S. reluctance to adapt to the metric system. Economically, a changeover would be costlier than simply educating people and relabeling. Containers would have to be redesigned and production retooled so that sizes would be in even numbers. (Would U.S. football have a first down with 9.144 meters to go?) Even for new products or those still under development, companies and countries are slow to reach agreement because they want to protect the investments they've already made. At best, international standards will come very slowly.

Cultural Considerations   Religious differences obviously limit the standardization of product offerings globally, such as the limitation of pork product sales by food franchises in Islamic countries. These franchises, such as McDonald's and Burger King, also add items to fit local tastes, such as squid oil on buns in Japan.[19] However, cultural differences affecting product demand may not be so easily discerned. Toyota failed to sell enough pickup trucks in the United States until it redesigned the interior with enough headroom for drivers to wear cowboy hats. Home Depot left the Chinese market after it could not overcome consumers' preference for hiring people to do jobs rather than embracing the do-it-yourself concept.[20] International food marketers substantially alter ingredients (especially fat, sodium, and sugar) to fit local tastes and requirements, such as Kellogg's All-Bran bar having more salt in the United States than in Mexico.

Economic Considerations

Income Level and Distribution   If a country has many consumers with low incomes, companies have an opportunity to sell to them differently than to higher-income consumers. For instance, in Peru, Unilever sells deodorants in aerosol cans to more affluent consumers, and it sells cream sachet in small containers to those with lower incomes.[21] Diageo and SABMiller have lowered beer prices to low-income consumers in several African countries by brewing with local ingredients, such as yams, and convincing governmental authorities to remove excise taxes because of the agricultural jobs created by the ingredient change.[22] When segmenting sales by economic levels, a company may need to distinguish its products by giving them different brand names, such as what Procter & Gamble does in China with both a Duracell and Nanfu brand of batteries.[23]

Infrastructure   Poor infrastructure may also require product alterations, such as making them to withstand rough terrain and utility outages. Whirlpool sells washing machine models in remote areas of India with rat guards to protect hoses, extra-strong parts to survive transportation on potholed roads, and heavy-duty wiring to cope with electrical ebbs and surges.[24] Japan, has adapted its excellent infrastructure to crowded conditions and high land prices, which limits sales of some large foreign automobile models (i.e., they are too wide to fit into elevators that carry cars to parking areas on upper floors or to make narrow turns on back streets).

ALTERATION COSTS

Some product alterations, such as package labeling, are cheaper to make than others, such as designing a different car model. Further, some will increase sales more than others, thus potential costs versus sales generation should be evaluated for each type of change.[25]

Margin notes:

Although some global product standardization would eliminate wasteful alterations, there is resistance because
- a changeover would be costly,
- people are familiar with the "old."

Examination of cultural differences may pinpoint possible product problems.

Personal incomes and infrastructures affect product demand, thus firms may
- aim product variations at different income levels,
- tailor products to compensate for infrastructure differences.

The cost of product alterations should be compared with their sales generation.

However, even packaging changes may necessitate costly research if the aim is to help build a certain product image in the minds of a target market. For example, packaging can partially sway consumers in buying decisions, but the image needed to do this may differ by target market.[26]

MNEs can compromise between products' uniformity and diversity by standardizing them a great deal while altering some characteristics. Whirlpool does this by putting the same basic mechanical parts in all its refrigerators while changing such features as doors and shelves for different countries.[27]

THE PRODUCT LINE: EXTENT AND MIX

Broadening the product line may gain distribution economies, but not all of a company's line has sales appeal everywhere.

When a firm introduces a range of its products abroad, the percentage share of sales for each commonly differs from the shares in its home country. For instance, a tire manufacturer may sell all its car tire sizes everywhere, but the share for each size depends on sales of different automobile models in each market. Cultural factors may also be important. Most of Nike's specialty sports shoes have sold well in China, but its running shoes have not. Why not? Running in China has been associated with unpopular school exercise programs and with people being chased.[28]

In many cases, not all an MNE's multiple products can generate sufficient sales to justify the cost of penetrating each market with each product. Even if they can, the company might offer only a portion of its product line, perhaps as an entry strategy or because of limited space and high inventory costs when handling a very broad product line. Walmart's Canadian stores, for instance, have only 20 percent of the merchandise variety available in its U.S. stores.[29]

Sales and Cost Considerations In reaching product-line decisions, managers should consider the sales and cost of having a large versus small family of products. Sometimes a firm must produce and sell a wide variety of products to gain distribution with large retailers. Further, if the sales per retailer are small, fixed distribution costs may cause delivery costs per sales unit to be high. In such a case, the company can broaden the product line it distributes, either by introducing a larger family of its products or by grouping sales of several manufacturers.

INTERNATIONAL PRICING COMPLEXITIES

A price must be low enough to gain sales but high enough to guarantee the flow of funds required to cover expenses and make sufficient profits to achieve long-term competitive viability.

POTENTIAL OBSTACLES IN INTERNATIONAL PRICING

Pricing is more complex internationally than domestically, and we'll now examine the major reasons.

Governmental price controls may
• set minimum or maximum prices,
• prohibit certain competitive pricing practices.

Government Intervention Every country has laws that affect the prices of goods. Minimum prices are usually set to prevent companies from eliminating competitors and gaining monopoly positions. Maximum prices are usually set so that poor consumers can buy products and services.

Some countries' consumers simply like certain products more and are willing to pay more for them.

Market Diversity Country-to-country variations in demand and competition create natural segments and limitations in pricing possibilities. In terms of culture, a seafood company would sell few sea urchins or tuna eyeballs in the United States at any price, but it can export them to Japan at a high price, where they are considered delicacies. In terms of competition, the more there is, the less discretion a firm has in setting its prices.

The weaker the competition, the more discretion a company has on its pricing strategy.

When a company has considerable pricing discretion, it may use any of the following tactics:

- A **skimming strategy**—charging a high price for a new product by aiming first at consumers willing to pay that much, then progressively lowering the price to sell to other consumers
- A **penetration strategy**—introducing a product at a low price to induce a maximum number of consumers to try it
- A **cost-plus strategy**—pricing at a desired margin over cost

Country-of-origin stereotypes also limit pricing possibilities. For example, exporters in developing economies must often compete primarily through low prices because of negative perceptions about their products' quality. The danger is that a lower price may weaken the product image even further.

Preference for cash versus credit buying affects demand.

Diversity in buying on credit affects sales, especially through impulse buying.[30] For example, the average consumers in some countries, such as Japan, are less willing to undertake debt (e.g., they have a feeling of insecurity when incurring debt) than consumers in other countries, such as the United States. In the former, it is harder to generate sales by offering credit.

CONCEPT CHECK

In Chapter 14 (pages 431–432), we discuss the importance of export intermediaries and the process of indirect selling (page 417) through independent companies that facilitate international trade.

Export Price Escalation   If standard markups occur within distribution channels, lengthening the channels or adding expenses somewhere in the system will further raise the price to the consumer—a situation known as *export price escalation*. Figure 17.2 shows price escalation in export sales.

Export prices generally rise by more than incremental transport and duty costs, thus exporters may have to lower margins to make sales.

There are two main implications of price escalation. Seemingly exportable products may turn out to be noncompetitive abroad if companies in the value chain use cost-plus pricing—which many do. To become competitive in exporting, a company may have to sell its product to intermediaries at a lower price or convince intermediaries to lower their margins to lessen the amount of escalation.

CONCEPT CHECK

In Chapter 9 (pages 282–283), we point out why foreign-exchange values fluctuate, and in Chapter 13 (pages 388–389), we describe how fluctuations affect companies' operations either positively or negatively.

Fluctuations in Currency Value   For companies accustomed to operating with one relatively stable currency, pricing in highly volatile currencies can be extremely troublesome. Managers should price to ensure the company enough funds to replenish its inventory and still make a profit. Otherwise, it may be making a "paper profit" while liquidating itself—that is, what shows on paper as a profit may result from the failure to adjust for inflation while the merchandise is in stock.

FIGURE 17.2   Why Cost-Plus Pricing Pushes Up Prices

Let's say that a product is being exported from Country A and imported into Country B for purchase by consumers there. Let's also say that both the producer/exporter and the importer/distributor tack on 50 percent markups to the prices they pay for the product. If you add in the costs of transport and tariffs, the product is substantially more expensive in Country B than in Country A—perhaps too expensive to be sold competitively.

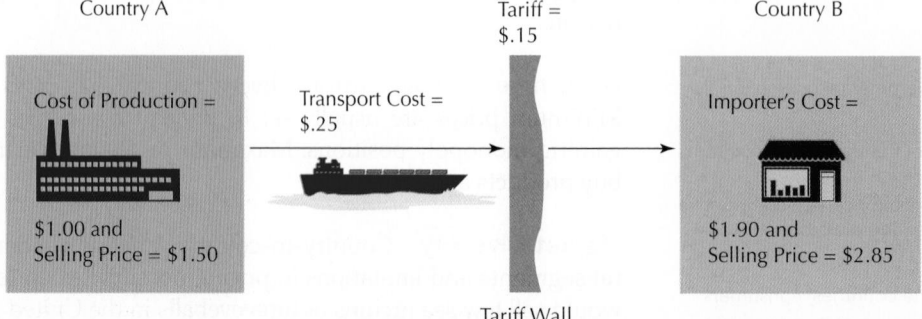

Two other pricing problems occur because of inflationary conditions:

1. The receipt of funds in a foreign currency that, when converted, buy less of the company's own currency than had been expected
2. The frequent readjustment of prices necessary to compensate for continual cost increases

In the first case, the company sometimes can specify within sales contracts an equivalency in some hard currency. For example, a U.S. firm's sale to a company in Venezuela may specify that payment be made in dollars or in bolívars at an equivalent price in terms of dollars at the time payment is made.

In the second case, frequent price increases may hamper the ability to quote prices very far in advance in the currency that is losing value. Further, it would be difficult to make vending-machine sales because of having to recalibrate machines and come up with coins or tokens that correspond to the new prices. Another alternative is to change the product's quality, which few firms are willing to do, or its size, which is what Coca-Cola did to its canned soft-drinks in Hong Kong when aluminum prices rose.[31]

Currency-value changes also affect pricing decisions for any product that has potential foreign competition. For example, when the U.S. dollar is strong, companies can sell non-U.S.-made goods more cheaply in the United States because their prices in dollars decrease. In such a situation, U.S. producers may have to accept a lower profit margin to be competitive. When the dollar is weak, however, producers in foreign countries may have to adjust their margins downward.

The Gray Market   The **gray market**, or **product diversion**, is the selling and handling of goods through unofficial distributors. Such unauthorized selling can undermine the longer-term viability of the distributorship system, induce a company's operations in different countries to compete with each other, and prevent companies from charging what the market will bear in each country. However, transport costs as a percentage of product costs are important in determining whether product diversion is feasible. If transport costs are a high percentage, such as for ice cream, large-scale movements across borders are impractical. But for many other products, the movements are practical. Let's say a firm sells its product in Asia at a lower price than in the United States because of different market conditions. If an unauthorized distributor buys it in Asia and resells it at a lower price in the United States, the authorized U.S. distributor either loses sales or can no longer sell at the U.S. market-bearing price. Traditionally, for example, publishers sold texts at substantially different prices in different countries, but the U.S. Supreme Court ruled the legality of buying lower-priced textbooks abroad to resell in the United States. In essence, maintaining large price differences among countries has become more difficult as consumers have gained access to more global price information and more access to buying abroad because of lower trade barriers.

Fixed Versus Variable Pricing   MNEs often negotiate their export prices with importers. Small firms, especially those from developing countries, frequently give price concessions too quickly, limiting their ability to negotiate on a range of marketing factors that affect their costs:

- Discounts for quantity or repeat orders
- Deadlines that increase production or transportation costs
- Credit and payment terms
- Service
- Supply of promotional materials
- Training of sales personnel or customers

Some people, regardless of culture, avoid price negotiation even when they know they may gain economically by doing so.[32] In essence, many people fear being perceived as too aggressive or too poor. Or, they may not want to take the time, preferring to develop long-term relationships that bargaining might upset. Regardless of cause, there is a substantial

---

Margin notes:

When companies' prices are significantly different among countries, consumers are tempted to buy in the cheapest country.

There are country-to-country differences in
- whether prices are fixed or bargained in stores,
- where and for what products bargaining occurs.

variation among countries in whether, where, and for what products consumers bargain in order to settle on an agreed price. In the United States, consumers commonly bargain for automobiles, real estate, and large orders of industrial supplies but not for grocery items. However, some auto dealerships sell only on a fixed-price basis, while bargaining for smaller items is growing as buyers more easily obtain alternative prices through the Internet. In contrast, consumers in most developing countries commonly bargain for both large and small items, but more routinely in traditional markets than in retail stores.[33]

> Markets' dominant companies have strong negotiating power.

Supplier Relations   Dominant companies with clout can get suppliers to offer lower prices, thereby gaining cost advantages over competitors. But they may lack this ability when entering foreign markets because of not dominating the market there. Walmart, Marks & Spencer, and Carrefour have such clout in their respective domestic markets, but they have been hard pressed to gain the same advantage when entering the others' home markets.

The Internet is also causing more companies to compete for the same business, especially for sales of largely undifferentiated materials. Thus, many industrial buyers are claiming large price decreases through Internet buying. However, sellers can improve their positions by negotiating and by combining the Internet with face-to-face interaction.[34]

SHOULD PROMOTION DIFFER AMONG COUNTRIES?

Promotion is the presentation of messages intended to help sell a product or service. The types and direction of messages and the methods of presentation may be extremely diverse, depending on the company, product, and country of operation.

THE PUSH–PULL MIX

Promotion may be **push**, which uses direct selling techniques, or **pull**, which relies on mass media. (The photo shows a street in Hong Kong lit with neon signs to pull customers to buy.) Most companies use combinations of both. For each product in each country, a company must determine the mix between push and pull within its total promotional budget.

One type of pull promotion is a sign in a public place. Here we see neon advertisements on a busy street in Hong Kong.

Source: Getty Images

Factors in Push–Pull Decisions Several factors help determine the mix of push and pull:

Push is more likely when

• self-service is not predominant,
• advertising is restricted,
• product price is a high portion of income.

• Type of distribution system
• Cost and availability of media to reach target markets
• Consumer attitudes toward sources of information
• Price of the product compared to incomes

Generally, the more tightly controlled the distribution system, the more likely a company is to emphasize a push strategy to distributors because it requires a greater effort to get them to handle a product. This is true where most distributors can carry few brands because they are small and highly fragmented, thereby forcing companies to concentrate on making their goods available.

Also affecting the push–pull mix is the amount of contact between salespeople and consumers. In a self-service situation, in which customers have few or no salespeople to turn to for opinions on products, it is more important for the company to use a pull strategy by advertising through mass media or at the point of purchase.

Finally, consumers react to word-of-mouth opinions, especially where uncertainty avoidance is high.[35] To enhance word-of-mouth opinions, companies need to persuade existing customers that their purchases have been of high quality and at reasonable prices, such as by providing after-sales support and service. Social media platforms are rapidly becoming more important in conveying independent experiences for products and services because they allow users to interact, such as by rating their recent hotel stays and sharing information about their experiences.

CONCEPT CHECK

In Chapter 2 (pages 84–85), we discuss the cultural concept of uncertainty avoidance.

SOME PROBLEMS IN INTERNATIONAL PROMOTION

Diverse national environments create varied promotional challenges. For example, over half of China's population is rural, most are poor, and many lack access to traditional media to view advertisements. Thus, PC makers such as Lenovo and Hewlett Packard promote in rural areas, such as in local markets, by providing variety shows and films to demonstrate their products.[36] In rural Nigeria, Kuwait's Mobile Telecommunications Company first tried direct marketing, but lost its billboards to thefts and found its salespeople facing too many dangers. The company then turned successfully to small shop owners—tailors, retailers, etc.—and established a mini-franchise system with them.[37]

In many areas, government regulations pose additional barriers, such as in Scandinavia where television cannot broadcast commercials aimed at children. In China, ads cannot interrupt dramas, thus they are all bunched together between shows, which companies claim make the ads less effective. Other countries may put legal constraints on what a company says. For instance, the United States allows pharmaceutical firms to advertise prescription drugs directly to consumers, but European countries do not. Thus, in the former, pharmaceutical companies describe physical symptoms, such as erectile dysfunction, in television ads and tell viewers to ask their physicians about a particular brand, such as Viagra or Cialis. However, Pfizer's and Eli Lilly's European ads simply tell TV viewers, without mentioning their brands, to talk with their physicians about problems.[38]

Finally, when a product's price compared to consumer income is high, consumers usually want more time and information before making a decision. In these situations, information is best conveyed in a personal selling situation that fosters two-way communication. Thus, in developing economies MNEs will often use push strategies for more products because of lower incomes.

Advantages of standardized advertising include

• some cost savings,
• better quality at the country level,
• a common image globally,
• rapid entry into different countries.

Advertising Standardization: Pro and Con Standardizing advertising among countries reduces costs, may improve the quality at the local level (because local agencies may lack expertise), prevents internationally mobile consumers from being confused by different images, and speeds the entry of products into different countries.

However, globally standardized advertising usually refers to *similarity* among markets rather than being *identical*. For example, Red Bull's ad campaigns are similar in that they focus on sports, but the sports differ among countries.[39] Standardization typically involves using the same ad agency globally. By doing this, MNEs such as Colgate and Tambrands can quickly introduce good ideas from one market into others without legal and ethical problems that could arise over agency copying. Other companies, like Procter & Gamble, prefer to use more than one agency to promote competition and to cover one agency's weak spots by drawing on another's strong points.

Finally, the issue of standardization in advertising raises problems in a few other areas—namely, *translation, legality,* and *message needs.*

CONCEPT CHECK

In Chapter 2 (pages 86–87), we emphasize the problems in translating messages and the role of nonverbal communications (pages 87–89) in comprehending messages.

Translation   Selling in a country with a different language necessitates translation unless the advertiser tries to communicate an aura of foreignness. Because voice dubbing of TV ads creates sound tracks that never quite correspond to lip movements, companies are turning to voice or print overlays of commercials in which actors do not speak.

Another type of advertisement dubbing involves product placement in books, movies, and television shows, especially those that are widely distributed internationally. Because the product may not be available everywhere, it may be replaced for given markets. *Spider-Man 2* had Cadbury Schweppes's Dr. Pepper logo on a refrigerator for U.S. screenings and PepsiCo's Mirinda logo in Europe.[40]

On the surface, translating a message would seem easy. However, some messages, particularly plays on words, don't translate—even between countries that have the same language. Sometimes an acceptable word or direct translation in one place has a nuance that is offensive, misleading, or meaningless in another. An additional issue lies in choosing the language when a country has more than one. For instance, many companies use Creole in Haiti to reach the general population but French to reach the upper class.

Differences in nations' values have led to advertising differences among them.

Legality   The legality of advertisements varies mainly because of diverse national views on consumer and competitive protection, civil rights promotion, standards of morality and behavior, and nationalism. For example, there are products that some societies view as being in sufficiently bad taste that they restrict their advertising.[41]

In terms of consumer protection, policies differ on the amount of deception permitted and what can be advertised to children. Mexico, for example, limits using TV advertisement of products high in sugar content directed at children.[42] The United Kingdom and the United States allow direct comparisons with competitive brands, while the Philippines prohibits them. Only a few countries regulate sexism in advertising. Elsewhere, governments restrict ads that might prompt misbehavior or law-breaking (such as promoting automobile speeds that exceed the speed limit), as well as those that show barely clad women.[43]

Effective promotional messages may be different among countries because of
- cultural factors,
- economic levels of target markets,
- stages of products in their life cycles.

Message Needs   An advertising theme may not be appropriate everywhere because of country differences in consumers' product awareness and perception, the people who make the purchasing decision, and what appeals are most important. At one time fewer Italians owned dishwashers than would be expected from Italian income levels because of a belief that buying for the sake of convenience reduces cleanliness; hence, a group of dishwasher manufacturers teamed up to advertise that dishwashers clean better because they use hotter water.[44] Because of economic differences, Home Depot promotes its U.S. stores by appealing to hobbyists, whereas in Mexico it promotes the cost savings for do-it-yourselfers.[45]

The reaction to messages may also vary. Leo Burnett Worldwide produced a public service ad to promote breast exams that showed an attractive woman being admired in a low-cut sundress. The voice-over message said, "If only women paid as much attention to their breasts as men do..." Japanese viewers found this a humorous way to draw attention to breast cancer, whereas French viewers found it offensive because cancer should not be viewed humorously.[46] Given the increase in television and Internet transmissions that reach audiences in multiple countries, advertisers must find common themes and messages that will appeal to potential consumers everywhere their ads are viewed.

Countries may differ in either the shape or the length of a product's life cycle. Thus, a product facing declining sales in one country may have growing or sustained sales in another. Consider cars: They are a mature product in Western Europe, in the late growth stage in South Korea, and in the early growth stage in India. At the mature stage, automobile companies must emphasize characteristics that encourage people to replace their still-functional cars, such as lifestyle, speed, and accessories. In the early growth stage, they need to appeal to first-time buyers who worry more about cost, so they emphasize fuel consumption and price.[47]

The growth in products' online availability through the Internet creates new promotional and distributional opportunities and challenges.

The Internet   Estimates vary widely on the current and future number of worldwide online households and the electronic commerce generated through online sales, but Internet ads may now account for about a quarter of advertising business.[48] The Internet has done more in recent years than any other innovation to alter international promotion. Through e-commerce, customers worldwide can quickly compare prices from different distributors, which drives prices down. Through the growing use of social media, they can obtain better information to compare the quality and reliability of products and distributors. The main characteristics of global online shoppers are they want convenience, they use e-mail and the Internet heavily, and they have favorable attitudes toward direct marketing and advertising.[49]

Opportunities   There are certainly many e-commerce success stories. These include promotion for direct sales as well as information to pre-sell and inform shoppers where they may buy the products. One such success story is the New Zealand prefab housing company Tristyle International, for which about 95 percent of sales are export and 40 percent are through the Internet.[50] Another is Lee Hung Fat Garment Factory of Hong Kong and Bangladesh. It flashes pictures of merchandise samples to apparel companies abroad that tinker with and return them so that it produces exactly what they want. For some products and services, such as airline tickets, hotel space, and music, the Internet has largely replaced traditional sales methods. But even here, companies may need to adapt to country differences, such as providing access through various languages.[51]

Problems   Global Internet sales are not without glitches. A company that wants to reach global markets may need to supplement its Internet sales with other means of promotion and distribution, which can be very expensive. Further, a switch to Internet sales may risk upsetting existing distributors and, if unsuccessful, make future sales more difficult.[52]

On the Internet, an MNE cannot as easily differentiate its marketing program for each country in which it sells even if it channels customers to local sites. In many instances, the same web ads and prices reach customers everywhere, even though different appeals and prices for different countries might yield more sales and profits. Making direct sales over the Internet requires expeditious delivery, which may require warehouses and service facilities abroad. Finally, the MNE's Internet ads and prices must comply with the laws of each country of sales. This is problematic because of the web's global reach. Clearly, although the Internet creates opportunities for companies to sell internationally, it also creates challenges for them.

INTERNATIONAL BRANDING STRATEGIES

A *brand* is an identifying mark for products or services. If it is legally registered, it is a trademark. A brand gives a product or service instant recognition and may save promotional costs. Because companies have spent heavily in the past to create brand awareness, many brands are worth billions of dollars and are the most valuable assets firms possess.[53] From a consumer standpoint, a brand conveys a perception of whether firms will deliver what they promise; however, the importance is more crucial in countries with strong cultural characteristics of uncertainty avoidance.[54]

Keep in mind that a company may use the same brand globally while altering the brand image for different markets. For example, individualistic cultures offer greater advantages in creating an image of innovativeness than collectivist cultures. However, within the latter, images of social responsibility apparently contribute more to brand commitment than in the former.[55]

GLOBAL BRAND VERSUS LOCAL BRANDS

International marketers must decide whether to adopt a global brand or use different brands for different countries.

Using the same brand name globally

- helps develop a common image,
- may increase consumers' demand if they think global products are better,
- is hampered by language differences,
- has a drawback in the case of acquisitions.

Advantages of a Global Brand   Some companies, such as Apple, use the same brand and logo for most of their products around the world. This helps develop a global image, especially for customers who travel internationally. In addition, there is evidence that the use of global brands helps identify companies as global players, which many consumers view more favorably.[56] Other companies, such as Nestlé, associate many of their products under the same family of brands, such as Nestea and Nescafé, to share the positive perception of the Nestlé name.

Some Problems with Global Brands   A number of problems are inherent in using global brands.

Language   A brand name may carry a different association in another language. GM renamed its Buick LaCrosse to Allure in Canada after discovering, through a pre-entry focus group, that the word was slang in Quebec for masturbation.[57] Coca-Cola uses global branding wherever possible, but given that the word *diet* in Diet Coke had a connotation of illness in Germany and Italy, the brand became Coca-Cola Light outside the United States.

Pronunciation presents other problems, since a foreign language may lack some of the sounds of a brand name, or give it a different meaning. Marcel Bich dropped the *h* from his name when branding Bic pens because of fearing mispronunciation in English. Microsoft's search engine Bing became Biying in China so that it sounded like the word for "seek and ye shall find" instead of "illness." IKEA, which uses Scandinavian names for its products, hired Thai speakers to modify its catalogue to prevent misinterpretation of names when pronounced in Thai.[58]

When alphabets use pictograms, such as in China, brands should both look and sound appealing. Thus, MNEs take great pains to ensure not only that the translation of their names is pronounced roughly the same in Mandarin or Cantonese Chinese as elsewhere but also that the brand name is meaningful in pictograms. Coca-Cola is pronounced *Ke-kou-ke-le* in Mandarin Chinese and means "tasty" and "fun." Tide became Tai-zi in Mandarin, which means "gets rid of dirt."[59] Companies seek names and prices using symbols considered lucky in China, such as one with eight strokes in it and displayed in red rather than blue.[60]

Brand Acquisition   Much international expansion is through acquisitions of companies with established brands, such as Bimbo's Sara Lee of various Brazilian coffee roasters. Although Sara Lee became the coffee-market leader in Brazil, stretching the promotional budget over many brands has been challenging.[61] Overall, the proportion of local to global brands is declining; however, companies lose the recognition and goodwill of strong local brands if they displace them.[62] Similarly, having a combination of global and local brands that appeal to different segments can sometimes be advantageous, such as those used for Anheuser-Busch InBev's beers.[63]

Images of products are affected by where they are made.

Country-of-Origin Images   Consumers have limited knowledge of the nationality of most brands, and they often misclassify the production origins.[64] Such confusion is compounded with the increased mixed source of the components that make up products. In addition, both the country of origin and the brand images interact so that a positive brand image can help overcome a negative country-of-origin image.[65]

Nevertheless, a minority of consumers, although an important segment, are influenced by their emotional affinity toward certain countries; their affinity affects their images of certain countries and buying decisions based on where products are made.[66]

But influences are complex, depending on such factors as type of product, the economic level of and nearness of the producing country to the consumers, consumers' national culture (such as effects of individualism versus collectivism), and consumers personalities (such as how materialistic they are).[67] Despite the complexity, companies may play up positive and play down negative country-of-origin images. For example, because many Japanese believe that clothing made abroad is superior to clothing made in Japan, Burberry has created separate labels for its products made in Japan and the United Kingdom. South African wineries, La Motte and Leopard's Leap, have a wine brand, L'Huguenot, for the Chinese market because the French-sounding name is perceived positively by Chinese consumers.[68]

Still, images can change. For many years various Korean firms sold abroad only under private labels or in contract with foreign companies. On the one hand, some of these, such as Samsung, now emphasize their own trade names and Korean product quality. On the other hand, the Korean LG Group, best known for its Gold Star brand, has introduced a line of high-end appliances with a European-sounding name, LG Tromm.[69]

Locational Origin of Names   One ongoing international legal debate concerns product names associated with location. The EU protects the names of many European products based on location names, such as Roquefort and Feta cheeses, Parma ham, and Chianti wine.[70] It has also pushed for protection against the foreign use of regulated names associated with wines, such as *clos, chateau, tawny, noble, ruby,* and *vintage.*[71]

Generic and Near-Generic Names   Companies want their brands to become household words, but not so much that they become **generic**, a situation whereby competitors can use the names to call their products. In the United States, the brand names Xerox and Kleenex are nearly synonymous with copiers and facial tissue, but they have nevertheless remained proprietary brands. Some other names that were once proprietary—cellophane, linoleum, Cornish hens—are now generic.

In this context, companies sometimes face differences among countries that may either stimulate or frustrate their sales. For example, *aspirin* and *Swiss Army knives* are proprietary names in Europe but generic in the United States—a situation that impairs European export sales of those products to the United States, since U.S. companies can produce them.

Side notes (left margin):

When the country of origin affects consumers' opinion of a product,

- a positive brand image may help overcome a negative country-of-origin image,
- these opinions can change over time.

If a brand name is used for a class of product, a company may lose its trademark.

Point

Should Home Governments Regulate Their Companies' Marketing in Developing Countries?

Point **Yes** MNEs advertise, promote, and sell products in developing markets that their home countries have banned. If they've made a decision not to sell these products domestically because of their dangers or ethical implications, they have a moral obligation to prevent the same consequences abroad. This statement may smack of extraterritoriality, but let's face it: Too many consumers in developing countries lack the education and reliable information to make intelligent decisions about products, and/or they are saddled with corrupt

political leaders who don't look after their interests. We must ensure that they spend on upright needs rather than on wants engendered by MNEs' clever promotion programs. If developed countries don't regulate to protect consumers in developing countries, who will?

Companies also export products that don't meet quality standards at home or are potentially dangerous. Take DDT: It's so dangerous to the environment that all developed countries banned its use, but exports to developing countries have continued. Or consider battery recycling:

Developed countries have pretty much abandoned that business because of strict antipollution requirements to prevent lead poisoning, which shows up only after slow, cumulative ingestion through the years. So now companies export the batteries to developing countries that have either weak or weakly enforced pollution laws.[72]

With the World Health Organization (WHO) estimating that tobacco is the leading cause of preventable death in the world, we have also attempted to limit tobacco use through warning labels and ads, restrictions on sales to minors, and smoking bans in certain public areas. While tobacco use has been declining in developed countries, it is burgeoning in developing ones, especially those in Africa, where tobacco companies have increased their promotions.[73]

MNEs also pay too little attention to the needs of consumers in developing markets. Instead, they primarily create products suitable to the needs of wealthier consumers who can afford them, but these products are often superfluous for low-income consumers, to whom MNEs introduce and promote them heavily. Thus, the poor end up buying products they don't need instead of spending their money on nutritional and health items. Bottled water, sold mainly in plastic bottles by such companies as Nestlé, Danone, Coca-Cola,

and PepsiCo, is an example. It is often no better than tap water (in fact, it often *is* tap water), but it sells for 10,000 times more in bottles that are thrown out and take 1,000 years to biodegrade.

Finally, MNEs spend little to make products to fit the needs of developing countries. Consider that little of the global health research budget is spent on diseases that account for most of the global disease burden—mainly those that largely bypass developed countries.[74] Instead of spending heavily on life-threatening illnesses like malaria, Chagas disease, and sleeping sickness, they spend on lifestyle treatments, such as penile erectile dysfunction and baldness. Although Ebola had long-plagued African countries, pharmaceutical companies spent little to develop a vaccine until there was danger of its spread to developed countries.[75] The U.S. Food and Drug Administration (FDA) did institute an incentive in 2008—faster approval of potential "blockbuster drugs"—for pharmaceutical companies that research previously neglected diseases. However, there is skepticism about whether faster approval is enough of an incentive.[76] Surely we can find the regulatory means to force companies to meet real needs in the developing world rather than concentrating on selling dangerous and superfluous products there.

Should Home Governments Regulate Their Companies' Marketing in Developing Countries?

Counterpoint **No** The answer here is education rather than limiting people's choices by regulating MNEs. In fact, there are many examples of behavior change in both consumers and governments when they learn the facts. For example, antismoking radio and television ads in a three-country African study showed a decrease in propensity to smoke.[77]

Your argument that products banned at home should not be sold abroad assumes that the home government knows best. Even among developed countries, there are different scientific opinions. For example, the EU produces many pesticides and chemicals that are banned for EU usage, but are allowed to be used in the United States.[78] Further, differences may reflect variations in a difference in morals rather than a problem of creating physical danger. For instance, some countries have banned the sale of the morning-after pill RU-486 on moral grounds. But to ban sales in other countries that accept a different morality would smack of cultural imperialism.

Conditions between rich and poor countries are sometimes so different that they need different regulations. Take your example of DDT exports. Developing countries are aware of DDT's adverse long-term effect on the environment, but in the short term many of them face mosquito cri-

Counterpoint

ses that cause Zika, dengue, chikungunya, and malaria.[79] When South Africa was persuaded to ban the use of DDT and turned instead to a different pesticide, the number of new malaria cases tripled in four years; renewing DDT spraying brought that number down again.[80] Until there is a better solution for mosquito controls, DDT bans will do more harm than good. Certainly, if one government has found a product dangerous, it should pass on this information to other governments; in terms of DDT and toxic materials exports, this is already being done.

Yes, tobacco companies are promoting more heavily in developing countries. Keep in mind, though, that a good part of that promotion is for smokeless tobacco products, which are safer than cigarettes and can help smokers stop.[81] In fact, Philip Morris is developing a product that will produce an aerosol without the combustion that causes most harm.[82] Nevertheless, if MNEs' home governments were to limit their companies' sales or promotion of tobacco abroad, developing countries' citizens would still be able to buy cigarettes. Many developing countries have indigenous tobacco companies, some of which are even government-owned, such as the China National Tobacco Company.

How far can we go to try to protect people? Obesity, considered a growing health problem in the developed world, is being attacked through education—the same way we should attack problems in developing countries. I can't imagine a widespread rationing or banning of sugars, fats, and carbohydrates. Certainly, products such as soft drinks and bottled water seem superfluous when people are ill-nourished and in poor health. But the lack of access to sanitary water is one of the world's biggest health problems, which the sale of soft drinks and bottled water are helping in the short term. In a longer term, Coca-Cola is working to distribute small scale purifying systems to mitigate the problem.[83] Moreover, there is no clear-cut means of drawing a line between people who can and can't afford these so-called superfluous products.

Companies *do* alter products to fit the needs of poor people—everything from less expensive packages to less

expensive products. The pharmaceutical firms you criticized for not attacking low-income health needs spend heavily to find solutions to diseases that attack *all* people, such as cancer and diabetes. In fact, they have seen, and expect to see, huge prescription drug growth in emerging markets.[84] However, they must recoup their expenses if they are to survive, so they concentrate on drugs for which they can be paid. Governmental research centers and nonprofit foundations are better candidates for solving the developing countries' health problems. Some are working jointly with pharmaceutical firms to find solutions, while the National Institutes of Health (NIH) in the United States has instituted a program to find treatments for some of the 6,800 diseases for which there is likely insufficient revenue to recoup research expenditures.[85]

DISTRIBUTION PRACTICES AND COMPLICATIONS

A company will not likely reach its sales potential unless its products are conveniently available. **Distribution** is the course—physical path or legal title—that goods take between production and consumption. This section discusses distributional differences and conditions within foreign countries.

DECIDING WHETHER TO STANDARDIZE

Because distribution reflects different country environments,

- it may vary substantially among countries,
- it is difficult to change.

Distribution is one of the most difficult marketing functions to standardize globally. Each country has its own distribution system, which is difficult to modify because of its intertwinement with the country's cultural, economic, and legal environments. In fact, most companies take a country's distribution system as a given and try to adapt to it. Although there are some large multinational distributors, such as Arrow and Grainger, wholesalers and retailers have generally lagged manufacturers and service companies' entries into foreign markets because of difficulty in breaking into these systems. Nevertheless, many retailers have more recently moved successfully abroad.

Some factors that influence countries' retail distribution include citizens' attitudes toward owning their own store, the cost of paying retail workers, legislation restricting store sizes and operating hours, laws on chain stores and individually owned stores, the trust owners have in employees, the efficacy of delivery systems, the quality of the infrastructure system, and the financial ability to carry large inventories. An example should illustrate how widespread differences are. Compare grocery distribution in Hong Kong with the United States: Hong Kong food stores carry a higher proportion of fresh goods, are smaller, sell less per customer, and are closer to each other, which means that companies selling canned, boxed, or frozen foods in Hong Kong encounter less demand per store, have to make smaller deliveries, and have a harder time fighting for shelf space.

At the same time, a company's system of distribution may give it strategic advantages not easily copied by competitors, such as Avon's selling directly through independent reps and Amazon.com's through Internet sales. Even these companies have had to adjust to national nuances. For instance, Avon does a thriving mail-order business in Japan because of the popularity of that distribution, has beauty counters in China because of regulations on house-to-house sales, has franchise centers in the Philippines because of infrastructure inefficiencies, and has beauty centers in Argentina because many customers want services when they purchase cosmetics.

INTERNALIZATION OR NOT?

Should companies handle their own distribution? Or should they contract other companies to do it for them?

Sales Volume and Cost   When sales volume is low, a company usually must rely on external distributors to be more economical. As sales grow, it may handle some distribution itself to gain more control. However, such internalization may still be difficult for small firms that lack necessary resources.

A company may enter a market gradually by limiting geographic coverage.

Nevertheless, companies may limit early distribution costs if they are able to sell regionally before moving nationally. Many products and markets lend themselves to this sort of gradual development. For example, many foreign companies enter the Chinese market by first going to Beijing, Shanghai, and Guanghou, then to provincial capitals, then to other large cities, and finally to smaller cities. Often, geographic barriers and poor internal transportation systems divide countries into very distinct markets. In fact, within developing countries most wealth and potential sales may lie in a few large metropolitan areas.

Factors Favoring Internalization   Circumstances conducive to internalization include not only high sales volume but also the following factors:

Distribution may be handled internally

- when companies have sufficient resources,
- when there is a need to deal directly with the customer because of the product's nature,
- when the customer is global,
- when the distribution form is a competitive advantage.

- When a product has the characteristic of high price, high technology, or the need for complex after-sales servicing (such as aircraft), the company will probably have to deal directly with the buyer, but may simultaneously use a distributor to identify sales leads.
- When the company deals with global customers, especially business-to-business (such as an auto-parts manufacturer selling original equipment to the same automakers in multiple countries), sales may go directly to the global customer.
- When the company's main competitive advantage is its distribution methods, it may control distribution abroad, such as Avon's direct selling through independent representatives.

DISTRIBUTION PARTNERSHIP

If a company wishes to collaborate with a distributor abroad, it can usually compare a number of potential companies. While trying to find the best distributors, it must also convince them to handle its products.

Which Distributors Are Best Qualified?   The choice of international distributor depends on the same criteria as for domestic options. These criteria include the distributor's financial strength, its good connections, the extent of its other business commitments, its current status (e.g., personnel, facilities, and equipment), and its reputation as an honest performer.

Distributors choose which companies and products to handle. Companies

- may need to give incentives,
- may use successful products as bait for new ones,
- must convince distributors that product and company are viable.

Promoting to Potential Distributors   Companies must evaluate potential distributors, but distributors must choose which companies and products to represent and emphasize. Wholesalers and retailers alike have limited storage facilities, display space, money for inventories, and transportation and personnel to move and sell merchandise, so they try to carry only those products with the greatest profit potential.

In some cases, distributors are tied into exclusive arrangements with manufacturers that impede new competitive entries. This is true in Japan, where many manufacturers have arrangements with thousands of distributors to sell only their products.

Any company that is new to a country and wants to introduce similar products to those that competitors are already selling may meet difficulty in finding distributors. Additionally, even established companies can find distribution difficult for new products, although they have the dual advantage of being known and being able to offer existing profitable lines only if distributors accept the new unproven goods. Companies may need to offer effective handling incentives (higher profit margins, after-sales servicing, promotional support, and so on). In the end, however, incentives will be of little use unless the distributors believe the company is reliable and its products viable.

DISTRIBUTION CHALLENGES AND OPPORTUNITIES

Although international distribution involves many challenges and opportunities, the following discussion highlights two: the need for after-sales service, and some often overlooked cost advantages and disadvantages.

Confidence in securing replacement parts and service are important for sales, especially for imported products.

How Reliable Is After-Sales Service? Consumers are reluctant to buy products that may require future replacement parts and service unless they feel sure that these will be readily available in good quality and at reasonable prices. This reluctance is especially keen for imported products because of concerns that distance and customs clearance will delay needed replacement parts. For fairly mature products, there are usually multiple service companies to which consumers can turn in case of problems. However, for products encompassing new technology, especially complex and expensive products, producers may face the downside of having to invest in or develop service centers. Nevertheless, the upside is that earnings from sales of parts and after-sales service may sometimes exceed those of the original product.

The question of after-sales service is especially important for the growing number of technologically oriented entrepreneurial companies from developing countries. Many face multiple problems in selling abroad because they are young, small, fairly unknown, perhaps suffering negative country-of-origin effects, and often assumed to be laggards in technological development.[86]

Hidden Distribution Costs and Gains Several factors often contribute to country differences in distribution costs.

Distribution costs increase when there is

- poor infrastructure,
- many levels in the distribution system,
- inefficient retail distribution,
- inadequate carrying of inventory by retailers.

Infrastructure Conditions Where roads and warehousing facilities are in bad condition, getting goods to consumers quickly, cheaply, and with minimum damage or loss is problematic. For example, Nigeria has no rail links to its ports, has fallen behind in road construction, and has poor connections between big and small cities.[87]

Levels in the Distribution System Where there are multitiered wholesalers that sell to each other (e.g., national wholesalers sell to regional ones, which sell to local ones, and so on) before the product reaches the retail level, each intermediary adds a markup and prices escalate. For example, Japan, though changing rapidly, has many more levels of distribution than, say, France and the United States.

CONCEPT CHECK

In Chapter 2 (pages 82 and 85), we describe societies in which people tend to distrust people outside their families.

Retail Inefficiencies Where low labor costs and owners' distrust of nonfamily members cause counter- rather than self-service merchandise examination, there is less productivity in serving customers. (In fact, some retailers require payment to a cashier before customers receive the merchandise.) On the one hand, the additional personnel add to retailing costs, and the added time people must be in the store means fewer people being served in the given space. On the other hand, most of these retailers tend to be small and dispersed near clients, which reduces the time, cost, and effort for customers to shop.[88] In addition, many retailers (mainly in developing economies) lack equipment that improves the efficiency of handling customers and reports, such as electronic scanners and payment systems linked to inventory-control records and to credit-card companies.

Inventory Stock-Outs Costs rise where governments restrict the ability of some retailers from using more productive distribution practices. For example, France, Germany, and Japan have laws protecting small retailers, effectively limiting the efficiencies large retail establishments can bring to sales. Most countries have patchwork systems that limit days or hours of operations because of religious observances or protection of employees from having to work late at night or on weekends. Although these systems serve social purposes, they limit retailers from covering the fixed cost of their space over more hours, and they usually pass costs on to consumers.

Where most retail establishments are small, there is little space to store inventory. Wholesalers must incur the cost of making small deliveries to many more establishments, sometimes visiting each retailer more frequently because of stock outages. However, these latter costs may be diminished through labor and transport cost savings that result from low-paid delivery personnel who may carry small quantities of merchandise on bicycles. (The following photo shows delivery by foot and bicycle in Vietnam.) Further, the retailers themselves incur lower costs because their inventory-carrying costs are low compared to sales.[89]

GAP ANALYSIS: A TOOL FOR HELPING TO MANAGE THE INTERNATIONAL MARKETING MIX

Emphasis in the marketing mix
- should be on the functions that account for major lost sales,
- may differ by country,
- may combine needs from different countries.

Although every element in the marketing mix—product, price, promotion, brand, and distribution—is important, the relative importance of one versus another may vary from product to product, place to place, and over time.

A company should calculate how well it is doing in each country, how it might do better, and how to gain synergy among marketing activities in different countries. One such tool is **gap analysis**, whereby a company estimates potential sales for a given type of product

Source: Arthur Greenberg/Alamy Stock Photo

FIGURE 17.3   Gap Analysis

Why aren't sales as high as they could be? That's the question asked by a company's managers when they undertake gap analysis. The arrow at the top represents total sales potential for all competitors during a given period. The arrow at A indicates actual sales. Notice that there's a gap between the product's potential and actual sales—the so-called usage gap. But there are other gaps as well. The arrow bracketing points A and B, for example, designates all sales lost by the company to its competitors—the gap, that is, between what the company did sell and what it could have sold if, for a variety of reasons, it hadn't lost so many sales to competitors. Finally, remember that in the real world, gap sizes will fluctuate.

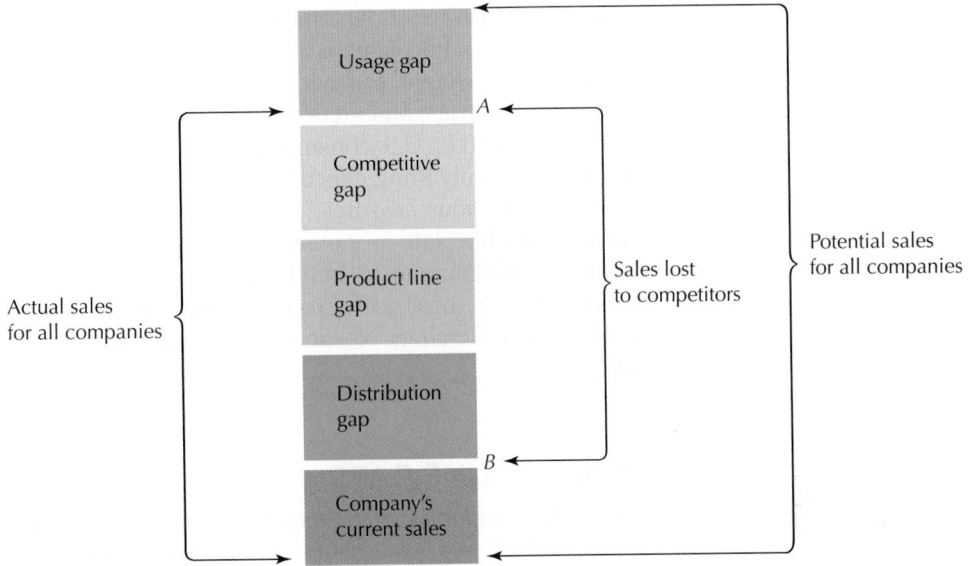

and compares how emphasis on different marketing mix elements can better help it serve prospective customers.[90]

The difference between total market potential and a company's sales is due to several types of gaps:

- *Usage*—collectively, all competitors sell less than the market potential
- *Product line*—the company lacks some product variations
- *Distribution*—the company misses coverage by geography or type of outlet
- *Competitive*—competitors' sales are not explained by product-line and distribution gaps

Figure 17.3 is a bar showing these four types of gaps. To construct such a bar, a company first needs to estimate the potential demand for all competitors in the country for a relevant period—say, for the next year or the next five years. This figure gives the height of the bar. Second, a company needs to estimate current sales by all competitors, which is point A. The space between point A and the top of the bar is a *usage gap*, meaning that this is the growth potential for all competitors in the market for the relevant period. Third, a company needs to plot its own current sales of the product, point B.

Finally, the company divides the difference between points A and B into types of gaps—distribution, product line, and competitive—based on its estimate of why sales are lost to competitors.

USAGE GAPS

Companies may have different-sized gaps in different markets. Large chocolate companies, for instance, have altered their marketing programs among countries because of this. In some markets, they have found less chocolate being consumed than expected on the basis of population and income levels. This has been the case in India, which has per capita consumption of less than one percent of that in Germany. Although low incomes and the inability to use certain animal fats (thus affecting taste) contribute to India's low consumption, it has been the world's fastest growth market in recent years. Why? Chocolate companies have developed small affordable chocolates to reach the masses, and they have promoted chocolate as a more hygienic and longer-lasting confection than alternative products.[91] Industry specialists estimate that in many developing economies, much of the population has never even tasted chocolate, leading companies to promote sales in those areas for chocolate in general.[92]

The U.S. market shows another type of usage gap. Nearly everyone in this market has tried most chocolate products, but per capita consumption has fallen because of concern about weight. Further, U.S. per capita consumption is much lower than in most European countries. Mars has concluded that the main reason for the different consumption is cultural (i.e., U.S. consumers usually take wine or flowers to dinner hosts, whereas Europeans usually bring chocolates). To counter this, Mars has a campaign of "Share your favorites with your favorites," to promote taking chocolate to friends and joining with them to eat chocolate at movies. Earlier, Nestlé promoted chocolate as an energy source for the sports-minded to build U.S. demand for chocolate. However, building general consumption is most useful to the market leader. With U.S. chocolate sales below those of Mars and Hershey, Nestlé actually benefited its competitors during its short-lived campaign.

PRODUCT-LINE GAPS

Chocolate companies have also found that they have product-line gaps. Several have recently added sugar-free, high cocoa content, and fair-traded chocolate products to their repertoire. In addition, they have added such ingredients as bacon, chia, green tea, and quinoa to some of their offerings.[93] Godiva has introduced specialty products in China to compete with local companies that sell theme products for the Chinese Zodiac year and for the Mid-Autumn Festival.[94]

DISTRIBUTION AND COMPETITIVE GAPS

A company's products may be sold in too few places, creating a gap in distribution. To combat this, Ferrero Rocher has recently emphasized product placement in more mainstream outlets. There also may be competitive gaps—sales by competitors that cannot be explained by differences between product lines and distribution. That is, competitors are selling more because of their prices, advertising campaigns, goodwill, or any of a host of other factors. In markets where per capita chocolate consumption is high, companies exert most of their efforts in gaining sales at the expense of competitors. For instance, Switzerland has the world's highest per capita consumption of chocolate. In that market, such competitors as Migros, Lindt, and Nestlé's Cailler go head to head in creating images of better quality.[95]

AGGREGATING COUNTRIES' PROGRAMS

Although gap analysis prioritizes elements in the marketing mix within countries, it is also possible to use the tool by aggregating needs among countries. Let's say the product-line gap is too small in a single country to justify the expense of developing a specific new product, such as a heat-resistant chocolate bar. Nevertheless, the combined market potential among several countries for this product may justify the product- and promotional-development costs. Thus, comparing the importance of the different elements within the marketing mix may help managers improve country-level performance along with enhancing synergy among the countries where they operate.

Looking to the Future
How Might International Market Segmentation Evolve?

Recall the discussion on how both demographics and psychographics affect market segmentation. How both of these will unfold in future years will likely affect international marketing. There are, of course, many more global trends that may affect future international marketing than we can possibly highlight (e.g., aging population, growing obesity, increasing use of social media), thus the following discussion highlights only one key demographic and one key psychographic area.

Income Demographics

Most projections are that disparities between the "haves" and "have-nots" will grow in the foreseeable future, both within and among countries. Furthermore, because haves will be more educated and more connected to the Internet, they will be better able to search globally for lower prices. Therefore, globally, the disparate purchasing power of the affluent segment will be even more than indicated by incomes.[96]

As discretionary income increases, some luxury products will become more commonplace (partly because it will take less work time to purchase them), and seemingly dissimilar products and services (such as cars, travel, jewelry, and art) will compete with each other for the same discretionary spending. Japan was the premier importer of luxury clothing during the 1980s and early 1990s, but competition from an array of other luxury services, such as spas and expensive restaurants, eroded those imports.[97] In addition, many Japanese consumers have moved down-market during Japan's stagnated economic growth, and there is speculation that they may not move up-market again when their economy improves. Nevertheless, because of better communications and rising educational levels of the haves, they will want more choices. However, market segments may not fall primarily along national lines. Rather, companies may depend more on identifying consumer niches that cut across country lines.

At the other extreme, because of the large number of poor people with little disposable income, companies will have opportunities to develop low-cost standardized products to fit the needs of the have-nots. In reality, low-income households collectively have considerable purchasing power and will likely spend mainly on housing, food, health care, education, communications, finance charges, and consumer goods.[98] Thus, companies will have conflicting opportunities: develop luxury to serve the haves and cut costs to serve the have-nots. Some producers are already responding to this market dichotomy. Frito-Lay calls it the "bifurcation" of the snack market and is emphasizing new products for the high and low ends, but not the middle.[99] The president of the Wine Academy of Spain pointed out this market split for wine sales in China. He indicated that there is no middle market; rather there is a high-end where people spend thousands of dollars per bottle as an investment or as an ostentatious drink and a low-end where people spend no more than the equivalent of a few dollars per bottle while buying in large containers.[100] Despite the growing proportions of haves and have-nots, demographers project that the actual numbers of people moving out of poverty levels and into middle-income levels will increase. This is largely because of population and income growth in a few low-income countries, especially in Asia. Such a shift raises questions: Will sales growth in poorer countries mainly be for products that are mature in industrial countries, such as many consumer electronics and household appliances? Or, will consumers in poorer countries leapfrog to newer products as they have done by bypassing landline phones and going directly to cellular ones?

Will National Markets Become Passé?

In addition to demographic differences, especially regarding income, attitudinal differences affect demand in general as well as for particular types of products and services. Although global communications are reaching far-flung populations, different people react differently to them. At least three—not mutually exclusive—types of personality traits interact and affect how potential consumers react.[101] They exist in all countries (thus creating a segment that cuts across the globe), but the portion of people who are strongly influenced by one versus the other presently varies by country. How these factors evolve will likely have a profound influence on the future of international marketing.

The first of the traits is **materialism**, which refers to the importance of acquiring possessions as a means of self-satisfaction and happiness, as well as for the appearance of success. There is evidence of this trait's growth and spread. However, there is also evidence that people who have always been affluent may exhibit lower materialistic behaviors than those who have recently become affluent, the so-called *nouveau riche*. The second of these traits is **cosmopolitanism**, which refers to openness to the world. While there is debate on whether this is a learned or an inborn trait, some of the characteristics include comparing oneself with what is in the whole world rather than with what is local. Cosmopolitanists may actually seek out foreign products and services. The third of these traits is **consumer ethnocentrism**, which refers to preference for local to global, such as seeking out local alternatives when buying products and services. ∎

CASE   Grameen Danone Foods in Bangladesh[102]

Professors Jon Jungbien Moon and John D. Daniels

In 1932, U.S. President Franklin D. Roosevelt referred to an impoverished person as "the forgotten man at the bottom [base] of the economic pyramid." Later, the term—shortened to "BoP"—became business jargon after publication in 2010 of *The Fortune at the Bottom of the Pyramid*.

Few places have more impoverished people than Bangladesh. With 169 million people in 2015, its per capita GDP at PPP was $3,581, with 43.3 percent of the population below the international poverty line of $1.25 per day. Thus, Bangladesh has conditions that correlate closely with poverty: an adult illiteracy rate of 42.3 percent, a high incidence of infectious diseases, a poor infrastructure, high underemployment, crowded conditions (imagine half the U.S. population squeezed into the state of Iowa), and more than its share of natural disasters—especially periodic flooding—that impede development. In the face of these ominous conditions, two companies—the Grameen Foundation from Bangladesh and Groupe Danone from France—formed a joint venture (JV) social business to serve Bangladesh's BoP.

What Is a Social Business?

Mohammad Yunus, founder of the Grameen Bank in 1974 and winner of the Nobel Peace Prize in 2006, originated the social business concept, which aims to generate social benefit by creating a sustainable business. The Grameen Danone Foods JV was established to make a profit but pay no dividends. All earnings are reinvested, except that investors may recoup their original capital input. Unlike NGOs, charities, and not-for-profit organizations, a social business must sustain itself by earning profits competitively rather than receiving new contributions to carry on.

The Grameen Bank and Foundation

The Grameen Bank (GB) began when Yunus lent $27 to a group of indigent villagers who repaid the money even though he had required no collateral from them. This small beginning, contrary to Bangladeshi bank practices, led to GB's microfinancing program. It has competed primarily with usurious money lenders who charge as much as 10 percent interest per day. GB's typical rate of 20 percent per year may sound high, but Bangladesh has had an inflation rate of nearly 9 percent, and GB supports many noninterest loans as well. Some banks outside Bangladesh, such as Citigroup and Deutsche Bank, have since used GB's example as a model.

Before GB, hardly any Bangladeshi loans went to women, and Yunus had to convince religious opposition that the Prophet Muhammad would have supported what he was doing. Today, about 97 percent of GB's loans go to women, and audits show a repayment rate of 98 percent. (Borrowers must repay a loan in order to get a new one.) GB uses repayments and interest to make additional loans and to support the Grameen Foundation's poverty-fighting projects. Its loans, which in 2015 came to almost $1.18 billion, have included initial financing for street vendors and construction of more than 600,000 houses. It provides more than

20,000 student loans and 50,000 scholarships per year. It has given noninterest loans to more than 70,000 beggars so they can sell trinkets during their house-to-house begging. The Foundation's activities have expanded into a variety of businesses, such as telephone service, solar power generation, and health care. The above photo shows a Grameen bank member collecting money from borrowers.

Groupe Danone

France's largest food company, Groupe Danone (spelled "Dannon" for the U.S. market) operates in four product divisions: dairy (world's largest, with Danone being almost a generic word for yogurt); bottled water (ranked second globally, including such brands as Evian and Volvic); baby food (second globally under the Blédine brand); and medical nutrition (largest in Europe). It operates worldwide and had 2015 sales of €22.4 billion ($25.2 billion). Before its JV with Grameen, it had no Bangladeshi operations. In fact, it aimed most of its products, such as its Activia and Actimel brands of yogurt, at higher-end consumers.

Why Invest in a Social Business?

Why would Danone, or anyone, want to invest in an operation that yields them no dividends or capital gains? Yunus contends that people are multidimensional and thus may desire more than economic gains for themselves. He points to business leaders (e.g., Carnegie, Gates, Rockefeller) who turned their attention to philanthropy after amassing large fortunes. Danone's JV participation fits this multidimensional vision. In fact, it has a history of socially responsible

behavior, with a corporate mission "to bring health through food to as many people as possible." Nevertheless, Danone must generate profits, and its management must answer to shareholders. The Bangladeshi JV could offer several potential economic advantages.

Maturing of Traditional Markets

The demand for Danone's products has been maturing in wealthier countries, which have been Danone's traditional markets. Hence, its management has been shifting more emphasis to poorer countries. Between 1999 and 2010, the share of its sales coming from LDCs increased from 6 percent to 49 percent. Yet, even there its sales have centered on affluent segments, about which its chairman, Frank Riboud, said, "It would be crazy to think only about the peak of the pyramid." Thus, Bangladesh could serve as a laboratory for learning about customers and ways of operating at the BoP.

Promoting LDC Growth

Critics complain that MNEs contribute to economic underdevelopment by pushing poor consumers to purchase superfluous products instead of nutritious food. In contrast, Danone's products are all healthful and sanitary. Although one company's successful marketing of such products is not likely to have a significant impact on development, it is a potential catalyst, which perhaps also leads to favorable publicity. Further, as BoP consumers move upward economically, they will have more to spend on other Danone products and may favor them because of their earlier experience. Riboud said, "When poverty is on the rise, my own growth prospects shrink. [This] means that combating poverty is good for my business."

Building Sales and Loyalty Abroad

Being perceived as socially responsible may improve business performance in various ways. However, there are an almost infinite number of competing ways to be socially responsible. The amount Danone invested in the JV was $500,000, a small outlay for a company of that size, and Danone stood to get the money back if the operation became sufficiently profitable. Moreover, the fact that it would become one of the first major corporations to invest in a social business could generate free positive publicity globally.

Preceding the Bangladeshi JV

At a 2005 lunch in Paris, Riboud asked Yunus what Danone might do to help the poor. When Yunus explained the social business concept, Riboud immediately said, "Let's do it," and the two shook hands on setting up their JV. Although this JV is one of the first social businesses established in partnership with a major MNE, Roosevelt's "forgotten man" was not completely forgotten in the interim. Many organizations have marketed to the BoP (most notably in India during the 1970s' heyday of the appropriate technology movement), with such devices as dung-powered stoves.

These experiences offer the following lessons for companies wishing to tap the BoP, especially with a nutritious product:

- **Price**—Low and stable prices help create and sustain sales, so companies gain an advantage by finding new means to cut and stabilize their own costs, which they then pass on to customers.
- **Product compatibility**—High nutrition at a low price alone is insufficient. Products must be compatible with the target market's accustomed habits and visually appealing and flavorful to them. So it is vital to pick the right products and adapt them to local markets.
- **Education**—Within some countries the BoP is largely illiterate, has low access to popular media, and is unconvinced about cause-and-effect scientific relationships. Hence, it may be important to reach people in this segment by nontraditional means, convince them that changes from nutrition are important and take time, and convey information that they will believe.
- **Promotion**—Publicity prior to the start of sales is quite valuable, so the use of opinion leaders (those that the target market group accepts) is essential in developing credibility.

- **Competition**—Given efforts to help the poor, competition may come from government programs, not-for-profit organizations, and charities. Thus, companies need to outperform this competition or find means of working cooperatively with it.

Strategic Thrust and Orientation

After their 2005 Paris handshake, the JV began production in less than two years. The partners started with a small rural factory to serve only its surrounding poverty-stricken area. Given the JV's social objective, the partners agreed that product and production would be as green as possible. Even though the factory is the size of only one percent of Danone's standard factories elsewhere, it has the latest equipment, treatment of both incoming and outgoing water, and solar panels to generate renewable energy.

Product Policies

The introductory plant and two more built by 2015 make only yogurt, a product of high nutritional value for children. It relies on efficient small-scale production and nearby supplies of the main ingredient (milk).

Through market testing, Danone decided to sell a sweeter and thinner yogurt, drinkable directly from the container (subsequent market feedback led the JV to include spoons as well). It fortifies the yogurt with 30 percent of the daily need for vitamin A, zinc, and iodine, and it uses biodegradable technology so that containers can be converted to fertilizer.

Pricing

To keep costs and prices low, the plant uses mostly local ingredients, mainly from small suppliers such as farmers with only one or two cows, who collect and deliver milk in jugs (thus saving refrigeration and transportation costs). Because of fluctuating milk prices, the JV negotiated longer-term contracts with farmers to better stabilize prices; hence, the JV pays higher than market price sometimes and less at other times. Fixed sales costs are kept low by selling only on commission (about 20 percent to saleswomen and 80 percent to small local stores). To minimize saleswomen's commissions, the company successfully suggested their selling additional products during house-to-house visits. Personnel costs have been kept low since completion of its start-up phase by employing only Bangladeshis. Although the yogurt plant lacks scale economies, its unit costs are equivalent to Danone's larger plants elsewhere.

MAP 17.1 Grameen Danone Foods Joint Venture

Groupe Dannon from France joined the Grameen Foundation to form a social business joint venture in Bangladesh. Subsequently, Group Dannone learned about serving the base of the pyramid and has transformed this knowledge to help it operate in Indonesia and Senegal.

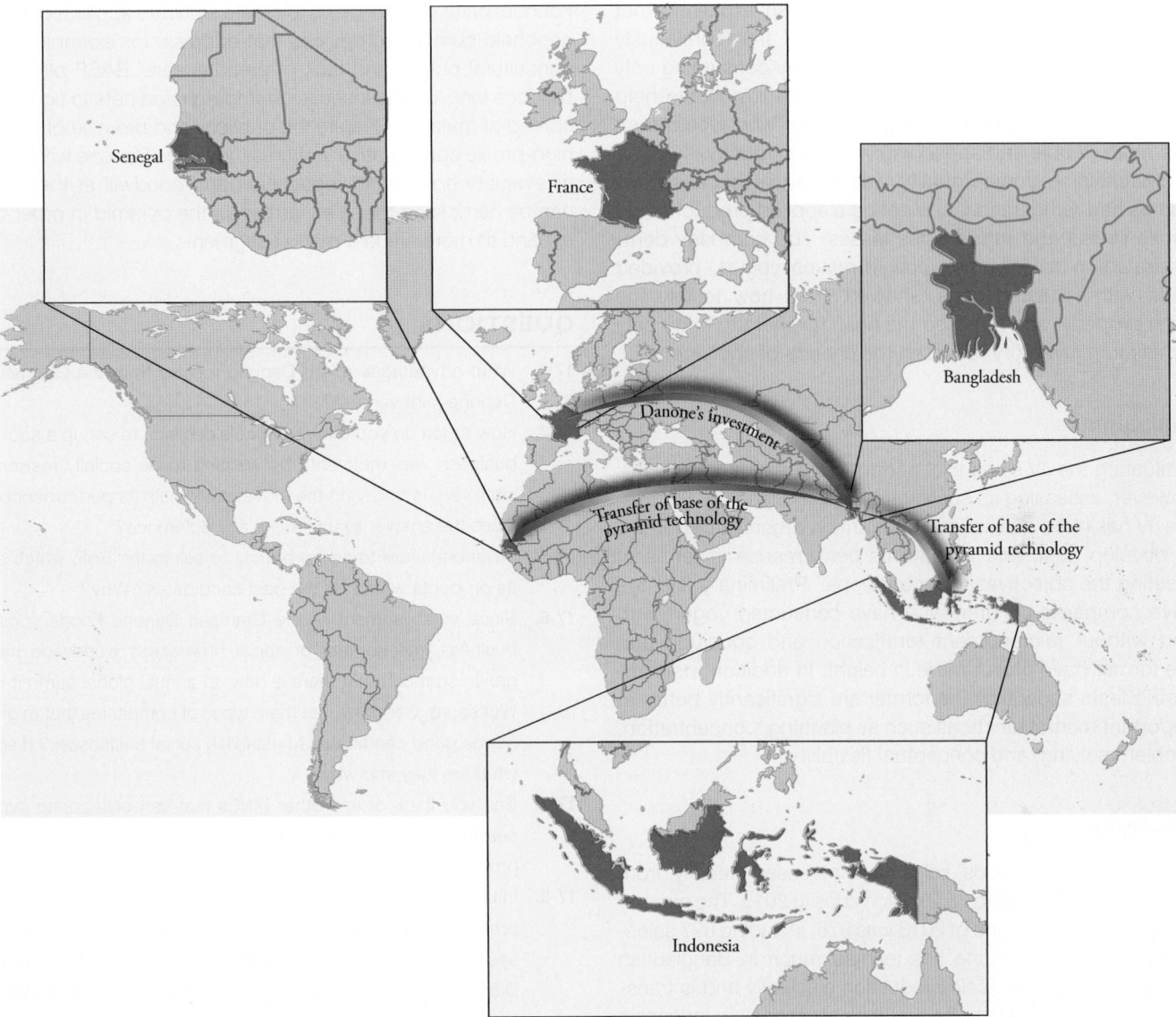

Promotion

Most promotion is word of mouth; however, one promotional event was noteworthy. Riboud arranged for the best-known Frenchman in Bangladesh, the soccer star Zinédine Zidane (Zizou), to visit the plant's opening, an event that made large headlines in newspapers throughout the country. While in Bangladesh, Zizou played with youth in the national stadium, signed the cornerstone of the plant, and contributed to instant national recognition for the new JV and its yogurt.

Branding

The JV name put Grameen first because of its high recognition. The yogurt brand is Shokti Doi, meaning "yogurt for power," and its symbol is a muscled lion that appears on the product and in ads. Lion-dressed mascots also visit youth areas to describe the value of eating yogurt.

Distribution

Bangladesh's high underemployment attracted more than enough women—mainly poor mothers from the target sales market—to work part time selling yogurt. However, the JV had to overcome a backlash similar to the one GB faced when lending to women; the complaint this time was about the impropriety of women going house-to-house. The next big task was to train the saleswomen on (1) the significance of selling yogurt other than to earn a commission and (2) the essentiality of the yogurt's quality and how to maintain it.

First, the significance for selling was primarily nourishment. The company engaged doctors who explained that children could regain any physical loss from previously deprived nutrition within 9 to 10 months by consuming only two cups of yogurt per week. Second, selling would help improve the economy by using suppliers who would then hire more people and spend within the community.

Maintaining yogurt quality was essential because few homes had refrigeration, and eating a spoiled product could cause illness and future sales losses. The company demonstrated to saleswomen how it makes yogurt, provided them with insulated bags, showed them how to use the bags properly, and stressed the need for them to carry only a minimum inventory to lessen the chance of spoilage.

Evaluation

Evaluating the JV's financial performance is straightforward; however, assessing its social effects is challenging. For this, the JV has hired a Swiss-based nutrition organization (GAIN) to develop, test, and validate its performance in terms of meeting the objectives for poor people. Preliminary findings have compared children who have consumed yogurt with and without micronutrient fortification and conclude that the former have grown more in height. In addition, psychometric tests show that the former are significantly better at important mental functions such as planning, concentration, problem solving, and conceptual flexibility.

The Future

Grameen Danone Foods' sales have increased steadily, from 150,000 cups in 2008 to 35.2 million cups in 2013. The number of employees at the end of 2013 was 976, including 697 saleswomen. Further, Danone has learned much in Bangladesh about running small-scale production efficiently and is transferring this knowledge to help with its operations in Indonesia

and Senegal. (Map 17.1 illustrates the international connections.) Inspired by this new model of collaboration, other major MNEs are establishing social businesses with the Grameen Foundation (e.g., Intel plans to create software applications on handheld computing devices that address, for example, low agricultural output and lack of prenatal care; BASF plans to produce long-lasting insecticide-impregnated nets to fight the spread of malaria). Despite the publicity and promise of these high-profile collaborative ventures, however, Danone will need to evaluate how brand recognition and goodwill at the BoP can be harnessed for sales farther up the pyramid in order to expand to more affluent market segments.

QUESTIONS

17-3. What advantages might Danone receive from the Grameen Danone joint venture?

17-4. How much do you think Danone's decision to set up a social business was motivated by wanting to be socially responsible versus believing the move would help its performance? Does the answer to this make any difference?

17-5. If Danone were to add products to sell to the BoP, which of its products would be the best candidates? Why?

17-6. Since establishment of the Grameen Danone Foods social business, the number of social businesses worldwide has grown so much that there is now an annual global summit in Wolfsburg, Germany. Are there types of companies that might not be good candidates to establish social businesses? If so, what are they and why?

17-7. Can you think of any other MNEs that can collaborate successfully with the Grameen Foundation and help solve specific problems in Bangladesh? How can they do this?

17-8. Initially, Grameen Danone Foods JV was expected to make a profit by 2012. Although no official numbers are published, it seems that they had not reached that point by 2016. Should Danone continue to invest in this JV? If so, what can be done to improve the financial outlook of the JV going forward?

MyLab Management

Go to **mymanagementlab.com** for the following Assisted-graded writing questions:

17-9 What marketing pitfalls might Danone face if it tries to duplicate its Bangladesh experience to serve BoP customers in other countries?

17-10 Assume a company, such as Danone, wishes eventually to serve all income segments within a country. What advantages and disadvantages might it encounter by first serving the BoP? How might it later deal with any disadvantages?

Endnotes

Scan for Endnotes or go to www.pearsonglobaleditions.com/Daniels

CHAPTER 18
Global Production and Supply Chains

OBJECTIVES

After studying this chapter, you should be able to

18-1   Define what is meant by global supply-chain management

18-2   Describe the different facets of global operations strategies

18-3   Show how global sourcing is an important aspect of global supply-chain and operations management

18-4   Explain how information technology is used in global operations and supply-chain management

18-5   Summarize how quality management is important in global operations and supply-chain management

MyLab Management®

Improve Your Performance!

When you see this icon ✪, visit **www.mymanagementlab.com** for activities that are applied, personalized, and offer immediate feedback.

A cheap thing doesn't lack defect, nor an expensive thing quality.

—Afghan proverb

Apple Phone. ▶

Source: alexeyboldin. 123rf.com

CASE   Apple's Global Supply Chain

How long does it take to get an iPhone?[1] In September 2012, Apple, the largest consumer electronics company in the world and the largest company in the United States in market capitalization, formally announced the iPhone 5, the sixth generation of the iPhone and successor to the popular iPhone 4S. The hype over the new phone was so high that preorders swamped Apple's ability to get enough phones from its factory in Zhengzhou, a city in the north-central region of China. Mandy Xiao was living in Provo, Utah, at the time and wanted to get the phone by Christmas of 2012, so she ordered the phone directly from Apple.com on December 5. The factory in Zhengzhou is actually owned by Taiwan-based Hon Hai Precision Industry Co. Ltd., also known as the Foxconn Technology Group. Given the Christmas rush and the fact that Zhengzhou was a little over 6,500 miles away, Mandy wasn't sure how long it would take to get her phone. But Apple's supply chain was fast. Mandy was able to track her phone's journey by UPS online from Zhengzhou to Incheon International Airport in Korea to Anchorage, Alaska, to her door in Provo, Utah—only two days after it was ordered. If you are going to compete today, you need to get the product to the consumer as soon as possible, and Apple excels at this, even when it's 6,500 miles away from the consumer.

APPLE'S ORIGINS

Apple's initial supply chain was relatively simple. In 1976, Steve Jobs and Steve Wozniak ("Woz") sold their first product, the Apple I computer, out of the Jobs' family garage in Cupertino, California. Woz was the designer and Jobs ran the business in the up-and-coming microcomputer industry. Jobs and Woz had to design the product, develop the operating system that made it work, manufacture it, and market it. Large auto companies like Ford and GM had the same issues, but they invested significant resources into building massive manufacturing facilities to supply the market. Unlike the auto companies, the new Apple Computer company was not a major manufacturer of products, but primarily an assembler of components supplied by other companies. However, Apple was extremely successful with this new venture, although the cost of the computer was quite high (since the company was in its infancy), volumes were not very high, and competition was not very strong.

What really changed the game was the entry of IBM into the market. IBM knew that to beat Apple, it needed to drive down costs as low as possible. Initially, IBM was a large vertically integrated company that produced most of its parts and components itself within the United States. In the early 1980s, however, IBM realized that it needed to use external suppliers for key components in an effort to create a cheaper alternative to the Apple II computer, the successor to Jobs' and Woz's successful Apple I computer. Then IBM outsourced its operating system to Microsoft and its microprocessor to Intel, and the race was on. By taking a close look at the value chain, IBM was able to modularize the industry so that Microsoft, for example, could sell its operating system to any company that wanted to use it, and Intel could develop semiconductors for a wide range of products for many different companies. This allowed them to achieve even greater economies of scale.

APPLE'S ADAPTATION

Apple adapted in many different ways, as did the entire consumer electronics industry. Apple's strength was in the design of new products that consumers wanted. However, it realized that it had to go far beyond just computers. Rather than just stick with personal computers, it branched off into a variety of mobile communication and media devices, portable music players, software, and cloud storage. Its products include the Apple Watch, iPhone, iPad, Mac, iPod, and the Apple TV, and it designs and manufactures its own products. Apple always comes up with cool stuff, and it is being pushed by new entrants in the market like Samsung. But it is still known for new ideas and new products—the strength of Steve Jobs and the organization he created before he died.

The big challenge is how to manufacture this wide range of products. Apple has assembly operations in Freemont, California; Cork, Ireland; and Singapore using components supplied by other companies. In 2012, it even announced that it was "reshoring" (also called onshoring) or bringing the manufacturing of some of its Macs back to the United States by investing $100 million in new facilities to assemble the computers. Even though Apple no longer manufactures its own components, it buys them from suppliers, what is also called supply chaining. Apple's decision to reshore some of its production is partly due to lower energy costs, rising wages in countries like China, a weaker U.S. dollar (at the time), quality control issues, and proximity to the large U.S. market. However, this is not a major shift in the way Apple manufactures all of its products.

THE RISE OF CONTRACT MANUFACTURING

Most of the components Apple uses come from multiple sources, but some are from single or limited sources, which can create supply problems. This is especially true when Apple uses some custom components that are not widely used in the industry but are used only for its products. Apple's search for reliable suppliers coincided with the emergence of Hon Hai Precision Industry Company, Ltd., widely known as Foxconn Technology Group. Foxconn was founded in Taiwan in 1976 by Terry Gou, about the same time Apple was founded. Gou began his company with a loan of $7,500 from his mother with a goal of increasing the affordability of electronics products by combining his expertise for mechanical and electrical parts with a low-cost solution. He started supplying parts to Atari and then traveled to the United States to develop relationships with U.S. companies. One of the companies that he won orders from was IBM. Gou arrived at just the right time. IBM's supply chain moved from being vertical to horizontal and from sourcing only domestically to sourcing internationally.

When Apple assembles products at its factory in Singapore, it is offshoring, meaning that it is moving a factory offshore from the United States to assemble products. The factory still belongs to Apple, but it may get parts and components from a variety of suppliers, mostly from Asia. Apple's relationship with Foxconn is different. As wages began to rise in Taiwan, many companies moved to the Philippines and Malaysia, but Foxconn invested in China, initially in Shenzhen but later in other cities where labor was plentiful and cheap. As it picked up more orders from abroad, it rose from a small company in Taiwan to the largest contract electronics manufacturer in the world, employing over 1 million people in China.

Although Foxconn supplies components to a variety of companies from all over the world, it is clear that Apple is its number one customer. In fact, when concerns arose in the first few months of 2013 over Apple's first quarter results, shares of Hon Hai fell by 14 percent, with similar results for shares of other Apple suppliers. However, when the first quarter results were released and Apple appeared to be doing just fine, the shares recovered their losses and posted gains. Such is the relationship between Apple and its suppliers.

When Tim Cook, the current CEO of Apple and successor to Steve Jobs, was brought into the company in 1997, he was asked by Jobs to clean up the manufacturing process. Manufacturing problems and excess inventory were a drag on corporate profits, cash flow, and therefore on funds available for investment in new products. As Cook worked to strengthen manufacturing, he developed strong supplier relations with companies throughout Asia, including Foxconn. The difference with Foxconn is that Apple was able to outsource the assembly of entire products, such as the iPhone 5 mentioned above, instead of just sourcing components that Apple could assemble at its own facilities. Rather than manufacture the product through offshoring in Ireland or Singapore, Apple was able to outsource the entire production process to Foxconn as a contract manufacturer. Apple designed the product with very tight specifications and worked with Foxconn and their suppliers to roll out new products, but Foxconn was responsible for the manufacture and delivery of the product to Apple. Now nearly all of Apple's hardware products are manufactured by outsourcing partners located primarily in Asia. A significant amount of the manufacturing is currently performed by a small number of contract manufacturers, like Foxconn, in single locations. Some of these partners are sole-sourced suppliers of components and manufacturers of many of Apple's products.

Although Foxconn became a very trusted contract manufacturer, Apple still has to work hard to make sure the quality of the product and components are exactly what it is looking for. It's one thing to control quality at your own assembly facilities, and it's quite another thing to make sure Foxconn's quality is high enough. Apple's strong relationship with Foxconn and other suppliers is the envy of the industry. However, contract manufacturing is not without its problems. News of Foxconn's problems with its employees at its facilities in China created PR problems for Apple. Workers were accusing Foxconn of forcing them to work long hours in poor conditions, and some employees even committed suicide by jumping from Foxconn buildings. As a result, Mr. Cook visited factories in China and insisted that Foxconn and other suppliers comply with Chinese labor laws and even higher international standards of worker safety. Apple became the first technology company to join the Fair Labor Association, and Apple began publishing the results of its audits on worker conditions in 2007. In 2012, Apple listed the names of 156 companies that supplied it with parts and other services used in manufacturing its products.

THE LAST PART OF THE SUPPLY CHAIN

In addition to designing and manufacturing good products, Apple needs to worry about marketing, the last part of the supply chain. When Mandy decided to buy her iPhone, she had lots of options. Apple sells its products worldwide through its retail stores, online stores (Mandy's choice), a direct sales force, and third-party cellular network carriers, wholesalers, retailers, and value-added retailers. The photo at the beginning of the chapter is an Apple retail store opened in Shanghai in 2011, only the second Apple store opened in China. As of 2016, there were 36 Apple stores in China, compared with only 8 in 2013. It sells its digital content through a variety of sources, including the iTunes Store. The key is to get the products from the point of manufacture to the final consumer, and 67 percent of Apple's revenues were from outside of the United States in 2016, compared with 40 percent in 2006. ■

QUESTIONS

✪ **18-1.** Although Apple's inbound logistics began with Apple controlling the assembly of its computers, it shifted to having suppliers acquire raw materials with contract manufacturers handling most of the production and assembly of final products. Why did they do this, and what are the major challenges Apple faces?

✪ **18-2.** Foxconn, a major contract manufacturer for Apple, is by far the largest ODM/EMS (original design manufacturer/ Electronics Manufacturing Services) company in the world, dwarfing U.S.-based Flextronics, which is the major manufacturer and assembler of Samsung phones. In 2013, Foxconn was contemplating opening operations in the United States. In what way could this be a challenge for Apple, Inc.?

GLOBAL SUPPLY-CHAIN MANAGEMENT

Most companies agree that effective supply-chain management is one of their most important tools in reducing costs and boosting revenue.[2] Our opening case on Apple illustrates dimensions of these supply-chain networks that link suppliers with manufacturers and customers. In the chapter, we will discuss the international dimensions of the global supply chain, focusing on the upstream processes of the purchasing function and supplier networks; operations strategy; the role of information technology in global supply-chain management; and quality management as it affects operations. The downstream process is covered primarily in Chapter 17.

WHAT IS SUPPLY-CHAIN MANAGEMENT?

Supply chain—the coordination of materials, information, and funds from the initial raw-material supplier to the ultimate customer.

As illustrated in Figure 18.1, the **supply chain** is the network that links together the different aspects of the value chain, from sourcing and procurement to conversion through operations to the final consumer.[3]

Supply-chain management refers to activities in the value chain that occur outside the company, whereas **operations management** (also known as **logistics management**) refers to internal activities. Suppliers can be part of the company's organizational structure, such as in a vertically integrated company, or they can be independent of it. For example, Foxconn, a contract manufacturer for Apple, has its own network of suppliers used in the manufacturing of Apple products in its factories in China. Suppliers can be located in the country where the manufacturing or assembly takes place, or they can be located elsewhere and ship materials to the final assembly facility or to an intermediate storage point. Manufacturing process output can be shipped directly to the customers or to a warehouse network and sold directly to the end consumer or to a distributor, wholesaler, or retailer, then on to the final consumer. As is the case in the supplier network, the output can be sold domestically or internationally.

Logistics (also called materials management)—that part of the supply-chain process that plans, implements, and controls the efficient, effective flow and storage of goods, services, and related information from the point of origin to the point of consumption in order to meet customers' requirements.

Most MNEs have excelled in their ability to manage their supply-chain networks. One of the best examples is Spanish Retailer Zara which is discussed in Chapter 12. Companies

FIGURE 18.1   An Integrated Global Supply Chain and Operations Strategy

Source: S. Thomas Foster, Scott Sampson, Cindy Wallin, and Scott Webb, *Managing Supply Chain and Operations: An Integrative Approach* (Pearson Education, Inc., 2016): 2.

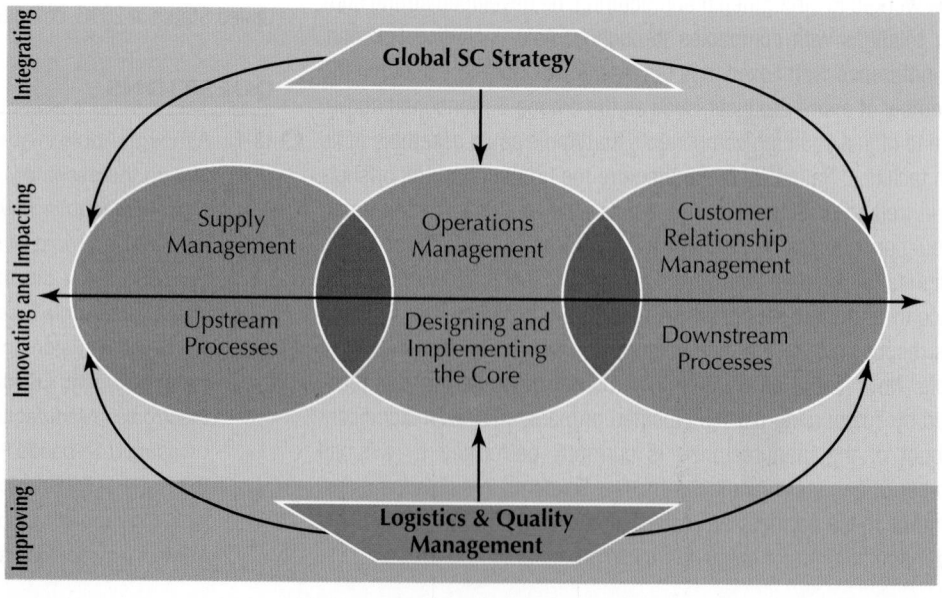

we study in this chapter are considered part of a global network that links together designers, suppliers, subcontractors, manufacturers, and customers. The supply-chain network is quite broad, and its coordination takes place through interactions between firms in the network.[4]

GLOBAL SUPPLY-CHAIN AND OPERATIONS MANAGEMENT STRATEGIES

Recall that Apple initially set up manufacturing facilities in China because of *location-specific advantages* (notably cheap labor and associated costs), choosing to enter the country through an agreement with Foxconn, its future contract manufacturer. This allowed Apple to focus on its *firm-specific assets* (innovation, product development, and marketing) and thus move away from vertical integration to become more effective by giving up more of the elements of the value chain to Foxconn.

Apple is not the only company to outsource manufacturing to others. Examples abound. Nike subcontracts its manufacturing, remaining basically a design and marketing firm. Rather than owning facilities in China to manufacture Barbie dolls, Mattel instead outsources the manufacturing to a Hong Kong–based company that invests in China.[5] As we note in Chapter 19, H&M purchases all of its fashion merchandise from external suppliers in Europe and Asia, rather than vertically integrating and establishing its own facilities.

OPERATIONS MANAGEMENT STRATEGY

One piece in the supply-chain strategy for both manufacturing and services is **operations**: the conversion of inputs into outputs. The success of a global operations strategy depends on four key factors: *compatibility, configuration, coordination,* and *control.*[6]

Compatibility   Compatibility in this context is the degree of consistency between the foreign investment decision and the company's competitive strategy. Some companies such as Walmart adopt a low-cost strategy. Others, like Apple, have adopted a differentiation strategy where they design products that are relatively unique. Some factors that companies must consider as they align their overall strategy with operations are

- *Efficiency/cost*—reduction of operational costs
- *Dependability*—degree of trust in a company's products, its delivery, and its price promises
- *Quality*—performance reliability, good service, speed of delivery, and dependable product maintenance
- *Innovation*—ability to develop new products and ideas
- *Flexibility*—ability of the production process to make a variety of products and adjust the volume of output.[7] For example, Wall's makes ice cream in China, including the Magnum Bar and the Cornetto, which are global brands for Unilever, Wall's parent company. However, Wall's found that it can produce some of its global brands during the winter when demand is down and ship them to South Africa and Australia during their summer, enabling the use of excess production facilities and reducing costs in markets outside China.[8]

Manufacturing Configuration   In the global supply chain, suppliers transform raw materials into parts which make up the inputs that go into the conversion of parts into final products in the operations management phase. The discussion below focuses on the manufacturing configuration of a company like Ford Motor Company that manufactures

CONCEPT CHECK

On page 354 in Chapter 12, we explain value as the underlying principle of strategy, defining it as "the measure of a firm's capability to sell what it makes for more than the costs incurred to make it."

Compatibility—the degree of consistency between FDI decisions and a company's competitive strategy.

CONCEPT CHECK

In discussing the process of "The Quest to Create Value" on pages 354 and 355 in Chapter 12, we explain that a firm that aspires to a position of cost leadership strives to be the low-cost producer in an industry for a given level of quality. This strategy, we observe, means that the firm adopts one of two tactics, both of which must be compatible with the structure of its value chain: (1) earning a profit higher than industry rivals by selling products at average industry prices or (2) capturing market share by selling products at prices below the industry average.

CONCEPT CHECK

Recall from page 365 in Chapter 12 our extended discussion of "Global Integration Versus Local Responsiveness" as an issue in configuring and coordinating a firm's value chain. We then proceed to explain how efforts to resolve this issue may contribute to the formulation of a global strategy or a multi-domestic strategy for international operations. Here we analyze ways in which this same issue can put pressure on specific strategic decisions about the configuration of manufacturing facilities.

automobiles worldwide. MNEs must consider three basic configurations in establishing a global manufacturing strategy:

Manufacturing configuration:
- Centralized manufacturing in one country
- Manufacturing facilities in specific regions to service those regions
- Multi-domestic facilities in each country

- *Centralized Manufacturing*—There are several options with a centralized strategy. MNEs may centralize their manufacturing in one plant, usually their home market, which services the entire world. A second option is they may have several plants in one country that service the domestic and international markets. A third is that they have factories that focus on a particular product which is sold worldwide. Ford doesn't have just one factory that produces all models, but it has different factories that produce different models. For example, Ford will manufacture the Ford Focus in a factory in Mexico, while the U.S. plant that was manufacturing the Focus will manufacture two other models.[9]

- *Regional Manufacturing*—Many companies use Asia as a regional hub for manufacturing. Hong Kong–based apparel maker, Tal Group, is one of Asia's largest suppliers of pants for Banana Republic and J. Crew, among other companies. It used to manufacture pants in China, but rising labor costs forced them to open factories in Malaysia and Vietnam. It still employs 4,000 workers in China to make shirts, so it has several manufacturing facilities in the region.[10] In this case, Tal Group's regional manufacturing strategy allows it to service clients outside of the region. BMW, Volkswagen AG, and Toyota Corporation have factories in the United States and Mexico to service clients in the North American region.[11] Most of the major auto manufacturers have set up manufacturing facilities in Mexico to service North America as well as other markets.[12]

Offshore manufacturing—any investment that takes place in a country other than the home country.

Nearshoring implies moving the supply chain closer to the home market, such as Mexico for U.S. firms or Prague for German firms.

Reshoring or onshoring means bringing back production to the home country from offshore locations.

Coordination is linking or integrating activities into a unified system.

- *Multi-Domestic Manufacturing*—As MNEs expand markets internationally, they may be forced to manufacture products in individual markets where they can be closer to consumers and meet individual needs. This is consistent with a multi-domestic strategy as discussed in Chapter 12.[13] This is the approach that Philips, the Dutch electronics company, used after World War II. Because there were barriers to entry in European countries, Philips had to manufacture on a country-by-country basis. As trade barriers dropped, they were able to rationalize their production in a regional manufacturing approach, but as the markets in the different countries grew, they found it made sense to have local manufacturing, even though there was a duplication of efforts.

Offshoring, Nearshoring, and Onshoring

Once a company decides to manufacture outside its home market, it is engaging in **offshore manufacturing**, as was the case when Apple set up manufacturing facilities in Singapore and Cork, Ireland. The main driver was cheap wages. As wages have continued to rise in China, companies moved to countries with even lower wages like Vietnam and Indonesia. Now, Africa is becoming popular as a low-wage destination.[14]

However, some companies have modified their offshore strategy by **nearshoring** (e.g., GM moved some of its manufacturing operations to Mexico to be closer to the U.S. market). Lower wages in Mexico compared with U.S. wages, coupled with NAFTA and the ability to have a closely aligned supply chain make it far more attractive to be located in Mexico than other markets that may have even cheaper wages but are farther from the U.S. market. Some MNEs have improved the efficiency of their operations so much that they have even moved back to their home countries, known as **reshoring** or **onshoring**.

CONCEPT CHECK

We discuss control on page 491 in Chapter 16 from the perspective of organization structure, coordination and control systems, and organizational culture. In explaining coordination and control systems, we explain that, regardless of its structure, the MNE must develop coordination and control mechanisms to prevent duplication of efforts, to coordinate resource allocation, and to ensure that company-wide operations benefit from ideas generated anywhere in the organization.

Control systems, such as organizational structure and performance measurement systems, ensure that managers implement company strategies.

Coordination and Control

Coordination and control fit well together. *Coordination* is the linking or integrating of activities into a unified system.[15] The activities include everything along the global supply chain, from purchasing to warehousing to shipment. It is hard to coordinate supplier relations and logistics activities if those issues are not considered when the manufacturing configuration is set up.

Once the company determines the manufacturing configuration it will use, it must adopt a control system to ensure that company strategies are carried out. *Control* can be the measuring of performance so a firm can respond appropriately to changing conditions. Another aspect of a control structure is the organizational structure, discussed in more detail in Chapter 16.

GLOBAL SOURCING

Sourcing—the process of a firm having inputs supplied to it from outside suppliers (both domestic and foreign) for the production process.

Global **sourcing** is the first step in the process of materials management, which includes obtaining a supply of inputs used in the production process, inventory management, and transportation between suppliers, manufacturers, and customers. Global sourcing and production strategies can be better understood by taking a look at Figure 18.2 which illustrates the basic operating-environment choices (home country or any foreign country) by stage in the production process.

Although global sourcing is often linked with high-tech and complex processes such as automobile manufacturing, global sourcing affects even the low-cost products we use and consume every day. Take U.S.-based Sara Lee's whole-grain white bread. To make this bread, Sara Lee acquires ingredients from a variety of suppliers, nearly a third of which are located in foreign countries. Its guar gum, used to keep the bread moist, is a powder that comes from the guar plant seedpods grown in India. Calcium propionate, a powdery mold inhibitor that is manufactured in several countries, is sourced in the Netherlands. Honey, used as a natural sweetener, is purchased from suppliers in the United States, China, Vietnam, Brazil, Uruguay, India, Canada, Mexico, and Argentina. Sara Lee sources from several different countries besides the United States because the U.S. supply can often run short. Flour enrichments to replenish the vitamins lost in the milling process come from China. Due to industry consolidation, suppliers of flour enrichments are limited. Beta-carotene, an artificial coloring used to provide color to the bread and crust, is sourced from Switzerland, though it is available in many countries. Vitamin D_3 is sourced from China, while wheat gluten comes from several countries, including France, Poland, Russia, the Netherlands, and Australia.[16]

With its ingredient sources spread all over the globe, Sara Lee must manage its supply chain carefully to ensure timeliness, safety, and quality. So it has centralized its global ingredients purchasing by consolidating its previously scattered procurement operations into a single division known as the "nerve center" located at company headquarters. Purchasing specialists monitor weather patterns, commodity trends, and energy prices. They also communicate and work closely with Sara Lee's diverse base of suppliers—in some cases, even investing money in suppliers' operations to ensure that they are complying with U.S. food safety standards.[17]

Companies can manufacture parts internally or purchase them from external manufacturers.

On the sourcing side, a company can manufacture parts internally or purchase parts from external (unrelated) manufacturers. It can also assemble its own products internally or subcontract to external firms; the manufacture of parts and final assembly may take place in its home country, the country in which it is trying to sell the product, or a third country.[18]

FIGURE 18.2 When a company wants to *source* raw materials, parts, or components as a function of its global strategy, it's faced with some key decisions. It may, for example, decide to source components at home, assemble them abroad, and then export the final product to the home market, to foreign markets, or to both.

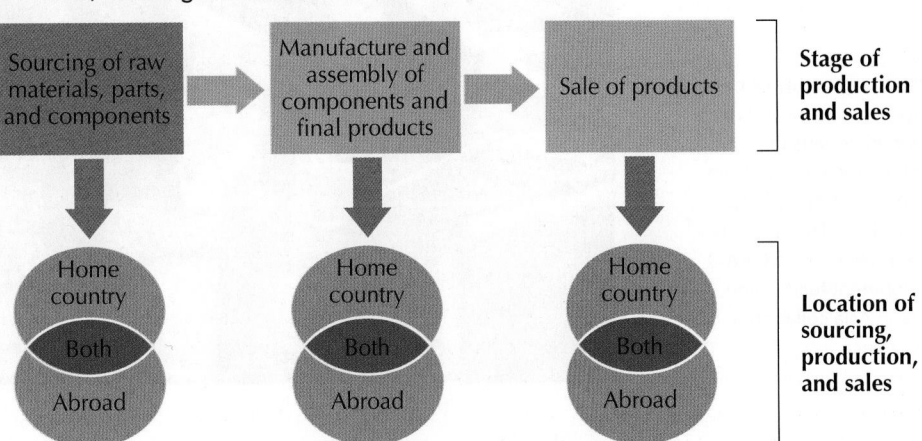

The term sourcing is used in a variety of ways. **Outsourcing**, for instance, refers to a situation in which one company externalizes a process or function to another company. This most often occurs with the IT function but is also being used in other areas, such as research, service centers, and even accounting and tax functions. In addition to offshore manufacturing, another type of offshoring occurs when a company moves part of its business processes outside its home country but internalizes the function rather than outsourcing it to another firm. An example would be setting up its own R&D facilities in another country or, say, a U.S.-based public accounting firm setting up a branch of its tax practice in India. Outsourcing can be domestic or offshore. Sometimes the entire operations can be shipped offshore using talent hired in that location.

Another way to look at outsourcing is **supply chaining** "which is a method of collaborating horizontally among suppliers, retailers, and customers to create value."[19] Zara, Walmart, and IKEA are three good examples of companies whose strategy is to engage in supply chaining with key suppliers from around the world to provide products for their customers. Supply chaining is slightly different from traditional outsourcing, which focuses more on a business process, but far more extensive and complicated since it relates more directly to the final product sold to customers. Apple's use of Foxconn as a **contract manufacturer** for products such as the iPhone is technically supply chaining, although it is similar to outsourcing since the entire manufacturing process is being handled by Foxconn. In Figure 18.1, a contract manufacturer like Foxconn not only assumes the upstream processes, but it also takes on some of the operations management functions since it also does the assembly.

Sourcing in the home country enables companies to avoid numerous problems such as language differences, long distances, lengthy supply lines, exchange-rate fluctuations, wars and insurrections, strikes, politics, tariffs, and complex transportation channels. However, for many companies, domestic sources may be unavailable or more expensive than foreign sources. In Japan, foreign procurement is critical because nearly all of the raw materials used in the manufacturing process such as uranium, bauxite, nickel, crude oil, iron ore, copper, and coking coal are imported. Japanese trading companies came into being expressly to acquire the raw materials needed to fuel Japan's manufacturing.

Supply chaining is a method of collaborating horizontally—among suppliers, retailers, and customers—to create value.

Contract manufacturers refer to companies such as Foxconn (the manufacturer of products for Apple).

Using domestic sources for raw materials and components allows a company to avoid problems with language differences, distance, currency, politics, and tariffs, as well as other problems.

Outsourcing occurs when a company transfers a portion of its work to outside suppliers, increasingly from countries with skilled, low-cost workers. This photo is an example of a software development team somewhere in Asia collaborating on a project.
Source: ProStockStudio/Shutterstock

WHY GLOBAL SOURCING?

Companies pursue global sourcing strategies for a number of reasons:

- To reduce costs through cheaper labor, laxer work rules, and lower land and facilities costs
- To improve quality
- To increase exposure to worldwide technology
- To improve the delivery-of-supplies process
- To strengthen the reliability of supply by supplementing domestic suppliers with foreign ones
- To gain access to materials that are only available abroad, possibly because of technical specifications or product capabilities
- To establish a presence in a foreign market
- To satisfy offset requirements
- To react to competitors' offshore sourcing practices[20]

These reasons are similar to the benefits to FDI discussed in Chapter 15. Whether the suppliers are company-owned or independent firms, MNEs can take advantage of the location-specific advantages in foreign countries.

In 2015, Abu Dhabi–owned Globalfoundries purchased from IBM a business that manufactured advanced microchips used in U.S. spy satellites, missiles, and combat jets. Globalfoundries has operations in Germany and Singapore in addition to IBM's former facilities in New York. One goal of the Pentagon was to globalize its supply chain in response to market trends and to reduce its costs. However, it still wanted the manufacture of the microchips to take place in New York until it can expand its supplier base. This is a good example of global sourcing in a unique business where cybersecurity is a real issue.[21]

In some ways, however, global sourcing is more expensive than domestic sourcing. For example, transportation and communications cost more. Given the longer length of supply lines, it often takes more time to get components from abroad, and lead times are less certain. This problem increases inventory carrying costs and makes it more difficult to get parts to the production site in time. If imported components come in with errors and need to be reworked, the cost per unit will rise, and some components may have to be shipped back to the supplier.

MAJOR SOURCING CONFIGURATIONS

Major outsourcing configurations include

- vertical integration,
- outsourcing through industrial clusters,
- other outsourcing.

Vertical Integration **Vertical integration** occurs when a company owns the entire supplier network, or at least a significant part of it as was the case with Apple before it began to outsource to suppliers and use contract manufacturers. The company may have to purchase raw materials from outside suppliers, but it produces the most expensive parts itself. Integrating vertically can reduce transaction costs by internalizing the different levels in the value chain.[22]

Industrial Clusters Utilizing **industrial clusters** is an alternative way to reduce transportation and transaction costs. Under clustering, buyers and suppliers locate close to each other to facilitate doing business. For example, the growth in auto manufacturers in Mexico has drawn suppliers to Mexico so they can be closer to their clients. Silicon Valley is a cluster of software firms that are taking advantage of research out of Stanford University and other high-tech firms in the IT supply chain.

Keiretsus Japanese *keiretsu* are groups of independent companies that work together to manage the flow of goods and services along the entire value chain.[23] Toyota's highly coordinated supplier network is among the most successful and well known of the Japanese *keiretsus* and a good example of industrial clustering. It borders on vertical integration because parts suppliers tend to set up shop close to Toyota's assembly operations, and Toyota usually has an ownership interest in them. The trusted relationships among companies in the *keiretsu* allow the companies to work closely together from the design phase onward, often sharing proprietary technology but also allowing each other the first right of refusal when new technology is developed. Changes in its global markets and price pressures resulting from the high cost of steel and the strong yen forced Toyota to start looking beyond its closely knit supplier base in Japan by pressuring its *keiretsu* suppliers to benchmark against China's cheaper suppliers. If the suppliers can't achieve low enough pricing, Toyota will be forced to court suppliers outside Japan.[24]

THE MAKE-OR-BUY DECISION

When it comes to production activities, MNE managers struggle with a *make-or-buy decision*: Which should be performed internally and which could be subcontracted to independent companies? In the case of subcontracting, a company must also decide whether the activities should be carried out in the home market or abroad. This often involves developing a strategy that might be a combination of outsourcing, offshoring, and/or supply chaining.

In deciding whether to make or buy, MNEs can focus on those parts of production that are critical to the product and that they are particularly good at making. They can outsource parts when suppliers have a distinct comparative advantage, such as greater scale, lower cost structure, or stronger performance incentives. They can also use outsourcing as an implied threat to underperforming employees: Improve, or we move the business elsewhere.[25] The MNE must determine the design and manufacturing capabilities of potential suppliers compared to its own capabilities. If the supplier has a clear advantage, management needs to decide what it would cost to catch up to the best suppliers and whether it would make sense to do so.

CONCEPT CHECK

As we explain on page 451 in Chapter 15, the resource-based view of the firm holds that every company has a unique combination of competencies. Here we suggest that make-or-buy decisions may depend on the extent to which a firm embraces this view, which may prompt it to concentrate internally on those activities that best fit its competencies while depending on other firms to supply products, services, or support activities for which it has lesser competency.

Make or buy—outsource or supply parts from internal production.

If MNEs outsource parts instead of sourcing them from internal production, they need to determine the degree of involvement with suppliers.

Should Firms Outsource Innovation?

Point

Point   **Yes** A firm should outsource innovative processes if it can maintain focus and position itself effectively in the roiling high-tech and electronics industries. More and more companies are coming to realize the advantages of doing so. Suppliers are taking on such responsibilities as designing and manufacturing prototypes, converting them into workable products, upgrading mature products, conducting quality tests, putting together user manuals, and selecting parts vendors. In 2011, 94 percent of the laptops in the world were designed by a small number of Taiwan-based original design manufacturers (ODMs), although they were often produced in China. The biggest companies are Quanta, Compai, Wistron, and Foxconn. The companies they supply include HP, Lenovo, Apple, Dell, and Acer. Even Boeing collaborated with an Indian company to develop software for its 787 Dreamliner jet.

Companies willing to outsource some R&D and technological designs can experience enormous cost savings. Although innovation is key to remaining competitive, more and more firms find that their internal R&D teams

aren't producing results that justify the large investments in them. Thus, in the face of demanding customers and relentless competition that pressures margins, managers must find a way to reduce costs or increase R&D productivity.

Outsourcing is a viable solution. Companies can save millions by simply buying designs rather than developing them in-house. For instance, using a predesigned platform for cell phones can reduce the costs of developing them from scratch—which takes approximately $10 million and 150 engineers—by 70 percent. Furthermore, demands by retailers and customers as well as uncertain future market trends require developing a costly range of product models. Third-party developers are better equipped to handle such costs, spreading them over many buyers and possessing the expertise to develop a variety of models from a single basic design.

Outsourcing also helps get products to market faster, which is crucial where products become commodities in a matter of months. Hewlett-Packard claims that by working with partners and suppliers on designs, it now gets a new concept to the market in 60 percent less time. Critics worry that by outsourcing technology, companies are outsourcing their fonts of competitive advantage; still, outsourcing certain design and development processes allows firms to focus more on their true core competencies. Few, if any, companies plan on completely eliminating their own R&D forces, and most insist they will continue with the more proprietary R&D work.

No one company can manage everything in-house. Even the chief technology officer of Nokia—a company that once prided itself on developing almost everything on its own—has stated, "Nobody can master it all." In fact, a recent survey of MNEs found that almost three-quarters of respondents believed they could boost innovation dramatically by collaborating with outsiders, even competitors.[26] The companies that will survive in the future are those able to efficiently and effectively control a network of partners and suppliers around the world.

Should Firms Outsource Innovation?

Counterpoint

No When it comes to outsourcing R&D, design, and development work, how does a firm know where to draw the line? How does it determine what is core intellectual property and what is commodity technology? The truth is, outsourcing turns the former into the latter, which becomes available to most anyone. Look at Toshiba. By working with South Korean chipmakers to develop its DRAM memory chips, it allowed the technology behind these components to become commoditized and is now struggling to stay ahead.[27]

Competitive advantage often depends on trade secrets that set a firm apart from its rivals. Outsourcing innovation enhances the risk that it will pass on these proprietary technologies to suppliers and partners, thereby fostering new competitors. Because suppliers rarely cooperate solely with one customer, the R&D they do for one can easily be transferred to another. Such was the case for Japanese company Sharp, which worked closely with suppliers to develop a "sixth-generation" plant for making larger flat panels for televisions. Unfortunately, its suppliers also work closely with Sharp's rivals, many of them Taiwanese companies, and not long after the completion of the plant, these competitors were constructing their own "Gen-6" facilities. Sharp tried to protect itself by secretly rewriting software on some equipment and fixing machinery in-house rather than having suppliers do it. However, in 2012, Foxconn of Taiwan bought 10 percent of Sharp and one of its factories in Japan that manufactures LCD displays.[28] In 2016, Foxconn completed the takeover of Sharp by investing $3.5 billion in the company which produces screens for Apple products. Foxconn was hoping that the investment will solidify its relationship with Apple even more.[29]

Suppliers and partners might also take the information and technology that have been shared with them and become competitors themselves. After Motorola hired Taiwanese company BenQ Corp. to design and manufacture its mobile phones, BenQ began selling the phones under its own brand name in the highly competitive Chinese market, causing Motorola to terminate the contract.

In addition to giving rise to new competitors, outsourcing innovation may cause firms to lose their competitive edge and the desire to invest in innovation. Although some assert that outsourcing certain development and design work allows companies to focus more on new innovative technologies, it more often prompts companies to decrease internal R&D investments and become lazy in their pursuit of future breakthroughs, relying too much on suppliers to do their work. Jim Andrew, senior vice president of Boston Consulting Group, warns, "If the innovation starts residing in the suppliers, you could incrementalize yourself to the point where there isn't much left."

High-tech and electronics firms that outsource their innovation processes risk losing the essence of their actual business, becoming mere marketing fronts for others. It also sends a bad message to investors, who might have difficulty finding intrinsic value in a company that owns little true intellectual property and whose profits from successful products are most likely being paid out in licensing fees to the companies that actually developed them.

Much has been made of manufacturing outsourcing in the past few decades, but outsourcing innovation poses a potentially greater threat to high-tech firms that see it as a shortcut to cost savings. Looking to immediate savings is shortsighted, and firms that do so will ultimately damage their competitive positions and lose viability as true industry players.[30]

QUESTION

1. Now that Apple purchases its iPhones and iPads from Foxconn, should it let Foxconn develop the new technology that goes in Apple's products so that they can focus more on marketing? Why or why not?

SUPPLIER RELATIONS

Supplier relationships are very important but sometimes complicated, especially for MNEs trying to manage them around the world. IKEA's global supply chain involves companies that employ over 600,000 people in more than 50 countries. Their suppliers' suppliers or sub-suppliers employ millions of other people. IKEA has established IWAY, a supplier Code of Conduct that focuses on a variety of issues, including energy and water sustainability, child labor, forced and bonded labor, and health and safety issues.[31] Apple's supplier responsibility report focuses on empowering workers, labor and human rights, health and safety, the environment, and accountability. The foundation of the supplier code of conduct is to ensure that workers have the right to safe and ethical working conditions. Apple uses not only its own auditors but third-party auditors as well. In 2015, it conducted 640 audits across its supply chain, over 20 percent of which were first-time audits.[32] The 2012 report discusses supplier accountability, including their audit program, and it also discloses its 17 final assembly facilities, including who the supplier is and what they assemble, and its top 200 suppliers which represent 97 percent of its procurement expenditures worldwide.

CONFLICT MINERALS

Conflict minerals are certain minerals that come from warring areas that generate revenues to fund conflicts.

A real challenge for U.S.-based MNEs is compliance with a provision in the Dodd–Frank Act that requires companies to disclose the use of certain minerals mined in war-torn or conflict areas, primarily in Africa. The minerals in question are titanium, tungsten, tin, and gold mined from ore and extracted from Congo or nine surrounding countries. The objective of the provision is to stamp out militias in these countries that are funded by the sale of the minerals.[33] Companies like Apple, Microsoft, and Intel have long supply lines, and they are under scrutiny to determine if their suppliers are using conflict minerals. The companies have to show that they are using their best judgment to do country-of-origin tests with their suppliers, but most are stopping short of stating that they are conflict free. In its 2015 Supplier Responsibility report, Apple goes to great lengths to show what it is doing to respond to Dodd–Frank. It provides a list of all of the "names, countries, and Conflict-Free Smelter Program participation status of the smelters and refiners in our supply chain."[34] Like most large MNEs, they use independent auditors to help determine if their suppliers are doing their best to avoid using conflict minerals, but it is impossible to verify that every product is conflict free.

THE PURCHASING FUNCTION

Global progression in the purchasing function:

- Domestic purchasing only
- Foreign buying based on need
- Foreign buying as part of a procurement strategy
- Integration of global procurement strategy

The purchasing agent is the link between a company's outsourcing decision and its supplier relationships. Just as companies go through stages of globalization, so does the purchasing agent's scope of responsibilities. Typically, purchasing goes through four phases before becoming "global":

1. Domestic purchasing only
2. Foreign buying based on need
3. Foreign buying as part of procurement strategy
4. Integration of global procurement strategy[35]

Phase 4 occurs when the company realizes the benefits that result from the integration and coordination of purchasing on a global basis and is most applicable to the MNE.

When purchasing becomes global, MNEs often face the centralize/decentralize dilemma. Should they allow each subsidiary to make every purchasing decision, or should they centralize all or some of them? The primary benefits of decentralization include increased control over purchases, better responsiveness to facility needs, and more effective use of local suppliers. The primary benefits of centralization are increased leverage with suppliers, better prices, eliminating administrative duplication, allowing purchasers to develop special-ized knowledge in purchasing techniques, reducing the number of orders processed, and enabling purchasing to build solid supplier relationships.[36]

INFORMATION TECHNOLOGY AND GLOBAL SUPPLY-CHAIN MANAGEMENT

A comprehensive supply-chain strategy is most effective with a strong commitment to infor-mation technology (IT), which aids in quick and efficient production, proficient inventory management, effective supplier communication, and customer satisfaction. In *The World is Flat*, Flattener #3 is workflow software.[37] Basically encompassing the standard protocols such as HTTP that allow computers to work with each other and business processes such as SAP, workflow software is critical for the supply-chain management process.

ELECTRONIC DATA INTERCHANGE (EDI)

The key to making a global information system work is getting the relevant information in a timely manner. Apple, for example, has established a B2B (business to business) gateway that all of its suppliers are required to use, which basically allows suppliers to share elec-tronic data with Apple. Many companies use **electronic data interchange (EDI)** to link sup-pliers, manufacturers, customers, and intermediaries, especially in the food-manufacturing and car-making industries, in which suppliers replenish in high volumes.

In a global context, EDI has been used to link exporters with customs to facilitate the quick processing of customs forms, thus speeding up cross-border deliveries. Walmart is known for its revolutionary use of EDI to connect its global suppliers to its inventory order-ing system.[38]

ENTERPRISE RESOURCE PLANNING/MATERIAL REQUIREMENTS PLANNING

The next wave of technology affecting the global supply chain was the implementation of IT packages known as **enterprise resource planning (ERP)**. Companies such as Oracle, Baan, PeopleSoft, and German software giant SAP introduced software to integrate everything in the back office (the part of the business dealing with internal matters, as opposed to the front office, which deals with the customer). ERP is essential for bringing together the infor-mation inside the firm with information from different geographic areas, but its inability to tie in to the customer and take advantage of e-commerce has been a problem.

An extension of ERP is *material requirements planning* (MRP), a computerized informa-tion system that addresses complex inventory situations and calculates the demand for parts from the production schedules of the companies that use them. DENSO, the Japanese auto parts supplier for Toyota, uses MRP extensively to calculate the demand for parts from the production schedules of the non-Toyota companies it supplies.

RADIO FREQUENCY ID (RFID)

A newer wave has recently swept the technology scene in the form of *radio frequency ID (RFID)*, a system that labels a product with an electronic tag that stores and transmits information on the product's origin, destination, and quantity. When electronic readers scan the tags by means of radio waves, the data can be rewritten or captured and sent to a computer-network database, which collects, organizes, stores, and moves the data—often in conjunction with an ERP system.

A key to making the global supply chain work is a good information system.

EDI (electronic data inter-change)—the electronic link-age of suppliers, customers, and third-party intermediaries to expedite documents and financial flows.

ERP (enterprise resource planning)—software that can link information flows from different parts of a business and from different geographic areas.

Material requirements planning (MRP)—computerized informa-tion system that addresses complex inventory situations and calculates the demand for parts from the production schedules of the companies that use the parts.

Radio frequency ID (RFID)—a system that labels prod-ucts with an electronic tag, which stores and transmits information regarding the product's origin, destination, and quantity.

Such real-time information allows manufacturers, suppliers, and distributors to keep track of products and components throughout their manufacturing processes and transportation networks, resulting in greater efficiency and more visibility along the supply chain. The use of RFID in the Las Vegas airport to track luggage has resulted in more accurate sorting, better tracking, and fewer lost bags.[39] In 2003, Walmart mandated that its top suppliers use RFID tags at the pallet level, predicting it could save billions of dollars for the entire retail industry through supply-chain efficiencies.[40] In 2010, it announced it would experiment with placing removable "smart tags" on individual garments such as jeans and underwear that would allow workers to use handheld scanners to identify exact inventory on the shelves or in the backroom. There are concerns over privacy, but RFID tags placed on removable labels or packaging is not as invasive as imbedding them in the clothing, which could then be tracked anywhere.[41] Apple even has an RFID app which can be purchased on iTunes and downloaded to an iPhone or iPad to display the location status of taggable items.

E-COMMERCE

CONCEPT CHECK

In discussing "Changing Times, Changing Organizations" on page 475 in Chapter 16, we observe that the Internet, which accelerates the spread of ideas throughout an organization, has created a new concept for organization structure. In other words, as a supremely efficient and effective means of organizing global knowledge, resources, and people, the Internet has inspired many people to imagine new ways of effectively organizing a company's resources (especially its people).

E-commerce—the use of the Internet to join together suppliers with companies and companies with customers.

Private technology exchange (PTX)—an online collaboration model that brings manufacturers, distributors, value-added resellers, and customers together to execute trading transactions.

The next technological wave linking together the parts of the global supply chain is **E-commerce**. Since Walmart moved its EDI-based infrastructure from traditional but expensive value-added networks (VANs) to the Internet, it has been good news for thousands of worldwide vendors. All of their transactions with Walmart are now web-based—a substantial cost savings for the MNE and its vendors.[42]

Extranets and Intranets   Companies with web-based systems usually establish an **extranet** for suppliers—a linkage to its information system via the Internet—so they can organize production and delivery of parts. Plugged into a company's customer database, the suppliers can keep track of changes in demand; plugged into the ordering process, they can track the progress of their orders from factory to doorstep.

The real attraction of the Internet in global supply-chain management is that it not only helps automate and speed up internal processes in a company through an **intranet**, but also spreads efficiency gains to the business systems of its customers and suppliers.[43] A recent development in technology is **private technology exchange (PTX)**, an online collaboration model that brings manufacturers, distributors, value-added resellers, and customers together through the Internet to execute trading transactions and share information about demand, production, availability, and more.

"The Digital Divide"   The challenge in global supply-chain management is that although some networks can be managed through the Internet, others—particularly in emerging markets—cannot because of the lack of technology or low Internet speeds. The use of the Internet varies by location and by industry. However, access to the Internet has grown in recent years. In December 2004, it was estimated that 12.7 percent of the global population was using the Internet; by December 2015, that had climbed to 46.4 percent.[44] Access to the Internet through cell phones has made a big difference in the general population, and the use of social media, such as Facebook, with over 1.5 billion users worldwide by April 2016, has provided another avenue for people to connect and shop online through the Internet.

The preceding discussion shows that IT can help companies manage their global supply chains but it must be carefully integrated into their overall strategy. Because IT is highly technical as well as a support to a company's lines of business, it is often difficult to align it with company strategy. This is especially true in the international arena, where personnel in different countries may be accustomed to their own IT systems and may have difficulty adopting a global IT format that will allow them to achieve some economies of scale as well as fully integrate it in the overall strategy.

QUALITY

Quality—meeting or exceeding the expectations of a customer.

An important aspect of all levels of the global supply chain is quality management, for service firms as well as manufacturers. **Quality** can be defined here as meeting or exceeding customer expectations. More specifically, it is conformance to specifications, value, fitness for use, support (provided by the company), and psychological impressions (image).[45] Quality involves careful design of a product or service and ensuring that an organization's systems can consistently produce the design.[46] For example, no one wants to buy computer software that has a lot of bugs, but the need to get software to market quickly may mean speeding it there as soon as possible and correcting errors later. In the airline industry, service is critical. Some airlines, such as Singapore Air, have developed a worldwide reputation for excellence in service—a distinct competitive advantage, especially when trying to attract the business traveler.

Quality failures can have serious ramifications for a company. Japan-based Takata Corporation manufactures motor vehicle seat belts, air bags, steering wheels, interior trims, and child restraint systems to major auto manufacturers worldwide. Although Honda is its largest customer, 14 Japanese, U.S., and European carmakers use its products. However, a major defect in Takata's air bags has resulted in 10 deaths and over 100 injuries in the United States alone. Even though far more lives have been saved by the deployment of air bags during crashes, the deaths and injuries that resulted from defective air bags have resulted in the largest and most complex safety recall in U.S. history, in addition to similar recalls worldwide.[47] The problem is that the faulty air bag's inflator can explode in a crash under certain conditions, shooting metal shards from the airbag that can be sprayed throughout the vehicle. It is estimated that over 85 million vehicles will have to be recalled. This has affected Takata's stock price and the company posted a $121 million loss in FY 2016. In addition, it has been trying to find a cash infusion to help pay for the recall. The quality issues have also strained relations with companies that use the air bags since the defective air bags are a blemish on their reputation.[48] The challenge is to figure out the source of the problem, when Takata first realized there was a problem, and when it notified Honda and other manufacturers.

ZERO DEFECTS

Zero defects—the refusal to tolerate defects of any kind.

Quality also refers to **zero defects**, an idea perfected by Japanese manufacturers who refuse to tolerate flaws of any kind, although the Takata example illustrates that nobody is perfect. Before this strong emphasis on getting rid of defects, many companies operated according to the premise of **acceptable quality level (AQL)**, which held that a few faulty products would be dealt with through repair facilities and service warranties. This type of manufacturing/operating environment required buffer inventories, rework stations, and expediting, with the goal of pushing through products as fast as possible and then dealing with the mistakes later. However, world-class companies prefer zero defects and they realize that taking quality seriously is the only way to beat the competition.[49] In the Takata case, imagine how difficult it would be to recall over 85 million vehicles.

Deming's 14 Points encompass the idea that the responsibility for quality resides within the policies and practices of managers.

In the late 1970s, when Japanese companies began to seriously outpace those in the United States in achieving high-quality products and processes, a new emphasis was placed on actively managing the operations that affect quality. One contributor to this focus on quality management, and one of the people who trained the Japanese in quality, was W. Edwards Deming. To espouse the idea that the responsibility for quality resides within the policies and practices of managers, Deming developed several suggestions on how companies could improve. His focus on quality was designed to reduce the variance in the manufacturing process through statistical control, design, and training and through the policies and practices of managers. He felt that higher quality would lead to lower costs and better acceptance by the consumer. His process for continuous improvement was to *plan* a process to correct problems, *do* or implement the plan, *check* to see how the improvements were progressing, and *act* to make sure the changes were permanent.

The emphasis on quality management has continued to provide a major source of competitive advantage and play a major role for companies across the globe. However, just as different countries possess different cultures, product preferences, and business practices, various regions of the world have approached the concept of quality management in various ways. The Japanese have long focused on lean production processes that eliminate waste and boost visibility, whereas the American approach has historically been more statistically based, and the Europeans have opted to concentrate more on quality standards.[50] These varying attitudes toward quality create a high level of complexity for MNEs with global operations.

LEAN MANUFACTURING AND TOTAL QUALITY MANAGEMENT (TQM)

One reason why companies might hesitate when considering whether to source parts from foreign suppliers is because of *lean manufacturing*, the process of reducing waste in all areas of the supply chain.[51] This concept was popularized by Toyota, and has been imitated worldwide. Because it relies on the efficiencies gained by reducing waste and defects, lean manufacturing is also closely tied to quality management.

Total quality management (TQM) is a process that stresses three principles: *customer satisfaction, continuous improvement,* and *employee involvement.*[52] The goal is to eliminate all defects. TQM often focuses on benchmarking world-class standards, product and service design, process design, and purchasing.[53] The center of the entire process, however, is customer satisfaction, the achievement of which may raise production costs. In TQM, quality means the product is so good that the customer wouldn't think of buying from anyone else.

TQM is a process of continuous improvement at every organizational level. It implies that the company is doing everything it can to achieve quality at every stage of the process. TQM does not use any specific production philosophy or require the use of other techniques, such as a just-in-time system for inventory delivery. Although benchmarking—determining the best processes used by the best companies—is an important part of TQM, it is not intended to be a goal. In essence, TQM means that a company will try to be better than the best.

Executives who have adopted the zero-defects philosophy of TQM claim that long-run production costs decline as defects decline. The continuous improvement process is also known as *kaizen,* which means identifying problems and enlisting employees at all levels to help eliminate those problems. The key is to make continuous improvement a part of every employee's daily work.

An important element of lean manufacturing is just-in-time (JIT) inventory management, which focuses on "reducing inefficiency and unproductive time in the production process to improve continuously the process and the quality of the product or service."[54] The JIT system gets raw materials, parts, and components to the buyer "just in time" for use, sparing companies the cost of storing large inventories.

That is what Dell hoped to accomplish in its Irish plant by having parts delivered just as they were to enter the production process and then go out the door to consumers as soon as the computers were built. However, the use of JIT means that parts must have few defects and must arrive on time. That is why companies need to develop solid supplier relationships to ensure good quality and delivery times if JIT is to work—and why industrial clustering is a popular way of linking more closely with suppliers.

Risks in Foreign Sourcing   Foreign sourcing can create big risks for companies that use lean manufacturing and JIT because interruptions in the supply line can cause havoc. MNEs are becoming expert at meeting the requirements of JIT—ships that take two weeks to cross the Pacific docking within an hour of scheduled arrival, factories that are able to more easily fill small orders, and so on. However, because of distances alone, the supply chain is open to more problems and delays.[55]

CONCEPT CHECK

Compare the concept of employee involvement as it's characterized here with the idea of coordination by mutual adjustment, which we discuss on page 494 in Chapter 16. Both approaches to coordination signal a willingness to coordinate value activities through a range of informal mechanisms, including means by which employees are encouraged to engage one another in decisions about matters of mutual importance.

Lean manufacturing—a productive system whose focus is on optimizing processes through the philosophy of continual improvement.

Total quality management (TQM)—a process that stresses customer satisfaction, employee involvement, and continuous improvement of quality. Its goal is to eliminate all defects.

Just-in-time (JIT) approach to inventory management—a system that sources raw materials and parts just as they are needed in the manufacturing process.

Many MNEs that have set up manufacturing and assembly facilities overseas to service local markets have practically forced their domestic parts suppliers to move overseas as well to allow them to continue with JIT manufacturing. That is why so many Japanese parts suppliers have moved to the United States and Mexico to be near their major customers.

A company's inventory management strategy determines the frequency of needed shipments. The less frequent the delivery, the more likely the need to store inventory somewhere. Because JIT requires delivery just as the inventory is to be used, some concession must be made for inventory arriving from foreign suppliers. Since DENSO, one of Toyota's major suppliers, is very close to Toyota's assembly plants in Japan, JIT allows the DENSO components to arrive a matter of a few minutes but no more than a few hours from when they are used.[56]

The Kanban System   One system pioneered by Toyota to facilitate its JIT strategies is the *kanban system*, named after the Japanese word for "card" or "visible record." Kanban cards are used to control the flow of production through a factory. In the system used by Toyota, components are shipped to a plant just before they need to go into production, where they are kept in a bin with an attached card identifying the quantity of items in the bin. When the assembly process begins, a production-order card signifies that a bin needs to be moved to the assembly line. When the bin is emptied, it is moved to a storage area and replaced with a full bin. The kanban card is then removed from the empty bin and is used to order a replacement from the supplier.

SIX SIGMA

Six Sigma is an effective statistical approach to quality management developed by Motorola and popularized by General Electric. As a highly focused system of quality control that scrutinizes a company's entire production system, it aims to eliminate defects, slash product cycle times, and cut costs across the board. The system uses data and rigorous statistical analysis to identify "defects" in a process or product, reduce variability, and achieve as close to zero defects as possible.[57]

Since being introduced by Motorola in the 1980s, Six Sigma has been adopted by many MNEs, including GE, GlaxoSmithKline, and Lockheed Martin. Although some have accused the program of diverting attention away from customers and squashing innovation, most of the 100 largest companies in the United States have embraced it.[58] Its main goal is defect reduction, and fewer defects should cause an improvement in yields, which should improve customer satisfaction and then lead to enhanced income. Given that Six Sigma is a metric designed to measure defects, some argue that it is most effective when used in conjunction with the Baldrige Criteria for Excellence or the European Quality Award.[59]

QUALITY STANDARDS

There are three different levels of quality standards: *general, industry-specific,* and *company-specific.* The first is a general standard, such as the Deming Award, which is presented to firms that demonstrate excellence in quality, or the Malcolm Baldrige National Quality Award, which is presented annually to companies that demonstrate quality strategies and achievements. However, even more important than awards is certification of quality.

General-Level Standards   The **International Organization for Standardization (ISO)** in Geneva was formed in 1947 to facilitate the international coordination and unification of industrial standards. From the beginning, it has partnered with the IEC (International Electrotechnical Commission), which is the originator of global technical standards. It also collaborates with the International Telecommunications Union and the World Trade Organization. As an NGO, the ISO represents a network of standard setters in 161 countries and has established over 21,000 international quality standards.[60]

It is hard to combine foreign sourcing and JIT production without having safety stocks of inventory on hand, which defeats the concept of JIT.

A *kanban* system facilitates JIT by using cards to control the flow of production through a factory.

Six Sigma—a quality control system aimed at eliminating defects, slashing product cycle times, and cutting costs across the board.

Levels of quality standards:
- General level—ISO 9000, Malcolm Baldrige National Quality Award
- Industry-specific level
- Company level

ISO 9000—a global set of quality standards intended to promote quality at every level of an organization.

ISO 14000—a quality standard concerned with environmental management.

ISO 9000 and ISO 14000

Even with more than 21,000 standards in the ISO, new ones are being published every year. The two main families of standards are ISO 9000, which describes the fundamentals of quality management systems, and ISO 14000, which addresses what the company does to improve its environmental performance. However, many different areas have ISO standards.

ISO 9000 is a set of universal standards for a quality assurance system that is accepted around the world. Applying uniformly to companies in any industry and of any size, it is intended to promote the idea of quality at every organizational level. Initially it was designed to harmonize technical norms within the EU. Now it is an important part of business operations throughout Europe. Under the ISO 9000 family of standards, companies must document how workers perform every function affecting quality and install mechanisms to ensure that they follow through on the documented routine. The documentation is generic and applicable to any organization that makes products or provides services. A major advantage of ISO 9000 is the documentation process, which not only requires workers to examine what they do to improve quality but also ensures continuity as workers change positions.

ISO certification entails a complex analysis of management systems and procedures, not just quality-control standards. Rather than judging the quality of a particular product, ISO evaluates the management of the manufacturing or service process according to the standards it has created in 20 domains, from purchasing to design to training. The operational principles of its management-system standards are: plan, do, check, and act (correct and improve plans), which is based on Deming's PDCA continuous improvement cycle. A company that wants to be ISO certified must fill out a report and submit to certification by a team of independent auditors.[61] The process can be expensive and time-consuming, as each site of a company must be separately certified. The ISO 14000 family of standards is designed to help companies establish high-quality environmental standards in terms of air, water, and soil; ensure that environmental standards are followed; and develop products and services that are environmentally friendly.

Non-European companies operating in Europe need to become ISO certified in order to maintain access to that market.

U.S. companies that operate in Europe seek ISO certification to maintain access to its market. When DuPont lost a major European contract to an ISO-certified European company, it decided to become certified. By doing so, not only was it able to position itself better in Europe, it also benefited from the experience of going through the certification process and focusing on quality in and of itself. Some European companies are so committed to ISO that they will not do business with a certified company if its suppliers are not also ISO certified. They want to be sure that quality flows back to every level of the supply chain.

Industry-Specific Standards

In addition to the general standards described earlier, there are industry-specific standards for quality, especially for suppliers to follow. Since ISO standards are relatively generic, some industries, such as the auto industry, have developed more specific ones to fit the industry. One such example is QS9000, which was initially required for any supplier of Ford and General Motors. However, it was eventually replaced by ISO/TS 16949:2009, which was more applicable to the auto industry. It is supposed to be used in conjunction with ISO 9001, and it defines the quality management system requirements for the design, development, production, installation, and service of automotive-related products.[62]

Company-Specific Standards

Individual companies also set their own standards for suppliers to meet if they are going to continue to supply them. Most large MNEs with large supply chains have set and published supply-chain standards, often in the context of a sustainability report. Apple's approach was noted above in the context of working with global suppliers. In the service sector, global public accounting firms, such as KPMG and PWC, have set high audit practices that it expects its affiliates around the world to use. This is always complicated since public accounting firms are an association of individual national partnerships operating under one name. However, the audit of a multinational client must be performed to high standards.

Looking to the Future
Uncertainty and the Global Supply Chain

Two competing ideas have been emphasized in this chapter: First, globalization has pushed companies to establish operations abroad or to outsource to foreign suppliers to reduce costs and be closer to markets; second, the longer the supply line, the greater the risk. Since September 11, 2001, the risks of longer supply lines have increased dramatically. At any time, global political events could completely disrupt a well-organized supply chain and put a company at risk. This was demonstrated more recently in 2011 with the earthquake and tsunami in Japan.

Because some of Sara Lee's suppliers have consolidated, there are fewer options for purchasing key ingredients for Sara Lee products. What if no supplier could deliver because of political events or safety/quality concerns? Ford Motor Company's announcement that the economic slowdown was forcing it to cut its suppliers by 50 percent created a ripple effect throughout the auto industry, since suppliers tend to supply many different companies.

As a supply chain stretches and uncertainty grows, companies have to become much better at scenario building so that viable contingencies are available. Maybe this means they will pursue more multi-domestic strategies to insulate their foreign operations from other countries and allow them to be more responsive to local consumers. However, as MNEs in the developed countries respond to competitive pressures to reduce costs, they will be forced to continue sourcing abroad, either in company-owned facilities or from third parties—at least until nobody can source abroad.

That's probably a little extreme, but the important thing is to continue to look at the "what-ifs." What if there is no secure air or ocean transportation available to move goods? What if the goods can move, but there are delays? What if terrorists begin to use the global supply chain of legitimate companies to contaminate products or move hazardous materials? Clearly, the future appears much more complicated than current or past conditions, so let the manager beware. Escalating costs in China, the manufacturing floor of the world, are causing many firms to look to other countries for cheaper sources of supply as well as closer to home for their sourcing decisions. ■

CASE   Nokero: Lighting the World[63]

Manuel G. Serapio, Associate Professor and IB Program Director, Business School and Faculty Director of the University of Colorado Denver CIBER prepared this case.

In June 2016, Steve Katsaros, founder and CEO of Nokero, was contemplating how to build on his company's accomplishments. Nokero, a marketer of solar light bulbs, has emerged as a successful born-global social enterprise. Since its establishment in 2010, Nokero had sold more than 1.4 million solar light bulbs to over 120 countries. The company has generated significant media attention. *CNN,*

The New York Times (online), *The Washington Post, Fast Company, Popular Mechanics, Popular Science, The Denver Post,* and *Engadget,* to name just a few, have featured Nokero's story of doing well by doing good as a provider of environmentally friendly solar lighting to the world's poor. Katsaros himself has been recognized for his humanitarian work. In April 2013, he was awarded the U.S. Patent Office's Patent for Humanity Award.

While Katsaros was very pleased with his company's overall performance to date, he was concerned with three fundamental questions. First, how should the company

Steve Katsaros, founder and ▶ CEO of Nokero, shows a group of children how his innovative solar light works.
Source: Courtesy of Steve Katsaros/ Nokero

(c) 2012 Nokero

grow? Specifically, what market segments should the company focus on for profitable growth? Several opportunities had propelled Nokero's sales since its establishment. The company has sold tens of thousands of solar bulbs in small and sample order sales through the company's website from thousands of customers in North America and abroad. Additionally, Nokero has entered into distributorship or dealer agreements in several countries. Finally, governments, international agencies, and nongovernmental organizations have partnered with or approached Nokero on collaborative social programs relating to environmental sustainability, renewable energy, poverty alleviation, and disaster and relief projects. Katsaros wanted to make sure that Nokero explores the best pathways for growth in both the social enterprise sector and commercial channels.

Second, where should the company grow? Currently, Nokero has pursued an opportunistic sales approach. The company's major customers are in diverse and dispersed locations in Kenya, Ghana, South Africa, Fiji, Mexico, India, Indonesia, Nigeria, Haiti, and other markets. Although practical business sense may dictate that international new ventures like Nokero focus on a few markets at a time, Katsaros was hesitant to pursue this approach since it contradicted the company's social mission of reaching out to as many people as possible that could benefit from Nokero's solar light bulbs.

Third, how should Nokero manage its supply chain to support the company's growth? Katsaros understood that growth brings a number of challenges that require Nokero to address critical global supply-chain issues effectively. How can the company serve different markets and customer segments that are dispersed in many countries? How can Nokero bring down sourcing, manufacturing, and distribution costs to make the product more affordable to its customers? What should the company do to address the "last mile issue" of reaching customers in the most remote locations?

The Nokero Story

Identifying the Opportunity

Nokero (short for "No Kerosene") was established by Steve Katsaros in order to develop safe and environmentally friendly solar products that eliminated the need for harmful and polluting fuels used for light and heat around the world and that are affordable to the customers who need them. Katsaros saw a significant opportunity in developing a solar light product to replace kerosene and diesel lanterns. Katsaros described the opportunity as follows:

> In many parts of the world, nonelectrified dwellings and workplaces are illuminated by kerosene or diesel lamps, candles or wood. There are electric options but most are expensive, or fragile, or don't have replaceable, rechargeable batteries.

More than 1.3 billion people live without electricity. Of these, 704 million people are in South Asia, 550 million in sub-Saharan Africa, and 225 million in Southeast Asia. Many of these people live in remote areas and rely on kerosene and diesel-fueled lanterns for their lighting. By substituting solar light bulbs for kerosene lanterns, these people are able to recoup their purchase price within a period of 12 days to 2 months, depending on market forces. Moreover, the replacement of kerosene lanterns with solar light bulbs generates significant environmental and health benefits. Every solar light that replaces a kerosene lantern saves three-quarters of a ton of CO_2 emissions over the five-year lifetime of the product. According to the World Bank, daily exposure to emissions from kerosene lanterns is like smoking two packs of cigarettes per day.

Inventing the Solution: The N100, N200, and N233

Katsaros invented the first Nokero light bulb (the Nokero N100) on January 24, 2010, drawing a sketch of the idea on a notepad. Four days later, he filed a U.S. patent on the N100 that was eventually granted in February 2011. Production on the light bulb commenced in June 2010 and the newest model, the N233, was introduced in November 2016.

The Nokero solar light bulb is a small, lightweight, portable light, shaped like a light bulb for easy identification. The bulb hangs in the sun to charge and can be hung or laid on its side at night. A "pivot" feature allows users to swivel the solar panel toward the sun to maximize charge capability. The bulb can be swiveled at night to direct light where needed. The LED lights are enclosed in the shatter resistant bulb, do not get hot, and produce an even light. (See the photo on the bottom page.)

The N233's brightness is 25 lumens on high illumination and 10 lumens on low illumination. The duration of light is 6–15 hours on one day's charge. While the brightness is not the same as traditional LED lighting, the N233's brightness is five times brighter than that of a kerosene lantern. The N233 is shatter- and rain-proof and built to last for five years.

Nokero sells the N233 in large quantity orders (e.g., over 1,000 light bulbs) for about $8.00 (FOB China). Sample sales are priced between $15 and $20 (depending on shipping costs). In response to strong market feedback for a low-price starter version of the Nokero solar bulbs, Katsaros has released a more basic version that sells for about half the price of the N233.

Building a Born-Global Company

A few weeks after developing the N100, Katsaros worked on Nokero's business model, package design, pricing, and manufacturing and distribution processes. In April 2010, he formed Nokero International Ltd., the operating company of Nokero.

The speed with which Nokero developed and manufactured the N100 and formed the business entity could be attributed to Katsaros' experience as an inventor and

Source: Courtesy of Steve Katsaros/Nokero

entrepreneur. He had previously licensed inventions to sports companies (e.g., Dynastar Skis, K2, and HaberVision) and built RevoPower, a motorized wheel for bicycles that gets 200 miles per gallon at 20 miles per hour. A BS Mechanical Engineering graduate from Purdue University, a Bard Center for Entrepreneurship (now the Jake Jabs Center for Entrepreneurship) certificate graduate recipient at the University of Colorado Denver, and a Collegiate Inventors Competition awardee, Katsaros is a patent agent registered with the U.S. Patent and Trademark Office which has issued him several patents for his previous inventions.

From the start, Nokero was a "born-global company" with customers in different parts of the world, and co-owners and supplier partners in Hong Kong and China. Katsaros partnered with three Hong Kong–based entrepreneurs to form Nokero International Ltd. in Hong Kong. These partners, associates of Katsaros in previous businesses, provided start-up capital that represented a minority equity interest in Nokero and helped Katsaros find a strong and reliable factory supplier in China. Nokero also leveraged the HK partners' connections with the factory supplier to secure a trade financing line from the supplier. The HK partners manage Nokero's operations, including overseeing the supplier factory in China; filling large orders directly from the factory; maintaining an outsourced fulfillment center in Shenzhen, China, to supply small and sample sales from all over the world; and managing the company's supply chain.

Nokero's Chinese supplier is an established factory that has significant experience and scale in consumer electronics. In solar-powered consumer electronic products alone, the supplier produces more than 30 million pieces of solar products every year. The supplier's clients include Costco, Walmart, Home Depot, Lowe's, and other major retail customers in the United States and Europe. Nokero maintains its headquarters in Denver, Colorado, where the company oversees sales and marketing, business development, web-based sales, and overall administration of the business.

Creating Groundswell Support

Widespread and favorable coverage by traditional and social media outlets has been instrumental in getting the Nokero story out to as many people as possible. A key moment came with a six-minute daytime television segment featuring Katsaros and Nokero with Ali Velshi on the CNN show "The Big Eye." Not only did the coverage reach a global audience, it helped legitimize Nokero to those who were interested in solar lighting in general and Nokero's products in particular.

Nokero has benefited from dozens of stories by traditional print media and TV networks and hundreds of stories from new and social media, including sources from abroad such as *O Globo* (Brazil), *Sydney Times* (Australia), Air France, and Sudwestrundfunk (Germany). In a story entitled "A Solar Light Bulb May Light the Way," *The New York Times* noted that "Where Nokero's bulb appears to break ground is in its design; it is small enough to carry, self-contained, highly durable and features a replaceable battery." In another article, "The Power of Light," *The Denver Post* lauded the environmental, health, and safety benefits of Nokero's products and the social entrepreneurial aspects of the company's business model. These major stories resulted in a boost in traffic to Nokero's website and new orders for samples, as well as inquiries from prospective distributors.

Social media, particularly blogs, have been a powerful way for the company to create community groundswell support. In July 2010, an influential London businessman offered support to the company, an offer that led to an endorsement of Nokero's products by popular soccer star Didier Drogba. Social media have also been instrumental in creating awareness and mobilizing community participation in social initiatives championed by Nokero and other partners. For example, Nokero has partnered with Project C.U.R.E. on a buy-give program. Under this program, customers who buy a solar light bulb from Nokero can give a second light bulb to Project C.U.R.E. that the latter will distribute to people in need throughout the world.

Similarly, filmmaker Kurt Mann's organization, American Green, brought light bulbs to Haiti to help victims who have been devastated by the country's earthquake. Nokero and American Green have jointly set up a program, "The Gift of Light," for people to donate light bulbs to Haiti. Mann also filmed a short video during one of his recent visits to Haiti to document how Nokero's products have helped the people of Haiti and the world's poor by providing ready access to light. Nokero and third parties have used this video widely to help tell the company's story. Nokero has also been quick to respond to natural calamities, such as Typhoon Haiyan in the Philippines or Hurricane Sandy in the U.S. East Coast, by donating solar bulbs to victims, as well as instituting a program that led to the donation of these solar bulbs.

Growing the Business

Opportunities in Working with Governments and International Organizations

Several governments, international nongovernmental organizations, and international agencies have approached Katsaros and Nokero on a number of potential large-scale partnerships and projects. The governments of Mexico and Congo are pursuing the idea of buying Nokero's products for distribution to people in their respective countries who are earning less than $2 per day (i.e., bottom of the pyramid consumers) and do not have access to electricity. Through a partner in the Philippines, Nokero is exploring how best to provide its solar light bulbs to school children from poor families who still rely on kerosene lanterns.

Nokero has also initiated discussions with international agencies, such as the United Nations, USAID, and various international foundations. While governments and international organization sales represent attractive opportunities for Nokero, they have posed three major challenges. First, the sales cycle in these organizations tends to be long and requires specialized skills and major business development resources. To address this challenge, Nokero has brought on board a consultant who is knowledgeable and has networked with these kinds of entities.

Second, the company would have to significantly scale production to fill larger orders from these governments. The governments that Nokero has been dealing with have talked about buying not thousands but *millions* of light bulbs. In addition, these governments are also likely to pressure Nokero to lower its price. Third, selling to these governments portends production and supply-chain challenges. Katsaros is also anticipating that governments that place large orders from Nokero would require the company to produce or assemble its products locally.

Opportunities in the Social Enterprise Sector

As previously mentioned, Nokero has been engaged in partnership programs with various social enterprises, such as Project C.U.R.E. (Commission on Urgent Relief and Equipment), Elephant Energy, Earthspark International, Shelterbox, Child Fund, and Power the World. As a case in point, Nokero and Project C.U.R.E. began the Lights for Life Campaign in 2010 whereby Nokero solar bulbs were added to the C.U.R.E. Kits for Kids (i.e., shoebox-sized kits of everyday health-care supplies, including bandages, antibiotic ointments, and insect repellent) and provided to parents who might not otherwise have access to an everyday medicine cabinet.

In contrast to working with governments and international organizations, partnerships with social enterprises entail a different set of challenges for Nokero. The programs championed by these partners are quite diverse, the customers that they serve are widely dispersed, and their order amounts tend to be smaller, although purchases are made more frequently. All of these considerations require different order and fulfillment mechanisms in Nokero's supply chain. While these processes may be more demanding, Katsaros is committed to working with micro-business and the social enterprise sector, since serving the people that these enterprises reach out to is at the core of Nokero's mission.

Opportunities in Commercial Channels

Nokero has driven sales through the commercial channel in two ways: through direct, web-based sales and through licensed distributors. Customers order directly through

Nokero's website (Nokero.com) and pay using a credit card or an account through PayPal. Once an order is placed and payment is verified, the order is added to a sales spreadsheet and is exported nightly to Nokero's fulfillment center, which handles the order deliveries. Nokero fills order using Hong Kong Post or Singapore Post. The customer can then log on to Nokero's website to track the shipment of their package and order history by entering the e-mail address that they used to place the order.

Since 2011, Nokero has been successful in selling tens of thousands of dollars of light bulbs to more than 120 countries through its website. Accordingly, one major opportunity that Katsaros sees in this channel is sales conversion (i.e., converting people who have placed sample orders to sign up as distributors). Nokero would like to put in place a strategy or process for such sales conversion other than a form on its website which invites people to apply to become distributors.

The company's largest customers are distributors, associations, and individuals that have ordered thousands of light bulbs, including Anzocare (South African Alternative Energy Association) and major individual distributors from India, Kenya, Zambia, Ghana, and Fiji. Additional distributors are in place in Afghanistan, Australia, Nigeria, Central America, Cote D' Ivoire, Mali, Burkina Faso, and Vietnam. Large commercial orders are filled directly from Nokero's factory in China via the port of Shenzhen, China. Nokero's outsourced fulfillment partner in Shenzhen, China, serves smaller orders.

Addressing Supply-Chain Issues

As previously mentioned, Katsaros understands that the success of Nokero's business hinges on its ability to address critical supply-chain issues. Katsaros and his Hong Kong partners must ensure that the company is ready to fill both large and concentrated orders from government and international organizations, as well as sample and small order sales from hundreds of customers that are geographically dispersed. At this point, Nokero needs to evaluate whether it should bring on board a second or third supplier that will support its major supplier partner in China. Moreover, it needs to evaluate the locations of the company's fulfillment centers.

In addition, Katsaros needs to address some operational issues related to supply-chain management. These include

1. *Payments and Pricing of Shipping Charges.* Currently, customers who order through the website pay by credit card or PayPal. However, PayPal is not accepted in all countries, particularly in some markets that represent attractive markets for Nokero in Asia and Africa. In addition, determining the correct amount to charge for shipping has been a challenge since Nokero's fulfillment center does not provide a live feed with updated international pricing of shipping charges, and in general it is extremely difficult to

reliably estimate the cost of shipping small orders to all the regions of the world.

2. *Order Tracking.* Tracking information usually stops once the package has left China (i.e., the Chinese factory location or fulfillment center in Shenzhen) making the tracking information limited and less useful.

3. *Timely Delivery.* Orders are filled and shipped in a timely manner from Nokero's factory and fulfillment center. However, the delivery process relies heavily on the timeliness and reliability of the postal system in the receiving country. In some instances, it has taken months for a sample or small order to be delivered to the customer.

4. *Last Mile Issue.* Often Nokero's customers are in remote locations that cannot be accessed by regular postal delivery. Even social enterprises and government organizations that partner with Nokero find it challenging to reach users in remote locations. The significance of the last mile issue is not just about getting the products to the needful users but educating them about product attributes and usage. As Katsaros noted, "this cannot be done through a website or a product manual, it is better if someone local can communicate with and demonstrate the products to users." To this end, Nokero is testing a model in Kenya where it has partnered with a Procter and Gamble distributor who has a strong reach and connections with customers in remote locations. Nokero has also hired a local employee to help with the communication and distribution of these products to Kenyan customers, as well as to work with its distributor. If successful, Nokero hopes to replicate this model in other markets.

Katsaros knows that the *growth* strategy that Nokero chooses to pursue will have important implications for the company's supply-chain strategy, processes, and probable results. In turn, generating greater efficiencies in distribution and the supply chain will be critical to Nokero's ability to lower its price and make its products more affordable to its customers. Katsaros wants to ensure that Nokero effectively addresses the key strategic and tactical issues related to the management of the company's supply chain, which will in turn help the company in anticipating and capitalizing on further and faster growth in the coming years.

QUESTIONS

18-3. What manufacturing strategy should Nokero pursue? Should it continue to supply all of its light bulb orders from a single factory location in China?

18-4. In terms of distribution networks, should Nokero maintain fulfillment warehouses in Africa, Asia, and Latin America? How should Nokero address the last mile issue of accessing people in the most remote locations?

MyLab Management

Go to **mymanagementlab.com** for the following Assisted-graded writing questions:

18-5 How should Nokero build its distribution footprint in international markets? What regions should it emphasize?

18-6 A number of potential distributors have asked Nokero for exclusive rights in key geographic markets. Should Nokero grant exclusive country distribution rights? What performance standards or metrics should Nokero put in place for distributors?

Endnotes

Scan for Endnotes or go to www.pearsonglobaleditions.com/Daniels

CHAPTER 19

Global Accounting and Financial Management

OBJECTIVES

After studying this chapter, you should be able to

19-1 Explain the crossroads of accounting and finance

19-2 Identify the major factors affecting the development of accounting objectives, standards, and practices

19-3 Describe international accounting standards and the process of global convergence

19-4 Demonstrate how companies account for foreign-currency transactions

19-5 Determine how companies can translate foreign-currency financial statements

19-6 List some of the key international finance functions

19-7 Show how companies protect against foreign-exchange risk

MyLab Management®

Improve Your Performance!

When you see this icon ⭐, visit **www.mymanagementlab.com** for activities that are applied, personalized, and offer immediate feedback.

Even between parents and children, money matters make strangers.

—Japanese proverb

Exchange rate trends displayed on a board at a foreign-exchange brokerage firm. ▼

Source: blueximages. 123rf.com

22,00		16,05 %		544,00	796,00	+
566,00	─	36,29 %		6.422,00	6.401,00	
6.827,00	+	31,74 %		65.646,00	64.922,00	+
4.243,00	+	229,81 %		6.546,00	6.693,00	
3.242,00	+	52,61 %		6.422,00	3.572,00	+
2.431,00	+	7,10 %		654,00	745,00	+
3.244,00	+	60,80 %		65.642,00	63.090,00	
12.927,00		24,46 %		64.565,00	55.245,00	
1.498,00	─	29,53 %		5.424,00	5.636,00	+
45.229,00	+	23,24 %		642,00	734,00	+
997,00	+	36,43 %		56.257,00	54.732,00	
528,00	+	38,92 %		6.796,00	6.798,00	+
6.928,00		0,58 %		643,00	834,00	─
6.798,00		48,13 %		48.447,00	39.643,00	─
8.864,00	+	61,66 %		87.995,00	80.354,00	+
1.282,00	+	3,36 %		7.653,00	7.934,00	+
4.920,00		7,19 %		73,00	127,00	
129,00	+	23,35 %		1.223,00	1.583,00	
6.582,00		18,68 %		32.124,00	31.844,00	

Parmalat: Europe's Enron

In January 2002, a European magazine published an article entitled "Enron: Could It Happen Here?" At the time the article was published, perhaps most people outside the United States would have answered "no" to that question.[1] In the wake of massive corporate frauds at Enron and WorldCom, there was a feeling outside the U.S. that such scandals were "an American problem" caused by the more aggressive business environment and practices there. However, a family-owned Italian firm was about to show the world that massive corporate scandals can happen anywhere.

A BRIEF BACKGROUND CHECK

In 1961, when Calisto Tanzi inherited his father's company at age 22, he directed it into dairy products and created the Parmalat brand. Inside two years, Parmalat had become the first Italian manufacturer of branded milk. In 1966, using packaging technology from Tetra Pak, Parmalat created its signature product: milk pasteurized at ultra-high temperatures (UHT), which gave it a shelf life of over six months. UHT milk provided the company with a technological competitiveness in the dairy industry, placing it ahead of its competition. In 1970, the law permitted the sale of whole milk in grocery stores, removing the limitation of specialty milk shops, and Parmalat quickly became Italy's dominant milk supplier.

The "Champion's Milk"

Parmalat also became known as the "champion's milk" after sponsoring the Ski World Cup and world-champion Formula One race-car driver Nicki Lauda in the 1970s. The company moved into new markets with the production of cheese, butter, and a variety of desserts near the end of the decade. As it increased in popularity, Parmalat also began international expansion through acquisitions in Germany and France, which marked the beginning of a global dairy empire.

The Pious Pioneer Sports Marketer

Calisto Tanzi, an almost legendary figure in Italy, was the author of this growth. It was he who discovered the power of sports marketing to make Parmalat a famous brand. He had friends in important government positions who helped pass laws favoring Parmalat. A pious Catholic, Tanzi was a generous benefactor who sponsored the restoration of Parma's eleventh-century basilica and funded its professional soccer team. And he seemed modest about his achievements. He didn't smoke, he drank little, and he drove his own Lexus. All throughout Parmalat's expansion, Tanzi maintained a paternalistic approach to the business.

Going Public and Going Global

In 1989, the firm was acquired by a holding company and changed its name to Parmalat Finanziaria SpA. Profits were healthy every year, and the balance sheet appeared strong, with large amounts of cash on hand. This allowed the milk giant to go public in Italy and raise capital in the United States and other countries by selling shares and issuing bonds. Parmalat used this new capital to expand into Latin America, where it dominated the dairy markets in Brazil, Argentina, Venezuela, and several other countries.

By the early 1990s, Parmalat was popular not only among grocery shoppers but also among investors and creditors, who deemed the firm a profitable business partner. Large international banks collected hefty fees by helping the company issue bonds, list stock in foreign markets, and raise capital to fund international acquisitions. As CFO Alberto Ferraris put it, "Outside my office, there was always a line of bankers, asking about new business." There was one problem, though: The profits that Parmalat reported were only an illusion created by a set of accounting manipulations.

ACCOUNTING ISSUES

One of the most interesting aspects of Parmalat's case is the simplicity of its fraudulent accounting (which was not quite as simple as the scheme suggested in Figure 19.1). The purpose of the fraud was straightforward: to hide operating losses so as not to disappoint investors and creditors. The core of the scheme was double billing to Italian supermarkets and other retailers. By standard accounting procedures, every time a product is shipped to a customer, a company records a receivable that it later expects to collect as cash. Because receivables count as sales revenue, Parmalat billed customers twice for each shipment, thus greatly enlarging its sales. The company used these inflated revenues as a means of securing loans from several international banks.

"Off-Balance-Sheet Financing"

By 1995, Parmalat was losing more than $300 million annually in Latin America alone. These continued operating losses caused company executives to search for more complex ways of masking the firm's true performance. Using a trick called "off-balance-sheet financing," executives set up three shell companies based in the Caribbean that pretended to sell Parmalat products. Parmalat would send them fake invoices and charge costs and fees to make the "sales" look legitimate, then write out a credit note for the amount the subsidiaries supposedly owed and use it to raise money at the banks.

Off-balance-sheet financing was also used to hide debts. The company transferred over half of its liabilities to the books of small subsidiaries based in offshore tax havens such as the Cayman Islands. This allowed Parmalat to present a "healthy" balance sheet and a profitable income statement to investors and creditors by hiding large amounts of debt and overstating sales revenue. In 2002, Parmalat reported liabilities of close to $8 billion on its consolidated balance sheet. In reality, the company had roughly $14 billion in debt.

The Art of Milking Growth

Taking advantage of its image, Parmalat issued bonds in the United States and Europe that were backed up by falsified assets, especially cash. "It was a reversal of logic," said the chief investigating magistrate after the scheme was discovered. Usually, companies take on debt to grow. But in Parmalat's case, "they had to grow to hide the debt." In other words, the company would obtain loans to pay off previous loans (which sounds a little like Greek sovereign debt). Investigators report that without the accounting manipulations, the company would have reported operating losses every year between 1990 and 2003. Clearly, Parmalat's milk carton was full of financial holes.

The circle of hiding operating losses by incurring increasingly larger amounts of debt eventually became hard to sustain. To perpetuate the fraud, Parmalat needed to continue incurring debt, paying interest on old debts with no real cash of its own, and finding new ways to create false sales. Alberto Ferraris, who was appointed CFO in March 2003, mentioned that "he couldn't understand why the company was paying so much to service its debt; the interest payments seemed far higher than warranted for the €5.4 billion in debt on the books."

By the late 1990s, auditors in Argentina and Brazil raised several red flags that pointed to problems with Parmalat's accounting. In early December 2003, the company failed to make a €150 million bond payment. This puzzled those familiar with the company because, according to the 2002 financial statements, Parmalat had plenty of cash on hand.

The fraud became public on December 19, 2003, when Grant Thornton LLP, the company's auditor, made a startling discovery. While auditing Bonlat, a fully owned subsidiary of Parmalat based in the Cayman Islands, the auditors contacted Bank of America to confirm a letter held by Bonlat in which the bank allegedly certified that the company had €3.95 billion in cash. Bank of America responded that such an account didn't exist. Investigators then swooped into Parmalat's headquarters to confiscate documents and computer hard drives, which uncovered the accounting tricks. On one hard drive, prosecutors found clues to the deception: "Account 999" contained details of secret transactions amounting to more than €8 billion.

THE CONSEQUENCES

Parmalat filed for bankruptcy protection on December 24, 2003. CEO Tanzi resigned and was detained by Italian authorities three days later and sent to prison, then subsequently confined to house arrest until September 27, 2004. Also accused of wrongdoing were Fausto Tonna, CFO during most of the period under investigation; Giovanni, Stefano, and Francesca Tanzi, the brother, son, and daughter of Calisto Tanzi; and other key employees believed to have been involved in the scheme.

Convicted

Initially, it was thought that misstatements were created only to hide operating losses; however, prosecutors demonstrated that the Tanzi family benefited financially from the fraud. For example, Calisto revealed that $638 million was moved to "a family-owned tourism business." In December 2008, he was finally sentenced to 10 years in jail for market rigging in a Milan court. In 2010 he was sentenced to another 18 years in prison by a judge in Parma for contributing to the company's demise. In 2012, the Public Prosecutor filed a motion for indictment against Calisto for hiding several valuable paintings from the prosecution that have since been seized to help pay for claims against him. Others have served or are serving jail time, and Stefano, Calisto's son, was tried and convicted in Switzerland on fraud and money-laundering charges and sentenced to 14 years in prison.

Enrico Bondi was appointed by the government as CEO of Parmalat to direct recovery efforts. As part of his campaign, he brought lawsuits against Grant Thornton and Deloitte, the auditors, for not performing the audit with proper care and not bringing their suspicions to the attention of management. In 2009 a judge in New York dismissed the case against Grant Thornton; in early 2011 the case was revived, but it was thrown out again.

Lawsuits, Rounds I and II

The lawsuits accuse the banks of ignoring the fraud to obtain fees from doing business with Parmalat. As mentioned earlier, these banks were instrumental in helping the company raise capital to fund its international expansion. The banks and the auditors deny any wrongdoing and claim they were victims of the scheme. Citigroup Inc., UBS AG, Deutsche Bank AG, and Morgan Stanley were involved in the Milan trial for "failing to have procedures that would have prevented crimes that contributed" to Parmalat's failure. As of mid-June 2007, Bondi has collected almost $900 million in settlements in Italy and the United States, but Parmalat lost its case against Citigroup and actually had to pay it damages.

Parmalat, in turn, has been sued by investors, banks, and other organizations. In the United States, the SEC filed a complaint against it on December 29, 2003, alleging that the company fraudulently raised money through bonds in the United States by overstating assets and understating liabilities. On July 30, 2004, Parmalat agreed to settle with the SEC without admitting or denying the claims. Parmalat won't be fined but has agreed to make changes to strengthen its board of directors and improve governance.

Restructuring

Besides the legal battles that have resulted from the fraud, Bondi's restructuring campaign calls for aggressive changes in Parmalat's organization. On March 29, 2004, the company announced it would narrow its focus in markets in Italy, Canada, Australia, South Africa, Spain, Portugal, Russia, and Romania and would pull out of other regions. However, in May 2007 Parmalat "agreed to sell its Spanish assets to Lacteos Siglo XXI." Latin American countries "with strong and profitable positions," such as Colombia, Nicaragua, and Venezuela, would be retained. In addition, Parmalat would cut its workforce from 32,000 to fewer than 17,000, slash the number of brands from 120 to 30, and concentrate on "healthy lifestyle" products.

By 2010 Parmalat had moved into Botswana, Cuba, Ecuador, Mozambique, Paraguay, Swaziland, and Zambia. It also has a presence through licensees in a number of countries. Recently the company has been focusing on higher value added products and has scheduled market testing to determine how much potential new products have in different geographic locations.

SO, WHAT'S THE BOTTOM LINE?

In Europe, the Parmalat scandal created deep concern among authorities. The European Commission suggested it would like to strengthen auditing standards by insisting that member countries introduce accounting-oversight boards similar to those in the United States. Many organizations have proposed reforms to prevent another scandal of such magnitude. One such reform considered was more transparency in the bond market in Europe—in other words, bond-price disclosure. However, "the [European Commission] has indicated that it will allow traders to police themselves instead of requiring the same data about bonds as for stocks."

From an accounting perspective, Parmalat joined the ranks of other European companies by adopting International Financial Reporting Standards published by the International Accounting Standards Board and adopted by the European Commission for their consolidated financial statements. In addition, global auditing firm PricewaterhouseCoopers has now become Parmalat's independent auditors. The hope is that these two moves will help convince investors that the company is moving in the right direction on the accounting side. Since the restructuring, Parmalat has risen from the ashes, is now listed again on the Milan stock exchange, and is Italy's biggest listed food company. At least it hasn't suffered Enron's fate.

Plus a Little Corporate Misgovernance

Even though the accounting moves described above were taken to help Parmalat recover, they are not enough. The fraud may have been perpetrated through a set of accounting tricks, but several issues converged to allow such manipulations to happen. One of the clearest deficiencies at Parmalat was its corporate governance system. As a family-owned business, the company was tightly controlled by insiders, especially Calisto Tanzi, who held the positions of CEO and chairman of the board of directors.

Most of the other board members were family members or managers of Parmalat, which prevented the company from having a strong, independent voice to stop the actions taken by management. In addition, Italian law allowed Parmalat to have two auditors instead of one. Grant Thornton was the main auditor, but Deloitte audited some of the subsidiaries, including Bonlat, where the fraud was uncovered. This arrangement made it more difficult for the auditors to have one clear, coherent picture of Parmalat's financial condition. (Neither of these auditors is used by Parmalat now.) Finally, and perhaps most importantly, management integrity failed. In the end, a manager determined to commit fraud will most likely succeed even in a very good governance system.

Parmalat is now taking the necessary steps to provide better corporate governance. Its managers are working hard to comply with the Italian Corporate Governance Code along with other general principles. The company has also created its own Code of Ethics, Code of Conduct, and Internal Dealing Code of Conduct. All employees are required to abide by the codes set in place. The 2012 Annual Report was audited by PricewaterhouseCoopers according to the rules set down by CONSOB, the Italian regulatory body that supervises companies and stock exchanges. Financial statements were prepared according to Italian accounting standards and IFRS as adopted by the European Union. The report was originally prepared in Italian, signed by Italian partner Massimo Rota, and translated into English for the convenience of international readers.

In the aftermath of Parmalat's fraud, investigators were left wondering how a few accounting numbers could fool so many people. One thing, however, was clear: Europe now had its very own version of Enron. ∎

QUESTIONS

19-1. How much of Parmalat's problems were due to bad accounting, and how much were due to fraud on the part of individuals in the company?

19-2. In the chapter, we discuss the difference in accounting standards in the U.S. and the rest of the world through IFRS. Do you think that it made a difference that Parmalat used IFRS instead of U.S. GAAP?

THE CROSSROADS OF ACCOUNTING AND FINANCE

CONCEPT CHECK

We discuss **foreign currency exchange rates** and the ways in which they affect the operations of an MNE in Chapter 7. Here we explain the responsibilities of the CFO in overseeing a company's closely related financial and accounting functions. As we'll see, financial management deals with the effects of exchange rates on such financial-statement items as receivables and payables.

As noted in Chapter 10, the Chief Financial Officer (CFO) of a company is responsible for overseeing the financial activities of a company.[2] Working under the CFO, the controller has responsibility for accounting-related activities, providing management with relevant and reliable information, and preparing information for the external users of financial information.

The accounting and finance functions are closely related, with each relying on the other to fulfill its responsibilities. The CFO relies on the controller, or chief accountant, to provide the right information for making decisions, while the internal audit staff ensures that corporate policies and procedures are followed. The internal auditors, the controller, and the CFO work closely with the external auditor to try to safeguard the assets of the business.

The actual and potential flow of assets across national boundaries complicates the finance and accounting functions. So MNEs must learn to cope with differing inflation rates, exchange-rate changes, currency controls, expropriation risks, customs duties, tax rates and methods of determining taxable income, levels of sophistication of local accounting personnel, and local as well as home-country reporting requirements.

WHAT DOES THE CONTROLLER CONTROL?

The controller is essential in providing information to financial decision-makers.

The role of the company controller is critical to providing useful and timely information to management and external stakeholders. Today's controller is engaged in a variety of activities outside the typical accounting and reporting functions that support the firm's general strategy such as evaluating potential acquisitions abroad, disposing of a subsidiary or a division, managing cash flow, hedging currency and interest-rate risks, tax planning, internal auditing, and helping to plan corporate strategy. As noted in Chapter 16, foreign managers and subsidiaries are usually evaluated at headquarters on the basis of data generated in the company's reporting system as set up and coordinated by the controller's office. The controller generates reports for internal consideration, local government needs, creditors, employees, suppliers, stockholders, and prospective investors while handling the effect of many different currencies and inflation rates on the statements and becoming familiar with different countries' accounting systems.

The controller of an international company must be concerned about a range of issues dealing with corporate strategy broader than just accounting issues.

DIFFERENCES IN FINANCIAL STATEMENTS INTERNATIONALLY

Both the form and the content of financial statements are different in different countries.

One problem an MNE faces is the varying accounting standards and practices around the world. Financial statements among countries differ in form (or format) and content (or substance). In terms of form, the balance sheets for U.S. companies are in the *balance format*:

$$\text{Assets} = \text{Liabilities} + \text{Shareholders' equity}$$

The balance sheet varies in the order of liquidity of the accounts presented. Some companies start with the least liquid assets (those that are harder to convert into cash quickly) and go to those that are most liquid (such as cash), whereas other companies start with the most liquid and progress to the least liquid assets (such as property, plants, and equipment). The former practice is very common among European companies such as Swedish retailer H&M; the latter is used by U.S.-based firms. In a slight twist, Parmalat from Italy uses the following format:

$$\text{Noncurrent assets} + \text{Current assets} = \text{Shareholders' equity} + \text{Noncurrent liabilities} + \text{Current liabilities}$$

The balance sheet for British retailer Marks and Spencer uses the following format, which is very common among British firms:

$$\text{Noncurrent assets} + \text{Current assets} - \text{Current liabilities} - \text{Noncurrent liabilities} = \text{Total equity}$$

DIFFERENCES IN THE CONTENT OF FINANCIAL INFORMATION

The types of financial information required in different countries can differ, while companies also have to consider who their audience is: Are they providing financial information only for the local market, or also for users from the broader global capital markets? Companies that list on stock exchanges usually provide an income statement, a balance sheet (also known as a statement of financial position), a statement of shareholders' equity, a cash-flow statement, and detailed footnotes in their annual report. The depth of disclosure of information, especially in footnotes, is a major issue in terms of content. Providers of financial information for the broader investing community need to consider the following three factors:

1. Language
2. Currency
3. Underlying GAAP on which the statements are based

> Major reporting issues:
> • Language
> • Currency
> • Underlying GAAP on which the financial statements are based

Language Differences   English tends to be the first choice of companies choosing to raise capital abroad. For example, German company Daimler issues financial statements in both German and English, while Sweden's H&M provides its annual reports in Swedish and English. Parmalat is interesting because its registered office is in Italy, its shares are traded on the Online Stock Market operated by the Borsa Italiana, and it is controlled by a French company that is part of the Lactalis Group, a French multinational dairy products company. It provides an annual report in English, although its financial statements are in euros, its major reporting currency. In addition to language, companies also have to deal with differences in terms.

> Major sources of influence are capital markets, the cultural and regulatory environments, global standards settings, and other users.

Currency Differences   Companies around the world prepare their financial statements in different currencies—Daimler's are in euros, H&M's in Swedish kronor, Coca-Cola in U.S. dollars, and so on. In its 2015 annual report, Adidas provided its financial information in euros, disclosed information on the firm's currency-translation policies, and gave average exchange rates for the U.S. dollar, the British pound, the Japanese yen, the Russian ruble, and the Chinese yuan to allow investors to make convenient translations from euros.[3]

Underlying GAAP   A major hurdle in raising capital in different countries is dealing with widely varying accounting and disclosure requirements. Although this problem is decreasing as more stock exchanges and countries allow the use of International Financial Reporting Standards (IFRS), some countries care more about those differences than others. Most countries also may apply one set of accounting standards for consolidated groups while using another set for the individual companies in the group. In this situation, the individual companies must use local accounting standards that are usually tied to legal requirements and are the basis for tax accounting. Consolidated financial statements, which are used for capital markets and not for tax purposes, are prepared by a different set of standards, such as IFRS. U.S. companies do not have the same situation. They disclose only consolidated financial statements, not individual company financial statements. There are some differences for tax accounting, but those differences are reconciled in the financial statements rather than as separate statements for each company in a group.

CONCEPT CHECK

In discussing "Legal Issues Facing International Companies" on p. 128 in Chapter 3, we survey the various ways in which local legal standards can affect the way foreign firms function on a day-to-day basis. Naturally, these standards include accounting standards, and here we emphasize that attitudes toward, and more importantly regulations concerning, accounting practices vary widely from country to country.

FACTORS AFFECTING ACCOUNTING OBJECTIVES, STANDARDS, AND PRACTICES

Figure 19.1 identifies some of the factors affecting the development of accounting standards and practices both domestically and internationally. Although all the factors shown are significant, their importance varies by country. Capital markets refer to equity and debt markets.

FIGURE 19.1 Sources of Influence on Accounting Standards and Practices

Every aspect of the accounting process is influenced by a variety of internal and external factors, and they're all potentially important. The degree of importance will vary by country.

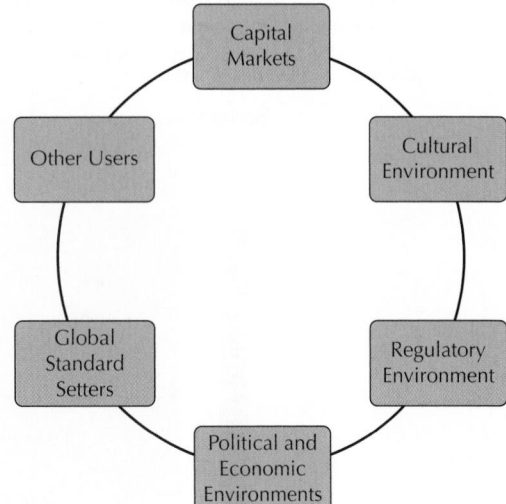

As noted in Chapter 10, lenders are considered to be bond holders, banks, and private equity funds. Equity market investors are influential in the United States and the United Kingdom, but creditors, primarily banks, have traditionally had more influence in Germany and Switzerland.

As we will discuss in more detail below, cultural issues cut across all countries and strongly influence the development of accounting. The regulatory environment, including legal and tax systems, is very influential, especially in countries with weak stock markets. However, the regulatory environment is also influential on stock markets. Certain international factors also have weight, such as former colonial influence, foreign investment, and the influence of regional economic agreements, such as the EU.

CULTURAL DIFFERENCES IN ACCOUNTING

The differences in measurement and disclosure practices among countries are of special interest to international investors. *Measurement* means how companies value assets, including inventory and fixed assets, whereas *disclosure* refers to how and what information companies provide and the level of detail and transparency.

Culture refers to learned norms based on the values, attitudes, and beliefs of a group of people. Much of the work on culture and accounting is initially based on Hofstede's research on the structural elements of culture, particularly those that most strongly affect behavior in the work situations of organizations and institutions.[4] Hofstede's work was extended into the accounting area by Gray, which resulted in country classifications according to disclosure and measurement principles—specifically, secrecy/transparency and optimism/conservatism.[5]

The Secrecy–Transparency/Optimism–Conservatism Matrix Figure 19.2 depicts the accounting practices of various groupings of countries within a matrix of the cultural values of secrecy–transparency and optimism–conservatism. With respect to accounting, secrecy and transparency indicate the degree to which companies disclose information to the public. In the past, countries such as Germany, Switzerland, and Japan tended to have less disclosure (illustrating the cultural value of secrecy) than did more transparent U.S. and British companies (Anglo-Saxon in Figure 19.2) due to their reliance on stock markets. The classification of countries in Figure 19.2 represents a point in time, but countries are always

---

Culture influences measurement and disclosure practices:

- Measurement—how to value assets
- Disclosure—the presentation of information and discussion of results

CONCEPT CHECK

Chapter 2 is devoted to illustrating the many ways in which local culture shapes the environment in which international business is conducted from country to country. Here we point out that culture also affects differences in approaches to accounting systems and policies. In Chapter 2, we cite Geert Hofstede among the researchers who've studied national differences in managerial attitudes and preferences, and here we use applications of Hofstede's findings to studies of work-situation behavior as a means of shedding light on the effect of cultural differences on accounting standards and practices.

FIGURE 19.2   A Disclosure/Assessment Matrix for National Accounting Systems

The vertical axis reflects practices according to transparency–secrecy (the extent to which companies in a country disclose information to the public). The horizontal axis reflects practices accounting to optimism–conservatism (the degree of caution taken by companies when it comes to valuing assets and recognizing income). Note that, not surprisingly, transparency and optimism tend to go hand in hand, as do secrecy and conservatism.

Source: Based on Lee H. Radebaugh, Sidney J. Gray, and Ervin L. Black, *International Accounting and Multinational Enterprises*, 6th ed. (New York: John Wiley & Sons, 2002): 51.

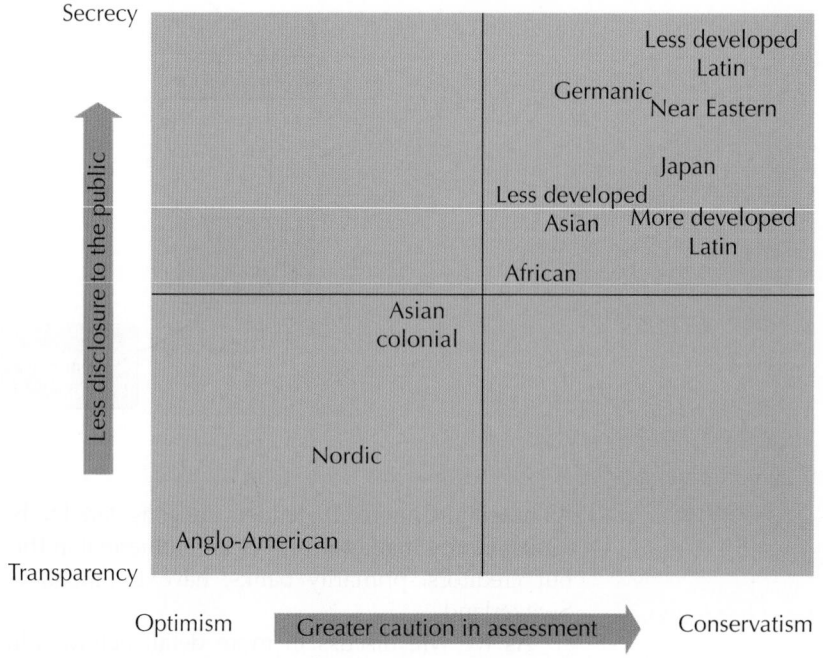

changing due to the increased importance of and demands by capital markets and the influence of IFRS. However, the importance of understanding where countries came from illustrates the complexity of moving everyone to one set of global accounting standards.

Optimism and conservatism (in an accounting sense, not political) are the degrees of caution companies exhibit in valuing assets and recognizing income. The more conservative countries tend to understate assets and income, whereas optimistic countries tend to be more liberal in their recognition of income. Historically, banks have been a primary source of funding for companies in countries with weak capital markets and a strong influence on tax accounting, so those companies tend to be very conservative both when recording profits that keep them from paying taxes and when declaring dividends to pile up cash reserves to service their bank debts. However, as German MNCs in particular outgrew the ability of banks to provide the majority of their funding needs, they were forced to adopt accounting standards and reporting practices more in line with global capital markets, becoming less secret and more transparent. In contrast, U.S. and British companies are more optimistic and want to show earning power to impress and attract investors.

> Secrecy and transparency refer to the degree to which corporations disclose information to the public. Optimism and conservatism refer to the degree of caution companies display in valuing assets and recognizing income.

> British and U.S. companies are optimistic when recognizing income, whereas Japanese and continental European companies are more conservative.

INTERNATIONAL STANDARDS AND GLOBAL CONVERGENCE

MUTUAL RECOGNITION VERSUS RECONCILIATION

Before the rise in importance of global capital markets and the move to a common set of accounting standards, it was common for many countries to apply the principle of **mutual recognition**, whereby a regulator, such as the German Stock Exchange, would accept financial statements provided in U.S. GAAP of a U.S. company wanting to list securities in Germany. Prior to the requirement in 2005 that EU companies provide financial statements prepared according to IFRS, some German companies such as Daimler and Deutsche Bank prepared their consolidated financial statements according to U.S. GAAP, as permitted at the time by German law. This made it easier for them to list on the New York Stock Exchange. However, they dropped this practice and moved to IFRS in 2007.

The United States uses two approaches: adoption of U.S. standards or the use of IFRS as established by the International Accounting Standards Board. If a foreign company prefers to list according to their home-country GAAP instead of U.S. GAAP or IFRS, they must provide a statement of **reconciliation**. In this case, the company usually lists American Depositary Receipts (ADRs) on a U.S. exchange and then reconciles its home-country GAAP with U.S. GAAP in a special statement called Form 20-F on net income and shareholders' equity. This is the approach Daimler used before it adopted U.S. GAAP for its consolidated financial statements. Since 2007, however, the SEC permits foreign issuers to list without a reconciliation statement as long as their financial statements are prepared in accordance with full IFRS. In response, the EU announced in 2008 that it would allow U.S. firms to continue to list on EU stock markets using U.S. GAAP, given the progress of convergence and the fact that U.S. GAAP and IFRS are essentially equivalent.[6]

Despite the many differences in accounting standards and practices around the world, a number of forces are leading to convergence:

- A movement to provide information compatible with the needs of investors

- The global integration of capital markets, which means easier and faster access to investment opportunities around the world and, therefore, the need for more comparable financial data

- The need of MNEs to raise capital outside their home-country capital markets while generating as few different financial statements as possible

- Regional political and economic harmonization, such as the efforts of the EU, which affect accounting as well as trade and investment issues

- Pressure from MNEs for more uniform standards to allow greater ease and reduced costs in general reporting in each country

THE FIRST STEPS IN ESTABLISHING IFRS

Established in 1973, the International Accounting Standards Committee (IASC), the forerunner of the IASB, began working toward harmonizing standards by issuing a set of International Accounting Standards (IAS) that they hoped anyone in the world could use. Its original standards had a strong capital-markets focus so that they could be used worldwide to facilitate the free flow of capital. With such a goal, the IASC tended to lean more toward the traditions of the United States and the United Kingdom rather than the legal- and tax-based systems of Germany and France, where funding was more the domain of banks than broadly based capital markets. The early standards were often very superficial, with too many options to capture the support of everyone.

The turning point in the significance of IAS came in 1995, when the **International Organization of Securities Commissions (IOSCO)** announced publicly it would endorse IAS if the IASC developed a set of core standards acceptable to it. IOSCO is significant because it comprises the regulators of most of the world's stock markets, including the SEC in the United States. In May 2000, the IASC completed a core set of standards acceptable to IOSCO, and securities market regulators began the process of convincing their standard setters to adopt these standards, called International Financial Reporting Standards (IFRS).

Major approaches to dealing with accounting and reporting differences:

- Mutual recognition
- Reconciliation to local GAAP
- Issue financial statements according to IFRS

Major forces leading to establishing global accounting standards:

- Investor orientation
- Global integration of capital markets
- MNEs' need for foreign capital
- Regional political and economic harmonization
- MNEs' desire to reduce accounting and reporting costs
- Convergence efforts of standards-setting bodies

The International Organization of Securities Commissions accepted a core set of accounting standards issued by the IASB in which securities regulators can be confident.

THE INTERNATIONAL ACCOUNTING STANDARDS BOARD

In March 2001, the IASC was reorganized into the International Accounting Standards Committee Foundation (now called the IFRS Foundation) and the International Accounting Standards Board (IASB). The IFRS Foundation is the parent entity of the IASB, which assumed the major standard-setting functions of the old IASC.[7] The IASB is composed of 14 members who are standard setters, preparers, auditors, users, and academics with broad geographic representation from the Asia/Oceania region, Europe, North America, Africa, and South America. Two members are "at large" instead of from a specific geographic area.[8]

International Financial Reporting Standards (IFRS)   When the IASB was organized, all of the old standards from the IASC were adopted, and the Board began to go through each one to upgrade them. Then the Board began to issue the new International Financial Reporting Standards; thus, when we use the term *IFRS*, we refer to the new standards as well as the old IAS.

The IASB is harmonizing accounting standards through issuing International Financial Reporting Standards (IFRS).

The objectives of the IFRS Foundation and the IASB include developing "a single set of high-quality, understandable, enforceable, and globally accepted international financial reporting standards (IFRSs) through its standard-setting body, the IASB, and [promoting] the use and rigorous application of those standards."[9] As of 2016, 120 countries require the use of IFRS for reporting by public companies, while most others permit their use in some cases. Of course, there is a difference between permitting and requiring, and that is a major issue. In 2016, the IASB published a detailed study of countries to determine the level of acceptance and usage of IFRS.[10]

FASB and IASB are trying to converge their standards through removing differences in existing standards and engaging in joint projects to develop new standards.

The Relationship Between the FASB and the IASB   The U.S. Financial Accounting Standards Board (FASB) and IASB have been working closely to achieve a convergence of accounting standards. In 2002, they issued the Norwalk Agreement, pledging their best efforts to remove individual differences between U.S. GAAP and IFRS and undertake joint projects to develop future standards.[11] Convergence implies a goal and a path to achieving it. The goal is to eliminate differences in accounting standards between FASB and the IASB. The convergence process (or path) takes several forms. Initially, the two Boards identified standards that could easily be converged. Once these standards were converged, they decided to jointly develop new standards where existing standards were too far apart. Finally, they identified entirely new standards which would be jointly developed.[12]

However, standard-setting in the United States depends on the cooperation of the Securities and Exchange Commission (SEC), whose mission is to "protect investors, maintain fair, orderly, and efficient markets, and facilitate capital formation."[13] Although the SEC does not set accounting standards, it empowers the FASB to do so because companies—both foreign and domestic—that want to raise capital in the United States must follow the SEC guidelines. Also, the SEC determines which accounting standards can be used by issuers on the U.S. stock exchanges as noted above. Convergence is complicated because it is both technical in terms of the quality of the standards as well as political.

The EU required adoption of IFRS in 2002, effective in 2005.

The European Response to Convergence   The main body of financial reporting requirements for limited liability companies in the EU consists of two directives issued by the European Council. Thus, it is important to understand that IFRS and interpretations must be approved by the European Parliament and the European Council and adopted as an official regulation by the European Commission to have legal standing in the EU.[14] This illustrates the importance of the political process in IFRS adoption. Prior to the development of the IASB, the EU was working to harmonize reporting practices to better coordinate financial markets. To enhance that process, it supported the efforts of the IASB and, in the spring of 2002, directed its member countries to adopt IFRS by 2005. In the case of the EU, this meant that 7,000 publicly listed companies started using IFRS for their consolidated financial statements in 2005.[15] The two main reasons for the EU to push IFRS were to allow it to influence IASB standards and to avoid funding and developing a competing standard-setting body.[16] By working with the

IASB, the EU would avoid relying on standards developed in the United States for capital market reporting. In one political decision, the EU suddenly made IFRS the most important set of accounting standards outside of standards issued by FASB in the United States.

The EU has adopted most of the standards as written, but has "carved out" or suspended the standard on financial instruments due largely to political pressure from French banks. Thus the EU has its own version of IFRS. As a result, European companies such as H&M, as described in the ending case, must state in their annual report that they apply IFRS "as adopted by the EU." That means that in the future, upon the EU's recommendation, its member companies can "opt out" or "carve out" certain standards, ending up with their own version of IFRS. Initial reactions of various parties to European firms' 2005 adoption of IFRS have been interesting. In fact, various interpretations and applications exist. Some firms use wide judgment in applying IFRS, while others use an adapted form with changes or alternative interpretations based on individual country accounting treatments.

Full application of IFRS in various countries and under various regulatory regimes is difficult to judge. The EU does not require companies to adhere to all IFRS, only those approved by the EU.

Point

Point **Yes** A major issue for investors around the world is obtaining reliable, comparable financial-statement information for company evaluation and comparison. Creditors and other users also need this information for making well-informed decisions on a global basis. As the composition of the business world has shifted from domestic economies to a global economy, the need for a single set of financial reporting standards has never been greater. IFRS are required for listed entities in many countries, such as all countries in the European Union, Canada, Australia, and New Zealand.

U.S. GAAP and IFRS are the two most recognized sets of standards today, and they are steadily becoming nearly identical to each other. The combined efforts of the IASB and the FASB in their convergence project have brought the two closer than ever before. The SEC currently allows foreign firms that list on U.S. exchanges to use IFRS for financial reporting and should allow U.S. firms as well. Not only would

Should U.S. Companies Be Allowed to Use IFRS?

this make the United States more a part of the global economy, its companies could also raise more capital because investors in countries that use it would be more familiar and able to keep up with the single international set of standards.

U.S. investors would also benefit. They would become more familiar with the international standards and would feel more apt to invest in international companies. As the gap between IFRS and U.S. GAAP shrinks, the quality of the financial information presented under IFRS will not be lower than it has been under GAAP.

Many U.S. firms with international operations use IFRS abroad, so allowing IFRS to be used for U.S. reporting would reduce the costs of accounting for and reporting information to users. In addition, U.S. companies that acquire foreign companies that use IFRS would find it easier to use IFRS for all operations rather than have to convert the results of their acquired companies from IFRS to U.S. GAAP for reporting purposes.

Should U.S. Companies Be Allowed to Use IFRS?

Counterpoint

Counterpoint **No** It is unrealistic to assume that IFRS would be appropriate for the unique U.S. economic environment. As the largest economy in the world, with the largest and most sophisticated capital market, the United States should have the most stringent and transparent financial reporting standards in the world. Many companies around the globe continue to prepare their financial information in accordance with U.S. GAAP because it has historically been the world's most reliable set of standards, designed to present information that is both relevant and trustworthy. IFRS are far less comprehensive than GAAP, and the standards, though oriented to capital markets, cannot take into account specific issues important to U.S. capital markets.

Allowing U.S. companies to use IFRS would impose tremendous costs on the nation's economy. Publicly traded firms would need trained employees proficient in IFRS application. U.S. accounting firms would be responsible for training their existing auditors in IFRS, hiring new employees and training them, or hiring existing IFRS experts. This training and/or hiring would impose tremendous burdens in both time and money on these firms, which would still be held responsible for meeting all the rigorous standards of the Public Company Accounting Oversight Board (PCAOB) and the Sarbanes–Oxley Act of 2002. Many contracts in the United States are based on U.S. GAAP, and it would be necessary to change nearly all of them to allow for the use of IFRS.

The differences between IFRS and U.S. GAAP, though growing more insignificant, still exist. The standards are not directly comparable, which could mean trouble for investors who may have difficulty seeing the differences. In addition, more than one set of IFRS seems to exist: (1) IFRS as issued by the IASB, (2) IFRS as adopted by the EU, and (3) IFRS as applied/adopted on an individual-country basis. How will investors ascertain which set is being used by various companies, and how will this information be comparable?

Just as politics enters into the adoption of IFRS in the EU, politics is important for U.S. GAAP. Since the SEC is a U.S. government entity whose five commissioners are appointed by the president,[17] it is impossible to believe that U.S. GAAP would be turned over to IFRS and the control of the IASB. Sovereignty, even over accounting, is not something the U.S. government would give up to an international organization over which it has some influence but not control.

TRANSACTIONS IN FOREIGN CURRENCIES

When a company operates outside the domestic market, it must concern itself with the proper recording and subsequent accounting of assets, liabilities, revenues, and expenses that are measured or denominated in foreign currencies. These transactions can result from the purchase and sale of goods and services as well as the borrowing and lending of foreign currency.

RECORDING TRANSACTIONS

Any time an importer has to pay for equipment or merchandise in a foreign currency, it must trade its own currency for that of the exporter to make the payment. Assume that Sundance Ski Lodge, a U.S. company, imports skis from a French supplier for €5,000 and agrees to pay in euros when the exchange rate is $1.4500/euro. Sundance records the following in its books:

Purchases	7,250	
Accounts payable		7,250
€ 5,000 @ 1.4500		

If Sundance pays immediately, there's no problem. But what happens if the exporter extends 30 days' credit to Sundance? If the rate changed to, say, $1.5000/euro by the time the payment was due, Sundance would record a final settlement as:

Accounts payable	7,250	
Foreign-exchange loss	250	
Cash		7,500

The merchandise stays at the original value of $7,250, but there is a difference between the dollar value of the account payable to the exporter ($7,250) and the actual number of dollars the importer must come up with to purchase the euros to pay the exporter ($7,500). The difference between the two accounts ($250) is the loss on foreign exchange and is recognized in the income statement.

Foreign-currency receivables and payables give rise to gains and losses whenever the exchange rate changes. Transaction gains and losses must be included in the income statement in the accounting period in which they arise.

The company that denominates the sale or purchase in the foreign currency (in this case, the importer) must recognize the gains and losses arising from foreign-currency transactions at the end of each accounting period. In the example here, assume that the end of the quarter has arrived and Sundance has still not paid the French exporter. The skis continue to be valued at $7,250, but the payable has to be updated to the new exchange rate of $1.5000/euro. The journal entry would be:

Foreign-exchange loss	250	
Accounts payable		250

The payable would now be worth $7,500. If settlement were made in the month following the end of the quarter and the exchange rate remained the same, the final entry would be:

Accounts payable	7,500	
Cash		7,500

If the U.S. company were an exporter and anticipated receiving foreign currency, the corresponding entries (using the same information as in the example here) would be:

Accounts receivable	7,250	
Sales		7,250
Cash	7,500	
Foreign-exchange gain		250
Accounts receivable		7,250

In this case, a gain results because the company received more cash than if it had collected its money immediately.

CORRECT PROCEDURES FOR U.S. COMPANIES

According to U.S. GAAP, U.S. companies must record the initial transaction at the spot exchange rate in effect on the transaction date and record receivables and payables on subsequent balance-sheet dates at the spot exchange rate on those dates. Any foreign-exchange gains and losses are recognized in the income statement in that period.[18] This is basically the same procedure required by the IASB as well as in IAS 21.[19]

TRANSLATING FOREIGN-CURRENCY FINANCIAL STATEMENTS

Even though U.S.-based MNEs receive reports originally developed in a variety of different currencies, they eventually must end up with one set of financial statements in U.S. dollars to help management and investors understand their worldwide activities in a common currency. The process of restating foreign-currency financial statements into U.S. dollars is called **translation**. The combination of all of these translated financial statements into one is **consolidation**. The same concept exists for other countries, such as a British-based MNE that has to come up with a set of financial statements in British pounds. For the sake of illustration, we use a U.S.-based MNE.

Translation in the United States is a two-step process:

1. *Recast foreign-currency financial statements into statements consistent with U.S. GAAP.*
2. *Translate all foreign-currency amounts into U.S. dollars.* FASB Statement No. 52 describes how companies must translate their foreign-currency financial statements into dollars. All U.S. companies, as well as foreign firms that list on a U.S. exchange, must use Statement No. 52.

TRANSLATION METHODS

Statement No. 52 and IAS 21, the relevant translation standards issued by the FASB and the IASB, respectively, are basically the same in how they require MNEs to translate their foreign-currency financial statements into the currency of the parent's country. For simplicity's sake, we continue to use the example of a U.S.-based MNE that must translate its foreign-currency financial statements into U.S. dollars.

The FASB requires that U.S. companies report foreign-currency transactions at the original spot exchange rate and that subsequent gains and losses on foreign-currency receivables or payables be put on the income statement. The same procedure must be followed according to IFRS.

Translation—the process of restating foreign-currency financial statements.

Consolidation—the process of combining the translated financial statements of a parent and its subsidiaries into one set of financial statements.

The functional currency is the currency of the primary economic environment in which the entity operates.

The current-rate method applies when the local currency is the functional currency.

The temporal method applies when the parent's reporting currency is the functional currency.

Two Methods: Current-Rate and Temporal   Both standards allow companies to use either of two methods in the translation process: the **current-rate method** (called the *closing rate method* under IFRS) or the **temporal method**. The one the company chooses depends on the **functional currency** of the foreign operation, which is the currency of the primary economic environment in which that entity operates. Whichever method a company uses, it has to determine the proper exchange rate to translate the foreign-currency balances into U.S. dollars.

For example, one of Coca-Cola's largest operations outside the United States is in Japan. Its primary economic environment is Japan, and its functional currency is the Japanese yen. FASB identifies several factors that can help management determine the functional currency: cash flows, sales prices, sales market data, expenses, financing, and transactions with other entities within the corporate group. If the cash flows and expenses are primarily in the foreign operation's currency, that is the functional currency; if they are in the parent's currency, that is the functional currency.

If the functional currency (the Japanese yen in the case of Coca-Cola) is that of the local operating environment (Japan), the company must use the current-rate method, which provides that it translates all assets and liabilities at the current exchange rate, which is the spot exchange rate on the balance-sheet date. All income-statement items are translated at the average exchange rate, and owners' equity is translated at the rates in effect when the company issued capital stock and accumulated retained earnings.

If the functional currency is the parent's currency, the MNE must use the temporal method, which provides that only monetary assets (cash, marketable securities, and receivables) and liabilities are translated at the current exchange rate. The company translates inventory, property, plants, and equipment at the historical exchange rates (the transaction rate in IASB terminology), which are the rates in effect when the assets were acquired. In general, the company translates most income-statement accounts at the average exchange rate, but it translates cost of goods sold and depreciation expense, as well as owners' equity, at the appropriate historical exchange rates.

Because companies can choose the translation method that's most appropriate for a particular foreign subsidiary, they don't have to pick just the temporal or the current-rate method. Coca-Cola faces this problem because it sells its products in over 200 countries and uses 71 different functional currencies.[20]

Figure 19.3 summarizes the selection of translation method, depending on the choice of functional currency. As in the preceding explanation, if the functional currency is the currency of the country where the foreign subsidiary is located, the current-rate method applies. If it is the reporting currency of the parent company, the temporal method applies.

FIGURE 19.3   Selecting a Translation Method

When an MNE receives reports from subsidiaries or branches located in different countries, the accounting department is faced with financial figures stated in different currencies. Accountants must translate these foreign-currency figures into amounts stated in the currency of the parent's home country. The functional currency, which may be either the currency of the economic environment in which the subsidiary or branch operates or the parent firm's currency, will determine the translation method that the company will use.

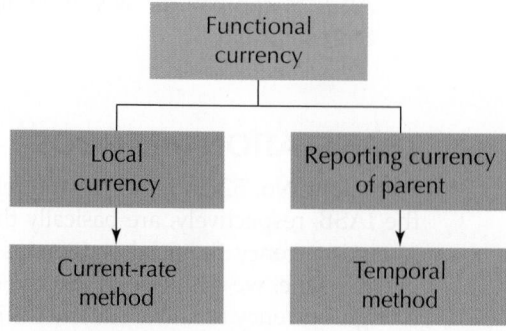

The Translation Process Tables 19.1 and 19.2 show a balance sheet and income statement developed under both approaches to compare the differences in translation methods. The beginning balance in retained earnings for both methods is assumed to be $40,000. The following exchange rates are used to perform the translation process in Tables 19.1 and 19.2:

- $1.5000—Historical exchange rate when fixed assets were acquired and capital stock issued
- $1.6980—Current exchange rate on December 31, 2014
- $1.5617—Average exchange rate during 2015
- $1.5606—Exchange rate during which the ending inventory was acquired
- $1.5600—Historical exchange rate for cost of goods sold

Because the foreign currency was rising in value (strengthening) between the time the capital stock was issued ($1.5000) and the end of the year ($1.6980), the balance sheet reflects a positive accumulated translation adjustment under the current-rate method. This is consistent with the idea that net assets were gaining value in a strong currency.

TABLE 19.1 Translating Foreign Currency: The Balance Sheet

	Foreign Currency	Temporal Method		Current-Rate Method	
		Rate	Dollars	Rate	Dollars
Cash	20,000	1.6980	33,960	1.6980	33,960
Accounts receivable	40,000	1.6980	67,920	1.6980	67,920
Inventories	40,000	1.5606	62,424	1.6980	67,920
Fixed assets	100,000	1.5000	150,000	1.6980	169,800
Accumulated depreciation	(20,000)	1.5000	(30,000)	1.6980	(33,960)
Total Assets	**180,000**		**284,304**		**305,960**
Accounts payable	30,000	1.6980	50,940	1.6980	50,940
Long-term debt	44,000	1.6980	74,712	1.6980	74,712
Capital stock	60,000	1.5000	90,000	1.5000	90,000
Retained earnings	46,000	*	68,652	*	77,481
Accumulated translation adjustment					12,507
Total Liabilities and Owners' Equity	**180,000**		**284,304**		**305,640**

Retained earnings is the U.S. dollar equivalent of all income earned in prior years retained in the business rather than distributed to shareholders plus this year's income. There is no single exchange rate used to translate retained earnings into dollars.

TABLE 19.2 Translating Foreign Currency: The Income Statement

	Foreign Currency	Temporal Method		Current-Rate Method	
		Rate	Dollars	Rate	Dollars
Sales	230,000	1.5617	359,191	1.5617	359,191
Expenses:					
Cost of goods sold	(110,000)	1.5600	(171,600)	1.5617	(171,787)
Depreciation	(10,000)	1.5000	(15,000)	1.5617	(15,617)
Other	(80,000)	1.5617	(124,936)	1.5617	(124,936)
Taxes	(6,000)	1.5617	(9,370)	1.5617	(9,370)
Translation gain (loss)			(9,633)		
Net Income	**24,000**		**28,652**		**37,481**

Note that under the temporal method, the ending retained earnings balance of $68,652 in Table 19.1 is found by subtracting the translated values of accounts payable, long-term debt, and capital stock from total assets. In Table 19.2, net income is found by subtracting the beginning retained earnings balance ($40,000) from the ending retained earnings balance ($68,652). When translating the income-statement accounts in Table 19.2, however, it is necessary to plug in the translation loss of $9,633 to get the net-income figure of $28,652. In the case of the current-rate method, net income is found in Table 19.2 by subtracting translated expenses from revenues. There is no translation gain or loss on the income statement, as will be explained below. On the balance sheet in Table 19.1, the retained earnings balance of $77,841 is found by adding net income ($37,481) to the beginning retained earnings balance ($40,000). However, total assets must equal total liabilities and owners' equity, so the accumulated translation adjustment of $12,507 must be plugged in to get the right total balance.

> With the current-rate method, the translation gain or loss is recognized in comprehensive income rather than net income, and therefore it goes to owners' equity. With the temporal method, the translation gain or loss is recognized on the income statement.

Disclosing Foreign-Exchange Gains and Losses   A major difference between the two translation methods is in the recognition of foreign-exchange gains and losses. Under the current-rate method, the gain or loss is called an *accumulated translation adjustment* and is taken to comprehensive income rather than net income, so it appears as a separate line item in owners' equity. This is important because the accumulated translation adjustment does not affect earnings per share, a key figure that financial analysts monitor. From a cultural perspective, this points out how important net income is to U.S.-based companies, which rely on the stock market as a major source of funding. Under the temporal method, the gain or loss is taken directly to net income and thus affects earnings per share.

INTERNATIONAL FINANCIAL ISSUES

In Chapter 10, we examined the finance function from the standpoint of global capital markets. In this section, we will discuss some of the important treasury functions, including capital budgeting, cash flows and global cash management, and foreign-exchange risk management.

CAPITAL BUDGETING IN A GLOBAL CONTEXT

> Capital budgeting—the process whereby MNEs determine which projects and countries will receive capital investment funds.

Capital budgeting is the technique that helps the MNE determine which projects and countries will receive its capital investment funds. The parent company must compare the net present value or internal rate of return of a potential foreign project with that of its other projects around the world to determine the best place to invest resources.

Methods of Capital Budgeting

> Capital budgeting techniques:
> - Payback period
> - Net present value of a project
> - Internal rate of return

Payback Period   One approach to capital budgeting is to determine the **payback period** of a project, or the number of years required to recover the initial investment made. This is typically done by estimating the annual after-tax free cash flow from the investment, determining the present value of the future cash flow for each year, and then determining how many years it will take to recoup the initial investment.

Net Present Value   A second approach is to determine the **net present value (NPV)** of a project, which is defined as follows:

$$NPV = \sum_{t=1}^{n} \frac{FCF_t}{(1 + k)^t} - IO$$

where FCF_t = the annual free cash flow in time period t

k = the appropriate discount rate; that is, the required rate of return or cost of capital

IO = the initial cash outlay

n = the project's expected life

The required rate of return is the rate the company must get from the project to justify the cost of raising the initial investment or at least maintaining the value of its common stock. If the NPV is positive, the project is also considered positive. If the NPV is negative, the company should not enter into the project.

Internal Rate of Return   A third approach is to compute the internal rate of return (IRR) of the project—the rate that equates the present value of future cash flows with the present value of the initial investment—and compare it with the required rate of return. If it is greater than the required rate of return, the investment is considered positive. However, the company then needs to compare the IRR with that of competing projects in other countries.

Several things are common about each of the methods. First, the firm needs to determine the free cash flows, which involves estimating those flows as well as bringing into the equation different tax rates from different countries. Second, in the case of both NPV and IRR, the company needs to determine what the required rate of return is.

MNEs need to determine free cash flows based on cash-flow estimates and tax rates in different countries and an appropriate required rate of return adjusted for risk.

Complications in Capital Budgeting   Several aspects of capital budgeting are unique to foreign-project assessment:

- Parent cash flows (those from the project back to the parent in the parent's currency) must be distinguished from project cash flows (those in local currency from the sale of goods and services). Will the decision be based on one, the other, or both?

- Remittance of funds to the parent, such as dividends, interest on loans, and payment of intracompany receivables and payables, is affected by differing tax systems, legal and political constraints on the movement of funds, local business norms, and differences in how financial markets and institutions function. In addition, tax systems affect free cash flows on the project, irrespective of the remittance issue.

- Differing rates of inflation must be anticipated by both the parent and the subsidiary because of their importance in causing changes in competitive position and cash flows over time.

- The parent must consider the possibility of unanticipated exchange-rate changes because of their direct effects on the value of cash flows and their indirect effects on the foreign subsidiary's competitive position.

- The parent company must evaluate political risk in a target market because political events can drastically reduce the value or availability of expected cash flows.

- The terminal value (the value of the project at the end of the budgeting period) is difficult to estimate because potential purchasers from host, home, or third countries—or from the private or public sector—may have widely divergent perspectives on the project's value. The terminal value is critical in determining the total cash flows from the project. The total cash outlay is partially offset by the terminal value—the amount of cash the parent company can get from the subsidiary or project if it eventually sells.[21]

Determine different cash flow scenarios or adjust the hurdle rate (the minimum required rate of return for a project).

Because of all the forces listed here, it's very difficult to estimate future cash flows. There are two ways to deal with the variations in future cash flows. One is to set out several different scenarios and then determine the payback period, net present value, or internal rate of return of the project. The other less appropriate approach is to adjust the hurdle rate, which is the minimum required rate of return the project must achieve for it to receive capital. The adjustment is usually made by increasing the hurdle rate above its minimal level. This is easier than estimating cash flows, but it is also the easy way out.

Once the budget is complete, the MNE must examine both the return in local currency and the return to the parent in dollars from cash flows. Examining the return in local currency will give management a chance to compare the project with other investment alternatives in the country. However, cash flows to the parent are important, since dividends are paid to shareholders from those flows. If the MNE cannot generate a sufficient return to the parent in the parent's currency, it will eventually fall behind in its ability to pay shareholders and pay off corporate debt. Finally, the decision must be made in the strategic context of the investment, not just the financial context.

INTERNAL SOURCES OF FUNDS

| Funds are working capital, or current assets minus current liabilities.

Although the term *funds* usually means "cash," it is used in a much broader sense in business and generally refers to working capital—that is, current assets minus current liabilities.[22] From a general perspective, funds come from the normal operations of a business (selling merchandise or services) as well as from financing activities, such as borrowing money, issuing bonds, or issuing shares. They are used to purchase fixed assets, pay employees, buy materials and supplies, and invest in marketable securities or long-term investments.

Cash Flows and the MNE   Cash flows in an MNE are significantly more complex than for a company that operates in a strictly domestic environment. An MNE that wants to expand operations or needs additional capital can look not only to the domestic and international debt and equity markets but also to sources within itself. The complexity of its internal sources is magnified because of the number of its subsidiaries and the diverse environments in which they operate.

| Sources of internal funds:
| • Loans
| • Investments through equity capital
| • Intercompany receivables and payables
| • Dividends

Figure 19.4 shows a parent company that has two foreign subsidiaries. All three may be increasing funds through normal operations that may be used on a company-wide basis, perhaps through loans. The parent can lend funds directly to one subsidiary or guarantee an outside loan to the other. Equity capital from the parent is another source of funds for the subsidiary.

Funds can also go from subsidiary to parent. A subsidiary could declare a dividend to the parent as a return on capital, or lend cash directly to it. If the subsidiary declared a dividend, the parent could lend the funds back. The dividend would not be tax deductible to the subsidiary, but it would be included as income to the parent, so the parent would have to pay tax on the dividend. If the subsidiary lent money to the parent, the interest paid by the parent would be tax deductible for the parent and taxable income for the subsidiary.

FIGURE 19.4   How the MNE Handles Its Funds (I): Internal Funds

Funds consist of working capital that comes from normal business operations and that may be used to purchase assets and materials, to pay employees, and to make investments. If the company is an MNE, funds may come from either parent or subsidiary operations, or both, and can be used by the parent to support either its own operations or those of its subsidiaries.

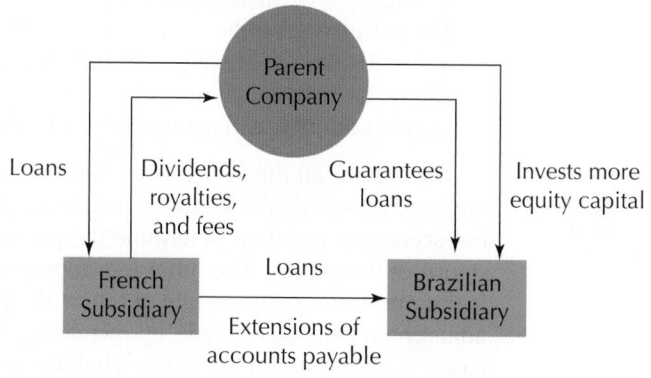

Merchandise, people, and financial flows can travel between subsidiaries, giving rise to receivables and payables. Companies can move money between and among related entities by paying quickly, or they can accumulate funds by deferring payment. They can also adjust the size of the payment by arbitrarily raising or lowering the price of intercompany transactions in comparison with the market price.

GLOBAL CASH MANAGEMENT

Managing cash effectively is a chief concern of the CFO, who must answer the following three questions:

1. What are the local and corporate system needs for cash?
2. How can the cash be withdrawn from subsidiaries and centralized?
3. Once the cash has been centralized, what should be done with it?

The cash manager, who reports to the treasurer, must collect and pay cash in the company's normal operational cycle and then deal with financial institutions. Before remitting any cash into the MNE's control center—whether at regional or headquarters level—the cash manager must first assess local cash needs through cash budgets and forecasts. Because the forecast projects the excess cash that will be available, the cash manager will know how much can be invested for short-term profits.

Once local cash needs are met, the cash manager must decide whether to allow the local manager to invest any excess cash or have it remitted to a central cash pool. If the cash is centralized, the manager must find a way to make the transfer. A cash dividend is the easiest way to distribute cash, but government restrictions may interfere. For example, foreign exchange controls may prevent the company from remitting as large a dividend as it would like. Cash can also be remitted through royalties, management fees, and repayment of principal and interest on loans.

Multilateral Netting   An important cash-management strategy is **netting** cash flows internationally. For example, an MNE with operations in four European countries could

> Cash budgets and forecasts are essential in assessing a company's cash needs. Dividends are a good source of intercompany transfers, but governments often restrict their free movement.

Brussels, Belgium is the home of the Grand Palace and is a major cash management center for MNEs operating in Europe. It's low tax rates coupled with its prime location, political and economic stability, access to international banking and communications, and a well-defined legal system make it ideal.

Source: S-F/Shutterstock

FIGURE 19.5 How the MNE Handles Its Funds (II): Multilateral Cash Flows

As the various subsidiaries of the MNE go about their business, cash can be transferred among them for a variety of reasons (e.g., in the form of loans or as proceeds from the sale of goods). Cash, of course, can flow in any direction, and if the MNE doesn't maintain some kind of cash-management center, each subsidiary must settle its accounts (receivables, payable, etc.) independently.

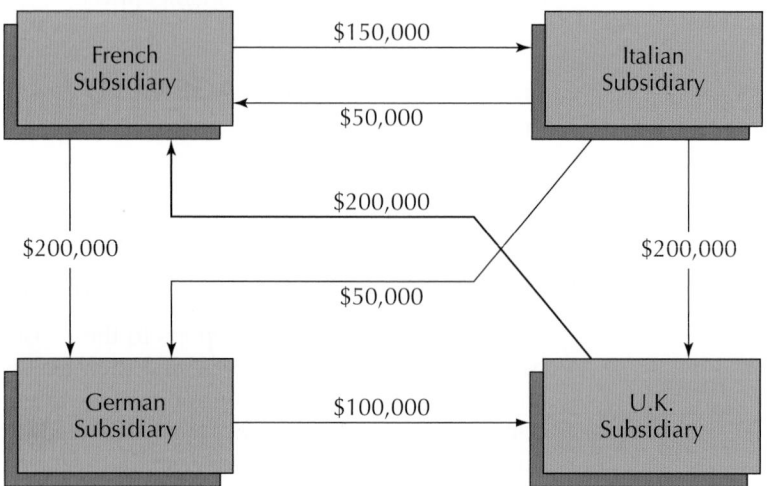

Multilateral netting—the process of coordinating cash inflows and outflows among the subsidiaries so that only net cash is transferred, reducing transaction costs.

Netting requires sophisticated software and good banking relationships in different countries.

have several different intercompany cash transfers resulting from loans, the sale of goods, licensing agreements, and so forth. In the illustration in Figure 19.5, for example, there are no fewer than seven different transfers among four subsidiaries. Among its special services, GPS Capital Markets Inc., helps clients determine their foreign-currency cash flows and assists them in developing strategies to net cash flows by minimizing the number of their foreign-currency transactions.

Table 19.3 identifies the total receivables, payables, and net position for each subsidiary. Rather than have each subsidiary settle its accounts independently with subsidiaries in other countries, many MNEs are establishing cash-management centers in one city (such as Brussels) to coordinate cash flows among subsidiaries from several countries.

Figure 19.6 illustrates how each subsidiary in a net payable position transfers funds to the central clearing account. The account manager then transfers funds to the accounts of the net receiver subsidiaries. In this example, only four transfers need to take place. The clearing account manager receives transaction information and computes the net position of each subsidiary at least monthly, then orchestrates the settlement process. The transfers

TABLE 19.3 How the MNE Handles Its Funds (III): Net Positions

Assume that these data are from the same MNE as the one introduced in Figure 19.5. Because the company has no cash-management center, *net positions*—the difference between *total receivables* and *total payables*—must be determined on a subsidiary-by-subsidiary basis.

Subsidiary	Total Receivables	Total Payables	Net Position
French	250,000	350,000	(100,000)
German	250,000	100,000	150,000
Italian	150,000	300,000	(150,000)
U.K.	300,000	200,000	100,000

FIGURE 19.6   How the MNE Handles Its Funds (IV): Multilateral Netting

Dissatisfied with the process represented in Figure 19.5, our MNE has now established a cash-management center—a *clearing account*—into which each subsidiary transfers its net cash. Naturally, the MNE may in turn distribute the total to support subsidiary operations.

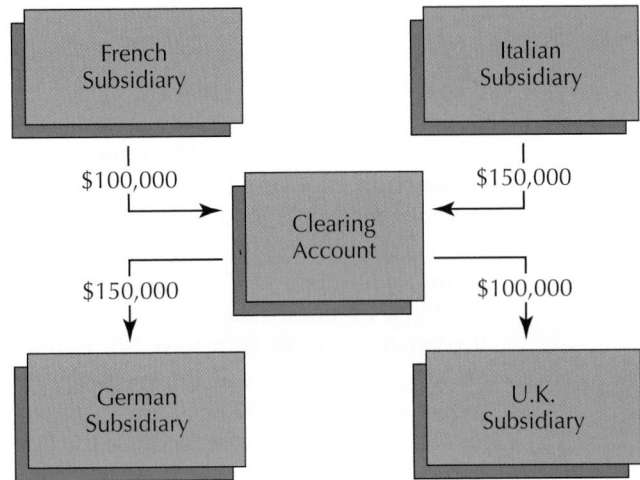

CONCEPT CHECK

In Chapter 8, we explain why it's important for MNEs to anticipate exchange-rate changes and make decisions about business activities that may be sensitive to those changes—decisions, for instance, about the sourcing of raw materials and components or the location of manufacturing and assembly facilities. We take up the same theme on p. 388 in Chapter 13, where we cite exchange-rate movement as just one factor that can affect wages in a particular country—and thus any advantage in labor-cost differences that a company might hope to gain from locating operations in that country.

Three types of foreign-exchange exposure:

• Translation
• Transaction
• Economic or operational

Translation exposure arises because the dollar value of the exposed asset or liability changes as the exchange rate changes.

take place in the payor's currency, and the foreign-exchange conversion takes place centrally. For netting to work, the company needs to match its cash needs with software that can track and transfer funds and with banking relationships that allow money to be moved among corporate entities.

FOREIGN-EXCHANGE RISK MANAGEMENT

As illustrated earlier, global cash-management strategy focuses on the flow of money for specific operating objectives. Another important objective of an MNE's financial strategy is to protect against the foreign-exchange risks of investing abroad. The strategies an MNE adopts to do this may mean the internal movement of funds as well as the use of one or more of the foreign-exchange instruments, such as options and forward contracts.

TYPES OF EXPOSURE

If all exchange rates were fixed in relation to one another, there would be no foreign-exchange risk. However, rates are not fixed, and currency values change frequently. A change in the exchange rate can result in three different exposures for a company: *translation, transaction,* and *economic* or *operational*.

Translation Exposure   Foreign-currency financial statements are translated into the reporting currency of the parent company (assumed to be USD for U.S. companies) so they can be combined with financial statements of other companies in the corporate group to form the consolidated financial statements. **Translation exposure** occurs because exposed accounts—those translated at the current exchange rate—either gain or lose value in dollars when the exchange rate changes.

Consider the example of a U.S. company with a subsidiary in Mexico. The subsidiary keeps its books in pesos, but it has to translate the financial statements into dollars so the parent can combine the results of the Mexican subsidiary with its operations from around the world. Assume the subsidiary has 900,000 pesos in the bank. So what is the effect of a change in the exchange rate on the dollar equivalent of the cash? If the exchange rate before the change was 18.5 pesos per dollar ($48,649) and the rate changes to 20 pesos per dollar (a weakening of the peso against the dollar), the cash would only be worth $45,000. The subsidiary still has pesos in the bank account, but the dollar equivalent of the peso has fallen, resulting in a loss. The gain or loss does not represent an actual cash flow effect because the pesos are only translated, not converted, into dollars. In addition, reported earnings can either rise or fall against the dollar because of the translation effect, which can affect earnings per share and stock prices.

> Transaction exposure arises when a transaction is denominated in a foreign currency and where the settlement gives rises to a cash flow gain or loss.

Transaction Exposure   Denominating a transaction in a foreign currency gives rise to **transaction exposure** because the company has accounts receivable or payable in foreign currency that must be settled eventually. Consider the example of a U.S. exporter delivering merchandise to a British importer for $500,000 when the exchange rate is $1.9000 per pound (equivalent to £263,158). If the exporter were to receive payment in dollars, there would be no immediate effect to the exporter if the dollar/pound exchange rate changed. If payment were to be received in pounds, however, the exporter might incur a foreign-exchange gain or loss. If the exchange rate when the exporter receives the pounds from the importer falls to $1.8800, the exporter would only receive $494,737, which would be a loss of $5,263. In this case, because the pound is falling in value, the exporter would receive fewer dollars from the sale after the change in the exchange rate. This would be an actual cash flow loss to the exporter.

> Economic, or operating, exposure arises from the effects of exchange-rate changes on
> - future cash flows,
> - the sourcing of parts and components,
> - the location of investments,
> - the competitive position of the company in different markets.

Economic (or Operating) Exposure   **Economic exposure**, also known as **operating exposure**, is the potential for change in expected cash flows that arises from the pricing of products, the sourcing and cost of inputs, and the location of investments. Pricing strategies have both immediate and long-term effects on cash flows. In the example above, if the exporter decides to receive payment in dollars, the foreign-exchange risk would pass to the importer. However, the *importer* would have to come up with more pounds at the new exchange rate (£265,957) than at the original exchange rate. Now, the importer can either sell the product at the original price and not earn as much profit, or it can raise the price and hope that consumers will be willing to pay it. The *exporter*, however, also has two choices. It can continue to sell the merchandise at the same price, or it can lower it. If it lowers the price, it will incur a lower profit margin. If it continues to sell at the same price, the importer will have to pay more for the merchandise, then decide what to do.

Another economic-exposure decision involves how to make investment decisions. In 2011, Volkswagen AG decided to open a factory in the United States to take advantage of the strong euro versus the dollar. Because of the strength of the euro, it had not been cost-competitive in the United States, and it realized that by opening a factory in Tennessee, it could take advantage of the strong euro as well as lower labor costs. Thus they were generating revenues in a weak currency and costs in a strong currency, severely affecting earnings. One of the economic solutions was to expand manufacturing operations in the United States to balance revenues and expenses in the same currency.[23]

EXPOSURE-MANAGEMENT STRATEGY

> To protect assets from exchange-rate risk, management needs to
> - define and measure exposure,
> - establish a reporting system,
> - adopt an overall policy on exposure management,
> - formulate hedging strategies.

To adequately protect assets against the risks from translation, transaction, and economic exposure to exchange-rate fluctuations, management must do the following:

- Define and measure exposure
- Organize and implement a reporting system that monitors exposure and exchange-rate movements
- Adopt a policy assigning responsibility for minimizing—or hedging—exposure
- Formulate strategies for hedging exposure

All three types of exposure must be monitored and measured separately.

Define and Measure Exposure

To develop a viable hedging strategy, an MNE must forecast the degree of exposure in each major currency in which it operates. Because the types differ, the actual exposure by currency must be tracked separately. For example, the firm should keep track of the translation exposure in Brazilian reals separately from the transaction exposure because it will result in an actual cash flow, whereas the translation exposure may not. Thus, the company generates one report for each type of exposure. It may also adopt different hedging strategies for the different types. Recall that GPS Capital Markets developed proprietary software, called FXpert, which not only conducts specialized audits of clients' foreign-exchange cash flows but proposes effective hedging strategies for improving them. Solutions may include such well-known hedging strategies as forwards, options, and futures contracts.

Exchange-rate movements are forecasted using in-house or external experts.

A key aspect of measuring exposure is forecasting exchange rates. A company should estimate and use ranges within which it expects a currency to vary over the forecasting period by developing in-house capabilities to monitor exchange rates or using economists who also try to obtain a consensus of exchange-rate movements from the banks they deal with. Their concern is to forecast the direction, magnitude, and timing of an exchange-rate change.

The reporting system should use both central control and input from foreign operations.

Organize and Implement a Reporting System

Once the company has decided how to define and measure exposure and estimate future exchange rates, it must create a reporting system that will assist in protecting it against risk. To achieve this goal, substantial participation from foreign operations must be combined with effective central control.

Hedging strategies can be operational or financial.

Formulate Hedging Strategies

Once a company has identified its level of exposure and determined which exposure is critical, it can hedge its position by adopting operational and/or financial strategies, each with cost-benefit as well as operational implications. The safest position is a balanced one in which exposed assets equal exposed liabilities.

Operational strategies include
- using local debt to balance local assets,
- taking advantage of leads and lags for intercompany payments.

Operational Hedging Strategies

The use of debt to balance exposure is an interesting strategy. Many companies "borrow locally," especially in weak-currency countries, because that helps them avoid foreign-exchange risk from borrowing in a foreign currency and balances their exposed position in assets and earnings. One problem with this strategy is that, because interest rates in weak-currency countries tend to be high, there must be a trade-off between the cost of borrowing and the potential loss from exchange-rate variations.

Protecting against loss from transaction exposure becomes complex. In dealing with foreign customers, it is always safest for the company to denominate the transaction in its own currency to avoid any foreign-exchange exposure. The risk shifts to the foreign customer that has to come up with the company's currency. Or the company could denominate purchases in a weaker currency and sales in a stronger one. If forced to make purchases in a strong currency and sales in a weak one, it could resort to contractual measures such as forward contracts or options, or it could try to balance its inflows and outflows through astute sales and purchasing strategies.

A lead strategy means collecting or paying early. A lag strategy means collecting or paying late.

Leads and Lags

Other operational strategies protect cash flows among related entities, such as a parent and subsidiaries. A **lead strategy** means either collecting foreign-currency receivables before they are due when the foreign currency is expected to weaken, or paying foreign-currency payables before they are due when it is expected to strengthen. With a **lag strategy**, a company either delays collection of foreign-currency receivables if that currency is expected to strengthen, or delays payables when it is expected to weaken. In other words, a company usually leads into and lags out of a hard currency and leads out of and lags into a weak one.

Sometimes an operational strategy means shifting assets overseas to take advantage of currency changes. As mentioned earlier, when the euro strengthened against the U.S. dollar, VW shifted some of its manufacturing to the United States.

Forward contracts can establish a fixed exchange rate for future transactions.

Using Derivatives to Hedge Foreign-Exchange Risk   In addition to the operational strategies just mentioned, a company may hedge exposure through *derivative* financial contracts such as forward contracts and options, with the most common hedge being a forward contract.

Consider a U.S. exporter selling goods to a British manufacturer for £1 million when the exchange rate is $1.9000 per £. If the exporter could collect the money right away and convert it into dollars, it would receive $1.9 million. However, if the exporter were not expected to receive payment for 90 days, it would be exposed to an exchange-rate change. One way to protect against this is to enter into a forward contract with a bank to deliver pounds and receive dollars at the forward rate of, say, $1.8500. In 90 days, the exporter would convert the pounds into dollars at $1.8500 and receive $1,850,000, which is less than it would have received at the initial spot rate. But if the pound had deteriorated even more in value, the exporter would still receive the $1.85 million. Also, the forward contract eliminates uncertainty.

Currency options can ensure access to foreign currency at a fixed exchange rate for a specific period of time.

A foreign-currency option is more flexible than a forward contract because it gives its purchaser the right, though not the obligation, to buy or sell a certain amount of foreign currency at a set exchange rate within a specified amount of time. In the same situation described above, the exporter would enter into an option contract with a trader to convert pounds into dollars at a certain exchange rate. For the cost of protection, the exporter pays a premium to the trader, which is like insurance. When the exporter receives the cash from the importer, it can decide whether to exercise the option. If the option gives it more money than the spot rate, the exporter will exercise the option. If not, it won't.

Looking to the Future
Will IFRS Become the Global Accounting Standard?

The future of accounting is complicated. It is clear that more jurisdictions use IFRS than U.S. GAAP for external financial reporting. However, the United States is no closer to allowing IFRS to be used for U.S. companies listing on U.S. stock exchanges. A major reason is that GAAP is far more comprehensive than IFRS, both in depth and breadth. Also, it responds more to the background, needs, and regulatory requirements of U.S. capital markets than do IFRS. The SEC is trying to figure out how to make it easier for U.S. MNEs to report financial information, improve disclosure, simplify financial reporting, and move toward a single global accounting standard.[24] This sounds almost impossible. However, one possibility would be to "drop the reconciliation requirement, letting companies supplement their U.S. financial reports with ones filed with U.S. regulators using international standards." As noted by the director of global accounting for Ford Motor Company, "we are concerned that providing both international accounting standards and U.S. GAAP financial data could be complicated."[25] Complicated, yes; impossible, no.

An important aspect of financial reporting in the United States is an independent auditing profession that examines internal control processes and ensures the accuracy of the financial records of a firm. A major concern with IFRS is the enforceability of the standards by an independent accounting profession. Simply generating a set of accounting rules is not enough if the auditing profession in each country is not good enough to verify the accuracy of the financial information. This can be seen in recent cases brought by the SEC against Chinese firms that are listing on the NYSE. U.S.-based audit firms use local Chinese auditors to perform audits of Chinese companies that list on the NYSE as well as on the Chinese subsidiaries of U.S. MNEs. The local Chinese audit firms would not provide documents to the SEC because Chinese law prohibited them from doing so. The SEC levied fines against the Big 4 PWC, Deloitte, KPMG, and E&Y and threatened to suspend the Chinese audit firms from auditing U.S. traded Chinese companies.[26]

The major vote in favor of U.S. GAAP is that half the world's stock market capitalization is located in the United States, and companies that want access to U.S. capital must play by U.S. rules. Americans have always felt that their standards were the best in the world and that it would be unfair for U.S. companies competing for cash in the U.S. market to allow foreign companies to list using IFRS. However, the decision by the SEC to allow foreign firms to list in the United States if they use full IFRS is a major game changer. As European stock markets continue to grow in importance, more European companies are choosing to list in Europe where they can use IFRS instead of in the United States where there are more regulatory requirements.

An additional complication to combining or converging IFRS and U.S. GAAP is the Sarbanes–Oxley Act of 2002. Requiring companies to establish solid internal controls over financial reporting, this legislation limits the types of services that may be performed by primary auditors in addition to the financial-statement audit, and requires the managers of publicly traded companies to assess internal controls and make a statement on this assessment, which must be examined and opined on by external auditors. Foreign issuers are required to abide by some of the key provisions of Sarbanes–Oxley, but they are given some concessions which decrease the burden on listed companies.[27] In addition, foreign issuers don't have to provide quarterly reports and they can file their annual reports as a 20-F.

The convergence project between the FASB and IASB may solve some of these problems in the long run. To its credit, the IASB has expanded coverage of key topics and has narrowed the alternatives available to companies. It has sold itself as based on *principles* rather than *rules,* although it is more accurate to say that the standards are simpler and less comprehensive. FASB and IASB are narrowing the differences in existing standards and developing new ones together. Now they jointly write new standards so that even the wording is the same. In addition, public accounting firms and publicly traded companies have several years of experience in adopting the requirements of Sarbanes–Oxley, so who knows what the future will bring?

Swedish-based H&M places trendy stores in trendy locations. This store in Liverpool, England, is one of H&M's 4000 stores in 61 countries.

Source: Julius Kielaitis/Alamy Stock Photo

CASE

H&M: The Challenges of Global Expansion and the Move to Adopt International Financial Reporting Standards

Hennes & Mauritz AB (also known as H&M), the Swedish MNE that is a fashion trendsetter, has a stated goal "to give customers unbeatable value by offering fashion and quality at the best price." It doesn't own any factories, but rather outsources production to independent suppliers, primarily in Asia and Europe. H&M also rents space from international and local landlords rather than owning its own stores.[28]

H&M is a major firm in the apparel retail market where fashion trends are critical and where goods move quickly. In this industry, the key buyers are consumers, the key suppliers are clothing manufacturers and wholesalers, designers are king, and a fast, well-organized supply chain is essential. Depending on the individual firm strategy, the apparel retail market doesn't have to be capital intensive, but the largest players in the industry are very international, both in retail footprint and suppliers. The biggest companies in the industry are U.S.-based The Gap; H&M; and Spain-based Industria de Diseno Textil, S.A. (Inditex), better known by its flagship brand, Zara. All three companies have different store brands: Gap, Banana Republic, Old Navy, and Athleta for The Gap; H&M, COS (collection of style), Monki, Weekday, and Cheap Monday for H&M; and Zara, Bershka, Pull and bear, Massimo Dutti, Stradivarius, Oysho, Zara Home and Uterque for Inditex.

Global Spread and Strategy

Both of H&M's competitors are very international. H&M operates about 4,000 stores in 61 markets, whereas The Gap operates 3,300 company stores and over 400 franchise stores worldwide, and Inditex operates in a network of over 7,000 stores in 85 countries. Zara has the largest geographic spread within Inditex with stores in 73 countries.

Hennes & Mauritz AB started as a single women's wear store in Sweden in 1947. Today, H&M's business is much broader and currently includes the sales of clothing, accessories, footwear, cosmetics, and home textiles. Although H&M is known as one of Sweden's premier MNEs, in 2015 it generated 17.6 percent of its sales in Germany, 12 percent in the United States, and 7.6 percent in the United Kingdom.

H&M and Zara have very different strategies. Zara delivers new products to its stores twice a week. Because of its highly organized supply chain, Zara only takes 10–15 days to go from design to the stores. Although it sources its apparel from around the world, it has adopted just-in-time manufacturing from the auto industry and established 14 highly automated Spanish factories where robots cut and dye fabrics creating the unfinished "gray goods" which are the foundation for their final products. It then takes the gray goods and outsources them to a network of small shops in Portugal and Spain to do the finish work. Store managers are constantly sending updated information on consumer demand so that they can move to the next hot fashion. The rule at Zara is that if you see it in the store and you like it, you'd better buy it because as soon as it is gone, you'll never see it again. Veteran Zara consumers keep track of when new shipments come in so they can buy the latest stuff. H&M is trendy, but it outsources production to a network of over 800 suppliers, 60 percent of which are in Asia. It offers a main collection twice a year in the spring and the fall with several sub-collections that allow it to bring in new trendy items. Longer lead time items are produced in Asia, whereas short lead time items are manufactured in Europe.

Currently the second-largest apparel retailer behind Inditex, H&M has met its target growth rate of 10–15 percent per year, with no plans of slowing its expansion—growing from 2,800 to 4,000 stores in the past three years. Despite its global presence, H&M is listed in the Stockholm Stock Exchange and Nasdaq Stockholm. H&M adopted the EU's version of IFRS and presents its financial statements in both English and Swedish. The financial statements are reported in Swedish kronor, which also serve as its functional currency. Because the retail industry is less capital intensive, most companies have no need to list in any foreign stock exchanges. Inditex lists only on the stock exchanges throughout its home country, Spain, including Madrid, Barcelona, Bilbao, and Valencia. Consistent with domestic listings, The Gap, which was founded in the United States in 1969, is listed solely on the NYSE.

The ability to list solely in the country in which a company is domiciled can simplify the financial reporting process by avoiding the need to present financial statements that adhere to the accounting rules of multiple countries. Ericsson, another popular Swedish MNE, required much more capital and was therefore listed on both the Stockholm exchange in Sweden as well as the NASDAQ in the United States as American Depositary Receipts. As a result, Ericsson has had to accommodate multiple accounting bodies and become more transparent in its reports because of its desire to raise capital on foreign exchanges.

The Gap, H&M, and Inditex come from different accounting and regulatory environments. In its 2015 annual report, H&M states that its consolidated accounts have been prepared in accordance with IFRS issued by the IASB and the interpretations provided by the IFRS Interpretations Committee. In addition, the IFRS that is used for its parent company reports are only those approved by the EU. Besides IFRS, H&M provides disclosures in accordance with the Swedish Financial Reporting Board's recommendation RFR 1. Both the parent company and consolidated balance sheets use the following format: fixed assets + current assets = equity + long term liabilities + current liabilities.

Given that Sweden is a member of the European Union, H&M was required to adopt IFRS as of 2005, which was a change from its past practices. Prior to that, H&M was using recommendations issued by the Swedish accounting standards setters which were largely based in International Accounting Standards, so the consolidated reports of H&M were already pretty much adjusted to IAS. In preparation for the switch from Swedish GAAP to IFRS, H&M began a transition process in 2003 and 2004 that was intensified in 2005. In its 2005 annual report, H&M reported that the greatest impact of the change was because of financial instruments and hedge accounting. H&M decided at that time to apply IAS 32 and IAS 39 on financial instruments. Prior to the adoption of these standards, H&M was holding derivatives for cash flow hedging, and gains and losses on derivatives were recognized when the hedged transaction took place. However, under IAS 39, all derivatives had to be recognized at fair value, so H&M commented that reported profit was probably going to be more volatile than it was when gains and losses on hedges were deferred and recognized outside the balance sheet. That is exactly the volatility that the European, especially French, banks wanted to avoid, resulting in the EU carving out the treatment of derivatives.

Before the Changeover to IFRS

Prior to the move to IFRS in 2006, H&M reported its financial results in compliance with Swedish GAAP—a bit of a mixture between Anglo-American accounting, which is driven by the capital markets, and Germanic accounting, which is driven by bank financing and taxation. Swedish reporting tends to be a little more transparent than German accounting but less transparent than Anglo-American accounting.

Issues of Transparency

One reason why Swedish accounting has been less transparent is its orientation to creditors, government, and tax authorities. In addition, because the Swedish Stock Exchange has become a focal point for listings by Nordic companies, the influential Swedish accounting profession has pushed for consolidated accounts to represent the needs of shareholders, whereas the parent-company accounts have reflected Swedish legal requirements. Swedish accounting tends to be very conservative due to the importance of taxes to fund extensive social welfare programs and the tendency of the Swedish government to use tax policies to influence investment in areas deemed important to the government and its social objectives.

Sweden and the EU

Since Sweden entered the EU, its accounting has evolved to incorporate EU accounting directives and philosophies. The Swedish government established an Accounting Standards Board (BFN) in 1976 to recommend accounting principles that fit within the framework of the Company Law. The Swedish Financial Accounting Council (RR) was established in 1991 to take over the role of the accounting profession in making recommendations on accounting practices, especially with respect to how to prepare an annual report according to the Annual Accounts Act. Now the standards are set by the Swedish Financial Reporting Board.

The Swedish Stock Exchange has supported the efforts of the profession, even though their recommendations are voluntary and subject to the Company Law. However, the decision by the EU to require firms to use IFRS for consolidated financial statements takes precedence over everything.

Conversion Costs

H&M didn't provide much information about the cost of converting to IFRS in 2005, but Ericsson did. Ericsson provided more information because it was listing on NASDAQ as well the Swedish Stock Exchange, so it had to provide Form 20F reconciliation between Swedish and U.S. GAAP. Because of its higher level of disclosure, Ericsson estimated that the conversion to IFRS in 2005 would result in a difference of about 1.5 billion Swedish kronor for 2004 net income and a difference of 5.7 billion kronor for equity as of January 1, 2005. Net income under Swedish GAAP would have been 17,539 million kronor under IFRS, compared with 19,024 million under Swedish GAAP. In addition, the recognition of cash on the balance sheet appears to be quite different under IFRS than it is under Swedish GAAP, with cash under IFRS being SEK46.1 billion less than cash under Swedish GAAP. From Ericsson's Form 20-F report, one can also see that cash at the end of 2004 was the same under U.S. GAAP and IFRS.

Costs of implementing IFRS are difficult to gauge. Many countries implemented national regulations that attempted alignment with IFRS (e.g., Sweden). Thus costs of implementation may have been spread out over several years because companies knew that full IFRS implementation was drawing near. Ericsson's management notes the following in the 2004 annual report:

> Because Swedish GAAP, in recent years, has been adapted to IFRS to a high degree and as the rules for first time adopters allows certain exemptions from full retrospective restatements, the transition from Swedish GAAP to IFRS is expected to have a relatively limited effect on our financial statements. Furthermore, we believe the conversion to IFRS will align our reporting more closely with US GAAP.

QUESTIONS

19-3. If an investor wants to compare the financial results of The Gap, Inditex, and H&M, what difference does it make that their financial statements are prepared according to different GAAP? Would you expect there to be a big difference between U.S. GAAP as used by The Gap and IFRS as used by H&M and Inditex?

19-4. What type of IFRS did H&M decide to disclose in its financial statements in 2005? In 2015?

MyLab Management

Go to **mymanagementlab.com** for the following Assisted-graded writing questions:

19-5   What are the major sources of influence on H&M's accounting standards and practices?

19-6   H&M says in its accounting policies that it uses IFRS as issued by the IASB for its consolidated accounts and, since its parent company is a company within the EU, only IFRS as approved by the EU are used in its financial statements. What difference does it make whether or not the financial statements are prepared according to full IFRS or IFRS as approved by the EU? Why does the EU insist on having a veto power over IFRS?

Endnotes

Scan for Endnotes or go to www.pearsonglobaleditions.com/Daniels

CHAPTER 20
Global Management of Human Resources

OBJECTIVES

After studying this chapter, you should be able to

20-1 Profile international human resource management

20-2 Distinguish the perspective of the expatriate

20-3 Differentiate the staffing frameworks used by MNEs

20-4 Describe expatriate selection

20-5 Appraise expatriate preparation

20-6 Summarize expatriate compensation

20-7 Profile expatriate repatriation

20-8 Describe expatriate failure

MyLab Management®

Improve Your Performance!

When you see this icon ⭐, visit **www.mymanagementlab.com** for activities that are applied, personalized, and offer immediate feedback.

A person does not seek luck; luck seeks the person.

—Turkish proverb

Source: Stephen Coburn. Shutterstock

Companies have been moving people around for centuries, capturing the benefits of putting the right person into the right job at the right place at the right time at the right pay for the right stretch. Contemporary market trends, strategic imperatives, and executive performance standards intensify this task. Today, career success requires, at the least, expanding your global awareness and, ideally, your experiential knowledge of the ways that the world works.

Globalization, by spurring trade, capital, and investment flows, expands the scope of the hundreds of thousands of existing subsidiaries that operate in the 214 markets that compose the global business environment. Each unit, established and emerging, requires executives who command the competencies to navigate economic complexities, cultural ambiguities, and political challenges, all the while maximizing the MNE's global efficiency and optimizing its local responsiveness. GE's Jeffrey Immelt explains, "A good global company does three things: It's a global sales company—meaning it's number one with customers all over the world, whether in Chicago or Paris or Tokyo. It's a global products company, with technologies, factories, and products made for the world, not just for a single region. And, most important, it's a global people company—a company that keeps getting better by capturing global markets and brains."[1]

By no means must one immediately pack up, say good-bye, and head abroad. For those who do, fear not, as an international assignment has many benefits (see Figure 20.1). Moreover, the word is out: A Gallup World Poll reports that 1.1 billion people, or one-quarter of the earth's adults, want to move temporarily to another country to find a higher paying job. Another 630 million aim to move abroad permanently.[2] Still, even if your career plans anchor you to your home market, globalizing markets encourage globalizing your mindset.

From Afghanistan to Zimbabwe, effective leadership increasingly calls for a global mindset. "You have to have an intuitive sense of how the world works and how people behave," says Paul Laudicina, vice president of A. T. Kearney.[3] Observed Daniel Meiland of Egon Zehnder International, an executive search firm, "The world is getting smaller, and markets are getting bigger. In my more than 25 years in the executive search profession, we've always talked about the global executive, but the need to find managers who can be effective in many different settings is growing ever more urgent. In addition to looking for intelligence, specific skills, and technical insights, MNEs are also looking for executives who are comfortable on the world stage."[4]

THE EXPATRIATE

MNEs often send managers to live and work in another country to run their foreign operations. Some, such as W. L. Gore and J&J, send only a few. Others, like Royal Dutch Shell and Wipro Technologies, send many. Unfortunately, few standards stipulate why, when, and where MNEs should use **expatriates** (a person who works outside their native country). Moreover, ambiguity complicates selecting the right expatriates, developing the right predeparture programs, designing the right compensation packages, setting the right stretch of time for the assignments, and determining the right way to reintegrate them into the home company when they complete their tour of duty.

The consequences of success and failure press MNEs to manage their human resources proactively. Honeywell, like many, begins developing potential expatriates years before they might head abroad. It assesses candidates' cross-cultural skills and prescribes training paths that anticipate likely points of culture shock. "We give them a horizon, a perspective, and, gradually, we tell them they are potentially on an international path," says Honeywell's VP of HR. "We want them to develop a cross-cultural intellect, what we call strategic accountability."[5] Honeywell might advise employees to network with experienced expatriates or improve their personal and professional resourcefulness. Nestlé leaves less to chance in developing its expatriate pipeline. High performers typically rotate through two stays at corporate headquarters in Vevey, Switzerland; the first early on in an individual's career and the other when one reaches middle management. The pace of globalization, particularly for MNEs in emerging economies like India, China, and the Philippines, accelerates preparation. Indeed, some managers identify expatriate candidates upon hire. Sanjay Joshi, chief executive of global programs at India's Wipro Technologies, notes, "A big part of our recruiting is telling people that they will get a chance to work abroad." This approach, he believes, improves the quality of new hires while fortifying the company's expatriate pipeline.[6]

NEW PLACES, NEW FACES, NEW WAYS

Figure 20.1 lists the benefits of working abroad. Enduring constants spotlight improving job prospects, engaging new challenges, boosting the quality of life, and increasing earning potential. Accomplished expatriates testify to the merits of the quest, describing how the experience changed their perception of business and their sense of self. Many note that working abroad pushed them, sometimes gently, sometimes harshly, to interpret situations differently. Galina Naumenko, of PwC Russia, says an international assignment "spurs global networking among employees, gives them an understanding of different cultures, and gets them thinking about alternative ways of approaching problems and solving them." Adds Michael Cannon-Brookes, head of strategy for IBM's Growth Markets, "You get very different thinking if you sit in Shanghai or São Paulo or Dubai than if you sit in New York."[7]

FIGURE 20.1 Top Benefits of the Expatriate Experience

Executives identify many benefits of their international assignments. Here we see leading personal and professional motivations.[8]

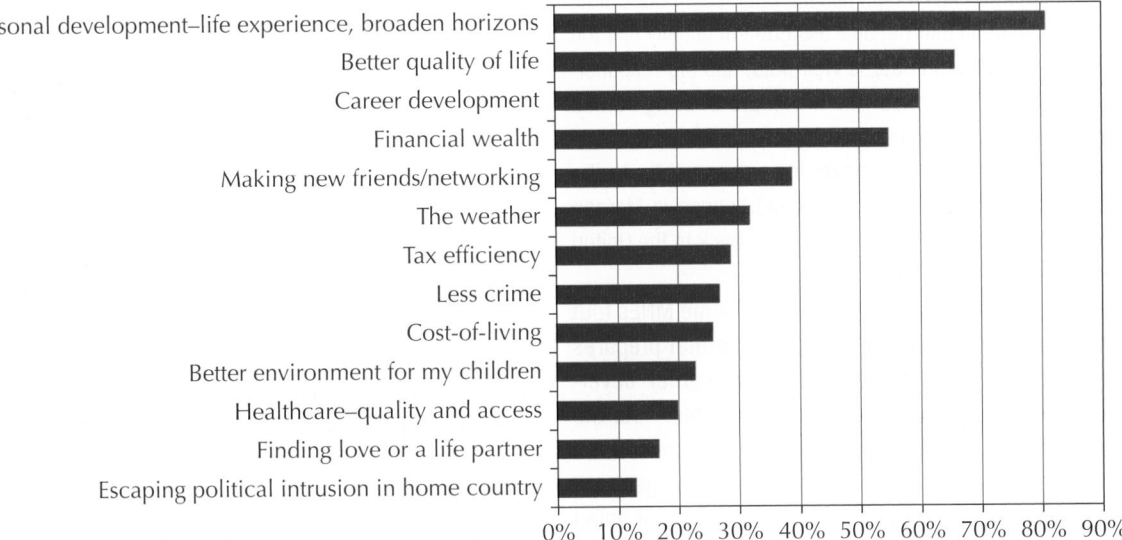

Working internationally compels employees to develop broader management repertoires. Consider Joan Pattle, a Microsoft manager who worked at headquarters in Seattle before accepting a post as product leader in Great Britain. Her U.K. job came with wider responsibilities, as she explains: "At home, my job was very strictly defined. I basically had to know everything about managing a database. But when I got to London, I was also in charge of direct marketing and press relations. I was exposed to a much broader set of experiences."[9] Similarly, Laura Anderson, a spokesperson for Intel, explains that an assignment in Hong Kong improved her sense of the company's business. In fact, several Asian media relations encounters opened her eyes. "For me," she says, "it was a tremendous growth experience."[10]

NEW PROBLEMS, NEW CHALLENGES

Notwithstanding the allure of adventure and rewards, the expatriate lifestyle is not for everyone. Difficulty adapting, no matter how strong the intent, explains nearly half of failed foreign assignments. Living and working abroad is tough. Cultural clashes, language difficulties, murky business practices, and social hazards rule out anything beyond a short-term visit for many. Other problems arise when a company asks an executive to transfer to a second- or third-tier city in a less preferred location. Moving from paradise to the wastelands, besides a tough sell, makes for a challenging experience.

The gap between life at home versus "over there" often fans professional, family, and personal problems. Expatriates routinely struggle with foreign cultures. Difficulty understanding and respecting differences, no matter how mundane, spiritual, or philosophical, causes expensive failures. To top it off, IB travel "is perhaps the most dangerous form of travel. Tourists wouldn't consider flying

into a Colombian war zone for a week, yet folks from oil, computer, pharmaceutical, agricultural, and telecom MNEs do it regularly."[11] Once there, merely frequenting high-profile hotels and restaurants is hazardous.

COMING HOME

Floating around the world are transpatirates, basically "expat lifers." Moving from assignment to assignment, whether with the same company or another, they plan never to return "home." Most, however, eventually do—they pack their bags, bid farewell to colleagues, board the plane, and return to a hero's welcome. A snap, right? Not so. In many cases, one gets everything but the big bash.

Repatriation—returning to one's country of origin—can prove disappointing, but need not. Tales of success confirm that career planning makes a big difference. Following a four-year assignment in Tokyo, Bryan Krueger returned to a promotion to president of Baxter Fenwal North America. When he left for Tokyo, his company had not guaranteed him a promotion upon his return. While he was away, however, he kept up to date with the goings-on at headquarters and visited the home office every few months to maintain his network. As he explains, "I was definitely proactive. Anyone who is not, does himself a disservice. I made a conscious effort to stay in touch, and it paid off."[12]

Still, not all executives share victory tales. A survey of repatriated executives who successfully completed their international assignments found that more than a third held temporary posts three months after returning home. Nearly 80 percent saw their new job as a demotion. More than 60 percent felt they had too few opportunities to leverage their international expertise. Some executives tolerate these outcomes. Others don't and move on.[13]

RISK AND RETURN

The choice to work abroad has a high upside, but a steep downside. On balance, the allure of an international assignment usually tips the scale. While overseas, an expatriate is well-paid, has big responsibilities, and commands high status. The adventure of living abroad makes an international career irresistible to some, effectively creating so-called "global nomads" who travel from one country to the next. For example, after stints in Singapore and London, a Morgan Stanley expat in India said, "I still don't want to go back to the United States. It's a big world—lots of things to see."[14]

Still, the risks of a career detour loom large. Some MNEs tout a foreign assignment as a meaningful experience that prepares managers for broader responsibilities—indeed, career development drives nearly a quarter of expat assignments.[15] As the reasoning goes, it improves skills and expertise, fosters cultural awareness, increases confidence in overcoming challenges, and enhances creativity through exposure to different ways of doing things. A neutral or negative career outcome, however, is not out of the question. As Tom Schiro of Deloitte & Touche observes, "Some MNEs just send somebody overseas and forget about them for two years."[16] Then, after returning, the company may be slow to reward a manager's successful experience with an expanded leadership role.

EMERGING STANDARDS

The expanding scale and scope of globalization triggers short supplies of talented executives. MNEs report difficulty finding skilled candidates, investing more time interviewing and hiring, and worrying about rivals poaching their high performers. Despite the global economic slowdown, shortages worsen. Manpower, a multinational human resource consulting firm, found that 34 percent of employers worldwide struggle to fill expatriate slots. According to the global consultancy McKinsey & Company, (1) only 43 percent of employers in leading markets such as Brazil, Germany, India, Mexico, Saudi Arabia, Turkey, and the United States can find enough skilled workers, (2) the world will be short 40 million college-educated workers in 2020, and (3) "there will be far too few workers with the advanced skills needed to drive a high productivity economy."[17] Shortages will amplify the value of a global mindset.

By changing the game, globalization also changes performance standards. Increasingly, MNEs regard international experience as the cornerstone of a high-impact career. Nearly 40 percent of *FTSE 100* companies have a foreign national as CEO, and about 70 percent have had a foreign assignment. Among the *Fortune 100*, the figures clock in at 10 percent and 33 percent, respectively.[18] At Procter & Gamble, nearly all of the company's top global executives have had a foreign assignment, and a good share were born outside the United States. Global awareness and experience are "ingredient[s] you must have if you aspire to be a global player in the long term," says P&G's HR director.[19] P&G expects its leaders to be both innovative and worldly; they cannot rise to the top without running operations in a foreign market.[20] Its German rival, Henkel, insists on the same, requiring executives to live in at least two different countries prior to promotion.[21] Boyden, an executive search firm, notes that nearly 3 of every 4 clients request international experience when seeking C-suite executives or board members; of those, roughly half now expect candidates' career records to show overseas experience.[22] Bluntly put, multinational experience is as essential as multifunctional and multiproduct experiences. Consequently, MNEs post high-potential executives overseas, giving them the opportunity to step up to the challenge, test their skills, and fine-tune their global mindset.

In summary, aspiring executives increasingly look abroad to move ahead. While perhaps overly hyped, personal ambition, environmental trends, market conditions, and workplace standards create situations where "the people with the top jobs in large corporations, even in the United States, will be those who have lived in several cultures and who can converse in at least two languages. Most CEOs will have had true global exposure, and their MNEs will be all the stronger for it."[23]

QUESTIONS

⭐ **20-1.** Identify three compelling reasons to pursue an expatriate assignment.

⭐ **20-2.** Explain why you would seek or, alternatively, avoid an expatriate assignment.

INTERNATIONAL HUMAN RESOURCE MANAGEMENT

Successful MNEs have clever strategies, effective organizations, efficient supply chains, sharp financial systems, and the like. Ultimately, though, success is a function of the people who start and sustain operations. The expanding global business web calls for executives who can manage interconnected operations across a diversity of markets. While directing global operations from the sanctuary of a home office, one can fall prey to misinterpreting international differences, with some executives seeing them as insurmountable while others view them

CONCEPT CHECK

Recall our discussion in Chapter 1 (page 50) of "The Forces Driving Globalization and IB," in which we identify several factors that create connections among people worldwide. The convergence of cultures, politics, and markets diminish the physical and psychic distances between countries. Here we suggest that this trend has begun to make the prospect of moving from one country to another a more attractive career plan.

IHRM refers to activities that staff the MNE's worldwide operations.

IHRM is more difficult for the MNE than its domestic counterpart due to

• environmental differences,
• strategic contingencies,
• organizational challenges.

as trivial. Managing design, manufacturing, marketing, and supply jobs worldwide calls for executives with experience in several functions in several regions—for example, overseeing a product from its design phase in Silicon Valley to production in Taiwan and then distributing it across Africa. These tasks, in isolation and totality, require talented executives.

Putting the right person in the right job in the right place at the right time for the right compensation for the right stretch takes us to the front lines of IB. From launching new ventures, rebuilding failing units, developing local expertise, filling skills gaps, setting technology platforms, or diffusing the organizational culture, the star of the show is an executive. Indeed, any successful or, for that matter, struggling strategy has an executive at its core. Quite simply, the focal point of IB is an executive facing challenges that often lead to transformational opportunities. The contest between challenge and opportunity, the focus of this chapter, is the spirit of a career in IB.[24]

International Human Resource Management (IHRM) shepherds an MNE's most valued assets—its people. IHRM organizes people within the MNE, developing policies and systems that improve individual productivity and collective performance. Opening and operating a business, whether a small-scale micronational or a vast multinational, requires finding people to implement the strategy, motivating them to perform well, upgrading their skills so they can move on to bigger challenges and, ultimately, retaining them.[25] IHRM directs these functions, minding the matters of staffing, training, performance evaluation, compensation, and retention given the requirements of the firm's strategy.

This chapter elaborates these issues, building on themes introduced in Chapter 12 and applied since to business functions and operating activities. We evaluate IHRM from the perspective that the successful MNE staffs its operations with skilled executives that are mission-led and principle-driven to leverage the company's core competencies while reconciling competing calls for global integration and local responsiveness. This perspective emphasizes that IHRM activities perform best when managers link them to the MNE's strategy (see Figure 20.2).

Unconditionally, IHRM is more difficult for the MNE than for its uni-national counterpart. Besides dealing with situations in the home market, IHRM adjusts policies and systems

FIGURE 20.2 Factors Influencing IHRM in IB

Successful MNEs consistently show that managing human resources, like managing finance, marketing, and supply chains, follows the requirements of the company's strategy. The key task centers on putting the right person in the right job in the right place at the right time for the right compensation for the right stretch—with the standard of "right" set by the MNE's strategy.

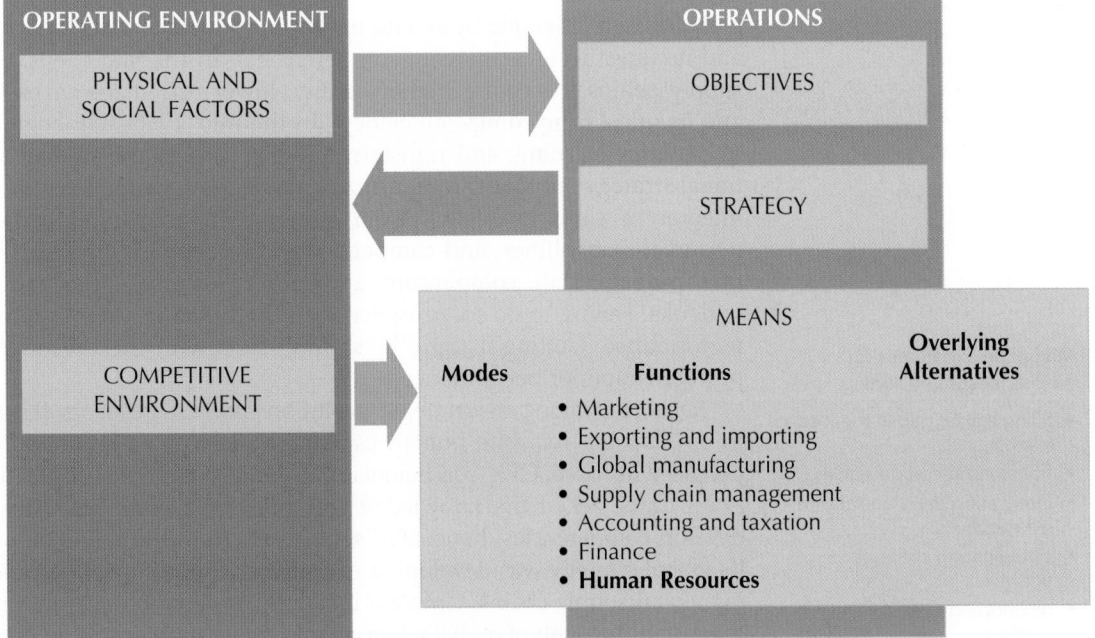

for differing political, cultural, legal, and economic circumstances. Preferred leadership styles and management practices, for example, often vary from country to country. Differences fan difficulties between people in different units—say, headquarters and local subsidiaries.[26] Neglected, they can turn great managers at home into ineffective ones overseas. Consequently, MNEs continually evaluate how to staff international operations and fine-tune the mix of recruiting, training, compensation, transfer, and repatriation programs.[27] Inevitably, some ask why executives put up with these aggravations. The short answer is that the megatrend of globalization demands doing so. The long answer is that in the face of globalization, successfully navigating these challenges creates value and fortifies competitiveness. Both answers highlight IHRM's mandate: Devise systems to develop and sustain a cadre of managers that lead the MNE to attain its vision.[28]

CONCEPT CHECK

A recurring theme of the text is the usefulness of adopting a strategic perspective. No matter if the topic involves political, legal, economic, or cultural dimensions of the marketplace, the quest for superior performance compels the MNE to link these trends, challenges, and consequences to its strategy.

IHRM policies that support the MNE's strategy generate high productivity and competitive advantage.

THE STRATEGIC ROLE OF IHRM

Anecdotes suggest and research confirms a powerful relationship between IHRM policies, executive expertise, and strategic performance.[29] GE's CEO, for example, sees global success as "truly about people, not about where the buildings are. You've got to develop people so they are prepared for leadership jobs and then promote them. That's the most effective way to become more global."[30] Ongoing study of MNEs in Asia, Europe, and the United States confirm that MNEs with superior human capital practices sustain high productivity, value creation, and competitive advantage.[31] On average, they consistently create greater value than those with run-of-the-mill IHRM practices.

Improving understanding of the link between human resources and company performance is correspondingly testing the thesis that superior performance creates the resources that then enable MNEs to develop superior IHRM practices. Analysis indicates the reverse: Superior IHRM is a key determinant of firm performance. Furthermore, the interaction between an MNE's strategy and its IHRM practices accounts for more variation in performance than does IHRM in isolation.[32] These relationships suggest IHRM is not a glorified euphemism for personnel management, concerned with administering routine employee processes and setting short-term employment policies. Rather, IHRM is a performance driver, identifying, developing, staffing, compensating, and retaining the executives that command the requisite skills and outlooks to direct the MNE.

A Case In Point: GE's Evolution　Looking at the role of IHRM in the context of GE's international evolution elaborates these ideas. Beginning in the 1980s, GE focused on globalizing its markets by selling existing products abroad (i.e., the international strategy and its quest to leverage core competencies). In the late 1980s, GE began globalizing its supply chains to acquire higher-quality, lower-priced resources (i.e., the global strategy and its quest to maximize efficiency). In the mid-1990s, GE began globalizing its intellect by seeking, learning, and transferring ideas throughout its operations (i.e., the transnational strategy and quest to optimize knowledge transfer, local responsiveness, and global integration simultaneously). Each strategy imposed unique demands for configuring resources, capabilities, and competencies. Correspondingly, each strategy required IHRM find, prepare, staff, compensate, and retain executives that had the requisite skills and outlooks. Failing to do so, irrespective of the brilliance of its strategy, would weaken GE's performance. Getting it right, by staffing slots with the executives with the "right stuff," powered superior performance.

Each stop along its strategic evolution saw GE reset its IHRM policies and systems to develop the requisite human capital. The key to its international strategy was staffing people who used GE's competencies to build competitive operations in foreign markets. Local units lacked the knowledge and skills to acquire resources, build capabilities, and develop competencies; hence, GE sent expats from the home office to fill gaps. The key to its global strategy was developing executives who optimized location economics in directing global supply chains. Growing linkages between local operations required coordinating the expanding web of global relationships; short supplies of the requisite executive talent in

MNEs use expatriates for various reasons, including

- filling a skills gap in the local market,
- transferring competencies,
- integrating decision-making perspectives,
- coordinating strategic activities,
- developing executive leaders

many subsidiaries spurred GE to fill gaps with experienced expats. Lastly, implementing its transnational strategy required posting expats that developed, transferred, and engaged ideas throughout global operations, irrespective of the business, function, or market source. This goal required posting different people to different operations in different countries to develop the requisite global outlook and leadership skills; hence, GE posted its best managers, no matter their nationality, to expat slots.

IHRM'S MISSION

An MNE's strategic evolution shapes how it engages IB. Each stage in GE's evolution, for instance, required IHRM align its policies and systems with the corresponding requirements of its strategy. CEO Jeffrey Immelt explains, "When I first joined General Electric [in 1982], globalization meant training the Americans to be global thinkers. So, Americans got the expat assignments. We still have many Americans living around the world, and that's good, but we shifted our emphasis in the late 1990s to getting overseas assignments for non-Americans. Now you see non-Americans doing new jobs, big jobs, and important jobs at every level and in every country."[33] Today, GE has a cadre of international managers with the expertise to acquire resources, build capabilities, and develop competencies that support superior performance.

GE's success, like that of many other MNEs profiled throughout this chapter, highlights IHRM's mission: find, staff, compensate, and retain executives with the qualifications needed to support and sustain the MNE's strategy. Done well, IHRM supports higher productivity, stronger competitiveness, and improving profitability. Done poorly, people problems undermine firm performance and diminish careers.

THE PERSPECTIVE OF THE EXPATRIATE

An executive perspective directs attention to the managerial activities that run international business operations.

One can evaluate IHRM from many perspectives, anchoring on the issue of job specification, recruitment, personnel planning, wages and salaries, benefits and incentives, labor relations, performance evaluation, etc. This chapter applies an executive perspective, centering on expatriate management. In the MNE, the tip of the operational spear is the executive running international operations. Virtually any successful or, for that matter, struggling strategy has executives at its core. Ultimately, it's the responsibility of executives to launch new ventures, rebuild failing units, develop local expertise, fill skills gaps, transfer core competencies, set technology platforms, and diffuse the organizational culture. Moreover, an executive perspective speaks to your likely interest in working internationally. Students often ask professors about the why, how, when, where, and what of careers in IB. This chapter sheds light on these questions.[34]

WHO'S WHO?

Classifying a foreign assignment, in terms of the executive's relative nationality, uses a range of terms, including

- expatriate,
- home-country national,
- parent-country national,
- third-country national,
- inpatriate,
- transpatriate,
- flexpatriate,
- reverse-expat.

This chapter looks at two broad types of executives: locals and expatriates. A **local** is hired by the MNE in his or her home country to staff the local operations; no special provisions apply to his or her work contract. A German national working in the Berlin office of a German MNE, for example, fits this profile. An **expatriate** (or "expat") is an executive sent to work temporarily in a country that is not his or her legal residence. There are various types of expatriates. A **home-country national**, also known as a **parent-country national**, is a citizen of the country where the firm is headquartered (i.e., a Brazilian national sent to the Argentinean subsidiary of her Brazilian MNE). A **third-country national** is neither a citizen of the home nor the host country (i.e., a Malaysian national running the Russian subsidiary of his Australian company). If the Malaysian executive is transferred to the MNE's Australian headquarters, he is then an **inpatriate**. Finally, a **transpatriate** refers to expat lifers who work an ongoing series of international assignments, plan never to return to headquarters, and in extreme cases, profess neither a corporate nor national "home."

TRENDS IN EXPATRIATE ASSIGNMENTS

Demand for expatriates escalates worldwide.[35] Consider that in 1990, there were approximately 3,000 MNC's worldwide. By 2010, there were 80,000 MNC's with 800,000 affiliates. Now, there are more than 100,000 MNC's running 900,000 affiliates.[36] Likewise, there are more than 25,000 MNEs headquartered in the emerging world; few existed a decade ago.[37] The emergence of fast-growing economies worldwide has led MNEs, both in established markets, like the United States and Germany, as well as emerging markets, such as China and India, to open subsidiaries in new, different locations. MNEs of all types struggle to staff subsidiaries. No matter where, no matter doing what, each unit of each MNE requires executive talent.

Shortages of talented executives, in light of flexible logistics and shifting markets, change the characteristics of the international assignment. The historical standard had been an executive posted to a host country for a three- to five-year assignment, with the plan of ultimately returning home. The notion of "a few years" increasingly gives way to a few months, a few weeks, or even a few days. So-called **commuter assignments** post an expatriate for a short span. In extreme cases, it comprises the workweek, with the expat returning home for the weekend—say, shuttling between Paris and Madrid. Notes an HR director, "Commuter assignments were nonexistent until ten years ago, but now they are much more common."[38] Doing so, as the photo below spotlights, put expats around the world in motion, moving here to there as they travel everywhere. Short-term assignments, besides far more economical than long-term tours, quickly transfer resources to local subsidiaries.[39] Moreover, face-time with coworkers, no matter how brief, promotes social relations that support innovation.[40] Increasingly, commuter assignments give rise to so-called **flexpatriates**, executives who run the commuter cycle for a longer span as they work "frequent flyer assignments."[41]

The Young, Old, and Restless   Besides duration, who goes abroad changes. Traditionally, expatriates were mid- and upper-level executives sent overseas to develop leadership potential and prepare for greater responsibilities. Effectively, international assignments were career stepping-stones for the MNE's best and brightest. This mindset still prevails in many MNEs. Xerox, for instance, rotates its rising stars through two- to four-year assignments; successfully passing this test makes one a C-level contender.[42] Increasingly, IHRM

> Short-term expatriate assignments, such as commuter and flexpatriates, are more common today than a decade ago.

Source: Rob Wilson/Shutterstock

Changing markets, growing cost consciousness, and evolving strategies are resetting notions of who is an expatriate—now, we see growing interest in the young, the old, and the restless.

expands expat searches to consider older employees, whose children have grown and whose spouses see an international assignment positively, and younger employees, who are single, more mobile, and eager to experience life abroad.[43] In 2014, for example, 46 percent of expats fell between 35 and 54 years old; 28 percent and 25 percent, respectively, were 18 to 34 and 55-plus.[44]

MNEs trade performance track records for long-term potential when posting younger managers to international assignments. For example, PricewaterhouseCoopers (PwC) offers its Early PwC International Challenge program (EPIC) to fast-track international assignments for its younger employees.[45] EPIC identifies high performers interested in working abroad. Candidates jump-start the process by completing an online assessment and consulting PwC's career pages. Then, if selected, the high performer departs for his chosen destination, completing a two-year assignment. Candidates, besides expediting career progression, improve executive skills and global orientation.[46] PwC benefits by fortifying the leadership pipeline.

Increasingly, university programs respond to and accelerate these trends. Schools worldwide internationalize their curricula, expand study-abroad options, offer joint degrees with foreign institutions, and recruit international students. Similarly, some students take the big plunge, heading abroad for college. Hong Kong University of Science and Technology's Business School, for example, had 16 nationalities in 2001, and almost all of them hailed from Asia. Now, it has more than 60 nationalities with many coming from outside Asia. The number of foreign students attending U.S. universities grew from 110,000 in 2001 to 524,000 in 2012, to nearly a million in 2016.[47] Similar change is afoot elsewhere, with Americans increasingly heading to overseas MBA programs. Explained one attending ESADE in Barcelona, "If you look at the world today, at the state of business, you see that bridges are being built and borders broken down. I desired to focus on global business to expand both my knowledge and my network."[48] Self-starting expatriates, heading abroad to pursue cultural, personal, and career experiences, refine interpretations.

CONCEPT CHECK

Chapter 12 (page 376) reported that search for superior competitive advantage pushes many to build a globally integrated enterprise that can implement increasingly sophisticated strategies. Consequently, they adjust their idea of an expatriate, fine-tuning the traditional notion of someone posted abroad for a lengthy tour as well as experimenting with novel formats that tinker with duration and design.

Expanding Scope of Women The gender dimension of expatriate selection evolves. In absolute terms, females compose roughly 20 percent of expatriates.[49] Relative growth has been far more dramatic. Since 2001, MNEs in the Asia–Pacific region have seen a sixteen-fold increase in women on international assignments, MNEs in North America have seen nearly a fourfold rise, and Europe has doubled its count. Surveys indicate that more than half of MNEs expect the number of female expatriates to increase, about a third believe the number will hold steady, and a handful see it declining. Reasoned an observer, "Going on expatriate placements can be an important step on the career ladder, and women are increasingly interested in taking these assignments."[50]

Growing Scope of Third-Country Nationals MNEs establish operations abroad in increasingly dissimilar markets—say, from the United States to Canada to England to India to Singapore to China to Vietnam. The changing workflow of globalization elevates the role of third-country nationals, who often have the outlook, resourcefulness, and versatility to run operations in diverse locales.[51] Longer term, the supply of skilled third-country nations will expand, especially in emerging economies. China has committed $250 billion to its university infrastructure, on top of already doubling its number of universities over the previous decade. It plans to produce 195 million college graduates by 2020.[52]

Short-term assignments boost the logistical appeal of third-country nationals—an executive living in Dubai, for instance, may spend Monday through Friday working in Mumbai, then return home for the weekend. Then, as the need arises for help in the MNE's Doha office, he easily changes his commute. "Fly In–Fly Out" mobility lets an MNE adroitly adapt its strategy, confident it has well-positioned executives to implement it. Data document the growing use of third-country nationals.[53] A generation ago, most expatriates were selected from the executive pool in the MNE's home country. In 2015, about 60 percent of international assignees relocated to or from the headquarters country; others relocated to or from a non-headquarters country.[54]

Reverse expats spend a predetermined amount of time at the company's home country operations before running emerging market operations.

Reverse Expatriates The rising importance of emerging markets refines our evolving ideas of expatriates. Historically, MNEs recruited executives in richer countries and assigned them to units in developing countries. Now, talented executives from emerging economies—so-called **reverse-expats**—are sent straight to richer countries to speed their development. They spend anywhere from a few weeks to a year in an operational unit before eventually returning home—where they often replace a traditionally defined, and usually higher-paid, expatriate.[55] Some tweak this option further. Goldman Sachs' Growth Markets Opportunity Program recruits high-potential Asians and Latin Americans that have earned an MBA from Western universities. It posts them to its New York or London offices for up to a year before expatriating them to emerging financial centers such as Singapore, São Paulo, and Hong Kong.[56]

THE ECONOMICS OF EXPATRIATES

Economic pressures and cost concerns spur companies to emphasize frequent business travel in lieu of a longer-term international assignment.

Expats, if anything, are expensive. Besides salary, relocation, taxation, housing, cost-of-living and education allowances means that an expat package runs two to three times an expat's annual pay.[57] Escalating expenses spur IHRM to contain costs; 75 percent of a worldwide sample report programs to reduce international assignment expenses.[58] In recourse, MNEs design short-term and commuter assignments in lieu of traditional, multiyear assignments. Rather than moving to foreign markets, executives travel far more often to far more places that lie farther from their home base. Presently, short-term posts (3 to 12 months) represent more than half of expat assignments.[59] Likewise, cost concerns accelerate deploying third-country nationals in place of parent-country executives. The latter often demand richer compensation packages and impose higher relocation costs.

Cost pressures encourage **localization**, whereby an expatriate retains the foreign assignment but accepts the status of a local hire and, correspondingly, a lower host-location salary. Some MNEs go with "expat-lite" slots that offer fewer benefits. In both cases, compensation is cut. IBM's "Project Match" added an interesting twist, offering terminated employees in the United States the option to move to a local unit in say, India, China, Brazil, Nigeria, Russia, provided the candidate has been a "satisfactory performer" and was "willing to work on local terms and conditions."[60] That is, one has the option to move abroad and preserve their job, but compensation will be set by the local pay scale. Granted, a few perks may be added to the package. Inevitably, though, total compensation falls.

THE ENDURING CONSTANT

Evolving trends in the global marketplace drive evolving ideas on staffing international operations. Still, there is an enduring constant: Running the hundreds of thousands of subsidiaries throughout the world requires a mix of talented, enterprising locals, parent-country execs, and third-country expatriates. So keen is demand that MNEs report ongoing shortages of expatriate talent for international assignments and, consequently, expand the pool to include the young, old, and restless.[61] Throughout it all, IHRM aims to staff the right person in the right job in the right place at the right time for the right compensation for the right stretch. Success drives strategy and sustainability. Failure erodes careers and diminishes performance.

STAFFING FRAMEWORKS IN THE MNE

Three perspectives anchor an MNE's staffing policy:

- Ethnocentrism
- Polycentricism
- Geocentrism

IHRM professionals apply **staffing frameworks** (a conceptual structure that helps solve complex issues) to organize expatriate policies and systems. A staffing framework identifies the optimal mix of local workers from the host nation, expatriates sent from the home country, and third-country nationals. It organizes selection, training, compensation, and repatriation guidelines in terms of the demands of the MNE's strategy. Recall from

Chapter 16, that high performance requires the right organization, a task that, in turn, requires the right sorts of executives to run the show. Research emphasizes the ethnocentric, polycentric, and geocentric staffing frameworks.

THE ETHNOCENTRIC FRAMEWORK

CONCEPT CHECK

Discussion of "Company and Management Orientations" in Chapter 2 (page 91) introduced the idea of polycentrism, ethnocentrism, and geocentrism to describe how MNEs and their managers approach foreign cultures. Here, we reintroduce these terms, highlighting the ways these "attitudes or orientations" influence an MNE's staffing framework.

Ethnocentrism is the conviction that one's preferred policies and procedures are the superior way to manage anyone, anywhere.

The ethnocentric framework fills key management positions with home-country nationals.

Ethnocentrism occurs when one group places itself at the top of a supposed hierarchy of relevant groups. Hence, the **ethnocentric framework** signifies the belief that the management principles and business practices used by headquarters are superior to those used in other countries. The proven success of the company's way of doing things, goes this reasoning, means there is little call to adapt people and processes to foreign markets.[62] Thus, the MNE fills executive positions in foreign units with home-country nationals (i.e., a Japanese MNE fills international slots with Japanese executives).

Advantages Home-office executives commonly explain there is no shortage of executive talent in a particular host country, just a shortage of people with the right mix of operational expertise, industry experience, and fluency with the company's preferred way of doing business. Thus, staffing overseas slots with parent-country executives has strategic, skills, and socialization advantages.

Strategic Advantages A firm earns success in its home market by uniquely bundling resources and capabilities to create proprietary core competencies. Success leads a firm to see its way of doing business as the superior means of creating value. Likewise, it sees international success as dependent on doing the same things, the same way, elsewhere. Headquarters concludes that executives who have performed successfully at home will do the same overseas. Thus, they adopt an ethnocentric staffing framework.

The growing importance of protecting ownership advantages spurs an MNE to safeguard its core competency. With it, the firm prospers; without it, the firm struggles. Headquarters prefers entrusting control of the company's "crown jewels" to those who will best protect them: namely, trustworthy colleagues from the home country. Earlier discussion of intellectual property explained that legal safeguards deter, but do not prevent, theft. The ethnocentric framework fortifies defenses by posting dependable home-country executives to vigilantly protect corporate assets.

Skills and Socialization Advantages Regulating the transfer of its core competencies is vital when they are difficult to articulate, specify, or standardize. For example, think of the challenge of codifying Apple's product-design and media expertise, Walmart's information-management and product-distribution systems, Ritz-Carlton's standards of service, or Honda's mastery of engine technology.[63] An ethnocentric framework offsets this problem by posting a home-country manager with technical knowledge and direct experience to local slots. Consider India's Wipro Technology, which has nearly 170,000 employees servicing over 900 of the *Fortune 1000* corporations with a presence in 175 countries. It uses more than 10,000 expats, most of whom are Indian, reasoning that they are best-prepared to spread the "Wipro Way." Explained Sanjay Joshi, chief executive of global programs, "We sprinkle Indians in new markets to help seed and set up the culture and intensity."[64] The HSBC Group long epitomized this outlook. For generations, most top executives came from a tight-knit cadre of elite expatriates who, in circulating among foreign operations, proactively dispersed the "DNA of the organization."[65]

Limitations MNEs have compelling rationales when asked why they rely on home-country nationals to run foreign operations. Yet, as the adage goes, vices are virtues taken to extreme. The same applies to the ethnocentric framework. Difficulties arise on several counts.

Workplace Tensions Ethnocentric staffing policies demotivate local workers. Consistently posting parent-country nationals sends the message to subsidiary personnel that all the smart, capable people live within a 25-mile radius of the home-office headquarters. Unless an expatriate transfers unique skills, local employees may resent someone they see as no more, perhaps less, qualified than themselves. Unchecked, resentment can lower productivity and increase turnover as locals sense a glass ceiling capping their careers. For instance, the preference among highly skilled Chinese professionals' to work in a domestic, rather than a foreign, company, increased significantly in just a few years; anecdotal evidence highlights the sense of greater upward mobility in local companies.[66]

> The ethnocentric staffing framework is vulnerable to problems arising from workplace, legal-political, and misreads and misfits tensions.

Legal-Political Tensions   An ethnocentric staffing policy can prove legally difficult and politically impractical. Employment law in countries worldwide regulates, sometimes lightly, sometimes strictly, the use of expatriates in place of locals. Host governments, alert to the importance of developing their workforce, prefer that subsidiaries hire locals. MNEs' plea that the special status of their operations prevents their doing so is often rejected. Governments then impose immigration laws or workplace regulations that prod MNEs to hire locals.

Misreads and Misfits Tensions   Force-fitting foreign operations to mimic the standards of the home office risks pounding square pegs into circular slots. Certainly, an MNE can make its foreign operations mirror the outward appearance of its home-country headquarters. Assigning home-office executives to foreign operations, however, does not automatically create a successful "mini-me" subsidiary. Consequently, an ethnocentric framework can prove detrimental, posting executives who misread markets and methods. In 2001, for example, Toyota aspired to sell one million cars a year in China within a decade. By 2012, data indicated serious shortfalls. Analysts reported Toyota had sorely misread the Chinese market, notably offering cars priced too high with too little *daqi* (Chinese consumers' perception of road presence). Toyota's solution to its ongoing China problem, a reflection of its traditional ethnocentric staffing policy, complicated problems. Explained a senior Toyota executive, "Our way of beefing up operations in China is to bring in more people from Japan. We should be localizing our business here, promoting Chinese managers, and listening more attentively to Chinese consumers. But we don't."[67]

THE POLYCENTRIC STAFFING FRAMEWORK

> The polycentric staffing framework looks to host-country nationals to manage local subsidiaries.

Polycentrism is the principle of organizing around different, but equivalently important political, social, or economic centers. Hence, the **polycentric staffing framework** acknowledges the business practices of foreign centers as philosophically and practically equivalent to those at home. Because business in the home country differs from that in foreign markets, and given intrinsic cross-national equivalency, IHRM adapts policies and systems to the host business environment. Thus, local executives from local units (e.g., home nationals staff headquarters, Russians run Russian subsidiaries, Mexicans run Mexican subsidiaries, and so on). In rare cases where home-office executives are posted to foreign subsidiaries, the working assumption is that their effectiveness requires immersing themselves in the ways of the local business environment.

Advantages   Staffing foreign operations with locals has strategic, economic, and political advantages.

Strategic Advantages   Proponents of polycentrism reason that local managers are stronger performers given their keener understanding of local customers, markets, and institutions. Interviews of 300 senior executives at global companies, for instance, found that more than 60 percent believed locals better understood the local operating environment and customers' needs than did they.[68] As Microsoft's former COO explains, "You want people who know the local situation, its value system, the way work gets done, the way people use technology in that particular country, and who the key competitors are.... If you send someone in fresh from a different region or country, they don't know those things."[69] Added Bill Gates, Microsoft's chairman, "It sends the wrong message to have a foreigner come over to run things."[70]

J&J's experiences spotlight related aspects. As a rule, locals run J&J's local subsidiaries. Each unit has substantial autonomy, commanding the freedom to act as it believes best given its read of the local market. Each unit performs as a small business, entrepreneurial in character and aware that success depends on its superior sense anticipating local customers' needs and delivering meaningful solutions. J&J's CEO explained that relying on locals to staff local operations "is a tremendous magnet for talent because it gives people room to grow and room to explore new ideas, thus developing their own skills and careers."[71] Likewise, fixing its Chinese market problems pushed Toyota to rethink its IHRM policy, deemphasizing its traditional ethnocentric approach in favor of greater localization. Explained a Toyota spokesperson, "We're promoting more local Chinese employees to management ranks and will continue to do so."[72]

Using host-country managers boosts local motivation and morale. Still, likely costs include gaps with global operations due to problems of accountability and allegiance.

Economic Advantages   A compelling motivation of the polycentric approach is its implications to expatriate economics. Hiring local managers eliminates the expense of posting expatriates to local slots. It is difficult to pinpoint the total cost of an expat assignment due to the range of relevant variables, running from financial incentives, housing, relocation, taxation, to cost-of-living and education allowances. A general rule is that the total annual cost is two to three times the expat's annual compensation.[73] Indirect administrative expenses boost this sum. For example, an expat slot generates more paperwork than an equivalent domestic slot. Setting policies and systems to administer the complicated circumstances of expatriate assignments requires, on average, twice as many HR professionals than needed for a non-expatriate slot.[74] Qualifying expat pay by the comparative expense of a local hire means an expat costs the employer much more than a local. Some see these stark economics encouraging staffing local operations with home-country nationals.

Political Advantages   Understandably, host governments prefer polycentric approaches. They see local managers as better citizens and stakeholders than expatriates, far more likely to champion national interests over global objectives. Activist officials often require the MNE hire locals, such as licensing requirements that prohibit expatriate accountants and lawyers or visa regulations that put a hard cap on the number of foreigners who can staff a local subsidiary. The polycentric framework neutralizes these impediments.

Limitations   A polycentric approach, by effectively decentralizing authority to local subsidiaries, fans organizational tensions on several counts.

Autonomy Tensions   Installing local executives in decision-making roles gives them opportunities to develop their skills and build thriving operations. Success supports growing resource independence from the parent that can turn the local subsidiary into a quasi-autonomous unit. Unchecked, an MNE risks devolving into a federation of loosely connected, largely autonomous national operations that pay little mind to headquarters. For instance, when J&J launched Tylenol in 1960 in the United States, the product was available to worldwide units shortly thereafter. However, the quasi-independent Japanese unit, despite duress from headquarters, did not begin selling it until 2000.[75]

Accountability and Allegiance Tensions   Dilemmas over allegiance emerge when host-country managers are loyal to local colleagues instead of their home-country bosses. In theory, local managers balance the competing demands of making sense of events from a local and the home-office view. In practice, however, national concerns often take precedence given the immediacy of local pressures.[76] Left to their own devices, local managers may respond to local circumstances in ways that then complicate integrating their activities with global operations.[77]

Motivation and Mobility Tensions There are few expatriate slots in the polycentric framework; again, the presumption is host-country nationals manage local subsidiaries, parent-country nationals run corporate headquarters, and a select few move between countries. Locals have scant opportunities to work outside their home country, effectively imposing a glass ceiling on their professional mobility. Consequently, local managers may see little incentive to study multinational business practices or identify ways to improve cross-national integration. The resulting single-country focus can isolate national subsidiaries as well as push enterprising executives, ambitious to work abroad, to quit.

THE GEOCENTRIC STAFFING FRAMEWORK

The geocentric framework posts the most qualified executives, regardless of nationality, to expatriate slots.

Geocentrism is a world-oriented set of attitudes and values that regards humanity as a single entity sharing universal outlooks and orientations. The **geocentric staffing framework** sees the blunt split of home-, host-, and third-country managers as needless divisions. Rather, it reasons the best way, wherever discovered, works everywhere, whenever applied. IHRM develops talented executives, regardless of their home nations or eventual host market, with the knowledge, skills, and abilities needed to get the job done. Reasoned GE's CEO, "It's more important to find the best people, wherever they may be, and develop them so that they can lead big businesses, wherever those may be."[78]

Advantages

The geocentric framework develops executives whose global mindset enables them to easily and effectively navigate cultures and countries.[79]

Strategic Advantages Geocentricity, and its advocacy of a global mindset, develops expats that command key competencies. They understand and interpret what is going on in a global situation, they decipher verbal and nonverbal messages and signals from people of different outlooks, and their flexibility helps them deal appropriately with different situations. They effectively implement global and, especially, transnational strategies, finding ways to exploit learning opportunities, transfer knowledge, and promote collaboration. As the CEO of Schering-Plough explains, "Good ideas can come from anywhere…the more places you are, the more ideas you will get. And the more ideas you get, the more places you can sell them and the more competitive you will be. Managing in many places requires a willingness to accept good ideas no matter where they come from—which means having a global attitude."[80]

Performance data confirm these effects. MNEs with diverse top teams are financial high performers, particularly those implementing ambitious global strategies with strong cross-cultural dimensions.[81] Promoting broader attitudes and values in the executive ranks promotes outlooks that bridge differences and champion collaboration. Too, developing a multinational management cadre reduces cultural myopia, improves team representativeness, and enhances market responsiveness.[82]

Limitations

A geocentric framework is tough to develop and costly to maintain. Professional and logistic tension complicate its effectiveness.

Professional Tensions Difficulty plagues expat development given the need for executives to retain a sense of identity in the face of increasing diversity. Working with groups marked by cultural diversity takes on a different vibe than with groups composed of people of similar ethnicities and nationalities.[83] Often, the mix of different perspectives generates creative breakthroughs. However, making sense of the various outlooks that potentially bear on a decision can prove overwhelming. Akin to the Tower of Babel, geocentrism can erode common cause as the clarity of the task is lost in a hodgepodge of dissimilar outlooks.[84]

The geocentric staffing framework is vulnerable to problems arising from professional and logistic tensions.

Logistics Tensions The geocentric framework imposes costly logistics. Exposing executives to different ideas in diverse places, given the quest to improve their global mindset, is expensive. Compensation and relocation costs escalate when transferring high-priced executives from country to country. Often the high pay and prestige enjoyed by those in the geocentric vanguard triggers resentment among the rank-and-file. The geocentric framework's preference for multiyear assignments runs counter to growing pressure to reduce expat expense via short-term posts and flexpatriate slots. Operationally, immigration laws and visa caps can hinder efficiently maneuvering executives among subsidiaries. In recourse, some advocate "think global, hire local" as a solution.[85]

WHICH STAFFING FRAMEWORK WHEN?

CONCEPT CHECK

Table 20.1 demonstrates a principle that we develop throughout this book: Although most of us are prone to determine the "one best way" of doing things, it's seldom a promising approach in IB. Likewise, this outlook applies to formulating a staffing strategy for international operations.

Table 20.1 summarizes the merits and drawbacks of the ethnocentric, polycentric, and geocentric frameworks. This typology applies a contingency perspective that optimizes staffing policies in terms of the requirements of the MNE's strategy. That is, expatriates drive an MNE's strategy: they launch new ventures, build management expertise, fill local skills gaps, transfer technology, and diffuse organization culture. Different strategies, whether international, localization, global, or transnational, impose different requirements. For example, nearly all MNEs prepare for global expansion by assessing the executive requirements of their strategic vision and mission. They then assess their pool of potential expatriates, identifying requisite outlooks and skills, and filling gaps.[86]

TABLE 20.1   Frameworks to Staff International Operations: Principles and Practices

The assumptions, advantages, drawbacks, and strategic fit of the leading staffing frameworks run the gamut. IHRM, keen to the requirements of the MNE's strategy, applies the most appropriate staffing framework. As they do, they mind various opportunities and trade-offs.

Framework	Assumptions	Advantages	Drawbacks	Strategic Fit
Ethnocentric	• The leadership ideals, management values, and workplace practices of one's company are superior to those elsewhere. • Headquarters makes key decisions and foreign subsidiaries implement them.	• Leverages and protects core competencies. • Promotes executives' international outlook. • Fills local skills gaps. • Transfers principles and practices of the company's culture.	• Fans dissent and demotivation among locals. • Discourages cultural empathy. • Managers may misread local innovations. • Alienates locals who prefer national orientation.	International Strategy, given its quest to leverage and safeguard the company's core competencies in foreign markets.
Polycentric	• Headquarters develops a vision and mission that local units adapt. • Responds to differences between home and host countries. • Superior competitiveness requires understanding local customers, markets, and institutions in the host market.	• Respects the unique merits of the local environment. • Local hires demand less compensation. • Local managers holding top jobs attract, motivate, and retain local employees. • Reduces the odds of expat failure. • Appeases host governments that prefer locals who champion local goals.	• Complicates coordinating and controlling value activities. • Isolates country operations. • Reduces the incentive among locals to engage a global perspective. • Creates agency dilemmas for quasi-autonomous country operations. • Promotes a single-nation focus among local staff.	Localization Strategy, given its quest to maximize the local responsiveness of foreign operations by adapting people, products, and processes to local standards.
Geocentric	• All nations are equal and possess inalienable characteristics that are neither superior nor inferior. • Headquarters and subsidiaries collaborate to identify, transfer, and diffuse best practices. • Ideas and innovations are found anywhere and everywhere—provided one is open to insights.	• Adroitly deal with different people with different outlooks in different countries. • Efficiently configures operations and expat staffs. • Leverages strategic scale and operational scope. • Promotes learning dynamics that develop, transfer, and leverage local ideas worldwide.	• Tough to develop, costly to run, hard to maintain. • Contrary to many countries' market development plans that champion local causes. • Difficult to find and fund qualified expatriates with a global mindset. • High status of global expats demotivates supporting players.	Global and Transnational Strategies, given the quest to optimize worldwide integration and local responsiveness.

EXPATRIATE SELECTION

CONCEPT CHECK

In Chapters 2, 3, and 4, we analyze the environments—cultural, political, legal, and economic—that frame international business operations. The variability in each context prevents setting absolute standards for running international operations. Here, we observe the implications of that variability to selecting expatriates. General guidelines more often than not take the place of absolute standards.

Developing high-performance expatriates requires identifying candidates who are interested in an international assignment, preparing them for the adventure, devising ways to motivate them, posting them to the appropriate job, and leveraging their improved skills when they are ready for their next position. IHRM steadily systematizes programs to perform these functions, starting with selection, and moving on sequentially through preparation, compensation, and repatriation. Screening executives to find those with the highest potential and greatest inclination for a foreign assignment anchors **expatriate selection** (see Figure 20.3).

Operationally, the challenge of expatriate selection is not finding candidates who are ready and willing to head abroad, but identifying those who are also able. IHRM lacks precise metrics that reliably predict the performance of a potential expatriate.[87] Some rely on hunch, sending someone who seems reasonably qualified. Failure though, is expensive. Avoiding this outcome, along with resolving escalating need to identify executives ready, willing, and able to go international, spurs IHRM to improve selection processes. Today, IHRM applies operational, cultural, and personality measures, commensurate with the prevailing staffing framework, to identify candidates. These screens, applied through objective evaluations and in-depth personal interviews, assess candidates on several dimensions. Anecdotes and analysis emphasize the following:[88]

Technical competency and operational expertise are key determinant of those executives that are posted to an expatriate slot.

TECHNICAL COMPETENCE

An enduring selection criteria is an executive's technical expertise, as indicated by past job performance, and his understanding of how to transfer it to the foreign unit.[89] Implementing a software system, orchestrating a marketing campaign, or launching ventures, for instance, often exceeds a subsidiary's competencies. Assigning a high-performance expatriate transfers the necessary expertise. Consequently, filling a technical or managerial skills gap in a foreign subsidiary determines nearly half of the executives sent abroad.[90] The sorts of sophisticated expertise typically needed means candidates have several years of high-performance line experience. Relatedly, IHRM routinely screens candidates by consulting coworkers, thereby reinforcing the importance of operational expertise. Finally, outstanding technical competence is often seen as signifying the self-confidence needed to succeed abroad.[91]

SELF-ORIENTATION

An expatriate assignment is marked by ambiguity, uncertainty, and risk. Thrust into challenging situations, an expat's effectiveness depends upon developing new knowledge, skills, and abilities. Facing ambiguities, one must organize interpretation and fortify decision-making.

FIGURE 20.3   Criteria for Identifying a Candidate for an Expatriate Assignment[92]

Challenged by physical, emotional, and social stress, one must reconcile choices and consequences. Hence, personal qualities, such as motivation, self-reliance, and conscientiousness help one start and move onward.[93] For instance, HSBC's selection process uses tests, interviews, and exercises to gauge a candidate's capacity for self-orientation. Still, HSBC evaluates intangible indicators, such as ambition and resilience. Explained its CEO,"We don't look so much at what or where people have studied, but rather at their drive, initiative, cultural sensitivity, and readiness to see the world as their oyster. Whether they've studied classics, economics, history, or languages is irrelevant. What matters are the skills and qualities necessary to be good, well-rounded executives in a highly international institution operating in a diverse set of communities."[94]

OTHERS-ORIENTATION

Orientation, both self and others, help expats

- manage ambiguity, uncertainty and risk,
- resolve physical, emotional and social stress,
- support effective communication,
- enhances interpersonal interactions.

International travelers note that new situations in new settings challenge their values and outlooks. Understanding how colleagues, customers, and competitors in the local market see events, rather than criticizing dissimilar perspectives, supports strong performance. Interpreting events in ways that reject stereotypes, preconceptions, and unrealistic expectations enables an expat to adapt messages to listeners' outlooks. Effective communication, an element of others-orientation, helps one go far in IB.[95] Likewise, others-orientation promotes cultural empathy, namely the ability to develop sincere, honest friendships with foreign nationals and the willingness to use, no matter how rudimentary, the host-country language. Others-orientation enhances one's interactions with people and, importantly, an understanding of why some went well while others did not. The records of successful expats indicate that they did not recoil from cultural differences, criticizing locals for their personal choices. Rather, they developed the necessary tools of communication, empathy, and diplomacy.[96]

RESOURCEFULNESS

Resourcefulness refers to a person's potential for

- self-maintenance situational flexibility,
- interpreting the immediate environment,
- developing productive workplace relationships.

The precise job descriptions found in the job bank of the home office inevitably give way to far broader responsibilities in foreign subsidiaries. Complicating matters is the fact that the expat usually lacks the battery of resources she commanded at the home office. The call to do many jobs simultaneously requires finding ways to interpret how locals engage the workplace, make decisions, tolerate uncertainty, use power, and build consensus. In addition, expats will confront different trade rules, investment regulations, and business practices. Resourcefulness enables one to make sense of odd situations and develop insightful solutions.

Executives in foreign subsidiaries usually assume a greater range of leadership roles than counterparts running similar-size home-country operations.

Fast-growing markets, for instance, have attracted many MNEs and, by extension, expatriates. More than a few hail from a rule of law environment (where rules governing business are straightforward directives, as in Germany), and move into a rule of man setting (where rules are seen more as flexible guidelines, as in China). One expat noted that in the West, "everything is transparent. If you want to obtain a license to do something, you don't need to spend money bribing an official or hiring a go-between: You just download the form from the Internet and apply."[97] Moving from the transparency of Germany to the opacity of China can prove daunting for those accustomed to following the straight and narrow. Resourcefulness, whether adapting to cultures, laws, or simply getting around town, shapes an expatriate's performance.

GLOBAL MINDSET

Figure 20.4 highlights the eclectic set of competencies, talents, and outlooks that shape an expat's success. Collectively, this data highlights the importance of a global mindset. Increasingly a precondition as well as an outcome of expatriate success, a global mindset reflects awareness of differences across countries coupled with a capacity to divine

FIGURE 20.4   Key Competencies of Expatriates

Surveys of the preferred competencies of expatriates consistently emphasize facets of executive outlook and international orientation. Effectively, technical skills open the door to an international assignment, but leadership skills and global mindset move one through it.[98]

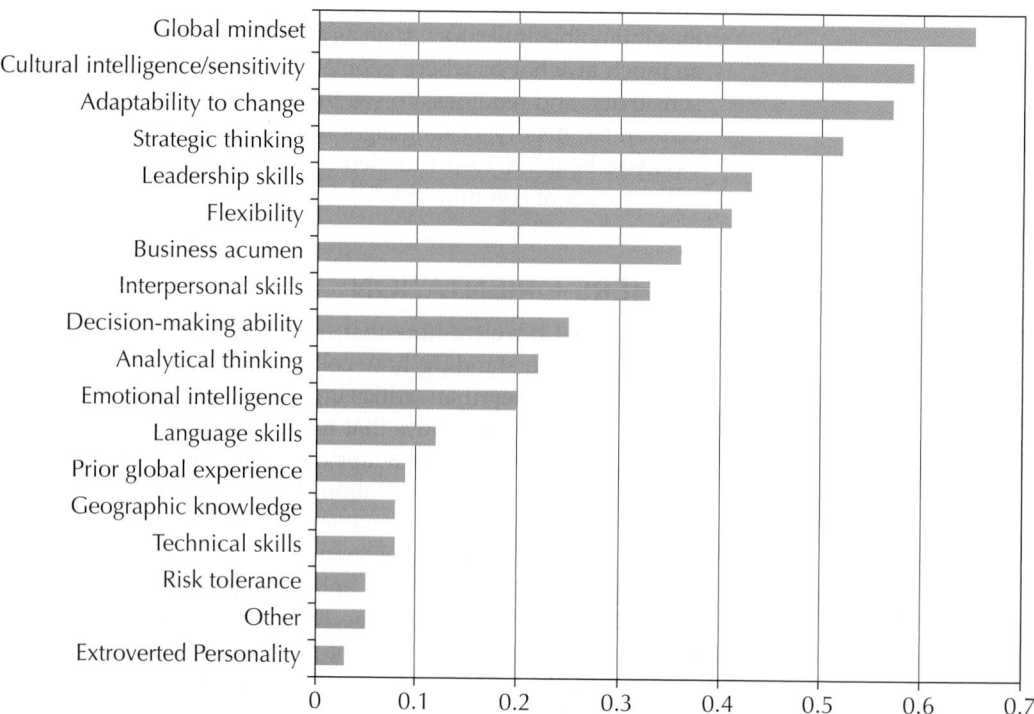

A global mindset helps successful expatriates see not a barren landscape, but a cornucopia of choices upon entering foreign markets.

overlapping principles. On this note, McKinsey & Co. concluded that whereas technical competence is a given, high-performance expatriates also have a particular mindset. Specifically, "When you look behind the success stories of leading globalizers, you find MNEs that have learned how to think differently from the herd. They seek out different information, process it in a different way, come to different conclusions, and make different decisions. Where others see threats and complexity, they see opportunity. Where others see a barren landscape, they see a cornucopia of choices."[99] Developing solutions requires switching from customary, even preferred methods, to alternative approaches. Making the switch depends on the expat's capacity to make sense of situations, adjusting her mindset given cues and circumstances, engaging the players and the processes, and insightfully responding.

EXPATRIATE PREPARATION AND DEVELOPMENT

Ideally, IHRIM begins preparing an executive for an international assignment long before she is slated to go. Too, IHRIM does not stop once she begins her new job; support systems carry on to optimize her performance. Often, circumstances prevent deliberative preparation. A foreign operation may be experiencing a technical meltdown, managerial impasse, or hostile takeover that requires headquarters immediately dispatch support. But, in a perfect world, IHRM has the flexibility to prepare and develop an executive for an international assignment.

Conventionally, IHRM focused on fitting an expat's technical know-how with the position's requirements. Functional expertise was seen as necessary and sufficient for high performance. Greater concern for the expat's business qualifications led IHRM to tailor preparation programs toward improving technical skills and administrative competencies. The matters of cultural awareness or resourcefulness were largely left up to the individual. Presumably, the manager interested in an international career would, through personal choices, travel abroad, monitor world events, and socialize with people of different ethnicities, cultures, and nationalities.[100]

CONCEPT CHECK

Improving understanding of the intricacies of international business operations, as we have seen in the previous chapters, along with increasingly sophisticated HRM programs has steadily reduced the rate of expatriate failure. Evidence confirms the importance of commanding a broad band of knowledge about institutions, markets, companies, and consumers.

FIGURE 20.5 Leading Concerns of Expatriates Ahead of Moving to Their Foreign Assignment

A foreign assignment is rich with opportunity yet, at the same time, fraught with challenges. Prior to heading abroad, executives worry about many issues. Anticipating and adjusting for the sorts of problems shown here improves the odds of a successful experience.[102]

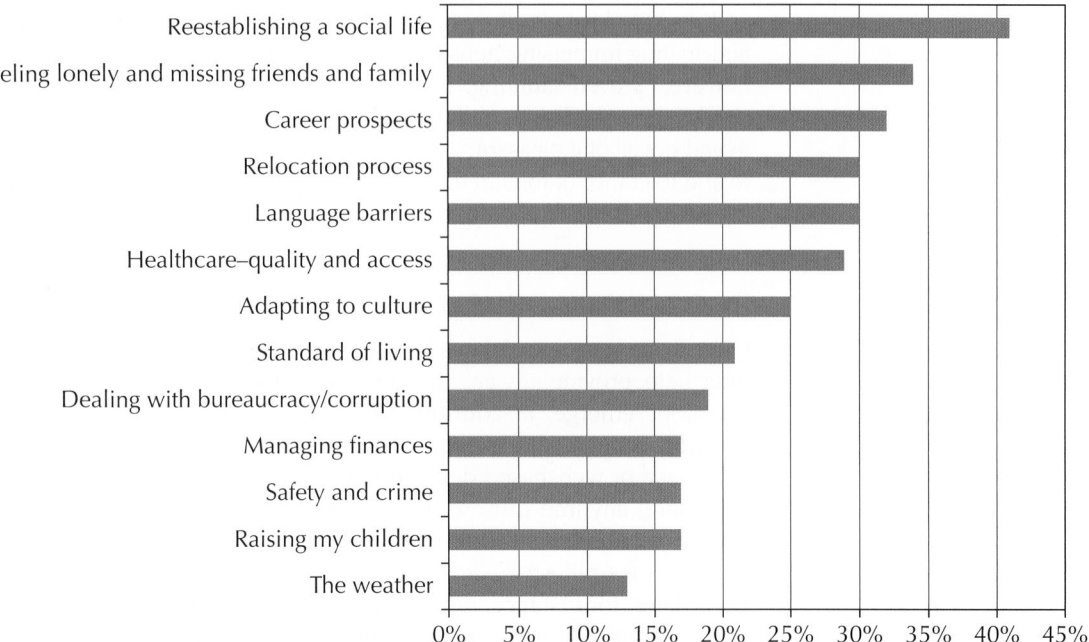

Performance records indicate that when eventually sent abroad, these sorts of managers often outperformed their less worldly counterparts.[101] The variability in performance among expatriates, by highlighting gaps in training and development, led MNEs to expand preparation and development beyond technical capabilities.

Today, rare is the foreign assignment that fails because IHRM misjudged a candidate's technical qualification. Improving understanding of working abroad finds that an executive's poor performance often follows from poor preparation for the lows of the international assignment. Unquestionably, as we saw in Figure 20.1, working abroad is often a stimulating experience. Still, expatriates run into difficulties that suppress, if not ruin, their workplace performance. Figure 20.5 identifies recurring stress points. Highlights, naturally, require little preparation. Stress points, however, do. Reestablishing a social life, overcoming loneliness, and reconciling with missing friends and family top the list. The challenge of building productive relationships with new, different colleagues, to say nothing of interacting with host nationals in a new cultural milieu, fans anxieties. These concerns show that improving cultural sensitivities and interpersonal skills improves the odds of successful adjustment and, by extension, a successful assignment.[103] IHRM translate this imperative into a two-stage program: preparation prior to departure, and then, once in-country, ongoing development.

PRE-DEPARTURE PREPARATION PROGRAMS

Host-country familiarization and cross-cultural orientation anchor most preparation programs.[104] A universal method is education about the way things work in the host country. Topics include politics, laws, economics, workplace practices, business etiquette, logistics options, and social situations. Instruction typically takes the form of roundtables, seminars, videos, web activities, and readings. Collectively, these materials provide general area studies, market analysis, operational overviews, and workplace profiles. Often, due to the expat's imminent departure, they compose the bulk of preparation.

Ideally, preparation includes cross-cultural training and rudimentary language lessons. Both help expatriates better navigate life in the host country. Cultural orientation highlights how differing ideas, attitudes, and beliefs influence workplace and social relations. These outlooks do

Expatriate preparation programs aim to transfer specific information about the host country as well as improve the executive's cultural sensitivity.

Culture shock is the anxiety and disorientation experienced when one moves into an unfamiliar culture.

not come naturally to all. Hence, preparing expats often requires helping them recognize gaps in their global mindset. Realization helps immunize them to **culture shock**—a soon-after-arrival dissatisfaction with the host society that can deteriorate into homesickness, irritability, arrogance, and disdain. Michelle Brown, for example, departed London for a job in Hong Kong, eagerly anticipating immersing herself in the new culture. The day-to-day practicalities of her new life, however, proved daunting. "I suppose I was quite naive, but Hong Kong was a complete culture shock," she says. "The humidity was insane, the smells made me ill, there was just so much to take in and not all of it pleasant."[105] Improving cross-cultural sensitivity boosts people's receptiveness to and tolerance of foreign environments.[106] Expats appreciate cross-cultural preparation; ongoing surveys consistently report that more than 80 percent see it as a good to great value.[107]

IN-COUNTRY DEVELOPMENT PROGRAMS

Once in-country, expatriates initially flow well in the workplace—colleagues and coworkers offer help, provide advice, and cut slack for the new guy. Gradually, ambiguous workplace situations emerge. In-country development efforts, often through mentorship programs, virtual meetings, and executive coaching, support the expatriate. Increasingly, MNEs use CD-based or web-based development programs, given that the expatriate can tap resources anywhere, anytime during an assignment.[108] Their economical convenience provides in-country reinforcement tools that can span the assignment.

Key to successfully transitioning to a foreign assignment, beyond workplace adjustments, is mastering the new ways of schooling, socializing, and shopping.

In terms of lifestyle, developing new routines in a different place can prove demanding. Expatriates, for instance, report big challenges arranging finances, health care, accommodations, and utilities in a host of locales, such as India, China, Brazil, Qatar, Russia, and Saudi Arabia. Notably easier, but still not the same as home, are South Africa, Canada, Thailand, and Australia.[109] Familiarizing expatriates and their families with host-country routines develops an understanding of the realities of daily life. The sooner they establish productive patterns of schooling, socializing, and shopping (to some, the "3Ss" of successful adjustment), the higher the odds of withstanding culture shock.

FAMILY MATTERS

Executives decline expatriate assignments for a variety of reasons, including compensation, security, and quality-of-life concerns. All pale in comparison to the influence of family and partner/spouse/children concerns—executives cite those reasons nearly 70 percent of the time they decline an expat offer.[110] Furthermore, a persistent cause of poor performance is the struggles an expatriate's spouse and children experience adapting to their new home. The foreign assignment is stressful for the expatriate, but the transfer can overwhelm the family. Challenges follow from education concerns, lifestyle adjustments, and family members' lingering regret about moving abroad. Expats warn of a recurring dynamic. Abrupt separation from friends, family, and career isolates the spouse and children. Many then look for companionship and reassurance from the expatriate whose job demands leave scant time to provide support. Sometimes slowly, sometimes quickly, but almost always, family harmony suffers as stress escalates. Unchecked, the expat's work performance declines because, "If the family starts to unravel, the employee will at some time start to unravel too."[111]

Increasingly, expatriate preparation and support activities include the spouse and family members.

IHRM tries workarounds, such as posting executives on short-term or commuter assignments, thereby avoiding uprooting families. Others advocate sending younger or older folks. Younger candidates are more likely single; motivated by adventure, career, and money; and less risk-averse. Alternatively, older candidates have grown children and more-agreeable partners.[112] An emerging trend is including families in predeparture preparation, particularly destination familiarization and cultural orientation programs. Similarly, proliferating dual career track family structures lead companies to extend support to spouses. Popular programs include language training, intercultural preparation, work permit advice, job finding fees, and career planning assistance. Some offer allowances for spousal support, club memberships, job possibilities, volunteer options, and support networks.

Point

English: Destined to Be the Global Language?

Point **Yes** The prevalence of English worldwide signals that learning a foreign language, while arguably worthwhile, is ultimately unnecessary. Inexorably, English ably performs as the *lingua franca* of the business world, providing a universal means for people who speak mutually unintelligible languages to communicate effectively. Presently, about a quarter of the world's population speaks some English, including the nearly 450 million who speak it as their mother tongue and the billions for whom it is a second language. Both counts steadily grow.[113] Too, when you get down to hard dollars, English rules. It accounts for a far larger share of world output than that represented by the proportion of native speakers. Though the first language of only 7 percent of the world's population, English speakers generate more than 40 percent of world output.

The Preferred Choice Situations in the European Union (EU), where more than half the population claims to be reasonably conversant in English, highlight common trends. Among Europeans born circa 1950, English, French, and German are equally common. But 15- to 24-year-olds are five times more likely to speak English as a foreign language than either German or French. Add native speakers to those who have learned it, and some 60 percent of young Europeans speak English "well or very well."[114] Many envision improving their competency; more than 70 percent in a survey of 16,000 people living in the EU agreed, "Everybody should speak English."

We see similar trends elsewhere. India has the second-largest fluent English-speaking population, after the United States; it will have the world's largest number of fluent English speakers within a decade. Hindi films, advertising billboards, and higher education are in English. Most well-paying jobs in India require some English competency.[115] In China, state employees younger than 40 must master a minimum of 1,000 English phrases.[116] The prevalence of English throughout the Arab world fans worry about the decline of Arabic. American universities reflect these general trends as well. Although they are aggressively internationalizing their curricula, fewer require foreign language training—currently 37 percent versus 53 percent in 2001. The share of university students enrolled in foreign language classes has dropped by half since 1960.[117]

The Default Choice Although English is not an official language in many countries, it is commonly taught as the second language. In the EU, 76 percent of schoolchildren study English, followed by French (32 percent), German (18 percent), and Spanish (8 percent). More than 90 percent

study English in Malta, Austria, Spain, Italy, Cyprus, Poland, Croatia, and France.[118] More than a quarter billion students in China study English; some begin as young as two, but all by kindergarten. More than a fifth of Japanese five-year-olds study English conversation. Argentina requires students from the fourth grade through high school to study English two hours per week. Chile mandates public schools begin teaching English in the fifth grade. English is the language of choice in the classrooms of many African countries. Countries worldwide aim to become bilingual in English in the next decade or two in the belief that "it's the language for international teaching. English allows students to be able to come from anyplace in the world and for our students to go everywhere."[119] In sum, with 2 billion people speaking or studying it today, we are on the verge of widespread diffusion of English language competency.[120]

The Online Choice Expanding English use gains from its predominance on the Internet. Ever so easily, one can conduct business worldwide using the English interface of one's preferred browser.[121] More than 80 percent of home pages on the web are in English. Heavyweight publications around the world, like *Der Spiegel* and *China Daily*, offer English-language websites. The growing sophistication of translation software makes foreign language competency a moot point for those who prefer using their local language on the Internet. Offline, workable, nearly flawless simultaneous-translation devices are now close-at-hand.[122]

Then again, the online choice may reset our notion of language. Rather than the phonetics or morphology of English, German, or Mandarin, people will master the semantics and syntax of Python, Java, or Ruby. The latter, forms of high-level programming languages, arguably better prepare people for a future in which the Internet is the foundation for nearly everything. Facebook, for instance, serves more than 1.5 billion customers in more than 150 nations through a website interface that is automatically translated into more than 100 languages.[123] Speaking a programming language that fits the digital pieces together, rather than conversing with foreigners in their native tongue, may prove to be the path to meaningful linguistic competency. As the director of government affairs of the Computing Research Association notes, "To be successful in the modern world, regardless of your occupation, requires a fluency in computers."[124]

The Only Choice MNEs respond in kind. *The Economist* reports that just under half of employers rate foreign language competency as important; it ranked well behind technical skills, leadership ability, and career development in assessing an expat candidate.[125] Airbus, SAP, Lenovo, Honda, Daimler-Chrysler, Renault, Lufthansa, Rakuten, Aventis, Samsung, and Microsoft, to name a few, mandate English as the corporate language.[126] Growing interest in programming languages, long considered arcane as well as uncool, may reset standards. Finally, some say

language proficiency is an easy but ultimately misleading proxy of a global mindset. As one CEO explains, "I've met many people who speak three or four languages, yet still have a very narrow view of the world. At the same time, I've come across people who speak only English but have a real passion and curiosity about the world and who are very effective in different cultures."[127]

English: Destined to Be the Global Language?

Counterpoint

No Learning another tongue is an indisputably enriching experience that has life-changing and mind-altering benefits. Studying another society, through the prism of its language, clarifies one's understanding of the world as well as a sense of self. Ultimately, international cooperation and collaboration requires people with foreign language proficiencies.

New Ways of Thinking Learning a foreign language changes the way you think, teaching you that there are several ways to express a concept, interpret an abstraction, and make sense of a situation.[128] Thinking differently, besides improving exchanges with stakeholders, sharpens business skills and expands global mindsets. Employees' foreign-language competency adds professional and personal value.[129] Managers that learn a foreign language discover new ways to make innovative contributions. Even if far from fluent, the willingness to communicate in the language of the locals builds productive rapport with colleagues. Others add that countries have different cultural and business expectations that one can only decipher through the local language.

Research suggests that learning a foreign language makes you smarter.[130] Bilingualism fortifies the brain's so-called executive function—basically, the command system that we use to plan, solve problems and puzzles, and manage cognitively demanding tasks. Bilinguals demonstrate sharper sensitivity to environmental circumstances and show greater efficiency solving problems. They sustain focus in the face of distractions, easily switch attention from one matter to another, and excel at organizing information.[131]

Cultural Imperatives Language helps people build, understand, and express emotions, values, and intentions. A vibrant national language, besides defining and sustaining culture, fortifies nationalism. Rising linguicide—the killing of a language—spurs cultures and countries to protect their legacies. First, the death rate is accelerating: on average, every 14 days a language passes on. By 2100, more than half of the 7,000 languages presently used will likely

Counterpoint

disappear.[132] Second, linguicide commonly follows from a community of speakers of the native language becoming bilingual in another language, then gradually shifting allegiance to the latter language until they cease using the former.

Linguicide compels cultures to defend their language. Canada's Official Languages Act promotes and protects the equal status of French and English. France relies on its *L'Académie française*, its official authority on usage, vocabulary, and grammar, to prevent the Anglicization of French. Proliferating *Arabizi*—switching back and forth from Arabic to English—sparks concern throughout the Middle East. Saudi Arabia prohibits the use of English to answer telephone calls in hotels, private companies, and government offices.[133] Likewise, China's General Administration of Press and Publication sees the invasion of English words and abbreviations in Chinese texts "abusing the language" and "severely damages the standard and purity of the Chinese language and disrupts the harmonious and healthy language and cultural environment, causing negative social impacts."[134] China bans mixing foreign language phrases, such as English words or abbreviations like GDP (gross domestic product), CPI (consumer price index), or WTO (World Trade Organization), in Chinese publications.[135] Lastly, deanglicization is a matter of national pride for some; India, for example, regarded Bombay as the corrupted English version of Mumbai and an unwanted legacy of British colonial rule. Hence, we now have Mumbai—and, for that matter, Kolkata, Bengaluru, and Chennai rather than Calcutta, Bangalore, and Madras.

New Networks Executives averse to learning a foreign language, besides signifying cross-cultural difficulties, exclude themselves from influential business networks, complicate relations with local officials, and slow socializing with workmates.[136] Working abroad is challenging; linguistic limitations worsen matters.[137] Microsoft's Joan Pattle noted that her inability to speak Turkish made for a lonely stint in Istanbul, explaining, "You can't really mix with the locals...use local transportation because you can't read any of the signs."[138] Symbolically, the effort to speak the local language, no matter how poorly, sends a subtle but essential message: We are equal.[139] Moreover, as anyone who has struggled to learn a foreign language can attest, unexpected benefits include a good dose of humility.

New Requirements Eventually, foreign language competency will be a competitive necessity. The expanding international links and intercultural connections in a globalizing world make linguistic skills crucial for getting many jobs and accelerating careers. Differentiating one's competencies, such as through linguistic skills, creates opportunities. The notion that the spread of English competency worldwide means those who already speak it need not worry is dubious. Marketplace trends will punish, not privilege, English-only speakers. They steadily lose the advantages that once came with being among the small number of native Anglophones who spoke the language of business. Bilinguals or multilinguals increasingly offer

the same as English monoglots, but also add innovative cognitive outlooks and broader international perspectives. Officials have begun institutionalizing incentives to support this movement. For instance, the EU's official language policy is "mother tongue plus two," whereby citizens are encouraged to learn two additional languages.[140]

Which One? Ultimately, one wonders, which foreign language should I study? One has many choices that are shaped by popularity, prevalence, and difficulty. Market trends clarify options for business players. Entrepreneurs may look around their hometown and go for fast-spreading languages such as Spanish, Mandarin, or Arabic. Those looking abroad quickly recognize that expatriate slot positions are migrating from the West to emerging economies. As MNEs struggle to place expatriates in these high-growth markets, proficiency in languages like Mandarin or Hindi will open opportunities.

EXPATRIATE COMPENSATION

All things being equal, compensation can determine the likelihood and success of an expatriate assignment. Pay too little, and people decline to go; if they do go, resentment often proves demotivating and hastens an early return. Pay them too much, and costs escalate, returns fall short, and inequities fan dissension. Too, more often than not, the higher the pay, the longer an expatriate assignment tends to last. Some managers, content to prolong a munificent lifestyle, are less than eager to return home.[141] Hence, compensation plays a decisive role in attracting, motivating, and retaining expatriates.

Ceteris paribus, compensation can make or break an expatriate's motivation.

Setting effective compensation systems that fairly reward executives here, there, and everywhere requires IHRM deal with a range of issues regarding differing pay levels, benefits, tax programs, and prerequisites. Should the MNE, for instance, pay executives in different countries according to the prevailing standards in each locale? Or should it set pay for each position on a global basis? What sorts of allowance should it offer? What might be the qualification standards? How should it resolve the impact of different tax policies on compensation? Further complicating these compensation choices is accommodating the different types of expatriates such as, long-term, short-term, commuter, flexpatriates, third-country nationals, that move among assignments worldwide.

"Keeping employees whole" spurs IHRM to offset features of the international assignment that negatively affect an expatriate's standard of living.

IHRM faces relentless pressure to economize the expense of an expatriate assignment. MNEs in the United States can easily spend great amounts on an expatriate during a three-year assignment. Practically, posting a $200,000-a-year American executive from Atlanta to São Paulo overnight triples her cost to her employer. Move her to high-cost locales like Hong Kong, Singapore, Luanda, or Zurich, and she becomes a million-dollar executive. Improving the return on investment on the expat calls for negotiating reasonable salaries. Several conditions shape the standards of reasonable.

- IHRM's mission is "keeping the expatiate whole," setting compensation so that working abroad does not impose additional costs that diminish one's standard of living.
- IHRM devises packages that convince an executive and family to go abroad, reflect the responsibility of the foreign assignment, and ensure that their after-tax income will not fall because of the foreign assignment.
- IHRM sets plans that preserve pay equity among peers, promote parity among expatriates, and ensure compensation competes with packages offered by rivals.

- IHRM delivers compensation packages that reconcile parent- and host-country financial, legal, and customary practices.
- IHRM devises efficiently administered compensation systems and policies.

These tasks are formidable and inexorably expand in line with the scale and scope of the MNEs international operations. IHRM, through trial and error as well as astute analytics, develops systems and methods that regularly meet the challenge.

TYPES OF COMPENSATION PLANS

MNEs generally manage expatriate compensation with variations of the **balance sheet approach**.[142] This approach organizes compensation plans so that an expatriate has the same living standard in the foreign post that he had at home, no matter where the assignment puts him.[143] In the spirit of "keeping one whole," its fundamental principle is *equalization*: an expatriate should neither overly prosper nor unduly suffer from working abroad.[144] The following methods implement variations of the balance sheet approach.

Home-Based Method This method bases expatriate compensation on the salary of a comparable job in the expat's hometown, thereby preserving equity with home-country colleagues as well as simplifying their eventual return. Salary is often set in the same manner as that for a domestic position, such as by a job evaluation or a competency-based plan, market surveys, merit, and incentives. It's the most prevalent compensation plan. Approximately 80 percent of MNEs apply it to short- and long-term assignments, especially for experienced mid- to senior-level expatriates.[145]

Headquarters-Based Method This method sets the expatriate's salary in the terms of a comparable job in the city where the MNE has its headquarters. For example, if a Boston-headquartered MNE posts expats to its offices in London, Santiago, and Jakarta, it would give each executive a salary structured in terms of the going wage in Boston. This plan recognizes the disruption of a foreign assignment and helps expatriates live as they had in their home country. This plan eases moving an expatriate from a low to a high cost post.

Host-Based Method Sometimes called *destination pricing, going rate,* or *localization,* this method bases expatriate compensation on the prevailing pay scales in the foreign locale. IHRM starts by setting the expatriate's salary in terms of a local executive with similar responsibilities. The expat then negotiates additional compensation in the form of cost-of-living allowances, home-country benefits, taxation relief, and so on. The host-based method compensates expatriates, relative to the home- and headquarters-based methods, the least. Although not beneficial to the employee, it reduces tension between an expatriate and typically lower-paid, host-country colleagues. Moreover, lower compensation expense improves the MNE's return on its investment. PwC uses the host-based method for expats involved in its EPIC program. It offsets lower pay with immigration aid, relocation planning, language study, and intercultural training.

Global Market Method Variability in the types, conditions, and duration of expatriate assignments, from traditional to commuter to flexpatriate, require IHRM tweak compensation methods. The global market approach views an international assignment as a continuous but an irregular activity. It recognizes that an expatriate, in the context of a commuter or flex assignment, irregularly works for different durations in the same or, sometimes, different countries. Implementing this approach requires designing flexible systems and sophisticated performance tracking that, in spite of logistical complications, keeps the expat whole.

The most common approach to determining expatriate compensation is the balance sheet approach.

Ideally, compensation neither overly rewards nor unduly punishes a person for accepting a foreign assignment.

Variations of the balance sheet approach to expatriate compensation include
- home-based method
- headquarters-based method
- host-based method
- global market method

Expatriate compensation packages typically incorporate many types of payments, allowances, provisions, and reimbursements.

Allowances give HRM the flexibility to tailor compensation plans to deal with special situations.

COMPONENTS OF EXPATRIATE COMPENSATION

The home-, headquarters-, and host-, and global market methods apply different goals and guidelines to set total compensation.[146] Commonly, expatriates negotiate their base salary, foreign-service premium, various allowances, fringe benefits, tax differentials, and benefits (see Table 20.2). Each dimension can significantly influence the total compensation.

The changing economics of expatriate assignments moderates compensation schemes. In particular, the mandate to contain costs pushes IHRM to review the link between aspects of selecting and classifying expatriates with compensation standards. Key points include:

Assignment Type The growing use of commuters and flexpatriates alters the compensation calculus. Short-term assignments typically do not trigger a change in pay or benefits, but add a per diem to regular pay.[147]

Supply Dynamics Growing numbers are willing to work most anywhere nowadays, motivated by career ambitions and personal quests. Some executives want to work abroad in order to turbocharge their career. Others see experiencing situations that expand their mindset, not financial gain, as the benefit of a foreign assignment.[148] In both cases, executives accept working abroad for lower pay. Consequently, many international assignments have "gone from being special and unique, with piles of money thrown at them, to being an everyday part of the company."[149] Foreign service premiums, likewise, have been phased out by many.[150]

TABLE 20.2 Components of Expatriate Compensation

Sending an executive on an international assignment imposes expensive logistics and considerable stress. MNEs adjust the total compensation package with the following sorts of allowances.

Dimension	Specification
Base Salary	An expat's base salary normally falls in the same range as that for a comparable job in the home country. It is paid either in the home-country currency or in the local currency.
Cost-of-Living	Ensures that expats don't suffer a decline in their standard of living due to the steep expense of a particular city (London or Lagos) or nation (Switzerland). Fair compensation reflects the cost of living in the assigned foreign city, accounting for its cost of goods and services, including housing, transportation, food, clothing, household goods, and entertainment.[151]
Foreign Service Premium	This cash incentive, a.k.a mobility premium, compensates an individual for the inconvenience of moving to a new country, living away from family and friends, dealing with the day-to-day challenges of the new culture, language, and workplace practices, and the reality that he will ultimately have to disrupt this life upon return. Long-term assignments often qualify for a mobility premium; short-term assignments rarely do.
Fringe Benefits	Various benefits supplement the expatriate's base salary, including health insurance, life coverage, education reimbursement, childcare and assistance reimbursement, and spouse support.[152]
Hardship	An expatriate assigned to a difficult environment or dangerous location typically negotiates a hardship allowance—a.k.a. combat pay. This allowance offsets the costs of security systems, ransom insurance, crisis response safeguards, or threat management programs.[153]
Housing	Allowance that enables the expatriate to replicate his accustomed standard of housing.[154]
Tax Differentials	Varying tax policies require that MNEs adjust compensation so that expatriates' after-tax income does not suffer from the taxes incurred during the foreign assignment. Tax equalization often proves a costly component of expatriate compensation.

IHRM tailors allowances to help an expatriate offset the difficulties of

- different standards of living,
- replicating preferred housing,
- supporting a trailing spouse,
- extraordinary safety or security hardships.

Redefining Markets Cost-reduction techniques redefine the compensation parameters of an international assignment. Many MNEs with operations in Europe now treat the continent as if it were one country. Others cut hardship allowances for locales that are far more hospitable than they once were, such as Prague, Shanghai, and Rio de Janeiro. Increasing globalization steadily reduces the number of hardship destinations.

COMPENSATION COMPLICATIONS

Setting compensation in evolving organizations that use several types of expatriates expands the parameters of analysis. IHRM, for instance, regularly resolves complications of the following sort.

CONCEPT CHECK

The expanding scale and scope of globalization, driven by increasing physical and cybernetic connectivity, increasingly blur the idea of expatriates. Where once foreigners seemed foreign, today they seem almost commonplace. Consequently, there is less need to pay people premiums to go to places that are increasingly alike.

Changing Standards The evolving dynamics of globalization require IHRM fine-tune compensation methods. The home-based method, for example, was designed to compensate employees and families transferred from Western-headquartered MNEs to slots throughout the world. Effectively, it based its cost of living indices and support allowances for moves from high-cost countries, such as England or the United States, to countries like Malaysia or Kenya.

Difficulties emerge when the path reverses—say, transferring an executive from inexpensive Manila to costly San Francisco. For example, Chinese expatriates tend not to enjoy lavish pay and benefits. China Unicom's managing director in Europe received his modest Chinese salary plus a small cost-of-living allowance during his foreign assignment. Combined, they totaled 30 percent of the local entry-level salary for his firm.[155] Hence, MNEs applying the balance sheet approach, particularly the home-based method, struggle to maintain pay equity and benefit consistency given the changing locales and demography of their expatriate populations.

MNEs struggle to equalize pay for the same type of job that is done by different people in different countries.

Consistency Concerns Systematizing pay and benefit programs while removing inconsistencies makes for fair and equitable compensation plans. Steadily, salaries for similar jobs vary less substantially among countries. Still, legal, cultural, and regulatory differences require tailoring performance-based pay by country and region. Differences especially challenge MNEs applying a geocentric staffing framework. Managing expatriates of multiple nationalities transferred from high to low or low to high cost markets quickly creates anomalies and exceptions. IHRM must determine if all managers who perform the same job, but in different locations, receive the same compensation.

Besides reducing the company's return on its investment, extreme pay disparities among managers doing similar jobs saps coworkers' motivation. An MNE with an ethnocentric or polycentric staffing policy, alternatively, has its own complications. It may have few expatriates today, but expanding internationalization complicates administering compensation packages on a case-by-case basis. Hence, even if few in number, effective IHRM calls for developing standards and systems. Then, throughout it all, IHRM must reconcile the dilemma of paying the expat just enough to persuade her to work abroad, but without sacrificing the standard of keeping her financially whole.[156]

EXPATRIATE REPATRIATION

IHRM drives a cycle of events: selection, preparation, compensation, and repatriation. The latter task is the process of reintegrating an expatriate into the home company upon completion of her foreign assignment, intact, and in good spirits. Success at each stage in the sequence, not just early on, supports a self-sustaining cycle. Returning employees share their knowledge, experiences, and enthusiasm with colleagues. High-performing coworkers, realizing the rewards of an international assignment, look abroad.

Repatriation works for many. Returning expatriates report that their international experience boosted career trajectories, led to faster promotions, improved performance ratings, and increased compensation. Others report repatriation falls short. Promotions never arrive, career

Repatriation returns an expatriate to his or her home country.

Returning home from a foreign assignment can be professionally rewarding. It is also marked by difficulties.

progression stalls, opportunities fade, and networks weaken.[157] A survey of expatriates who had successfully completed their overseas assignments found that a third held temporary assignments three months after returning home. Of these, 80 percent saw their new jobs as demotions and some 60 percent saw few opportunities to leverage their international expertise. Frustrated, former high flyers left for other companies—the 15-year average switch runs around 20 percent.[158] But, spun differently, 80 percent of returning expats remain with their employer.[159]

REPATRIATION CHALLENGES

IHRM, focused on boosting success rates, identifies recurring stress points.[160] Consistently, job placement dominates an expatriate's concerns, followed by changes in personal finances and readjusting to life at home.

Repatriation tends to trigger work, financial, and social adjustment difficulties.

Career Progression Pressed to pinpoint where repatriation breakdowns begin, expats target the difficulty of returning to the right job. "People who have spent two years working in different ways across varied markets and cultures are not always happy to return to the same desk and the same prospects," concludes one report. Others add that "in this vacuum of direction, many have a career 'wobble,' and then leave via a recruitment market in which their experience is seen as increasingly valuable."[161] More than half of returning expatriates report that their employer had been vague about career progression. Others noted returning home to less challenging jobs and finding former peers have been promoted above them. Colleagues occasionally question whether they've maintained cutting-edge market knowledge and technical skills during their exotic "vacation." They may struggle to rejoin the office network. Resentment often builds as executives reason that they have worked hard to progress professionally, taken one for the team, and deserve praise and promotion.

The principal cause of repatriation frustrations is finding the right job for the returning executive.

A recurring repatriation difficulty is "out of sight overseas" deteriorates into "out of mind back home." This fear leads some fast-tracking executives to decline an international assignment. Going abroad effectively means leaving the power center for the periphery. Explains one executive, "MNEs station people abroad and then forget about them. If anything, advancement is even more difficult for the expat when he returns to headquarters, having missed out on opportunities to network with top management."[162] This situation plays havoc in business cultures, especially those anchored in collectivism, where face time with influential executives shapes promotions.

Reverse culture shock occurs when one experiences anxiety when returning to one's own culture.

Changes in Personal Finances Returning home significantly alters the expat's finances. Many enjoy rich benefits during an international assignment, living in exclusive neighborhoods, sending children to prestigious schools, employing domestic help, socializing with elites, and still saving a good amount. Returning home to a reasonable compensation plan with far fewer privileges can prove demoralizing.

CONCEPT CHECK

Chapters 3 and 4 note political, legal, and economic factors that contribute to the changing profile of high-growth markets. Chapter 17 discusses new wrinkles in global manufacturing strategies and strategies in supply-chain management that respond to this changing profile. These trends lead some MNEs to preempt repatriation problems by changing their expatriate-staffing policies to recruit more locals to run local operations.

Personal Readjustment Return challenges repatriates to readjust to home life.[163] Problems emerge as they, and their families, experience reverse culture shock. Upon returning to the United States, one said, "I loved the culture so much in Peru. My feelings don't fit my own beliefs anymore. This is my home, but it doesn't make sense."[164] Depending on the length of the international assignment, repatriates may need to relearn what they once took for granted about hometown life. Meantime, children may struggle to fit into school, while spouses may feel isolated or out of touch with the career or friends they left behind.

IMPROVING REPATRIATION

IHRM notes the importance of effective repatriation. Most have formal repatriation policies, organize workshops, and link return strategies to career management.[165] Some find ways to create opportunities for the expatriate to utilize her international experience, providing recognition after the assignment, supporting the family's transition, and providing greater choices of new assignments. Still, repatriation demands jam many employers into difficult situations. An expat's office cannot sit vacant while she is abroad. Mergers, acquisitions, divestures, and restructurings change a company's plans and, by extension, those it had for the expatriate. Likewise, permitting repatriated employees to bump their "replacements" on return solves one problem, but creates another.

IHRM studies and solves repatriation complications precisely because the greater the difficulties that repatriates confront, the greater the difficulty in convincing others to accept international assignments. Some MNEs pledge that repatriates will return to jobs at least as good as those they originally left. Others integrate foreign assignments into career planning, developing mentoring programs to safeguard the expat's career. PwC's EPIC program installs safety nets, promising participants "unrivaled support mechanisms" to safeguard their careers.[166] Personal career management is as vital to being selected for a foreign assignment as it is to returning home triumphantly. IHRM advises expats to manage the cycle, encouraging them to regularly revisit the home office, either in person or online, to sustain networks. Passivity is hazardous. Navigating repatriation requires a keen sense of its positive and negative aspects—before departure, while abroad, and particularly before transitioning home.[167]

EXPATRIATE FAILURE

The best-laid plans, as we all know, often go awry. Similarly, MNEs fall prey when they select their best and brightest executives, invest in their development, send them abroad, compensate them well, and watch them fail. Sometimes expatriate failure is the result of poor assignment planning, putting the wrong person in the wrong job at the wrong time with the wrong expectations. Other times it comes as a surprise, as personal circumstances disrupt what many saw as a sure thing. In either case, plans get twisted. **Expatriate failure**, narrowly defined, is a manager's premature return home due to poor operational performance. Broadly defined, it is the breakdown of IHRM's expatriate management systems.

The improving sophistication of expatriate selection processes has reduced the rate of expatriate failure.

In the 1980s, performance problems brought nearly a third of American expatriates assigned to advanced countries home early; the failure rate was twice that for those posted to less-hospitable countries. Today, approximately 5 percent of expats fail to complete their assignment.[168] Leading causes include quitting to work elsewhere, family concerns, spouse/partner dissatisfaction, inadequate job performance, organizational restructuring, and internal transfer. Difficulty adjusting to the host culture and quality of life, once commonplace concerns, are increasingly anomalies given the expanding connectivity of globalization.

THE COSTS OF FAILURE

Expatriate failure is operationally costly, professionally detrimental, and personally stressful.

The continuing decline in expatriate failure testifies to the improving sophistication of IHRM's talent to select, prep, and post the right individual to the right job. The decline is cause for celebration, but it does not signify mission accomplished. The financial and personal costs of failure, no matter how infrequent, are significant. Moreover, some worry about a possible rise in failure rates. Expansion into emerging economies puts expats into markets that test their resourcefulness to deal with fundamentally different environments. Already, we see escalating difficulties. China and India, today's leading hotbeds of expat slots, top the list of locations with the highest failure rates.[169] The average cost of failure runs as high as three times the expat's annual domestic salary plus the cost of relocation.[170] Total financial costs are often eye-opening when one accounts for the time and money spent on selection, preparation, logistics, lost productivity, and damage control. An incalculable cost is the personal implications of professional failure to the formerly high-performing executive's self-confidence and leadership potential. Finally, there is the consequence of the hardship on the spouse and family.[171]

A leading cause of expatriate failure is the difficulty the partner/spouse and family experience in adapting to the foreign assignment.

THE WILDCARD

Some folks, despite best-intentions, do not adjust well to working abroad. In theory, an ideal expatriate's technical qualification, self-confidence, resourcefulness, and global mind-set make her effective anywhere and everywhere.[172] For some, this ideal rings hollow given struggles overcoming the operational and lifestyle challenges of the assignment. Sadly, awareness of differences, as one might hear from an executive about to depart Boston for Bangkok, does not confirm the capacity to adapt to the odd, strange, and different.[173] Displacement can lead to nostalgia, culture shock, and depression. Notwithstanding the glamour and rewards, the expatriate lifestyle moves some far beyond their comfort zone. Then, no matter the degree of preparation, a sought-after adventure devolves into a nerve-wracking exile.[174]

Looking to the Future

I'm Going Where? The Changing Locations of International Assignments

A generation ago, expatriates, by and large, flocked to the premier business centers of the flourishing markets of Europe, North America, and Japan.[175] Looking down the road signals big changes in the geography of expatriate assignments. Western MNEs are reorienting their strategies toward countries that once were off the beaten path. The rising importance of emerging economies, particularly in fast-growing Africa, Asia, and South America, leads them to open and expand operations there. Meanwhile, back in their home markets, Western MNEs downscale operations and reduce headcounts. At Unilever, for example, emerging markets generate more than 60 percent of sales. In the United States, companies such as GE, Microsoft, IBM, Walmart, and Citibank reset operations, relocating activities to emerging markets.

Changing corporate configurations drive all sorts of change. Consider the matter of hotel rooms in Africa. Its long-dormant but now fast-growing markets attract an increasing number of expats of all sorts, including commuters, flexpatriates, and long-termers. Consequently, hotel chains are fast-tracking new facilities across Africa. Marriott, a U.S. hotel group, plans 50 hotels in Africa by 2020, a 600 percent increase. Accor, a French counterpart, plans another 5,000 rooms in 30 hotels spanning the continent. Other global hotel brands are scouting sites in African capitals.[176]

As multinationals reset battle lines, they redeploy their troops. In the 1990s, for example, U.S. companies added 4.4 million workers in the United States versus 2.7 million abroad. In contrast, during the 2000s they cut their workforces in the United States by nearly 3 million, while concurrently boosting employment overseas by 2.4 million. Asked about the shift, GE's chief executive replied, "Today we go to Brazil, we go to China, we go to India, because that's where the customers are."[177] Correspondingly, MNEs reorganize their executives, moving those that had worked in the West to business centers in the East. Cisco combined all of its emerging-markets activities into a single unit, "Cisco East" in Bengaluru, and transferred a high-ranking executive with the auspicious title of Chief Globalization Officer. Moreover, the pace of change accelerates—executives at 17 MNEs reported that "just 2 percent of their top 200 employees were located in Asian emerging markets that would, in the years ahead, account for more than one-third of total sales."[178]

Changing Career Strategies

The allure of emerging markets extends beyond companies. Graduates face slow-growing business and saturated executive markets in mature Western economies. Many see better chances getting promoted, to say nothing about starting a career, in Panama City, Shanghai, Lagos, or Mumbai than in New York, Tokyo, Paris, or London. "A lot of my friends are going to Asia and Latin America to do their internships," said a student at a prominent U.S. business school. "It may be outside their comfort zone, but they see getting some experience there as helpful, since that's where many of the jobs will be."[179] Then again, let's not forget about the magnetic draw of working abroad to young people; a survey of 4,200 graduates in

44 countries found that 80 percent wanted to work internationally.[180]

Rather than patiently waiting for opportunities, students jump-start the process and head straight to the markets they see powering the future. While compelling for graduates with cultural links to foreign locales as well as those with relevant language fluency, the siren call of opportunity also attracts those with limited cultural experience and linguistic skills.[181] Growing economies, lower costs of living, higher after-tax compensation, and the chance to bypass years spent in dues-paying entry-level jobs prove irresistible.

Full Speed Ahead

As sales, growth, labor, and executive opportunity migrate from the West to emerging economies, we anticipate a radical reset of the geography of expatriate assignments and activities. Data already confirms the trend is underway: China, Brazil, the United Arab Emirates, Hong Kong, India, and Singapore are leading destinations for expats.[182] Not far behind are Thailand, Malaysia, Kenya, and Nigeria. Finally, keep in mind that the flow is not one way. Emerging market MNEs increasingly post expatriates to run operations in Western markets.[183] ∎

CASE Tel-Comm-Tek: Selecting the Managing Director of its Indian Subsidiary[184]

In May 2016, Mark Hopkins, managing director of Tel-Comm-Tek (TCT) India, a subsidiary of a U.S. MNE, announced his retirement. During his tenure, Hopkins had overseen the rising growth, market share, and profitability of the Indian operation. Upon his announcement, TCT began searching for his replacement.

TCT manufactures office equipment, such as photocopiers, laser printers, and document shredders, in 13 countries that are then sold worldwide. Most recently, it reported sales in 83 countries. TCT entered India in 2005, initially relying on local agents to sell and service its imported products. Increasing sales led TCT to open a marketing subsidiary in New Delhi in 2010. TCT's sales have steadily risen, in tandem with the booming Indian IT industry. Forecasts saw sales accelerating, fueled by demand from local companies, such as Infosys, Tata, and Wipro. TCT USA projected India's becoming the center point of its expanding Asian operations. In 2015, TCT made plans to add a local manufacturing facility to its Indian operations.

India: An Emerging Juggernaut

Fast Growth

Some see India developing into the world's next big industrial power. This view leads many MNEs to expand their Indian operations. For example, IBM, a longtime customer of TCT, has steadily boosted its Indian headcounts from a handful in 1998 to approximately 150,000 today. TCT expects India's growth will push its total sales past those of the United States by 2024.

Improving Infrastructure

The expanding Indian transportation network spurred expanding TCT India's strategy. Improving highways, railways, and ports boost logistic efficiencies. Management sees TCT India becoming a vital link in its global supply chain and, longer term, the hub of its Asian network.

Political Economy

From 1947 through 1990, India had a centrally planned economy. Government control, rather than free-market ideals, led to the notorious "License Raj," a situation marked by extensive regulations that were administered by an opaque bureaucracy. In 1991, a balance-of-payments crisis forced India's hand. The government began liberalizing the economy, scrapping burdensome regulations and boosting investment, trade, and operating freedom. Its transition, an ongoing process, stabilized the economy and improves India's market attractiveness. Confident of continuing liberalization, TCT decided to invest in a manufacturing unit.

Labor Laws

Notwithstanding steady deregulation, India's restrictive labor laws pose problems. They prohibit companies, for example, from letting manufacturing workers clock more than 54 hours of overtime in any three-month period—even if workers are willing. India's Industrial Disputes Act requires a company employing 100 or more workers get the state's authorization before firing anyone, no matter how dire the situation.[185] Permission typically hinges on extensive negotiations and settlements. Consequently, "companies think twice, 10 times, before they hire new people," said the CEO of India's Hero Group.[186]

Industry Regulation

Various laws, largely designed to protect the millions of small enterprises operating in scattered villages, restrict MNEs from competing in many Indian industries. High tariffs pose other challenges. Instituted long ago to promote domestic production, they still apply to many imports. Minimizing tariff exposure spurs TCT to make products locally.

Legal Legacies

Although a functioning democracy, corruption mars India's business environment. Transparency International 2015, for instance, ranked it 85 of 175 countries in terms of the misuse of public power for private benefit.[187] Its legal system, though endorsing the rule of law, struggles with the problems posed by its vast bureaucracy—a legacy of its centrally planned economy and the infamous License Raj. Regulatory transparency has improved, but has far to go. High-tech MNEs have struggled to protect intellectual property rights.

Damn the Torpedoes, Full Speed Ahead

In early 2017, TCT began building a factory in Bengaluru, the center of India's Silicon Valley. The plant will make entry-level to high-end laser printers, with the first production run set for March 2018. Local shortages of quality components require initially sourcing inputs from TCT's U.S. facilities. Several of these inputs face high tariffs. Ultimately, TCT India plans to make these parts locally.

TCT India initially planned to hire 75 to 90 workers to run its assembly line. It anticipates no problems recruiting skilled labor given demographic and educational circumstances. For example, when the South Korean conglomerate LG looked to staff 458 assembly-line jobs at its just-opened Indian factory, it required applicants to have at least 15 years of education—a condition that translates into having both high school and technical college certification. Too, preferring a young workforce, LG sought workers with some, but not much, previous experience. Ultimately, some 55,000 people qualified for interviews. Likewise, millions regularly apply for slots at prominent Indian IT MNEs.[188]

TCT enlisted a Japanese engineering firm to supervise construction of its Bengaluru plant. Upon completion, Gary Kent will temporarily move from TCT's USA laser printer factory in the role of production supervisor. He will jointly report to TCT's U.S. headquarters as well as TCT India's managing director in New Delhi (the position made vacant by Hopkins's retirement). Once the plant is certified, Mr. Kent will return to the United States and his replacement will report directly to the managing director of TCT India.

Selecting the Managing Director

TCT applies a geocentric staffing framework, mixing home-, host-, and third-country nationals to staff international operations. It fills executive vacancies by promoting the best-qualified candidate from within; a key criteria is openness to developing a global mindset. It also rotates managers among its foreign and U.S. locations, believing that international experience is a key facet of leadership. Generally, ambitious executives must successfully complete an expatriate assignment before contending for a C-level position.

The Candidates

TCT USA charged its Asian Regional Office to select the Managing Director for TCT India. The Director commissioned a committee, consisting of manufacturing, marketing, logistics, and administrative representatives, to rank order the following candidates:

Atasi Das
Source: Shutterstock

- **Atasi Das:** Born in the United States, Das joined TCT nine years ago after earning her MBA from a university in New England. At 38, she has successfully moved between staff and line positions and assumed broader responsibilities in strategic planning. For two years, she was the assistant director of a midsized product group. Her performance regularly earns excellent ratings. Currently, she directs supply-chain logistics from TCT's home office. Upon joining TCT, she stated her goal was to work internationally, pointing to her undergraduate major in international management. She has reiterated her interest in international responsibilities and her interest in continuing with TCT, but was not averse to looking elsewhere. She speaks Hindi and is unmarried. Her parents, who now live in the United States, are first-generation immigrants from India. She has relatives in India's northern states, Kashmir and Punjab.

Brett Harrison
Source: EDHAR/Shutterstock

- **Brett Harrison:** Harrison, 44, has spent 15 years with TCT running both line activities and supervising staff. His superiors consider him a seasoned executive poised to move into upper-level management. For the past three years, he has worked in the Singapore-based Asian Regional Office and regularly tours TCT's Asian operations. He and his wife, along with their two teenage children, have traveled to India a few times and are familiar with its geography, politics, customs, and outlooks. The Harrisons know other expats in the Bengaluru region. Mrs. Harrison works as the marketing director for the Singapore subsidiary of a Japanese pharmaceutical company. It presently does not have an operating unit in India.

Jalan Bukit Seng
Source: Ajay Bhaskar/Shutterstock

- **Jalan Bukit Seng:** Seng, 52, is the managing director of TCT's assembly operation in Malaysia. A citizen of Singapore, he has spent his career in Singapore or Malaysia. He regularly commutes to various TCT factories, helping to upgrade assembly systems and supervising equipment refits. He earned an undergraduate and MBA degrees from the National University of Singapore and speaks Singapore's four official languages—Malay, English, Mandarin, and Tamil. His performance reviews are consistently positive, with a periodic ranking of excellent. Seng is unmarried but has family members in Singapore and Malaysia.

Ravi Desai
Source: ansar80/Shutterstock

- **Ravi Desai:** Currently an assistant managing director in TCT India, Desai oversees local market activity. A citizen of India, he has spent 11 years with TCT, primarily working in India, but also working, short-term, in the Japanese and Australian units as a flexpatriate. Now 37, he holds an MBA from the prestigious Indian Institute of Management. He is married, has two children (ages 2 and 7), and speaks English and Hindi as well. His wife, also a native of India, neither works outside the home nor speaks English.

Saumitra Chakraborty
Source: Ashwin/Shutterstock

- **Saumitra Chakraborty:** At 36, Chakraborty is an executive assistant to the departing managing director in India. He has held that position since joining TCT India upon graduating from Oxford University. He consistently earns a job performance rating of excellent in customer relationship management. He has increased TCT India's sales, largely owing to his connections with prominent Indian families and government officials, along with his skillfulness in the ways of the Indian business environment. Besides speaking India's main languages of English and Hindi, Chakraborty is the only candidate who speaks Kannada (the local language of Bengaluru). Presently, he lacks line experience.

Tom Wallace
Source: Andresr/Shutterstock

- **Tom Wallace:** A 30-year TCT veteran, Wallace has broad technical skills and sales experience. He has worked with Gary Kent on supply-chain projects in the United States. Although he has never worked abroad, he has periodically toured TCT's foreign operations. He recently expressed interest in an expatriate slot. His superiors typically rate his performance as excellent. Wallace is set to retire in seven years. He and his wife speak only English. They have three adult children who live with their own families in the United States. Presently, Wallace manages a U.S. unit that is a little larger than the present size of TCT India. The merger of his unit with another TCT division will eliminate his current position in nine months.

QUESTIONS

⭐ **20-3.** Identify the key advantage of each of the six candidates. Identify their key limitation. Rank-order the candidates, from the most to least qualified, for the position of Managing Director of TCT India.

⭐ **20-4.** What operational and personal challenges might the person you recommend encounter if named managing director?

20-5. What steps would you recommend your preferred candidate take to manage those challenges?

20-6. What are the pros and cons of posting a foreign national versus an Indian-born candidate to the position of Managing Director?

MyLab Management

Go to **mymanagementlab.com** for the following Assisted-graded writing questions:

20-7 How should the compensation package differ if TCT U.S. opted for a short-term versus long-term expatriate assignment?

20-8 What benefits might result by appointing two different individuals to the position of co-managing director of TCT India – effectively, one person would supervise sales and customer relations while the other would supervise manufacturing. Each slot would command equal positional authority and each person would be charged to co-manage with his or her counterpart. What benefits issues might result from this arrangement? What problems, if any, might occur?

Endnotes

Scan for Endnotes or go to www.pearsonglobaleditions.com/Daniels

Glossary

Absolute advantage: A free trade theory holding that different countries produce different things more efficiently than others.

Acceptable quality level (AQL): A concept of quality control whereby managers are willing to accept a certain level of production defects, which are dealt with through repair facilities and service centers.

Acquired advantage: An explanation of a country's competitive advantage based on either product or process technology.

Acquired group memberships: An individual affiliation not determined by birth, such as religion, political membership, and profession.

Active income: Income of a CFC that is derived from the active conduct of a trade or business, as specified by the U.S. Internal Revenue Code.

Ad valorem duty or tariff: A tax placed on the value of goods shipped internationally.

Advance import deposit: A form of foreign-exchange convertibility control where the government tightens control of import licenses and requires importers to make a deposit with the central bank.

American Depositary Receipt (ADR): A negotiable certificate issued by a U.S. bank in the United States to represent the underlying shares of a foreign corporation's stock held in trust at a custodian bank in the foreign country.

American terms: The practice of using the direct quote for exchange rates.

Andean Community (CAN): A South American form of economic integration involving Bolivia, Colombia, Ecuador, and Peru.

Arbitrage: The process of buying and selling foreign currency at a profit that results from price discrepancies between or among markets.

Arm's-length price: A price between two companies that do not have an ownership interest in each other.

Ascribed group membership: An individual affiliation determined by birth, such as gender, family, age, ethnicity, and race.

Asia Pacific Economic Cooperation (APEC): A cooperation formed by 21 countries that border the Pacific Rim in Asia and the Americas to promote multilateral economic cooperation in trade and investment in the Pacific Rim.

Association of South East Asian Nations (ASEAN): A free trade area involving the Asian countries of Brunei, Cambodia, Indonesia, Laos, Malaysia, Myanmar, the Philippines, Singapore, Thailand, and Vietnam.

Ascribed group memberships: An individual affiliation determined by birth, such as gender, family, age, ethnicity, and race.

Balance of payments: Statement that summarizes all economic transactions between a country and the rest of the world during a given period of time.

Balance sheet approach: Compensation plan that sets expatriate salaries to equalize purchasing power across countries.

Bank for International Settlements (BIS): A bank in Basel, Switzerland, that facilitates transactions among central banks; it is effectively the central banks' central bank.

Base currency: The currency whose value is implicitly 1 when a quote is made between two currencies; for example, if the Brazilian real is trading at 3.8 reals (reais) per dollar, the dollar is the base currency and the real is the quoted currency.

Bargaining school theory: A premise that the terms of a foreign investor's operations depend on how much the investor and host country need each other.

Base of the Pyramid: The billions of people living on less than a few dollars per day yet who some see as the next market frontier of the global economy.

Bicultural: A description of someone who has internalized two different national cultures.

Bid (buy) rate: The amount a trader is willing to pay for foreign exchange.

Bilateral integration: A form of integration between two countries in which they agree to cooperate more closely, usually in the form of tariff reductions, but often in other areas as well.

Black market: The foreign-exchange market that lies outside the official market.

Born-global companies: Companies that start out with a global focus, usually because of their founders' international experience and knowledge of foreign markets through advances in communications.

Boundaries: In terms of political environments, an official or perceived point of separation that defines the boundary of a nation. In terms of organization structure, horizontal constraints that follow from having specific employees only do specific jobs in specific units as well as the vertical constraints that separate employees into specific levels of a precisely stipulated command-and-control hierarchy.

Boundarylessness: State whereby companies build organizations that eliminate the vertical, horizontal, and external boundaries that impede information flows and hinder developing relationships.

Bretton Woods Agreement: An agreement among IMF countries to promote exchange-rate stability and to facilitate the international flow of currencies.

BRICs: An acronym referring to the nations of Brazil, Russia, India, and China that reflect their vanguard status as emerging economies.

Bureaucratic control: System whereby an organization uses centralized authority to install rules and procedures to govern activities.

Capability: A distinct type of resource that improves the productivity of related resources owned by the firm.

Capitalism: An economic system characterized by private ownership, pricing, production, and distribution of goods.

Caribbean Community (CARICOM): A customs union in the Caribbean region.

Carry trade: Borrow a currency at a low interest rate and invest it in a currency with a higher interest rate.

Centralization: The degree to which high-level managers, usually above the country level, make strategic decisions and delegate them to lower levels for implementation.

Civil law system: A legal system based on a detailed set of laws that are organized into a code; countries with a civil law system, also called a codified legal system, include Germany, France, and Japan.

Civil law: A body of rules that delineate private rights and remedies, and govern disputes between individuals in such areas as contracts, property, and family.

Chicago Mercantile Exchange (CME) Group: The CME Group is the world's leading and most diverse derivatives marketplace, dealing in future and options products for a wide variety of asset classes, including foreign exchange.

Clan control: System whereby an MNE relies on shared values among employees to idealize and enforce preferred behaviors.

Cluster effect: Follows from the congregation of buyers and sellers of a particular good or service in a certain locale; they, in turn, induce other buyers and sellers to relocate there.

Code of conduct: A set of principles guiding the actions of MNEs in their contacts with societies.

Collaborative arrangements: Companies' working together, such as in joint ventures, licensing agreements, management contracts, minority ownership, and long-term contractual arrangements.

Collectivism: Perspective that the needs of the group take precedence over the needs of the individual; encourages dependence on the organization.

Command economy: An economic system in which the political authorities make major decisions regarding the production and distribution of goods and services.

Commercial law: The area of law that governs the broad areas of business, commerce, and consumer transactions.

Common law system: A legal system based on tradition, precedent, and custom and usage, in which the courts interpret the law based on those conventions; found in the United Kingdom and former British colonies.

Common market: A form of regional economic integration in which countries abolish internal tariffs, use a common external tariff, and abolish restrictions on factor mobility.

Communism: A form of totalitarianism initially theorized by Karl Marx in which the political and economic systems are virtually inseparable.

Commuter assignment: One where the expatriate travels between his home and host country at frequent intervals.

Comparable access argument: Also known as a fairness argument, it holds that industries are entitled to the same access to foreign markets as foreign industries have to theirs.

Comparative advantage: A free trade argument that global efficiency gains may result from trade if a country specializes in what it can produce most efficiently, even though other countries' may have an absolute advantage.

Compound duty: A tariff based on both a valuation and the number of units traded.

Concentrated configuration: The design of a value chain whereby a particular activity is performed in one geographic location and serves the world from it.

Concentration strategy: A company first moves to only one or a few foreign countries, not going elsewhere until it develops a very strong involvement and competitive position.

Configuration: To set up, arrange, and disperse value activities to the ideal locations around the world so that the company can start and sustain operations.

Confirmed letter of credit: A letter of credit to which a bank in the exporter's country adds its guarantee of payment.

Consolidation: An accounting process in which financial statements of related entities, such as a parent and its subsidiaries, are combined to yield a unified set of financial statements; in the process, transactions among the related enterprises are eliminated so that the statements reflect transactions with outside parties.

Contract manufacturer: A company that is responsible for manufacturing and delivering a product on behalf of another company with which it is contracted.

Constitutional law: Law that is created and changed by the people.

Consortium: An organization owned by more than two firms.

Consumer ethnocentrism: Preference for local to global, such as seeking out local alternatives when buying products and services.

Control systems: Process by which managers compare performance to plans, identify differences, and, where found, assess the basis for the gap and implement corrective action; ensure that activities are completed in ways that support the company's strategy.

Controlled foreign corporation (CFC): A foreign corporation of which more than 50 percent of the voting stock is owned by U.S. shareholders (taxable entities that own at least 10 percent of the voting stock of the corporation).

Convergence: Efforts by the FASB and IASC to move toward a common global set of accounting standards.

Coopetition: Refers to situations in which competing firms collaborate on some portions of their operations.

Coordination by mutual adjustment: System whereby managers interact extensively with counterparts in setting common goals.

Coordination by plan: System that relies on general goals and detailed objectives to coordinate activities.

Coordination by standardization: System whereby rules and procedures apply to units worldwide, thereby enforcing consistency in the performance of activities in geographically dispersed units.

Coordination systems: Systems that synchronize the work responsibilities of the value chain so that the company uses its resources efficiently and makes decisions effectively.

Core competency: A special outlook, skill, capability, or technology that runs through the firm's operations, weaving together disparate value activities into an integrated value chain; Managers bundle resources and capabilities to create a core competency.

Core values: Values so strong that they are not negotiable.

Cosmopolitanism: Openness to the world, thus high acceptance of foreign products.

Cost leadership: Strategy whereby a firm sells its products at the average industry price to earn a profit higher than that of rivals or below the average industry prices to capture market share.

Cost-plus strategy: Pricing at a desired margin over cost.

Countertrade (or offsets): A requirement that an exporter create value in the importing country, such as by transferring technology or receiving payment in the importing country's merchandise. An umbrella term for several sorts of trade, such as barter or offset, in which the seller accepts goods or services, rather than currency or credit, as payment.

Country-similarity theory: A trade theory that organizations place earlier and stronger emphasis on those countries most similar to their own.

Country of origin: Where products or services are created, which affects trade in that consumers may prefer to buy goods produced in one country rather than another usually because of quality perceptions or because of nationalism.

Criminal law: Body of laws dealing with crimes against the public and members of the public.

Cross-licensing: An arrangement whereby companies exchange technology or other intangible property rather than compete with each other on every product in every market.

Cross rate: An exchange rate between two currencies used in the spot market and computed from the exchange rate of each currency in relation to a third currency, usually the U.S. dollar.

Cultural collision: A situation whereby contact among divergent cultures creates problems.

Cultural distance: A measurement based on cultural factors that indicates the relative similarity of countries culturally.

Cultural imperialism: The imposition of certain elements from an alien culture.

Culture: The shared values, attitudes, and beliefs of a group of individuals.

Culture shock: The frustration resulting from having to absorb a vast array of new cultural cues and expectations.

Currency swap: The exchange of principal and interest payments between two currencies.

Current-rate method: A method of translating foreign-currency financial statements that is used when the functional currency is that of the local operating environment.

Customary law system: A legal system anchored in the wisdom of daily experience or great spiritual or philosophical traditions.

Customs broker: The profession that involves helping importers and exporters clear shipments through a nation's customs agencies.

Deal-focus (DF) culture: A culture in which people are primarily task oriented rather than relationship oriented.

Decentralization: The degree to which lower-level managers, usually at or below the country level, make and implement strategic decisions.

Deflation: A decrease in the general price level of goods and services; often caused by a reduction in the supply of money or credit.

Democracy Index: An index compiled by the Economist Intelligence Unit that assesses the state of democracy in many states based on 60 indicators.

Democracy: A political system that relies on citizens' participation in the decision-making process.

Deontological approach: An approach which asserts that moral reasoning occurs independent of consequences.

Dependencia theory: A theory holding that emerging economies have practically no power in their dealings with MNEs.

Derivative: A foreign-exchange instrument such as an option or futures contract that derives its value from the underlying currency.

Developed economy: An economy marked by a comparatively higher standard of living, advanced technological infrastructure, and broader range of productive activities relative to developing economies.

Developing country: A developing country is typically marked by low industrialization and low standard of living relative to other countries; also referred to as a less developed country or underdeveloped country.

Diamond of national competitive advantage: A theory showing four features as important for countries' competitive superiority: demand conditions; factor conditions; related and supporting industries; and firm strategy, structure, and rivalry.

Differentiation: A business strategy in which a company tries to gain a competitive advantage by providing a unique product or service, or providing a unique brand of customer service.

Digitization: The conversion of paper and other media in existing collections to digital form.

Direct exports: Products sold to an independent party outside of the exporter's home country.

Direct quote: A quote expressed in terms of the number of units of the domestic currency given for one unit of a foreign currency.

Dispersed configuration: The design of a value chain whereby a particular activity is performed in many geographic locations and serves the world market from any to all of its units.

Distribution: The course—physical path or legal title—that goods take between production and consumption.

Diversification strategy: In the context of IB location, it describes a company's rapid movement into many foreign markets, gradually increasing its commitment within each one.

Divesting: This is also called harvesting. It is the process of reducing commitments in some countries because they have poorer performance prospects than do others.

Divisional structures: An organization that contains separate divisions based around individual product lines or based on the geographic areas of the markets served.

Draft (or commercial bill of exchange): An instrument of payment in international business that instructs the importer to forward payment to the exporter.

Dumping: Exporting below cost or below the home-country price.

Duty: A tax levied on a good shipped internationally (also known as a tariff).

Dynamic effect: The overall growth in the market and the impact on a company of expanding production and achieving greater economies of scale.

E-commerce: The use of the Internet to join together suppliers with companies and companies with customers.

Economic exposure (operating exposure): The potential for change in expected cash flows that arises from the pricing of products, the sourcing and cost of inputs, and the location of investments.

Economic Freedom Index: The systematic measurement of economic freedom in countries throughout the world; sponsored by the Heritage Foundation and the *Wall Street Journal*.

Economic freedom: The absence of government coercion or constraint on the production, distribution, or consumption of goods and services beyond the extent necessary for citizens to protect and maintain liberty.

Economic integration: Political and economic agreements among nations in which preference is given to member countries, especially as they relate to the reduction of trade barriers.

Economic system: The system concerned with the allocation of scarce resources.

Economies of scale: The lowering of cost per unit as output increases because of allocation of fixed costs over more units produced.

Economy in transition: Economy applying structural transformations that aim to institute market-based principles and practices.

Effective tariff: An argument that the manufactured portion of products from developing countries pay higher tariffs in developed countries than the stated tariff because the raw material component would have come in duty free.

Electronic data interchange (EDI): The electronic movement of money and information via computers and telecommunications equipment.

Embargo: A specific type of quota that prohibits all trade.

Emerging economies: Countries with developing economies, often experiencing rapid growth and offering lucrative investment opportunities, but also characterized by political instability and high risk.

Emerging economy: An economy that is experiencing rapid growth, expanding industrialization, and improving standard of living.

Enterprise resource planning (ERP): Software that can link information flows from different parts of a business and from different geographic areas.

Equity alliance: A collaborative arrangement in which at least one of the companies takes an ownership position (almost always minority) in the other(s).

Escalation of commitment: The more time and money companies invest in examining an alternative, the more likely they are to accept it, regardless of its merits.

Essential-industry argument: A rationale for protectionism contending that nations should apply trade restrictions to protect crucial domestic industries so that they are not dependent on foreign supplies during hostile political periods.

Ethnocentrism: A conviction that one's own practices are superior to those in other countries.

Ethnocentric framework: A staffing approach in which all key management positions, whether in the home country or abroad, are filled by home-country nationals.

Euro: The common currency of the European Union, although not all members have adopted the euro.

Eurobond: A bond sold in a country other than the one in whose currency it is denominated.

Eurocredit: A loan, line of credit, or other form of medium- or long-term credit on the Eurocurrency market that has a maturity of more than one year.

Eurocurrency: Any currency that is banked outside of its country of origin.

Eurocurrency market: An international wholesale market that deals in Eurocurrencies.

Eurodollars: U.S. dollars banked outside of the United States.

Euroequity market: The market for shares sold outside the boundaries of the issuing company's home country.

European Central Bank (ECB): Established July 1, 1998, the ECB is responsible for setting the monetary policy and for managing the exchange-rate system for all of Europe since January 1, 1999.

European Monetary System (EMS): A cooperative foreign-exchange agreement involving many members of the EU and designed to promote exchange-rate stability within the EU.

European Monetary Union (EMU): An agreement by participating European Union member countries that consists of three stages coordinating economic policy and culminating with the adoption of the euro.

European terms: The practice of using the indirect quote for exchange rates.

European Union (EU): A form of regional economic integration among countries in Europe that involves a free trade area, a customs union, and the free mobility of factors of production that is working toward political and economic union. It is governed by the European Commision, the European Council, the European Parliament, and the Court of Justice.

Exchange rate: The price of one currency in terms of another currency.

Expatriate: An expatriate, often reduced to "expat," is a person temporarily or permanently working in a country other than that of his or her country of origin.

Expatriate failure: Narrowly defined, it is the manager's premature return home due to poor performance. Broadly defined, it is the failure of the MNE's selection policies to identify individuals who succeed abroad.

Expatriate selection: The process of screening executives to find those with the greatest inclination and highest potential for a foreign assignment.

Experience effect: The more experience a firm has in producing a particular good or service, the lower are its costs.

Export intermediaries: Individuals or companies that assume responsibility for different combinations of finding overseas buyers, sourcing and shipping products, and getting paid on the behalf of a manufacturer. The export intermediary may be a commissioned agent, an export management company (EMC), an export trading company (ETC), an export agent, or a re-marketer.

Export plan: Specification of the key issues that shape the success of exporting.

Export tariffs: Taxes collected on exports by the exporting country.

Exporting: The sale of goods or services produced by a company based in one country to customers that reside in a different country.

Export-led development: A country's promotion of industries with export potential so as to increase economic growth.

Extranet: The use of the Internet to link a company with outsiders.

Extraterritoriality: The extension by a government of the application of its laws to foreign operations of companies.

Factor mobility theory: A theory focusing on why production factors move internationally, the effects of those movements on transforming factor endowments, and their impact on world trade.

Factor proportions theory: A theory maintaining that differences in countries' proportional endowments of labor, land, and capital explain differences in these endowments' costs and, thus, the export of products using abundant and cheaper inputs.

Favorable balance of trade: A country is exporting more than it imports.

FDI: An acronym for foreign direct investment.

Financial Accounting Standards Board (FASB): The private-sector organization that sets financial accounting standards in the United States.

First-mover advantage: Being first into a country enables a firm to more easily gain the best partners, best locations, and best suppliers.

Fisher Effect: The theory about the relationship between inflation and interest rates; for example, if the nominal interest rate in one country is lower than that in another, the first country's inflation should be lower so that the real interest rates will be equal.

Five-forces model: A framework used to assess industry structure and business strategy in estimating the potential for profitability.

Flexpatriates: An employee who conducts an international assignment through frequent international business travel from his home market rather than relocating to the host market.

Foreign bond: A bond sold outside of the borrower's country but denominated in the currency of the country of issue.

Foreign Corrupt Practices Act (FCPA): A law that criminalizes certain types of payments by U.S. companies, such as bribes to foreign government officials.

Foreign direct investment: This is sometimes referred to simply as *direct investment*. It is an operation in which an investor holds a controlling interest in a foreign company.

Foreign exchange: Checks and other instruments for making payments in another country's currency.

Foreign exchange control: A requirement that an individual or company must apply to government authorities for permission to buy foreign currency above some determined threshold amount.

Foreign-exchange market: The market where foreign exchange is traded; usually banks, nonbank financial institutions, and exchanges, such as the CME.

Forward discount: The amount by which the forward rate in a foreign currency is less than the spot rate, that is, the foreign currency is expected to weaken in the future.

Forward premium: The amount by which the forward rate in a foreign currency is greater than the spot rate, that is, the foreign currency is expected to strengthen in the future.

Franchising: A contract in which a company assists another on a continuous basis and allows use of its trademark.

Freight forwarder: A company that facilitates the movement of goods from one country to another.

Functional currency: The currency of the primary economic environment in which an entity operates; useful in helping a firm determine how to translate its foreign currency financial statements into the current of the parent company.

Functional structure: An organization that is structured according to functional areas of business.

Fundamental forecasting: A forecasting tool that uses trends in economic variables to predict future exchange rates.

Future orientation: A willingness to delay gratification in order to reap more in the future.

Futures contract: An agreement between two parties to buy or sell a particular currency at a particular price on a particular future date, as specified in a standardized contract to all participants in that currency futures exchange.

FX swap: A simultaneous spot and forward transaction in foreign exchange.

Gap analysis: A tool used by a company to estimate potential sales for a given type of product and compare how emphasis on different marketing mix elements accounts for shortcomings in reaching the potential.

General Agreement on Tariffs and Trade (GATT): A global arrangement aimed at reducing barriers to trade, both tariff and nontariff; at the signing of the Uruguay round, the GATT was designated to become the World Trade Organization (WTO).

Generally Accepted Accounting Principles (GAAP): The accounting standards accepted by the accounting profession in each country as required for the preparation of financial statements for external users.

Generic: A situation whereby a branded product enters the public domain so that competitors can use the name for their products.

Geocentrism: A process of integrating home- and host-country practices as well as introducing some entirely new ones.

Geocentric staffing framework: Staffing perspective that seeks the best people for key jobs throughout the organization, regardless of nationality.

Gini coefficient: A measure of the extent to which the distribution of income deviates from a perfectly equal distribution.

Global integration: The unification of distinct national economic systems into one global market.

Global strategy: A strategy that increases profitability by achieving cost reductions from experience curves and location economies.

Globality: The state of affairs where one competes with everyone, from everywhere, for everything.

Globalization: The widening and deepening of interdependent relationships among people from different nations. The term sometimes refers to the elimination of barriers to international movements of goods, services, capital, technology, and people that influence the integration of world economies.

Glorecalization: A portmanteau of **Glo**balization-**Re**gionalization-Lo**calization;** champions consistent global values and customized local tactics within a regional context.

Go-no-go decisions: Examining one opportunity at a time and pursuing it if it meets some threshold criteria.

Gray market: It is also called product diversion and refers to the selling and handling of goods through unofficial distributors.

Great by choice: The principle that managers' choices are the basis of building and sustaining a high-performance enterprise in unpredictable, tumultuous, and fast-moving times.

Green economics: Transdisciplinary field that studies the interdependence and coevolution of human economies and natural ecosystems.

Gross national income (GNI): Formerly referred to as Gross national product.

Gross national product (GNP): The total of incomes earned by residents of a country, regardless of where the productive assets are located.

Gulf Cooperation Council: A group of Middle-Eastern, oil-rich Arab countries that includes Bahrain, Saudi Arabia, Kuwait, Oman, Qatar, and the UAE.

Happynomics: Evaluating a country's performance and potential by directly considering peoples' life satisfaction.

Hard currency: A currency that is freely traded without many restrictions and for which there is usually strong external demand; often called a freely convertible currency.

Harvesting: This is also called divesting. It is the process of reducing commitments in some countries because they have poorer performance prospects than do others.

Hedge fund: An investment fund available to a limited number of investors that is managed more aggressively than mutual funds.

Hierarchy-of-needs theory: A motivation theory that people try to fulfill lower-level needs before moving on to higher-level ones.

High-context cultures: Where most people tend to understand and regard indirect information as pertinent.

Home-country nationals: Expatriate employees who are citizens of the country in which the company is headquartered.

Idealism: A preference to establish overall principles before trying to resolve small issues.

Import or export license: A country's requirement that importers or exporters secure governmental permission before transacting trade. The license often controls access to foreign exchange at a government-specified exchange rate.

Import substitution: The restriction of imports to boost local production of products that would otherwise be imported.

Import tariffs: Taxes on traded goods imposed by the country in which international shipments enter.

Importing: The purchase of products by a company based in one country from sellers that reside in another.

Income distribution: The distribution of national income among groups of individuals, households, social classes, or factors of production.

Incremental internationalization: The view that as a company gains experience, resources, and confidence, it progressively exports to increasingly distant and dissimilar countries.

Indirect exports: Exports that are not handled directly by the manufacturer or producer but through an export agent, freight forwarder, or 3PL.

Indirect quote: An exchange rate given in terms of the number of units of the foreign currency for one unit of the domestic currency.

Individualism: A construct comparing people's preference to fulfill leisure time, build friendships, and improve skills independently and outside the organization as opposed to collectively and within the organization.

Industrial policy: This is also known as a strategic trade policy. It is one in which a government identifies target industries to develop to be internationally competitive.

Industrialization argument: A trade protection argument that, although a country may develop an inefficient and non-globally competitive industrial sector, it will achieve economic growth by protecting the industrial sector so that the unemployed and underemployed people can work in industry.

Industry organization (IO) paradigm: Field of economics that studies the strategic behavior of firms, the structure of markets, and their interactions.

Industry structure: The makeup of an industry: its number of sellers and their size distribution, the nature of the product, and the extent of barriers to entry.

Infant-industry argument: It holds that a government should shield an emerging industry from foreign competition by guaranteeing it a large share of the domestic market until it can compete on its own.

Inflation: A general and progressive increase in prices.

Inpatriate: An expatriate transferred from a foreign operation to the MNE's headquarters country.

Institutions: Systems of established and prevalent social rules that structure social interactions, such as language, money, law, systems of weights and measures, table manners and organizations.

Integrated cost leadership/differentiation strategy: Simultaneously pursue providing unique but comparatively inexpensive goods or services by combining elements of the cost leadership and differentiation strategy.

Integration-responsiveness (IR) grid: Schema that helps managers measure the global and local pressures that influence the configuration and coordination of value chains.

Intellectual property (IP): Property in the form of patents, trademarks, service marks, trade names, trade secrets, and copyrights.

Intellectual property right (IPR): Ownership rights to intangible assets, such as patents, trademarks, copyrights, and know-how.

Interbank transactions: Foreign-exchange transactions that take place between commercial banks.

Internalization: Control through self-handling of foreign operations, primarily because such control is less expensive than to contract with an external organization.

Interest arbitrage: Investing in debt instruments in different countries to take advantage of interest differentials. The investment is "covered" if the investor converts money into foreign exchange at the spot rate, invests it in the foreign market at a higher interest rate, and enters into a forward contract so that it can convert principle and interest back into the home currency and earn more than if that money had been invested in the home currency.

International Accounting Standards Board (IASB): The international private-sector organization based in London that sets financial accounting standards for worldwide use.

International Financial Reporting Standards (IFRS): A set of accounting standards issued by the International Accounting Standards Board (IASB) and adopted by many countries, especially those in the European Union.

International Fisher Effect (IFE): The theory that the relationship between interest rates and exchange rates implies that the currency of the country with the lower interest rate will strengthen in the future.

International human resource management (IHRM): The staffing function of the organization; includes the activities of human resources planning, recruitment, selection, performance appraisal, compensation, retention, and labor relations.

International Monetary Fund (IMF): A multi-governmental association organized in 1945 to promote exchange-rate stability and to facilitate the international flow of currencies.

International Organization of Securities Commissions (IOSCO): An international organization of securities regulators that supports the efforts of the IASB to establish comprehensive accounting standards.

International strategy: The effort of managers to create value by transferring core competencies from the home market to foreign markets in which local competitors lack those competencies.

Intranet: The use of the Internet to link together the different divisions and functions inside a company.

Jamaica Agreement: A 1976 agreement among countries that permitted greater flexibility of exchange rates, basically formalizing the break from fixed exchange rates.

Joint venture: An operation in which two or more companies share ownership. (There are also non-equity joint ventures.)

Kyoto Protocol: An international agreement among countries to reduce the emission of greenhouse gases which was replaced by the Paris Agreement in 2015/2016.

Lag strategy: An operational strategy that involves either delaying collection of foreign-currency receivables if the currency is expected to strengthen or delaying payment of foreign-currency payables if the currency is expected to weaken; the opposite of a lead strategy.

Laissez-faire: The concept of minimal government intervention in a society's economic activity.

Lead strategy: An operational strategy that involves either collecting foreign-currency receivables before they are due when the currency is expected to weaken or paying foreign-currency payables before they are due when the currency is expected to strengthen; the opposite of a lag strategy.

Learning effect: The more times a task has been performed, the less time is required on each subsequent iteration, thereby improving productivity.

Legal system: The rules that regulate behavior, the processes that enforce the laws of a country, and the procedures used to resolve grievances.

Letter of credit (L/C): A precise document by which the importer's bank extends credit to the importer and agrees to pay the exporter.

Leverage: The amount of debt used to finance a firm's assets.

Liability of foreignness: Foreign companies' lower survival rate in comparison to local companies for many years after they begin operations.

License for trade: *See* import or export license.

Licensing agreements: Contracts whereby firms allow others to use some assets, such as trademarks, patents, copyrights, or expertise.

Local content: A term used in trade agreements which refers to the percentage of a product which is produced in the member countries to the agreement. Preferential tariff provisions often depend on the amount of local or regional content included in a product.

Location advantages: Cost advantages arising from performing a value activity in the optimal location.

Local responsiveness: The process of disaggregating a standardized whole into differentiated parts to improve responsiveness to local market circumstances.

Localization strategy: An approach that emphasizes responsiveness to the unique conditions prevailing in different national markets.

Localization: Process whereby an expatriate retains a foreign assignment provided she accepts the status, and corresponding compensation, of a local hire.

Location economies: Cost advantages arising from performing a value activity in the optimal location.

Logistics (or materials) management: That part of the supply chain process that plans, implements, and controls the efficient, effective flow and storage of goods, services, and related information from the point of origin to the point of consumption, to meet customers' requirements; sometimes called materials management.

London Interbank Offered Rate (LIBOR): The interest rate for large interbank loans of Eurocurrencies. It is the benchmark interest rate for many different types of loans, including home mortgages.

Low-context cultures: Where people generally regard as relevant only firsthand information that bears directly on the subject at hand.

Management contracts: Arrangements in which a company provides personnel to perform management functions for another organization.

Market capitalization: A common measure of the size of a stock market, which is computed by multiplying the total number of shares of stock listed on the exchange by the market price per share.

Market control: System whereby an MNE uses external market mechanisms to establish internal performance benchmarks and standards.

Market economy: An economic system in which resources are allocated and controlled by consumers who "vote" by buying goods; emphasizes minimal government involvement.

Masculinity–femininity index: A construct measuring attitudes toward achievement and the roles expected of genders.

Materialism: The importance of acquiring possessions as a means of self-satisfaction and happiness, as well as for the appearance of success.

Matrix structure: A structure in which foreign units report (by product, function, or area) to more than one group, each of which shares responsibility over the foreign unit.

Mercosur: A major regional group in South America that includes Argentina, Brazil, Paraguay, Uruguay, and Venezuela that is hampered by internal political issues.

Mercantilism: A trade theory holding that a country's wealth is measured by its holdings of "treasure," which usually means its gold.

Merchandise exports and imports: Tangible products—goods—that are respectively sent *out* of and brought *into* a country.

Mission: Statement that defines the business, its objectives, and its approach to achieve them.

Mixed economy: An economic system characterized by some mixture of market and command economies; balances public and private ownership of factors of production.

Mixed legal system: A legal system that emerges when two or more legal systems function in a country.

Mixed structure: A structure that integrates various aspects of classical structures.

MNC: An acronym for multinational corporation or multinational company and a synonym for multinational enterprise.

MNE: An acronym for multinational enterprise.

Monochronic: A term to describe cultures in which most people normally prefer to work sequentially, such as finishing transactions with one customer before dealing with another.

Most-favored-nation (MFN) clause: A GATT (and now a WTO) requirement that a trade concession that is given to one country must be given to all other countries. Also known as "trade without discrimination."

Multicultural: Description of someone who has internalized more than two national cultures.

Multinational corporation or company (MNC): A synonym for a multinational enterprise (MNE).

Multinational enterprise (MNE): Usually signifies any company with foreign direct investments.

Multiple exchange-rate system: A means of foreign-exchange control whereby the government sets different exchange rates for different kinds of transactions.

Mutual recognition: The principle that a foreign registrant that wants to list and have its securities traded on a foreign stock exchange need only provide information prepared according to the GAAP of the registrant's country.

NASDAQ: The second-largest stock market in the United States that trades in equities, commodities, options, and futures. In the Nordic countries, it owns and operates the exchanges in Denmark, Finland, Iceland, Sweden, and has an exchange for commodities derivatives in Norway. It is known in the region as NASDAQ OMX.

Natural advantage: A reason for a competitive advantage in production that comes from countries' climatic conditions, access to certain natural resources, or availability of certain labor forces.

Nearshoring: This applies to bringing back or setting up production or services in a country close to the home country, often in a country that shares a common border.

Neoclassical structure: Applies different devices to resolve the shortcomings, such as conformity, rigidity, bureaucracy, and authoritarianism, often found in the classical formats of functional and divisional structures.

Neomercantilism: The running of a favorable balance of trade to achieve some social or political objective.

Net present value (NPV): The sum of the present values of the annual cash flows minus the initial investment.

Netting: The transfer of funds from subsidiaries in a net payable position to a central clearing account and from there to the accounts of the net receiver subsidiaries.

Network structure: Neoclassical structure whereby a small core organization outsources value activities to linked firms whose core competencies support greater innovation.

Non-tradable goods: Products and services that are seldom practical to export because of high transportation costs.

Normativism: A theory stating that universal standards of behavior (based on people's own values) exist that all cultures should follow, making nonintervention unethical.

North American Free Trade Agreement (NAFTA): A free trade agreement involving the United States, Canada, and Mexico that went into effect on January 1, 1994.

NYSE:ICE: Also known as Intercontinental Exchange Inc., ICE owns and operates 23 regulated exchanges in the United States, Canada, and Europe, including the New York Stock Exchange and various derivatives exchanges. NYSE is the largest stock market in the world.

Offsets: *See* countertrade.

Offer (sell): The amount for which a foreign-exchange trader is willing to sell a currency.

Offshore financial centers (OFCs): Cities or countries that provide large amounts of funds in currencies other than their own and are used as locations in which to raise and accumulate cash.

Offshore financing: The provision of financial services by banks and other agents to nonresidents.

Offshoring: The dependence on production in a foreign country, usually by shifting from a domestic source.

Offshore manufacturing: Any investment that takes place in a country other than the home country.

Oligopolistic reaction: In IB, it is a situation in which managers may purposely crowd a market to prevent competitors from gaining advantages there that they can use to improve their positions elsewhere.

Onshoring: Relocating operations from a foreign to a domestic location.

Operations: The conversion of inputs into outputs.

Operations management: Activities in the value chain that occur within the company.

Optimum-tariff theory: The imposition of an import tariff that leads a foreign producer to lower its export price.

Option: A foreign-exchange instrument that gives the purchaser the right, but not the obligation, to buy or sell a certain amount of foreign currency at a set exchange rate within a specified amount of time.

Organizational culture: The shared meaning and beliefs that shape how employees interpret information, make decisions, and implement actions.

Organization of Petroleum Exporting Countries (OPEC): A producers' alliance among 13 petroleum-exporting countries that attempt to agree on oil production and pricing policies.

Organization structure: The formal arrangement of roles, responsibilities, and relationships within an organization.

Organization: The specification of the framework for work, development of the systems that coordinate and control what work is done, and the cultivation of a common workplace culture among employees.

Outright forward transaction: A forward contract that is not connected to a spot transaction.

Outsourcing: Where one company contracts with another company to perform certain functions, including manufacturing and back-office operations. May be done in the company's home country or in another country (nearshoring oroffshoring).

Pacific Alliance: A regional economic group in Latin America composed of Mexico, Colombia, Peru, and Chile. It is more favorable to trade and investment than other regional groups in South America.

Par value: The benchmark value of a currency, originally quoted in terms of gold or the U.S. dollar and now quoted in terms of Special Drawing Rights.

Parent-country nationals: An expatriate sent from her or his home country to live and work in another.

Payback period: The number of years required to recover the initial investment made.

Peg: To fix a currency's exchange rate to some benchmark, such as another currency.

Penetration strategy: Introducing a product at a low price to induce a maximum number of consumers to try it.

Peripheral values: Those values that are less dominant and more pliable than core values.

Planning: A comprehensive process that determines how the firm can best achieve its goals. An industry is composed of those companies engaged in a particular type of enterprise.

Political freedom index: An annual index created by The Freedom House to assess the degree of political freedom in various nations.

Political freedom: The right to participate freely in the political process.

Political ideology: The body of complex ideas, theories, and aims that constitute a socio-political program.

Political risk: Potential changes in political conditions that may cause a company's operating positions to deteriorate.

Political spectrum: A conceptual structure that specifies and organizes various types of political ideologies.

Political system: The system designed to integrate a society into a viable, functioning unit.

Polycentric staffing framework: A staffing policy whereby a company relies on host country nationals to manage operations in their own country, while parent-country nationals staff corporate headquarters.

Polychronic: A term to describe cultures where most people are more comfortable when working simultaneously on a variety of tasks (multitasking).

Poverty: Multidimensional condition in which a person or community lacks the essentials for a minimum standard of well-being and life.

Power distance: A measurement of employee preferences of interaction between superiors and subordinates.

Pragmatic: Describes cultures in which people focus more on details than on abstract principles.

Primary activities: The line activities that compose the value chain. Specifically, inbound logistics, operations, outbound logistics, marketing, and service.

Private technology exchange (PTX): An online collaboration model that brings manufacturers, distributors, value-added resellers, and customers together to execute trading transactions and to share information about demand, production, availability, and more.

Product diversion: It is also called the gray market and refers to the selling and handling of goods through unofficial distributors.

Product life cycle (PLC) theory of trade: The theory states that the production location of certain manufactured products shifts as they go through their life cycle, particularly from developed to developing countries.

Protectionism: The collective, governmental actions to influence international trade.

Pull: A type of promotion that relies on mass media.

Purchasing power parity (PPP): A theory that explains exchange-rate changes as being based on differences in price levels in different countries. Also, the number of units of a country's currency to buy the same products or services in the domestic market that US$1 would buy in the United States.

Push: A type of promotion that uses direct selling techniques.

Quality: Meeting or exceeding the expectations of a customer.

Quota: A quantity limit of a product's import or export in a given time frame, typically per year.

Reconciliation: The process required in U.S. capital markets where a company from a foreign country reconciles its home country GAAP with U.S. GAAP.

Regional integration: A form of integration in which a group of countries located in the same geographic proximity decide to cooperate.

Relationship-focus (RF) culture: A culture that puts dealings with friends ahead of business dealings.

Relativism: A theory stating that ethical truths depend on the groups holding them, making intervention by outsiders unethical. The belief that behavior has meaning and can be judged only in its specific cultural context.

Repatriation: An expatriate's return to his or her home country.

Reshoring: Firms' bringing operations back to their home countries from abroad and is sometimes called rightshoring.

Resource-based view: Each company has a unique combination of resources, capabilities, and competencies.

Resources: Inputs, owned or controlled by the MNE, that support its production process.

Reverse culture shock: The trauma of adjusting to one's own country after having become partial to aspects of life abroad that are not options back home.

Reverse-expat: A local manager who directs a Western-based company's emerging-market business and is rotated through some of the company's established operations outside of that market before returning home.

Rightsourcing: Also known as reshoring is the process of shifting production from abroad to the home country.

Royalties: Payments for the use of some assets, such as trademarks, patents, copyrights, or expertise.

Rule of law: The principle that every member of a society must follow the same laws.

Rule of man: Notion that the word and whim of the ruler, no matter how arbitrary, are law.

Scanning: A process in which managers examine many countries broadly—using information that is readily available, inexpensive, and fairly comparable—to narrow detailed analysis and travel to only the most promising ones.

Serendipity: Refers to the trigger of so-called accidental exporters who, responding to happenstance or odd circumstances, enter overseas markets by chance.

Service exports and imports: Non-merchandise international earnings. They are also referred to as invisibles.

Shadow economy: Illicit economic activity, such as counterfeiting or unlicensed services, that exists alongside a country's official economy; also called the underground, informal, or parallel economy.

Sight draft: A commercial bill of exchange that requires payment to be made as soon as it is presented to the party obligated to pay.

Silent language: The exchange of messages through a host of nonspoken and nonwritten cues.

Six Sigma: A highly focused system of quality control that uses data and rigorous statistical analysis to identify "defects" in a process or product, reduce variability, and achieve as close to zero defects as possible.

Skimming strategy: Charging a high price for a new product by aiming first at consumers willing to pay that much, then progressively lowering the price to sell to other consumers.

Small and medium-sized enterprise (SME): Companies whose headcount or sale turnover falls below certain thresholds; in the United States, companies that employ fewer than 500 employees. Commonly expressed as "SME."

Smithsonian Agreement: A 1971 agreement among countries that resulted in the devaluation of the U.S. dollar, revaluation of other world currencies, a widening of exchange-rate flexibility, and a commitment on the part of all participating countries to reduce trade restrictions; superseded by the Jamaica Agreement of 1976.

Socialism: A system based on public ownership of the means of production and distribution of wealth.

Soft (or weak) currency: A currency that is usually not fully convertible. Often these currencies are unstable and not very liquid.

Sourcing: The strategy that a company pursues in purchasing materials, components, and final products; sourcing can be from domestic and foreign locations and from inside and outside the company.

Sovereignty: A country's freedom to "act locally" and without externally imposed restrictions.

Sovereign wealth fund (SWF): A pool of money from a country's reserve which is set aside for investment purposes; usually related to natural resources such as oil.

Specific duty: A tariff assessed on a per-unit basis.

Special drawing right (SDR): A unit of account issued to countries by the International Monetary Fund to expand their official reserves bases.

Speculation: The buying or selling of foreign currency with the prospect of great risk and high return.

Spillover effect: A marketing program in one country that results in product awareness elsewhere, particularly in an adjacent country.

Spot rate: An exchange rate quoted for immediate delivery of foreign currency, usually within two business days.

Spot transactions: Foreign exchange transactions involving the exchange of currency the second day after the date on which the two foreign-exchange traders agree to the transaction.

Spread: In the forward market, the difference between the spot rate and the forward rate; in the spot market, the difference between the bid (buy) and offer (sell) rates quoted by a foreign-exchange trader.

Staffing framework: A systems view that articulates the internal structures and mechanisms of human resource management.

Stakeholders: The collection of groups, including stockholders, employees, customers, and society at large, that a company must satisfy to be successful.

State capitalism: An economic system whereby the state decides how, when, and where assets will be valued and resources allocated.

Static effect: The shifting of resources from inefficient to efficient companies as trade barriers fall.

Strategic alliance: Refers simply to companies' working together, such as in joint ventures and licensing agreements. However, the term sometimes refers to an agreement that is of critical importance to a partner or one that does not involve joint ownership.

Strategic trade policy: Also known as an industrial policy. It is one in which a government identifies target industries to develop to be internationally competitive.

Strategy: An integrated and coordinated set of commitments of actions that reflects the company's present situation, identifies the direction it should go, and determines how it will get there.

Subpart F (or passive) income: Income of a CFC that comes from sources other than those connected with the active conduct of a trade or business, such as holding company income.

Supply chain: The coordination of materials, information, and funds from the initial raw material supplier to the ultimate customer.

Supply-chaining: Collaborating horizontally among suppliers, relailers, and customers to create value.

Support activities: The general infrastructure of the firm that anchors the day-to-day execution of the primary activities of the value chain.

Sustainability: The ability to meet the needs of the present without compromising the ability of future generations to meet their own needs, while taking into account what is best for the people and the environment.

Syndication: Cooperation by a lead bank and several other banks to make a large loan to a public or private organization.

Tariff: A tax levied on a good shipped internationally.

Technical forecasting: A forecasting tool that uses past trends in exchange rates themselves to spot future trends in rates.

Teleological approach: An approach based on the idea that decisions are made based on the consequences of the action.

Temporal method: A method of translating foreign-currency financial statements used when the functional currency is that of the parent company.

Terms currency: In a foreign exchange quote, the base currency is 1 and the terms currency gives you the number of units of that currency per one unit of the base currency. If a foreign exchange trader quotes USD/JPY, the dollar is the base currency and the yen is the terms currency. The quote will give you the number of Japanese yen per U.S. dollar. The quote is also shown as USDJPY=X.

Terms of trade: The quantity of imports that a given quantity of a country's exports can buy.

Theocratic law: A situation whereby a nation's legal system is based on whatever religious text the ruling religion abides by.

Theory of country size: Countries with larger land masses usually depend less on trade than smaller ones.

Third Wave of Democratization: Expression to capture the collective set of nations that moved from nondemocratic to democratic political systems during the 1970s through the 1990s.

Third-country national: An expatriate who is neither a citizen of the country in which he or she is working nor a citizen of the country where the company is headquartered.

Third-party logistics (3PL): Agents that develop state-of-the-art technology to help companies understand trade practices, identify opportunities, manage risks, and shepherd exports and imports from buyers to sellers.

Time draft: A commercial bill of exchange calling for payment to be made at some time after delivery.

TNC: An acronym for transnational company, a term used by the United Nations to refer to a multinational enterprise.

Total quality management (TQM): The process that a company uses to achieve quality, where the goal is elimination of all defects.

Totalitarian system: A political system characterized by the absence of widespread participation in decision making and suppression of political and civil freedoms.

Trade deficit: A country is importing more than it is exporting.

Trade surplus: A country is exporting more than it is importing.

TQM: *See* Total quality management.

Trans-Pacific Partnership: A potential regional economic trade group involving the United States, Australia, Brunei, Canada, Chile, Japan, Malaysia, Mexico, New Zealand, Peru, Singapore, and Vietnam.

Transaction exposure: Foreign-exchange risk arising because a company has outstanding accounts receivable or accounts payable that are denominated in a foreign currency.

Transit tariffs: Taxes charged by countries through which international shipments move.

Translation: The restatement of financial statements from one currency to another.

Translation exposure: An exposure that occurs because exposed accounts—those translated at the balance-sheet or current exchange rate—either gain or lose value when the exchange rate changes.

Transnational company: A term used by the United Nations to refer to a multinational enterprise.

Transnational strategy: Configuring a value chain to exploit location economies as well as coordinate activities to leverage core competencies while simultaneously responding to local pressures.

Transpatriate: An expatriate "lifer" who tends to work in several countries over time and who has no true corporate "home."

Turnkey operations: Construction projects performed under contract and transferred to owners when they're operational.

Uncertainty avoidance: A country trait whereby most people feel uncomfortable with ambiguity.

Unemployment rate: The percentage of the workforce that is unemployed at any given date.

Unfavorable balance of trade: A country is importing more than it is exporting.

United Nations Conference on Trade and Development (UNCTAD): A UN body that has been especially active in dealing with the relationships between developing and industrialized countries with respect to trade.

Unity-of-command principle: An unbroken chain of command and communication should flow from the CEO to the entry-level worker.

Utilitarianism: A consequences-based approach to moral reasoning that judges an action to be right if it does the most good to the most people.

Value chain: The collective activities that occur as a product moves from raw materials through production to final distribution; the disaggregation of value creation.

Value: A measure of a firm's capability to sell what it makes for more than the costs incurred to make it; the ultimate purpose of strategy.

VER: *See* voluntary export restraint.

Vertical differentiation: The specification of the degrees of centralization and decentralization of decision-making in an organization.

Vertical integration: The control of the different stages as a product moves from raw materials through production to final distribution.

Virtual organization: A form of company that acquires strategic capabilities by creating a temporary network of independent companies, suppliers, customers, and even rivals.

Vision: The idealization of what an MNE firm wants to be. It expresses, in broad terms, its ultimate goal.

Voluntary export restraint (VER): A quota variation whereby a country voluntarily reduces its companies' exports to another country.

World Trade Organization (WTO): The 125-member successor to GATT that is charged with reducing tariff and nontariff barriers to trade in goods, services, and investment among member nations.

Zero defects: The elimination of defects, which results in the reduction of manufacturing costs and an increase in consumer satisfaction.

Company and Trademarks Index

Page references with "*f*" refer to figures, page references with "*m*" refer to maps, and page references with "n" refer to endnotes cited by number.

Name Index

Page references with "*f*" refer to figures, page references with "*m*" refer to maps, and page references with "n" refer to endnotes cited by number.

Subject Index

Page references with "*f*" refer to figures, page references with "*m*" refer to maps, and page references with "n" refer to endnotes cited by number.